Baseball America PROSPECT HANDBOOK

PUBLISHED BY
Baseball America Inc.

EDITORS
Jim Callis, Will Lingo

ASSOCIATE EDITORS
Josh Boyd, Allan Simpson

CONTRIBUTING WRITERS
Bill Ballew, Mike Berardino, Pat Caputo, Jeff Fletcher, Jim Ingraham,
Will Kimmey, Michael Levesque, Jack Magruder, John Manuel, Drew Olson,
John Perrotto, Tracy Ringolsby, Phil Rogers, Casey Tefertiller

PHOTO EDITOR
Alan Matthews

EDITORIAL ASSISTANTS
Mark Derewicz, Gary Martin

DESIGN & PRODUCTION
Phillip Daquila, Matthew Eddy, Linwood Webb

STATISTICAL CONSULTANT
SportsTicker
Boston

COVER PHOTO
Mark Teixeira by Rick Battle

BaseBall america

President: Catherine Silver
Publisher: Lee Folger
Editor: Allan Simpson
Managing Editor: Will Lingo
Executive Editor: Jim Callis
Design & Production Director: Phillip Daquila

BaseballAmerica.com

Contents

Foreword by Billy Beane 5
Introduction 6
Profiling Prospects 7
Minor League Depth Charts 8
Organization Talent Rankings 9
Top 50 Prospects 10

Anaheim Angels 14
Arizona Diamondbacks 30
Atlanta Braves 46
Baltimore Orioles 62
Boston Red Sox 78
Chicago Cubs 94
Chicago White Sox 110
Cincinnati Reds 126
Cleveland Indians 142
Colorado Rockies 158
Detroit Tigers 174
Florida Marlins 190
Houston Astros 206
Kansas City Royals 222
Los Angeles Dodgers 238
Milwaukee Brewers 254
Minnesota Twins 270
Montreal Expos 286
New York Mets 302
New York Yankees 318
Oakland Athletics 334
Philadelphia Phillies 350
Pittsburgh Pirates 366
St. Louis Cardinals 382
San Diego Padres 398
San Francisco Giants 414
Seattle Mariners 430
Tampa Bay Devil Rays 446
Texas Rangers 462
Toronto Blue Jays 478

Bonus History 494
2003 Draft Prospects 498
Minor League Top Prospects 502
Winter League Top Prospects 505

Index 506

Foreword

When you get right down to it, running a baseball team isn't about knowing what a player *has done*. It's about knowing what he *will do*. Of course, anyone who loves baseball—whether they're executives or fans or media—will talk about how Player A hit 30 home runs last year, and argue endlessly about whether that contribution was more valuable than Player B's 3.68 ERA. But when you're piecing together a baseball team, what you care about most is how those players will perform *next year*, when they might wear your uniform and cash your $4.5 million checks. You must project into the future to be successful.

When it comes to prospects, no one looks into that crystal ball better than the people at Baseball America. Whether the player is a first-round draft pick or a nondrafted free agent, a newcomer in Rookie ball or an established blue-chipper dominating Double-A, Baseball America surveys the field of future big leaguers every two weeks and reports on them more thoroughly and more intelligently than anyone else. They'll tell you who can play and who can't and, more important, why.

This book is their crowning achievement. Now in its third year, the Baseball America Prospect Handbook gives every baseball executive a one-stop reference source on the top 30 prospects in every organization—from personal data and career statistics to a top-notch appraisal of tools. That's 900 scouting reports, plus signing bonus data and more. Of course, no organization is successful without its own database of information and scouting reports, but you'd be surprised how often the Prospect Handbook provides invaluable facts and figures when a minor leaguer comes up in trade talks.

These pages give you a peek into baseball's future. Hundreds of the players profiled here will play in the major leagues someday. Some will be all-stars, some will not. The only sure thing is that you'll be glad you did your homework beforehand.

Billy Beane
General Manager
Oakland Athletics

Introduction

Work at Baseball America for a little while and you'll never have to worry about passion for baseball. Never mind the people actually on the staff; BA readers continually amaze us with their fervor for following the game at every level.

Witness an e-mail sent to me—on Christmas Day, no less—that laid out in amazing detail the track record of our Top 100 Prospects lists. Apparently this reader had gotten into a debate with a friend about the validity of prospect analysis. The reader said we provided significant insight about the futures of players, while his friend said we were no better than blind men groping in a dark room.

Well, 11 parts and 35,000 words later, our reader concluded that we did, in fact, have a good idea of what we were talking about.

But I didn't need to tell you that. You're holding the best book about prospects in the known universe. You don't need to be told that by reading the 900 scouting reports in this book, you have more insight into the best prospects in the game.

We can't tell you which of the players in this book will be superstars and which will be washouts. But we can give you our best predictions. More important, we'll give you all the information we could find about each player, and you can make up your own mind.

It's easy for anyone with a computer to crank out a top 10 (or 20 or 30) list. What sets our lists apart is the work that goes into them. We talk to general managers, scouting directors, farm directors, scouts, managers, coaches and other people in the game. Then we spend hours researching, writing, editing and proofreading. What ends up on the pages that follow speaks for itself.

As usual, the Prospect Handbook was a massive undertaking made possible only by the great work of our editorial staff and correspondents, as well as our crack production team. And as usual, we weren't willing to leave well enough alone. Additions to this year's book include expanded statistics, with opponent batting average for pitchers and on-base and slugging percentage for hitters.

We also added depth charts for every organization's minor league system. These present the prospects at a glance, so you can see where they'll line up, as well as providing the names of promising players even beyond the top 30s.

Remember that for the purposes of this book, a prospect is anyone who is still rookie-eligible under Major League Baseball guidelines (no more than 50 innings pitched or 130 at-bats), without regard to service time. Players are listed with the organizations they were with on Jan. 28, so you'll find Jason Romano with the Dodgers and Luke Allen with the Rockies— the last deal that made it into the book.

The third Prospect Handbook is the best yet, so jump right in and see what we have in store for you this year.

Will Lingo
Managing Editor

DEDICATION
To the memory of my mom, Bonnie Boyd
Who encouraged me to follow my dreams, and whose spirit still inspires me every day.
May 13, 1944–June 18, 2002
—Josh Boyd

Profiling Prospects

Among all the scouting lingo you'll come across in this book, perhaps no terms are more telling and prevalent than "profile" and "projection."

When scouts evaluate a player, their main objective is to identify—or project—what the player's future role will be in the major leagues. Each organization has its own philosophy when it comes to grading players, so we talked to scouts from several teams to provide general guidelines.

The first thing to know is what scouts are looking for. In short, tools. These refer to the physical skills a player needs to be successful in the major leagues. For a position player, the five basic tools are hitting, hitting for power, fielding, arm strength and speed. For a pitcher, the tools are based on the pitches he throws. Each pitch is graded, as well as a pitcher's control, delivery and durability.

For most teams, the profiling system has gone through massive changes in recent years because of the offensive explosion in baseball. Where arm strength and defense used to be a must in the middle of the diamond, there has been an obvious swing toward finding players who can rake, regardless of their gloves. In the past, players like Jeff Kent and Alfonso Soriano wouldn't have been accepted as second baseman, but now they are the standard for offensive-minded second baseman.

While more emphasis is placed on hitting—which also covers getting on base—fielding and speed are still at a premium up the middle. As teams sacrifice defense at the corner outfield slots, they look for a speedy center fielder to make up ground in the alleys. Most scouts prefer at least a 55 runner (on the 20-80 scouting scale; see chart) at short and center field, but as power increases at those two positions, running comes down (see Rich Aurilia, Jim Edmonds). Shortstops need range and at least average arm strength, and second basemen need to be quick on the pivot. Teams are more willing to put up with an immobile corner infielder if he can mash.

The Scouting Scale

When grading a player's tools, scouts use a standard 20-80 scale. When you read that a pitcher throws an above-average slider, it can be interpreted as a 60 pitch, or a plus pitch. Plus-plus is 70, or well-above-average, and so on. Scouts don't throw 80s around very freely. Here's what each grade means:

80	Outstanding
70	Well-above-average
60	Above-average
50	Major league average
40	Below-average
30	Well-below-average
20	Poor

Arm strength is the one tool moving way down preference lists. For a catcher, it was always the No. 1 tool, but with fewer players stealing and the slide step helping to shut down running games, scouts are looking for more offensive production from the position. Receiving skills, including game-calling, blocking pitches and release times, can make up for the lack of a plus arm.

On the mound, it doesn't just come down to pure stuff. While a true No. 1 starter on a first-division team should have a couple of 70 or 80 pitches in his repertoire, like Curt Schilling and Randy Johnson, they also need to produce 250-plus innings, 35 starts and 15-plus wins.

A player's overall future potential is also graded on the 20-80 scale, though some teams use a letter grade. This number is not just the sum of his tools, but rather a profiling system and a scout's ultimate opinion of the player.

70-80 (A): This category is reserved for the elite players in baseball. This player will be a perennial all-star, the best player at his position, one of the top five starters in the game or a frontline closer. Alex Rodriguez, Barry Bonds and Pedro Martinez reside here.

60-69 (B) You'll find all-star-caliber players here: No. 2 starters on a championship club and first-division players. See Mike Mussina, Miguel Tejada and Alfonso Soriano.

55-59 (C+) The majority of first-division starters are found in this range, including quality No. 2 and 3 starters, frontline set-up men and second-tier closers.

50-54 (C) Solid-a verage everyday major leaguers. Most are not first-division regulars. This group also includes No. 4 and 5 starters.

45-49 (D+) Fringe everyday players, backups, some no. 5 starters, middle relievers, pinch-hitters and one-tool players.

40-44 (D) Up-and-down roster fillers, situational relievers and 25th players.

38-39 (O) Organizational players who provide depth for the minor leagues but are not considered future major leaguers.

20-37 (NP) Not a prospect.

MinorLeague**Depth**Charts

AN OVERVIEW

A new feature of the Prospect Handbook is a depth chart of every organization's minor league talent. This shows you at a glance where a system's strengths and weaknesses lie and provides even more prospects beyond an organization's top 30. Each depth chart is accompanied by analysis of the system, as well as where it ranks in baseball (see facing page for the complete list). The rankings are based on our judgment of the quality and quantity of talent in each system, with higher marks to organizations that have more high-ceiling prospects or a deep system. The best systems have both.

To help you better understand why players are slotted at particular positions, we show you here what scouts look for in the ideal candidate at each spot, with individual tools ranked in descending order.

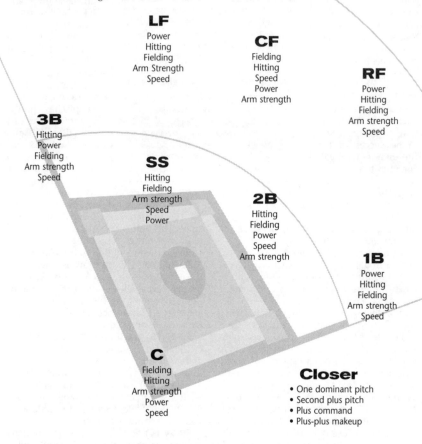

LF
Power
Hitting
Fielding
Arm Strength
Speed

CF
Fielding
Hitting
Speed
Power
Arm strength

RF
Power
Hitting
Fielding
Arm strength
Speed

3B
Hitting
Power
Fielding
Arm strength
Speed

SS
Hitting
Fielding
Arm strength
Speed
Power

2B
Hitting
Fielding
Power
Speed
Arm strength

1B
Power
Hitting
Fielding
Arm strength
Speed

C
Fielding
Hitting
Arm strength
Power
Speed

Closer
• One dominant pitch
• Second plus pitch
• Plus command
• Plus-plus makeup

Starting Pitchers

No. 1
• Two plus-plus pitches
• Average third and fourth pitch
• Plus-plus command
• Durability
• Plus makeup

No. 2
• Two plus pitches
• Average third pitch
• Above-average command
• Durability
• Average makeup

No. 3
• Solid-average velocity
• Above-average secondary pitches
• Average command
• Durability

Nos. 4-5
• Average stuff across the board
• Ability to pitch in relief
• Consistent breaking pitch

TalentRankings

		2002	2001	2000	1999
1	**Cleveland Indians**	20	26	19	4
	Trades and good drafts have shot the Tribe up the charts.				
2	**Atlanta Braves**	7	5	4	1
	As their rankings show, the Braves consistently find and produce talent.				
3	**Chicago Cubs**	1	2	16	26
	All that's left for the Cubs is to translate prospects into big league wins.				
4	**Minnesota Twins**	6	15	10	10
	Twins' big league breakthrough should be sustained by a deep system.				
5	**Anaheim Angels**	17	25	29	30
	Talent that sparked their World Series win is just the crest of a wave.				
6	**Toronto Blue Jays**	13	17	8	4
	Blue Jays will try to win for less, and have the young talent to do it.				
7	**Philadelphia Phillies**	11	12	17	21
	Perennially bad Phillies system continues its steady climb up.				
8	**Florida Marlins**	10	9	2	2
	In spite of other problems, Marlins continue to bring in talent.				
9	**Seattle Mariners**	2	4	24	20
	A step back after the 2001 dream season was inevitable.				
10	**Tampa Bay Devil Rays**	15	6	13	29
	Can Lou Piniella be patient with the Rays' young talent?				
11	**San Francisco Giants**	12	22	28	22
	Underappreciated system has several pitchers who could help soon.				
12	**Detroit Tigers**	18	18	25	16
	Dave Dombrowski has quickly restored some hope in Detroit.				
13	**New York Mets**	27	20	22	23
	An otherwise moribund system has flash at the top, led by Jose Reyes and Scott Kazmir.				
14	**Los Angeles Dodgers**	25	28	23	24
	A new commitment to player development is already paying dividends.				
15	**Chicago White Sox**	9	1	6	12
	Big league graduations have sapped the organization's depth.				
16	**Milwaukee Brewers**	26	30	30	27
	The Brewers have a lot of problems, but the farm system isn't one of them anymore.				
17	**New York Yankees**	5	7	1	3
	Big-money foreign signings prevented an even more severe nosedive.				
18	**Pittsburgh Pirates**	22	19	14	15
	Affiliates had a winning record for the second time in 34 years.				
19	**Texas Rangers**	8	13	7	8
	Grady Fuson has a lot of holes to fill behind Mark Teixeira.				
20	**San Diego Padres**	4	8	11	5
	Black hole on the big league roster sucked prospects from the system.				
21	**Arizona Diamondbacks**	23	29	12	18
	Failed premium draft picks have been offset by diamonds in the rough.				
22	**Oakland Athletics**	19	11	3	6
	A's will look to 2002 draft haul to replenish a system thinned by trades.				
23	**Houston Astros**	3	10	9	11
	Injuries and disappointing performances hit the Astros hard.				
24	**Cincinnati Reds**	14	3	20	28
	Most of the Reds' premium prospects come with big question marks.				
25	**Colorado Rockies**	24	16	26	25
	They may finally have figured out how to develop pitchers for Coors Field.				
26	**Kansas City Royals**	21	14	5	13
	Lots of help needed in KC, but this system doesn't have much to give.				
27	**Boston Red Sox**	28	24	21	17
	End of the Duquette regime means this ranking could finally turn around.				
28	**St. Louis Cardinals**	30	23	27	9
	They deal a lot of their prospects away, but it's a system that works.				
29	**Montreal Expos**	16	21	15	7
	New owner will find that MLB has left a picked-over carcass on the farm.				
30	**Baltimore Orioles**	29	27	18	19
	Organization finally gets its desperately needed new administration.				

Top 50 Prospects

If nothing else, a collection of top 50 lists proves that reasonable people can disagree. These are the personal top 50s for the four people who oversee Baseball America's prospect rankings, giving you a glimpse at each person's preferences.

The biggest issue this year is how to value the two newest Yankees: Hideki Matsui and Jose Contreras. Both are probably as close to locks as you can get at being big league contributors, but you have to weigh that against their career value. Assuming both players reach their full potential in the major leagues, would you rather have 15 years of Mark Teixeira or five years of Hideki Matsui? How likely is either player to fulfill that potential? You can see how we weighed that question in the pages that follow. It's all part of what makes prospect rating fun.

Rocco Baldelli

These lists are snapshots after the end of winter ball and before spring training, and they would probably change the next time we put them together. From lists like these, we assemble a consensus list, argue about it, run it by more people in the industry and argue about it some more. It ends up as our annual Top 100 Prospects list that comes out in March, the list that we consider the best compilation of prospects in the game.

Allan Simpson

1. Mark Teixeira, 3b, Rangers	26. Sean Burnett, lhp, Pirates
2. Rocco Baldelli, of, Devil Rays	27. Rafael Soriano, rhp, Mariners
3. Jose Reyes, ss, Mets	28. Xavier Nady, of, Padres
4. Jesse Foppert, rhp, Giants	29. Bryan Bullington, rhp, Pirates
5. Gavin Floyd, rhp, Phillies	30. Hee Seop Choi, 1b, Cubs
6. Joe Mauer, c, Twins	31. Aaron Heilman, rhp, Mets
7. Hideki Matsui, of, Yankees	32. Jose Castillo, ss, Pirates
8. Hanley Ramirez, ss, Red Sox	33. Joe Borchard, of, White Sox
9. Francisco Rodriguez, rhp, Angels	34. Scott Hairston, 2b, Diamondbacks
10. Scott Kazmir, lhp, Mets	35. Wilson Betemit, ss/3b, Braves
11. Jose Contreras, rhp, Yankees	36. Juan Rivera, of, Yankees
12. Miguel Cabrera, 3b, Marlins	37. Brad Nelson, 1b, Brewers
13. Jason Stokes, 1b, Marlins	38. Bobby Jenks, rhp, Angels
14. Brandon Phillips, 2b/ss, Indians	39. Shin-Soo Choo, of, Mariners
15. Adam Wainwright, rhp, Braves	40. Mike Gosling, lhp, Diamondbacks
16. Jeremy Bonderman, rhp, Tigers	41. Dewon Brazelton, rhp, Devil Rays
17. Casey Kotchman, 1b, Angels	42. Aaron Cook, rhp, Rockies
18. Victor Martinez, c, Indians	43. Kris Honel, rhp, White Sox
19. Rich Harden, rhp, Athletics	44. Mike Jones, rhp, Brewers
20. John VanBenschoten, rhp, Pirates	45. Jeremy Guthrie, rhp, Indians
21. Justin Morneau, 1b, Twins	46. Cliff Lee, lhp, Indians
22. Josh Hamilton, of, Devil Rays	47. John Buck, c, Astros
23. B.J. Upton, ss, Devil Rays	48. Andy Marte, 3b, Braves
24. Jose Lopez, ss, Mariners	49. Adrian Gonzalez, 1b, Marlins
25. Michael Cuddyer, of, Twins	50. Bubba Nelson, rhp, Braves

Will Lingo

1. Mark Teixeira, 3b, Rangers
2. Jose Contreras, rhp, Yankees
3. Jose Reyes, ss, Mets
4. Rocco Baldelli, of, Devil Rays
5. Brandon Phillips, ss/2b, Indians
6. Joe Mauer, c, Twins
7. Hideki Matsui, of, Yankees
8. Jesse Foppert, rhp, Giants
9. Joe Borchard, of, White Sox
10. Francisco Rodriguez, rhp, Angels
11. Adam Wainwright, rhp, Braves
12. Miguel Cabrera, 3b, Marlins
13. Gavin Floyd, rhp, Phillies
14. Victor Martinez, c, Indians
15. Michael Cuddyer, of, Twins
16. Rafael Soriano, rhp, Mariners
17. Jason Stokes, 1b, Marlins
18. Scott Kazmir, lhp, Mets
19. Hee Seop Choi, 1b, Cubs
20. Justin Morneau, 1b, Twins
21. Jeremy Bonderman, rhp, Tigers
22. John VanBenschoten, rhp, Pirates
23. Brad Nelson, 1b, Brewers
24. Rich Harden, rhp, Athletics
25. Hanley Ramirez, ss, Red Sox

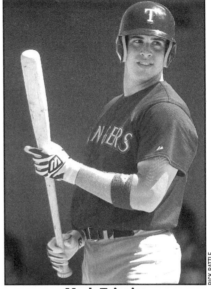

RICK BATTLE

Mark Teixeira

26. B.J. Upton, ss, Devil Rays
27. Dustin McGowan, rhp, Blue Jays
28. Zack Greinke, rhp, Royals
29. Chris Snelling, of, Mariners
30. Bryan Bullington, rhp, Pirates
31. Aaron Heilman, rhp, Mets
32. Juan Rivera, of, Yankees
33. Cliff Lee, lhp, Indians
34. Michael Restovich, of, Twins
35. Casey Kotchman, 1b, Angels
36. Colby Lewis, rhp, Rangers
37. John Buck, c, Astros
38. Aaron Cook, rhp, Rockies
39. Mike Gosling, lhp, Diamondbacks
40. Xavier Nady, of, Padres
41. Jerome Williams, rhp, Giants
42. Sean Burnett, lhp, Pirates
43. Adrian Gonzalez, 1b, Marlins
44. Andy Sisco, lhp, Cubs
45. Dontrelle Willis, lhp, Marlins
46. Jayson Werth, of/c, Blue Jays
47. Franklyn German, rhp, Tigers
48. Jason Lane, of, Astros
49. Mike McDougal, rhp, Royals
50. Bobby Jenks, rhp, Angels

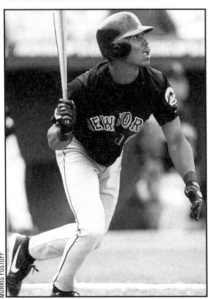

MORRIS FOSTOFF

Jose Reyes

LARRY GOREN

Francisco Rodriguez

DIAMOND IMAGES

Brandon Phillips

Jim Callis

1. Mark Teixeira, 3b, Rangers	26. Mike Restovich, of, Twins
2. Jose Contreras, rhp, Yankees	27. Joe Borchard, of, White Sox
3. Joe Mauer, c, Twins	28. Josh Hamilton, of, Devil Rays
4. Jesse Foppert, rhp, Giants	29. Chris Snelling, of, Mariners
5. Rocco Baldelli, of, Devil Rays	30. Jose Lopez, ss, Mariners
6. Brandon Phillips, ss/2b, Indians	31. Cliff Lee, lhp, Indians
7. Jose Reyes, ss, Mets	32. Travis Hafner, 1b, Indians
8. Michael Cuddyer, of, Twins	33. Dontrelle Willis, lhp, Marlins
9. Scott Kazmir, lhp, Mets	34. Brad Nelson, 1b, Brewers
10. Hideki Matsui, of, Yankees	35. Aaron Cook, rhp, Rockies
11. Jeremy Bonderman, rhp, Tigers	36. Angel Guzman, rhp, Cubs
12. Gavin Floyd, rhp, Phillies	37. Jonathan Figueroa, lhp, Dodgers
13. Casey Kotchman, 1b, Angels	38. Macay McBride, lhp, Braves
14. Francisco Rodriguez, rhp, Angels	39. Andy Sisco, lhp, Cubs
15. Victor Martinez, c, Indians	40. Shin-Soo Choo, of, Mariners
16. Hee Seop Choi, 1b, Cubs	41. Sean Burnett, lhp, Pirates
17. Justin Morneau, 1b, Twins	42. Rich Harden, rhp, Athletics
18. Jason Stokes, 1b, Marlins	43. Dustin McGowan, rhp, Blue Jays
19. Scott Hairston, 2b, Diamondbacks	44. John VanBenschoten, rhp, Pirates
20. Hanley Ramirez, ss, Red Sox	45. Jerome Williams, rhp, Giants
21. B.J. Upton, ss, Devil Rays	46. Adrian Gonzalez, 1b, Marlins
22. Colby Lewis, rhp, Rangers	47. James Loney, 1b, Dodgers
23. Miguel Cabrera, 3b, Marlins	48. Franklyn German, rhp, Tigers
24. Adam Wainwright, rhp, Braves	49. Jeff Mathis, c, Angels
25. Rafael Soriano, rhp, Mariners	50. Andy Marte, 3b, Braves

Josh Boyd

1. Rocco Baldelli, of, Devil Rays
2. Mark Teixeira, 3b, Rangers
3. Joe Mauer, c, Twins
4. Jose Reyes, ss, Mets
5. Jose Contreras, rhp, Yankees
6. Jesse Foppert, rhp, Giants
7. Gavin Floyd, rhp, Phillies
8. Brandon Phillips, 2b/ss, Indians
9. Miguel Cabrera, 3b, Marlins
10. Scott Kazmir, lhp, Mets
11. Francisco Rodriguez, rhp, Angels
12. Casey Kotchman, 1b, Angels
13. Justin Morneau, 1b, Twins
14. Brad Nelson, 1b, Brewers
15. Sean Burnett, lhp, Pirates
16. Michael Cuddyer, of, Twins
17. Jeff Mathis, c, Angels
18. Colby Lewis, rhp, Rangers
19. Hideki Matsui, of, Yankees
20. Jason Stokes, 1b, Marlins
21. James Loney, 1b, Dodgers
22. Victor Martinez, c, Indians
23. Jonathan Figueroa, lhp, Dodgers
24. B.J. Upton, ss, Devil Rays
25. Bobby Jenks, rhp, Angels
26. Andy Marte, 3b, Braves
27. John VanBenschoten, rhp, Pirates
28. Franklyn German, rhp, Tigers
29. Adrian Gonzalez, 1b, Marlins
30. Hanley Ramirez, ss, Red Sox
31. Johan Santana, rhp, Angels
32. Dontrelle Willis, lhp, Marlins
33. Adam Wainwright, rhp, Braves
34. Scott Hairston, 2b, Diamondbacks
35. Hee Seop Choi, 1b, Cubs
36. Rich Harden, rhp, Athletics
37. Michael Restovich, of, Twins
38. Felix Pie, of, Cubs
39. Clint Everts, rhp, Expos
40. Wilson Betemit, ss, Braves
41. Cliff Lee, lhp, Indians
42. Travis Hafner, 1b, Indians
43. John Patterson, rhp, Diamondbacks
44. Joe Borchard, of, White Sox
45. Rafael Soriano, rhp, Mariners
46. Jerome Williams, rhp, Giants
47. Jeremy Bonderman, rhp, Tigers
48. Dustin McGowan, rhp, Blue Jays
49. Angel Guzman, rhp, Cubs
50. Mike Hinckley, lhp, Expos

Joe Mauer

Gavin Floyd

ANAHEIM
ANGELS

TOP 30 PROSPECTS

1. Francisco Rodriguez, rhp
2. Casey Kotchman, 1b
3. Bobby Jenks, rhp
4. Jeff Mathis, c
5. Johan Santana, rhp
6. Dallas McPherson, 3b
7. Joe Saunders, lhp
8. Rich Fischer, rhp
9. Joe Torres, lhp
10. Chris Bootcheck, rhp
11. Steven Shell, rhp
12. Rafael Rodriguez, rhp
13. Brendan Donnelly, rhp
14. Derrick Turnbow, rhp
15. Jake Woods, lhp
16. Nathan Haynes, of
17. Robb Quinlan, of
18. Quan Cosby, of
19. Nick Touchstone, lhp
20. Brian Specht, ss
21. Eric Aybar, ss
22. Alfredo Amezaga, ss
23. Alberto Callaspo, 2b
24. Kevin Jepsen, rhp
25. Phil Wilson, rhp
26. Nick Kimpton, of
27. Mike Brunet, rhp
28. Chone Figgins, 2b
29. Jared Abruzzo, c
30. Tommy Murphy, ss

By Josh Boyd

Just a year ago the Angels franchise was in disarray. Disney couldn't find a buyer after putting the team on the market. Contraction was a possibility. Anaheim agreed to trade team leader and pending free agent Darin Erstad to the White Sox for Jon Garland and Chris Singleton before ownership pulled the plug for marketing reasons. Shortly thereafter, team president Tony Tavares resigned.

But general manager Bill Stoneman never wavered. He put the pieces in place for manager Mike Scioscia to lead an improbable run to the 2002 World Series title.

While the Angels may not have been even the most talented team in franchise history, their character was the biggest difference from their predecessors, who were notorious for late-season collapses.

Anaheim's never-say-die approach was best illustrated by its Game Six comeback against the Giants in the World Series. But the Angels were riding the Rally Monkey's magic before the rest of the nation realized what was going on, as they stayed in a heated American League West race even as the Athletics went on a 20-game winning streak.

Anaheim should remain a contender. The club's nucleus is tied up with long-term con-tracts, and Disney has increased the payroll to $84 million, though the franchise remains up for sale.

Stoneman has shown a knack for turning spare parts such as shortstop David Eckstein and relievers Brendan Donnelly and Ben Weber into vital cogs. With a larger budget and an improved farm system, he won't be forced to sift through the bargain bin as often.

Scouting director Donny Rowland followed up a fruitful 2001 draft that produced Casey Kotchman, Jeff Mathis and Dallas McPherson with another solid effort in 2002. First-rounder Joe Saunders should move quickly, and several pitchers who were taken with later picks could emerge.

No. 1 prospect Francisco Rodriguez leads the new wave of home-grown talent, already having made a name for himself by dominating in October. Troy Percival's eventual replacement, Rodriguez will shorten games for Scioscia and bridge the gap to Percival in 2003.

Another young righthander stepped up for the Angels with the season on the line, and should be a fixture in the rotation. John Lackey became the first rookie since Pittsburgh's Babe Adams in 1909 to win Game Seven of the World Series.

OrganizationOverview

General Manager: Bill Stoneman. **Farm Director:** Tony Reagins. **Scouting Director:** Donny Rowland.

2002 PERFORMANCE

Class	Farm Team	League	W	L	Pct.	Finish*	Manager(s)
Majors	Anaheim	American	99	63	.611	3rd (14)	Mike Scioscia
Triple-A	Salt Lake Stingers	Pacific Coast	78	66	.542	3rd (16)	Mike Brumley
Double-A	Arkansas Travelers	Texas	51	89	.364	8th (8)	Doug Sisson
High A	Rancho Cucamonga Quakes	California	52	88	.371	10th (10)	Bobby Meacham
Low A	Cedar Rapids Kernels	Midwest	81	58	.583	3rd (14)	Todd Claus
Rookie	Provo Angels	Pioneer	38	38	.500	4th (8)	Tom Kotchman
Rookie	AZL Angels	Arizona	28	28	.500	t-3rd (7)	Brian Harper
OVERALL 2002 MINOR LEAGUE RECORD			328	367	.472	22nd (30)	

*Finish in overall standings (No. of teams in league)

ORGANIZATION LEADERS

BATTING   *Minimum 250 At-Bats
*AVG	Rick Short, Salt Lake	.356
R	Chone Figgins, Salt Lake	100
H	Robb Quinlan, Salt Lake	176
TB	Robb Quinlan, Salt Lake	293
2B	Jeff Mathis, Cedar Rapids	41
3B	Chone Figgins, Salt Lake	18
HR	Michael O'Keefe, Arkansas	21
	Carlos Duncan, Arkansas/Rancho Cucamonga	21
RBI	Robb Quinlan, Salt Lake	112
BB	Dallas McPherson, Cedar Rapids	78
SO	Brian Specht, Arkansas	129
SB	Kenny James, Arkansas	40

PITCHING   #Minimum 75 Innings
W	Johan Santana, Cedar Rapids	14
L	Three tied at	14
#ERA	Francisco Rodriguez, Salt Lake/Arkansas	2.27
G	Bart Miadich, Salt Lake	59
CG	Rich Fischer, Rancho Cucamonga/Arkansas.	5
SV	Joel Peralta, Arkansas/Cedar Rapids	27
IP	Rich Fischer, Arkansas/Rancho Cucamonga	176
BB	Bobby Jenks, Arkansas/Rancho Cucamonga	90
SO	Pedro Liriano, Rancho Cucamonga	176

BEST TOOLS

Best Hitter for Average	Casey Kotchman
Best Power Hitter	Dallas McPherson
Fastest Baserunner	Quan Cosby
Best Athlete	Quan Cosby
Best Fastball	Bobby Jenks
Best Curveball	Francisco Rodriguez
Best Slider	Johan Santana
Best Changeup	Joe Saunders
Best Control	Rich Fischer
Best Defensive Catcher	Jeff Mathis
Best Defensive Infielder	Tommy Murphy
Best Infield Arm	Tommy Murphy
Best Defensive Outfielder	Quan Cosby
Best Outfield Arm	Jason Coulie

PROJECTED 2006 LINEUP

Catcher	Jeff Mathis
First Base	Casey Kotchman
Second Base	Adam Kennedy
Third Base	Troy Glaus
Shortstop	David Eckstein
Left Field	Garret Anderson
Center Field	Darin Erstad
Right Field	Dallas McPherson
Designated Hitter	Tim Salmon
No. 1 Starter	Jarrod Washburn

Robb Quinlan   **Bart Miadich**

No. 2 Starter	John Lackey
No. 3 Starter	Bobby Jenks
No. 4 Starter	Johan Santana
No. 5 Starter	Ramon Ortiz
Closer	Francisco Rodriguez

TOP PROSPECTS OF THE DECADE

1993	Tim Salmon, of
1994	Brian Anderson, lhp
1995	Andrew Lorraine, lhp
1996	Darin Erstad, of
1997	Jarrod Washburn, lhp
1998	Troy Glaus, 3b
1999	Ramon Ortiz, rhp
2000	Ramon Ortiz, rhp
2001	Joe Torres, lhp
2002	Casey Kotchman, 1b

TOP DRAFT PICKS OF THE DECADE

1993	Brian Anderson, lhp
1994	McKay Christensen, of
1995	Darin Erstad, of
1996	Chuck Abbott, ss (2)
1997	Troy Glaus, 3b
1998	Seth Etherton, rhp
1999	John Lackey, rhp (2)
2000	Joe Torres, lhp
2001	Casey Kotchman, 1b
2002	Joe Saunders, lhp

ALL-TIME LARGEST BONUSES

Troy Glaus, 1997	$2,250,000
Joe Torres, 2000	$2,080,000
Casey Kotchman, 2001	$2,075,000
Joe Saunders, 2002	$1,825,000
Chris Bootcheck, 2000	$1,800,000

MinorLeague**Depth**Chart

ANAHEIM ANGELS

5 RANK

From the World Series to the depth of a budding farm system, everything suddenly clicked last year for one of the game's traditional underachievers. The Angels boast a largely homegrown lineup at the big league level, along with premium prospects in the minors and a balance between pitchers and position players. Under Donny Rowland's direction, the scouting staff has beefed up the organization with three good drafts while re-establishing a solid Latin American connection. The potential impact of Casey Kotchman, Jeff Mathis and Dallas McPherson from the 2001 draft heads a wave of talent that should be capable of keeping the Angels in contention for years.

Note: Depth charts prepared by Josh Boyd. Numbers in parentheses indicate prospect rankings.

LF
Mike O'Keefe
Barry Wesson
Caleb Maher
Josh Gray

CF
Nathan Haynes (16)
Quan Cosby (18)
Nick Kimpton (26)

RF
Robb Quinlan (17)
Greg Porter
Jordan Renz

3B
Dallas McPherson (6)
Matt Brown

SS
Eric Aybar (21)
Alfredo Amezaga (22)
Tommy Murphy (30)
Juan Batista
Javy Rodriguez

2B
Brian Specht (20)
Alberto Callaspo (23)
Chone Figgins (28)
J.T. Turner
H.J. Kendrick

1B
Casey Kotchman (2)
Chris Walston

C
Jeff Mathis (4)
Jared Abruzzo (29)
Jose Molina
Wil Nieves
Ryan Budde
Alex Dvorsky

RHP

Starters	Relievers
Bobby Jenks (3)	Francisco Rodriguez (1)
Johan Santana (5)	Brendan Donnelly (13)
Rich Fischer (8)	Derrick Turnbow (14)
Chris Bootcheck (10)	Mike Brunet (27)
Steven Shell (11)	Bart Miadich
Rafael Rodriguez (12)	Ronnie Ray
Kevin Jepsen (24)	Carlos Morban
Phil Wilson (25)	
Steve Green	
James Holcomb	
Matt Hensley	
Austin Bilke	
Anthony Reed	
Dave Wolensky	

LHP

Starters	Relievers
Joe Saunders (7)	Ambrionix Delgadillo
Joe Torres (9)	
Jake Woods (15)	
Nick Touchstone (19)	
Kyle Pawelczyk	
Scott Hindman	
Dan Mozingo	
Micah Posey	

DraftAnalysis

2002 Draft

Best Pro Debut: LHP Joe Saunders (1) went 5-2, 2.80 overall and was even better after a promotion to low Class A, going 3-1, 1.88 in five outings. SS Javy Rodriguez (5) advanced even further, hitting .254 with 19 steals in high Class A. C Alex Dvorsky (26) was a Rookie-level Pioneer League all-star after batting .321-9-52.

Best Athlete: 2B Howard Kendrick (10) has a live body, and the Angels are excited about his potential with the bat after he hit .318 in Rookie ball.

Best Pure Hitter: Kendrick is instinctive at the plate and is a switch-hitter. The Angels considered taking him in the first six rounds, but gambled that he'd last a little later.

Best Raw Power: OF Jordan Renz (4) or 1B Chris Walston (6), neither of whom homered in his first pro summer. Renz has a higher ceiling, while Walston–who set a California prep record with 22 homers last spring–has more loft in his swing.

Fastest Runner: Kendrick and OF Aaron Peel (11) are solid average to plus runners.

Best Defensive Player: Rodriguez does not have a classic shortstop body, but he's effective and could be a good second baseman if he has to move. His arm will play at any position, as he threw 91-93 mph while pitching for Miami in 2001 fall practice.

Best Fastball: RHP Kevin Jepsen (2) has little effort to his delivery and touched 98 mph during the spring. He worked at 94-95 after signing.

Best Breaking Ball: Jepsen's slider has been clocked as high as 91 mph. RHP James Holcomb (8), who has touched 94 mph, also has a plus curveball.

Most Intriguing Background: 3B Jake Mathis' (28) younger brother Jeff was an Angels supplemental first-rounder in 2001 and is one of the game's best catching prospects. OF **Jason Sugden's** (35) great-great-grandfather Joe Sugden worked in baseball for 65 years.

RODGER WOOD

Sugden

Closest To The Majors: Saunders was one of the most polished pitchers available, and he's left-handed to boot. He commands an average fastball and plus changeup to both sides of the plate.

Best Late-Round Pick: LHP Nick Touchstone (18) turned down a six-figure bonus from the Yankees as a draft-and-follow. He has a low-90s fastball and, when it's on, a tight power curveball. The Angels signed Touchstone and LHP Scott Hindman (22)–both touch 95 mph–from the Cape Cod League on the same day last summer.

The One Who Got Away: Compared to Shawn Green, OF Ryan Broderick (20) would have been a much higher pick had he not missed his senior season with a hip injury. He's now at Southern California.

Assessment: After one of the game's best drafts in 2001, the Angels had another solid effort. They added several good lefthanders, including Kyle Pawelczyk (3), another draft-and-follow who re-entered the draft.

2001 Draft

1B Casey Kotchman (1) and C Jeff Mathis (1) are among the minors' best prospects at their positions. The hits kept on coming with 3B Dallas McPherson (2), RHP Steven Shell (2) and LHP Jake Woods (3).   **Grade: A**

2000 Draft

LHP Joe Torres (1) and RHPs Chris Bootcheck (1) and Bobby Jenks (5) all have high ceilings. This grade will rise as they come closer to reaching them.   **Grade: C+**

1999 Draft

The Angels didn't have a first-round pick, but did quite nicely with top pick John Lackey (2). SSs Brian Specht (9) and Alfredo Amezaga (13) and OF Robb Quinlan (10) also have a shot to contribute.   **Grade: B**

1998 Draft

Anaheim didn't sign the best player it picked, SS Bobby Crosby (34). RHP Seth Etherton's (1) career has been wrecked by a shoulder injury.   **Grade: D**

Note: Draft analysis prepared by Jim Callis. Numbers in parentheses indicate draft rounds.

. . . Rodriguez made veteran hitters look foolish with his electrifying two-pitch arsenal.

Francisco Rodriguez rhp

Born: Jan. 7, 1982.
Ht.: 6-0. **Wt.:** 170.
Bats: R. **Throws:** R.
Career Transactions: Signed out of Venezuela by Angels, Sept. 24, 1998.

Rodriguez has been a fixture on prospect lists since the Angels signed him for $900,000 in 1998. Yet it wasn't until instructional league after the 2001 season that the Angels decided he could be their future closer. He showed his overpowering stuff as a starter, but shoulder and elbow problems kept him from surpassing 114 innings. His career took off when he moved to the bullpen in 2002 and his arm proved resilient. His September callup produced 5⅔ dominant innings, and that's all it took to put him in manager Mike Scioscia's postseason plans. Rodriguez became the youngest pitcher in 32 years to pitch in the World Series and the youngest ever to pick up a victory. He went 5-1, 1.93 with 28 strikeouts in 19 postseason innings.

Despite spending most of the season in the minors, Rodriguez emerged as Scioscia's go-to reliever in critical playoff situations. He made veteran hitters look foolish with his electrifying two-pitch arsenal. His lightning-quick arm generates 94-96 mph velocity on his fastball with explosive late life. Rodriguez tightened the hard rotation on his breaking ball and became more consistent locating it. He can throw it for a strike to either side of the plate or bury it in the dirt, and hitters have a difficult time reading the pitch until it's too late. Scouts are split on whether it's a slider or curveball. Rodriguez alters his grip and changes the tilt on the pitch, creating a true slider break or a sweepy curveball arc. Righthanders stand little chance when he's on. Rodriguez made his biggest strides in maturity, mound presence and conditioning.

Though his across-the-body delivery creates deception and leverage, his mechanics and frame could be considered red flags. Considering Rodriguez' history of arm problems, the Angels would be wise to preserve his arm. Unflappable and confident on the mound, he still overthrows at times. Scouts already compare the Rodriguez-Troy Percival tandem to John Wetteland and an up-and-coming Mariano Rivera. Like Rivera, Rodriguez' is the heir apparent as closer.

Year	Club (League)	Class	W	L	ERA	G	GS	CG	SV	IP	H	R	ER	HR	BB	SO	AVG
1999	Butte (Pio)	R	1	1	3.31	12	9	1	0	52	33	21	19	1	21	69	.179
	Boise (NWL)	A	1	0	5.40	1	1	0	0	5	3	4	3	0	1	6	.150
2000	Lake Elsinore (Cal)	A	4	4	2.81	13	12	0	0	64	43	29	20	2	32	79	.189
2001	Rancho Cucamonga (Cal)	A	5	7	5.38	20	20	1	0	114	127	72	68	13	55	147	.277
2002	Arkansas (TL)	AA	3	3	1.96	23	0	0	9	41	32	13	9	2	15	61	.206
	Salt Lake (PCL)	AAA	2	3	2.57	27	0	0	6	42	30	13	12	1	13	59	.204
	Anaheim (AL)	MAJ	0	0	0.00	5	0	0	0	6	3	0	0	0	2	13	.167
MAJOR LEAGUE TOTALS			0	0	0.00	5	0	0	0	6	3	0	0	0	2	13	.167
MINOR LEAGUE TOTALS			16	18	3.71	96	42	2	15	318	268	152	131	19	137	421	.225

2. Casey Kotchman, 1b

Born: Feb. 22, 1983. **Ht.:** 6-3. **Wt.:** 210. **Bats:** L. **Throws:** L. **School:** Seminole (Fla.) HS. **Career Transactions:** Selected by Angels in first round (13th overall) of 2001 draft; signed July 28, 2001.

The son of longtime Angels scout and minor league manager Tom Kotchman, Casey shot straight to the top of this list a year ago. After he led Seminole High to a No. 1 national ranking, the Angels popped him with the 13th overall pick. Kotchman is from the same classic mold as Will Clark and Mark Grace. He doesn't have the same picturesque stroke, but Kotchman combines rhythm and timing with bat speed and explosive contact. He has plenty of gap power now and projects to hit for above-average home run power as he matures. He has mastered the strike zone, and while there's some effort to his stroke, he rarely swings and misses. He's equally outstanding on defense. Kotchman played in just 10 games for low Class A Cedar Rapids after June, and has had each of his first two seasons cut short by wrist injuries. It shouldn't be a long-term concern, but he needs to prove his durability over the course of a full season. Kotchman returned to the Cedar Rapids lineup in time for the Midwest League playoffs and showed no ill effects by hitting .389. If healthy, he could be batting third in the Angels lineup by 2005.

Year	Club (League)	Class	AVG	G	AB	R	H	2B	3B	HR	RBI	BB	SO	SB	SLG	OBP
2001	Angels (AZL)	R	.600	4	15	5	9	1	0	1	5	3	2	0	.867	.632
	Provo (Pio)	R	.500	7	22	6	11	3	0	0	7	2	0	0	.636	.542
2002	Cedar Rapids (Mid)	A	.281	81	288	42	81	30	1	5	50	48	37	2	.444	.390
MINOR LEAGUE TOTALS			.311	92	325	53	101	34	1	6	62	53	39	2	.477	.411

3. Bobby Jenks, rhp

Born: March 14, 1981. **Ht.:** 6-3. **Wt.:** 240. **Bats:** R. **Throws:** R. **School:** Inglemoor HS, Bothell, Wash. **Career Transactions:** Selected by Angels in fifth round of 2000 draft; signed June 13, 2000.

After an encouraging stint in big league spring training, Jenks was suspended for team violations at midseason. Subsequently demoted from Double-A Arkansas to extended spring training, he worked hard and finished 2002 by leading the Arizona Fall League in strikeouts for the second straight season. With an overpowering fastball that has hit 102 mph, Jenks is on the verge of harnessing his explosive stuff. He works in the mid- to upper 90s and added a two-seamer in the AFL. His power curveball is among the best breaking pitches in the minors, and he gained the confidence to throw it for strikes in Arizona. His arm action is clean and effortless. Jenks needs consistency on and off the field. He has to establish a rhythm on the mound and repeat his delivery. He has a feel for his changeup, but doesn't trust it enough to throw it for strikes. Jenks will return to Double-A if he can build off his fall success in spring training. Scouts compare his dominant repertoire and frame to a young Curt Schilling. If he doesn't develop command, his stuff might allow him to become a closer.

Year	Club (League)	Class	W	L	ERA	G	GS	CG	SV	IP	H	R	ER	HR	BB	SO	AVG
2000	Butte (Pio)	R	1	7	7.86	14	12	0	0	53	61	57	46	2	44	42	.290
2001	Cedar Rapids (Mid)	A	3	7	5.27	21	21	0	0	99	90	74	58	10	64	98	.245
	Arkansas (TL)	AA	1	0	3.60	2	2	0	0	10	8	5	4	0	5	10	.200
2002	Arkansas (TL)	AA	3	6	4.66	10	10	1	0	58	49	34	30	2	44	58	.234
	Rancho Cucamonga (Cal)	A	3	5	4.82	11	10	1	0	65	50	42	35	4	46	64	.212
MINOR LEAGUE TOTALS			11	25	5.46	58	55	2	0	285	258	212	173	18	203	272	.243

4. Jeff Mathis, c

Born: March 31, 1983. **Ht.:** 6-0. **Wt.:** 180. **Bats:** R. **Throws:** R. **School:** Marianna (Fla.) HS. **Career Transactions:** Selected by Angels in first round (33rd overall) of 2001 draft; signed June 5, 2001.

Mathis grabbed scouts' attention as fellow 2001 first-rounder Alan Horne's personal catcher in high school. Mathis spent most of his time between shortstop and the mound, hitting .506 while posting a 0.95 ERA. The Angels considered him with the 13th overall pick, where they snagged Casey Kotchman, and signed Mathis for $850,000. Mathis' strong hands and plus bat speed allow him to drive the ball with power into the gaps, and eventually will produce home runs. He's a premium athlete with an aggressive nature and above-average tools behind the plate. He already shows advanced receiving skills, a plus arm and a quick release. One scout said Mathis' makeup is off the charts. Mathis needs minor adjustments at the plate in pitch recognition and situational hitting. Freak injuries–a broken hand in 2001 and broken cheekbone in 2002–ended his first two pro years, and he was worn down during the last month of his first full season. Mathis offers a unique combination of tools for a catcher and has the potential to be a two-way asset. He should move up the ladder rapidly alongside Kotchman.

Year	Club (League)	Class	AVG	G	AB	R	H	2B	3B	HR	RBI	BB	SO	SB	SLG	OBP
2001	Angels (AZL)	R	.304	7	23	1	7	1	0	0	3	2	4	0	.348	.346
	Provo (Pio)	R	.299	22	77	14	23	6	3	0	18	11	13	1	.455	.387
2002	Cedar Rapids (Mid)	A	.287	128	491	75	141	41	3	10	73	40	75	7	.444	.346
MINOR LEAGUE TOTALS			.289	157	591	90	171	48	6	10	94	53	92	8	.442	.351

5. Johan Santana, rhp

Born: Nov. 28, 1983. **Ht.:** 6-2. **Wt.:** 170. **Bats:** R. **Throws:** R. **Career Transactions:** Signed out of Dominican Republic by Angels, Sept. 2, 2000.

STEVE MOORE

Santana has grown two inches and added 20 pounds since signing for $700,000–and he's getting bigger. After leading the Rookie-level Arizona League in strikeouts in 2001, he finished third in the Midwest League last year. Licey manager and Red Sox advance scout Dave Jauss called Santana the best young prospect in the Dominican League. The ball screams out of Santana's hand, coming in as high as 98 mph. He pitches in the mid-90s and flirts with the upper 90s. He made progress with his plus slider last season and has the makings of an above-average changeup. With the help of pitching instructors Howie Gershberg and Mike Butcher, Santana eliminated the head jerk in his delivery. Santana has good control, filling the strike zone with three quality pitches, and needs to fine-tune his command to move the ball to different quadrants. He occasionally tips his changeup by slowing his arm speed. Similar to a young Ramon Martinez, Santana has frontline stuff and a projectable picher's frame. He'll head to Class A Rancho Cucamonga's rotation at the start of 2003.

Year	Club (League)	Class	W	L	ERA	G	GS	CG	SV	IP	H	R	ER	HR	BB	SO	AVG
2001	Angels (AZL)	R	3	2	3.22	10	9	1	0	59	40	27	21	0	35	69	.184
	Provo (Pio)	R	2	1	7.71	4	4	0	0	19	19	17	16	1	12	22	.247
2002	Cedar Rapids (Mid)	A	14	8	4.16	27	27	0	0	147	133	75	68	10	48	146	.240
MINOR LEAGUE TOTALS			19	11	4.21	41	40	1	0	224	192	119	105	11	95	237	.226

6. Dallas McPherson, 3b

Born: July 23, 1980. **Ht.:** 6-4. **Wt.:** 210. **Bats:** L. **Throws:** R. **School:** The Citadel. **Career Transactions:** Selected by Angels in second round of 2001 draft; signed June 18, 2001.

JOHN SPEAR

In the Angels' evaluation system, only three points separated McPherson from 2001 first-rounders Casey Kotchman and Jeff Mathis. Anaheim considered all of them with the No. 13 pick and managed to land all three. Several teams also coveted McPherson as a pitcher because he showed mid-90s velocity in the Cape Cod League. There's tremendous violence in McPherson's swing, which generates the best raw power in the system. He'll develop more game power as he harnesses his stroke, and he has shown improvement in that regard. Content to go to the opposite field in college, he's now pulling pitches with more authority. At third base, he sports an above-average arm and soft hands. McPherson didn't play third base much in college, and it showed in 2002. He has to improve his footwork and square up to take advantage of his arm strength, but they are subtle adjustments. Some scouts think McPherson is headed for first base or right field, and with Troy Glaus locked up at the hot corner, that would make sense. He could find himself in Double-A by the end of 2003 and knocking on the door in Anaheim in 2004.

Year	Club (League)	Class	AVG	G	AB	R	H	2B	3B	HR	RBI	BB	SO	SB	SLG	OBP
2001	Provo (Pio)	R	.395	31	124	30	49	11	0	5	29	12	22	1	.605	.449
2002	Cedar Rapids (Mid)	A	.277	132	499	71	138	24	3	15	88	78	128	30	.427	.381
MINOR LEAGUE TOTALS			.300	163	623	101	187	35	3	20	117	90	150	31	.462	.393

7. Joe Saunders, lhp

Born: June 16, 1981. **Ht.:** 6-3. **Wt.:** 200. **Bats:** L. **Throws:** L. **School:** Virginia Tech. **Career Transactions:** Selected by Angels in first round (12th overall) of 2002 draft; signed June 10, 2002.

Saunders was raw when the Phillies drafted him in the fifth round out of high school, but three years later he emerged as one of the most polished college lefties available. He went 12th overall in June and signed a predraft deal worth $1.825 million. Saunders can spot his 89-94 mph fastball to both sides of the plate, and he adds and subtracts from the velocity. He's aggressive inside. His best pitch is his changeup, which drops off the table and is thrown with the same arm speed as his fastball. Operating with a sound delivery and repeatable arm action, he has above-average command and action to all three of his offerings. If Saunders can improve the consistency of the break on his curveball, he could flash three plus pitches. If his curve doesn't come around, he may toy with a cutter. Because he isn't overpowering, he'll have to continue to be fine with his pitchers. Saunders is similar to Jarrod Washburn but more advanced at the same stage. He could join a prospect-laden rotation in Rancho Cucamonga and reach Double-A in the second half of 2003.

Year	Club (League)	Class	W	L	ERA	G	GS	CG	SV	IP	H	R	ER	HR	BB	SO	AVG
2002	Provo (Pio)	R	2	1	3.62	8	8	0	0	32	40	19	13	1	11	21	.305
	Cedar Rapids (Mid)	A	3	1	1.88	5	5	0	0	29	16	7	6	2	9	27	.168
MINOR LEAGUE TOTALS			5	2	2.80	13	13	0	0	61	56	26	19	3	20	48	.248

8. Rich Fischer, rhp

Born: Oct. 21, 1980. **Ht.:** 6-3. **Wt.:** 180. **Bats:** R. **Throws:** R. **School:** San Bernardino Valley (Calif.) JC. **Career Transactions:** Selected by Angels in 21st round of 2000 draft; signed June 9, 2000.

Fischer pitched all of 11 innings in junior college, but area scout Tim Corcoran liked his arm strength and action as a shortstop. He was solid in 2001, his first full season on the mound, and led the minors with four shutouts while finishing third in complete games and sixth in strikeouts in 2002. Fischer has made impressive progress. He pitches in the low 90s with severe finish to his fastball, and he tops out at 95 mph. He works with a plus changeup and above-average command, rare for a converted position player. He honed his delivery, improving his curveball life and depth. He uses his aggressive demeanor to go after hitters. Fischer occasionally drops his elbow when throwing his curve, causing it to flatten. His arm works free and easy, but the Angels should be cautious with his workload because he wasn't conditioned to throw many innings as an amateur. Though they're deep in pitching and received inquiries about him at the trade deadline, the Angels hung onto Fischer. He has lots of room for growth in velocity and approach.

Year	Club (League)	Class	W	L	ERA	G	GS	CG	SV	IP	H	R	ER	HR	BB	SO	AVG
2000	Butte (Pio)	R	3	5	5.91	18	13	1	1	70	103	63	46	8	26	45	.338
2001	Cedar Rapids (Mid)	A	9	7	4.20	20	20	2	0	131	131	73	61	8	33	97	.261
2002	Rancho Cucamonga (Cal)	A	7	8	3.50	19	19	5	0	131	118	61	51	14	29	138	.239
	Arkansas (TL)	AA	1	3	4.23	7	7	0	0	45	40	22	21	8	10	36	.233
MINOR LEAGUE TOTALS			20	23	4.28	64	59	8	1	376	392	219	179	38	98	316	.266

9. Joe Torres, lhp

Born: Sept. 3, 1982. **Ht.:** 6-2. **Wt.:** 180. **Bats:** L. **Throws:** L. **School:** Gateway HS, Kissimmee, Fla. **Career Transactions:** Selected by Angels in first round (10th overall) of 2000 draft; signed June 21, 2000.

Torres has gone the wrong way since ranking No. 1 on this list after his debut season. He hasn't approached the 96 mph he hit in 2000, though he made strides in 2002 despite pitching without his best stuff. Torres spent most of 2002 at 87-88 mph, touching 91, which forced him to a finesse approach. From a low three-quarters release point and with whiplike arm action, he creates effective arm-side run and sink on his fastball. His curveball has the potential to be a double-plus pitch. He has outstanding work habits. Because his delivery went haywire, Torres spent the offseason in yoga classes to gain flexibility. He lost arm speed and extension out front, costing him velocity on his fastball and bite on his curveball. His changeup is slightly below-average. Angels scouts were impressed with Torres during offseason workouts and expect him to show up in spring training looking more like the pitcher they signed to a $2.08 million bonus. If things click for him in high Class A, he'll catapult his way back into the system's upper echelon.

Year	Club (League)	Class	W	L	ERA	G	GS	CG	SV	IP	H	R	ER	HR	BB	SO	AVG
2000	Boise (NWL)	A	4	1	2.54	11	10	0	0	46	27	17	13	0	23	52	.170
2001	Cedar Rapids (Mid)	A	0	3	5.82	4	4	0	0	17	16	12	11	0	14	14	.258
	Provo (Pio)	R	2	2	4.02	9	8	0	0	31	32	20	14	2	15	39	.260
2002	Cedar Rapids (Mid)	A	11	8	3.52	25	25	0	0	133	125	73	52	7	66	87	.251
MINOR LEAGUE TOTALS			17	14	3.56	49	47	0	0	227	200	122	90	9	118	192	.237

10. Chris Bootcheck, rhp

Born: Oct. 24, 1978. **Ht.:** 6-5. **Wt.:** 200. **Bats:** R. **Throws:** R. **School:** Auburn University. **Career Transactions:** Selected by Angels in first round (20th overall) of 2000 draft; signed Sept. 13, 2000.

Bootcheck, whose father Dan pitched in the Tigers system in the 1970s, started 2002 in Double-A. Despite a subpar performance, he earned a promotion to Triple-A Salt Lake, where he improved under pitching coach Mike Butcher. Bootcheck was at his best in the Pacific Coast League playoffs, fanning 16 in 11 innings. A good athlete, Bootcheck could have played Division I basketball. He's lean and loose on the mound, with a sound delivery and an arm that works well. He regained some velocity and established a two-seam fastball while tightening his cutter. His fastball touches 94 mph and sits in the 89-92 range. Bootcheck fell in love with his changeup after relying heavily on an 86-87 mph darting slider in college, and it cost him some of his aggressiveness. His breaking ball isn't as sharp as it was at Auburn. Bootcheck will return to Triple-A, where the Angels hope he'll maintain a power mindset while working with Butcher for a full season. Bootcheck could be a solid No. 4 starter in the big leagues.

Year	Club (League)	Class	W	L	ERA	G	GS	CG	SV	IP	H	R	ER	HR	BB	SO	AVG
2001	Rancho Cucamonga (Cal)	A	8	4	3.93	15	14	1	0	87	84	45	38	11	23	86	.251
	Arkansas (TL)	AA	3	3	5.45	6	6	1	0	36	39	25	22	3	11	22	.265
2002	Arkansas (TL)	AA	8	7	4.81	19	19	3	0	116	130	68	62	11	35	90	.277
	Salt Lake (PCL)	AAA	4	3	3.88	9	9	1	0	58	64	29	25	5	16	38	.283
MINOR LEAGUE TOTALS			23	17	4.45	49	48	6	0	297	317	167	147	30	85	236	.269

11. Steven Shell, rhp

Born: March 10, 1983. **Ht.:** 6-5. **Wt.:** 190. **Bats:** R. **Throws:** R. **School:** El Reno (Okla.) HS. **Career Transactions:** Selected by Angels in third round of 2001 draft; signed June 17, 2001.

Shell had the look of a raw high school product when he made his pro debut in 2001, but scouts coveted him for his effortless delivery and clean arm action. He was the best pitcher in Anaheim's minor league camp last spring, which prompted his jump to low Class A for his first full season. Shell won his first three starts and remained consistent for most of the summer before suffering from elbow soreness in August. The Angels kept him out of game action, though he was throwing bullpens at full strength during the Midwest League playoffs. His 89-93 mph fastball appears even quicker because the ball comes out of his hand so easily. Scouts project his velocity to increase to 92-95 as he fills out his flat-chested, lean frame. He added a two-seam fastball to complement his riding four-seamer and started getting a lot of groundouts. His spike curveball has plus potential with good, late depth. He still needs to gain consistency with it, however, as he occasionally guides the pitch, which causes it to roll instead of bite. He shows a feel for an average changeup. Still inexperienced, Shell must develop a game plan on the mound and learn how to put hitters away. When he figures that out, one veteran scout says, Shell has an opportunity to be better than Johan Santana. He'll head to high Class A in 2003 and should progress one level at a time.

Year	Club (League)	Class	W	L	ERA	G	GS	CG	SV	IP	H	R	ER	HR	BB	SO	AVG
2001	Angels (AZL)	R	1	0	0.00	3	0	0	0	4	1	0	0	0	2	3	.077
	Provo (Pio)	R	0	3	7.17	14	4	0	1	38	52	31	30	3	15	33	.331
2002	Cedar Rapids (Mid)	A	11	4	3.72	22	21	1	0	121	119	59	50	12	26	86	.255
MINOR LEAGUE TOTALS			12	7	4.43	39	25	1	1	163	172	90	80	15	43	122	.270

12. Rafael Rodriguez, rhp

Born: Sept. 24, 1984. **Ht.:** 6-1. **Wt.:** 170. **Bats:** R. **Throws:** R. **Career Transactions:** Signed out of Dominican Republic by Angels, July 20, 2001.

Discovered by Dominican scout Leo Perez, Rodriguez signed for $780,000 after scouting director Donny Rowland and international scouting supervisor Clay Daniel watched him throw during a workout. Rodriguez made his pro debut last summer after pitching in instructional league following the 2001 season. At 17, he was among the youngest players in the minors. Rodriguez has outstanding arm speed and touched 97 mph during his short stay in the Arizona League. His fastball regularly dwells in the 91-95 range, though commanding his heater to both sides of the plate is still an issue. Rodriguez tends to rush his delivery and his mechanics as a whole need some tinkering. His slider can be downright nasty with tight spin and late bite in the zone. He shows a feel for a deceptive changeup by maintaining his fastball arm speed. The Angels don't plan on pushing Rodriguez, who pitched in their Dominican instructional program during the offseason. He has a chance to open 2003 in low Class A, which would be a big jump.

Year	Club (League)	Class	W	L	ERA	G	GS	CG	SV	IP	H	R	ER	HR	BB	SO	AVG
2002	Angels (AZL)	R	2	1	3.99	8	8	0	0	38	37	19	17	4	20	50	.255
	Provo (Pio)	R	1	1	5.96	6	6	0	0	26	26	17	17	3	14	25	.268
MINOR LEAGUE TOTALS			3	2	4.78	14	14	0	0	64	63	36	34	7	34	75	.260

13. Brendan Donnelly, rhp

Born: July 4, 1971. **Ht.:** 6-3. **Wt.:** 200. **Bats:** R. **Throws:** R. **School:** Mesa State (Colo.) College. **Career Transactions:** Selected by White Sox in 27th round of 1992 draft; signed June 9, 1992 . . . Released by White Sox, April 16, 1993 . . . Signed by Cubs, June 16, 1993 . . . Released by Cubs, March 29, 1994 . . . Signed by independent Ohio Valley (Frontier), July 1994 . . . Signed by Reds, March 4, 1995 . . . Granted free agency, Oct. 16, 1998; re-signedby Reds, March 15, 1999 . . . Released by Reds, April 3, 1999 . . . Signed by independent Nashua (Atlantic), May 1999 . . . Contract purchased by Devil Rays from Nashua, May 15, 1999 . . . Released by Devil Rays, Aug. 12, 1999 . . . Signed by Pirates, Aug. 18, 1999 . . . Released by Pirates, Aug. 25, 1999 . . . Signed by Blue Jays, Aug. 26, 1999 . . . Released by Blue Jays, July 28, 2000 . . . Signed by Cubs, Aug. 10, 2000 . . . Granted free agency, Oct. 15, 2000 . . . Signed by Angels, Jan. 20, 2001.

Though he's not a rookie by service time, Donnelly qualifies for this list because at 49⅔ innings he hasn't exceeded the playing-time limit of 50. Entering 2002, he wasn't considered much more than a journeyman. After he was released six times—including once by Tampa Bay to make room for "The Rookie," Jim Morris—and making two trips to independent leagues, a big league cameo, let alone prospect status, didn't appear to be in Donnelly's future. He has been around so long that Angels minor league hitting instructor Bobby Magallanes remembers facing him during his minor league career. Donnelly pitched well in spring training, earning a look in middle relief in April. He returned to Triple-A as his velocity dipped and it wasn't until July, when he tossed 12 scoreless innings out of the Angels bullpen, that he regained his low- to mid-90s heat and pitched in meaningful innings. By the end of the year, he was the main set-up man for Troy Percival. After persevering in the minors for a decade, Donnelly is aggressive on the mound. One of the turning points for him was altering the grip on his upper-80s slider. His command and control also improved. He displays the confidence to challenge major league hitters. While Francisco Rodriguez may steal his eighth-inning role, Donnelly will be an important bullpen workhorse in Anaheim.

Year	Club (League)	Class	W	L	ERA	G	GS	CG	SV	IP	H	R	ER	HR	BB	SO	AVG
1992	White Sox (GCL)	R	0	3	3.67	9	7	0	1	42	41	25	17	0	21	31	.256
1993	Geneva (NY-P)	A	4	0	6.28	21	3	0	1	43	39	34	30	4	29	29	.242
1994	Ohio Valley (Fron)	IND	1	1	2.63	10	0	0	0	14	13	5	4	1	4	20	.250
1995	Charleston, (SAL)	A	1	1	1.19	24	0	0	12	30	14	4	4	0	7	33	.139
	Winston-Salem (Car)	A	1	2	1.02	23	0	0	2	35	20	6	4	1	14	32	.167
	Indianapolis (AA)	AAA	1	1	23.63	3	0	0	0	3	7	8	7	2	2	1	.500
1996	Chattanooga (SL)	AA	1	2	5.52	22	0	0	0	29	27	21	18	4	17	22	.237
1997	Chattanooga (SL)	AA	6	4	3.27	62	0	0	6	83	71	43	30	6	37	64	.228
1998	Chattanooga (SL)	AA	2	5	2.98	38	0	0	13	45	43	16	15	4	24	47	.247
	Indianapolis (IL)	AAA	4	1	2.65	19	1	0	0	37	29	16	11	3	16	39	.212
1999	Nashua (Atl)	IND	0	0	3.00	3	0	0	0	3	1	1	1	1	3	4	.125
	Durham (IL)	AAA	5	5	3.05	37	1	0	2	62	53	23	21	5	18	61	.240
	Altoona (EL)	AA	0	0	7.71	2	0	0	1	2	4	2	2	0	2	0	.571
	Syracuse (IL)	AAA	0	1	2.89	5	0	0	0	9	8	4	3	1	4	9	.242
2000	Syracuse (IL)	AAA	4	6	5.48	37	0	0	0	43	47	34	26	5	27	34	.278
	Iowa (PCL)	AAA	0	3	7.56	9	0	0	1	17	25	19	14	3	6	14	.338
2001	Arkansas (TL)	AA	4	1	2.48	27	0	0	12	29	21	8	8	2	13	37	.200
	Salt Lake (PCL)	AAA	5	1	2.40	29	0	0	1	41	38	11	11	4	8	50	.245
2002	Salt Lake (PCL)	AAA	4	0	3.48	25	0	0	6	34	27	13	13	5	11	42	.213
	Anaheim (AL)	MAJ	1	1	2.17	46	0	0	1	50	32	13	12	2	19	54	.184
MAJOR LEAGUE TOTALS			1	1	2.17	46	0	0	1	50	32	13	12	2	19	54	.184
MINOR LEAGUE TOTALS			42	36	3.60	392	12	0	58	585	514	287	234	49	256	545	.235

14. Derrick Turnbow, rhp

Born: Jan. 25, 1978. **Ht.:** 6-3. **Wt.:** 210. **Bats:** R. **Throws:** R. **School:** Franklin (Tenn.) HS. **Career Transactions:** Selected by Phillies in fifth round of 1997 draft; signed July 4, 1997 . . . Selected by Angels from Phillies in major league Rule 5 draft, Dec. 13, 1999.

There's still time for Turnbow to pay dividends. After spending all of 2000 in a mopup role in the Anaheim bullpen, his last two seasons have been marred by injuries. He broke the ulna in his right arm three starts into 2001, but his 99 mph fastballs indicated he was set to return last spring. Just when things were looking up, he experienced a setback and had pins permanently set in his ailing forearm. He spent a second straight season rehabbing and hit his stride by mid-August. Turnbow was up to 98 mph in the Arizona Fall League, and showed the resilience to hit 96 with just one day of rest. He has a second out pitch in his slider, though it's not reliable yet. He lacks a quality third offering. Turnbow is taller in his delivery than when he first joined the organization, allowing him to use more of a downhill plane on his pitches. The injuries have taken their toll on his arm action, which isn't as fluid as it once was. If he can hold up over a full season, the Angels' stockpile of late-inning power relievers could make him expendable. When he's right, he draws comparisons to Matt Anderson. Turnbow's command might prevent him from ever pitching in the ninth inning, however.

Year	Club (League)	Class	W	L	ERA	G	GS	CG	SV	IP	H	R	ER	HR	BB	SO	AVG
1997	Martinsville (Appy)	R	1	3	7.40	7	7	0	0	24	34	29	20	5	16	7	.354
1998	Martinsville (Appy)	R	2	6	5.01	13	13	1	0	70	66	44	39	7	26	45	.249
1999	Piedmont (SAL)	A	12	8	3.35	26	26	4	0	161	130	67	60	10	53	149	.221
2000	Anaheim (AL)	MAJ	0	0	4.74	24	1	0	0	38	36	21	20	7	36	25	.254
2001	Arkansas (TL)	AA	0	0	2.57	3	3	0	0	14	12	4	4	0	5	11	.240
2002	Angels (AZL)	R	0	1	4.50	3	3	0	0	8	5	5	4	0	3	12	.161
	Rancho Cucamonga (Cal)	A	0	0	5.25	13	0	0	0	12	16	11	7	1	9	14	.320
MAJOR LEAGUE TOTALS			0	0	4.74	24	1	0	0	38	36	21	20	7	36	25	.254
MINOR LEAGUE TOTALS			15	18	4.17	65	52	5	0	289	263	160	134	23	112	238	.244

15. Jake Woods, lhp

Born: Sept. 3, 1981. **Ht.:** 6-1. **Wt.:** 190. **Bats:** L. **Throws:** L. **School:** Bakersfield (Calif.) JC. **Career Transactions:** Selected by Angels in third round of 2001 draft; signed June 13, 2001.

Woods became the third pitcher in three years drafted in the top three rounds out of Bakersfield JC, with Colby Lewis (Rangers, 1999) and Phil Dumatrait (Red Sox, 2000) preceding Woods. Woods broke Dumatrait's school record for strikeouts as a sophomore. Cut from a similar mold as big league lefties Mike Stanton and Terry Mulholland, Woods doesn't project to add much more velocity to his 87-92 mph fastball. While his ceiling isn't considered high, most scouts believe there's little risk involved in profiling Woods as a back-of-the-rotation starter or middle reliever. He's already a polished strike-thrower. His fastball features run and sink, offering a good complement to his best pitch—a plus curveball—and average changeup. Woods operates with a full-throttle delivery, expending a lot of effort on every pitch, which could limit his workload down the road. He averaged less than six innings per start last year. The Angels plan to keep him in the rotation in high Class A this season.

Year	Club (League)	Class	W	L	ERA	G	GS	CG	SV	IP	H	R	ER	HR	BB	SO	AVG
2001	Provo (Pio)	R	4	3	5.29	15	14	1	0	65	70	41	38	6	29	84	.275
2002	Cedar Rapids (Mid)	A	10	5	3.05	27	27	1	0	153	128	66	52	12	54	121	.228
MINOR LEAGUE TOTALS			14	8	3.72	42	41	2	0	218	198	107	90	18	83	205	.243

16. Nathan Haynes, of

Born: Sept. 7, 1979. **Ht.:** 5-9. **Wt.:** 170. **Bats:** L. **Throws:** L. **School:** Pinole Valley HS, Pinole, Calif. **Career Transactions:** Selected by Athletics in first round (32nd overall) of 1997 draft; signed June 14, 1997 . . . Traded by Athletics with OF Jeff DaVanon and RHP Elvin Nina to Angels for RHP Omar Olivares and 2B Randy Velarde, July 29, 1999.

Injuries have limited Haynes to just one full season in the last four. He was out of action for most of 1999 with a career-threatening sports hernia, and he missed three weeks in 2000 with wrist and shoulder injuries. He has had arthroscopic surgery on both knees and last spring, when he was making a good impression in big league camp, he tore a ligament in his left thumb and didn't return until June. Haynes is still a plus runner. While scouts can't figure out why he doesn't steal more bases, he uses his speed effectively to track down balls in center field. At the plate, Haynes hits line drives but lacks pop. Because he hasn't developed into a more disciplined hitter to hit atop the order, and his sub-.400 career slugging percentage isn't enough for a corner, he profiles as a reserve outfielder. For all his injuries, he has six years under his belt and is still just 23. It's back to Triple-A in 2003, unless Haynes can show he's capable of handling Orlando Palmeiro's duties as an extra outfielder and left-handed pinch-hitter.

Year	Club (League)	Class	AVG	G	AB	R	H	2B	3B	HR	RBI	BB	SO	SB	SLG	OBP
1997	Athletics (AZL)	R	.278	17	54	8	15	1	0	0	6	7	9	5	.296	.381
	Southern Oregon (NWL)	A	.280	24	82	18	23	1	1	0	9	26	21	19	.317	.459
1998	Modesto (Cal)	A	.252	125	507	89	128	13	7	1	41	54	139	42	.312	.328
1999	Visalia (Cal)	A	.310	35	145	28	45	7	1	1	14	17	27	12	.393	.392
	Lake Elsinore (Cal)	A	.327	26	110	19	36	5	5	1	15	12	19	10	.491	.395
	Erie (EL)	AA	.158	5	19	3	3	1	0	0	0	5	5	0	.211	.360

			AVG	G	AB	R	H	2B	3B	HR	RBI	BB	SO	SB	SLG	OBP
2000	Erie (EL)	AA	.254	118	457	56	116	16	4	6	43	33	107	37	.346	.315
2001	Arkansas (TL)	AA	.310	79	316	49	98	11	5	5	23	32	65	33	.424	.379
2002	Rancho Cucamonga (Cal)	A	.280	11	50	6	14	0	0	0	2	4	8	6	.280	.345
	Salt Lake (PCL)	AAA	.283	67	283	37	80	14	6	2	12	12	53	10	.396	.313
MINOR LEAGUE TOTALS			.276	507	2023	313	558	69	29	16	165	202	453	174	.362	.348

17. Robb Quinlan, of

Born: March 17, 1977. **Ht.:** 6-1. **Wt.:** 200. **Bats:** R. **Throws:** R. **School:** University of Minnesota. **Career Transactions:** Selected by Angels in 10th round of 1999 draft; signed June 10, 1999.

After setting the Minnesota single-season home run record with 24 as a junior, Quinlan was overlooked in the 1998 draft. He showed scouts he could swing a wood bat by leading the Northwoods League in homers that summer, then led the Big 10 Conference in batting (.413) and RBIs (84) and was league MVP as a senior. The Angels, who also selected him in the 56th round out of high school, finally took him in the 10th round. Quinlan has continued to hit and won MVP honors in the short-season Northwest League in his pro debut and again in the Pacific Coast League last year. Quinlan, whose older brother Tom spent parts of four seasons in the majors, has good bat speed and uses the whole field. He's the type of player who grows on you, according to one scout who compared Quinlan to Dustan Mohr and Shane Spencer. The Angels will give him the opportunity to grow in front of their eyes in spring training. Quinlan's lack of speed and arm strength limit him in the outfield, and he's not gifted with the glove in the infield. He played third base earlier in his career and saw time at first base in 2002. With the Angels re-signing Brad Fullmer, Quinlan's shot at a DH role may have evaporated.

Year	Club (League)	Class	AVG	G	AB	R	H	2B	3B	HR	RBI	BB	SO	SB	SLG	OBP
1999	Boise (NWL)	A	.322	73	295	51	95	20	1	9	77	35	52	5	.488	.400
2000	Lake Elsinore (Cal)	A	.317	127	482	79	153	35	5	5	85	67	82	6	.442	.396
2001	Arkansas (TL)	AA	.295	129	492	82	145	33	7	14	79	53	84	0	.476	.366
2002	Salt Lake (PCL)	AAA	.333	136	528	95	176	31	13	20	112	41	93	8	.555	.376
MINOR LEAGUE TOTALS			.317	465	1797	307	569	119	26	48	353	196	311	19	.492	.383

18. Quan Cosby, of

Born: Dec. 23, 1982. **Ht.:** 5-10. **Wt.:** 180. **Bats:** B. **Throws:** R. **School:** Mart (Texas) HS. **Career Transactions:** Selected by Angels in sixth round of 2001 draft; signed June 6, 2001.

Cosby is one of the top all-around athletes in baseball. He was the first player in Texas prep football history to earn all-state honors at three positions (quarterback, defensive back and kick returner) in consecutive seasons. He amassed 6,177 yards of offense between his junior and senior seasons and scored 48 touchdowns in leading Mart High to the state 2-A title as a senior. He also won 2-A championships in the 100 meters (10.46 seconds) and 200 meters (21.31), and managed to find time to hit close to .500 and steal 81 bases in 82 attempts. He also can bench-press 370 pounds. Both of his brothers, including twin Quincy, were also standouts on the gridiron for Mart. Quan turned down an opportunity to play wide receiver at the University of Texas to sign a baseball-only deal worth $850,000. Cosby has blown away scouts and pleasantly surprised the Angels with the progress he has made since signing. He was untested as an amateur, and most scouts saw more raw tools than baseball skills. Yet he showed a good idea at the plate last year by reaching base at a .404 clip. He has made impressive strides in reading and recognizing pitches, though he still needs to make more consistent contact. Angels scouts rave about Cosby's aptitude and intelligence as much as his tools. He has pull-power potential batting righthanded, while he looks to be more of a line-drive hitter from the left. He also has improved in center field, where he has outstanding range. His arm strength is below-average but is getting better and could be average as he loosens his arm. With Cosby's ability to get on base and his top-of-the-line speed, the Angels envision him as a top-of-the-order threat, though they realize he is a long way from the majors.

Year	Club (League)	Class	AVG	G	AB	R	H	2B	3B	HR	RBI	BB	SO	SB	SLG	OBP
2001	Angels (AZL)	R	.243	41	148	21	36	4	1	0	8	9	40	8	.284	.289
2002	Provo (Pio)	R	.302	76	291	66	88	9	4	0	29	45	62	22	.361	.404
MINOR LEAGUE TOTALS			.282	117	439	87	124	13	5	0	37	54	102	30	.335	.367

19. Nick Touchstone, lhp

Born: Nov. 19, 1981. **Ht.:** 6-5. **Wt.:** 220. **Bats:** L. **Throws:** L. **School:** Okaloosa-Walton (Fla.) CC. **Career Transactions:** Selected by Angels in 18th round of 2002 draft; signed Oct. 2, 2002.

Touchstone turned down a six-figure bonus as a Yankees 2001 draft-and-follow and went to the Cape Cod League to improve his status after lasting until the 18th round of the 2002 draft. He had a 1.69 ERA with 33 strikeouts in 32 innings on the Cape, prompting the Angels to up their offer to $300,000. They signed Touchstone and another hard-throwing lefty, Scott Hindman (22nd round, Princeton), out of the Cape on the same day. In addition to first-rounder Joe Saunders, Touchstone and Hindman, the Angels addressed an organization weakness with an influx of promising southpaws last summer. The group included 2001 draft-and-follow Micah Posey and 2002 third-rounder Kyle Pawelczyk. Saunders aside, Touchstone leads the group with a fastball that has been clocked as high as 95 mph. He also flashes an above-average curveball. His power arm action isn't as clean as the silky smooth Pawelczyk, which has led to some command problems. Touchstone could launch his pro career in low Class A this year if he performs well in spring training performances. His command will dictate how quickly he advances.

Year	Club (League)	Class	W	L	ERA	G	GS	CG	SV	IP	H	R	ER	HR	BB	SO	AVG
					Has Not Played—Signed 2003 Contract												

20. Brian Specht, ss

Born: Oct. 19, 1980. **Ht.:** 5-11. **Wt.:** 170. **Bats:** B. **Throws:** R. **School:** Doherty HS, Colorado Springs. **Career Transactions:** Selected by Angels in ninth round of 1999 draft; signed July 14, 1999.

Specht has been rushed since spurning a commitment to Baylor for a $600,000 bonus. He began his pro career in high Class A, unusual for a player less than a year removed from high school. He skyrocketed to No. 3 on this list after his debut but has been hampered by shoulder problems ever since. Some scouts compare Specht to Adam Kennedy because his future is predicated on his ability as an offensive middle infielder. While Kennedy hit .309 in the minors, though, Specht has a career .255 average. He has a smooth stroke from both sides of the plate, though it occasionally collapses, leading to lazy fly balls to the opposite field. The Angels plan to keep him at shortstop until he proves he can't handle the position. He's steady in the field, catching what he gets to, but won't make many spectacular plays. His arm strength, which was a plus, is now short on tough plays in the hole or up the middle. His defense will be a half-grade better if he moves across the bag to second base. After having arthroscopic surgery on his labrum, Specht might miss the first week of spring training.

Year	Club (League)	Class	AVG	G	AB	R	H	2B	3B	HR	RBI	BB	SO	SB	SLG	OBP
2000	Lake Elsinore (Cal)	A	.269	89	334	70	90	22	5	2	35	52	80	25	.383	.370
2001	Rancho Cucamonga (Cal)	A	.242	65	264	45	64	13	6	7	31	24	78	17	.417	.312
	Arkansas (TL)	AA	.265	45	155	14	41	9	2	2	15	13	32	2	.387	.325
2002	Arkansas (TL)	AA	.248	126	476	64	118	24	4	13	60	49	129	18	.397	.321
MINOR LEAGUE TOTALS			.255	325	1229	193	313	68	17	24	141	138	319	62	.396	.333

21. Eric Aybar, ss

Born: Jan. 14, 1984. **Ht.:** 5-11. **Wt.:** 160. **Bats:** B. **Throws:** R. **Career Transactions:** Signed out of Dominican Republic by Angels, Feb. 4, 2002.

Aybar's older brother Willy signed with the Dodgers in January 2000 for a then-Dominican record $1.4 million bonus. Two years later, with less fanfare, the Angels landed Eric for $100,000. He got his career off to a tremendous start by finishing among the top 10 in the Rookie-level Pioneer League in hitting, triples, runs and total bases. Aybar is a natural shortstop with above-average feet and hands. His arm is solid average and he's capable of making accurate throws on the run from different angles. A plus runner, Aybar needs to improve his technique to be a successful basestealer at higher levels. Offensively, he has good bat speed and a nice stroke from both sides of the plate. He tends to be too much of a free swinger, and the Angels have him working on bunting to take advantage of his wheels. He'll move up to low Class A this year and probably will need a full year at every level.

Year	Club (League)	Class	AVG	G	AB	R	H	2B	3B	HR	RBI	BB	SO	SB	SLG	OBP
2002	Provo (Pio)	R	.326	67	273	64	89	15	6	4	29	21	43	15	.469	.395
MINOR LEAGUE TOTALS			.326	67	273	64	89	15	6	4	29	21	43	15	.469	.395

22. Alfredo Amezaga, ss

Born: Jan. 16, 1978. **Ht.:** 5-10. **Wt.:** 160. **Bats:** B. **Throws:** R. **School:** St. Petersburg (Fla.) JC. **Career Transactions:** Selected by Angels in 13th round of 1999 draft; signed June 4, 1999.

Ranked as the organization's No. 6 prospect a year ago, Amezaga didn't have much go his way in 2002. Adam Kennedy and David Eckstein cemented their roles as the Angels' double-play combo, and while Amezaga went 7-for-13 during his brief time in the majors, Anaheim chose the faster Chone Figgins for the 25th spot on its postseason roster. The Angels credit Amezaga with handling the decision well and soaking up valuable experience from the bench throughout the championship run. Some scouts still project him as an everyday player, while others think he profiles better in a utility role. He understands his limitations and plays the little game well. He uses his speed and bat control to make things happen. Amezaga's instincts and ability to play shortstop should give him the slight edge over Figgins in the long run, though he needs more offensive consistency.

Year	Club (League)	Class	AVG	G	AB	R	H	2B	3B	HR	RBI	BB	SO	SB	SLG	OBP
1999	Butte (Pio)	R	.294	8	34	11	10	2	0	0	5	5	5	6	.353	.400
	Boise (NWL)	A	.322	48	205	52	66	6	4	2	29	23	29	14	.420	.402
2000	Lake Elsinore (Cal)	A	.279	108	420	90	117	13	4	4	44	63	70	73	.357	.374
2001	Arkansas (TL)	AA	.312	70	285	50	89	10	5	4	21	22	55	24	.425	.370
	Salt Lake (PCL)	AAA	.250	49	200	28	50	5	4	1	16	14	45	9	.330	.307
2002	Salt Lake (PCL)	AAA	.251	128	518	77	130	25	7	6	51	45	100	23	.361	.317
	Anaheim (AL)	MAJ	.538	12	13	3	7	2	0	0	2	0	1	1	.692	.538
MAJOR LEAGUE TOTALS			.538	12	13	3	7	2	0	0	2	0	1	1	.692	.538
MINOR LEAGUE TOTALS			.278	411	1662	308	462	61	24	17	166	172	304	149	.374	.352

23. Alberto Callaspo, 2b

Born: April 19, 1983. **Ht.:** 5-10. **Wt.:** 160. **Bats:** R. **Throws:** R. **Career Transactions:** Signed out of Venezuela by Angels, Feb. 16, 2001.

Signed out of Venezuela by Amador Arias and Carlos Porte, Callaspo finished third in the Rookie-level Dominican Summer League with a .356 average in 2001. He continued to hit in his U.S. debut, leading the Pioneer League in hits, triples and runs. He combined with Eric Aybar to form what Provo manager Tom Kotchman called the best double-play combination he's had during his long career. Callaspo demonstrates a more advanced approach than Aybar at the plate. He works the count and is tough to strike out, though his ability to make contact limits his chances of drawing walks. His bat-handling skills include bunting. Callaspo has average speed and good baserunning instincts. He's not quite as flashy as Aybar in the field, but Callaspo has quick, sure hands and a solid arm. The two should move up the ladder together a level at a time, unless Callaspo hits enough to prompt a midseason jump at some point. They're both set to play in low Class A this year.

Year	Club (League)	Class	AVG	G	AB	R	H	2B	3B	HR	RBI	BB	SO	SB	SLG	OBP
2001	Angels (DSL)	R	.356	66	275	55	98	11	4	2	39	22	16	14	.447	.403
2002	Provo (Pio)	R	.338	70	299	70	101	16	10	3	60	17	14	13	.488	.374
MINOR LEAGUE TOTALS			.347	136	574	125	199	27	14	5	99	39	30	27	.469	.388

24. Kevin Jepsen, rhp

Born: July 26, 1984. **Ht.:** 6-3. **Wt.:** 210. **Bats:** R. **Throws:** R. **School:** Bishop Manogue HS, Sparks, Nev. **Career Transactions:** Selected by Angels in second round of 2002 draft; signed July 10, 2002.

The Anaheim scouting staff was on hand to watch the hype around Jepsen explode last spring. Crosschecker Mark Russo was in a frenzy when Jepsen registered 98 mph with a fastball and 91 with a slider. National supervisor Hank Sargent saw Jepsen touch 95 as a snowstorm brewed in another outing. Word spread fast as Jepsen's stock soared throughout the scouting community, and the Angels were thrilled to land him in the second round. After signing for $745,000, Jepsen topped out at 94 in the Arizona League but was just getting his arm back into top shape as the season ended. He's primarily a two-pitch power arm, and his delivery borders on maximum effort. Jepsen is a project, as his slider, changeup and command all need to improve, but his arm strength is intriguing. His future could be in the bullpen, but he'll stay in the rotation for now to build stamina and hone his arsenal. He's likely headed for Provo this summer after extended spring training.

Year	Club (League)	Class	W	L	ERA	G	GS	CG	SV	IP	H	R	ER	HR	BB	SO	AVG
2002	Angels (AZL)	R	1	3	6.84	8	5	0	0	26	29	22	20	3	12	19	.274
MINOR LEAGUE TOTALS			1	3	6.84	8	5	0	0	26	29	22	20	3	12	19	.274

25. Phil Wilson, rhp

Born: April 1, 1981. **Ht.:** 6-8. **Wt.:** 220. **Bats:** R. **Throws:** R. **School:** Poway (Calif.) HS. **Career Transactions:** Selected by Angels in third round of 1999 draft; signed Aug. 8, 1999.

For the second straight season, Wilson was forced to dig his way out of a hole after a horrific start. He made enough progress to earn a promotion to Double-A, but things went downhill from there. Wilson never showed his best stuff in 2002, and his season ended in August when he had arthroscopic elbow surgery. Maintaining and repeating his delivery has been the biggest issue for the gangly Wilson, who has sprouted four inches since he was a high school senior. He occasionally flies open in his delivery and leaves his arm lagging behind, which keeps his pitches up in the strike zone. He pitched mostly at 88-91 mph with sinking life last year and sank to 85 when he struggled. When he's on his game, he works in the low 90s. Wilson's command should improve as he learns to repeat his delivery, but for now control is an issue. He uncorked 18 wild pitches last year. Wilson's slurvy slider and changeup are decent offerings with average potential. He had a strained muscle in his right arm in high school, then shouldered a heavy workload during his first two years in the system. That may have contributed to his elbow soreness last season. To regain his prospect status, he has to stay healthy, improve his command and prove he can get Double-A hitters out.

Year	Club (League)	Class	W	L	ERA	G	GS	CG	SV	IP	H	R	ER	HR	BB	SO	AVG
2000	Cedar Rapids (Mid)	A	8	5	3.41	21	21	1	0	129	114	61	49	9	49	82	.238
	Lake Elsinore (Cal)	A	3	0	1.96	6	6	0	0	41	32	9	9	1	10	33	.212
2001	Rancho Cucamonga (Cal)	A	8	10	5.23	26	26	1	0	160	173	102	93	15	55	134	.276
	Arkansas (TL)	AA	1	1	11.37	2	2	0	0	6	10	12	8	1	6	5	.333
2002	Rancho Cucamonga (Cal)	A	5	5	5.53	14	14	1	0	86	93	62	53	13	29	71	.269
	Arkansas (TL)	AA	2	4	7.17	7	7	0	0	43	57	37	34	10	14	15	.315
MINOR LEAGUE TOTALS			27	25	4.75	76	76	3	0	466	479	283	246	49	163	340	.264

26. Nick Kimpton, of

Born: Oct. 27, 1983. **Ht.:** 6-1. **Wt.:** 170. **Bats:** L. **Throws:** L. **Career Transactions:** Signed out of Australia by Angels, Jan. 21, 2001.

Signed out of Australia by scout Grant Weir, Kimpton also pitched as an amateur. His bat is the reason he has become a favorite of general manager Bill Stoneman, though. Kimpton began last year in extended spring training and then started slowly at the plate. He skipped a level to become the youngest everyday player in the Midwest League. He has a good feel for the bat head, with loose wrists and sneaky pop. He shows the ability to drive the ball the other way, along with occasional pull power. But he's lean and physically immature, often looking overmatched at the plate. Angels scouts project his power to develop as he fills out, and some liken him to a young version of Steve Finley or Brady Anderson. Kimpton bunts effectively and is a plus runner. He's capable in all three outfield spots, with good instincts and enough arm for right field. He'll return to low Class A for a full season at age 19.

Year	Club (League)	Class	AVG	G	AB	R	H	2B	3B	HR	RBI	BB	SO	SB	SLG	OBP
2001	Angels (AZL)	R	.269	49	186	30	50	4	2	0	23	21	39	9	.312	.354
2002	Cedar Rapids (Mid)	A	.262	93	302	51	79	12	4	0	26	42	61	20	.328	.358
MINOR LEAGUE TOTALS			.264	142	488	81	129	16	6	0	49	63	100	29	.322	.357

27. Mike Brunet, rhp

Born: March 5, 1977. **Ht.:** 6-2. **Wt.:** 160. **Bats:** R. **Throws:** R. **School:** Pasco-Hernando (Fla.) CC. **Career Transactions:** Selected by Angels in fifth round of 1997 draft; signed Aug. 2, 1997 . . . On disabled list, June 20-Sept. 29, 2000 . . . On disabled list, June 15-Sept. 10, 2001.

Multiple back and elbow operations limited Brunet to 14 innings in his first four seasons. He missed all of 2000-01 recovering from back surgery and returned at full strength as a closer last year. He was exposed to the major league Rule 5 draft, and despite the fears of Angels scouts wasn't selected. Brunet attracted attention with his lightning-quick arm and 92-96 mph gas. His secondary stuff—a short, quick slider and diving splitter—is devastating on lefties, who managed a .151 average. His slider features such a late, abrupt break that it's often mistaken for his splitter. Brunet was handled with kid gloves last year. He never pitched on consecutive days, and a strict pitch count limited him to one-inning stints. With major league-caliber stuff, Brunet could make up for lost time provided he stays healthy.

Year	Club (League)	Class	W	L	ERA	G	GS	CG	SV	IP	H	R	ER	HR	BB	SO	AVG
1998	Boise (NWL)	A	0	0	10.80	4	0	0	0	3	4	4	4	1	3	4	.250
1999	Butte (Pio)	R	1	0	1.69	9	0	0	3	11	8	2	2	1	4	12	.205
2000					Did Not Play—Injured												
2001					Did Not Play—Injured												
2002	Rancho Cucamonga (Cal)	A	0	1	3.57	39	0	0	16	40	39	16	16	5	11	50	.252
MINOR LEAGUE TOTALS			1	1	3.64	52	0	0	19	54	51	22	22	7	18	66	.243

28. Chone Figgins, 2b

Born: Jan. 22, 1978. **Ht.:** 5-9. **Wt.:** 150. **Bats:** B. **Throws:** R. **School:** Brandon (Fla.) HS. **Career Transactions:** Selected by Rockies in fourth round of 1997 draft; signed June 9, 1997 . . . Traded by Rockies to Angels for OF Kimera Bartee, July 13, 2001.

When Anaheim acquired Figgins (whose first name is pronounced "shawn") from the Rockies for Kimera Bartee, a journeyman outfielder, the transaction barely attracted a mention in either city. Figgins wasn't considered much more than a fringe prospect in Colorado, and Bartee had failed to establish any kind of consistency since reaching the majors with the Tigers in 1996. Figgins broke through last year and found himself as the 25th man on the Angels' postseason roster, while the Rockies let Bartee go after the 2001 season. Figgins' game is predicated on his speed and quickness on the bases and in the field. Drafted as a shortstop, he moved to second base after making 45 errors in 1999. His arm is slightly below-average and his hands are decent, but he has work to do to become an average defender. At the plate, he's similar to Bip Roberts with pedestrian bat speed and little power. Figgins is capable of pulling line drives into the gaps for doubles and triples. He has double-plus raw speed but could be more aggressive. As a pinch-runner in the World Series, he made several mistakes on the bases. Figgins has a future as a utility infielder.

Year	Club (League)	Class	AVG	G	AB	R	H	2B	3B	HR	RBI	BB	SO	SB	SLG	OBP
1997	Rockies (AZL)	R	.280	54	214	41	60	5	6	1	23	35	51	30	.374	.386
1998	Portland (NWL)	A	.283	69	269	41	76	9	3	1	26	24	56	25	.349	.345
1999	Salem (Car)	A	.239	123	444	65	106	12	3	0	22	41	86	27	.279	.306
2000	Salem (Car)	A	.278	134	522	92	145	26	14	3	48	67	107	37	.398	.358
2001	Carolina (SL)	AA	.220	86	332	41	73	14	5	2	25	40	73	27	.310	.306
	Arkansas (TL)	AA	.268	39	138	21	37	12	2	0	12	14	26	7	.384	.329
2002	Salt Lake (PCL)	AAA	.305	125	511	100	156	25	18	7	62	53	83	39	.466	.364
	Anaheim (AL)	MAJ	.167	15	12	6	2	1	0	0	1	0	5	2	.250	.167
MAJOR LEAGUE TOTALS			.167	15	12	6	2	1	0	0	1	0	5	2	.250	.167
MINOR LEAGUE TOTALS			.269	630	2430	401	653	103	51	14	218	274	482	192	.370	.342

29. Jared Abruzzo, c

Born: Nov. 15, 1981. **Ht.:** 6-3. **Wt.:** 220. **Bats:** B. **Throws:** R. **School:** El Capitan HS, Lakeside, Calif. **Career Transactions:** Selected by Angels in second round of 2000 draft; signed June 20, 2000.

Abruzzo was overshadowed by Scott Heard when they were rival catchers at San Diego high schools, and Heard went one round ahead of him in the 2000 draft. Three years later, however, Abruzzo has made significantly greater strides toward the majors. The Angels signed him for $687,500 to keep him away from Louisiana State. He spent 2002 as one of the youngest backstops in the California League, where he shared time with the defensive-minded Ryan Budde. Though Abruzzo has above-average arm strength, he must improve his overall receiving skills. He has the work ethic necessary to get better, but some scouts say he's too hard on himself. He shows good pop from both sides of the plate, and unlike most reserve catchers it may be his bat rather than his defense that will carry him to the big leagues. He went to the Angels' Dominican instructional league program to work on building his confidence and concentration. With Jeff Mathis charging hard from the lower levels, Abruzzo will face stiff competition come spring training. He'll either platoon again with Budde in Double-A or back up Mathis and DH in high Class A this year.

Year	Club (League)	Class	AVG	G	AB	R	H	2B	3B	HR	RBI	BB	SO	SB	SLG	OBP
2000	Butte (Pio)	R	.255	62	208	46	53	11	0	8	45	61	58	1	.423	.423
2001	Cedar Rapids (Mid)	A	.241	87	323	41	78	20	0	10	53	44	104	1	.396	.340
	Rancho Cucamonga (Cal)	A	.208	28	101	13	21	1	0	2	13	9	30	1	.277	.270
2002	Rancho Cucamonga (Cal)	A	.244	101	385	53	94	27	0	16	53	30	124	1	.439	.300
MINOR LEAGUE TOTALS			.242	278	1017	153	246	59	0	36	164	144	316	4	.406	.339

30. Tommy Murphy, ss

Born: Aug. 27, 1979. **Ht.:** 6-0. **Wt.:** 180. **Bats:** R. **Throws:** R. **School:** Florida Atlantic University. **Career Transactions:** Selected by Angels in third round of 2000 draft; signed July 5, 2000.

Selected by scouting directors as Baseball America's 2000 preseason All-America shortstop, Murphy projected as a first-round pick. His draft status faded as he batted .319 with aluminum, raising questions about his ability to hit pro pitching. After signing for $440,000, he hasn't erased those doubts. He made progress last season, his second as a switch-hitter, from the left side of the plate. Carrying a .188 average into June, Murphy hit .311 in his last 325 at-bats. His average rose as he became more consistent with his lefthanded stroke. He improved in situational hitting, especially behind in the count, and with his zone recognition. He still lacks power and strikes out too much. Murphy's athleticism is what gets scouts going. He's the best defensive infielder in the system, and not many prospects can match his arm strength, which rates a 70 on the 20-80 scouting scale. He's a well-above-average runner with good basestealing ability. The Angels hoped to build confidence by sending Murphy back to low Class A last year, and they believe they accomplished that. Now it's time to challenge the 23-year-old, and they'd be ecstatic if he reaches Double-A by the end of the year. If Murphy continues to make progress with his hitting approach, his defense and speed can carry him to the majors as no worse than a versatile utilityman.

Year	Club (League)	Class	AVG	G	AB	R	H	2B	3B	HR	RBI	BB	SO	SB	SLG	OBP
2000	Boise (NWL)	A	.225	55	213	38	48	18	1	2	25	15	52	14	.347	.291
2001	Cedar Rapids (Mid)	A	.204	74	280	32	57	15	3	4	31	16	94	7	.321	.259
	Rancho Cucamonga (Cal)	A	.190	50	200	16	38	8	0	0	11	5	69	7	.230	.214
2002	Cedar Rapids (Mid)	A	.270	128	485	72	131	20	2	3	48	40	115	31	.338	.324
MINOR LEAGUE TOTALS			.233	307	1178	158	274	61	6	9	115	76	330	59	.317	.284

ARIZONA
DIAMONDBACKS

TOP 30 PROSPECTS
1. Scott Hairston, 2b
2. Mike Gosling, lhp
3. Lyle Overbay, 1b
4. John Patterson, rhp
5. Brandon Webb, rhp
6. Edgar Gonzalez, rhp
7. Sergio Santos, ss
8. Chad Tracy, 3b
9. Brian Bruney, rhp
10. Luis Terrero, of
11. Tim Olson, ss/of
12. Chris Snyder, c
13. Oscar Villarreal, rhp
14. Adriano Rosario, rhp
15. Jesus Cota, of/1b
16. Jose Valverde, rhp
17. Brian Barden, 3b
18. Brad Cresse, c
19. Dustin Nippert, rhp
20. Bill White, lhp
21. Andrew Good, rhp
22. Jared Doyle, lhp
23. Marland Williams, of
24. Robby Hammock, c/of
25. Beltran Perez, rhp
26. Alex Cintron, ss/2b
27. Lance Cormier, rhp
28. Greg Aquino, rhp
29. Josh Kroeger, of
30. Jerry Gil, ss

By Jack Magruder

After watching the Diamondbacks get beat up for 97 losses during their inaugural 1998 season, team owner Jerry Colangelo embarked on a four-year plan to win immediately. The trigger was a $119 million foray into the free-agent market that included the signings of Randy Johnson, Steve Finley, Greg Swindell and Todd Stottlemyre. Arizona understood its young farm system wouldn't be able to produce enough talent to compete soon enough to suit its taste.

At the major league level, the Diamondbacks got the results they desired. They've enjoyed four straight winning seasons, including three play-off appearances and the 2001 World Series championship.

The Diamondbacks believed that when they changed direction their system would be ready to supply a steady stream of talent by 2003 or 2004. There are signs that part of the plan is falling in place. While Arizona remains a veteran team, the upper levels of the farm system appear to have a growing reservoir of talent. That dovetails nicely with the next phase of Arizona's blueprint: to build through the system and with trades, with occasional free-agent signings.

Second baseman Junior Spivey and righthanders John Patterson and Mike Koplove made big league contributions in 2002, signaling the first charge of the minor leaguers. Spivey, a 30th-rounder from 1996, became the first Arizona draft choice to turn in a season-long, quality performance, hitting .301-16-78 with 11 steals. Patterson and Koplove became valuable assets in part-time duty last year, and both figure prominently in the team's plans for 2003 and beyond. Patterson will get every chance to make the rotation after the loss of four reliable arms over the winter. Koplove, who was so good that he was overworked in the second half of last season, will continue as a set-up specialist.

The organization used Erubiel Durazo in a trade to bring in Elmer Dessens to plug into the rotation. Lyle Overbay is expected to take over full-time at first base after batting .345 on his trek through the minors. Lefthander Mike Gosling and righthander Brandon Webb lead the next wave of pitchers.

"We have a lot of people who could come to camp and compete for a job in 2003," general manager Joe Garagiola Jr. said. That's the first time the Diamondbacks have been able to say that, though it's exactly what they were hoping all along.

Organization Overview

General Manager: Joe Garagiola, Jr. **Farm Director:** Tommy Jones. **Scouting Director:** Mike Rizzo.

2002 PERFORMANCE

Class	Farm Team	League	W	L	Pct.	Finish*	Manager(s)
Majors	Arizona	National	98	64	.605	2nd (16)	Bob Brenly
Triple-A	Tucson Sidewinders	Pacific Coast	73	68	.518	7th (16)	Al Pedrique
Double-A	El Paso Diablos	Texas	76	62	.551	2nd (8)	Chip Hale
High A	Lancaster Jet Hawks	California	63	77	.450	8th (10)	S. Scarsone/B. Plummer
Low A	South Bend Silver Hawks	Midwest	52	87	.374	14th (14)	Dick Schofield
Short-season	Yakima Bears	Northwest	23	53	.303	8th (8)	Mike Aldrete
Rookie	Missoula Osprey	Pioneer	35	41	.461	t-6th (8)	Jerry Hairston
OVERALL 2002 MINOR LEAGUE RECORD			322	388	.454	27th (30)	

*Finish in overall standings (No. of teams in league)

ORGANIZATION LEADERS

BATTING
*Minimum 250 At-Bats

*AVG	Scott Hairston, Lancaster/South Bend	.345
R	Scott Hairston, Lancaster/South Bend	99
H	Lyle Overbay, Tucson	180
TB	Scott Hairston, Lancaster/South Bend	285
2B	Scott Hairston, Lancaster/South Bend	46
3B	Victor Hall, El Paso/Lancaster	13
HR	Scott Hairston, Lancaster/South Bend	22
RBI	Lyle Overbay, Tucson	109
BB	Andy Green, Tucson/Lancaster	69
SO	Josh Kroeger, Lancaster	136
SB	Marland Williams, Yakima	51

PITCHING
#Minimum 75 Innings

W	Stephen Randolph, Tucson	15
L	Ryan Holsten, South Bend	13
#ERA	Edgar Gonzalez, Lancaster/South Bend	2.63
G	Javier Lopez, El Paso	61
CG	Edgar Gonzalez, Lancaster/South Bend	4
SV	Bret Prinz, Tucson/Lancaster	18
IP	Andrew Good, El Paso	178
BB	Stephen Randolph, Tucson	81
SO	Edgar Gonzalez, Lancaster/South Bend	131

BEST TOOLS

Best Hitter for Average	Lyle Overbay
Best Power Hitter	Sergio Santos
Fastest Baserunner	Marland Williams
Best Athlete	Marland Williams
Best Fastball	Brian Bruney
Best Curveball	John Patterson
Best Slider	Oscar Villareal
Best Changeup	Mike Gosling
Best Control	Edgar Gonzalez
Best Defensive Catcher	Chris Snyder
Best Defensive Infielder	Jerry Gil
Best Infield Arm	Jerry Gil
Best Defensive Outfielder	Luis Terrero
Best Outfield Arm	Luis Terrero

PROJECTED 2006 LINEUP

Catcher	Chris Snyder
First Base	Lyle Overbay
Second Base	Scott Hairston
Third Base	Chad Tracy
Shortstop	Sergio Santos
Left Field	Luis Gonzalez

Victor Hall

Stephen Randolph

Center Field	Luis Terrero
Right Field	Junior Spivey
No. 1 Starter	Curt Schilling
No. 2 Starter	Mike Gosling
No. 3 Starter	John Patterson
No. 4 Starter	Byung-Hyun Kim
No. 5 Starter	Brandon Webb
Closer	Brian Bruney

TOP PROSPECTS OF THE DECADE

1997	Travis Lee, 1b
1998	Travis Lee, 1b
1999	Brad Penny, rhp
2000	John Patterson, rhp
2001	Alex Cintron, ss
2002	Luis Terrero, of

TOP DRAFT PICKS OF THE DECADE

1996	Nick Bierbrodt, lhp
1997	Jack Cust, 1b
1998	Darryl Conyer, of (3)
1999	Corey Myers, ss
2000	Mike Schultz, rhp (2)
2001	Jason Bulger, rhp
2002	Sergio Santos, ss

ALL-TIME LARGEST BONUSES

Travis Lee, 1996	$10,000,000
John Patterson, 1996	$6,075,000
Byung-Hyun Kim, 1999	$2,000,000
Corey Myers, 1999	$2,000,000
Mike Gosling, 2001	$2,000,000

MinorLeagueDepthChart

ARIZONA DIAMONDBACKS

RANK 21

The Diamondbacks reached the postseason in three of their five years of existence with little help from a farm system that was regarded as the weakest in baseball two years ago. With an aging big league club and few blue-chip players on the horizon, there were worries about the future, but late bloomers like Erubiel Durazo, Junior Spivey and Lyle Overbay—all products of the maligned Donnie Mitchell scouting era—provided a boost. Arizona has hit more on low-round finds than with top draft picks Nick Bierbrodt, Jack Cust, Darryl Conyer, Corey Myers, Mike Schultz and Jason Bulger—who have combined to play eight games in the big leagues. Current scouting director Mike Rizzo has energized the system with three promising drafts.

Note: Depth charts prepared by Josh Boyd. Numbers in parentheses indicate prospect rankings.

LF
Jesus Cota (15)
Josh Kroeger (29)
Jarred Ball

CF
Luis Terrero (10)
Marland Williams (23)
Lino Garcia
Jay Garthwaite

RF
Doug Devore
Brian Gordon

3B
Chad Tracy (8)
Brian Barden (17)

SS
Sergio Santos (7)
Tim Olson (11)
Jerry Gil (30)
Joandry Berroa

2B
Scott Hairston (1)
Alex Cintron (26)
Matt Kata
Andy Green

1B
Lyle Overbay (3)
Corey Myers
Jeff Stanek

C
Chris Snyder (12)
Brad Cresse (18)
Robby Hammock (24)
Craig Ansman

RHP

Starters	Relievers
John Patterson (4)	Brian Bruney (9)
Brandon Webb (5)	Jose Valverde (16)
Edgar Gonzalez (6)	Greg Aquino (28)
Oscar Villarreal (13)	Jesus Silva
Adriano Rosario (14)	Jason Bulger
Dustin Nippert (19)	Corbey Medlin
Andrew Good (21)	Brandon Medders
Beltran Perez (25)	Jay Belflower
Lance Cormier (27)	Jeremy Ward
John Allender	
Mike Schultz	
Enrique Gonzalez	
Phil Stockman	
Ryan Holsten	
Justin Wechsler	
Matt Henrie	

LHP

Starters	Relievers
Mike Gosling (2)	Stephen Randolph
Bill White (20)	Chris Cervantes
Jared Doyle (22)	Doug Slaten
Chris Capuano	
Mark Rosen	
Tetsya Yamaguchi	

DraftAnalysis

2002 Draft

Best Pro Debut: Players almost never make all-star teams in high Class A in their draft year, but 3B Brian Barden (6) was an exception after hitting .335-8-46 in the California League. LHP Jared Doyle (3) went 4-4, 2.87, earning all-star honors in the short-season Northwest League. RHP Dustin Nippert (15) went 4-2, 1.65 with a 77-9 strikeout-walk ratio in 55 innings in Rookie ball.

Best Athlete: Barden is the best from the 2002 draft crop, but he's not in the class of OF Marland Williams, a 2001 draft-and-follow who's exceptional.

Best Pure Hitter: SS Sergio Santos (1) saw his stock dip as a senior. He got a rap for being a hot dog and unsignable, but the Diamondbacks couldn't be more pleased after he hit .272-9-37 in Rookie ball. His bat gets through the strike zone in a flash.

Best Raw Power: Santos drove balls out in every direction during a workout at Bank One Ballpark. The Diamondbacks say his power with wood grades out as an 80 on the 20-80 scouting scale.

Fastest Runner: Williams is a pure basestealer who's capable of running the 60-yard dash in 6.25 seconds. From the draft; Santos is the best runner at 6.8 seconds.

Best Defensive Player: The Diamondbacks rated Chris Snyder (2) as the best defensive catcher in the draft. He has some pop and hit .258-9-44 in the Cal League.

Best Fastball: Nippert pitched his way out of West Virginia's rotation, but area scout Greg Lonigro stayed on him because he's 6-foot-7 and was throwing in the low 90s. After

signing, Nippert's command improved and his velocity jumped to 98 mph. He worked at 93-96. Doyle topped out at 95, while LHP Mark Rosen (5) has reached 94–exceptional for a 17-year-old southpaw.

Best Breaking Ball: Rosen and Nippert both have power curveballs.

Most Intriguing Background: RHP Sam Smith's (19) grandfather Bob Smith pitched for four years in the majors. Doyle and his twin brother Nathan, a shortstop, helped James Madison to a school-record 44 victories in the spring.

Rosen

Closest To The Majors: Snyder, because of his defensive skills and bat, plus Arizona's need for catching help. Santos could move quickly for a high school hitter and may move to high Class A in 2003.

Best Late-Round Pick: Nippert.

The One Who Got Away: C Ryan Mahoney (8) has a strong 6-foot-4 frame and offers lefthanded power. He's at South Carolina, which has the top college catching prospect for 2003 in Landon Powell.

Assessment: The Diamondbacks signed just two high school players for the second straight year, but this time they landed premium talents in Santos and Rosen. They continue to focus on collegians to boost a thinned-out system, and Snyder, Doyle and Barden could rush through the minors.

2001 Draft

RHP Jason Bulger (1) looks like a bust. But 2B Scott Hairston (3) has been one of the best hitters in the minors since turning pro, and LHP Mike Gosling (2) and 3B Chad Tracy (7) also should reach Bank One Ballpark quickly. **Grade: A**

2000 Draft

The Diamondbacks had no first-rounder and C Brad Cresse (5) has faded after a brilliant start. But SS Tim Olson (7), RHPs Brandon Webb (8) and Brian Bruney (12) and draft-and-follow 1B/OF Jesus Cota (14) are a solid bunch. **Grade: C+**

1999 Draft

Overdrafting 1B/3B Corey Myers (1) rather than taking Ben Sheets fourth overall was a colossal blunder. Another first-rounder, RHP Casey Daigle, didn't work out either, but the Diamondbacks salvaged their starting 1B in Lyle Overbay (18). **Grade: C+**

1998 Draft

Lacking picks in the first two rounds, Arizona might as well have skipped round three rather than take OF Daryl Conyer, who no longer plays baseball. It did find some late-round bullpen help with RHPs Bret Prinz (18) and Mike Koplove (29). **Grade: C**

Note: Draft analysis prepared by Jim Callis. Numbers in parentheses indicate draft rounds.

... Hairston is even more valuable because of the exceptional wallop he provides for his position.

Scott
Hairston 2b

Born: May 25, 1980.
Ht.: 6-1. **Wt.:** 190.
Bats: R. **Throws:** R.
School: Central Arizona JC.
Career Transactions: Selected by Diamondbacks in third round of 2001 draft; signed June 15, 2001.

Hairston wasn't born with a bat in his hand—but he could have been. His baseball gene is as dominant as that of any Bell or Boone in the game. Hairston's grandfather Sam was a fixture in the Negro Leagues before getting a taste of the majors in 1951. His father Jerry Sr. was a 14-year major leaguer who managed the White Sox' Rookie-level Arizona League affiliate in 2002. His uncle John got four big league at-bats in 1969, while his brother Jerry Jr. starts at second base for the Orioles. Scott has the tools to surpass all of them. He won the Arizona junior college triple crown in 2001, then tied for the minor league lead with 73 extra-base hits and topped the Midwest League with a .426 on-base percentage in his first full pro season. One MWL manager compared him to Gary Sheffield.

Hairston is a strong, solidly built athlete with the physique of a running back. With a short, compact stroke, he can turn around any fastball and drive pitches to all parts of the ballpark. When pitchers stopped throwing him strikes at low Class A South Bend, he adjusted and took walks. Hairston has a good eye and above-average speed. While he is not the basestealing threat his brother is, he could swipe 10-15 bases a season. He's out of the Jeff Kent mold, a power-first second baseman made even more valuable because of the exceptional wallop he provides for his position.

Hairston spent at least four days a week in the Arizona Fall League working on his defense, especially on turning the double play. He has the tools for second base—quick hands, good range, adequate arm—but most who saw him in the Midwest League projected him as a left fielder. One scout who covered the league said he didn't see Hairston put any effort into his defense, let alone run out a grounder, but the Diamondbacks don't have any questions about his makeup. They also don't doubt he'll be able to stay at second base.

After tearing up three levels in two seasons, Hairston will continue his ascent at Double-A El Paso this year. If he continues his fast progress, he could reach Triple-A Tucson by the end of the season. Arizona incumbent Junior Spivey was a 2002 all-star, but the Diamondbacks will get both in the lineup when the time comes by moving one to the outfield.

Year	Club (League)	Class	AVG	G	AB	R	H	2B	3B	HR	RBI	BB	SO	SB	SLG	OBP
2001	Missoula (Pio)	R	.347	74	291	81	101	16	6	14	65	38	50	2	.588	.432
2002	South Bend (Mid)	A	.332	109	394	79	131	35	4	16	72	58	74	9	.563	.426
	Lancaster (Cal)	A	.405	18	79	20	32	11	1	6	26	6	16	1	.797	.442
MINOR LEAGUE TOTALS			.346	201	764	180	264	62	11	36	163	102	140	12	.597	.430

2. Mike Gosling, lhp

Born: Sept. 23, 1980. **Ht.:** 6-2. **Wt.:** 200. **Bats:** L. **Throws:** L. **School:** Stanford University. **Career Transactions:** Selected by Diamondbacks in second round of 2001 draft; signed Aug. 1, 2001.

Because teams were wary of Gosling's agent, Scott Boras, the Diamondbacks gambled that they could get him in the second round of the 2001 draft. They were correct, and signed him for $2 million—the largest bonus outside the first round that year. In his pro debut last year, he won 14 games in Double-A in the hitter-friendly Texas League. Gosling has a great understanding of his craft. He can spot his low-90s fastball on both sides of the plate, and it has a natural tail that makes it tough for hitters to make solid contact. He has command of both a slider and a curveball, and he changes speeds well. There have been minor issues with Gosling's durablilty, delivery and control in the past, but he answered them in 2002. About all he needs is further refinement with his command and more pro innings. Despite his limited experience, Gosling has an outside chance to make the Arizona rotation in 2003. It's more likely that he'll begin the season in Triple-A, but he could be the first starter summoned if the Diamondbacks need reinforcements.

Year	Club (League)	Class	W	L	ERA	G	GS	CG	SV	IP	H	R	ER	HR	BB	SO	AVG
2002	El Paso (TL)	AA	14	5	3.13	27	27	2	0	167	149	66	58	7	62	115	.238
MINOR LEAGUE TOTALS			14	5	3.13	27	27	2	0	167	149	66	58	7	62	115	.238

3. Lyle Overbay, 1b

Born: Jan. 28, 1977. **Ht.:** 6-2. **Wt.:** 210. **Bats:** L. **Throws:** L. **School:** University of Nevada. **Career Transactions:** Selected by Diamondbacks in 18th round of 1999 draft; signed June 8, 1999.

Though he set several Nevada and Big West Conference records, Overbay wasn't drafted until his senior year—and even then he lasted until the 18th round because scouts didn't think he profiled well at any position. He has made other teams pay for the oversight, becoming the first short-season player to drive in 100 runs and batting .345 in four pro seasons. Overbay is a line-drive machine, similar to Sean Casey and Mark Grace. He has a sweet, short stroke and adeptly uses the entire field. He has consistently produced tons of doubles in the minors, and he has the build to develop more over-the-fence power. The Grace comparisons don't entirely work because Overbay doesn't draw as many walks and isn't particularly smooth around first base. Scouts who saw him in the Triple-A Pacific Coast League didn't think his approach was conducive to hitting home runs. Now 26, he never has been young for his league. Overbay's promise was a major reason the Diamondbacks decided to trade Erubiel Durazo in a four-team deal that allowed them to upgrade their rotation with Elmer Dessens. Overbay will start at first base for Arizona and benefit from Grace's veteran counsel.

Year	Club (League)	Class	AVG	G	AB	R	H	2B	3B	HR	RBI	BB	SO	SB	SLG	OBP
1999	Missoula (Pio)	R	.343	75	306	66	105	25	7	12	101	40	53	10	.588	.418
2000	South Bend (Mid)	A	.332	71	259	47	86	19	3	6	47	27	36	9	.498	.397
	El Paso (TL)	AA	.352	62	244	43	86	16	2	8	49	28	39	3	.533	.420
2001	El Paso (TL)	AA	.352	138	532	82	187	49	3	13	100	67	92	5	.528	.423
	Arizona (NL)	MAJ	.500	2	2	0	1	0	0	0	0	0	1	0	.500	.500
2002	Tucson (PCL)	AAA	.343	134	525	83	180	40	0	19	109	42	86	0	.528	.396
	Arizona (NL)	MAJ	.100	10	10	0	1	0	0	0	1	0	5	0	.100	.100
MAJOR LEAGUE TOTALS			.167	12	12	0	2	0	0	0	1	0	6	0	.167	.167
MINOR LEAGUE TOTALS			.345	480	1866	321	644	149	15	58	406	204	306	27	.534	.411

4. John Patterson, rhp

Born: Jan. 30, 1978. **Ht.:** 6-5. **Wt.:** 180. **Bats:** R. **Throws:** R. **School:** West Orange-Stark HS, Orange, Texas. **Career Transactions:** Selected by Expos in first round (fifth overall) of 1996 draft . . . Granted free agency . . . Signed by Diamondbacks, Nov. 7, 1996.

The fifth overall pick in 1996 by the Expos, Patterson became a free agent because Montreal didn't properly tender him a contract. He signed with Arizona for $6.075 million and pitched well until needing Tommy John surgery in May 2000. He improved steadily last season and the Diamondbacks won four of his five big league starts. Patterson has worked diligently to return to his pre-injury form and made a breakthrough in 2002. He regained the shoulder-to-shoetops curveball that always has been his best pitch. He can buckle hitters with the bender while buzzing them with a 93 mph fastball that he locates well. He loves to compete. Patterson's fastball still hasn't quite returned to its previous 95-96 mph range, though he was consistently in the low 90s last season. Missing much of 2000 and 2001 cost him time to work on the development of his changeup. A spot in Arizona's rotation is Patterson's for the taking this spring. Even if his old velocity never returns, he learned to pitch without his best stuff while recovering from surgery and is the better for it now.

Year	Club (League)	Class	W	L	ERA	G	GS	CG	SV	IP	H	R	ER	HR	BB	SO	AVG
1997	South Bend (Mid)	A	1	9	3.23	18	18	0	0	78	63	32	28	3	34	95	.221
1998	High Desert (Cal)	A	8	7	2.83	25	25	0	0	127	102	54	40	12	42	148	.217
1999	El Paso (TL)	AA	8	6	4.77	18	18	2	0	100	98	61	53	16	42	117	.256
	Tucson (PCL)	AAA	1	5	7.04	7	6	0	0	31	43	26	24	3	18	29	.331
2000	Tucson (PCL)	AAA	0	2	7.80	3	2	0	0	15	21	14	13	1	9	10	.323
2001	Lancaster (Cal)	A	0	0	5.79	2	2	0	0	9	9	6	6	3	3	9	.243
	El Paso (TL)	AA	1	2	4.26	5	5	0	0	25	30	15	12	2	9	19	.297
	Tucson (PCL)	AAA	2	7	5.85	13	12	0	0	68	82	50	44	9	31	40	.301
2002	Tucson (PCL)	AAA	10	5	4.23	19	18	0	0	113	117	59	53	14	45	104	.265
	Arizona (NL)	MAJ	2	0	3.23	7	5	0	0	31	27	11	11	7	7	31	.235
MAJOR LEAGUE TOTALS			2	0	3.23	7	5	0	0	31	27	11	11	7	7	31	.235
MINOR LEAGUE TOTALS			31	43	4.34	110	106	2	0	566	565	317	273	63	233	571	.259

5. Brandon Webb, rhp

Born: May 9, 1979. **Ht.:** 6-3. **Wt.:** 190. **Bats:** R. **Throws:** R. **School:** University of Kentucky. **Career Transactions:** Selected by Diamondbacks in eighth round of 2000 draft; signed June 6, 2000.

Webb set the Kentucky single-season strikeout record (since broken by Athletics first-rounder Joe Blanton) in 2000, the year Arizona drafted him in the eighth round. After being shut down with a tired arm in his first pro summer, he has been solid ever since. He ranked fourth in the Texas League in both ERA and strikeouts last year. Webb's fastball tops out at 94-95 mph but is best at 92, where it really sinks. He also has a heavy slider, and his stuff reminds scouts of Bob Wickman's. His two-seam fastball can be so dominant that he could rely on it almost exclusively. With 40 hit batters and 23 wild pitches over the last two seasons, it's obvious Webb still has work to do to master his command. His pitches have such live, late movement that he can be difficult to catch. He just began to incorporate a changeup into his repertoire last year. Like his former El Paso teammate Mike Gosling, Webb has an outside chance to make the Diamondbacks roster in 2003. He could be used as either a starter or a long reliever. Whatever the case, he should be a major league mainstay in the near future.

Year	Club (League)	Class	W	L	ERA	G	GS	CG	SV	IP	H	R	ER	HR	BB	SO	AVG
2000	Diamondbacks (AZL)	R	0	0	9.00	1	1	0	0	1	2	1	1	0	0	3	.400
	South Bend (Mid)	A	0	0	3.24	12	0	0	2	17	10	7	6	0	9	18	.172
2001	Lancaster (Cal)	A	6	10	3.99	29	28	0	0	162	174	90	72	9	44	158	.276
2002	El Paso (TL)	AA	10	6	3.14	26	25	1	0	152	141	66	53	4	59	122	.247
	Tucson (PCL)	AAA	0	1	3.86	1	1	0	0	7	5	3	3	0	4	5	.200
MINOR LEAGUE TOTALS			16	17	3.58	69	55	1	2	339	332	167	135	13	116	306	.258

6. Edgar Gonzalez, rhp

Born: Feb. 23, 1983. **Ht.:** 6-0. **Wt.:** 220. **Bats:** R. **Throws:** R. **Career Transactions:** Signed out of Dominican Republic by Diamondbacks, April 18, 2000 . . . Returned from restricted list, April 4, 2002.

Signed at 17 for a mere $3,500, Gonzalez was sent home from the Rookie-level Dominican Summer League because of homesickness. He returned to the Diamondbacks last April and threw a no-hitter in his second low Class A start. He was even better after a promotion to high Class A Lancaster. His roll continued into the offseason, as he led the Mexican Pacific League in wins (eight) and ERA (1.89). Unlike most true four-pitch pitchers, Gonzalez can reach the mid-90s with his fastball. He was clocked at 96 mph in the ninth inning of one of his starts at South Bend. His slider is his second-best pitch, and he has a curveball and changeup. Gonzalez has great feel for altering the speed of his pitches. He wants the ball in big situations. Gonzalez isn't lacking much beyond experience. If he can improve his command within the strike zone, he has the stuff to dominate hitters. Counting winter ball, he racked up 250 innings in a nine-month period, so Arizona should monitor his 2003 workload carefully. Gonzalez looks ready to make the jump to Double-A. If he keeps developing this rapidly, he could be in Arizona by September.

Year	Club (League)	Class	W	L	ERA	G	GS	CG	SV	IP	H	R	ER	HR	BB	SO	AVG
2002	South Bend (Mid)	A	11	8	2.91	23	23	4	0	151	141	66	49	4	34	110	.246
	Lancaster (Cal)	A	3	0	0.78	4	4	0	0	23	24	7	2	1	3	21	.264
MINOR LEAGUE TOTALS			14	8	2.63	27	27	4	0	174	165	73	51	5	37	131	.248

7. Sergio Santos, ss

Born: July 4, 1983. **Ht.:** 6-3. **Wt.:** 200. **Bats:** R. **Throws:** R. **School:** Mater Dei HS, Hacienda Heights, Calif. **Career Transactions:** Selected by Diamondbacks in first round (27th overall) of 2002 draft; signed June 26, 2002.

Santos may have been the victim of overexposure. He was identified as a top prospect by the time he was a high school sophomore, and scouts expected more than he delivered as a senior. Arizona drafted him 27th overall and used a $1.4 million bonus to sign him away from a scholarship to Southern California. Santos has prodigious power, which he displayed by driving balls to all parts of the park in a private workout at Bank One Ballpark prior to the 2002 draft. He hadn't shown consistent pop in high school. Santos has a compact swing and can make adjustments. His instincts and makeup are solid, and they enhance his average speed and defensive tools. His arm strength is a plus. Santos still has to learn to play balls off wood bats, and his 28 errors ranked third in the Pioneer League. Considering his size and that he's still growing, he probably will get too big for shortstop and have to move to second or third base. His swing can get long, hampering his ability to make contact. Santos has enough power for any position and will be a middle-of-the-order hitter in the majors, perhaps as early as 2005. He'll spend this year in Class A.

Year	Club (League)	Class	AVG	G	AB	R	H	2B	3B	HR	RBI	BB	SO	SB	SLG	OBP
2002	Missoula (Pio)	R	.272	54	202	38	55	19	2	9	37	29	49	6	.520	.367
MINOR LEAGUE TOTALS			.272	54	202	38	55	19	2	9	37	29	49	6	.520	.367

8. Chad Tracy, 3b

Born: May 22, 1980. **Ht.:** 6-2. **Wt.:** 190. **Bats:** L. **Throws:** R. **School:** East Carolina University. **Career Transactions:** Selected by Diamondbacks in seventh round of 2001 draft; signed June 9, 2001.

The Diamondbacks had inside information on Tracy, because area scout Howard McCullough's son Clayton played with him at East Carolina. In his first full season, Tracy stayed above .400 in Double-A through early June. He tailed off because of a shoulder injury, but still led the Texas League in batting, hits and doubles and was the league's player of the year. Tracy is a classic line-drive hitter. He has a short, compact swing and takes the ball where it's pitched. He makes contact with ease and can fight off pitches until he gets one to his liking. With his stroke and knowledge, he should add more home run power in time. A first baseman in his first two years of college, Tracy remains a work in progress at the hot corner and made 26 errors last season. He puts the bat on the ball so effortlessly that he cuts into his walk totals. He didn't need surgery, but his shoulder problem cost him a chance to play in the Arizona Fall League. Tracy will begin 2003 in Triple-A as Matt Williams plays out the end of his five-year contract. Craig Counsell may provide competition, but Tracy could be Arizona's starter in 2004.

Year	Club (League)	Class	AVG	G	AB	R	H	2B	3B	HR	RBI	BB	SO	SB	SLG	OBP
2001	Yakima (NWL)	A	.278	10	36	2	10	1	0	0	5	3	5	1	.306	.350
	South Bend (Mid)	A	.340	54	215	43	73	11	0	4	36	19	19	3	.447	.393
2002	El Paso (TL)	AA	.344	129	514	80	177	39	5	8	74	38	51	2	.486	.389
MINOR LEAGUE TOTALS			.340	193	765	125	260	51	5	12	115	60	75	6	.467	.388

9. Brian Bruney, rhp

Born: Feb. 17, 1982. **Ht.:** 6-3. **Wt.:** 220. **Bats:** R. **Throws:** R. **School:** Warrenton (Ore.) HS. **Career Transactions:** Selected by Diamondbacks in 12th round of 2000 draft; signed June 6, 2000.

Bruney was only 17 when he signed as a raw talent from a town of 2,200 on the tip of northwest Oregon. Credit the scouting department for finding him and the development staff for refining him into a closer prospect. He dominated in the Arizona Fall League after a strong 2002 season, not allowing a run in 16 appearances. Bruney routinely hit 99 mph with his fastball in his first two years in the organization. He now works more in the mid-90s, and the pitch has natural cutting action, making it that much more difficult to hit. His slider has improved, and his most important achievement has been refining a consistent delivery. Control has been a problem at times for Bruney, though as he has grown he has learned he doesn't have to throw 99 mph every pitch to be successful. His average of 3.1 walks per nine innings last year was by far the best ratio of his career. He doesn't have much of an offspeed pitch, but he rarely needs one. If Matt Mantei can't stay healthy and Byung-Hyun Kim gets his wish to become a starter, Bruney could become Arizona's closer in the near future. He needs at least one more year of minor league apprenticeship first.

Year	Club (League)	Class	W	L	ERA	G	GS	CG	SV	IP	H	R	ER	HR	BB	SO	AVG
2000	Diamondbacks (AZL)	R	4	1	6.48	20	2	0	2	25	21	23	18	2	29	24	.221
2001	South Bend (Mid)	A	1	4	4.13	26	0	0	8	33	24	19	15	1	19	40	.205
	Yakima (NWL)	A	1	2	5.14	15	0	0	2	21	19	14	12	2	11	28	.226
2002	South Bend (Mid)	A	4	3	1.68	37	0	0	10	48	37	15	9	1	17	54	.210
	El Paso (TL)	AA	0	2	2.92	10	0	0	0	12	11	5	4	1	4	14	.268
MINOR LEAGUE TOTALS			10	12	3.75	108	2	0	22	139	112	76	58	7	80	160	.218

10. Luis Terrero, of

Born: May 18, 1980. **Ht.:** 6-2. **Wt.:** 190. **Bats:** B. **Throws:** R. **Career Transactions:** Signed out of Dominican Republic by Diamondbacks, Sept. 27, 1997.

Terrero ranked No. 1 on this list a year ago and has as much all-around upside as anyone in the system. But he has been plagued by injuries throughout his five-year pro career, including hamstring problems, a broken hamate bone and a fractured ankle. Though his 104 games in 2002 were a career high, he still spent nearly a month on the disabled list. A gifted physical specimen, Terrero is long and chiseled. He has power to all fields and runs like a deer. With his long strides he gobbles up ground both in the outfield alleys and while on the bases. He has a strong arm and has been a major league-ready center fielder since starring in the 2000 Hall of Fame Game at Cooperstown. Terrero has had trouble staying on the field long enough to develop a consistent approach at the plate. He has trouble recognizing and adjusting to breaking pitches, and he does a poor job of controlling the strike zone. He has the speed to steal 30 bases a year, but his instincts aren't there yet. Terrero has all the tools to be a major league center fielder for a decade. He has been on the radar screen so long that it's easy to forget that he's just 22. He should start the season at Triple-A Tucson.

Year	Club (League)	Class	AVG	G	AB	R	H	2B	3B	HR	RBI	BB	SO	SB	SLG	OBP
1998	Diamondbacks (DSL)	R	.231	56	169	19	39	7	1	2	15	13	44	9	.320	.301
1999	Missoula (Pio)	R	.287	71	272	74	78	13	7	8	40	32	91	27	.474	.365
2000	High Desert (Cal)	A	.190	19	79	10	15	3	1	0	1	3	16	5	.253	.229
	Missoula (Pio)	R	.261	68	276	48	72	10	0	8	44	10	75	23	.384	.305
2001	South Bend (Mid)	A	.157	24	89	4	14	2	0	1	8	0	29	3	.213	.176
	Yakima (NWL)	A	.317	11	41	7	13	2	1	0	0	2	8	0	.415	.349
	Lancaster (Cal)	A	.451	19	71	16	32	9	1	4	11	1	14	5	.775	.466
	El Paso (TL)	AA	.299	34	147	29	44	13	3	3	8	4	45	9	.490	.331
2002	El Paso (TL)	AA	.286	104	360	49	103	20	6	8	54	23	89	18	.442	.342
MINOR LEAGUE TOTALS			.273	406	1504	256	410	79	20	34	181	88	411	99	.420	.325

11. Tim Olson, ss/of

Born: Aug. 1, 1978. **Ht.:** 6-2. **Wt.:** 200. **Bats:** R. **Throws:** R. **School:** University of Florida. **Career Transactions:** Selected by Diamondbacks in seventh round of 2000 draft; signed June 14, 2000.

Like Darin Erstad, Olson is a native of North Dakota who made his way south to fashion his career. He first attended Hutchinson (Kan.) Community College, where he was clocked at 93 mph as a pitcher, and then went to Florida, where he was the outstanding player in a 2000 NCAA regional at Baylor. Olson is a gifted athlete with gap power. While tinkering with his stance in the Arizona Fall League, he still managed to hit .374 with eight doubles and six stolen bases in 31 games. He's an above-average runner who has the ability to steal 15 bases a year. He has a good arm at shortstop and a feel for the position. His athleticism also makes him one of the organization's best defenders at both third base and the outfield (his primary college position). Like a lot of young hitters, Olson needs to refine his plate discipline and make pitchers come to him. The Diamondbacks plan to keep Olson at shortstop unless he plays his way off the position. He'll start there in Triple-A this year.

Year	Club (League)	Class	AVG	G	AB	R	H	2B	3B	HR	RBI	BB	SO	SB	SLG	OBP
2000	South Bend (Mid)	A	.218	68	261	37	57	14	2	2	26	15	49	15	.310	.281
2001	Lancaster (Cal)	A	.289	61	239	36	69	12	4	6	32	14	49	13	.448	.336
	El Paso (TL)	AA	.317	46	167	29	53	13	0	2	24	11	36	4	.431	.378
2002	El Paso (TL)	AA	.273	126	433	61	118	24	2	10	64	27	91	9	.406	.337
MINOR LEAGUE TOTALS			.270	301	1100	163	297	63	8	20	146	67	225	41	.396	.330

12. Chris Snyder, c

Born: Feb. 12, 1981. **Ht.:** 6-3. **Wt.:** 220. **Bats:** R. **Throws:** R. **School:** University of Houston. **Career Transactions:** Selected by Diamondbacks in second round of 2002 draft; signed June 16, 2002.

Snyder immediately became the best catch-and-throw guy in the organization after he signed. That's a testament to his skills behind the plate rather than a shot at the rest of the catchers in the system. A big man with a Carlton Fisk-type body, Snyder is mobile and quick with soft hands. He receives the ball well and already has learned how to frame pitches on the corners. He uses his feet well and does a fine job of blocking balls in the dirt. His arm strength is good, and his release is quick and accurate. Snyder also has all the intangibles teams want in a catcher. He calls his own game, as he did at Houston, and has strong leadership traits. The loft in his stroke bodes well for his power, which he displayed often during his pro debut in high Class A. Snyder's swing can get long, which hurts his ability to make contact and hit for average. Rod Barajas was the Diamondbacks' first homegrown catcher to reach the majors, and Snyder has a chance to be the second. He'll spend most of 2003 in Double-A.

Year	Club (League)	Class	AVG	G	AB	R	H	2B	3B	HR	RBI	BB	SO	SB	SLG	OBP
2002	Lancaster (Cal)	A	.258	60	217	31	56	16	0	9	44	25	54	0	.456	.337
MINOR LEAGUE TOTALS			.258	60	217	31	56	16	0	9	44	25	54	0	.456	.337

13. Oscar Villarreal, rhp

Born: Nov. 22, 1981. **Ht.:** 6-0. **Wt.:** 170. **Bats:** L. **Throws:** R. **Career Transactions:** Signed out of Mexico by Diamondbacks, Nov. 6, 1998.

There is no questioning Villarreal's toughness. He sustained a hairline fracture of his right thumb when struck by a line drive in a late April start in Double-A and still made his next two starts—in pain all the while—before letting the organization know about the injury. Until he got hurt, he was the most dominant pitcher in the Texas League, going 4-1, 1.26 with scoreless streaks of 11 and 19 innings. Villarreal features an 89-92 mph fastball and the best slider in the system, yet his changeup may be his most effective pitch. He throws all his pitches for strikes and improved his command within the zone in 2002. Villarreal missed a month before returning, and afterward he didn't baffle hitters as much as he had before the injury. He'll try to find that groove again when he begins 2003 in Triple-A.

Year	Club (League)	Class	W	L	ERA	G	GS	CG	SV	IP	H	R	ER	HR	BB	SO	AVG
1999	Diamondbacks (AZL)	R	1	5	3.78	14	11	0	0	64	64	39	27	1	25	51	.260
2000	Tucson (PCL)	AAA	1	0	2.08	2	0	0	0	4	6	1	1	0	2	4	.353
	South Bend (Mid)	A	1	3	4.41	13	5	0	0	33	37	19	16	0	17	30	.274
	Diamondbacks (AZL)	R	0	0	9.00	1	0	0	0	1	2	1	1	0	0	1	.400
	High Desert (Cal)	A	0	2	3.65	9	4	0	0	25	24	20	10	4	14	18	.253
2001	El Paso (TL)	AA	6	9	4.41	27	27	0	0	141	154	96	69	10	63	108	.274
2002	El Paso (TL)	AA	6	3	3.74	14	12	1	0	84	73	36	35	2	26	85	.233
	Tucson (PCL)	AAA	3	3	4.36	10	10	0	0	64	68	33	31	8	22	40	.278
MINOR LEAGUE TOTALS			18	25	4.11	90	69	1	0	416	428	245	190	25	169	337	.265

14. Adriano Rosario, rhp

Born: May 16, 1985. **Ht.:** 6-2. **Wt.:** 190. **Bats:** R. **Throws:** R. **Career Transactions:** Signed out of Dominican Republic by Diamondbacks, June 13, 2002.

A month before the 2002 draft, Arizona scouting director Mike Rizzo got an urgent call from Latin American scouting coordinator Junior Noboa, asking him to come to the Dominican Republic. Rosario had hit 96 mph on the first pitch of his workout for the Diamondbacks and later reached 98 mph. Arizona made sure it signed him, paying a bonus of $400,000. The initial plan was to keep him in the Rookie-level Dominican Summer League, but he was so dominant that he earned a late-season look at Missoula. While his statistics weren't as gaudy in the United State, he still touched 99 mph and pitched at 95. He also showed a Francisco Rodriguez-style power slider that sat at 87-88 mph, and he threw strikes. What's scary is there's still room for projection because he's so young, long and lean. Rosario is developing a curveball and changeup to give hitters something offspeed to worry about. He could move quickly once he figures those secondary pitches out.

Year	Club (League)	Class	W	L	ERA	G	GS	CG	SV	IP	H	R	ER	HR	BB	SO	AVG
2002	Diamondbacks (DSL)	R	3	1	2.05	10	10	1	0	57	41	16	13	0	7	57	.193
	Missoula (Pio)	R	1	2	6.30	4	4	0	0	20	26	15	14	0	3	14	.321
MINOR LEAGUE TOTALS			4	3	3.16	14	14	1	0	77	67	31	27	0	10	71	.229

15. Jesus Cota, of/1b

Born: Nov. 7, 1981. **Ht.:** 6-3. **Wt.:** 220. **Bats:** L. **Throws:** R. **School:** Pima (Ariz.) CC. **Career Transactions:** Selected by Diamondbacks in 14th round of 2000 draft; signed May 28, 2001.

Like the traded Erubiel Durazo, Cota is a native of Hermosillo, Mexico, who hits left-handed and honed his skills at the high school and junior college levels in Tucson. The comparisons extend further. Cota has a strong, short stroke similar to Durazo's, and is tearing up the minors just like Durazo did. Cota won the Pioneer League triple crown in his pro debut and led the high Class A California League in RBIs in his first full season. He still chases pitches and doesn't have Durazo's strike-zone discipline, but he thrives with runners in scoring position. Cota has power to all fields and can turn around the best fastballs. He was disciplined for not running out a ball late in the 2002 season but seemed to learn from the benching. Cota moved from first base midway through the year after 1999 first-round pick Corey Myers was moved from third base to first, and showed he could play left field adequately. He's limited in terms of athleticism and speed, so he'll never be a standout defender. He's ready for Double-A in 2003.

Year	Club (League)	Class	AVG	G	AB	R	H	2B	3B	HR	RBI	BB	SO	SB	SLG	OBP
2001	Missoula (Pio)	R	.368	75	272	74	100	22	0	16	71	56	52	2	.625	.476
2002	Lancaster (Cal)	A	.280	135	540	73	151	33	3	16	101	38	121	0	.441	.325
MINOR LEAGUE TOTALS			.309	210	812	147	251	55	3	32	172	94	173	2	.502	.380

16. Jose Valverde, rhp

Born: July 24, 1979. **Ht.:** 6-4. **Wt.:** 220. **Bats:** R. **Throws:** R. **Career Transactions:** Signed out of Dominican Republic by Diamondbacks, Jan. 31, 1997.

A big, strapping flamethrower from Baseball City, D.R.—San Pedro de Macoris—Valverde was clocked at 100 mph during spring training in 2002 and claims to have thrown 101 in the Texas League the year before. That's all well and good. But after being added to the 40-man roster in November 2001, Valverde had a lost season in his first crack at Triple-A. He relied almost exclusively on his power fastball but had trouble with location, and the veteran hitters in the Pacific Coast League had no trouble timing him and sending his heat in the other direction. Control is his main issue. He hasn't learned to spot his fastball on the edges of the plate. He also hasn't developed a reliable second pitch, though he has worked on a cutter and a slider. He needs something to keep hitters from cheating on his fastball. It got to the point last season that the Diamondbacks would remove Valverde after a good inning rather than risk him losing confidence by getting hit around in a second inning. He has spent time on the disabled list in each of the last three years with shoulder (2000), elbow (2001) and back ailments (2002), and has never pitched more than 51 innings in a season. His top-notch velocity keeps Valverde on the radar screen, though he still has plenty to prove in Triple-A.

Year	Club (League)	Class	W	L	ERA	G	GS	CG	SV	IP	H	R	ER	HR	BB	SO	AVG
1997	Diamondbacks (DSL)	R	0	0	5.30	14	0	0	0	19	20	12	11	1	13	19	.267
1998	Diamondbacks (DSL)	R	1	3	1.75	23	4	0	7	51	31	14	10	2	22	56	.169
1999	Diamondbacks (AZL)	R	1	2	4.08	20	0	0	8	29	34	21	13	1	10	47	.274
	South Bend (Mid)	A	0	0	0.00	2	0	0	0	3	2	0	0	0	2	3	.250
2000	South Bend (Mid)	A	0	5	5.40	31	0	0	14	32	31	20	19	1	25	39	.254
	Missoula (Pio)	R	1	0	0.00	12	0	0	4	12	3	0	0	0	4	24	.075
2001	El Paso (TL)	AA	2	2	3.92	39	0	0	13	41	36	19	18	1	27	72	.225
2002	Tucson (PCL)	AAA	2	4	5.85	49	0	0	5	48	45	33	31	8	23	65	.250
MINOR LEAGUE TOTALS			7	16	3.93	190	4	0	51	234	202	119	102	14	126	325	.226

17. Brian Barden, 3b

Born: April 2, 1981. **Ht.:** 5-11. **Wt.:** 190. **Bats:** R. **Throws:** R. **School:** Oregon State University. **Career Transactions:** Selected by Diamondbacks in sixth round of 2002 draft; signed June 9, 2002.

A late bloomer in high school, Barden didn't receive many scholarship offers and signed with Oregon State after the Beavers noticed him in a summer tournament. He became a two-time all-Pacific-10 Conference third baseman, and pulled off something even rarer after signing last June. Despite missing the first half of the season, he made the California League all-star team. Barden doesn't have a classic power hitter's body but has a compact stroke that produces gap power. He makes continual adjustments at the plate and seldom gives away at-bats. He has a great mental approach, never getting too high or too low. Barden looks like a future Gold Glover at third base and scouts consider him similar to David Bell. If he continues to hit as he did in his debut, Barden will give Chad Tracy a run for the right to succeed Matt Williams at the hot corner in Arizona.

Year	Club (League)	Class	AVG	G	AB	R	H	2B	3B	HR	RBI	BB	SO	SB	SLG	OBP
2002	Yakima (NWL)	A	.333	4	15	5	5	1	0	0	2	1	1	0	.400	.412
	Lancaster (Cal)	A	.335	64	269	58	90	19	1	8	46	16	63	3	.502	.370
MINOR LEAGUE TOTALS			.335	68	284	63	95	20	1	8	48	17	64	3	.496	.373

18. Brad Cresse, c

Born: July 31, 1978. **Ht.:** 6-2. **Wt.:** 210. **Bats:** R. **Throws:** R. **School:** Louisiana State University. **Career Transactions:** Selected by Diamondbacks in fifth round of 2000 draft; signed June 19, 2000.

The son of longtime Dodgers bullpen coach Mark Cresse and the godson of Hall of Famer Tommy Lasorda, Cresse has cooled off since his scintillating 2000 performance. He led NCAA Division I with 30 homers and drove in the College World Series-winning run for Louisiana State, then hit 17 homers in 48 high Class A games after signing. He has a power stroke and previously showed the ability to make adjustments, but he struggled at the plate in 2002 as he was shuttled between Double-A and Triple-A. The Diamondbacks also believe his offensive woes were related to a conscious effort to improve his defense, which was successful. He improved his catch-and-throw skills, increasing his success against basestealers to 39 percent, up from 27 percent in 2001. His footwork and accuracy on throws got better, and he grew more adept at game-calling—something catchers don't do at LSU. Cresse could reassert himself as a prospect in Triple-A if he learns to not put so much pressure on himself and let his natural gifts work for him.

Year	Club (League)	Class	AVG	G	AB	R	H	2B	3B	HR	RBI	BB	SO	SB	SLG	OBP
2000	High Desert (Cal)	A	.324	48	173	35	56	7	0	17	56	17	50	0	.659	.402
	El Paso (TL)	AA	.262	15	42	9	11	1	0	1	10	6	12	0	.357	.385
2001	El Paso (TL)	AA	.289	118	429	55	124	39	1	14	81	44	116	0	.483	.373
2002	Tucson (PCL)	AAA	.270	36	126	23	34	10	0	2	14	4	38	0	.397	.306
	El Paso (TL)	AA	.229	66	240	25	55	15	0	3	24	16	74	1	.329	.282
MINOR LEAGUE TOTALS			.277	283	1010	147	280	72	1	37	185	87	290	1	.460	.350

19. Dustin Nippert, rhp

Born: May 6, 1981. **Ht.:** 6-7. **Wt.:** 210. **Bats:** R. **Throws:** R. **School:** West Virginia University. **Career Transactions:** Selected by Diamondbacks in 15th round of 2002 draft; signed June 9, 2002.

Like Randy Johnson but with a much lower profile, Nippert never got comfortable with his gangly body and quality stuff while pitching in college. He began the 2002 college season in West Virginia's rotation, but pitched his way into the bullpen. Diamondbacks area scout Greg Lonigro stayed on Nippert because he's 6-foot-7 and threw in the low 90s. After Arizona signed him, Nippert tinkered with his three-quarters delivery, lengthening his stride and achieving immediate impact. His velocity improved to the mid-90s with a high of 98 mph, and his command got dramatically better. With a power curveball, he might have as good a 1-2 punch as any pitcher in the system, and he's intelligent on the mound. Nippert still has to refine his changeup but the Diamondbacks don't believe he's a fluke. They may give him a chance to prove that by jumping him three levels to high Class A this year.

Year	Club (League)	Class	W	L	ERA	G	GS	CG	SV	IP	H	R	ER	HR	BB	SO	AVG
2002	Missoula (Pio)	R	4	2	1.65	17	11	0	0	55	42	12	10	2	9	77	.208
MINOR LEAGUE TOTALS			4	2	1.65	17	11	0	0	55	42	12	10	2	9	77	.208

20. Bill White, lhp

Born: Nov. 20, 1978. **Ht.:** 6-4. **Wt.:** 210. **Bats:** L. **Throws:** L. **School:** Jacksonville State University. **Career Transactions:** Selected by Diamondbacks in third round of 2000 draft; signed June 28, 2000.

White led NCAA Division I with an average of 16.0 strikeouts per nine innings at Jacksonville State in 2000. A big, strong lefthander, White uses a sharp curveball as his out pitch and owns a 91-92 mph fastball with nice life. He has shown only flashes of his ability in his three pro seasons, however, because of various physical ailments. He was shut down for most of 2000 with a tired arm, slightly tore his labrum late in 2001 and had his wrist broken by a liner last year. White should be ready for spring training, where he'll compete for a starting job in Double-A. The Diamondbacks still believe in him and want him to stay healthy so he can make some progress with his changeup and his control.

Year	Club (League)	Class	W	L	ERA	G	GS	CG	SV	IP	H	R	ER	HR	BB	SO	AVG
2000	Diamondbacks (AZL)	R	0	1	6.00	4	1	0	0	6	3	4	4	0	5	9	.158
	South Bend (Mid)	A	0	0	3.38	1	1	0	0	3	3	1	1	0	3	5	.273
2001	South Bend (Mid)	A	9	3	3.80	19	19	0	0	111	90	53	47	9	53	103	.224
	El Paso (TL)	AA	0	4	4.54	7	7	0	0	38	38	23	19	2	20	26	.275
2002	Yakima (NWL)	A	0	1	9.35	3	3	0	0	9	10	9	9	2	10	11	.278
	Lancaster (Cal)	A	0	3	10.24	6	6	0	0	19	31	23	22	4	16	15	.369
MINOR LEAGUE TOTALS			9	12	4.94	40	37	0	0	186	175	113	102	17	107	169	.254

21. Andrew Good, rhp

Born: Sept. 19, 1979. **Ht.:** 6-3. **Wt.:** 170. **Bats:** R. **Throws:** R. **School:** Rochester (Mich.) HS. **Career Transactions:** Selected by Diamondbacks in eighth round of 1998 draft; signed June 29, 1998 . . . On disabled list, April 6-Sept. 8, 2000.

Good's performance stands out more than his tools. He was the organization's minor league pitcher of the year in 1999, but tore up his elbow in 2000 and had Tommy John surgery. He won 10 games while rebuilding his arm strength in 2001 and 13 more in Double-A last year. Good understands the art of pitching as well as anyone in the system. While his fastball tops out at 90 mph, he locates it well and mixes in curveballs and changeups. He can throw any pitch in any count and specializes in keeping hitters off balance. Good is expected to keep moving up the ladder, with a spot in the Triple-A rotation on the horizon. It's possible that his savvy could land him in Arizona in the next year or two.

Year	Club (League)	Class	W	L	ERA	G	GS	CG	SV	IP	H	R	ER	HR	BB	SO	AVG
1998	Diamondbacks (AZL)	R	1	3	4.28	9	8	0	0	34	46	25	16	1	7	25	.324
	South Bend (Mid)	A	0	1	3.00	2	0	0	0	6	7	4	2	0	1	6	.280
1999	South Bend (Mid)	A	11	10	4.10	27	27	0	0	154	160	80	70	9	42	146	.268
2000						Did Not Play—Injured											
2001	Lancaster (Cal)	A	8	6	4.80	19	18	0	0	101	108	63	54	12	27	104	.267
	El Paso (TL)	AA	2	3	5.88	10	9	0	0	57	79	44	37	2	20	46	.324
2002	El Paso (TL)	AA	13	6	3.54	28	27	2	0	178	170	89	70	21	26	127	.248
MINOR LEAGUE TOTALS			35	29	4.23	95	89	2	0	529	570	305	249	45	123	454	.272

22. Jared Doyle, lhp

Born: Jan. 30, 1981. **Ht.:** 6-0. **Wt.:** 190. **Bats:** L. **Throws:** L. **School:** James Madison University. **Career Transactions:** Selected by Diamondbacks in third round of 2002 draft; signed June 15, 2002.

Doyle and his twin brother Nathan led James Madison to a school-record 44 victories last spring. Jared led the Colonial Athletic Association with 11 wins, while Nathan, a shortstop, tied for top honors with 14 homers. Nathan wasn't drafted, but Jared went in the third round and made the short-season Northwest League all-star team in his pro debut. He excelled as both a reliever and a starter at Yakima. Doyle has a low-90s fastball that maxes out at 95 mph, a quality curveball and a changeup that may be his best pitch. He's not afraid to throw strikes and has a good idea of what he wants to accomplish. He keeps the ball down, giving up only one home run in 63 pro innings. Given his makeup, he should be able to handle high Class A if Arizona decides to skip him a level.

Year	Club (League)	Class	W	L	ERA	G	GS	CG	SV	IP	H	R	ER	HR	BB	SO	AVG
2002	Yakima (NWL)	A	4	4	2.87	16	8	0	1	63	44	24	20	1	29	70	.198
MINOR LEAGUE TOTALS			4	4	2.87	16	8	0	1	63	44	24	20	1	29	70	.198

23. Marland Williams, of

Born: June 22, 1981. **Ht.:** 5-9. **Wt.:** 170. **Bats:** R. **Throws:** R. **School:** North Florida CC. **Career Transactions:** Selected by Diamondbacks in 36th round of 2001 draft; signed May 10, 2002.

A draft-and-follow from 2001, Williams is the fastest player and best athlete in the system. He was recruited out of high school as a wide receiver by Florida and Florida State, but instead chose to pursue baseball. The 2002 Florida community college player of the year, he has one exceptional tool: speed. He has been timed consistently between 6.25 and 6.3 seconds in the 60-yard dash and is explosive. He's at full speed in one step and has a good understanding of how to steal bases. Little wonder, then, that he led the Northwest League with eight triples and 51 steals (in 58 attempts). The rest of Williams' game is raw. While he hit 14 home runs at North Florida, he has just enough pop to get himself in trouble. The Diamondbacks want him to make more contact and hit more balls on the ground to best utilize his jets. He's a legitimate center fielder, covering ground to both sides with an average arm. Arizona will be patient with his development.

Year	Club (League)	Class	AVG	G	AB	R	H	2B	3B	HR	RBI	BB	SO	SB	SLG	OBP
2002	Yakima (NWL)	A	.246	70	280	46	69	4	8	3	17	27	86	51	.350	.311
MINOR LEAGUE TOTALS			.246	70	280	46	69	4	8	3	17	27	86	51	.350	.311

24. Robby Hammock, c/of

Born: May 13, 1977. **Ht.:** 5-11. **Wt.:** 180. **Bats:** R. **Throws:** R. **School:** University of Georgia. **Career Transactions:** Selected by Diamondbacks in 23rd round of 1998 draft; signed June 3, 1998.

Hammock had always hit since signing in 1998, but last year he established himself as a jack of all trades capable of filling three roles—backup catcher, corner infielder, corner outfielder—with one roster spot. His ascent through the minors was slowed by a severe bone bruise in his right wrist in 2000. Once he returned, Brad Cresse cut into Hammock's time behind the plate. He alternated between catcher, outfield and third base last year. Hammock uses a short stroke, makes good contact, has solid power and does a fine job of recognizing pitches. He threw out 40 percent of basestealers in 2002 and showed agility at every position he played. The Diamondbacks believe he could become their answer to Eli Marrero after some time in Triple-A.

Year	Club (League)	Class	AVG	G	AB	R	H	2B	3B	HR	RBI	BB	SO	SB	SLUG	OBP
1998	Lethbridge (Pio)	R	.286	62	227	46	65	14	2	10	56	28	34	5	.498	.367
1999	High Desert (Cal)	A	.332	114	379	80	126	20	7	9	72	47	63	3	.493	.403
2000	High Desert (Cal)	A	.353	40	136	25	48	15	1	3	23	27	24	3	.544	.455
	El Paso (TL)	AA	.250	45	140	22	35	5	1	1	15	11	25	1	.321	.305
2001	El Paso (TL)	AA	.162	26	74	6	12	5	0	0	4	7	18	2	.230	.235
	South Bend (Mid)	A	.248	34	125	16	31	3	2	2	14	14	21	5	.352	.324
	Lancaster (Cal)	A	.311	45	190	33	59	11	3	4	36	16	42	3	.463	.378
2002	El Paso (TL)	AA	.290	122	441	68	128	28	4	11	73	43	68	5	.447	.358
MINOR LEAGUE TOTALS			.294	488	1712	296	504	101	20	40	293	193	295	27	.447	.368

25. Beltran Perez, rhp

Born: Oct. 24, 1981. **Ht.:** 6-2. **Wt.:** 150. **Bats:** R. **Throws:** R. **Career Transactions:** Signed out of Dominican Republic by Diamondbacks, Feb. 2, 1999.

Perez hit a bump in the road for the first time in 2002 after three solid seasons in the lower minors, where he went 23-6 while working his way up from the Dominican Summer League through low Class A. He had trouble adjusting to the hitter's parks and more advanced opponents in Double-A. Perez has the stuff to be successful. He has a quality slider and an even better changeup, and his fastball tops out at 91-92 mph. He can throw his pitches for strikes in just about any count, his location is outstanding and he has a mature mental approach. That's why the Diamondbacks tried to jump him two levels, and though that didn't work, he was back to his old self once he was allowed to catch his breath in high Class A during August. With his tall, lean build, Arizona envisions him putting on weight and adding velocity, but he has gained just four pounds in the last two years. He might be best off by returning to high Class A and getting off to a quick start this year.

Year	Club (League)	Class	W	L	ERA	G	GS	CG	SV	IP	H	R	ER	HR	BB	SO	AVG
1999	Diamondbacks (DSL)	R	6	0	2.45	18	0	0	0	29	24	12	8	1	9	31	.216
2000	Diamondbacks (AZL)	R	5	1	5.81	11	4	0	0	48	61	37	31	1	25	47	.321
	High Desert (Cal)	A	0	1	3.60	2	2	0	0	10	8	4	4	3	5	11	.211
2001	South Bend (Mid)	A	12	4	2.81	27	27	2	0	160	142	59	50	10	35	157	.236
2002	El Paso (TL)	AA	3	8	5.47	20	19	1	0	97	114	70	59	10	33	77	.292
	Lancaster (Cal)	A	3	2	2.51	5	5	0	0	32	31	11	9	1	3	30	.263
MINOR LEAGUE TOTALS			29	16	3.85	83	57	3	0	377	380	193	161	26	110	353	.262

26. Alex Cintron, ss/2b

Born: Dec. 17, 1978. **Ht.:** 6-2. **Wt.:** 180. **Bats:** B. **Throws:** R. **School:** Mech Tech, Yabucoa, P.R. **Career Transactions:** Selected by Diamondbacks in 36th round of 1997 draft; signed June 15, 1997.

Cintron ranked No. 1 on this list two years ago, but the Diamondbacks have beefed up their system considerably since then and he has not moved forward in his development. Cintron continues to hit for average, but that represents the extent of his offensive contributions because he hasn't added hitting homers or drawing walks to his repertoire. He has added 30 pounds since signing, and while he's gotten stronger the extra bulk has cut into his speed and his range at shortstop. Cintron is adequate at short, second base and third base (his regular position over the winter in Puerto Rico). He no longer is Arizona's shortstop of the future, but he does have potential value as a utilityman or injury replacement. Cintron could make the Diamondbacks big league roster if they decide to carry seven infielders, or he could play second base opposite Tim Olson in Triple-A.

Year	Club (League)	Class	AVG	G	AB	R	H	2B	3B	HR	RBI	BB	SO	SB	SLG	OBP
1997	Diamondbacks (AZL)	R	.197	43	152	23	30	6	1	0	20	21	32	1	.250	.301
	Lethbridge (Pio)	R	.333	1	3	0	1	0	0	0	0	0	1	0	.333	.333
1998	Lethbridge (Pio)	R	.264	67	258	41	68	11	4	3	34	20	32	8	.372	.319
1999	High Desert (Cal)	A	.307	128	499	78	153	25	4	3	64	19	65	15	.391	.333
2000	El Paso (TL)	AA	.301	125	522	83	157	30	6	4	59	29	56	9	.404	.336
2001	Tucson (PCL)	AAA	.292	107	425	53	124	24	3	3	35	15	48	9	.384	.315
	Arizona (NL)	MAJ	.286	8	7	0	2	0	1	0	0	0	0	0	.571	.286
2002	Tucson (PCL)	AAA	.322	85	351	53	113	22	3	4	26	11	33	9	.436	.345
	Arizona (NL)	MAJ	.213	38	75	11	16	6	0	0	4	12	13	0	.293	.322
MAJOR LEAGUE TOTALS			.220	46	82	11	18	6	1	0	4	12	13	0	.317	.319
MINOR LEAGUE TOTALS			.292	556	2210	331	646	118	21	17	238	115	267	51	.388	.328

27. Lance Cormier, rhp

Born: Aug. 19, 1980. **Ht.:** 6-1. **Wt.:** 190. **Bats:** R. **Throws:** R. **School:** University of Alabama. **Career Transactions:** Selected by Diamondbacks in fourth round of 2002 draft; signed June 6, 2002.

Cormier is similar to Andrew Good, another pitcher who relies more on guile than over-powering stuff. He set several school records in four seasons at Alabama, and signed with Arizona last June after turning down Houston as a 10th-rounder a year earlier. Cormier's changeup is his top pitch, and he throws an 88-92 mph fastball, a curveball and a slider. He has command of all four pitches to all four quadrants of the strike zone. In his pro debut, he issued just two walks in 29 innings. Cormier pitched mainly in relief after signing because he had worked 129 innings with the Crimson Tide during the spring, but he'll move back to the rotation this year in Class A.

Year	Club (League)	Class	W	L	ERA	G	GS	CG	SV	IP	H	R	ER	HR	BB	SO	AVG
2002	Yakima (NWL)	A	0	0	27.00	1	0	0	0	1	4	4	3	0	0	3	.500
	South Bend (Mid)	A	3	0	2.93	11	3	0	1	28	29	9	9	1	2	17	.259
MINOR LEAGUE TOTALS			3	0	3.77	12	3	0	1	29	33	13	12	1	2	20	.275

28. Greg Aquino, rhp

Born: Jan. 11, 1979. **Ht.:** 6-1. **Wt.:** 150. **Bats:** R. **Throws:** R. **Career Transactions:** Signed out of Dominican Republic by Diamondbacks, Nov. 8, 1995.

Aquino has gone through major changes since signing in 1995. He spent his first 3½ years as a shortstop before batting .160 in two tries at low Class A. His offensive struggles and his strong arm prompted a move to the mound in 1999. He also played under the surname Valera before last season. Aquino's fastball registers 96-97 mph consistently and he has more than adequate control for a power pitcher. His main problem is that he lacks a decent second pitch to keep hitters off his heater. The Diamondbacks remain hopeful he'll improve his slider and changeup, and they're comfortable with his development to this point. He'll probably start 2003 in high Class A.

Year	Club (League)	Class	AVG	G	AB	R	H	2B	3B	HR	RBI	BB	SO	SB	SLG	OBP
1996	Diamondbacks (DSL)	R	.200	58	160	21	32	3	0	0	9	22	11	7	.219	.308
1997	Diamondbacks (DSL)	R	.289	53	180	39	52	9	0	0	14	18	21	3	.339	.355
	South Bend (Mid)	A	.185	8	27	2	5	2	0	0	2	0	7	0	.259	.185
1998	Diamondbacks (AZL)	R	.282	45	163	20	46	11	1	0	11	7	34	2	.362	.310
1999	South Bend (Mid)	A	.156	53	186	18	29	4	2	0	10	9	46	1	.199	.199
2000	South Bend (Mid)	A	.000	29	0	1	0	0	0	0	0	0	0	0	.000	.000
MINOR LEAGUE TOTALS			.229	246	716	101	164	29	3	0	46	56	119	13	.278	.289

Year	Club (League)	Class	W	L	ERA	G	GS	CG	SV	IP	H	R	ER	HR	BB	SO	AVG
1999	Diamondbacks (AZL)	R	1	2	3.79	13	2	0	0	19	17	11	8	0	13	20	.246
2000	South Bend (Mid)	A	5	7	4.46	29	18	0	0	119	119	67	59	9	56	93	.260
2001	Lancaster (Cal)	A	2	5	8.14	25	4	0	0	42	59	40	38	7	24	39	.331
	Yakima (NWL)	A	4	2	3.30	8	8	0	0	46	39	18	17	2	14	39	.229
2002	Yakima (NWL)	A	1	1	2.06	6	6	0	0	35	26	9	8	0	17	34	.213
	Lancaster (Cal)	A	4	1	3.67	8	8	0	0	49	50	20	20	3	18	50	.267
MINOR LEAGUE TOTALS			17	18	4.35	89	46	0	0	310	310	165	150	21	142	275	.262

29. Josh Kroeger, of

Born: Aug. 31, 1982. **Ht.:** 6-3. **Wt.:** 210. **Bats:** L. **Throws:** L. **School:** Scripps Ranch HS, San Diego. **Career Transactions:** Selected by Diamondbacks in fourth round of 2000 draft; signed June 6, 2000.

Kroeger has regressed offensively as he has moved through the minors, and his strike-zone judgment completely fell apart in 2002. However, the Diamondbacks still see plenty of potential. Kroeger was just 17 when he signed, turning down a football scholarship to play wide receiver at NCAA Division II Truman State (Mo.). He's athletic and has raw power, but he continues to struggle with pitch recognition and is overly aggressive. He gets himself out rather than making pitchers work to do so. Kroeger is a natural right fielder, with the arm strength and range to play there. He has acceptable speed but hasn't refined his basestealing instincts. He needs to repeat high Class A this year.

Year	Club (League)	Class	AVG	G	AB	R	H	2B	3B	HR	RBI	BB	SO	SB	SLG	OBP
2000	Diamondbacks (AZL)	R	.297	54	222	40	66	9	3	4	28	21	41	5	.419	.359
2001	South Bend (Mid)	A	.274	79	292	36	80	15	1	3	37	18	49	4	.363	.324
2002	Lancaster (Cal)	A	.235	133	497	63	117	20	7	7	58	23	136	2	.346	.274
MINOR LEAGUE TOTALS			.260	266	1011	139	263	44	11	14	123	62	226	11	.367	.308

30. Jerry Gil, ss

Born: Oct. 14, 1982. **Ht.:** 6-3. **Wt.:** 180. **Bats:** R. **Throws:** R. **Career Transactions:** Signed out of Dominican Republic by Diamondbacks, Nov. 5, 1999.

For six weeks last year, the Northwest League saw flashes of the Jerry Gil who commanded a $767,500 bonus in 1999. He was brilliant at times in Yakima and looked like a five-tool player. He's easily the best defender and has the strongest arm among the system's infielders, and has been since he signed. But he has been slow to develop any understanding of the strike zone, as his career 224-26 strikeout-walk ratio attests, or any real approach at the plate. Scouts often wonder what he could be thinking in the batter's box. Gil has well above-average speed and is a basestealing threat—if he can get on base. Injuries sabotaged his 2002 season. He missed a month at high Class A with a quadriceps strain, and a sore elbow caused him to tail off in the NWL. The Diamondbacks still have confidence in his physical gifts and probably will return him to the California League in 2003.

Year	Club (League)	Class	AVG	G	AB	R	H	2B	3B	HR	RBI	BB	SO	SB	SLG	OBP
2000	Missoula (Pio)	R	.225	58	227	24	51	10	2	0	20	11	63	7	.286	.266
2001	South Bend (Mid)	A	.215	105	363	40	78	14	5	2	31	8	103	19	.298	.240
2002	Lancaster (Cal)	A	.216	10	37	4	8	0	0	1	4	1	11	1	.297	.237
	Yakima (NWL)	A	.250	65	224	21	56	11	2	2	28	6	47	14	.344	.274
MINOR LEAGUE TOTALS			.227	238	851	89	193	35	9	5	83	26	224	41	.307	.256

ATLANTA
BRAVES

TOP 30 PROSPECTS

1. Adam Wainwright, rhp
2. Wilson Betemit, ss
3. Andy Marte, 3b
4. Bubba Nelson, rhp
5. Macay McBride, lhp
6. Jeff Francoeur, of
7. Carlos Duran, of
8. Scott Thorman, 1b
9. Brett Evert, rhp
10. Gonzalo Lopez, rhp
11. Horacio Ramirez, lhp
12. Kelly Johnson, ss
13. Adam LaRoche, 1b
14. Bryan Digby, rhp
15. Zach Miner, rhp
16. Jung Bong, lhp
17. Gregor Blanco, of
18. Dan Meyer, lhp
19. Trey Hodges, rhp
20. Ryan Langerhans, of
21. Anthony Lerew, rhp
22. Blaine Boyer, rhp
23. Richard Lewis, 2b
24. Chris Waters, lhp
25. Andy Pratt, lhp
26. John Ennis, rhp
27. Matt Wright, rhp
28. Brian McCann, c
29. Matt Belisle, rhp
30. Bill McCarthy, of

By Bill Ballew

Most teams only dream of the type of rebuilding project the Braves are facing.

Riding the crest of 11 straight division titles, the longest playoff run in the history of pro sports, Atlanta entered the offseason with aces Tom Glavine and Greg Maddux testing free agency and uncertainty on the right side of its infield. The Braves made their first move by acquiring lefthander Mike Hampton from the Marlins. Florida will pay $30 million toward his 2003-05 salaries, with Atlanta responsible for just $5.5 million. Then Glavine signed with the Mets for three years and $35 million. He expressed disappointment that the Braves didn't make a stronger effort to keep him.

Concerned that he might not be able to re-sign Maddux, general manager John Schuerholz offered him arbitration, then added veterans Russ Ortiz (in a trade with the Giants) and Paul Byrd (as a free agent). After Maddux accepted arbitration, Schuerholz wasn't going to be able to follow owner AOL Time Warner's edict to cut payroll from the $111 million it spent in 2002.

In a stunning move that weakened the Braves and strengthened a division rival, Schuerholz traded Kevin Millwood to the Phillies for backup catcher Johnny Estrada. Schuerholz laid the blame on baseball economics, but it was his own overaggressiveness in trying to maintain a strong pitching staff that doomed him.

Schuerholz made his final move in signing Robert Fick to play first base, after the Tigers nontendered him. In spite of all the changes, though, it's not all doom and gloom in Atlanta. The Braves still have Maddux. John Smoltz re-emerged as a top closer and few teams can match the outfield of Chipper and Andruw Jones, plus Gary Sheffield. The farm system remains one of the best in the game. If Atlanta needs another starter in 2003, Trey Hodges and Jung Bong are waiting in the wings. More pitching help is less than two years away in Adam Wainwright, Bubba Nelson and others. The Braves also have a deep stock of position players.

The lower reaches of the minors are healthy after three strong drafts by scouting director Roy Clark. Atlanta's complex in the Dominican Republic also continues to pay dividends, offsetting the shrinking of the farm system from seven to six affiliates in 2002.

Organization Overview

General Manager: John Schuerholz. Farm Director: Dayton Moore. Scouting Director: Roy Clark.

2002 PERFORMANCE

Class	Farm Team	League	W	L	Pct.	Finish*	Manager
Majors	Atlanta	National	101	59	.631	1st (16)	Bobby Cox
Triple-A	Richmond Braves	International	75	67	.528	7th (14)	Fredi Gonzalez
Double-A	Greenville Braves	Southern	65	69	.485	7th (10)	Brian Snitker
High A	Myrtle Beach Pelicans	Carolina	79	61	.564	3rd (8)	Randy Ingle
Low A	†Macon Braves	South Atlantic	66	74	.471	t-10th (16)	Lynn Jones
Rookie	Danville Braves	Appalachian	37	31	.544	5th (10)	Ralph Henriquez
Rookie	GCL Braves	Gulf Coast	28	32	.467	t-8th (14)	Rick Albert
OVERALL 2002 MINOR LEAGUE RECORD			350	334	.512	12th (30)	

*Finish in overall standings (No. of teams in league). †Franchise will move to Rome, Ga., for 2003.

ORGANIZATION LEADERS

BATTING
*Minimum 250 At-Bats
*AVG	Adam LaRoche, Greenville/Myrtle Beach	.317
R	Gregor Blanco, Macon	87
H	Carlos Duran, Macon	144
TB	Andy Marte, Macon	240
2B	Scott Thorman, Macon	38
3B	Adam Stern, Myrtle Beach	10
	Carlos Duran, Macon	10
HR	Mike Hessman, Richmond	26
RBI	Andy Marte, Macon	105
BB	Gregor Blanco, Macon	85
SO	Gregor Blanco, Macon	120
SB	Adam Stern, Myrtle Beach	40
	Gregor Blanco, Macon	40

PITCHING
#Minimum 75 Innings
W	Trey Hodges, Richmond	15
L	Brett Evert, Greenville/Myrtle Beach	13
ERA	Ray Aguilar, Myrtle Beach/Danville	1.57
G	Ray Beasley, Richmond	64
CG	Daniel Curtis, Greenville/Myrtle Beach	4
SV	Kevin Barry, Myrtle Beach	26
	Billy Sylvester, Richmond/Greenville	26
IP	Chris Waters, Myrtle Beach	183
BB	Adam Wainwright, Myrtle Beach	66
SO	Adam Wainwright, Myrtle Beach	167

BEST TOOLS

Best Hitter for Average	Adam LaRoche
Best Power Hitter	Scott Thorman
Fastest Baserunner	Gregor Blanco
Best Athlete	Jeff Francoeur
Best Fastball	Bryan Digby
Best Curveball	Bubba Nelson
Best Slider	Macay McBride
Best Changeup	Jung Bong
Best Control	Dan Curtis
Best Defensive Catcher	Jose Salas
Best Defensive Infielder	T.J. Pena
Best Infield Arm	Wilson Betemit
Best Defensive Outfielder	Jeff Francoeur
Best Outfield Arm	Adam Stern

PROJECTED 2006 LINEUP

Catcher	Javy Lopez
First Base	Chipper Jones
Second Base	Rafael Furcal
Third Base	Andy Marte
Shortstop	Wilson Betemit
Left Field	Gary Sheffield
Center Field	Andruw Jones
Right Field	Jeff Francoeur
No. 1 Starter	Adam Wainwright

Adam LaRoche   Ray Aguilar

No. 2 Starter	Russ Ortiz
No. 3 Starter	Bubba Nelson
No. 4 Starter	Macay McBride
No. 5 Starter	Mike Hampton
Closer	John Smoltz

TOP PROSPECTS OF THE DECADE

1993	Chipper Jones, ss
1994	Chipper Jones, ss
1995	Chipper Jones, ss/3b
1996	Andruw Jones, of
1997	Andruw Jones, of
1998	Bruce Chen, lhp
1999	Bruce Chen, lhp
2000	Rafael Furcal, ss
2001	Wilson Betemit, ss
2002	Wilson Betemit, ss

TOP DRAFT PICKS OF THE DECADE

1993	Andre King, of (2)
1994	Jacob Shumate, rhp
1995	*Chad Hutchinson, rhp
1996	A.J. Zapp, 1b
1997	Troy Cameron, ss
1998	Matt Belisle, rhp (2)
1999	Matt Butler, rhp (2)
2000	Adam Wainwright, thp
2001	Macay McBride, lhp
2002	Jeff Francoeur, of

* Did not sign.

ALL-TIME LARGEST BONUSES

Jeff Francoeur, 2002	$2,200,000
Matt Belisle, 1998	$1,750,000
Jung Bong, 1997	$1,700,000
Macay McBride, 2001	$1,340,000
Adam Wainwright, 2001	$1,250,000
Josh Burrus, 2001	$1,250,000

MinorLeague**Depth**Chart

ATLANTA BRAVES

RANK 2

The Braves rebuilt their franchise through scouting and player development in the early 1990s, and have managed to keep the cupboards nearly full ever since, while supplementing the parent club with the talent to win 11 straight National League East titles. Amazingly, the Braves' philosophy hasn't varied much over the years. Their emphasis has been on power arms along the lines of Adam Wainwright and international prospects such as Wilson Betemit and Andy Marte. Betemit lost his foothold atop the organization's prospect list with a disappointing, injury-plagued 2002 season, but he still has a lofty ceiling.

Note: Depth charts prepared by Josh Boyd. Numbers in parentheses indicate prospect rankings.

LF
Gregor Blanco (17)
Josh Burrus

CF
Jeff Francoeur (6)
Carlos Duran (7)
Ryan Langerhans (20)
Ardley Jansen
Miguel Mota
Adam Stern

RF
Billy McCarthy (30)
Cory Aldridge

3B
Andy Marte (3)
Kelly Johnson (12)
Mike Hessman
Cole Barthel

SS
Wilson Betemit (2)
Luis Hernandez
Ramon Castro
T.J. Pena

2B
Richard Lewis (23)
Joanthan Schuerholz
Nick Green

1B
Scott Thorman (8)
Adam LaRoche (13)
James Jurries
Yaron Peters

C
Brian McCann (28)
Lee Evans
Kyle Roat

RHP

Starters	Relievers
Adam Wainwright (1)	Bryan Digby (14)
Bubba Nelson (4)	Blaine Boyer (22)
Brett Evert (9)	Matt McClendon
Gonzalo Lopez (10)	Kevin Barry
Zach Miner (15)	Ralph Roberts
Trey Hodges (19)	Bill Sylvester
Anthony Lerew (21)	Jose Capellan
John Ennis (26)	Efigenio Peralta
Matt Wright (27)	Francisco Arteaga
Matt Belisle (29)	Chris Spurling
Kyle Davies	Ray Aguilar
Daniel Curtis	Charlie Morton
Joe Dawley	
Steve Russell	

LHP

Starters	Relievers
Macay McBride (5)	Andy Pratt (25)
Horacio Ramirez (11)	
Jung Bong (16)	
Dan Meyer (18)	
Chris Waters (24)	

DraftAnalysis

2002 Draft

Best Pro Debut: Managers rated OF Jeff Francoeur (1) the top prospect in the Rookie-level Appalachian League after he batted .327-8-31. LHP Fernando Tadefa (19) led the Appy League with 16 saves.

Best Athlete: Francoeur was a standout defensive back in high school and gave up a Clemson football grant. 2B Mike Grasso (11) was a wide receiver at Rhode Island before transferring to Albany to focus on baseball.

Best Pure Hitter: In 1999, 1B James Jurries (6) beat out Mark Teixeira for BA's Freshman of the Year award. Jurries is gifted with the bat and hit .290-5-30 in high Class A.

Best Raw Power: Francoeur matched Andruw Jones and Javy Lopez in batting practice at Turner Field. 1B Yaron Peters (10) finished second in NCAA Division I with 29 homers and tied for third with 95 RBIs.

Fastest Runner: Francoeur flies through the 60-yard dash in 6.43 seconds. Grasso and SS Jon Schuerholz (8) also run well.

Best Defensive Player: Francoeur has center-field range and a plus arm. C **Brian McCann** (2) has good catch-and-throw skills and is working on his agility.

Best Fastball: LHP Dan Meyer (1) has an 89-93 mph fastball that's as notable for its sink as its velocity. RHP Mike Mueller (16), a converted outfielder, throws nearly as hard.

Best Breaking Ball: RHP Charlie Morton's (3) curveball. As Morton fills out his 6-foot-4, 180-pound frame, his fastball could jump from the high 80s to the mid-90s.

Most Intriguing Background: Schuerholz' father John is Atlanta's general manag-

er. RHPs Michael (14) and Steven Reiss (25) are identical twins from Canada. C/RHP Kris Harvey's (5) father Bryan was a two-time all-star as a closer. McCann's brother Brad is a third-base prospect who joined Harvey at Clemson, and McCann's father Howard was once Marshall's baseball coach. RHP Paul Bush (25) was NAIA player of the year after going 13-1, 1.63 for Georgia Southwestern.

BOB LIBBY

McCann

Closest To The Majors: Meyer or Jurries, who could surface in Double-A in 2003. Meyer, the Braves' highest-drafted college player since they took Mike Kelly No. 2 in 1991, has an advanced feel for pitching and a plus changeup.

Best Late-Round Pick: The Braves were glad to get Peters, the Southeastern Conference player of the year, in the 10th round.

The One Who Got Away: SS Tyler Greene (2) was one of the draft's best pure shortstops and could be a first-round pick after three years at Georgia Tech. After missing Greene the Braves made a run at LHP Tim Cunningham (23), who returned to Stanford.

Assessment: The Braves weren't scared off by Francoeur's price and signed him for $2.2 million. They missed on Greene and RHP Patrick Clayton (7)–products of the local East Cobb youth program–as well as Harvey and Nick Starnes (9). No other club lost as many picks in the first 10 rounds.

2001 Draft

The Braves had three first-rounders and used them all on homestate products. LHP Macay McBride looks like a star, while 2B Richard Lewis is off to a decent start and 3B Josh Burrus has struggled. **Grade: B**

2000 Draft

Atlanta went 3-for-4 on first-rounders, hitting on RHP Adam Wainwright, 1B Scott Thorman and SS Kelly Johnson and missing on 2B Aaron Herr. RHP Bubba Nelson (2) led the minors in ERA in 2002. RHPs Bryan Digby (2) and Zach Miner (4) and 1B Adam LaRoche (29) all rank among the system's top prospects. **Grade: A**

1999 Draft

The Braves are hoping Brett Evert (7) recovers from shoulder problems, because they dealt their best two picks: RHP Andrew Brown (6) and LHP Ben Kozlowski (12). **Grade: C+**

1998 Draft

Atlanta again didn't have a first-round pick, and failed to sign a future one in RHP Ryan Karp (8). RHP Matt Belisle (2) has been sidetracked by back problems and draft-and-follow RHP Tim Spooneybarger (29) was traded. **Grade: C**

Note: Draft analysis prepared by Jim Callis. Numbers in parentheses indicate draft rounds.

... Wainwright has an excellent mound presence and can be intimidating with his downward angle to the plate.

Adam
Wainwright rhp

Born: Aug. 30, 1981.
Ht.: 6-6. **Wt.:** 190.
Bats: R. **Throws:** R.
School: Glynn Academy, Brunswick, Ga.
Career Transactions: Selected by Braves in first round (29th overall) of 2000 draft; signed June 12, 2000.

The 29th overall pick in the 2000 draft, Wainwright has lived up to the Braves' early projections. He was the strikeout leader in the high Class A Carolina League–where managers rated him the league's No. 3 prospect–and earned a spot in the Futures Game last season. Since signing, he has been ranked the No. 2 prospect in the Rookie-level Gulf Coast League and No. 1 in the Rookie-level Appalachian and low Class A South Atlantic leagues. In 2001, he set a Macon record and led the SAL with 184 strikeouts.

Few pitchers are more projectable than Wainwright. His tall body and loose arm action should allow him to add velocity as he continues to mature and develop. He reached 96 mph during the Futures Game and sat in the 90-93 mph range last season at Myrtle Beach. His fastball, rated the best in the Carolina League by managers, has outstanding movement and frequently fools hitters. Wainwright is nearly as successful with his hard curveball, though he has yet to master consistency and feel with it. He also throws strikes with his solid changeup. Wainwright has an excellent mound presence and can be intimidating with his downward angle to the plate. He works both sides of the dish well and has a solid idea of what he wants to accomplish with every pitch. Wainwright needs to get stronger and improve his stamina by intensifying his offseason conditioning. He has faded in the past two seasons. He went 8-3, 2.24 during the first four months of the 2002 season before going 1-3, 6.32 in his final seven starts. While he has ranked among the minor league leaders in strikeouts the last two years, Wainwright could be more aggressive in the strike zone. With his lanky body, he has difficulty repeating his delivery, resulting in a loss of control and rhythm. His over-the-top delivery gives hitters a good view of the ball, so he needs to add deception.

Wainwright has the ingredients to be a top-of-the-rotation starter, but the Braves don't want to rush him. His ETA in Atlanta is 2004, and he should spend most of 2003 at Double-A Greenville. If Wainwright continues to perform as he has, though, he could force Atlanta's hand.

Year	Club (League)	Class	W	L	ERA	G	GS	CG	SV	IP	H	R	ER	HR	BB	SO	AVG
2000	Braves (GCL)	R	4	0	1.13	7	5	0	0	32	15	5	4	1	10	42	.136
	Danville (Appy)	R	2	2	3.68	6	6	0	0	29	28	13	12	3	2	39	.252
2001	Macon (SAL)	A	10	10	3.77	28	28	1	0	165	144	89	69	9	48	184	.230
2002	Myrtle Beach (Car)	A	9	6	3.31	28	28	1	0	163	149	67	60	7	66	167	.240
MINOR LEAGUE TOTALS			25	18	3.35	69	67	2	0	389	336	174	145	20	126	432	.229

TOM PRIDDY

2. Wilson Betemit, ss

Born: Nov. 2, 1981. **Ht.:** 6-3. **Wt.:** 190. **Bats:** B. **Throws:** R. **Career Transactions:** Signed out of Dominican Republic by Braves, July 28, 1996.

Considered one of the top prospects in baseball, Betemit struggled mightily in 2002 at Triple-A Richmond. He hit just .198 during the first three months and made 21 errors in 93 games. A strained back, bruised foot and sprained ankle hurt his performance. Betemit remains a five-tool athlete whose skills are still blossoming. He hits to all fields from both sides of the plate and is adding power. He has a live body with easy actions toward the ball and good bat speed with excellent extension. Scouts believe he'll hit 20 homers and steal 25 bases annually in the big leagues. Betemit can make the spectacular play but also can be lackadaisical on defense. He fields the ball too close to his body at times, and he lets the ball play him instead of being aggressive. The accuracy of his strong arm is unpredictable. His plate discipline has never been strong. After having an outside shot at winning Atlanta's shortstop job last spring, Betemit will return to Triple-A in 2003. He must prove that 2002 was a fluke and a move to third base isn't needed.

Year	Club (League)	Class	AVG	G	AB	R	H	2B	3B	HR	RBI	BB	SO	SB	SLG	OBP
1997	Braves (GCL)	R	.212	32	113	12	24	6	1	0	15	9	32	0	.283	.270
1998	Braves (GCL)	R	.220	51	173	23	38	8	4	5	16	20	49	6	.399	.301
1999	Danville (Appy)	R	.320	67	259	39	83	18	2	5	53	27	63	6	.463	.383
2000	Jamestown (NY-P)	A	.331	69	269	54	89	15	2	5	37	30	37	3	.457	.393
2001	Myrtle Beach (Car)	A	.277	84	318	38	88	20	1	7	43	23	71	8	.412	.324
	Greenville (SL)	AA	.355	47	183	22	65	14	0	5	19	12	36	6	.514	.394
	Atlanta (NL)	MAJ	.000	8	3	1	0	0	0	0	0	0	2	3	1	.000	.400
2002	Richmond (IL)	AAA	.245	93	343	43	84	17	1	8	34	34	82	8	.370	.312
	Braves (GCL)	R	.263	7	19	2	5	4	0	0	2	5	2	1	.474	.417
MAJOR LEAGUE TOTALS			.000	8	3	1	0	0	0	0	0	2	3	1	.000	.400
MINOR LEAGUE TOTALS			.284	450	1677	233	476	102	11	35	219	160	372	38	.420	.345

3. Andy Marte, 3b

Born: Oct. 21, 1983. **Ht.:** 6-1. **Wt.:** 180. **Bats:** R. **Throws:** R. **Career Transactions:** Signed out of Dominican Republic by Braves, Sept. 12, 2000.

Marte hit just .200 in the Appalachian League in 2001 after signing for $600,000 the previous September. But he proved to be a bargain last year by pacing the South Atlantic League in RBIs and ranking second in home runs and extra-base hits. Managers also rated him the SAL's best defensive third baseman. Marte has quick wrists that allow him to turn on most fastballs. He has power to all fields, makes impressive adjustments to all types of pitches and refuses to concede any at-bat. Marte possesses quick reflexes, soft hands and a strong arm. He also has impressive maturity for a teenager. His speed is average. Despite being a plus defender, Marte can become careless in the field. He also tends to give up on pitches on the outer half of the plate, limiting his overall coverage of the dish. He could stand to draw a few more walks. Because the Braves lack depth at the hot corner, Marte is in position to move rapidly through the system. He should start the 2003 season in high Class A and could move up to Double-A at midseason.

Year	Club (League)	Class	AVG	G	AB	R	H	2B	3B	HR	RBI	BB	SO	SB	SLG	OBP
2001	Danville (Appy)	R	.200	37	125	12	25	6	0	1	12	20	45	3	.272	.306
2002	Macon (SAL)	A	.281	126	488	69	137	32	4	21	105	41	114	2	.492	.339
MINOR LEAGUE TOTALS			.264	163	613	81	162	38	4	22	117	61	159	5	.447	.332

4. Bubba Nelson, rhp

Born: Aug. 26, 1981. **Ht.:** 6-2. **Wt.:** 200. **Bats:** R. **Throws:** R. **School:** Riverdale Baptist HS, Upper Marlboro, Md. **Career Transactions:** Selected by Braves in second round of 2000 draft; signed June 23, 2000.

In 2001, his first full season, Nelson went 9-2 in the first half at Macon but lost six of his last nine decisions. He avoided such inconsistency last year, leading the minors with a 1.66 ERA and holding opponents to a .197 average. Nelson is a great competitor who allows the natural nasty movement of his pitches to work for him. His heavy fastball sits at 91-94 mph and induces plenty of grounders. His two-seamer has improved since he added the pitch in 2001. His strikeout pitch is a hard slider, and he's most consistent with a plus curveball he throws any time in the count. When he struggles, Nelson gets caught in between his curveball and slider, which causes his breaking pitches to flatten. He should avoid the problem when he gains more consistency with his arm slot. His changeup could use refinement. The Braves believe Nelson is on the verge of being ready for the big leagues. While he could be the first pitcher from Atlanta's heralded 2000 draft class to reach the majors, he'll open 2003 in Double-A.

Year	Club (League)	Class	W	L	ERA	G	GS	CG	SV	IP	H	R	ER	HR	BB	SO	AVG
2000	Braves (GCL)	R	3	2	4.23	12	6	1	0	45	40	24	21	2	13	54	.233
2001	Macon (SAL)	A	12	8	3.93	25	24	2	0	151	144	76	66	16	57	154	.252
2002	Myrtle Beach (Car)	A	11	5	1.72	23	23	0	0	136	98	37	26	4	44	105	.202
	Braves (GCL)	R	0	0	0.00	3	3	0	0	5	1	0	0	0	1	7	.063
MINOR LEAGUE TOTALS			26	15	3.02	63	56	3	0	336	283	137	113	22	115	320	.227

5. Macay McBride, lhp

RODGER WOOD

Born: Oct. 24, 1982. **Ht.:** 5-11. **Wt.:** 180. **Bats:** L. **Throws:** L. **School:** Screven County HS, Sylvania, Ga. **Career Transactions:** Selected by Braves in first round (24th overall) of 2001 draft; signed June 6, 2001.

The Braves planned to start McBride at Rookie-level Danville last year before injuries hit Macon hard in early April. He proceeded to lead the South Atlantic League in ERA and earn most valuable pitcher honors. He won nine of his last 10 decisions and didn't allow an earned run in 11 of his 25 starts. The 24th overall pick in 2001, McBride has outstanding arm strength and impressive command. He throws a heavy, low-90s fastball along with a plus slider with excellent late break. His 12-to-6 curveball and changeup improved over the course of last season. McBride discovered how to set up hitters in 2002, and by the end of the season he was breaking bats with his changeup. He's aggressive yet maintains his composure on the mound. McBride is polished and mainly requires more experience. He'll focus on improving the finer points of pitching, such as holding runners on base and getting to pitcher's counts. While McBride will begin 2003 in high Class A, there's no doubt he's on a fast track to the major leagues. Few lefthanders at any level can match his stuff.

Year	Club (League)	Class	W	L	ERA	G	GS	CG	SV	IP	H	R	ER	HR	BB	SO	AVG
2001	Braves (GCL)	R	4	4	3.76	13	11	0	0	55	51	30	23	0	23	67	.248
2002	Macon (SAL)	A	12	8	2.12	25	25	2	0	157	119	49	37	6	48	138	.209
MINOR LEAGUE TOTALS			16	12	2.54	38	36	2	0	212	170	79	60	6	71	205	.219

6. Jeff Francoeur, of

BILL SETLIFF

Born: Jan. 8, 1984. **Ht.:** 6-4. **Wt.:** 200. **Bats:** R. **Throws:** R. **School:** Parkview HS, Lilburn, Ga. **Career Transactions:** Selected by Braves in first round (23rd overall) of 2002 draft; signed July 8, 2002.

The 23rd overall pick last June, Francoeur made a seamless transition from high school to pro ball. He was the Appalachian League's No. 1 prospect. A prep All-America defensive back, he passed up a football scholarship from Clemson to sign for a Braves-record $2.2 million bonus. Francoeur impresses scouts as much with his character as he does with his tools. And he's loaded with tools, starting with 6.43-second speed in the 60-yard dash and solid baserunning instincts. He has a plus arm and the ability and instincts to play all three outfield positions. He drives the ball to all fields and makes rapid adjustments. His swing is smooth and features little wasted movement. Experience is the biggest thing lacking for Francoeur. As he focuses on baseball, he'll understand how pitchers are trying to set him up at the plate and how to read them while getting leads. Francoeur is a natural leader with a tremendous drive to reach the big leagues. Several Braves officials said he could top this list at the end of 2003, which he'll begin at Rome, the organization's new low Class A affiliate.

Year	Club (League)	Class	AVG	G	AB	R	H	2B	3B	HR	RBI	BB	SO	SB	SLG	OBP
2002	Danville (Appy)	R	.327	38	147	31	48	12	1	8	31	15	34	8	.585	.395
MINOR LEAGUE TOTALS			.327	38	147	31	48	12	1	8	31	15	34	8	.585	.395

7. Carlos Duran, of

Born: Dec. 27, 1982. **Ht.:** 6-1. **Wt.:** 160. **Bats:** L. **Throws:** L. **Career Transactions:** Signed out of Venezuela by Braves, July 29, 1999.

Macon featured one of the better outfields in low Class A last year, with Duran joined by Gregor Blanco, Angelo Burrows and Greg Miller. Duran combined his speed and hitting to lead the South Atlantic League in triples while ranking fourth in hits and fifth in runs. Duran has incredible instincts that enhance his natural tools. He has a smooth swing and the speed to allow him to create havoc on the basepaths. He continues to add power and could hit 20 home runs annually. Defensively, he owns a strong arm and gets good jumps on balls hit into the gaps. Opposing managers liked the way he carried himself last year. Duran must understand the importance of playing with intensity at all times. He gave away too many at-bats last season because he lacks patience. He has to work deeper counts to see more advantageous pitches. He also needs to learn the nuances of basestealing after being caught 17 times in 40 attempts. The Braves are in no hurry to push Duran, who will move up to high Class A this year. He has the potential to be an all-star if he can refine all five of his tools.

Year	Club (League)	Class	AVG	G	AB	R	H	2B	3B	HR	RBI	BB	SO	SB	SLG	OBP
2000	Chico Canonico (VSL)	R	.306	54	196	48	60	12	6	8	41	18	28	13	.551	.378
2001	Braves (GCL)	R	.304	54	204	35	62	10	3	2	17	12	30	16	.412	.349
2002	Macon (SAL)	A	.270	132	534	86	144	22	10	7	50	29	80	23	.388	.312
MINOR LEAGUE TOTALS			.285	240	934	169	266	44	19	17	108	59	138	52	.427	.334

8. Scott Thorman, 1b

Born: Jan. 6, 1982. **Ht.:** 6-3. **Wt.:** 200. **Bats:** L. **Throws:** R. **School:** Preston HS, Cambridge, Ontario. **Career Transactions:** Selected by Braves in first round (30th overall) of 2000 draft; signed June 19, 2000 . . . On disabled list, June 19-Sept. 18, 2001.

Drafted with the 30th overall pick in 2000, Thorman missed all of 2001 after shoulder surgery. He made up for lost time last year, putting together a 21-game hitting streak while leading the South Atlantic League in doubles and tying for second in extra-base hits. No one in the organization has more raw power than Thorman. He struggled early last season while trying to crush every pitch before realizing the ball naturally jumps off his bat. He has a smooth, easy swing with a slight uppercut. A pitcher in high school with a mid-90s fastball, Thorman maintains a strong arm. After moving from third base to first in 2002, he showed quick feet and good hands. He also runs out every ball. Despite making a successful shift to first base, Thorman still is learning the position. While his passion for the game is obvious, channeling his emotions will enable him to get the most out of his abilities on a consistent basis. Thorman's offensive potential, not to mention his hustle and determination, could make him Atlanta's long-term answer at first base. He'll climb a step to high Class A this season.

Year	Club (League)	Class	AVG	G	AB	R	H	2B	3B	HR	RBI	BB	SO	SB	SLG	OBP
2000	Braves (GCL)	R	.227	29	97	15	22	7	1	1	19	12	23	0	.351	.330
2001			Did Not Play—Injured													
2002	Macon (SAL)	A	.294	127	470	57	138	38	3	16	82	51	83	2	.489	.367
MINOR LEAGUE TOTALS			.282	156	567	72	160	45	4	17	101	63	106	2	.466	.361

9. Brett Evert, rhp

Born: Oct. 23, 1980. **Ht.:** 6-6. **Wt.:** 200. **Bats:** L. **Throws:** R. **School:** North Salem (Ore.) HS. **Career Transactions:** Selected by Braves in seventh round of 1999 draft; signed June 9, 1999.

His ailing shoulder led the Braves to shut Evert down in late July 2001, but he proved healthy and durable last season. He started well in Double-A to earn Futures Game recognition, then slumped and was sent to high Class A. Evert's fastball gets into the low 90s and has natural movement. His curveball is also a plus pitch, featuring a tight spin and a hard, 12-to-6 drop. He continues to make progress with his changeup, which should be at least an average pitch. His command had been excellent before slipping in 2002. Evert's struggles began when his mechanics got out of whack. With his gangly frame, he must maintain control of his body and repeat his delivery. He also needs to keep his pitches down in the strike zone more often. The Braves admit that they may have overreacted last July when they sent Evert down to Myrtle Beach. But they wanted him to work with pitching coach Bruce Dal Canton, who got him back on track. Expected to begin 2003 in Double-A, Evert could be as close as a half-season away from Atlanta.

Year	Club (League)	Class	W	L	ERA	G	GS	CG	SV	IP	H	R	ER	HR	BB	SO	AVG
1999	Braves (GCL)	R	5	3	2.03	13	10	0	0	49	37	17	11	0	9	39	.208
2000	Macon (SAL)	A	1	4	4.64	7	7	0	0	43	53	27	22	7	9	29	.298
	Jamestown (NY-P)	A	8	3	3.38	15	15	0	0	77	92	52	29	6	19	64	.288
2001	Macon (SAL)	A	1	0	0.74	6	6	0	0	36	25	5	3	0	3	34	.182
	Myrtle Beach (Car)	A	7	2	2.24	13	13	1	0	72	63	25	18	4	15	75	.226
2002	Greenville (SL)	AA	5	8	4.90	16	15	1	0	94	94	59	51	15	35	84	.263
	Myrtle Beach (Car)	A	3	5	3.75	10	10	1	0	58	53	30	24	3	21	51	.241
MINOR LEAGUE TOTALS			30	25	3.32	80	76	3	0	429	417	215	158	35	111	376	.250

10. Gonzalo Lopez, rhp

Born: Oct. 6, 1983. **Ht.:** 6-2. **Wt.:** 170. **Bats:** R. **Throws:** R. **Career Transactions:** Signed out of Nicaragua by Braves, July 8, 2000.

Lopez discovered the ups and downs of playing in a full-season league at 18. He posted his sixth win of the season on July 8 with a five-hit shutout at South Georgia, but had only one more win the rest of the season. He faded in August, though that couldn't erase the impression he made in 2002. One day Lopez could have three plus pitches. His lively fastball averages 93 mph, his curveball has its moments and his changeup is effective. He's advanced for a teenager, both in the quality of his stuff and his command. While his curveball has potential, Lopez lost it during the second half of last season. As a result, he relied almost exclusively on his fastball and paid the price. He needs to improve the spin and depth of his curve, and he did make some progress with the pitch in instructional league. He also must use his changeup and the bottom half of the strike zone more often. Some people have misgivings about his makeup. At 19, Lopez figures to be one of the Carolina League's youngest pitchers in 2003. If he can mature both on and off the mound, his ceiling is unlimited.

Year	Club (League)	Class	W	L	ERA	G	GS	CG	SV	IP	H	R	ER	HR	BB	SO	AVG
2001	Braves (GCL)	R	5	4	2.45	12	11	0	0	59	44	17	16	2	10	69	.208
2002	Macon (SAL)	A	7	10	3.10	28	27	1	0	157	134	72	54	11	51	130	.233
MINOR LEAGUE TOTALS			12	14	2.92	40	38	1	0	216	178	89	70	13	61	199	.226

11. Horacio Ramirez, lhp

Born: Nov. 24, 1979. **Ht.:** 6-1. **Wt.:** 170. **Bats:** L. **Throws:** L. **School:** Inglewood (Calif.) HS. **Career Transactions:** Selected by Braves in fifth round of 1997 draft; signed June 6, 1997.

After placing second in the Carolina League with 15 wins in 2000, Ramirez threw just three games in 2001 before succumbing to Tommy John surgery. The lefthander made a rapid recovery by excelling in Double-A during the second half of last season. Ramirez won seven of his last eight decisions and tossed at least six innings in eight of final 10 outings. He capped that effort with a strong showing in the Arizona Fall League. Ramirez is a solid four-pitch pitcher with excellent command and good poise. His fastball sits in the low 90s, and he complements it with a natural cut fastball with a sharp break. His curveball is effective when he repeats his delivery, and his changeup has shown steady development and added depth. Ramirez fought through a dead-arm period shortly after reporting to Greenville last June. While he has made impressive progress in his rehabilitation, he must continue to rebuild his arm strength. From a pitching standpoint, regaining the feel of his curveball on a consistent basis is a must. Pitchers typically make their greatest strides during their second season back from reconstructive elbow surgery. With that in mind, the Braves feel Ramirez is close to pitching in Turner Field. He'll be evaluated closely in spring training, and could reach at Atlanta at some point this year after starting in Triple-A.

Year	Club (League)	Class	W	L	ERA	G	GS	CG	SV	IP	H	R	ER	HR	BB	SO	AVG
1997	Braves (GCL)	R	3	3	2.25	11	8	0	0	44	30	13	11	1	18	61	.192
1998	Macon (SAL)	A	1	7	5.86	12	12	0	0	55	70	50	36	8	16	38	.310
	Eugene (NWL)	A	2	7	6.31	16	8	0	0	56	84	51	39	4	17	39	.346
1999	Macon (SAL)	A	6	3	2.67	17	14	1	0	78	70	30	23	6	25	43	.248
2000	Myrtle Beach (Car)	A	15	8	3.22	27	26	3	0	148	136	57	53	14	42	125	.242
2001	Greenville (SL)	AA	1	1	4.91	3	3	0	0	15	17	8	8	2	8	17	.309
2002	Macon (SAL)	A	0	2	6.00	2	1	0	0	6	11	10	4	0	2	5	.355
	Greenville (SL)	AA	9	5	3.03	16	16	0	0	92	85	41	31	5	32	64	.253
MINOR LEAGUE TOTALS			37	36	3.74	104	88	4	0	494	503	260	205	40	160	392	.266

12. Kelly Johnson, ss

Born: Feb. 22, 1982. **Ht.:** 6-1. **Wt.:** 180. **Bats:** L. **Throws:** R. **School:** Westwood HS, Austin. **Career Transactions:** Selected by Braves in first round (38th overall) of 2000 draft; signed June 12, 2000.

Johnson made a major splash in 2001, his first full season of pro ball, earning top-prospect honors in the South Atlantic League. His jump to high Class A last year was not as smooth, as he struggled for the first time before regaining his swing in July. Johnson is an offensive infielder with above-average pop and the ability to drive the ball to all fields. His power numbers were hurt last year by the large dimensions and constant breeze blowing in from center at Myrtle Beach's Coastal Federal Field. His quick hands will allow him to hit for both power and average once he quits out-thinking himself and trusts his natural ability. While he has improved defensively, Johnson's range and arm strength rate no better than average at shortstop and could lead to a move to third base. That said, he has the ability to become an impact player in the major leagues. He'll make the jump to Double-A in 2003.

Year	Club (League)	Class	AVG	G	AB	R	H	2B	3B	HR	RBI	BB	SO	SB	SLG	OBP
2000	Braves (GCL)	R	.269	53	193	27	52	12	3	4	29	24	45	6	.425	.349
2001	Macon (SAL)	A	.289	124	415	75	120	22	1	23	66	71	111	25	.513	.404
2002	Myrtle Beach (Car)	A	.255	126	482	62	123	21	5	12	49	51	105	12	.394	.325
MINOR LEAGUE TOTALS			.271	303	1090	164	295	55	9	39	144	146	261	43	.445	.361

13. Adam LaRoche, 1b

Born: Nov. 6, 1979. **Ht.:** 6-3. **Wt.:** 180. **Bats:** L. **Throws:** L. **School:** Seminole State (Okla.) CC. **Career Transactions:** Selected by Braves in 29th round of 2000 draft; signed June 21, 2000.

LaRoche made the greatest leap among any player in the Atlanta organization last year. Returning to high Class A after a mediocre showing there in 2001, he was the Carolina League's most productive all-around hitter outside of Rockies prospect Brad Hawpe. He earned a promotion to Double-A and led the Braves system with a .317 average. LaRoche has a solid baseball background. His father Dave earned two all-star berths during a 14-year major league career, and his brother Jeff used to pitch in the Rockies system. LaRoche took his turn on the mound as a two-way player at Seminole State JC, where he earned MVP honors at the 2000 Junior College World Series. While several teams were interested in LaRoche as a pitcher, the Braves are reaping the rewards for allowing him to hit. LaRoche attacks pitches with his aggressive approach. Beginning with a wide-open stance, his swing creates a natural lift thanks to his excellent weight transfer and his ability to use his hands well. He makes good contact, though he doesn't draw an abundance of walks and has yet to show true first-base power. His timing gets out of whack on occasion, which hurts his consistency. He has a laid-back personality that allows him to handle adversity well. CL managers rated him the league's best defensive first baseman, and the Braves believe he could become a Gold Glover. LaRoche isn't a good runner, which limits him to first base. LaRoche will get an extended look in spring training. While a trip to Triple-A appears likely, he could be a major league surprise as a potential backup to Robert Fick.

Year	Club (League)	Class	AVG	G	AB	R	H	2B	3B	HR	RBI	BB	SO	SB	SLG	OBP
2000	Danville (Appy)	R	.308	56	201	38	62	13	3	7	45	24	46	4	.507	.381
2001	Myrtle Beach (Car)	A	.251	126	471	49	118	31	0	7	47	30	108	10	.361	.305
2002	Myrtle Beach (Car)	A	.336	69	250	30	84	17	0	9	53	27	37	0	.512	.406
	Greenville (SL)	AA	.289	45	173	17	50	9	0	4	19	19	38	1	.410	.363
MINOR LEAGUE TOTALS			.287	296	1095	134	314	70	3	27	164	100	229	15	.430	.352

14. Bryan Digby, rhp

Born: Dec. 31, 1981. **Ht.:** 6-2. **Wt.:** 190. **Bats:** R. **Throws:** R. **School:** McIntosh HS, Peachtree City, Ga. **Career Transactions:** Selected by Braves in second round of 2000 draft; signed June 9, 2000.

The 2002 season could have been a major disappointment in Digby's development. He came down with a shoulder impingement in April and pitched just 26 innings. But he recovered in time to report to instructional league, where he made outstanding progress working with roving pitching instructor Rick Adair. Under Adair's guidance, Digby shortened his arm action. Previously, his delivery was so long that the hitters could see the ball behind Digby, which led to poor command. The more compact motion is easier for him to repeat, which has led to increased consistency and confidence. Digby continued to excel after making a late trip to the Arizona Fall League. He throws a hard sinker in the low 90s. If he can maintain his new mechanics and continue to develop a better feel for his slider and changeup, the Braves believe he can move rapidly. Digby projects as a power reliever, though he likely will continue to start this year in Class A in order to get as many innings as possible.

Year	Club (League)	Class	W	L	ERA	G	GS	CG	SV	IP	H	R	ER	HR	BB	SO	AVG
2000	Braves (GCL)	R	1	3	7.33	10	3	0	0	27	28	28	22	3	21	34	.257
2001	Danville (Appy)	R	3	5	3.38	12	12	1	0	61	52	33	23	2	32	49	.222
	Macon (SAL)	A	1	0	1.13	3	1	0	0	8	3	1	1	0	7	6	.120
2002	Macon (SAL)	A	1	2	6.20	7	3	0	0	20	25	16	14	0	16	16	.313
	Braves (GCL)	R	0	0	7.50	3	2	0	0	6	9	5	5	0	5	5	.346
MINOR LEAGUE TOTALS			6	10	4.77	35	21	1	0	123	117	83	65	5	81	110	.247

15. Zach Miner, rhp

Born: March 12, 1982. **Ht.:** 6-3. **Wt.:** 190. **Bats:** R. **Throws:** R. **School:** Palm Beach Gardens (Fla.) HS. **Career Transactions:** Selected by Braves in fourth round of 2000 draft; signed Sept. 1, 2000.

Miner quietly put together one of the strongest seasons in the organization last year, a fact disguised somewhat by his 8-9 record. Considered a first-round talent in 2000, Minor lasted until the fourth round because of signability questions surrounding his commitment to the University of Miami. He signed for a $1.2 million bonus and has lived up to projections. He has a mature approach to pitching along with quality stuff that's continuing to develop along with his body. Miner has an easy and smooth delivery that produces 90-91 mph sinkers. He also throws a solid slider and a good changeup that made significant improvement in 2002. Miner also mirrors other pitchers in the organization with his burning competitiveness and unwillingness to give in to hitters. His greatest need is to add strength, which will make his overall stuff that much better. Miner was gassed at the end of last season and got in trouble when he left pitches up in the strike zone. The Braves believe those adjustments will take place naturally as Miner heads to high Class A this year.

Year	Club (League)	Class	W	L	ERA	G	GS	CG	SV	IP	H	R	ER	HR	BB	SO	AVG
2001	Jamestown (NY-P)	A	3	4	1.89	15	15	0	0	91	76	26	19	6	16	68	.226
2002	Macon (SAL)	A	8	9	3.28	29	28	1	0	159	143	73	58	10	51	131	.243
MINOR LEAGUE TOTALS			11	13	2.78	44	43	1	0	250	219	99	77	16	67	199	.237

16. Jung Bong, lhp

Born: July 15, 1980. **Ht.:** 6-3. **Wt.:** 170. **Bats:** L. **Throws:** L. **Career Transactions:** Signed out of Korea by Braves, Nov. 6, 1997.

Few pitchers created a louder buzz during the Arizona Fall League than Bong. The lefthander continued his impressive August at Greenville by displaying a plus-plus changeup and solid overall command in the AFL. The Korean had opened the season on a steady note in Double-A before making an emergency start in Atlanta on April 23, allowing five earned runs in six innings and taking a loss against Arizona. Bong then fell apart upon his return to the Southern League, losing six straight starts. He was demoted to the bullpen in order to focus on his control and aggressiveness, then re-entered the rotation in August and went 3-1, 1.14 in his last five outings. In addition to his superb changeup with excellent fade and sink, the athletic Bong has a low-90s fastball that touches 94 mph, plus an improving curveball. He needs to command his fastball better and continue to develop his curve. Based on his development over the past two seasons, Bong has the potential to be a fine No. 3 or 4 starter. He's slated for Triple-A in 2003.

Year	Club (League)	Class	W	L	ERA	G	GS	CG	SV	IP	H	R	ER	HR	BB	SO	AVG
1998	Braves (GCL)	R	1	1	1.49	11	10	0	0	48	31	9	8	2	14	56	.195
1999	Macon (SAL)	A	6	5	3.98	26	20	0	1	109	111	61	48	8	50	100	.266
2000	Macon (SAL)	A	7	7	4.23	20	19	0	0	113	119	65	53	4	45	90	.275
	Myrtle Beach (Car)	A	3	1	2.18	7	6	0	0	41	33	14	10	1	7	37	.220
2001	Myrtle Beach (Car)	A	13	9	3.00	28	28	0	0	168	151	67	56	7	47	145	.245
2002	Greenville (SL)	AA	7	8	3.25	27	17	0	2	122	136	59	44	6	45	107	.286
	Atlanta (NL)	MAJ	0	1	7.50	1	1	0	0	6	8	5	5	0	2	4	.320
MAJOR LEAGUE TOTALS			0	1	7.50	1	1	0	0	6	8	5	5	0	2	4	.320
MINOR LEAGUE TOTALS			37	31	3.28	119	100	0	3	601	581	275	219	28	208	535	.258

17. Gregor Blanco, of

Born: Dec. 12, 1983. **Ht.:** 5-11. **Wt.:** 170. **Bats:** L. **Throws:** L. **Career Transactions:** Signed out of Venezuela by Braves, July 4, 2000.

Blanco opened eyes throughout the organization with a strong showing during instructional league in 2001 before continuing to impress in low Class A in 2002, his first season in the United States. The Venezuela native struggled early as an 18-year-old in the South Atlantic League, hitting .219 through May 23. He then heated up and improved to a season-best .282 in late July before tiring over the final month. Blanco's plus speed and knack for getting on base make him a potential leadoff man. He hit into just two double plays last year and tied Adam Stern for the organization lead in stolen bases. Blanco hits southpaws and righthanders equally well and showed surprising power at times. Still, he tends to swing for the fences more than he should instead of perfecting the small-ball aspects of the game, particularly bunting. A good outfielder with an above-average arm, Blanco's biggest need is to mature. Some SAL managers didn't like the way he carried himself last year, but the Braves believe he'll grow up as he gets older and continues to adjust to the United States. He'll play in high Class A this year.

Year	Club (League)	Class	AVG	G	AB	R	H	2B	3B	HR	RBI	BB	SO	SB	SLG	OBP
2001	Braves 2 (DSL)	R	.330	58	215	45	71	6	10	0	18	31	31	21	.451	.422
2002	Macon (SAL)	A	.271	132	468	87	127	14	9	7	36	85	120	40	.385	.392
MINOR LEAGUE TOTALS			.290	190	683	132	198	20	19	7	54	116	151	61	.406	.401

18. Dan Meyer, lhp

Born: July 3, 1981. **Ht.:** 6-3. **Wt.:** 190. **Bats:** R. **Throws:** L. **School:** James Madison University. **Career Transactions:** Selected by Braves in first round (34th overall) of 2002 draft; signed June 7, 2002.

Atlanta scouting director Roy Clark said he believes the Braves got a steal when they grabbed Meyer with the 34th overall pick last June. Clark also said he would have taken Meyer with his first pick, 23rd overall, had Jeff Francoeur not been available. The highest-drafted collegian by the Braves since they took Mike Kelly second overall in 1991, Meyer ranked as the No. 8 prospect in the Appalachian League in his pro debut. He projects as either a middle-of-the-rotation starter or a key bullpen lefthander. Meyer has an 89-93 mph fastball with great late movement and sink. His best pitch is a plus straight changeup that scouts say is better than that of most big leaguers. He also has a hard slider that has shown steady development and should become a third plus pitch. Meyer does a fine job of mixing his pitches, which also include a curveball and splitter, and shows an outstanding feel for pitching. Scouts love Meyer's lanky body, loose arm and sound mechanics. It wouldn't be a surprise if Meyer started to move fast through the organization and landed as high as Double-A during 2003.

Year	Club (League)	Class	W	L	ERA	G	GS	CG	SV	IP	H	R	ER	HR	BB	SO	AVG
2002	Danville (Appy)	R	3	3	2.74	13	13	1	0	66	47	22	20	4	18	77	.198
MINOR LEAGUE TOTALS			3	3	2.74	13	13	1	0	66	47	22	20	4	18	77	.198

19. Trey Hodges, rhp

Born: June 29, 1978. **Ht.:** 6-3. **Wt.:** 180. **Bats:** R. **Throws:** R. **School:** Louisiana State University. **Career Transactions:** Selected by Braves in 17th round of 2000 draft; signed June 21, 2000.

ESPN's Chris Berman sometimes says that all wide receiver Cris Carter does is score touchdowns. Hodges is the Braves' version of Carter: All he does is win. Since undergoing major shoulder surgery while at Louisiana State, Hodges won the deciding game and the MVP award at the 2000 College World Series and has earned 15 minor league wins in each of his two full pro seasons. He was the Carolina League co-pitcher of the year in 2001 and led the Triple-A International League in wins last season. The trend continued during his first taste of the big leagues last September, as Hodges had two victories while making four relief appearances. His success stems from baffling hitters instead of overpowering them. His best pitch is a plus slider that he throws at any time in the count. He has outstanding command of that offering as well as an 88-91 mph fastball that sneaks up on hitters. Hodges' changeup continues to improve but still needs additional depth. Hodges eats innings with his consistency. The Braves' signing of Paul Byrd probably ended Hodges' chances of being their fifth starter, but he could pitch out of the bullpen while awaiting an opportunity.

Yr	Club (League)	Class	W	L	ERA	G	GS	CG	SV	IP	H	R	ER	HR	BB	SO	AVG
2000	Jamestown (NY-P)	A	0	2	5.95	13	2	0	0	20	22	14	13	3	12	13	.278
2001	Myrtle Beach (Car)	A	15	8	2.76	26	26	1	0	173	156	64	53	13	18	139	.237
2002	Richmond (IL)	AAA	15	9	3.19	28	28	1	0	172	158	66	61	9	56	116	.247
	Atlanta (NL)	MAJ	2	0	5.40	4	0	0	0	12	16	7	7	2	2	6	.348
MAJOR LEAGUE TOTALS			2	0	5.40	4	0	0	0	12	16	7	7	2	2	6	.348
MINOR LEAGUE TOTALS			30	19	3.13	67	56	2	0	365	336	144	127	25	86	268	.244

20. Ryan Langerhans, of

Born: Feb. 20, 1980. **Ht.:** 6-3. **Wt.:** 190. **Bats:** L. **Throws:** L. **School:** Round Rock (Texas) HS. **Career Transactions:** Selected by Braves in third round of 1998 draft; signed June 28, 1998.

The numbers have been slow to come for Langerhans, but he continues to push forward and is closer to the majors than any of the Braves' outfield prospects. He made a one-day cameo in Atlanta on April 28 after B.J. Surhoff blew out his anterior cruciate ligament. Langerhans subsequently battled a knee injury of his own and slumped in Double-A before finishing well in August and in the Arizona Fall League. His defense is unquestioned, as he has the instincts and enough speed for any outfield position and the arm strength to handle right field. He also runs the bases well, works counts to draw walks and projects to hit 20 homers annually. The lone concern is whether he'll hit enough at the major league level, especially after he batted just .184 against lefthanders last year. The Braves say that Langerhans, whose father John was a second-round pick of the Twins in 1968 and was Ryan's high school coach, will be at least an average everyday outfielder in the majors, though he will need at least a full season in Triple-A.

Year	Club (League)	Class	AVG	G	AB	R	H	2B	3B	HR	RBI	BB	SO	SB	SLG	OBP
1998	Braves (GCL)	R	.277	43	148	15	41	10	4	2	19	19	38	2	.439	.357
1999	Macon (SAL)	A	.268	121	448	66	120	30	1	9	49	52	99	19	.400	.352
2000	Myrtle Beach (Car)	A	.212	116	392	55	83	14	7	6	37	32	104	25	.329	.286
2001	Myrtle Beach (Car)	A	.287	125	450	66	129	30	3	7	48	55	104	22	.413	.374
2002	Greenville (SL)	AA	.251	109	391	57	98	23	2	9	62	68	83	10	.389	.366
	Atlanta (NL)	MAJ	.000	1	1	0	0	0	0	0	0	0	0	0	.000	.000
MAJOR LEAGUE TOTALS			.000	1	1	0	0	0	0	0	0	0	0	0	.000	.000
MINOR LEAGUE TOTALS			.258	514	1829	259	471	107	17	33	215	226	428	78	.389	.347

21. Anthony Lerew, rhp

Born: Oct. 28, 1982. **Ht.:** 6-3. **Wt.:** 215. **Bats:** L. **Throws:** R. **School:** Northern HS, Wellsville, Pa. **Career Transactions:** Selected by Braves in 11th round of 2001 draft; signed June 6, 2001.

Lerew was an unheralded 11th-round draft pick before breaking out with a performance that earned him co-pitcher-of-the-year honors in the Appalachian League. He ranked second in the Appy League in wins and ERA, and fourth in strikeouts. Using a 92-94 mph fastball with good movement, a hard breaking ball and a solid changeup, Lerew allowed no more than one run in 10 of his 14 starts at Danville. He has impressive size for a 20-year-old at 6-foot-3 and 215 pounds and mixes his offerings with the savvy of a veteran. The Braves rave about Lerew's makeup and the way he comprehends and responds to instruction. He's working on becoming more consistent with his breaking pitch and doing a better job of spotting his pitches in the strike zone. Based on his development thus far, Lerew could be on the verge of blossoming into an even better pitcher. His next step will be low Class A in 2003.

Year	Club (League)	Class	W	L	ERA	G	GS	CG	SV	IP	H	R	ER	HR	BB	SO	AVG
2001	Braves (GCL)	R	1	2	2.92	12	7	0	0	49	43	25	16	3	14	40	.228
2002	Danville (Appy)	R	8	3	1.73	14	14	0	0	83	60	23	16	2	25	75	.205
MINOR LEAGUE TOTALS			9	5	2.18	26	21	0	0	132	103	48	32	5	39	115	.214

22. Blaine Boyer, rhp

Born: July 11, 1981. **Ht.:** 6-3. **Wt.:** 190. **Bats:** R. **Throws:** R. **School:** Walton HS, Marietta, Ga. **Career Transactions:** Selected by Braves in third round of 2000 draft; signed June 13, 2000.

Boyer had a rough initiation into low Class A last year, giving up 13 earned runs in his first 13 innings. Yet just as it appeared that a demotion might be necessary, he bordered on untouchable. Boyer put together 16 straight scoreless outings and allowed just 11 earned runs in his last 57 innings, then continued to make progress during instructional league. Boyer has two plus pitches: a heavy fastball that has been clocked as high as 95 mph and a sharp-breaking curveball. During instructional league, he had more consistency with his curve and did a better job of incorporating a developing changeup into his repertoire. After showing a lack of concentration as a starter in 2001, Boyer displayed the makeup to develop as a power closer. He must do a better job of mixing his pitches, which should occur once he polishes all of his offerings and builds confidence. Boyer also battles with his control as well as the consistency of his release point. Nevertheless, his progress at Macon was impressive, leaving the Braves interested to see what develops in high Class A this year.

Year	Club (League)	Class	W	L	ERA	G	GS	CG	SV	IP	H	R	ER	HR	BB	SO	AVG
2000	Braves (GCL)	R	1	3	2.51	11	5	0	1	32	24	16	9	0	19	27	.200
2001	Danville (Appy)	R	4	5	4.32	13	12	0	0	50	48	35	24	4	19	57	.250
2002	Macon (SAL)	A	5	9	3.07	43	0	0	1	70	52	30	24	0	39	73	.207
MINOR LEAGUE TOTALS			10	17	3.36	67	17	0	2	153	124	81	57	4	77	157	.220

23. Richard Lewis, 2b

Born: June 29, 1980. **Ht.:** 6-1. **Wt.:** 190. **Bats:** R. **Throws:** R. **School:** Georgia Tech. **Career Transactions:** Selected by Braves in first round (40th overall) of 2001 draft; signed June 14, 2001.

Second base has been a revolving door in Atlanta since the retirement of Mark Lemke. Veterans Quilvio Veras and Bret Boone were acquired and discarded, youngster Marcus Giles and Mark DeRosa have been inconsistent, and Keith Lockhart has been nothing more than a stopgap. Lewis could become the long-term answer. The unspectacular Lewis is a Bobby Cox type of player, a steady performer who plays solid defense and does the little things necessary to win. The 40th overall pick in the 2001 draft after playing multiple infield positions at Georgia Tech, Lewis has settled at second base as a pro. He has good range and a strong arm for the position. He looks a little stiff on plays to his right, yet turns the double play well and was the most surehanded second baseman in the Carolina League last year, committing eight errors in 124 games. An excellent baserunner with surprising speed that helped him swipe 31 bags in 41 attempts, Lewis has solid gap power and continues to incorporate more power in his game. He needs to get stronger but should be a consistent No. 2, 7 or 8 hitter with the ability to bunt and hit-and-run. He's scheduled to begin 2003 in Double-A and could reach Atlanta sometime during the next two seasons.

Year	Club (League)	Class	AVG	G	AB	R	H	2B	3B	HR	RBI	BB	SO	SB	SLG	OBP
2001	Jamestown (NY-P)	A	.242	71	285	37	69	7	1	4	27	20	50	16	.316	.298
2002	Myrtle Beach (Car)	A	.279	130	484	82	135	23	4	2	51	55	80	31	.355	.359
MINOR LEAGUE TOTALS			.265	201	769	119	204	30	5	6	78	75	130	47	.341	.337

24. Chris Waters, lhp

Born: Aug. 17, 1980. **Ht.:** 6-0. **Wt.:** 170. **Bats:** L. **Throws:** L. **School:** South Florida CC. **Career Transactions:** Selected by Braves in fifth round of 2000 draft; signed June 7, 2000.

Durability is one of the keys to success in developing a minor league pitcher, and Waters hasn't missed a start while being able to prove his worth by making consistent progress over his three pro seasons. He ranked fourth in the minors in innings last year, when he led Myrtle Beach in wins and ranked fifth in the Carolina League in ERA. Waters doesn't have an overwhelming pitch, but he has three solid ones: a 90-92 mph fastball, a curveball and a changeup. He has fine overall command of his pitches, thanks to a fluid delivery he repeats on a regular basis. While Waters' stuff is as consistent as any pitcher in the organization, he must understand that every pitch he throws should have a purpose. Waters also needs to become steadier with his control. Though he allowed just 43 walks last year, he needs to cut down on his hit batters (24) and wild pitches (12). Some fine-tuning remains on the agenda for him this year in Double-A.

Year	Club (League)	Class	W	L	ERA	G	GS	CG	SV	IP	H	R	ER	HR	BB	SO	AVG
2000	Danville (Appy)	R	5	3	3.91	13	13	1	0	69	64	33	30	4	29	73	.255
2001	Macon (SAL)	A	8	6	3.35	25	24	3	0	148	131	71	55	14	52	78	.239
2002	Myrtle Beach (Car)	A	13	7	2.76	28	28	2	0	183	154	63	56	12	43	103	.230
MINOR LEAGUE TOTALS			26	16	3.18	66	65	6	0	399	349	167	141	30	124	254	.237

25. Andy Pratt, lhp

Born: Aug. 27, 1979. **Ht.:** 6-0. **Wt.:** 180. **Bats:** L. **Throws:** L. **School:** Chino Valley (Ariz.) HS. **Career Transactions:** Selected by Rangers in ninth round of 1998 draft; signed June 8, 1998 . . . Traded by Rangers to Braves for LHP Ben Kozlowski, April 9, 2002.

The Braves surprised a lot of people last spring when they gave up lefthander Ben Kozlowski to get Pratt, whom the Rangers designated for assignment when they got in a 40-man roster bind. The consensus was that Kozlowski was the better prospect to begin with, and he didn't need to be protected on the 40-man roster. The trade now looks even worse, as Kozlowski blossomed in 2002 and widened the gap between him and Pratt, who lost his first seven decisions in the Atlanta system. Pratt eventually regained his command and eventually received a cup of coffee with Atlanta in September. Pratt is a finesse pitcher who has added velocity in the past year, as his fastball now sits in the low 90s. He also throws a cut fastball, a curveball and a changeup. He does an excellent job of mixing his pitches while painting the outside corners. The Braves aren't sure what his long-term role will be, especially after watching Pratt pitch exceptionally well in Puerto Rico over the winter. He could earn a job in the Atlanta bullpen with an impressive spring, but chances are he'll begin 2003 in the Triple-A rotation.

Year	Club (League)	Class	W	L	ERA	G	GS	CG	SV	IP	H	R	ER	HR	BB	SO	AVG
1998	Rangers (GCL)	R	4	3	3.86	12	8	0	0	56	49	25	24	4	14	49	.238
1999	Savannah (SAL)	A	4	4	2.89	13	13	1	0	72	66	30	23	4	16	100	.242
2000	Charlotte (FSL)	A	7	4	2.72	16	16	2	0	93	68	37	28	8	26	95	.203
	Tulsa (TL)	AA	1	6	7.22	11	11	0	0	52	66	48	42	7	33	42	.303
2001	Tulsa (TL)	AA	8	10	4.61	27	26	3	0	168	175	99	86	18	57	132	.268
2002	Greenville (SL)	AA	4	9	4.26	20	18	1	0	93	92	54	44	5	44	67	.262
	Richmond (IL)	AAA	4	2	3.10	6	6	1	0	41	35	15	14	2	9	36	.232
	Atlanta (NL)	MAJ	0	0	6.75	1	0	0	0	1	1	1	1	0	4	1	.200
MAJOR LEAGUE TOTALS			0	0	6.75	1	0	0	0	1	1	1	1	0	4	1	.200
MINOR LEAGUE TOTALS			32	38	4.09	105	98	8	0	574	551	308	261	48	199	521	.252

26. John Ennis, rhp

Born: Oct. 17, 1979. **Ht.:** 6-5. **Wt.:** 220. **Bats:** R. **Throws:** R. **School:** Monroe HS, Panorama City, Calif. **Career Transactions:** Selected by Braves in 14th round of 1998 draft; signed June 18, 1998.

Like Jung Bong and Ryan Langerhans, Ennis had a one-game stint in the majors last year. He made his debut on April 11 against the Phillies, allowing two earned runs in four innings while making an emergency start in place of Albie Lopez. Ennis spent the rest of the year in Double-A. He knows how to set up hitters with his three-pitch repertoire, which includes a low-90s fastball, a hard curveball and a changeup. He'll also throw a slider on occasion to give hitters another something else to think about. Upgrading the overall consistency of his pitches and working on the little things such as fielding and holding runners are on his to-do list. He'll be promoted to Triple-A for 2003.

Year	Club (League)	Class	W	L	ERA	G	GS	CG	SV	IP	H	R	ER	HR	BB	SO	AVG
1998	Braves (GCL)	R	0	3	4.62	8	2	0	0	25	30	16	13	0	6	18	.288
1999	Danville (Appy)	R	4	3	5.07	13	13	0	0	66	71	46	37	7	21	60	.272
2000	Macon (SAL)	A	7	4	2.55	18	16	0	0	99	77	37	28	5	25	105	.209
2001	Myrtle Beach (Car)	A	6	8	3.58	25	25	1	0	138	111	63	55	12	45	144	.219
2002	Greenville (SL)	AA	9	9	4.18	26	26	0	0	149	131	79	69	7	62	103	.243
	Atlanta (NL)	MAJ	0	0	4.50	1	1	0	0	4	5	2	2	0	3	1	.385
MAJOR LEAGUE TOTALS			0	0	4.50	1	1	0	0	4	5	2	2	0	3	1	.385
MINOR LEAGUE TOTALS			26	27	3.81	90	82	1	0	477	420	241	202	31	159	430	.236

27. Matt Wright, rhp

Born: March 13, 1982. **Ht.:** 6-4. **Wt.:** 220. **Bats:** R. **Throws:** R. **School:** Robinson HS, Waco, Texas. **Career Transactions:** Selected by Braves in 21st round of 2000 draft; signed June 21, 2000.

Wright had to wonder what else could go wrong during the first half of 2002. He suffered through every type of bad luck imaginable while losing his first seven decisions in low Class A. His maturity and determination allowed him to turn his season around, as he won 10 of his last 11 decisions. Wright has better stuff that would be expected from a former 21st-round pick, beginning with a low-90s fastball that he works to both sides of the plate. His changeup is solid and continues to show more consistency and fade. Wright's third option is a power curveball that could develop into an above-average pitch if he can maintain his release point when throwing it. Wright has made steady progress in the organization by applying instruction and making the necessary adjustments. Added physical maturity will enable him to become stronger and develop into a potential No. 4 starter in the major leagues. He'll spend this year in high Class A.

Year	Club (League)	Class	W	L	ERA	G	GS	CG	SV	IP	H	R	ER	HR	BB	SO	AVG
2000	Braves (GCL)	R	0	2	0.86	12	0	0	4	21	8	5	2	0	11	30	.113
2001	Danville (Appy)	R	3	5	3.72	14	14	1	0	73	60	40	30	4	26	89	.221
2002	Macon (SAL)	A	10	8	3.18	26	25	0	0	153	135	68	54	11	60	146	.236
MINOR LEAGUE TOTALS			13	15	3.14	52	39	1	4	246	203	113	86	15	97	265	.222

28. Brian McCann, c

Born: Feb. 20, 1984. **Ht.:** 6-3. **Wt.:** 190. **Bats:** L. **Throws:** R. **School:** Duluth (Ga.) HS. **Career Transactions:** Selected by Braves in second round of 2002 draft; signed July 11, 2002.

The weakest position in the Braves organization is catcher, which could lead to a rapid ascent for McCann, provided the 64th overall pick in the 2002 draft remains behind the plate. McCann's calling card is his offensive potential, including some of the best raw power in the system. The son of former Marshall head coach Howard McCann, Brian has a textbook swing and an impressive approach to hitting. His quick wrists allow him to turn on any pitch and he drives the ball to all fields. He needs to make more consistent contact and do better against breaking balls. McCann has catch-and-throw tools, but he also has a thick lower body. He needs to improve his footwork and agility. He does a good job of calling a game. After signing late in the summer, McCann reported to the Gulf Coast League out of shape. The Braves say McCann can develop into a frontline receiver, though others see him as a power-hitting first baseman. Regardless, if his bat lives up to expectations he could move quickly up the ladder. He'll begin this year in low Class A.

Year	Club (League)	Class	AVG	G	AB	R	H	2B	3B	HR	RBI	BB	SO	SB	SLG	OBP
2002	Braves (GCL)	R	.220	29	100	9	22	5	0	2	11	10	22	0	.330	.295
MINOR LEAGUE TOTALS			.220	29	100	9	22	5	0	2	11	10	22	0	.330	.295

29. Matt Belisle, rhp

Born: June 6, 1980. **Ht.:** 6-3. **Wt.:** 190. **Bats:** B. **Throws:** R. **School:** McCallum HS, Austin. **Career Transactions:** Selected by Braves in second round of 1998 draft; signed Aug. 23, 1998 . . . On disabled list, April 5-Sept. 4, 2001.

Belisle had difficulty gaining any consistency last season, mainly because he missed all of 2001 after having surgery to repair a ruptured disc in his back. While he looked strong during instructional league in the fall of 2001, his rustiness was apparent as he tried to make the jump to Double-A after never pitching above low Class A previously. Belisle can be overpowering when his mechanics are in sync. His fastball registers in the low 90s and touches 95 mph. He also has good control of his changeup and curveball. Belisle is strong and athletic, but he looked a little stiff last year compared to the past. He struggled against left-handers, who batted .282 against him. While he threw strikes with all his pitches, he couldn't locate them in the zone like he wanted. The Braves hope that with Belisle now a full year removed from back surgery, he'll get back to where he was before the injury. A return to Double-A is likely for Belisle to begin 2003.

Year	Club (League)	Class	W	L	ERA	G	GS	CG	SV	IP	H	R	ER	HR	BB	SO	AVG
1999	Danville (Appy)	R	2	5	4.67	14	14	0	0	71	86	50	37	3	23	60	.291
2000	Macon (SAL)	A	9	5	2.37	15	15	1	0	102	79	37	27	7	18	97	.216
	Myrtle Beach (Car)	A	3	4	3.43	12	12	0	0	79	72	32	30	5	11	71	.246
2001									Did Not Play—Injured							
2002	Greenville (SL)	AA	5	9	4.35	26	26	1	0	159	162	91	77	18	39	123	.261
MINOR LEAGUE TOTALS			19	23	3.74	67	67	2	0	412	399	210	171	33	91	351	.253

30. Bill McCarthy, of

Born: Dec. 2, 1979. **Ht.:** 6-2. **Wt.:** 200. **Bats:** R. **Throws:** R. **School:** Rutgers University. **Career Transactions:** Selected by Braves in sixth round of 2001 draft; signed June 10, 2001.

McCarthy joined Adam Stern and Mailon Kent, fellow Braves college outfielders selected in the 2001 draft, in spending his first full pro season in high Class A. He outperformed Stern and Kent, leading Myrtle Beach in doubles, RBIs and total bases. McCarthy has good pop and drives the ball to all fields. He stands close to the plate, which allows him to cover the full strike zone and also makes him a magnet for pitches (he was hit 23 times last year). He runs well on the basepaths and is steady in the outfield, committing only one error last year. McCarthy's arm is strong enough for right field, but his power potential isn't quite what big league clubs want at the position. He's not fast enough to play center in the majors, though he does get good jumps on balls. McCarthy has the tools and the makeup to play in the majors if he continues to improve his all-around game. His development will continue this year in Double-A.

Year	Club (League)	Class	AVG	G	AB	R	H	2B	3B	HR	RBI	BB	SO	SB	SLG	OBP
2001	Jamestown (NY-P)	A	.295	74	285	38	84	17	2	2	39	20	47	7	.389	.351
2002	Myrtle Beach (Car)	A	.305	128	442	52	135	26	4	11	65	38	88	6	.457	.386
MINOR LEAGUE TOTALS			.301	202	727	90	219	43	6	13	104	58	135	13	.431	.373

BALTIMORE
ORIOLES

TOP 30 PROSPECTS

1. Erik Bedard, lhp
2. Darnell McDonald, of
3. Daniel Cabrera, rhp
4. Luis Jimenez, 1b/of
5. Rommie Lewis, lhp
6. Mike Fontenot, 2b
7. Richard Stahl, lhp
8. John Maine, rhp
9. Tripper Johnson, 3b
10. Eli Whiteside, c
11. Corey Shafer, of
12. Bryan Bass, ss
13. Val Majewski, of
14. Dave Crouthers, rhp
15. Kurt Birkins, lhp
16. Steve Bechler, rhp
17. Aaron Rakers, rhp
18. Doug Gredvig, 1b
19. Paul Henry, rhp
20. Eric DuBose, lhp
21. Ed Rogers, ss
22. Keith Reed, of
23. Arturo Rivas, of
24. Matt Riley, lhp
25. Tommy Arko, c
26. Beau Hale, rhp
27. Mike Paradis, rhp
28. Hayden Penn, rhp
29. Richard Bartlett, rhp
30. Chris Smith, lhp

By Will Lingo

Peter Angelos finally decided he had seen enough. After a fifth straight losing season in Baltimore, the worst attendance in the 10-year history of Camden Yards, and the worst minor league winning percentage in baseball, the Orioles had become an embarrassment. And that's not to mention the end of a 42-year affiliation with Triple-A Rochester.

So Angelos forced out Syd Thrift and replaced him with a two-headed general manager: Jim Beattie will be the team's executive vice president of baseball operations and Mike Flanagan vice president of baseball operations. One of their first acts was to reassign farm director Don Buford and hire Doc Rodgers from the Reds to replace him. Scouting director Tony DeMacio, who has been in his job since December 1998, had his contract renewed.

The decision seemed to reflect a feeling that talent is coming into the organization but had not been handled correctly. No story illustrated the problems better than the case of lefthander Erik Bedard. He was having a great 2002 season at Double-A Bowie, but in a June game against Akron was sent out to pitch the eighth inning even though he was at or over his prescribed pitch count, sources said. He recorded two outs but then grabbed his arm on a pitch, and a trainer led him straight to the clubhouse. He had Tommy John surgery in September. The Orioles later reassigned Bowie manager Dave Cash and pitching coach Tom Burgmeier. Bedard's injury unfortunately was not an isolated event. Other promising pitchers such as Josh Cenate, Beau Hale, Matt Riley, Luis Rivera, Chris Smith and Richard Stahl have all dealt with serious arm problems.

It remains to be seen how the two-man GM idea will work. It won't be hard to improve on the past few years. The trade deadline deals Thrift made in 2000 when the Orioles were unloading veterans, for instance, are likely to yield nothing.

The problem was that a once-proud franchise simply had no direction. The Orioles have produced one significant position player (Jerry Hairston) since Cal Ripken in 1982 and one pitcher (Sidney Ponson) since Mike Mussina in 1991. Several times in 2002, the Orioles played without a single player drafted and developed in their system.

Changes were finally made, but it's not clear how long it will take the new regime to rebuild not only the team on the field but the image of the franchise.

Organization Overview

General Managers: Jim Beattie/Mike Flanagan. **Farm Director:** Doc Rodgers. **Scouting Director:** Tony DeMacio.

2002 PERFORMANCE

Class	Farm Team	League	W	L	Pct.	Finish*	Manager(s)
Majors	Baltimore	American	67	95	.414	11th (14)	Mike Hargrove
Triple-A	†Rochester Red Wings	International	55	89	.382	14th (14)	Andy Etchebarren
Double-A	Bowie Baysox	Eastern	55	85	.393	11th (12)	Dave Cash/Dave Stockstill
High A	Frederick Keys	Carolina	47	92	.338	8th (8)	Jack Voigt
Low A	Delmarva Shorebirds	South Atlantic	76	64	.543	4th (16)	Joe Ferguson
Short-season	Aberdeen IronBirds	New York-Penn	31	45	.408	11th (14)	Joe Almaraz
Rookie	Bluefield Orioles	Appalachian	45	23	.662	1st (10)	Bien Figueroa
Rookie	GCL Orioles	Gulf Coast	24	36	.400	12th (14)	Jesus Alfaro
OVERALL 2002 MINOR LEAGUE RECORD			333	434	.434	30th (30)	

*Finish in overall standings (No. of teams in league)   †Affiliate will be in Ottawa (International) in 2003.

ORGANIZATION LEADERS

BATTING
*Minimum 250 At-Bats
*AVG	Neal Stephenson, Aberdeen	.310
R	Tripper Johnson, Delmarva	73
H	Darryl Brinkley, Rochester	145
TB	Darnell McDonald, Rochester/Bowie	212
2B	Tripper Johnson, Delmarva	32
3B	Three tied at	7
HR	Alex Gordon, Frederick/Delmarva	18
RBI	Doug Gredvig, Bowie	80
BB	Tripper Johnson Delmarva	62
SO	Bryan Bass, Delmarva	146
SB	Napolean Calzado, Bowie	42

PITCHING
#Minimum 75 Innings
W	Rich Bartlett, Frederick/Delmarva	12
L	Jay Spurgeon, Rochester	14
#ERA	Dave Farren, Delmarva/Aberdeen	2.95
G	Lesli Brea, Rochester	60
CG	Kurt Birkins, Delware	3
SV	Rommie Lewis, Delmarva	25
IP	Steve Bechler, Rochester/Bowie	173
BB	Cory Morris, Frederick/Delmarva	67
SO	Jancy Andrade, Frederick/Delmarva	152

BEST TOOLS

Best Hitter for Average	Luis Jimenez
Best Power Hitter	Doug Gredvig
Fastest Baserunner	Tim Raines Jr.
Best Athlete	Darnell McDonald
Best Fastball	Daniel Cabrera
Best Curveball	Erik Bedard
Best Slider	Eric DuBose
Best Changeup	Kurt Birkins
Best Control	Ben Knapp
Best Defensive Catcher	Eli Whiteside
Best Defensive Infielder	Ed Rogers
Best Infield Arm	Eddy Garabito
Best Defensive Outfielder	Darnell McDonald
Best Outfield Arm	Keith Reed

PROJECTED 2006 LINEUP

Catcher	Eli Whiteside
First Base	Luis Jimenez
Second Base	Mike Fontenot
Third Base	Tripper Johnson
Shortstop	Bryan Bass
Left Field	Corey Shafer
Center Field	Darnell McDonald
Right Field	Jay Gibbons
Designated Hitter	Val Majewski
No. 1 Starter	Erik Bedard
No. 2 Starter	Rodrigo Lopez

Alex Gordon

Dave Farren

No. 3 Starter	Daniel Cabrera
No. 4 Starter	Rommie Lewis
No. 5 Starter	Sidney Ponson
Closer	Jorge Julio

TOP PROSPECTS OF THE DECADE

1993	Brad Pennington, lhp
1994	Jeffrey Hammonds, of
1995	Armando Benitez, rhp
1996	Rocky Coppinger, rhp
1997	Nerio Rodriguez, rhp
1998	Ryan Minor, 3b
1999	Matt Riley, lhp
2000	Matt Riley, lhp
2001	Keith Reed, of
2002	Richard Stahl, lhp

TOP DRAFT PICKS OF THE DECADE

1993	Jay Powell, rhp
1994	Tommy Davis, 1b (2)
1995	Alvie Shepherd, rhp
1996	Brian Falkenborg, rhp (2)
1997	Jayson Werth, c
1998	Rick Elder, of
1999	Mike Paradis, rhp
2000	Beau Hale, rhp
2001	Chris Smith, lhp
2002	*Adam Loewen, lhp

*Has not signed.

ALL-TIME LARGEST BONUSES

Beau Hale, 2000	$2,250,000
Chris Smith, 2001	$2,175,000
Darnell McDonald, 1997	$1,900,000
Richard Stahl, 1999	$1,795,000
Mike Paradis, 1999	$1,700,000

MinorLeague**Depth**Chart

BALTIMORE ORIOLES

RANK 30

The Orioles' front-office makeover, which resulted in the hiring of co-general managers Jim Beattie and Mike Flanagan in the offseason, has to address player development first and foremost. The minor league system had the worst winning percentage in the game last year (.434) and mirrors the big league situation in that the organization lacks impact talent. Injuries have ravaged many of the farm's best players, including No. 1 prospect Erik Bedard and 2001 first-rounder Chris Smith. Tony DeMacio retained his position as scouting director and is highly respected by his peers, but new farm director Doc Rodgers has a big challenge in front of him.

Note: Depth charts prepared by Josh Boyd. Numbers in parentheses indicate prospect rankings.

LF
Val Majewski (13)
Ray Cabrera

CF
Darnell McDonald (2)
Arturo Rivas (23)
Tim Raines Jr

RF
Keith Reed (22)
Tim Gilhooly

3B
Tripper Johnson (9)
Napolean Calzado
Carlos Rijo

SS
Bryan Bass (12)
Ed Rogers (21)
Brandon Fahey

2B
Mike Fontenot (6)
Eddy Garabito
Omar Rogers

1B
Luis Jimenez (4)
Corey Shafer (11)
Doug Gredvig (18)
Dustin Yount
Alex Gordon

C
Eli Whiteside (10)
Tommy Arko (25)
Ryan Hubele
Mike Russell

RHP

Starters	Relievers
Daniel Cabrera (3)	Aaron Rakers (17)
John Maine (8)	Paul Henry (19)
Dave Crouthers (14)	Mike Paradis (27)
Steve Bechler (16)	Freddy Deza
Beau Hale (26)	Ben Knapp
Hayden Penn (28)	Jayme Sperring
Richard Bartlett (29)	Luis Rivera
Joe Coppinger	Eddy Rodriguez
Ryan Keefer	Dave Farren
Jacobo Sequea	
Matt Bolander	
Richal Acosta	

LHP

Starters	Relievers
Erik Bedard (1)	Eric DuBose (20)
Rommie Lewis (5)	Richard Salazar
Richard Stahl (7)	Scott Rice
Kurt Birkins (15)	
Matt Riley (24)	
Chris Smith (30)	
Trevor Caughey	
Jacobo Meque	

DraftAnalysis

2002 Draft

Best Pro Debut: RHP John Maine (6) struggled with his command all spring, going 5-8, 5.61 as a UNC Charlotte junior. He straightened himself out after signing, going 2-1, 1.45 with a 60-7 strikeout-walk ratio in 43 innings. Short-season and Class A hitters batted just .172 against him.

Best Athlete: RHP Hayden Penn (5) showed Division I basketball potential before committing to baseball. At 6-foot-3, he's projectable and already touches 94 mph on occasion. OF Zach Davis (28) has a chiseled physique but is raw. LHP Adam Loewen (1), the fourth overall pick who headed to Chipola (Fla.) JC, also could have been a first-round pick as a power-hitting outfielder. He could have been mentioned in most of these categories had he signed.

Best Pure Hitter: OF Val Majewski (3) regained his stroke when he stopped trying to hit homers to impress scouts.

Best Raw Power: OF Corey Shafer (2) was one of the best lefthanded power hitters in the draft. He also has a nice swing, so he won't be a one-dimensional hitter.

Fastest Runner: SS Levi Robinson (34) isn't a burner, but he's a plus runner whose first-step quickness and instincts make him even more dangerous on the bases.

Best Defensive Player: OF Tim Gilhooly's (4) arm and range are both assets in right field. SS/2B Gera Alvarez (16) is solid at both middle-infield positions and projects as a useful utilityman who can hit a little and steal an occasional base.

Best Fastball: Maine works in the low 90s and tops out at 95 mph. RHP Paul Henry (7), who had more success as a shortstop than a closer at Ball State, saw his fastball peak at 94 after becoming a full-time pitcher. Loewen throws in the low to mid-90s at 18.

Best Breaking Ball: Until Loewen's hard 12-to-6 curveball becomes Baltimore property, this distinction belongs to Henry's hard slider.

Most Intriguing Background: Loewen is the highest-drafted Canadian ever. 3B Brandon Fahey's (12) father Bill caught for 11 years in the majors.

Majewski

Closest To The Majors: If Maine throws strikes and performs as he did last summer, the Orioles won't be able to hold him back.

Best Late-Round Pick: OF Neal Stephenson (17) has a nice lefthanded swing and batted .310-3-40 in short-season ball. LHP Jason Cierlik (23) has an average fastball and shows flashes of a plus curveball.

The One Who Got Away: Baltimore lost the rights to just two significant players, both of whom have high ceilings. RHP Mark McCormick (11) hit 98 mph last spring but didn't show much control of his pitches or his emotions. He's at Baylor.

Assessment: While the Orioles signed some promising players, it won't be a successful draft if they don't sign Loewen as a draft-and-follow in May. A compensation pick won't be much of a consolation prize.

2001 Draft

The Orioles' three first-rounders are off to disappointing starts, as LHP Chris Smith's career already has been jeopardized by shoulder problems and 2B Mike Fontenot and SS Bryan Bass have been lackluster with the bat. LHP Rommie Lewis (5) might be a star, though, and RHP Dave Crouthers (3) and C Eli Whiteside (6) also show promise.   **Grade: B**

2000 Draft

RHP Beau Hale (1) has been dreadful, while fellow first-rounder 3B Tripper Johnson (1) has one of the system's top bats. Draft-and-follow Kurt Birkins (33) was a nice pickup.   **Grade: C**

1999 Draft

Seven first-rounders should amount to more than this crop ever will. At least LHP Erik Bedard (6) has become the system's best prospect—though he won't pitch in 2003 after blowing out his elbow.   **Grade: C+**

1998 Draft

If you're scoring at home, OFs Rick Elder and Manon Tucker (both lost in the Rule 5 minor league draft in December) make that 14 first-rounders in four years, one projected big league regular among them.   **Grade: F**

Note: Draft analysis prepared by Jim Callis. Numbers in parentheses indicate draft rounds.

... When healthy, Bedard has the stuff to be a top-of-the-rotation starter.

Erik
Bedard lhp

Born: March 6, 1979.
Ht.: 6-1. **Wt.:** 180.
Bats: L. **Throws:** L.
School: Norwalk (Conn.) CC.
Career Transactions: Selected by Orioles in sixth round of 1999 draft; signed June 8, 1999.

RODGER WOOD

How obscure is Erik Bedard's hometown? It doesn't even exist. Noted in the Orioles media guide as hailing from Naum, Ontario, Bedard is actually from Navan, a small farming community just east of Ottawa that's renowned for its vegetables. Bedard didn't start playing baseball until he was 13, his high school did not have a team, and he never made a youth traveling squad. He walked on at Norwalk (Conn.) CC as a tall, skinny guy who could throw a curveball. He ate a lot and worked out a lot, adding strength and velocity, and got noticed at the 1999 Junior College Division III World Series. After the Orioles signed Bedard, he pitched well at every stop and was at his best in 2002, dominating at Double-A Bowie. After nearly making the big league club out of spring training, he made his major league debut April 17, becoming the 200th Canadian big leaguer. His dream season came to a sudden end June 26 when he blew out his arm in a game against Akron after he exceeded his mandated pitch count. Baysox manager Dave Cash and pitching coach Tom Burgmeier were reassigned shortly thereafter. Bedard tried rest but had Tommy John surgery in September when the pain persisted.

When healthy, Bedard has the stuff to be a top-of-the-rotation starter. His fastball sits at 92 mph, and his snappy curveball is his best pitch. It was how he got hitters out as a youngster, when he was considered a runt. He pitches well to both sides of the plate and shows no fear of hitters. The first big leaguer he faced was the Yankees' Jason Giambi, and though Giambi got a hit, Bedard broke his bat. His changeup is solid and he throws all of his pitches for strikes. After shoulder problems bothered him in 2001, Bedard faces a much bigger challenge. He is unlikely to get back on a mound in the 2003 season. If his arm is sound, Bedard will need more experience in how to get better hitters out.

Bedard was on a path toward starting 2003 in the Baltimore rotation but now is on the list of Orioles pitching casualties. While Tommy John surgery shouldn't threaten his career, it does significantly alter his timetable. If everything goes well, he'll be back in 2004.

Year	Club (League)	Class	W	L	ERA	G	GS	CG	SV	IP	H	R	ER	HR	BB	SO	AVG
1999	Orioles (GCL)	R	2	1	1.86	8	6	0	0	29	20	7	6	1	13	41	.192
2000	Delmarva (SAL)	A	9	4	3.57	29	22	1	2	111	98	48	44	2	35	131	.233
2001	Frederick (Car)	A	9	2	2.15	17	17	0	0	96	68	27	23	4	26	130	.198
	Orioles (GCL)	R	0	1	3.00	2	2	0	0	6	4	2	2	0	3	7	.200
2002	Bowie (EL)	AA	6	3	1.97	13	12	0	0	69	43	18	15	0	30	66	.176
	Baltimore (AL)	MAJ	0	0	13.50	2	0	0	0	1	2	1	1	0	0	1	.500
MAJOR LEAGUE TOTALS			0	0	13.50	2	0	0	0	1	2	1	1	0	0	1	.500
MINOR LEAGUE TOTALS			26	11	2.60	69	59	1	2	311	233	102	90	7	107	375	.206

2. Darnell McDonald, of

Born: Nov. 17, 1978. **Ht.:** 5-11. **Wt.:** 210. **Bats:** R. **Throws:** R. **School:** Cherry Creek HS, Englewood, Colo. **Career Transactions:** Selected by Orioles in first round (26th overall) of 1997 draft; signed Aug. 8, 1997.

One of the most celebrated athletes in the 1997 draft, McDonald passed up a Texas football scholarship to sign with the Orioles for $1.9 million. It looked as if he made the wrong career choice until 2002, when the proverbial light bulb seemed to go off. His brother Donzell played for the Royals in 2002 and has signed to play for the Braves in 2003. McDonald has as much athleticism as you could hope for. He translated that into performance when he started to understand hitting and the strike zone, showing patience, getting leverage in his swing and using all fields. In addition, better performance gave him confidence. McDonald can run and steal bases, but it's not clear he has enough speed to play center field in the big leagues. His power, while improved, also might be short for a corner outfielder. He'll need to improve in one area or the other to be an everyday player. The Orioles showed patience with McDonald, if only because of the money invested in him, and it finally paid off. He's likely to return to Triple-A to start 2003, and if he shows further improvement he could be in the big leagues to stay sometime during the season.

Year	Club (League)	Class	AVG	G	AB	R	H	2B	3B	HR	RBI	BB	SO	SB	SLG	OBP
1998	Delmarva (SAL)	A	.261	134	528	87	138	24	5	6	44	33	117	35	.360	.308
	Frederick (Car)	A	.222	4	18	3	4	2	0	1	2	3	6	2	.500	.333
1999	Frederick (Car)	A	.266	130	507	81	135	23	5	6	73	61	92	26	.367	.347
2000	Bowie (EL)	AA	.242	116	459	59	111	13	5	6	43	29	87	11	.331	.290
2001	Bowie (EL)	AA	.282	30	117	16	33	7	1	3	21	9	28	3	.436	.336
	Rochester (IL)	AAA	.238	104	391	37	93	19	2	2	35	29	75	13	.312	.291
2002	Bowie (EL)	AA	.292	37	144	21	42	9	1	4	15	22	27	9	.451	.393
	Rochester (IL)	AAA	.289	91	332	43	96	21	6	6	35	32	78	11	.443	.353
MINOR LEAGUE TOTALS			.261	646	2496	347	652	118	25	34	268	218	510	110	.369	.323

3. Daniel Cabrera, rhp

Born: May 28, 1981. **Ht.:** 6-8. **Wt.:** 220. **Bats:** R. **Throws:** R. **Career Transactions:** Signed out of Dominican Republic by Orioles, March 11, 1999.

After two years in the Rookie-level Dominican Summer League, Cabrera came to the United States in 2001 and didn't show much in the Rookie-level Gulf Coast League, leading his team in walks with 39. He turned that around in 2002 with a jump in velocity and results. Cabrera has a nearly unlimited ceiling, as his fastball has touched 97 mph and sits in the mid-90s. He has a hard breaking ball and a decent changeup that he simply hasn't needed yet. He is a big kid who has grown into his body. With Cabrera's body and mechanics coming together, scouts have mentioned names like Randy Johnson and J.R. Richard in comparisons. Command is still an issue for Cabrera, though it improved last season. He tries to overpower every hitter and will have to learn how to attack them more subtly and keep his pitch counts lower. He also needs to tighten up his breaking ball, which he calls a curve and the organization calls a slider. In some ways Cabrera profiles as a potential closer, but the Orioles want him to start until he proves he can't. He'll make his first foray into full-season ball at low Class A Delmarva in 2003.

Year	Club (League)	Class	W	L	ERA	G	GS	CG	SV	IP	H	R	ER	HR	BB	SO	AVG
1999	Orioles (DSL)	R	2	4	4.71	14	10	1	0	57	60	42	30	3	42	74	.260
2000	Orioles (DSL)	R	8	1	2.52	12	10	2	0	71	45	26	20	3	38	44	.167
2001	Orioles (GCL)	R	2	3	5.53	12	7	0	0	41	31	29	25	1	39	36	.215
2002	Bluefield (Appy)	R	5	2	3.28	12	12	0	0	60	52	25	22	0	25	69	.234
MINOR LEAGUE TOTALS			17	10	3.80	50	39	3	0	230	188	122	97	7	144	223	.217

4. Luis Jimenez, 1b/of

Born: May 7, 1982. **Ht.:** 6-4. **Wt.:** 230. **Bats:** L. **Throws:** L. **Career Transactions:** Signed out of Venezuela by Athletics, Jan. 18, 1999 . . . Released by Athletics, Sept. 26, 2001 . . . Signed by Orioles, Oct. 29, 2001 . . . Granted free agency, Oct. 15, 2002; re-signed by Orioles, Oct. 27, 2002.

Jimenez spent three seasons in the Athletics organization before he was released in 2001, reportedly because of a confrontation with a coach. The Orioles have been happy with him on the field and off, and he won the Rookie-level Appalachian League batting title in 2002. Jimenez is a natural hitter, with a level swing and bat speed that should produce power to all fields. The ball jumps off his bat, and he showed the ability to make adjustments as the season went on. He runs better than average for a player his size and shows good baserunning instincts. Any questions about Jimenez' past have been resolved to the Orioles' satisfaction. He'll have to keep his body in good shape and avoid gaining weight. He has to avoid trying to pull everything, which causes his swing to get long. Over the long haul he'll focus on first base, where he has good footwork, and less on the outfield. Much like Rodrigo Lopez provided a pleasant surprise in the big leagues, Jimenez fell into the Orioles' laps and now is one of their best batting prospects. He could start out at either of Baltimore's Class A affiliates to begin 2003.

Year	Club (League)	Class	AVG	G	AB	R	H	2B	3B	HR	RBI	BB	SO	SB	SLG	OBP
1999	Athletics East (DSL)	R	.212	34	104	9	22	2	2	0	11	13	25	1	.269	.300
2000	Athletics East (DSL)	R	.285	59	214	45	61	7	4	5	37	39	45	3	.425	.400
2001	Athletics (AZL)	R	.214	24	70	8	15	1	1	0	12	8	23	2	.257	.280
2002	Bluefield (Appy)	R	.375	51	176	40	66	13	1	8	42	33	33	9	.597	.474
MINOR LEAGUE TOTALS			.291	168	564	102	164	23	8	13	102	93	126	15	.429	.391

5. Rommie Lewis, lhp

Born: Sept. 2, 1982. **Ht.:** 6-6. **Wt.:** 200. **Bats:** L. **Throws:** L. **School:** Newport HS, Bellevue, Wash. **Career Transactions:** Selected by Orioles in fourth round of 2001 draft; signed June 9, 2001.

Lewis was an easy choice as the low Class A South Atlantic League's all-star closer in his first full season. The bigger question was why he was in the bullpen at all when he owns one of the organization's top arms. The Orioles put Lewis in the bullpen after he was drafted in 2001 to ease his acclimation to pro ball. He performed well in the role and they made him the closer at Delmarva, where he overpowered hitters with a 93 mph fastball that has improved since he signed. He has great command for his experience level and already can locate the ball where he wants in the strike zone. Lewis has a decent curveball and changeup, but he didn't get to use them enough working in relief so they still need improvement. With his frame and stuff, some in the organization feel strongly that he should be a starter. It's not clear at this point where Lewis will pitch in 2003 or in what role. He'll be at one of the Orioles' Class A affiliates, and whether he moves to the rotation could be determined by the offseason changes that take place in the front office.

Year	Club (League)	Class	W	L	ERA	G	GS	CG	SV	IP	H	R	ER	HR	BB	SO	AVG
2001	Orioles (GCL)	R	1	1	2.14	10	7	0	0	34	37	16	8	3	6	27	.276
	Frederick (Car)	A	0	1	9.00	1	0	0	0	4	8	7	4	1	1	2	.400
2002	Delmarva (SAL)	A	1	2	2.15	53	0	0	25	71	50	19	17	1	20	77	.198
MINOR LEAGUE TOTALS			2	4	2.40	64	7	0	25	109	95	42	29	5	27	106	.233

6. Mike Fontenot, 2b

Born: June 9, 1980. **Ht.:** 5-8. **Wt.:** 170. **Bats:** L. **Throws:** R. **School:** Louisiana State University. **Career Transactions:** Selected by Orioles in first round (19th overall) of 2001 draft; signed Sept. 5, 2001.

Fontenot signed for $1.3 million as a draft-eligible sophomore in 2001 and didn't take the field until 2002. He was picked for the midseason California League-Carolina League all-star game but did not play because of a broken finger on his throwing hand. He was one of the few players in the Arizona Fall League who hadn't played above Class A. The Orioles see Fontenot as an offensive sparkplug at second base, capable of hitting for average with occasional pop. He has a strong, compact body and should be fine defensively, though he committed 25 errors last season. Even given that he was adjusting from aluminum bats and gorilla ball at Louisiana State to the pro game, Fontenot still was miscast as a leadoff hitter. He didn't have much of an idea at the plate and needs to get a better awareness of the strike zone and projects more as a No. 2 hitter. He rushed throws and didn't set his feet well, problems that can be corrected. Considering it was his first pro season, Fontenot showed promise and was much better by the end of the season. He'll take the next step to Double-A in 2003.

Year	Club (League)	Class	AVG	G	AB	R	H	2B	3B	HR	RBI	BB	SO	SB	SLG	OBP
2002	Frederick (Car)	A	.264	122	481	61	127	16	4	8	53	42	117	13	.364	.333
MINOR LEAGUE TOTALS			.264	122	481	61	127	16	4	8	53	42	117	13	.364	.333

7. Richard Stahl, lhp

Born: April 11, 1981. **Ht.:** 6-7. **Wt.:** 220. **Bats:** R. **Throws:** L. **School:** Newton HS, Covington, Ga. **Career Transactions:** Selected by Orioles in first round (18th overall) of 1999 draft; signed Aug. 31, 1999.

The organization's top prospect a year ago, Stahl was supposed to take off in 2002 and put his history of nagging injuries behind. It didn't work out that way, as he made just two starts before having surgery to remove a bone spur at the top of his left shoulder in July. The spur was stretching the tendons in his shoulder. Stahl was back to full health by the end of instructional league, where his fastball velocity returned to the mid-90s. His curveball also has the potential to be a plus pitch. He already has filled out his big frame significantly since signing, adding nearly 40 pounds of muscle. Taking the ball every five days would do wonders for Stahl, who has pitched 78 innings combined in the last two seasons. The good news is that his injuries appear to be caused by his growing body, not any arm problems. Whatever the case, he needs innings to start smoothing out his rough edges. Stahl has completed all of his rehabilitation and goes into spring training ready to take over a rotation spot. High Class A Frederick is his likely starting point.

Year	Club (League)	Class	W	L	ERA	G	GS	CG	SV	IP	H	R	ER	HR	BB	SO	AVG
2000	Delmarva (SAL)	A	5	6	3.34	20	20	0	0	89	97	47	33	3	51	83	.280
2001	Delmarva (SAL)	A	2	3	2.67	6	6	0	0	34	24	15	10	3	15	31	.205
	Frederick (Car)	A	1	1	1.95	6	6	1	0	32	26	13	7	1	15	24	.232
	Orioles (GCL)	R	0	0	0.00	1	1	0	0	2	1	0	0	0	1	1	.167
2002	Delmarva (SAL)	A	1	1	5.59	2	2	0	0	10	10	8	6	3	5	9	.278
MINOR LEAGUE TOTALS			9	11	3.02	35	35	1	0	167	158	83	56	10	87	148	.256

8. John Maine, rhp

Born: May 8, 1981. **Ht.:** 6-4. **Wt.:** 190. **Bats:** R. **Throws:** R. **School:** UNC Charlotte. **Career Transactions:** Selected by Orioles in sixth round of 2002 draft; signed July 5, 2002.

Maine was Conference USA's 2001 pitcher of the year, but he had a disappointing junior season and fell to the sixth round, a round that has been good to the Orioles. In addition to Maine, the organization found Bedard and Eli Whiteside as sixth-rounders in the last four years. The Orioles have brought in an intriguing group of college arms in the last few years, and Maine has the best raw stuff of the group. His fastball sits at 92-93 mph and can go higher, and he throws it with great sink. He also has a hard slider that's a great pitch when it's on. Maine has a big, loose frame, and he runs into problems when his mechanics get out of whack. His long arm action in college worried scouts and gave him command problems, but the Orioles say they haven't seen that from him as a pro. He needs to work on a changeup. A strong competitor with the stuff to back it up, Maine will open the season in high Class A. He could move through the organization quickly if he continues to dominate.

Year	Club (League)	Class	W	L	ERA	G	GS	CG	SV	IP	H	R	ER	HR	BB	SO	AVG
2002	Aberdeen (NY-P)	A	1	1	1.74	4	2	0	0	10	6	2	2	0	3	21	.154
	Delmarva (SAL)	A	1	1	1.36	6	5	0	0	33	21	8	5	0	4	39	.178
MINOR LEAGUE TOTALS			2	2	1.45	10	7	0	0	43	27	10	7	0	7	60	.172

9. Tripper Johnson, 3b

Born: April 28, 1982. **Ht.:** 6-1. **Wt.:** 200. **Bats:** R. **Throws:** R. **School:** Newport HS, Bellevue, Wash. **Career Transactions:** Selected by Orioles in first round (32nd overall) of 2000 draft; signed June 26, 2000.

After a promising debut and a disappointing follow-up campaign, Johnson got back on track in his first taste of full-season ball. A teammate of Rommie Lewis at Newport High (the same school that also produced Todd Hollandsworth, Ron Romanick, Cliff Pastornicky and Mike Campbell), Johnson had a storybook prep career in baseball, basketball and football. The Seattle Times chose him as its 2000 male athlete of the year. Johnson is an all-around athlete who doesn't stand out in any one aspect but is solid in all areas. He showed a much better idea at the plate and made consistent, solid contact, again encouraging the Orioles that he can develop above-average power. The organization expects that many of the doubles he hit in 2002 can become home runs as he matures and compares him to Ken Caminiti. While Johnson showed enough improvement on defense to indicate he'll be able to stay at third base, he still needs to get better. He also must continue to develop his strike-zone judgment. Johnson is a quiet, steady player who goes about his business in a professional manner every day. He's not likely to draw the hype of other prospects but is as good a bet as any to make it to the big leagues. He'll move up to high Class A in 2003.

Year	Club (League)	Class	AVG	G	AB	R	H	2B	3B	HR	RBI	BB	SO	SB	SLG	OBP
2000	Orioles (GCL)	R	.306	48	180	22	55	5	3	2	33	13	38	7	.400	.355
2001	Bluefield (Appy)	R	.261	43	157	24	41	6	1	2	26	11	37	4	.350	.312
2002	Delmarva (SAL)	A	.260	136	493	73	128	32	6	11	71	62	88	19	.416	.349
MINOR LEAGUE TOTALS			.270	227	830	119	224	43	10	15	130	86	163	30	.400	.344

10. Eli Whiteside, c

Born: Oct. 22, 1979. **Ht.:** 6-2. **Wt.:** 200. **Bats:** R. **Throws:** R. **School:** Delta State (Miss.) University. **Career Transactions:** Selected by Orioles in sixth round of 2001 draft; signed June 7, 2001.

RICH ABEL

The Orioles drafted Whiteside after he was an NCAA Division II all-American at Delta State and took the team to the semifinals of the D-II College World Series. He was to continue his fast pace in the Arizona Fall League last year, but a hairline fracture to his hamate bone put him on the shelf. The Orioles drafted Whiteside for his defense. He's got a country-strong body that's well suited for the rigors of catching, plus good feet and good technique behind the plate. He records mitt-to-glove times of less than 2.0 seconds on throws to second base. What has made him a prospect is his bat, which has been better than expected. Whiteside is still learning how to handle pitchers, and on offense he'll need to develop more power to become a premium player. He had less success throwing out basestealers in 2002 (31 percent) than in his pro debut (41 percent). In an organization that could use a few pleasant surprises, Whiteside has been one. He's a blue-collar worker who could be in the big leagues within a year. He'll open 2003 in Double-A.

Year	Club (League)	Class	AVG	G	AB	R	H	2B	3B	HR	RBI	BB	SO	SB	SLG	OBP
2001	Delmarva (SAL)	A	.250	61	212	30	53	11	0	7	28	9	45	1	.401	.300
2002	Frederick (Car)	A	.259	80	313	34	81	19	0	8	42	14	57	0	.396	.296
	Bowie (EL)	AA	.263	27	99	11	26	5	0	2	11	4	18	0	.374	.311
MINOR LEAGUE TOTALS			.256	168	624	75	160	35	0	17	81	27	120	1	.394	.300

11. Corey Shafer, of

Born: Dec. 17, 1982. **Ht.:** 6-3. **Wt.:** 210. **Bats:** L. **Throws:** L. **School:** Choctaw (Okla.) HS. **Career Transactions:** Selected by Orioles in second round of 2002 draft; signed Aug. 14, 2002.

Shafer had one of the best lefthanded power bats in the 2002 draft, surpassed among high school players only by Prince Fielder, the Brewers' first-round pick, and Jeff Clement, the national prep career home run leader. (Clement is now at the University of Southern California, and his college commitment was the main reason he lasted until the Twins took him in the 12th round.) The Yankees had watched Shafer closely, sending as many as five scouts in to see him, so Baltimore grabbed him in the second round before the Yankees made a pick. He signed too late to play last summer. Power is the name of the game for Shafer, who generates his pop with a big, strong frame and an aggressive and fluid stroke. His bat will have to carry him, and it should. The Orioles compare him to Ryan Klesko as well as former big leaguer Dan Pasqua. He looked good in instructional league and even showed that he might be able to stay in left field. He's not a baseclogger but isn't a great runner and could end up at first base. Even though he hasn't taken the field yet in an official game, Shafer has generated excitement in an organization that needs players with breakout tools.

Year	Club (League)	Class	AVG	G	AB	R	H	2B	3B	HR	RBI	BB	SO	SB	SLG	OBP
Has Not Played—Signed 2003 Contract																

12. Bryan Bass, ss

Born: April 12, 1982. **Ht.:** 6-1. **Wt.:** 180. **Bats:** B. **Throws:** R. **School:** Seminole (Fla.) HS. **Career Transactions:** Selected by Orioles in first round (31st overall) of 2001 draft; signed July 13, 2001.

Bass turned down a football scholarship from Alabama so he could sign with the Orioles for a $1.15 million bonus in 2001. He grew up in Alabama but moved to Florida in his draft year to get more exposure. A transfer snafu made him ineligible, though teams still knew about his tools and he went 31st overall. Bass, whose brothers Jayson and Kevin were outfielders in the Cubs system, followed a successful pro debut with a disastrous first full season, as he led the organization in strikeouts and errors (38). He's still a baseball rat who likes to do two things: play baseball and fish. To improve, he needs to stop chasing high pitches and offspeed stuff. The organization worked with him in instructional league to shorten his stroke from the left side and make him understand the importance of just putting the ball into play. In the field and at the plate, Bass has to control his aggression so his tools will translate into performance. On some days he looks all right at shortstop, and on others he doesn't. In the long run, he'll probably end up at third base. Bass came to the organization with a reputation of being cocky, but the Orioles haven't seen that. He loves to play the game and never has a bad day at the park. Baltimore might have more success with a hands-off approach with Bass. He could go back to low Class A in 2003 to get a chance to taste success again.

Year	Club (League)	Class	AVG	G	AB	R	H	2B	3B	HR	RBI	BB	SO	SB	SLG	OBP
2001	Orioles (GCL)	R	.297	21	74	12	22	3	6	0	7	5	25	4	.500	.333
	Bluefield (Appy)	R	.324	19	71	17	23	6	1	5	20	10	17	0	.648	.407
2002	Delmarva (SAL)	A	.221	130	457	60	101	20	7	6	59	40	146	15	.335	.299
MINOR LEAGUE TOTALS			.243	170	602	89	146	29	14	11	86	55	188	19	.392	.316

13. Val Majewski, of

Born: June 19, 1981. **Ht.:** 6-2. **Wt.:** 200. **Bats:** R. **Throws:** L. **School:** Rutgers University. **Career Transactions:** Selected by Orioles in third round of 2002 draft; signed July 22, 2002.

Like Rutgers teammate Bobby Brownlie, Majewski had a disappointing junior season and it hurt him in the 2002 draft. He didn't sign until the end of July, after Orioles owner Peter Angelos got involved in negotiations. The Orioles were pleased with what they saw after he signed, as he earned a promotion to low Class A. He's a complete player with a line-drive swing from the left side, a balanced approach and good knowledge of the strike zone. He likes to put the ball in play and has a knack for doing so, putting together a 12-game hitting streak at Aberdeen. The question mark is power. His quest for it led to his struggles at Rutgers, but he showed more at Aberdeen. He played first base in his first two years of college but moved to the outfield last year, and he even playing center in the minors. He profiles as a corner outfielder, where his arm and athletic ability should make him at least an average defender. He also runs well for his size. Majewski will play in Class A in 2003, and where he starts the season will be determined by how he plays in spring training.

Year	Club (League)	Class	AVG	G	AB	R	H	2B	3B	HR	RBI	BB	SO	SB	SLG	OBP
2002	Aberdeen (NY-P)	A	.300	31	110	22	33	7	4	1	15	13	14	8	.464	.376
	Delmarva (SAL)	A	.118	7	17	2	2	0	0	1	3	1	1	0	.294	.158
MINOR LEAGUE TOTALS			.276	38	127	24	35	7	4	2	18	14	15	8	.441	.347

14. Dave Crouthers, rhp

Born: Dec. 18, 1979. **Ht.:** 6-3. **Wt.:** 200. **Bats:** R. **Throws:** R. **School:** Southern Illinois University-Edwardsville. **Career Transactions:** Selected by Orioles in third round of 2001 draft; signed June 7, 2001.

Crouthers was drafted out of Southern Illinois-Edwardsville, where he was the team's cleanup hitter and broke school records for both RBIs and pitching strikeouts. He was also a teammate of fellow Orioles minor leaguer Aaron Rakers. A converted shortstop with low mileage on his arm, Crouthers has a big frame and easy arm action. He already throws 92-94 mph with a decent slider and changeup. He's also an excellent athlete who repeats his delivery well. But he is a project because of his inexperience on the mound. Crouthers still is refining his pitches and trying to develop consistent command, so nuances like how to attack hitters are still in his future. Expect Crouthers to take a level-to-level path through the minors, which will put him in high Class A for 2003. His lack of refinement makes him risky and could lead to an eventual move to the bullpen, but his arm definitely bears watching.

Year	Club (League)	Class	W	L	ERA	G	GS	CG	SV	IP	H	R	ER	HR	BB	SO	AVG
2001	Bluefield (Appy)	R	2	3	4.43	10	10	1	0	45	41	28	22	7	18	45	.243
2002	Delmarva (SAL)	A	8	6	3.34	25	25	1	0	129	117	66	48	4	58	108	.243
MINOR LEAGUE TOTALS			10	9	3.62	35	35	2	0	174	158	94	70	11	76	153	.243

15. Kurt Birkins, lhp

Born: Aug. 11, 1980. **Ht.:** 6-2. **Wt.:** 180. **Bats:** L. **Throws:** L. **School:** Los Angeles Pierce JC. **Career Transactions:** Selected by Orioles in 33rd round of 2000 draft; signed May 25, 2001.

Birkins was a draft-and-follow sign out of Los Angeles Pierce JC, where Barry Zito spent a year during his college career. Birkins originally attended UCLA but left after his freshman season in 1999 and took a year off. He intended to return to the Bruins but the Orioles drafted him, so he went to Pierce instead. He became a top juco prospect and signed for

$400,000. In his first full pro season, Birkins was part of the Delmarva staff that featured some of the organization's best arms. He can touch the low 90s with his sinking fastball but usually pitches in the high 80s. His curveball and changeup are both solid pitches. His best attribute is his approach to pitching, as he has a good feel for how to attack hitters and is a strong competitor. Birkins is a converted outfielder who continues to smooth out his mechanics. He made mechanical refinements last year to help his command, and they also could improve his velocity. He'll move up to high Class A for 2003, and he profiles as an innings-eating starter.

Year	Club (League)	Class	W	L	ERA	G	GS	CG	SV	IP	H	R	ER	HR	BB	SO	AVG
2001	Orioles (GCL)	R	2	1	2.05	5	4	0	0	22	13	5	5	2	3	24	.167
	Bluefield (Appy)	R	4	1	2.92	6	6	0	0	37	28	14	12	2	5	42	.206
2002	Delmarva (SAL)	A	9	7	3.51	27	25	3	0	144	140	66	56	10	46	102	.257
MINOR LEAGUE TOTALS			15	9	3.24	38	35	3	0	203	181	85	73	14	54	168	.239

16. Steve Bechler, rhp

Born: Nov. 18, 1979. **Ht.:** 6-2. **Wt.:** 230. **Bats:** R. **Throws:** R. **School:** South Medford HS, Medford, Ore.
Career Transactions: Selected by Orioles in third round of 1998 draft; signed June 5, 1998.

Bechler completed a steady progression through the organization by making his major league debut last September. He made three appearances before pulling his hamstring as he ran to cover first against the Red Sox, which kept him from pitching again. Illustrating Bechler's bulldog mentality, he tried to pitch through the pain. Illustrating that he still has a lot to learn, Bechler gave up a grand slam to Trot Nixon. Before that, he overcame a 0-7 start at Triple-A Rochester to pitch well in the second half of the season and go 6-5, 3.21 in his last 15 starts. Bechler's fastball is 91-94 mph, and his out pitch is a solid knuckle-curve. In addition to improving his mechanics, Bechler also has matured as he has moved through the minors. He'll have to refine his command to make it in the big leagues, however. The Orioles hope he recognizes the mistakes he made in the majors and will learn from them. He'll compete for a spot in the Baltimore rotation in spring training but is more likely to return to Triple-A at the organization's new affiliate in Ottawa.

Yea	Club (League)	Class	W	L	ERA	G	GS	CG	SV	IP	H	R	ER	HR	BB	SO	AVG
1998	Orioles (GCL)	R	2	4	2.72	9	9	0	0	50	51	22	15	4	8	39	.259
1999	Delmarva (SAL)	A	8	12	3.54	26	26	1	0	152	137	69	60	12	58	139	.239
2000	Frederick (Car)	A	8	12	4.83	27	27	2	0	162	179	98	87	19	57	137	.278
2001	Frederick (Car)	A	5	2	2.27	13	13	1	0	83	73	24	21	3	22	71	.244
	Rochester (IL)	AAA	1	1	15.95	2	2	0	0	7	14	14	13	4	5	6	.359
	Bowie (EL)	AA	3	5	3.08	12	12	2	0	79	63	31	27	14	15	58	.217
2002	Bowie (EL)	AA	2	1	3.42	4	4	0	0	24	28	11	9	2	6	13	.304
	Rochester (IL)	AAA	6	11	4.09	24	24	2	0	150	154	78	68	15	52	77	.265
	Baltimore (AL)	MAJ	0	0	13.50	3	0	0	0	5	6	7	7	3	4	3	.300
MAJOR LEAGUE TOTALS			0	0	13.50	3	0	0	0	5	6	7	7	3	4	3	.300
MINOR LEAGUE TOTALS			35	48	3.82	117	117	8	0	707	699	347	300	73	223	540	.257

17. Aaron Rakers, rhp

Born: Jan. 22, 1977. **Ht.:** 6-3. **Wt.:** 200. **Bats:** R. **Throws:** R. **School:** Southern Illinois University-Edwardsville.
Career Transactions: Selected by Orioles in 23rd round of 1999 draft; signed June 7, 1999.

Rakers (pronounced ROCK-ers) played at Southern Illinois-Edwardsville with Dave Crouthers, and he has been a successful reliever as a pro despite a fastball that's fringe average. Some in the organization compare him to Greg McMichael. After sharing closing duties at Bowie in 2001, Rakers missed the first seven weeks of the 2002 season recovering from surgery to remove bone chips from his elbow. He returned to Double-A in June and put together an impressive season, then made up for some lost innings in the Arizona Fall League. Rakers' fastball is straight and tops out at 90 mph, but he has an out pitch in his splitter. He does lose consistency with his splitter at times, however. Rakers has added a slider as he tries to find a weapon to make him more effective against lefthanders, who hit .274 against him last year. He also needs to refine his command. Pitchers with Rakers' stuff have to prove themselves every step of the way. He'll get his next opportunity in the Triple-A bullpen.

Year	Club (League)	Class	W	L	ERA	G	GS	CG	SV	IP	H	R	ER	HR	BB	SO	AVG
1999	Bluefield (Appy)	R	0	0	2.57	3	0	0	0	7	5	2	2	1	3	12	.200
	Delmarva (SAL)	A	4	1	1.42	18	0	0	8	25	9	6	4	0	13	38	.108
2000	Frederick (Car)	A	1	1	1.55	26	0	0	8	41	23	8	7	2	12	57	.163
	Bowie (EL)	AA	3	2	2.79	24	0	0	8	29	20	11	9	5	10	21	.194
2001	Bowie (EL)	AA	4	4	2.39	51	0	0	14	60	53	21	16	8	20	74	.227
2002	Bowie (EL)	AA	5	1	2.06	36	0	0	10	48	39	12	11	3	12	45	.232
MINOR LEAGUE TOTALS			17	9	2.10	158	0	0	48	210	149	60	49	19	70	247	.198

18. Doug Gredvig, 1b

Born: Aug. 25, 1979. **Ht.:** 6-3. **Wt.:** 230. **Bats:** R. **Throws:** R. **School:** Sacramento CC. **Career Transactions:** Selected by Orioles in fifth round of 2000 draft; signed June 9, 2000.

Gredvig emerged as a prospect in 2001 after leading the high Class A Carolina League with 20 home runs and 57 extra-base hits, but his follow-up in Double-A against more advanced pitching was less impressive. He was set to get more experience against quality pitchers in the Arizona Fall League, but he aggravated an Achilles tendon injury after the season. Gredvig still offers the best power in the Orioles system and is one of the organization's hardest workers. He has a quiet approach at the plate and a power swing with natural loft. He cut down on his strikeouts and walked a bit more in 2002, but Baltimore wants his power to return. His biggest area of improvement last year was on defense. Though he committed 11 errors, he should be able to stay at first base rather than DH. But if he's to get to the big leagues, it will be for his bat. He needs to improve against righthanders, against whom he hit .242 last year (compared to .347 versus lefties). Some in the organization describe him as a working man's player, the type of prospect who toils without fanfare and suddenly shows up in the big leagues. Gredvig will probably get another chance at Double-A to open 2003 to see if that's really the case.

Year	Club (League)	Class	AVG	G	AB	R	H	2B	3B	HR	RBI	BB	SO	SB	SLG	OBP
2000	Orioles (GCL)	R	.444	2	9	0	4	0	0	0	1	0	1	0	.444	.444
	Delmarva (SAL)	A	.220	56	186	28	41	12	0	6	24	35	48	3	.382	.347
2001	Frederick (Car)	A	.254	129	484	71	123	35	2	20	62	37	125	2	.459	.313
2002	Bowie (EL)	AA	.275	129	465	48	128	22	1	14	80	46	94	2	.417	.345
MINOR LEAGUE TOTALS			.259	316	1144	147	296	69	3	40	167	118	268	7	.429	.333

19. Paul Henry, rhp

Born: June 27, 1981. **Ht.:** 6-3. **Wt.:** 190. **Bats:** R. **Throws:** R. **School:** Ball State University. **Career Transactions:** Selected by Orioles in seventh round of 2002 draft; signed July 8, 2002.

Like Dave Crouthers, Henry was a two-way player in college who will focus on pitching as a pro. Henry, a shortstop/closer at Ball State, was overshadowed there by two first-round pitchers from the 2002 draft: No. 1 overall pick Bryan Bullington, who went to the Pirates, and Luke Hagerty, who went 32nd overall to the Cubs. Scouts were divided over Henry's pro role, but the Orioles went with his loose arm and 92-94 mph fastball. He worked mostly as a closer at Rookie-level Bluefield, but he'll go into a rotation in 2003. The organization has been impressed with Henry since he showed up in a coat and tie to sign his contract. He has a much better idea of how to pitch than Crouthers because he has more experience. He's a cerebral, competitive player, and Baltimore compares his approach to Orel Hershiser's. He has the makings of an above-average slider but has to develop a changeup and learn how to miss bats. Because he has a good feel for pitching to go with his big arm, Henry could move quickly. He'll open 2003 in low Class A.

Year	Club (League)	Class	W	L	ERA	G	GS	CG	SV	IP	H	R	ER	HR	BB	SO	AVG
2002	Bluefield (Appy)	R	2	1	4.71	16	0	0	3	21	25	11	11	2	9	31	.291
MINOR LEAGUE TOTALS			2	1	4.71	16	0	0	3	21	25	11	11	2	9	31	.291

20. Eric DuBose, lhp

Born: May 15, 1976. **Ht.:** 6-3. **Wt.:** 230. **Bats:** L. **Throws:** L. **School:** Mississippi State University. **Career Transactions:** Selected by Athletics in first round (21st overall) of 1997 draft; signed June 23, 1997 . . . Claimed on waivers by Indians from Athletics, Sept. 8, 2000 . . . Claimed on waivers by Tigers from Indians, Sept. 22, 2000 . . . Released by Tigers, March 31, 2001 . . . Signed by Orioles, Jan. 28, 2002.

DuBose was an All-American at Mississippi State and a first-round pick by the Athletics in 1997. He flashed great stuff and was regarded as one of Oakland's top prospects, but injuries threatened his career. He was waived twice in September 2000 and didn't even play in 2001 after getting released by the Tigers that March. He had surgery in April 2001 to repair his left labrum and rotator cuff. The Orioles brought him to major league spring training last year, but shoulder stiffness eliminated what small chance he had of making the club. The club did hold on to him and sent him to Double-A. He got over early shoulder tightness to stay healthy and pitch well. DuBose was getting ready for the Arizona Fall League when the Orioles called him up in September, after Yorkis Perez went on the 60-day disabled list to open a spot on the 40-man roster. He made his major league debut with a scoreless inning against the Blue Jays. DuBose kept his spot on the 40-man in the offseason and will compete for a big league bullpen spot in the spring. DuBose now throws 88-90 mph with a curveball and changeup, and he added a slider last season. The Orioles won't try to make him any more than a lefty specialist out of the bullpen for now.

Year	Club (League)	Class	W	L	ERA	G	GS	CG	SV	IP	H	R	ER	HR	BB	SO	AVG
1997	S. Oregon (NWL)	A	1	0	0.00	3	1	0	0	10	5	0	0	0	6	15	.152
	Visalia (Cal)	A	1	3	7.04	10	9	0	0	38	43	37	30	4	28	39	.270
1998	Visalia (Cal)	A	6	1	3.38	17	10	0	1	72	56	34	27	5	35	85	.212
	Huntsville (SL)	AA	7	6	2.70	14	14	1	0	83	86	37	25	2	34	66	.273
1999	Midland (TL)	AA	4	2	5.49	21	14	0	1	77	89	57	47	10	44	68	.295
2000	Midland (TL)	AA	5	1	4.13	18	0	0	0	28	25	16	13	1	18	20	.227
	Visalia (Cal)	A	0	1	1.69	5	0	0	1	11	8	2	2	0	5	12	.200
2001	Did Not Play—Injured																
2002	Rochester (IL)	AAA	0	0	27.00	1	0	0	0	0	1	2	1	0	2	0	.333
	Bowie (EL)	AA	5	3	2.51	41	0	0	3	65	46	21	18	2	21	66	.198
	Baltimore (AL)	MAJ	0	0	3.00	4	0	0	0	6	7	2	2	1	1	4	.304
MAJOR LEAGUE TOTALS			0	0	3.00	4	0	0	0	6	7	2	2	1	1	4	.304
MINOR LEAGUE TOTALS			29	17	3.81	130	48	1	6	385	359	206	163	24	193	371	.246

21. Ed Rogers, ss

Born: Aug. 29, 1978. **Ht.:** 6-1. **Wt.:** 170. **Bats:** R. **Throws:** R. **Career Transactions:** Signed out of Dominican Republic by Orioles, Nov. 7, 1997.

Expectations for Rogers have fallen a long way since the Orioles compared him to Nomar Garciaparra and Derek Jeter after the 2000 season. Even though he put together a decent Double-A season in 2002, Rogers' stock fell again when it turned out he was three years older than originally believed, making him 24 at season's end. Still, his tools make him the organization's best (and perhaps only) pure shortstop prospect. He can play defense at any level with smooth actions, an above-average arm and good range. Rogers has developed a better understanding of what he needs to do to be a successful hitter, and he projects to be a .260-.270 hitter with 10 homers a year. His strike-zone judgment still needs a lot of work, though, and his walk totals continue to decline. He struggles to handle offspeed pitches. If he can improve on that and continue to play strong defense, he still has a major league future. Rogers is likely to open the season in Triple-A, but the Orioles might decide to send him back to Double-A to see if he can get off to a hot start.

Year	Club (League)	Class	AVG	G	AB	R	H	2B	3B	HR	RBI	BB	SO	SB	SLG	OBP
1998	Orioles (DSL)	R	.289	58	194	33	56	9	2	2	27	26	29	8	.387	.373
1999	Orioles (GCL)	R	.288	53	177	34	51	5	1	1	19	23	22	20	.345	.379
2000	Delmarva (SAL)	A	.274	80	332	46	91	14	5	5	42	22	63	27	.392	.317
	Bowie (EL)	AA	.286	13	49	4	14	3	0	1	8	3	15	1	.408	.321
2001	Bowie (EL)	AA	.199	53	191	11	38	10	1	0	13	6	40	10	.262	.231
	Frederick (Car)	A	.260	73	292	39	76	20	3	8	41	14	47	18	.432	.310
2002	Bowie (EL)	AA	.261	112	422	59	110	26	2	11	57	16	70	14	.410	.300
	Baltimore (AL)	MAJ	.000	5	3	0	0	0	0	0	0	0	0	0	.000	.000
MAJOR LEAGUE TOTALS			.000	5	3	0	0	0	0	0	0	0	0	0	.000	.000
MINOR LEAGUE TOTALS			.263	442	1657	226	436	87	14	28	207	110	286	98	.383	.316

22. Keith Reed, of

Born: Oct. 8, 1978. **Ht.:** 6-4. **Wt.:** 210. **Bats:** R. **Throws:** R. **School:** Providence College. **Career Transactions:** Selected by Orioles in first round (23rd overall) of 1999 draft; signed June 19, 1999.

No. 1 on this list two years ago, Reed continues to offer a maddening combination of outstanding athletic ability and inconsistent performance. Drafted as a 20-year-old out of Providence, Reed was pushed up the system in his first three seasons even though he had relatively little baseball experience and had been more of a basketball player growing up in the Northeast. After not being protected on the 40-man roster after the 2001 season, Reed finally spent an entire season in one place in 2002, but the results weren't encouraging in Double-A. He hasn't established a consistent approach at the plate. The Orioles worked with him again in instructional league to make adjustments so he can better handle breaking balls, as well as using the middle of the field and not trying to pull everything. He still has plenty of tools, particularly on defense, where he covers a lot of ground and has the best outfield arm in the organization. If he doesn't hit, though, it won't matter. Reed probably will get another shot at Double-A to start 2003.

Year	Club (League)	Class	AVG	G	AB	R	H	2B	3B	HR	RBI	BB	SO	SB	SLG	OBP
1999	Bluefield (Appy)	R	.188	4	16	2	3	0	0	0	0	1	3	0	.188	.235
	Delmarva (SAL)	A	.258	61	240	36	62	14	3	4	25	22	53	3	.392	.326
2000	Delmarva (SAL)	A	.290	70	269	43	78	16	1	11	59	25	56	20	.480	.358
	Frederick (Car)	A	.235	65	243	33	57	10	1	8	31	21	58	9	.383	.303
2001	Frederick (Car)	A	.270	72	267	28	72	14	0	7	29	13	57	8	.401	.305
	Bowie (EL)	AA	.254	18	67	7	17	3	0	1	8	6	10	2	.343	.315
	Rochester (IL)	AAA	.311	20	74	11	23	7	1	2	11	5	14	1	.514	.354
2002	Bowie (EL)	AA	.246	137	488	57	120	20	1	15	64	40	107	3	.383	.314
MINOR LEAGUE TOTALS			.260	447	1664	217	432	84	7	48	227	133	358	46	.405	.321

23. Arturo Rivas, of

Born: Feb. 2, 1984. **Ht.:** 6-0. **Wt.:** 190. **Bats:** R. **Throws:** R. **Career Transactions:** Signed out of Venezuela by Orioles, Oct. 18, 2000.

Rivas, who signed with the Orioles when he was 16, skipped the Rookie league in his native Venezuela and came straight to the United States to make his professional debut in 2001, making him the youngest player in the system at the time. Rivas played well at Bluefield last season, encouraging the organization that he's a potential impact player. It's much too early to call him a five-tool prospect, but all five of his tools have potential. Rivas is athletic with good speed. His best tool might be his arm, which helped him lead Appalachian League outfielders with five double plays in 2002. He also shows good power potential. The key will be how he develops as a hitter. He has little knowledge of the strike zone or how to hit breaking pitches at this point, though he did improve a lot in a year. Some in the organization also have questioned his work habits. Rivas probably will make his full-season debut in low Class A this season if he has a good spring training.

Year	Club (League)	Class	AVG	G	AB	R	H	2B	3B	HR	RBI	BB	SO	SB	SLG	OBP
2001	Bluefield (Appy)	R	.147	11	34	4	5	0	0	0	2	5	13	4	.147	.286
	Orioles (GCL)	R	.308	8	26	6	8	1	0	0	2	4	5	2	.346	.412
2002	Bluefield (Appy)	R	.272	55	213	45	58	11	1	8	34	19	47	11	.446	.342
MINOR LEAGUE TOTALS			.260	74	273	55	71	12	1	8	38	28	65	17	.399	.342

24. Matt Riley, lhp

Born: Aug. 2, 1979. **Ht.:** 6-1. **Wt.:** 200. **Bats:** L. **Throws:** L. **School:** Sacramento CC. **Career Transactions:** Selected by Orioles in third round of 1997 draft; signed May 28, 1998 . . . On disabled list, April 1-Nov. 19, 2001.

Riley sat atop this list in 1999 and 2000, but it all fell apart in big league camp the latter year. He didn't perform well and lost more points for his immature behavior. He injured his elbow late in the season and required Tommy John surgery. After missing all of 2001, Riley was erratic in his return to action last season in Double-A. Perhaps more important, though, he pitched the entire season with few problems. He did miss a start with a blister on his thumb and was shut down a bit early with shoulder soreness, but overall his arm seemed sound. The organization considered sending him to the Arizona Fall League but decided to give him the winter off. Riley showed flashes of the form that made him a top prospect, which includes a mid-90s fastball and a curveball that's one of the best breaking pitches in the organization. But his mechanics were often out of whack, which meant he lost velocity on his fastball, didn't have the sharp break on his curve and couldn't develop consistent command. He improved when roving pitching coordinator Dave Schmidt took over as Bowie's pitching coach at midseason, and in his next-to-last start of the season he struck out 10, walked one and gave up two hits in 6 1/3 innings against Erie. Riley is still just 23, so the Orioles will be patient with him as he tries to return to form. They may send him back to Double-A to open the season.

Year	Club (League)	Class	W	L	ERA	G	GS	CG	SV	IP	H	R	ER	HR	BB	SO	AVG
1998	Delmarva (SAL)	A	5	4	1.19	16	14	0	0	83	42	19	11	0	44	136	.152
1999	Frederick (Car)	A	3	2	2.61	8	8	0	0	52	34	19	15	5	14	58	.188
	Bowie (EL)	AA	10	6	3.22	20	20	3	0	126	113	53	45	13	42	131	.241
	Baltimore (AL)	MAJ	0	0	7.36	3	3	0	0	11	17	9	9	4	13	6	.378
2000	Rochester (IL)	AAA	0	2	14.14	2	2	0	0	7	15	12	11	3	4	8	.417
	Bowie (EL)	AA	5	7	6.08	19	14	2	1	74	74	56	50	9	49	66	.262
2001					Did Not Play—Injured												
2002	Bowie (EL)	AA	4	10	6.34	22	22	0	0	109	136	84	77	12	48	105	.306
MAJOR LEAGUE TOTALS			0	0	7.36	3	3	0	0	11	17	9	9	4	13	6	.378
MINOR LEAGUE TOTALS			27	31	4.17	87	80	5	1	451	414	243	209	42	201	504	.245

25. Tommy Arko, c

Born: July 28, 1982. **Ht.:** 6-2. **Wt.:** 210. **Bats:** R. **Throws:** R. **School:** Cooper HS, Abilene, Texas. **Career Transactions:** Selected by Orioles in third round of 2000 draft; signed June 9, 2000.

Even though it was his third season in Rookie ball, Arko generated some buzz with his 14 home runs at Bluefield. He earned a late promotion to Delmarva and looked overmatched in his short stint there. Still just 20, Arko has a lot of maturing to do, both physically and emotionally. He doesn't have much of an idea of what he's doing at the plate, but when he gets hold of the ball he can hit it a long way. His plate discipline has improved but still has a long way to go. He also has a great body for a catcher. Defensively, Arko has a good arm, though his feet are sluggish. He's a below-average runner. The biggest concern about him, though, is his attitude. He's hard on himself and it's not clear he's committed to the game. Arko is likely to either put his tools together and become a top prospect or completely wash out. We'll get an indication in 2003 when he returns to low Class A.

Year	Club (League)	Class	AVG	G	AB	R	H	2B	3B	HR	RBI	BB	SO	SB	SLG	OBP
2000	Orioles (GCL)	R	.205	37	127	12	26	6	2	1	11	18	42	0	.307	.305
2001	Bluefield (Appy)	R	.194	36	124	16	24	4	1	5	16	13	47	0	.363	.271
2002	Delmarva (SAL)	A	.127	22	63	5	8	3	0	0	0	7	28	0	.175	.236
	Bluefield (Appy)	R	.265	57	181	41	48	11	0	14	37	35	58	0	.558	.387
MINOR LEAGUE TOTALS			.214	152	495	74	106	24	3	20	64	73	175	0	.396	.320

26. Beau Hale, rhp

Born: Dec. 1, 1978. **Ht.:** 6-2. **Wt.:** 200. **Bats:** R. **Throws:** R. **School:** University of Texas. **Career Transactions:** Selected by Orioles in first round (14th overall) of 2000 draft; signed Aug. 18, 2000.

It's been all downhill for Hale since he led Texas to the College World Series and became a first-round pick in 2000. He didn't make his professional debut until 2001 after signing late and has battled injuries in both of his pro seasons, though none of the ailments has been considered serious. Both his shoulder and elbow have bothered him at times. Hale was shut down a couple of times last season with muscle soreness, and he had been afraid to rear back and let a pitch go until the latter part of 2002. He had poor results in high Class A but pitched well after a promotion to Double-A—before getting shut down again. Hale threw 95-97 mph in college but has not approached that velocity as a pro, throwing around 89-92. His changeup might be his best pitch now, and he needs time to work on his breaking stuff. He has thrown a slider and a curveball. His mechanics and arm strength are obviously areas of concern as well. Hale has done a very good job of throwing strikes but also has been very hittable. He'll probably head back to Double-A to open 2003. The Orioles would just like to see the healthy and confident pitcher they drafted.

Year	Club (League)	Class	W	L	ERA	G	GS	CG	SV	IP	H	R	ER	HR	BB	SO	AVG
2001	Frederick (Car)	A	1	2	1.32	5	5	1	0	34	30	8	5	1	4	30	.236
	Bowie (EL)	AA	1	5	5.11	12	12	0	0	62	74	39	35	8	15	40	.306
2002	Frederick (Car)	A	8	8	5.02	22	22	0	0	131	157	83	73	8	27	79	.297
	Bowie (EL)	AA	2	0	0.84	2	2	0	0	11	11	2	1	0	3	6	.256
MINOR LEAGUE TOTALS			12	15	4.32	41	41	1	0	237	272	132	114	17	49	155	.289

27. Mike Paradis, rhp

Born: May 3, 1978. **Ht.:** 6-3. **Wt.:** 190. **Bats:** R. **Throws:** R. **School:** Clemson University. **Career Transactions:** Selected by Orioles in first round (13th overall) of 1999 draft; signed June 22, 1999.

At the beginning of the Arizona Fall League season, Paradis looked like he had finally figured things out. He led Maryvale starters in ERA but then gave up nine earned runs in two starts, covering seven innings, and ended up with a 4.15 ERA and more walks than strikeouts. That's the story of Paradis' career so far. There are nights when he causes scouts to wonder why he's still in the minor leagues, but too many others when he can't seem to find the plate. He's a sinker/slider pitcher whose stuff is among the best in the organization when it's on. He works at 92-93 mph and throws a curveball and changeup that can be very good. The problem is Paradis is high-strung and needs everything to be perfect. When things go wrong, he can implode and pitch himself into trouble. If he's spotting his fastball and getting his hard slider over, he can be unhittable. He just needs the confidence to do it, as well as the realization that he doesn't have to strike out every hitter. He may be better suited for bullpen work, but he'll get a chance in the Triple-A rotation.

Year	Club (League)	Class	W	L	ERA	G	GS	CG	SV	IP	H	R	ER	HR	BB	SO	AVG
1999	Delmarva (SAL)	A	0	1	15.00	2	2	0	0	3	3	5	5	0	4	6	.273
2000	Delmarva (SAL)	A	6	5	3.99	18	18	0	0	97	95	53	43	5	49	81	.251
	Frederick (Car)	A	2	5	4.17	8	8	1	0	45	55	24	21	1	24	32	.302
2001	Bowie (EL)	AA	8	13	4.71	27	26	1	0	138	157	98	72	13	62	108	.279
2002	Bowie (EL)	AA	8	13	5.64	27	27	1	0	152	174	108	95	12	66	94	.291
MINOR LEAGUE TOTALS			24	37	4.89	82	81	3	0	435	484	288	236	31	205	321	.279

28. Hayden Penn, rhp

Born: Oct. 13, 1984. **Ht.:** 6-3. **Wt.:** 180. **Bats:** R. **Throws:** R. **School:** Santata HS, Santee, Calif. **Career Transactions:** Selected by Orioles in fifth round of 2002 draft; signed Aug. 1, 2002.

Penn is a rangy athlete who generated interest from NCAA Division I basketball programs. He committed to San Diego State in baseball but signed with the Orioles instead. The team didn't sign him until August because of budget concerns, so he'll make his pro debut in 2003. Penn has a live arm with a fastball that ranges from the low to mid-90s and a hard slider. His build, which one scout compared to Todd Stottlemyre's, offers good projection. He's very much a work in progress, though. Penn had a mediocre senior season in high school and was inconsistent because of his mechanics, which caused his velocity and control to vary wildly. His slider needs work and his changeup is virtually nonexistent right now. The Orioles will start him in extended spring training and just get him used to playing baseball every day before sending him to one of their short-season clubs. He has a high ceiling if he can harness his arm.

Year	Club (League)	Class	W	L	ERA	G	GS	CG	SV	IP	H	R	ER	HR	BB	SO	AVG
								Has Not Played—Signed 2003 Contract									

29. Richard Bartlett, rhp

Born: Oct. 6, 1981. **Ht.:** 6-3. **Wt.:** 210. **Bats:** R. **Throws:** R. **School:** Kamiakin HS, Kennewick, Wash. **Career Transactions:** Selected by Orioles in third round of 2000 draft; signed June 20, 2000.

Bartlett hadn't shown much in his first two seasons in the Orioles organization, but he got off to a great start in low Class A in 2002, winning five times in April. Baltimore pushed him to high Class A, where he struggled for one of the worst teams in the minors. Bartlett is a thinking-man's pitcher with a good idea of what to do on the mound. His fastball is a bit below average at 87-88 mph, but he throws strikes and mixes his pitches well. He also throws a slider and changeup and has command of all three pitches. He's competitive and very particular with his stuff. He would be better served by rearing back and throwing more, as he sometimes thinks too much. Because of his stuff, he has to be on his game every time out to avoid getting knocked around. His frame suggests that he could add velocity as he matures, and he profiles as a middle-of-the-rotation starter who piles up innings. He'll get another shot at high Class A to start the season.

Year	Club (League)	Class	W	L	ERA	G	GS	CG	SV	IP	H	R	ER	HR	BB	SO	AVG
2000	Orioles (GCL)	R	0	4	4.31	10	9	0	0	40	46	25	19	2	21	32	.301
2001	Delmarva (SAL)	A	5	9	4.53	19	18	0	0	95	109	54	48	6	30	60	.293
2002	Delmarva (SAL)	A	6	0	2.63	9	8	0	0	48	45	16	14	1	16	33	.243
	Frederick (Car)	A	6	10	5.35	18	18	1	0	99	116	72	59	12	29	57	.293
MINOR LEAGUE TOTALS			17	23	4.46	56	53	1	0	282	316	167	140	21	96	182	.286

30. Chris Smith, lhp

Born: Dec. 10, 1979. **Ht.:** 5-11. **Wt.:** 210. **Bats:** L. **Throws:** L. **School:** Cumberland (Tenn.) University. **Career Transactions:** Selected by Orioles in first round (seventh overall) of 2001 draft; signed June 12, 2001.

Smith took a big risk in college, jumping from Florida State to Cumberland (Tenn.), an NAIA program, so he could prove himself as a pitcher. It worked out well, as he threw 94 mph and became the seventh overall pick in the 2001 draft. Not much has worked out since then, though, even as the Orioles took a cautious approach with him. After he signed for $2.175 million just a week after the 2001 draft, Smith was held back from pitching until the last 10 days of the season, when he threw two innings. He got into a regular throwing program in instructional league but reported weakness in his shoulder. Orthopedic specialist Dr. James Andrews examined Smith late in 2001, and an MRI didn't reveal any structural damage. A club official blamed the discomfort on mild tendinitis. After extended spring training, Smith made five starts in Rookie ball, where he couldn't find his usual velocity and his control was completely out of whack. Doctors finally found a labrum tear and performed surgery, and Smith is expected to be ready to pitch this season. If healthy, Smith has an exciting arm, but the injury has cost him much-needed development time as well as casting doubt on his future. His curveball, changeup and command all need plenty of work.

Year	Club (League)	Class	W	L	ERA	G	GS	CG	SV	IP	H	R	ER	HR	BB	SO	AVG
2001	Orioles (GCL)	R	0	0	0.00	2	0	0	0	2	2	2	0	0	1	0	.222
2002	Bluefield (Appy)	R	0	3	11.45	5	5	0	0	11	12	14	14	1	21	4	.300
MINOR LEAGUE TOTALS			0	3	9.69	7	5	0	0	13	14	16	14	1	22	4	.286

BOSTON
RED SOX

TOP 30 PROSPECTS

1. Hanley Ramirez, ss
2. Kelly Shoppach, c
3. Kevin Youkilis, 3b
4. Freddy Sanchez, ss/2b
5. Phil Dumatrait, lhp
6. Manny Delcarmen, rhp
7. Billy Simon, rhp
8. Jon Lester, lhp
9. Jorge de la Rosa, lhp
10. Aneudis Mateo, rhp
11. Michael Goss, of
12. Dustin Brown, c/of
13. Scott White, 3b
14. Andy Shibilo, rhp
15. Kason Gabbard, lhp
16. Rene Miniel, rhp
17. Chris Smith, rhp
18. Anastacio Martinez, rhp
19. Chad Spann, 3b
20. Matt White, lhp
21. Earl Snyder, 1b
22. Paul Stewart, rhp
23. Juan Cedeno, lhp
24. Denny Tussen, rhp
25. Tyler Pelland, lhp
26. David Pahucki, rhp
27. Charlie Weatherby, rhp
28. Brett Bonvechio, 1b
29. Javier Lopez, lhp
30. Angel Santos, 2b

By Jim Callis

After the Red Sox failed to lure Billy Beane from Oakland, they made 28-year-old Theo Epstein the youngest general manager in major league history in November. Touted by Beane and others as one of the brightest young executives in the game, Epstein built a diverse resume with the Orioles and Padres. As he tries to end the Red Sox' championship drought, he can build on the number of positive changes that have occured since John Henry's ownership group assumed control of the franchise in February.

While the Red Sox won 93 games and stayed in playoff contention for much of 2002, their thin farm system isn't ready to help them trim a bloated, nine-figure payroll. Team president Larry Lucchino vowed that player development and scouting would serve as the foundation in Boston, and the Red Sox have made several moves toward that goal.

Scouting director David Chadd and director of international scouting Luis Eljaua arrived from the Marlins, Henry's former club. Epstein came to the organization from the Padres, where he had worked under Lucchino. Before his promotion from assistant GM, his main task was working with Ben Cherington, who was promoted to farm director, to oversee the revitalization of the minor league system. The Red Sox hired short-season manager Orv Franchuk from the Athletics to be their minor league hitting coordinator, and scout Mark Wasinger from the Padres to evaluate the entire system. Franchuk is noted for his ability to teach plate discipline, and fits the Sox' new emphasis on on-base percentage that starts at the top with Henry. Another proponent of OBP is another new hire, senior adviser Bill James, who popularized the statistical analysis of baseball. Bill Lajoie, a respected judge of talent, was brought in from the Brewers to serve as a special assistant to Epstein.

All of these people have their work cut out for them to pump life into a farm system that grew fallow in the final years of former GM Dan Duquette's reign. The Red Sox ranked 28th among the 30 organizations with a .454 minor league winning percentage in 2002. Epstein was able to deal mid-level prospects Josh Thigpen, Josh Hancock and Tony Blanco to shore up the right side of his infield with Jeremy Giambi and Todd Walker, though the Phillies and Reds were motivated by concerns other than talent in those trades.

OrganizationOverview

General Manager: Theo Epstein. **Farm Director:** Ben Cherington. **Scouting Director:** David Chadd.

2002 PERFORMANCE

Class	Team	League	W	L	Pct.	Finish*	Manager
Majors	Boston	American	93	69	,574	t-5th (14)	Grady Little
Triple-A	Pawtucket Red Sox	International	60	84	.417	11th (14)	Buddy Bailey
Double-A	†Trenton Thunder	Eastern	63	77	.450	t-9th (12)	Ron Johnson
High A	Sarasota Red Sox	Florida State	62	74	.456	10th (12)	Billy Gardner
Low A	Augusta GreenJackets	South Atlantic	69	67	.507	8th (16)	Arnie Beyeler
Short-season	Lowell Spinners	New York-Penn	34	41	.453	8th (14)	Mike Boulanger
Rookie	GCL Red Sox	Gulf Coast	26	34	.433	11th (14)	John Sanders
OVERALL 2002 MINOR LEAGUE RECORD			314	377	.454	28th (30)	

*Finish in overall standings (No. of teams in league). †Affiliate will be in Portland (Eastern) in 2003.

ORGANIZATION LEADERS

BATTING
*Minimum 250 At-Bats
*AVG	Hanley Ramirez, GCL Red Sox/Lowell	.352
R	Freddy Sanchez, Pawtucket/Trenton	85
H	Freddy Sanchez, Pawtucket/Trenton	157
TB	Freddy Sanchez, Pawtucket/Trenton	215
2B	Kelly Shoppach, Sarasota	35
3B	Tonayne Brown, Trenton	9
HR	Shane Andrews, Pawtucket	22
RBI	Wilton Veras, Pawtucket/Trenton	83
BB	Kevin Youkilis, Trenton/Sarsota	93
SO	Steve Lomasney, Pawtucket/Trenton	148
SB	Freddy Sanchez, Pawtucket/Trenton	24

PITCHING
#Minimum 75 Innings
W	Isauro Pineda, Trenton	9
	Alex Solano, Sarasota	9
L	Matt Thompson, Sarasota	14
#ERA	Brian Adams, Trenton/Sarasota	2.11
G	Tim Young, Pawtucket	57
CG	Four tied at	2
SV	Jason Howell, Augusta	16
IP	Don Wengert, Pawtucket	169
BB	Anastacio Martinez, Trenton	75
SO	Manny Delcarmen, Augusta	136

BEST TOOLS

Best Hitter for Average	Kevin Youkilis
Best Power Hitter	Juan Diaz
Fastest Baserunner	Michael Goss
Best Athlete	Michael Goss
Best Fastball	Manny Delcarmen
Best Curveball	Phil Dumatrait
Best Slider	Andy Shibilo
Best Changeup	Chris Elmore
Best Control	Chris Elmore
Best Defensive Catcher	Kelly Shoppach
Best Defensive Infielder	Freddy Sanchez
Best Infield Arm	Tony Blanco
Best Defensive Outfielder	Jeremy Owens
Best Outfield Arm	Carlos Rodriguez

PROJECTED 2006 LINEUP

Catcher	Kelly Shoppach
First Base	Kevin Youkilis
Second Base	Freddy Sanchez
Third Base	Hanley Ramirez
Shortstop	Nomar Garciaparra
Left Field	Manny Ramirez
Center Field	Johnny Damon
Right Field	Trot Nixon
Designated Hitter	Jeremy Giambi
No. 1 Starter	Pedro Martinez

Wilton Veras   Don Wengert

No. 2 Starter	Derek Lowe
No. 3 Starter	Phil Dumatrait
No. 4 Starter	Manny Delcarmen
No. 5 Starter	Casey Fossum
Closer	Jorge de la Rosa

TOP PROSPECTS OF THE DECADE

1993	Frank Rodriguez, rhp
1994	Trot Nixon, of
1995	Nomar Garciaparra, ss
1996	Donnie Sadler, ss
1997	Nomar Garciaparra, ss
1998	Brian Rose, rhp
1999	Dernell Stenson, of
2000	Steve Lomasney, c
2001	Dernell Stenson, of/1b
2002	Seung Song, rhp

TOP DRAFT PICKS OF THE DECADE

1993	Trot Nixon, of
1994	Nomar Garciaparra, ss
1995	Andy Yount, rhp
1996	Josh Garrett, rhp
1997	John Curtice, lhp
1998	Adam Everett, ss
1999	Rick Asadoorian, of
2000	Phil Dumatrait, lhp
2001	Kelly Shoppach, c (2)
2002	Jon Lester, lhp (2)

ALL-TIME LARGEST BONUSES

Adam Everett, 1998	$1,725,000
Rick Asadoorian, 1999	$1,725,000
Phil Dumatrait, 2000	$1,250,000
Robinson Checo, 1996	$1,150,000
Sang-Hoon Lee, 1999	$1,050,000

MinorLeague**Depth**Chart

BOSTON RED SOX

RANK 27

When the Red Sox filed their 40-man roster in November, it included just 28 players. That was a telling commentary on the lack of talent in the upper levels of the farm system. Though devoid of depth, the Sox have done an effective job of dealing minor leaguers for established major leaguers. New general manager Theo Epstein has incorporated a new philosophy, blending performance with tools, which can only help an organization that has not produced much homegrown talent. The new regime also pledges a renewed commitment to player development and scouting in the U.S. and Latin America, efforts that suffered as the team was combing the Far East in recent years.

Note: Depth charts prepared by Josh Boyd. Numbers in parentheses indicate prospect rankings.

LF
Dernell Stenson

CF
Michael Goss (11)
Antron Seiber
Jeremy Owens

RF
Justin Sherrod

3B
Kevin Youkilis (3)
Scott White (13)
Chad Spann (19)
John Hattig
Luis Herrera

SS
Hanley Ramirez (1)
Kenny Perez

2B
Freddy Sanchez (4)
Angel Santos (30)
Eric West
Melvin Dorta
Melvin Reyes

1B
Earl Snyder (21)
Brett Bonvechio (28)
Juan Diaz

C
Kelly Shoppach (2)
Dustin Brown (12)
Edgar Martinez
Alberto Concepcion
Chris Coste

LHP

Starters
Phil Dumatrait (5)
Jon Lester (8)
Kason Gabbard (15)
Juan Cedeno (23)
Tyler Pelland (25)

Relievers
Jorge de la Rosa (9)
Matt White (20)
Javier Lopez (29)
Juan Perez
Chris Elmore

RHP

Starters
Manny Delcarmen (6)
Billy Simon (7)
Aneudis Mateo (10)
Chris Smith (18)
Paul Stewart (22)
Denny Tussen (24)
David Pahucki (26)
Junior Frias
Mat Thompson
Luis Mendoza
Olivio Astacio

Relievers
Andy Shibilo (14)
Rene Miniel (16)
Anastacio Martinez (18)
Charlie Weatherby (27)
Kevin Huang
Justin Kaye
Hansel Izquierdo
Ryo Kumagai
Felix Villegas
Dan Generelli

DraftAnalysis

2002 Draft

Best Pro Debut: OF Mike Goss (11) hit .398 with 14 steals in 21 short-season games before dislocating his pinky sliding into second base. RHP John Priola (14) doesn't have an above-average pitch, but he did go 3-0, 2.54 with 13 saves and a 33-5 strikeout-walk ratio in 46 short-season innings.

Best Athlete: Goss was a wide receiver and kick returner for Jackson State's football team. LHP Jon Lester (2) could have been an early pick as a position player thanks to his bat and speed, and he was a basketball standout in high school. SS Chad Spann (5) was a high school quarterback.

Best Pure Hitter: 3B Scott White (3) or Spann. Some scouts said White had a bit of a hitch in his swing, but the Red Sox say it's a timing mechanism and don't plan any changes yet. His pitch recognition is a plus.

Best Raw Power: C Alberto Concepcion (21) edges White and Spann now, though they could pass him as they mature.

Fastest Runner: Goss has basestealing instincts to go with 6.4-6.45 second speed in the 60-yard dash.

Best Defensive Player: White moves well to both sides and has a strong arm at third base.

Best Fastball: Lester and RHP Brandon Moss (8) both reached 93 mph in high school, with Lester having more projection for the future. The Red Sox have elected to use the versatile Moss as a middle infielder.

Best Breaking Ball: RHP Chris Smith (4) has a power curveball to go with an average fastball and an advanced under-

standing of pitching.

Most Intriguing Background: Unsigned RHP Brian Bannister's (45) father Floyd won 134 big league games and led the American League in strikeouts in 1982. Floyd was the No. 1 pick in the June 1976 draft.

Closest To The Majors: Smith, the lone college player Boston drafted in the first nine rounds.

Best Late-Round Pick: Concepcion, the Pacific-10 Conference player of the year, was a Padres second-round pick

RICH ABEL

Smith

out of high school. He slid three years later because of questions about his catching ability and his makeup, but the Red Sox say he just needs to improve his footwork.

The One Who Got Away: RHP Jason Neighborgall (7) may have better stuff than Josh Beckett did at the same point, but teams were leery of paying him Beckett money. He's part of a Georgia Tech recruiting class rated as the best in the nation.

Assessment: It took most of the summer, but the Red Sox were able to bring in Lester, White and Pelland, all of whom were challenging signs. First-year scouting director David Chadd didn't have the benefit of a first-round pick but got a first-round talent in Lester. Neighborgall would have been a coup for a club trying to rebuild its farm system, but his price was just too high.

2001 Draft

Despite not having a first-rounder and failing to sign LHP Matt Chico (2), the Red Sox still came up with three of their best prospects: C Kelly Shoppach (2), 3B Kevin Youkilis (8) and RHP Billy Simon (9). **Grade: B**

2000 Draft

Boston started well with LHP Phil Dumatrait (1) and RHP Manny Delcarmen (2), now its top two pitching prospects. SS Freddy Sanchez (11), since-traded RHP Josh Thigpen (16) and draft-and-follows LHP Kason Gabbard (29) and C Dustin Brown (35) were uncovered in later rounds. **Grade: B**

1999 Draft

LHP Casey Fossum (1) is promising, but fellow first-rounders OF Rick Asadoorian and RHP Brad Baker faded before being traded. OF Lew Ford (12) is intriguing—and was dealt to Minnesota. **Grade: C+**

1998 Draft

The Red Sox rue not signing 3B Mark Teixeira (1) and LHP Ben Kozlowski (26). Draft-and-follow RHP Dennis Tankersley (38) went to San Diego in a deal for Ed Sprague. **Grade: C+**

Note: Draft analysis prepared by Jim Callis. Numbers in parentheses indicate draft rounds.

... Ramirez is a legitimate five-tool shortstop who has instincts to go with his athletic talents.

Hanley
Ramirez, ss

Born: Dec. 23, 1983.
Ht.: 6-1. **Wt.:** 170.
Bats: B. **Throws:** R.
Career Transactions: Signed out of Dominican Republic by Red Sox, July 2, 2000.

Ramirez rocketed from obscurity to the top of the list over the course of the 2002 season. In his 2001 pro debut, he led Boston's Rookie-level Dominican Summer League affiliate with a .345 average and earned the organization's player of the year award for that club, but otherwise escaped attention. After arriving in the United States, he didn't stay anonymous for long. Managers rated him the best prospect in both the Rookie-level Gulf Coast and the short-season New York-Penn leagues, and he led the GCL in slugging percentage. Though it's risky to place labels on a player before he even reaches full-season ball, managers and scouts already are comparing Ramirez to such players as Nomar Garciaparra, Vladimir Guerrero, Alex Rodriguez and Alfonso Soriano. The best parallel at this point is Soriano.

Ramirez is a legitimate five-tool shortstop who has instincts to go with his athletic talents. Signed as a switch-hitter, he was so advanced from the right side that he had no need to hit lefthanded. Ramirez has quick hands and the ball jumps off his bat. Against Mets first-round pick Scott Kazmir, he drilled a 96 mph fastball off the wall. Ramirez recognizes pitches, can hit the breaking ball and uses the whole field. He's mechanically sound and doesn't chase pitches out of the strike zone. Ramirez projects to be a plus hitter for both average and power in the big leagues; he's also an above-average runner. Defensively, he has soft hands and supplements an average arm with a quick release. His footwork improved over the course of the season.

The Red Sox have some concerns that the hype has come too fast for Ramirez, who was sent home early from instructional league for disciplinary reasons. He knows he's good, and can be immature and selfish. While he has lots of potential, he'll need to keep working hard to realize it. Ramirez rarely swings and misses, to the detriment of working deep counts and drawing walks. Though Boston has no need to rush him, Ramirez will determine how much time he needs in the minors. He'll start 2003 at low Class A Augusta but could force a mid-season promotion if he continues to dominate.

Year	Club(League)	Class	AVG	G	AB	R	H	2B	3B	HR	RBI	BB	SO	SB	SLG	OBP
2001	Red Sox (DSL)	R	.345	54	197	32	68	18	2	5	34	15	22	13	.533	.397
2002	Red Sox (GCL)	R	.341	45	164	29	56	11	3	6	26	16	15	8	.555	.402
	Lowell (NY-P)	A	.371	22	97	17	36	9	2	1	19	4	14	4	.536	.400
MINOR LEAGUE TOTALS			.349	121	458	78	160	38	7	12	79	35	51	25	.541	.400

KEN BABBITT

2. Kelly Shoppach, c

Born: April 29, 1980. **Ht.:** 6-1. **Wt.:** 210. **Bats:** R. **Throws:** R. **School:** Baylor University. **Career Transactions:** Selected by Red Sox in second round of 2001 draft; signed Aug. 17, 2001.

RICK BATTLE

Shoppach was the Red Sox' top draft pick in 2001, when they didn't have a first-rounder. He signed late for $737,500 and didn't make his pro debut until 2002, when he went directly to high Class A and was a Florida State League all-star. September surgery to repair a small tear in his rotator cuff prevented him from attending the Arizona Fall League. Shoppach stands out most for his catch-and-throw skills, and managers rated him the FSL's best defensive catcher. He used a strong arm and quick release to throw out 33 percent of basestealers. He also moves well behind the plate and possesses natural leadership abilities. Shoppach already could drive the ball to the opposite field and started to develop pull power in 2002. His ability to draw walks fits with Boston's new philosophy. His shoulder injury naturally is a concern, but the Red Sox expect Shoppach to be able to catch in games by late May. He'll need to make more consistent contact at higher levels. Shoppach will spend 2003 at Double-A Portland, solely as a DH at the outset. Jason Varitek's contract expires in 2004, after which Shoppach should be able to take over.

Year	Club (League)	Class	AVG	G	AB	R	H	2B	3B	HR	RBI	BB	SO	SB	SLG	OBP
2002	Sarasota (FSL)	A	.271	116	414	54	112	35	1	10	66	59	112	2	.432	.369
MINOR LEAGUE TOTALS			.271	116	414	54	112	35	1	10	66	59	112	2	.432	.369

3. Kevin Youkilis, 3b

Born: March 15, 1979. **Ht.:** 6-1. **Wt.:** 220. **Bats:** R. **Throws:** R. **School:** University of Cincinnati. **Career Transactions:** Selected by Red Sox in eighth round of 2001 draft; signed June 11, 2001.

RICK BATTLE

Undrafted as a Cincinnati junior in 2000, Youkilis impressed scouts in the Cape Cod League that summer and went in the eighth round a year later. He has turned out to be more than just a senior sign, compiling a .457 on-base percentage and reaching Double-A in his first 1½ seasons as a pro. Youkilis has an extraordinary eye at the plate and consistently produces hits and walks. Though he doesn't have a live body, he's more athletic than he looks. His feet, hands and work ethic will allow him to be a solid average third baseman. Though he started to lift pitches more frequently in Double-A, Youkilis may not hit more than 15-20 homers annually. While he moves better than expected, he's still not fast. His arm is more notable for its accuracy than its strength. Youkilis' on-base abilities fit Boston's approach more than all-star Shea Hillenbrand's do. Youkilis will spend the year in Triple-A, and may move to first base or left field in the majors unless Hillenbrand is traded.

Year	Club (League)	Class	AVG	G	AB	R	H	2B	3B	HR	RBI	BB	SO	SB	SLG	OBP
2001	Lowell (NY-P)	A	.317	59	183	52	58	14	2	3	28	70	28	4	.464	.512
	Augusta (SAL)	A	.167	5	12	0	2	0	0	0	0	3	3	0	.167	.375
2002	Augusta (SAL)	A	.283	15	53	5	15	5	0	0	6	13	8	0	.377	.433
	Sarasota (FSL)	A	.295	76	268	45	79	16	0	3	48	49	37	0	.388	.422
	Trenton (EL)	AA	.344	44	160	34	55	10	0	5	26	31	18	5	.500	.462
MINOR LEAGUE TOTALS			.309	199	676	136	209	45	2	11	108	166	94	9	.430	.457

4. Freddy Sanchez, ss/2b

Born: 21 Dec. 1977. **Ht.:** 5-11. **Wt.:** 180. **Bats:** R **Throws:** R. **School:** Oklahoma City University. **Career Transactions:** Selected by Red Sox in 11th round of 2000 draft; signed June 14, 2000

After leading all minor league shortstops with a .334 average in 2001, Sanchez proved that performance was no fluke. He made the Double-A Eastern League all-star team, was Triple-A Pawtucket's player of the year and drilled a two-run single in his first big league at-bat. Sanchez has excellent hand-eye coordination and the ability to make consistent line-drive contact and hit for gap power. His instincts enhance his physical skills at the plate, on the bases and in the field. He has a solid average arm at shortstop and reads balls well off the bat. The knock on Sanchez always has been that he lacks pure shortstop range, though that's a moot point with Garciaparra in Boston. The Red Sox believe Sanchez could play short if needed. After making strides with his selectivity in Double-A, he regressed in Triple-A and the majors. Sanchez was the frontrunner for the Red Sox' second-base job until they traded for Todd Walker. Now he'll get more time to improve in Triple-A and could ease into the majors in a utility role. Walker becomes a free agent after the 2003 season, so Sanchez could be the starter in 2004.

Year	Club (League)	Class	AVG	G	AB	R	H	2B	3B	HR	RBI	BB	SO	SB	SLG	OBP
2000	Lowell (NYP)	A	.288	34	132	24	38	13	2	1	14	9	16	2	.439	.347
	Augusta (SAL)	A	.303	30	109	17	33	7	0	0	15	11	19	4	.367	.372
2001	Sarasota (FSL)	A	.339	69	280	40	95	19	4	1	24	22	30	5	.446	.388
	Trenton (EL)	AA	.326	44	178	25	58	20	0	2	19	9	21	3	.472	.363
2002	Trenton (EL)	AA	.328	80	311	60	102	23	1	3	38	37	45	19	.437	.403
	Pawtucket (INT)	AAA	.301	45	183	25	55	10	1	4	28	12	21	5	.432	.350
	Boston (AL)	Majors	.188	12	16	3	3	0	0	0	2	2	3	0	.188	.278
MINOR LEAGUE TOTALS			.319	302	1193	191	381	92	8	11	138	100	152	38	.438	.377
MAJOR LEAGUE TOTALS			.188	12	16	3	3	0	0	0	2	2	3	0	.188	.278

5. Phil Dumatrait, lhp

Born: July 12, 1981. **Ht.:** 6-2. **Wt.:** 170. **Bats:** R. **Throws:** L. **School:** Bakersfield (Calif.) JC. **Career Transactions:** Selected by Red Sox in first round (22nd overall) of 2000 draft; signed July 10, 2000.

With the 22nd pick in the 2000 draft, Boston seriously considered Jason Stokes before balking at his $2.5 million price tag. Instead they took Dumatrait, who blossomed suddenly after not being drafted as a high school senior in 1999, and signed him for $1.275 million. While Stokes is now a top slugging prospect with the Marlins, Dumatrait has become the Red Sox' top pitching prospect. Dumatrait's plus-plus curve-ball is the best breaking pitch in the Boston system. The new Red Sox front office values pitchers' approaches as well as pure stuff, and Dumatrait has a very good feel for his craft. His fastball is a solid average offering at 89-92 mph. His curve is an out pitch, but Dumatrait sometimes uses it too much at the expense of his changeup, which needs refinement. He also has to tweak his command after it got away from him a little bit at high Class A Sarasota. The Red Sox haven't had a homegrown lefty win in double digits since Tom Bolton in 1990. Dumatrait, who's headed back to high Class A, is the best hope to end that drought if Casey Fossum can't.

Year	Club (League)	Class	W	L	ERA	G	GS	CG	SV	IP	H	R	ER	HR	BB	SO	AVG
2000	Red Sox (GCL)	R	0	1	1.65	6	6	0	0	16	10	6	3	0	12	12	.172
2001	Red Sox (GCL)	R	3	0	2.76	8	8	0	0	33	27	10	10	0	9	33	.229
	Lowell (NY-P)	A	1	1	3.48	2	2	0	0	10	9	4	4	0	4	15	.225
2002	Augusta (SAL)	A	8	5	2.77	22	22	1	0	120	109	44	37	5	47	108	.249
	Sarasota (FSL)	A	0	2	3.86	4	4	0	0	14	10	9	6	0	15	16	.192
MINOR LEAGUE TOTALS			12	9	2.79	42	42	1	0	194	165	73	60	5	87	184	.234

6. Manny Delcarmen, rhp

Born: Feb. 16, 1982. **Ht.:** 6-2. **Wt.:** 190. **Bats:** R. **Throws:** R. **School:** West Roxbury (Mass.) HS. **Career Transactions:** Selected by Red Sox in second round of 2000 draft; signed Aug. 22, 2000.

The first inner-city Boston high schooler drafted since 1966, Delcarmen has the highest ceiling of any player in the system. As a result, the Red Sox are handling him carefully. After he threw 136 innings while being kept on strict pitch counts in 2002, he was told to skip instructional league and not do any throwing in the offseason. Delcarmen has a 92-94 mph fastball that can touch 95-96. He also has a curveball that is a plus pitch at times. He's a tough competitor who, while not completely polished, is fairly advanced considering his age and background. Convincing Delcarmen that he needs to throw his changeup has been a challenge. He'd rather go after hitters with his fastball, an approach that isn't going to work at the higher levels. He sometimes slows down his arm speed when he throws his changeup, letting hitters know what's coming. In 2003, Delcarmen will be part of a high Class A rotation that also will include Phil Dumatrait. Delcarmen is at least 2½ years from Boston.

Year	Club (League)	Class	W	L	ERA	G	GS	CG	SV	IP	H	R	ER	HR	BB	SO	AVG
2001	Red Sox (GCL)	R	4	2	2.54	11	8	0	1	46	35	16	13	0	19	62	.211
2002	Augusta (SAL)	A	7	8	4.10	26	24	0	0	136	124	77	62	15	56	136	.242
MINOR LEAGUE TOTALS			11	10	3.71	37	32	0	1	182	159	93	75	15	75	198	.234

7. Billy Simon, rhp

Born: Nov. 11, 1982. **Ht.:** 6-6. **Wt.:** 220. **Bats:** R. **Throws:** R. **School:** Wellington HS, West Palm Beach, Fla. **Career Transactions:** Selected by Red Sox in ninth round of 2001 draft; signed July 27, 2001.

Simon is part of the Wellington High pipeline that also includes recent first-round picks Bobby Bradley, Sean Burnett and Justin Pope. Simon projected as an early pick in 2001, but slid to the ninth round because he was committed to Louisiana State. The Red Sox signed him for $325,000, about fourth-round money. At 6-foot-6, Simon throws on a downward plane that makes it tough for hitters to get good swings against him. In his brief pro career, opponents have batted .189 without a homer against him. His fastball has plus velocity (90-92 mph) and life, with late sink. He throws a hard, overhand curveball and has a good feel for pitching. Simon has made progress with his changeup but still has work to do. His overall package is promising and his biggest need is experience. He has pitched just 42 innings since signing. Simon was the most impressive pitcher in Boston's instructional league camp, so he could develop quicker than expected. He'll open 2003 in low Class A.

Year	Club (League)	Class	W	L	ERA	G	GS	CG	SV	IP	H	R	ER	HR	BB	SO	AVG
2001	Red Sox (GCL)	R	0	0	1.00	3	3	0	0	9	6	2	1	0	1	7	.207
2002	Red Sox (GCL)	R	1	1	1.64	6	5	0	0	22	12	6	4	0	5	24	.156
	Lowell (NY-P)	A	0	1	1.64	3	3	0	0	11	10	6	2	0	6	12	.238
MINOR LEAGUE TOTALS			1	2	1.50	12	11	0	0	42	28	14	7	0	12	43	.189

8. Jon Lester, lhp

Born: Jan. 7, 1984. **Ht.:** 6-3. **Wt.:** 200. **Bats:** L. **Throws:** L. **School:** Bellarmine Prep, Puyallup, Wash. **Career Transactions:** Selected by Red Sox in second round of 2002 draft; signed Aug. 13, 2002.

Lacking a first-round pick in 2002 because they signed free agent Johnny Damon, the Red Sox landed a first-round talent in Lester with their first choice, 57th overall. He signed for $1 million, the only seven-figure bonus outside the first round. He was a legitimate prospect as a first baseman, though pro teams preferred him as a pitcher. He also was a standout basketball player in high school. Lester is an athletic lefthander along the lines of Mark Langston, which allows him to repeat his delivery with ease and bodes well for his command. Lester throws 88-93 mph, and his fastball has room to grow because he has a projectable body and easy arm action. His changeup is his second-best pitch, and his curveball showed promise in instructional league. Lester's curve needs the most work. He also threw a slider in high school, but Boston prefers that its young pitchers focus initially on curveballs. Though he's talented, he's also raw at this point. The Red Sox will proceed slowly with Lester. He'll probably begin 2003 in extended spring training before joining the Rookie-level Gulf Coast League team in June.

Year	Club (League)	Class	W	L	ERA	G	GS	CG	SV	IP	H	R	ER	HR	BB	SO	AVG
2002	Red Sox (GCL)	R	0	1	13.50	1	1	0	0	1	5	6	1	0	1	1	.714
MINOR LEAGUE TOTALS			0	1	13.50	1	1	0	0	1	5	6	1	0	1	1	.714

9. Jorge de la Rosa, lhp

Born: April 5, 1981. **Ht.:** 6-1. **Wt.:** 190. **Bats:** L. **Throws:** L. **Career Transactions:** Signed out of Mexico by Diamondbacks, March 20, 1998 . . . Contract purchased by Monterrey (Mexican) from Diamondbacks, April 2, 2000 . . . Contract purchased by Red Sox from Monterrey, Feb. 22, 2001.

The Diamondbacks signed de la Rosa in 1998 but sold him to the Monterrey Sultans two years later. When Arizona's working agreement with Monterrey expired, the Sultans kept de la Rosa's rights, then saw his velocity jump to the mid-90s in winter ball. Boston signed him for $600,000 in February 2001, and former general manager Dan Duquette dubbed him "the Mexican John Rocker." Moved to the rotation in 2002 to get more innings, de la Rosa still maintained a 92-94 mph fastball. He also throws a hard breaking ball and made strides with his changeup. For two consecutive seasons, de la Rosa has pitched well in high Class A before getting hammered in Double-A. He must gain better command of his pitches and more consistency with his changeup to succeed against more advanced hitters. The Red Sox will give de la Rosa a third crack at Double-A in 2002, continuing to use him as a starter to give him more mound time. His best long-term fit may be as a power lefty out of the bullpen.

Year	Club (League)	Class	W	L	ERA	G	GS	CG	SV	IP	H	R	ER	HR	BB	SO	AVG
1998	Diamondbacks (DSL)	R	1	0	4.50	13	0	0	1	14	8	7	7	3	8	21	.160
1999	Diamondbacks (AZL)	R	0	0	3.21	8	0	0	2	14	12	5	5	1	3	17	.226
	High Desert (Cal)	A	0	0	0.00	2	0	0	0	3	1	0	0	0	2	3	.100
	Missoula (Pio)	R	0	1	7.98	13	0	0	2	15	22	17	13	2	9	14	.333
2000	Monterrey (Mex)	AAA	3	2	6.28	37	0	0	1	39	38	27	27	2	32	50	.257
2001	Sarasota (FSL)	A	0	1	1.21	12	0	0	2	30	13	7	4	0	12	27	.127
	Trenton (EL)	AA	1	3	5.84	29	0	0	0	37	56	35	24	4	20	27	.348
2002	Sarasota (FSL)	A	7	7	3.65	23	23	1	0	121	105	53	49	10	52	95	.231
	Trenton (EL)	AA	1	2	5.50	4	4	0	0	18	17	12	11	0	9	15	.239
MINOR LEAGUE TOTALS			13	16	4.35	141	27	1	8	290	272	163	140	22	147	269	.244

10. Aneudis Mateo, rhp

Born: Oct. 3, 1982. **Ht.:** 6-4. **Wt.:** 210. **Bats:** R. **Throws:** R. **Career Transactions:**
Signed out of Dominican Republic by Red Sox, March 17, 2000.

Mateo has a friendly rivalry with Billy Simon, and followed him from
the Gulf Coast League to short-season Lowell in 2002. The two are similar, though Mateo isn't as consistent or as physically mature as Simon.
Boston's GCL pitcher of the year, Mateo is long and lanky, and he's tough
to hit because he's deceptive and commands the strike zone. He gets
good, late sink on a fastball with average velocity, and he has done a fine
job of polishing his curveball. He also has a good feel for throwing a
changeup and altering speeds on his fastball. At 6-foot-4 and 180 pounds, he's projectable
and should add velocity. Though he's the most advanced of a promising crop of Dominican
pitchers that also includes Juan Cedeno, Junior Frias and Denny Tussen, Mateo still will
need a few years to develop.

Year	Club (League)	Class	W	L	ERA	G	GS	CG	SV	IP	H	R	ER	HR	BB	SO	AVG
2000	Red Sox (DSL)	R	2	4	3.27	9	7	0	0	33	38	16	12	2	5	34	.275
2001	Red Sox (GCL)	R	0	1	0.00	3	2	0	0	8	6	4	0	0	0	6	.200
2002	Red Sox (GCL)	R	4	3	1.76	11	11	2	0	51	45	14	10	1	11	45	.232
	Lowell (NY-P)	A	2	0	1.45	3	3	0	0	19	8	3	3	1	2	13	.133
MINOR LEAGUE TOTALS			8	8	2.04	26	23	2	0	110	97	37	25	4	18	98	.230

11. Michael Goss, of

Born: Sept. 26, 1980. **Ht.:** 5-11. **Wt.:** 210. **Bats:** L. **Throws:** L. **School:** Jackson State University. **Career
Transactions:** Selected by Red Sox in 11th round of 2002 draft; signed June 19, 2002.

Goss might have gone as high as the fifth round in the 2002 draft had his NFL potential
as a kick returner not made teams wary. More of a wide receiver/return specialist than a baseball player at Jackson State, Goss slipped to the 11th round—the same round when Boston
grabbed Freddy Sanchez two years earlier. Goss got off to an electrifying start at Lowell, hitting .397 with 14 steals in 21 games, before dislocating a finger on a headfirst slide. He's an
exciting player, the fastest guy (6.4 to 6.45 seconds in the 60-yard dash) and the best athlete in the system, but he's also raw and isn't going to make it to Boston overnight. Goss,
the only real prospect among the system's outfielders, does understand what he needs to do
at the plate. His game is about speed, not strength, and he knows line drives and ground
balls play to his strong suit. His plate discipline needs improvement, and he's not going to
be a viable leadoff hitter unless he learns to draw a walk. Goss steals bases and runs down
fly balls on pure speed, and he'll have to learn how to make better reads and get better
jumps. His arm is below-average but playable in center field because he gets to balls quickly. He'll spend his first full pro season in low Class A.

Year	Club (League)	Class	AVG	G	AB	R	H	2B	3B	HR	RBI	BB	SO	SB	SLG	OBP
2002	Lowell (NY-P)	A	.398	21	83	9	33	2	1	0	10	4	15	14	.446	.438
MINOR LEAGUE TOTALS			.398	21	83	9	33	2	1	0	10	4	15	14	.446	.438

12. Dustin Brown, c/of

Born: June 19, 1982. **Ht.:** 6-0. **Wt.:** 180. **Bats:** R. **Throws:** R. **School:** Yavapai (Ariz.) JC. **Career
Transactions:** Selected by Red Sox in 35th round of 2000 draft; signed May 25, 2001.

Former scouting director Wayne Britton was high on three draft-and-follows from 2000
who signed in 2001: Brown, lefthander Kason Gabbard and first baseman Brett Bonvechio
all looked promising in 2002. Brown surprised the organization with his reluctance to
catch at the beginning of the season, so he spent some time in the outfield in the Gulf
Coast League, where he was the team's player of the year. He since has realized his quickest path to the majors is behind the plate and isn't resisting any longer. GCL managers

compared him to former Twins standout Brian Harper because of Brown's line-drive stroke, but he has the potential for more upside. Brown should develop at least average power as learns how to get pitches he can drive, and he already works counts well. He's also a better defender than Harper was, throwing out 37 percent of basestealers in 2002 and showing agility behind the plate. Though Brown will play some right field in low Class A in 2003 because the Red Sox also want to get Alberto Concepcion time at catcher, his future is as a backstop. That said, Kelly Shoppach will provide a formidable obstacle in the future.

Year	Club (League)	Class	AVG	G	AB	R	H	2B	3B	HR	RBI	BB	SO	SB	SLG	OBP
2001	Red Sox (GCL)	R	.254	36	126	15	32	5	4	0	14	7	24	1	.357	.289
2002	Red Sox (GCL)	R	.321	45	159	28	51	12	2	1	20	23	24	11	.440	.404
	Lowell (NY-P)	A	.282	21	78	12	22	3	1	0	12	8	20	1	.346	.371
MINOR LEAGUE TOTALS			.289	102	363	55	105	20	7	1	46	38	68	13	.391	.359

13. Scott White, 3b

Born: Oct. 18, 1983. **Ht.:** 6-3. **Wt.:** 190. **Bats:** R. **Throws:** R. **School:** Walton HS, Marietta, Ga. **Career Transactions:** Selected by Red Sox in third round of 2002 draft; signed Aug. 13, 2002.

White is a product of the nation's best youth baseball program, East Cobb in suburban Atlanta. East Cobb alumni included 2002 first-round picks Jeremy Hermida (Marlins) and Jeff Francoeur (Braves), and White went two rounds later. His pro debut was delayed until 2003 because he took all summer before signing for $825,000, the second-highest bonus in the third round. At 6-foot-3 and 190 pounds, White will need a year or two to develop physically. His eye at the plate excites an organization with a new focus on discipline, and he drew raves for taking pitches inches off the black in instructional league. He has raw power and solid defensive skills at third base. Before the draft, some scouts were concerned by a slight hitch in his swing, but the Red Sox say it serves as a timing mechanism and they have no plans to mess with it. In all likelihood, he'll start 2003 in extended spring training before going to the Gulf Coast League in June.

Year	Club (League)	Class	AVG	G	AB	R	H	2B	3B	HR	RBI	BB	SO	SB	SLG	OBP
	Has Not Played—Signed 2003 Contract															

14. Andy Shibilo, rhp

Born: Sept. 16, 1976. **Ht.:** 6-7. **Wt.:** 220. **Bats:** R. **Throws:** R. **School:** Pepperdine University. **Career Transactions:** Selected by Cardinals in 23rd round of 1998 draft; signed June 5, 1998 . . . Released by Cardinals, March 30, 2000 . . . Signed by independent Lehigh Valley (Atlantic), April 2000 . . . Signed by Padres, March 4, 2001 . . . Traded by Padres with LHP Alan Embree to Red Sox for RHP Brad Baker and RHP Dan Giese, June 23, 2002.

Not only did the Red Sox add Alan Embree from San Diego in June, but they also got more bullpen help by getting Shibilo in the deal. One of several Padres reclamation prospects from independent ball, Shibilo cuts an imposing figure on the mound at 6-foot-7. His velocity dipped slightly to 90-93 mph in 2002, yet he remained effective because his fastball has late sinking life. He gets inside on batters, breaking bats and generating ugly swings. His slider is solid average and gives him a second plus pitch at times. Shibilo further helps himself by being stingy with walks and homers. His biggest weakness is a slow delivery that makes him an easy target for stolen bases, but his funky motion also makes him hard to hit, so the Red Sox don't want to adjust it too much. He toys with a splitter and throws an occasional changeup, but for the most part he's a fastball/slider pitcher. Spring training will determine whether he begins 2003 in Triple-A or the majors.

Year	Club (League)	Class	W	L	ERA	G	GS	CG	SV	IP	H	R	ER	HR	BB	SO	AVG
1998	New Jersey (NY-P)	A	4	4	3.45	9	9	0	0	47	51	21	18	2	8	54	.268
	Peoria (Mid)	A	1	3	8.51	7	7	0	0	31	42	30	29	2	11	22	.339
1999	Peoria (Mid)	A	4	13	5.11	27	24	2	0	136	157	105	77	10	41	96	.283
2000	Lehigh Valley (Atl.)	IND	11	13	4.02	27	26	11	0	179	173	99	80	10	61	128	.255
2001	Lake Elsinore (Cal)	A	10	2	1.96	60	0	0	15	83	66	24	18	4	27	105	.216
2002	Mobile (SL)	AA	4	3	4.89	29	0	0	0	42	49	26	23	2	16	42	.301
	Trenton (EL)	AA	1	0	3.19	21	0	0	6	31	27	11	11	1	7	34	.233
	Pawtucket (IL)	AAA	0	1	5.19	6	0	0	0	9	9	7	5	0	2	9	.265
MINOR LEAGUE TOTALS			24	26	4.31	159	40	2	21	378	401	224	181	21	112	362	.269

15. Kason Gabbard, lhp

Born: April 8, 1982. **Ht.:** 6-4. **Wt.:** 200. **Bats:** L. **Throws:** L. **School:** Indian River (Fla.) CC. **Career Transactions:** Selected by Red Sox in 29th round of 2000 draft; signed May 27, 2001.

A 29th-round pick out of high school in 2000, Gabbard spent a year at Indian River before signing as a draft-and-follow. He got off to an auspicious start in 2002, his first full pro season, not giving up more than two earned runs in any of seven low Class A starts. Then his elbow began to bother him and he didn't pitch again until instructional league. Gabbard had elbow surgery before he turned pro, and he needed another operation to clean out bone chips. He returned for instructional league, though he was shut down before it ended when his elbow got tired. If he can stay healthy, Gabbard offers a lot of promise. He threw 90-92 mph in instructional league in 2001, though his velocity sat more at 87-89 last year. At 6-foot-4, he should be able to maintain a plus fastball, and he already achieves nice sink with the pitch. His curveball and changeup also should be at least solid average, and his approach rates higher than that. Because he barely has pitched as a pro, the Red Sox will move slowly and send him back to low Class A in 2003.

Year	Club (League)	Class	W	L	ERA	G	GS	CG	SV	IP	H	R	ER	HR	BB	SO	AVG
2001	Red Sox (GCL)	R	0	1	5.65	6	6	0	0	14	11	11	9	1	9	17	.208
2002	Augusta (SAL)	A	0	4	1.89	7	7	0	0	38	31	14	8	0	7	31	.221
MINOR LEAGUE TOTALS			0	5	2.92	13	13	0	0	52	42	25	17	1	16	48	.218

16. Rene Miniel, rhp

Born: April 26, 1979. **Ht.:** 6-2. **Wt.:** 170. **Bats:** R. **Throws:** R. **Career Transactions:** Signed out of Dominican Republic by Red Sox, Jan. 15, 1998.

Miniel entered 2002 as Boston's second-best pitching prospect, trailing only Seung Song, who went to the Expos as part of the Cliff Floyd trade in July. By then, Miniel's status had taken a major hit. During the spring, he turned out to be two years older than previously believed, making his strong 2001 showing in the low Class A South Atlantic League less impressive. Though his fastball reached the low 90s, it never returned to the 94-96 mph range he showed consistently in the SAL. He regressed with his secondary pitches, a curveball and a changeup, and didn't miss as many bats as he had in the past. Some Red Sox officials think he's destined for the bullpen, and he may move there in 2003 because the team plans on pushing many of its top pitching prospects to high Class A. Miniel still gets natural cutting action on his fastball and there's some hope his velocity will bounce back. Boston officials said he worked too hard the previous offseason and asked him to take this winter off.

Year	Club (League)	Class	W	L	ERA	G	GS	CG	SV	IP	H	R	ER	HR	BB	SO	AVG
1998	Red Sox (DSL)	R	4	5	1.85	13	11	1	0	73	58	34	15	4	27	38	.223
1999	Red Sox (GCL)	R	1	2	4.06	21	0	0	1	38	40	28	17	2	16	37	.256
2000	Red Sox (GCL)	R	2	4	4.00	21	1	0	7	38	36	37	21	16	1	31	.274
2001	Augusta (SAL)	A	8	4	2.73	27	23	0	0	122	93	49	37	1	38	114	.211
2002	Sarasota (FSL)	A	7	10	4.51	26	26	0	0	128	125	72	64	11	39	78	.257
MINOR LEAGUE TOTALS			22	25	3.38	108	61	1	8	396	353	204	149	19	141	298	.239

17. Chris Smith, rhp

Born: April 9, 1981. **Ht.:** 6-2. **Wt.:** 200. **Bats:** R. **Throws:** R. **School:** UC Riverside. **Career Transactions:** Selected by Red Sox in fourth round of 2002 draft; signed June 10, 2002.

In his final start for UC Riverside, Smith struck out 15 UC Irvine batters to eclipse former Indians first-rounder Daron Kirkreit's school records for whiffs in a game and a season (127). He also pushed his innings total for his junior season to 136, fifth among Division I pitchers who didn't pitch in the postseason. Smith was a little gassed after he signed, but he still showed decent stuff to go with good command. He mostly threw his fastball in the high 80s, and he could creep into the 90s after resting this offseason. Smith's curveball is his best pitch, and his changeup should give him a solid third offering in time. His best attribute is his feel for pitching, which allows him to win even when he's not at his best. He doesn't have as high a ceiling as most pitchers on this list, but he should develop more rapidly and reach the majors sooner than most. Boston will challenge him with a promotion to high Class A to begin his first full pro season.

Year	Club (League)	Class	W	L	ERA	G	GS	CG	SV	IP	H	R	ER	HR	BB	SO	AVG
2002	Lowell (NY-P)	A	3	3	4.13	14	14	0	0	57	54	29	26	3	14	50	.245
MINOR LEAGUE TOTALS			3	3	4.13	14	14	0	0	57	54	29	26	3	14	50	.245

18. Anastacio Martinez, rhp

Born: Nov. 3, 1978. **Ht.:** 6-2. **Wt.:** 180. **Bats:** R. **Throws:** R. **Career Transactions:** Signed out of Dominican Republic by Red Sox, Jan. 6, 1998.

Martinez, like Miniel, is another Dominican who fell out of the top 10 because his age jumped two years while his performance declined. He did keep his spot on Boston's 40-man roster, though that wasn't much of an accomplishment considering the team initially protected just 28 players. Martinez routinely got hammered in Double-A as his control deteriorated—he led the Eastern League in walks—and didn't handle adversity well. He succeeded when he had his mechanics in sync and more than one pitch working for him, but that happened infrequently. Martinez dials his fastball up to 95 mph with little effort. At times he'll show a hard curveball, but it's inconsistent, and his changeup has not developed. With his power arm and lack of feel for starting, he's a prime candidate to convert to relieving when he returns to Double-A in 2003.

Year	Club (League)	Class	W	L	ERA	G	GS	CG	SV	IP	H	R	ER	HR	BB	SO	AVG
1998	Red Sox (DSL)	R	0	1	13.50	2	2	0	0	7	13	11	10	0	7	8	.433
	Red Sox (GCL)	R	2	3	3.18	12	10	0	0	51	45	28	18	2	12	50	.232
1999	Augusta (SAL)	A	2	4	6.30	10	10	0	0	40	44	37	28	7	18	36	.262
	Lowell (NY-P)	A	0	3	3.68	11	11	0	0	51	61	36	21	4	18	43	.289
2000	Augusta (SAL)	A	9	6	4.64	23	23	0	0	120	130	69	62	8	50	107	.279
	Red Sox (GCL)	R	0	1	9.45	2	1	0	0	7	15	9	7	0	3	1	.441
2001	Sarasota (FSL)	A	9	12	3.35	25	24	1	0	145	130	69	54	12	39	123	.236
2002	Trenton (EL)	AA	5	12	5.31	27	27	0	0	139	152	98	82	12	75	127	.276
MINOR LEAGUE TOTALS			27	42	4.53	112	108	1	0	560	590	357	282	45	222	495	.268

19. Chad Spann, 3b

Born: Oct. 25, 1983. **Ht.:** 6-1. **Wt.:** 190. **Bats:** R. **Throws:** R. **School:** Southland Academy, Buena Vista, Ga. **Career Transactions:** Selected by Red Sox in fifth round of 2002 draft; signed June 10, 2002.

Drafted two rounds later than No. 13 prospect Scott White, Spann shares much in common with him. Both are Georgia products playing the hot corner after Spann moved from shortstop, and both have power potential and defensive upside. A high school quarterback, Spann is more athletic than White but isn't as advanced at the plate because he faced the lowest level of prep competition in Georgia. Spann will be one of the main projects for new minor league hitting coordinator Orv Franchuk. He has tremendous bat speed but needs better pitch recognition and patience. Defensively, he's more agile and has a slightly better arm than White does. Like White, he'll begin 2003 in extended spring training. Spann could return to the Gulf Coast League because White is a better candidate for the New York-Penn League if Boston decides to split them up.

Year	Club (League)	Class	AVG	G	AB	R	H	2B	3B	HR	RBI	BB	SO	SB	SLG	OBP
2002	Red Sox (GCL)	R	.222	57	203	20	45	8	3	6	28	12	37	1	.379	.271
MINOR LEAGUE TOTALS			.222	57	203	20	45	8	3	6	28	12	37	1	.379	.271

20. Matt White, lhp

Born: Aug. 19, 1977. **Ht.:** 6-1. **Wt.:** 180. **Bats:** R. **Throws:** L. **School:** Clemson University. **Career Transactions:** Selected by Indians in 15th round of 1998 draft; signed June 15, 1998 . . . Selected by Red Sox from Indians in major league Rule 5 draft, Dec. 16, 2002.

The Red Sox were active in the major league Rule 5 draft at the Winter Meetings, picking up three players and losing two. The Tigers took lefthander Wil Ledezma and the Reds grabbed righthander Jerome Gamble, who would have figured into the upper half of this list. They still bear watching because both have histories of injuries and need to pitch rather than be buried on a big league roster, so Boston could get both of them back. Of the players they picked up, the Red Sox figure to keep Adrian Brown as a fifth outfielder and either White or Javier Lopez as a second bullpen lefty behind Alan Embree. White hit the wall as a starter in Double-A before switching to the bullpen last June, and the move gave the Massachusetts native's career new life. He posted a 2.14 ERA in relief and carried his success over in the Dominican League. As a starter, White's best pitch was his changeup and he regularly threw his fastball in the high 80s. As a reliever, he saw his stuff suddenly jump and the Red Sox think he can be more than just a one- or two-batter lefty specialist. White now works at 90-93 mph and has more velocity on his slider, giving him multiple weapons to combat righthanders. He has improved control as well. White has added bulk in recent years, and Boston will work with him to loosen his delivery. The Indians liked him, but because they acquired so many prospects in 2002 they couldn't find room for him on their 40-man roster. Because he has a stronger repertoire, White has a better chance to stick than Lopez.

Year	Club (League)	Class	W	L	ERA	G	GS	CG	SV	IP	H	R	ER	HR	BB	SO	AVG
1998	Watertown (NY-P)	A	3	2	4.28	6	6	0	0	27	31	19	13	4	11	24	.295
	Burlington (Appy)	R	4	1	1.94	8	8	0	0	46	34	14	10	0	24	47	.210
1999	Columbus (SAL)	A	3	10	5.29	19	18	1	0	95	99	67	56	12	31	75	.266
2000	Kinston (Car)	A	11	9	4.07	28	26	2	0	144	136	76	65	14	63	115	.257
2001	Akron (EL)	AA	8	10	4.81	25	25	0	0	144	151	84	77	18	60	72	.277
2002	Akron (EL)	AA	6	2	3.93	27	11	0	1	89	97	42	39	9	39	63	.280
	Buffalo (IL)	AAA	0	0	4.76	7	1	0	0	17	23	13	9	1	6	12	.319
MINOR LEAGUE TOTALS			35	34	4.30	120	95	3	1	563	571	315	269	58	234	408	.268

21. Earl Snyder, 3b/1b

Born: May 6, 1976. **Ht.:** 6-0. **Wt.:** 200. **Bats:** R. **Throws:** R. **School:** University of Hartford. **Career Transactions:** Selected by Mets in 36th round of 1998 draft; signed June 5, 1998 . . . Traded by Mets with LHP Billy Traber to Indians, Dec. 13, 2001, completing trade in which Indians sent 2B Roberto Alomar, LHP Mike Bacsik and 1B Danny Peoples to Mets for OF Matt Lawton, OF Alex Escobar, RHP Jerrod Riggan and two players to be named (Dec. 11, 2001) . . . Claimed on waivers by Red Sox from Indians, Jan. 17, 2003.

Boston won't get Jeff Bagwell back, but it did land the second-best corner infielder out of the University of Hartford when it claimed Snyder off waivers from the Indians. Snyder, who broke several of Bagwell's school records, won two team MVP awards and one organization player-of-the-year honor in his three full seasons with the Mets. New York sent him to Cleveland in the Roberto Alomar trade before the 2002 season. Snyder's best attribute is his power, and he never has hit fewer than 20 homers in any of his four full seasons. He hits for a decent average and draws a few walks but doesn't stand out in either category. The same is true of his work on the bases and in the field, where he has played first base, third base and the corner outfield spots in the minors. The Red Sox will evaluate him in spring training, and though his role with the organization was unclear after he was designated for assignment, he could at least be a good Triple-A insurance policy.

Year	Club (League)	Class	AVG	G	AB	R	H	2B	3B	HR	RBI	BB	SO	SB	SLG	OBP
1998	Pittsfield (NY-P)	A	.252	71	262	39	66	8	1	11	40	23	60	0	.416	.316
1999	Capital City (SAL)	A	.267	136	486	73	130	25	4	28	97	55	117	2	.508	.339
2000	St. Lucie (FSL)	A	.282	134	514	84	145	36	0	25	93	57	127	4	.498	.358
2001	Binghamton (EL)	AA	.281	114	405	69	114	35	2	20	75	58	111	4	.526	.374
	Norfolk (IL)	AAA	.474	6	19	5	9	3	0	0	3	3	1	0	.632	.565
2002	Buffalo (IL)	AAA	.263	110	400	69	105	29	1	19	66	43	96	0	.483	.341
	Cleveland (AL)	MAJ	.200	18	55	5	11	2	0	1	4	6	21	0	.291	.279
MAJOR LEAGUE TOTALS			**.200**	**18**	**55**	**5**	**11**	**2**	**0**	**1**	**4**	**6**	**21**	**0**	**.291**	**.279**
MINOR LEAGUE TOTALS			**.273**	**571**	**2086**	**339**	**569**	**136**	**8**	**103**	**374**	**239**	**512**	**10**	**.494**	**.350**

22. Paul Stewart, rhp

Born: Oct. 21, 1978. **Ht.:** 6-5. **Wt.:** 220. **Bats:** R. **Throws:** R. **School:** Garner (N.C.) HS. **Career Transactions:** Selected by Brewers in sixth round of 1996 draft; signed July 1, 1996 . . . Granted free agency, Oct. 15, 2002 . . . Signed by Red Sox, Nov. 12, 2002.

The Red Sox also delved more heavily into the minor league free-agent market this off-season. Their best pickup was Stewart, who finally learned how to pitch in his seventh season in the Brewers system. He entered 2002 with a career 36-50, 5.00 record as a pro, and got hammered in his first five starts at Huntsville, dropping his lifetime Double-A mark to 1-12, 7.39. Suddenly, everything came together for him and he went 12-4, 2.29 in 22 starts, including a 102-32 strikeout-walk ratio in 142 innings. At 6-foot-5 and 240 pounds, Stewart has plenty of mound presence. If he can continue to pound the strike zone with his low-90s sinker and demonstrate command of his other three pitches (curveball, slider, changeup), he'll be quite a find. Stewart will get his first taste of Triple-A in 2003.

Year	Club (League)	Class	W	L	ERA	G	GS	CG	SV	IP	H	R	ER	HR	BB	SO	AVG
1996	Ogden (Pio)	R	1	4	7.83	12	9	0	0	44	47	49	38	11	26	39	.266
1997	Ogden (Pio)	R	5	6	5.31	15	15	1	0	81	88	59	48	13	30	82	.267
1998	Beloit (Mid)	A	8	10	4.90	26	25	1	0	143	164	99	78	22	45	114	.286
1999	Stockton (Cal)	A	10	11	3.96	27	25	5	0	170	171	90	75	18	61	117	.262
2000	Huntsville (SL)	AA	1	7	6.13	10	10	0	0	47	75	36	32	5	22	30	.379
	Mudville (Cal)	A	2	4	4.40	17	10	0	0	59	56	32	29	6	31	61	.246
2001	High Desert (Cal)	A	9	8	5.16	28	27	0	0	152	169	106	87	23	64	127	.280
2002	Huntsville (SL)	AA	12	9	3.28	27	27	2	0	162	147	69	59	12	42	124	.245
MINOR LEAGUE TOTALS			**48**	**59**	**4.68**	**162**	**148**	**9**	**0**	**858**	**917**	**540**	**446**	**110**	**321**	**694**	**.273**

23. Juan Cedeno, lhp

Born: Aug. 19, 1983. **Ht.:** 6-1. **Wt.:** 160. **Bats:** L. **Throws:** L. **Career Transactions:** Signed out of Dominican Republic by Red Sox, Jan. 5, 2001.

In general, Twins farmhands, who also train in Fort Myers, Fla., dominated their Red Sox counterparts in instructional league. One of Boston's few highlights came when Cedeno blew away Joe Mauer, one of the game's best prospects, in two different confrontations. By the end of instructional league, Cedeno was touching 95 mph and had made major strides with his curveball. A wiry 6-foot-1 athlete with huge hands and long fingers that impart a good deal of spin on his pitches, he physically resembles fellow Dominican Pedro Martinez. Cedeno's whippy arm action allows him to generate his velocity. He has huge feet and is still growing, so there's a lot of projectability to him. He needs a lot of time to develop his pitches and his command—both throwing strikes and spotting his pitches within the zone—but he's certainly intriguing.

Year	Club (League)	Class	W	L	ERA	G	GS	CG	SV	IP	H	R	ER	HR	BB	SO	AVG
2001	Red Sox (DSL)	R	3	3	3.38	14	14	0	0	64	45	30	24	0	37	77	.198
2002	Red Sox (GCL)	R	2	5	4.19	11	7	0	0	43	55	31	20	1	12	32	.297
MINOR LEAGUE TOTALS			5	8	3.70	25	21	0	0	107	100	61	44	1	49	109	.243

24. Denny Tussen, rhp

Born: April 25, 1983. **Ht.:** 6-0. **Wt.:** 140. **Bats:** R. **Throws:** R. **Career Transactions:** Signed out of Dominican Republic by Red Sox, Oct. 9, 1999.

Tussen looks even more like Pedro Martinez than Juan Cedeno does. He has a slighter build than Cedeno, very long fingers and throws from a low three-quarters angle like Martinez does, even dropping down sidearm on occasion. After missing all of 2001 because of elbow surgery, Tussen mainly worked out of the bullpen in the Gulf Coast League in 2002. He throws an effortless 92-94 mph and is something to behold when he's throwing strikes and working down in the zone. He tries to throw a curveball, but Martinez may be the only pitcher to have much success doing so from that arm slot. Tussen's breaking ball is slurvy and he may be better off with a slider. The Red Sox prefer their young pitchers to throw a curveball, and because he's coming back from elbow problems Tussen hasn't been asked to try a slider yet. While it's too early to get excited about Tussen, his upside is considerable.

Year	Club (League)	Class	W	L	ERA	G	GS	CG	SV	IP	H	R	ER	HR	BB	SO	AVG
2000	Red Sox (DSL)	R	3	2	2.32	12	8	0	0	54	57	29	14	0	10	38	.251
2001					Did Not Play—Injured												
2002	Red Sox (GCL)	R	2	2	2.60	12	3	0	0	52	48	28	15	1	15	37	.246
MINOR LEAGUE TOTALS			5	4	2.45	24	11	0	0	106	105	57	29	1	25	75	.249

25. Tyler Pelland, lhp

Born: Oct. 9, 1983. **Ht.:** 6-0. **Wt.:** 190. **Bats:** R. **Throws:** L. **School:** Mount Abraham HS, Bristol, Ver. **Career Transactions:** Selected by Red Sox in ninth round of 2002 draft; signed Aug. 17, 2002.

The Red Sox didn't draft as many New England players in 2002 as they had in the past. The exception was Pelland, one of the region's top prospects. Because he was committed to Clemson—one of Pelland's high school coaches is the brother of Tigers coach Jack Leggett—he lasted until the ninth round, about five lower than expected. Pelland is a stocky 6-footer, though that doesn't prevent him from reaching the low 90s. Like Juan Cedeno and Denny Tussen, he's very much a project. Pelland's curveball and changeup are below-average, and he'll have to develop more movement on his fastball. He throws with effort and won't add much if any velocity, so making those improvements is critical. He signed late and won't make his pro debut until June. He'll start his career in the Gulf Coast League after spending two months in extended spring training.

Year	Club (League)	Class	W	L	ERA	G	GS	CG	SV	IP	H	R	ER	HR	BB	SO	AVG
				Has Not Played—Signed 2003 Contract													

26. David Pahucki, rhp

Born: Oct. 17, 1980. **Ht.:** 6-2. **Wt.:** 210. **Bats:** R. **Throws:** R. **School:** Siena College. **Career Transactions:** Selected by Red Sox in 23rd round of 2002 draft; signed June 10, 2002.

Pahucki had an up-and-down career at Siena yet was consistent in his 2002 pro debut. Pahucki won the first nine decisions of his college career, then lost 12 of his next 17 and saw his ERA balloon to 7.40 as a junior. He rebounded to go 6-4, 3.16 as a senior, finishing as the Saints' career leader in wins and strikeouts. After turning pro, he didn't allow more than one earned run in any of his first six starts and in nine of 13 overall. Pahucki relies on finesse more than pure stuff. He doesn't have a consistent plus pitch. His fastball sits in the high 80s, though he reached 93 mph with a four-seamer in instructional league. His curveball and changeup are generally average. Pahucki's strength is his fastball command, and he can locate all of his pitches with precision. His profile reminds new Red Sox general manager Theo Epstein of Brian Lawrence, whom Epstein championed when he worked for the Padres. Pahucki probably will start 2003 in low Class A.

Year	Club (League)	Class	W	L	ERA	G	GS	CG	SV	IP	H	R	ER	HR	BB	SO	AVG
2002	Lowell (NY-P)	A	1	2	1.84	9	9	0	0	44	31	11	9	1	8	48	.194
	Augusta (SAL)	A	2	1	4.15	4	4	0	0	22	24	10	10	0	7	15	.286
MINOR LEAGUE TOTALS			3	3	2.60	13	13	0	0	66	55	21	19	1	15	63	.225

27. Charlie Weatherby, rhp

Born: Dec. 23, 1978. **Ht.:** 6-0. **Wt.:** 200. **Bats:** R. **Throws:** R. **School:** UNC Wilmington. **Career Transactions:** Selected by Red Sox in 21st round of 2001 draft; signed June 11, 2001.

Weatherby pitched at East Carteret (N.C.) High, which produced 1991 No. 1 overall draft pick Brien Taylor, and earned all-Colonial Athletic Association honors as a UNC Wilmington senior in 2001. In 2002, his first full pro season, he showed the Red Sox better stuff than they expected. Moved to the bullpen on a full-time basis, he started throwing 92-94 mph and overmatched righthanders with his splitter. His slider has a chance to become average. Weatherby didn't pitch as well in high Class A or the Arizona Fall League, and at 23 he was old for low Class A, so he still has to prove himself. He's not big and there's some effort to his delivery, and he lacks an offspeed pitch. More important, he must improve his location within the strike zone. How he performs in 2003, when he should reach Double-A at some point, will show if he's a legitimate prospect.

Year	Club (League)	Class	W	L	ERA	G	GS	CG	SV	IP	H	R	ER	HR	BB	SO	AVG
2001	Lowell (NY-P)	A	2	3	3.02	13	10	0	0	51	45	21	17	0	15	41	.239
2002	Augusta (SAL)	A	4	0	2.92	17	0	0	4	25	20	8	8	2	5	23	.213
	Sarasota (FSL)	A	0	3	4.57	17	0	0	9	22	23	15	11	1	5	17	.267
MINOR LEAGUE TOTALS			6	6	3.34	47	10	0	13	97	88	44	36	3	25	81	.239

28. Brett Bonvechio, 1b

Born: Nov. 13, 1982. **Ht.:** 6-1. **Wt.:** 190. **Bats:** L. **Throws:** R. **School:** West Valley (Calif.) JC. **Career Transactions:** Selected by Red Sox in 37th round of 2000 draft; signed May 27, 2001.

Boston took Bonvechio in the 37th round out of high school in 2000, then liked his bat enough to give him a six-figure bonus as a draft-and-follow after he spent a year in junior college. The Red Sox still are enthusiastic about his offense promise but haven't seen as much of it as they would have liked. He broke a thumb in his first pro summer and was bothered by a hamate bruise in his wrist last year, limiting him to a total of 172 at-bats in two seasons. Bonvechio has a sweet lefthanded stroke, power potential and has shown a willingness to take walks. The injuries have kept him from working on his strength and conditioning, and he could improve rapidly if he stays healthy. Bonvechio played mostly first base in 2002 and Boston would like to return him to third base, where he played as an amateur and in his pro debut. He has enough arm for the position, but needs to work on his first-step quickness and agility. He has a chance to open 2003 in low Class A.

Year	Club (League)	Class	AVG	G	AB	R	H	2B	3B	HR	RBI	BB	SO	SB	SLG	OBP
2001	Red Sox (GCL)	R	.217	19	69	4	15	5	1	1	5	9	12	0	.362	.304
2002	Red Sox (GCL)	R	.291	30	103	19	30	11	1	3	24	14	24	0	.505	.373
MINOR LEAGUE TOTALS			.262	49	172	23	45	16	2	4	29	23	36	0	.448	.345

29. Javier Lopez, lhp

Born: July 11, 1977. **Ht.:** 6-4. **Wt.:** 200. **Bats:** L. **Throws:** L. **School:** University of Virginia. **Career Transactions:** Selected by Diamondbacks in fourth round of 1998 draft; signed June 6, 1998 . . . Selected by Red Sox from Diamondbacks in major league Rule 5 draft, Dec. 16, 2002.

Like Matt White, Lopez is a major league Rule 5 pick who resurrected his career last season and will compete for the job as the second bullpen lefty in 2003. Lopez was shelled for his first four years in the minors, compiling a 5.69 ERA. The Diamondbacks moved him to the bullpen in 2001, which didn't solve anything. They switched him to a sidearm delivery in 2002, which proved to be just what he needed. Lopez sliced his Double-A ERA from 7.43 the year before to 2.72 and was death to lefthanders, who went just 7-for-60 (.117) with one extra-base hit (a double) and 23 strikeouts against him. He continued to pitch well in his native Puerto Rico over the winter. Lopez throws a mid-80s fastball, variations off his slider and a changeup. He mixes arm angles and velocities, and alternates his slider between a hard breaking ball and a sweeping pitch. Lopez will have to prove that he can keep big league righthanders at bay, and if he does in spring training he could break camp with the Red Sox.

Year	Club (League)	Class	W	L	ERA	G	GS	CG	SV	IP	H	R	ER	HR	BB	SO	AVG
1998	South Bend (Mid)	A	2	4	6.55	16	9	0	0	44	60	36	32	2	30	31	.328
1999	South Bend (Mid)	A	4	6	6.00	20	20	0	0	99	122	74	66	9	43	70	.300
2000	High Desert (Cal)	A	4	8	5.22	30	21	0	2	136	152	87	79	14	57	98	.288
2001	El Paso (TL)	AA	1	0	7.43	22	1	0	0	40	64	39	33	6	14	21	.370
	Lancaster (Cal)	A	1	3	2.63	17	0	0	1	24	30	9	7	2	5	18	.313
2002	El Paso (TL)	AA	2	2	2.72	61	0	0	6	46	34	16	14	3	16	47	.204
MINOR LEAGUE TOTALS			14	23	5.34	166	51	0	9	390	462	261	231	36	165	285	.297

30. Angel Santos, 2b

Born: Aug. 14, 1979. **Ht.:** 5-11. **Wt.:** 170. **Bats:** B. **Throws:** R. **School:** Miguel Melendez Munoz HS, Cayey, P.R.. **Career Transactions:** Selected by Red Sox in fourth round of 1997 draft; signed July 26, 1997.

Santos is an offensive-minded second baseman in an organization that isn't looking for one. The Red Sox traded for Todd Walker during the offseason, and Freddy Sanchez will be ready to take over if Walker departs as a free agent following the 2003 season. Santos has enough pop to hit 30 doubles and reach double digits in homers annually. A switch-hitter, he generates most of his power from the left side, hitting 23 of his 24 homers the last two years against righthanders. He draws enough walks to satisfy the new Boston administration but needs to make more contact. He's an above-average runner, though a sprained ligament in his right knee slowed him in 2002. Sanchez has improved at turning the double play, but he has stiff hands that limit him defensively. He might have a future with the Red Sox as a utilityman, though the club also moved to strengthen that position by dealing for Cesar Crespo.

Year	Club (League)	Class	AVG	G	AB	R	H	2B	3B	HR	RBI	BB	SO	SB	SLG	OBP
1997	Red Sox (GCL)	R	.183	17	60	8	11	1	0	0	7	7	11	8	.200	.261
1998	Red Sox (GCL)	R	.351	23	77	14	27	5	1	0	13	13	10	7	.442	.435
	Lowell (NY-P)	A	.245	28	102	19	25	4	1	1	12	9	12	2	.333	.306
1999	Augusta (SAL)	A	.270	130	466	83	126	30	2	15	55	62	88	25	.440	.360
2000	Trenton (EL)	AA	.258	80	275	32	71	17	2	3	32	32	60	18	.367	.335
2001	Trenton (EL)	AA	.271	129	510	75	138	32	0	14	52	54	106	26	.416	.343
	Pawtucket (IL)	AAA	.200	4	15	1	3	1	0	0	2	1	4	1	.267	.235
	Boston (AL)	MAJ	.125	9	16	2	2	1	0	0	1	2	7	0	.188	.211
2002	Pawtucket (IL)	AAA	.260	102	350	40	91	15	2	10	50	38	70	12	.400	.332
MAJOR LEAGUE TOTALS			.125	9	16	2	2	1	0	0	1	2	7	0	.188	.211
MINOR LEAGUE TOTALS			.265	513	1855	272	492	105	8	43	223	216	361	99	.400	.343

CHICAGO
CUBS

UBS
TM

TOP 30 PROSPECTS

1. Hee Seop Choi, 1b
2. Angel Guzman, rhp
3. Andy Sisco, lhp
4. Felix Pie, of
5. Nic Jackson, of
6. Francis Beltran, rhp
7. Luke Hagerty, lhp
8. Brendan Harris, 3b/2b
9. David Kelton, 3b/1b
10. Todd Wellemeyer, rhp
11. Jae-Kuk Ryu, rhp
12. Justin Jones, lhp
13. Felix Sanchez, lhp
14. Luis Montanez, ss/2b
15. Alfredo Francisco, 3b
16. Steve Smyth, lhp
17. Billy Petrick, rhp
18. Matt Bruback, rhp
19. Ricky Nolasco, rhp
20. John Webb, rhp
21. Chadd Blasko, rhp
22. Brian Dopirak, 1b
23. Brandon Sing, of/1b
24. Jason Wylie, rhp
25. Renyel Pinto, lhp
26. J.J. Johnson, of
27. Carmen Pignatiello, lhp
28. Ray Sadler, of
29. Russ Rohlicek, lhp
30. Jon Leicester, rhp

By Jim Callis

On the heels of an 88-74 season, the Cubs had postseason aspirations in 2002. Those were quickly doused as Chicago went 67-95 to extend its streak without consecutive winning seasons to 30 years.

Don Baylor's dismissal was the first move made by Jim Hendry when he was promoted from vice president of player personnel to general manager on July 5. That was a reward for Hendry rebuilding the farm system during his six years as farm and/or scouting director. The system remains the hope and the future for the Cubs, who have been burned by the last two mega-contracts they handed out to free agents (Todd Hundley, Moises Alou). Though Corey Patterson has yet to mature and Juan Cruz stumbled last season, Chicago's prospect depth gives plenty of cause for optimism.

Cubs affiliates combined for a .529 winning percentage in 2002, the seventh-best mark in baseball. Chicago is loaded at the lower levels, reflected by their championships in the short-season Northwest and Rookie-level Arizona leagues, and a near-miss in the low Class A Midwest League.

Mark Prior needed just nine minor league starts before advancing to Wrigley Field, where he was often spectacular. Fellow rookie Carlos Zambrano also crashed the rotation and had his moments. Hee Seop Choi and Bobby Hill conquered Triple-A, and all that remains is for them to solidify the right side of Chicago's infield in 2003. The Cubs also had several new faces blossom into prospects. Six-foot-9 left-hander Andy Sisco blew away NWL hitters, while multi-tooled center fielder Felix Pie shared MVP honors in the AZL. Brendan Harris became the latest candidate to fill the void at third base.

Chicago bolstered its store of talent last year through several avenues. Alfredo Francisco, another hot-corner possibility, signed out of the Dominican Republic in February. With six extra draft picks in June, the Cubs had a banner draft—even if they don't sign first-rounder Bobby Brownlie. And with the big league team going nowhere, the Cubs used veterans Jeff Fassero, Tom Gordon, Roberto Machado and Bill Mueller in trades.

Hendry's best offseason moves didn't involve players, though, as he targeted Dusty Baker as his top managerial candidate, waited for the postseason to end and landed him quickly. The Cubs also lured Gary Hughes, one of game's top scouts, from the Reds to become a special assistant.

OrganizationOverview

General Manager: Jim Hendry. **Farm Director:** Oneri Fleita. **Scouting Director:** John Stockstill.

2002 PERFORMANCE

Class	Farm Team	League	W	L	Pct.	Finish*	Manager(s)
Majors	Chicago	National	67	95	.414	14th (16)	D. Baylor/B. Kimm
Triple-A	Iowa Cubs	Pacific Coast	71	73	.493	11th (16)	B. Kimm/P. Listach
Double-A	West Tenn Diamond Jaxx	Southern	73	67	.521	4th (10)	Bobby Dickerson
High A	Daytona Cubs	Florida State	64	73	.467	8th (12)	Dave Trembley
Low A	Lansing Lugnuts	Midwest	74	65	.532	5th (14)	Julio Garcia
Short-season	Boise Hawks	Northwest	49	27	.645	+1st (8)	Steve McFarland
Rookie	AZL Cubs	Arizona	35	21	.625	+1st (7)	Carmelo Martinez
OVERALL MINOR LEAGUE RECORD			366	326	.529	7th (30)	

*Finish in overall standings (No. of teams in league).   +League champion.

ORGANIZATION LEADERS

BATTING
*Minimum 250 At-Bats
*AVG	Brendan Harris, West Tenn/Daytona	.328
R	Hee Seop Choi, Iowa	94
H	Brendan Harris, West Tenn/Daytona	157
TB	Brendan Harris, West Tenn/Daytona	255
2B	Brendan Harris, West Tenn/Daytona	39
3B	Felix Pie, Boise/AZL Cubs	13
HR	Julio Zuleta, Iowa	31
RBI	Julio Zuleta, Iowa	104
BB	Hee Seop Choi, Iowa	95
SO	Dave Kelton, West Tenn	129
SB	Ryan Theriot, Lansing	32
	Ray Sadler, West Tenn/Daytona	32

PITCHING
#Minimum 75 Innings
W	Angel Guzman, Daytona/Lansing	11
L	Chris Gissell, Iowa	12
#ERA	Angel Guzman, Daytona/Lansing	2.19
G	Dave Hooten, West Tenn	65
CG	Three tied at	2
SV	Francis Beltran, West Tenn	23
IP	Matt Bruback, West Tenn	174
BB	Ben Ford, Iowa	73
SO	Matt Bruback, West Tenn	158

BEST TOOLS

Best Hitter for Average	Brendan Harris
Best Power Hitter	Hee Seop Choi
Fastest Baserunner	Dwaine Bacon
Best Athlete	Felix Pie
Best Fastball	Francis Beltran
Best Curveball	Angel Guzman
Best Slider	Francis Beltran
Best Changeup	Angel Guzman
Best Control	Sergio Mitre
Best Defensive Catcher	Eliezer Alfonzo
Best Defensive Infielder	Ronny Cedeno
Best Infield Arm	Brendan Harris
Best Defensive Outfielder	Mike Mallory
Best Outfield Arm	Jackson Melian

PROJECTED 2006 LINEUP

Catcher	Damian Miller
First Base	Hee Seop Choi
Second Base	Bobby Hill
Third Base	Brendan Harris
Shortstop	Luis Montanez
Left Field	Corey Patterson
Center Field	Felix Pie
Right Field	Sammy Sosa
No. 1 Starter	Mark Prior
No. 2 Starter	Kerry Wood

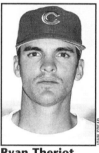 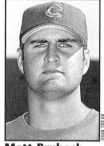

JOHN SPEAR   JOHN SPEAR

Ryan Theriot   Matt Bruback

No. 3 Starter	Matt Clement
No. 4 Starter	Angel Guzman
No. 5 Starter	Andy Sisco
Closer	Francis Beltran

TOP PROSPECTS OF THE DECADE

1993	Jessie Hollins, rhp
1994	Brooks Kieschnick, of
1995	Brooks Kieschnick, of
1996	Brooks Kieschnick, of
1997	Kerry Wood, rhp
1998	Kerry Wood, rhp
1999	Corey Patterson, of
2000	Corey Patterson, of
2001	Corey Patterson, of
2002	Mark Prior, rhp

TOP DRAFT PICKS OF THE DECADE

1993	Brooks Kieschnick, of
1994	Jayson Peterson, rhp
1995	Kerry Wood, rhp
1996	Todd Noel, rhp
1997	Jon Garland, rhp
1998	Corey Patterson, of
1999	Ben Christensen, rhp
2000	Luis Montanez, ss
2001	Mark Prior, rhp
2002	*Bobby Brownlie, rhp

*Has not signed

ALL-TIME LARGEST BONUSES

Mark Prior, 2001	$4,000,000
Corey Patterson, 1998	$3,700,000
Luis Montanez, 2000	$2,750,000
Jae-Kuk Ryu, 2001	$1,600,000
Bobby Hill, 2000	$1,425,000

MinorLeague**Depth**Chart

CHICAGO CUBS

RANK 3

The Cubs' minor league talent has ranked among the top three organizations in the game for each of the last three years, and was No. 1 a year ago. They've continued to bolster the lower levels through strong drafts and a flourishing Latin American program, while promoting frontline prospects Mark Prior, Corey Patterson, Bobby Hill, Hee Seop Choi, Carlos Zambrano and Juan Cruz to Chicago. Now the trick will be for the Cubs to translate all the potential into performance at the big league level. The only real weakness in the system is a lack of pure middle-infield talent, as Ronny Cedeno faltered last year and Luis Montanez has yet to live up to his potential.

Note: Depth charts prepared by Josh Boyd. Numbers in parentheses indicate prospect rankings.

LF
Brandon Sing (23)
Aron Weston
Jason Fransz

CF
Felix Pie (4)
Nic Jackson (5)
Ray Sadler (28)
Adam Greenberg
Mike Mallory

RF
J.J. Johnson (26)
Jackson Melian

3B
Brendan Harris (8)
David Kelton (9)
Alfredo Francisco (15)
Matt Craig

SS
Ronny Cedeno
Ryan Theriot
Nate Frese

2B
Luis Montanez (14)
Matt Creighton
Jemel Spearman
Robinson Chirinos

1B
Hee Seop Choi (1)
Brian Dopirak (22)
Kevin Collins
Brad Bouras
Micah Hoffpauir

C
Jeff Goldbach
Eli Alfonzo

RHP
Starters
Angel Guzman (2)
Todd Wellemeyer (10)
Jae-Kuk Ryu (11)
Billy Petrick (17)
Matt Bruback (18)
Ricky Nolasco (19)
John Webb (20)
Jason Wylie (24)
Sergio Mitre
Wilton Chavez
Mike Nannini
Ben Christensen

Relievers
Francis Beltran (6)
Chadd Blasko (21)
Jon Leicester (30)
Matt Clanton
Scott Chiasson
Jared Blasdell
Jeff Verplancke
Eric Brown

LHP
Starters
Andy Sisco (3)
Luke Hagerty (7)
Justin Jones (12)
Felix Sanchez (13)
Steve Smyth (16)
Renyel Pinto (25)
Carmen Pignatiello (27)
Russ Rohlicek (29)
Aaron Krawiec
Rich Hill

Relievers
Will Ohman
Ferenc Jonejan

DraftAnalysis

2002 Draft

Best Pro Debut: LHP Justin Jones (2) was the top pitching prospect in the Rookie-level Arizona League, while LHP Luke Hagerty (1) was second-best in the short-season Northwest League. Both struck out more hitters than they allowed to reach base. OF Micah Hoffpauir (13), SS Jemel Spearman (16) and 3B Donnie Hood (18) earned league all-star honors, with Spearman leading the AZL in runs (46) and steals (29).

Best Athlete: 3B Matt Craig (3) or OF Jason Fransz (8). RHP Billy Petrick (3) was one of the top long-snapper recruits in the nation but gave up a Washington State football scholarship to sign with the Cubs.

Best Pure Hitter: OF Adam Greenberg (9) hit .384 in 21 high Class A games.

Best Raw Power: 1B Brian Dopirak (2) didn't homer in 21 pro games, but he was considered the top power hitter in the draft. His swing and approach need refinement.

Fastest Runner: The Cubs repeatedly clocked OF Chris Walker (6) from the right side of the plate to first base in 3.85 seconds, which is rare speed. He and Spearman were teammates at Georgia Southern.

Best Defensive Player: SS/2B Joey Monahan (7) or Greenberg.

Best Fastball: Before he came down with biceps tendinitis, RHP Bobby Brownlie (1) threw 94-97 mph. He passed up his senior season at Rutgers as he continued to negotiate with the Cubs. Among players who signed, the 6-foot-8 Hagerty threw in the mid-90s more consistently in the NWL than he did in college. RHP **Chadd Blasko** (1) topped out in

the same range in college, while Petrick reached that level in instructional league.

Best Breaking Ball: Jones' curveball is a shade better than Hagerty's slider, and both improved their breaking stuff as pros. Brownlie's curveball is a cut above either of those.

JEFF GOLDEN

Blasko

Most Intriguing Background: Monahan's brother Shane played briefly with the Mariners, and his father Hartland spent seven seasons in the NHL. His grandfather, Boom-Boom Geoffrion, won six Stanley Cups and a place in the hockey hall of fame. C Alan Rick's (4) father Sam is the baseball coach at St. John's River (Fla.) CC.

Closest To The Majors: For now, it's Hagerty. Assuming Brownlie signs and is healthy, he might not need much more time than Mark Prior took to reach Wrigley Field.

Best Late-Round Pick: Hood, who batted .279-12-42 and may get a look as a catcher.

The One Who Got Away: OF Shawn Scobee (5) should be one of college baseball's top freshman hitters at Cal State Fullerton.

Assessment: The Cubs will have arguably the best college pitcher from each of the last two drafts if they sign Brownlie to go with Mark Prior. They'll still have a good harvest if that doesn't work out, as they used supplemental first-round choices on Hagerty, Blasko and RHP Matt Clanton and had extra picks in the next three rounds.

2001 Draft

RHP Mark Prior (1), who needed just nine starts in the minors, makes this draft by himself. LHP Andy Sisco (2) and 3B/2B Brendan Harris (5) have considerable upside as well. Just imagine if they had signed SS Khalil Greene (14) and 1B Wes Whisler (41).　　**Grade: A**

2000 Draft

2B Bobby Hill already is starting in Chicago, and SS Luis Montanez (1), OF Nic Jackson (3) and RHP Todd Wellemeyer (4) are working their way toward him. LHP Dontrelle Willis (8) blossomed after being dealt to the Marlins.　　**Grade: A**

1999 Draft

LHP Steve Smyth (4) overcame shoulder surgery to reach the majors in 2002. But RHP Ben Christensen (1) may not be able to overcome shoulder and elbow problems.　　**Grade: C**

1998 Draft

3B Eric Hinske (17) was BA's 2002 Rookie of the Year, albeit for Toronto after being traded. OF Corey Patterson (1) and 3B/1B David Kelton (2) tailed off last year but still have a lot of promise.　　**Grade: A**

Note: Draft analysis prepared by Jim Callis. Numbers in parentheses indicate draft rounds.

... Choi is more than just a one-dimensional slugger.

Hee Seop
Choi 1b

Born: March 16, 1979.
Ht.: 6-5. **Wt.:** 240.
Bats: L. **Throws:** L.
Career Transactions: Signed
out of Korea by Cubs, March 4, 1999.

Choi became the first Korean position player to sign with a major league team when he agreed to a $1.2 million bonus. He homered in the quarterfinals and semifinals of the 1998 World Championships in Italy—as a 19-year-old—and hasn't stopped hitting since arriving in the United States. He led the Arizona Fall League in homers in 2000 but was way-laid in 2001 by severe inflammation in his right hand. Healthy again last year, he was one of the most dangerous hitters in the Triple-A Pacific Coast League and made his major league debut in September. He played only sporadically because manager Bruce Kimm was more concerned with Fred McGriff becoming the first big leaguer to reach 30 homers with five different teams. Choi did hit his first two big league homers, then starred in the AFL again after the season.

The top power hitter in the system, Choi launches balls to all fields. He shortened his swing last year without sacrificing any pop. Even better, he's more than just a one-dimensional slugger. He hits for average because he combines the ability to make adjustments with patience at the plate. Choi led the PCL in walks last year. He initially struggled against left-handers but conquered them in Triple-A. For his size, Choi moves well. He should be a solid-average to plus defender at first base. Because he's big and has some uppercut to his swing, some questioned Choi's ability to hit inside fastballs, and whether he'd do damage against quality pitching rather than just feast on mistakes. Others pointed to his approach and ability to use the entire ballpark and weren't concerned. At 6-foot-5 and 240 pounds, Choi will have to watch his body. He still has work to do defensively, particularly with his footwork and receiving skills.

Though McGriff wasn't re-signed, the Cubs traded for Eric Karros (and Mark Grudzielanek) in the offseason. That deal was more about exchanging bad contracts (Chicago dumped Todd Hundley) than consigning Choi to the bench. Choi and Bobby Hill should man the right side of Chicago's infield for years to come. They'll ease into starting roles in 2003, with Karros and Grudzielanek serving as insurance.

Year	Club (League)	Class	AVG	G	AB	R	H	2B	3B	HR	RBI	BB	SO	SB	SLG	OBP
1999	Lansing (Mid)	A	.321	79	290	71	93	18	6	18	70	50	68	2	.610	.422
2000	Daytona (FSL)	A	.296	96	345	60	102	25	6	15	70	37	78	4	.533	.369
	West Tenn (SL)	AA	.303	36	122	25	37	9	0	10	25	25	38	3	.623	.419
2001	Iowa (PCL)	AAA	.229	77	266	38	61	11	0	13	45	34	67	5	.417	.313
2002	Iowa (PCL)	AAA	.287	135	478	94	137	24	3	26	97	95	119	3	.513	.406
	Chicago (NL)	MAJ	.180	24	50	6	9	1	0	2	4	7	15	0	.320	.281
MAJOR LEAGUE TOTALS			.180	24	50	6	9	1	0	2	4	7	15	0	.320	.281
MINOR LEAGUE TOTALS			.286	423	1501	288	430	87	15	82	307	241	370	17	.528	.386

2. Angel Guzman, rhp

Born: Dec. 14, 1981. **Ht.:** 6-2. **Wt.:** 180. **Bats:** R. **Throws:** R. **Career Transactions:**
Signed out of Venezuela by Royals, March 4, 1999 . . . Contract voided, June 24, 1999
. . . Signed by Cubs, Nov. 12, 1999.

The Cubs thought Guzman was headed for a breakout 2002 season,
and they were correct. In his first taste of full-season ball, he breezed
through two Class A leagues and led Chicago minor leaguers in wins (11)
and ERA (2.19). That earned him a nonroster invitation to big league
camp. After his promotion to high Class A Daytona, Guzman regained
the curveball he had when he signed three years earlier. At times, all three
of his pitches graded as 70 on the 20-80 scouting scale. He also throws a 91-96 mph fastball
with explosive sinking life and the best changeup in the system. He's athletic, throws strikes
and has a feel for pitching. His delivery is effortless. Guzman needs only to make subtle
adjustments, such as improving his location within the strike zone and pitching inside more
often. Maintaining the curveball he had in the second half of 2002 would be huge. Guzman
is set to begin the year at Double-A West Tenn. Some Cubs officials believe he could move
from there to Wrigley Field as quickly as Mark Prior did last season.

Year	Club (League)	Class	W	L	ERA	G	GS	CG	SV	IP	H	R	ER	HR	BB	SO	AVG
2000	La Pradera (VSL)	R	1	1	1.93	7	6	0	0	33	24	13	7	0	5	25	.197
2001	Boise (NWL)	A	9	1	2.23	14	14	0	0	77	68	27	19	2	19	63	.233
2002	Lansing (Mid)	A	5	2	1.89	9	9	1	0	62	42	18	13	3	16	49	.186
	Daytona (FSL)	A	6	2	2.39	16	15	1	0	94	99	34	25	2	33	74	.268
MINOR LEAGUE TOTALS			21	6	2.17	46	44	2	0	265	233	92	64	7	73	211	.231

3. Andy Sisco, lhp

Born: Jan. 13, 1983. **Ht.:** 6-9. **Wt.:** 250. **Bats:** L. **Throws:** L. **School:** Eastlake HS,
Sammamish, Wash. **Career Transactions:** Selected by Cubs in second round of 2001
draft; signed June 26, 2001.

The Cubs may have found not one but two No. 1 starters in the 2001
draft. After taking Mark Prior No. 2 overall, they also landed Sisco in the
second round. A former defensive end who turned down football scholarships from several Pacific-10 Conference schools, Sisco signed for $1
million. He was the short-season Northwest League's No. 1 prospect and
strikeout leader in 2002. Because he's an intimidating 6-foot-9 lefthander,
Sisco draws inevitable comparisons to Randy Johnson—and he's much more polished than
Johnson was at the same age. Sisco made impressive strides with his mechanics last year,
when he regularly threw 90-96 mph. Besides his arm, he also earns high marks for his athleticism, feel, poise and work ethic. Sisco still needs to make his delivery and his pitches
more consistent. He has a slurvy breaking ball that should become a curveball once he
maintains a higher arm slot. He throws his splitter too often and needs to develop a true
changeup. His command can be shaky and lead to high pitch counts. Chicago's strength is
pitching from top to bottom, so Sisco won't be rushed. He'll open 2003 at low Class A
Lansing and won't see Wrigley Field before late 2005.

Year	Club (League)	Class	W	L	ERA	G	GS	CG	SV	IP	H	R	ER	HR	BB	SO	AVG
2001	Cubs (AZL)	R	1	0	5.24	10	7	0	0	34	36	28	20	1	10	31	.267
2002	Boise (NWL)	A	7	2	2.43	14	14	0	0	78	51	23	21	3	39	101	.188
MINOR LEAGUE TOTALS			8	2	3.29	24	21	0	0	112	87	51	41	4	49	132	.214

4. Felix Pie, of

Born: Feb. 8, 1985. **Ht.:** 6-2. **Wt.:** 160. **Bats:** L. **Throws:** L. **Career Transactions:**
Signed out of Dominican Republic by Cubs, July 3, 2001.

The Cubs touted Pie as their top position-player signing on the international market in 2001, and Pie went out and proved them right in
2002. In his pro debut, Pie led the Arizona League in triples and extra-
base hits en route to being named the Rookie league's co-MVP and No. 1
prospect. He played on championship teams in the AZL and at short-season Boise. The top all-around athlete in the system, Pie already shows
four tools. His best at the moment is speed, which allows him to steal
bases and cover plenty of ground in center field. He also shows a solid arm. For a teenager,
Pie has an advanced approach at the plate. Pie has a quick bat and he's wiry strong, and he's
already capable of driving the ball into the gaps. His enthusiasm is another plus. Pie just
needs time. With more experience, he'll make more contact and learn the art of basesteal-

ing. As he fills out his frame, he should develop at least average home run power. Chicago won't rush him, so Pie might go to extended spring training before returning to Boise. He's three or four years away from the majors.

Year	Club (League)	Class	AVG	G	AB	R	H	2B	3B	HR	RBI	BB	SO	SB	SLG	OBP
2002	Cubs (AZL)	R	.321	55	218	42	70	16	13	4	37	21	47	17	.569	.385
	Boise (NWL)	A	.125	2	8	1	1	1	0	0	1	1	1	0	.250	.222
MINOR LEAGUE TOTALS			.314	57	226	43	71	17	13	4	38	22	48	17	.558	.379

5. Nic Jackson, of

Born: Sept. 25, 1979. **Ht.:** 6-3. **Wt.:** 200. **Bats:** L. **Throws:** R. **School:** University of Richmond. **Career Transactions:** Selected by Cubs in third round of 2000 draft; signed June 20, 2000.

Since signing, Jackson has been fully healthy for only the 2001 season—when managers rated him the most exciting player in the high Class A Florida State League. In his draft year of 2000, he had a ligament injury in his right middle finger. Last season he fouled two pitches off his right leg, fracturing his right shin, and didn't play after May 11. Jackson is athletic in the mold of fellow University of Richmond product Brian Jordan. He hits for average and power, runs well and can play all three outfield positions capably. His worst tool is probably his arm, but it's solid average and doesn't keep him from projecting as a right fielder. Jackson lost a year of development. He tried to make up at-bats in the Mexican Pacific League this winter, but tweaked a hamstring and left at midseason. He's still refining his plate discipline. With several outfielders pushing their way up from high Class A, Jackson could begin 2003 in Triple-A. The Cubs expect him to reach the majors at some point in 2004, and he could make it easy to decline Moises Alou's $11.5 million option for 2005.

Year	Club (League)	Class	AVG	G	AB	R	H	2B	3B	HR	RBI	BB	SO	SB	SLG	OBP
2000	Eugene (NWL)	A	.255	74	294	39	75	12	7	6	47	22	64	25	.405	.308
2001	Daytona (FSL)	A	.296	131	503	87	149	30	6	19	85	39	96	24	.493	.355
2002	West Tenn (SL)	AA	.290	32	131	18	38	9	1	3	20	6	23	8	.443	.329
MINOR LEAGUE TOTALS			.282	237	928	144	262	51	14	28	152	67	183	57	.458	.337

6. Francis Beltran, rhp

Born: Nov. 29, 1979. **Ht.:** 6-5. **Wt.:** 220. **Bats:** R. **Throws:** R. **Career Transactions:** Signed out of Dominican Republic by Cubs, Nov. 15, 1996.

Though he had a 5.02 ERA in five pro seasons, Chicago protected Beltran on its 40-man roster after the 2001 season. He showed why last year, when he emerged as a dominant closer in Double-A and reached the majors. At the Futures Game, Beltran threw 96 mph and struck out Joe Borchard and Jason Stokes with sliders. Managers rated Beltran's 95-98 mph fastball the best in the Double-A Southern League. No one in the Cubs system has a better heater or slider. He throws the latter pitch in the mid-80s. He also uses a splitter to give hitters something else to think about it. Beltran didn't have as much success as a starter because his changeup and command were spotty. He doesn't need the changeup now, but he does need to improve his control, both in terms of throwing strikes and locating pitches within the zone. Though his age was revised upward eight months last spring, that didn't alter his prospect status. While with the Cubs, Beltran showed he needed more seasoning. After Chicago signed Mark Guthrie, Mike Remlinger and Dave Veres as free agents, Beltran will go to Triple-A Iowa.

Year	Club (League)	Class	W	L	ERA	G	GS	CG	SV	IP	H	R	ER	HR	BB	SO	AVG
1997	Cubs (AZL)	R	0	1	3.42	16	0	0	1	24	27	18	9	1	8	17	.276
1998	Cubs (AZL)	R	1	1	5.55	12	5	0	0	36	49	23	22	1	14	26	.343
1999	Cubs (AZL)	R	0	1	0.00	7	0	0	2	11	5	3	0	0	1	8	.139
	Eugene (NWL)	A	0	2	8.36	16	0	0	0	28	41	32	26	2	14	28	.331
2000	Lansing (Mid)	A	1	1	9.68	16	0	0	0	18	24	22	19	0	19	16	.338
	Eugene (NWL)	A	2	2	2.68	25	0	0	8	44	28	16	13	1	20	52	.178
2001	Daytona (FSL)	A	6	9	5.00	21	18	0	0	95	93	62	53	10	40	72	.251
2002	West Tenn (SL)	AA	2	2	2.59	39	0	0	23	42	28	14	12	2	19	43	.192
	Chicago (NL)	MAJ	0	0	7.50	11	0	0	0	12	14	11	10	2	16	11	.311
MAJOR LEAGUE TOTALS			0	0	7.50	11	0	0	0	12	14	11	10	2	16	11	.311
MINOR LEAGUE TOTALS			12	19	4.68	152	23	0	34	296	295	190	154	17	135	262	.258

7. Luke Hagerty, lhp

Born: April 1, 1981. **Ht.:** 6-7. **Wt.:** 230. **Bats:** R. **Throws:** L. **School:** Ball State University. **Career Transactions:** Selected by Cubs in first round (32th overall) of 2002 draft; signed June 27, 2002.

Hagerty played second fiddle to No. 1 overall pick Bryan Bullington at Ball State and to Bobby Brownlie in Chicago's 2002 draft. While the Cubs still hadn't signed Brownlie in January, their sense of urgency was reduced by Hagerty's performance in his pro debut. He was more consistent than he was in college and looks like a steal for where he went (32nd overall) and what he signed for ($1.15 million). He'll need time to develop, but Hagerty oozes potential as a strong 6-foot-7 lefthander. He throws 88-94 mph with late life, and he projects to add velocity. His slider is average at times and should give him a second plus pitch once he refines it. For a pitcher his size, Hagerty has fairly smooth mechanics and throws without effort, which gives him good command. Hagerty was up and down during the spring at Ball State, which is why he fell from the top half of the first round. His changeup has a ways to go, and his fastball and slider also need work. But all the ingredients are there. The pitching-rich Cubs have the luxury of letting Hagerty move at his own timetable. They'll probably start him at low Class A in 2003.

Year	Club (League)	Class	W	L	ERA	G	GS	CG	SV	IP	H	R	ER	HR	BB	SO	AVG
2002	Boise (NWL)	A	5	3	1.13	10	10	0	0	48	32	15	6	2	15	50	.189
MINOR LEAGUE TOTALS			5	3	1.13	10	10	0	0	48	32	15	6	2	15	50	.189

8. Brendan Harris, 3b/2b

Born: Aug. 26, 1980. **Ht.:** 6-1. **Wt.:** 190. **Bats:** R. **Throws:** R. **School:** College of William & Mary. **Career Transactions:** Selected by Cubs in fifth round of 2001 draft; signed July 21, 2001.

Area scout Billy Swoope has a knack for finding talented hitters at Virginia colleges. After cutting his pro debut short to work toward his government concentration degree at William & Mary—which he completed in December 2002—Harris was spectacular in his first full season. Playing through a nagging knee injury, he hit .328 and reached Double-A. Harris has supplanted David Kelton as the system's top pure hitter and best hope to end the Curse of Ron Santo. He hits for gap power and, unlike Kelton, has demonstrated the ability to play the hot corner. Managers rated Harris the Florida State League's best defensive third baseman and he has the strongest infield arm among Cubs farmhands. An all-New York basketball player in high school, he also offers athleticism and speed. He can play second base if needed. Harris has a fiery temper that sometimes gets the best of him. Then again, his drive allowed him to play through his knee problems, which didn't require surgery, and recover from a .217 April last year. He'll begin 2003 as a Double-A third baseman but could push for a quick promotion. He should be in Chicago's lineup somewhere by the end of 2004.

Year	Club (League)	Class	AVG	G	AB	R	H	2B	3B	HR	RBI	BB	SO	SB	SLG	OBP
2001	Lansing (Mid)	A	.274	32	113	25	31	5	1	4	22	17	26	5	.442	.370
2002	Daytona (FSL)	A	.329	110	425	82	140	35	6	13	54	43	57	16	.532	.395
	West Tenn (SL)	AA	.321	13	53	8	17	4	1	2	11	2	5	1	.547	.345
MINOR LEAGUE TOTALS			.318	155	591	115	188	44	8	19	87	62	88	22	.516	.386

9. David Kelton, 3b/1b

Born: Dec. 17, 1979. **Ht.:** 6-3. **Wt.:** 200. **Bats:** R. **Throws:** R. **School:** Troup County HS, La Grange, Ga. **Career Transactions:** Selected by Cubs in second round of 1998 draft; signed June 3, 1998.

How Kelton fared in 2002 is in the eye of the beholder. In his sixth pro season, he still didn't make it to Triple-A and had continued difficulty playing third base. On the other hand, at 22 he wasn't old for Double-A, led the Southern League in homers, RBIs and extra-base hits, and managers rated him the league's best batting prospect. Kelton owns a pure swing and there's little doubt that he can hit .275 with 20-25 homers in the majors. He has the hands, range and quickness for third base, and perhaps to become an average outfielder. Kelton never has looked comfortable at third, where his bat would fit best. He had shoulder surgery in high school, and he has had mechanical and mental problems throwing from the hot corner as a pro. He played just six games there in Double-A last year, and committed 11 errors in 43 games at third in Mexico this winter. Offensively, he needs to tighten his strike zone. The Cubs plan to send Kelton to Triple-A to play third base, his clearest path to the big leagues. If he can't cut it defensively or Brendan Harris is ready for a promotion, Kelton may have to move again.

Year	Club (League)	Class	AVG	G	AB	R	H	2B	3B	HR	RBI	BB	SO	SB	SLG	OBP
1998	Cubs (AZL)	R	.265	50	181	39	48	7	5	6	29	23	58	16	.459	.353
1999	Lansing (Mid)	A	.269	124	509	75	137	17	4	13	68	39	121	22	.395	.322
2000	Daytona (FSL)	A	.268	132	523	75	140	30	7	18	84	38	120	7	.455	.317
2001	West Tenn (SL)	AA	.313	58	224	33	70	9	4	12	45	24	55	1	.549	.378
2002	West Tenn (SL)	AA	.261	129	498	68	130	28	6	20	79	52	129	12	.462	.332
MINOR LEAGUE TOTALS			.271	493	1935	290	525	91	26	69	305	176	483	58	.452	.333

10. Todd Wellemeyer, rhp

Born: Aug. 30, 1978. **Ht.:** 6-3. **Wt.:** 200. **Bats:** R. **Throws:** R. **School:** Bellarmine (Ky.) University. **Career Transactions:** Selected by Cubs in fourth round of 2000 draft; signed June 10, 2000.

Wellemeyer might not have played college baseball if Bellarmine hadn't offered him a last-minute scholarship, and he didn't get much exposure until he pitched in the Coastal Plain League in 1999. Though he was raw, the Cubs picked him in the fourth round in 2000 and haven't been disappointed. He has improved each year and was an Arizona Fall League all-star after last season. Wellemeyer always has shown arm strength, and he pitches at 90-95 mph with his fastball. He upsets hitters' timing with a changeup that features splitter action. In 2002, he made significant strides with his command and his slider. One scout who saw him in the AFL compared him to Todd Stottlemyre, though not as athletic. The biggest thing Wellemeyer needs to do is maintain the consistency he started to show with his control and breaking ball. He missed a month last summer with back problems, but should be ready for spring training. Wellemeyer likely will begin 2003 in Double-A, where he pitched better last year than his ERA would indicate. Because the Cubs have so many starters, his long-term role might be as a reliever.

Year	Club (League)	Class	W	L	ERA	G	GS	CG	SV	IP	H	R	ER	HR	BB	SO	AVG
2000	Eugene (NWL)	A	4	4	3.67	15	15	0	0	76	62	35	31	3	33	85	.225
2001	Lansing (Mid)	A	13	9	4.16	27	27	1	0	147	165	85	68	14	74	167	.288
2002	Daytona (FSL)	A	2	4	3.79	14	14	0	0	74	63	33	31	7	19	87	.230
	West Tenn (SL)	AA	3	3	4.70	8	8	1	0	46	33	25	24	2	18	37	.204
MINOR LEAGUE TOTALS			22	20	4.04	64	64	2	0	343	323	178	154	26	144	376	.251

11. Jae-Kuk Ryu, rhp

Born: May 30, 1983. **Ht.:** 6-3. **Wt.:** 180. **Bats:** R. **Throws:** R. **Career Transactions:** Signed out of Korea by Cubs, June 1, 2001.

The last major signee for former Pacific Rim coordinator Leon Lee, who's now coaching with Japan's Orix Blue Wave, Ryu has been impressive since agreeing to a $1.6 million bonus in June 2001. He was untouchable in the Arizona League that summer, and easily held his own as one of the youngest pitchers in the Northwest League last year. Ryu initially struggled after a late-season promotion to the low Class A Midwest League, but he came on in the playoffs to win his first start and strike out 10 in 5⅔ innings in his second. Ryu throws a 90-96 mph fastball on a nice downward plane, and his curveball gives him a second plus pitch. He uses both a deceptive splitter and a changeup to keep hitters off balance. His mechanics are smooth and he has decent command. At this point, Ryu just needs more innings to refine his command and improve the consistency of all his pitches. He doesn't use his fastball as much as he should. Ryu didn't know how to prepare and lacked a place to work out when he returned to Korea after the 2001 season, so he wasn't fully ready for spring training in 2002. Those situations have been rectified, so he could make even more progress this year, which he'll start back in low Class A.

Year	Club (League)	Class	W	L	ERA	G	GS	CG	SV	IP	H	R	ER	HR	BB	SO	AVG
2001	Cubs (AZL)	R	1	0	0.61	4	3	0	0	15	11	2	1	0	5	20	.196
2002	Boise (NWL)	A	6	1	3.57	10	10	0	0	53	45	28	21	1	25	56	.223
	Lansing (Mid)	A	1	2	7.11	5	4	0	0	19	26	16	15	1	8	21	.333
MINOR LEAGUE TOTALS			8	3	3.84	19	17	0	0	87	82	46	37	2	38	97	.244

12. Justin Jones, lhp

Born: Sept. 25, 1984. **Ht.:** 6-4. **Wt.:** 180. **Bats:** L. **Throws:** L. **School:** Kellam HS, Virginia Beach. **Career Transactions:** Selected by Cubs in second round of 2002 draft; signed June 25, 2002.

Because he hailed from the same area as B.J. Upton, the No. 2 overall pick in the 2002 draft, Jones often pitched in front of scouting directors and national crosscheckers last spring. Jones performed unevenly yet still went in the second round based on his pro-jectability. He didn't waste any time delivering on his potential after signing. He won the Arizona League ERA title as his fastball jumped from 86-91 mph to 90-93. His curveball became more consistent and he wasn't afraid to throw it at any count. He also showed tremendous poise for a 17-year-old. Jones still needs to refine his slurvy slider, changeup and control, and he has plenty of time to do so. He should add velocity as he fills out his lanky 6-foot-4, 180-pound frame. The Cubs have been searching for quality lefthanded starters for years, and they have three intriguing ones coming through the pipeline in Andy Sisco, Luke Hagerty and Jones.

Year	Club (League)	Class	W	L	ERA	G	GS	CG	SV	IP	H	R	ER	HR	BB	SO	AVG
2002	Cubs (AZL)	R	3	1	1.80	11	11	0	0	50	31	12	10	0	18	63	.181
	Boise (NWL)	A	1	0	1.80	1	1	0	0	5	4	1	1	0	3	4	.211
MINOR LEAGUE TOTALS			4	1	1.80	12	12	0	0	55	35	13	11	0	21	67	.184

13. Felix Sanchez, lhp

Born: Aug. 3, 1981. **Ht.:** 6-3. **Wt.:** 180. **Bats:** R. **Throws:** L. **Career Transactions:** Signed out of Dominican Republic by Cubs, Sept. 15, 1998.

Entering 2002, Cubs officials believed that Angel Guzman and Sanchez were poised for breakout years. Sanchez wasn't as spectacular as Guzman, who rocketed to No. 2 on this list, but he excelled when shifted to the bullpen in August. Blister problems precipitated the move and he'll return to the rotation in 2002, but he may have given a glimpse of his future when he topped out at 96-97 mph and earned four saves in the Midwest League playoffs. As a starter, Sanchez worked mainly at 92-94 and struggled with his below-average slider. Though he has a decent changeup and throws strikes, he sometimes got hit hard because opponents didn't respect his stuff. Sanchez limited lefties to a .237 average and one extra-base hit (a double) in 76 at-bats, but needs better stuff to combat righthanders. If he can't improve his slider—and some scouts question his ability to do so—the Cubs eventually may just let him deal heat as a late-inning reliever.

Year	Club (League)	Class	W	L	ERA	G	GS	CG	SV	IP	H	R	ER	HR	BB	SO	AVG
1999	Cubs (DSL)	R	1	3	3.28	7	7	0	0	25	27	18	9	1	9	27	.273
2000	Cubs (DSL)	R	4	2	3.15	13	13	0	0	54	45	26	19	2	15	61	.223
2001	Cubs (AZL)	R	2	5	4.01	12	9	0	0	61	57	38	27	2	22	55	.250
	Boise (NWL)	A	2	0	1.56	3	3	0	0	17	11	4	3	0	10	16	.180
2002	Lansing (Mid)	A	6	6	4.15	26	21	0	2	119	130	67	55	7	44	101	.286
MINOR LEAGUE TOTALS			15	16	3.68	61	53	0	2	276	270	153	113	12	100	260	.259

14. Luis Montanez, ss/2b

Born: Dec. 15, 1981. **Ht.:** 6-2. **Wt:** 180. **Bats:** R. **Throws:** R. **School:** Coral Park HS, Miami. **Career Transactions:** Selected by Cubs in first round (third overall) of 2000 draft; signed June 6, 2000.

The No. 3 pick in the 2000 draft, Montanez has been promoted aggressively, reaching high Class A at age 20. In each of his two full seasons, he has started slowly before finishing with a strong second half. In 2002, he batted .240 through June 11 and .287 afterward. He's still viewed as an offensive middle infielder, with differing viewpoints as to whether he'll wind up at shortstop or second base. Montanez has the arm and hands to play either position, but he doesn't have the speed and range typical of most shortstops. He has made 64 errors in 213 games at short the last two seasons, many coming on errant throws. He looked good when he played second base for the first time as a pro last year. Since he won the Arizona League MVP award in his pro debut, Montanez' offensive production has leveled off as he has been challenged. He has good juice in his bat for a middle infielder, and his plate discipline improved last year. He should continue to improve, especially if the Cubs give him a chance to catch his breath. Montanez will play in Double-A at age 21 this year.

Year	Club (League)	Class	AVG	G	AB	R	H	2B	3B	HR	RBI	BB	SO	SB	SLG	OBP
2000	Cubs (AZL)	R	.344	50	192	50	66	16	7	2	37	25	42	11	.531	.438
	Lansing (Mid)	A	.138	8	29	2	4	1	0	0	0	3	6	0	.172	.219
2001	Lansing (Mid)	A	.255	124	499	70	127	33	6	5	54	34	121	20	.375	.316
2002	Daytona (FSL)	A	.265	124	487	69	129	21	5	4	59	44	89	14	.353	.333
MINOR LEAGUE TOTALS			.270	306	1207	191	326	71	18	11	150	106	258	45	.386	.341

15. Alfredo Francisco, 3b

Born: Aug. 27, 1984. **Ht.:** 6-3. **Wt.:** 180. **Bats:** R. **Throws:** R. **Career Transactions:** Signed out of Dominican Republic by Cubs, Feb. 1, 2002.

The Cubs' three-decade search for a successor to Ron Santo continues. If Brendan Harris and David Kelton don't pan out, Francisco gives them another hope. Signed in February 2002, he came straight to the United States for his pro debut, playing in the Arizona League at age 17. As would be expected, he was quite raw but showed flashes of considerable talent. While he was at times overmatched because he had never faced anything approaching the quality of pro pitching, Francisco's upside was obvious. He's athletic, uses a short swing and has power potential that he'll tap into if he gets stronger and learns the strike zone. Defensively, he has soft hands, a strong arm and solid footwork. He'll need time to adjust to the United States and to pro ball. As a result, Francisco likely will start this year in extended spring training before joining Boise or the AZL Cubs in June.

Year	Club (League)	Class	AVG	G	AB	R	H	2B	3B	HR	RBI	BB	SO	SB	SLG	OBP
2002	Cubs (AZL)	R	.266	48	188	23	50	6	1	1	24	9	58	1	.324	.296
	Lansing (Mid)	A	.000	2	7	0	0	0	0	0	0	0	2	0	.000	.000
MINOR LEAGUE TOTALS			.256	50	195	23	50	6	1	1	24	9	60	1	.313	.286

16. Steve Smyth, lhp

Born: June 3, 1978. **Ht.:** 6-1. **Wt.:** 200. **Bats:** L. **Throws:** L. **School:** University of Southern California. **Career Transactions:** Selected by Cubs in fourth round of 1999 draft; signed June 8, 1999.

Smyth led the Southern League in ERA and was on the verge of a callup in 2001 when he came down with shoulder problems. He had surgery to tighten his capsule and clean up fraying in his rotator cuff, which also cost him the first month of the 2002 season. While he made his big league debut last year, Smyth's stuff didn't come quite all the way back and he was exhausted by the end of the season. His command was fine as usual, but his fastball usually sat at 87-89 mph, down from the low 90s. He throws both a slider and curveball, and his breaking pitches were breaking too early. Smyth also has an average changeup. He got shelled with the Cubs, especially by righthanders, who hit .351 and slugged .727 against him. Given the winter to rest and put the surgery further behind him, he should be at full strength again in 2003. Chicago has signed lefties Shawn Estes, Mark Guthrie and Mike Remlinger as free agents this offseason, which probably means Smyth is destined for Triple-A.

Year	Club (League)	Class	W	L	ERA	G	GS	CG	SV	IP	H	R	ER	HR	BB	SO	AVG
1999	Eugene (NWL)	A	1	1	4.38	5	5	0	0	25	29	17	12	2	7	14	.293
	Lansing (Mid)	A	5	3	6.93	10	10	0	0	51	68	40	39	5	30	46	.333
2000	Daytona (FSL)	A	8	8	3.25	24	23	1	0	138	134	62	50	9	57	100	.255
2001	West Tenn (SL)	AA	9	3	2.54	18	18	3	0	120	110	38	34	9	40	93	.246
2002	West Tenn (SL)	AA	4	4	3.58	11	11	0	0	73	62	34	29	7	18	74	.228
	Iowa (PCL)	AAA	3	2	5.81	6	6	0	0	31	35	21	20	4	10	25	.287
	Chicago (NL)	MAJ	1	3	9.35	8	7	0	0	26	34	28	27	9	10	16	.321
MAJOR LEAGUE TOTALS			1	3	9.35	8	7	0	0	26	34	28	27	9	10	16	.321
MINOR LEAGUE TOTALS			30	21	3.78	74	73	4	0	438	438	212	184	36	162	352	.262

17. Billy Petrick, rhp

Born: April 29, 1984. **Ht.:** 6-6. **Wt.:** 220. **Bats:** R. **Throws:** R. **School:** Morris (Ill.) HS. **Career Transactions:** Selected by Cubs in third round of 2002 draft; signed July 19, 2002.

The seventh player drafted by Chicago in 2002, Petrick is the third member of that crop to appear on this list. The Cubs believe they got excellent third-round value in the home-state product, who turned down a Washington State football scholarship as one of the nation's top long-snapper recruits. After signing for $459,500, Petrick won the Arizona League championship game and reached 95 mph in instructional league. During the season, he usually pitched at 88-92 with heavy life. He should throw harder more consistently as he fills out his athletic 6-foot-5 frame. His arm action is loose and easy, which allows him to throw strikes. Petrick also shows the aptitude to spin a curveball and use a changeup. Because the Cubs have a logjam of starters ready for their two Class A clubs, he'll probably pitch at Boise in 2003.

Year	Club (League)	Class	W	L	ERA	G	GS	CG	SV	IP	H	R	ER	HR	BB	SO	AVG
2002	Cubs (AZL)	R	2	1	1.71	6	6	0	0	32	21	8	6	0	6	35	.189
MINOR LEAGUE TOTALS			2	1	1.71	6	6	0	0	32	21	8	6	0	6	35	.189

18. Matt Bruback, rhp

Born: Jan. 12, 1979. **Ht.:** 6-7. **Wt.:** 210. **Bats:** R. **Throws:** R. **School:** Manatee (Fla.) JC. **Career Transactions:** Selected by Cubs in 47th round of 1997 draft; signed May 16, 1998.

Selected out of a Texas high school in 1997 as a raw draft-and-follow, Bruback piqued the Cubs' interest by throwing 94-97 mph at Manatee (Fla.) CC. He might have been a first-round pick in 1998 if they hadn't signed him before the draft. Since refining his mechanics, he now throws in the low 90s and doesn't have as high a ceiling. But he did make major strides with his command and confidence last year, which enabled him to lead the Southern League in strikeouts and crack Chicago's 40-man roster for the first time. Bruback's changeup is his second-best pitch, and his slider became a more reliable option in 2002. His next step is to solve lefthanders, who batted .280 against him last year. He's erratic defensively with a career .839 fielding percentage. Bruback has struggled in his first exposure to each full-season level, a trend he'll hope to avoid this year in Triple-A.

Year	Club (League)	Class	W	L	ERA	G	GS	CG	SV	IP	H	R	ER	HR	BB	SO	AVG
1998	Williamsport (NY-P)	A	2	7	3.93	14	14	0	0	66	62	46	29	2	45	43	.248
1999	Lansing (Mid)	A	9	8	5.40	25	25	0	0	135	151	92	81	15	87	118	.286
2000	Lansing (Mid)	A	4	2	2.93	9	9	2	0	55	49	23	18	2	19	36	.230
	Daytona (FSL)	A	5	5	4.85	18	18	0	0	89	101	57	48	6	50	69	.294
2001	Daytona (FSL)	A	6	3	3.00	14	14	0	0	84	70	33	28	3	21	87	.223
	West Tenn (SL)	AA	2	5	9.00	9	9	0	0	38	58	44	38	3	20	43	.345
2002	West Tenn (SL)	AA	9	7	3.16	28	28	0	0	174	157	70	61	9	48	158	.243
MINOR LEAGUE TOTALS			37	37	4.25	117	117	2	0	642	648	365	303	40	290	554	.263

19. Ricky Nolasco, rhp

Born: Dec. 13, 1982. **Ht.:** 6-2. **Wt.:** 220. **Bats:** R. **Throws:** R. **School:** Rialto (Calif.) HS. **Career Transactions:** Selected by Cubs in fourth round of 2001 draft; signed July 31, 2001.

He hasn't attracted nearly the attention of fellow 2002 draftees Mark Prior and Andy Sisco, but Nolasco has started his pro career with a flourish. The younger brother of Brewers minor league righthander Dave Nolasco, he tied for the Boise lead in wins last year as part of a talented rotation that also included Sisco, Luke Hagerty and Jae-Kuk Ryu. Nolasco can touch 96 mph but is better off working in the lower 90s and getting more sink with a two-seam fastball. He throws over the top, so he doesn't have a lot of natural life on his pitches. The velocity fluctuates on his promising curveball, though that might be more by accident than by design. Nolasco has solid command but his changeup requires more work. Already filled out at 6-foot-2 and 220 pounds, he doesn't project to add more velocity and must watch his conditioning. He's ready to make his full-season debut in 2003.

Year	Club (League)	Class	W	L	ERA	G	GS	CG	SV	IP	H	R	ER	HR	BB	SO	AVG
2001	Cubs (AZL)	R	1	0	1.50	5	4	0	0	18	11	3	3	0	5	23	.175
2002	Boise (NWL)	A	7	2	2.48	15	15	0	0	91	72	32	25	1	25	92	.214
MINOR LEAGUE TOTALS			8	2	2.32	20	19	0	0	109	83	35	28	1	30	115	.208

20. John Webb, rhp

Born: May 23, 1979. **Ht.:** 6-3. **Wt.:** 200. **Bats:** R. **Throws:** R. **School:** Manatee (Fla.) CC. **Career Transactions:** Selected by Cubs in 19th round of 1999 draft; signed June 16, 1999.

Like Matt Bruback a product of Manatee (Fla.) CC, Webb emerged in the shadows of Juan Cruz at Lansing in 2000 before succumbing to Tommy John surgery the following season. Before he hurt his elbow, Webb threw a low-90s sinker, a plus slider and a changeup. He showed the same quality of stuff only sporadically in 2002 as he worked his way back to full strength. He tired toward the end of the season after he was promoted to Double-A. Webb competes hard and learned to pitch at less than his best, which should help him once his pitches and his command bounce back as expected this year. More of a shortstop as an amateur, Webb is athletic and even was used as a pinch-hitter last year. He'll return to Double-A in 2003.

Year	Club (League)	Class	W	L	ERA	G	GS	CG	SV	IP	H	R	ER	HR	BB	SO	AVG
1999	Cubs (AZL)	R	0	0	3.58	18	0	0	3	33	33	20	13	0	8	39	.246
	Eugene (NWL)	A	1	0	0.00	2	0	0	1	4	1	0	0	0	1	3	.077
2000	Lansing (Mid)	A	7	6	2.47	21	21	1	0	135	125	53	37	4	40	108	.250
	Daytona (FSL)	A	1	1	4.76	4	2	0	1	17	17	11	9	1	3	18	.250
2001	Daytona (FSL)	A	1	1	5.40	5	4	0	0	20	23	13	12	0	7	20	.280
2002	Daytona (FSL)	A	5	3	3.43	10	10	1	0	58	43	23	22	3	23	65	.207
	West Tenn (SL)	AA	4	5	4.52	11	11	0	0	62	52	33	31	5	22	45	.231
MINOR LEAGUE TOTALS			19	16	3.41	71	48	2	5	328	294	153	124	13	104	298	.239

21. Chadd Blasko, rhp

Born: March 9, 1981. **Ht.:** 6-6. **Wt.:** 210. **Bats:** R. **Throws:** R. **School:** Purdue University. **Career Transactions:** Selected by Cubs in first round (36th overall) of 2002 draft; signed Aug. 31, 2002.

After two so-so years at Purdue, Blasko pitched himself into 2002's supplemental first round with a strong summer in the Cape Cod and a solid junior season. Like many Scott Boras clients, Blasko held out for all of his first pro summer. After signing for $1.05 million, he reported to instructional league. The Cubs didn't get much of a look at him because he was hit in the foot by a line drive while shagging balls in the outfield in his first week. Blasko's main weapon is a 90-96 mph fastball. Still projectable at 6-foot-6 and 205 pounds, he could dial his fastball up a couple of more notches as he gets stronger. He'll need to flesh out the rest of his repertoire. Blasko supplements his heat with a splitter, slider, curveball and changeup. He has a long arm action that worried some scouts, but it hasn't hampered his command and Chicago has no immediate plans to change him. He'll compete for a spot in the low Class A rotation during spring training.

Year	Club (League)	Class	W	L	ERA	G	GS	CG	SV	IP	H	R	ER	HR	BB	SO	AVG
					Has Not Played—Signed 2003 Contract												

22. Brian Dopirak, 1b

Born: Dec. 20, 1983. **Ht.:** 6-4. **Wt.:** 220. **Bats:** R. **Throws:** R. **School:** Dunedin (Fla.) HS. **Career Transactions:** Selected by Cubs in second round of 2002 draft; signed Aug. 4, 2002.

Despite bidding goodbye to Fred McGriff and his 478 career home runs, the Cubs have no shortage of power-hitting first basemen. Starting with Hee Seop Choi, McGriff's heir apparent, their list also includes Brad Bouras, Kevin Collins and Micah Hoffpauir. David Kelton and Brandon Sing also ended the season at first base. Choi has the most usable power, but no one in the system has more home run potential than Dopirak, a 2002 second-rounder. Considered to have the most raw pop in the 2002 draft, Dopirak didn't homer in his pro debut. He's going to have to adjust his approach, as he's a free swinger who doesn't make consistent contact. Before the draft, scouts described him as a hit-or-miss player who could hit 50 homers in the majors or top out in Double-A. They also thought he needed to spend more time on conditioning and less on showing off his tattoos. Dopirak's lightning-quick bat will have to carry him, because he's rough at first base or in left field. His development will require patience, which probably means sending him to Boise in 2003.

Year	Club (League)	Class	AVG	G	AB	R	H	2B	3B	HR	RBI	BB	SO	SB	SLG	OBP
2002	Cubs (AZL)	R	.253	21	79	10	20	4	0	0	6	6	23	0	.304	.306
MINOR LEAGUE TOTALS			.253	21	79	10	20	4	0	0	6	6	23	0	.304	.306

23. Brandon Sing, of/1b

Born: March 13, 1981. **Ht.:** 6-4. **Wt.:** 210. **Bats:** R. **Throws:** R. **School:** Joliet (Ill.) West HS. **Career Transactions:** Selected by Cubs in 20th round of 1999 draft; signed July 31, 1999.

More than one Chicago official compares Sing to Richie Sexson because he's tall, rangy and offers plenty of power. He tied for fourth in the Florida State League in homers last year. His .248 average was his career high for a full-season league, though he did offer hope for improvement by showing better plate discipline. Sexson put up roughly similar statistics at the same age, though in Double-A. Sing is agile and has arm strength, but he's still in search of a defensive home. A shortstop in high school, he played third base for his first 2½ years as a pro before the Cubs decided his struggles there were detracting from his bat. He spent the end of 2001 at first base, then played most of 2002 on the outfield corners (more in left field than right) before returning to first in August. At some point he'll have to step up his offensive production regardless of where he settles. Sing will move up to Double-A in 2003.

Year	Club (League)	Class	AVG	G	AB	R	H	2B	3B	HR	RBI	BB	SO	SB	SLG	OBP
1999	Cubs (AZL)	R	.265	17	68	4	18	4	1	2	12	5	16	1	.441	.311
2000	Eugene (NWL)	A	.229	61	218	29	50	11	1	9	28	35	75	4	.413	.339
2001	Lansing (Mid)	A	.245	121	417	54	102	27	2	16	50	46	109	3	.434	.328
2002	Daytona (FSL)	A	.248	125	440	65	109	18	5	18	64	64	96	5	.434	.348
MINOR LEAGUE TOTALS			.244	324	1143	152	279	60	9	45	154	150	296	13	.430	.337

24. Jason Wylie, rhp

Born: May 27, 1981. **Ht.:** 6-5. **Wt.:** 220. **Bats:** R. **Throws:** R. **School:** University of Utah. **Career Transactions:** Selected by Cubs in 12th round of 2002 draft; signed June 6, 2002.

Wylie is the most pleasant surprise from a potentially outstanding 2002 Cubs draft. His size and projectability were obvious, but he also went 13-11, 7.14 in three years as a starter at Utah, so he lasted until the 12th round. He threw 90-91 during the spring, with scouts predicting he one day could reach 95 mph. Wylie did just that as a a reliever after signing, topping out at 94-95. He can make his fastball sink or bore in on righthanders. He also throws a slider, curveball and changeup and showed a better feel for pitching than the Cubs might have expected. Wylie finished two of Boise's three wins in a sweep of the Northwest League playoffs. Chicago would like to move him back into the rotation this year, but that might be difficult because its Class A teams are overloaded with starting candidates.

Year	Club (League)	Class	W	L	ERA	G	GS	CG	SV	IP	H	R	ER	HR	BB	SO	AVG
2002	Boise (NWL)	A	1	1	1.99	24	0	0	11	41	26	9	9	1	7	44	.187
MINOR LEAGUE TOTALS			1	1	1.99	24	0	0	11	41	26	9	9	1	7	44	.187

25. Renyel Pinto, lhp

Born: July 8, 1982. **Ht.:** 6-4. **Wt.:** 190. **Bats:** L. **Throws:** L. **Career Transactions:** Signed out of Dominican Republic by Cubs, Jan. 31, 1999.

Pinto has some power in his left arm but doesn't display it consistently. Julio Garcia, his Midwest League manager the last two years, has seen him touch 93-94 mph. One member of the Cubs front office says he never has seen Pinto show that kind of velocity, while another has watched him top out at 96. Pinto recovered from mild elbow problems that bothered him in 2001, but he wasn't able to handle high Class A at the beginning of last season because his secondary pitches aren't effective. Throwing from a deceptive, low three-quarters delivery, he's tough for lefthanders to pick up. They batted .224 and went homerless in 98 at-bats against Pinto in 2002. If he can't develop a couple of pitches to complement his fastball, a move to the bullpen may be in his future. That could happen as early as 2003, because competition for spots in the high Class A rotation will be spirited.

Year	Club (League)	Class	W	L	ERA	G	GS	CG	SV	IP	H	R	ER	HR	BB	SO	AVG
1999	Cubs (DSL)	R	4	5	4.38	13	13	1	0	64	70	35	31	5	22	62	.289
2000	Cubs (AZL)	R	0	2	6.30	9	4	0	0	30	42	29	21	3	16	23	.326
2001	Lansing (Mid)	A	4	8	5.22	20	20	1	0	88	94	64	51	9	44	69	.278
2002	Daytona (FSL)	A	3	3	5.51	7	7	0	0	33	45	23	20	5	11	24	.338
	Lansing (Mid)	A	7	5	3.31	17	16	0	0	98	79	39	36	9	28	92	.221
MINOR LEAGUE TOTALS			18	23	4.58	66	60	2	0	312	330	190	159	31	121	270	.275

26. J.J. Johnson, of

Born: Nov. 3, 1981. **Ht.:** 6-2. **Wt.:** 190. **Bats:** R. **Throws:** R. **School:** Greenbrier HS, Evans, Ga. **Career Transactions:** Selected by Cubs in sixth round of 2000 draft; signed June 10, 2000.

For three straight years, one of the Cubs' better offensive prospects has been hampered by a hand injury. Following Nic Jackson and Hee Seop Choi, Johnson was the victim in 2002. After winning top-prospect honors and the MVP award in the Northwest League the year before, he never got untracked because of a severe bone bruise in his right hand. He was hit by pitches on the hand twice early in the year, which affected his ability to grip the bat and to throw. Johnson insisted on playing through that injury as well as later hamstring troubles, with dismal results. He has the swing, bat speed and whole-field approach to hit for power and average, assuming he tightens his strike zone. Johnson also has average speed and an arm suitable for right field. He may return to low Class A to start 2003 in order to boost his confidence.

Year	Club (League)	Class	AVG	G	AB	R	H	2B	3B	HR	RBI	BB	SO	SB	SLG	OBP
2000	Cubs (AZL)	R	.316	44	177	27	56	9	4	3	43	12	19	3	.463	.354
2001	Boise (NWL)	A	.317	70	287	55	91	15	5	7	61	20	50	18	.477	.362
2002	Lansing (Mid)	A	.240	112	420	58	101	25	2	2	56	38	89	7	.324	.308
MINOR LEAGUE TOTALS			.281	226	884	140	248	49	11	12	160	70	158	28	.402	.334

27. Carmen Pignatiello, lhp

Born: Sept. 12, 1982. **Ht.:** 6-0. **Wt.:** 170. **Bats:** R. **Throws:** L. **School:** Providence Catholic HS, Frankfurt, Ill. **Career Transactions:** Selected by Cubs in 20th round of 2000 draft; signed June 28, 2000.

Pignatiello won a gold medal with the U.S. national 18-and-under team at the 1999 World Junior Championships and was the 2000 Illinois high school player of the year. He came out of the same Providence Catholic High program that produced big leaguer Bryan Rekar and White Sox 2001 first-rounder Kris Honel. But Pignatiello doesn't throw hard and was committed to Mississippi State, which enabled Chicago to draft him in the 20th round. He has made consistent progress since signing. His fastball ranges from 82-88 mph, though the Cubs could see him developing an average fastball if he gets stronger. Pignatiello pitches better than his velocity because he's not afraid to pitch inside and does a fine job of commanding his curveball and changeup, both of which are average. Given his stuff, he draws the inevitable comparisons to Jamie Moyer and Kirk Rueter. It's difficult to project Pignatiello starting for the Cubs because of all the quality arms ahead of him, but it also would be foolish to bet against him. He'll continue proving himself this year in high Class A.

Year	Club (League)	Class	W	L	ERA	G	GS	CG	SV	IP	H	R	ER	HR	BB	SO	AVG
2000	Cubs (AZL)	R	4	1	4.46	9	3	0	0	36	48	26	18	1	13	32	.314
2001	Boise (NWL)	A	7	3	3.00	16	12	0	1	78	70	37	26	2	22	83	.230
2002	Lansing (Mid)	A	9	11	3.17	27	27	1	0	167	152	76	59	10	51	139	.240
MINOR LEAGUE TOTALS			20	15	3.29	52	42	1	1	282	270	139	103	13	86	254	.248

28. Ray Sadler, of

Born: Sept. 19, 1980. **Ht.:** 6-1. **Wt.:** 200. **Bats:** R. **Throws:** R. **School:** Hill (Texas) JC. **Career Transactions:** Selected by Cubs in 30th round of 1999 draft; signed May 30, 2000.

A cousin of Rangers utilityman Donnie Sadler, Ray has a more well-rounded game than his speedy relative. He's a rare player in that his tools have improved as he has risen through the minors since signing as a draft-and-follow out of Hill JC. Sadler is now stronger, faster and quicker. He has 65 speed on the 20-80 scouting scale, getting from the right side of the plate to first base in 4.15 seconds. He has improved his play in center field and can play any of the three outfield spots. Sadler's line-drive approach, hitting ability and speed are well-suited for a leadoff role, but his plate discipline needs improvement. He has gap power and can handle good fastballs. He'll spend 2003 in Double-A.

Year	Club (League)	Class	AVG	G	AB	R	H	2B	3B	HR	RBI	BB	SO	SB	SLG	OBP
2000	Cubs (AZL)	R	.339	42	165	32	56	5	5	1	27	16	27	4	.448	.395
2001	Lansing (Mid)	A	.341	94	378	74	129	27	3	10	50	22	58	18	.508	.378
2002	Daytona (FSL)	A	.286	112	462	81	132	31	1	11	47	27	91	30	.429	.333
	West Tenn (SL)	AA	.067	10	30	4	2	1	0	0	1	5	5	2	.100	.263
MINOR LEAGUE TOTALS			.308	258	1035	191	319	64	9	22	125	70	181	54	.451	.357

29. Russ Rohlicek, lhp

Born: Dec. 26, 1979. **Ht.:** 6-5. **Wt.:** 220. **Bats:** R. **Throws:** L. **School:** Long Beach State University. **Career Transactions:** Selected by Astros in sixth round of 2001 draft; signed June 25, 2001 . . . Traded by Astros with two players to be named to Cubs for RHP Tom Gordon, Aug. 22, 2002; Cubs acquired RHP Mike Nannini and RHP Travis Anderson to complete trade (Sept. 11, 2002).

The Cubs' 67-95 record last year was a major disappointment, but their fall from grace did allow them to trade veteran spare parts for minor league depth. Acquisitions of note included righthanded relievers Jared Blasdell (from the Cardinals in a trade for Jeff Fassero) and Jeff Verplancke (Giants for Bill Mueller), and athletic outfielders Jackson Melian (Brewers for Roberto Machado) and Aron Weston (Pirates for two minor leaguers). The best of the lot was Rohlicek, who came from the Astros in an August deal for Tom Gordon. Rohlicek showed a live arm and a pro body at Long Beach State but little command of his pitches. He has improved significantly as a pro, showing much more consistency with his low-90s fastball, slider and changeup. He also has added a cut fastball. Rohlicek throws from a deceptive low three-quarters arm angle, but needs to maintain his arm slot on his offspeed pitches. Strong and durable, he has been compared to Denny Neagle. He'll pitch in high Class A this year.

Year	Club (League)	Class	W	L	ERA	G	GS	CG	SV	IP	H	R	ER	HR	BB	SO	AVG
2001	Pittsfield (NY-P)	A	4	1	2.74	12	9	0	1	43	32	28	13	0	37	33	.208
2002	Michigan (Mid)	A	9	5	2.98	25	25	0	0	151	148	58	50	10	36	95	.256
	Lansing (Mid)	A	0	2	6.92	2	2	0	0	13	12	10	10	3	6	11	.250
MINOR LEAGUE TOTALS			13	8	3.18	39	36	0	1	207	192	96	73	13	79	139	.246

30. Jon Leicester, rhp

Born: Feb. 7, 1979. **Ht.:** 6-2. **Wt.:** 220. **Bats:** R. **Throws:** R. **School:** University of Memphis. **Career Transactions:** Selected by Cubs in 11th round of 2000 draft; signed June 19, 2000.

Given Leicester's career record and 2002 Arizona Fall League performance (8.29 ERA, .341 opponent average), the Cubs' decision to add him to their 40-man roster might seem curious. Given that he has one of the best arms in the system and that several clubs had expressed interest in him, though, the move makes sense. Leicester missed time last year with a sore arm and blisters, but threw 92-95 mph when he was 100 percent. He's still working on the rest of his game. His curveball has its moments but also reverts to a slurve, and his changeup isn't effective. Leicester's lack of confidence doesn't help him throw strikes. He'll try to put it all together this year in Double-A.

Year	Club (League)	Class	W	L	ERA	G	GS	CG	SV	IP	H	R	ER	HR	BB	SO	AVG
2000	Eugene (NWL)	A	1	5	5.44	17	7	0	0	50	47	36	30	4	22	31	.247
2001	Lansing (Mid)	A	9	10	5.29	28	27	1	0	153	182	117	90	16	58	109	.297
2002	Daytona (FSL)	A	2	3	3.97	20	14	0	0	82	77	43	36	2	48	57	.248
	West Tenn (SL)	AA	2	2	4.61	5	4	0	0	27	24	16	14	1	13	18	.231
MINOR LEAGUE TOTALS			14	20	4.91	70	52	1	0	312	330	212	170	23	141	215	.271

CHICAGO
WHITE SOX

TOP 30 PROSPECTS

1. Joe Borchard, of
2. Miguel Olivo, c
3. Anthony Webster, of
4. Kris Honel, rhp
5. Jon Rauch, rhp
6. Corwin Malone, lhp
7. Andy Gonzalez, ss
8. Felix Diaz, rhp
9. Arnie Munoz, lhp
10. Royce Ring, lhp
11. Neal Cotts, lhp
12. Micah Schnurstein, 3b
13. Dave Sanders, lhp
14. Ryan Wing, lhp
15. Brian West, rhp
16. Brian Miller, rhp
17. Tim Hummel, ss/2b
18. Daniel Haigwood, lhp
19. Pedro Lopez, 2b
20. Jason Stumm, rhp
21. Jeremy Reed, of
22. Josh Stewart, lhp
23. Edwin Almonte, rhp
24. Wyatt Allen, rhp
25. Heath Phillips, lhp
26. Josh Rupe, rhp
27. Edwin Yan, 2b
28. Dennis Ulacia, lhp
29. Franklin Francisco, rhp
30. Thomas Brice, of

By Phil Rogers

With a pulse barely detectable at midseason, the White Sox decided it was time for another purge of veterans. Turning to young kids may not have become an annual ritual, but it's always an option.

In this case, out went old-timers such as Sandy Alomar Jr. (though he was brought back), Royce Clayton, Ray Durham and Kenny Lofton. In came the fresh legs of Joe Borchard, Joe Crede, Willie Harris, D'Angelo Jimenez and Miguel Olivo. After running in place for four months, the Sox belatedly kicked it into gear. A 22-12 finish in 2002 allowed Jerry Manuel's team, which had been picked by many to win the American League Central, to save some face with an 81-81 record. More important, it set a positive tone for 2003.

For years, the White Sox have been hyping their young pitchers. Mark Buehrle, Jon Garland and Dan Wright all established themselves as big league starters before turning 24, but many others struggled to fulfill their potential. The untold story was the wave of position players getting ready to arrive.

Crede, who hit .302-36-100 between Triple-A Charlotte and Chicago last year, figures to be a fixture at third base during this decade. Borchard, a switch-hitting outfielder with lots of power, and Olivo, a cannon-armed catcher, should join him by the second half of 2003, if not Opening Day. Harris and Jimenez, infielders acquired in 2002 trades, also will get opportunities to earn regular playing time.

Under general manager Ken Williams, the White Sox often have traded minor leaguers for veterans. He regretted the deal that sent righthanders Josh Fogg, Sean Lowe and Kip Wells to Pittsburgh for Todd Ritchie last year. But Williams is likely to be happier about the January deal that brought Bartolo Colon from the Expos, which makes the Sox favorites in the AL Central again, along with the Twins.

There are still good arms who could help soon, led by lefthander Corwin Malone, 6-foot-11 righthander Jon Rauch and relievers Dave Sanders and Edwin Almonte.

While the Sox miss the contributions of productive scout George Bradley, who died of a heart attack in 2002, their farm and scouting departments remain the best part of the organization. Director of player personnel Duane Shaffer, farm director Bob Fontaine and scouting director Doug Laumann know players and where to find them.

Organization Overview

General Manager: Ken Williams. Farm Director: Bob Fontaine. Scouting Director: Doug Laumann.

2002 PERFORMANCE

Class	Farm Team	League	W	L	Pct.	Finish*	Manager
Majors	Chicago	American	81	81	.500	7th (14)	Jerry Manuel
Triple-A	Charlotte Knights	International	55	88	.385	13th (14)	Nick Capra
Double-A	Birmingham Barons	Southern	79	61	.564	+1st (10)	Wally Backman
High A	Winston-Salem Warthogs	Carolina	50	90	.357	7th (8)	Razor Shines
Low A	Kannapolis Intimidators	South Atlantic	66	74	.471	t-11th (16)	John Orton
Rookie	Bristol Sox	Appalachian	43	25	.632	+2nd (10)	Nick Leyva
Rookie	†AZL White Sox	Arizona	27	29	.482	5th (7)	Jerry Hairston
OVERALL 2002 MINOR LEAGUE RECORD			320	367	.466	24th (30)	

*Finish in overall standings (No. of teams in league). +League champion. †Affiliate will be in Great Falls (Pioneer) in 2003.

ORGANIZATION LEADERS

BATTING
*Minimum 250 At-Bats
*AVG	Aaron Miles, Birmingham	.322
R	Danny Sandoval, Birmingham	86
H	Aaron Miles, Birmingham	171
TB	Aaron Miles, Birmingham	239
2B	Aaron Miles, Birmingham	39
3B	Miguel Olivo, Birmingham	10
HR	Joe Crede, Charlotte	24
RBI	Ryan Hankins, Birmingham	72
BB	Scott Bikowski, Birmingham	58
	Eric Storey, Kannapolis	58
SO	Darron Ingram, Charlotte/Birmingham	162
SB	Edwin Yan, Winston-Salem	88

PITCHING
#Minimum 75 Innings
W	Ryan Wing, Kannapolis	12
L	Heath Phillips, Winston-Salem	16
#ERA	Josh Fields, Win.-Salem/Kannapolis	2.51
G	Gary Majewski, Birmingham	57
	Josh Fields, Win.-Salem/Kannapolis	57
CG	Heath Phillips, Winston-Salem	5
SV	Joe Valentine, Birmingham	36
IP	Heath Phillips, Winston-Salem	179
BB	Corwin Malone, Birmingham	89
SO	Kris Honel, Winston-Salem/Kannapolis	160

BEST TOOLS

Best Hitter for Average	Anthony Webster
Best Power Hitter	Joe Borchard
Fastest Baserunner	Edwin Yan
Best Athlete	Andy Gonzalez
Best Fastball	Brian Miller
Best Curveball	Arnie Munoz
Best Slider	Dave Sanders
Best Changeup	Edwin Almonte
Best Control	Daniel Haigwood
Best Defensive Catcher	Miguel Olivo
Best Defensive Infielder	Pedro Lopez
Best Infield Arm	Jason Dellaero
Best Defensive Outfielder	Mike Spidale
Best Outfield Arm	Joe Borchard

PROJECTED 2006 LINEUP

Catcher	Miguel Olivo
First Base	Paul Konerko
Second Base	D'Angelo Jimenez
Third Base	Joe Crede
Shortstop	Andy Gonzalez
Left Field	Joe Borchard
Center Field	Anthony Webster
Right Field	Magglio Ordonez
Designated Hitter	Frank Thomas
No. 1 Starter	Bartolo Colon

TYLER BOLDEN   TYLER BOLDEN

Aaron Miles   **Gary Majewski**

No. 2 Starter	Mark Buehrle
No. 3 Starter	Dan Wright
No. 4 Starter	Jon Garland
No. 5 Starter	Kris Honel
Closer	Royce Ring

TOP PROSPECTS OF THE DECADE

1993	Jason Bere, rhp
1994	James Baldwin, rhp
1995	Scott Ruffcorn, rhp
1996	Chris Snopek, ss/3b
1997	Mike Cameron, of
1998	Mike Caruso, ss
1999	Carlos Lee, 3b
2000	Kip Wells, rhp
2001	Jon Rauch, rhp
2002	Joe Borchard, of

TOP DRAFT PICKS OF THE DECADE

1993	Scott Christman, lhp
1994	Mark Johnson, c
1995	Jeff Liefer, 3b
1996	*Bobby Seay, lhp
1997	Jason Dellaero, ss
1998	Kip Wells, rhp
1999	Jason Stumm, rhp
2000	Joe Borchard, of
2001	Kris Honel, rhp
2002	Royce Ring, lhp

*Did not sign

ALL-TIME LARGEST BONUSES

Joe Borchard, 2000	$5,300,000
Jason Stumm, 1999	$1,750,000
Royce Ring, 2002	$1,600,000
Kris Honel, 2001	$1,500,000
Kip Wells, 1998	$1,495,000

MinorLeagueDepthChart

CHICAGO WHITE SOX

RANK 15

The White Sox' depth isn't what it was a couple of years ago, when their minor league talent was rated the best in the game and Baseball America had made the White Sox the 2000 Organization of the Year. That is due in large part to their success at graduating prospects to the big leagues. Last year, though, they tried to rush 2000 Minor League Player of the Year Jon Rauch back from shoulder surgery and it cost them. Aside from Joe Borchard, who needs more seasoning in Triple-A, and catcher Miguel Olivo, the system doesn't have much talent that's near major league-ready. With pitchers occupying 20 of the 30 places on the organization's top prospects list, that is clearly the deepest position in the organization.

Note: Depth charts prepared by Josh Boyd. Numbers in parentheses indicate prospect rankings.

LF
Thomas Brice (30)

CF
Anthony Webster (3)
Jeremy Reed (21)
Mike Spidale
Chris Young

RF
Joe Borchard (1)
Daylan Holt

3B
Micah Schnurstein (12)

SS
Andy Gonzalez (7)
Jorge Nunez
Guillermo Reyes
Danny Sandoval

2B
Tim Hummel (17)
Pedro Lopez (19)
Edwin Yan (27)
Aaron Miles
Leonard Luna

1B
Casey Rogowski

C
Miguel Olivo (2)
Charlie Lisk
Chris Stewart

LHP

Starters	Relievers
Corwin Malone (6)	Arnie Munoz (9)
Neal Cotts (11)	Royce Ring (10)
Ryan Wing (14)	Dave Sanders (13)
Daniel Haigwood (18)	Dennis Ulacia (28)
Josh Stewart (22)	Tom Jacquez
Heath Phillips (25)	Byeong An
Tim Bittner	Ryan Meaux
Ryan Rodriguez	Paulino Reynoso
	Felix Arellan

RHP

Starters	Relievers
Kris Honel (4)	Jason Stumm (20)
Jon Rauch (5)	Edwin Almonte (23)
Felix Diaz (8)	Josh Rupe (26)
Brian West (15)	Franklin Francisco (29)
Brian Miller (16)	Kyle Kane
Wyatt Allen (24)	Jon Adkins
Sean Tracey	Todd Deininger
Mitch Wylie	Julio Castro
Brandon McCarthy	Jason Dellaero
Dario Ortiz	Brian Sager

DraftAnalysis

2002 Draft

Best Pro Debut: Managers rated unheralded 3B Micah Schnurstein (7) as the No. 2 prospect in the Rookie-level Arizona League. He hit .332-3-48 and led the circuit with 48 RBIs and a league-record 26 doubles. LHP Daniel Haigwood (16) topped the AZL in wins and went 8-4, 2.28. OF **Jeremy Reed** (2) hit .319 with 17 steals in low Class A.

Best Athlete: 1B Eric Keefner (22) played linebacker for Arizona State as a freshman before transferring to Mesa (Ariz.) CC. An Astros fourth-round pick out of high school, he has size, strength and speed but needs to get the football stiffness out of his body. Reed has decent all-around tools, and the White Sox considered him the best college outfielder in the draft.

Best Pure Hitter: Reed batted .366 to lead Team USA in the summer of 2001. Australian OF Thomas Brice (24) has masterful bat control and hit .480 in his first nine pro games before injuring his shoulder. He finished with a .327 average in Rookie ball.

Best Raw Power: Keefner and OF Seth Morris (21) are strong but have to make more contact. 3B Edgar Varela (31) may be a safer bet after hitting .330-8-40 in Rookie ball. Draft-and-follow OF Tom Collaro has more pop than any of them.

Fastest Runner: Reed runs a 6.75-second 60-yard dash. On a bunt, he gets from the left side to first base in 3.8 seconds.

Best Defensive Player: Schnurstein or Reed.

Best Fastball: RHP Todd Deininger (9) throws 91-94 mph with sink. For sheer velocity, RHP Rick Hummel's (32) fastball touches 96 but isn't as lively or consistent.

Best Breaking Ball: LHP Royce Ring (1) repeats a curveball that grades as a 55 on the 20-80 scouting scale. RHP Josh Rupe (3) uses a violent delivery to unleash curves that range from a 30 to a 70.

Reed

Most Intriguing Background: Haigwood won the first 43 decisions of his high school career before losing in the Arkansas 2-A semifinals last spring. 2B Anthony Manuel's (48) father Jerry manages the White Sox, while C Jeremy Paul's (46) brother Josh catches for Chicago. Neither signed.

Closest To The Majors: Ring, a first-team All-America closer at San Diego State, throws three pitches for strikes, including a 91-92 mph fastball. He's lefthanded and the Sox need bullpen help, which aids his cause.

Best Late-Round Pick: Haigwood's velocity is slightly below-average, but he misses bats because he's so deceptive.

The One Who Got Away: SS Chris Getz (6) has all-around tools but needs to develop. He'll benefit from attending Wake Forest.

Assessment: The White Sox have drafted conservatively since signing Joe Borchard for $5.3 million in 2000. They targeted pitching, using 11 of their first 14 picks on arms, but may have uncovered hidden gems in Schnurstein, Haigwood and Brice.

2001 Draft

RHP Kris Honel (1), SS Andy Gonzalez (5) and OF Anthony Webster (15) all rank among the White Sox' top seven prospects. Keep an eye on LHP Ryan Wing (2) too.   **Grade: B+**

2000 Draft

OF Joe Borchard (1) just may justify his record $5.3 million bonus. SS/2B Tim Hummel (2) could factor into Chicago's infield soon.   **Grade: B**

1999 Draft

This crop could produce as many as 11 major league pitchers in Jason Stumm (1), Matt Ginter (1), Brian West (1), Danny Wright (2), Jon Rauch (3), Josh Stewart (5), Dave Sanders (6), Dennis Ulacia (8), Corwin Malone (9) and the since-traded Matt Guerrier (10) and Joe Valentine (26). Of four first-rounders, only RHP Rob Purvis (1) has been a disappointment. The Sox did fail to sign dynamic 2Bs Bobby Hill (2) and Scott Hairston (18).   **Grade: A**

1998 Draft

Draft-and-follow LHP Mark Buehrle (38) has been a revelation. RHPs Kip Wells (1) and Josh Fogg (3) were used in a disastrous deal for Todd Ritchie, but Chicago did hold on to OF Aaron Rowand (1) and LHP Hector Almonte (26).   **Grade: A**

Note: Draft analysis prepared by Jim Callis. Numbers in parentheses indicate draft rounds.

... Borchard is a superior athlete who has serious power from both sides of the plate.

Joe
Borchard of

Born: Nov. 25, 1978.
Ht.: 6-5. **Wt.:** 220.
Bats: B. **Throws:** R.
School: Stanford University.
Career Transactions: Selected by White Sox in first round (12th overall) of 2000 draft; signed Aug. 8, 2000.

RON VESELY

In September, when Borchard could have been beginning his rookie season as an NFL quarterback taken early in the first round of the football draft, he was finishing up his second full season as a full-time baseball player with a cameo in the big leagues. The White Sox gave him a record $5.3 million bonus to earn that commitment. Borchard hasn't smoothed all the rough ends of his game as fast as Chicago had hoped but still shows tremendous potential. His 2002 season began late after he broke a bone in his right foot during spring training, but he recovered fast and played in 133 games. He looked at place in a big league clubhouse, both during spring training and at the end of the regular season. The Sox believe he will bring valuable leadership skills once he's there on a full-time basis.

Borchard is a superior athlete who has serious power from both sides of the plate. He has an uncanny ability to come through in big situations. He has a strong arm, which he once showed by throwing five touchdown passes for Stanford against UCLA. He isn't a basestealer but runs well for a big man, circling the bases on an inside-the-park homer at Kauffman Stadium in September. The Sox appreciate how hard he has worked to improve. Strikeouts are a part of the package with Borchard, who struggled at times with breaking pitches in 2002. He'll almost certainly strike out 150-plus times if he's a regular and could lead the league in whiffs if he doesn't get a better idea of the strike zone. He has played center field for two seasons but is considered a marginal outfielder. He might benefit from a move to a corner spot, his eventual destination.

The Sox face a difficult decision with Borchard. He's ready to contribute in the big leagues but they must determine if he'd benefit from at least another half-season at Triple-A Charlotte. Many scouts believe he would, pointing to his ratio of almost three strikeouts for every walk in 2002. Borchard went to winter ball in the hopes of improving his chances to stick in the spring. With Magglio Ordonez in right, Borchard will play either left field or center once he becomes a permanent part of Chicago's lineup. He could get an immediate opportunity if center fielder Aaron Rowand comes back slowly from injuries suffered in an offseason dirt bike crash.

Year	Club (League)	Class	AVG	G	AB	R	H	2B	3B	HR	RBI	BB	SO	SB	SLG	OBP
2000	White Sox (AZL)	R	.414	7	29	3	12	4	0	0	8	4	4	0	.552	.485
	Winston-Salem (Car)	A	.288	14	52	7	15	3	0	2	7	6	9	0	.462	.377
	Birmingham (SL)	AA	.227	6	22	3	5	0	1	0	3	3	8	0	.318	.308
2001	Birmingham (SL)	AA	.295	133	515	95	152	27	1	27	98	67	158	5	.509	.384
2002	Winston-Salem (Car)	A	.000	2	3	1	0	0	0	0	0	6	0	0	.000	.667
	Charlotte (IL)	AAA	.272	117	438	62	119	35	2	20	59	49	139	2	.498	.349
	Chicago (AL)	MAJ	.222	16	36	5	8	0	0	2	5	1	14	0	.389	.243
MAJOR LEAGUE TOTALS			.222	16	36	5	8	0	0	2	5	1	14	0	.389	.243
MINOR LEAGUE TOTALS			.286	279	1059	171	303	69	4	49	175	135	318	7	.498	.372

2. Miguel Olivo, c

Born: July 15, 1978. **Ht.:** 6-0. **Wt.:** 180. **Bats:** R. **Throws:** R. **Career Transactions:** Signed out of Dominican Republic by Athletics, Sept. 30, 1996 . . . Traded by Athletics to White Sox, Dec. 12, 2000, completing trade in which White Sox sent RHP Chad Bradford to Athletics for a player to be named (Dec. 7, 2000).

Olivo's cannon arm always has drawn attention, and the White Sox believe they've helped him develop into a solid hitter as well. He has climbed through the minors slowly, spending the last two seasons in Double-A after two in high Class A. He led Birmingham to the Southern League championship, winning playoff MVP honors with four homers, then went deep off Andy Pettitte in his first big league at-bat. Olivo's arm is as strong as any in the big leagues, including that of Pudge Rodriguez. He's a solid hitter who has improved his approach, becoming somewhat more selective. He has excellent speed for a catcher. He not only had 29 steals while playing for ultra-aggressive Birmingham manager Wally Backman, but also led the team with 10 triples. While he has shown power at times in his career, Olivo's extra-base numbers dropped in his second Double-A season. He'll have to continue to improve his receiving skills and ability to handle major league pitchers. With Mark Johnson gone to Oakland, Olivo has a good chance of opening the season in Chicago with a solid spring training performance. Veteran Josh Paul doesn't have nearly the upside he does.

Year	Club (League)	Class	AVG	G	AB	R	H	2B	3B	HR	RBI	BB	SO	SB	SLG	OBP
1997	Athletics East (DSL)	R	.271	63	221	37	60	11	4	6	57	34	36	6	.439	.362
1998	Athletics (AZL)	R	.311	46	164	30	51	11	3	2	23	8	43	2	.451	.356
1999	Modesto (Cal)	A	.305	73	243	46	74	13	6	9	42	21	60	4	.519	.363
2000	Modesto (Cal)	A	.282	58	227	40	64	11	5	5	35	16	53	5	.441	.332
	Midland (TL)	AA	.237	19	59	8	14	2	0	1	9	5	15	0	.322	.297
2001	Birmingham (SL)	AA	.259	93	316	45	82	23	1	14	55	37	62	6	.472	.347
2002	Birmingham (SL)	AA	.306	106	359	51	110	24	10	6	49	40	66	29	.479	.381
	Chicago (AL)	MAJ	.211	6	19	2	4	1	0	1	5	2	5	0	.421	.286
MAJOR LEAGUE TOTALS			.211	6	19	2	4	1	0	1	5	2	5	0	.421	.286
MINOR LEAGUE TOTALS			.286	458	1589	257	455	95	29	43	270	161	335	52	.464	.356

3. Anthony Webster, of

Born: April 10, 1983. **Ht.:** 6-0. **Wt.:** 190. **Bats:** L. **Throws:** R. **School:** Riverside HS, Parsons, Tenn. **Career Transactions:** Selected by White Sox in 15th round of 2001 draft; signed June 16, 2001.

An outstanding high school tailback, Webster picked baseball over football and is proving his instincts to be as good as his ability. Despite rough edges and a lack of amateur pedigree, he has come out firing as a pro, hitting .330 in his first two pro seasons while scoring 96 runs in 116 games. He led Bristol to the Rookie-level Appalachian League title. Webster is reminiscent of a young Marquis Grissom, though he's still learning how to put his explosive speed and his raw power to use on a diamond. He's a natural hitter and made tremendous strides in his approach in 2002, drawing as many walks as strikeouts. He plays the game with a vengeance. Despite his strength, Webster has one homer in two pro seasons. He lacks experience, which sometimes leads to him trying to force the action in center field. He'll have to prove he can hit the quality breaking pitches he'll see in full-season leagues. Webster will open 2003 as a teenager at low Class A Kannapolis. He's a good candidate for step-by-step development but has the talent to force his way upward quickly if he continues to play like he has thus far. All the tools are there for him to develop into an all-star.

Year	Club (League)	Class	AVG	G	AB	R	H	2B	3B	HR	RBI	BB	SO	SB	SLG	OBP
2001	White Sox (AZL)	R	.307	55	225	38	69	9	7	0	30	9	33	18	.409	.332
2002	Bristol (Appy)	R	.352	61	244	58	86	7	3	1	30	38	38	16	.418	.448
MINOR LEAGUE TOTALS			.330	116	469	96	155	16	10	1	60	47	71	34	.414	.396

4. Kris Honel, rhp

Born: Nov. 7, 1982. **Ht.:** 6-5. **Wt.:** 190. **Bats:** R. **Throws:** R. **School:** Providence Catholic HS, New Lenox, Ill. **Career Transactions:** Selected by White Sox in first round (16th overall) of 2001 draft; signed June 14, 2001.

Honel is a rare package for a Chicago team—an elite prospect who knew the way to the city's ballparks before signing a contract. He grew up in the city's southwest suburbs before going 16th overall in the 2001 draft, the highest an Illinois prep pitcher had been taken since Bob Kipper went eighth in 1982. Honel has the basic package that scouts look for, starting with a low-90s fastball and a breaking ball that keeps hitters off his heater. His velocity was down a little in 2002 but was still plenty good because of his command of other pitches. His knuckle-curve, which acts like a slider, might be his best pitch. His fastball is rarely straight, often getting devastating late movement. A shortfall in experience is about the only remaining issue. Honel made strides with his mound presence in 2002 and showed that the elbow problems he developed late in 2001 were nothing to be overly concerned about. Honel will start 2003 at high Class A Winston-Salem. He could be in the mix for Comiskey Park by late 2004, but the Sox haven't gotten great results from recent prospects they rushed to the big leagues, including Jon Garland, Jon Rauch, Kip Wells and Dan Wright.

Year	Club (League)	Class	W	L	ERA	G	GS	CG	SV	IP	H	R	ER	HR	BB	SO	AVG
2001	White Sox (AZL)	R	2	0	1.80	3	1	0	0	10	9	3	2	0	3	8	.257
	Bristol (Appy)	R	2	3	3.13	8	8	0	0	46	41	19	16	4	9	45	.240
2002	Kannapolis (SAL)	A	9	8	2.82	26	26	0	0	153	128	57	48	12	52	152	.228
	Winston-Salem (Car)	A	0	0	1.69	1	1	0	0	5	3	2	1	0	3	8	.150
MINOR LEAGUE TOTALS			13	11	2.81	38	36	0	0	215	181	81	67	16	67	213	.230

5. Jon Rauch, rhp

Born: Sept. 27, 1978. **Ht.:** 6-11. **Wt.:** 230. **Bats:** R. **Throws:** R. **School:** Morehead State University. **Career Transactions:** Selected by White Sox in third round of 1999 draft; signed June 9, 1999.

Coming off shoulder surgery that sidelined him for most of 2001, Rauch inexplicably was pushed by the White Sox. GM Ken Williams erred by allowing him to win a big league job out of spring training, and manager Jerry Manuel exacerbated a bad situation by sitting him for two weeks in April without getting him into a game. Rauch didn't get into a rhythm until the second half. The tallest pitcher in major league history, Rauch parlays his height into unusual arm angles on all his pitches. He's seemingly on top of batters when he releases a pitch, allowing his 91-92 mph fastballs to look much harder. More than just a power pitcher, he has a smooth delivery and throws strikes with two above-average breaking balls. Rauch is something of a frontrunner, pitching very well when he hits on all cylinders but vulnerable to big innings. His control wasn't as sharp as it had been before surgery, though that may have been due to how he was handled. Unlike in 2002, Rauch goes to spring training believing he's ready to pitch in the big leagues. The prospect of that happening diminished when the White Sox traded for Bartolo Colon. It's more likely that he will be headed back to Triple-A, as Chicago may want him to get on a roll before turning to him again.

Year	Club (League)	Class	W	L	ERA	G	GS	CG	SV	IP	H	R	ER	HR	BB	SO	AVG
1999	Bristol (Appy)	R	4	4	4.45	14	9	0	2	57	65	44	28	4	16	66	.269
	Winston-Salem (Car)	A	0	0	3.00	1	1	0	0	6	4	3	2	1	3	7	.174
2000	Winston-Salem (Car)	A	11	3	2.86	18	18	1	0	110	102	49	35	10	33	124	.249
	Birmingham (SL)	AA	5	1	2.25	8	8	2	0	56	36	18	14	4	16	63	.179
2001	Charlotte (IL)	AAA	3	5	5.79	6	6	0	0	28	28	20	18	8	7	27	.248
2002	Chicago (AL)	MAJ	2	1	6.59	8	6	0	0	29	28	26	21	7	14	19	.248
	Charlotte (IL)	AAA	7	8	4.28	19	19	1	0	109	91	60	52	14	42	97	.226
MAJOR LEAGUE TOTALS			2	1	6.59	8	6	0	0	29	28	26	21	7	14	19	.248
MINOR LEAGUE TOTALS			28	19	3.66	66	61	4	2	366	326	194	149	41	117	384	.234

6. Corwin Malone, lhp

Born: July 3, 1980. **Ht.:** 6-3. **Wt.:** 200. **Bats:** R. **Throws:** L. **School:** Thomasville (Ala.) HS. **Career Transactions:** Selected by White Sox in ninth round of 1999 draft; signed June 7, 1999.

After making huge strides in 2001, the one-time linebacker slowed down in 2002, mostly because of control problems. He might have done his best pitching of the season in a March 31 exhibition at Pacific Bell Park, where he blew away the Giants en route to Double-A Birmingham, where he had finished the previous year. Elbow problems ended Malone's season after 22 starts. Malone has the ability to overpower hitters with a fastball that can climb to 93 mph. His natural deception earns him comparisons to Vida Blue. His curveball has tremendous snap on it when his mechanics are under control. He's athletic and coaches rave about his eagerness to learn. Malone tried to throw fewer fastballs in 2002 and paid for it. He didn't command the strike zone as he had the year before, and his walks rose as his strikeouts dipped. He spent much of spring training working on his changeup and seemed to force it into his arsenal, at the cost of too often falling behind in the count. The White Sox believe Malone will be completely healthy in 2003, when he's expected to earn a spot in the Triple-A rotation. He showed improvement after deciding to be more aggressive, and if he gets off to a fast start could join the Chicago rotation if needed in the second half.

Year	Club (League)	Class	W	L	ERA	G	GS	CG	SV	IP	H	R	ER	HR	BB	SO	AVG
1999	White Sox (AZL)	R	0	2	8.00	10	0	0	0	18	16	19	16	1	16	24	.219
2000	Burlington (Mid)	A	2	3	4.90	38	1	0	0	72	67	52	39	4	60	82	.244
2001	Kannapolis (SAL)	A	11	4	2.00	18	18	2	0	112	83	30	25	2	44	119	.208
	Winston-Salem (Car)	A	0	1	1.72	5	5	0	0	37	25	10	7	1	10	38	.192
	Birmingham (SL)	AA	2	0	2.33	4	4	0	0	19	8	5	5	2	12	20	.127
2002	Birmingham (SL)	AA	10	7	4.71	22	22	0	0	124	116	77	65	6	89	89	.248
MINOR LEAGUE TOTALS			25	17	3.70	97	50	2	0	382	315	193	157	16	231	372	.224

7. Andy Gonzalez, ss

Born: Dec. 15, 1981. **Ht.:** 6-2. **Wt.:** 180. **Bats:** R. **Throws:** R. **School:** Florida Air Academy, Melbourne, Fla. **Career Transactions:** Selected by White Sox in fifth round of 2001 draft; signed June 16, 2001.

An all-around athlete, Gonzalez opened eyes immediately after being drafted. He and fellow 2001 pick Anthony Webster have made a smooth transition to pro ball and should continue climbing the ladder together. Gonzalez has the tools to last as a shortstop and is a dangerous hitter who has batted .298 as a pro with 75 RBIs in 114 games. While balls jump off his bat, his best tool might be his arm. Some clubs considered drafting Gonzalez as a pitcher. He covers ground well at shortstop and has improved his fundamentals greatly since being drafted. Because the Sox opted to give him time in extended spring training in 2002, Gonzalez hasn't had to face a year-long grind of playing games. He's expected to develop some power but went deep just once in 2002. Gonzalez' stock will soar if he goes to low Class A and duplicates his Rookie-ball success. He could move quickly in a system that lacks middle-infield depth and gives the Sox a chance for their first homegrown regular at shortstop since Bucky Dent in 1976.

Year	Club (League)	Class	AVG	G	AB	R	H	2B	3B	HR	RBI	BB	SO	SB	SLG	OBP
2001	White Sox (AZL)	R	.323	48	189	33	61	18	1	5	30	15	36	13	.508	.382
2002	Bristol (Appy)	R	.280	66	254	48	71	17	0	1	45	32	43	5	.358	.358
MINOR LEAGUE TOTALS			.298	114	443	81	132	35	1	6	75	47	79	18	.422	.368

8. Felix Diaz, rhp

Born: July 27, 1980. **Ht.:** 6-1. **Wt.:** 170. **Bats:** R. **Throws:** R. **Career Transactions:** Signed out of Dominican Republic by Giants, March 20, 1998 . . . Traded by Giants with LHP Ryan Meaux to White Sox for OF Kenny Lofton, July 28, 2002.

Once considered the crown jewel of San Francisco's increased efforts in Latin America, Diaz was deemed expendable among a wealth of power righthanders in the organization. The White Sox landed him in a deadline deal for Kenny Lofton. Diaz throws gas. He often works in the mid-90s and has a hard slider that he throws in the mid-80s. His changeup is also a plus pitch. He has all the pitches he needs to dominate. Durability is a major question for Diaz, who missed time with a tender arm in 2001 and an ankle injury in 2002. He generates tremendous arm speed from a slight body and hasn't stayed healthy for an entire season. He aged one year in baseball's birthdate crackdown, but he still wasn't old for Double-A. The sky's the limit for Diaz and his low-mileage arm. It's possible the White Sox will move him to the bullpen, hoping he'll become another Francisco Rodriguez, but for now he'll get a chance to climb as a starter. If he doesn't open in Triple-A, he should be there at season's end, trying to put himself in Chicago's 2004 plans.

Year	Club (League)	Class	W	L	ERA	G	GS	CG	SV	IP	H	R	ER	HR	BB	SO	AVG
1998	Giants (DSL)	R	0	4	7.55	14	5	0	0	39	52	44	33	4	26	34	.306
1999	Giants (DSL)	R	0	0	0.75	3	3	0	0	12	6	2	1	0	7	19	.150
2000	Giants (AZL)	R	3	4	4.16	11	11	0	0	63	56	35	29	0	16	58	.232
	Salem-Keizer (NWL)	A	0	1	8.10	3	0	0	0	3	6	6	3	2	1	2	.400
2001	Hagerstown (SAL)	A	1	4	3.66	15	12	0	0	52	49	27	21	4	16	56	.245
2002	Shreveport (TL)	AA	3	5	2.70	12	12	1	0	60	54	22	18	1	23	48	.240
	Birmingham (SL)	AA	4	0	3.48	7	6	0	0	31	25	14	12	4	8	30	.207
MINOR LEAGUE TOTALS			11	18	4.05	65	49	1	0	260	248	150	117	15	97	247	.245

9. Arnie Munoz, lhp

Born: June 21, 1982. **Ht.:** 5-9. **Wt.:** 170. **Bats:** L. **Throws:** L. **Career Transactions:** Signed out of Dominican Republic by White Sox, Dec. 20, 1998.

Because the baby-faced Munoz isn't intimidating and has been used in the thankless role of middle relief, he has escaped attention. But there's no overlooking his results. He asserted himself by pitching well in Class A in 2001, then skipped a level and was unfazed by Double-A as a teenager. He pitched lights out in the Dominican this winter. There aren't many minor league curveballs better than the Zito-esque one Munoz possesses. His fastball parks in the 87-89 range and can be run up to 91 when needed. Those two pitches alone can make him unhittable for all but the best lefthanders. An improved changeup and a consistent sinker help him attack righties. His pickoff move freezes runners. Munoz wears down after 30-40 pitches, losing his arm angle, which flattens out his pitches. He has averaged 4.6 walks per nine innings as pro, though he cut that mark to 3.6 in 2002. While a stop in Triple-A is likely, Munoz could give the White Sox the same second-half lift they received when Mark Buehrle joined the bullpen in 2000. Munoz should occupy a set-up role, but it's not far-fetched to project him as a middle-of-the-rotation starter.

Year	Club (League)	Class	W	L	ERA	G	GS	CG	SV	IP	H	R	ER	HR	BB	SO	AVG
1999	White Sox (AZL)	R	0	2	5.25	14	0	0	1	12	13	10	7	1	8	12	.255
2000	Burlington (Mid)	A	2	3	6.81	22	0	0	0	38	45	34	29	2	25	44	.294
2001	Kannapolis (SAL)	A	6	3	2.49	60	0	0	12	80	41	24	22	2	42	115	.161
2002	Birmingham (SL)	AA	6	0	2.61	51	0	0	6	72	62	29	21	6	29	78	.231
MINOR LEAGUE TOTALS			14	8	3.51	147	0	0	19	202	161	97	79	11	104	249	.221

10. Royce Ring, lhp

Born: Dec. 21, 1980. **Ht.:** 6-0. **Wt.:** 220. **Bats:** L. **Throws:** L. **School:** San Diego State University. **Career Transactions:** Selected by White Sox in first round (18th overall) of 2002 draft; signed June 10, 2002.

Armed with a mid-90s fastball and a theme song (Metallica's "Sad But True"), Ring was one of the best shows in college baseball in 2002. He made a name for himself by sprinting in from the bullpen, pawing at the mound and then throwing as hard as possible. That formula helped him set San Diego State records for saves in a season and career, and got him drafted 16th overall in June. Ring is a perpetual motion machine who comes at hitters. His low-90s fastball can be an overpowering pitch. His curveball and changeup are also effective. He wants the ball with the game on the line. His control isn't considered a major problem, but Ring will get to Comiskey Park quicker if he cuts down on his walks. His weight was an issue at San Diego State and bears watching. College closers drafted in the first round don't have the greatest history as pros, but Ring could be the exception to that rule. The Sox hope he'll take the fast track to the majors, but there's a crowd of lefty relievers ahead of him, headed by Damaso Marte, Dave Sanders and Arnie Munoz. Ring could open 2003 in Double-A and may get a look in Chicago in September.

Year	Club (League)	Class	W	L	ERA	G	GS	CG	SV	IP	H	R	ER	HR	BB	SO	AVG
2002	White Sox (AZL)	R	0	0	0.00	3	0	0	0	5	2	0	0	0	0	9	.118
	Winston-Salem (Car)	A	2	0	3.91	21	0	0	5	23	20	11	10	2	11	22	.247
MINOR LEAGUE TOTALS			2	0	3.21	24	0	0	5	28	22	11	10	2	11	31	.224

11. Neal Cotts, lhp

Born: March 25, 1980. **Ht.:** 6-2. **Wt.:** 200. **Bats:** L. **Throws:** L. **School:** Illinois State University. **Career Transactions:** Selected by Athletics in second round of 2001 draft; signed June 13, 2001 . . . Traded by Athletics with OF Daylan Holt to White Sox, Dec. 16, 2002, completing trade in which the Athletics sent RHP Billy Koch, two players to be named and cash to White Sox for RHP Keith Foulke, RHP Joe Valentine and C Mark Johnson (Dec. 3, 2002).

Cotts was a 2001 second-round pick from Illinois State, the highest selection in school history. He returned to his home state in December in a trade that saw the Athletics and White Sox swap closers Keith Foulke and Billy Koch. Though Cotts' fastball barely breaks 90 mph, he has averaged 11.1 strikeouts per nine innings as a pro. He changes speeds with aplomb and hitters have great difficulty making sound contact. He pitched most of 2002 using just a fastball and changeup before he began working on his curveball. The curve showed great improvement late in the season and during instructional league. That third pitch will be critical if he's to remain a starter. He also needs better control. Cotts will work on both those areas in Double-A this year.

Year	Club (League)	Class	W	L	ERA	G	GS	CG	SV	IP	H	R	ER	HR	BB	SO	AVG
2001	Vancouver (NWL)	A	1	0	3.09	9	7	0	0	35	28	14	12	2	13	44	.215
	Visalia (Cal)	A	3	2	2.32	7	7	0	0	31	27	14	8	0	15	34	.225
2002	Modesto (Cal)	A	12	6	4.12	28	28	0	0	138	123	72	63	5	87	178	.239
MINOR LEAGUE TOTALS			16	8	3.67	44	42	0	0	204	178	100	83	7	115	256	.233

12. Micah Schnurstein, 3b

Born: July 18, 1984. **Ht.:** 6-1. **Wt.:** 200. **Bats:** R. **Throws:** R. **School:** Basic HS, Henderson, Nev. **Career Transactions:** Selected by White Sox in seventh round of 2002 draft; signed June 7, 2002.

Schnurstein wasn't expected to go as high as the seventh round in the 2002 draft, but he more than justified Chicago's faith by destroying the Rookie-level Arizona League. He hit the ball as hard as any player in the AZL, as nearly half his hits went for extra bases, including a league-record 26 doubles. He also played a solid third base. Schnurstein is a pure hitter who pounds the ball. His home run power should improve as he gains strength. While he started 2002 as a second baseman, he made a smooth transition to the hot corner. He has soft hands and enough arm for the position. The stocky Schnurstein doesn't run well. He could stand to improve his patience at the plate, but the White Sox aren't complaining about the initial results of his aggressive approach. Extended spring training and a second year in a short-season league are possibilities for Schnurstein, but don't be surprised if he hits his way onto the Kannapolis roster. He'd join Anthony Webster, Andy Gonzalez and Pedro Lopez in a lineup that should produce runs. Schnurstein has the potential to develop into a Phil Nevin clone.

Year	Club (League)	Class	AVG	G	AB	R	H	2B	3B	HR	RBI	BB	SO	SB	SLG	OBP
2002	White Sox (AZL)	R	.332	50	205	28	68	26	1	3	48	12	34	1	.512	.373
MINOR LEAGUE TOTALS			.332	50	205	28	68	26	1	3	48	12	34	1	.512	.373

13. Dave Sanders, lhp

Born: Aug. 29, 1979. **Ht.:** 6-0. **Wt.:** 200. **Bats:** L. **Throws:** L. **School:** Barton County (Kan.) CC. **Career Transactions:** Selected by White Sox in sixth round of 1999 draft; signed July 12, 1999.

The White Sox' 1999 draft just keeps looking deeper and deeper in regards to pitching. It has already produced big leaguers in Matt Ginter, Danny Wright and Jon Rauch and delivered prospects Jason Stumm, Brian West, Dennis Ulacia, Corwin Malone, Matt Guerrier (traded to the Pirates for Damaso Marte) and Joe Valentine (dealt to the Athletics in the Keith Foulke-Billy Koch exchange). Sanders and fellow lefty Josh Stewart are the latest pitchers from the 1999 draft to open eyes, thanks to their performances in Double-A and the Arizona Fall League. Sanders made the most of his second season in Birmingham, joining Arnie Munoz to give the Barons two lefthanded bullpen weapons. He used a power slider and a 90-91 mph fastball to average nearly a strikeout per inning. He worked three perfect innings of relief in the 12-inning victory that wrapped up a Southern League title, then led the AFL in ERA. He'll move up to Triple-A in 2003 and could join the White Sox sooner than might be expected.

Year	Club (League)	Class	W	L	ERA	G	GS	CG	SV	IP	H	R	ER	HR	BB	SO	AVG
1999	White Sox (AZL)	R	1	0	1.10	7	1	0	1	16	12	3	2	0	6	26	.207
2000	Winston-Salem (Car)	A	3	2	5.21	51	0	0	6	48	39	35	28	4	39	50	.215
2001	Birmingham (SL)	AA	3	0	2.65	36	0	0	0	34	27	12	10	1	25	25	.227
2002	Birmingham (SL)	AA	3	1	1.84	47	0	0	0	64	56	17	13	3	28	61	.234
MINOR LEAGUE TOTALS			10	3	2.94	141	1	0	7	162	134	67	53	8	98	162	.224

14. Ryan Wing, lhp

Born: Feb. 1, 1982. **Ht.:** 6-2. **Wt.:** 170. **Bats:** L. **Throws:** L. **School:** Riverside (Calif.) CC. **Career Transactions:** Selected by White Sox in second round of 2001 draft; signed July 23, 2001.

Mononucleosis limited Wing to one outing after he signed in 2001, but his 2002 season was worth waiting for. He led Kannapolis in victories and kept getting better as the season went on. Sox coaches rave about Wing's arm. He throws in the low-90s with hard, sinking action on his fastball, and he has an excellent slider. His delivery gives him some natural deception and he has an arm angle that makes him extremely tough on lefthanders. He has shown a willingness to knock hitters off the plate. Wing doesn't yet have the command and polish of some of the organization's other lefties—Josh Stewart, Dennis Ulacia and Heath Phillips, to name three—but he has a better arm than just about any of them except for Corwin Malone.

Year	Club (League)	Class	W	L	ERA	G	GS	CG	SV	IP	H	R	ER	HR	BB	SO	AVG
2001	Bristol (Appy)	R	1	0	9.00	1	0	0	0	1	1	1	1	0	0	2	.200
2002	Kannapolis (SAL)	A	12	7	3.78	25	21	0	0	124	111	64	52	6	60	109	.240
MINOR LEAGUE TOTALS			13	7	3.83	26	21	0	0	125	112	65	53	6	60	111	.239

15. Brian West, rhp

Born: Aug. 4, 1980. **Ht.:** 6-4. **Wt.:** 230. **Bats:** R. **Throws:** R. **School:** West Monroe (La.) HS. **Career Transactions:** Selected by White Sox in first round (35th overall) of 1999 draft; signed July 1, 1999.

A staple on the White Sox prospect list since 2000, West has climbed through the system one rung at a time. He hasn't yet had a winning season but has proven to be a durable starter. His total of 149 innings last year was his low as a pro. He's a large-framed guy who once was targeted by major-college football programs as a defensive end. Though the Sox see lots of upside in him, he hasn't been an all-star since pitching in the low Class A Midwest League in 2000. West throws a two-seam fastball that reaches the low 90s and features lots of movement, and he has developed an outstanding changeup. He sometimes struggles to put away hitters, however, and his ratio of strikeouts per nine innings fell from 6.9 in high Class A to 5.5 in Double-A. He continues to work on his curveball. A repeat of Double-A isn't out of the question at least to open the 2003 season, as West faded down the stretch in 2002 and lost five of his final six starts.

Year	Club (League)	Class	W	L	ERA	G	GS	CG	SV	IP	H	R	ER	HR	BB	SO	AVG
1999	White Sox (AZL)	R	0	1	13.50	2	0	0	0	5	10	7	7	0	2	3	.500
	Bristol (Appy)	R	1	2	10.50	8	1	0	2	18	26	25	21	4	14	17	.317
2000	Burlington (Mid)	A	8	9	3.78	24	24	0	0	148	146	81	62	3	73	90	.261
	Winston-Salem (Car)	A	0	1	11.37	2	2	0	0	6	10	12	8	2	6	3	.323
2001	Winston-Salem (Car)	A	7	12	3.46	28	28	3	0	169	179	75	65	11	70	130	.281
2002	Birmingham (SL)	AA	9	11	4.34	27	26	0	0	149	129	91	72	9	71	91	.236
MINOR LEAGUE TOTALS			25	36	4.27	91	81	3	2	495	500	291	235	29	236	334	.267

16. Brian Miller, rhp

Born: Oct. 18, 1982. **Ht.:** 6-3. **Wt.:** 200. **Bats:** R. **Throws:** R. **School:** Charlotte (Mich.) HS. **Career Transactions:** Selected by White Sox in 20th round of 2001 draft; signed Aug. 15, 2001.

Questions about signability caused Miller to slide in the 2001 draft, but there are few doubts about his arm. He's looking like a major coup for area scout Nathan Durst and scouting director Doug Laumann, who got the deal done. Miller was rated as the top prep pitcher in Michigan in 2001 but indicated that he had made a firm commitment to Michigan State. The Sox negotiated hard to get him signed just before classes began. He started his pro career in extended spring training in 2002, then turned in a solid performance in the Appalachian League, winning a team-high seven games to help Bristol to the championship. Miller has a power arm and a pitcher's body. He has gained strength and velocity since signing, with his fastball jumping from the low 90s to the mid-90s. His changeup was a good pitch when he signed and has improved. Miller has yet to be tested in full-season leagues, but few pitchers in the organization have a higher ceiling.

Year	Club (League)	Class	W	L	ERA	G	GS	CG	SV	IP	H	R	ER	HR	BB	SO	AVG
2002	Bristol (Appy)	R	7	3	4.30	13	13	0	0	61	57	32	29	3	30	63	.251
MINOR LEAGUE TOTALS			7	3	4.30	13	13	0	0	61	57	32	29	3	30	63	.251

17. Tim Hummel, ss/2b

Born: Nov. 18, 1978. **Ht.:** 6-2. **Wt.:** 195. **Bats:** R. **Throws:** R. **School:** Old Dominion University. **Career Transactions:** Selected by White Sox in second round of 2000 draft; signed June 21, 2000.

Following a disappointing season in Triple-A, Hummel found his stride again in the

Arizona Fall League. In his second year in the AFL, he hit .303 and had the best walk-strike-out ratio in the league (18-10). The Sox hope he can continue that trend when he returns for a second tour of the International League. He's considered a textbook hitter with a unusually pure righthanded stroke. But he couldn't get himself going until late 2002 and slipped behind D'Angelo Jimenez and Willie Harris in the organization's pecking order. Hummel, an All-America shortstop at Old Dominion, had been considered the likely successor to Ray Durham before Harris and Jimenez were acquired in trades. He constantly has been juggled between shortstop, second base and even third. He's a reliable fielder up the middle—which showed as he made one error in 28 games between short and second in the AFL—but lacks the speed and range of a typical shortstop. His first order of business in 2003 is to re-establish himself as a possible No. 2 hitter.

Year	Club (League)	Class	AVG	G	AB	R	H	2B	3B	HR	RBI	BB	SO	SB	SLG	OBP
2000	Burlington (Mid)	A	.326	39	144	22	47	9	1	1	21	21	20	8	.424	.411
	Winston-Salem (Car)	A	.327	27	98	15	32	7	0	1	9	13	12	1	.429	.416
2001	Birmingham (SL)	AA	.290	134	524	83	152	33	6	7	63	62	69	14	.416	.364
2002	Charlotte (IL)	AAA	.260	142	523	55	136	33	0	4	41	51	95	6	.346	.332
MINOR LEAGUE TOTALS			.285	342	1289	175	367	82	7	13	134	147	196	29	.389	.361

18. Daniel Haigwood, lhp

Born: Nov. 19, 1983. **Ht.:** 6-2. **Wt.:** 190. **Bats:** B. **Throws:** L. **School:** Midland HS, Batesville, Ark. **Career Transactions:** Selected by White Sox in 16th round of 2002 draft; signed June 4, 2002.

Scouts love radar guns, but even so it's hard to figure how Haigwood slipped through the cracks. He was dominant throughout his high school career, winning his first 43 decisions and not allowing an earned run as a senior before losing 5-3 in the Arkansas state 2-A semifinals. His playoff run included a no-hitter and a 16-strikeout performance in which he threw 78 of 94 pitches for strikes. Yet Haigwood slid deep into the 2002 draft, only in part because he was committed to the University of Arkansas. The White Sox found he wanted to play pro ball, however, and it's no wonder why. He was outstanding in the Arizona League, leading the league in wins and showing fine command. Haigwood isn't overpowering but can hit 90 with his fastball. He complements it with a plus curveball—it was rated the best at the Perfect Game predraft showcase in May—and has learned to throw a two-seam fastball. He should increase velocity as he matures. His changeup needs work but he can throw it for strikes. Scouts give him high marks for his pitching acumen, saying he has a natural feel for setting up hitters. Haigwood probably is headed for the low Class A South Atlantic League in 2003. If he keeps this up, a lot of teams are going to be kicking themselves for getting scared off such an obvious pick.

Year	Club (League)	Class	W	L	ERA	G	GS	CG	SV	IP	H	R	ER	HR	BB	SO	AVG
2002	White Sox (AZL)	R	8	4	2.28	14	14	0	0	75	69	31	19	2	26	74	.244
MINOR LEAGUE TOTALS			8	4	2.28	14	14	0	0	75	69	31	19	2	26	74	.244

19. Pedro Lopez, 2b

Born: April 28, 1984. **Ht.:** 6-1. **Wt.:** 160. **Bats:** R. **Throws:** R. **Career Transactions:** Signed out of Dominican Republic by White Sox, Sept. 14, 2000.

Signed at age 16, Lopez twice has excelled in short-season leagues. He's a career .316 hitter and an outstanding defensive player. Signed as a shortstop, he mostly has played second base with the more highly regarded Andy Gonzalez playing alongside him. Lopez has range, soft hands, quick reflexes and the toughness to hang in on the double-play pivot. He cut his error total down from 19 to six in his second pro season. Lopez has unusual bat control for such a young player. He's difficult to strike out, uses the whole field and is an excellent bunter. He has good speed and could develop into a 40-steal man. He'll tackle a full-season league for the first time in 2003 but should have no problems continuing his promising development.

Year	Club (League)	Class	AVG	G	AB	R	H	2B	3B	HR	RBI	BB	SO	SB	SLG	OBP
2001	White Sox (AZL)	R	.312	50	199	26	62	11	3	1	19	16	24	12	.412	.359
2002	Bristol (Appy)	R	.319	63	260	42	83	11	0	0	35	20	27	22	.362	.370
MINOR LEAGUE TOTALS			.316	113	459	68	145	22	3	1	54	36	51	34	.383	.365

20. Jason Stumm, rhp

Born: April 13, 1981. **Ht.:** 6-2. **Wt.:** 215. **Bats:** R. **Throws:** R. **School:** Centralia (Wash.) HS. **Career Transactions:** Selected by White Sox in first round (15th overall) of 1999 draft; signed June 21, 1999.

Stumm might as well wear a jersey that says "Handle With Care." A former all-everything in three sports, he has been plagued by arm injuries since opting for a baseball career. He was slow to recover from Tommy John surgery in 2000, working just 52 innings the last two years, and underwent shoulder surgery after the 2002 season. He'll be sidelined for the first part of this season. Before surgery, Stumm threw 96-97 mph and was beginning to develop his secondary pitches. The White Sox had limited him to a maximum of two innings in his 22 outings in 2002 and for a time were encouraged by the results. His velocity appeared all the way back but it came at the expense of a shoulder injury. The Sox root for him because he's a good kid and a proven winner, but the odds against him seem to grow every year.

Year	Club (League)	Class	W	L	ERA	G	GS	CG	SV	IP	H	R	ER	HR	BB	SO	AVG
1999	White Sox (AZL)	R	0	0	3.27	3	2	0	0	11	13	8	4	2	3	9	.310
	Burlington (Mid)	A	3	3	5.32	10	10	0	0	44	47	31	26	4	27	33	.276
2000	Burlington (Mid)	A	2	7	4.61	13	13	2	0	66	66	46	34	6	30	62	.262
2001	White Sox (AZL)	R	0	2	2.25	4	4	0	0	12	6	4	3	0	5	12	.154
2002	Kannapolis (SAL)	A	0	1	2.25	22	0	0	5	40	37	10	10	1	12	45	.245
MINOR LEAGUE TOTALS			5	13	4.00	52	29	2	5	173	169	99	77	13	77	161	.258

21. Jeremy Reed, of

Born: June 15, 1981. **Ht.:** 6-0. **Wt.:** 180. **Bats:** L. **Throws:** L. **School:** Long Beach State University. **Career Transactions:** Selected by White Sox in second round of 2002 draft; signed June 25, 2002.

A former Alaska League MVP and Team USA batting leader, Reed is your basic Dave Martinez starter kit. He played mostly first base in his first two seasons at Long Beach State but was drafted as an outfielder and played the outfield exclusively at Kannapolis, where his .319 average was almost 30 points higher than any teammate. Reed is a line-drive hitter who uses the entire park. He has limited power but could develop more because of his solid grasp of hitting. Reed has good speed and is aggressive on the bases, stretching singles into doubles. He's not a blazer but could steal 30-40 bases a season. Reed played some center field in his pro debut but fits better in right. He's an interesting guy, especially for an organization that hasn't had much luck with lefthanded hitters.

Year	Club (League)	Class	AVG	G	AB	R	H	2B	3B	HR	RBI	BB	SO	SB	SLG	OBP
2002	Kannapolis (SAL)	A	.319	57	210	37	67	15	0	4	32	11	24	17	.448	.377
MINOR LEAGUE TOTALS			.319	57	210	37	67	15	0	4	32	11	24	17	.448	.377

22. Josh Stewart, lhp

Born: Dec. 5, 1978. **Ht.:** 6-3. **Wt.:** 205. **Bats:** L. **Throws:** L. **School:** Memphis University. **Career Transactions:** Selected by White Sox in fifth round of 1999 draft; signed June 7, 1999.

Stewart earned a 40-man roster spot with a breakout season in 2002 as he helped his teams win Southern League and Arizona Fall League championships. He especially opened eyes in the AFL, where he was second to White Sox teammate David Sanders with a 0.81 ERA and won the title game, allowing only one unearned run over six innings. Though there's nothing overly impressive about Stewart's stuff, his overall package reminds some of Mike Sirotka, the lefty who won 15 games for the 2000 Sox before tearing his labrum. Command and confidence are Stewart's keys. He throws in the high 80s and has a plus curveball. He changes speeds, moves the ball in and out on hitters and works at the bottom of the strike zone. Stewart needs to follow up with a strong 2003 season in Triple-A to put himself in the big league picture, either with the White Sox or for an interested organization elsewhere.

Year	Club (League)	Class	W	L	ERA	G	GS	CG	SV	IP	H	R	ER	HR	BB	SO	AVG
1999	Bristol (Appy)	R	1	0	1.50	5	0	0	1	18	13	5	3	0	5	25	.206
	Burlington (Mid)	A	2	0	7.28	16	0	0	1	30	32	25	24	6	21	35	.283
2000	Burlington (Mid)	A	9	9	4.57	25	25	1	0	138	157	84	70	14	58	82	.290
2001	Winston-Salem (Car)	A	4	6	3.82	12	12	1	0	64	64	41	27	6	28	38	.258
	Birmingham (SL)	AA	3	4	6.67	16	16	0	0	82	110	68	61	7	42	47	.330
2002	Birmingham (SL)	AA	11	7	3.53	26	26	1	0	150	145	65	59	11	56	92	.255
MINOR LEAGUE TOTALS			30	26	4.56	100	79	3	2	482	521	288	244	44	210	319	.279

23. Edwin Almonte, rhp

Born: Dec. 17, 1976. **Ht.:** 6-3. **Wt.:** 200. **Bats:** R. **Throws:** R. **School:** St. Francis (N.Y.) College. **Career Transactions:** Selected by White Sox in 26th round of 1998 draft; signed June 6, 1998.

In an organization that should understand the value of an excellent changeup—thank you, Keith Foulke—Almonte should be well positioned. But at his age, the clock is ticking loudly. He has climbed without a hitch, leading the minors with a total of 62 saves the last two seasons. But Almonte hasn't performed well in front of big league manager Jerry Manuel, getting rocked last spring when he arrived after a heavy workload in winter ball.

Almonte's fastball rarely hits 90 mph but is set up by a dynamite changeup that he almost never telegraphs. He also has a slider and generally throws strikes with all his pitches. Almonte grew up on the streets of New York, where he developed lots of mental toughness. The Sox would have been well advised to give Almonte a look last September but limited callups in a cost-cutting move. If there's not going to be a place for Almonte on the staff in 2003, the Sox should move him elsewhere. He's ready to help someone.

Year	Club (League)	Class	W	L	ERA	G	GS	CG	SV	IP	H	R	ER	HR	BB	SO	AVG
1998	White Sox (AZL)	R	0	0	0.93	5	0	0	0	10	6	5	1	0	1	8	.171
	Bristol (Appy)	R	3	0	3.38	8	3	0	0	27	29	14	10	3	4	26	.271
1999	Burlington (Mid)	A	9	12	3.03	37	5	2	5	116	107	48	39	5	28	85	.239
2000	Winston-Salem (Car)	A	3	1	3.16	33	7	0	2	77	66	32	27	2	20	73	.227
	Birmingham (SL)	AA	1	3	4.54	7	6	0	0	40	45	22	20	5	9	21	.304
2001	Birmingham (SL)	AA	1	4	1.49	54	0	0	36	66	58	16	11	4	16	62	.228
2002	Charlotte (IL)	AAA	2	3	2.24	50	0	0	26	60	52	16	15	6	12	56	.236
MINOR LEAGUE TOTALS			19	23	2.80	194	21	2	69	395	363	153	123	25	90	331	.242

24. Wyatt Allen, rhp

Born: April 12, 1980. **Ht.:** 6-4. **Wt.:** 205. **Bats:** R. **Throws:** R. **School:** University of Tennessee. **Career Transactions:** Selected by White Sox in first round (39th overall) of 2001 draft; signed June 26, 2001.

Despite his periodic flashes of brilliance, most organizations considered Allen a project coming out of college. The White Sox knew his erratic delivery needed a lot of work but were intrigued by his arm and took him 39th overall in the 2001 draft. They still like his ceiling but were disappointed that Allen didn't prove to be a quicker study in his first full season as a pro. His season was not a washout, as he made 29 starts and worked more than 167 innings. But he had 86 walks and didn't miss many bats, so there's much work to be done. Allen hasn't shown the velocity he had at Tennessee—he was clocked at 97 mph in the Cape Cod League after his sophomore season—but mostly needs to continue working on his curveball and changeup. He's likely to return to high Class A unless he shows signs of a breakthrough in spring training.

Year	Club (League)	Class	W	L	ERA	G	GS	CG	SV	IP	H	R	ER	HR	BB	SO	AVG
2001	Kannapolis (SAL)	A	4	5	3.16	12	11	2	0	63	60	29	22	4	16	45	.253
2002	Winston-Salem (Car)	A	8	9	4.45	28	28	1	0	162	163	91	80	15	80	110	.263
	Charlotte (IL)	AAA	0	1	9.00	1	1	0	0	5	6	5	5	2	6	2	.300
MINOR LEAGUE TOTALS			12	15	4.20	41	40	3	0	229	229	125	107	21	102	157	.261

25. Heath Phillips, lhp

Born: March 24, 1982. **Ht.:** 6-3. **Wt.:** 205. **Bats:** L. **Throws:** L. **School:** Lake City (Fla.) CC. **Career Transactions:** Selected by White Sox in 10th round of 2000 draft; signed May 12, 2001.

Don't judge Phillips by his 8-23 career record. He has pitched in bad luck for teams that have given him minimal run support. He led Sox minor leaguers with 179 innings in 2002 and was dominant at times, working five complete games with three shutouts. His polish in outings like those has prompted comparisons to Mark Buehrle, another quick study. But Phillips doesn't have quite the command that turned Buehrle into a big winner at a young age. He throws a lot of strikes with a high-80s fastball that has good movement, and a slider that keeps righthanded hitters off balance. It will be interesting to see how effective Phillips can be when he's on a strong team with a good bullpen. The Sox hope that situation presents itself when he arrives in Double-A this year.

Year	Club (League)	Class	W	L	ERA	G	GS	CG	SV	IP	H	R	ER	HR	BB	SO	AVG
2001	Kannapolis (SAL)	A	2	7	3.64	14	12	1	0	72	74	36	29	1	18	54	.276
2002	Winston-Salem (Car)	A	6	16	3.52	28	28	5	0	179	184	82	70	17	50	112	.268
MINOR LEAGUE TOTALS			8	23	3.55	42	40	6	0	251	258	118	99	18	68	166	.270

26. Josh Rupe, rhp

Born: Aug. 18, 1982. **Ht.:** 6-2. **Wt.:** 180. **Bats:** R. **Throws:** R. **School:** Louisburg (N.C.) JC. **Career Transactions:** Selected by White Sox in third round of 2002 draft; signed June 14, 2002.

Rupe was drafted as a project. After he signed, the White Sox limited his work while overhauling his mechanics, similar to the program they drew up for Corwin Malone. Rupe just needs to harness his live arm. He has a 91-93 mph fastball, but his best pitch is an old-fashioned, Nolan Ryan-style overhand curveball that starts out at the top of the strike zone and ends up at the knees. Bristol manager Nick Leyva called it the best breaking pitch he's seen from a young pitcher in years. He also has strong makeup. Rupe sometimes looks mechanical on the mound as he tries to learn his delivery. He'll need a lot of innings to be able to repeat the changes that Sox coaches have implemented. Until he figures it all out, control will be an issue. Rupe probably will spend 2003 as a starter in low Class A.

Year	Club (League)	Class	W	L	ERA	G	GS	CG	SV	IP	H	R	ER	HR	BB	SO	AVG
2002	Bristol (Appy)	R	3	3	5.26	17	2	0	0	38	38	23	22	4	22	40	.260
MINOR LEAGUE TOTALS			3	3	5.26	17	2	0	0	38	38	23	22	4	22	40	.260

27. Edwin Yan, 2b

Born: Feb. 18, 1982. **Ht.:** 6-0. **Wt.:** 160. **Bats:** B. **Throws:** R. **Career Transactions:** Signed out of Dominican Republic by Pirates, Jan. 4, 1999 . . . Traded by Pirates with LHP Damaso Marte to White Sox for RHP Matt Guerrier, March 27, 2002.

This guy can fly. Some in the White Sox organization even believe Yan could steal bases standing up. He led the minors with 88 steals in 107 attempts last year. Yan's batting average slipped from .283 in low Class A to only .253 after he was promoted to high Class A. Despite his speed, the switch-hitting Yan hasn't become more than a singles hitter. He needs to gain strength, especially in his upper body. He's athletic and has above-average range at second base but needs work on his fundamentals. He always has been willing to work. He will be tested by Double-A pitchers but needs to make only minor adjustments with the advantage his speed gives him. Drawing more walks would help, because his value comes from what he can do once he gets on base.

Year	Club (League)	Class	AVG	G	AB	R	H	2B	3B	HR	RBI	BB	SO	SB	SLG	OBP
1999	Pirates (DSL)	R	.300	69	250	61	75	6	1	3	21	49	49	48	.368	.424
2000	Pirates (GCL)	R	.357	12	42	10	15	0	1	0	1	12	8	5	.405	.500
2001	Hickory (SAL)	A	.283	128	446	58	126	8	4	2	24	42	62	56	.332	.347
2002	Winston-Salem (Car)	A	.253	132	490	78	124	6	7	4	35	42	57	88	.318	.312
MINOR LEAGUE TOTALS			.277	341	1228	207	340	20	13	9	81	145	176	197	.336	.356

28. Dennis Ulacia, lhp

Born: April 2, 1981. **Ht.:** 6-1. **Wt.:** 185. **Bats:** L. **Throws:** L. **School:** Monsignor Pace HS, Opa Locka, Fla. **Career Transactions:** Selected by White Sox in eighth round of 1999 draft; signed, June 16, 1999.

This is getting confusing. In three full seasons as a pro, Ulacia has gone from mediocre to brilliant and back again to mediocre. The lack of consistency has dropped him behind several other lefthanders in the White Sox system. He seemed poised for a big year at Double-A in 2002 but instead pitched himself out of the rotation by year's end. It's possible he was overextended in 2001, when he followed 180 regular-season innings with a stint in the Southern League playoffs that included a four-hit shutout. Ulacia struggled to maintain his velocity last season, which gave him problems as hitters began to sit on his breaking ball and his changeup. His changeup still needs improvement, and he must also have a consistent fastball to help him mix speeds. He was vulnerable to home runs despite being based in a pitcher's park, and allowed opponents to bat .299 against him. Ulacia is a polished pitcher, however, and with his knowledge can rebound quickly if he's able to regain the low-90s fastball he had in 2001.

Year	Club (League)	Class	W	L	ERA	G	GS	CG	SV	IP	H	R	ER	HR	BB	SO	AVG
1999	White Sox (AZL)	R	3	2	3.79	8	8	0	0	38	36	19	16	2	11	52	.250
2000	Burlington (Mid)	A	4	14	4.73	28	28	1	0	148	157	109	78	8	67	111	.271
2001	Kannapolis (SAL)	A	8	1	2.43	15	15	0	0	89	68	25	24	6	36	93	.216
	Winston-Salem (Car)	A	5	3	3.64	10	10	4	0	64	57	27	26	2	26	47	.248
	Charlotte (IL)	AAA	1	0	2.57	1	1	1	0	7	6	2	2	1	1	3	.231
	Birmingham (SL)	AA	1	1	2.25	3	3	0	0	20	11	7	5	1	5	18	.155
2002	Birmingham (SL)	AA	6	14	4.82	28	25	0	1	146	173	95	78	15	51	88	.299
MINOR LEAGUE TOTALS			28	35	4.02	93	90	6	1	512	508	284	229	35	197	412	.261

29. Franklin Francisco, rhp

Born: Sept. 11, 1979. **Ht.:** 6-2. **Wt.:** 180. **Bats:** R. **Throws:** R. **Career Transactions:** Signed out of Dominican Republic by Red Sox, Dec. 15, 1996 . . . On disabled list, June 1-Aug. 15, 1997 . . . Traded to White Sox with LHP Byeong An for Bob Howry, July 31, 2002.

Francisco had a stressful year in 2002 and didn't handle it well. He was outstanding the season before, starring as a low Class A closer, and he ended up as the No. 10 prospect in the Red Sox organization—admittedly a much thinner system than the White Sox. Perhaps because Francisco turned out to be nine months older than previously listed, the Red Sox skipped him past high Class A. That didn't work, as Francisco self-destructed in Double-A because of wildness. He re-established himself after a demotion, but then pitched poorly as a starter after he came to Chicago in a trade for Bobby Howry. Francisco has moved back and forth from the rotation to the bullpen during his career and could be heading back to relief in 2003. He's better in that role because his lack of a changeup isn't as much of a drawback. While Francisco can hit 95 mph and has a curveball, he can't be successful working behind in the count. The White Sox will give him lots of attention in spring training but may not have much patience if he can't throw more strikes.

Year	Club (League)	Class	W	L	ERA	G	GS	CG	SV	IP	H	R	ER	HR	BB	SO	AVG
1997					Did Not Play—Injured												
1998	Red Sox (DSL)	R	0	5	10.31	16	13	0	0	48	44	66	55	4	76	53	.243
1999	Red Sox (GCL)	R	2	4	4.56	12	7	0	0	53	58	39	27	3	35	48	.275
2000	Red Sox (GCL)	R	0	0	18.00	1	0	0	0	1	2	3	2	0	2	1	.400
2001	Augusta (SAL)	A	4	3	2.91	37	0	0	2	68	40	25	22	3	30	90	.168
2002	Trenton (EL)	AA	2	2	5.63	9	0	0	0	16	10	13	10	0	16	18	.172
	Sarasota (FSL)	A	1	5	2.55	16	10	0	0	53	33	19	15	1	27	58	.185
	Winston-Salem (Car)	A	0	4	8.06	6	6	0	0	26	31	23	23	3	18	25	.310
MINOR LEAGUE TOTALS			9	23	5.23	97	36	0	2	265	218	188	154	14	204	293	.225

30. Thomas Brice, of

Born: Aug. 24, 1981. **Ht.:** 6-5. **Wt.:** 210. **Bats:** L. **Throws:** L. **School:** Faulkner State (Ala.) JC. **Career Transactions:** Selected by White Sox in 24th round of 2002 draft; signed June 7, 2002.

White Sox area scout Warren Hughes learned about Brice, a fellow Australian, and stashed him at Faulkner State CC for a year before the team drafted him in the 24th round last June. Though Brice was a two-way player who touched 91 mph in junior college, Chicago wanted him for his bat. Brice's cricket background Down Under helped him develop his hand-eye coordination and has made him an excellent low-ball hitter. Mirroring cricket, he would take batting practice at Faulkner State with the pitcher just 50 feet away, serving up balls on the bounce—and Brice would drill liners all over the field. One Sox official compared his stroke to John Olerud's. Though he was limited by a minor shoulder injury, Brice had no difficulty adjusting to Rookie ball in his pro debut. He's a decent athlete with enough arm for right field, though the White Sox were working on his throwing over the winter. They think he's a year or two away from an overall breakthrough.

Year	Club (League)	Class	AVG	G	AB	R	H	2B	3B	HR	RBI	BB	SO	SB	SLG	OBP
2002	Bristol (Appy)	R	.327	29	98	11	32	4	1	0	20	10	11	1	.388	.395
MINOR LEAGUE TOTALS			.327	29	98	11	32	4	1	0	20	10	11	1	.388	.395

CINCINNATI
REDS

REDS

TOP 30 PROSPECTS

1. Chris Gruler, rhp
2. Bobby Basham, rhp
3. Wily Mo Pena, of
4. Edwin Encarnacion, 3b/ss
5. Dustin Moseley, rhp
6. Ty Howington, lhp
7. Ricardo Aramboles, rhp
8. Brandon Larson, 3b
9. Josh Hall, rhp
10. Mark Schramek, 3b
11. Luke Hudson, rhp
12. Josh Thigpen, rhp
13. Stephen Smitherman, of
14. Joey Votto, 3b/c
15. Dane Sardinha, c
16. Justin Gillman, rhp
17. Jerome Gamble, rhp
18. Daylan Childress, rhp
19. Rainer Olmedo, ss/2b
20. Gookie Dawkins, ss/2b
21. William Bergolla, 2b/ss
22. Tony Blanco, 3b
23. Alan Moye, of
24. Miguel Perez, c
25. Chris Booker, rhp
26. Alex Farfan, rhp
27. Kyle Edens, rhp
28. Jesse Gutierrez, 1b/c
29. Blake Williams, rhp
30. Hector Tiburcio, ss

By Josh Boyd

Three years ago, the Reds acquired one of the game's best and most recognizable players. Over the last two seasons, they've added two of baseball's brightest young prospects in baseball to their outfield. In 2003, they'll move into the Great American Ballpark. So why aren't things rosy in Cincinnati?

While revenue will increase, ownership isn't planning to put much of that money into an already tight payroll. Jim Bowden, baseball's second-longest-tenured general manager, still has to look for creative ways to field a contender. The Reds' budget constraints have reduced him to combing the bargain basement for reclamation projects.

Last year, with the Reds within reach of their first division title since 1995, Bowden was thwarted by ownership in his attempts to acquire pitching. He got Ryan Dempster but wasn't allowed to add the salary of Chuck Finley or Scott Rolen. Bowden settled for Shawn Estes and Brian Moehler, who went a combined 3-7, 6.69 as Cincinnati fell by the wayside.

Now more than ever, the Reds need to rely on their farm system to supply major leaguers at low cost. It has already delivered Adam Dunn and Austin Kearns, products of a terrific 1998 draft, to flank Ken Griffey in the outfield. The team is counting on third baseman Brandon Larson, a 1997 first-rounder, to finally pay dividends in 2003. While the lineup looks promising, especially if Griffey stays healthy, the pitching is another issue. Elmer Dessens' departure weakens an already shaky rotation. Prospect Luke Hudson isn't far away from helping the bullpen, but the Reds may rush youngsters Bobby Basham, Dustin Moseley, Ty Howington and Ricardo Aramboles out of necessity.

A tense, political atmosphere in the front office led to the exodus of several executives in the offseason. Director of pro scouting Gary Hughes, one of the game's best judges of talent, took a similar job with the Cubs. Doc Rodgers, who had been reassigned from assistant GM to special assistant, became Baltimore's farm director.

Kasey McKeon, who had been bumped down from scouting director to major league scout, joined the Rockies as a special assistant to the GM. DeJon Watson, who preceded McKeon as scouting director and selected both Dunn and Kearns before being demoted to a big league scout, joined the Indians as director of pro scouting.

Organization Overview

General Manager: Jim Bowden. **Farm Director:** Tim Naehring. **Scouting Director:** Leland Maddox.

2002 PERFORMANCE

Class	Farm Team	League	W	L	Pct.	Finish*	Manager
Majors	Cincinnati	National	78	84	.481	10th (16)	Bob Boone
Triple-A	Louisville RiverBats	International	79	65	.549	6th (14)	Dave Miley
Double-A	Chattanooga Lookouts	Southern	60	80	.429	9th (10)	Phillip Wellman
High A	†Stockton Ports	California	89	51	.636	+1st (10)	Jayhawk Owens
Low A	Dayton Dragons	Midwest	73	67	.521	7th (14)	Donnie Scott
Rookie	Billings Mustangs	Pioneer	38	37	.507	3rd (8)	Rick Burleson
Rookie	GCL Reds	Gulf Coast	30	30	.500	7th (14)	Edgar Caceras
OVERALL MINOR LEAGUE RECORD			369	330	.527	8th (30)	

*Finish in overall standings (No. of teams in league). +League champion. †Affiliate will be in Potomac (Carolina) in 2003.

ORGANIZATION LEADERS

BATTING
Minimum 250 At-Bats
- *AVG Brandon Larson, Louisville 340
- R Raul Gonzalez, Louisville 91
- Andrew Beattie, Chattanooga/Stockton 91
- H Noochie Varner, Dayton 160
- TB Stephen Smitherman, Stockton 246
- 2B Stephen Smitherman, Stockton 36
- 3B Noochie Varner, Dayton 12
- HR Brandon Larson, Louisville 25
- RBI Kevin Witt, Louisville 107
- BB Andrew Beattie, Chattanooga/Stockton 71
- SO Kevin Witt, Louisville 140
- SB Noochie Varner, Dayton 37

PITCHING
#Minimum 75 Innings
- W Three tied at 13
- L Three tied at 10
- #ERA Andy Boutwell, Stockton/Dayton 2.28
- G Trever Miller, Louisville 65
- CG Bobby Basham, Dayton 4
- SV Nathan Cotton, Dayton 34
- IP Ryan Mottl, Stockton 180
- BB John Koronka, Chattanooga/Stockton 87
- SO Josh Hall, Chattanooga/Stockton 167

BEST TOOLS

- Best Hitter for Average .... Mark Schramek
- Best Power Hitter .... Wily Mo Pena
- Fastest Baserunner .... Wily Mo Pena
- Best Athlete .... Wily Mo Pena
- Best Fastball .... Chris Gruler
- Best Curveball .... Dustin Moseley
- Best Slider .... Bobby Basham
- Best Changeup .... Ricardo Aramboles
- Best Control .... Bobby Basham
- Best Defensive Catcher .... Dane Sardinha
- Best Defensive Infielder .... Rainer Olmedo
- Best Infield Arm .... Edwin Encarnacion
- Best Defensive Outfielder .... Wily Mo Pena
- Best Outfield Arm .... Wily Mo Pena

PROJECTED 2006 LINEUP

- Catcher .... Jason LaRue
- First Base .... Sean Casey
- Second Base .... Aaron Boone
- Third Base .... Edwin Encarnacion
- Shortstop .... Felipe Lopez
- Left Field .... Adam Dunn
- Center Field .... Ken Griffey
- Right Field .... Austin Kearns
- No. 1 Starter .... Chris Gruler
- No. 2 Starter .... Bobby Basham

Kevin Witt   **Nathan Cotton**

- No. 3 Starter .... Dustin Moseley
- No. 4 Starter .... Ryan Dempster
- No. 5 Starter .... Chris Reitsma
- Closer .... Scott Williamson

TOP PROSPECTS OF THE DECADE

- 1993 .... Willie Greene, 3b
- 1994 .... Pokey Reese, ss
- 1995 .... Pokey Reese, ss
- 1996 .... Pokey Reese, ss
- 1997 .... Aaron Boone, 3b
- 1998 .... Damian Jackson, ss/2b
- 1999 .... Rob Bell, rhp
- 2000 .... Gookie Dawkins, ss
- 2001 .... Austin Kearns, of
- 2002 .... Austin Kearns, of

TOP DRAFT PICKS OF THE DECADE

- 1993 .... Pat Watkins, of
- 1994 .... C.J. Nitkowski, lhp
- 1995 .... Brett Tomko, rhp (2)
- 1996 .... John Oliver, of
- 1997 .... Brandon Larson, ss/3b
- 1998 .... Austin Kearns, of
- 1999 .... Ty Howington, lhp
- 2000 .... David Espinosa, ss
- 2001 .... *Jeremy Sowers, lhp
- 2002 .... Chris Gruler, rhp

*Did not sign.

ALL-TIME LARGEST BONUSES

- Chris Gruler, 2002 .... $2,500,000
- Austin Kearns, 1998 .... $1,950,000
- Ty Howington, 1999 .... $1,750,000
- Brandon Larson, 1997 .... $1,330,000
- Alejandro Diaz, 1999 .... $1,175,000

MinorLeagueDepthChart

CINCINNATI REDS

RANK 24

The Reds move into a new ballpark, but the euphoria that generally accompanies such moves isn't apparent in Cincinnati. General manager Jim Bowden enters the final year of his contract, and the organization has been affected by the instability that led to the departure of several top player personnel officials. The 2002 draft brought top prospect Chris Gruler, but his future is clouded by a frayed rotator cuff. The Reds again had difficulty signing their top picks but say they got the best college and high school bats with Mark Schramek and Joey Votto. Brandon Larson should join the big league lineup at third base, but his impact will be considerably less than the Reds last two prospect graduates: Adam Dunn and Austin Kearns.

Note: Depth charts prepared by Josh Boyd. Numbers in parentheses indicate prospect rankings.

LF
Stephen Smitherman (13)
Alan Moye (23)
Eyoxy Esparragoza

CF
Alejandro Diaz

RF
Wily Mo Pena (3)
Tiago Campos

3B
Edwin Encarnacion (4)
Brandon Larson (8)
Mark Schramek (10)
Tony Blanco (22)

SS
Rainer Olmedo (19)
Hector Tiburcio (30)

2B
Gookie Dawkins (20)
William Bergolla (21)
Kevin Howard
Damaso Espino
Andy Beattie

1B
Travis Wong

C
Joey Votto (14)
Dane Sardinha (15)
Miguel Perez (24)
Jesse Gutierrez (28)

LHP

Starters
Ty Howington (6)
Camilo Vasquez
Casey DeHart

Relievers
Cleris Severino
Jan Granado
Nick Brannon
Paul Darnell

RHP

Starters
Chris Gruler (1)
Bobby Basham (2)
Dustin Moseley (5)
Ricardo Aramboles (7)
Josh Hall (9)
Justin Gillman (16)
Blake Williams (29)
O.J. King
Brian Reith
Steve Kelly
David Gil
Ryan Mottl
Scott Dunn
Rafael German

Relievers
Luke Hudson (11)
Josh Thigpen (12)
Jerome Gamble (17)
Daylan Childress (18)
Chris Booker (25)
Alex Farfan (26)
Kyle Edens (27)
Brett Gray
Nathan Cotton
Wascar Serrano
Don Gemmell
Andy Boutwell
Brandon Culp
Corey Wachman

DraftAnalysis

2002 Draft

Best Pro Debut: 1B Travis Wong (48) hit .310-10-45 and led the Rookie-level Gulf Coast League in homers, while C Joey Votto (2) batted .269-9-33 and led the GCL with 25 extra-base hits. OF Chris Denorfia (19) hit .327 with 18 steals and reached Double-A.

Best Athlete: 3B Mark Schramek (1) has solid tools across the board, and 3B Kevin Howard (5) offers everything except for power. Denorfia also has a good package of tools, though his speed is his only true plus.

Best Pure Hitter: Schramek is an outstanding hitter whose .416 average led the Southland Conference. Howard is the runner-up. Votto has a chance to hit for average and power.

Best Raw Power: Votto over Wong and 1B Walter Olmstead (6), who was bothered by a scratched cornea in his first summer.

Fastest Runner: Denorfia runs the 60-yard dash in 6.7 seconds.

Best Defensive Player: Schramek, the Southland's defensive player of the year as well as its MVP, or Howard. Denorfia and SS Troy Cairns (46) are also solid.

Best Fastball: RHP Chris Gruler (1) threw 90-94 mph all year and peaked at 97. RHP Corey Wachman (7) showed a 94-96 mph fastball in a predraft workout at Cinergy Field and usually works at 90-94. RHP Kyle Edens (3) sits at 92-93 mph and was clocked at 97 during the spring.

Best Breaking Ball: Gruler has a true 12-to-6 hammer curveball. Edens and RHP O.J. King (8) have plus sliders.

Most Intriguing Background: Schra-mek became so frustrated with the Reds that he went to Japan to try out for the Orix Blue Wave. He didn't want to commit to a nine-year deal with a $40,000 bonus. He agreed to a deal with the independent Atlantic League's Long Island Ducks before finally signing with the Reds. RHP Mayque Quintero (31) is a Cuban defector drafted out of the independent Western League. His stuff hasn't lived up to pre-draft reports. Unsigned SS Jose Enrique Cruz' (13) father Jose held most of the Astros' career batting records before Jeff Bagwell and Craig Biggio came along, and his brother Jose played for the Blue Jays. RHP Jonathan George's (16) uncle Will scouts for the Rockies.

King

Closest To The Majors: Gruler is advanced for a high school pitcher and had his moments in low Class A. Schramek and Edens should move quickly as well.

Best Late-Round Pick: Denorfia.

The One Who Got Away: Cruz has five-tool potential but battled injuries his first two seasons at Rice.

Assessment: Cincinnati signed Gruler quickly for $2.5 million, and he proved he wasn't just a signability pick. The always cost-conscious Reds went heavily for college seniors and took all fall figuring out how to work Schramek, Edens, LHP Camilo Vazquez (4) and Howard into the budget.

2001 Draft

The Reds had no intention of signing LHP Jeremy Sowers (1), not the best way to start off a draft. At least RHP Bobby Basham (7) has started to emerge in a big way.   **Grade: C+**

2000 Draft

Since-traded 2B David Espinosa (1) and C Dane Sardinha (2) signed big league contracts without bonuses but haven't met expectations. RHP Dustin Moseley (1), LHP Ryan Snare (2) and OF Stephen Smitherman (23) have been better, though Snare was dealt to Florida.   **Grade: B**

1999 Draft

LHP Ty Howington (1) can boost this grade if he can get healthy. 1B/OF Ben Broussard (2) broke into pro ball with a bang but has leveled off and is now with Cleveland.   **Grade: C**

1998 Draft

Few teams have started a draft in better fashion than Cincinnati did with OFs Austin Kearns (1) and Adam Dunn (2). RHP Josh Hall (7) is a sleeper. The Reds signed LHPs Bobby Madritsch (6) and Cory Stewart (27), released them after they got hurt, then saw them become quality prospects with other teams after playing in independent leagues.   **Grade: A**

Note: Draft analysis prepared by Jim Callis. Numbers in parentheses indicate draft rounds.

. . . Johnny Bench said Gruler's break-ing ball and changeup were better than Tom Seaver's.

Chris
Gruler rhp

Born: Sept. 11, 1983.
Ht.: 6-3. **Wt.:** 200.
Bats: R. **Throws:** R.
School: Liberty Union HS, Brentwood, Calif.
Career Transactions: Selected by Reds in first round (3rd overall) of 2002 draft; signed June 5, 2002.

The Reds' scouting contingent was split on which high school pitcher to draft with the third overall pick in 2002: Gruler or Scott Kazmir. Then-scouting director Kasey McKeon led the Kazmir bandwagon, but he was outnumbered. The consensus in the game was that Kazmir had a higher ceiling, but his price tag was considered much higher as well. Gruler, who got a club-record $2.5 million bonus, wasn't purely a signability pick, though. After his predraft workout in Cinergy Field, Johnny Bench said Gruler's breaking ball and changeup were better than Tom Seaver's. Gruler's stock soared in the months leading up to the draft, as his velocity increased from the upper 80s to the mid-90s.

With nine Reds scouts on hand for his final prep start, he hit 95 mph in the seventh inning. He finished with a 4-3, 1.49 record for a poor team, showing his dominance by fanning 135 in 66 innings. Upon reporting to Rookie-level Billings, Gruler was shut down after his first start as a minor precaution. He threw pain-free for the rest of the season, highlighted by six no-hit innings in the low Class A Midwest League. But he experienced shoulder soreness during instructional league and doctors discovered fraying in his rotator cuff. Instead of having surgery, Gruler was ordered not to throw for two months and concentrated on rebuilding his shoulder strength.

Gruler already has two plus pitches to go with a clean and effortless delivery. His fastball explodes out of his hand and he consistently pumped 89-94 mph fastballs with boring action in on righties. He snaps off nasty curveballs from the same arm slot, generating hard downward bite through the zone. While he toyed with a splitter in high school, Gruler shelved it in favor of a changeup. He has been a sponge since signing, soaking up knowledge from veteran pitching instructor Sammy Ellis and video work. The biggest hurdle for Gruler to overcome is his rotator-cuff injury. The fear is that while he has avoided surgery for now, an operation is inevitable. As for his arsenal, he needs to hone the command of his fastball and continue to develop his changeup.

Gruler's shoulder ailment could keep him out of action until May, and the Reds will monitor his pitch counts closely. Provided he returns at full strength, he'll likely return to low Class A Dayton after a stint in extended spring training. He should move fast starting in 2004.

Year	Club (League)	Class	W	L	ERA	G	GS	CG	SV	IP	H	R	ER	HR	BB	SO	AVG
2002	Billings (Pio)	R	0	0	1.08	4	4	0	0	17	11	3	2	1	6	11	.183
	Dayton (Mid)	A	0	1	5.60	7	7	0	0	27	23	19	17	2	16	31	.228
MINOR LEAGUE TOTALS			0	1	3.89	11	11	0	0	44	34	22	19	3	22	42	.211

2. Bobby Basham, rhp

Born: March 7, 1980. **Ht.:** 6-3. **Wt.:** 200. **Bats:** R. **Throws:** R. **School:** University of Richmond. **Career Transactions:** Selected by Reds in seventh round of 2001 draft; signed July 18, 2001.

A former backup quarterback at Richmond, Basham posted an ugly 0-7, 6.39 record as a Spiders junior but showed enough the previous summer in the Cape Cod League to intrigue the Reds. They've allowed him to attend spring classes in each of the last two years, so he didn't report to Dayton until late May last year. He hurled three consecutive shutouts at Dayton—including two 78-pitch outings—and finished the year with a dominating performance in the high Class A California League championship game. Basham has made a rapid transition from raw thrower to pitcher. He had a two-week spring training but showed tremendous aptitude by incorporating mechanical adjustments on the fly. He fills the zone with a lively 90-93 mph fastball, devastating two-plane slider, plus knuckle-curve and fosh changeup. He has a slightly complex delivery, so Basham will have to work hard to maintain consistency. He worked with Dayton pitching coach Ted Power to correct his flaws. Basham will start the year at Double-A Chattanooga. After an encouraging trip to the Arizona Fall League, he could get through the upper levels in a hurry.

Year	Club (League)	Class	W	L	ERA	G	GS	CG	SV	IP	H	R	ER	HR	BB	SO	AVG
2001	Billings (Pio)	R	1	2	4.85	6	6	0	0	30	36	23	16	2	17	37	.300
2002	Dayton (Mid)	A	6	4	1.64	13	13	4	0	88	64	25	16	4	9	97	.195
MINOR LEAGUE TOTALS			7	6	2.45	19	19	4	0	117	100	48	32	6	26	134	.223

3. Wily Mo Pena, of

Born: Jan. 23, 1982. **Ht.:** 6-3. **Wt.:** 210. **Bats:** R. **Throws:** R. **Career Transactions:** Signed out of Dominican Republic by Yankees, July 15, 1998 . . . Traded by Yankees to Reds for OF Michael Coleman and 3B Drew Henson, March 21, 2001.

Pena had deals with the Marlins and Mets nixed by the commissioner's office before he turned 16. He eventually signed a four-year major league pact for $3.7 million with the Yankees, then was traded to the Reds for Drew Henson. He tore his hamstring in the Arizona Fall League and had surgery that will keep him out at the beginning of spring training. Pena is often compared to Sammy Sosa at the same stage of their careers. He owns similar raw power and may have more than anyone in the minors. He put on a home run display at Miller Park before the Futures Game last year. Pena is the fastest athlete in the system, and he projects as a prototypical right fielder with a cannon arm. His plus-plus bat speed allows him to crush any fastball. His biggest weakness is his contract. Pena has to be kept on the 25-man roster or be exposed to waivers, where he certainly would be lost. He needs more minor league at-bats because he's ultra-aggressive and hasn't grasped the idea of selectivity yet, but he's not going to get them. The Reds may buy a little time by sending Pena to the minors on a rehab assignment. After that, he'll have to learn on the job in the major leagues while sitting behind Adam Dunn, Ken Griffey and Austin Kearns.

Year	Club (League)	Class	AVG	G	AB	R	H	2B	3B	HR	RBI	BB	SO	SB	SLG	OBP
1999	Yankees (GCL)	R	.247	45	166	21	41	10	1	7	26	12	54	3	.446	.323
2000	Greensboro (SAL)	A	.205	67	249	41	51	7	1	10	28	18	91	6	.361	.268
	Staten Island (NY-P)	A	.301	20	73	7	22	1	2	0	10	2	23	2	.370	.354
2001	Dayton (Mid)	A	.264	135	511	87	135	25	5	26	113	33	177	26	.485	.327
2002	Chattanooga (SL)	AA	.255	105	388	47	99	23	1	11	47	36	126	8	.405	.330
	Cincinnati (NL)	MAJ	.222	13	18	1	4	0	0	1	1	0	11	0	.389	.222
MAJOR LEAGUE TOTALS			.222	13	18	1	4	0	0	1	1	0	11	0	.389	.222
MINOR LEAGUE TOTALS			.251	372	1387	203	348	66	10	54	224	101	471	45	.430	.318

4. Edwin Encarnacion, 3b/ss

Born: Jan. 7, 1983. **Ht.:** 6-1. **Wt.:** 170. **Bats:** R. **Throws:** R. **School:** Manuela Toro HS, Caguas, P.R. **Career Transactions:** Selected by Rangers in ninth round of 2000 draft; signed June 12, 2000 . . . Traded by Rangers with OF Ruben Mateo to Reds for RHP Rob Bell, June 15, 2001.

The Rangers considered Encarnacion a throw-in to the Rob Bell-Ruben Mateo trade two years ago, but the Reds insisted on his inclusion in the deal. He has blossomed while Bell and Mateo have floundered. Encarnacion's athleticism enticed the Reds into moving him to shortstop late in 2002. Encarnacion combines outstanding bat speed with natural loft in his swing to drive the ball with authority. He covers the plate well and can make hard

ROGER WOOD

contact even on pitches out of the zone. His hands are quick at the plate and in the field, and his arm is the best in the system. While he has the tools—plus arm strength, first-step quickness and great hands—to be an asset in the field, Encarnacion committed 40 errors last year. He tends to rush his throws, and needs to square up and get his feet set. He's a slightly below-average runner. His bat will be even more dangerous when he stops trying to pull everything and displays more patience. He was originally drafted as a shortstop, so it's not out of the realm of possibility for Encarnacion to stay there. Most scouts believe he's better suited for third base, and his bat will allow him to play there.

Year	Club (League)	Class	AVG	G	AB	R	H	2B	3B	HR	RBI	BB	SO	SB	SLG	OBP
2000	Rangers (GCL)	R	.311	51	177	31	55	6	3	0	36	21	27	3	.379	.381
2001	Savannah (SAL)	A	.306	45	170	23	52	9	2	4	25	12	34	3	.453	.355
	Dayton (Mid)	A	.162	9	37	2	6	2	0	1	6	1	5	0	.297	.184
	Billings (Pio)	R	.261	52	211	27	55	8	2	5	26	15	29	8	.389	.307
2002	Dayton (Mid)	A	.282	136	518	80	146	32	4	17	73	40	108	25	.458	.338
MINOR LEAGUE TOTALS			.282	293	1113	163	314	57	11	27	166	89	203	39	.426	.337

5. Dustin Moseley, rhp

JOHN SPEAR

Born: Dec. 26, 1981. **Ht.:** 6-4. **Wt.:** 200. **Bats:** R. **Throws:** R. **School:** Arkansas HS, Texarkana, Ark. **Career Transactions:** Selected by Reds in first round (34th overall) of 2000 draft; signed Nov. 22, 2000.

Moseley signed for $930,000 as a 2000 supplemental first-rounder, but because the Reds ran out of money in their draft budget, the deal wasn't finalized until the start of their 2001 fiscal calendar in November. His late start hasn't bothered him at all. Moseley has shown a great feel for pitching since his high school days. His fluid delivery and arm action allow him to fire three pitches for strikes. His fastball is gaining velocity, and he'll dial his two-seamer up to 92-93 mph. He regularly sits at 90-91 with good life. His 76 mph curveball is a plus pitch, ranking with Josh Hall's for the system's best. Moseley has improved his mechanics and does a better job staying back over the rubber. He shows a good feel for his changeup, but could improve it and incorporate it more frequently. He also has worked hard to develop his lower-body strength this offseason. Moseley got knocked around after his promotion to Double-A, so he'll return there in 2003. He'll be part of a prospect-laden rotation that will include Bobby Basham, Ty Howington, Ricardo Aramboles and Hall.

Year	Club (League)	Class	W	L	ERA	G	GS	CG	SV	IP	H	R	ER	HR	BB	SO	AVG
2001	Dayton (Mid)	A	10	8	4.20	25	25	0	0	148	158	83	69	10	42	108	.271
2002	Stockton (Cal)	A	6	3	2.74	14	14	2	0	89	60	28	27	3	21	80	.188
	Chattanooga (SL)	AA	5	6	4.13	13	13	0	0	81	91	47	37	5	37	52	.293
MINOR LEAGUE TOTALS			21	17	3.77	52	52	2	0	317	309	158	133	18	100	240	.255

6. Ty Howington, lhp

RODGER WOOD

Born: Nov. 4, 1980. **Ht.:** 6-5. **Wt.:** 220. **Bats:** B. **Throws:** L. **School:** Hudson's Bay HS, Vancouver, Wash. **Career Transactions:** Selected by Reds in first round (14th overall) of 1999 draft; signed Nov. 1, 1999.

Considered the top southpaw in the 1999 draft, Howington has been stymied by injuries since signing for $1.75 million. He overcame arthroscopic elbow surgery in the spring of 2001 but wasn't as successful trying to work through shoulder tendinitis last year. He was shut down in April, returned in June, then had his season end in early August. The Reds expect Howington to regain the velocity on his plus fastball. He threw 92-94 mph prior to 2002, when he still got to 89 with a dead arm. His pitches have life down in the strike zone. He flashes an above-average curveball and good fading changeup. Howington's mechanical flaws are probably the root of his injuries. He was cutting his delivery off, putting unnecessary stress on his arm. More consistent mechanics not only will keep him healthy, but also will improve the quality of his three pitches. Howington was back throwing darts in instructional league, hitting 89-91 mph without pain. At 22, he's still on schedule and will try to re-establish himself in Double-A.

Year	Club (League)	Class	W	L	ERA	G	GS	CG	SV	IP	H	R	ER	HR	BB	SO	AVG
2000	Dayton (Mid)	A	5	15	5.27	27	26	0	0	142	150	91	83	7	86	119	.275
2001	Dayton (Mid)	A	4	0	1.15	6	6	1	0	39	15	7	5	0	9	47	.116
	Mudville (Cal)	A	3	2	2.43	7	7	0	0	37	33	18	10	2	20	44	.234
	Chattanooga (SL)	AA	1	3	3.27	7	7	0	0	41	36	18	15	3	24	38	.240
2002	Chattanooga (SL)	AA	1	5	5.12	15	15	1	0	65	65	39	37	5	33	51	.261
	Stockton (Cal)	A	1	1	3.09	2	2	0	0	12	7	6	4	1	4	9	.171
MINOR LEAGUE TOTALS			15	26	4.13	64	63	2	0	336	306	179	154	18	176	308	.244

7. Ricardo Aramboles, rhp

Born: Dec. 4, 1981. **Ht.:** 6-4. **Wt.:** 220. **Bats:** R. **Throws:** R. **Career Transactions:** Signed out of Dominican Republic by Marlins, July 2, 1996 . . . Contract voided, Dec. 3, 1997 . . . Signed by Yankees Feb. 26, 1998 . . . Traded by Yankees to Reds for RHP Mark Wohlers, June 30, 2001.

Like Wily Mo Pena, Aramboles signed with the Yankees after Major League Baseball voided his first contract with the Marlins because he was too young. He had Tommy John surgery in 1999 and was traded for Mark Wohlers in 2001. Aramboles hasn't been able to get through a full season since 2000. Last year, he strained a thumb ligament swinging a bat in spring training and came down with a tender elbow during the season. Aramboles has major league-caliber stuff. His deceptive changeup is a plus pitch and makes his 92-94 mph fastball that much better. He backs those pitches up with a power 78 mph curveball with depth. He has a big league body, but Aramboles must prove he can withstand a full season without injury. He has a good delivery and clean arm action, but needs to gain more consistency with it. He has worked with pitching instructor Sammy Ellis to fine-tune his mechanics. He was on the cusp of the majors last spring and could impress the big league staff in the same manner again. Aramboles might be better served getting consistent innings in Double-A before being rushed. He was at full strength in instructional league.

Year	Club (League)	Class	W	L	ERA	G	GS	CG	SV	IP	H	R	ER	HR	BB	SO	AVG
1997	Marlins (DSL)	R	1	1	1.71	8	2	0	0	21	15	7	4	0	7	14	.200
1998	Yankees (GCL)	R	2	1	2.93	10	9	0	0	40	33	14	13	0	13	44	.231
	Oneonta (NY-P)	A	1	0	1.50	1	1	0	0	6	4	2	1	1	1	8	.190
1999	Yankees (GCL)	R	2	3	3.89	9	7	0	0	35	35	18	15	1	14	42	.276
	Greensboro (SAL)	A	1	2	2.34	6	6	1	0	35	25	9	9	1	12	34	.205
2000	Greensboro (SAL)	A	5	13	4.31	25	25	2	0	138	150	81	66	12	47	150	.274
2001	Tampa (FSL)	A	7	2	4.06	12	11	0	0	69	72	37	31	5	19	59	.271
	Columbus (IL)	AAA	1	3	3.04	4	4	0	0	24	26	11	8	2	4	14	.283
	Chattanooga (SL)	AA	0	2	8.00	2	1	0	0	9	12	8	8	1	0	5	.324
	Dayton (Mid)	A	1	2	3.66	4	4	0	0	20	23	8	8	2	4	9	.299
2002	Chattanooga (SL)	AA	1	0	3.13	4	4	0	0	23	22	8	8	0	8	22	.268
MINOR LEAGUE TOTALS			22	29	3.68	85	74	3	0	418	417	203	171	25	129	401	.262

8. Brandon Larson, 3b

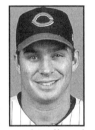

Born: May 24, 1976. **Ht.:** 6-0. **Wt.:** 210. **Bats:** R. **Throws:** R. **School:** Louisiana State University. **Career Transactions:** Selected by Reds in first round (14th overall) of 1997 draft; signed July 22, 1997.

After transferring to Louisiana State from Blinn (Texas) Junior College for his junior season, Larson finished second in NCAA Division I to Rice's Lance Berkman with 40 homers and was the College World Series MVP in 1997. Years of battling through knee, ankle and wrist surgeries slowed his progress as a pro and led to his removal from the 40-man last spring. Then his bat heated up at Triple-A Indianapolis. Larson is a dead-red fastball hitter, geared to yank heat out of the park. He made adjustments to hit offspeed stuff last year and became a more complete hitter when he started using the whole field. He also had laser eye surgery, which coincided with his improved pitch recognition. He's average at the hot corner. Larson is a full-effort hacker with a lot of pre-swing movement. He has an aggressive, power hitter's mentality that doesn't lend itself to working counts and still leaves him susceptible to offspeed pitches. After trading Todd Walker, the Reds will move Aaron Boone to second base to make room for Larson at third. At 26, he needs to seize his opportunity.

Year	Club (League)	Class	AVG	G	AB	R	H	2B	3B	HR	RBI	BB	SO	SB	SLUG	OBP
1997	Chattanooga (SL)	AA	.268	11	41	4	11	5	1	0	6	1	10	0	.439	.279
1998	Burlington (Mid)	A	.221	18	68	5	15	3	0	2	9	4	16	2	.353	.264
1999	Rockford (Mid)	A	.300	69	250	38	75	18	1	13	52	25	67	12	.536	.367
	Chattanooga (SL)	AA	.285	43	172	28	49	10	0	12	42	10	51	4	.552	.332
2000	Chattanooga (SL)	AA	.272	111	427	61	116	26	0	20	64	31	122	15	.473	.330
	Louisville (FSL)	AAA	.286	17	63	11	18	7	1	2	4	4	16	0	.524	.328
2001	Louisville (IL)	AAA	.255	115	424	61	108	22	2	14	55	24	123	5	.415	.312
	Cincinnati (NL)	MAJ	.121	14	33	2	4	2	0	0	1	2	10	0	.182	.171
2002	Louisville (IL)	AAA	.340	80	297	47	101	20	1	25	69	24	70	1	.667	.393
	Cincinnati (NL)	MAJ	.275	23	51	8	14	2	0	4	13	6	10	1	.549	.362
MAJOR LEAGUE TOTALS			.214	37	84	10	18	4	0	4	14	8	20	1	.405	.290
MINOR LEAGUE TOTALS			.283	464	1742	255	493	111	6	88	301	123	475	39	.505	.338

9. Josh Hall, rhp

Born: Dec. 16, 1980. **Ht.:** 6-2. **Wt.:** 190. **Bats:** R. **Throws:** R. **School:** E.C. Glass HS, Lynchburg, Va. **Career Transactions:** Selected by Reds in seventh round of 1998 draft; signed June 11, 1998 . . . On disabled list, June 16-Sept. 13, 1999.

The Reds agreed to a trade that would have sent Hall and position prospects Alan Moye and David Espinosa to the Rangers for Kenny Rogers last July, but Rogers nixed it. Hall had a minor knee injury in high school and had reconstructive shoulder surgery that cost him all of 1999 and most of 2000. Since then, he has emerged as one of Cincinnati's best pitching prospects without much fanfare. Hall is similar to Dustin Moseley. Neither is overpowering, though Hall has touched 94 mph. His fastball is usually average at 88-90, but he keeps it down and hits his spots with pinpoint command. His 12-to-6 curveball is a strikeout pitch, and his changeup is also a plus offering. He's poised on the mound with a feel for pitching that belies his youth. Hall has little margin for error and will have to continue to be fine with his control. His feel for his offspeed pitches is so advanced that he should be able to keep hitters off balance without blowing them away. Hall was forced to rebuild his mechanics after surgery, and farm director Tim Naehring said his rehab could be used as a blueprint for injured arms. Hall should return to Double-A and could find himself in Triple-A before the end of 2003.

Year	Club (League)	Class	W	L	ERA	G	GS	CG	SV	IP	H	R	ER	HR	BB	SO	AVG
1998	Billings (Pio)	R	5	4	5.00	14	14	1	0	81	89	53	45	6	33	50	.276
1999								Did Not Play—Injured									
2000	Reds (GCL)	R	0	5	10.57	6	6	0	0	15	26	25	18	2	13	20	.371
2001	Dayton (Mid)	A	11	5	2.65	22	22	2	0	132	117	52	39	4	39	122	.232
2002	Stockton (Cal)	A	4	0	2.27	7	7	1	0	44	31	13	11	1	13	51	.194
	Chattanooga (SL)	AA	7	8	3.75	22	22	1	0	132	140	75	55	7	50	116	.276
MINOR LEAGUE TOTALS			27	22	3.74	71	71	5	0	404	403	218	168	20	148	359	.258

10. Mark Schramek, 3b

Born: June 2, 1980. **Ht.:** 6-2. **Wt.:** 190. **Bats:** L. **Throws:** R. **School:** University of Texas-San Antonio. **Career Transactions:** Selected by Reds in first round (40th overall) of 2002 draft; signed Dec. 18, 2002.

The Reds say they landed the best college hitter available in the draft by taking Schramek, the Southland Conference's 2002 MVP and defensive player of the year, with the 40th overall pick. That didn't stop them from taking a hardline negotiating approach, which spurred Schramek to work out for Japan's Orix Blue Wave and to sign with the independent Atlantic League's Long Island Ducks. The Reds finally got him in December for $200,000, which tied for the lowest bonus in the first three rounds. Schramek has a pure line-drive stroke with quickness and strength through the zone. He has the defensive tools to project as a potential Gold Glover at third base. The Reds coveted his arm as a pitcher in high school, and it's still an asset from the hot corner. Schramek tore the anterior cruciate ligament in his left knee during the 2001 Southland Conference tournament, had reconstructive surgery and played last season with a brace. That caused some teams to back off of him, but scouts say he has regained his mobility and has no lingering effects. Schramek should hit the ground running at the Reds' new high Class A Potomac affiliate. The Reds have little doubt he'll hit for average at any level.

Year	Club (League)	Class	AVG	G	AB	R	H	2B	3B	HR	RBI	BB	SO	SB	SLG	OBP
			Has Not Played—Signed 2003 Contract													

11. Luke Hudson, rhp

Born: May 2, 1977. **Ht.:** 6-3. **Wt.:** 190. **Bats:** R. **Throws:** R. **School:** University of Tennessee. **Career Transactions:** Selected by Rockies in fourth round of 1998 draft; signed June 5, 1998 . . . Traded by Rockies with LHP Gabe White to Reds for LHP Dennys Reyes and 2B Pokey Reese, Dec. 18, 2001.

Hudson was part of two national championship youth teams and won consecutive California state high school titles in 1994-95. He spurned an Orioles fifth-round offer out of high school to attend Tennessee, where he posted a 6.82 ERA in his draft year (1998) yet still went in the fourth round. He joined the Reds in the Pokey Reese trade with Colorado in December 2001. Hudson's fastball sat in the 91-93 mph range when he was a starter, but after moving to the bullpen last year he should be able to reach the mid-90s consistently. His curveball is a tight knee-buckler. Command always has been an issue for Hudson. He still hasn't learned to locate his fastball to both sides of the plate, which is what prompted his shift to relief. His changeup velocity is too close to his fastball, though he doesn't need the change as much out of the bullpen. He made strides with his delivery last year. General manager Jim Bowden was a proponent of moving Hudson to the pen. He could settle into the role and break camp as part of the Reds staff.

Year	Club (League)	Class	W	L	ERA	G	GS	CG	SV	IP	H	R	ER	HR	BB	SO	AVG
1998	Portland (NWL)	A	3	6	4.74	15	15	0	0	80	68	46	42	8	51	82	.226
1999	Asheville (SAL)	A	6	5	4.30	21	20	1	0	88	89	47	42	10	24	96	.265
2000	Salem (Car)	A	5	8	3.27	19	19	2	0	110	101	47	40	9	34	80	.246
2001	Carolina (SL)	AA	7	12	4.20	29	28	1	0	165	159	90	77	19	68	145	.250
2002	Louisville (IL)	AAA	5	9	4.51	30	17	0	3	118	102	64	59	6	57	129	.233
	Cincinnati (NL)	MAJ	0	0	4.50	3	0	0	0	6	5	5	3	1	6	7	.227
MAJOR LEAGUE TOTALS			0	0	4.50	3	0	0	0	6	5	5	3	1	6	7	.227
MINOR LEAGUE TOTALS			26	40	4.18	114	99	4	3	560	519	294	260	52	234	532	.245

12. Josh Thigpen, rhp

Born: June 27, 1982. **Ht.:** 6-4. **Wt.:** 190. **Bats:** R. **Throws:** R. **School:** Rogers HS, Greenville, Ala. **Career Transactions:** Selected by Red Sox in 16th round of 2000 draft; signed July 11, 2000 . . . Traded by Red Sox to Reds with 3B Tony Blanco, Dec. 16, 2002, completing trade in which Red Sox acquired 2B Todd Walker from Reds for two players to be named (Dec. 12, 2002).

An all-Alabama performer in baseball, basketball and football in high school, Thigpen is one of the system's better athletes. He joined the Reds in a December cost-cutting trade that sent Todd Walker to the Red Sox. In 2002, Thigpen developed a knot in the back of his shoulder that sidelined him sporadically and relegated him to the bullpen and strict pitch counts for much of the year. He came on in the final month, with a 1.08 ERA, 23 strikeouts and a .143 opponent average in 25 innings. Thigpen's fastball sits at 93 mph and is capable of reaching 96. His solid-average curveball returned by the end of the season. While he's very much a work in progress, his athleticism should enable him to repeat his delivery and develop command. Thigpen has spent relatively little time pitching, dividing himself among three sports in high school and working a total of 125 innings in three pro seasons. As a result he's raw. His changeup and control are rudimentary, and he lacks touch. If Thigpen can make the transition from two-pitch thrower to three-pitch pitcher, he can be a frontline starter. He'll begin 2003 in high Class A.

Year	Club (League)	Class	W	L	ERA	G	GS	CG	SV	IP	H	R	ER	HR	BB	SO	AVG
2000	Red Sox (GCL)	R	0	1	15.00	2	0	0	0	3	3	5	5	1	6	2	.300
2001	Red Sox (GCL)	R	4	2	2.52	10	6	0	1	39	20	15	11	1	14	44	.153
2002	Augusta (SAL)	A	6	6	3.92	25	9	0	2	83	76	45	36	5	45	87	.252
MINOR LEAGUE TOTALS			10	9	3.74	37	15	0	3	125	99	65	52	7	65	133	.224

13. Stephen Smitherman, of

Born: Sept. 1, 1978. **Ht.:** 6-4. **Wt.:** 230. **Bats:** R. **Throws:** R. **School:** University of Arkansas-Little Rock. **Career Transactions:** Selected by Reds in 23rd round of 2000 draft; signed June 7, 2000.

Smitherman was a 23rd-round find by area scout Jimmy Gonzales, who also signed Scott Williamson and four other players among the Reds' top 30: Dustin Moseley, Mark Schramek, Daylan Childress and Jesse Gutierrez. Gonzales saw something in Smitherman, who hit a disappointing .326-9-53 as an Arkansas-Little Rock senior and has transformed himself into a prospect with three productive seasons in the low minors. Despite playing his home games last year at high Class A Stockton's Billy Herbert Field, a graveyard for righthanded power hitters, Smitherman finished among the California League leaders in average, hits, doubles and RBIs. He was the MVP of the playoffs, batting .522 to lead the Ports to the championship. An impressive physical specimen, he hits from an open stance and dives into the plate with an aggressive approach. This often leaves him vulnerable to getting tied up by pitches in on his hands. When he closes up early, he drives the ball to all fields. He displays good strike-zone awareness at times but needs to do so more consistently. Smitherman is athletic and runs well for his size. Below-average arm strength will relegate him to left field, but he has improved his routes and ability to cut off ground balls. He's a diabetic but that hasn't limited him. To this point, the Reds have asked him to prove himself one level at a time, and he has done so. A good spring showing could earn him a trip to Triple-A.

Year	Club (League)	Class	AVG	G	AB	R	H	2B	3B	HR	RBI	BB	SO	SB	SLG	OBP
2000	Billings (Pio)	R	.316	70	301	61	95	16	5	15	65	23	67	14	.551	.373
2001	Dayton (Mid)	A	.280	134	497	89	139	45	2	20	73	43	113	16	.499	.348
2002	Stockton (Cal)	A	.313	128	482	78	151	36	1	19	99	39	126	17	.510	.362
MINOR LEAGUE TOTALS			.301	332	1280	228	385	97	8	54	237	105	306	47	.516	.359

14. Joey Votto, 3b/c

Born: Sept. 10, 1983. **Ht.:** 6-3. **Wt.:** 200. **Bats:** L. **Throws:** R. **School:** Richview Collegiate Institute, Toronto. **Career Transactions:** Selected by Reds in second round of 2002 draft; signed June 5, 2002.

The Reds signed Votto to a $600,000 deal on day two of the draft. He had a tremendous predraft workout in Cinergy Field, highlighted by catching advice from Johnny Bench and home runs into the second deck against 91 mph fastballs. His fluid lefthanded stroke with natural loft and raw power also garnered predraft looks from the Yankees and Angels. Votto moved to catcher in the summer of 2001 and caught just 15 games in high school. Primarily a third baseman as an amateur, he spent most of his time in his pro debut there. He led the Rookie-level Gulf Coast League with 25 extra-base hits in 50 games. Votto has outstanding bat speed and demonstrates good hitting instincts. He shows a feel for hitting the ball to all fields. Defensively, some scouts question if he'll be able to stay behind the plate. He has a good arm and receives the ball well, but has a lot of room for improvement on footwork and glove-to-hand transfer. He threw out four of 18 basestealers in the GCL. The Reds want him to concentrate on hitting adjustments before stressing his defensive development. A strong spring effort could propel him to low Class A.

Year	Club (League)	Class	AVG	G	AB	R	H	2B	3B	HR	RBI	BB	SO	SB	SLG	OBP
2002	Reds (GCL)	R	.269	50	175	29	47	13	3	9	33	21	45	7	.531	.342
MINOR LEAGUE TOTALS			.269	50	175	29	47	13	3	9	33	21	45	7	.531	.342

15. Dane Sardinha, c

Born: April 8, 1979. **Ht.:** 6-0. **Wt.:** 210. **Bats:** R. **Throws:** R. **School:** Pepperdine University. **Career Transactions:** Selected by Reds in second round of 2000 draft; signed Sept. 1, 2000.

Sardinha signed a major league deal for $1.75 million that included no bonus, another concession to the Reds' budget machinations. He has two younger brothers in the minors: Bronson, one of the best hitters in the Yankees system; and Duke, a Rockies third baseman. Dane's .221 average in two years of pro ball underscores his biggest weakness, but the Reds remain confident he'll come on offensively. They were encouraged by his Arizona Fall League performance (.311-4-24), but that was only 101 at-bats. He did start to shake his aluminum-bat approach and learned to stay back and trust his hands and strength. He has a two-piece swing, where his upper and lower body don't quite work together. He needs to tone down his aggressiveness and develop more patience. Sardinha likely won't hit for much of an average, but the reason most scouts still consider him a prospect is his advanced catch-and-throw skills. He's adept at framing pitches, and he has soft hands and a quick transfer. He threw out 37 percent of basestealers last year. He's slated for a return to Double-A, where the Reds would love to see Sardinha carry over his AFL progress.

Year	Club (League)	Class	AVG	G	AB	R	H	2B	3B	HR	RBI	BB	SO	SB	SLG	OBP
2001	Mudville (Cal)	A	.235	109	422	45	99	24	2	9	55	12	97	0	.365	.259
2002	Chattanooga (SL)	AA	.206	106	394	34	81	20	0	4	40	14	114	0	.287	.234
MINOR LEAGUE TOTALS			.221	215	816	79	180	44	2	13	95	26	211	0	.327	.246

16. Justin Gillman, rhp

Born: June 27, 1983. **Ht.:** 6-2. **Wt.:** 180. **Bats:** R. **Throws:** R. **School:** Mosley HS, Panama City, Fla. **Career Transactions:** Selected by Reds in second round of 2001 draft; signed June 26, 2001.

Primarily an infielder until his junior year in high school, Gillman didn't attract scouts' attention until he took the mound and started throwing 88 mph. His velocity jumped into the low 90s before the 2001 draft, and he showed a tremendous feel for pitching. After signing for $625,000 as a second-round pick, he dominated in his pro debut in the Gulf Coast League thanks to his command of three pitches. He would have pitched in the Midwest League playoffs had Dayton not been eliminated quickly. He returned to low Class A last year, but went down in May with elbow trouble that required Tommy John surgery. Gillman will start 2003 in extended spring training and probably won't see game action until instructional league. The history of the ligament-replacement operation suggests he'll regain his explosive 90-93 mph fastball and plus curveball. He also had shown a promising changeup. The good news is that he'll still be just 20 when he returns at full strength in 2004.

Year	Club (League)	Class	W	L	ERA	G	GS	CG	SV	IP	H	R	ER	HR	BB	SO	AVG
2001	Reds (GCL)	R	4	2	1.75	9	7	0	0	36	19	10	7	1	11	38	.156
	Billings (Pio)	R	1	0	0.00	1	1	0	0	6	0	1	0	0	5	2	.000
2002	Dayton (Mid)	A	1	3	3.49	7	7	0	0	39	29	17	15	3	17	30	.209
MINOR LEAGUE TOTALS			6	5	2.45	17	15	0	0	81	48	28	22	4	33	70	.173

17. Jerome Gamble, rhp

Born: April 5, 1980. **Ht.:** 6-2. **Wt.:** 200. **Bats:** R. **Throws:** R. **School:** Benjamin Russell HS, Alexander City, Ala. **Career Transactions:** Selected by Red Sox in fourth round of 1998 draft; signed June 9, 1998 . . . Selected by Reds from Red Sox in major league Rule 5 draft, Dec. 16, 2002.

The Reds approached the Red Sox about acquiring Gamble in a trade last summer, and couldn't pass up the opportunity to take him in the Rule 5 draft. Two years ago Gamble was considered to have the best raw arm in the Boston system, though he had been limited to 31 appearances because of elbow problems. The news didn't get any better in 2001, when he pitched just three times before requiring Tommy John surgery. When he returned in mid-2002, he was on strict pitch counts and never went past five innings. He was dominant in his short stints, and his quality stuff returned. Gamble again was throwing 92-94 mph with ease, and his hard curveball came back. He doesn't throw his changeup for strikes yet, but he believes in the pitch and throws it with the same arm slot as his fastball. Gamble was to be turned loose as a high Class A starter in 2003. He'll have to stay on Cincinnati's 25-man roster all year or be offered back to the Red Sox, who hope they'll be able to reclaim him.

Year	Club (League)	Class	W	L	ERA	G	GS	CG	SV	IP	H	R	ER	HR	BB	SO	AVG
1998	Red Sox (GCL)	R	2	3	4.43	11	6	0	1	43	33	24	21	4	19	49	.204
1999	Lowell (NY-P)	A	1	0	1.75	5	5	0	0	26	18	7	5	1	9	37	.196
2000	Augusta (SAL)	A	5	3	2.52	15	15	0	0	79	69	26	22	1	32	71	.235
2001	Sarasota (FSL)	A	0	0	7.88	3	2	0	1	8	11	8	7	0	4	7	.333
2002	Augusta (SAL)	A	1	2	1.82	14	14	0	0	49	34	12	10	2	22	42	.192
MINOR LEAGUE TOTALS			9	8	2.86	48	42	0	2	204	165	77	65	8	86	206	.218

18. Daylan Childress, rhp

Born: July 31, 1978. **Ht.:** 6-1. **Wt.:** 200. **Bats:** R. **Throws:** R. **School:** McLennan (Texas) CC. **Career Transactions:** Selected by Reds in fifth round of 2001 draft; signed June 6, 2001.

Childress pitched in the same McLennan CC rotation in 2001 as Sean Henn, who signed with the Yankees for a draft-and-follow record $1.701 million bonus. Childress flashed a mid-90s fastball and agreed to a predraft deal worth $40,000, the lowest bonus among fifth-rounders. The Reds tinkered with Childress' mechanics, but he didn't take to the adjustments until last season. Once he did, scouts noticed a significant difference in his repertoire. Childress pitches with a fluid arm action and has sacrificed a little velocity—his fastball now ranges from 89-93 mph—for more life down in the strike zone. Strictly a fastball/slider pitcher in college, he added a changeup that now grades as his best pitch. Reds scout Jimmy Gonzales, who signed him, describes the pitch's movement as "cartoon-like." Childress' slider has tight rotation but is still erratic, as is his control at times. His aggressive makeup leads some scouts to project him as a reliever down the road, and his mid-90s velocity could return in a shorter role. He has added 15 pounds of lower-body muscle during the offseason, which will help him continue to amass innings as a starter in high Class A this year.

Year	Club (League)	Class	W	L	ERA	G	GS	CG	SV	IP	H	R	ER	HR	BB	SO	AVG
2001	Billings (Pio)	R	6	1	3.55	14	8	0	1	63	59	32	25	4	17	54	.246
2002	Dayton (Mid)	A	9	10	3.51	28	27	1	0	169	147	82	66	7	68	152	.233
MINOR LEAGUE TOTALS			15	11	3.53	42	35	1	1	232	206	114	91	11	85	206	.237

19. Rainer Olmedo, ss/2b

Born: May 31, 1981. **Ht.:** 5-11. **Wt.:** 150. **Bats:** B. **Throws:** R. **Career Transactions:** Signed out of Venezuela by Reds, Jan. 21, 1999.

Olmedo draws comparisons to Omar Vizquel for his flashy glovework. He has outstanding actions, soft hands and plus arm strength. He gets careless at times, but cut his errors from 40 in 2001 to 25 last season. After Olmedo batted .237 against righthanders in 2000, the Reds decided to make him switch-hitter. A natural righty, he has batted .255 and .260 as a lefty the last two years, but his righthanded production has suffered as a result. Olmedo is a slap hitter who lacks power and gets the bat knocked out of his hands by overpowering stuff. He made more consistent contact last year and showed more patience at the plate. He's a solid-average runner who will be a threat on the bases once he improves his reads and jumps. His work ethic is as good as any player in the organization. Olmedo could move up to Double-A, but it wouldn't be a bad idea to return to high Class A at the start of 2003.

Year	Club (League)	Class	AVG	G	AB	R	H	2B	3B	HR	RBI	BB	SO	SB	SLG	OBP
1999	Reds (GCL)	R	.236	54	195	30	46	12	1	1	19	12	28	13	.323	.281
2000	Dayton (Mid)	A	.255	111	369	50	94	19	1	4	41	30	70	17	.344	.309
2001	Mudville (Cal)	A	.244	129	536	57	131	23	4	0	28	24	121	38	.302	.285
2002	Chattanooga (SL)	AA	.247	132	478	62	118	21	1	3	30	53	86	15	.314	.331
MINOR LEAGUE TOTALS			.247	426	1578	199	389	75	7	8	118	119	305	83	.318	.305

20. Gookie Dawkins, ss/2b

Born: May 12, 1979. **Ht.:** 6-1. **Wt.:** 180. **Bats:** R. **Throws:** R. **School:** Newberry (S.C.) HS. **Career Transactions:** Selected by Reds in second round of 1997 draft; signed June 8, 1997.

In 2002, Dawkins spent time in Double-A for the fourth straight year and made his third consecutive trip to the Arizona Fall League. Once rated ahead of Adam Dunn and Austin Kearns as the organization's top prospect after his breakthrough 1999 season, he hasn't developed offensively. Once regarded as the heir apparent to Barry Larkin at shortstop, he looks more like he'll have to settle for a utility role. Dawkins can run and field, though he stole a career-low nine bags last season. He has quick hands, good range and an above-average arm that's very accurate. At the plate, however, he struggles to stay back and recognize pitches. He doesn't strike the ball with authority, and he hasn't improved his plate discipline either. Dawkins is out of options, so he'll need to win a spot on the Cincinnati bench this spring.

Year	Club (League)	Class	AVG	G	AB	R	H	2B	3B	HR	RBI	BB	SO	SB	SLG	OBP
1997	Billings (Pio)	R	.241	70	253	47	61	5	0	4	37	30	38	16	.308	.315
1998	Burlington (Mid)	A	.264	102	367	52	97	7	6	1	30	37	60	37	.324	.332
1999	Rockford (Mid)	A	.272	76	305	56	83	10	6	8	32	35	38	38	.423	.346
	Chattanooga (SL)	AA	.364	32	129	24	47	7	0	2	13	14	17	15	.465	.427
	Cincinnati (NL)	MAJ	.143	7	7	1	1	0	0	0	0	0	4	0	.143	.250
2000	Chattanooga (SL)	AA	.231	95	368	54	85	20	6	6	31	40	71	22	.367	.310
	Cincinnati (NL)	MAJ	.220	14	41	5	9	2	0	0	3	2	7	0	.268	.256
2001	Chattanooga (SL)	AA	.226	104	394	59	89	16	3	8	40	32	88	14	.343	.285
2002	Cincinnati (NL)	MAJ	.125	31	48	2	6	2	0	0	0	6	21	2	.167	.222
	Chattanooga (SL)	AA	.271	40	155	21	42	10	1	1	12	25	28	5	.368	.372
	Louisville (IL)	AAA	.251	47	167	14	42	5	2	0	8	12	34	2	.305	.302
MAJOR LEAGUE TOTALS			.167	52	96	8	16	4	0	0	3	8	32	2	.208	.238
MINOR LEAGUE TOTALS			.255	566	2138	327	546	80	24	30	203	225	374	149	.357	.326

21. William Bergolla, 2b/ss

Born: Feb. 4, 1983. **Ht.:** 6-0. **Wt.:** 170. **Bats:** R. **Throws:** R. **Career Transactions:** Signed out of Venezuela by Reds, Nov. 15, 1999.

Bergolla's sweet, natural stroke stood out to Reds assistant scouting director Johnny Almaraz at a Venezuela tryout camp in 1999. Bergolla started last year as one of the youngest everyday players in the Midwest League. While he wasn't overmatched, he spent the second half of the year in the Rookie-level Pioneer League, where he finished third in hitting. Bergolla uses his hands well, and scouts like the way the ball comes off his bat. They see that as a sign he'll find the gaps more frequently as he fills out his wiry frame. Showing more patience also would help. Bergolla is a solid-average runner down the line and even better once he gets going. He demonstrates a good feel for taking extra bases. Bergolla's arm is average, but some scouts question if he can stay at shortstop. He projects as an above-average second baseman with good hands, though he needs to improve his footwork on grounders and double-play pivots. He'll be tested in low Class A again this year.

Year	Club (League)	Class	AVG	G	AB	R	H	2B	3B	HR	RBI	BB	SO	SB	SLG	OBP
2000	Cagua (VSL)	R	.372	13	43	6	16	3	2	0	5	8	3	1	.535	.481
	Reds (GCL)	R	.182	8	22	2	4	0	0	0	0	4	2	3	.182	.308
2001	Billings (Pio)	R	.323	57	232	47	75	5	3	4	24	24	21	22	.422	.387
2002	Dayton (Mid)	A	.248	68	274	38	68	13	1	3	23	16	36	13	.336	.291
	Billings (Pio)	R	.352	53	210	35	74	9	1	3	29	24	26	16	.448	.408
MINOR LEAGUE TOTALS			.303	199	781	128	237	30	7	10	81	76	88	55	.398	.364

22. Tony Blanco, 3b

Born: Nov. 10, 1981. **Ht.:** 6-1. **Wt.:** 170. **Bats:** R. **Throws:** R. **Career Transactions:** Signed out of Dominican Republic by Red Sox, July 2, 1998 . . . Traded with RHP Josh Thigpen to Red Sox, Dec. 16, 2002, completing trade in which Reds sent 2B Todd Walker to Red Sox for two players to be named (Dec. 12, 2002).

Considered the top position player in the Red Sox system the previous two years, Blanco saw his stock fall considerably in 2002. He fell behind Shea Hillenbrand and Kevin Youkilis on Boston's depth chart before being included in a December trade for Todd Walker. Blanco still has impressive power tools. His pop and infield arm remained the class of the Boston organization until the trade. But he has hit just .248 in two years of full-season ball, and his 148-23 strikeout-walk ratio during that time is even more disturbing. The Red Sox worked extensively with him and he showed signs of making adjustments in batting practice, but Blanco didn't carry his lessons into game action. His swing gets too long, and he flies open in his stance trying to pull pitches way out of the park. After shoulder problems cost him time in 2001, he missed the first two months of 2002 when an errant pitch broke his left hand in spring training. He doesn't move especially well at third base, but he does have a cannon for an arm. With Mark Schramek ticketed for high Class A this year, Blanco may have to take a step back to low Class A.

Year	Club (League)	Class	AVG	G	AB	R	H	2B	3B	HR	RBI	BB	SO	SB	SLG	OBP
1999	Red Sox (DSL)	R	.277	67	249	36	69	12	5	8	41	29	65	12	.462	.366
2000	Red Sox (GCL)	R	.384	52	190	32	73	13	1	13	50	18	38	6	.668	.442
	Lowell (NY-P)	A	.143	9	28	1	4	1	0	0	0	2	12	1	.179	.226
2001	Augusta (SAL)	A	.265	96	370	44	98	23	2	17	69	17	78	1	.476	.308
2002	Sarasota (FSL)	A	.221	65	244	22	54	13	2	6	32	6	70	2	.365	.250
MINOR LEAGUE TOTALS			.276	289	1081	135	298	62	10	44	192	72	263	22	.474	.332

23. Alan Moye, of

Born: Oct. 8, 1982. **Ht.:** 6-2. **Wt.:** 200. **Bats:** R. **Throws:** R. **School:** Pine Tree HS, Longview, Texas. **Career Transactions:** Selected by Reds in third round of 2001 draft; signed June 9, 2001.

Moye wasn't highly touted entering his senior year of high school in 2001. The baseball competition in east Texas isn't highly regarded by scouts, and his parents, both educators, were expected to steer him to Baylor. He also was a standout wide receiver, which took away from his time on the diamond. The Reds were delighted when they were able to draft him in the third round and sign him for $400,000. He's a special athlete built along the lines of a young Eric Davis, which is why the Rangers tried to acquire Moye last July in a trade that Kenny Rogers vetoed. Moye was the most improved player in the system last year and was the standout in Cincinnati's 2002 instructional league program. He applies his wiry strength at the plate, where the ball takes off upon contact, as well as on the bases and in the outfield. While he's a plus runner, Moye needs to use his speed more effectively on the diamond. His strike-zone knowledge also is undeveloped. The Reds expect him to adjust quickly, starting this year in low Class A.

Year	Club (League)	Class	AVG	G	AB	R	H	2B	3B	HR	RBI	BB	SO	SB	SLG	OBP
2001	Reds (GCL)	R	.287	48	171	24	49	9	2	2	18	8	34	12	.398	.330
2002	Billings (Pio)	R	.261	43	157	20	41	6	4	5	22	9	47	3	.446	.324
MINOR LEAGUE TOTALS			.274	91	328	44	90	15	6	7	40	17	81	15	.421	.327

24. Miguel Perez, c

Born: Sept. 25, 1983. **Ht.:** 6-3. **Wt.:** 190. **Bats:** R. **Throws:** R. **Career Transactions:** Signed out of Venezuela by Reds, Nov. 15, 2000.

Signed by Reds international scouting director Jorge Oquendo, Perez made an impressive U.S. debut in the Gulf Coast League last year. Now Cincinnati has him slotted behind Joey Votto and Dane Sardinha on its catching depth chart. His defensive tools also rank a close second to Sardinha. Perez threw out 31 percent of basestealers last year, a rate scouts expect to rise as he learns to harness his plus arm strength. He tends to drop his arm angle, causing his throws to tail and lose carry. A simple adjustment with his footwork and more experience should help him become a menacing presence behind the plate. Perez doesn't produce much power now, but he's an aggressive hitter with a knack for putting the ball in play. He needs to shorten his stroke. Coming off an encouraging instructional league stint, he has a chance to jump all the way to low Class A this year.

Year	Club (League)	Class	AVG	G	AB	R	H	2B	3B	HR	RBI	BB	SO	SB	SLG	OBP
2001	Cagua (VSL)	R	.331	48	163	20	54	3	1	0	19	12	33	6	.362	.377
2002	Cagua (VSL)	R	.213	34	108	14	23	4	0	2	18	9	23	1	.306	.320
	Reds (GCL)	R	.360	26	86	12	31	1	0	0	11	2	9	3	.372	.396
MINOR LEAGUE TOTALS			.303	108	357	46	108	8	1	2	48	23	65	10	.347	.363

25. Chris Booker, rhp

Born: Dec. 9, 1976. **Ht.:** 6-3. **Wt.:** 230. **Bats:** R. **Throws:** R. **School:** Monroe County HS, Monroeville, Ala. **Career Transactions:** Selected by Cubs in 20th round of 1995 draft; signed June 15, 1995 . . . Traded by Cubs with RHP Ben Shaffar to Reds for OF Michael Tucker, July 20, 2001 . . . On disabled list, April 4-Sept. 17, 2002.

Booker has pitched all of 16 innings for the Reds since being acquired from the Cubs in a mid-2001 deal for Michael Tucker. Nevertheless, Cincinnati placed the fireballer on its 40-man roster in the offseason to protect him from the Rule 5 draft. Booker missed all of 2002 after spring surgery to repair a torn labrum. Before he got hurt, his stature and upper-90s fastball reminded observers of Lee Smith. His splitter, slider and command all needed refinement, but it was easy to project him helping the Reds bullpen in the not-too-distant future. Now Booker's timetable may be pushed back as far as 2004. He likely won't return to the mound until spring training, though he showed his range of motion and flexibility were back in instructional league last October.

Year	Club (League)	Class	W	L	ERA	G	GS	CG	SV	IP	H	R	ER	HR	BB	SO	AVG
1995	Cubs (GCL)	R	3	2	2.76	13	7	0	1	42	36	22	13	0	16	43	.232
1996	Daytona (FSL)	A	0	0	0.00	1	1	0	0	2	1	1	0	0	3	2	.125
	Williamsport (NY-P)	A	4	6	5.31	14	14	0	0	61	57	51	36	2	51	52	.246
1997	Williamsport (NY-P)	A	1	5	3.35	24	3	0	1	46	39	20	17	2	25	60	.234
1998	Rockford (Mid)	A	1	2	3.36	44	1	0	4	64	47	32	24	2	53	78	.212
1999	Daytona (FSL)	A	2	5	3.95	42	0	0	6	73	72	45	32	6	37	68	.254
2000	Daytona (FSL)	A	0	2	2.28	31	0	0	10	28	25	12	7	0	14	34	.238
	West Tenn (SL)	AA	1	0	3.68	12	0	0	0	15	10	8	6	1	12	21	.189
2001	West Tenn (SL)	AA	2	6	4.33	45	0	0	1	52	39	29	25	7	36	76	.205
	Chattanooga (SL)	AA	2	0	3.94	16	0	0	1	16	13	7	7	1	11	25	.217
2002								Did Not Play—Injured									
MINOR LEAGUE TOTALS			16	28	3.77	242	26	0	24	399	339	227	167	21	258	459	.230

26. Alex Farfan, rhp

Born: Jan. 6, 1983. **Ht.:** 6-3. **Wt.:** 200. **Bats:** R. **Throws:** R. **Career Transactions:** Signed out of Venezuela by Reds, June 15, 2000.

Farfan garnered attention last summer when he moved to the bullpen during his U.S. debut and lit up radar guns with 96-97 mph readings. General manager Jim Bowden included him among the organization's top up-and-coming arms. Right now, however, Farfan is little more than an arm-strength guy. He threw in the low 80s when he signed in June 2000 and since has added 25 pounds to his projectable frame. His primary objective in instructional league was to work on his secondary pitches. He is trying to develop a consistent arm speed and grip on his changeup and slider. Farfan was one of 55 pitchers invited to the Reds' minor league advanced development program in February to get a head start on spring training. He could skip a level and begin 2003 in low Class A.

Year	Club (League)	Class	W	L	ERA	G	GS	CG	SV	IP	H	R	ER	HR	BB	SO	AVG
2000	Cagua (VSL)	R	0	4	12.15	8	3	0	0	13	17	24	18	0	16	11	.327
2001	Cagua (VSL)	R	0	2	3.74	16	5	0	2	34	22	19	14	0	37	26	—
2002	Reds (GCL)	R	3	4	5.18	20	5	0	4	40	28	28	23	3	20	31	.194
MINOR LEAGUE TOTALS			3	10	5.69	44	13	0	6	87	67	71	55	3	73	68	—

27. Kyle Edens, rhp

Born: Jan. 25, 1980. **Ht.:** 5-10. **Wt.:** 200. **Bats:** R. **Throws:** R. **School:** Baylor University. **Career Transactions:** Selected by Reds in third round of 2002 draft; signed Nov. 6, 2002.

Edens played with Mark Schramek at San Antonio's James Madison High, and like Schramek was one of the more attractive college seniors in the 2002 draft. He didn't sign until November so the Reds could fit his $300,000 bonus—the lowest in the third round—into their 2003 budget. Undrafted in 2001, he turned heads when he was clocked at 96-97 mph in Baylor's season opener at Minute Maid Park last February. Edens didn't maintain that velocity throughout the college season, but he sat at 93 mph and flirted with the mid-90s while tying for the Big 12 Conference lead with 14 saves. He's similar to Scott Williamson (another Big 12 product) in stature, stuff, aggressive mentality and the effort in his delivery. Edens is a two-pitch guy with a slider that breaks 15 inches. He occasionally mixes in a decent changeup, giving the Reds hope he can handle a starting assignment, if for no other reason than to accumulate innings. He'll make his pro debut in Class A this year.

Year	Club (League)	Class	W	L	ERA	G	GS	CG	SV	IP	H	R	ER	HR	BB	SO	AVG
					Has Not Played—Signed 2003 Contract												

28. Jesse Gutierrez, 1b/c

Born: June 16, 1978. **Ht.:** 6-2. **Wt.:** 190. **Bats:** R. **Throws:** R. **School:** St. Mary's (Texas) University. **Career Transactions:** Selected by Reds in 20th round of 2001 draft; signed June 6, 2001.

Gutierrez led NCAA Division I with an .855 slugging percentage at Texas-Pan American in 2000, then transferred to St. Mary's and led Division II with 28 homers the following year. He also hit two homers in his final game, earning MVP honors as the Rattlers won the national title. Reds area scout Jimmy Gonzales saw Gutierrez launch six home runs in a doubleheader for St. Mary's and was impressed with his electric bat speed. He makes good contact for a power hitter, though his plate discipline slipped in 2002 when he got his first exposure to full-season ball. Primarily a first baseman in college, Gutierrez has experience behind the plate, and the Reds project his value soaring as he learns the nuances of catching. He has good arm strength, but has to work on the fundamentals and shortening his release. He threw out 24 percent of basestealers last year and didn't commit an error in 33 games as a catcher. Gutierrez spent the offseason in a conditioning program at IMG's

Baseball Academy in Bradenton, Fla., in preparation to handle the catching chores at Stockton.

Year	Club (League)	Class	AVG	G	AB	R	H	2B	3B	HR	RBI	BB	SO	SB	SLG	OBP
2001	Billings (Pio)	R	.294	72	269	45	79	21	0	16	61	29	43	1	.550	.369
2002	Dayton (Mid)	A	.273	123	458	51	125	28	1	13	66	32	78	2	.424	.324
MINOR LEAGUE TOTALS			.281	195	727	96	204	49	1	29	127	61	121	3	.470	.341

29. Blake Williams, rhp

Born: Feb. 22, 1979. **Ht.:** 6-5. **Wt.:** 210. **Bats:** R. **Throws:** R. **School:** Southwest Texas State University. **Career Transactions:** Selected by Cardinals in first round (24th overall) of 2000 draft; signed July 19, 2000 . . . Selected by Reds from Cardinals in major league Rule 5 draft, Dec. 16, 2002.

Williams was one of the biggest surprises in the major league phase of the Rule 5 draft in December after missing most of the season recovering from Tommy John surgery. He had the operation in July 2001 and returned to the mound ahead of schedule. He may have come back too soon, though, making just two starts before being shut down with a mild case of tendinitis. The Cardinals wouldn't let him return to the mound as a precaution, and possibly in an attempt to hide him from the Rule 5 draft. All three of Cincinnati's big league Rule 5 picks came with disclaimers, as Luke Prokopec is recovering from arthroscopic shoulder surgery and Jerome Gamble is a member of the Tommy John fraternity. The 24th overall pick in the 2000 draft, Williams began his pro career in promising fashion before being sidelined. When healthy, he has an average fastball, a plus curveball, a developing changeup and good command. His delivery was considered clean before the injury, and because he didn't rely solely on arm strength—though he touched the mid-90s in college—he should be able to recover his form. The Reds' reports had Williams at 100 percent during the offseason.

Year	Club (League)	Class	W	L	ERA	G	GS	CG	SV	IP	H	R	ER	HR	BB	SO	AVG
2000	New Jersey (NY-P)	A	3	1	1.59	6	6	0	0	28	20	7	5	1	9	25	.202
2001	Potomac (Car)	A	4	10	2.43	17	17	2	0	107	82	43	29	12	30	92	.211
2002	New Jersey (NY-P)	A	0	1	1.69	2	2	0	0	5	2	1	1	1	1	8	.111
MINOR LEAGUE TOTALS			7	12	2.23	25	25	2	0	141	104	51	35	14	40	125	.206

30. Hector Tiburcio, ss

Born: June 11, 1981. **Ht.:** 6-0. **Wt.:** 150. **Bats:** B. **Throws:** R. **Career Transactions:** Signed out of Dominican Republic by Reds, Oct. 15, 1999.

Tiburcio ranked 27th on this list a year ago, under the name of Danny Mateo. In addition to his change of identity, Tiburcio also turned out to be 14 months older than previously reported. He still remains an intriguing prospect because of his raw tools and phenomenal defensive ability. His pure shortstop actions are nearly as good as Rainer Olmedo's. Tiburcio has soft hands, quickness to go with raw speed, the ability to make plays on the move and a plus arm to boot. He needs to play more under control after committing 32 errors in 52 games at shortstop last year. As with Olmedo, his bat is questionable. Tiburico must learn the importance of working counts and showing plate discipline. A switch-hitter, he's aggressive at the plate with a decent swing and projectable gap power. He'll move slowly until he develops more offensively.

Year	Club (League)	Class	AVG	G	AB	R	H	2B	3B	HR	RBI	BB	SO	SB	SLG	OBP
2000	Reds (DSL)	R	.242	48	153	34	37	2	4	1	17	23	28	13	.327	.362
2001	Reds (GCL)	R	.244	53	180	29	44	6	0	1	14	15	48	27	.294	.323
	Billings (Pio)	R	.556	4	9	1	5	0	0	0	2	0	3	0	.556	.556
2002	Reds (GCL)	R	.240	9	25	6	6	1	0	0	1	2	2	3	.280	.321
	Billings (Pio)	R	.259	48	185	33	48	7	3	2	14	17	39	16	.362	.324
MINOR LEAGUE TOTALS			.254	162	552	103	140	16	7	4	48	57	120	59	.330	.338

CLEVELAND
INDIANS

TOP 30 PROSPECTS

1. Brandon Phillips, ss/2b
2. Victor Martinez, c
3. Cliff Lee, lhp
4. Jeremy Guthrie, rhp
5. Travis Hafner, 1b
6. Ricardo Rodriguez, rhp
7. Grady Sizemore, of
8. Billy Traber, lhp
9. Brian Tallet, lhp
10. Jason Davis, rhp
11. Corey Smith, 3b
12. Francisco Cruceta, rhp
13. Alex Escobar, of
14. J.D. Martin, rhp
15. Josh Bard, c
16. Dan Denham, rhp
17. Johnny Peralta, ss
18. Travis Foley, rhp
19. Matt Whitney, 3b
20. Luis Garcia, of/1b
21. Alex Herrera, lhp
22. Fernando Cabrera, rhp
23. Ben Broussard, 1b/of
24. Sean Smith, rhp
25. Ryan Church, of
26. Covelli Crisp, of
27. Chris de la Cruz, ss
28. Micah Schilling, 2b
29. Carl Sadler, lhp
30. Brian Slocum, rhp

By Jim Ingraham

Few clubs have made such a radical mid-season change as the Indians did in 2002. After starting the season with the dubious premise that they could remain a contender while rebuilding, club executives scrubbed that notion by late June and embarked on a full-blown detonation of the roster. With a series of veterans-for-prospects trades, Cleveland said good-bye to an era that included six American League Central titles in seven years.

The Indians spent the second half of the season replenishing their minor league system and evaluating the young players they acquired in those trades. They now have more prospect depth than any franchise in the game.

The midseason deals landed five players who made 2002 Top 10 Prospects lists with their previous organization: Expos infielder Brandon Phillips and outfielder Grady Sizemore, Dodgers righthander Ricardo Rodriguez, Cardinals outfielder/first baseman Luis Garcia and Reds first baseman/outfielder Ben Broussard. Cleveland also got players whose stock rose during the season. Then they acquired first baseman Travis Hafner from the Rangers in an offseason trade. He immediately became the organization's best power prospect. That influx of talent, coupled with emerging prospects already in the system and products of a strong 2002 draft, give the Indians hope their rebuilding can be completed sooner rather than later.

With the new players comes a new manager, Eric Wedge, whose background is in player development. He served Cleveland as a minor league manager for the last six years and has worked with many of the prospects.

Expectations for 2003 will be way down, especially with the departure of Jim Thome as a free agent to the Phillies. The Indians would be content if Wedge can work several of the young players into key roles and have them show progress by the end of the season.

General manager Mark Shapiro's administration enters its second year hoping it will be quieter and less eventful than its first. The turbulent 2002 season included the firing of manager Charlie Manuel, the death of longtime trainer Jimmy Warfield, injuries to several key players, a failed effort to retain Thome, and the acknowledgment that the club's yearly waltz to a division title is no longer a given. It's time to look at kids, lots and lots of kids.

Organization Overview

General Manager: Mark Shapiro. **Farm Director:** John Farrell. **Scouting Director:** John Mirabelli.

2002 PERFORMANCE

Class	Farm Team	League	W	L	Pct.	Finish*	Manager(s)
Majors	Cleveland	American	74	88	.457	9th (14)	C. Manuel/J. Skinner
Triple-A	Buffalo Bisons	International	87	57	.604	2nd (14)	Eric Wedge
Double-A	Akron Aeros	Eastern	93	48	.660	1st (12)	Brad Komminsk
High A	Kinston Indians	Carolina	74	65	.532	4th (8)	Ted Kubiak
Low A	†Columbus RedStixx	South Atlantic	79	60	.568	3rd (16)	Torey Lovullo
Short-season	Mahoning Valley Scrappers	New York-Penn	46	30	.605	5th (14)	Chris Bando
Rookie	Burlington Indians	Appalachian	29	39	.426	8th (10)	Rouglas Odor
OVERALL 2002 MINOR LEAGUE RECORD			408	299	.577	1st (30)	

*Finish in overall standings (No. of teams in league).   †Franchise will move to Eastlake, Ohio, for 2003.

ORGANIZATION LEADERS

BATTING
*Minimum 250 At-Bats
*AVG	Victor Martinez, Akron	.336
R	Victor Martinez, Akron	84
H	Chris Coste, Buffalo	152
TB	Victor Martinez, Akron	255
2B	Victor Martinez, Akron	40
3B	Zach Sorensen, Buffalo	12
HR	Victor Martinez, Akron	22
RBI	Victor Martinez, Akron	85
BB	J.J. Sherrill, Columbus	65
SO	Corey Smith, Kinston	141
SB	Alex Requena, Kinston	72

PITCHING
#Minimum 75 Innings
W	Billy Traber, Buffalo/Akron	17
L	Jake Dittler, Columbus	11
#ERA	Marcos Mendoza, Akron/Kinston	1.61
G	Ryan Larson, Buffalo/Akron/Kinston	56
CG	Three tied at	2
SV	Lee Gronkiewicz, Columbus	27
IP	Billy Traber, Buffalo/Akron	162
BB	Dan Denham, Columbus	65
SO	Travis Foley, Columbus	138

BEST TOOLS

Best Hitter for Average	Victor Martinez
Best Power Hitter	Travis Hafner
Fastest Baserunner	Alex Requena
Best Athlete	Brandon Phillips
Best Fastball	Jason Davis
Best Curveball	Francisco Cruceta
Best Slider	Cliff Lee
Best Changeup	Jeremy Guthrie
Best Control	Billy Traber
Best Defensive Catcher	Josh Bard
Best Defensive Infielder	Ivan Ochoa
Best Infield Arm	Brandon Phillips
Best Defensive Outfielder	Jody Gerut
Best Outfield Arm	Ryan Church

PROJECTED 2006 LINEUP

Catcher	Victor Martinez
First Base	Travis Hafner
Second Base	Brandon Phillips
Third Base	Corey Smith
Shortstop	Johnny Peralta
Left Field	Grady Sizemore
Center Field	Alex Escobar
Right Field	Luis Garcia
Designated Hitter	Matt Whitney
No. 1 Starter	C.C. Sabathia

Chris Coste   Ryan Larson

No. 2 Starter	Cliff Lee
No. 3 Starter	Jeremy Guthrie
No. 4 Starter	Ricardo Rodriguez
No. 5 Starter	Billy Traber
Closer	Danys Baez

TOP PROSPECTS OF THE DECADE

1993	Manny Ramirez, of
1994	Manny Ramirez, of
1995	Jaret Wright, rhp
1996	Bartolo Colon, rhp
1997	Bartolo Colon, rhp
1998	Sean Casey, 1b
1999	Russell Branyan, 3b
2000	C.C. Sabathia, lhp
2001	C.C. Sabathia, lhp
2002	Corey Smith, 3b

TOP DRAFT PICKS OF THE DECADE

1993	Daron Kirkreit, rhp
1994	Jaret Wright, rhp
1995	David Miller, 1b/of
1996	Danny Peoples, 1b/of
1997	Tim Drew, rhp
1998	C.C. Sabathia, lhp
1999	Will Hartley, c (2)
2000	Corey Smith, 3b
2001	Dan Denham, rhp
2002	Jeremy Guthrie, rhp

ALL-TIME LARGEST BONUSES

Danys Baez, 1999	$4,500,000
Jeremy Guthrie, 2002	$3,000,000
Dan Denham, 2001	$1,860,000
Tim Drew, 1997	$1,600,000
Corey Smith, 2000	$1,375,000

MinorLeagueDepthChart

CLEVELAND INDIANS

RANK 1

The Indians were a perennial contender in the American League in the 1990s, though they never won a World Series. They sacrificed minor league talent in their quest for a title to such a degree that their farm system ranked among the weakest in the game. All that has changed as new general manager Mark Shapiro is rebuilding the organization from the bottom up, through trades and the draft. He dealt veterans for prospects en masse last year, with 10 of the organization's top 20 prospects coming in trades. Scouting director John Mirabelli has had a slew of extra draft picks to stock the lower levels, and his 2001 and 2002 efforts ranked among the best in the game. The Latin American program is also stronger than it's ever been.

Note: Depth charts prepared by Josh Boyd. Numbers in parentheses indicate prospect rankings.

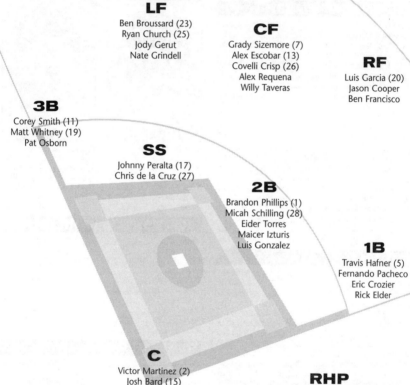

LF
Ben Broussard (23)
Ryan Church (25)
Jody Gerut
Nate Grindell

CF
Grady Sizemore (7)
Alex Escobar (13)
Covelli Crisp (26)
Alex Requena
Willy Taveras

RF
Luis Garcia (20)
Jason Cooper
Ben Francisco

3B
Corey Smith (11)
Matt Whitney (19)
Pat Osborn

SS
Johnny Peralta (17)
Chris de la Cruz (27)

2B
Brandon Phillips (1)
Micah Schilling (28)
Eider Torres
Maicer Izturis
Luis Gonzalez

1B
Travis Hafner (5)
Fernando Pacheco
Eric Crozier
Rick Elder

C
Victor Martinez (2)
Josh Bard (15)

RHP

Starters	Relievers
Jeremy Guthrie (4)	Alberto Garza
Ricardo Rodriguez (6)	Jose Vargas
Jason Davis (10)	Hank Thoms
Francisco Cruceta (12)	David Elder
J.D. Martin (14)	
Dan Denham (16)	
Travis Foley (18)	
Fernando Cabrera (22)	
Sean Smith (24)	
Brian Slocum (30)	
Jake Dittler	
Kyle Denney	
Ryan Larson	
Nick Moran	
Matthew Haynes	
Jim Ed Warden	

LHP

Starters	Relievers
Cliff Lee (3)	Alex Herrera (21)
Billy Traber (8)	Carl Sadler (29)
Brian Tallet (9)	Chris Cooper
Mariano Gomez	Victor Kleine
Lance Carraciolli	Mike Hernandez
Shane Wallace	
Keith Ramsey	

DraftAnalysis

2002 Draft

Best Pro Debut: OF Ben Francisco (5) hit .349-3-23 with 22 steals, leading the short-season New York-Penn League in batting and runs (55). LHP Keith Ramsey (10) gave the Indians a second NY-P all-star, going 6-3, 2.04 with a 71-10 strikeout-walk ratio. LHP Shea Douglas (32) used his plus-plus change-up to go 3-1, 1.29 with a 51-10 K-BB ratio. He had two scoreless appearances in the low Class A South Atlantic League playoffs.

Best Athlete: Francisco does everything but hit homers and may stay in center field. OF Nathan Panther's (15) lefthanded bat, speed and arm strength are all intriguing.

Best Pure Hitter: 2B Micah Schilling's (1) swing evokes memories of another Louisiana prep star, Will Clark. Schilling was bothered by a bone chip in his left elbow after signing and batted .206 in Rookie ball. 3B Matt Whitney (1) also has a nice stroke.

Best Raw Power: OF Jason Cooper (3) never got the most of his power in three years at Stanford. The Indians are letting him use the leg lift he had in high school and encouraging him to pull more pitches.

Fastest Runner: Panther, a 6.6-second runner in the 60-yard dash.

Best Defensive Player: Though 3B Pat Osborn (2) tore the labrum in both his shoulders, the Indians believe his arm is bouncing back. He's agile at the hot corner.

Best Fastball: RHP Jeremy Guthrie (1) works at 90-95 mph, a tick ahead of RHP Brian Slocum (2).

Best Breaking Ball: LHP Michael Hernandez' (6) power slider will help him move quickly. Ramsey's slider is his best pitch.

Most Intriguing Background: 1B Bill Peavey's (11) brother Pat signed with the Astros as a 33rd-rounder. Their great-grandmother Hazel Hotchkiss Wightman, after whom tennis' Wightman Cup is named, won six U.S. singles tennis titles. Ramsey's great-uncle John Ramsey was a public-address announcer for the Dodgers. Cooper was Stanford's backup punter as a freshman. C Clayton McCullough's (22) father Howard scouts for the Diamondbacks.

Whitney

Closest To The Majors: Guthrie may follow Danys Baez' path to the majors. Baez spent little more than a year in the minors before reaching Cleveland, and Guthrie has an even better feel for pitching.

Best Late-Round Pick: Panther has a higher ceiling than Ramsey but will need a lot more seasoning.

The One Who Got Away: The Indians signed their first 16 picks. They hoped to steer slugging OF Curt Mendoza (19) to a junior college, but he's at San Diego State.

Assessment: With four extra picks, Cleveland got two of the best college arms (Guthrie and Slocum) sandwiching two of the best high school bats (Whitney and Schilling). The Indians added plenty of talent deeper in the draft, and got first-round quality in RHP Sean Smith as a draft-and-follow.

2001 Draft

RHPs Dan Denham (1) and J.D. Martin (1) still have time to regain the form they showed in their pro debuts. As for the two other first-rounders, RHP Alan Horne didn't sign and OF Michael Conroy hasn't hit. RHPs Travis Foley (4) and Sean Smith (16, draft-and-follow) have come on since signing. **Grade: C+**

2000 Draft

3B Corey Smith (1) and LHP Brian Tallet (2) have made decent progress. LHP Derek Thompson (1) was lost to the Dodgers in the December major league Rule 5 draft. **Grade: C+**

1999 Draft

One of the worst drafts ever kicked off with no first-round pick, then C Will Hartley (2), who was out of baseball within two years. This could have been salvaged with the signing of 3B Jeff Baker (4). **Grade: F**

1998 Draft

LHP C.C. Sabathia (1) is at the heart of Cleveland's rebuilding effort. RHP Ryan Drese (5) fizzled before he was traded this offseason. **Grade: A**

Note: Draft analysis prepared by Jim Callis. Numbers in parentheses indicate draft rounds.

... Phillips' confidence and flair some- times annoy opponents. But he enjoys playing the game and doesn't hide it.

ED WOLFSTEIN

Brandon
Phillips ss/2b

Born: June 28, 1981.
Ht.: 5-11. **Wt.:** 180.
Bats: R. **Throws:** R.
School: Redan HS, Stone Mountain, Ga.
Career Transactions: Selected by Expos in second round of 1999 draft; signed June 21, 1999 ... Traded by Expos with 1B Lee Stevens, OF Grady Sizemore and LHP Cliff Lee to Indians for RHP Bartolo Colon and a player to be named, June 27, 2002; Expos acquired RHP Tim Drew to complete trade (June 28, 2002).

Of all the prospects the Indians reeled in with trades in 2002, Phillips was clearly the biggest trophy. Rated the Expos' No. 1 prospect before the season, he was the marquee name in the package the Indians acquired for Bartolo Colon. After settling in at Triple-A Buffalo, Phillips flashed the five-tool ability that has always excited scouts. He earned a big league cameo in September and made several eye-popping plays at second base, his new position. He moved from shortstop in deference to Omar Vizquel.

Phillips is a premier athlete who projects as an all-star at either middle-infield postion. As a shortstop, Phillips has drawn comparisons to a young Barry Larkin or Derek Jeter. Hitting out of a Jeff Bagwell-style crouch, Phillips has the bat speed and athletic skill to be a top-of-the-order hitter. Few middle infielders offer his combination of hitting for average and power. He has average range and plus arm strength at shortstop, and those tools play even better at second base. Phillips also has a charisma that stamps him as a special player. His confidence and flair sometimes annoy opponents. But he enjoys playing the game and doesn't hide it.

Phillips sometimes tries to do too much. He'll overswing when ahead in the count. He needs to drive the ball to right-center to counter the adjustments pitchers have made to attack his holes. He's still learning how to turn the double play as a second baseman. Most important is his weight transfer as he comes across the bag, which can lead to him short-hopping throws to first. Phillips will get a long look for Cleveland's second-base job, especially with incumbent Ricky Gutierrez a question mark following spinal surgery. Even if he returns to Triple-A, it won't be long before he joins the Indians for good.

Year	Club (League)	Class	AVG	G	AB	R	H	2B	3B	HR	RBI	BB	SO	SB	SLG	OBP
1999	Expos (GCL)	R	.290	47	169	23	49	11	3	1	21	15	35	12	.408	.358
2000	Cape Fear (SAL)	A	.242	126	484	74	117	17	8	11	72	38	97	23	.378	.306
2001	Jupiter (FSL)	A	.284	55	194	36	55	12	2	4	23	38	45	17	.428	.414
	Harrisburg (EL)	AA	.298	67	265	35	79	19	0	7	36	12	42	13	.449	.337
2002	Harrisburg (EL)	AA	.327	60	245	40	80	13	2	9	35	16	33	6	.506	.380
	Ottawa (IL)	AAA	.257	10	35	1	9	4	0	1	5	2	6	0	.457	.297
	Buffalo (IL)	AAA	.283	55	223	30	63	14	0	8	27	14	39	8	.453	.321
	Cleveland (AL)	MAJ	.258	11	31	5	8	3	1	0	4	3	6	0	.419	.343
MAJOR LEAGUE TOTALS			.258	11	31	5	8	3	1	0	4	3	6	0	.419	.343
MINOR LEAGUE TOTALS			.280	420	1615	239	452	90	15	41	219	135	297	79	.430	.344

2. Victor Martinez, c

Born: Dec. 23, 1978. **Ht.:** 6-2. **Wt.:** 160. **Bats:** B. **Throws:** R. **Career Transactions:** Signed out of Venezuela by Indians, July 15, 1996.

Martinez has won back-to-back batting titles and MVP awards in the high Class A Carolina and Double-A Eastern leagues–as a switch-hitting catcher. In 2002, he also led the EL in slugging percentage, on-base percentage and runs. Martinez is a natural hitter with tremendous strike-zone discipline and an uncanny ability to produce from either side of the plate. He rarely swings and misses. His power numbers jumped in 2002 as he got stronger. He has shown an ability to pick the pitch and count that allow him to drive the ball. Martinez' skills at calling a game and blocking and receiving pitches are also major league ready. Martinez' throwing needs work. It's a matter of getting his footwork and arm action aligned. He struggles to stay mechanically consistent, which led to him throwing out just two of 13 big leaguers who tried to steal on him in September. Martinez could battle Josh Bard for a big league job, but he'll more likely begin the year in Triple-A. He's Cleveland's long-term catcher and a future all-star.

Year	Club (League)	Class	AVG	G	AB	R	H	2B	3B	HR	RBI	BB	SO	SB	SLG	OBP
1997	Maracay 1 (VSL)	R	.344	53	122	21	42	12	0	0	26	32	11	6	.443	.474
1998	Guacara 2 (VSL)	R	.269	55	160	28	43	13	0	1	27	32	14	8	.369	.404
1999	Mahoning Valley (NY-P)	A	.277	64	235	37	65	9	0	4	36	27	31	0	.366	.346
2000	Kinston (Car)	A	.217	26	83	9	18	7	0	0	8	11	5	1	.301	.313
	Columbus (SAL)	A	.371	21	70	11	26	9	1	2	12	11	6	0	.614	.452
2001	Kinston (Car)	A	.329	114	420	59	138	33	2	10	57	39	60	3	.488	.394
2002	Akron (EL)	AA	.336	121	443	84	149	40	0	22	85	58	62	3	.576	.417
	Cleveland (AL)	MAJ	.281	12	32	2	9	1	0	1	5	3	2	0	.406	.333
MAJOR LEAGUE TOTALS			.281	12	32	2	9	1	0	1	5	3	2	0	.406	.333
MINOR LEAGUE TOTALS			.314	454	1533	249	481	123	3	39	251	210	189	21	.474	.400

3. Cliff Lee, lhp

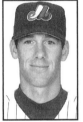

Born: Aug. 30, 1978. **Wt.:** 190. **Bats:** L. **Throws:** L. **School:** University of Arkansas. **Career Transactions:** Selected by Expos in fourth round of 2000 draft; signed July 6, 2000 . . . Traded by Expos with 1B Lee Stevens, SS Brandon Phillips and OF Grady Sizemore to Indians for RHP Bartolo Colon and a player to be named, June 27, 2002; Expos acquired RHP Tim Drew to complete trade (June 28, 2002).

After coming to the Indians in the Bartolo Colon deal, Lee jumped from Double-A to Triple-A to the big leagues, getting rave reviews at each level. Lee is a rare pitcher who can win without his best stuff. And when he's on, watch out. His fastball sits at 91-93 mph, his slider has good late action, and his curveball and changeup give hitters something else to worry about. Lee is so smooth that hitters don't get a good read on his pitches until they're halfway to the plate. Lee's velocity was down to the high 80s in September, probably because his innings jumped in 2002. He just needs to adjust to the majors and appreciate the importance of every pitch. Lee is a candidate to win one of the openings in the rotation behind C.C. Sabathia. He, Billy Traber and Brian Tallet give Cleveland three advanced southpaws, and Lee has the most upside.

Year	Club (League)	Class	W	L	ERA	G	GS	CG	SV	IP	H	R	ER	HR	BB	SO	AVG
2000	Cape Fear (SAL)	A	1	4	5.24	11	11	0	0	45	50	39	26	1	36	63	.281
2001	Jupiter (FSL)	A	6	7	2.79	21	20	0	0	110	78	43	34	13	46	129	.199
2002	Harrisburg (EL)	AA	7	2	3.23	15	15	0	0	86	61	31	31	12	23	105	.197
	Akron (EL)	AA	2	1	5.40	3	3	0	0	17	11	11	10	1	10	18	.180
	Buffalo (IL)	AAA	3	2	3.77	8	8	0	0	43	36	18	18	7	22	30	.229
	Cleveland (AL)	MAJ	0	1	1.74	2	2	0	0	10	6	2	2	0	8	6	.171
MAJOR LEAGUE TOTALS			0	1	1.74	2	2	0	0	10	6	2	2	0	8	6	.171
MINOR LEAGUE TOTALS			19	16	3.57	58	57	0	0	300	236	142	119	34	137	345	.215

4. Jeremy Guthrie, rhp

Born: April 8, 1979. **Ht.:** 6-1. **Wt.:** 195. **Bats:** R. **Throws:** R. **School:** Stanford University. **Career Transactions:** Selected by Indians in first round (22nd overall) of 2002 draft; signed Oct. 3, 2002.

It took about four months, but the Indians signed Guthrie to a four-year, $4 million major league contract. The deal included a $3 million signing bonus, a club record for a drafted player. The negotiations prevented him from pitching in the minors, so he debuted in the Arizona Fall League. Guthrie is an advanced pitcher. His fastball is in the 92-93 mph range and will touch 95 at times, and his slider and changeup are plus pitches. He has a strong, compact body and commands all his pitches well. He's mature beyond his years, thanks in part to a two-year Mormon mission in Spain. Guthrie faded late in 2001, his first year back from Spain, so there were some questions about his durability. But he answered those by finishing strong in 2002 and didn't miss a start in two years at Stanford. His 158 innings in 2002 were the most by a college pitcher. He's 23, so there's not a lot of room for projection, but he's plenty good as is. Guthrie likely will begin his pro career at Double-A Akron, unless the Indians decide to send him to the warmer climate of high Class A Kinston for the first month. It won't be a surprise if he reaches Cleveland by the end of 2003.

Year	Club (League)	Class	W	L	ERA	G	GS	CG	SV	IP	H	R	ER	HR	BB	SO	AVG
									Has Not Played—Signed 2003 Contract								

5. Travis Hafner, 1b

JOHN SPEAR

Born: June 3, 1977. **Ht.:** 6-3. **Wt.:** 240. **Bats:** L. **Throws:** R. **School:** Cowley County (Kan.) CC. **Career Transactions:** Selected by Rangers in 31st round of 1996 draft; signed June 2, 1997 . . . Traded by Rangers with RHP Aaron Myette to Indians for C Einar Diaz and RHP Ryan Drese, Dec. 6, 2002.

The December trade that brought Hafner to Cleveland couldn't have worked out better for the player or the team. The Indians saved $4.65 million and cleared the catching job for Victor Martinez and Josh Bard by sending Einar Diaz to Texas. And Hafner, who had a premium bat but no clear path to regular playing time with the slugger-laden Rangers, immediately becomes Cleveland's replacement for Jim Thome. One member of the Texas front office directly compared him to Thome a month before the trade and said Hafner's offensive upside rivaled that of Rangers farmhand Mark Teixeira, the best hitting prospect in the game. Hafner always used the whole field, and as his plate discipline has improved he has unleashed his power by working himself into favorable counts and learning to pull the ball. He's a grinder who has learned to hang tough against lefthanders and knows the value of a walk. He led the minors with a .463 on-base percentage in 2002 while walking more than he struck out. Only nagging wrist injuries, including a broken wrist in 2001, have slowed him offensively since he signed as a draft-in-follow in 1997—days after earning tournament MVP honors while leading Cowley County to the national junior college title. Defensively, he's not a slug, but Hafner's footwork can be awkward. He'll have to work to be adequate.

Year	Club (League)	Class	AVG	G	AB	R	H	2B	3B	HR	RBI	BB	SO	SB	SLG	OBP
1997	Rangers (GCL)	R	.286	55	189	38	54	14	0	5	24	24	45	7	.439	.375
1998	Savannah (SAL)	A	.237	123	405	62	96	15	4	16	84	68	139	7	.412	.351
1999	Savannah (SAL)	A	.292	134	480	94	140	30	4	28	111	67	151	5	.546	.387
2000	Charlotte (FSL)	A	.346	122	436	90	151	34	1	22	109	67	86	0	.580	.447
2001	Tulsa (TL)	AA	.282	88	323	59	91	25	0	20	74	59	82	3	.545	.396
2002	Oklahoma (PCL)	AAA	.342	110	401	79	137	22	1	21	77	79	76	2	.559	.463
	Texas (AL)	MAJ	.242	23	62	6	15	4	1	1	6	8	15	0	.387	.329
MAJOR LEAGUE TOTALS			.242	23	62	6	15	4	1	1	6	8	15	0	.387	.329
MINOR LEAGUE TOTALS			.299	632	2234	422	669	140	10	112	479	364	579	24	.521	.407

6. Ricardo Rodriguez, rhp

Born: May 21, 1978. **Ht.:** 6-3. **Wt.:** 160. **Bats:** R. **Throws:** R. **Career Transactions:** Signed out of Dominican Republic by Dodgers, Sept. 2, 1996 . . . Traded by Dodgers with LHP Terry Mulholland and RHP Francisco Cruceta to Indians for RHP Paul Shuey, July 28, 2002.

Acquired from the Dodgers for Paul Shuey, Rodriguez was the Dodgers' top prospect a year ago. Some scouts even rated Francisco Cruceta, who also was included in the trade, ahead of him. That transaction looks like a heist in Cleveland's favor. Rodriguez has the demeanor and talent to pitch at the front of a rotation. He loves to pitch inside—he drilled eight batters in seven big league games—and challenge hitters. His 92-95 mph fastball has above-average sink, and his slider is a strikeout pitch. Because of his aggressiveness, Rodriguez becomes too fastball-oriented with the game on the line. He got off to a slow start in 2002, which was attributed to too many innings in winter ball. Rodriguez is a strong candidate for the Cleveland rotation in 2003. There are four openings in the rotation, and he's the best righthander among the candidates, which works in his favor.

Year	Club(League)	Class	W	L	ERA	G	GS	CG	SV	IP	H	R	ER	HR	BB	SO	AVG
1997	Dodgers (DSL)	R	1	2	6.40	12	10	0	0	32	42	39	23	6	26	20	.316
1998	Dodgers (DSL)	R	1	1	3.55	13	9	1	0	33	28	19	13	2	34	36	.239
1999	Dodgers (DSL)	R	3	2	3.43	9	9	0	0	42	34	22	16	2	18	51	.227
2000	Great Falls (Pio)	R	10	3	1.88	15	15	2	0	96	66	32	20	2	23	129	.192

Year	Club (League)	Class	W	L	ERA	G	GS	CG	SV	IP	H	R	ER	HR	BB	SO	AVG
2001	Vero Beach (FSL)	A	14	6	3.21	26	26	2	0	154	133	67	55	13	60	154	.232
2002	Jacksonville (SL)	AA	5	4	1.99	11	11	2	0	68	56	21	15	4	13	44	.224
	Las Vegas (PCL)	AAA	1	0	3.86	2	2	0	0	12	13	5	5	1	5	7	.295
	Buffalo (IL)	AAA	3	1	3.60	4	4	0	0	25	26	10	10	1	7	14	.271
	Cleveland (AL)	MAJ	2	2	5.66	7	7	0	0	41	40	27	26	5	18	24	.255
MAJOR LEAGUE TOTALS			2	2	5.66	7	7	0	0	41	40	27	26	5	18	24	.255
MINOR LEAGUE TOTALS			38	19	3.06	92	86	7	0	462	398	215	157	31	186	455	.233

7. Grady Sizemore, of

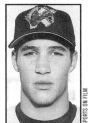

Born: Aug. 2, 1982. **Ht.:** 6-2. **Wt.:** 200. **Bats:** L. **Throws:** L. **School:** Cascade HS, Everett, Wash. **Career Transactions:** Selected by Expos in third round of 2000 draft; signed June 16, 2000 . . . Traded by Expos with 1B Lee Stevens, SS Brandon Phillips and LHP Cliff Lee to Indians for RHP Bartolo Colon and a player to be named, June 27, 2002; Expos acquired RHP Tim Drew to complete trade (June 28, 2002).

The third player among the organization's top seven prospects who was acquired in the Bartolo Colon trade, Sizemore stepped up his offensive production after switching organizations. If the Expos hadn't given him a $2 million signing bonus as a 2000 third-round pick, he'd be playing college football at Washington. Extremely confident, Sizemore is one of the most advanced hitters in the system. He's an above-average runner with the ability to cover center field, and he controls the strike zone well. He proved to be a natural, Kirk Gibson-style leader at Kinston and backed up his confidence by repeatedly coming through in the clutch. Sizemore's arm is his biggest weakness. He has a fringe arm for center, though his range and instincts should keep him at the position. He has yet to show the power the Indians expect will come, which may be related to his middle-of-the-field approach. Just 20, Sizemore is one of the most exciting position players Cleveland has had in years. He'll start the 2003 season in Double-A and could be ready for the majors by mid-2004.

Year	Club (League)	Class	AVG	G	AB	R	H	2B	3B	HR	RBI	BB	SO	SB	SLG	OBP
2000	Expos (GCL)	R	.293	55	205	31	60	8	3	1	14	23	24	16	.376	.380
2001	Clinton (Mid)	A	.268	123	451	64	121	16	4	2	61	81	92	32	.335	.381
2002	Brevard County (FSL)	A	.258	75	256	37	66	15	4	0	26	36	41	9	.348	.351
	Kinston (Car)	A	.343	47	172	31	59	9	3	3	20	33	30	14	.483	.451
MINOR LEAGUE TOTALS			.282	300	1084	163	306	48	14	6	121	173	187	71	.369	.385

8. Billy Traber, lhp

Born: Sept. 18, 1979. **Ht.:** 6-5. **Wt.:** 200. **Bats:** L. **Throws:** L. **School:** Loyola Marymount University. **Career Transactions:** Selected by Mets in first round (16th overall) of 2000 draft; signed Sept. 5, 2000 . . . Traded by Mets with 1B Earl Snyder to Indians, Dec. 13, 2001, completing trade in which Indians sent 2B Roberto Alomar, LHP Mike Bacsik and 1B Danny Peoples to Mets for OF Matt Lawton, OF Alex Escobar, RHP Jerrod Riggan and two players to be named (Dec. 11, 2001).

Alex Escobar was the biggest name acquired from the Mets for Roberto Alomar, but Traber's importance was reinforced when Escobar missed all of 2002 with a knee injury. While other pitching prospects were called up to Cleveland in September, Traber was not, in order to save a spot on the 40-man roster and to ease his workload. Pure and simple, Traber is a winner. He finished second in the minors with 17 wins. He isn't overpowering but has a variety of pitches and an unorthodox delivery. He's a strike thrower with good life and movement on all his pitches, making it tough for hitters to make hard contact. His fastball has below-average velocity at 87-88 mph, but its movement and Traber's delivery make it a solid pitch. His curveball and splitter are also reliable. Traber's changeup is his weakest pitch, and he needs it against righthanders. The Mets discovered ligament damage in his elbow after drafting him, but he has been durable to date as a pro. Yet another candidate for the Opening Day rotation, Traber should make his major league debut at some point in 2003.

Year	Club (League)	Class	W	L	ERA	G	GS	CG	SV	IP	H	R	ER	HR	BB	SO	AVG
2001	St. Lucie (FSL)	A	6	5	2.66	18	18	0	0	102	85	36	30	2	23	79	.223
	Binghamton (EL)	AA	4	3	4.43	8	8	0	0	43	50	25	21	4	13	45	.296
	Norfolk (IL)	AAA	0	1	1.29	1	1	0	0	7	5	3	1	0	0	0	.192
2002	Akron (EL)	AA	13	2	2.76	18	17	2	0	108	99	38	33	8	20	82	.243
	Buffalo (IL)	AAA	4	3	3.29	9	9	0	0	55	58	22	20	3	12	33	.276
MINOR LEAGUE TOTALS			27	14	3.01	54	53	2	0	314	297	124	105	17	68	239	.249

9. Brian Tallet, lhp

Born: Sept. 21, 1977. **Ht.:** 6-7. **Wt.:** 200. **Bats:** L. **Throws:** L. **School:** Louisiana State University. **Career Transactions:** Selected by Indians in second round of 2000 draft; signed Aug. 1, 2000.

Tallet threw six shutout innings against Boston on Sept. 16 to win his first big league start. His performance wasn't a surprise, considering he pitched in pressure games at Louisiana State, including the championship game of the 2000 College World Series. He's similar to Billy Traber with more velocity and less control. Tallet has absolutely no fear. He throws an 89-91 mph fastball, a slider and a changeup. He commands all his offerings and on a given night, any of the three could be his No. 1 pitch. Savvy and fearless, he enjoys throwing inside. He has no problem getting righthanders out and actually has more trouble with lefties. At 6-foot-7, maintaining his mechanics can be a challenge for Tallet at times, and he's an easy mark for basestealers. Opponents succeeded on 20 of 27 steal attempts in 2002. Tallet is in the mix for a spot in the 2003 rotation. Because Cleveland has an abundance of lefthanders, it's possible his long-term role with the Indians might be in the bullpen.

Year	Club (League)	Class	W	L	ERA	G	GS	CG	SV	IP	H	R	ER	HR	BB	SO	AVG
2000	Mahoning Valley (NY-P)	A	0	0	1.15	6	6	0	0	16	10	2	2	0	3	20	.172
2001	Kinston (Car)	A	9	7	3.04	27	27	2	0	160	134	62	54	12	38	164	.224
2002	Akron (EL)	AA	10	1	3.08	18	16	1	0	102	93	41	35	9	32	73	.243
	Buffalo (IL)	AAA	2	3	3.07	8	7	0	0	44	47	17	15	1	16	25	.281
	Cleveland (AL)	MAJ	1	0	1.50	2	2	0	0	12	9	3	2	0	4	5	.214
MAJOR LEAGUE TOTALS			1	0	1.50	2	2	0	0	12	9	3	2	0	4	5	.214
MINOR LEAGUE TOTALS			21	11	2.96	59	56	3	0	322	284	122	106	22	89	282	.236

10. Jason Davis, rhp

Born: May 8, 1980. **Ht.:** 6-6. **Wt.:** 190. **Bats:** R. **Throws:** R. **School:** Cleveland State (Tenn.) JC. **Career Transactions:** Selected by Indians in 21st round of 1999 draft; signed May 18, 2000.

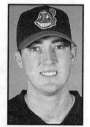

A basketball player in junior college, Davis signed as a draft-and-follow. He won 14 games at low Class A Columbus in 2001, his first full season as a pro. He ended 2002 by pitching well in three big league appearances after starting the year in high Class A. Though he's 6-foot-6, Davis is the most athletic pitcher in the organization and is adept at fielding his position and controlling the running game. He also might have the best arm in the system. He works in the 93-95 mph range with a heavy fastball and will touch 98. A workhorse, he also has an above-average splitter. Davis' slider needs more work, but it's coming. He needs to learn to use both sides of the plate with his fastball and work inside against righthanders. As good as his stuff is, he gets hit more often than he should. A better changeup also would help him. Unlike most of the candidates for Cleveland's rotation, Davis hasn't pitched in Triple-A. Some time in Buffalo to smooth out his secondary pitches and approach might be beneficial.

Year	Club (League)	Class	W	L	ERA	G	GS	CG	SV	IP	H	R	ER	HR	BB	SO	AVG
2000	Burlington (Appy)	R	4	4	4.40	10	10	0	0	45	48	27	22	5	16	35	.276
2001	Columbus (SAL)	A	14	6	2.70	27	27	1	0	160	147	72	48	9	51	115	.243
2002	Kinston (Car)	A	3	6	4.15	17	17	1	0	100	107	64	46	7	31	68	.272
	Akron (EL)	AA	6	2	3.51	10	10	0	0	59	63	26	23	2	16	45	.278
	Cleveland (AL)	MAJ	1	0	1.84	3	2	0	0	15	12	3	3	1	4	11	.218
MAJOR LEAGUE TOTALS			1	0	1.84	3	2	0	0	15	12	3	3	1	4	11	.218
MINOR LEAGUE TOTALS			27	18	3.44	64	64	2	0	364	365	189	139	23	114	263	.261

11. Corey Smith, 3b

Born: April 15, 1982. **Ht.:** 6-1. **Wt.:** 200. **Bats:** R. **Throws:** R. **School:** Piscataway (N.J.) HS. **Career Transactions:** Selected by Indians in first round (26th overall) of 2000 draft; signed June 15, 2000.

The measure of how much talent Cleveland has added is reflected by the fact that Smith was the organization's top prospect a year ago but fell out of the top 10 after a decent season in high Class A. He started 2002 quickly, batting .308 in April, but hit just .241 afterward. Smith shows tremendous explosiveness at the plate and in the field. He generates terrific bat speed and has the ability to drive the ball. He projects to hit for a decent average with lots of doubles and homers. At third base, he shows good range and plenty of arm. The Indians like his hard-nose attitude. He has made progress drawing walks, but Smith still strikes out too much. He needs to refine his two-strike approach. Smith also led Carolina

League third basemen with 34 errors because he gets too aggressive and makes poor throws. He just needs to relax defensively. Third base is the most unsettled position on the big league club, but Smith won't be rushed. He'll start the 2003 season in Double-A and probably won't be ready for Cleveland until 2005.

Year	Club (League)	Class	AVG	G	AB	R	H	2B	3B	HR	RBI	BB	SO	SB	SLG	OBP
2000	Burlington (Appy)	R	.256	57	207	21	53	8	2	4	39	27	50	8	.372	.339
2001	Columbus (SAL)	A	.260	130	500	59	130	26	5	18	85	37	149	10	.440	.312
2002	Kinston (Car)	A	.255	134	505	71	129	29	2	13	67	59	141	7	.398	.341
MINOR LEAGUE TOTALS			.257	321	1212	151	312	63	9	35	191	123	340	25	.411	.329

12. Francisco Cruceta, rhp

Born: July 4, 1981. **Ht.:** 6-2. **Wt.:** 170. **Bats:** R. **Throws:** R. **Career Transactions:** Signed out of Dominican Republic by Dodgers, May 20, 1999 . . . Traded by Dodgers with LHP Terry Mulholland and RHP Ricardo Rodriguez to Indians for RHP Paul Shuey, July 28, 2002.

Acquired from the Dodgers in the midseason trade for Paul Shuey, Cruceta was something of an unknown quantity coming into 2002. That began to change when he pitched well in spring training, and he gained further notoriety when he tossed a no-hitter in April. He turned in a strong performance after changing organizations and was quite impressive in instructional league, where he had 20 strikeouts and no walks in 15 innings. Cruceta's fastball sits at 92-94 mph. He also throws a solid average major league changeup, and two types of breaking balls, a slider, and a hard-breaking curve. Cruceta commands his breaking stuff better than his fastball. He's not wild, but he tends to elevate his fastball. He also needs to find a consistent arm slot for both his breaking pitches. He tends to vary the angle depending on whether he's throwing a slider or curve, and that's something quality major league hitters will pick up on. Cruceta is projected as a starter, but with his stuff and durability he also might fit in the bullpen. He'll start the 2003 season in the Double-A rotation.

Year	Club (League)	Class	W	L	ERA	G	GS	CG	SV	IP	H	R	ER	HR	BB	SO	AVG
1999	Dodgers (DSL)	R	3	2	7.56	14	1	0	0	25	33	34	21	4	15	21	.308
2000	Dodgers (DSL)	R	4	2	3.31	21	6	0	3	49	33	29	18	1	36	49	.180
2001	Dodgers (DSL)	R	0	4	1.50	11	9	0	0	48	35	24	8	1	24	47	.200
2002	South Georgia (SAL)	A	8	5	2.80	20	20	3	0	113	98	42	35	7	34	111	.231
	Kinston (Car)	A	2	0	2.50	7	7	0	0	40	31	13	11	2	25	37	.217
MINOR LEAGUE TOTALS			17	13	3.05	73	43	3	3	274	230	142	93	15	134	265	.223

13. Alex Escobar, of

Born: Sept. 6, 1978. **Ht.:** 6-1. **Wt.:** 180. **Bats:** R. **Throws:** R. **Career Transactions:** Signed out of Venezuela by Mets, July 1, 1995 . . . Traded by Mets with OF Matt Lawton, RHP Jerrod Riggan and two players to be named to Indians for 2B Roberto Alomar, LHP Mike Bacsik and 1B Danny Peoples, Dec. 11, 2001; Indians acquired LHP Billy Traber and 1B Earl Snyder to complete trade (Dec. 13, 2001) . . . On disabled list, April 1-Sept. 30, 2002.

The first sign that 2002 wasn't going to be the Indians' year came in the first week of exhibition games. Escobar, the key prospect to come over from the Mets in the Roberto Alomar trade, blew out his left knee making a catch in the outfield and required season-ending reconstructive knee surgery. He should be 100 percent, or close to it, by the start of spring training, but he lost a full season when he needed to re-establish himself following a disappointing 2001 performance. Escobar has tremendous athletic ability, and is a well-rounded player offensively and defensively. He has the range, speed, and arm for all three outfield positions, and offers Cleveland a much-needed righthanded bat. He has the potential to hit .265-.285 and be at least a 20-20 man. Escobar's high strikeout totals were an ongoing source of concern for the Mets. His ability to get over the knee injury may be as big a challenge mentally as physically, and how the injury affects his speed and range in the outfield remains to be seen. Assuming he's ready physically, Escobar will come to training camp and compete for a starting job, most likely in right field.

Year	Club (League)	Class	AVG	G	AB	R	H	2B	3B	HR	RBI	BB	SO	SB	SLG	OBP
1996	Mets (GCL)	R	.360	24	75	15	27	4	0	0	10	4	9	7	.413	.410
1997	Kingsport (Appy)	R	.194	10	36	6	7	3	0	0	3	3	8	1	.278	.250
	Mets (GCL)	R	.247	26	73	12	18	4	1	1	11	10	17	0	.370	.341
1998	Capital City (SAL)	A	.310	112	416	90	129	23	5	27	91	54	133	49	.584	.393
1999	Mets (GCL)	R	.375	2	8	1	3	2	0	0	1	1	2	0	.625	.444
	St. Lucie (FSL)	A	.667	1	3	1	2	0	0	1	3	1	1	1	1.667	.600
2000	Binghamton (EL)	AA	.288	122	437	79	126	25	7	16	67	57	114	24	.487	.375
2001	Norfolk (IL)	AAA	.267	111	397	55	106	21	4	12	52	35	146	18	.431	.327
	New York (NL)	MAJ	.200	18	50	3	10	1	0	3	8	3	19	1	.400	.245
2002							Did Not Play—Injured									
MAJOR LEAGUE TOTALS			.200	18	50	3	10	1	0	3	8	3	19	1	.400	.245
MINOR LEAGUE TOTALS			.289	408	1445	259	418	82	17	57	238	165	430	100	.488	.366

14. J.D. Martin, rhp

Born: Jan. 2, 1983. **Ht.:** 6-4. **Wt.:** 170. **Bats:** R. **Throws:** R. **School:** Burroughs HS, Ridgecrest, Calif. **Career Transactions:** Selected by Indians in first round (35th overall) of 2001 draft; signed June 20, 2001.

After the Indians made him a supplemental first-round pick, Martin exploded on the pro scene with eye-catching numbers (1.38 ERA, 71-11 strikeout-walk ratio) at Rookie-level Burlington. He wasn't as dominant in his first full season, though he won 14 games to lead a talented Columbus staff. He has outstanding command of all his pitches, which include an 87-88 mph fastball, a changeup, an overhand curve and a big, sweeping slider. Martin showed an intuitive feel for pitching that was remarkable for a teenager. Unlike many young pitchers, he has to be encouraged to throw his fastball more. He used it just half of the time during some games last year, and Cleveland wants him to up that mark to 65-70 percent. The gangly Martin had some stamina problems, which caused his velocity to drop at mid-season. But he eventually gained a second wind and the velocity returned near the end of the season. He needs to get stronger in order to at least maintain his velocity on his fastball. He'll move up a level to high Class A in 2003.

Year	Club (League)	Class	W	L	ERA	G	GS	CG	SV	IP	H	R	ER	HR	BB	SO	AVG
2001	Burlington (Appy)	R	5	1	1.38	10	10	0	0	46	26	9	7	3	11	72	.164
2002	Columbus (SAL)	A	14	5	3.90	27	26	0	0	138	141	76	60	12	46	131	.266
MINOR LEAGUE TOTALS			19	6	3.28	37	36	0	0	184	167	85	67	15	57	203	.242

15. Josh Bard, c

Born: March 30, 1978. **Ht.:** 6-3. **Wt.:** 200. **Bats:** B. **Throws:** R. **School:** Texas Tech. **Career Transactions:** Selected by Rockies in third round of 1999 draft; signed Aug. 12, 1999 . . . Traded by Rockies with OF Jody Gerut to Indians for OF Jacob Cruz, June 2, 2001.

When the Indians acquired Bard as part of a trade that sent Jacob Cruz to the Rockies in the middle of the 2001 season, the transaction drew little notice. But Bard started opening eyes immediately with his leadership and game-calling ability. Last year, he drew raves from veteran Terry Mulholland the first time he caught Mulholland. Bard has an innate feel for determining what his batterymate's strength is on a given day, and he can help guide a pitcher through rough spots. He also does a solid job of combating the running game. Offensively, Bard has made tremendous strides. From the left side, he has gone from a dead-pull hitter to one who uses the entire field. He has learned how to pick pitches he can drive. Bard won't be a top run producer, but he has enough bat to be an everyday catcher for a first-division team. (That said, he doesn't have enough bat to hold off Victor Martinez once Martinez is ready.) Bard needs to get stronger, in order to prove he can handle catching 120 games a year. After Einar Diaz was traded to the Rangers, Bard became the Opening Day starter behind the plate.

Year	Club (League)	Class	AVG	G	AB	R	H	2B	3B	HR	RBI	BB	SO	SB	SLG	OBP
2002	Salem (Car)	A	.285	93	309	40	88	17	0	2	25	32	33	3	.359	.352
	Colo. Spr. (PCL)	AAA	.235	4	17	0	4	0	0	0	1	0	2	0	.235	.235
2001	Carolina (SL)	AA	.258	35	124	14	32	13	0	1	24	19	23	0	.387	.359
	Akron (EL)	AA	.278	51	194	26	54	11	0	4	25	16	27	0	.397	.338
	Mahoning Valley (NY-P)	A	.273	13	44	7	12	4	0	2	8	6	2	0	.500	.373
	Buffalo (IL)	AAA	.000	1	4	0	0	0	0	0	0	0	1	0	.000	.000
2002	Buffalo (IL)	AAA	.297	94	344	36	102	26	2	6	53	20	45	0	.436	.332
	Cleveland (AL)	MAJ	.222	24	90	9	20	5	0	3	12	4	13	0	.378	.255
MAJOR LEAGUE TOTALS			.222	24	90	9	20	5	0	3	12	4	13	0	.378	.255
MINOR LEAGUE TOTALS			.282	291	1036	123	292	71	2	15	136	93	133	3	.398	.342

16. Dan Denham, rhp

Born: Dec. 24, 1982. **Ht.:** 6-2. **Wt.:** 190. **Bats:** R. **Throws:** R. **School:** Deer Valley HS, Antioch, Calif. **Career Transactions:** Selected by Indians in first round (17th overall) of 2001 draft; signed July 7, 2001.

Denham's $1.86 million bonus in 2001 was the largest the Indians gave a draft pick until Jeremy Guthrie received $3 million last year. Though his numbers weren't overwhelming, Denham had a huge year in 2002 in terms of acclimating himself to the pro game. He went through some challenging times and grew mentally. There are still some mechanical issues he needs to address in order to repeat his delivery. He's not all over the place but he needs to improve his command. His fastball ranges from 91-93 mph, with occasional bursts to 94. He also throws a curveball, slider and changeup. He must refine his changeup to develop a weapon against lefthanders, who hit .314 against him last year. Denham also needs to make continued mental adjustments, such as learning how to take errors made behind him in stride. He'll move up a level to high Class A this year.

Year	Club (League)	Class	W	L	ERA	G	GS	CG	SV	IP	H	R	ER	HR	BB	SO	AVG
2001	Burlington (Appy)	R	0	4	4.40	8	8	0	0	31	30	21	15	5	26	31	.256
2002	Columbus (SAL)	A	9	8	4.76	28	28	0	0	125	123	76	66	7	65	109	.265
MINOR LEAGUE TOTALS			9	12	4.69	36	36	0	0	155	153	97	81	12	91	140	.263

17. Johnny Peralta, ss

Born: May 28, 1982. **Ht.:** 6-1. **Wt.:** 180. **Bats:** R. **Throws:** R. **Career Transactions:** Signed out of Dominican Republic by Indians, April 14, 1999.

Because they have a wealth of middle infielders, the Indians sent Peralta to the Arizona Fall League to play third base. His ultimate position has yet to be determined, though his thick build probably will mean he'll have to move off shortstop. Offensively, he had a break-out year in 2002, raising his average 41 points, more than doubling his home run production and cutting his strikeouts by more than a third. Peralta can hit any fastball. He's steady defensively, with excellent hands and plenty of arm for shortstop or third base. His range is fringe average at best and he's a below-average runner who lacks quick reactions to the ball. Cleveland will continue to play him at shortstop until he outgrows or proves he can't handle the position. Because the Indians have third-base options, he may wind up at second base as part of a double-play combo with Brandon Phillips. Peralta will open this year in Triple-A.

Year	Club (League)	Class	AVG	G	AB	R	H	2B	3B	HR	RBI	BB	SO	SB	SLG	OBP
1999	Indians (DSL)	R	.303	62	208	48	63	14	6	6	43	33	49	14	.514	.397
2000	Columbus (SAL)	A	.241	106	349	52	84	13	1	3	34	59	102	7	.309	.352
2001	Kinston (Car)	A	.240	125	441	57	106	24	2	7	47	58	148	4	.351	.328
2002	Akron (EL)	AA	.281	130	470	62	132	28	5	15	62	45	97	4	.457	.343
MINOR LEAGUE TOTALS			.262	423	1468	219	385	79	14	31	186	195	396	29	.399	.348

18. Travis Foley, rhp

Born: March 11, 1983. **Ht.:** 6-1. **Wt.:** 180. **Bats:** R. **Throws:** R. **School:** Butler HS, Louisville. **Career Transactions:** Selected by Indians in fourth round of 2001 draft; signed June 13, 2001.

Foley went three rounds after Dan Denham and J.D. Martin in the 2001 draft, but he was considerably tougher to hit than they were last year at Columbus. Foley has good stuff and his mental toughness may be even more impressive. He has good command of his fastball, which sits at 90-91 mph, and is aggressive with it. He also has an overhand, 12-to-6 curve-ball that could use some shortening. Foley also has a good feel for his changeup and uses it well. It's a big part of his repertoire, and he needs it because it helps determine the success of his fastball. As Foley continues to move up levels, he'll have to improve the late action on all his pitches. He'll also need to get better at controlling the running game. Foley will start 2003 in the Kinston rotation with Denham and Martin.

Year	Club (League)	Class	W	L	ERA	G	GS	CG	SV	IP	H	R	ER	HR	BB	SO	AVG
2001	Burlington (Appy)	R	2	3	2.80	10	10	0	0	45	26	16	14	4	15	59	.171
2002	Columbus (SAL)	A	13	4	2.82	26	26	1	0	137	108	47	43	9	44	138	.215
MINOR LEAGUE TOTALS			15	7	2.81	36	36	1	0	182	134	63	57	13	59	197	.205

19. Matt Whitney, 3b

Born: Feb. 13, 1984. **Ht.:** 6-4. **Wt.:** 190. **Bats:** R. **Throws:** R. **School:** Palm Beach Gardens (Fla.) HS. **Career Transactions:** Selected by Indians in first round (33rd overall) of 2002 draft; signed June 14, 2002.

One of the most highly regarded high school hitters in the 2002 draft, Whitney somehow lasted until the supplemental first round. He's one of the more exciting position players to enter the organization in years. He reached double figures in home runs at Burlington, showing power to all fields. He showed some susceptibility to breaking balls early, but his temperament and even-keel approach allowed him to adjust. He recognizes what pitchers are trying to do against him. Though he's big, he's athletic enough that he doesn't clog the bases and has good range at third base. Whitney tends to push the ball on his throws, but that can be fixed with a minor adjustment. He fits the profile for a corner infielder and has no glaring weaknesses. He'll begin his first full season in low Class A.

Year	Club (League)	Class	AVG	G	AB	R	H	2B	3B	HR	RBI	BB	SO	SB	SLG	OBP
2002	Burlington (Appy)	R	.286	45	175	33	50	12	1	10	33	18	49	5	.537	.359
	Columbus (SAL)	A	.111	6	18	0	2	0	0	0	0	3	4	0	.111	.238
MINOR LEAGUE TOTALS			.269	51	193	33	52	12	1	10	33	21	53	5	.497	.347

20. Luis Garcia, of/1b

Born: Nov. 5, 1978. **Ht.:** 6-4. **Wt.:** 180. **Bats:** R. **Throws:** R. **Career Transactions:** Signed out of Mexico by Red Sox, March 14, 1996 . . . Loaned by Red Sox to Monterrey (Mexican), April 30-Sept. 20, 1999 . . . Traded by Red Sox with OF Rick Asadoorian and 1B Dustin Brisson to Cardinals for RHP Dustin Hermanson, Dec. 15, 2001 . . . Traded by Cardinals with a player to be named to Indians for LHP Chuck Finley, July 19, 2002; Indians acquired OF Covelli Crisp to complete trade (Aug. 5, 2002).

After getting him from the Red Sox when they dumped Dustin Hermanson in December 2001, the Cardinals used Garcia to get Chuck Finley from the Indians last July. A graceful athlete, Garcia has the most raw power of any hitter in the Cleveland system except Travis Hafner. He has shown an ability to hit in the .280-.300 range and doesn't strike out as much as most sluggers. He'll have to prove himself against the better breaking balls he'll see at higher levels. Garcia needs to stay on pitches longer and fight his urge to pull everything. The ball comes off his bat better than any hitter in the Indians organization, and he has good plate discipline. He doesn't strike out as much as a typical power hitter. He spent time at first base and three outfield positions in 2002, and his best fit may be in right field. A former pitcher, he has enough arm to play there. He also showed good actions and soft hands at first base. He'll see time at first and in the outfield this year in Triple-A.

Year	Club (League)	Class	W	L	ERA	G	GS	CG	SV	IP	H	R	ER	HR	BB	SO	AVG
1996	Astros/Red Sox (DSL)	R	2	0	3.75	14	0	0	0	24	13	12	10	1	23	17	.148
1997	Red Sox (DSL)	R	0	3	5.91	4	3	0	0	11	10	10	7	1	7	12	.204
	Red Sox (GCL)	R	1	2	2.87	8	1	0	1	16	12	10	5	0	10	18	.203
1998	Red Sox (DSL)	R	0	0	0.00	3	0	0	0	8	3	0	0	0	4	7	.111
MINOR LEAGUE TOTALS			3	5	3.38	29	4	0	1	59	38	32	22	2	44	54	.170

Year	Club (League)	Class	AVG	G	AB	R	H	2B	3B	HR	RBI	BB	SO	SB	SLG	OBP
1998	Red Sox (DSL)	R	.212	54	189	31	40	6	2	8	32	27	33	3	.392	.312
1999	Mexico (AZL)	R	.330	50	188	35	62	9	6	13	40	22	31	1	.649	.398
2000	Augusta (SAL)	A	.260	128	493	72	128	27	5	20	77	51	112	8	.456	.329
2001	Sarasota (FSL)	A	.303	65	267	38	81	14	1	12	44	18	61	2	.498	.348
	Trenton (EL)	AA	.310	63	229	35	71	20	1	14	45	28	68	0	.590	.384
2002	New Haven (EL)	AA	.266	88	308	42	82	16	1	12	37	32	59	3	.442	.335
	Akron (EL)	AA	.289	39	166	24	48	9	0	6	21	13	27	1	.452	.343
MINOR LEAGUE TOTALS			.278	487	1840	277	512	101	16	85	296	191	391	18	.489	.346

21. Alex Herrera, lhp

Born: Nov. 5, 1976. **Ht.:** 5-11. **Wt.:** 170. **Bats:** L. **Throws:** L. **Career Transactions:** Signed out of Venezuela by Indians, July 4, 1997.

Herrera wasn't as overwhelming last year as he was in his breakout year of 2001, but he was solid and continued to move toward the majors as a power lefty reliever. He has a mid-90s fastball and a slider that can be devastating at times. When he keeps his mechanics together and allows his slider to work for him, Herrera can be a dominating pitcher. Like most power pitchers, Herrera sometimes struggles with his command and has a tendency to overthrow. He needs to harness his emotions and concentrate on repeating his delivery. Though he's lefthanded he doesn't hold runners well; basestealers went 13-for-13 against him in 2002. He has more than enough stuff to get both lefties and righties out, and he showed well in five late-season appearances with Cleveland. He'll go to spring training and compete for a job in the big league bullpen.

Year	Club (League)	Class	W	L	ERA	G	GS	CG	SV	IP	H	R	ER	HR	BB	SO	AVG
1998	Guacara 2 (VSL)	R	7	4	2.30	18	11	0	3	74	70	34	19	2	17	68	.251
1999	San Felipe (VSL)	R	3	2	1.28	16	9	0	5	56	42	19	8	2	20	74	.202
2000	Columbus (SAL)	A	4	3	3.43	20	0	0	0	42	41	25	16	1	21	41	.263
	Kinston (Car)	A	0	1	2.32	17	0	0	1	31	28	11	8	1	19	40	.239
	Akron (EL)	AA	0	0	0.00	2	0	0	0	1	2	1	0	0	1	1	.400
2001	Kinston (Car)	A	4	0	0.60	28	0	0	3	60	36	6	4	1	18	83	.171
	Akron (EL)	AA	3	0	2.83	15	0	0	2	29	24	9	9	1	9	22	.229
2002	Akron (EL)	AA	0	2	3.38	30	0	0	5	61	47	24	23	8	30	65	.212
	Buffalo (IL)	AAA	0	1	11.57	5	0	0	0	7	10	9	9	0	8	5	.345
	Cleveland (AL)	MAJ	0	0	0.00	5	0	0	0	5	3	0	0	0	1	5	.158
MAJOR LEAGUE TOTALS			0	0	0.00	5	0	0	0	5	3	0	0	0	1	5	.158
MINOR LEAGUE TOTALS			21	13	2.39	151	20	0	19	362	300	138	96	16	143	399	.225

22. Fernando Cabrera, rhp

Born: Nov. 16, 1981. **Ht.:** 6-4. **Wt.:** 170. **Bats:** R. **Throws:** R. **School:** Disciples of Christ Academy, Bayamon, P.R. **Career Transactions:** Selected by Indians in 10th round of 1999 draft; signed Aug. 23, 1999.

Cabrera began to emerge in 2002, averaging more than a strikeout per inning for the second straight year and reaching Double-A at age 20. While he has been used as a starter in his three years in the organization, he projects as a power reliever. His fastball consistently reaches 93-96 mph and he can command it to both sides of the plate. Cabrera needs to refine his mechanics and improve his control of his slider and splitter. His changeup isn't an asset at this point, and his ability to hold runners is weak. Though he's still raw, he did hold lefthanders to a .204 average last year. He'll open 2003 in the Double-A rotation but likely will be moved to the bullpen either this year or next.

Year	Club (League)	Class	W	L	ERA	G	GS	CG	SV	IP	H	R	ER	HR	BB	SO	AVG
2000	Burlington (Appy)	R	3	7	4.61	13	13	0	0	68	64	42	35	4	20	50	.252
2001	Columbus (SAL)	A	5	6	3.61	20	20	0	0	95	89	49	38	7	37	96	.242
2002	Kinston (Car)	A	6	8	3.52	21	21	0	0	110	83	48	43	7	40	107	.206
	Akron (EL)	AA	1	2	5.33	7	4	0	1	27	26	16	16	1	12	29	.252
MINOR LEAGUE TOTALS			15	23	3.96	61	58	0	1	300	262	155	132	19	109	282	.232

23. Ben Broussard, 1b/of

Born: Sept. 24, 1976. **Ht.:** 6-3. **Wt.:** 220. **Bats:** L. **Throws:** L. **School:** McNeese State University. **Career Transactions:** Selected by Reds in second round of 1999 draft; signed June 2, 1999 . . . Traded by Reds to Indians for 3B Russell Branyan, June 7, 2002.

Yet another of the many prospects the Indians added during 2002, Broussard was acquired from Cincinnati in a trade for Russell Branyan. With the presence of Jim Thome at first base, Broussard was moved to the outfield following the deal. The transition didn't go especially well, because at times he seemed so occupied with learning the outfield that it detracted from his hitting. He's an offensive-minded player with the power to hit 20-25 homers, similar to Brian Daubach but with a better batting eye. Broussard went from a gap-to-gap approach to more of a pull hitter by the end of the season. First base is still Broussard's best position. He handles himself well around the bag and has soft hands. As a left fielder, his best tool is his arm. He still needs work at that position, as well as on his overall strength and conditioning. When Thome signed with the Phillies, Broussard had a good chance to replace him until the Indians traded for Travis Hafner. He still figures into the big league picture somewhere.

Year	Club (League)	Class	AVG	G	AB	R	H	2B	3B	HR	RBI	BB	SO	SB	SLG	OBP
1999	Billings (Pio)	R	.407	38	145	39	59	11	2	14	48	34	30	1	.800	.527
	Clinton (Mid)	A	.550	5	20	8	11	4	1	2	6	3	4	0	1.150	.609
	Chattanooga (SL)	AA	.213	35	127	26	27	5	0	8	21	11	41	1	.441	.291
2000	Chattanooga (SL)	AA	.255	87	286	64	73	8	4	14	51	72	78	15	.458	.413
2001	Mudville (Cal)	A	.245	30	102	14	25	5	0	5	21	16	31	0	.441	.360
	Chattanooga (SL)	AA	.320	100	353	81	113	27	0	23	69	61	69	10	.592	.428
2002	Louisville (IL)	AAA	.273	57	187	31	51	14	1	11	30	31	50	4	.535	.396
	Buffalo (IL)	AAA	.242	42	153	30	37	8	0	5	21	24	30	0	.392	.354
	Cleveland (AL)	MAJ	.241	39	112	10	27	4	0	4	9	7	25	0	.384	.292
MAJOR LEAGUE TOTALS			.241	39	112	10	27	4	0	4	9	7	25	0	.384	.292
MINOR LEAGUE TOTALS			.288	394	1373	293	396	82	8	82	267	252	333	31	.539	.409

24. Sean Smith, rhp

Born: Oct. 13, 1983. **Ht.:** 6-4. **Wt.:** 180. **Bats:** R. **Throws:** R. **School:** Sacramento (Calif.) CC. **Career Transactions:** Selected by Indians in 16th round of 2001 draft; signed May 29, 2002.

One of the more coveted draft-and-follows in 2002, Smith signed for $1.1 million after spending a year at Sac City. After a decent pro debut, he really hit his stride in instructional league. Smith's fastball sat at 89-90 mph last summer and was clocked as high as 94 during the spring. He has a very good feel for his curveball and changeup, and his command of those offspeed pitches is what sets him apart from other pitchers his age. His poise and polish are uncanny for a teenager. The next step in Smith's development will be improving his overall physical strength. His workload will be closely monitored, as is being done with J.D. Martin, another similarly built pitcher with great promise. Smith will compete for a spot in the low Class A rotation during spring training.

Year	Club (League)	Class	W	L	ERA	G	GS	CG	SV	IP	H	R	ER	HR	BB	SO	AVG
2002	Burlington (Appy)	R	1	1	3.24	10	9	0	0	33	29	14	12	1	12	29	.236
MINOR LEAGUE TOTALS			1	1	3.24	10	9	0	0	33	29	14	12	1	12	29	.236

25. Ryan Church, of

Born: Oct. 14, 1978. **Ht.:** 6-1. **Wt.:** 190. **Bats:** L. **Throws:** L. **School:** University of Nevada. **Career Transactions:** Selected by Indians in 14th round of 2000 draft; signed June 7, 2000.

Church has quietly plugged along and become a viable prospect. He began his college career as a pitcher before hurting his arm, and he's still developing at the plate. He's a little too pull-conscious now and needs to use the whole field. He does strike out a lot and his plate discipline deteriorated once he reached Double-A. However, Church projects to hit 20-25 home runs, which would be a luxury for a center fielder. Though he's no more than an average runner, Church is athletic enough and gets good enough jumps on balls to play center at Jacobs Field. He easily has the strongest arm of any outfielder in the Indians system. As he has advanced, he has shown a pattern of struggling early at each new level before making adjustments. He'll vie for a spot in the Triple-A outfield this spring, but may have to return to Akron. Either way, he's a candidate for a September callup to Cleveland.

Year	Club (League)	Class	AVG	G	AB	R	H	2B	3B	HR	RBI	BB	SO	SB	SLG	OBP
2000	Mahoning Valley (NY-P)	A	.298	73	272	51	81	16	5	10	65	38	49	11	.504	.396
2001	Columbus (SAL)	A	.287	101	363	64	104	23	3	17	76	54	79	4	.507	.385
	Kinston (Car)	A	.241	24	83	16	20	7	0	5	15	18	23	1	.506	.379
2002	Kinston (Car)	A	.326	53	181	30	59	12	1	10	30	31	51	4	.569	.433
	Akron (EL)	AA	.296	71	291	39	86	17	4	12	51	12	58	1	.505	.325
MINOR LEAGUE TOTALS			.294	322	1190	200	350	75	13	54	237	153	260	21	.515	.381

26. Covelli Crisp, of

Born: Nov. 1, 1979. **Ht.:** 6-0. **Wt.:** 180. **Bats:** B. **Throws:** R. **School:** Los Angeles Pierce JC. **Career Transactions:** Selected by Cardinals in seventh round of 1999 draft; signed June 7, 1999 . . . Traded by Cardinals to Indians, Aug. 5, 2002, completing trade in which Indians sent LHP Chuck Finley to Cardinals for 1B Luis Garcia and a player to be named (July 19, 2002).

The Cardinals' 2001 minor league player of the year, Crisp came to the Indians in a trade for Chuck Finley. Crisp is athletic, no surprise considering that his father boxed, his mother was a world-class sprinter and his sister is an ice skater. His best tool is his speed, and if he could walk more often and hit more balls on the ground, he'd be a fine leadoff man. He understands that's his role in the big leagues, and does show a knack for bunting and handling the bat. Defensively, Crisp has a below-average arm and was put on an offseason throwing and lifting program to address that deficiency. He needs to get a better feel for the strength of big league hitters, which will help him improve his jumps and reads on fly balls. He has a tendency to play a shallow center field, and balls get driven over his head more than they should. Crisp's bat fits better in center than on a corner, so getting better on defense is crucial. He and incumbent Milton Bradley are the leading candidates to start in center for Cleveland this year.

Year	Club (League)	Class	AVG	G	AB	R	H	2B	3B	HR	RBI	BB	SO	SB	SLG	OBP
1999	Johnson City (Appy)	R	.258	65	229	55	59	5	4	3	22	44	41	27	.354	.379
2000	New Jersey (NY-P)	A	.239	36	134	18	32	5	0	0	14	11	22	25	.276	.301
	Peoria (Mid)	A	.276	27	98	14	27	9	0	0	7	16	15	7	.367	.377
2001	Potomac (Car)	A	.306	139	530	80	162	23	3	11	47	52	64	39	.423	.368
2002	New Haven (EL)	AA	.301	89	355	61	107	16	1	9	47	36	56	26	.428	.365
	Akron (EL)	AA	.406	7	32	9	13	1	0	1	4	3	3	4	.531	.457
	Cleveland (AL)	MAJ	.260	32	127	16	33	9	2	1	9	11	19	4	.386	.314
	Buffalo (IL)	AAA	.238	4	21	3	5	1	0	0	2	0	2	1	.286	.238
MAJOR LEAGUE TOTALS			.260	32	127	16	33	9	2	1	9	11	19	4	.386	.314
MINOR LEAGUE TOTALS			.289	367	1399	240	405	60	8	24	143	162	203	129	.395	.364

27. Chris de la Cruz, ss

Born: May 3, 1982. **Ht.:** 6-0. **Wt.:** 160. **Bats:** B. **Throws:** R. **Career Transactions:** Signed out of Dominican Republic by Indians, May 7, 2001.

A smooth, switch-hitting shortstop who reminds some of a young Tony Fernandez, de la Cruz is another addition to the bulging list of shortstop prospects in the organization. In his first year in the United States, he finished fourth in the Rookie-level Appalachian League batting race. He also showed some gap power, though he'll need to draw a few more walks to become an effective leadoff hitter. De la Cruz is a solid average runner and has the potential to steal 20-25 bases in the majors. He has loose actions and plenty of arm for short. He always seems to be in the right place at the right time and has an innate feel for the game. De la Cruz will get his first taste of full-season ball in 2003.

Year	Club (League)	Class	AVG	G	AB	R	H	2B	3B	HR	RBI	BB	SO	SB	SLG	OBP
2001	Indians (DSL)	R	.284	62	243	30	69	8	4	0	21	24	24	9	.350	.349
2002	Burlington (Appy)	R	.367	43	180	33	66	7	6	1	12	17	27	13	.489	.422
MINOR LEAGUE TOTALS			.319	105	423	63	135	15	10	1	33	41	51	22	.409	.380

28. Micah Schilling, 2b

Born: Dec. 27, 1982. **Ht.:** 5-11. **Wt.:** 180. **Bats:** L. **Throws:** R. **School:** Silliman Institute, Clinton, La. **Career Transactions:** Selected by Indians in first round (41st overall) of 2002 draft; signed June 23, 2002.

Matt Whitney and Schilling were considered two of the most advanced high school hitters in the 2002 draft, and the Indians landed both of them as supplemental first-round picks. Schilling is an aggressive hitter who scouts said had one of the sweetest swings to come out of Louisiana since Will Clark. Schilling hyperextended his elbow swinging the bat at Burlington, which hampered him offensively. He has gap power and uses the whole field well. He sometimes tries to do too much, but once he learned to relax in instructional league, the hits started to come. Schilling is only adequate defensively. He needs to work on his footwork around second base, and his agility and quickness bear watching because there's a chance he could outgrow second base. If that happens, he still has enough bat to play elsewhere. Schilling again will form a double-play combination with Chris de la Cruz in 2003, this time in low Class A.

Year	Club (League)	Class	AVG	G	AB	R	H	2B	3B	HR	RBI	BB	SO	SB	SLG	OBP
2002	Burlington (Appy)	R	.206	33	126	13	26	6	1	0	10	15	39	5	.270	.303
MINOR LEAGUE TOTALS			.206	33	126	13	26	6	1	0	10	15	39	5	.270	.303

29. Carl Sadler, lhp

Born: Oct. 11, 1976. **Ht.:** 6-2. **Wt.:** 180. **Bats:** L. **Throws:** L. **School:** Taylor County HS, Perry, Fla. **Career Transactions:** Selected by Expos in 34th round of 1996 draft; signed June 14, 1996 . . . Released by Expos, April 1, 1998 . . . Signed by Indians, April 3, 1998 . . . On disabled list, April 3-Sept. 5, 1998.

Released by the Expos after two seasons because he had elbow problems, Sadler was signed by the Indians two days later. Cleveland let him move at his own pace, and he missed all of 1998 and most of 1999 while trying to come back from two surgeries. He moved to the bullpen in 2000 and emerged unexpectedly last year. Sadler's fastball jumped from 90 to 94 mph in 2002, giving him a second plus pitch to go with his curveball. He commands both well, though he'll sometimes fall in a rut and rely on one at the expense of the other. He needs to use both pitches to be effective. He's probably no more than a lefty specialist, but he was effective in that role in the major leagues and wasn't rattled by his first callup. He's a strong candidate to make Cleveland's Opening Day roster.

Year	Club (League)	Class	W	L	ERA	G	GS	CG	SV	IP	H	R	ER	HR	BB	SO	AVG
1996	Expos (GCL)	R	2	2	3.89	17	3	0	1	37	41	24	16	2	12	24	.268
1997	Expos (GCL)	R	0	2	4.35	9	3	0	0	21	26	11	10	0	5	14	.313
	Vermont (NY-P)	A	2	2	4.21	7	6	0	0	36	33	20	17	2	23	27	.239
1998					Did Not Play—Injured												
1999	Burlington (Appy)	R	1	0	3.13	5	5	0	0	23	18	10	8	0	10	22	.220
	Mahoning Valley (NY-P)	A	0	1	31.50	1	1	0	0	2	8	7	7	0	3	3	.571
2000	Mahoning Valley (NY-P)	A	0	0	3.00	5	0	0	0	6	5	2	2	0	3	3	.238
	Columbus (SAL)	A	1	3	6.61	10	0	0	0	16	20	13	12	0	7	21	.303
2001	Kinston (Car)	A	6	0	1.88	27	2	0	2	62	51	19	13	2	18	78	.216
	Akron (EL)	AA	2	3	6.50	11	0	0	0	18	23	16	13	1	9	14	.303
2002	Akron (EL)	AA	4	1	2.33	21	0	0	2	46	39	12	12	0	12	37	.229
	Buffalo (IL)	AAA	1	1	1.93	12	0	0	1	19	19	7	4	1	8	13	.268
	Cleveland (AL)	MAJ	1	2	4.43	24	0	0	0	20	15	10	10	2	11	23	.211
MAJOR LEAGUE TOTALS			1	2	4.43	24	0	0	0	20	15	10	10	2	11	23	.211
MINOR LEAGUE TOTALS			19	15	3.58	125	20	0	6	287	283	141	114	8	110	256	.255

30. Brian Slocum, rhp

Born: March 27, 1981. **Ht.:** 6-4. **Wt.:** 190. **Bats:** R. **Throws:** R. **School:** Villanova University. **Career Transactions:** Selected by Indians in second round of 2002 draft; signed June 21, 2002.

Slocum reminds some Indians officials of Charles Nagy. Both came from Big East Conference schools and were quiet, intelligent, headstrong competitors. Where they differ is that Slocum throws much harder than Nagy did. Slocum touches 95 mph on occasion and his fastball explodes on hitters. He has the makings of a good changeup, though he needs to tighten his slider. He throws strikes and limited short-season New York-Penn League hitters to a .230 average and one homer in his pro debut. More important, he put to rest any questions about his durability. Slocum missed the 2001 season with a sore shoulder—though he avoided surgery—and pitched through biceps tendinitis in 2002. He has the chance to skip a level and go to high Class A this year.

Year	Club (League)	Class	W	L	ERA	G	GS	CG	SV	IP	H	R	ER	HR	BB	SO	AVG
2002	Mahoning Valley (NY-P)	A	5	2	2.60	11	11	0	0	55	47	19	16	1	14	48	.230
MINOR LEAGUE TOTALS			5	2	2.60	11	11	0	0	55	47	19	16	1	14	48	.230

COLORADO
ROCKIES

TOP 30 PROSPECTS

1. Aaron Cook, rhp
2. Chin-Hui Tsao, rhp
3. Rene Reyes, of/1b
4. Jason Young, rhp
5. Choo Freeman, of
6. Jayson Nix, 2b
7. Jeff Baker, 3b
8. Zach Parker, lhp
9. Jeff Francis, lhp
10. Brad Hawpe, 1b
11. Ubaldo Jimenez, rhp
12. Oscar Materano, ss
13. Garrett Atkins, 3b
14. Ching-Lung Lo, rhp
15. Tony Miller, of
16. Matt Holliday, of
17. J.D. Closser, c
18. Chris Buglovsky, rhp
19. Mike Esposito, rhp
20. Brian Fuentes, lhp
21. Jack Cust, of
22. Pablo Ozuna, 2b/of
23. Cory Vance, lhp
24. Clint Barmes, ss
25. Luke Allen, of
26. Javier Colina, 2b/3b
27. Cory Sullivan, of
28. Ryan Kibler, rhp
29. Ben Crockett, rhp
30. Jose Vasquez, of

By Tracy Ringolsby

Two winters after shelling out $172 million to sign free-agent lefthanders Mike Hampton and Denny Neagle to provide a veteran foundation for the Rockies rotation, general manager Dan O'Dowd's focus turned to unloading both Hampton and Neagle. Reality had set in.

Hampton and Neagle never came close to meeting expectations. And more important, the Rockies realized in the long term they're better off with quality young pitchers. They're faring better trying to establish themselves than veterans have done trying to adapt to Coors Field. The first indication came in 2001 with the arrival of Shawn Chacon. In 2002, Jason Jennings was National League rookie of the year, Denny Stark also received votes and No. 1 prospect Aaron Cook made four quality starts in September.

"If you put the right people together, we could develop a very good staff here," O'Dowd said. "Is it all going to happen in 2003? Probably not. But there's going to be excitement with the disappointment. There are at least two kids on every (minor league) staff that we look at and feel are going to be big league pitchers. We should have a steady flow of pitchers coming through."

This season, the Rockies figure Jason Young will be ready to make a move to the big leagues. Chin-Hui Tsao, who showed he was recovered from Tommy John surgery with a strong second half in high Class A, could surface late in the season. "We have more pitchers closer to the big leagues than we have in past years," said Rick Mathews, promoted during the offseason from roving pitching coordinator to major league bullpen coach. "Consequently, that's going to give Dan more opportunities and options with the salary structure he has to deal with."

Colorado's supply of position players isn't as close to harvest, but some are on the way. Outfielder Jack Cust and utilitymen Pablo Ozuna and Jason Romano could capture reserve roles this spring. By 2004, higher-ceiling players should be knocking on the door.

The nucleus of the teams that won the high Class A Carolina League in 2001 and a Double-A Southern League first-half division title in 2002 move to Triple-A this year. The most promising among that group are outfielders Rene Reyes, Choo Freeman and Matt Holliday; third baseman Garrett Atkins; shortstop Clint Barmes; and second baseman Javier Colina.

Organization Overview

General Manager: Dan O'Dowd. Farm Director: Bill Geivett. Scouting Director: Bill Schmidt

2002 PERFORMANCE

Class	Farm Team	League	W	L	Pct.	Finish*	Manager(s)
Majors	Colorado	National	73	89	.451	12th (16)	Buddy Bell/Clint Hurdle
Triple-A	Colorado Springs Sky Sox	Pacific Coast	58	86	.403	15th (16)	Chris Cron
Double-A	†Carolina Mudcats	Southern	65	71	.478	8th (10)	P.J. Carey
High A	#Salem Avalanche	Carolina	74	66	.529	5th (8)	Stu Cole
Low A	Asheville Tourists	South Atlantic	64	74	.464	12th (16)	Joe Mikulik
Short-season	Tri-City Dust Devils	Northwest	40	36	.526	5th (8)	Ron Gideon
Rookie	Casper Rockies	Pioneer	35	41	.461	t-6th (8)	Darron Cox
OVERALL 2002 MINOR LEAGUE RECORD			336	374	.473	21st (30)	

*Finish in overall standings (No. of teams in league). †Affiliate will be in Tulsa (Texas) in 2003. #Affiliate will be in Visalia (California) in 2003.

ORGANIZATION LEADERS

BATTING
*Minimum 250 At-Bats
*AVG	Brad Hawpe, Salem	.347
R	Tony Miller, Asheville	109
H	Cory Sullivan, Salem	161
TB	Brad Hawpe, Salem	264
2B	Cory Sullivan, Salem	42
3B	Jorge Piedra, Salem	13
HR	Jack Cust, Colorado Springs	23
RBI	Brad Hawpe, Salem	97
BB	Tony Miller, Asheville	88
SO	Justin Lincoln, Salem	145
SB	Tony Miller, Asheville	50

PITCHING
#Minimum 75 Innings
W	Zach Parker, Asheville	16
L	Gerrit Simpson, Salem/Asheville	15
#ERA	Aaron Cook, Colorado Springs/Carolina	2.37
G	Matt Whiteside, Colorado Springs	60
CG	Aaron Cook, Colorado Springs/Carolina	3
SV	Matt Whiteside, Colorado Springs	26
IP	Scott Dohmann, Salem	170
BB	Cory Vance, Carolina	76
SO	Jason Young, Colorado Springs/Carolina	150

BEST TOOLS

Best Hitter for Average	Garrett Atkins
Best Power Hitter	Ryan Shealy
Fastest Baserunner	Tony Miller
Best Athlete	Choo Freeman
Best Fastball	Aaron Cook
Best Curveball	Ubaldo Jimenez
Best Slider	Chris Buglovsky
Best Changeup	Ryan Cameron
Best Control	Chin-Hui Tsao
Best Defensive Catcher	Dan Conway
Best Defensive Infielder	Oscar Materano
Best Infield Arm	Oscar Materano
Best Defensive Outfielder	Cory Sullivan
Best Outfield Arm	Rene Reyes

PROJECTED 2006 LINEUP

Catcher	J.D. Closser
First Base	Todd Helton
Second Base	Jayson Nix
Third Base	Jeff Baker
Shortstop	Juan Uribe
Left Field	Preston Wilson
Center Field	Choo Freeman
Right Field	Rene Reyes
No. 1 Starter	Aaron Cook
No. 2 Starter	Jason Jennings
No. 3 Starter	Jason Young

JOHN SPEAR

Jack Cust　　　**Matt Whiteside**

No. 4 Starter	Zach Parker
No. 5 Starter	Jeff Francis
Closer	Chin-Hui Tsao

TOP PROSPECTS OF THE DECADE

1993	David Nied, rhp
1994	John Burke, rhp
1995	Doug Million, lhp
1996	Derrick Gibson, of
1997	Todd Helton, 1b
1998	Todd Helton, 1b
1999	Choo Freeman, of
2000	Choo Freeman, of
2001	Chin-Hui Tsao, rhp
2002	Chin-Hui Tsao, rhp

TOP DRAFT PICKS OF THE DECADE

1993	Jamey Wright, rhp
1994	Doug Million, lhp
1995	Todd Helton, 1b
1996	Jake Westbrook, rhp
1997	Mark Mangum, rhp
1998	Choo Freeman, of
1999	Jason Jennings, rhp
2000	*Matt Harrington, rhp
2001	Jayson Nix, ss
2002	Jeff Francis, lhp

*Did not sign.

ALL-TIME LARGEST BONUSES

Jason Young, 2000	$2,750,000
Chin-Hui Tsao, 1999	$2,200,000
Jeff Francis, 2002	$1,850,000
Jason Jennings, 1999	$1,675,000
Choo Freeman, 1998	$1,400,000
Ching-Lung Lo, 2001	$1,400,000

MinorLeagueDepthChart

COLORADO ROCKICKS

RANK 25

Developing homegrown pitchers Shawn Chacon and Jason Jennings over the last two years gives the Rockies hope in mile-high Coors Field. Jennings' stuff isn't spectacular, but his heavy sinker, which also is top prospect Aaron Cook's best pitch, is one of the prerequisites in the Coors Survival Guide. But it's no guarantee of success. The organization's focus on drafting and developing pitchers that fit the Coors Field mold has often come at the expense of securing frontline position players, though the Rockies were able to land two potential first-round talents last year in ninth overall pick Jeff Francis and fourth-rounder Jeff Baker, who slid out of the first three rounds because of signability issues.

Note: Depth charts prepared by Josh Boyd. Numbers in parentheses indicate prospect rankings.

LF
Rene Reyes (3)
Matt Holliday (16)
Jack Cust (21)
Trey George

CF
Choo Freeman (5)
Tony Miller (15)
Cory Sullivan (27)
Jason Frome
Brian Barre

RF
Luke Allen (25)
Jose Vasquez (30)
Jorge Piedra
Trey George
Sean Barker
Ryan Spilborghs

3B
Jeff Baker (7)
Garrett Atkins (13)

SS
Oscar Materano (12)
Ronnie Merrill

2B
Jayson Nix (6)
Pablo Ozuna (22)
Clint Barmes (24)
Javier Colina (26)

1B
Brad Hawpe (10)
Ryan Shealy
Nick Gretz
Ross Gload

C
J.D. Closser (17)
Neil Wilson
Garret Gentry
Dan Conway

LHP
Starters
Zach Parker (8)
Jeff Francis (9)
Cory Vance (23)

Relievers
Brian Fuentes (20)
Josh Kalinowski
Michael Davies
Isaac Pavlik
Tim Christman

RHP
Starters
Aaron Cook (1)
Chin-Hui Tsao (2)
Jason Young (4)
Ubaldo Jimenez (11)
Ching-Lung Lo (14)
Chris Buglovsky (18)
Mike Esposito (19)
Ryan Kibler (28)
Ben Crockett (29)
Ryan Cameron
Gerrit Simpson
Scott Dohmann
Justin Hampson
Kip Bouknight
Doug Johnson

Relievers
Cam Esslinger
William Vazquez
Manuel Corpas
Ryan Speier
Jentry Beckstead

DraftAnalysis

2002 Draft

Best Pro Debut: 1B Ryan Shealy (11) was the Rookie-level Pioneer League MVP, hitting .368-19-70 and leading the circuit in homers, RBIs, on-base percentage (.497) and slugging (.714). OF Brian Barre (13) hit .300-9-35 with 11 steals to join Shealy on the Pioneer all-star team, and LHP Isaac Pavlik (10) earned similar honors in the short-season Northwest League, where he went 5-1, 1.13. LHP Jeff Francis (1) and RHP Steve Reba (21) also posted sub-2.00 ERAs.

Best Athlete: OF Sean Barker (6) is 6-foot-3, 225 pounds with five-tool potential.

Best Pure Hitter: 3B Jeff Baker (4) was the best all-around college hitter in the draft, though a poor start to his season and rumors that he wanted Mark Teixeira money knocked him out of the first round.

Best Raw Power: Baker set the Clemson career home run record, but Shealy can jolt the ball a little farther.

Fastest Runner: OF Mitsuru Sakamoto (24) goes from the left side of the plate to first base in 4.05 seconds.

Best Defensive Player: Baker's hands and arm give him a chance to become a Gold Glove third baseman. C Neil Wilson (5) is agile and advanced for a high school kid in his first full year behind the plate.

Best Fastball: RHP Doug Johnson (5) maxes out at 94 mph, just ahead of Francis, Pavlik and RHP Mike Esposito (12).

Best Breaking Ball: Johnson can hit the mid-80s at times with his slider.

Most Intriguing Background: Sakamoto is believed to be the first Japanese player drafted by a major league club. 3B Duke Sardinha (19) has brothers playing in the Reds (Dane) and Yankees (Bronson) systems. Unsigned OF Tyler Littlehales (45) is a wide receiver at Colorado. In 2001, Francis was MVP of the National Baseball Congress World Series and unsigned RHP Micah Owings (2) was MVP of the Connie Mack World Series.

Shealy

Closest To The Majors: Francis and Baker are on an express route to Coors Field, and both may begin 2003 in high Class A. RHP Ben Crockett (3), Shealy and Esposito are California League candidates as well.

Best Late-Round Pick: Shealy or Esposito. Shealy was a fifth-round pick out of high school by the Rockies. Esposito, who had Tommy John surgery in 2000, would have gone much higher had he been more consistent last spring.

The One Who Got Away: Owings, who nearly broke the national prep home run record, had more arm strength than any pitcher Colorado signed. He should be a two-way star at Georgia Tech.

Assessment: Francis was a bit of a signability pick, but he has lots of upside. Unlike most teams, the Rockies weren't afraid to go above slot money to get later picks such as Baker ($2 million major league contract) and Esposito ($750,000 bonus).

2001 Draft

2B Jayson Nix (1) and OF Tony Miller (10) look decent thus far, but no one else has distinguished himself.   **Grade: C**

2000 Draft

RHP Matt Harrington (1) didn't sign and neither did OF Michael Vick (30), who unlike Harrington went on to better things. In between, the Rockies found RHP Jason Young (2), 3B Garrett Atkins (5), 1B Brad Hawpe (11) and draft-and-follow LHP Zach Parker (21).   **Grade: C+**

1999 Draft

RHP Jason Jennings (1) has shown that pitchers can succeed at Coors Field. C Josh Bard (3) would be starting for Colorado—if he hadn't been given to Cleveland in a trade for Jacob Cruz. Unsigned RHP Bobby Brownlie (26) would look nice in the rotation, too.   **Grade: B**

1998 Draft

RHP Matt Roney (1), OF Choo Freeman (1) and C Jeff Winchester (1) floundered for a while, though Roney (since lost to the Tigers in the major league Rule 5 draft) and especially Freeman recovered in 2002. OF Juan Pierre (13) was dealt so Colorado could dump Mike Hampton's contract, while RHP Luke Hudson (4) was given away to the Reds.   **Grade: C**

Note: Draft analysis prepared by Jim Callis. Numbers in parentheses indicate draft rounds.

... Cook's calling card is a heavy sinker that ranges from 93-96 mph.

Aaron
Cook rhp

Born: Feb. 8, 1979.
Ht.: 6-3. **Wt.:** 170.
Bats: R. **Throws:** R.
School: Hamilton (Ohio) HS.
Career Transactions: Selected by Rockies in second round of 1997 draft; signed July 13, 1997.

After spending five years without getting past high Class A Salem, Cook moved quickly up the ladder last year. He started 2002 at Double-A Carolina, where managers voted him the Southern League's best pitching prospect. After a brief visit to Triple-A Colorado Springs, he finished the season with the Rockies. He turned in quality starts in his first four attempts. Colorado decided to shut him down in mid-September after he reached 195 innings, a career high. Cook led the system with a 2.37 ERA, pitched in the Futures Game at midseason and was the organization's minor league pitcher of the year.

Cook is a power pitcher with command. His calling card is a heavy sinker that ranges from 93-96 mph. He also uses a four-seam fastball that hits 96-98 mph. He shows stamina, carrying his velocity into late innings and working at least 155 innings in the last three seasons. Cook has an exceptional 85-89 mph slurve that looks like a forkball with its late explosion. He refined his mechanics in 2001 and has a compact and smooth delivery that helped his command and velocity. He's an excellent athlete. Cook has to continue to work on his offspeed pitch, particularly with the challenge of Coors Field, where varying speeds is mandatory. He can get lazy with his slurve, mostly when he is ahead in the count. He has a tendency to try to overpower hitters when he gets ahead in the count instead of just getting them out. For a pitcher with such electric stuff, Cook doesn't miss as many bats as would be expected.

Colorado is counting on Cook to fill a rotation spot and pick up where Jason Jennings left off. It was no coincidence he was limited to 36 innings in the majors last season—keeping him rookie-eligible. Cook eventually will take over as the Rockies' No. 1 starter.

Year	Club (League)	Class	W	L	ERA	G	GS	CG	SV	IP	H	R	ER	HR	BB	SO	AVG
1997	Rockies (AZL)	R	1	3	3.13	9	8	0	0	46	48	27	16	1	17	35	.261
1998	Portland (NWL)	A	5	8	4.88	15	15	1	0	79	87	50	43	8	39	38	.275
1999	Asheville (SAL)	A	4	12	6.44	25	25	2	0	122	157	99	87	17	42	73	.310
2000	Asheville (SAL)	A	10	7	2.96	21	21	4	0	143	130	54	47	10	23	118	.241
	Salem (Car)	A	1	6	5.44	7	7	1	0	43	52	33	26	4	12	37	.297
2001	Salem (Car)	A	11	11	3.08	27	27	0	0	155	157	73	53	4	38	122	.263
2002	Carolina (SL)	AA	7	2	1.42	14	14	2	0	95	73	24	15	4	19	58	.213
	Colorado Springs (PCL)	AAA	4	4	3.78	10	10	1	0	64	67	40	27	6	18	32	.264
	Colorado (NL)	MAJ	2	1	4.54	9	5	0	0	36	41	18	18	4	13	14	.295
MAJOR LEAGUE TOTALS			2	1	4.54	9	5	0	0	36	41	18	18	4	13	14	.295
MINOR LEAGUE TOTALS			43	53	3.78	128	127	11	0	747	771	400	314	54	208	513	.265

2. Chin-Hui Tsao, rhp

Born: June 2, 1981. **Ht.:** 6-2. **Wt.:** 170. **Bats:** R. **Throws:** R. **Career Transactions:** Signed out of Taiwan by Rockies, Oct. 7, 1999.

Tsao was the Rockies' first significant signee from Asia, getting a then-franchise-record $2.2 million in 1999. He was the low Class A South Atlantic League's pitcher of the year in his 2000 pro debut, but had Tommy John surgery in 2001 and missed the first half of last season. While sidelined, Tsao worked on learning English and making other cultural adjustments. He made a solid return in 2002, though he was shut down with forearm tightness late in the year. Tsao still shows a plus fastball, reaching 91-96 mph last year. His changeup is excellent, and he showed his pitching aptitude in how quickly he mastered the pitch. His hard slider is a quality pitch as well. Tsao also has considerable poise, which comes from being Taiwan's ace during international competition. Staying healthy is Tsao's main challenge. His stuff, command and makeup are beyond reproach. Tsao will open the season at Colorado's new Double-A Tulsa affiliate. He figures to move to Triple-A at midseason and make his big league debut before the end of the year. He has the overpowering stuff to close games, but with his variety of pitches he likely will battle Cook for the eventual No. 1 spot in the rotation.

Year	Club (League)	Class	W	L	ERA	G	GS	CG	SV	IP	H	R	ER	HR	BB	SO	AVG
2000	Asheville (SAL)	A	11	8	2.73	24	24	0	0	145	119	54	44	8	40	187	.220
2001	Salem (Car)	A	0	4	4.67	4	4	0	0	17	23	11	9	1	5	18	.333
2002	Tri-City (NWL)	A	0	0	0.00	3	3	0	0	11	6	2	0	0	2	16	.150
	Salem (Car)	A	4	2	2.09	9	9	0	0	47	34	13	11	3	12	45	.204
MINOR LEAGUE TOTALS			15	14	2.61	40	40	0	0	221	182	80	64	12	59	266	.223

3. Rene Reyes, of/1b

Born: Feb. 21, 1978. **Ht.:** 5-11. **Wt.:** 210. **Bats:** B. **Throws:** R. **Career Transactions:** Signed out of Venezuela by Rockies, Aug. 29, 1996 . . . On disabled list, April 6-Sept. 29, 2000.

Signed as a catcher, Reyes was MVP of the Rookie-level Arizona League during his U.S. debut in 1998. He since has moved to first base and then the outfield. After missing all of 2000 following knee surgery, he came back to be the South Atlantic League MVP in 2001. Reyes has tremendous hitting instincts and power from both sides of the plate. He's athletic, which allows him to play all three outfield positions as well as first base, and leads to speculation he could wind up at third base. Reyes hasn't always put out and has to be challenged. Teammate Tino Sanchez made a breakthrough with him last year in Double-A, and Reyes hit .323-7-27 in the final two months after he started showing up for voluntary extra work. He needs to use his hands better to handle inside pitches and could draw more walks. His body has matured, so he won't be the basestealer some projected him to be two years ago. Reyes could move into the big league mix at some point in 2003 after opening the year in Triple-A. His versatility will enhance his chances.

Year	Club (League)	Class	AVG	G	AB	R	H	2B	3B	HR	RBI	BB	SO	SB	SLG	OBP
1997	Guacara 1 (VSL)	R	.220	38	82	8	18	2	2	1	9	7	14	1	.329	.281
1998	Rockies (AZL)	R	.429	49	177	40	76	9	4	5	39	8	15	16	.610	.493
1999	Rockies (AZL)	R	.361	22	97	21	35	4	4	1	20	4	14	6	.515	.398
	Asheville (SAL)	A	.350	40	160	26	56	6	1	3	19	6	22	1	.456	.377
2000					Did Not Play—Injured											
2001	Asheville (SAL)	A	.322	128	484	71	156	27	2	11	61	28	80	53	.455	.371
2002	Carolina (SL)	AA	.292	123	455	64	133	33	4	14	54	29	69	10	.475	.339
MINOR LEAGUE TOTALS			.326	400	1455	230	474	81	17	35	202	82	214	87	.477	.374

4. Jason Young, rhp

Born: Sept. 28, 1979. **Ht.:** 6-5. **Wt.:** 210. **Bats:** R. **Throws:** R. **School:** Stanford University. **Career Transactions:** Selected by Rockies in second round of 2000 draft; signed Sept. 26, 2000.

Young signed for a club-record $2.75 million as a second-round pick in 2000. He made his pro debut the following year, when he pitched in the Futures Game but also was shut down with a tender elbow. He pitched a full season in 2002, meeting all expectations, returning to the Futures Game and reaching Triple-A. Young has a full assortment of pitches. He uses all four quadrants of the strike zone with his fastball. He has a four-seamer that sits at 92 mph and a two-seamer that ranges from 87-90 mph with decent sink.

His Vulcan changeup works well for him, and his curveball is a good pitch. Young needs to get stronger so he can work deeper into games. His curveball can get loose at times. He could create deception in his delivery, which is a bit deliberate. Young used to throw 94 mph when he was at Stanford, and while that velocity could come back, it hasn't since he had shoulder soreness with the Cardinal. Young likely will open the season in Triple-A. He should make it to Coors Field for keeps at some point in 2003.

Year	Club (League)	Class	W	L	ERA	G	GS	CG	SV	IP	H	R	ER	HR	BB	SO	AVG
2001	Salem (Car)	A	6	7	3.44	17	17	2	0	105	104	47	40	8	28	91	.259
2002	Carolina (SL)	AA	7	4	2.64	14	14	1	0	89	71	30	26	1	30	76	.219
	Colorado Springs (PCL)	AAA	6	5	4.97	13	13	0	0	80	87	52	44	10	38	74	.272
MINOR LEAGUE TOTALS			19	16	3.63	44	44	3	0	273	262	129	110	19	96	241	.251

5. Choo Freeman, of

Born: Oct. 20, 1979. **Ht.:** 6-2. **Wt.:** 200. **Bats:** R. **Throws:** R. **School:** Dallas Christian HS, Mesquite, Texas. **Career Transactions:** Selected by Rockies in first round (36th overall) of 1998 draft; signed July 13, 1998.

A wide receiver who set a Texas high school record with 50 touchdown catches, Freeman turned down a Texas A&M football scholarship to sign for $1.4 million. His development has been slow, but he established himself defensively in 2001 and broke out with his bat and became a Southern League all-star last year. Freeman has the speed to cover the ground in center field, and the power potential to play on the corners if needed. He uses the entire field as a hitter and can use his wheels to take the extra base. His plate discipline improved immensely in 2002. Freeman's arm strength has improved but remains below-average. Despite his speed, he lacks the instincts to be a base-stealer. He needs to show more confidence in his two-strike approach at the plate. For all his power potential, his career high for extra-base hits is 40. This is a key season for Freeman, who heads to Triple-A and must build off his solid 2002 effort. He has the skills to be a run-producing center fielder with the type of range the Rockies need at Coors Field, but it likely will be mid-2004 before he arrives in the big leagues to stay.

Year	Club (League)	Class	AVG	G	AB	R	H	2B	3B	HR	RBI	BB	SO	SB	SLG	OBP
1998	Rockies (AZL)	R	.320	40	147	35	47	3	6	1	24	15	25	14	.442	.391
1999	Asheville (SAL)	A	.274	131	485	82	133	22	4	14	66	39	132	16	.423	.363
2000	Salem (Car)	A	.266	127	429	73	114	18	7	5	54	37	104	16	.375	.326
2001	Salem (Car)	A	.240	132	517	63	124	16	5	8	42	31	108	19	.337	.292
2002	Carolina (SL)	AA	.291	124	430	81	125	18	6	12	64	64	101	15	.444	.400
MINOR LEAGUE TOTALS			.270	554	2008	334	543	77	28	40	250	186	470	80	.396	.341

6. Jayson Nix, 2b

Born: Aug. 26, 1982. **Ht.:** 5-11. **Wt.:** 180. **Bats:** R. **Throws:** R. **School:** Midland (Texas) HS. **Career Transactions:** Selected by Rockies in first round (44th overall) of 2001 draft; signed July 14, 2001.

Nix' older brother Laynce, 22, is an outfielder in the Rangers system. Jayson was a standout pitcher and shortstop in high school. He was the MVP of the Texas 5-A state championship in 2001, earning a save in the semifinals and tossing a complete game in the deciding game. He moved to second base in 2002, his first full pro season, and was a South Atlantic League all-star. Nix is a ballplayer. He has a feel for how to play the game and isn't intimidated. As a 19-year-old he hit in the No. 3 slot on a team of older players, and he had 23 more RBIs than any of his Asheville teammates. Nix uses the whole field and shows power. He stays back on pitches well, which allows him to handle offspeed stuff. He made major defensive strides last year and excels at making the double-play pivot. Nix has a strong body, but his range is a little short at second base. He should be able to make adjustments as he gets more comfortable with the position. His biggest need is to ease up on himself. Nix will open the season at Colorado's new high Class A Visalia affiliate. He could force his way to Double-A before season's end.

Year	Club (League)	Class	AVG	G	AB	R	H	2B	3B	HR	RBI	BB	SO	SB	SLG	OBP
2001	Casper (Pio)	R	.294	42	153	28	45	10	1	5	24	21	43	1	.471	.385
2002	Asheville (SAL)	A	.246	132	487	73	120	29	2	14	79	62	105	14	.400	.340
MINOR LEAGUE TOTALS			.258	174	640	101	165	39	3	19	103	83	148	15	.417	.351

7. Jeff Baker, 3b

Born: June 22, 1981. **Ht.:** 6-2. **Wt.:** 205. **Bats:** R. **Throws:** R. **School:** Clemson University. **Career Transactions:** Selected by Rockies in fourth round of 2002 draft; signed Sept. 27, 2002

Baker might have the highest ceiling of any college player in the 2002 draft, but a so-so junior season, his poor history with wood bats and rumors that he wanted at least $4 million to sign hurt his standing. The Rockies gambled a fourth-round pick and waited him out. He signed in October for a $2 million major league contract but received just $50,000 up front. Baker has a quick bat and huge power, which could make him a force in Coors Field. He already has learned patience at the plate after facing an abnormal amount of breaking and offspeed pitches in college. Originally a shortstop, he outgrew the position but has the soft hands and plus arm to play well at third base. Baker has some length and an uppercut in his swing, so he'll have to close the holes. He swings hard and will need to make concessions against better breaking balls at higher levels. After hitting .216 in two summers using wood bats with Team USA, he'll have to prove he can do damage without aluminum. Baker figures to make his pro debut in high Class A. The best hitting prospect drafted by the Rockies since Todd Helton, he'll move as quickly as his bat allows.

Year	Club (League)	Class	AVG	G	AB	R	H	2B	3B	HR	RBI	BB	SO	SB	SLG	OBP
	Has Not Played—Signed 2003 Contract															

8. Zach Parker, lhp

Born: Aug. 19, 1981. **Ht.:** 6-2. **Wt.:** 200. **Bats:** R. **Throws:** L. **School:** San Jacinto (Texas) JC. **Career Transactions:** Selected by Rockies in 21st round of 2000 draft; signed May 27, 2001.

Parker turned down Louisiana State to sign as a draft-and-follow out of San Jacinto JC, and he might be the best Gators lefty since Andy Pettitte. Limited in his 2001 pro debut by a tired arm after a heavy workload at San Jac, Parker rebounded in 2002. He led the system in wins and innings. Parker's top pitch is an 88-93 mph sinker, and he throws it on a tough downward plane. He has good fade on his changeup, and throws it with fastball arm speed to keep hitters from picking it up. He has a hanging pickoff move that is a borderline balk. Parker's breaking ball has nice velocity, though it doesn't have the depth of a curveball or the late break of a slider. Parker's command is a game-by-game proposition. If he finds the plate in the first inning, he'll dominate. If not, he doesn't know how to adjust. He's a good athlete but gets himself in trouble by trying to rush things as a fielder. Parker has the ability to skip high Class A and jump directly to Double-A. He projects as a solid middle-of-the-rotation southpaw.

Year	Club (League)	Class	W	L	ERA	G	GS	CG	SV	IP	H	R	ER	HR	BB	SO	AVG
2001	Casper (Pio)	R	1	2	7.52	8	8	0	0	26	42	26	22	2	12	19	.389
2002	Asheville (SAL)	A	16	7	4.01	28	28	1	0	168	174	89	75	11	64	119	.274
MINOR LEAGUE TOTALS			17	9	4.48	36	36	1	0	195	216	115	97	13	76	138	.290

9. Jeff Francis, lhp

Born: Jan. 8, 1981. **Ht.:** 6-5. **Wt.:** 200. **Bats:** L. **Throws:** L. **School:** University of British Columbia. **Career Transactions:** Selected by Rockies in first round (ninth overall) of 2002 draft; signed June 19, 2002.

Francis burst onto the prospect scene in the summer of 2001, when he was the player of the year and top prospect in the Alaska League, then threw 14 shutout innings to capture MVP honors and lead the Anchorage Glacier Pilots to the title at the National Baseball Congress World Series. After going ninth overall in the 2002 draft and signing for a prearranged $1.85 million bonus, he had his pro debut cut short when a line drive hit him in the face in the Asheville dugout. Francis has a solid assortment of pitches. He has a low-90s fastball, a slurvy breaking ball that is more slide than curve, and a changeup with the potential to be a plus pitch. He has an easy arm action, above-average command and a good feel for pitching. Most of all, Francis needs to mature physically. With added upper-body strength, he could pitch deeper into games and add velocity. He also must tighten his slurve. Francis returned to the mound during instructional league and showed no after-effects from his injury. He showed enough in his brief time as a pro to earn the right to start in high Class A this year.

Year	Club (League)	Class	W	L	ERA	G	GS	CG	SV	IP	H	R	ER	HR	BB	SO	AVG
2002	Tri-City (NWL)	A	0	0	0.00	4	3	0	0	11	5	0	0	0	4	16	.143
	Asheville (SAL)	A	0	0	1.80	4	4	0	0	20	16	6	4	2	4	23	.232
MINOR LEAGUE TOTALS			0	0	1.17	8	7	0	0	31	21	6	4	2	8	39	.202

10. Brad Hawpe, 1b

RODGER WOOD

Born: June 22, 1979. **Ht.:** 6-3. **Wt.:** 190. **Bats:** L. **Throws:** L. **School:** Louisiana State University. **Career Transactions:** Selected by Rockies in 11th round of 2000 draft; signed June 21, 2000.

Hawpe won a College World Series title with Louisiana State in 2000, when he tied the NCAA Division I record with 36 doubles. He had a breakthrough season in 2002, leading the high Class A Carolina League in batting, walks, on-base percentage, slugging and total bases (264). He was promoted to Double-A for the Southern League playoffs. Hawpe can hit for both average and power. He uses all fields and has shown he can handle all types of pitching at the lower levels. He recognizes the value of a walk, which will help him adjust against quality pitchers in the upper minors. Hawpe was old for the CL last year and had his eyes opened by the pitching in Venezuela, where he batted .238 before straining a ribcage muscle. He's average at best as a first baseman and is a below-average runner, which will make playing left field more of a challenge. Double-A will be a proving ground for Hawpe in 2003. With Todd Helton locking up first base in Colorado, Hawpe may get more exposure in the outfield after seeing time there in Venezuela.

Year	Club (League)	Class	AVG	G	AB	R	H	2B	3B	HR	RBI	BB	SO	SB	SLG	OBP
2000	Portland (NWL)	A	.288	62	205	38	59	19	2	7	29	40	51	2	.502	.398
2001	Asheville (SAL)	A	.267	111	393	78	105	22	3	22	72	59	113	7	.506	.363
2002	Salem (Car)	A	.347	122	450	87	156	38	2	22	97	81	84	1	.587	.447
MINOR LEAGUE TOTALS			.305	295	1048	203	320	79	7	51	198	180	248	10	.540	.406

11. Ubaldo Jimenez, rhp

Born: Jan. 22, 1984. **Ht.:** 6-2. **Wt.:** 160. **Bats:** R. **Throws:** R. **Career Transactions:** Signed out of Dominican Republic by Rockies, April 25, 2001.

Though Jimenez posted a 6.53 ERA in the Rookie-level Pioneer League, the more important numbers were his age (18), velocity (90-95 mph) and strikeouts (65 in 62 innings). His down-breaking curveball—the best in the system and similar to Shawn Chacon's—passed the altitude test at Casper, which bodes well for his future at Coors. His overall command took a big step forward in 2002, another positive sign. At this point, Jimenez needs to get innings under his belt and become a more consistent pitcher. He's a competitor but must develop a stronger mound presence. He shows sign of a changeup, though it's still a work in progress. Now that he has a year in the United States under his belt, he should be ready for low Class A. He has the stuff to be a frontline starter in the majors.

Year	Club (League)	Class	W	L	ERA	G	GS	CG	SV	IP	H	R	ER	HR	BB	SO	AVG
2001	Rockies (DSL)	R	2	5	4.88	13	13	0	0	48	41	36	26	1	44	36	.225
2002	Rockies (DSL)	R	2	0	0.00	3	3	0	0	18	10	1	0	0	6	25	.152
	Casper (Pio)	R	3	5	6.53	14	14	0	0	62	72	46	45	6	29	65	.288
MINOR LEAGUE TOTALS			7	10	4.98	30	30	0	0	128	123	83	71	7	79	126	.247

12. Oscar Materano, ss

Born: Nov. 18, 1981. **Ht.:** 6-1. **Wt.:** 190. **Bats:** R. **Throws:** R. **Career Transactions:** Signed out of Venezuela by Rockies, July 18, 1998.

Materano was a short-season Northwest League all-star last year, when he led Tri-City in homers and RBIs despite being the youngest everyday player on the club. Even so, his glove is ahead of his bat, as he's the top defensive infielder and owns the strongest infield arm in the system. He's an excellent athlete with great body control and fine instincts. His arm and hands allow him to make spectacular plays at shortstop. Materano has a quick bat but needs to tighten his strike zone to have a better chance at the plate. Still young, he needs to maintain his focus, particularly on defense. The latest Latin shortstop produced by the Rockies, Materano hopes to follow Neifi Perez and Juan Uribe to Colorado. He'll play this year in low Class A.

Year	Club (League)	Class	AVG	G	AB	R	H	2B	3B	HR	RBI	BB	SO	SB	SLG	OBP
1999	Universidad (VSL)	R	.220	44	159	8	35	11	2	0	26	11	44	2	.314	.280
2000	Rockies (AZL)	R	.243	31	115	19	28	3	3	0	13	10	25	5	.322	.331
2001	Casper (Pio)	R	.251	69	271	34	68	11	0	6	38	9	59	5	.358	.291
2002	Tri-City (NWL)	A	.259	68	270	38	70	14	0	9	40	11	61	7	.411	.293
MINOR LEAGUE TOTALS			.247	212	815	99	201	39	5	15	117	41	189	19	.362	.295

13. Garrett Atkins, 3b

Born: Dec. 12, 1979. **Ht.:** 6-2. **Wt.:** 190. **Bats:** R. **Throws:** R. **School:** UCLA. **Career Transactions:** Selected by Rockies in fifth round of 2000 draft; signed June 22, 2000.

Atkins, who had a school-record 33-game hitting streak at UCLA, hit .317 as a first baseman in his first two pro seasons. With Todd Helton in Colorado, the Rockies decided to move Atkins to third base last year in Double-A, where he also made offensive adjustments. Pitchers overpowered him inside early in the season, but he sped up his hands by setting up on his back leg and moving closer to the plate. He's a pure hitter with good hand-eye coordination and the ability to stay back against offspeed stuff. As solid as Atkins' hitting fundamentals are, he needs to show more power to be a corner infielder. He has 24 homers as a pro and slugged a career-low .406 in 2002. Atkins has the arm strength for third base, but erratic footwork costs him accuracy on his throws. He'll continue his conversion to the hot corner in Triple-A this season, and he now faces competition within the system from Jeff Baker.

Year	Club (League)	Class	AVG	G	AB	R	H	2B	3B	HR	RBI	BB	SO	SB	SLUG	OBP
2000	Portland (NWL)	A	.303	69	251	34	76	12	0	7	47	45	48	2	.434	.411
2001	Salem (Car)	A	.325	135	465	70	151	43	5	5	67	74	98	6	.471	.421
2002	Carolina (SL)	AA	.271	128	510	71	138	27	3	12	61	59	77	6	.406	.345
MINOR LEAGUE TOTALS			.298	332	1226	175	365	82	8	24	175	178	223	14	.436	.388

14. Ching-Lung Lo, rhp

Born: Aug. 20, 1985. **Ht.:** 6-6. **Wt.:** 190. **Bats:** R. **Throws:** R. **Career Transactions:** Signed out of Taiwan by Rockies, Oct. 20, 2001.

Lo, perhaps better known by his nickname "Dragon," made his pro debut last year at 16. Not only did he have to deal with being the youngest player in U.S. pro ball, but he also faced cultural adjustments. He signed for $1.4 million out of Taiwan's Koio Yuan High, the same school that produced Chin-Hui Tsao. He held his own in the Pioneer League even though the Rockies wouldn't let him throw his slider and splitter, his two liveliest pitches, until he gets stronger. Colorado closely monitored his development as he worked with an 88-90 mph sinker and a plus changeup. Maturing physically and adapting to pitching on a regular basis are Lo's points of emphasis for now. He spent the winter working out in Denver, where he benefited from the presence of Tsao. Lo most likely will return to Casper in 2003.

Year	Club (League)	Class	W	L	ERA	G	GS	CG	SV	IP	H	R	ER	HR	BB	SO	AVG
2002	Casper (Pio)	R	2	4	3.20	14	9	0	0	45	44	22	16	3	22	21	.246
MINOR LEAGUE TOTALS			2	4	3.20	14	9	0	0	45	44	22	16	3	22	21	.246

15. Tony Miller, of

Born: Aug. 18, 1980. **Ht.:** 5-9. **Wt.:** 180. **Bats:** R. **Throws:** R. **School:** University of Toledo. **Career Transactions:** Selected by Rockies in 10th round of 2001 draft; signed June 7, 2001.

A defensive back at the University of Toledo, Miller has adjusted quickly to pro ball. In his first full season, he led the system in runs, walks and steals, a testament to his leadoff skills. He's a Marquis Grissom-type athlete who also will offer some pop atop a batting order. He's a hard worker who often works in the batting cage after games. Miller's inexperience shows against breaking balls, and he sometimes chases high fastballs. He also gets too pull-conscious at times. Miller has a strong arm for center field and the speed to track balls down. He does rely on his wheels a little too much at times, but he has started to take better routes. He could jump to Double-A in 2003, certainly at midseason if not on Opening Day.

Year	Club (League)	Class	AVG	G	AB	R	H	2B	3B	HR	RBI	BB	SO	SB	SLG	OBP
2001	Casper (Pio)	R	.306	70	268	68	82	17	3	10	34	41	63	28	.504	.399
2002	Asheville (SAL)	A	.283	129	501	109	142	23	4	17	48	88	129	50	.447	.396
MINOR LEAGUE TOTALS			.291	199	769	177	224	40	7	27	82	129	192	78	.467	.397

16. Matt Holliday, of

Born: Jan. 10, 1980. **Ht.:** 6-4. **Wt.:** 230. **Bats:** R. **Throws:** R. **School:** Stillwater (Okla.) HS. **Career Transactions:** Selected by Rockies in seventh round of 1998 draft; signed July 24, 1998.

Twice the Rockies have shown their belief in Holliday's potential. They gave him an $840,000 bonus out of high school to get him to pass up the opportunity to play quarterback at Oklahoma State. When Florida and Tennessee approached him about returning to football in 2001, Colorado signed him to a six-year deal with a minimum guarantee of $700,000. The wait, however, continues for Holliday to transform his power potential into reality. He has hit only 49 home runs in 478 pro games. His power comes through in batting practice, but he needs to keep his swing short and use his hands more. The son of Oklahoma State baseball coach Tom Holliday and the nephew of Rockies scout Dave Holliday, Matt has the strength to hit at least 30 homers a season. He has come a long way in converting from third base to left field, and has built up his arm strength to above-average for left field. He has good basestealing instincts despite ordinary speed. Holliday could return to Double-A Tulsa to open 2003.

Year	Club (League)	Class	AVG	G	AB	R	H	2B	3B	HR	RBI	BB	SO	SB	SLG	OBP
1998	Rockies (AZL)	R	.342	32	117	20	40	4	1	5	23	15	21	2	.521	.413
1999	Asheville (SAL)	A	.264	121	444	76	117	28	0	16	64	53	116	10	.435	.350
2000	Salem (Car)	A	.274	123	460	64	126	28	2	7	72	43	74	11	.389	.335
2001	Salem (Car)	A	.275	72	255	36	70	16	1	11	52	33	42	11	.475	.358
2002	Carolina (SL)	AA	.276	130	463	79	128	19	2	10	64	67	102	16	.391	.375
MINOR LEAGUE TOTALS			.277	478	1739	275	481	95	6	49	275	211	355	50	.423	.359

17. J.D. Closser, c

Born: Jan. 15, 1980. **Ht.:** 5-10. **Wt.:** 170. **Bats:** B. **Throws:** R. **School:** Monroe HS, Alexandria, Ind. **Career Transactions:** Selected by Diamondbacks in fifth round of 1998 draft; signed June 28, 1998 . . . Traded by Diamondbacks with OF Jack Cust to Rockies for LHP Mike Myers, Jan. 7, 2002.

Outfielder Jack Cust was the more ballyhooed prospect the Rockies received from the Diamondbacks for Mike Myers in January 2001, but Closser looks like he'll turn out to be more valuable. He's easily the most advanced catching prospect in the system. A switch-hitter with power from both sides of the plate, Closser spent the bulk of his time last year batting cleanup for Carolina. He shows good patience, though at times he becomes too pull-conscious. Closser relishes working with pitchers. He has natural quickness and arm strength, but he sometimes overthrows and hurts his accuracy. He threw out just 26 percent of basestealers in 2002. After splitting catching duties with Jason Dewey last year, Closser will get the bulk of the playing time in Triple-A in 2003. He should arrive in the big leagues next season.

Year	Club (League)	Class	AVG	G	AB	R	H	2B	3B	HR	RBI	BB	SO	SB	SLG	OBP
1998	Diamondbacks (AZL)	R	.313	45	150	26	47	13	2	4	21	37	36	3	.507	.453
	South Bend (Mid)	A	.214	4	14	3	3	1	0	0	2	2	7	0	.286	.313
1999	South Bend (Mid)	A	.241	52	174	29	42	8	0	3	27	34	37	0	.339	.363
	Missoula (Pio)	R	.324	76	275	73	89	22	0	10	54	71	57	9	.513	.458
2000	South Bend (Mid)	A	.224	101	331	54	74	19	1	8	37	60	61	6	.360	.347
2001	Lancaster (Cal)	A	.291	128	468	85	136	26	6	21	87	65	106	6	.506	.377
2002	Carolina (SL)	AA	.283	95	315	43	89	27	1	13	62	44	69	9	.498	.369
MINOR LEAGUE TOTALS			.278	501	1727	313	480	116	10	59	290	313	373	33	.459	.389

18. Chris Buglovsky, rhp

Born: Nov. 22, 1979. **Ht.:** 6-2. **Wt.:** 160. **Bats:** L. **Throws:** R. **School:** College of New Jersey. **Career Transactions:** Selected by Rockies in third round of 2000 draft; signed June 14, 2000.

An all-New Jersey performer in soccer as well as baseball in high school, Buglovsky established multiple school records at the College of New Jersey, an NCAA Division III program. He's athletic and stronger than his slender build would indicate. He has a resilient arm and hasn't missed a start since turning pro. His size still leads to questions about his durability, so he could wind up in the bullpen. Buglovsky's fastball ranges from 88-92 mph with excellent movement down in the zone. His best pitch is a hard slider that runs up to 87 mph. His changeup is inconsistent and his curveball needs a lot of work, two more reasons that relieving could be in his future. Buglovsky must control the running game better, and he gets particularly lazy with runners on second base. He's headed for Double-A this year.

Year	Club (League)	Class	W	L	ERA	G	GS	CG	SV	IP	H	R	ER	HR	BB	SO	AVG
2000	Portland (NWL)	A	5	5	2.63	14	12	0	0	65	50	30	19	5	32	50	.212
2001	Asheville (SAL)	A	8	10	4.08	26	26	0	0	143	158	83	65	14	32	119	.273
2002	Salem (Car)	A	9	9	3.12	27	27	1	0	165	161	68	57	12	58	126	.259
MINOR LEAGUE TOTALS			22	24	3.40	67	65	1	0	373	369	181	141	31	122	295	.257

19. Mike Esposito, rhp

Born: Aug. 27, 1981. **Ht.:** 6-0. **Wt.:** 190. **Bats:** R. **Throws:** R. **School:** Arizona State University. **Career Transactions:** Selected by Rockies in 12th round of 2002 draft; signed Aug. 29, 2002.

Esposito was a Reds fifth-round pick out of high school. Entering 2002, he projected to go in the top two rounds of the draft despite having Tommy John surgery as a freshman two years earlier. He battled a sore arm throughout last spring, which coupled with his bonus demands caused him to slip all the way to the 12th round. When the Rockies failed to sign second-rounder Micah Owings, who opted to attend Georgia Tech, they spent that money on Esposito, who got a $750,000 bonus. As a 5-foot-11 righthander with a history of arm trouble, he's not exactly a scout's dream. But Esposito does have an 88-93 mph fastball and the makings of a plus changeup. His curveball can be a hammer at times, and he has an average slider. The biggest question, obviously, is his durability. He'll probably start his pro career in low Class A.

Year	Club (League)	Class	W	L	ERA	G	GS	CG	SV	IP	H	R	ER	HR	BB	SO	AVG
	Has Not Played—Signed 2003 Contract																

20. Brian Fuentes, lhp

Born: Aug. 9, 1975. **Ht.:** 6-4. **Wt.:** 220. **Bats:** L. **Throws:** L. **School:** Merced (Calif.) JC. **Career Transactions:** Selected by Mariners in 25th round of 1995 draft; signed May 26, 1996 . . . Traded by Mariners with RHP Jose Paniagua and RHP Dennis Stark to Rockies for 3B Jeff Cirillo, Dec. 15, 2001.

Fuentes was part of the Jeff Cirillo trade with Seattle. He was a conventional over-the-top pitcher whose career was headed nowhere until the Mariners had him drop to a much lower arm slot in 2001. Fuentes' motion is now similar to a Frisbee thrower's, giving him excellent deception. He has a consistent 90 mph fastball, impressive velocity for a sub-mariner. He throws a slider that he can run in on righthanders. Control is a problem when Fuentes doesn't get regular work, but if he pitches four times a week he's usually fine. He can hold his own against righties, allowing managers the luxury of using him as more than just a lefty specialist. Fuentes should be the primary southpaw in the Colorado bullpen this year.

Year	Club (League)	Class	W	L	ERA	G	GS	CG	SV	IP	H	R	ER	HR	BB	SO	AVG
1996	Everett (NWL)	A	0	1	4.39	13	2	0	0	27	23	14	13	2	13	26	.230
1997	Wisconsin (Mid)	A	6	7	3.56	22	22	0	0	119	84	52	47	6	59	153	.203
1998	Lancaster (Cal)	A	7	7	4.17	24	22	0	0	119	121	73	55	8	81	137	.273
1999	New Haven (EL)	AA	3	3	4.95	15	14	0	0	60	53	36	33	5	46	66	.255
2000	New Haven (EL)	AA	7	12	4.51	26	26	1	0	140	127	80	70	7	70	152	.246
2001	Tacoma (PCL)	AAA	3	2	2.94	35	0	0	6	52	35	19	17	4	25	70	.206
	Seattle (AL)	MAJ	1	1	4.63	10	0	0	0	12	6	6	6	2	8	10	.171
2002	Colorado Springs (PCL)	AAA	3	3	3.70	41	0	0	1	49	44	25	20	0	32	61	.246
	Colorado (NL)	MAJ	2	0	4.73	31	0	0	0	27	25	14	14	4	13	38	.250
MAJOR LEAGUE TOTALS			3	1	4.70	41	0	0	0	38	31	20	20	6	21	48	.230
MINOR LEAGUE TOTALS			29	35	4.07	176	86	1	7	564	487	299	255	32	326	665	.240

21. Jack Cust, of

Born: Jan. 16, 1979. **Ht.:** 6-1. **Wt.:** 200. **Bats:** L. **Throws:** R. **School:** Immaculata HS, Somerville, N.J. **Career Transactions:** Selected by Diamondbacks in first round (30th overall) of 1997 draft; signed July 14, 1997 . . . Traded by Diamondbacks with C J.D. Closser to Rockies for LHP Mike Myers, Jan. 7, 2002.

Cust has been a darling of statistical analysts for a while, and Athletics general manager Billy Beane reportedly coveted him last offseason. Instead it was the Rockies who acquired him for Mike Myers after the Diamondbacks tired of Cust's offense-only approach. He led the system in homers and was named MVP of the Triple-A all-star game in 2002, but also had his least productive season since his pro debut and often looked helpless in the majors. Cust has big-time power to all parts of the park, but after six years as a pro he still hasn't learned to turn on balls with regularity. He's an extremely patient hitter who's not afraid to take pitchers deep in the count and draws lots of walks. He also takes too many close pitches, which result in strikeouts, and he doesn't expand his zone in RBI situations. Arizona thought he was indifferent toward playing defense and moved him from first base to the outfield so he'd be involved in fewer plays. While Cust did work more last year on his outfield play, he has no speed and little in the way of instincts. Ideally, he'd be a DH with an American League club.

Year	Club (League)	Class	AVG	G	AB	R	H	2B	3B	HR	RBI	BB	SO	SB	SLG	OBP
1997	Diamondbacks (AZL)	R	.306	35	121	26	37	11	1	3	33	31	39	2	.488	.447
1998	South Bend (Mid)	A	.242	16	62	5	15	3	0	0	4	5	20	0	.290	.294
	Lethbridge (Pio)	R	.345	73	223	75	77	20	2	11	56	86	71	6	.601	.530
1999	High Desert (Cal)	A	.334	125	455	107	152	42	3	32	112	96	145	1	.651	.450
2000	El Paso (TL)	AA	.293	129	447	100	131	32	6	20	75	117	150	12	.526	.440
2001	Tucson (PCL)	AAA	.278	135	442	81	123	24	2	27	79	102	160	6	.525	.415
	Arizona (NL)	MAJ	.500	3	2	0	1	0	0	0	0	1	0	0	.500	.667
2002	Colorado Springs (PCL)	AAA	.265	105	359	74	95	24	0	23	55	83	121	6	.524	.407
	Colorado (NL)	MAJ	.169	35	65	8	11	2	0	1	8	12	32	0	.246	.295
MAJOR LEAGUE TOTALS			.179	38	67	8	12	2	0	1	8	13	32	0	.254	.309
MINOR LEAGUE TOTALS			.299	618	2109	468	630	156	14	116	414	520	706	42	.551	.439

22. Pablo Ozuna, 2b/of

Born: Aug. 25, 1974. **Ht.:** 6-0. **Wt.:** 160. **Bats:** R. **Throws:** R. **Career Transactions:** Signed out of Dominican Republic by Cardinals, April 8, 1996 . . . Traded by Cardinals with RHP Braden Looper and LHP Armando Almanza to Marlins for SS Edgar Renteria, Dec. 14, 1998 . . . On disabled list, March 23-Nov. 13, 2001 . . . Traded by Marlins with OF Preston Wilson, C Charles Johnson and LHP Vic Darensbourg to Rockies for LHP Mike Hampton and OF Juan Pierre , Nov. 16, 2002.

When the Marlins traded Edgar Renteria to the Cardinals in December 1998, Ozuna was the key player they received in return. When the Rockies dumped Mike Hampton's contract on the Marlins last November, they got Ozuna, but he was mostly an afterthought. Once viewed as Luis Castillo's eventual replacement at second base, Ozuna's stock took a hit last spring when he was found to be four years older than his listed age. That news came after he missed the entire 2001 season following left wrist surgery. Ozuna remains a tremendous hitter for average, with the ability to put almost any pitch in play, but he doesn't have much pop and has grown less patient each year. His basestealing prowess, a big part of the package when he was in the St. Louis system, has lessened in importance despite his outstanding speed. He has stiff hands in the field, booting routine plays too often to be trusted with the everyday job at second. His instincts remain questionable. He played 23 games in center field for Triple-A Calgary and showed decent ability at tracking balls. His arm is average. He'll get a chance to make the Rockies this spring as a utility player.

Year	Club (League)	Class	AVG	G	AB	R	H	2B	3B	HR	RBI	BB	SO	SB	SLG	OBP
1996	Cardinals (DSL)	R	.363	74	295	57	107	12	4	6	60	23	19	18	.492	.415
1997	Johnson City (Appy)	R	.323	56	232	40	75	13	1	5	24	10	24	23	.453	.351
1998	Peoria (Mid)	A	.357	133	538	122	192	27	10	9	62	29	56	62	.494	.400
1999	Portland (EL)	AA	.281	117	502	62	141	25	7	7	46	13	50	31	.400	.315
2000	Portland (EL)	AA	.308	118	464	74	143	25	6	7	59	40	55	35	.433	.368
	Florida (NL)	MAJ	.333	14	24	2	8	1	0	0	0	0	2	1	.375	.333
2001					Did Not Play—Injured											
2002	Florida (NL)	MAJ	.277	34	47	4	13	2	2	0	3	1	3	1	.404	.300
	Calgary (PCL)	AAA	.326	77	261	37	85	16	1	7	33	17	37	16	.475	.371
MAJOR LEAGUE TOTALS			.296	48	71	6	21	3	2	0	3	1	5	2	.394	.311
MINOR LEAGUE TOTALS			.324	575	2292	392	743	118	29	41	284	132	241	185	.455	.369

23. Cory Vance, lhp

Born: June 20, 1979. **Ht.:** 6-1. **Wt.:** 190. **Bats:** L. **Throws:** L. **School:** Georgia Tech. **Career Transactions:** Selected by Rockies in fourth round of 2000 draft; signed July 17, 2000.

After spending 2002 in Double-A, Vance was working out in September, getting ready for the Arizona Fall League. He suddenly was summoned by the Rockies, who were running out of pitchers, and got a two-game cup of coffee. He's not spectacular but he's a consistent winner, leading the Atlantic Coast Conference in victories in 2000 and reaching double figures in each of his two full pro sesons. He keeps hitters off balance with his offspeed pitches, a downer curveball and a changeup that he can turn over. If Vance can learn to throw his sinker in hitter's counts, he has a chance to start in the majors. He needs to command that two-seam fastball—which works best at 86-88 mph but will hit 91—better and trust it more often. Vance is an excellent athlete who fields his position, holds runners and even swings the bat well. He'll make the move to Triple-A in 2003.

Year	Club (League)	Class	W	L	ERA	G	GS	CG	SV	IP	H	R	ER	HR	BB	SO	AVG
2000	Portland (NWL)	A	0	2	1.11	7	3	0	0	24	11	5	3	1	8	26	.138
2001	Salem (Car)	A	10	8	3.10	26	26	1	0	154	129	65	53	9	65	142	.232
2002	Carolina (SL)	AA	10	8	3.77	25	25	1	0	150	142	73	63	8	76	114	.256
	Colorado (NL)	MAJ	0	0	6.75	2	1	0	0	4	4	3	3	2	4	1	.267
MAJOR LEAGUE TOTALS			0	0	6.75	2	1	0	0	4	4	3	3	2	4	1	.267
MINOR LEAGUE TOTALS			20	18	3.26	58	54	2	0	329	282	143	119	18	149	282	.237

24. Clint Barmes, ss

Born: March 6, 1979. **Ht.:** 6-0. **Wt.:** 170. **Bats:** R. **Throws:** R. **School:** Indiana State University. **Career Transactions:** Selected by Rockies in 10th round of 2000 draft; signed June 9, 2000.

A center fielder at Indiana State, Barmes was converted to a middle infielder and was considered a potential utility player until last season. The Rockies sent several of their top prospects to Carolina, and were pleasantly surprised when Barmes emerged alongside them. He made the Southern League all-star team and shows Rich Aurilia potential. The only negative came when he was hit by a pitch and broke his left hand, ending his season in early August. Barmes more than doubled his previous career home run total and may even have enough bat to play third base. His biggest weakness at the plate is sliders on the outer half of the plate. Barmes has plus speed to go with the agility and range to play shortstop. He also has a solid average arm. Barmes will make the jump to Triple-A this year, and the thin air at Colorado Springs could really enhance his power.

Year	Club (League)	Class	AVG	G	AB	R	H	2B	3B	HR	RBI	BB	SO	SB	SLG	OBP
2000	Portland (NWL)	A	.282	45	181	37	51	6	4	2	16	18	28	12	.392	.361
	Asheville (SAL)	A	.173	19	81	11	14	4	0	0	4	10	13	4	.222	.269
2001	Asheville (SAL)	A	.260	74	285	40	74	14	1	5	24	17	37	21	.368	.314
	Salem (Car)	A	.248	38	121	17	30	3	3	0	9	15	20	4	.322	.350
2002	Carolina (SL)	AA	.272	103	438	62	119	23	2	15	60	31	72	15	.436	.329
MINOR LEAGUE TOTALS			.260	279	1106	167	288	50	10	22	113	91	170	56	.383	.328

25. Luke Allen, of

Born: Aug. 4, 1978. **Ht.:** 6-2. **Wt.:** 220. **Bats:** L. **Throws:** R. **School:** Newton County HS, Covington, Ga. **Career Transactions:** Signed as nondrafted free agent by Dodgers, Aug. 4, 1996 . . . Traded by Dodgers to Rockies for OF/2B Jason Romano, Jan. 27, 2003.

The Dodgers shifted Allen from third base to right field in 2001 after he had committed a total of 80 errors during the previous two years. Allen was signed for his offensive potential, but his development was temporarily stunted when he spent parts of four seasons in Double-A. He bulked up too much and lost a lot of his flexibility. He loosened up his frame by toning his body in 2002. It paid off as he showed better bat control and plate discipline, though he still didn't produce the power expected from a right fielder. Allen boosted his value with an impressive winter performance in the Dominican (.316-7-35 in 152 at-bats), and the Rockies traded for him in January. Still, some scouts aren't sure of his role in the big leagues. Some think he'll show more power as he learns which pitches to drive, and he's a proven hitter for average. Others think he's too pull-conscious, though he does hang in well against southpaws. Allen's raw arm strength grades out as a 70 on the standard 20-80 scouting scale. With no apparent openings in Colorado for him right now, he'll head back to Triple-A for 2003.

Year	Club (League)	Class	AVG	G	AB	R	H	2B	3B	HR	RBI	BB	SO	SB	SLG	OBP
1997	Great Falls (Pio)	R	.345	67	258	50	89	12	6	7	40	19	53	12	.519	.390
1998	San Bernardino (Cal)	A	.298	105	399	51	119	25	6	4	46	30	93	18	.421	.349
	San Antonio (TL)	AA	.333	23	78	9	26	3	1	3	10	6	16	1	.513	.381
1999	San Antonio (TL)	AA	.281	137	533	90	150	16	12	14	82	44	102	14	.435	.336
2000	San Antonio (TL)	AA	.265	90	339	55	90	15	5	7	60	40	71	14	.401	.340
2001	Jacksonville (SL)	AA	.290	125	486	74	141	32	6	16	73	42	111	13	.479	.345
	Las Vegas (PCL)	AAA	.222	2	9	1	2	1	0	0	0	0	0	0	.333	.222
2002	Las Vegas (PCL)	AAA	.329	137	501	85	165	28	3	12	78	56	77	4	.469	.395
	Los Angeles (NL)	MAJ	.143	6	7	2	1	1	0	0	0	2	3	0	.286	.333
MAJOR LEAGUE TOTALS			.143	6	7	2	1	1	0	0	0	2	3	0	.286	.333
MINOR LEAGUE TOTALS			.300	686	2603	415	782	132	39	63	389	237	523	76	.454	.358

26. Javier Colina, 2b/3b

Born: Feb. 15, 1979. **Ht.:** 6-1. **Wt.:** 190. **Bats:** R. **Throws:** R. **Career Transactions:** Signed out of Venezuela by Rockies, June 5, 1997.

Since the Rockies signed Andres Galarraga on the eve of the 1992 expansion draft, they've had a presence in Venezuela. Finally, it's starting to show in their system. Outfielder Rene Reyes is their best position prospect, while Oscar Materano is their top infield defender. Another Venezuelan to watch is Colina, who won the batting title in an abbreviated winter season in his native country's league with a .355 average. He has primarily played second base in the minors but spent the winter at third base. He can drive the ball but has yet to show the power teams look for at the hot corner. When Colina is swinging the bat well he uses all fields, but he still gets into funks where he tries to pull everything. He needs to show better discipline at the plate. Colina is better at third base, where his hands and arm serve him well, than at second, where he lacks quick feet. He'll probably return to Triple-A in 2003, at least to start the season.

Year	Club (League)	Class	AVG	G	AB	R	H	2B	3B	HR	RBI	BB	SO	SB	SLG	OBP
1997	Guacara 1 (VSL)	R	.246	26	65	4	16	2	1	0	8	5	14	3	.308	.296
1998	Rockies (AZL)	R	.320	44	169	28	54	6	2	6	39	18	30	9	.485	.387
1999	Asheville (SAL)	A	.302	124	516	70	156	37	3	6	81	26	101	12	.421	.339
2000	Carolina (SL)	AA	.217	130	429	34	93	12	1	2	35	44	81	5	.263	.292
2001	Carolina (SL)	AA	.042	7	24	0	1	0	0	0	2	0	10	0	.042	.042
	Salem (Car)	A	.285	113	439	67	125	33	7	9	58	22	61	9	.453	.324
2002	Carolina (SL)	AA	.272	35	136	17	37	6	1	1	17	7	21	4	.353	.310
	Colorado Springs (PCL)	AAA	.245	95	322	40	79	23	3	4	30	22	53	0	.373	.295
MINOR LEAGUE TOTALS			.267	574	2100	260	561	119	18	28	270	144	371	42	.381	.317

27. Cory Sullivan, of

Born: Aug. 20, 1979. **Ht.:** 6-0. **Wt.:** 180. **Bats:** L. **Throws:** L. **School:** Wake Forest University. **Career Transactions:** Selected by Rockies in seventh round of 2001 draft; signed June 7, 2001.

With his uncanny knowledge of how to play the game enhancing his tools, Sullivan has Mark Kotsay potential. After starring as a two-way player at Wake Forest, he reported to full-season Class A and has put up solid stats for two years. There's nothing spectacular about Sullivan, but he has solid tools across the board. He's a spray hitter with doubles power. Adding lift to his swing could produce more homers. He makes consistent contact but could use some more walks. Sullivan has the ability to steal bases and is a quality center fielder. He has a plus arm for the position, and as a college pitcher he was clocked at 87-89 mph. Sullivan will take the next step to Double-A this year and should be ready for the majors by the end of the following season.

Year	Club (League)	Class	AVG	G	AB	R	H	2B	3B	HR	RBI	BB	SO	SB	SLG	OBP
2001	Asheville (SAL)	A	.275	67	258	36	71	12	1	5	22	25	56	13	.388	.344
2002	Salem (Car)	A	.288	138	560	90	161	42	6	12	67	36	70	26	.448	.340
MINOR LEAGUE TOTALS			.284	205	818	126	232	54	7	17	89	61	126	39	.429	.341

28. Ryan Kibler, rhp

Born: Sept. 17, 1980. **Ht.:** 6-2. **Wt.:** 180. **Bats:** R. **Throws:** R. **School:** King HS, Tampa. **Career Transactions:** Selected by Rockies in second round of 1999 draft; signed June 17, 1999.

After leading the organization with 14 wins and a 2.15 ERA in 2001, Kibler ranked as the No. 4 prospect in the organization. Last year, his victories were cut in half while his ERA more than doubled, and he has tumbled down the list of pitchers in Colorado's plans. This year will be a major challenge for him to reaffirm his prospect status. He's such a competitor that the Rockies believe he may have pushed himself too hard when teammates Aaron Cook and Jason Young started so well at Carolina last year. Kibler isn't the same type of pitcher they are. He's more of a finesse guy, relying on a sinker that tops out at 90 mph and a circle changeup. A slider serves as his third pitch. Kibler's command fell off last year and he didn't fool many Double-A hitters. He has a tendency to drag his arm in his delivery, which flattens his pitches and puts strain on his shoulder. Despite his struggles, he may move to Triple-A at the start of this season.

Year	Club (League)	Class	W	L	ERA	G	GS	CG	SV	IP	H	R	ER	HR	BB	SO	AVG
1999	Rockies (AZL)	R	6	2	2.55	14	14	2	0	81	77	35	23	3	14	55	.248
	Portland (NWL)	A	0	0	21.60	1	1	0	0	3	8	8	8	1	4	4	.471
2000	Asheville (SAL)	A	10	14	4.41	26	26	0	0	155	173	107	76	9	67	110	.276
2001	Asheville (SAL)	A	3	5	2.93	10	10	1	0	61	50	26	20	3	27	59	.226
	Salem (Car)	A	7	0	1.55	11	11	0	0	76	53	19	13	0	16	61	.194
	Carolina (SL)	AA	4	1	2.11	8	8	1	0	47	38	17	11	0	19	41	.216
2002	Carolina (SL)	AA	7	8	4.91	25	25	0	0	143	158	98	78	6	64	59	.280
MINOR LEAGUE TOTALS			37	30	3.64	95	95	4	0	567	557	310	229	22	211	389	.255

29. Ben Crockett, rhp

Born: Dec. 19, 1979. **Ht.:** 6-3. **Wt.:** 200. **Bats:** R. **Throws:** R. **School:** Harvard University. **Career Transactions:** Selected by Rockies in third round of 2002 draft; signed June 17, 2002.

It's somewhat surprising that the Rockies landed Crockett with a third-round pick in 2002. He generated some first-round buzz in 2001 but went in the 10th round to the Red Sox. While many expected Crockett to sign with his hometown team, Boston lowballed him and he returned to Harvard for his senior season. The Athletics were believed to have interest in Crockett as a bargain for one of their seven first-round picks but passed him up. He set several Crimson school records, including marks for strikeouts in a game (17), season (117) and career (263), and helped them to two NCAA regional appearances. Crockett tore a ligament in his right elbow his junior year, but decided against surgery and turned in his second straight dominating Cape Cod League effort that summer. He has good command but must throw better strikes after low Class A torched him for a .372 average. Crockett has a 90-92 mph fastball and maintains his velocity deep into games. His changeup could become a plus pitch, while his curveball needs considerable work. He'll pitch in Class A this year.

Year	Club (League)	Class	W	L	ERA	G	GS	CG	SV	IP	H	R	ER	HR	BB	SO	AVG
2002	Tri-City (NWL)	A	0	1	2.88	7	6	0	0	25	26	8	8	2	3	21	.263
	Asheville (SAL)	A	2	3	7.36	6	6	0	0	29	51	25	24	4	6	18	.372
MINOR LEAGUE TOTALS			2	4	5.30	13	12	0	0	54	77	33	32	6	9	39	.326

30. Jose Vasquez, of

Born: Dec. 28, 1982. **Ht.:** 6-3. **Wt.:** 220. **Bats:** L. **Throws:** L. **School:** Booker HS, Sarasota, Fla. **Career Transactions:** Selected by Rockies in 16th round of 2000 draft; signed June 7, 2000.

A converted first baseman, Vasquez is one of the more intriguing prospects in the Rockies system. He's far from a polished player but has awesome power potential. Vasquez hits the ball a long way and does it with an easy swing, but he doesn't hit the ball often enough. He has 291 strikeouts in 203 pro games and led his league in whiffs in his first two years as a pro. He was on pace to make it three in a row, but a nagging hip injury bothered him throughout 2002. Vasquez must learn to recognize offspeed pitches to have a chance to translate his raw potential into results. He hasn't adapted quickly to the outfield, though his throwing has improved. Vasquez figures to return to low Class A this year.

Year	Club (League)	Class	AVG	G	AB	R	H	2B	3B	HR	RBI	BB	SO	SB	SLG	OBP
2000	Rockies (AZL)	R	.311	46	177	37	55	12	5	5	38	27	73	10	.520	.411
2001	Casper (Pio)	R	.232	64	228	40	53	6	3	14	39	27	96	1	.469	.332
2002	Asheville (SAL)	A	.223	93	319	44	71	20	2	6	36	30	122	4	.354	.302
MINOR LEAGUE TOTALS			.247	203	724	121	179	38	10	25	113	84	291	15	.431	.339

DETROIT
TIGERS

TOP 30 PROSPECTS

1. Jeremy Bonderman, rhp
2. Preston Larrison, rhp
3. Franklyn German, rhp
4. Omar Infante, ss/2b
5. Eric Munson, 1b/3b
6. Scott Moore, ss
7. Nook Logan, of
8. Rob Henkel, lhp
9. Brent Clevlen, of
10. Anderson Hernandez, ss
11. Chad Petty, lhp
12. Cody Ross, of
13. Matt Coenen, lhp
14. Andy Van Hekken, lhp
15. Jack Hannahan, 3b
16. Andres Torres, of
17. Kenny Baugh, rhp
18. Curtis Granderson, of
19. Humberto Sanchez, rhp
20. Michael Woods, 2b
21. Travis Chapman, 3b
22. Wil Ledezma, lhp
23. Adrian Burnside, lhp
24. David Espinosa, 2b
25. Ryan Raburn, 3b
26. Matt Pender, rhp
27. Maxim St. Pierre, c
28. Roberto Novoa, rhp
29. Shane Loux, rhp
30. Juan Tejeda, 1b

By Pat Caputo

The Tigers keep waiting for their minor league system to become the foundation of a resurgence at the major league level. Detroit went into a rebuilding mode in 1996 when general manager Randy Smith was hired, and the effort bogged down to the point that Smith was fired after the team lost its first six games in 2002.

Weighed down by a number of long-term contracts, Dave Dombrowski, the team president who named himself to replace Smith as GM, has decided another overhaul is in order. Dombrowski hasn't necessarily been unhappy with what he has seen from the system. Detroit has good depth in the minors, but he decided the franchise lacked potential impact players who could lead the Tigers to a championship.

That's why he was quick to trade the club's most valuable commodity, Jeff Weaver, to the Yankees last July in a three-way deal with Oakland. Detroit landed first baseman Carlos Pena, righthander Jeremy Bonderman and closer Franklyn German.

Pena hit .253-12-36 in 75 games with the Tigers, making enough of an impression for the organization to view him as its first baseman of the future. Bonderman, the first high school junior ever drafted when he went in 2001's first round, fared well as a teenager in high Class A in 2002, his pro debut. He jumps to the top of the Tigers' prospect list and adds to the organization's strength, which is starting pitching. German, a hard-throwing closer, ranks third and gives the Tigers an option if Matt Anderson, the No. 1 overall pick in 1997, isn't able to bounce back from a shoulder tear that sidelined him for most of 2002.

Among homegrown players, Detroit used rookies Omar Infante and Ramon Santiago as its double-play combination in late September. The Tigers haven't developed their own middle-infield tandem since Lou Whitaker and Alan Trammell came up in 1977.

While Detroit has drafted well in recent years, its efforts have been hindered by injuries. First-round picks Matt Wheatland (2000) and Kenny Baugh (2001), both righthanders, had shoulder surgery and missed all of 2002. Two other highlights from a strong 2001 draft, second baseman Michael Woods (supplemental first round) and third baseman Ryan Raburn (fifth), were limited to just 40 games each because of physical ailments.

OrganizationOverview

General Manager: Dave Dombrowski. **Farm Director:** Steve Boros. **Scouting Director:** Greg Smith.

2002 PERFORMANCE

Class	Farm Team	League	W	L	Pct.	Finish*	Manager(s)
Majors	Detroit	American	55	106	.342	t-13th (14)	Phil Garner/Luis Pujols
Triple-A	Toledo Mud Hens	International	81	63	.563	4th (14)	Bruce Fields
Double-A	Erie Sea Wolves	Eastern	52	89	.369	12th (12)	Kevin Bradshaw
High A	Lakeland Tigers	Florida State	69	70	.496	7th (12)	Gary Green
Low A	West Michigan Whitecaps	Midwest	83	57	.593	2nd (14)	Phil Regan
Short-season	Oneonta Tigers	New York-Penn	47	27	.635	2nd (14)	Randy Ready
Rookie	GCL Tigers	Gulf Coast	23	37	.383	13th (14)	Howard Bushong
OVERALL MINOR LEAGUE RECORD			355	343	.509	13th (30)	

*Finish in overall standings (No. of teams in league).

ORGANIZATION LEADERS

BATTING   *Minimum 250 At-Bats
*AVG	Craig Monroe, Toledo	.321
R	Juan Francia, West Michigan	94
H	Juan Tejeda, West Michigan	157
TB	Juan Tejeda, West Michigan	236
2B	Ryan Jackson, Toledo	35
3B	David Mattle, West Michigan	10
HR	Eric Munson, Toledo	24
RBI	Juan Tejeda, West Michigan	106
BB	Eric Munson, Toledo	77
SO	Jason Knoedler, West Michigan	145
SB	Nook Logan, Lakeland	55

PITCHING   #Minimum 75 Innings
W	Chad Petty, West Michigan	15
L	Kevin Lidle, Erie/Lakeland	14
#ERA	Homero Rivera, Toledo/Erie	3.07
G	Jason Birtwell, West Michigan	58
CG	Shane Loux, Toledo	5
SV	Mike Kobow, West Michigan	31
IP	Andy Van Hekken, Toledo/Erie	183
BB	Tommy Marx, Lakeland	83
SO	Matt Coenen, West Michigan	141

BEST TOOLS

Best Hitter for Average	Curtis Granderson
Best Power Hitter	Eric Munson
Fastest Baserunner	Nook Logan
Best Athlete	Robbie Sovie
Best Fastball	Franklyn German
Best Curveball	Rob Henkel
Best Slider	Jeremy Bonderman
Best Changeup	Preston Larrison
Best Control	Andy Van Hekken
Best Defensive Catcher	Maxim St. Pierre
Best Defensive Infielder	Anderson Hernandez
Best Infield Arm	Anderson Hernandez
Best Defensive Outfielder	Nook Logan
Best Outfield Arm	Cody Ross

PROJECTED 2006 LINEUP

Catcher	Brandon Inge
First Base	Carlos Pena
Second Base	Omar Infante
Third Base	Scott Moore
Shortstop	Ramon Santiago
Left Field	Dmitri Young
Center Field	Nook Logan
Right Field	Brent Clevlen
Designated Hitter	Eric Munson
No. 1 Starter	Jeremy Bonderman

Juan Tejeda   **Andy Van Hekken**

No. 2 Starter	Preston Larrison
No. 3 Starter	Nate Cornejo
No. 4 Starter	Rob Henkel
No. 5 Starter	Chad Petty
Closer	Franklyn German

TOP PROSPECTS OF THE DECADE

1993	Greg Gohr, rhp
1994	Justin Thompson, lhp
1995	Tony Clark, 1b
1996	Mike Drumright, rhp
1997	Mike Drumright, rhp
1998	Juan Encarnacion, of
1999	Gabe Kapler, of
2000	Eric Munson, 1b/c
2001	Brandon Inge, c
2002	Nate Cornejo, rhp

TOP DRAFT PICKS OF THE DECADE

1993	Matt Brunson, ss
1994	Cade Gaspar, rhp
1995	Mike Drumright, rhp
1996	Seth Greisinger, rhp
1997	Matt Anderson, rhp
1998	Jeff Weaver, rhp
1999	Eric Munson, c/1b
2000	Matt Wheatland, rhp
2001	Kenny Baugh, rhp
2002	Scott Moore, ss

ALL-TIME LARGEST BONUSES

Eric Munson, 1999	$3,500,000
Matt Anderson, 1997	$2,505,000
Scott Moore, 2002	$2,300,000
Matt Wheatland, 2000	$2,150,000
Kenny Baugh, 2001	$1,800,000

MinorLeagueDepthChart

DETROIT TIGERS

Dave Dombrowski arrived last year, quickly assumed the general manager's reins from Randy Smith and set out to mold a team for the future. Suddenly the Tigers are a team on the upswing. Some questioned dealing staff ace Jeff Weaver to the Yankees, but Dombrowski netted a sweet-swinging, young first baseman with power in Carlos Pena, Weaver's eventual replacement in the rotation in Jeremy Bonderman, and a potential power closer in Franklyn German. A January deal with the Marlins, Dombrowski's former club, landed three more prospects. The only real setback in the minors in 2002 centered on righthanders Matt Wheatland and Kenny Baugh, first-round picks in 2000 and 2001 who missed the season with injuries.

Note: Depth charts prepared by Josh Boyd. Numbers in parentheses indicate prospect rankings.

LF
Cody Ross (12)
Curtis Granderson (18)
Noochie Varner
Craig Monroe
Robbie Sovie
Dave Mattle

CF
Nook Logan (7)
Andres Torres (16)
Bo Flowers
Corey Richardson

RF
Brent Clevlen (9)
Neil Jenkins

3B
Scott Moore (6)
Jack Hannahan (15)
Travis Chapman (21)
Ryan Raburn (25)
Juan Gonzalez

SS
Omar Infante (4)
Anderson Hernandez (10)
Donald Kelly

2B
Michael Woods (20)
David Espinosa (24)
Juan Francia

1B
Eric Munson (5)
Juan Tejada (30)

C
Maxim St. Pierre (27)
Mike Rabelo

RHP
Starters
Jeremy Bonderman (1)
Preston Larrison (2)
Kenny Baugh (17)
Humberto Sanchez (19)
Matt Pender (26)
Shane Loux (29)
Matt Wheatland
Jeremy Johnson
Joel Zumaya
Ross Koenig
Jason Moates

Relievers
Franklyn German (3)
Roberto Novoa (28)
Fernando Rodney
Matt Roney
Jorge Cordova
John Birtwell

LHP
Starters
Rob Henkel (8)
Chad Petty (11)
Matt Coenen (13)
Andy Van Hekken (14)
Tim Kalita
Kevin McDowell
Tommy Marx
Rikki Johnston

Relievers
Wil Ledezma (22)
Adrian Burnside (23)
Eric Eckenstahler
Pedro Feliciano

DraftAnalysis

2002 Draft

Best Pro Debut: OF Curtis Granderson (3) hit .344-3-34 to win MVP honors in the short-season New York-Penn League. LHP Corey Hamman (12) allowed one earned run and had a 26-3 strikeout-walk ratio in 25 innings between the NY-P and high Class A Lakeland. OF Brent Clevlen (2) batted .330-3-21 in the Rookie-level Gulf Coast League.

Best Athlete: The Tigers loaded up on athletes, grabbing SS Scott Moore (1) and OFs Clevlen, Granderson, Robbie Sovie (4), Bo Flowers (5) and Wilton Reynolds (7) with six of their first eight picks. Sovie stands out as a Georgia high school football and track star who had a scholarship to play safety for Western Carolina. Clevlen and Flowers were high school quarterbacks, and Flowers was pursued by several college football programs.

Best Pure Hitter: Granderson finished second in the NCAA Division I (.483) and NY-P batting races. Moore is three years behind him but could hit for a higher average down the road.

Best Raw Power: Moore or Flowers.

Fastest Runner: Sovie can run the 60 in 6.3 seconds and was the fastest premium prospect in the draft.

Best Defensive Player: C Luke Carlin (10) has a strong arm and is agile behind the plate. He was a volleyball and lacrosse star while growing up in Canada.

Best Fastball: RHP Joel Zumaya (11) started topping out at 93 mph last spring, and his fastball jumped again to 94-97 after he signed. He went 2-1, 1.93 with a 46-11 K-BB ratio in 37 Rookie-ball innings. RHP Matt Pender (3) and seven-figure draft-and-follow RHP Humberto Sanchez both reach the mid-90s and also have good curveballs.

Best Breaking Ball: 6-foot-8 RHP Troy Pickford (8) has a low-80s slider to go with an 88-93 mph fastball.

RICH ABEL

Granderson

Most Intriguing Background: Sovie was a three-sport star in high school even after reconstructive knee surgery that cost him all of the 2001 baseball season. Hamman was the MVP of the 2000 NCAA Division III College World Series, winning the championship game for Montclair State (N.J.). 1B Drew Caravella (23) was the Division III player of the year and won the D-III batting title with a .534 average.

Closest To The Majors: Granderson doesn't have an obvious weakness and would be a nice fit in Comerica Park.

Best Late-Round Pick: Zumaya.

The One Who Got Away: RHP Anthony Reyes (13) would have been an early first-round pick had he not been sidetracked by elbow tendinitis. Detroit signed 16 of its first 17 picks, but never was close to prying Reyes away from his senior season at Southern California.

Assessment: The Tigers wanted to deepen their stock of position players and did just that. They found four promising arms in Pender, Pickford, Zumaya and Sanchez.

2001 Draft

At the end of the 2001 season, this looked like the best draft of the year. Then RHP Kenny Baugh (1), 2B Michael Woods (1) and 3B Ryan Raburn (5) all got hurt. Others to watch include RHP Preston Larrison (2), LHP Matt Coenen (3), 3B Jack Hannahan (4) and draft-and-follow RHP Humberto Sanchez (31). **Grade: C+**

2000 Draft

RHP Matt Wheatland (1) has pitched just 69 innings in three years because of finger and shoulder problems. LHP Chad Petty (2) and OF Nook Logan (3) are intriguing long-term projects. **Grade: C**

1999 Draft

1B Eric Munson (1) was supposed to reach the majors quickly but still hasn't found his niche. OF Cody Ross (4) is an overachiever who keeps putting up numbers. **Grade: C**

1998 Draft

RHP Jeff Weaver (1) quickly became the Tigers' ace before they traded him, and Brandon Inge (2) is their long-term catcher. They're still waiting on RHP Nate Cornejo (1) and OF Andres Torres (4). **Grade: B**

Note: Draft analysis prepared by Jim Callis. Numbers in parentheses indicate draft rounds.

. . . Bonderman has maturity beyond his age, three above-average pitches and competitive makeup.

Jeremy
Bonderman rhp

Born: Oct. 28, 1982.
Ht.: 6-2. **Wt.:** 210.
Bats: R. **Throws:** R.
School: Pacso (Wash.) HS.
Career Transactions: Selected by Athletics in first round (26th overall) of 2001 draft; signed Aug. 22, 2001 . . . Traded by Athletics to Tigers, Aug. 22, 2002, completing three-way trade in which Tigers received 1B Carlos Pena, RHP Franklin German and a player to be named from Athletics, Athletics received LHP Ted Lilly, RHP Jason Arnold and OF John-Ford Griffin from Yankees and Yankees received RHP Jeff Weaver from Tigers, July 6, 2002.

BILL NICHOLS

Bonderman was acquired from Oakland along with first baseman Carlos Pena and closer Franklyn German in a three-way trade that sent Jeff Weaver, Detroit's top player and 1998 first-round pick, to the Yankees. The trade was made in July, but the Tigers couldn't official- ly acquire Bonderman until one year after his original signing (Aug. 22, 2001). He was in the news the previous summer as well, when he became the first player ever drafted after his junior year in high school. He was eligible because he was 18 and had received his GED diploma. Bonderman didn't make his pro debut until 2002 because he signed late, and Oakland challenged him by sending him straight to high Class A. Considering his age and experience, he was spectacular. He hadn't even pitched much in instructional league in 2001, logging just three innings.

Bonderman has every tool to be a No. 1 starter in the major leagues. His fastball is consis- tently in the 92-94 mph range with movement, and there are times when he throws harder. His slider is sharp and he commands it well. Given his limited experience, Bonderman also has made excellent progress with his changeup. He's competitive and wants the ball, displaying a bulldog mentality on the mound. He has a strong frame, which bodes well for his durability. To reach his potential, Bonderman will need better command of his pitches, particularly his fastball. When he falls behind in the count, at times he comes in with less than his best stuff over the heart of the plate. He gave up 18 homers in 157 innings in 2002. Bonderman got better each month of the season until fading in August, so he'll have to get accustomed to the long grind of pro ball.

Though Bonderman is just 20, the Tigers have no intention of bringing him along slow- ly. Barring injury or a poor performance during spring training, he'll begin 2003 at Double- A Erie. Bonderman has maturity beyond his age, three above-average pitches and a ground- ed and competitive makeup. It's not inconceivable that he could reach the majors late in the season, though 2004 is a more likely timetable.

Year	Club (League)	Class	W	L	ERA	G	GS	CG	SV	IP	H	R	ER	HR	BB	SO	AVG
2002	Modesto (Cal)	A	9	8	3.61	25	25	1	0	145	129	77	58	15	55	160	.233
	Lakeland (FSL)	A	0	1	6.00	2	2	1	0	12	11	8	8	3	4	10	.262
MINOR LEAGUE TOTALS			9	9	3.79	27	27	2	0	157	140	85	66	18	59	170	.235

2. Preston Larrison, rhp

Born: Nov. 19, 1980. **Ht.:** 6-4. **Wt.:** 210. **Bats:** R. **Throws:** R. **School:** University of Evansville. **Career Transactions:** Selected by Tigers in second round of 2001 draft; signed July 13, 2001.

Projected as a first-round pick in 2001, Larrison had a disappointing junior year at Evansville and scouts questioned his competitive nature. The Tigers were delighted to get him in the second round. After a shoulder ailment early in 2002, he overmatched Class A Florida State League hitters in the second half. He went 7-3, 1.25 in his final 12 starts. Larrison has an outstanding changeup and sets it up with a heavy, 91-93 mph sinker. Not only is his changeup deceptive and lively, but he's also able to throw it for strikes anytime during the count. At this stage, Larrison's breaking ball doesn't match the quality of his fastball and changeup. His shoulder woes cost him a month early in the season and raised durability concerns. He dominated the Cape Cod League in 2000 but couldn't back it up the following spring, so he must prove he can carry his success from 2002 to 2003. Larrison will join Jeremy Bonderman in the Double-A Erie rotation to begin 2003. If he fares well, Larrison will move up to Triple-A Toledo and could see Comerica Park by the end of the year.

Year	Club (League)	Class	W	L	ERA	G	GS	CG	SV	IP	H	R	ER	HR	BB	SO	AVG
2001	Oneonta (NY-P)	A	1	3	2.47	10	8	0	0	47	37	22	13	1	21	50	.208
2002	Lakeland (FSL)	A	10	5	2.39	21	19	3	0	120	86	39	32	6	45	92	.200
MINOR LEAGUE TOTALS			11	8	2.42	31	27	3	0	168	123	61	45	7	66	142	.202

3. Franklyn German, rhp

Born: Jan. 20, 1980. **Ht.:** 6-4. **Wt.:** 260. **Bats:** R. **Throws:** R. **Career Transactions:** Signed out of Dominican Republic by Athletics, July 2, 1996 . . . Traded by Athletics to Tigers with 1B Carlos Pena and a player to be named as part of three-way trade in which Athletics received LHP Ted Lilly, RHP Jason Arnold and OF John-Ford Griffin from Yankees and Yankees received RHP Jeff Weaver from Tigers, July 6, 2002; Tigers acquired RHP Jeremy Bonderman from Athletics to complete trade (Aug. 22, 2002).

Part of the Jeff Weaver trade with the Athletics and Yankees, German had 30 saves between three levels and two organizations in 2002. Signed as a 16-year-old out of the Dominican Republic, he made slow but consistent progress before a breakthrough in winter ball after the 2001 season. German combines a 96 mph fastball with an excellent splitter. If he gets ahead in the count, hitters generally have no chance against the splitter. He averaged 12.2 strikeouts per nine innings and didn't allow a homer in 2002. For a large pitcher, German's mechanics are smooth and consistent. He's athletic for his size. German is a two-pitch pitcher without a good offspeed pitch, so he has to work as a short reliever. At times, he struggles to throw strikes. German pitched well before the Tigers called him up last September. He'll probably open 2003 as a setup man for Matt Anderson, and he could take over if Anderson gets hurt or is ineffective.

Year	Club (League)	Class	W	L	ERA	G	GS	CG	SV	IP	H	R	ER	HR	BB	SO	AVG
1997	Athletics West (DSL)	R	8	3	2.33	13	13	5	0	89	66	33	23	2	31	80	.208
1998	Athletics (AZL)	R	2	1	6.13	14	12	0	0	54	69	43	37	5	18	46	.317
1999	S. Oregon (NWL)	A	3	5	5.99	15	15	0	0	74	89	52	49	10	45	58	.306
2000	Modesto (Cal)	A	5	5	5.50	17	14	0	0	72	88	55	44	4	37	52	.307
	Vancouver (NWL)	A	1	0	1.77	9	2	0	0	20	13	4	4	0	10	20	.173
2001	Visalia (Cal)	A	2	4	3.98	53	0	0	19	63	67	34	28	7	31	93	.262
2002	Midland (TL)	AA	1	1	3.05	37	0	0	16	41	28	14	14	0	27	59	.194
	Toledo (IL)	AAA	1	1	1.59	23	0	0	13	23	15	4	4	0	7	31	.188
	Detroit (AL)	MAJ	1	0	0.00	7	0	0	1	7	3	0	0	0	2	6	.150
MAJOR LEAGUE TOTALS			1	0	0.00	7	0	0	1	7	3	0	0	0	2	6	.150
MINOR LEAGUE TOTALS			23	20	4.19	181	56	5	48	436	435	239	203	28	206	439	.261

4. Omar Infante, ss/2b

Born: Dec. 26, 1981. **Ht.:** 6-0. **Wt.:** 150. **Bats:** R. **Throws:** R. **Career Transactions:** Signed out of Venezuela by Tigers, April 28, 1999.

After leading all shortstops in the upper minors with a .302 average in 2001, Infante slipped to .268 in Triple-A in 2002. He hit just .221 through early May before going on the disabled list with a back injury. He also had a tough time overcoming the death of his father. That came three years after his brother Asdrubal, who pitched in the Tigers system, was shot to death in a robbery. A fluid infielder, Infante has good range and excellent actions. He played second base during a September callup and made the switch without a hitch. He turns the double play well. At the plate, Infante drives the ball the opposite way with authority. He's a dedicated and hard-working player with an intense approach. Infante isn't going to hit for power, so he'll have to get on base. He must prove he can pull an inside pitch or major league pitchers will work him tight all the time. Infante needs to be more consistent in the field. He lacks the speed of a typical big league shortstop. Infante played well in September and should make Detroit's Opening Day roster as the starter at either middle-infield spot.

Year	Club (League)	Class	AVG	G	AB	R	H	2B	3B	HR	RBI	BB	SO	SB	SLG	OBP
1999	Tigers (GCL)	R	.268	25	97	11	26	4	0	0	7	4	11	4	.309	.294
2000	Lakeland (FSL)	A	.274	79	259	35	71	11	0	2	24	20	29	11	.340	.324
	West Michigan (Mid)	A	.229	12	48	7	11	0	0	0	5	5	7	1	.229	.327
2001	Erie (EL)	AA	.302	132	540	86	163	21	4	2	62	46	87	27	.367	.355
2002	Toledo (IL)	AAA	.268	120	436	49	117	16	8	4	51	28	49	19	.369	.309
	Detroit (AL)	MAJ	.333	18	72	4	24	3	0	1	6	3	10	0	.417	.360
MAJOR LEAGUE TOTALS			.333	18	72	4	24	3	0	1	6	3	10	0	.417	.360
MINOR LEAGUE TOTALS			.281	368	1380	188	388	52	12	8	149	103	183	62	.354	.330

5. Eric Munson, 1b/3b

Born: Oct. 3, 1977. **Ht.:** 6-3. **Wt.:** 220. **Bats:** L. **Throws:** R. **School:** University of Southern California. **Career Transactions:** Selected by Tigers in first round (third overall) of 1999 draft; signed June 24, 1999.

The third overall pick in the 1999 draft, Munson was a catcher at Southern California but that's no longer an option. A back injury in 2000 slowed his progress considerably. He was hitting .196 midway through 2002 but heated up after the Tigers traded for fellow first baseman Carlos Pena in July. Munson has a classic lefthanded hitting stroke. He has exceptionally quick hands and generates a lot of bat speed, giving him plus power to all fields. He shows patience at the plate, drawing a good number of walks. Munson struggles when he becomes pull-conscious, and there are extended periods when he strikes out too much. Some coaches and scouts question his drive. Though managers rated him the International League's best defensive first baseman and he has improved, he's not much more than adequate. Before his second-half turnaround, Munson was on the verge of wearing out his welcome in Detroit. With a logjam at first base, he spent the off-season learning to play third base. If Munson becomes more consistent, the Tigers will get his bat in their lineup.

Year	Club (League)	Class	AVG	G	AB	R	H	2B	3B	HR	RBI	BB	SO	SB	SLG	OBP
1999	Lakeland (FSL)	A	.333	2	6	0	2	0	0	0	1	1	1	0	.333	.429
	West Michigan (Mid)	A	.266	67	252	42	67	16	1	14	44	37	47	3	.504	.378
2000	Jacksonville (SL)	AA	.252	98	365	52	92	21	4	15	68	39	96	5	.455	.348
	Detroit (AL)	MAJ	.000	3	5	0	0	0	0	0	1	0	1	0	.000	.000
2001	Erie (EL)	AA	.260	142	519	88	135	35	1	26	102	84	141	0	.482	.371
	Detroit (AL)	MAJ	.152	17	66	4	10	3	1	1	6	3	21	0	.273	.188
2002	Toledo (IL)	AAA	.262	136	477	77	125	30	4	24	84	77	114	1	.493	.367
	Detroit (AL)	MAJ	.186	18	59	3	11	0	0	2	5	6	11	0	.288	.269
MAJOR LEAGUE TOTALS			.162	38	130	7	21	3	1	3	12	9	33	0	.269	.220
MINOR LEAGUE TOTALS			.260	445	1619	259	421	102	10	79	299	238	399	9	.482	.366

6. Scott Moore, ss

Born: Nov. 17, 1983. **Ht.:** 6-2. **Wt.:** 180. **Bats:** L. **Throws:** R. **School:** Cypress HS, Long Beach, Calif. **Career Transactions:** Selected by Tigers in first round (eighth overall) of 2002 draft; signed June 4, 2002.

Moore drew comparisons to Eric Chavez and Chipper Jones while emerging as the top prospect in Southern California. He signed quickly for $2.3 million, the third-highest bonus in club history. Despite wrist and back problems, he performed well in his pro debut in the Rookie-level Gulf Coast League. Moore has a smooth lefthanded stroke and considerable power potential. He already has a live bat that will enable him to move to third base if needed. As an infielder, he shows soft hands and above-average arm strength. He does not have normal shortstop speed, but he's a solid average runner. Like most young hitters, Moore could use a little more patience at the plate. His range as a shortstop is below-average and almost certainly will prompt a move to the hot corner. Moore will begin his first full season at low Class A Michigan as a shortstop. That's a position of considerable depth in the Detroit system, but Tigers officials would rather keep him at shortstop as long as possible. They don't want to move him to the hot corner and then possibly shift him back down the road.

Year	Club (League)	Class	AVG	G	AB	R	H	2B	3B	HR	RBI	BB	SO	SB	SLG	OBP
2002	Tigers (GCL)	R	.293	40	133	18	39	6	2	4	25	10	31	1	.459	.349
MINOR LEAGUE TOTALS			.293	40	133	18	39	6	2	4	25	10	31	1	.459	.349

7. Nook Logan, of

Born: Nov. 28, 1979. **Ht.:** 6-2. **Wt.:** 180. **Bats:** B. **Throws:** R. **School:** Copiah-Lincoln (Miss.) CC. **Career Transactions:** Selected by Tigers in third round of 2000 draft; signed July 8, 2000.

Drafted out of junior college as a shortstop, Logan was moved to center field in instructional league after his first pro season. The Tigers also have made him a switch-hitter. He's a prolific basestealer, finishing second in the low Class A Midwest League with 61 in 2001 and leading the Florida State League with 55 in 2002. Logan has excellent speed and good instincts as a basestealer. His wheels also made his transition to center field go easily. He covers a lot of ground and throws well. Logan made strides as a hitter during the second half of 2002, making more consistent contact and beginning to bunt for hits. Logan needs to get stronger. He rarely turns on a pitch and pulls it. He needs to understand his speed and defense are his tickets to the majors. Logan must learn to bunt better and hit the ball on the ground more consistently to take advantage of his quickness. He makes too many errors in center field. The Tigers long have had a void in center field, and Logan is the primary candidate to fill it. He's probably two more years away though, and he'll begin 2003 in Double-A.

Year	Club (League)	Class	AVG	G	AB	R	H	2B	3B	HR	RBI	BB	SO	SB	SLG	OBP
2000	Tigers (GCL)	R	.279	43	136	29	38	2	2	0	14	31	36	20	.324	.412
	Lakeland (FSL)	A	.333	11	42	4	14	1	0	0	3	2	13	2	.357	.364
2001	West Michigan (Mid)	A	.262	128	522	82	137	19	8	1	27	53	129	67	.335	.330
2002	Lakeland (FSL)	A	.269	124	506	75	136	14	7	2	26	40	111	55	.336	.321
MINOR LEAGUE TOTALS			.269	306	1206	190	325	36	17	3	70	126	289	144	.335	.338

8. Rob Henkel, lhp

Born: Aug. 3, 1978. **Ht.:** 6-2. **Wt.:** 210. **Bats:** R. **Throws:** L. **School:** UCLA. **Career Transactions:** Selected by Marlins in third round of 2000 draft; signed Sept. 19, 2000 . . . Traded by Marlins to Tigers with RHP Gary Knotts and LHP Nate Roberston for RHP Jerrod Fuell and LHP Mark Redman, Jan. 11, 2003.

Henkel was the key to the trade that sent Mark Redman to Florida in January. Though the other two players Detroit acquired—lefthander Nate Robertson and righthander Gary Knotts—have major league experience and high upsides, they don't have the ceiling that Henkel does. After signing for $650,000 in September 2000, he spent nearly a year fighting a balky shoulder that caused his velocity to drop from 93-95 mph to the low 80s. Having already survived Tommy John surgery, he worked hard to strengthen the shoulder and gradually saw his velocity climb back up to 88-92 mph. He dominated the Florida State League in 2002 and earned a midseason promotion to Double-A. When he's on, Henkel brandishes a late-breaking knuckle-curve that can be close to unhittable. Combined with a deceptive delivery, his hook is hard for hitters to pick up and makes his fastball work that much better. He did a better job of integrating his changeup last season, giving him three solid weapons for the first time. A sociology major, Henkel tends to overanalyze his performance. With his history of arm problems, the Marlins often gave him a few extra days between starts. His delivery is high-maintenance, he still overthrows at times and his changeup needs more work. Florida planned on giving Henkel a look in big league camp as a swingman, but Detroit will evaluate him as a starter. He's more likely to open the year in Triple-A, but with his maturity and advanced knowledge, he probably won't need much more seasoning.

Year	Club (League)	Class	W	L	ERA	G	GS	CG	SV	IP	H	R	ER	HR	BB	SO	AVG
2001	Marlins (GCL)	R	1	3	1.52	9	8	0	0	30	17	9	5	0	11	38	.156
	Utica (NY-P)	A	0	0	4.32	3	3	0	0	8	7	4	4	0	6	11	.212
	Kane County (Mid)	A	0	0	4.50	1	1	0	0	4	6	3	2	0	1	2	.316
2002	Jupiter (FSL)	A	8	3	2.51	14	12	0	0	75	55	22	21	4	22	82	.206
	Portland (EL)	AA	5	4	3.86	13	13	0	0	70	54	31	30	6	27	68	.212
MINOR LEAGUE TOTALS			14	10	2.98	40	37	0	0	187	139	69	62	10	67	201	.204

9. Brent Clevlen, of

Born: Oct. 27, 1983. **Ht.:** 6-2. **Wt.:** 190. **Bats:** R. **Throws:** R. **School:** Westwood HS, Cedar Park, Texas. **Career Transactions:** Selected by Tigers in second round of 2002 draft; signed July 23, 2002.

Clevlen tore up the 2001 Area Code Games but couldn't quite live up to that performance as a high school senior. Mentioned as a possible pick in the middle of the first round, he lasted until the second and agreed to an $805,000 bonus. An all-district quarterback, he also pitched and out-dueled No. 5 overall pick Clint Everts (Expos) in the Texas 5-A playoffs. For a high school player, Clevlen is a polished hitter. He can hit the ball to all fields and battles pitchers throughout the count. He can turn on a ball with power. A right fielder, he has sure hands and a strong arm. Clevlen has average speed at best. His range in the outfield is limited because he sometimes gets bad jumps and takes poor routes to balls. He's a good but not great athlete, so his bat will have to carry him to the majors. Like Scott Moore, Clevlen will make the jump to low Class A in 2003. West Michigan's Fifth Third Ballpark is tough on hitters and they'll both be young for the Midwest League.

Year	Club (League)	Class	AVG	G	AB	R	H	2B	3B	HR	RBI	BB	SO	SB	SLG	OBP
2002	Tigers (GCL)	R	.330	28	103	14	34	2	3	3	21	8	24	2	.495	.372
MINOR LEAGUE TOTALS			.330	28	103	14	34	2	3	3	21	8	24	2	.495	.372

10. Anderson Hernandez, ss

Born: Oct. 30. **Ht.:** 5-9. **Wt.:** 150. **Bats:** B. **Throws:** R. **Career Transactions:** Signed out of Dominican Republic by Tigers, April 23, 2001.

Because he was 18 when he signed out of the Dominican Republic in April 2001, Hernandez has been pushed through the system. He made his pro debut in the Gulf Coast League and jumped to Lakeland for his first full season. Hernandez has handled the challenges well. A brilliant fielder, Hernandez is the best defensive shortstop in the organization. That's saying something with Omar Infante and Ramon Santiago on hand. Hernandez has excellent range, extraordinary arm strength and soft hands. As a hitter, he held his own in 2002 despite being young for the Florida State League. More quick than fast, he has average baserunning speed. A switch-hitter, Hernandez seldom turns on pitches or pulls the ball with authority. He hits everything to the opposite field, particularly while hitting lefthanded. He also needs a better understanding of the strike zone. For all of his brilliance with the glove, Hernandez still makes too many errors. He tends to sulk after poor performances. Hernandez will be one of the youngest regular position players in Double-A at age 20. He'll move as quickly as his bat allows.

Year	Club (League)	Class	AVG	G	AB	R	H	2B	3B	HR	RBI	BB	SO	SB	SLG	OBP
2001	Tigers (GCL)	R	.264	55	216	37	57	5	11	0	18	13	38	34	.389	.303
	Lakeland (FSL)	A	.190	7	21	2	4	0	1	0	1	0	8	0	.286	.190
2002	Lakeland (FSL)	A	.259	123	410	52	106	13	7	2	42	33	102	16	.339	.310
MINOR LEAGUE TOTALS			.258	185	647	91	167	18	19	2	61	46	148	50	.354	.304

11. Chad Petty, lhp

Born: Feb. 17, 1982. **Ht.:** 6-4. **Wt.:** 200. **Bats:** L. **Throws:** L. **School:** Chalker HS, West Farmington, Ohio. **Career Transactions:** Selected by Tigers in second round of 2000 draft; signed June 12, 2000.

Petty has pitched well since recovering from the arm problems he experienced during his first spring training in 2001. He has gone 21-11 the last two seasons, being named the top prospect in the Gulf Coast League in 2001 and holding up for 28 starts in low Class A in 2002. Petty throws 89-91 mph consistently with some movement on his fastball. He has a fine breaking ball for a young pitcher, a cross between a curveball and a slider. He's athletic and has a good feel for pitching. Durability is no longer a question now that he does a better job of staying in shape. Petty's changeup is weak and will need a lot of work. There are concerns about the way he prepares on the days he's not pitching. There are times when Petty loses command of his fastball, and he will have to cut down on his walks. He hits a lot of batters and throws too many wild pitches. Petty will move up to high Class A in 2003. The Tigers feel no sense of urgency to rush him and want to give him time to mature.

Year	Club (League)	Class	W	L	ERA	G	GS	CG	SV	IP	H	R	ER	HR	BB	SO	AVG
2000	Tigers (GCL)	R	2	3	3.00	9	7	1	0	39	31	18	13	0	20	38	.218
2001	Tigers (GCL)	R	6	0	1.11	12	10	2	0	57	35	11	7	2	13	52	.171
	Oneonta (NY-P)	A	0	1	2.84	1	1	0	0	6	6	5	2	0	2	0	.250
2002	West Michigan (Mid)	A	15	10	3.24	28	28	3	0	161	155	73	58	4	77	119	.255
MINOR LEAGUE TOTALS			23	14	2.73	50	46	6	0	264	227	107	80	6	112	209	.232

12. Cody Ross, of

Born: Dec. 23, 1980. **Ht.:** 5-11. **Wt.:** 180. **Bats:** R. **Throws:** L. **School:** Carlsbad (N.M.) HS. **Career Transactions:** Selected by Tigers in fourth round of 1999 draft; signed June 12, 1999.

The question about Ross is not whether he's a future major leaguer, but how high his ceiling is. He has been productive and had his best season last year in Double-A. From a tools standpoint, he has power and runs the bases well. His arm is strong and accurate enough that the Tigers considered making him a pitcher when they drafted him. At the same time, Ross doesn't have one overwhelming tool. He's not big and his listed height is generous. Some scouts say Ross is as good as he's going to get. Others think his Craig Biggio intensity will allow him to become a big league regular. His future probably lies at a corner outfield spot, though Ross did help his cause by showing he can play center field last season. Ross will open 2003 in Triple-A but could push for major league playing time in the second half.

Year	Club (League)	Class	AVG	G	AB	R	H	2B	3B	HR	RBI	BB	SO	SB	SLG	OBP
1999	Tigers (GCL)	R	.218	42	142	19	31	8	3	4	18	16	28	3	.401	.304
2000	West Michigan (Mid)	A	.267	122	434	71	116	17	9	7	68	55	83	11	.396	.356
2001	Lakeland (FSL)	A	.276	127	482	84	133	34	5	15	80	44	96	28	.461	.337
2002	Erie (EL)	AA	.280	105	400	73	112	28	3	19	72	44	86	16	.508	.352
MINOR LEAGUE TOTALS			.269	396	1458	247	392	87	20	45	238	159	293	58	.449	.344

13. Matt Coenen, lhp

Born: March 13, 1980. **Ht.:** 6-6. **Wt.:** 230. **Bats:** L. **Throws:** L. **School:** Charleston Southern University. **Career Transactions:** Selected by Tigers in second round of 2001 draft; signed July 12, 2001.

The Tigers liked Coenen's size and velocity when they drafted him in 2001. While he hasn't lived up to the 93 mph radar gun readings he flashed in college and in the Cape Cod League, he has proven to be refined. He showed a good feel for pitching in 2002, winning 14 games in low Class A during his first full pro season. In order to move up the ladder, Coenen must become a three-pitch pitcher. His fastball isn't overpowering, as he usually throws around 88 mph and tops out at 91. He has a slurvy breaking ball that he commands well, but he needs an improved changeup. Coenen uses a three-quarters delivery that gives his pitches some movement, but it doesn't look like he ever will be overpowering. To set up his breaking ball, Coenen will need command of his fastball early in the count. He'll move up to high Class A this season.

Year	Club (League)	Class	W	L	ERA	G	GS	CG	SV	IP	H	R	ER	HR	BB	SO	AVG
2001	Oneonta (NY-P)	A	2	2	3.04	10	9	1	1	47	44	26	16	1	16	37	.237
2002	West Michigan (Mid)	A	14	8	3.38	28	28	2	0	165	148	69	62	6	65	141	.240
MINOR LEAGUE TOTALS			16	10	3.30	38	37	3	1	213	192	95	78	7	81	178	.239

14. Andy Van Hekken, lhp

Born: July 31, 1979. **Ht.:** 6-3. **Wt.:** 170. **Bats:** R. **Throws:** L. **School:** Holland (Mich.) HS. **Career Transactions:** Selected by Mariners in third round of 1998 draft; signed June 26, 1998 . . . Traded by Mariners to Tigers, June 26, 1999, as part of trade in which Tigers sent OF Brian Hunter to Mariners for two players to be named (April 21, 1999); Tigers acquired OF Jerry Amador to complete trade (Aug. 26, 1999).

Van Hekken battled back from a slow start last season to reestablish himself as a top prospect in the eyes of Tigers officials. He solidified their belief in him by shutting out the Indians in his major league debut in September. But that game also created concern because Van Hekken's fastball averaged 83 mph and didn't top 85. This much the Tigers know about Van Hekken: He has a big league curveball, an excellent feel for pitching and knows how to win games. He's athletic and does the little things well, and he has a strong makeup. The only question surrounding him is whether he throws hard enough to be effective in the majors. His fastball does have good movement and he's able to make it tail back over the outside of the plate against righthanders. He works the outer half of the plate well against righties and is effective against lefties because of his curve. Showing an improved changeup in spring training would help his chances of making the Opening Day rotation.

Year	Club (League)	Class	W	L	ERA	G	GS	CG	SV	IP	H	R	ER	HR	BB	SO	AVG
1998	Mariners (AZL)	R	6	3	4.43	11	8	0	0	41	34	23	20	1	18	55	.214
1999	Oneonta (NY-P)	A	4	2	2.15	11	10	0	0	50	44	17	12	3	16	50	.230
2000	West Michigan (Mid)	A	16	6	2.45	26	25	3	1	158	139	48	43	3	37	126	.232
2001	Lakeland (FSL)	A	10	4	3.17	19	19	2	0	111	105	43	39	8	33	82	.252
	Erie (EL)	AA	5	0	4.69	8	8	0	0	48	63	29	25	5	8	29	.320
2002	Erie (EL)	AA	4	7	3.83	21	21	1	0	134	138	69	57	10	34	97	.270
	Toledo (IL)	AAA	5	0	1.82	7	7	1	0	49	41	14	10	4	11	19	.228
	Detroit (AL)	MAJ	1	3	3.00	5	5	1	0	30	38	13	10	2	6	5	.311
MAJOR LEAGUE TOTALS			1	3	3.00	5	5	1	0	30	38	13	10	2	6	5	.311
MINOR LEAGUE TOTALS			50	22	3.14	103	98	7	1	591	564	243	206	34	157	458	.250

15. Jack Hannahan, 3b

Born: March 4, 1980. **Ht.:** 6-2. **Wt.:** 200. **Bats:** L. **Throws:** R. **School:** University of Minnesota. **Career Transactions:** Selected by Tigers in third round of 2001 draft; signed June 20, 2001.

Like Joe Mauer, the No. 1 overall pick in the 2001 draft, Hannahan was a baseball and football star at St. Paul's Cretin-Derham Hall. But Hannahan has taken a much more difficult path. He developed a drinking problem as an adolescent and was kicked off the Cretin-Derham baseball team for drinking in the 10th grade. His trials continued, including arrests and blackouts, before he finally sought help in July 2000, entered a treatment facility and got sober. He came back for his junior year at Minnesota and became the Big 10 Conference player of the year. When the Tigers selected Hannahan out of Minnesota, they figured they had landed an advanced prospect. They were right, as he got to Double-A within a year. But once he got to Erie, Hannahan hit the wall and didn't perform up to expectations. One of the reasons Hannahan advanced quickly was because he showed patience at the plate, didn't chase bad pitches and used the entire field. In Double-A, he was less selective and less successful. The knock against him is that he doesn't have typical power for a corner infielder, and he may have hurt himself by trying to beat that rap. He'll have to hit for a high average to be an effective major league hitter at third base. Defensively, Hannahan is excellent. He has soft hands and a good throwing arm. He lacks speed, but is a fluid athlete otherwise. He'll get a second chance at Double-A this year.

Year	Club (League)	Class	AVG	G	AB	R	H	2B	3B	HR	RBI	BB	SO	SB	SLG	OBP
2001	Oneonta (NY-P)	A	.291	14	55	11	16	4	1	0	8	5	7	2	.400	.333
	West Michigan (Mid)	A	.318	46	170	24	54	11	0	1	27	26	39	4	.400	.409
2002	Lakeland (FSL)	A	.272	66	246	28	67	11	1	6	42	36	44	9	.398	.362
	Erie (EL)	AA	.239	65	226	17	54	12	1	3	20	21	50	2	.341	.309
MINOR LEAGUE TOTALS			.274	191	697	80	191	38	3	10	97	88	140	17	.380	.355

16. Andres Torres, of

Born: Jan. 26, 1978. **Ht.:** 5-10. **Wt.:** 180. **Bats:** B. **Throws:** R. **School:** Miami-Dade CC North. **Career Transactions:** Selected by Tigers in fourth round of 1998 draft; signed June 23, 1998.

Torres got his shot in the major leagues last season and was underwhelming. He didn't make enough contact or get on base frequently enough to make much use of his speed, and his throwing arm was a problem in center field. He played better in Triple-A but still wasn't the player the Tigers hoped he would be at this point. They believe he has gotten too big, bulking up considerably from when he was drafted as a raw project who had more experience with track than with baseball during his youth in Puerto Rico. His skills aren't designed for a power game and he must accept that his ticket is playing small ball. He needs to put more balls in play and learn to bunt better to take advantage of his blazing wheels. Torres sometimes takes odd routes to balls, but he has the tools to become an above-average center fielder if his throwing arm recovers. He once had a solid average arm, but he had shoulder surgery in 2001 and his throws lacked strength and carry last year. His mechanics also looked awkward. Detroit may have found its center fielder and leadoff man with an offseason trade for Eugene Kingsale, so Torres likely will get more time in Triple-A.

Year	Club (League)	Class	AVG	G	AB	R	H	2B	3B	HR	RBI	BB	SO	SB	SLG	OBP
1998	Jamestown (NY-P)	A	.234	48	192	28	45	2	6	1	21	25	50	13	.323	.323
1999	West Michigan (Mid)	A	.236	117	407	72	96	20	5	2	34	92	116	39	.324	.385
2000	Lakeland (FSL)	A	.296	108	398	82	118	11	11	3	33	63	82	65	.402	.399
	Jacksonville (SL)	AA	.148	14	54	3	8	0	0	0	0	5	14	2	.148	.220
2001	Erie (EL)	AA	.294	64	252	54	74	16	3	1	23	36	50	19	.393	.391
2002	Toledo (IL)	AAA	.266	115	462	80	123	17	8	4	42	53	116	42	.364	.345
	Detroit (AL)	MAJ	.200	19	70	7	14	1	1	0	3	6	16	2	.243	.266
MAJOR LEAGUE TOTALS			.200	19	70	7	14	1	1	0	3	6	16	2	.243	.266
MINOR LEAGUE TOTALS			.263	466	1765	319	464	66	33	11	153	274	428	180	.356	.368

17. Kenny Baugh, rhp

Born: Feb. 5, 1979. **Ht.:** 6-4. **Wt.:** 190. **Bats:** R. **Throws:** R. **School:** Rice University. **Career Transactions:** Selected by Tigers in first round (11th overall) of 2001 draft; signed June 5, 2001 . . . On disabled list, April 5-Sept. 4, 2002.

The Tigers expected Baugh to move quickly when they chose him 11th overall in 2001, after he was the Western Athletic Conference pitcher of the year as a Rice senior. He quickly advanced to Double-A in his first pro summer, throwing well in five starts before being shut down with a tired arm. The problem is that he hasn't pitched since because of shoulder woes. After rest initially was prescribed, he needed arthroscopic surgery on his labrum. When he's right, Baugh has a fastball that usually sits around 90 mph with sinking action.

He has touched 95 but gets more movement when he doesn't light up the radar gun. His changeup has progressed nicely, but his curveball is terribly inconsistent. At times it's a plus pitch and at others it's not even close. Regaining his health and improving his curve to the point that he can depend on it are the keys for Baugh. He knows how to work both sides of the plate and sets up hitters for his offspeed pitches late in the count. He's expected to be 100 percent for spring training. If that's the case, Baugh likely will begin the season in Double-A.

Year	Club (League)	Class	W	L	ERA	G	GS	CG	SV	IP	H	R	ER	HR	BB	SO	AVG
2001	West Michigan (Mid)	A	2	1	1.59	6	6	0	0	34	31	14	6	0	10	39	.238
	Erie (EL)	AA	1	3	2.97	5	5	1	0	30	23	16	10	5	6	30	.207
2002					Did Not Play—Injured												
MINOR LEAGUE TOTALS			3	4	2.24	11	11	1	0	64	54	30	16	5	16	69	.224

18. Curtis Granderson, of

Born: March 16, 1981. **Ht.:** 6-1. **Wt.:** 180. **Bats:** L. **Throws:** R. **School:** University of Illinois-Chicago. **Career Transactions:** Selected by Tigers in third round of 2002 draft; signed June 28, 2002.

After finishing second in NCAA Division I in hitting with a .483 batting average at Illinois-Chicago, Granderson did the same in the short-season New York-Penn League. He finished runner-up with a .344 average and won league MVP honors. Granderson has a quick, compact batting stroke and drives the ball hard from gap to gap. He has yet to flash a lot of power, but organization officials see that coming. The Tigers love Granderson's makeup. He's a hard worker and a team player. He's neither very fast nor very athletic, and his arm strength is ordinary. Detroit envisions him as a left fielder, and to get there he'll have to continue to hit and develop more pop. He'll begin 2003 in low Class A, where West Michigan's Fifth Third Ballpark will provide a stern test.

Year	Club (League)	Class	AVG	G	AB	R	H	2B	3B	HR	RBI	BB	SO	SB	SLG	OBP
2002	Oneonta (NY-P)	A	.344	52	212	45	73	15	4	3	34	20	35	9	.495	.417
MINOR LEAGUE TOTALS			.344	52	212	45	73	15	4	3	34	20	35	9	.495	.417

19. Humberto Sanchez, rhp

Born: May 28, 1983. **Ht.:** 6-6. **Wt.:** 230. **Bats:** R. **Throws:** R. **School:** Connors State (Okla.) JC. **Career Transactions:** Selected by Tigers in 31st round of 2001 draft; signed May 27, 2002.

A high school star in the Bronx, Sanchez attended Rockland (N.Y.) Community College and had surgery to remove scar tissue from his elbow two months before the 2001 draft. Undeterred, the Tigers selected him and monitored him as a draft-and-follow. After he transferred to Connors State, he blossomed into a possible first-round pick before Detroit signed him for a $1 million bonus. He pitched well at short-season Oneonta despite spending two stints on the disabled list with a right shoulder strain and right biceps strain. Sanchez, who resembles Jose Mesa, usually works in the low 90s with his fastball and touches 95. Besides velocity, his fastball also has good sink. He throws both a curveball and slider, and both are solid pitches. His changeup is excellent at times, though it's inconsistent. Sanchez carries a lot of weight on his frame and there are some concerns about his conditioning. While he shows four quality pitches at times, he needs to command them better. He's expected to begin 2003 in low Class A and will be promoted quickly if he shows early progress.

Year	Club (League)	Class	W	L	ERA	G	GS	CG	SV	IP	H	R	ER	HR	BB	SO	AVG
2002	Oneonta (NY-P)	A	2	2	3.62	9	9	0	0	32	29	18	13	1	21	26	.244
MINOR LEAGUE TOTALS			2	2	3.62	9	9	0	0	32	29	18	13	1	21	26	.244

20. Michael Woods, 2b

Born: Sept. 11, 1980. **Ht.:** 6-1. **Wt.:** 200. **Bats:** R. **Throws:** R. **School:** Southern University. **Career Transactions:** Selected by Tigers in second round of 2001 draft; signed June 29, 2001.

The Tigers were surprised Woods was available with the 32nd overall pick in 2001 because he had been projected to go in the middle of the first round. After a respectable debut, he began 2002 in high Class A. In his first plate appearance of the season, Woods walked and then stole second base—injuring his knee in the process. After returning from arthroscopic surgery, he struggled to find consistency before hurting his other knee and needing another operation. Neither injury is expected to hinder Woods in the long term, but the missed playing time set him back. He's a strong athlete with average speed. His quick hands generate a lot of bat speed, and he has exceptional power potential for a middle infielder. He also has drawn a high number of walks in his brief time as a pro. Woods has soft hands and a solid arm for second base, though he's not especially fluid and needs to smooth out his rough edges defensively. Because 2002 was a lost season, Woods will return to Lakeland in 2003.

Year	Club (League)	Class	AVG	G	AB	R	H	2B	3B	HR	RBI	BB	SO	SB	SLG	OBP
2001	Oneonta (NY-P)	A	.270	9	37	6	10	2	0	0	3	4	5	5	.324	.357
	West Michigan (Mid)	A	.270	44	163	30	44	8	4	0	17	32	44	13	.368	.401
2002	Lakeland (FSL)	A	.225	33	111	20	25	6	4	2	11	28	25	7	.405	.385
	Tigers (GCL)	R	.286	7	21	2	6	1	1	0	2	3	6	3	.429	.375
MINOR LEAGUE TOTALS			.256	93	332	58	85	17	9	2	33	67	80	28	.380	.389

21. Travis Chapman, 3b

Born: June 5, 1978. **Ht.:** 6-2. **Wt.:** 180. **Bats:** R. **Throws:** R. **School:** Mississippi State University. **Career Transactions:** Selected by Phillies in 17th round of 2000 draft; signed June 18, 2000 . . . Selected by Indians from Phillies in major league Rule 5 draft, Dec. 16, 2002 . . . Sold by Indians to Tigers, Dec. 16, 2002.

With Dean Palmer playing just 61 games over the last two seasons, the Tigers bought third-base insurance in the major league Rule 5 draft. During his first two pro seasons, Chapman looked like nothing more than a solid organizational player, hitting for average but showing little power for a third baseman. Philadelphia wanted him to play winter ball after the 2001 season, but Chapman decided he would be better served by working on his strength and conditioning. The Phillies assented and a bulked-up Chapman nearly tripled his career home run total in 2002. It's a testament to his strong work ethic and makeup. Chapman shows a disciplined approach at the plate and has average tools across the board. He's solid defensively at third, where he does everything well but little exceptionally. After the Phillies signed David Bell as a free agent, they decided not to protect Chapman on the 40-man roster. He projects as a useful corner utility player in the majors, and that's the role Detroit will use him in this season.

Year	Club (League)	Class	AVG	G	AB	R	H	2B	3B	HR	RBI	BB	SO	SB	SLG	OBP
2000	Phillies (GCL)	R	.188	9	32	3	6	3	1	0	5	4	4	0	.344	.308
	Batavia (NY-P)	A	.316	49	174	23	55	10	2	1	28	12	24	0	.414	.379
2001	Clearwater (FSL)	A	.307	96	329	39	101	22	0	4	50	44	39	3	.410	.400
	Reading (EL)	AA	.182	7	22	3	4	0	0	1	3	0	5	0	.318	.250
2002	Reading (EL)	AA	.301	136	478	64	144	35	1	15	76	54	77	3	.473	.388
MINOR LEAGUE TOTALS			.300	297	1035	132	310	70	4	21	162	114	149	6	.436	.385

22. Wil Ledezma, lhp

Born: Jan. 21, 1981. **Ht.:** 6-3. **Wt.:** 150. **Bats:** L. **Throws:** L. **Career Transactions:** Signed out of Venezuela by Red Sox, April 3, 1998 . . . Selected by Tigers from Red Sox in major league Rule 5 draft, Dec. 16, 2002.

The Tigers wound up with three players in the major league phase of the Rule 5 draft, though Ledezma was the only one they selected themselves. In addition to acquiring Travis Chapman, they also added righthander Matt Roney from the Rockies via the Pirates. Ledezma has tremendous upside but has been hampered by injuries. He emerged as a prospect when he made his U.S. debut in 1999, before his elbow began bothering him in the middle of the next season. Ledezma had a stress fracture in his left elbow, which kept him out from late July 2000 until April 2002. He pitched well in five low Class A starts, before a nagging lower back strain sidelined him again. Ledezma did return for an August appearance in the Gulf Coast League, and was 100 percent for instructional league and the Venezuelan League after the season. In Venezuela, he pitched for Magallanes manager Phil Regan, who doubles as a skipper in the Tigers system. Before Ledezma went down, he was throwing 93-94 mph from a deceptive angle and showed a consistently hard curveball. His lack of innings has made it hard to develop a changeup. His 41-8 strikeout-walk ratio in 27 innings in 2002 is indicative of his ceiling. Boston planned to return him to low Class A, so Detroit may have a difficult time keeping him on its 25-man roster all season. If the Tigers can't, the Red Sox almost certainly will take him back for half the $50,000 Rule 5 draft price.

Year	Club (League)	Class	W	L	ERA	G	GS	CG	SV	IP	H	R	ER	HR	BB	SO	AVG
1998	Red Sox (DSL)	R	2	4	4.40	11	11	0	0	47	38	28	23	0	38	34	.228
1999	Red Sox (GCL)	R	5	1	3.30	13	6	0	1	57	57	28	21	2	20	52	.233
2000	Augusta (SAL)	A	2	4	5.13	14	14	0	0	53	51	33	30	3	36	60	.256
2001					Did Not Play—Injured												
2002	Augusta (SAL)	A	2	2	3.80	5	5	0	0	24	23	10	10	0	8	38	.250
	Red Sox (GCL)	R	0	0	6.00	1	0	0	0	3	4	2	2	0	0	3	.308
MINOR LEAGUE TOTALS			11	11	4.21	44	36	0	1	184	167	101	86	5	102	187	.242

23. Adrian Burnside, lhp

Born: March 15, 1977. **Ht.:** 6-3. **Wt.:** 210. **Bats:** R. **Throws:** L. **Career Transactions:** Signed out of Australia by Dodgers, July 12, 1995 . . . Selected by Reds from Dodgers in major league Rule 5 draft, Dec. 13, 1999 . . . Returned to Dodgers, March 14, 2000 . . . Traded by Dodgers with RHP Mike Fetters to Pirates for LHP Terry Mulholland, July 31, 2001 . . . Traded by Pirates with two players to be named to Tigers for 1B Randall Simon, Nov. 25, 2002; Tigers acquired RHP Roberto Novoa (Dec. 16, 2002) as one of two players.

When the Tigers decided they had several first-base options and didn't want to go to arbitration with Randall Simon, they traded him to the Pirates for three minor leaguers. Burnside, who has been traded twice and claimed in the major league Rule 5 draft once, was the most advanced of the prospects. Though 26, he hasn't pitched above Double-A and has been stuck at that level for the last three seasons. Yet Burnside intrigues scouts because he's a lefthander who consistently tops 90 mph and sometimes reaches the mid-90s. He also flashes an excellent slider. His problem is that he lacks command. His changeup and overall feel for pitching also leave something to be desired. Primarily a starter throughout his career, he may have more of a future as a reliever. Burnside should get his first crack at Triple-A in 2003.

Year	Club (League)	Class	W	L	ERA	G	GS	CG	SV	IP	H	R	ER	HR	BB	SO	AVG
1996	Great Falls (Pio)	R	1	3	6.80	14	5	0	0	41	44	35	31	3	38	33	.278
1997	Yakima (NWL)	A	6	3	4.93	15	13	0	0	66	67	53	36	9	49	66	.262
1998	San Bernardino (Cal)	A	1	10	7.81	21	12	0	0	78	97	79	68	6	48	65	.309
	Yakima (NWL)	A	1	4	4.05	8	6	0	0	33	27	21	15	0	30	34	.223
1999	San Bernardino (Cal)	A	10	9	4.17	26	22	0	0	132	124	69	61	7	55	129	.249
2000	San Antonio (TL)	AA	6	5	2.90	17	17	0	0	93	73	40	30	6	55	82	.223
2001	Jacksonville (SL)	AA	4	3	2.66	13	12	0	0	68	44	21	20	6	30	67	.181
	Altoona (EL)	AA	0	2	3.62	6	6	0	0	32	28	15	13	3	14	32	.235
2002	Altoona (EL)	AA	6	9	4.55	32	23	0	0	131	120	70	66	18	67	122	.242
MINOR LEAGUE TOTALS			35	48	4.54	152	116	0	0	674	624	403	340	58	386	630	.247

24. David Espinosa, 2b

Born: Dec. 16, 1981. **Ht.:** 6-2. **Wt.:** 190. **Bats:** B. **Throws:** R. **School:** Gulliver Prep, Miami. **Career Transactions:** Selected by Reds in second round of 2000 draft; signed, Sept. 1, 2000 . . . Traded by Reds with two players to be named to Tigers for RHP Brian Moehler, 3B Matt Boone and cash, July 23, 2002; Tigers acquired OF Noochie Varner (Aug. 30, 2002) and RHP Jorge Cordova (Sept. 24, 2002) to complete trade.

Rated as one of the best infield prospects in the 2000 draft, Espinosa lasted 23 picks because of signability concerns. The Reds had blown most of their signing budget before the draft, so they signed him to a unique deal: an eight-year, major league contract worth a guaranteed $2.75 million, but with no up-front bonus money. He showed the potential to be a dynamic leadoff hitter while in the Cincinnati system, but his defensive shortcomings led the Reds to include him in a trade for Brian Moehler last July. Espinosa didn't play after switching organizations because of back spasms; the Tigers were aware of his condition and don't believe it will linger. Espinosa offers size, budding strength and good bat speed. He appreciates the value of a walk and has basestealing speed. He's still raw, however, as he strikes out and gets caught stealing too often. He's even less refined as a middle infielder and already has proven he can't play shortstop. His footwork has led to throwing problems, and some scouts believe Espinosa would fit better in center field. Detroit contemplated making that move, but kept him at second base in instructional league and he played relatively well. With a good spring, he could open 2003 in Double-A.

Year	Club (League)	Class	AVG	G	AB	R	H	2B	3B	HR	RBI	BB	SO	SB	SLG	OBP
2001	Dayton (Mid)	A	.262	122	493	88	129	29	8	7	37	55	120	15	.396	.340
2002	Stockton (Cal)	A	.245	95	367	71	90	13	7	7	44	62	104	26	.376	.356
MINOR LEAGUE TOTALS			.255	217	860	159	219	42	15	14	81	117	224	41	.387	.347

25. Ryan Raburn, 3b

Born: April 17, 1981. **Ht.:** 6-0. **Wt.:** 180. **Bats:** R. **Throws:** R. **School:** South Florida CC. **Career Transactions:** Selected by Tigers in fifth round of 2001 draft; signed June 20, 2001.

After an excellent pro debut in 2001, Raburn dislocated his hip in an all-terrain vehicle accident during the offseason. There was concern that his career was in jeopardy and he was expected to miss all of 2002. He returned ahead of schedule, playing in 48 games, but his production was down considerably. His live bat started to come around again during instructional league. The brother of Brewers infield prospect Johnny Raburn, Ryan has a short stroke, good pitch recognition and power to all fields. He has a long way to go defensively and made 15 errors in 23 games at third base last season. He has a strong arm and good hands, but poor footwork causes fielding and throwing problems. He'll spend the season with one of Detroit's Class A affiliates.

Year	Club (League)	Class	AVG	G	AB	R	H	2B	3B	HR	RBI	BB	SO	SB	SLG	OBP
2001	Tigers (GCL)	R	.155	19	58	4	9	2	0	1	5	9	19	2	.241	.300
	Oneonta (NY-P)	A	.363	44	171	25	62	17	8	8	42	17	42	1	.696	.418
2002	Tigers (GCL)	R	.300	8	30	4	9	3	1	1	5	3	7	0	.567	.364
	West Michigan (Mid)	A	.220	40	150	27	33	10	1	6	28	16	46	0	.420	.306
MINOR LEAGUE TOTALS			.276	111	409	60	113	32	10	16	80	45	114	3	.521	.355

26. Matt Pender, rhp

Born: June 11, 1981. **Ht.:** 6-5. **Wt.:** 210. **Bats:** R. **Throws:** R. **School:** Kennesaw State (Ga.) University.
Career Transactions: Selected by Tigers in third round of 2002 draft; signed June 28, 2002.

After he took his teams to College World Series at the junior college and NCAA Division II levels the last two years, the Tigers drafted Pender with a 2002 third-round pick they received from the Mets as compensation for free agent Roger Cedeno. Considered a project despite his college background, Pender was more refined than Detroit expected. In his first pro summer, he displayed good command of his fastball while making progress with his off-speed pitches. Scouts compare him to Andy Ashby because he has a loose, lanky frame and a fluid motion. Pender's fastball has good life and consistently hits 90-92 mph. His curve-ball is a plus pitch at times but is inconsistent, and his changeup has a long way to go. The main thing Tigers coaches have been working on with Pender is getting him to trust his abil-ity. When he gets in trouble, it's often because he's being too fine with his fastball early in the count. Pender will begin this season in low Class A.

Year	Club (League)	Class	W	L	ERA	G	GS	CG	SV	IP	H	R	ER	HR	BB	SO	AVG
2002	Oneonta (NY-P)	A	2	2	2.31	9	9	0	0	39	34	16	10	1	12	35	.234
MINOR LEAGUE TOTALS			2	2	2.31	9	9	0	0	39	34	16	10	1	12	35	.234

27. Maxim St. Pierre, c

Born: April 17, 1980. **Ht.:** 6-0. **Wt.:** 170. **Bats:** R. **Throws:** R. **School:** Col. de Levis HS, Montreal. **Career Transactions:** Selected by Tigers in 26th round of 1997 draft; signed June 16, 1997.

After a slow growth curve, St. Pierre took a big step forward last season. He set career bests in home runs and RBIs while reaching Double-A, and he continued to make strides as a receiver. After the season, he played well in the Arizona Fall League. Because St. Pierre pro-gressed so much, the Tigers didn't hesitate to trade Michael Rivera to the Padres for Eugene Kingsale. St. Pierre has above-average arm strength. The knock on him in the past was that he didn't get rid of the ball quickly enough, but his release was quicker last season. St. Pierre frames pitches well and has good hands. As a hitter, St. Pierre sometimes tries to pull the ball too much, and his swing tends to get long. When he hits to all fields, he's more pro-ductive. There are some coaches and front-office officials in the Tigers organization who view St. Pierre as a potential everyday catcher in the major leagues. Others remain skeptical because he doesn't show much power, and see his ceiling as a backup with decent defensive skills. St. Pierre will go to Triple-A to start 2003 and could get his first taste of the majors later in the season.

Year	Club (League)	Class	AVG	G	AB	R	H	2B	3B	HR	RBI	BB	SO	SB	SLG	OBP
1997	Tigers (GCL)	R	.244	20	41	3	10	1	0	0	3	3	8	2	.268	.340
1998	Tigers (GCL)	R	.385	31	104	18	40	3	0	2	15	15	12	6	.471	.467
1999	Oneonta (NY-P)	A	.251	51	175	12	44	7	0	1	22	11	29	9	.309	.305
2000	West Michigan (Mid)	A	.249	73	229	41	57	10	1	2	28	42	37	2	.328	.373
2001	Lakeland (FSL)	A	.248	99	330	42	82	15	0	4	43	43	50	2	.330	.338
2002	Lakeland (FSL)	A	.256	55	195	20	50	12	0	4	27	13	30	2	.379	.324
	Erie (EL)	AA	.266	60	207	24	55	9	0	3	28	17	31	0	.353	.320
	Toledo (IL)	AAA	.000	1	2	0	0	0	0	0	1	0	0	0	.000	.000
MINOR LEAGUE TOTALS			.263	390	1283	160	338	57	1	16	167	144	197	23	.347	.346

28. Roberto Novoa, rhp

Born: Aug. 15, 1979. **Ht.:** 6-5. **Wt.:** 200. **Bats:** R. **Throws:** R. **Career Transactions:** Signed out of Dominican Republic by Pirates, July 3, 1999 . . . Traded by Pirates to Tigers, Dec. 16, 2002, as part of trade in which Tigers sent 1B Randall Simon to Tigers for LHP Adrian Burnside and two players to be named (Nov. 25, 2002).

The first of two players to be named in the Randall Simon trade, Novoa has a live arm but also some negatives. After a solid U.S. debut in 2001, Novoa was found to be two years older than originally thought. He also was hammered in low Class A, forcing him to repeat the short-season level. Novoa has a mid-90s fastball and a hard, biting slider. Unlike many young power pitchers, Novoa consistently throws strikes. He needs better command within the strike zone, as he tends to try to get away with high fastballs that can be hit. Novoa's changeup is decent but must be fine-tuned in order to give him the offspeed pitch he needs to complement his hard stuff. Some Pirates officials said they thought Novoa could be a dominant closer, but the Tigers will keep him as a starter in low Class A this year.

Year	Club (League)	Class	W	L	ERA	G	GS	CG	SV	IP	H	R	ER	HR	BB	SO	AVG
2000	Pirates (DSL)	R	4	6	4.15	13	13	1	0	82	99	65	38	5	29	44	.289
2001	Williamsport (NY-P)	A	5	5	3.39	14	13	1	0	80	76	40	30	4	20	55	.255
2002	Hickory (SAL)	A	1	5	5.48	10	10	0	0	43	61	30	26	2	15	29	.335
	Williamsport (NY-P)	A	8	3	3.65	12	12	0	0	67	62	32	27	4	8	56	.240
MINOR LEAGUE TOTALS			18	19	4.01	49	48	2	0	271	298	167	121	15	72	184	.276

29. Shane Loux, rhp

Born: Aug. 31, 1979. **Ht.:** 6-2. **Wt.:** 230. **Bats:** R. **Throws:** R. **School:** Highland HS, Gilbert, Ariz. **Career Transactions:** Selected by Tigers in second round of 1997 draft; signed June 14, 1997.

After turning down an Arizona State scholarship to sign with the Tigers, Loux had an impressive pro debut (.129 opponent average) in the Gulf Coast League in 1997—so impressive that he has had trouble living up to it ever since. Yet he has won a total of 21 games in Triple-A the last two seasons and is still just 23. Loux had arthroscopic elbow surgery following the 2000 season and pitched without his usual velocity in 2001 in a gritty effort. He continued to struggle in the first half of last year, with a 6.40 ERA through mid-June, before making a dramatic turnaround. He threw shutouts in three of his next four starts and had a 3.11 ERA in his final 12 outings. When he's pitching well, Loux works both sides of the plate with a 90 mph sinker, a good changeup and a curveball. He's competitive, which works both for and against him. There were concerns about Loux' conditioning earlier in his career, but he has addressed those issues and gotten in better shape. Loux was hit hard when called to the major leagues for the first time in September, hurting his chances of making Detroit's rotation in 2003.

Year	Club (League)	Class	W	L	ERA	G	GS	CG	SV	IP	H	R	ER	HR	BB	SO	AVG
1997	Tigers (GCL)	R	4	1	0.84	10	9	1	0	43	19	7	4	0	10	33	.129
1998	West Michigan (Mid)	A	7	13	4.64	28	28	2	0	157	184	96	81	13	52	88	.291
1999	West Michigan (Mid)	A	1	3	6.27	8	8	0	0	47	55	39	33	5	16	43	.293
	Lakeland (FSL)	A	6	5	4.05	17	17	0	0	91	92	48	41	8	47	52	.264
2000	Lakeland (FSL)	A	0	1	1.80	1	1	0	0	5	2	1	1	0	3	6	.133
	Jacksonville (SL)	AA	12	9	3.82	26	26	2	0	158	150	78	67	12	55	130	.254
2001	Toledo (IL)	AAA	10	11	5.78	28	27	2	0	151	203	111	97	22	73	72	.325
2002	Toledo (IL)	AAA	11	10	4.72	26	26	5	0	158	196	94	83	11	38	87	.307
	Detroit (AL)	MAJ	0	3	9.00	3	3	0	0	14	19	16	14	4	3	7	.317
MAJOR LEAGUE TOTALS			0	3	9.00	3	3	0	0	14	19	16	14	4	3	7	.317
MINOR LEAGUE TOTALS			51	53	4.52	144	142	12	0	810	901	474	407	71	294	511	.283

30. Juan Tejeda, 1b

Born: Jan. 26, 1982. **Ht.:** 6-2. **Wt.:** 190. **Bats:** R. **Throws:** R. **Career Transactions:** Signed out of Dominican Republic by Tigers, July 7, 1999.

In his first exposure to full-season ball, Tejeda led the Midwest League with 106 RBIs last season. He has produced throughout his four years in the organization and is advanced for a young hitter. He understands the strike zone, makes consistent contact and uses all fields. Tejeda's 11 homers last year aren't indicative of his power. West Michigan's Fifth Third Ballpark is a hitter's nightmare, and he hit .256-3-43 there compared to .342-8-63 on the road. Tejeda is a purely offensive player. He's not athletic and has poor footwork at first base. His bat will have to carry him as he continues his progression through the minors, which will take him to high Class A this year.

Year	Club (League)	Class	AVG	G	AB	R	H	2B	3B	HR	RBI	BB	SO	SB	SLG	OBP
1999	Tigers (DSL)	R	.276	42	152	26	42	9	2	5	26	14	33	1	.461	.360
2000	Tigers (DSL)	R	.312	66	260	52	81	20	3	10	46	16	45	2	.527	.374
2001	Tigers (GCL)	R	.295	50	173	17	51	8	1	4	37	8	32	0	.422	.344
2002	West Michigan (Mid)	A	.300	137	524	68	157	34	6	11	106	60	89	5	.450	.372
MINOR LEAGUE TOTALS			.298	295	1109	163	331	71	12	30	215	98	199	8	.465	.367

FLORIDA
MARLINS

TOP 30 PROSPECTS

1. Miguel Cabrera, 3b
2. Jason Stokes, 1b
3. Adrian Gonzalez, 1b
4. Dontrelle Willis, lhp
5. Jeremy Hermida, of
6. Don Levinski, rhp
7. Justin Wayne, rhp
8. Blaine Neal, rhp
9. Will Smith, of
10. Josh Wilson, ss
11. Ryan Snare, lhp
12. Ronald Belizario, rhp
13. Denny Bautista, rhp
14. Chip Ambres, of
15. Kevin Hooper, ss/2b
16. Abraham Nunez, of
17. Eric Reed, of
18. Victor Prieto, rhp
19. Robert Andino, ss
20. Scott Olsen, lhp
21. Josh Willingham, 1b/3b
22. Ryan Jorgensen, c
23. Yorman Bazardo, rhp
24. Jesus Medrano, 2b
25. Juan Nova, rhp
26. Josh Johnson, rhp
27. Garrett Berger, rhp
28. Wes Anderson, rhp
29. Allen Baxter, rhp
30. Franklyn Gracesqui, lhp

By Mike Berardino

I n the strangest winter swap since Mike Kekich and Fritz Peterson traded wives, children and family dogs, John Henry handed over the Marlins to former Expos owner Jeffrey Loria.

Henry went on to use his $158.5 million golden parachute to buy the Red Sox, while Loria and stepson David Samson, the Marlins' new president, were left to pick up the pieces of a broken South Florida market. They took over less than a week before the start of spring training, and missteps were plentiful along the way. Florida wound up 29th in attendance, and even that required the last-day purchase of 15,000 tickets by an anonymous "benefactor" to clip the reviled Expos by an average of seven fans.

Even so, the Marlins would have ranked third in Pacific Coast League attendance, trailing the Sacramento River Cats and the Memphis Redbirds. The Mexican League's Saltillo Sarape Makers also outdrew the Marlins.

On the field, prospects were better. The major league club finished 79-83 under new manager Jeff Torborg, who came south from Montreal with dozens of other employees on the baseball side. The fourth-place finish was disappointing but understandable considering the stream of key injuries to such players as Josh Beckett, A.J. Burnett, Alex Gonzalez and Brad Penny.

In the minors, an already solid collection of talent was augmented through a trio of trades. Lefty Dontrelle Willis and catcher Ryan Jorgensen came from the Cubs in a controversial deal near the end of spring training. Willis was the Marlins minor league pitcher of the year after going 12-2, 1.83 at two Class A stops.

At midseason, trades that sent Ryan Dempster to Cincinnati and Cliff Floyd to Montreal netted young pitchers Don Levinski, Justin Wayne and Ryan Snare. Wayne, a former first-rounder out of Stanford, received a September callup and the other two aren't too far away.

As he had in Montreal, Loria showed a willingness to spend in the draft. Outfielder Jeremy Hermida received a $2.0125 million bonus as the 11th overall pick and did nothing to disappoint. Second-rounder Robert Andino, a slick-fielding shortstop, signed for $750,000 and the Marlins had signed 17 of their top 20 picks.

Two more key additions came in the front office, as former Devil Rays scouting director Dan Jennings and former Rockies farm director Mike Hill came aboard.

OrganizationOverview

General Manager: Larry Beinfest. **Farm Director:** Marc DelPiano. **Scouting Director:** Stan Meek.

2002 PERFORMANCE

Class	Farm Team	League	W	L	Pct.	Finish*	Manager
Majors	Florida	National	79	83	.488	9th (16)	Jeff Torborg
Triple-A	†Calgary Cannons	Pacific Coast	67	71	.486	12th (16)	Dean Treanor
Double-A	#Portland Sea Dogs	Eastern	63	77	.450	t-9th (12)	Eric Fox
High A	Jupiter Hammerheads	Florida State	81	57	.587	2nd (14)	Luis Dorante
Low A	@Kane County Cougars	Midwest	64	75	.460	10th (14)	Steve Phillips
Short-season	Jamestown Jammers	New York-Penn	32	42	.432	10th (14)	Johnny Rodriguez
Rookie	GCL Marlins	Gulf Coast	31	29	.517	6th (14)	Jesus Campos
OVERALL 2002 MINOR LEAGUE RECORD			338	351	.491	18th (30)	

*Finish in overall standings (No. of teams in league). †Franchise will move to Albuquerque for 2003.
#Affiliate will be in Carolina (Southern) in 2003. @Affiliate will be in Greensboro (South Atlantic) in 2003.

ORGANIZATION LEADERS

BATTING *Minimum 250 At-Bats
*AVG	Jason Stokes, Kane County	.341
R	Brian Banks, Calgary	90
H	Will Smith, Jupiter	164
TB	Will Smith, Jupiter	260
2B	Miguel Cabrera, Jupiter	43
3B	Will Smith, Jupiter	12
HR	Jason Stokes, Kane County	27
RBI	Adrian Gonzalez, Portland	96
BB	Jesus Medrano, Portland	79
	Pat Magness, Jupiter	79
SO	Matt Padgett, Portland	131
SB	Charles Frazier, Jupiter/Kane County	48

PITCHING #Minimum 75 Innings
W	Rob Henkel, Portland/Jupiter	13
L	Phil Akens, Kane County	15
#ERA	Dontrelle Willis, Jupiter/Kane County	1.83
G	Mike Flannery, Jupiter	58
CG	Three tied at	3
SV	Mike Flannery, Jupiter	26
IP	Nate Robertson, Portland	163
BB	Omar Ortiz, Portland	70
SO	Rob Henkel, Portland/Jupiter	150

BEST TOOLS

Best Hitter for Average	Adrian Gonzalez
Best Power Hitter	Jason Stokes
Fastest Baserunner	Eric Reed
Best Athlete	Chip Ambres
Best Fastball	Ronald Belizario
Best Curveball	Ryan Snare
Best Slider	Blaine Neal
Best Changeup	Justin Wayne
Best Control	Dontrelle Willis
Best Defensive Catcher	Ryan Jorgensen
Best Defensive Infielder	Kevin Hooper
Best Infield Arm	Miguel Cabrera
Best Defensive Outfielder	Eric Reed
Best Outfield Arm	Abraham Nunez

PROJECTED 2006 LINEUP

Catcher	Ivan Rodriguez
First Base	Adrian Gonzalez
Second Base	Luis Castillo
Third Base	Miguel Cabrera
Shortstop	Josh Wilson
Left Field	Jason Stokes
Center Field	Juan Encarnacion
Right Field	Jeremy Hermida
No. 1 Starter	Josh Beckett

Jesus Medrano   Nate Robertson

No. 2 Starter	A.J. Burnett
No. 3 Starter	Dontrelle Willis
No. 4 Starter	Brad Penny
No. 5 Starter	Don Levinski
Closer	Tim Spooneybarger

TOP PROSPECTS OF THE DECADE

1993	Nigel Wilson, of
1994	Charles Johnson, c
1995	Charles Johnson, c
1996	Edgar Renteria, ss
1997	Felix Heredia, lhp
1998	Mark Kotsay, of
1999	A.J. Burnett, rhp
2000	A.J. Burnett, rhp
2001	Josh Beckett, rhp
2002	Josh Beckett, rhp

TOP DRAFT PICKS OF THE DECADE

1993	Marc Valdes, rhp
1994	Josh Booty, 3b
1995	Jaime Jones, of
1996	Mark Kotsay, of
1997	Aaron Akin, rhp
1998	Chip Ambres, of
1999	Josh Beckett, rhp
2000	Adrian Gonzalez, 1b
2001	Garrett Berger, rhp
2002	Jeremy Hermida, of

ALL-TIME LARGEST BONUSES

Josh Beckett, 1999	$3,625,000
Adrian Gonzalez, 2000	$3,000,000
Livan Hernandez, 1996	$2,500,000
Jason Stokes, 2000	$2,027,000
Jeremy Hermida, 2002	$2,012,000

MinorLeague**Depth**Chart

FLORIDA MARLINS

RANK 8

After the Marlins swapped front offices with the Expos before last season, it's not surprising they have continued to emphasize scouting and player development, with a priority on premium athletes, high-ceiling high school bats and lefthanded pitching. The new administration inherited a strong crop of prospects and made trades with the Cubs, Expos and Reds that brought in pitchers like Dontrelle Willis, Don Levinski, Justin Wayne and Ryan Snare. If Fred Ferreira can rediscover the magic touch that enabled him to sign players like Vladimir Guerrero on the international market, it will be a nice supplement to the steady drafts of unheralded scouting director Jim Fleming and his successor Stan Meek.

Note: Depth charts prepared by Josh Boyd. Numbers in parentheses indicate prospect rankings.

LF
Will Smith (9)
Kenny Berkenbosch

CF
Chip Ambres (14)
Eric Reed (17)
Charles Frazier
Anthony Brewer
Xavier Arroyo

RF
Jeremy Hermida (5)
Abraham Nunez (16)
Ulysses Powel

3B
Miguel Cabrera (1)

SS
Josh Wilson (10)
Robert Andino (19)
Wilson Valdez
Rex Rundgren

2B
Kevin Hooper (15)
Jesus Medrano (24)
Kevin Randel

1B
Jason Stokes (2)
Adrian Gonzalez (3)
Pat Magness

C
Josh Willingham (21)
Ryan Jorgensen (22)
Patrick Arlis
Angel Molina

LHP
Starters
Dontrelle Willis (4)
Scott Olsen (20)
Frailyn Tejada

Relievers
Ryan Snare (11)
Franklyn Gracesqui (30)
Geoff Goetz
Oswaldo Mairena
Todd Moser

RHP
Starters
Don Levinski (6)
Justin Wayne (7)
Ronald Belizario (12)
Denny Bautista (13)
Victor Prieto (18)
Josh Johnson (26)
Garrett Berger (27)
Wes Anderson (28)
Allen Baxter (29)
Jason Grilli
Jose Cueto
Randy Messenger
Nate Bump
Phil Akens

Relievers
Blaine Neal (8)
Yorman Bazardo (23)
Juan Nova (25)
Lincoln Holdzkom
Ryan Warpinski
Jon Asahina
Manny Esquivia

DraftAnalysis

2002 Draft

Best Pro Debut: OF Eric Reed (9) has no problem hitting with wood. The 2001 Cape Cod League batting champ hit .317 with 26 steals in his first pro summer while reaching low Class A.

Best Athlete: OF Jeremy Hermida (1) has one of the best high school bats since Eric Chavez, and he's an average runner with a strong arm. Reed can fly. OF Xavier Arroyo (7) has a wide array of tools and was Puerto Rico's top-rated prospect.

Best Pure Hitter: Hermida has a classic swing and an advanced approach. After batting .224 in the Rookie-level Gulf Coast League, he improved to .319 when challenged with a promotion to the short-season New York-Penn League.

Best Raw Power: 1B Robert Word (10) has more sock now but will be passed by Hermida, who's 3½ years younger.

Fastest Runner: Reed has 75 speed on the 20-80 scouting scale. He can get to first base from the left side in 3.85 seconds.

Best Defensive Player: The Marlins rated SS Robert Andino (2) as the best defensive shortstop in the entire draft. He threw 92 mph off a mound, and has terrific hands and actions to go with solid range. He made just two errors in 18 pro games.

Best Fastball: RHP **Ryan Warpinski** (8) has rebounded from two elbow surgeries at Texas A&M to throw his sinker up to 93-94 mph. RHP Jimmy deMontel (12) has a similar fastball but not the feel for pitching.

Best Breaking Ball: RHP Trevor Hutchinson (3), who's still holding out

though he's out of college eligibility, has a top-notch slider. Until Hutchinson signs, RHP Josh Johnson's (4) slider is the top breaking ball in the class.

RODGER WOOD

Warpinski

Most Intriguing Background: Hutchinson's brother Chad is a former Cardinals bonus baby and two-sport star at Stanford who gave up baseball last year and is now a quarterback for the Dallas Cowboys. Unsigned C Nick Hundley's (5) father Tim is an assistant football coach at the University of Washington.

Closest To The Majors: Take your pick between former Texas A&M teammates Warpinski and Reed, though Hutchinson is further along than both.

Best Late-Round Pick: SS/2B Kevin Randel (13) is a gamer who can do a little of everything. He started switch-hitting again after signing and showed more pop than the Marlins expected, hitting .277-7-27 in the NY-P. He's patient at the plate, drawing 49 walks in 69 games.

The One Who Got Away: Hundley has catch-and-throw skills, is athletic and has power potential. He's attending Arizona.

Assessment: At one point Hermida was considered by teams with two of the first four picks, and getting him at No. 11 may look like a steal for Florida in a couple of years. The rest of the crop looks ordinary, though signing Hutchinson would help.

2001 Draft

The Marlins didn't have a first-round pick. Worse, their top two choices, RHP Garrett Berger (2) and Allen Baxter (3), already have suffered serious elbow injuries.   **Grade: D**

2000 Draft

1Bs Adrian Gonzalez (1) and Jason Stokes (2) and OF Will Smith (6) all look like big league mashers. LHP Rob Henkel (3) was traded to Detroit this offseason.   **Grade: A**

1999 Draft

The No. 2 overall pick, RHP Josh Beckett (1) is looking a lot better than the two selections who sandwiched him (Josh Hamilton, Eric Munson). SS Josh Wilson (2) and SS/2B Kevin Hooper (8) are making their way toward Florida.   **Grade: A**

1998 Draft

Football star/OF Chip Ambres (1) has developed slowly, and the Marlins signed no one else of note.   **Grade: D**

Note: Draft analysis prepared by Jim Callis. Numbers in parentheses indicate draft rounds.

. . . Cabrera projects to hit for average and power, with annual totals of 35-40 homers not out of the question.

Miguel
Cabrera 3b

Born: April 18, 1983.
Ht.: 6-2. **Wt.:** 180.
Bats: R. **Throws:** R.
Career Transactions:
Signed out of Venezuela by
Marlins, July 2, 1999.

MORRIS FOSTOFF

Signed for a Venezuelan-record $1.9 million bonus, Cabrera grew up with a diamond just beyond his backyard, and his instincts show as much. He was called up from the winter parallel league in his homeland at age 18 and has been a key member of the Aragua Tigers the past two winters. He's the youngest player to appear in the Futures Game in the four years of the event, achieving the distinction in 2001 in Seattle and returning last year in Milwaukee. Cabrera benefited from playing with roommate Adrian Gonzalez at low Class A Kane County in 2001. Gonzalez helped him achieve a comfort level with a foreign language and strange land. Some wondered how Cabrera would fare when Gonzalez jumped ahead to Double-A last year, but Cabrera stood out at high Class A Jupiter.

Signed as a shortstop, Cabrera moved to third base last spring and fared well. He's a below-average runner but is quick on his feet and has drawn comparisons to countryman Andres Galarraga in that regard. He has soft hands and a plus arm that's accurate and ranks as the best among the system's infielders. Cabrera's line-drive swing has produced more doubles than homers so far. While some of his teammates were frustrated by hitting in the Florida State League, Cabrera took his doubles off the wall and stayed positive. He projects to hit for both average and power, with annual totals of 35-40 homers not out of the question down the road. He loves to play, doesn't get too emotional and constantly works to get better.

While he has a good grasp of the strike zone, Cabrera should accept more walks and lay off breaking balls out of the zone. He isn't much of a threat on the bases, though he's an instinctive baserunner. He was plagued by a lower-back problem in 2001 but had no relapses last season. Having outgrown shortstop, Cabrera could get too big for third base if he continues to add bulk and wind up at first base, which would give the organization a perplexing logjam.

With Mike Lowell two seasons from free agency, Cabrera is poised to take over at third base by 2005, if not sooner. He'll start the year at Florida's new Double-A Carolina affiliate.

Year	Club (League)	Class	AVG	G	AB	R	H	2B	3B	HR	RBI	BB	SO	SB	SLG	OBP
2000	Marlins (GCL)	R	.260	57	219	38	57	10	2	2	22	23	46	1	.352	.344
	Utica (NY-P)	A	.250	8	32	3	8	2	0	0	6	2	6	0	.313	.294
2001	Kane County (Mid)	A	.268	110	422	61	113	19	4	7	66	37	76	3	.382	.328
2002	Jupiter (FSL)	A	.274	124	489	77	134	43	1	9	75	38	85	10	.421	.333
MINOR LEAGUE TOTALS			.269	299	1162	179	312	74	7	18	169	100	213	14	.391	.332

2. Jason Stokes, 1b

Born: Jan. 23, 1982. **Ht.:** 6-4. **Wt.:** 220. **Bats:** R. **Throws:** R. **School:** Coppell (Texas) HS. **Career Transactions:** Selected by Marlins in second round of 2000 draft; signed Aug. 29, 2000.

After signing late for a $2.027 million bonus in 2000, Stokes worked hard to make a transition to left field in 2001 but was waylaid by back and hamstring problems. He exploded last year, leading the low Class A Midwest League in batting and homers, and the entire minor leagues in slugging, despite a painful cyst on his left wrist. He could lean on his massive power, but Stokes wants to be a complete player. He hits to all fields and shows a good understanding of the strike zone and pitchers' tactics. He runs out pop flies like a super-sized David Eckstein. He has worked hard on his defense, and while he will never be nimble, won't hurt a club at first base. After fighting through injuries the last two years, Stokes' durability is in question. His arm is average at best and his speed is below-average, though not bad for his size. Stokes had wrist surgery, which included a bone graft, but should be ready for spring training. He'll probably start 2003 in high Class A. Adrian Gonzalez' superior defense makes it likely Stokes will play left field when both are big league regulars, perhaps in 2005.

Year	Club (League)	Class	AVG	G	AB	R	H	2B	3B	HR	RBI	BB	SO	SB	SLG	OBP
2001	Utica (NY-P)	A	.231	35	130	12	30	2	1	6	19	11	48	0	.400	.299
2002	Kane County (Mid)	A	.341	97	349	73	119	25	0	27	75	47	96	1	.645	.421
MINOR LEAGUE TOTALS			.311	132	479	85	149	27	1	33	94	58	144	1	.578	.389

3. Adrian Gonzalez, 1b

Born: May 8, 1982. **Ht.:** 6-2. **Wt.:** 190. **Bats:** L. **Throws:** L. **School:** Eastlake HS, Chula Vista, Calif. **Career Transactions:** Selected by Marlins in first round (first overall) of 2000 draft; signed June 6, 2000.

Signability played a large part in Gonzalez' selection as the No. 1 pick in 2000, but his performance has quieted the skeptics and justified his $3 million bonus. Older brother Edgar is a third baseman in the Devil Rays system. Their father David was a first baseman in Mexican semipro leagues into his early 40s. Gonzalez skipped high Class A and thrived after overcoming a slow start at Double-A Portland. He uses the whole field, fills the gaps, enjoys RBI situations and projects to add more power down the road. Comparisons to a young Rafael Palmeiro appear apt. Gonzalez also has Gold Glove potential with soft hands, plus range and a daring nature. Gonzalez may have been too power-conscious at the start of 2002, uncharacteristically getting himself out by expanding his zone. His speed is below-average. He made 16 errors last year, most of them due to poor concentration. With the emergence of Stokes, Gonzalez has competition to be the Marlins' future first baseman. He's ticketed for Triple-A Albuquerque, though he may miss the start of spring training after he had surgery to repair torn cartilage in his wrist in December.

Year	Club (League)	Class	AVG	G	AB	R	H	2B	3B	HR	RBI	BB	SO	SB	SLG	OBP
2000	Marlins (GCL)	R	.295	53	193	24	57	10	1	0	30	32	35	0	.358	.397
	Utica (NY-P)	A	.310	8	29	7	9	3	0	0	3	7	6	0	.414	.444
2001	Kane County (Mid)	A	.312	127	516	86	161	37	1	17	103	57	83	5	.486	.382
2002	Portland (EL)	AA	.266	138	508	70	135	34	1	17	96	54	112	6	.437	.344
MINOR LEAGUE TOTALS			.291	326	1246	187	362	84	3	34	232	150	236	11	.445	.371

4. Dontrelle Willis, lhp

Born: Jan. 12, 1982. **Ht.:** 6-4. **Wt.:** 200. **Bats:** L. **Throws:** L. **School:** Encinal HS, Alameda, Calif. **Career Transactions:** Selected by Cubs in eighth round of 2000 draft; signed July 6, 2000 . . . Traded by Cubs with RHP Julian Tavarez, RHP Jose Cueto and C Ryan Jorgensen to Marlins for RHP Antonio Alfonseca and RHP Matt Clement, March 27, 2002.

Willis was the key player in the spring trade that sent Matt Clement and Antonio Alfonseca to the Cubs. His stock rocketed as he dominated two Class A leagues. He was shut down with a bruised triceps, but he threw on the side at instructional league without incident. Willis creates excellent deception with an unorthodox delivery he says he learned from his mother as a child. Throwing from a low three-quarters arm slot, he induces lots of groundballs and awkward swings. His improved fastball tops out at 93 mph, and he can cut it and sink it. He added depth to his slurvy breaking ball and gets sink out of his changeup as well. His command is excellent and he rarely leaves balls up in the zone. Willis' slider tends to flatten out and his changeup is inconsistent. He must pitch inside to righthanders more effectively. After his injury, Willis learned he wasn't doing his shoulder exercises correctly. His delivery can be violent and his fielding must improve. After opening eyes throughout his new organization, Willis figures to return to high Class A to start 2003.

Year	Club (League)	Class	W	L	ERA	G	GS	CG	SV	IP	H	R	ER	HR	BB	SO	AVG
2000	Cubs (AZL)	R	3	1	3.86	9	1	0	0	28	26	15	12	0	8	22	.245
2001	Boise (NWL)	A	8	2	2.98	15	15	0	0	94	76	36	31	1	19	77	.217
2002	Kane County (Mid)	A	10	2	1.83	19	19	3	0	128	91	29	26	3	21	101	.200
	Jupiter (FSL)	A	2	0	1.80	5	5	0	0	30	24	7	6	2	3	27	.216
MINOR LEAGUE TOTALS			23	5	2.42	48	40	3	0	279	217	87	75	6	51	227	.212

5. Jeremy Hermida, of

Born: Jan. 30, 1984. **Ht.:** 6-4. **Wt.:** 200. **Bats:** L. **Throws:** R. **School:** Wheeler HS, Marietta, Ga. **Career Transactions:** Selected by Marlins in first round (11th overall) of 2002 draft; signed July 5, 2002.

The Marlins were ecstatic when Hermida was available 11th overall last June. Rated the best pure high school hitter available, he signed for $2.0125 million. A natural righthanded hitter, Hermida was converted into a lefty at age 4 by his father. Hermida has practiced with a wood bat since he was 13 and counts former big leaguer Terry Harper among his tutors. Some scouts called Hermida the best high school hitter since Eric Chavez. Others compared his body type to a young Andy Van Slyke. Marlins assistant general manager Jim Fleming sees a young Paul O'Neill, while Hermida identifies more with Shawn Green. He has a smooth, quick stroke and excellent instincts. His speed and rightfield arm are average. He loves to play and has a great disposition. Hermida jumps at pitches from time to time. He must grow into his power, though the Marlins fully expect that to come. After a standout debut at short-season Jamestown, Hermida figures to begin 2003 at Florida's new low Class A Greensboro affiliate. His success will dictate how quickly he moves.

Year	Club (League)	Class	AVG	G	AB	R	H	2B	3B	HR	RBI	BB	SO	SB	SLG	OBP
2002	Marlins (GCL)	R	.224	38	134	15	30	7	3	0	14	15	25	5	.321	.316
	Jamestown (NY-P)	A	.319	13	47	8	15	2	1	0	7	7	10	1	.404	.407
MINOR LEAGUE TOTALS			.249	51	181	23	45	9	4	0	21	22	35	6	.343	.340

6. Don Levinski, rhp

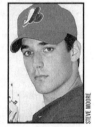

Born: Oct. 20, 1982. **Ht.:** 6-4. **Wt.:** 200. **Bats:** R. **Throws:** R. **School:** Weimar (Texas) HS. **Career Transactions:** Selected by Expos in second round of 2001 draft; signed Aug. 4, 2001 . . . Traded by Expos to Marlins, Aug. 5, 2002, completing trade in which Marlins sent OF Cliff Floyd, 2B Wilton Guerrero, RHP Claudio Vargas and cash to Expos for RHP Carl Pavano, LHP Graeme Lloyd, RHP Justin Wayne, 2B Mike Mordecai and a player to be named (July 11, 2002).

Levinski came south from Montreal along with Justin Wayne in the Cliff Floyd trade. In his final start with the Expos, Levinski's velocity dropped into the mid-80s and an MRI later revealed a slight rotator-cuff tear. The Marlins opted to keep him in the deal and subsequent tests showed a strain rather than a tear. After being shut down for the final month of 2002, Levinski threw a handful of bullpens at instructional league and was healthy. His heavy sinker arrives at 88-93 mph with hard, late life. When he's in a groove, he can almost get by with his fastball alone. He also features a power curve and a solid changeup. He has a sound delivery that he repeats with ease. He has a quiet personality but is competitive and confident. Walks have been a concern as Levinski learns to command his darting arsenal. After last year's health scare, he'll need to prove he can stay in the rotation for a full season. He also must use his changeup more often. Having dominated the Midwest League for four months, Levinski will probably open 2003 at Jupiter. His maturity and repertoire make him a candidate to move quickly.

Year	Club (League)	Class	W	L	ERA	G	GS	CG	SV	IP	H	R	ER	HR	BB	SO	AVG
2001	Expos (GCL)	R	0	0	3.46	3	3	0	0	13	15	5	5	1	7	15	.300
2002	Clinton (Mid)	A	12	6	3.02	21	21	1	0	119	92	48	40	6	55	125	.212
MINOR LEAGUE TOTALS			12	6	3.06	24	24	1	0	132	107	53	45	7	62	140	.221

7. Justin Wayne, rhp

Born: April 16, 1979. **Ht.:** 6-3. **Wt.:** 200. **Bats:** R. **Throws:** R. **School:** Stanford University. **Career Transactions:** Selected by Expos in first round (fifth overall) of 2000 draft; signed July 20, 2000 . . . Traded by Expos with RHP Carl Pavano, LHP Graeme Lloyd, 2B Mike Mordecai and a player to be named to Marlins for OF Cliff Floyd, 2B Wilton Guerrero, RHP Claudio Vargas and cash, July 11, 2002; Marlins acquired RHP Don Levinski to complete trade (Aug. 5, 2002).

Wayne is a favorite of Jeffrey Loria, whose Expos drafted him fifth overall in 2000 and gave him a Montreal-record $2.95 million bonus. After being reunited with Loria in the Cliff Floyd trade, Wayne struggled in Triple-A before showing flashes in a five-start September audition in the majors. Wayne pitches at 87-90 mph and keeps hitters off-balance with pinpoint control and an intelligent approach. He throws four pitches for strikes, including a plus curveball, a plus slider and a changeup that's the best in the system. His velocity climbed to 92-93 mph in the majors. His slider sometimes gets flat, and Wayne will go for long stretches without trusting his curve. Though he's a fitness nut, he missed a few starts with shoulder tendinitis and needs to get stronger. A perfectionist, he tends to nibble and overanalyze his performance. After getting his first taste of the majors, Wayne will get a legitimate shot at making the Florida rotation this spring.

Year	Club (League)	Class	W	L	ERA	G	GS	CG	SV	IP	H	R	ER	HR	BB	SO	AVG
2000	Jupiter (FSL)	A	0	3	5.81	5	5	0	0	26	26	22	17	2	11	24	.263
2001	Jupiter (FSL)	A	2	3	3.02	8	7	0	0	42	31	16	14	0	9	35	.204
	Harrisburg (EL)	AA	9	2	2.62	14	14	2	0	93	87	28	27	4	34	70	.248
2002	Harrisburg (EL)	AA	5	2	2.37	17	17	0	0	99	74	41	26	7	32	47	.213
	Portland (EL)	AA	3	3	4.85	7	7	1	0	43	43	26	23	3	13	30	.269
	Calgary (PCL)	AAA	0	1	6.35	2	2	0	0	11	8	8	8	3	6	10	.195
	Florida (NL)	MAJ	2	3	5.32	5	5	0	0	24	22	16	14	3	13	16	.244
MAJOR LEAGUE TOTALS			2	3	5.32	5	5	0	0	24	22	16	14	3	13	16	.244
MINOR LEAGUE TOTALS			19	14	3.30	53	52	3	0	313	269	141	115	19	105	216	.234

8. Blaine Neal, rhp

Born: April 6, 1978. **Ht.:** 6-5. **Wt.:** 200. **Bats:** L. **Throws:** R. **School:** Bishop Eustace HS, Pennsauken, N.J. **Career Transactions:** Selected by Marlins in fourth round of 1996 draft; signed July 13, 1996.

Signed for $350,000, Neal developed slowly because of elbow problems in his first two years as a pro. The Marlins tried him at first base without success and nearly released him after the 1998 season. After arthroscopic surgery to remove several bone spurs and shave down part of a bone to relieve pressure on a nerve, Neal hasn't looked back. Neal employs a fastball that touches 98 mph and stays at 93-95 with late movement. He has a short, tight slider and a strong pitcher's frame with wide back muscles. His arm bounces back well and he's a ferocious competitor. Neal's delivery is somewhat stiff and he overthrows his fastball at times. There's still some doubt whether Neal projects as a full-fledged closer or a two-inning set-up man. If nothing else, Neal got a chance to work on his frequent-flier account last season. He had four separate stints with the Marlins, going back and forth on the shuttle to Calgary. He pitched well at both places, showing enough potential to earn a full shot in a set-up role this year.

Year	Club (League)	Class	AVG	G	AB	R	H	2B	3B	HR	RBI	BB	SO	SB	SLG	OBP
1998	Utica (NY-P)	A	.190	53	121	13	23	4	0	0	13	23	32	2	.223	.329
MINOR LEAGUE TOTALS			.190	53	121	13	23	4	0	0	13	23	32	2	.223	.329

Year	Club (League)	Class	W	L	ERA	G	GS	CG	SV	IP	H	R	ER	HR	BB	SO	AVG
1996	Marlins (GCL)	R	1	1	4.60	7	5	0	1	29	32	18	15	1	6	15	.274
1997	Marlins (GCL)	R	4	1	3.63	10	0	0	1	22	24	11	9	1	11	19	.267
1999	Kane County (Mid)	A	4	2	2.32	26	0	0	6	31	21	8	8	2	10	31	.200
2000	Brevard County (FSL)	A	2	2	2.15	41	0	0	11	54	40	27	13	1	24	65	.200
2001	Portland (EL)	AA	2	3	2.36	54	0	0	21	53	43	17	14	1	21	45	.218
	Florida (NL)	MAJ	0	0	6.75	4	0	0	0	5	7	4	4	0	5	3	.304
2002	Calgary (PCL)	AAA	3	1	2.90	29	0	0	11	31	27	11	10	2	15	26	.233
	Florida (NL)	MAJ	3	0	2.73	32	0	0	0	33	32	12	10	1	14	33	.248
MAJOR LEAGUE TOTALS			3	0	3.29	36	0	0	0	38	39	16	14	1	19	36	.257
MINOR LEAGUE TOTALS			16	10	2.81	167	5	0	51	221	187	92	69	8	87	201	.227

9. Will Smith, of

Born: Oct. 23, 1981. **Ht.:** 6-1. **Wt.:** 180. **Bats:** L. **Throws:** R. **School:** Palo Verde HS, Tucson. **Career Transactions:** Selected by Marlins in sixth round of 2000 draft; signed June 9, 2000.

Smith set the Arizona high school record for career home runs and seems to be growing into his power at the pro level. Despite an unorthodox stance that has been described as Yastrzemski Lite, he continues to stand conventional wisdom on its head. Forget what Smith does as the ball makes it way to home plate. Once it gets there, his bat almost always is in the correct hitting position. He loves to play and appears to be a born hitter with no holes in his swing. The new Marlins regime challenged him to work on other parts of his game, and he made significant progress in those areas. His arm and speed are average. Smith has a tendency to pull off the ball against lefties, but made progress during instructional league after opening his stance. He could draw more walks and needs to get stronger. His arm has improved from below-average, but he remains a so-so corner outfielder at best. After cleaning up in his first three seasons, Smith will go to Double-A. If he stays as serious about the rest of his game as he is about his hitting, his swing could raise major league eyebrows in 2004.

Year	Club (League)	Class	AVG	G	AB	R	H	2B	3B	HR	RBI	BB	SO	SB	SLG	OBP
2000	Marlins (GCL)	R	.368	54	204	37	75	21	2	2	34	26	24	7	.520	.440
2001	Kane County (Mid)	A	.280	125	535	92	150	26	2	16	91	32	74	4	.426	.324
2002	Jupiter (FSL)	A	.299	133	549	84	164	30	12	14	73	31	75	8	.474	.336
MINOR LEAGUE TOTALS			.302	312	1288	213	389	77	16	32	198	89	173	19	.461	.348

10. Josh Wilson, ss

Born: March 26, 1981. **Ht.:** 6-1. **Wt.:** 160. **Bats:** R. **Throws:** R. **School:** Mount Lebanon (Pa.) HS. **Career Transactions:** Selected by Marlins in third round of 1999 draft; signed June 5, 1999.

As the son of Mike Wilson, head baseball coach at Duquesne University, Josh's instincts and makeup are beyond reproach. The rest of his game is catching up as well. He still gets a little too pull-conscious at times, hitting too many balls in the air, but projects to add enough pop to become a Jay Bell/Jeff Blauser middle infielder. While he had a somewhat disappointing season in high Class A, he still showed a line-drive stroke and the ability to make consistently hard contact. He needs to show more patience, however, working deeper counts and drawing more walks. While the previous Marlins regime started playing him at second base with an eye toward the future, those who inherited Wilson view him as a legitimate shortstop. He teamed on the left side of Jupiter's infield with Miguel Cabrera, who made the move from shortstop to third. Wilson has soft hands, quick feet, solid range and an above-average arm. Tall and thin, he still needs to add upper-body strength and is just an average runner and poor basestealer. But he's getting better all the time and already carries himself with the confidence of a future big leaguer.

Year	Club (League)	Class	AVG	G	AB	R	H	2B	3B	HR	RBI	BB	SO	SB	SLG	OBP
1999	Marlins (GCL)	R	.266	53	203	29	54	9	4	0	27	24	36	14	.350	.352
2000	Kane County (Mid)	A	.269	13	52	2	14	3	1	1	6	3	14	0	.423	.316
	Utica (NY-P)	A	.344	66	259	43	89	13	6	3	43	29	47	9	.475	.418
2001	Kane County (Mid)	A	.285	123	506	65	144	28	5	4	61	28	60	17	.383	.325
2002	Jupiter (FSL)	A	.256	111	398	51	102	17	1	11	50	28	67	7	.387	.318
	Portland (EL)	AA	.341	12	41	5	14	3	0	2	5	2	6	0	.561	.372
MINOR LEAGUE TOTALS			.286	378	1459	195	417	73	17	21	192	114	230	47	.402	.345

11. Ryan Snare, lhp

Born: Feb. 8, 1979. **Ht.:** 6-0. **Wt.:** 190. **Bats:** L. **Throws:** L. **School:** University of North Carolina. **Career Transactions:** Selected by Reds in second round of 2000 draft; signed Aug. 11, 2000 . . . Traded by Reds with OF Juan Encarnacion and 2B Wilton Guerrero to Marlins for RHP Ryan Dempster, July 11, 2002.

Snare had a busy year, bouncing between the rotation and the bullpen, getting traded for the first time and making stops in three different minor league towns. He gets by with solid command and an 88-91 mph fastball that has decent movement, but it's a knee-buckling curveball that distinguishes him. It's the best breaking pitch in the system. Snare's changeup is improving but he doesn't throw it enough, in part because of the way he was used. He isn't afraid to throw inside to righthanders. The Marlins aren't sure whether he projects as a starter or a Mike Stanton-style set-up man, but it's a nice dilemma to have. Snare has an aggressive nature and an intense personality. He tends to overthrow at times and must continue to work on controlling his emotions. A planned trip to the Arizona Fall League was canceled when Snare reported a tired arm late in the season. He could break into the Florida bullpen at some point this season.

Year	Club (League)	Class	W	L	ERA	G	GS	CG	SV	IP	H	R	ER	HR	BB	SO	AVG
2001	Dayton (Mid)	A	9	5	3.05	21	20	0	0	115	101	45	39	7	37	118	.238
2002	Stockton (Cal)	A	8	2	3.07	13	13	0	0	82	74	36	28	4	18	81	.238
	Chattanooga (SL)	AA	0	0	3.00	5	0	0	0	6	5	3	2	1	3	4	.263
	Portland (EL)	AA	4	2	3.44	11	9	0	0	55	46	25	21	6	19	52	.224
MINOR LEAGUE TOTALS			21	9	3.14	50	42	0	0	258	226	109	90	18	77	255	.236

12. Ronald Belizario, rhp

Born: Dec. 31, 1982. **Ht.:** 6-2. **Wt.:** 148. **Bats:** R. **Throws:** R. **Career Transactions:** Signed out of Venezuela by Marlins, Aug. 2, 1999.

Signed the same week as fellow countryman Miguel Cabrera, Belizario came to the Marlins with significantly less fanfare. His signing bonus was less than $60,000, compared to the Venezuelan-record $1.9 million Cabrera received, but both are on track for the big leagues. Blessed with what some consider the loosest arm in the organization, Belizario pitches at 90-93 mph and has touched 98. Everything he throws moves, especially his two-seam fastball with hard, boring action. He still throws both a curveball and slider, both of which are solid average, and his changeup is improving as he tinkers with different grips. He has a fun-loving personality, loves to compete and enjoys being on the mound. He'll overthrow at times, which makes his fastball straighten out, and he occasionally loses focus. Just 148 pounds upon signing, he now needs to firm up a somewhat soft frame. He eventually could wind up as a closer, but for now he'll continue to pile up innings and experience in high Class A.

Year	Club (League)	Class	W	L	ERA	G	GS	CG	SV	IP	H	R	ER	HR	BB	SO	AVG
2000	Universidad (VSL)	R	2	3	7.39	17	5	0	6	35	37	34	29	1	18	27	.253
2001	Marlins (GCL)	R	4	6	2.34	13	10	1	0	73	62	29	19	4	20	54	.229
2002	Kane County (Mid)	A	6	5	3.46	23	22	1	0	140	131	67	54	4	56	98	.247
MINOR LEAGUE TOTALS			12	14	3.69	53	37	2	6	249	230	130	102	9	94	179	.243

13. Denny Bautista, rhp

Born: Oct. 23, 1982. **Ht.:** 6-5. **Wt.:** 170. **Bats:** R. **Throws:** R. **Career Transactions:** Signed out of Dominican Republic by Marlins, April 11, 2000.

After streaking to No. 3 on the Marlins' prospect list a year ago, Bautista fell back with an uneven season marred by visa troubles that delayed his arrival at spring training. Trying to make up for lost time, he overthrew and wound up missing six weeks with shoulder tendinitis. Mentored back home in the Dominican Republic by the Brothers Martinez, Pedro and Ramon, Bautista can be headstrong at times. After getting hurt, though, he accepted suggestions to tone down his violent delivery and stopped trying to throw everything through a brick wall. He pitched at 92-94 mph, a tick down from the 96 mph he reached in the past, and commanded his curveball and changeup much better in the second half. He proved more efficient while on a 75-pitch limit, coaxing groundballs instead of going for strikeouts and taking pressure off his arm. He can be overly emotional on the mound when he struggles and still must improve his fielding and attention to detail, but his ceiling remains high. Largely on Pedro Martinez' advice, Bautista signed with the Marlins for about $350,000. That could yet turn out to be a tremendous bargain.

Year	Club (League)	Class	W	L	ERA	G	GS	CG	SV	IP	H	R	ER	HR	BB	SO	AVG
2000	Marlins (GCL)	R	6	2	2.43	11	11	2	0	63	49	24	17	1	17	58	.209
	Marlins (DSL)	R	0	1	2.57	3	3	0	0	14	11	6	4	2	9	17	.216
	Utica (NY-P)	A	0	0	3.60	1	1	0	0	5	4	3	2	0	2	5	.222
2001	Kane County (Mid)	A	3	1	4.35	8	7	0	0	39	43	21	19	2	14	20	.281
	Utica (NY-P)	A	3	1	2.08	7	7	0	0	39	25	16	9	0	6	31	.174
2002	Jupiter (FSL)	A	4	6	4.99	19	15	0	0	88	80	52	49	6	40	79	.242
MINOR LEAGUE TOTALS			16	11	3.62	49	44	2	0	249	212	122	100	11	88	210	.228

14. Chip Ambres, of

Born: Dec. 19, 1979. **Ht.:** 6-1. **Wt.:** 190. **Bats:** R. **Throws:** R. **School:** West Brook HS, Beaumont, Texas. **Career Transactions:** Selected by Marlins in first round (27th overall) of 1998 draft; signed Aug. 3, 1998.

Coming off surgery to repair a broken right fibula, Ambres had a frustrating debut in high Class A. Playing with a metal plate in his leg, Ambres' batting average and confidence suffered as he struggled to hit in the Florida State League's heavy air and sprawling ballparks. Sensing an opportunity, several college football programs swooped into re-recruit the former prep quarterback. Ambres, who received a $1.5 million bonus to turn down a football scholarship from Texas A&M, opted to stick it out. A five-day session at instructional league with roving hitting coordinator John Mallee got Ambres back on the right track as he headed to the Arizona Fall League, where he quickly earned the nickname "Baby Hunter," as in Torii. At Mallee's urging, Ambres toned down his pronounced leg kick and spread out his stance, which helped him keep his bat in the zone longer. Ambres remains one of the best athletes in the system and is more selective than most, but he's no longer viewed as a future leadoff hitter. Nor is he likely to be a big-time basestealer, despite above-average speed. His arm is good enough to play center field. His work ethic and makeup are beyond question as he prepares for his first taste of Double-A.

Year	Club (League)	Class	AVG	G	AB	R	H	2B	3B	HR	RBI	BB	SO	SB	SLG	OBP
1999	Marlins (GCL)	R	.353	37	139	29	49	13	3	1	15	25	19	22	.511	.452
	Utica (NY-P)	A	.267	28	105	24	28	3	6	5	15	21	25	11	.552	.388
2000	Kane County (Mid)	A	.231	84	320	46	74	16	3	7	28	52	72	26	.366	.342
2001	Kane County (Mid)	A	.265	96	377	79	100	26	8	5	41	53	81	19	.416	.369
2002	Jupiter (FSL)	A	.236	123	509	88	120	25	7	9	37	57	98	23	.365	.323
MINOR LEAGUE TOTALS			.256	368	1450	266	371	83	27	27	136	208	295	101	.406	.357

15. Kevin Hooper, ss/2b

Born: Dec. 7, 1976. **Ht.:** 5-10. **Wt.:** 160. **Bats:** R. **Throws:** R. **School:** Wichita State University. **Career Transactions:** Selected by Marlins in eighth round of 1999 draft; signed June 3, 1999.

While clubs scramble to find the next David Eckstein, the Marlins believe they already have theirs in Hooper. Like Eckstein, Hooper beats opponents as much with his brain and heart as with his body. He looks immature, both facially and physically, but then so does Eckstein. Both have excellent speed and soft hands, but Hooper has a much better arm than Eckstein and may have better range as well. Like Eckstein, Hooper is willing to take pitches and fights off those he can't handle. He won't get plunked quite as often, but Hooper will give himself up to advance runners and is forever dropping flares into short right field for singles. His 31-game hitting streak at Calgary was the second-longest in the minors last year. Routinely clocked at 4.08 seconds from home to first, Hooper needs to improve his basestealing instincts to take full advantage of his speed. After seeing more time at second base in Double-A, he convinced the new regime he could handle the everyday grind at shortstop. With incumbent Alex Gonzalez returning from shoulder surgery and veterans Andy Fox and Mike Mordecai around as well, Hooper appears to be blocked in his path to the majors. He could break in through a utility role.

Year	Club (League)	Class	AVG	G	AB	R	H	2B	3B	HR	RBI	BB	SO	SB	SLG	OBP
1999	Utica (NY-P)	A	.280	73	289	52	81	18	6	0	22	39	35	14	.384	.370
2000	Kane County (Mid)	A	.249	123	457	73	114	25	6	3	38	73	83	17	.350	.359
2001	Kane County (Mid)	A	.292	17	65	11	19	2	0	0	4	11	13	3	.323	.390
	Portland (EL)	AA	.308	117	468	70	144	19	6	2	39	59	78	24	.387	.392
2002	Calgary (PCL)	AAA	.288	117	452	70	130	21	3	2	38	34	51	17	.361	.341
MINOR LEAGUE TOTALS			.282	447	1731	276	488	85	21	7	141	216	260	75	.367	.367

16. Abraham Nunez, of

Born: Feb. 5, 1977. **Ht.:** 6-2. **Wt.:** 180. **Bats:** B. **Throws:** R. **Career Transactions:** Signed out of Dominican Republic by Diamondbacks, Aug. 22, 1996 . . . Traded by Diamondbacks to Marlins, Dec. 14, 1999, completing trade in which Diamondbacks sent RHP Vladimir Nunez, RHP Brad Penny and a player to be named to Marlins for RHP Matt Mantei (July 9, 1999).

Nunez spent the last three years in the organization's top 10, but that was before he was found to be three years older than his listed age. Once considered a five-tool player with star potential, he now has some wondering if he'll ever be more than an extra outfielder with tantalizing skills. He still has plus power, good speed and the best arm in the system, but he strikes out too much, has a long swing and shows little aptitude for making adjustments at the plate. He struggles most from the left side, and there's some thought he might be better off sticking with his righthanded swing exclusively. He has much more power from the left side but far better plate coverage from the right. He had his best season as a basestealer last year, but his overall instincts remain in question. One Marlins insider describes him as Bernie Williams waiting to happen, but so far there has been little indication all that potential will ever translate into production. After spending a full season in Triple-A, Nunez should get a chance to make the majors in a reserve role. He has the arm and range to play all three outfield spots.

Year	Club (League)	Class	AVG	G	AB	R	H	2B	3B	HR	RBI	BB	SO	SB	SLG	OBP
1997	Diamondbacks (AZL)	R	.305	54	213	52	65	17	4	0	21	26	40	3	.423	.384
	Lethbridge (Pio)	R	.167	2	6	2	1	0	0	0	1	1	0	0	.167	.286
1998	South Bend (Mid)	A	.255	110	364	44	93	14	2	9	47	67	81	12	.379	.371

1999	High Desert (Cal)	A	.273	130	488	106	133	29	6	22	93	86	122	40	.492	.378
2000	Portland (EL)	AA	.276	74	221	39	61	17	3	6	42	44	64	8	.462	.392
	Brevard County (FSL)	A	.194	31	103	17	20	4	0	1	9	28	34	11	.262	.376
2001	Portland (EL)	AA	.240	136	467	75	112	14	9	17	53	83	155	26	.418	.357
2002	Calgary (PCL)	AAA	.250	129	428	68	107	24	5	21	60	51	112	31	.477	.329
	Florida (NL)	MAJ	.118	19	17	2	2	0	0	0	1	0	5	0	.118	.118
MAJOR LEAGUE TOTALS			.118	19	17	2	2	0	0	0	1	0	5	0	.118	.118
MINOR LEAGUE TOTALS			.259	666	2290	403	592	119	29	76	326	386	608	131	.435	.365

17. Eric Reed, of

Born: Dec. 2, 1980. **Ht.:** 5-11. **Wt.:** 170. **Bats:** L. **Throws:** L. **School:** Texas A&M University. **Career Transactions:** Selected by Marlins in ninth round of 2002 draft; signed June 6, 2002.

Reed plummeted in the 2002 draft after a poor junior season, but the Marlins put more stock in what he did in the Cape Cod League, where he won the batting title with a .365 average the summer before. Considered perhaps the strongest player on the Texas A&M team, Reed can bench press upwards of 270 pounds despite a wiry frame. Marlins assistant general manager Jim Fleming has a theory that stronger hitters may struggle with metal bats, and Reed, who has 3 percent body fat, apparently qualifies. Signed for $85,000 as a ninth-round pick, Reed is close to an 80 runner on the 20-80 scouting scale. He has blazing speed to first and in the outfield. He's an excellent bunter, even with two strikes, but needs to refine his basestealing skills, which the Marlins expect he'll be able to do. Some consider him a poor man's Ichiro Suzuki. Reed can change a game with his speed, slapping balls the other way and beating out the occasional routine three-hopper to shortstop. Developing more patience would allow him to draw more walks, a must for a player who can create such havoc on the bases. Reed figures to have some gap power as he increases his understanding at the plate, though he had just seven extra-base hits in 71 pro games and just 14 extra-base hits (one homer) in 133 college contests. In the field, he's already capable of jaw-dropping plays. He has an above-average arm and tremendous range. He may start 2003 back in low Class A, where he hit .360 in a short stint at the end of last season.

Year	Club (League)	Class	AVG	G	AB	R	H	2B	3B	HR	RBI	BB	SO	SB	SLG	OBP
2002	Jamestown (NY-P)	A	.308	60	250	35	77	5	1	0	17	17	30	19	.336	.348
	Kane County (Mid)	A	.360	12	50	11	18	1	0	0	2	3	11	7	.380	.396
MINOR LEAGUE TOTALS			.317	72	300	46	95	6	1	0	19	20	41	26	.343	.356

18. Victor Prieto, rhp

Born: April 24, 1983. **Ht.:** 6-2. **Wt.:** 170. **Bats:** R. **Throws:** R. **Career Transactions:** Signed out of Venezuela by Marlins, July 2, 1999.

One of many intriguing prospects signed out of Venezuela by former Marlins scout Miguel Garcia, Prieto took a huge leap forward in his first U.S. season. After posting two strong years in the Rookie-level Venezuelan Summer League, Prieto showed a classic delivery and quick arm action last year in the Rookie-level Gulf Coast League. He was dominant after he got over a bout with shoulder soreness. The ball jumps out of his hand and he touches 95 mph with good movement. He needs to choose between a hard curveball and a slider, both of which have severe tilt, and he has the makings of an outstanding changeup. He has a tendency to overthrow at times. With Prieto's frame, thin almost to the point of being frail, his health must be monitored carefully. He was shut down a couple of times with a tired arm and needs to add more strength. He likely will start 2003 in extended spring training, followed by his first taste of short-season Jamestown. While Prieto is still raw, his ceiling is high.

Year	Club (League)	Class	W	L	ERA	G	GS	CG	SV	IP	H	R	ER	HR	BB	SO	AVG
2000	Universidad (VSL)	R	5	3	3.36	14	10	0	0	59	67	30	22	1	32	65	.293
2001	Ciudad Alianza (VSL)	R	2	2	3.19	13	5	0	0	31	19	14	11	0	21	34	—
2002	Marlins (GCL)	R	4	2	3.16	8	7	1	0	31	14	17	11	0	19	21	.135
MINOR LEAGUE TOTALS			11	7	3.26	35	22	1	0	121	100	61	44	1	72	120	—

19. Robert Andino, ss

Born: April 25, 1984. **Ht.:** 6-0. **Wt.:** 170. **Bats:** R. **Throws:** R. **School:** Southridge HS, Miami. **Career Transactions:** Selected by Marlins in second round of 2002 draft; signed Aug. 4, 2002.

Only B.J. Upton rated higher among shortstops on the Marlins' 2002 draft board, so they were pleased to grab Andino 50 picks after Upton went second overall. After a two-month holdout, he signed for $750,000, nearly $4 million less than Upton got from the Devil Rays. At this point, Andino's glove is far ahead of his bat, but there's reason to believe the gap will narrow once he adds strength and experience. Taking groundballs alongside the rehabbing Alex Gonzalez during instructional league, Andino wowed Florida's brass with his similarly smooth actions and soft hands. He can make the routine plays as well as the tough ones, has a plus arm and excellent defensive instincts. Some compare him to a young Pokey Reese. At the plate, Andino has good bat speed but jumps at too many pitches and gets out of kilter with his leg kick. He needs to cut down on his swing, which would help him get out of the box faster and add a few leg hits. His speed is just average. The son of a former professional player in Puerto Rico, Andino must improve his overall concentration and discipline because he tends to drift.

Year	Club (League)	Class	AVG	G	AB	R	H	2B	3B	HR	RBI	BB	SO	SB	SLG	OBP
2002	Marlins (GCL)	R	.259	9	27	2	7	0	0	0	2	5	6	3	.259	.364
	Jamestown (NY-P)	A	.167	9	36	2	6	1	1	0	3	1	9	1	.250	.189
MINOR LEAGUE TOTALS			.206	18	63	4	13	1	1	0	5	6	15	4	.254	.271

20. Scott Olsen, lhp

Born: Jan. 12, 1984. **Ht.:** 6-4. **Wt.:** 170. **Bats:** L. **Throws:** L. **School:** Crystal Lake (Ill.) South HS. **Career Transactions:** Selected by Marlins in 6th round of 2002 draft; signed June 9, 2002.

Olsen flew into the system under the radar, lasting until the sixth round when the Marlins nabbed him on the recommendation of Scot Engler, their scout of the year. Olsen, who signed for $146,000, is a tall, projectable lefty with a loose arm and an easy delivery. He has a skinny frame that could stand to add another 15-20 pounds. He had some mechanical problems in high school, especially throwing across his body and falling off toward third base, but minor league pitching coach Jeff Schwarz fixed him in a hurry. Olsen wowed the Marlins during instructional league. He tops out at 91 mph with good sink but projects to add velocity. His slider is decent and his changeup already has gone from below average to average. In time he could have three plus pitches. Olsen still must improve his emotional maturity, overall command and his breaking ball, but there's a lot to like about him.

Year	Club (League)	Class	W	L	ERA	G	GS	CG	SV	IP	H	R	ER	HR	BB	SO	AVG
2002	Marlins (GCL)	R	2	3	2.96	13	11	0	0	52	39	18	17	0	17	50	.204
MINOR LEAGUE TOTALS			2	3	2.96	13	11	0	0	52	39	18	17	0	17	50	.204

21. Josh Willingham, 1b/3b/of/c

Born: Feb. 17, 1979. **Ht.:** 6-1. **Wt.:** 200. **Bats:** R. **Throws:** R. **School:** University of North Alabama. **Career Transactions:** Selected by Marlins in 17th round of 2000 draft; signed June 8, 2000.

Blocked at third base by Miguel Cabrera and at first by Jason Stokes and Adrian Gonzalez, Willingham agreed to try catching at instructional league. In just three weeks, he improved by leaps and bounds, showing enough potential behind the plate to jump-start his career possibilities. He figures to return to high Class A as Jupiter's starting catcher this year, but early signs point to a strong arm and an aptitude for blocking balls. A shortstop at the University of North Alabama, he caught in high school and even tried left field at Jupiter. Willingham is selective at the plate, with good power to all fields and fine instincts on the bases and everywhere else. He has stolen successfully 81 percent of the time as a pro despite average speed at best. He missed six weeks last year with a fractured cheekbone after getting beaned in the face, but he showed no signs of fear upon his return. A classic tough guy, he isn't arrogant or cocky but carries himself confidently. Some have compared him to Mike Kinkade, another good-hitting third baseman in the minors who moved behind the plate to speed his path to the majors. Willingham's ceiling appears to be higher.

Year	Club (League)	Class	AVG	G	AB	R	H	2B	3B	HR	RBI	BB	SO	SB	SLG	OBP
2000	Utica (NY-P)	A	.263	65	205	37	54	16	0	6	29	39	55	9	.429	.400
2001	Kane County (Mid)	A	.259	97	320	57	83	20	2	7	36	53	85	24	.400	.382
2002	Jupiter (FSL)	A	.274	107	376	72	103	21	4	17	69	63	88	18	.487	.394
MINOR LEAGUE TOTALS			.266	269	901	166	240	57	6	30	134	155	228	51	.443	.391

22. Ryan Jorgensen, c

Born: May 4, 1979. **Ht.:** 6-2. **Wt.:** 200. **Bats:** R. **Throws:** R. **School:** Louisiana State University. **Career Transactions:** Selected by Cubs in seventh round of 2000 draft; signed June 22, 2000 . . . Traded by Cubs with RHP Julian Tavarez, RHP Jose Cueto and LHP Dontrelle Willis to Marlins for RHP Antonio Alfonseca and RHP Matt Clement, March 27, 2002.

Recognizing a dearth of young catchers in the organization, the new Marlins regime was pleased when the Cubs agreed to include Jorgensen in a late-spring deal for four minor leaguers, including Dontrelle Willis. Bothered by a sprained ankle early in the year, Jorgensen still hit much better than expected at the outset. His batting average came back to earth, but the former Louisiana State backup (to Diamondbacks prospect Brad Cresse) still showed enough behind the plate to earn a midseason promotion to Double-A. An excellent catch-and-throw guy, Jorgensen blocks balls, takes pride in his game-calling and works well with pitchers. He has added strength and shown signs of developing some gap power, though he still tends to pull off balls and get a little long with his swing. If he can hit .250 with 10 homers annually in the majors, that might be enough to warrant a starting job. His receiving skills are that good. This year he'll return to Double-A, where he has hit just .178 the past two seasons in 253 at-bats.

Year	Club (League)	Class	AVG	G	AB	R	H	2B	3B	HR	RBI	BB	SO	SB	SLG	OBP
2000	Eugene (NWL)	A	.300	41	130	17	39	10	2	1	23	17	27	2	.431	.380
2001	Daytona (FSL)	A	.282	54	188	24	53	12	1	8	29	23	39	1	.484	.366
	West Tenn (SL)	AA	.119	32	109	8	13	4	0	2	7	11	38	0	.211	.195
2002	Jupiter (FSL)	A	.260	60	223	26	58	16	0	3	35	24	38	4	.372	.335
	Portland (EL)	AA	.222	41	144	15	32	4	0	2	14	12	33	3	.292	.287
MINOR LEAGUE TOTALS			.246	228	794	90	195	46	3	16	108	87	175	10	.372	.322

23. Yorman Bazardo, rhp

Born: July 11, 1984. **Ht.:** 6-2. **Wt.:** 170. **Bats:** R. **Throws:** R. **Career Transactions:** Signed out of Venezuela by Marlins, July 19, 2000.

Signed for $85,000 out of Venezuela by former Marlins scout Miguel Garcia, Bazardo has shown an electrifying arm that ranks among the best in the system. He has touched 96 mph with an improving power curve, though he still tries to overthrow and sees his stuff flatten out when he does. His delivery can get out of whack at times as well, but that should be remedied with experience. Tall and long-limbed, Bazardo remains raw. After he was used as a starter in the Venezuelan Summer League, the new Marlins regime stuck him in the bullpen at Jamestown. Bazardo proved dominant at times in that role, but at other also was surprisingly hittable considering his stuff and enviable pitcher's frame. He likely will start this year in low Class A, where he figures to remain in the bullpen. The Marlins found him to be more comfortable and effective in a two-inning relief role. Quiet and still learning to speak English, Bazardo is a fairly happy-go-lucky and needs to get more aggressive. His makeup is considered a plus.

Year	Club (League)	Class	W	L	ERA	G	GS	CG	SV	IP	H	R	ER	HR	BB	SO	AVG
2001	Ciudad Alianza (VSL)	R	7	2	2.43	12	12	1	0	70	59	26	19	0	18	62	—
2002	Jamestown (NY-P)	A	5	0	2.72	25	0	0	6	36	39	11	11	0	6	26	.275
MINOR LEAGUE TOTALS			12	2	2.53	37	12	1	6	107	98	37	30	0	24	88	.275

24. Jesus Medrano, 2b

Born: Sept. 11, ·1978. **Ht.:** 6-0. **Wt.:** 180. **Bats:** R. **Throws:** R. **School:** Bishop Amat HS, La Puente, Calif. **Career Transactions:** Selected by Marlins in 11th round of 1997 draft; signed June 19, 1997.

After two years in high Class A, Medrano made a solid transition to Double-A and held his own. He received a scare in August, when he was struck in the temple by an errant throw during pregame work. He missed a couple of weeks while recovering from a concussion, then was able to report to the Arizona Fall League as planned. Few players in the system utilize their speed better than Medrano. He's a good bunter with a line-drive stroke and a willingness to move runners. He shows a solid grasp of the strike zone and knows how to work counts and draw walks, but he also stays aggressive early in the count. If he sees something he likes, he'll jump on it. For his career Medrano has been successful on 80 percent of his steal attempts. He exudes confidence on the basepaths but still gets jammed too much at the plate, where pitchers sometimes take advantage of his weak frame. After seeing 21 games at shortstop in 2001, he played exclusively at second last year. He made just 14 errors, his career-low for a full-season league. Medrano has earned a shot at Triple-A in 2003.

Year	Club (League)	Class	AVG	G	AB	R	H	2B	3B	HR	RBI	BB	SO	SB	SLG	OBP
1997	Marlins (GCL)	R	.279	40	111	20	31	4	0	0	16	19	18	16	.315	.391
1998	Marlins (GCL)	R	.286	48	175	42	50	11	1	2	15	21	30	26	.394	.367
1999	Kane County (Mid)	A	.274	118	445	64	122	26	5	5	46	36	92	42	.389	.331
2000	Brevard County (FSL)	A	.219	117	466	56	102	18	3	3	46	48	98	32	.290	.293
2001	Brevard County (FSL)	A	.251	124	454	93	114	15	2	1	32	51	81	61	.300	.331
2002	Portland (EL)	AA	.297	116	414	77	123	27	6	3	32	79	82	39	.413	.411
MINOR LEAGUE TOTALS			.262	563	2065	352	542	101	17	14	187	254	401	216	.348	.346

25. Juan Nova, rhp

Born: March 11, 1984. **Ht.:** 6-2. **Wt.:** 170. **Bats:** R. **Throws:** R. **Career Transactions:** Signed out of Dominican Republic by Marlins, Aug. 8, 2000.

In terms of pure arm strength, Nova is among the more intriguing Marlins prospects. He has topped out at 95 mph and pitches at 92-93 with a fastball that can be overpowering at times. His secondary pitches need work, however. His slider remains too loose and slurvy to be an effective weapon. His changeup is a long way away. He speaks virtually no English, so his understanding of the mental side of his craft has developed slowly. He remains raw in terms of fielding and holding runners, but when it comes time to fire toward home, he's impressive. Nova has a strong, solid body and showed a better feel for pitching inside to righthanders last year. He has an aggressive personality and seemed to enjoy pitching in short relief. Considering that, the Marlins might leave him in the bullpen, stretching him out to two or three innings at a time as he works to round out his repertoire.

Year	Club (League)	Class	W	L	ERA	G	GS	CG	SV	IP	H	R	ER	HR	BB	SO	AVG
2001	Marlins (DSL)	R	4	7	4.50	15	14	0	0	74	87	56	37	2	18	35	.279
2002	Marlins (GCL)	R	1	2	1.11	22	0	0	7	32	26	8	4	1	6	23	.217
MINOR LEAGUE TOTALS			5	9	3.47	37	14	0	7	106	113	64	41	3	24	58	.262

26. Josh Johnson, rhp

Born: Jan. 31, 1984. **Ht.:** 6-7. **Wt.:** 220. **Bats:** L. **Throws:** R. **School:** Jenks HS, Tulsa. **Career Transactions:** Selected by Marlins in fourth round of 2002 draft; signed June 8, 2002.

Once considered as a possible late first-round pick for 2002, Johnson had a disappointing high school senior season and slid to Florida in the fourth round. Troubled by shoulder tendinitis after signing for $300,000, Johnson was shut down and returned fully healthy after a rehab period. Despite his impressive size, he's not a power pitcher. He commands his 88-92 mph fastball, which has good movement in both the two- and four-seam variety. Considering his frame, he projects to add velocity. Johnson also has shown a good feel for a hard curveball. His changeup shows signs of becoming a plus pitch as well. A pulled hip flexor limited his showing during instructional league but he still impressed the Marlins. Johnson tends to be around the plate almost too much, as he allows more hits than he should. Some in the organization also say he needs to become less passive, though his make-up and intelligence are considered pluses.

Year	Club (League)	Class	W	L	ERA	G	GS	CG	SV	IP	H	R	ER	HR	BB	SO	AVG
2002	Marlins (GCL)	R	2	0	0.60	4	3	0	0	15	8	3	1	0	3	11	.154
MINOR LEAGUE TOTALS			2	0	0.60	4	3	0	0	15	8	3	1	0	3	11	.154

27. Garrett Berger, rhp

Born: May 11, 1983. **Ht.:** 6-2. **Wt.:** 260. **Bats:** R. **Throws:** R. **School:** Carmel (Ind.) HS. **Career Transactions:** Selected by Marlins in second round of 2001 draft; signed Aug. 12, 2001 . . . On disabled list, June 18-Sept. 30, 2002.

Nicknamed "Chunk" after one of the characters from "The Goonies," Berger is well on his way back from Tommy John surgery. Signed for $795,000 as the Marlins' top pick (second round) in 2001, he injured his elbow during his first instructional league. Berger worked hard to return to the mound by instructional league last fall. He was able to get in games and threw a number of bullpens, far ahead of schedule. Dedicated and intelligent, Berger is a disciple of former Rangers pitching coach Tom House. Berger loves to talk mechanics and knows far more about pitching than most players his age. His velocity has yet to return to its mid-90s peak, as he was topping out at 91 mph last fall. His slider is solid, but the Marlins would like to see him junk his forkball in favor of a straight change. Berger, a barrel-chested sort who wears a size 52 coat, has worked to smooth out a stiff delivery. He needs to incorporate his legs more and stop relying so much on his upper body. He comes from an athletic family as his two older sisters are scholarship softball players at the University of Florida.

Year	Club (League)	Class	W	L	ERA	G	GS	CG	SV	IP	H	R	ER	HR	BB	SO	AVG
2002		Did Not Play—Injured															

28. Wes Anderson, rhp

Born: Sept. 10, 1979. **Ht.:** 6-4. **Wt.:** 170. **Bats:** R. **Throws:** R. **School:** Pine Bluff (Ark.) HS. **Career Transactions:** Selected by Marlins in 14th round of 1997 draft; signed Aug. 18, 1997.

Once considered among the jewels of the Marlins system, Anderson has been on the slow road back from shoulder surgery in September 2001. Anderson had arthroscopic surgery to repair an 85 percent tear in his labrum and minor fraying in his rotator cuff. He made it back for four starts in the Gulf Coast League and saw limited action in instructional league last year. He still has his fluid delivery, once compared to that of John Smoltz, but his fastball topped out at 91 mph. That's still a few ticks down from the 94 mph he showed before surgery. Though given complete medical clearance, he threw relatively few sliders last year as he remained tentative on the mound. Anderson's slider was a plus pitch in the past, but he got by with his fastball and a solid changeup. Earnest and eager, he tends to put too much pressure on himself. If he continues to progress, he could start the year in high Class A and make it to Double-A at some point.

Year	Club (League)	Class	W	L	ERA	G	GS	CG	SV	IP	H	R	ER	HR	BB	SO	AVG
1998	Marlins (GCL)	R	5	2	1.39	11	11	1	0	65	44	25	10	0	18	66	.196
1999	Kane County (Mid)	A	9	5	3.21	23	23	2	0	137	111	55	49	8	51	134	.222
2000	Brevard County (FSL)	A	6	9	3.42	22	21	0	0	116	108	55	44	5	66	91	.245
2001	Brevard County (FSL)	A	1	6	5.63	8	8	0	0	32	48	26	20	3	21	17	.353
	Marlins (GCL)	R	0	1	27.00	1	1	0	0	0	3	2	1	1	1	0	.600
2002	Marlins (GCL)	R	0	1	3.00	4	4	0	0	15	15	6	5	0	3	7	.268
MINOR LEAGUE TOTALS			21	24	3.18	69	68	3	0	365	329	169	129	17	160	315	.241

29. Allen Baxter, rhp

Born: July 6, 1983. **Ht.:** 6-4. **Wt.:** 210. **Bats:** R. **Throws:** R. **School:** Varina HS, Sandston, Va. **Career Transactions:** Selected by Marlins in third round of 2001 draft; signed June 14, 2001.

Baxter roared into prospect status a year ago, debuting at No. 5 in the organization after a dazzling first season of pro ball. Four starts into 2002, however, reality struck. He threw a pitch for Kane County and felt a strange sensation in his elbow. He threw a couple of more pitches and still felt odd, walking off the mound for what would be the last time all year. Baxter had Tommy John surgery on his elbow and is shooting for a full return by instructional league 2003. Before the injury, he pitched at 90-91 mph and hit 95 on several occasions. Club officials raved about the Kevin Brown-style movement on both his two- and four-seam fastballs. Baxter's curveball already was a plus pitch, and his changeup was advanced. Baxter has a prototypical pitcher's frame that has drawn comparisons to Curt Schilling and Kerry Wood. He signed quickly for $450,000, in part because he had no major college options. He still needs to add maturity, and some in the organization would like to see him display more outward desire.

Year	Club (League)	Class	W	L	ERA	G	GS	CG	SV	IP	H	R	ER	HR	BB	SO	AVG
2001	Marlins (GCL)	R	2	3	2.38	9	7	0	0	34	25	13	9	0	8	40	.207
	Utica (NY-P)	A	0	0	3.60	1	1	0	0	5	3	2	2	0	3	5	.176
2002	Kane County (Mid)	A	0	2	3.06	4	4	0	0	18	19	9	6	0	8	15	.288
MINOR LEAGUE TOTALS			2	5	2.70	14	12	0	0	57	47	24	17	0	19	60	.230

30. Franklyn Gracesqui, lhp

Born: Aug. 20, 1979. **Ht.:** 6-5. **Wt.:** 210. **Bats:** B. **Throws:** L. **School:** George Washington HS, New York. **Career Transactions:** Selected by Blue Jays in 21st round of 1998 draft; signed June 7, 1998 . . . Selected by Marlins from Blue Jays in minor league Rule 5 draft, Dec. 16, 2002.

With the January trade that sent Rob Henkel and Nate Robertson to the Tigers for starter Mark Redman, the Marlins system lost two of its most intriguing lefties. They were able to deal from a position of depth, to some extent, thanks to a couple of pickups in the Triple-A phase of December's Rule 5 draft: Gracesqui and Eric Reynolds. Just a year before, Gracesqui had earned a spot on Toronto's 40-man roster. His large frame alone makes him imposing and intriguing, as does his fastball, which has reached 93-94 mph. A Dominican Republic native who attended the same New York high school as countryman Manny Ramirez, Gracesqui also has a slider that's tough to pick up out of his three-quarters delivery. Gracesqui, who projects as a useful situational reliever, still must refine his command but already has shown the ability to dominate lefthanders at times. For his career, he has averaged better than a strikeout per inning.

Year	Club (League)	Class	W	L	ERA	G	GS	CG	SV	IP	H	R	ER	HR	BB	SO	AVG
1998	St. Catharines (NY-P)	A	1	0	6.61	11	0	0	0	16	16	12	12	2	12	19	.242
1999	St. Catharines (NY-P)	A	2	3	5.05	15	10	0	1	46	44	30	26	4	41	45	.253
2000	Medicine Hat (Pio)	R	0	1	2.63	8	4	0	0	24	15	11	7	1	21	20	.185
	Hagerstown (SAL)	A	0	1	4.91	3	1	0	0	7	4	4	4	1	9	6	.174
2001	Charleston, WV (SAL)	A	2	8	3.17	35	2	0	1	65	60	40	23	1	34	66	.245
	Dunedin (FSL)	A	1	0	0.00	4	0	0	0	6	2	0	0	0	8	6	.125
2002	Tennessee (SL)	AA	4	2	4.64	41	0	0	1	43	40	26	22	3	34	48	.258
	Dunedin (FSL)	A	2	1	2.49	10	0	0	1	22	15	8	6	1	11	25	.192
MINOR LEAGUE TOTALS			12	16	3.92	127	17	0	4	229	196	131	100	13	170	235	.234

HOUSTON
ASTROS

TOP 30 PROSPECTS

1. John Buck, c
2. Jason Lane, of
3. Brad Lidge, rhp
4. Jimmy Barrett, rhp
5. Chris Burke, 2b/ss
6. Tommy Whiteman, ss
7. Rodrigo Rosario, rhp
8. Hector Gimenez, c
9. Chad Qualls, rhp
10. Santiago Ramirez, rhp
11. Derick Grigsby, rhp
12. Henri Stanley, of
13. Anthony Pluta, rhp
14. Gavin Wright, of
15. Jeriome Robertson, lhp
16. Manny Santillan, rhp
17. Miguel Saladin, rhp
18. Victor Hall, of
19. Greg Miller, lhp
20. Fernando Nieve, rhp
21. Mitch Talbot, rhp
22. Rory Shortell, rhp
23. Ramon German, 3b
24. Ruddy Lugo, rhp
25. Adam Everett, ss
26. D.J. Houlton, rhp
27. Charlton Jimerson, of
28. Matt Albers, rhp
29. Brooks Conrad, 2b
30. Jason Alfaro, 3b

By Jim Callis

After finishing with the best record in the National League and winning Baseball America's Organization of the Year award in 2001, the Astros slipped last year. Their performance at the major and minor league levels was disappointing.

A strong farm system was supposed to feed a big league club expected to contend for its fifth NL Central title in six years. Neither happened, as Houston underachieved and finished 13 games behind the Cardinals. Shortstop Adam Everett and third baseman Morgan Ensberg broke camp as starters but quickly played their way out of those jobs. Lefthander Carlos Hernandez won five games in the first two months but just two afterward as he battled shoulder problems that persisted into the offseason. Jason Lane and Kirk Saarloos showed flashes, and Brandon Puffer and Ricky Stone had their moments. But Houston needed more and didn't get it.

The story was the same in the minors, as the Astros didn't match their previous standards. Their six affiliates combined to win at a .535 clip, the fifth-best record in baseball. But after capturing seven championships over the previous four years, Houston farm clubs came up empty in 2002.

Houston also stumbled in the draft. With a strike possible, Astros owner Drayton McLane declared a midsummer embargo on signing picks. The club eventually signed its top three selections but didn't get to see them in game action, and fifth-rounder Pat Misch returned to Western Michigan.

Houston has moved to upgrade the quality of its minor league affiliates in recent years, and its arrangement with Double-A Round Rock has been a huge success on and off the field. In order to play in another top facility, Lexington's Applebee's Park, the Astros fielded two low Class A teams for two years, at the expense of having a high Class A club. The set-up wasn't too troublesome in 2001, but it created problems last year. Some of Houston's best prospects struggled because they had to skip a level and go from low Class A to Double-A. The situation has been rectified for 2003, as the Astros established a new agreement with high Class A Salem.

Houston's stock hasn't tumbled like Enron's, which relinquished its ballpark naming rights in 2002. But an organization that ranked among the best in both the majors and minors a year earlier has fallen back toward the middle of the pack.

OrganizationOverview

General Manager: Gerry Hunsicker. Farm Director: Tim Purpura. Scouting Director: David Lakey.

2002 PERFORMANCE

Class	Farm Team	League	W	L	Pct.	Finish*	Manager
Majors	Houston	National	84	78	.519	6th (16)	Jimy Williams
Triple-A	New Orleans Zephyrs	Pacific Coast	75	69	.521	t-5th(16)	Chris Maloney
Double-A	Round Rock Express	Texas	75	65	.536	4th (8)	Jackie Moore
Low A	†Michigan Battle Cats	Midwest	79	61	.564	4th (14)	John Massarelli
Low A	Lexington Legends	South Atlantic	81	59	.579	2nd (16)	J.J. Cannon
Short-season	Tri-City Valley Cats	New York-Penn	27	48	.360	13th (14)	Ivan DeJesus
Rookie	Martinsville Astros	Appalachian	41	26	.612	3rd (10)	Jorge Orta
OVERALL MINOR LEAGUE RECORD			378	328	.535	5th (30)	

*Finish in overall standings (No. of teams in league).   †High Class A affiliate will be in Salem (Carolina) in 2003.

ORGANIZATION LEADERS

BATTING
*Minimum 250 At-Bats
*AVG	Royce Huffman, Round Rock	.322
R	Brooks Conrad, Michigan	94
	Mike Rodriguez, Michigan	94
H	Royce Huffman, Round Rock	168
TB	Henri Stanley, Round Rock	247
2B	Five tied at	36
3B	Brooks Conrad, Michigan	14
HR	Three tied at	16
RBI	Brooks Conrad, Michigan	94
	Todd Self, Michigan	94
BB	Henri Stanley, Round Rock	72
SO	Charlton Jimerson, Lexington	168
SB	Eric Bruntlett, New Orleans/Round Rock	36

PITCHING
#Minimum 75 Innings
W	Mike Burns, Michigan	14
	D.J. Houlton, Michigan	14
L	Anthony Pluta, Michigan	13
	Chad Qualls, Round Rock	13
#ERA	Kirk Saarloos, New Orleans/Round Rock	1.54
G	Tom Shearn, New Orleans	57
CG	Mike Burns, Michigan	3
SV	Miguel Saladin, New Orleans/Round Rock	24
IP	Mike Burns, Michigan	181
BB	Anthony Pluta, Michigan	83
SO	Chad Qualls, Round Rock	142

BEST TOOLS

Best Hitter for Average	Jason Lane
Best Power Hitter	Jason Lane
Fastest Baserunner	Charlton Jimerson
Best Athlete	Charlton Jimerson
Best Fastball	Anthony Pluta
Best Curveball	Eny Cabreja
Best Slider	Brad Lidge
Best Changeup	Brandon Roberson
Best Control	Mike Burns
Best Defensive Catcher	John Buck
Best Defensive Infielder	Adam Everett
Best Infield Arm	Jason Alfaro
Best Defensive Outfielder	Charlton Jimerson
Best Outfield Arm	Gavin Wright

PROJECTED 2006 LINEUP

Catcher	John Buck
First Base	Jeff Bagwell
Second Base	Chris Burke
Third Base	Jeff Kent
Shortstop	Tommy Whiteman
Left Field	Lance Berkman
Center Field	Jason Lane
Right Field	Richard Hidalgo

Brooks Conrad   **Anthony Pluta**

No. 1 Starter	Roy Oswalt
No. 2 Starter	Wade Miller
No. 3 Starter	Carlos Hernandez
No. 4 Starter	Tim Redding
No. 5 Starter	Jimmy Barrett
Closer	Billy Wagner

TOP PROSPECTS OF THE DECADE

1993	Todd Jones, rhp
1994	Phil Nevin, 3b
1995	Brian Hunter, of
1996	Billy Wagner, lhp
1997	Richard Hidalgo, of
1998	Richard Hidalgo, of
1999	Lance Berkman, of
2000	Wilfredo Rodriguez, lhp
2001	Roy Oswalt, rhp
2002	Carlos Hernandez, lhp

TOP DRAFT PICKS OF THE DECADE

1993	Billy Wagner, lhp
1994	Ramon Castro, c
1995	Tony McKnight, rhp
1996	Mark Johnson, rhp
1997	Lance Berkman, 1b
1998	Brad Lidge, rhp
1999	Mike Rosamond, of
2000	Robert Stiehl, rhp
2001	Chris Burke, ss
2002	Derick Grigsby, rhp

ALL-TIME LARGEST BONUSES

Chris Burke, 2001	$2,125,000
Robert Stiehl, 2000	$1,250,000
Derick Grigsby, 2002	$1,125,000
Brad Lidge, 1998	$1,070,000
Lance Berkman, 1997	$1,000,000

MinorLeague**Depth**Chart

HOUSTON ASTROS

RANK 23

The Astros were hitting on all cylinders in 2001 when they claimed Baseball America's Organization of the Year award. Nothing worked out quite as well in 2002, both at the major and minor league levels, causing Houston's talent ranking to slide 20 spots. Not having an affiliate at the high Class A level last year was a leading cause of their problems, as several prospects didn't handle a two-level jump well. John Buck, Jason Lane, Chris Burke, Brad Lidge, Anthony Pluta and Morgan Ensberg all struggled more than expected. Shoulder injuries to lefties Carlos Hernandez (2002) and Wilfredo Rodriguez (2000), both former No. 1 prospects in the organization, are a cause for concern.

Note: Depth charts prepared by Josh Boyd. Numbers in parentheses indicate prospect rankings.

LF
Jason Lane (2)
Henri Stanley (12)
Mike Rodriguez
Hamilton Sarabia
Fehlandt Lentini

CF
Gavin Wright (14)
Victor Hall (18)
Charlton Jimerson (27)

RF
Mike Hill
Kyle Logan
Mike Rosamond

3B
Ramon German (23)
Jason Alfaro (30)

SS
Tommy Whiteman (6)
Adam Everett (25)
Eric Bruntlett
Osvaldo Fernando

2B
Chris Burke (5)
Brooks Conrad (29)
Dave Matranga
Jon Helquist

1B
Todd Self
Royce Huffman
Tony Acevedo

C
John Buck (1)
Hector Gimenez (8)

RHP
Starters
Jimmy Barrett (4)
Rodrigo Rosario (7)
Chad Qualls (9)
Derick Grigsby (11)
Anthony Pluta (13)
Manny Santillan (16)
Fernando Nieve (20)
Mitch Talbot (21)
Rory Shortell (22)
D.J. Houlton (26)
Matt Albers (28)
Mike Burns
Cory Doyne
Joey DeLeon
Nick Roberts
Robert Stiehl
Chance Douglass

Relievers
Brad Lidge (3)
Santiago Ramirez (10)
Miguel Saladin (17)
Ruddy Lugo (24)
James Lira
Juan Campos
J.P. Duran
Jared Gothreaux
Brandon Roberson
Monte Mansfield
Andres Astacio

LHP
Starters
Jeriome Robertson (15)
Greg Miller (19)
Eny Cabrera
Julio Salazar

Relievers
Mike Gallo
Mark McLemore

DraftAnalysis

2002 Draft

Best Pro Debut: RHP Daniel Freeman (17) went 9-1, 2.96 to lead the Rookie-level Appalachian League in wins. His curveball is his best pitch, and he does a nice job of spotting his 87-88 mph sinker.

Best Athlete: 3B/OF Nick Covarrubias (13) doesn't have a standout tool, but he doesn't have a below-average one either. SS Andy Topham (9) and OF Dustin Hawkins (37) are also good athletes.

Best Pure Hitter: The Astros weren't able to sign 1B/OF Scott Robinson (7), but they control his rights because he went to Palomar (Calif.) JC rather than San Diego State. Covarrubias and 3B Pat Peavey (33) are the best hitters Houston signed.

Best Raw Power: OF Jason Reuss (11) has plus-plus power to all fields but struck out 41 times in his first 93 pro at-bats.

Fastest Runner: Hawkins gets from the left side to first base in 4.1 seconds.

Best Defensive Player: Topham or C Randy McGarvey (26).

Best Fastball: RHP Derick Grigsby (1), the first junior college player drafted, is all power. He pitches at 93-94 mph and reaches 96 with his fastball, and his slider peaks at 86 mph. The Astros focused on hard throwers. RHPs Mitch Talbot (2) and J.P. Duran (6) can touch 95 and RHPs Rory Shortell (3) and Chance Douglass (12) are right behind.

Best Breaking Ball: Duran's curveball is slightly nastier than the sliders of Grigsby and RHP Jared Gothreaux (16).

Most Intriguing Background: Unsigned OF Shawn Williams' (35) father Jimy man-

ages the Astros. Unsigned 1B Freddie Thon's (43) father Frankie scouted Puerto Rico for the club, while his uncle Dickie was an all-star shortstop for Houston. Reuss' father Jerry won 220 games in the majors, while Robin-son's dad Bruce was a big league catcher. Peavey's brother Bill signed with the Angels as an 11th-round pick. Hazel Hotch-kiss Wightman, their great-grandmother, was a U.S. tennis champion.

Freeman

Closest To The Majors: Shortell reminds the Astros of Shane Reynolds. He's advanced, with two legitimate pitches (fastball, curveball), and just needs fine-tuning.

Best Late-Round Pick: Douglass fell in the draft because he came down with shoulder tendinitis and was committed to Rice. Gothreaux, a 6-footer with a plus fastball and slider, is reminiscent of Jeff Brantley. The Astros have had success with short righties.

The One Who Got Away: RHP Brad Chedister (10) has a strong 6-foot-4, 210-pound build and hit 97 mph during a workout. He ended up at Louisiana Tech.

Assessment: Because of the team's temporary embargo on signing draft picks, the top three choices–Grigsby, Talbot and Shortell–have yet to make their pro debuts. Houston, which has done a fine job of developing arms, took pitchers with its first six picks.

2001 Draft

RHP Kirk Saarloos (3) reached the majors soon after Mark Prior but doesn't have the same ceiling. 2B/SS Chris Burke (1) figured to move fast but hit the wall in Double-A.   **Grade: C**

2000 Draft

This draft looked better a year ago, before RHP Robert Stiehl (1) missed a full season following rotator-cuff surgery and RHPs Chad Qualls (2) and Anthony Pluta (3) and SS Tommy Whiteman (6) all struggled.   **Grade: C+**

1999 Draft

OF Jason Lane (6) has made up for the disappointment of OF Mike Rosamond (1) and just needs a spot in the Houston lineup. RHP Jimmy Barrett (3) may wind up becoming the best starting pitcher in the system.   **Grade: B**

1998 Draft

RHP Brad Lidge (1) finally stayed healthy and reached the majors in 2002, while C John Buck (7) is the Astros' top prospect. 3B Morgan Ensberg (9) failed a trial as their starting third baseman, but draft-and-follow Gavin Wright (34) eventually may plug their hole in center field. RHP Mike Nannini (1) hit the wall in Double-A and was traded.   **Grade: B**

Note: Draft analysis prepared by Jim Callis. Numbers in parentheses indicate draft rounds.

... Few catching prospects can match Buck's all-around package.

John Buck C

Born: July 7, 1980.
Ht.: 6-3. **Wt.:** 210.
Bats: R. **Throws:** R.
School: Taylorsville (Utah) HS.
Career Transactions: Selected by Astros in seventh round of 1998 draft; signed June 11, 1998.

Area scout Doug Deutsch has signed six major leaguers, including 2002 revelation Kirk Saarloos and otherwise overlooked college seniors Morgan Ensberg and Jason Lane. But his biggest find may prove to be Buck. He was raw when he signed but has made quick adjustments to pro ball. Perhaps more than any player, Buck was hurt by Houston's lack of a high Class A club the past two years. The transition was made more difficult when, on the first pitch he caught of the 2002 season, he was hit on the back of his left hand by the hitter's bat. Buck was unable to grip a bat properly in the early part of the season and posted his worst offensive numbers since short-season ball in 1999. Nevertheless, he made the Texas League's postseason all-star team.

Few catching prospects can match Buck's all-around package. He projects as a .275 hitter with 20 homers in the major leagues now that he has learned to turn on fastballs and recognize breaking pitches. His defense grades out better than his offense. Buck has plus arm strength and threw out 36 percent of basestealers last year. His receiving skills are solid, though he can make further improvements on balls outside of the strike zone. Buck's makeup may be his greatest strength. He's a student of the game who takes charge of a pitching staff. He believes that making his pitchers more successful is a huge part of his job. Somehow while catching games in the Texas heat, Buck put on 15 pounds between May and the end of the season. The extra weight made him sluggish in August and in the Arizona Fall League, where his swing lengthened and his offense tapered off. He's becoming a base-clogger and spent the offseason working on his flexibility and agility. Since he started hitting for power, Buck has been more aggressive going after pitches early in the count, but he should be able to recapture the plate discipline he had earlier.

Buck figures to spend 2003 in Triple-A New Orleans, one of the tougher hitter's parks in the offense-oriented Pacific Coast League. Brad Ausmus' contract expires after the season, and the Astros hope Buck can carry at least part of the big league load in 2004.

Year	Club (League)	Class	AVG	G	AB	R	H	2B	3B	HR	RBI	BB	SO	SB	SLG	OBP
1998	Astros (GCL)	R	.286	36	126	24	36	9	0	3	15	13	22	2	.429	.362
1999	Auburn (NY-P)	A	.245	63	233	36	57	17	0	3	29	25	48	7	.356	.328
	Michigan (Mid)	A	.100	4	10	1	1	1	0	0	0	2	3	0	.200	.250
2000	Michigan (Mid)	A	.282	109	390	57	110	33	0	10	71	55	81	2	.444	.374
2001	Lexington (SAL)	A	.275	122	443	72	122	24	1	22	73	37	84	4	.483	.345
2002	Round Rock (TL)	AA	.263	120	448	48	118	29	3	12	89	31	93	2	.422	.314
MINOR LEAGUE TOTALS			.269	454	1650	238	444	113	4	50	277	163	331	17	.433	.342

2. Jason Lane, of

Born: Dec. 22, 1976. **Ht.:** 6-2. **Wt.:** 210. **Bats:** R. **Throws:** L. **School:** University of Southern California. **Career Transactions:** Selected by Astros in sixth round of 1999 draft; signed June 7, 1999.

Unlike most players, Lane has accepted and handled tougher defensive assignments as he has risen through the minors. He broke in as a first base-man, moved to the corners of the outfield and spent 2002 as a center field-er. While his run of three consecutive league RBI titles and two straight league MVPs ended, he had a solid year and looked good in his big league debut. Lane projects as a .275-.280 hitter with 25-30 homers. He has enough power and bat speed to take good fastballs out of the park. He has improved all facets of his outfield play and has a solid-average arm that's also accurate. He also runs well for his size. Lane needs to improve his pitch selection and draw more walks. He has gotten better going back on balls, but he's still more serviceable than a standout in center. Best suited for right field, Lane is better than Lance Berkman in center and ready for a big league job. If the Astros move Craig Biggio to the outfield, he might have to come off the bench in 2003.

Year	Club (League)	Class	AVG	G	AB	R	H	2B	3B	HR	RBI	BB	SO	SB	SLG	OBP
1999	Auburn (NY-P)	A	.279	74	283	46	79	18	5	13	59	38	46	6	.516	.366
2000	Michigan (Mid)	A	.299	133	511	98	153	38	0	23	104	62	91	20	.509	.375
2001	Round Rock (TL)	AA	.316	137	526	103	166	36	2	38	124	61	98	14	.608	.407
2002	New Orleans (PCL)	AAA	.272	111	426	65	116	36	2	15	83	31	90	13	.472	.328
	Houston (NL)	MAJ	.290	44	69	12	20	3	1	4	10	10	12	1	.536	.375
MAJOR LEAGUE TOTALS			.290	44	69	12	20	3	1	4	10	10	12	1	.536	.375
MINOR LEAGUE TOTALS			.294	455	1746	312	514	128	9	89	370	192	325	53	.531	.372

3. Brad Lidge, rhp

Born: Dec. 23, 1976. **Ht.:** 6-5. **Wt.:** 200. **Bats:** R. **Throws:** R. **School:** University of Notre Dame. **Career Transactions:** Selected by Astros in first round (17th overall) of 1998 draft; signed July 2, 1998.

Lidge entered 2002 with the best arm in the system and a checkered medical history that included nearly as many surgeries (three) as pro wins (four). Houston planned to make him a full-time reliever to keep him healthy but two things happened: New Orleans needed him in its rota-tion, and he more than doubled his career innings total without hurting his arm. He did pull an abdominal muscle and required offseason arthro-scopic surgery to repair a minor cartilage tear in his left knee. Lidge's slider is as good as any in the game. It's unhittable and has so much life that it often gets splitter. His velocity dipped in 2002, but he still showed enough juice at 92-94 mph. Getting regular innings allowed him to improve his changeup to combat lefthanders. Though he stayed rel-atively healthy last year, Lidge has lost so much time to injuries that he'll have to be a reliev-er unless his command takes a major jump forward. That's not terrible, but his ceiling as a starter would be huge. He has closer stuff and continues to parallel Robb Nen, who had a sim-ilar injury history in the minors. Barring injury, Lidge should make the Astros this spring.

Year	Club (League)	Class	W	L	ERA	G	GS	CG	SV	IP	H	R	ER	HR	BB	SO	AVG
1998	Quad City (Mid)	A	0	1	3.27	4	4	0	0	11	10	5	4	0	5	6	.227
1999	Kissimmee (FSL)	A	0	2	3.38	6	6	0	0	21	13	8	8	0	11	19	.183
2000	Kissimmee (FSL)	A	2	1	2.81	8	8	0	0	42	28	14	13	3	15	46	.190
2001	Round Rock (TL)	AA	2	0	1.73	5	5	0	0	26	21	5	5	1	7	42	.219
2002	Round Rock (TL)	AA	1	1	2.45	5	0	0	0	11	9	4	3	0	3	18	.220
	Houston (NL)	MAJ	1	0	6.23	6	1	0	0	9	12	6	6	0	9	12	.333
	New Orleans (PCL)	AAA	5	5	3.39	24	19	0	0	112	83	47	42	9	47	110	.206
MAJOR LEAGUE TOTALS			1	0	6.23	6	1	0	0	9	12	6	6	0	9	12	.333
MINOR LEAGUE TOTALS			10	10	3.03	52	42	0	0	223	164	83	75	13	88	241	.205

4. Jimmy Barrett, rhp

Born: June 7, 1981. **Ht.:** 6-2. **Wt.:** 190. **Bats:** R. **Throws:** R. **School:** Fort Hill HS, Cumberland, Md. **Career Transactions:** Selected by Astros in third round of 1999 draft; signed June 25, 1999.

Barrett spent two years in the Rookie-level Appalachian League and two more in low Class A, but his breakthrough in 2002 was worth the wait. He became more committed to his offseason workout program and the results showed. Barrett's velocity, secondary pitches and command all improved. He missed time in April with back spasms but was fine after-ward. Barrett, who threw 89-92 mph in 2001, got his fastball back up to

95 with an easy arm action that belies how hard he throws. His curveball gained consistency and he showed signs of eventually mastering a changeup. Barrett also throws a natural cutter. He stopped being hard on himself and let his natural ability take over, which helped him immensely. Now that he's accomplished the broad strokes, Barrett needs to work on the nuances of pitching. He can throw his fastball for strikes but needs to locate it better within the strike zone. He also must show he can handle a level the first time around. Barrett will move up to Houston's new high Class A Salem affiliate this season. He reminds one scout of Jason Isringhausen without the power curveball.

Year	Club (League)	Class	W	L	ERA	G	GS	CG	SV	IP	H	R	ER	HR	BB	SO	AVG
1999	Martinsville (Appy)	R	0	1	4.42	6	3	0	0	18	15	9	9	0	10	12	.227
2000	Martinsville (Appy)	R	6	2	4.73	13	13	0	0	67	60	37	35	4	32	72	.239
2001	Michigan (Mid)	A	10	5	4.48	27	25	1	0	131	122	76	65	12	62	98	.242
2002	Lexington (SAL)	A	9	5	2.81	27	22	0	1	134	112	53	42	13	40	131	.230
MINOR LEAGUE TOTALS			25	13	3.88	73	63	1	1	350	309	175	151	29	144	313	.236

5. Chris Burke, 2b/ss

STEVE MOORE

Born: March 11, 1980. **Ht.:** 5-11. **Wt.:** 180. **Bats:** R. **Throws:** R. **School:** University of Tennessee. **Career Transactions:** Selected by Astros in first round (10th overall) of 2001 draft; signed June 22, 2001.

Burke seemed ready for Double-A. The Southeastern Conference player of the year and the 10th overall pick in 2001, he went straight to low Class A and hit .300 in his pro debut. But he struggled at Round Rock throughout last year and regressed in most areas. Burke has the tools and makeup to be the leadoff hitter Houston needs. His bat and speed are above-average. Though he messed up his approach trying to adapt to the Texas League, he did a better job of using the whole field, bunting and learning to relax in instructional league. He covers a lot of ground at either second base or shortstop. To bat first in the lineup, Burke will have to draw more walks. His stolen-base instincts were disappointing during the season but looked better in instructional league. His arm isn't quite enough for shortstop, and even at second base he sometimes has trouble throwing quickly or from odd angles. In a perfect world, Burke would have started 2002 in high Class A, but the Astros didn't have an affiliate there. He'll probably repeat Double-A at the beginning of this year and make his big league debut toward the end of 2004.

Year	Club (League)	Class	AVG	G	AB	R	H	2B	3B	HR	RBI	BB	SO	SB	SLG	OBP
2001	Michigan (Mid)	A	.300	56	233	47	70	11	6	3	17	26	31	21	.438	.376
2002	Round Rock (TL)	AA	.264	136	481	66	127	19	8	3	37	39	61	16	.356	.330
MINOR LEAGUE TOTALS			.276	192	714	113	197	30	14	6	54	65	92	37	.382	.345

6. Tommy Whiteman, ss

RODGER WOOD

Born: July 14, 1979. **Ht.:** 6-3. **Wt.:** 170. **Bats:** R. **Throws:** R. **School:** University of Oklahoma. **Career Transactions:** Selected by Astros in sixth round of 2000 draft; signed June 16, 2000.

A Native American whose given name is Owner of Outstanding Horses, Whiteman is the first pro athlete from the Crow Nation. Like Chris Burke, he had difficulty with the jump from low Class A to Double-A in 2002. Whiteman, who missed a month with a hamstring injury, rebounded in the Arizona Fall League, where he earned all-star honors by hitting .330 and making just two errors in 26 games. He's an offensive shortstop who's better suited than Burke for the position because he has a stronger arm. Whiteman flashes all five tools, including the ability to hit for average and gap power. He's not fazed by power fastballs. Tall and rangy, he gobbles up grounders at short. Whiteman is 23 and has yet to prove he can hit above low Class A. To do so, he probably will have to draw more walks. He sometimes drops his arm slot and flips his throws on routine plays, hurting his accuracy. Burke and Whiteman will be teammates at Round Rock again this year. Whiteman will get most of the time at shortstop and occasionally will play third base. He might have enough bat for the hot corner if he has to play there full-time down the road.

Year	Club (League)	Class	AVG	G	AB	R	H	2B	3B	HR	RBI	BB	SO	SB	SLG	OBP
2000	Auburn (NY-P)	A	.250	70	232	33	58	10	3	1	22	22	52	7	.332	.318
2001	Lexington (SAL)	A	.319	114	389	58	124	26	8	18	57	34	106	17	.566	.380
	Round Rock (TL)	AA	.250	4	16	1	4	0	0	1	1	0	5	0	.438	.294
2002	Round Rock (TL)	AA	.179	15	56	3	10	2	1	0	5	4	17	1	.250	.246
	Lexington (SAL)	A	.303	90	350	50	106	29	2	10	49	36	66	6	.483	.374
MINOR LEAGUE TOTALS			.290	293	1043	145	302	67	14	30	134	96	246	31	.467	.356

7. Rodrigo Rosario, rhp

Born: Dec. 14, 1977. **Ht.:** 6-2. **Wt.:** 160. **Bats:** R. **Throws:** R. **Career Transactions:** Signed out of Dominican Republic by Astros, July 6, 1996.

Rosario's 2002 got off to an inauspicious start when his birthdate was revealed to be two years earlier than previously believed. That meant his breakout year at low Class A Lexington came when he was 23. Nevertheless, Rosario didn't have the same trouble Houston's other top prospects did making the jump to Double-A. Rosario throws four pitches, all of which come in at the knees or lower, and at times each can be above-average. His most trustworthy weapon is a 91-95 mph fastball with late sink and boring action. His slurvy curveball is his No. 2 pitch, and he also employs a slider and a changeup. He must get stronger after coming down with a tired arm at midseason last year. Rosario likes to vary his arm angle, but when he drops down too low his breaking stuff flattens out and misses the strike zone more often. He needs to decide on a third pitch and use it more often. Rosario didn't bounce all the way back this winter in his native Dominican Republic, where he had a 23.63 ERA in three appearances. If healthy, he'll advance to Triple-A and could reach Houston by the end of the year.

Year	Club (League)	Class	W	L	ERA	G	GS	CG	SV	IP	H	R	ER	HR	BB	SO	AVG
1997	Astros (DSL)	R	6	4	2.46	15	14	0	0	91	63	30	25	2	24	81	.195
1998	Astros (GCL)	R	2	2	4.12	13	12	0	0	68	61	36	31	6	30	65	.245
	Auburn (NY-P)	A	0	0	0.00	2	0	0	0	2	0	0	0	0	3	2	.000
1999	Martinsville (Appy)	R	5	5	4.69	14	14	0	0	79	78	46	41	9	32	86	.267
2000	Auburn (NY-P)	A	5	6	3.45	14	14	0	0	76	67	36	29	3	32	67	.232
2001	Lexington (SAL)	A	13	4	2.14	30	21	1	2	147	105	46	35	8	36	131	.198
2002	Round Rock (TL)	AA	11	6	3.11	26	23	0	0	130	106	56	45	5	59	94	.222
MINOR LEAGUE TOTALS			42	27	3.13	114	98	1	2	593	480	250	206	33	216	526	.222

8. Hector Gimenez, c

Born: Sept. 28, 1982. **Ht.:** 5-10. **Wt.:** 180. **Bats:** B. **Throws:** R. **Career Transactions:** Signed out of Venezuela by Astros, July 2, 1999.

A Rookie-level Venezuelan League all-star in 2001, Gimenez was no less impressive during his U.S. debut last year. He went directly to low Class A, where managers rated him the best defensive catcher in the South Atlantic League, and hit well with the exception of a 5-for-40 slump in May. He missed four weeks with a groin injury. Some Astros officials think Gimenez is a better defensive catcher than John Buck, though that's not the consensus opinion. Gimenez, who threw out 32 percent of basestealers in 2002, has at least as much arm strength and a better release. He also receives and moves well. Gimenez' strong wrists and quick bat give him power from both sides of the plate. Gimenez still has a lot to learn about plate discipline. He tends to chase high pitches out of the strike zone. He has below-average speed but has sound instincts on the bases. Ticketed for high Class A in 2003, Gimenez will move one level at a time through the system. If he's as good as he looked last year and Buck also delivers on his promise, the Astros will have some very attractive options behind the plate.

Year	Club (League)	Class	AVG	G	AB	R	H	2B	3B	HR	RBI	BB	SO	SB	SLG	OBP
2000	Venoco (VSL)	R	.297	34	91	9	27	8	0	1	13	12	21	0	.418	.396
2001	Venoco (VSL)	R	.278	42	144	27	40	12	3	5	34	26	30	4	.507	.388
2002	Lexington (SAL)	A	.263	85	297	41	78	16	1	11	42	25	78	2	.434	.320
MINOR LEAGUE TOTALS			.273	161	532	77	145	36	4	17	89	63	129	6	.451	.353

9. Chad Qualls, rhp

Born: Aug. 17, 1978. **Ht.:** 6-5. **Wt.:** 200. **Bats:** R. **Throws:** R. **School:** University of Nevada. **Career Transactions:** Selected by Astros in second round of 2000 draft; signed Aug. 16, 2000.

Add Qualls to the list of Astros prospects who could have used time in high Class A last year. After leading the low Class A Midwest League with 15 wins in his 2001 pro debut, Qualls lost his first six Double-A decisions. He led the Texas League in strikeouts but also finished second in losses and walks. Qualls is a sinker/slider pitcher and both are quality offerings. Righthanders have little chance when he throws his slider from a three-quarters angle. He can reach the mid-90s, but he's more affective burying his fastball low in the zone at 90-93. Once Qualls figures out command—both throwing strikes and locating his pitches within the zone—he'll be in the majors. He's not mechanically sound, though he's strong enough to fight through it. He made progress under Round Rock pitching coach Mike Maddux. Qualls can get too predictable, relying too much on his slider while eschewing his changeup, and hasn't solved lefties yet. Qualls may return to Double-A in 2003, though he won't be able to work with Maddux, who's now Milwaukee's pitching coach. His long-term role may come in relief because of his stuff and his command.

Year	Club (League)	Class	W	L	ERA	G	GS	CG	SV	IP	H	R	ER	HR	BB	SO	AVG
2001	Michigan (Mid)	A	15	6	3.72	26	26	3	0	162	149	77	67	8	31	125	.239
2002	Round Rock (TL)	AA	6	13	4.36	29	29	0	0	163	174	92	79	9	67	142	.273
MINOR LEAGUE TOTALS			21	19	4.04	55	55	3	0	325	323	169	146	17	98	267	.256

10. Santiago Ramirez, rhp

Born: Aug. 15, 1978. **Ht.:** 5-11. **Wt.:** 180. **Bats:** R. **Throws:** R. **Career Transactions:** Signed out of Dominican Republic by Astros, June 23, 1997.

Ramirez didn't make it past low Class A in his first five pro seasons, but his six scoreless outings for the Dominican Republic at the November 2001 World Cup showed he might be ready to turn the corner. He didn't just turn it; he blew right past it and reached Triple-A in 2002. His age was revised upward two years but it isn't a major issue now that he's so close to Houston. Ramirez always has shown arm strength. He has a 92-93 mph fastball that he can pump up to 95, and he locates his heater well. He didn't succeed as a starter because he had no breaking ball, but he has found consistency with a hard curveball. He needs a good pitching coach and catcher to keep him focused, and Ramirez had two of the best last year at Round Rock with Mike Maddux and John Buck. He still has to gain more feel for his curveball and slider. In all likelihood, Ramirez will open 2003 in Triple-A to build up his confidence. By the end of the year, he could be forming a dynamic set-up trio with Octavio Dotel and Brad Lidge in Houston.

Year	Club (League)	Class	W	L	ERA	G	GS	CG	SV	IP	H	R	ER	HR	BB	SO	AVG
1997	Astros (DSL)	R	4	1	2.65	15	2	0	0	34	26	13	10	1	6	24	.217
1998	Astros (DSL)	R	6	5	2.17	14	13	0	0	83	64	32	20	1	18	62	.203
1999	Martinsville (Appy)	R	2	1	1.45	25	0	0	17	31	26	9	5	1	14	35	.232
2000	Michigan (Mid)	A	3	3	6.07	23	0	0	5	30	27	28	20	6	32	22	.245
	Auburn (NY-P)	A	3	6	4.25	20	9	0	2	53	36	34	25	3	39	57	.197
2001	Lexington (SAL)	A	8	2	3.63	45	0	0	4	79	69	35	32	2	28	85	.237
2002	Round Rock (TL)	AA	5	2	2.56	33	0	0	4	63	45	19	18	3	26	73	.199
	New Orleans (PCL)	AAA	2	0	3.38	18	0	0	1	21	17	8	8	2	11	15	.221
MINOR LEAGUE TOTALS			33	20	3.15	193	24	0	33	395	310	178	138	19	174	373	.216

11. Derick Grigsby, rhp

Born: June 30, 1982. **Ht.:** 6-0. **Wt.:** 190. **Bats:** R. **Throws:** R. **School:** Northeast Texas CC. **Career Transactions:** Selected by Astros in first round (29th overall) of 2002 draft; signed Aug. 11, 2002.

Grigsby came out of Marshall (Texas) High a year ahead of fireballer Colt Griffin, who was more of a first baseman when they were teammates. Grigsby attended the University of Texas as a freshman in 2001, but he pitched just 11 innings before leaving school when his mother unexpectedly died during routine surgery. He transferred to Northeast Texas CC, where he became the top junior college prospect in the 2002 draft. Grigsby signed late for $1.125 million, missing the regular season thanks to Astros owner Drayton McLane's temporary draft embargo. On the day of Houston's first instructional league workout, he learned that his father had been seriously injured in an accident while riding a motorcycle Grigsby had bought him with part of his bonus money. By the time his father recovered and Grigsby returned, his arm wasn't in shape, so Houston hasn't seen much of him on the mound since he turned pro. At Northeast Texas, Grigsby routinely threw 95-96 mph with a smooth arm action, and he also showed a power slider. His changeup and command will need much more work, and he's quite raw. The Astros are going to take their time with Grigsby and will decide where to send him this year after seeing more of him this spring. It's possible he'll go to extended spring training before reporting to either short-season Tri-City or Rookie-level Martinsville in June.

Year	Club (League)	Class	W	L	ERA	G	GS	CG	SV	IP	H	R	ER	HR	BB	SO	AVG
						Has Not Played—Signed 2003 Contract											

12. Henri Stanley, of

Born: Dec. 15, 1977. **Ht.:** 5-10. **Wt.:** 190. **Bats:** L. **Throws:** L. **School:** Clemson University. **Career Transactions:** Signed as nondrafted free agent by Astros, June 15, 2000.

Stanley was a Clemson senior in 2000 when he made a brief impression on the Astros at an early-season tournament. Then he lost his starting job and teams passed him over in the draft. Houston was having trouble in its early negotiations with fifth-round outfielder Jake Whitesides when scouting director David Lakey happened to see Stanley playing in the College World Series on an airport television. The Astros decided to sign him for insurance as a nondrafted free agent and haven't regretted it. His performance in 2002, when Stanley led the Texas League with a .542 slugging percentage and posted a .408 on-base percentage for the second straight year, earned him a spot on the 40-man roster. He handles the bat well, as he's able to bunt, hit-and-run or drive the ball into the gaps as needed. He also led the TL in triples (10) and extra-base hits (62). Stanley runs well and hard, which combined with his ability to draw walks makes him a potentially exciting leadoff hitter. His makeup is another plus, and not getting drafted has only made him try harder. Stanley covers enough ground to play center field, though his instincts aren't the best and he relies on his speed to compensate for mistakes. His arm is well-below-average and probably will force him to left field in the major leagues. Triple-A is next for Stanley, who could help Houston as an extra outfielder later in 2003.

Year	Club (League)	Class	AVG	G	AB	R	H	2B	3B	HR	RBI	BB	SO	SB	SLG	OBP
2000	Martinsville (Appy)	R	.248	46	165	34	41	8	6	4	20	25	37	10	.442	.347
2001	Michigan (Mid)	A	.300	114	400	75	120	24	12	14	76	73	84	30	.525	.408
2002	Round Rock (TL)	AA	.314	127	456	90	143	36	10	16	72	72	85	14	.542	.408
MINOR LEAGUE TOTALS			.298	287	1021	199	304	68	28	34	168	170	206	54	.519	.398

13. Anthony Pluta, rhp

Born: Oct. 28, 1982. **Ht.:** 6-2. **Wt.:** 190. **Bats:** R. **Throws:** R. **School:** Las Vegas (Nev.) HS. **Career Transactions:** Selected by Astros in third round of 2000 draft; signed Aug. 22, 2000.

In a season of disappointments, no player in the Astros system fell short of expectations more than Pluta. After a strong pro debut, Pluta made a lateral move to low Class A Michigan. Repeating a level and owning the best arm in the system should have been the ingredients for a dominant season, but instead he had the worst ERA and allowed the most homers (18) in the Midwest League. Pluta's arm strength was still evident, as he sat at 94 mph and was clocked at 97 in the seventh inning of one game. At times, he showed a plus hard curveball and feel for a changeup. But all too often, Pluta pitched as if velocity was all that mattered. He tries to overpower hitters, which causes him to fly open in his delivery and lose command and life on his pitches. There's a lot of effort to his delivery, and Pluta needs to dial it down a couple of notches and focus on finding the strike zone. He briefly got on track in June but fell apart again afterward. In the long term, he may be best off pitching in relief and trying to blow away hitters for an inning or two. For now, the Astros will continue to try to polish him up as a starter in high Class A.

Year	Club (League)	Class	W	L	ERA	G	GS	CG	SV	IP	H	R	ER	HR	BB	SO	AVG
2001	Lexington (SAL)	A	12	4	3.20	26	26	0	0	132	107	52	47	7	86	138	.231
2002	Michigan (Mid)	A	11	13	5.92	28	28	1	0	143	155	100	94	18	83	120	.277
MINOR LEAGUE TOTALS			23	17	4.61	54	54	1	0	275	262	152	141	25	169	258	.256

14. Gavin Wright, of

Born: May 6, 1979. **Ht.:** 6-2. **Wt.:** 180. **Bats:** R. **Throws:** R. **School:** Blinn (Texas) JC. **Career Transactions:** Selected by Astros in 33rd round of 1998 draft; signed May 21, 1999.

For the first time in three years, Wright avoided injuries and got past low Class A in 2002. Shoulder, wrist and hamstring problems hampered him in 2000-01, and he seemed to lose his enthusiasm in his second year at Michigan. Wright played with passion last year, however, performing consistently throughout the South Atlantic League season and batting .316 in the Texas League playoffs. As he has gotten stronger, Wright has lost a step but still runs above-average. His defense and arm are plus tools as well, and he's equally capable in center and right field. The key for Wright last year was working with minor league hitting coordinator Pat Roessler to get his entire body in sync during his swing. He also changed his approach, enabling him to make more contact. Wright doesn't try to hit homers but shows power to the opposite field. He just needs to add a little more patience at the plate. Set to return to Double-A, he's a 20-20 player in the making.

Year	Club (League)	Class	AVG	G	AB	R	H	2B	3B	HR	RBI	BB	SO	SB	SLG	OBP
1999	Martinsville (Appy)	R	.309	61	236	37	73	17	3	2	29	25	46	31	.432	.376
2000	Michigan (Mid)	A	.288	43	163	22	47	10	5	2	19	18	37	10	.448	.355
2001	Michigan (Mid)	A	.273	100	392	68	107	17	6	8	52	28	76	26	.408	.326
2002	Lexington (SAL)	A	.296	128	517	73	153	23	6	8	57	40	92	21	.410	.346
	Round Rock (TL)	AA	.333	2	9	2	3	0	0	0	2	0	2	0	.333	.364
MINOR LEAGUE TOTALS			.291	334	1317	202	383	67	20	20	159	111	253	88	.418	.347

15. Jeriome Robertson, lhp

Born: March 30, 1977. **Ht.:** 6-1. **Wt.:** 190. **Bats:** L. **Throws:** L. **School:** Exeter Union (Calif.) HS. **Career Transactions:** Selected by Astros in 24th round of 1995 draft; signed Aug. 22, 1995.

Robertson made steady progress that culminated with a spot on the 40-man roster following a Texas League all-star season in 1999. He pitched poorly in 2000 and was converted to relief in 2001 and wasn't protected after either season. Neither time did he draw a nibble in the Rule 5 draft. Moved back to the rotation last year, Robertson adjusted his approach with spectacular results. He was the Pacific Coast League pitcher of the year after leading the circuit in ERA and innings. Managers rated his command the best in the PCL. Robertson's fastball tops out at 90 mph, and he finally decided to use it to set up his other pitches rather than trying (unsuccessfully) to strike out hitters with it. Spotting his fastball made his plus changeup even better, and Robertson's slider was better than it had been. He also throws an offspeed curveball but hangs it too often. He won't be an all-star, but he'll be a major leaguer, something that seemed unlikely a year earlier. Robertson will compete for a job in the back of Houston's rotation but may fit better in the bullpen, where the Astros don't have a lefty in front of closer Billy Wagner.

Year	Club (League)	Class	W	L	ERA	G	GS	CG	SV	IP	H	R	ER	HR	BB	SO	AVG
1996	Astros (GCL)	R	5	3	1.72	13	13	1	0	78	51	20	15	2	15	98	.181
	Kissimmee (FSL)	A	0	0	2.57	1	1	0	0	7	4	4	2	0	1	2	.154
1997	Quad City (Mid)	A	11	8	4.07	26	25	2	1	146	151	86	66	12	56	135	.261
1998	Kissimmee (FSL)	A	10	10	3.70	28	28	2	0	175	185	83	72	13	53	131	.276
1999	Jackson (TL)	AA	15	7	3.06	28	28	1	0	191	184	81	65	22	45	133	.253
2000	Kissimmee (FSL)	A	2	1	4.66	5	5	1	0	29	28	19	15	1	5	13	.248
	Round Rock (TL)	AA	2	2	4.13	11	10	0	0	61	62	36	28	8	18	30	.257
	New Orleans (PCL)	AAA	1	7	7.07	9	9	0	0	50	64	42	39	10	23	27	.323
2001	Round Rock (TL)	AA	5	1	3.91	57	0	0	3	74	89	33	32	10	21	72	.296
2002	New Orleans (PCL)	AAA	12	8	2.55	27	27	2	0	180	160	59	51	13	45	114	.238
	Houston (NL)	MAJ	0	2	6.52	11	1	0	0	10	13	8	7	4	5	6	.394
MAJOR LEAGUE TOTALS			0	2	6.52	11	1	0	0	10	13	8	7	4	5	6	.394
MINOR LEAGUE TOTALS			63	47	3.50	205	146	9	4	991	978	463	385	91	282	755	.257

16. Manny Santillan, rhp

Born: Aug. 20, 1979. **Ht.:** 6-0. **Wt.:** 200. **Bats:** R. **Throws:** R. **Career Transactions:** Signed out of Dominican Republic by Astros, Oct. 2, 1996.

Santillan signed as a catcher and spent his first three years as a pro behind the plate. He showed good defensive skills but little offensively, never getting above the Mendoza line. The Astros converted him to pitching in 2000, easing him in as a reliever before turning him loose as a starter in 2002. The results were exciting, as Santillan dominated the South Atlantic League until being shut down with a sore elbow in June. He didn't require surgery after being diagnosed with a stress reaction where the bones collide in the joint. Santillan began the season averaging 89-91 mph with his fastball and gradually threw harder, reaching 96 before being shut down. He made progress with his mechanics but still needs more work. A smoother delivery would be good for his velocity and health. Santillan already commands his fastball well, which is why he overmatched low Class A hitters. His slider is terribly inconsistent but is a plus pitch when it's on. His changeup is further away. Santillan took the winter off rather than pitch in his native Dominican Republic, and should be able to start 2003 in high Class A.

Year	Club (League)	Class	AVG	G	AB	R	H	2B	3B	HR	RBI	BB	SO	SB	SLG	OBP
1997	Astros (DSL)	R	.175	27	80	6	14	2	0	0	7	5	24	0	.200	.241
1998	Astros (DSL)	R	.136	31	88	8	12	1	0	1	8	12	16	2	.182	.245
1999	Martinsville (Appy)	R	.181	21	72	13	13	3	1	2	9	4	21	2	.333	.224
MINOR LEAGUE TOTALS			.163	79	240	27	39	6	1	3	24	21	61	4	.233	.238

Year	Club (League)	Class	W	L	ERA	G	GS	CG	SV	IP	H	R	ER	HR	BB	SO	AVG
2000	Martinsville (Appy)	R	1	0	4.76	19	0	0	1	23	21	18	12	1	24	20	.253
2001	Lexington (SAL)	A	6	5	3.54	38	7	0	1	97	83	43	38	4	43	90	.237
2002	Lexington (SAL)	A	5	5	2.06	14	14	1	0	96	73	27	22	4	28	76	.211
MINOR LEAGUE TOTALS			12	10	3.01	71	21	1	2	215	177	88	72	9	95	186	.227

17. Miguel Saladin, rhp

Born: May 22, 1975. **Ht.:** 5-11. **Wt.:** 190. **Bats:** R. **Throws:** R. **Career Transactions:** Signed out of Dominican Republic by Astros, Dec. 1, 1995.

Saladin's age was revised upward from 23 to 26 before the 2002 season, so the Astros sent him to Double-A to see how he'd respond. Managers rated him the top relief prospect in the Texas League, ahead of his set-up man, Santiago Ramirez. Houston re-signed him as a minor league free agent after the season ended and immediately put him on the 40-man roster. A converted infielder who moved to the mound in 1997, Saladin pumps 93-95 mph fastballs by hitters. He sometimes makes mistakes up in the zone, but Double-A hitters couldn't take advantage. His second pitch is a hard, big-breaking slider, but he doesn't always throw it for strikes. Despite his success, he's not as aggressive as a typical closer. If Saladin develops consistency and command, he won't spend much time in Triple-A this year.

Year	Club (League)	Class	AVG	G	AB	R	H	2B	3B	HR	RBI	BB	SO	SB	SLG	OBP
1996	Astros/Red Sox (DSL)	R	.244	39	135	13	33	3	0	0	19	6	18	9	.267	.280
1997	Astros (DSL)	R	.250	8	16	2	4	0	0	0	2	2	5	0	.250	.333
* MINOR LEAGUE TOTALS			.250	100	152	15	38	3	0	0	22	8	23	9	.270	.290

* Includes stats as a pitcher

Year	Club (League)	Class	W	L	ERA	G	GS	CG	SV	IP	H	R	ER	HR	BB	SO	AVG
1997	Astros (DSL)	R	1	2	2.04	13	0	0	0	18	19	13	4	0	12	15	.250
1998	Astros (DSL)	R	2	4	3.22	17	5	0	2	45	42	20	16	1	24	45	.258
1999	Auburn (NY-P)	A	1	4	7.13	8	0	0	0	18	23	19	14	1	7	10	.303
	Martinsville (Appy)	R	1	0	5.06	11	0	0	1	16	24	12	9	1	4	19	.338
2000	Auburn (NY-P)	A	2	3	0.68	27	0	0	4	40	32	19	3	0	20	42	.211
2001	Michigan (Mid)	A	7	3	2.93	46	0	0	11	74	72	27	24	2	24	66	.253
2002	Round Rock (TL)	AA	4	5	2.06	53	0	0	24	57	36	18	13	4	25	46	.185
	New Orleans (PCL)	AAA	0	0	4.50	2	0	0	0	2	3	1	1	0	1	2	.375
MINOR LEAGUE TOTALS			18	21	2.82	177	5	0	42	268	251	129	84	9	117	245	.245

18. Victor Hall, of

Born: Sept. 16, 1980. **Ht.:** 5-11. **Wt.:** 170. **Bats:** L. **Throws:** L. **School:** Monroe HS, Sepulveda, Calif. **Career Transactions:** Selected by Diamondbacks in 12th round of 1998 draft; signed June 3, 1998 . . . Selected by Rockies from Diamondbacks in major league Rule 5 draft, Dec. 16, 2002 . . . Traded by Rockies to Astros for RHP Nelson Cruz, Dec. 16, 2002.

A high school track star who didn't play baseball until his senior year, Hall used his meager 12th-round bonus to buy a batting cage for his backyard. His development has been steady yet slow, but the Astros saw enough potential to trade Nelson Cruz to get him from the Rockies, who selected him from the Diamondbacks in the major league Rule 5 draft at the Winter Meetings. Assuming Houston carries him on its 25-man roster all year so it can retain him, Hall will be the best defensive outfielder on the big league club. He has exceptional range in center field and an average arm. He'll need more time in the minors after 2003, but the Astros hope he'll hit enough so he can be a viable center fielder for the long term. Hall understands his role. He has blazing speed and does whatever he can to reach base. Cognizant of his lack of power, he hits the ball on the ground and draws walks. Hall doesn't need to bulk up, but he does need to get stronger so he can handle quality pitching.

Year	Club (League)	Class	AVG	G	AB	R	H	2B	3B	HR	RBI	BB	SO	SB	SLG	OBP
1998	Diamondbacks (AZL)	R	.188	28	101	10	19	1	1	0	10	10	29	14	.218	.272
1999	Diamondbacks (AZL)	R	.365	27	104	19	38	2	1	0	14	13	25	10	.404	.442
	Missoula (Pio)	R	.279	34	147	27	41	4	0	0	11	15	30	18	.306	.359
2000	South Bend (Mid)	A	.232	41	164	19	38	4	5	2	16	13	41	12	.354	.296
	Missoula (Pio)	R	.307	70	241	70	74	7	9	3	26	77	38	47	.448	.479
2001	South Bend (Mid)	A	.275	113	415	82	114	13	12	0	39	52	71	60	.364	.362
2002	Lancaster (Cal)	A	.278	91	352	72	98	10	8	3	32	47	72	26	.378	.373
	El Paso (TL)	AA	.286	38	161	18	46	4	5	0	12	6	23	7	.373	.322
MINOR LEAGUE TOTALS			.278	442	1685	317	468	45	41	8	160	233	329	194	.367	.374

19. Greg Miller, lhp

Born: Sept. 30, 1979. **Ht.:** 6-5. **Wt.:** 210. **Bats:** L. **Throws:** L. **School:** Aurora (Ill.) West HS. **Career Transactions:** Selected by Red Sox in fifth round of 1997 draft; signed July 2, 1997 . . . Traded by Red Sox with SS Adam Everett to Astros for OF Carl Everett, Dec. 15, 1999.

The Astros system is light on lefthanded starters, with only Jeriome Robertson, Miller and Eny Cabreja sticking out on their full-season clubs in 2002. Miller had been Houston's most advanced southpaw starter, but Robertson has passed him after Miller lost significant time the last two seasons. Bothered by shoulder tendinitis and a strained lower back in 2001, he had arthroscopic shoulder surgery that October to address a bone spur underneath his labrum. He began 2002 in extended spring and didn't make it to Double-A until mid-June. He regained his form by August, pitching at 88-92 mph with his fastball and doing a fine job of changing speeds with his effective curveball. His changeup was working as well, and he threw occasional sliders. He's one of several pitchers who benefited from working with former Round Rock pitching coach Mike Maddux. Miller isn't overpowering, but he throws strikes and keeps hitters off balance. He had a mild setback when he left the Venezuelan League because his back flared up, though the Astros think homesickness may have played a part in his decision. He'll head to Triple-A and hope to turn in a full season in 2003.

Year	Club (League)	Class	W	L	ERA	G	GS	CG	SV	IP	H	R	ER	HR	BB	SO	AVG
1997	Red Sox (GCL)	R	0	2	3.72	4	4	0	0	10	8	6	4	0	6	6	.235
1998	Red Sox (GCL)	R	6	0	2.49	11	7	0	0	43	33	18	12	2	18	47	.205
1999	Augusta (SAL)	A	10	6	3.10	25	25	1	0	137	109	54	47	8	56	146	.220
2000	Kissimmee (FSL)	A	10	8	3.70	24	24	1	0	146	131	63	60	13	46	109	.239
	Round Rock (TL)	AA	0	0	0.00	2	0	0	0	2	0	0	0	0	1	2	.000
2001	Round Rock (TL)	AA	5	3	3.25	14	14	0	0	55	38	22	20	3	35	37	.197
2002	Round Rock (TL)	AA	3	6	5.00	14	12	0	0	68	77	44	38	6	20	51	.274
MINOR LEAGUE TOTALS			34	25	3.53	94	86	2	0	462	396	207	181	32	182	398	.230

20. Fernando Nieve, rhp

Born: July 15, 1982. **Ht.:** 6-0. **Wt.:** 190. **Bats:** R. **Throws:** R. **Career Transactions:** Signed out of Venezuela by Astros, May 11, 1999.

Though he has pitched just one game above Rookie ball, the Astros nearly protected Nieve on their 40-man roster and felt fortunate not to lose him in the Rule 5 draft. He ranked second among Appalachian League starters in opponent average (.185) last year and made progress in instructional league. With an easy arm action, Nieve tops out in the mid-90s and pitches at 91-93. His slider ranges from sharp to slurvy, while his offspeed curveball and changeup are works in progress. He needs to maintain his arm slot in order to have command and crispness on his pitches. Nieve is too passive, at times acting like all he needs to do is light up the radar guns. Houston will look for him to mature this year in low Class A.

Year	Club (League)	Class	W	L	ERA	G	GS	CG	SV	IP	H	R	ER	HR	BB	SO	AVG
1999	La Pradera (VSL)	R	0	6	4.55	11	7	0	0	32	31	22	16	0	16	41	—
2000	Venoco (VSL)	R	3	4	2.71	14	13	0	0	80	56	29	24	5	28	64	.199
2001	Martinsville (Appy)	R	4	2	3.79	12	8	1	0	38	27	20	16	2	21	49	.197
2002	Martinsville (Appy)	R	4	1	2.39	13	13	0	0	68	46	23	18	5	27	60	.185
	Lexington (SAL)	A	0	1	6.00	1	1	0	0	3	6	5	2	0	0	2	.353
MINOR LEAGUE TOTALS			11	14	3.10	51	42	1	0	220	166	99	76	12	92	216	.198

21. Mitch Talbot, rhp

Born: Oct. 17, 1983. **Ht.:** 6-2. **Wt.:** 170. **Bats:** R. **Throws:** R. **School:** Canyon View, HS, Cedar City, Utah. **Career Transactions:** Selected by Astros in second round of 2002 draft; signed Aug. 20, 2002.

Talbot could form an all-Utah battery with John Buck in four or five years. The Major League Scouting Bureau gave Talbot the highest grade among Beehive State prospects last year, and he enhanced his draft status by announcing he wouldn't go on a two-year Mormon mission. Because of the club's temporary draft embargo, Talbot has yet to make his pro debut. He did impress the Astros during instructional league, resembling a young Ron Darling with his effortless delivery, arm action and feel for three pitches. Talbot pitched at 88 mph in instructional league, but during the spring he sat at 91-92 and touched 95. His fastball has a lot of run and sink. He also throws a tight curveball and a changeup that's advanced for his age. Talbot's command and competitiveness also earn high marks. He likely will begin 2003 in extended spring and make his debut at Tri-City or Martinsville in June.

Year	Club (League)	Class	W	L	ERA	G	GS	CG	SV	IP	H	R	ER	HR	BB	SO	AVG
	Has Not Played—Signed 2003 Contract																

22. Rory Shortell, rhp

Born: June 3, 1981. **Ht.:** 6-3. **Wt.:** 200. **Bats:** R. **Throws:** R. **School:** San Diego State University. **Career Transactions:** Selected by Astros in third round of 2002 draft; signed Aug. 15, 2002.

Another victim of owner Drayton McLane's freeze on signing draft choices, Shortell is the most advanced pitcher signed by Houston last year. The Astros think he has a chance to move nearly as quickly as 2001 third-rounder Kirk Saarloos, who reached the majors less than a year after he signed. Of course, Saarloos had the benefit of pitching in his draft summer. Drafted in the fourth round out of high school by the Red Sox, Shortell pitched and played the middle infield as a San Diego State freshman. He gave up hitting as a sophomore but didn't really blossom until last spring. Shortell wasn't overpowering in instructional league but threw 92-93 mph for the Aztecs. Both his curveball and slider have a hard downward break. Houston also likes his poise on the mound. He throws with a short arm action but at least that creates deception. The Astros believe Shortell just needs some fine-tuning, mainly improving his changeup and learning to miss more bats than he has in the past. He could begin his pro career in high Class A.

Year	Club (League)	Class	W	L	ERA	G	GS	CG	SV	IP	H	R	ER	HR	BB	SO	AVG
	Has Not Played—Signed 2003 Contract																

23. Ramon German, 3b

Born: Jan. 15, 1980. **Ht.:** 5-11. **Wt.:** 160. **Bats:** B. **Throws:** R. **Career Transactions:** Signed out of Dominican Republic by Astros, Jan. 19, 1997.

Houston's two best hopes for a homegrown third baseman regressed in 2002. Morgan Ensberg failed in his first extended shot at the majors. German, doomed to return to Lexington by the organization's lack of a high Class A affiliate, didn't build off the rapid improvement he showed in 2001 and missed two months with a broken finger. He hit .264 with seven homers in April before pitchers realized he was trying to pull everything. He batted .232 with four homers the rest of the way, piling up more strikeouts (62) than hits (56). Pitchers took advantage of his lack of discipline. German has power and doesn't have to try to hit the ball 500 feet. He has yet to adapt to changing speeds or learn how to cover the lower half of the strike zone. He did improve at third base, showing good reactions and increased agility. His infield arm remained one of the strongest in the system. When he moves up to high Class A this year, the Astros would like to see German learn the strike zone, improve his overall concentration and watch his weight more carefully.

Year	Club (League)	Class	AVG	G	AB	R	H	2B	3B	HR	RBI	BB	SO	SB	SLG	OBP
1997	Astros (DSL)	R	.255	33	98	16	25	7	0	0	8	18	15	3	.327	—
1998	Astros (DSL)	R	.276	51	181	28	50	16	1	3	27	21	25	3	.425	.353
1999	Astros (DSL)	R	.289	69	249	48	72	23	1	9	47	41	44	19	.498	.396
2000	Martinsville (Appy)	R	.320	59	225	42	72	24	1	7	44	23	64	16	.529	.384
2001	Lexington (SAL)	A	.265	129	461	72	122	37	3	13	93	55	107	21	.443	.352
2002	Lexington (SAL)	A	.241	86	328	46	79	15	1	11	49	43	77	15	.393	.328
MINOR LEAGUE TOTALS			.272	427	1542	252	420	122	7	43	268	201	332	77	.423	.360

24. Ruddy Lugo, rhp

Born: May 22, 1980. **Ht.:** 6-0. **Wt:** 190. **Bats:** R. **Throws:** R. **School:** Xaverian HS, Brooklyn. **Career Transactions:** Selected by Brewers in third round of 1999 draft; signed June 21, 1999 . . . Traded by Brewers to Dodgers, June 1, 2001, completing trade in which Dodgers sent OF Devon White to Brewers for OF Marquis Grissom and a player to be named (Feb. 25, 2001) . . . Traded by Dodgers to Astros for Daryle Ward, Jan. 25, 2003.

The younger brother of Astros shortstop Julio Lugo, Ruddy showed promise as an athletic two-way player in high school. He was compared to Frankie Rodriguez, another highly touted two-way prospect who came up through the New York City prep ranks. Like Rodriguez, Lugo expressed interest in continuing to both hit and pitch as a pro, but the Brewers drafted him with the intention of using him as a pitcher. Acquired in the Devon White-Marquis Grissom trade, Lugo fires low- to mid-90s heat that gets on hitters in a hurry. He has a diverse arsenal of pitches, featuring a fastball that cuts, runs or sinks, breaking balls from different angles and an above-average changeup. He has a quick arm and uses his athleticism well on the mound, but some scouts think the flat plane to his fastball and curve will affect his success at higher levels. He'll return to Double-A, where he finished 2002.

Year	Club (League)	Class	W	L	ERA	G	GS	CG	SV	IP	H	R	ER	HR	BB	SO	AVG
1999	Ogden (Pio)	R	1	2	7.88	6	6	0	0	24	35	23	21	2	12	26	.340
2000	Ogden (Pio)	R	5	5	3.44	16	16	1	0	92	82	48	35	7	52	88	.253
2001	Beloit (Mid)	A	1	0	0.60	10	0	0	5	15	10	1	1	0	6	20	.192
	Wilmington (SAL)	A	0	2	3.77	16	0	0	2	31	29	14	13	2	13	23	.259
2002	Vero Beach (FSL)	A	8	2	2.38	22	9	1	1	87	68	28	23	5	26	77	.217
	Jacksonville (SL)	AA	3	1	4.05	11	2	0	1	33	34	15	15	3	13	23	.274
MINOR LEAGUE TOTALS			18	12	3.45	81	33	2	9	282	258	129	108	19	122	257	.251

25. Adam Everett, ss

Born: Feb. 2, 1977. **Ht.:** 6-0. **Wt.:** 160. **Bats:** R. **Throws:** R. **School:** University of South Carolina. **Career Transactions:** Selected by Red Sox in first round (12th overall) of 1998 draft; signed Aug. 4, 1998 . . . Traded by Red Sox with LHP Greg Miller to Astros for OF Carl Everett, Dec. 15, 1999.

When the Astros acquired Everett from Boston in a December 1999 trade, they expected that he'd be their regular shortstop by now. He did win the job in spring training last year but couldn't hold it. He was farmed out three weeks into the season after batting .189, and didn't do much better when he got a second chance after Julio Lugo broke his left forearm. A 2000 U.S. Olympian, Everett had the best Triple-A performance of his career last year, but it was his third try at that level and little consolation. He can handle the bat and make contact, but his plate discipline has regressed and pitchers still get him out by pounding him inside with fastballs. Everett did improve working with New Orleans batting coach Gary Gaetti and spent the offseason trying to get stronger. Whether he'll ever hit enough remains in question. His defense is beyond reproach, however, as he has the complete package. If he could stay in the lineup, Everett would contend for Gold Gloves thanks to his range, arm, hands and instincts. The Astros were happy to learn he has an extra option remaining, and he'll return to Triple-A unless he impresses them with his bat in spring training.

Year	Club (League)	Class	AVG	G	AB	R	H	2B	3B	HR	RBI	BB	SO	SB	SLG	OBP
1998	Lowell (NY-P)	A	.296	21	71	11	21	6	2	0	9	11	13	2	.437	.407
1999	Trenton (EL)	AA	.263	98	338	56	89	11	0	10	44	41	64	21	.385	.356
2000	New Orleans (PCL)	AAA	.245	126	453	82	111	25	2	5	37	75	100	13	.342	.363
2001	New Orleans (PCL)	AAA	.249	114	441	69	110	20	8	5	40	39	74	24	.365	.330
	Houston (NL)	MAJ	.000	9	3	1	0	0	0	0	0	0	1	1	.000	.000
2002	Houston (NL)	MAJ	.193	40	88	11	17	3	0	0	4	12	19	3	.227	.297
	New Orleans (PCL)	AAA	.275	88	345	51	95	16	7	2	25	24	59	12	.380	.331
MAJOR LEAGUE TOTALS			.187	49	91	12	17	3	0	0	4	12	20	4	.220	.288
MINOR LEAGUE TOTALS			.258	447	1648	269	426	78	19	22	155	190	310	72	.369	.348

26. D.J. Houlton, rhp

Born: Aug. 12, 1979. **Ht.:** 6-4. **Wt.:** 220. **Bats:** R. **Throws:** R. **School:** University of the Pacific. **Career Transactions:** Selected by Astros in 11th round of 2001 draft; signed June 9, 2001.

The Astros have a few finesse righthanders who have had success, including Mike Burns (2.49 ERA, Midwest League-best 181 innings in 2002) and Nick Roberts (team-high 12 wins at Round Rock). The best is Houlton, one of six players among the top 30 signed as a college senior—an Astros specialty. (The others are Jason Lane, Chad Qualls, Henri Stanley, Charlton Jimerson and Todd Self). Some Houston officials cite his curveball as his best pitch, while others give the nod to his changeup. What is certain is that Houlton's prime asset is his ability to change speeds and spot his stuff around the strike zone. He has a deceptive delivery that makes hitters react as if his average fastball were in the low 90s. Houlton also throws a slider, but it's slurvy and it detracts from his other pitches. He trusted his stuff more last year than he did in his 2001 pro debut. He'll have to prove himself at every level and will get a chance in high Class A this year.

Year	Club (League)	Class	W	L	ERA	G	GS	CG	SV	IP	H	R	ER	HR	BB	SO	AVG
2001	Martinsville (Appy)	R	5	4	2.50	13	13	1	0	72	67	24	20	7	7	71	.240
	Michigan (Mid)	A	0	1	5.40	1	1	0	0	5	7	5	3	0	1	4	.304
2002	Michigan (Mid)	A	14	5	3.14	35	16	0	2	141	120	57	49	12	30	138	.223
MINOR LEAGUE TOTALS			19	10	2.98	49	30	1	2	218	194	86	72	19	38	213	.231

27. Charlton Jimerson, of

Born: Sept. 22, 1979. **Ht.:** 6-3. **Wt.:** 200. **Bats:** R. **Throws:** R. **School:** University of Miami. **Career Transactions:** Selected by Astros in fifth round of 2001 draft; signed June 23, 2001.

If Jimerson can put everything together, he could be the next Eric Davis. That might be a tall task, but it's impossible to count him out considering his background. His mother was a crack addict who often abandoned Jimerson and his younger brother, while his father was abusive toward his mom and became homeless. Jimerson's older sister took care of her younger siblings, and Jimerson passed up the Astros as a 25th-round pick out of high school to attend Miami on an academic scholarship. He made the baseball team as a walk-on, playing sparingly for 3½ years while completing his computer-science degree. Jimerson finally earned regular playing time toward the end of 2001, and parlayed it into the College World Series Most Outstanding Player award and fifth-round draft status. He's the best athlete and top defensive outfielder in the system. His combination of power and speed is exciting, and he has a quick bat. Jimerson's makeup is exceptional, and he and Henri Stanley play harder than any of Houston's minor leaguers. That can be a detriment when Jimerson is at the plate, because he's too aggressive and has little grasp of the strike zone. He must do better at laying off high fastballs, identifying and reacting to breaking pitches, and making adjustments once he figures out what pitchers are trying to do to him. He made progress in fits and starts during the 2002 season and showed positive signs in instructional league. Jimerson has a strong arm but is working on his throwing mechanics. The Astros may send him back to low Class A to get him on the right track. He might not become another Davis, but Houston hopes he can at least become Preston Wilson with better center-field defense.

Year	Club (League)	Class	AVG	G	AB	R	H	2B	3B	HR	RBI	BB	SO	SB	SLG	OBP
2001	Pittsfield (NY-P)	A	.234	51	197	35	46	12	1	9	31	18	79	15	.442	.304
2002	Lexington (SAL)	A	.228	125	439	65	100	22	4	14	57	36	168	34	.392	.295
MINOR LEAGUE TOTALS			.230	176	636	100	146	34	5	23	88	54	247	49	.407	.298

28. Matt Albers, rhp

Born: Jan. 20, 1983. **Ht.:** 6-1. **Wt.:** 210. **Bats:** L. **Throws:** R. **School:** San Jacinto (Texas) JC. **Career Transactions:** Selected by Astros in 23rd round of 2001 draft; signed May 31, 2002.

The Astros selected Albers out of a suburban Houston high school in 2001 and signed him as a draft-and-follow after he spent a year at San Jacinto JC, where he went to the Junior College World Series. He's something to behold because he has a short, somewhat soft frame at 6 feet and 210 pounds—with an electric right arm attached. Albers is still raw, but his potential is obvious. He throws a 91-95 mph fastball, a slider that has its moments and a changeup. He can be inconsistent with his release point and needs to firm up his body, but he'll shoot up the prospect list and through the minors if he figures it all out. Albers sent a positive sign to the Astros by shedding 12 pounds before reporting to instructional league. Houston won't rush him, so he could begin 2003 in extended spring training before reporting to short-season ball.

Year	Club (League)	Class	W	L	ERA	G	GS	CG	SV	IP	H	R	ER	HR	BB	SO	AVG
2002	Martinsville (Appy)	R	2	3	5.13	13	13	0	0	60	61	38	34	2	38	72	.274
MINOR LEAGUE TOTALS			2	3	5.13	13	13	0	0	60	61	38	34	2	38	72	.274

29. Brooks Conrad, 2b

Born: Jan. 16, 1980. **Ht.:** 5-11. **Wt.:** 180. **Bats:** B. **Throws:** R. **School:** Arizona State University. **Career Transactions:** Selected by Astros in eighth round of 2001 draft; signed June 18, 2001.

Every organization is looking for its own David Eckstein these days, and Conrad is Houston's. He's a short second baseman who doesn't have any overwhelming tools but gets the job done, exuding hustle all the while. In his first full pro season, Conrad led the Midwest League in runs and triples. He was a catalyst for Michigan in the No. 2 spot in the order. A switch-hitter who's better from the left side, Conrad gets on base and has surprising gap power for his size. His pure speed is average, but he runs better than that because he goes all out and has tremendous instincts. Defensively, he's a little stiff at second base and has a so-so arm. He needs to build up his stamina after fading in August. The Astros will send Conrad to high Class A and see if he can continue to overachieve in 2003. With his makeup, they think he'll at least become a big league utilityman.

Year	Club (League)	Class	AVG	G	AB	R	H	2B	3B	HR	RBI	BB	SO	SB	SLG	OBP
2001	Pittsfield (NY-P)	A	.280	65	232	41	65	16	5	4	39	26	52	14	.444	.375
2002	Michigan (Mid)	A	.287	133	499	94	143	25	14	14	94	62	102	18	.477	.368
MINOR LEAGUE TOTALS			.285	198	731	135	208	41	19	18	133	88	154	32	.466	.370

30. Jason Alfaro, 3b

Born: Nov. 29, 1977. **Ht.:** 5-10. **Wt.:** 190. **Bats:** R. **Throws:** R. **School:** Hill (Texas) JC. **Career Transactions:** Selected by Astros in 22nd round of 1997 draft; signed June 30, 1997.

Drafted as a two-way player out of Hill JC, Alfaro pitched four games in his first pro summer before becoming a full-time infielder. He spent three years as a shortstop and another as a utilityman, never doing much with the bat. In spring training 2002, he made his stance more upright so he could see the ball better and tried to adopt a more disciplined approach. Bingo. Alfaro became a Texas League all-star, hitting .314 (59 points above his previous average) with 16 homers (one less than he hit in his first 403 pro games). He showed power to almost all areas of the field and doubled his career high for walks. He also has average speed and good instincts on the bases. The Astros compare him to Keith Ginter, whom they traded to the Brewers for Mark Loretta last August, but Alfaro isn't as pull-conscious and is more flexible defensively. Alfaro has top-of-the-line arm strength that translated well to the hot corner when he moved there full-time last year. He also showed good hands, leading TL third basemen with a .963 fielding percentage. He's still a little inconsistent and needs to read balls better at third. Alfaro was 24 and repeating Double-A last year, so he has to prove that his breakthrough wasn't a fluke. If he's for real, he has more offensive upside than most of the position players on this list. Projected as Houston's regular Triple-A third baseman in 2003, Alfaro will get time at second base and in the outfield if Morgan Ensberg is sent to New Orleans.

Year	Club (League)	Class	AVG	G	AB	R	H	2B	3B	HR	RBI	BB	SO	SB	SLUG	OBP
1997	Astros (GCL)	R	.265	34	102	8	27	5	0	2	13	8	14	6	.373	.324
1998	Astros (GCL)	R	.242	47	178	20	43	8	0	1	18	11	24	5	.303	.286
1999	Michigan (Mid)	A	.271	118	473	74	128	25	4	5	50	23	62	5	.372	.302
2000	Kissimmee (FSL)	A	.250	117	460	58	115	20	1	7	41	25	63	2	.343	.287
2001	Round Rock (TL)	AA	.243	87	284	26	69	16	2	2	29	7	40	2	.335	.264
2002	Round Rock (TL)	AA	.314	124	455	71	143	36	2	16	74	50	75	11	.508	.393
MINOR LEAGUE TOTALS			.269	527	1952	257	525	110	9	33	225	124	278	31	.385	.315

KANSAS CITY
ROYALS

TOP 30 PROSPECTS

1. Zack Greinke, rhp
2. Angel Berroa, ss
3. Jimmy Gobble, lhp
4. Ken Harvey, 1b
5. Mike MacDougal, rhp
6. Alexis Gomez, of
7. Colt Griffin, rhp
8. Kyle Snyder, rhp
9. Andres Blanco, ss
10. Jeremy Hill, rhp
11. Ryan Bukvich, rhp
12. Danny Christensen, lhp
13. Ruben Gotay, 2b
14. Alejandro Machado, ss
15. Mike Tonis, c
16. Brad Voyles, rhp
17. Ian Ferguson, rhp
18. Wes Obermueller, rhp
19. David DeJesus, of
20. Roscoe Crosby, of
21. Jeff Austin, rhp
22. Ronny Paulino, c
23. D.J. Carrasco, rhp
24. James Shanks, of
25. Byron Gettis, of
26. Chris Tierney, lhp
27. Adam Donachie, c
28. Dusty Wrightsman, rhp
29. Danny Tamayo, rhp
30. Micah Kaaihue, 1b

By Will Kimmey

The Royals haven't enjoyed a winning season since 1994. They lost a franchise-record 100 games in 2002. Though owner David Glass expects the team to get back to .500 in 2003, the streak of losing seasons likely will reach double figures.

"You have to be realistic," said Allard Baird, the general manager since June 2000. "We're in a rebuilding mode. But I've said many times, rebuilding should not be used as an excuse to lose or an acceptance of losing. We have two guys who are impact players in Carlos Beltran and Mike Sweeney. The key will be pitching."

It's a sentiment that recalls 1997. The Royals started that season with impact outfielders Johnny Damon and Jermaine Dye in place and Beltran and Sweeney on the way. Adding to the young nucleus of position players, Kansas City spent its top pick on righthander Dan Reichert and added three more pitchers with first-round choices in 1998. Not one has established himself as a serviceable major league starter.

The Royals spent four more first-round picks on arms in 1999, but Jay Gehrke was a bust and injuries slowed Kyle Snyder, Mike MacDougal and Jimmy Gobble. The trio is on track to reach the majors soon, however. Kansas City hopes they can join home-grown products Jeremy Affeldt and Runelvys Hernandez in the rotation, with the club's most recent first-rounders, Colt Griffin and Zack Greinke, arriving later. If all that happens, it would signal a much-needed mound turnaround. The Royals were 29th in the majors with a 5.21 ERA in 2002 and haven't finished better than 25th since 1999.

Kansas City also could use an infusion of offense after finishing 11th in the American League with 4.55 runs a game. But the organization has little position-player talent in the upper minors beyond shortstop Angel Berroa, first baseman Ken Harvey and outfielder Alexis Gomez.

While Kansas City's system is one of the thinnest in the game, Baird has beefed up the scouting department, especially in the pro staff and Latin American operations.

"Patience isn't accepting mediocrity," Baird said. "It just means there will be bumps and grinds. When we lose 100 games, you could put some stopgap veterans out there and we probably win some more games, but we want to get the young guys experience and start that learning curve."

Organization Overview

General Manager: Allard Baird. **Farm Director:** Muzzy Jackson. **Scouting Director:** Deric Ladnier.

2002 PERFORMANCE

Class	Farm Team	League	W	L	Pct.	Finish*	Manager(s)
Majors	Kansas City	American	62	100	.383	12th (14)	T. Muser/J. Mizerock/T. Pena
Triple-A	Omaha Royals	Pacific Coast	76	68	.528	4th (16)	Bucky Dent
Double-A	Wichita Wranglers	Texas	80	59	.576	1st (8)	Keith Bodie
High A	Wilmington Blue Rocks	Carolina	89	51	.636	1st (8)	Jeff Garber
Low A	Burlington Bees	Midwest	68	71	.489	9th (16)	Joe Szekely
Short-season	†Spokane Indians	Northwest	29	47	.382	7th (8)	Tom Poquette
Rookie	†GCL Royals	Gulf Coast	22	38	.367	14th (14)	Lloyd Simmons
OVERALL MINOR LEAGUE RECORD			364	334	.521	10th (30)	

*Finish in overall standings (No. of teams in league).   †Royals will have two affiliates in Rookie-level Arizona League in 2003.

ORGANIZATION LEADERS

BATTING
*Minimum 250 At-Bats
*AVG	Chan Perry, Wichita	.316
R	Ruben Gotay, Burlington	87
	Tydus Meadows, Wichita/Wilmington	87
H	James Shanks, Burlington	152
TB	Ruben Gotay, Burlington	232
2B	Ruben Gotay, Burlington	42
3B	Donzell McDonald, Omaha	15
HR	Kit Pellow, Omaha	27
RBI	Ruben Gotay, Burlington	83
BB	Richard Paz, Wichita	81
SO	Jon Guzman, Burlington	159
SB	Patrick Hallmark, Wichita	42

PITCHING
#Minimum 75 Innings
W	Ian Ferguson, Wichita/Wilmington	18
L	Mike Stodolka, Burlington	14
	Chris Tierney, Burlington	14
#ERA	Kris Wilson, Omaha/Wich./Wilmington	2.08
G	Jeremy Hill, Wichita	56
CG	Three tied at	2
SV	Jeremy Hill, Wichita	19
IP	Ian Ferguson, Wichita/Wilmington	185
BB	Colt Griffin, Wilmington/Burlington	87
SO	Ian Ferguson, Wichita/Wilmington	141

BEST TOOLS

Best Hitter for Average	Ken Harvey
Best Power Hitter	Micah Kaaihue
Fastest Baserunner	Alexis Gomez
Best Athlete	Roscoe Crosby
Best Fastball	Colt Griffin
Best Curveball	Jimmy Gobble
Best Slider	Mike MacDougal
Best Changeup	Danny Tamayo
Best Control	Zack Greinke
Best Defensive Catcher	Mike Tonis
Best Defensive Infielder	Andres Blanco
Best Infield Arm	Angel Berroa
Best Defensive Outfielder	David DeJesus
Best Outfield Arm	Alexis Gomez

PROJECTED 2006 LINEUP

Catcher	Mike Tonis
First Base	Mike Sweeney
Second Base	Alejandro Machado
Third Base	Ruben Gotay
Shortstop	Angel Berroa
Left Field	David DeJesus
Center Field	Carlos Beltran
Right Field	Alexis Gomez
Designated Hitter	Ken Harvey
No. 1 Starter	Zack Greinke

Ruben Gotay   **Mike Stodolka**

No. 2 Starter	Jimmy Gobble
No. 3 Starter	Runelvys Hernandez
No. 4 Starter	Jeremy Affeldt
No. 5 Starter	Miguel Ascencio
Closer	Jeremy Hill

TOP PROSPECTS OF THE DECADE

1993	Johnny Damon, of
1994	Jeff Granger, lhp
1995	Johnny Damon, of
1996	Jim Pittsley, rhp
1997	Glendon Rusch, lhp
1998	Dee Brown, of
1999	Carlos Beltran, of
2000	Dee Brown, of
2001	Chris George, lhp
2002	Angel Berroa, ss

TOP DRAFT PICKS OF THE DECADE

1993	Jeff Granger, lhp
1994	Matt Smith, lhp/1b
1995	Juan LeBron, of
1996	Dee Brown, of
1997	Dan Reichert, rhp
1998	Jeff Austin, rhp
1999	Kyle Snyder, rhp
2000	Mike Stodolka, lhp
2001	Colt Griffin, rhp
2002	Zack Greinke, rhp

ALL-TIME LARGEST BONUSES

Jeff Austin, 1998	$2,700,000
Mike Stodolka, 2000	$2,500,000
Zack Greinke, 2002	$2,475,000
Colt Griffin, 2001	$2,400,000
Kyle Snyder, 1999	$2,100,000

MinorLeagueDepthChart

KANSAS CITY ROYALS

RANK 26

The small-market Royals depend on their farm system for success. Unfortunately, it hasn't provided much help as the big league club has continued to struggle. The Royals haven't been able to develop first-round picks like Jeff Austin, Dee Brown, Dan Reichert, Mike Stodolka and Chris George. A high-risk 2001 draft produced a wild card in Colt Griffin, who has averaged a walk an inning, and Roscoe Crosby, who hasn't had a professional at-bat. The Royals were pleased with the turnaround of Mike MacDougal over the winter and see him as their next closer. But the organization has a laundry list of needs, and the front office hasn't been able to fill them despite dealing off the likes of Johnny Damon and Jermaine Dye.

Note: Depth charts prepared by Josh Boyd. Numbers in parentheses indicate prospect rankings.

LF
David DeJesus (19)
Tydus Meadows

CF
Roscoe Crosby (20)
James Shanks (24)

RF
Alexis Gomez (6)
Byron Gettis (25)
Jonathan Guzman

3B
Jarrod Patterson
Justin Gemoll
Matt Ferrera

SS
Angel Berroa (2)
Andres Blanco (9)
Don Murphy

2B
Ruben Gotay (13)
Alejandro Machado (14)
Elvis Pena
Angel Sanchez

1B
Ken Harvey (4)
Micah Kaaihue (30)
David Jensen
Chad Santos

C
Mike Tonis (15)
Ronny Paulino (22)
Adam Donachie (26)
Matt Tupman
Luis Gonzalez
Scott Walter

RHP

Starters	Relievers
Zack Greinke (1)	Mike MacDougal (5)
Colt Griffin (7)	Jeremy Hill (10)
Kyle Snyder (8)	Ryan Bukvich (11)
Ian Ferguson (17)	Brad Voyles (16)
Wes Obermueller (18)	D.J. Carrasco (23)
Dusty Wrightsman (28)	Jeff Austin (21)
Danny Tamayo (29)	Barry Armitage
Shawn Sedlacek	Ryan Baerlocher
Brian Sanches	Mike Natale
Carlos Rosa	Kyle Colton
Ambiorix Burgos	
Ira Brown	

LHP

Starters	Relievers
Jimmy Gobble (3)	Brian Shackelford
Danny Christensen (12)	
Chris Tierney (26)	
Mike Stodolka	

DraftAnalysis

2002 Draft

Best Pro Debut: OF Tim Frend (23), who owns several career records at Davidson, hit .326-2-34 and finished second in the short-season Northwest League in hitting and on-base percentage (.412). LHP Danny Christensen (4) went 2-0, 1.10 in six starts after his promotion to the NWL.

Best Athlete: RHP Zack Greinke (1) went sixth overall and had early-round possibilities as a catcher or third baseman. OF Kenard Springer (8) starred as a football running back and basketball guard in high school.

Best Pure Hitter: SS Don Murphy (5) or 1B David Jensen (3), though neither has the bat of unsigned SS Brandon Jones (6), whom the Royals will pursue as a draft-and-follow.

Best Raw Power: 1B Micah Kaaihue (15), the top-rated prospect from Hawaii last spring. Springer has promising power as well but isn't polished as a hitter.

Fastest Runner: OF Leon Stephens (32) is a 4.0-second runner from the left side of the plate. He's also more advanced as a hitter than expected. He just needs to make more contact to take advantage of his speed.

Best Defensive Player: Cs Adam Donachie (2), Matt Tupman (9) and Rusty Meyer (13) all are defensively gifted backstops who will have to prove they can hit.

Best Fastball: Greinke kept his velocity all year long, hitting 96 mph during the spring and 95 during the high Class A Carolina League playoffs. RHP Jonah Bayliss (7) topped out at 94 in college.

Best Breaking Ball: Greinke's curveball is better than his slider, and both are quality

Frend

pitches. So is his changeup, and he commands his entire arsenal well.

Most Intriguing Background: Unsigned OF J.J. Brown (26) is a cousin of Cubs outfielder Roosevelt Brown, who was originally signed by the Braves and area scout Deric Ladnier–who's now Kansas City's scouting director. Unsigned OF Michael Hernandez' (27) brother Johnny is an outfielder in the Cardinals system.

Closest To The Majors: Greinke pitched this winter in Puerto Rico, a rare move for a pitcher straight out of high school. He likely will begin this season where he finished the last one, in high Class A. Whichever catcher hits the most will move quickly, and right now that's Tupman.

Best Late-Round Pick: Kaaihue was committed to attending Nebraska before the club wooed him for two days at Kauffman Stadium. As soon as he signed, he asked if he could catch an immediate flight to the Rookie-level Gulf Coast League.

The One Who Got Away: RHP Cesar Carillo (33) took his 90-92 mph fastball and tight curveball to the University of Miami.

Assessment: Greinke became the best prospect in the system on the day he signed. Kansas City hasn't had much luck drafting position players recently and needs some of these guys to come through.

2001 Draft

The Royals spent $2.4 million on RHP Colt Griffin (1), who may have terminal wildness, and another $1.75 million on football star/OF Roscoe Crosby (2), who has yet to play in a pro game. Not the best recipe for small-market success.   **Grade: D**

2000 Draft

LHP Mike Stodolka (1) has bombed, while C Mike Tonis (2) has been injured. RHPs Ryan Bukvich (11) and Ian Ferguson (21) and draft-and-follow 2B Ruben Gotay (31) have picked up some of the slack, with Ferguson leading the minors in victories last year.   **Grade: C**

1999 Draft

Kyle Snyder and Mike MacDougal and LHP Jimmy Gobble all look like worthwhile first-rounders. The same can't be said of RHP Jay Gehrke (1), who was released. 1B Ken Harvey (5) should crack the lineup this year. The Royals should have kept 2B Mark Ellis (9) and signed RHP Bryan Bullington (37), who became the No. 1 overall pick in 2002.   **Grade: B+**

1998 Draft

There's still hope for LHP Chris George (1) but not much for his fellow first-rounders, RHPs Jeff Austin and Matt Burch.   **Grade: C**

Note: Draft analysis prepared by Jim Callis. Numbers in parentheses indicate draft rounds.

... The Royals considered Greinke the most polished high school arm in the 2002 draft.

Zack
Greinke rhp

Born: Oct. 21, 1983.
Ht.: 6-2. **Wt.:** 190.
Bats: R. **Throws:** R.
School: Apopka HS, Orlando.
Career Transactions: Selected by Royals in first round (sixth overall) of 2002 draft; signed July 13, 2002.

Greinke entered his high school senior season as a projected second- or third-round pick–as either a pitcher or third baseman. He never hit less than .444 in high school, producing 31 homers and 144 RBIs in four seasons. When scouts saw that his strong infield arm provided 96 mph heat from the mound last spring, though, his future was set. Greinke became more committed to pitching and went 9-2, 0.55 with 118 strikeouts and eight walks in 63 innings. He turned down a Clemson scholarship to sign with the Royals for a $2.475 million bonus as the sixth overall pick. Because the Royals had no instructional league and Greinke got in just 12 innings last summer, they sent him to pitch in the Puerto Rican League over the winter. Though such an assignment is almost unheard of, Greinke handled it well and was regarded as one of the league's top prospects. Guy Hansen, a former Royals scout who now works for the Braves and was Greinke's pitching coach at Mayaguez, said Greinke was a cross between David Cone and Bret Saberhagen, with Cone's breaking ball and Saberhagen's mechanics and command. Hansen also had high praise for Greinke's polished approach to pitching and his ability to accept and implement instruction.

Despite his inexperience on the mound, Greinke commands four above-average pitches. His fastball sits between 91 and 93 mph, and he likes to move it in and out on hitters. He also has a slider with good tilt, along with a curveball and changeup. Because he has plenty of athleticism, a compact delivery and easy arm action, Greinke may increase his velocity as he progresses. If that happens, he would profile as a No. 1 starter. Greinke's infield experience makes him a good fielding pitcher who holds runners well. Though he has four pitches, Greinke rarely uses all of them in a given outing. He usually has two working at a time and tends to stick with them. Because he barely pitched after signing, the biggest key for Greinke is to get experience in game situations and continue to build his arm strength. He needs to work on pitching down in the strike zone more. He also needs to improve the command of his secondary pitches.

The Royals considered Greinke the most polished high school arm in the 2002 draft. Based on his performance in Puerto Rico, where he had a 2.45 ERA in 26 innings, Greinke could start the season in high Class A. While Greinke's stuff isn't as overwhelming as 2001 first-rounder Colt Griffin's, he's a workaholic who studies hitters and figures to succeed with his intellect and command.

Year	Club (League)	Class	W	L	ERA	G	GS	CG	SV	IP	H	R	ER	HR	BB	SO	AVG
2002	Royals (GCL)	R	0	0	1.93	3	3	0	0	5	3	1	1	0	3	4	.200
	Spokane (NWL)	A	0	0	7.71	2	2	0	0	5	9	4	4	0	0	5	.391
	Wilmington (Car)	A	0	0	0.00	1	0	0	0	2	1	0	0	0	0	0	.167
MINOR LEAGUE TOTALS			0	0	3.97	6	5	0	0	12	13	5	5	0	3	9	.295

2. Angel Berroa, ss

Born: Jan. 27, 1978. **Ht.:** 6-0. **Wt.:** 170. **Bats:** R. **Throws:** R. **Career Transactions:** Signed out of Dominican Republic by Athletics, Aug. 14, 1997 . . . Traded by Athletics with C A.J. Hinch and cash to Royals, as part of three-way trade in which Athletics acquired OF Johnny Damon, SS Mark Ellis and a player to be named from Royals and RHP Cory Lidle from Devil Rays, Royals acquired RHP Roberto Hernandez from Devil Rays, and Devil Rays acquired OF Ben Grieve and a player to be named or cash from Athletics, Jan. 8, 2001.

After coming from the Athletics, Berroa led all minor league shortstops with 60 extra-base hits in 2001 and was the Royals' top prospect. He missed two months in 2002 after arthroscopic knee surgery in April and then battled nagging back, leg and hamstring injuries for the remainder of a disappointing season. He also turned out to be two years older than previously thought. Berroa has the tools to become a standout defensive shortstop, with great hands, plus arm strength and range. He also shows solid instincts for the game and a good work ethic. He has a quick bat and some pop. Berroa got a little homer-happy last season as he tried to pull everything. He needs to improve his pitch recognition and plate discipline. He makes errors because he's aggressive and rushes plays, so that should stop as he matures. Whether he's ready, the shortstop job is Berroa's to lose in spring training after Neifi Perez was released.

Year	Club (League)	Class	AVG	G	AB	R	H	2B	3B	HR	RBI	BB	SO	SB	SLG	OBP
1998	Athletics West (DSL)	R	.245	58	196	51	48	7	4	8	37	25	37	4	.444	.338
1999	Athletics (AZL)	R	.290	46	169	42	49	11	4	2	24	16	26	11	.438	.371
	Midland (TL)	AA	.059	4	17	3	1	1	0	0	0	0	2	0	.118	.059
2000	Visalia (Cal)	A	.277	129	429	61	119	25	6	10	63	30	70	11	.434	.337
2001	Wilmington (Car)	A	.317	51	199	43	63	18	4	6	25	9	41	10	.538	.382
	Wichita (TL)	AA	.296	80	304	63	90	20	4	8	42	17	55	15	.467	.373
	Kansas City (AL)	MAJ	.302	15	53	8	16	2	0	0	4	3	10	2	.340	.339
2002	Omaha (PCL)	AAA	.215	77	297	37	64	11	4	8	35	15	84	6	.360	.277
	Kansas City (AL)	MAJ	.227	20	75	8	17	7	1	0	5	7	10	3	.347	.301
MAJOR LEAGUE TOTALS			.258	35	128	16	33	9	1	0	9	10	20	5	.344	.317
MINOR LEAGUE TOTALS			.269	445	1611	300	434	93	26	42	226	112	315	57	.438	.340

3. Jimmy Gobble, lhp

Born: July 19, 1981. **Ht.:** 6-3. **Wt.:** 190. **Bats:** L. **Throws:** L. **School:** John S. Battle HS, Bristol, Va. Career Transactions: Selected by Royals in first round (43rd overall) of 1999 draft; signed June 21, 1999.

After two promising seasons, Gobble battled injuries in 2002. A right groin tear forced him to the disabled list for three weeks in June. Four starts after he returned, he had shoulder soreness, which didn't turn out to be anything major. That scare, coupled with more groin pain, led the Royals to shut him down in July. Like many lefthanded pitching prospects, Gobble is compared to Tom Glavine. Few live up to the hype, but Gobble has a chance because he operates with three quality pitches, including a low-90s fastball. His curveball is the best in the system and his deceptive changeup is more than a show-me pitch. Gobble doesn't have a major weakness and just needs to stay healthy. Against more advanced hitters he'll have to make adjustments, such as tightening his big-breaking curve and locating his fastball with more precision. Had he stayed healthy, Gobble was in line for a September callup. He's ticketed for Triple-A Omaha to start 2003.

Year	Club (League)	Class	W	L	ERA	G	GS	CG	SV	IP	H	R	ER	HR	BB	SO	AVG
1999	Royals (GCL)	R	0	0	2.70	4	1	0	0	7	6	3	2	0	5	8	.222
2000	Charleston, WV (SAL)	A	12	10	3.66	25	25	3	0	145	144	75	59	10	34	115	.256
2001	Wilmington (Car)	A	10	6	2.55	27	27	0	0	162	134	58	46	8	33	154	.226
2002	Wichita (TL)	AA	5	7	3.38	13	13	0	0	69	71	29	26	3	19	52	.267
MINOR LEAGUE TOTALS			27	23	3.12	69	66	3	0	383	355	165	133	21	91	329	.245

4. Ken Harvey, 1b

Born: March 1, 1978. **Ht.:** 6-2. **Wt.:** 240. **Bats:** R. **Throws:** R. **School:** University of Nebraska. **Career Transactions:** Selected by Royals in fifth round of 1999 draft; signed June 4, 1999.

Harvey tried a new stance similar to Jeff Bagwell's in 2002. He batted .277—58 points off his previous career low—but everything came together for him in the Arizona Fall League. He was the league MVP after setting records for batting (.479), slugging (.752) and on-base percentage (.537). Harvey uses a unique grip, overlapping his hands as he goes into his trigger mechanism, with his right hand covering half of his left. With his inside-out, line-drive swing, Harvey smokes the ball up the middle and to the opposite field. He could add power as he learns which pitches to drive in specific counts. Despite putting in plenty of work on his defense, Harvey will struggle to become an average first baseman. He lacks first-step quickness, which also rules out a switch to left field, and his hands are stiff. He doesn't walk much, more because of his ability to make contact than a poor eye. His weight is a concern. Harvey has one above-average tool, but he has left no question he can rake. His AFL campaign should catapult him into Kansas City's 2003 plans as a DH.

Year	Club (League)	Class	AVG	G	AB	R	H	2B	3B	HR	RBI	BB	SO	SB	SLG	OBP
1999	Spokane (NWL)	A	.397	56	204	49	81	17	0	8	41	23	30	7	.598	.477
2000	Wilmington (Car)	A	.335	46	164	20	55	10	0	4	25	14	29	0	.470	.411
2001	Wilmington (Car)	A	.380	35	137	22	52	9	1	6	27	13	21	3	.591	.455
	Wichita (TL)	AA	.338	79	314	54	106	20	3	9	63	18	60	3	.506	.372
	Kansas City (AL)	MAJ	.250	4	12	1	3	1	0	0	2	0	4	0	.333	.250
2002	Omaha (PCL)	AAA	.277	128	488	75	135	30	1	20	75	42	87	8	.465	.342
MAJOR LEAGUE TOTALS			.250	4	12	1	3	1	0	0	2	0	4	0	.333	.250
MINOR LEAGUE TOTALS			.328	344	1307	220	429	86	5	47	231	110	227	21	.510	.392

5. Mike MacDougal, rhp

Born: March 5, 1977. **Ht.:** 6-4. **Wt.:** 190. **Bats:** B. **Throws:** R. **School:** Wake Forest University. **Career Transactions:** Selected by Royals in first round (25th overall) of 1999 draft; signed July 1, 1999.

MacDougal's 2001 major league debut ended after he sustained a skull fracture when struck in the head by Carlos Beltran's bat during a game. He lost the feeling in his right arm for a time, and still has occasional numbness in his fingertips. This may have contributed to his control problems in 2002, when he was shut down for six weeks. MacDougal pumps his fastball into the mid-90s with plus life and was clocked at 100 mph or better six times in winter ball in Puerto Rico, where he was also rated the league's top prospect. His darting slider is one of the nastiest in the system, and he has shown a feel for a curveball and changeup. Command is a major issue, though it was better over the winter, and learning to harness his electric arsenal has been tough. His inability to repeat his delivery is the main problem, and the life on his pitches makes it even harder. But after MacDougal's winter assignment, he's ready to compete for the big league closer's job

Year	Club (League)	Class	W	L	ERA	G	GS	CG	SV	IP	H	R	ER	HR	BB	SO	AVG
1999	Spokane (NWL)	A	2	2	4.47	11	11	0	0	46	43	25	23	3	17	57	.251
2000	Wilmington (Car)	A	9	7	3.92	26	25	0	1	145	115	79	63	5	76	129	.219
	Wichita (TL)	AA	0	1	7.71	2	2	0	0	12	16	10	10	0	7	9	.356
2001	Omaha (PCL)	AAA	8	8	4.68	28	27	1	0	144	144	90	75	13	76	110	.259
	Kansas City (AL)	MAJ	1	1	4.70	3	3	0	0	15	18	10	8	2	4	7	.290
2002	Omaha (PCL)	AAA	3	5	5.60	12	10	0	0	53	52	42	33	4	55	30	.265
	Wichita (TL)	AA	1	1	3.06	4	4	1	0	18	11	12	6	1	24	14	.193
	Royals (GCL)	R	0	0	3.00	1	1	0	0	3	1	1	1	0	0	3	.273
	Wilmington (Car)	A	0	1	1.08	5	0	0	2	8	3	4	1	1	5	10	.107
	Kansas City (AL)	MAJ	0	1	5.00	6	0	0	0	9	5	5	5	0	7	10	.161
MAJOR LEAGUE TOTALS			1	2	4.81	9	3	0	0	24	23	15	13	2	11	17	.247
MINOR LEAGUE TOTALS			23	25	4.45	89	80	2	3	429	387	263	212	27	260	362	.244

6. Alexis Gomez, of

Born: Aug. 6, 1980. **Ht.:** 6-2. **Wt.:** 180. **Bats:** L. **Throws:** L. **Career Transactions:** Signed out of Dominican Republic by Royals, Feb. 21, 1997.

An outstanding athlete, Gomez was a volleyball star in the Dominican Republic. He resembles a more slender Carlos Beltran with similar tools, albeit less raw power. Gomez was hitting .402 in late May in Double-A until he came down with chicken pox and missed two weeks. He had his best offensive season because he learned to use the whole field, shortened his stroke and worked deeper counts. He handled breaking balls, which had been a bugaboo. Gomez generates plenty of bat speed and hit more homers than he had in his entire career. He has plus speed and slightly above-average arm strength. Gomez can steal bases, but needs to improve his jumps. He was caught stealing on 40 percent of his attempts in 2002. His athleticism allows him to track down balls in center field, but he can be erratic because he doesn't have great instincts. Gomez is rough around the edges, but he has improved every year and should continue to do so in Triple-A in 2003.

Year	Club (League)	Class	AVG	G	AB	R	H	2B	3B	HR	RBI	BB	SO	SB	SLG	OBP
1997	Royals (DSL)	R	.351	64	248	51	87	12	9	0	42	33	52	9	.472	.430
1998	Royals (DSL)	R	.283	67	233	51	66	11	3	1	34	50	46	17	.369	.421
1999	Royals (GCL)	R	.276	56	214	44	59	12	1	5	31	32	48	13	.411	.371
2000	Wilmington (Car)	A	.254	121	461	63	117	13	4	1	33	45	121	21	.306	.322

		Class	AVG	G	AB	R	H	2B	3B	HR	RBI	BB	SO	SB	OBP	SLG
2001	Wilmington (Car)	A	.302	48	169	29	51	8	2	1	9	11	43	7	.391	.348
	Wichita (TL)	AA	.281	83	342	55	96	15	6	4	34	27	70	16	.395	.337
2002	Wichita (TL)	AA	.295	114	461	72	136	21	8	14	75	45	84	36	.466	.359
	Kansas City (AL)	MAJ	.200	5	10	0	2	0	0	0	0	0	2	0	.200	.200
MAJOR LEAGUE TOTALS			.200	5	10	0	2	0	0	0	0	0	2	0	.200	.200
MINOR LEAGUE TOTALS			.288	553	2128	365	612	92	33	26	258	243	464	119	.398	.364

7. Colt Griffin, rhp

Born: Sept. 29, 1982. **Ht.:** 6-4. **Wt.:** 200. **Bats:** R. **Throws:** R. **School:** Marshall (Texas) HS. **Career Transactions:** Selected by Royals in first round (ninth overall) of 2001 draft; signed Aug. 8, 2001 . . . On disabled list, April 5-Sept. 30, 2001.

Griffin was recruited as a first baseman by Louisiana Tech before he was clocked at 98 mph in 2001. He became the first documented high school pitcher to reach 100 mph and parlayed that into a $2.4 million bonus. While Griffin can dial his fastball into the upper 90s with ease, he often doesn't know where it's going. He's trying to strike a balance between velocity and command, so he has abandoned his two-seamer and kept his four-seamer at 93-94 mph. His slider is a potentially dominant pitch once he develops a feel for it. He also employs a circle change. Griffin still has major control issues and finished fourth in the minors in walks in 2002. For all his stuff, he didn't miss many bats, either. He needs to hone his delivery and avoid overthrowing. His slider flattens out when he drops his elbow. Griffin could be a dominant starter if he harnesses his control. Or he could become a tremendous bust. Command will be his point of emphasis in high Class A in 2003.

Year	Club (League)	Class	W	L	ERA	G	GS	CG	SV	IP	H	R	ER	HR	BB	SO	AVG
2001	Spokane (NWL)	A	0	1	27.00	3	2	0	0	2	4	7	7	0	7	0	.364
2002	Burlington (Mid)	A	6	6	5.36	19	19	0	0	91	75	60	54	1	82	66	.233
	Wilmington (Car)	A	0	1	3.86	3	0	0	0	5	3	2	2	0	5	3	.214
MINOR LEAGUE TOTALS			6	8	5.81	25	21	0	0	98	82	69	63	1	94	69	.236

8. Kyle Snyder, rhp

Born: Sept. 9, 1977. **Ht.:** 6-8. **Wt.:** 220. **Bats:** B. **Throws:** R. **School:** University of North Carolina. **Career Transactions:** Selected by Royals in first round (seventh overall) of 1999 draft; signed June 8, 1999 . . . On disabled list, April 5-Sept. 30, 2001.

Snyder was the Northwest League's top prospect in his pro debut but pitched just two innings in the next two years. Coming back from Tommy John surgery in September 2000, he slowly worked his way back into form in 2002. Snyder has regained the velocity on his fastball, which sits between 90-94 mph, and he continues to throw on a tough downhill plane. His curveball, which rivals Gobble's, and changeup can be plus pitches. He throws strikes, and his outstanding makeup helped him battle through his injury adversity. Snyder should use his curveball and changeup more often. While rehabbing, he focused on tossing a few solid innings or working on a certain pitch, rather than winning games. He has yet to show he can handle higher pitch counts. Because of his elbow problems, Snyder no longer throws his splitter, which was a plus pitch. Snyder remains a wild card because of his health. He made encouraging progress in the AFL and seems to be regaining the form that made him a coveted prospect. He'll begin 2003 in Double-A.

Year	Club (League)	Class	W	L	ERA	G	GS	CG	SV	IP	H	R	ER	HR	BB	SO	AVG
1999	Spokane (NWL)	A	1	0	4.13	7	7	0	0	24	20	13	11	1	7	25	.220
2000	Royals (GCL)	R	0	0	0.00	1	1	0	0	2	1	0	0	0	0	4	.143
	Wilmington (Car)	A	0	0	0.00	1	1	0	0	0	0	1	0	0	1	0	.000
2001					Did Not Play—Injured												
2002	Wilmington (Car)	A	0	2	2.98	15	15	0	0	48	49	19	16	1	11	48	.261
	Wichita (TL)	AA	2	2	4.21	6	6	0	0	26	21	12	12	4	7	18	.226
MINOR LEAGUE TOTALS			3	4	3.51	30	30	0	0	100	91	45	39	6	26	95	.240

9. Andres Blanco, ss

Born: April 11, 1984. **Ht.:** 5-10. **Wt.:** 150. **Bats:** B. **Throws:** R. **Career Transactions:** Signed out of Venezuela by Royals, Aug. 2, 2000.

Angel Berroa should have Kansas City's shortstop job for at least a few years. Blanco is the only player in the system with the skills to challenge him, and he's not nearly as advanced. For all the defensive accolades Berroa earns, Blanco might be even better. Blanco has the hands, range, actions and instincts for shortstop. He's steadier than Berroa while making the flashy diving stops and deep-in-the-hole throws. He's an above-average runner who can steal bases, with good bat speed and the strength to become a pesky, slap-hitting leadoff batter with gap power. For all his tools, Blanco is still weak offensively at this point and needs to add muscle to his slight frame. He also could stand to improve his pitch selection, as he's a bit of a free swinger. Gomez made the jump from the Rookie-level Gulf Coast League to high Class A in 2000, and the Royals will see if Blanco can pull off the same feat in 2003. He held his own in a brief stint there in 2002. If he learns to walk more and can hit in the .275 range, Blanco will enjoy a productive career as a major league shortstop.

Year	Club (League)	Class	AVG	G	AB	R	H	2B	3B	HR	RBI	BB	SO	SB	SLG	OBP
2001	Royals (DSL)	R	.298	54	188	39	56	0	3	0	16	28	23	9	.330	.411
2002	Royals (GCL)	R	.249	52	193	27	48	8	0	0	14	15	29	16	.290	.315
	Wilmington (Car)	A	.308	5	13	2	4	1	0	0	0	1	4	0	.385	.357
MINOR LEAGUE TOTALS			.274	111	394	68	108	9	3	0	30	44	56	25	.312	.364

10. Jeremy Hill, rhp

Born: Aug. 8, 1977. **Ht.:** 5-11. **Wt.:** 200. **Bats:** R. **Throws:** R. **School:** W.T. White HS, Dallas. **Career Transactions:** Selected by Royals in fifth round of 1996 draft; signed June 4, 1996.

After hitting .229 in five seasons as a catcher, Hill and his live arm moved to the other end of the battery in instructional league following the 2000 season. When he hit 95 mph, the conversion became permanent. He has drawn comparisons to Troy Percival, another catcher-turned-closer. Hill has unconventional mechanics–he leans backward before delivering pitches to generate more velocity–but he has no trouble repeating his delivery and it's tough for hitters to pick up. His quick arm action allows his explosive fastball to peak at 98-99 mph. He's aggressive in going after hitters, but his background as a catcher reminds him that changing speeds also can be effective. Hill's curveball was scrapped for a slider. His progress with that pitch will determine whether he pitches the seventh or ninth inning. He still needs to throw the slider with more conviction and velocity, and he needs to throw strikes more consistently. After pitching in the Dominican League over the winter, Hill should make the Royals' bullpen out of spring training.

Year	Club (League)	Class	AVG	G	AB	R	H	2B	3B	HR	RBI	BB	SO	SB	SLG	OBP
1996	Royals (GCL)	R	.178	31	90	4	16	6	0	0	4	12	17	0	.244	.286
1997	Spokane (NWL)	A	.283	60	187	35	53	12	1	3	29	25	53	1	.406	.366
1998	Lansing (Mid)	A	.240	86	288	25	69	12	1	4	37	15	75	4	.330	.285
1999	Wilmington (Car)	A	.234	92	304	37	71	12	1	4	27	38	75	2	.319	.329
2000	Wilmington (Car)	A	.197	99	299	33	59	12	2	3	26	33	84	1	.281	.281
MINOR LEAGUE TOTALS			.229	368	1168	134	268	54	5	14	123	123	304	8	.320	.309

Year	Club (League)	Class	W	L	ERA	G	GS	CG	SV	IP	H	R	ER	HR	BB	SO	AVG
2001	Burlington (Mid)	A	0	2	1.51	40	0	0	12	48	22	11	8	2	25	66	.138
	Wilmington (Car)	A	4	0	0.73	9	0	0	2	12	10	2	1	0	8	13	.233
2002	Wichita (TL)	AA	4	7	2.36	56	0	0	19	76	61	26	20	4	32	80	.221
	Kansas City (AL)	MAJ	0	1	3.86	10	0	0	0	9	8	4	4	1	8	7	.235
MAJOR LEAGUE TOTALS			0	1	3.86	10	0	0	0	9	8	4	4	1	8	7	.235
MINOR LEAGUE TOTALS			8	9	1.91	105	0	0	33	136	93	39	29	6	65	159	.194

11. Ryan Bukvich, rhp

Born: May 13, 1978. **Ht.:** 6-2. **Wt.:** 250. **Bats:** R. **Throws:** R. **School:** University of Mississippi. **Career Transactions:** Selected by Royals in 11th round of 2000 draft; signed June 9, 2000.

Bukvich began his college career at Division II Delta State (Miss.) before transferring to Mississippi, where he pitched poorly for two years and was academically ineligible as a senior. Area scout Mark Willoughby remembered Bukvich's arm strength and got the Royals to take a flier on him in the 2000 draft. Bukvich started the 2002 season by not allowing an earned run in his first 17 appearances, and didn't give up any runs after a promotion to Triple-A. His .131 opponents average was the lowest among minor league relievers. Bukvich throws a heavy fastball at 92-96 mph but needs a reliable second pitch to succeed in the majors. He must develop more consistency with his slurvy slider or improve his below-average splitter. Bukvich also struggled mightily with command in the majors, delivering first-pitch strikes to less than half the batters he faced. When he did find the plate he often served up meatballs, so he needs to throw more quality strikes as well. Bukvich has an outside shot at winning Kansas City's closer job in a spring-training competition with fellow rookies Mike MacDougal and Jeremy Hill. More likely, Bukvich will wind up as a set-up man.

Year	Club (League)	Class	W	L	ERA	G	GS	CG	SV	IP	H	R	ER	HR	BB	SO	AVG
2000	Spokane (NWL)	A	2	0	0.64	10	0	0	2	14	5	1	1	0	9	15	.111
	Charleston (SAL)	A	0	0	1.88	11	0	0	4	14	6	3	3	0	7	17	.128

Kansas City Royals

Year	Club (League)	Class	W	L	ERA	G	GS	CG	SV	IP	H	R	ER	HR	BB	SO	AVG
	Wilmington (Car)	A	0	1	18.00	2	0	0	0	2	3	4	4	0	5	3	.375
2001	Wilmington (Car)	A	0	1	1.72	37	0	0	13	58	41	16	11	1	31	80	.194
	Wichita (TL)	AA	0	0	3.75	7	0	0	0	12	9	6	5	2	2	14	.200
2002	Wichita (TL)	AA	1	1	1.31	23	0	0	8	34	17	8	5	0	15	47	.145
	Omaha (PCL)	AAA	1	0	0.00	12	0	0	8	14	4	0	0	0	7	17	.093
	Kansas City (AL)	MAJ	1	0	6.12	26	0	0	0	25	26	19	17	2	19	20	.277
MAJOR LEAGUE TOTALS			1	0	6.12	26	0	0	0	25	26	19	17	2	19	20	.277
MINOR LEAGUE TOTALS			4	3	1.76	102	0	0	35	148	85	38	29	3	76	193	.165

12. Danny Christensen, lhp

Born: Aug. 10, 1983. **Ht.:** 6-2. **Wt.:** 200. **Bats:** L. **Throws:** L. **School:** Xaverian HS, Brooklyn. **Career Transactions:** Selected by Royals in fourth round of 2002 draft; signed June 8, 2002.

Born and raised in Brooklyn, Christensen doesn't drive and uses a passport for identification in lieu of a driver's license. He made himself a top draft prospect with a marked improvement on the mound as a high school senior. That earned him a $308,000 bonus as a fourth-round pick. Christensen works with an 85-90 mph fastball that tails, sinks and occasionally reaches 92 mph. An offseason conditioning program could help him increase his velocity. His curveball and changeup are both potential plus pitches. He understands when to use his circle changeup and has a good overall feel for pitching. Christensen needs to be able to control his sweeping curveball better and throw more strikes with it. And while he can command his fastball, he must learn how to work both sides of the plate more effectively. His mechanics are nearly perfect and he hides the ball well. With a bulldog mentality on the mound, Christensen is similar to 2002 first-rounder Zack Grienke. Both are polished for prep pitchers and could advance rapidly. Christensen, who profiles as a middle-of-the-rotation starter, should start 2003 in low Class A. Jumping a level to high Class A isn't out of the question either, based on his strong showing at short-season Spokane, as well as his makeup and the Royals' willingness to aggressively promote young prospects.

Year	Club (League)	Class	W	L	ERA	G	GS	CG	SV	IP	H	R	ER	HR	BB	SO	AVG
2002	Royals (GCL)	R	1	3	3.10	7	6	0	0	29	20	13	10	2	14	28	.196
	Spokane (NWL)	A	2	0	1.10	6	6	0	0	33	24	6	4	3	14	23	.198
MINOR LEAGUE TOTALS			3	3	2.04	13	12	0	0	62	44	19	14	5	28	51	.197

13. Ruben Gotay, 2b

Born: Dec. 25, 1982. **Ht.:** 5-11. **Wt.:** 160. **Bats:** B. **Throws:** R. **School:** Indian Hills (Iowa) CC. **Career Transactions:** Selected by Royals in 31st round of 2000 draft; signed May 28, 2001.

He might not ooze tools and projectability, but Gotay continues to produce the offensive numbers to force his way into the organization's plans. He demonstrates great field awareness and instincts, which allow him to play above the sum of his physical tools. Gotay followed up a solid debut by leading the Midwest League in doubles and extra-base hits in 2002, his first full pro season. He has gap power and uses the whole field. A switch-hitter, Gotay was significantly better from the left side, hitting 91 points higher (.313 versus .222) with eight of his nine homers. He has average speed at best and must work on his baserunning. Because he doesn't run as well as the typical middle infielder, he only has average range at second base. His fielding has improved, though he still needs work on his double-play pivot. Gotay has a tendency to wait for throws on top of the base rather than coming through it as he receives the ball. The Royals like his bat, but Gotay will have to keep proving himself at each level, continuing in high Class A this year.

Year	Club (League)	Class	AVG	G	AB	R	H	2B	3B	HR	RBI	BB	SO	SB	SLG	OBP
2001	Royals (GCL)	R	.315	52	184	29	58	15	1	3	19	26	22	5	.457	.398
2002	Burlington (Mid)	A	.285	133	509	87	145	42	9	9	83	73	110	5	.456	.377
MINOR LEAGUE TOTALS			.293	185	693	116	203	57	10	12	102	99	132	10	.456	.383

14. Alejandro Machado, ss

Born: April 26, 1982. **Ht.:** 6-0. **Wt.:** 160. **Bats:** R. **Throws:** R. **Career Transactions:** Signed out of Venezuela by Braves, July 2, 1998 . . . Traded by Braves with RHP Brad Voyles to Royals for SS Rey Sanchez, July 31, 2001.

The Royals got Machado from the Braves for Rey Sanchez, and he projects as a similar middle infielder. Machado's average arm may relegate him to second base, especially in an organization with strong-armed and slick-fielding Angel Berroa and Andres Blanco already at shortstop. Even so, Machado's hands and range allow him to play a smooth second base, with the exception of being a little rough around the bag when turning the double play. Despite missing time with a groin pull, he made great strides at the plate in high Class A, batting .366 in the final three months to finish third in the Carolina League batting race. Machado is a spray hitter who rarely drives the ball, but he can handle the bat well and should hit for average. His ability to bunt and hit-and-run makes him a prime candidate for a No. 2 hitter if he can learn to draw more walks. His speed is a tick above average at best, so he won't be a huge basestealing threat at the upper levels. He should take a step up to Double-A in 2003 and could be in Kansas City by 2004.

Year	Club (League)	Class	AVG	G	AB	R	H	2B	3B	HR	RBI	BB	SO	SB	SLG	OBP
1999	Braves (GCL)	R	.278	56	223	45	62	11	0	0	14	20	22	19	.327	.348
2000	Danville (Appy)	R	.341	61	217	45	74	6	2	0	16	53	29	30	.387	.477
2001	Macon (SAL)	A	.271	82	306	43	83	6	3	1	24	34	56	20	.320	.368
	Burlington (Mid)	A	.239	28	109	17	26	5	0	0	11	10	16	5	.284	.311
2002	Wilmington (Car)	A	.314	101	325	53	102	9	1	2	29	27	43	20	.366	.381
MINOR LEAGUE TOTALS			.294	328	1180	203	347	37	6	3	94	144	166	94	.343	.385

15. Mike Tonis, c

Born: Feb. 9, 1979. **Ht.:** 6-3. **Wt.:** 220. **Bats:** R. **Throws:** R. **School:** University of California. **Career Transactions:** Selected by Royals in second round of 2000 draft; signed July 12, 2000.

Tonis rivals Devil Rays outfield prospect Josh Hamilton for the frequency of his hospital visits. Tonis had knee surgery after the 2001 season, forcing him to miss the Arizona Fall League. When he reported to spring training, his shoulder was so sore that he couldn't even throw the ball 90 feet. Shoulder surgery kept him out of action until August, when he headed to the Gulf Coast League to DH and get some at-bats. After homering in his first at-bat, Tonis was hit by a pitch that broke his jaw in his fifth game, ending his season. Tonis shows good power potential and could develop into a 15-20 home run catcher, but he never has hit for a high average because of poor plate discipline. He's a below-average runner. Defensively, he can catch and throw in the majors right now with his above-average arm and soft hands. He gunned down 39 percent of basestealers in 2001. Tonis also calls a good game. Look for him to start 2003 in Double-A. The selection of Ronny Paulino in the major league Rule 5 draft probably quiets any chance that Tonis would get a midseason promotion. If he can stay healthy, Tonis could be starting for Kansas City at some point in 2004.

Year	Club (League)	Class	AVG	G	AB	R	H	2B	3B	HR	RBI	BB	SO	SB	SLG	OBP
2000	Charleston (SAL)	A	.200	28	100	10	20	8	0	0	17	9	22	1	.280	.268
	Omaha (PCL)	AAA	.500	2	8	1	4	0	0	0	3	0	3	0	.500	.500
2001	Wilmington (Car)	A	.252	33	123	15	31	8	0	3	18	15	34	0	.390	.343
	Wichita (TL)	AA	.270	63	226	36	61	11	1	9	43	22	41	1	.447	.344
2002	Royals (GCL)	R	.176	6	17	2	3	0	0	1	3	2	3	0	.353	.300
MINOR LEAGUE TOTALS			.251	132	474	64	119	27	1	13	84	48	103	2	.395	.328

16. Brad Voyles, rhp

Born: Dec. 30, 1976. **Ht.:** 6-1. **Wt.:** 190. **Bats:** R. **Throws:** R. **School:** Lincoln Memorial (Tenn.) University. **Career Transactions:** Selected by Braves in 45th round of 1998 draft; signed June 7, 1998 . . . Traded by Braves with SS Alejandro Machado to Royals for SS Rey Sanchez, July 31, 2001.

A year after shooting from high Class A to the majors, Voyles spent 2002 on the Omaha-to-Kansas City shuttle, spending three stints with each club. Unlike most relievers, he has three pitches he can work with. His fastball, which can reach 95 mph, is more effective at 90-91 with good sinking action. He also has a plus changeup and an effective curveball. Voyles displays plenty of bravado on the mound, but sometimes his determination turns to stubbornness. He thought he could throw his heater by major league hitters—and found out the hard way he can't. Voyles gets in trouble when he falls behind in counts and elevates his fastball. He's much more effective when he works backward and starts hitters with his changeup. Voyles needs to improve the command of his fastball, but he'll battle for a spot in the Royals' all-prospect bullpen with Jeremy Hill, Mike MacDougal and Ryan Bukvich in 2003.

Year	Club (League)	Class	W	L	ERA	G	GS	CG	SV	IP	H	R	ER	HR	BB	SO	AVG
1998	Eugene (NWL)	A	0	0	3.09	7	0	0	0	12	9	5	4	0	10	22	.209
1999	Macon (SAL)	A	3	3	2.98	38	0	0	14	51	27	21	17	0	39	65	.151
	Myrtle Beach (Car)	A	1	1	2.25	5	0	0	0	12	7	3	3	1	9	13	.175
2000	Myrtle Beach (Car)	A	5	2	1.11	39	0	0	19	57	21	8	7	1	25	70	.115
2001	Myrtle Beach (Car)	A	0	0	0.00	2	0	0	1	2	0	0	0	0	1	3	.000
	Greenville (SL)	AA	0	0	1.08	15	0	0	6	17	11	3	2	0	10	25	.193
	Wichita (TL)	AA	1	0	0.00	11	0	0	4	15	8	0	0	0	10	19	.163
	Kansas City (AL)	MAJ	0	0	3.86	7	0	0	0	9	5	4	4	1	8	6	.161
2002	Omaha (PCL)	AAA	3	4	4.18	26	0	0	5	32	29	15	15	2	22	34	.248
	Kansas City (AL)	MAJ	0	2	6.51	22	0	0	1	28	31	21	20	5	18	26	.284
MAJOR LEAGUE TOTALS			0	2	5.84	29	0	0	1	37	36	25	24	6	26	32	.257
MINOR LEAGUE TOTALS			13	10	2.19	143	0	0	49	198	112	55	48	4	126	251	.166

17. Ian Ferguson, rhp

Born: Aug. 23, 1979. **Ht.:** 6-4. **Wt.:** 220. **Bats:** R. **Throws:** R. **School:** Regis (Colo.) University. **Career Transactions:** Selected by Royals in 21st round of 2000 draft; signed June 9, 2000.

Ferguson stands 6-foot-4 and led the organization in strikeouts, but don't mistake him for a power pitcher. He relies on pinpoint command and changing speeds to keep hitters off balance. It worked wonders in 2002, as he walked three or more hitters in game just three times while leading the minors in victories and improving his pro record to 36-14. His 185 innings pitched ranked second in the minors. Ferguson used to work mostly off his 88-89 mph sinker, but he improved in 2002 when he sharpened his curveball, which now projects as a plus pitch. His changeup also improved, but it still isn't major league average and he doesn't use it enough. Ferguson probably needs to hone that third pitch to be effective in the big leagues, where he likely will be a back-of-the-rotation starter. Ferguson can deliver strikes, even with his curveball, in any count. However, he sometimes leaves his fastball too high in the zone, where it gets pounded. His makeup, professionalism and feel for pitching all rate high. Given the state of the Kansas City staff, he could claim a spot in the rotation, or at least in long relief, at some point this year.

Year	Club (League)	Class	W	L	ERA	G	GS	CG	SV	IP	H	R	ER	HR	BB	SO	AVG
2000	Spokane (NWL)	A	5	6	3.28	15	15	0	0	71	76	38	26	6	16	66	.269
2001	Burlington (Mid)	A	3	2	5.28	10	10	0	0	58	62	39	34	9	10	30	.282
	Wilmington (Car)	A	10	3	3.83	18	18	0	0	96	85	47	41	5	27	72	.235
2002	Wilmington (Car)	A	12	1	2.39	17	17	0	0	109	100	36	29	2	20	81	.248
	Wichita (TL)	AA	6	2	2.61	11	11	2	0	76	60	24	22	7	17	60	.217
MINOR LEAGUE TOTALS			36	14	3.33	71	71	2	0	411	383	184	152	29	90	309	.248

18. Wes Obermueller, rhp

Born: Dec. 22, 1976. **Ht.:** 6-2. **Wt.:** 190. **Bats:** R. **Throws:** R. **School:** University of Iowa. **Career Transactions:** Selected by Royals in second round of 1999 draft; signed June 22, 1999.

Often talked about in the same breath as Ian Ferguson because they posted similar numbers in 2002, Obermueller possesses better overall stuff but lacks Ferguson's feel for pitching. Obermueller had shoulder surgery in 2000, experienced more shoulder soreness in 2001 and wasn't ready to resume a full workload until last year. Getting more frequent work allowed him to improve his delivery. Drafted as a college senior, Obermueller was primarily an outfielder at Iowa. His repertoire is average across the board with the exception of his slider, which has developed into a plus pitch. Obermuller throws 86-92 mph with average command and enjoys success working the inside half of the plate. He also uses a changeup. Though his slider rates as his best pitch, Obermueller doesn't have much success putting hitters away with it or any other pitches. Developing a knockout pitch and maintaining a more consistent arm slot—he often drifts too high with his release point in a quest for more movement on his pitches—rank atop Obermuelller's to-do list if he's to push his way into Kansas City's rotation or bullpen in 2003.

Year	Club (League)	Class	W	L	ERA	G	GS	CG	SV	IP	H	R	ER	HR	BB	SO	AVG
1999	Royals (GCL)	R	2	1	2.58	11	7	0	0	38	33	16	11	2	12	39	.228
2000	Charleston (SAL)	A	3	0	1.14	8	7	0	0	32	19	6	4	0	5	29	.174
2001	Wilmington (Car)	A	0	2	3.08	20	6	0	0	38	38	15	13	3	16	28	.266
2002	Wilmington (Car)	A	5	0	2.76	8	4	0	0	46	38	14	14	1	14	44	.228
	Wichita (TL)	AA	9	5	2.90	17	17	0	0	106	98	39	34	6	40	65	.250
	Kansas City (AL)	MAJ	0	2	11.74	2	2	0	0	8	14	10	10	3	2	5	.378
MAJOR LEAGUE TOTALS			0	2	11.74	2	2	0	0	8	14	10	10	3	2	5	.378
MINOR LEAGUE TOTALS			19	8	2.64	64	41	0	0	259	226	90	76	12	87	205	.236

19. David DeJesus, of

Born: Dec. 20, 1979. **Ht.:** 6-0. **Wt.:** 170. **Bats:** L. **Throws:** L. **School:** Rutgers University. **Career Transactions:** Selected by Royals in fourth round of 2000 draft; signed Aug. 22, 2000 . . . On disabled list, April 5-Sept. 30, 2001.

It took him two years to make his pro debut, but the hard-nosed DeJesus never gave in to injuries. He sustained a hairline fracture in his right elbow sliding into second base in his last college game at Rutgers. After signing in August 2000, DeJesus slightly tore a ligament in his left elbow five days into instructional league. During spring training in 2001, he felt a pop in the elbow and soon thereafter had Tommy John surgery. Finally healthy in 2002, DeJesus got off to a hot start in high Class A before cooling off in Double-A. He makes solid contact, shows good plate discipline and will take a walk. He's a gap hitter who probably won't hit more than 10-15 homers annually, but his above-average speed should allow him to steal 15-20 bases. He had a good showing in the Arizona Fall League. Defensively, DeJesus can play all three outfield positions well and his arm, which is currently below-average, should improve. If he can stay healthy and keep overachieving, DeJesus might play his way into a fourth outfielder's role in the majors. He'll start this year in Double-A.

Year	Club (League)	Class	AVG	G	AB	R	H	2B	3B	HR	RBI	BB	SO	SB	SLG	OBP
2001					Did Not Play—Injured											
2002	Wilmington (Car)	A	.296	87	334	69	99	22	6	4	41	48	42	15	.434	.400
	Wichita (TL)	AA	.253	25	79	7	20	5	2	2	15	8	10	3	.443	.347
MINOR LEAGUE TOTALS			.288	112	413	76	119	27	8	6	56	56	52	18	.436	.390

20. Roscoe Crosby, of

Born: Feb. 6, 1983. **Ht.:** 6-2. **Wt.:** 200. **Bats:** L. **Throws:** R. **School:** Union (S.C.) HS. **Career Transactions:** Selected by Royals in second round of 2001 draft; signed July 25, 2001 . . . On disabled list, April 7-Sept. 30, 2002.

The Royals spent $1.75 million in bonus money on Crosby in 2001 and have yet to receive anything aside from medical bills. Crosby reported to Spokane after signing but didn't play because of a right elbow injury that forced him to DH as a high school senior. Then he headed off to Clemson, where he caught 27 passes and four touchdowns as a freshman wide receiver. (His NFL potential and elbow problems were the prevailing reasons the consensus best athlete in the 2001 draft lasted until the second round.) After completing his freshman year, Crosby reported to extended spring training. He was able to hit but the elbow continued to bother him, so Crosby had Tommy John surgery. He hasn't been able to display the blend of speed and power that had the Royals comparing him to a young Ken Griffey. He still offers tremendous upside, but his potential to reach it has diminished thanks to the two-year layoff, combined with his time lost to football and his inferior high school competition. He spent the fall rehabbing and didn't attend classes at Clemson but plans to continue his football career. Getting 500 at-bats a year would go a long way toward improving Crosby's game and standing as a prospect.

Year	Club (League)	Class	AVG	G	AB	R	H	2B	3B	HR	RBI	BB	SO	SB	SLG	OBP
2002					Did Not Play—Injured											

21. Jeff Austin, rhp

Born: Oct. 19, 1976. **Ht.:** 6-0. **Wt.:** 180. **Bats:** R. **Throws:** R. **School:** Stanford University. **Career Transactions:** Selected by Royals in first round (fourth overall) of 1998 draft; signed Feb. 20, 1999.

Austin won Baseball America's College Player of the Year award in 1998, the same year the Royals selected him fourth overall and paid him a club-record $2.7 million bonus. He sailed through the minors until he reached Triple-A. His curveball, which was his money pitch at Stanford but now is no better than average, and 88 mph fastball weren't enough, and Austin looked like a complete first-round bust until the Royals sent him to the bullpen in May 2001. The change of roles added velocity to his fastball, which now reaches the low- to mid-90s, but his command of the pitch still rates below-average. Austin is throwing a hard slider more than his curve now. He went away from the slider in college and starting using it more as he searched for a pitch to help him retire more advanced hitters. It ranks as a borderline plus pitch, and his changeup is fringe average. Austin will have a shot to make the Royals as a bullpen arm, and his starter's background could lead him to a swing role. His ultimate ceiling now looks like that of a set-up man, and he rates behind relievers such as Mike MacDougal, Jeremy Hill and Ryan Bukvich.

Year	Club (League)	Class	W	L	ERA	G	GS	CG	SV	IP	H	R	ER	HR	BB	SO	AVG
1999	Wilmington (Car)	A	7	2	3.77	18	18	0	0	112	108	52	47	10	39	97	.255
	Wichita (TL)	AA	3	1	4.46	6	6	0	0	34	40	19	17	1	11	21	.284
2000	Wichita (TL)	AA	2	2	2.93	6	6	1	0	43	33	16	14	3	4	31	.210
	Omaha (PCL)	AAA	7	9	4.48	23	19	1	0	127	150	85	63	16	35	57	.299
2001	Omaha (PCL)	AAA	3	7	6.88	28	8	0	2	71	89	56	54	14	27	55	.314
	Kansas City (AL)	MAJ	0	0	5.54	21	0	0	0	26	27	17	16	4	14	27	.273
2002	Kansas City (AL)	MAJ	0	0	4.91	10	0	0	0	11	14	6	6	0	6	6	.318
	Omaha (PCL)	AAA	4	0	3.27	39	0	0	2	52	54	24	19	2	15	44	.263
MAJOR LEAGUE TOTALS			0	0	5.35	31	0	0	0	37	41	23	22	4	20	33	.287
MINOR LEAGUE TOTALS			26	21	4.38	120	57	2	4	439	474	252	214	46	131	305	.277

22. Ronny Paulino, c

Born: April 21, 1981. **Ht.:** 6-3. **Wt.:** 210. **Bats:** R. **Throws:** R. **Career Transactions:** Signed out of Dominican Republic by Pirates, Dec. 29, 1997 . . . Selected by Royals from Pirates in major league Rule 5 draft, Dec. 16, 2002.

Paulino couldn't make the Pirates' 40-man roster and wouldn't have appeared on the Pittsburgh prospect list, but the Royals were happy to grab him in the major league Rule 5 draft. He did well when he repeated high Class A in 2002, earning Carolina League all-star honors and driving in the championship-clinching run in the playoffs. Paulino has plus power potential but needs more at-bats to gain better recognition of breaking balls, which give him trouble. Defensively, Paulino is ready to catch and throw in the majors. He has a plus arm and is equally adept at receiving and blocking pitches. He's agile for his size, though there's concern that he'll add more weight and lose some of his flexibility. Royals manager Tony Pena is intrigued by the young catcher's skills and will be available to tutor him on a daily basis. Paulino heads into the season as Brent Mayne's backup, though the Royals might need to carry a third catcher if Paulino can't adjust to major league pitching.

Year	Club (League)	Class	AVG	G	AB	R	H	2B	3B	HR	RBI	BB	SO	SB	SLG	OBP
1998	Pirates (DSL)	R	.235	53	170	18	40	5	0	4	26	17	27	6	.335	.318
1999	Pirates (GCL)	R	.253	29	83	6	21	2	4	1	13	8	19	1	.410	.319
2000	Hickory (SAL)	A	.289	88	301	38	87	16	2	6	39	27	71	3	.415	.354
2001	Lynchburg (Car)	A	.290	103	352	30	102	16	1	6	51	36	76	4	.392	.353
2002	Lynchburg (Car)	A	.262	119	442	63	116	26	2	12	55	39	87	2	.412	.321
MINOR LEAGUE TOTALS			.272	392	1348	155	366	65	9	29	184	127	280	16	.398	.336

23. D.J. Carrasco, rhp

Born: April 12, 1977. **Ht.:** 6-1. **Wt.:** 210. **Bats:** R. **Throws:** R. **School:** Pima (Ariz.) CC. **Career Transactions:** Selected by Orioles in 26th round of 1997 draft; signed Aug. 4, 1997 . . . Released by Orioles, June 14, 1998 . . . Signed by Indians, June 18, 1998 . . . Released by Indians, Aug. 21, 1998 . . . Signed by Pirates, March 29, 1999 . . . Selected by Royals from Pirates in major league Rule 5 draft, Dec. 16, 2002.

Carrasco came out of nowhere to emerge as a prospect in 2002, leading the Carolina League with 29 saves and 55 appearances. The Royals liked what they saw of Carrasco in the Carolina-California League midseason all-star game and followed him throughout the year. His strong numbers in the Arizona Fall and Mexican Pacific leagues during the offseason clinched the team's decision to grab him in the major league Rule 5 draft. Carrasco was a position player at Pima CC and didn't take it well when the coaching staff moved him to the mound. That attitude contributed to Carrasco being released by the Orioles and Indians earlier in his career. Though he will turn 26 as the 2003 season opens and has thrown just 20 innings above high Class A, the Royals believe Carrasco is finally getting the hang of pitching. His best pitch is a plus slider that was considered the best in the Pittsburgh system. His fastball sits at 91-93 mph. Carrasco has solid command of both pitches, and he can drop down and throw them from a sidearm slot to freeze hitters in two-strike counts. He's ticketed to open the season in the Kansas City bullpen, which already is crowded with young arms.

Year	Club (League)	Class	W	L	ERA	G	GS	CG	SV	IP	H	R	ER	HR	BB	SO	AVG
1998	Watertown (NY-P)	A	1	1	5.40	13	1	0	2	32	36	23	19	3	14	38	.281
1999	Williamsport (NY-P)	A	4	2	2.96	18	4	0	0	52	43	20	17	2	23	49	.236
	Lynchburg (Car)	A	0	1	6.35	2	0	0	0	6	9	8	4	0	3	4	.360
2000	Hickory (SAL)	A	5	4	1.34	27	0	0	6	40	35	10	6	0	20	40	.236
	Lynchburg (Car)	A	1	0	3.48	8	0	0	2	10	8	5	4	1	8	10	.222
	Altoona (EL)	AA	1	1	8.36	9	0	0	0	14	16	14	13	0	13	10	.296
2001	Lynchburg (Car)	A	4	0	1.50	22	0	0	7	36	18	7	6	0	14	40	.145
	Altoona (EL)	AA	2	2	4.14	27	1	0	1	37	34	22	17	2	25	35	.239
2002	Lynchburg (Car)	A	4	4	1.61	55	0	0	29	73	52	18	13	1	18	83	.205
MINOR LEAGUE TOTALS			22	15	2.98	181	6	0	47	299	251	127	99	9	138	309	.230

24. James Shanks, of

Born: Jan. 26, 1979. **Ht.:** 6-0. **Wt.:** 180. **Bats:** R. **Throws:** R. **School:** Solomon HS, North Augusta, S.C. **Career Transactions:** Selected by Royals in 21st round of 1998 draft; signed June 5, 1998.

Shanks starred in baseball, basketball and football in high school, but his actions off the field drew even more attention. He was expelled from one high school after being accused of possessing crack cocaine on campus, and from another for smoking marijuana before a basketball tournament. The Royals also suspended him for much of the 2000 season for undisclosed reasons. A cousin of Cubs outfield prospect J.J. Johnson, Shanks faced him last year in the Midwest League. On the field, Shanks shows plenty of tools. He rates as a plus runner and defender. He has the raw strength to drive balls all over the park and the speed to run down everything in center field and be a threat on the basepaths. Shanks led Burlington in stolen bases and batting. Despite the high average, he doesn't make consistent contact and struck out almost twice as much as he walked. He should follow his offensive partner in crime, Ruben Gotay, to high Class A in 2003.

Year	Club (League)	Class	AVG	G	AB	R	H	2B	3B	HR	RBI	BB	SO	SB	SLG	OBP
1998	Royals (GCL)	R	.264	42	144	21	38	9	0	0	13	18	26	10	.326	.355
1999	Spokane (NWL)	A	.258	69	260	41	67	9	0	0	29	19	52	19	.292	.314
2000						Did Not Play										
2001	Spokane (NWL)	A	.295	67	251	39	74	7	3	0	13	21	50	24	.347	.361
2002	Burlington (Mid)	A	.295	126	515	81	152	26	4	6	53	51	94	26	.396	.362
MINOR LEAGUE TOTALS			.283	304	1170	182	331	51	7	6	108	109	222	79	.354	.351

25. Byron Gettis, of

Born: March 13, 1980. **Ht.:** 6-0. **Wt.:** 240. **Bats:** R. **Throws:** R. **School:** Cahokia (Ill.) HS. **Career Transactions:** Signed as nondrafted free agent by Royals, June 29, 1998.

Gettis continued his slow but steady progression with a strong season as he repeated high Class A. It fell in line with the rest of his career: He generally struggles in his first crack at a level and then shows significant improvement the next year. A former University of Minnesota quarterback recruit, Gettis is the cousin of former NFL linebacker Dana Howard. He's a strong athlete whose baseball skills were raw when the Royals signed him. Managers rated him the Carolina League's best defensive outfielder in 2002, and noted his strong right-field arm. Gettis tweaked his approach at the plate in 2002, taking more pitches and using the opposite field. While his weight can be a concern, he runs well for his size but doesn't show the power one might expect. The Royals say if Gettis continues to improve as a hitter, the homers will come down the line. Gettis will move to Double-A in 2003, and he'll need to pick up the pace if he's to reach the majors before he turns 25.

Year	Club (League)	Class	AVG	G	AB	R	H	2B	3B	HR	RBI	BB	SO	SB	SLG	OBP
1998	Royals (GCL)	R	.216	27	88	11	19	2	0	0	4	4	20	0	.239	.247
1999	Royals (GCL)	R	.316	28	95	20	30	6	2	5	21	17	21	3	.579	.424
	Charleston, WV (SAL)	A	.295	43	149	19	44	7	2	2	13	10	36	10	.409	.361
2000	Wilmington (Car)	A	.155	30	97	13	15	2	0	0	10	13	33	2	.175	.265
	Charleston, WV (SAL)	A	.215	94	344	43	74	18	3	5	50	31	95	11	.328	.284
2001	Burlington (Mid)	A	.314	37	140	26	44	9	2	5	26	14	25	4	.514	.385
	Wilmington (Car)	A	.251	82	303	34	76	21	2	6	51	20	70	4	.393	.321
2002	Wilmington (Car)	A	.283	120	449	76	127	33	2	8	70	48	103	10	.419	.364
MINOR LEAGUE TOTALS			.258	461	1665	242	429	98	13	31	245	157	403	44	.388	.337

26. Chris Tierney, lhp

Born: Sept. 1, 1983. **Ht.:** 6-6. **Wt.:** 200. **Bats:** L. **Throws:** L. **School:** Lockport (Ill.) HS. **Career Transactions:** Selected by Royals in seventh round of 2001 draft; signed July 10, 2001.

Tierney's 14 losses in 2002 might have tied teammate Mike Stodolka for the second-most losses in the Midwest League, but his record didn't indicate how well Tierney pitched, especially late in the season. He allowed just six earned runs over his last seven starts, reaching the seventh inning six times and collecting four wins. At 6-foot-6, he throws his fastball on a steep downhill plane. It's an average pitch but he shows plus command of it. Tierney was throwing 86-87 mph early in 2002, but improved his velocity over the course of the year and reached 90-92. His changeup blossomed into a solid-average pitch with future plus potential. He has the command and confidence to throw it with a full count. Tierney's curveball has a nice, tight rotation, but he struggles with his release point, and by extension, his command of it at times. His arm works easy and he repeats his delivery well, especially for a pitcher of his size. Tierney needs to get quicker to the plate because basestealers take advantage of him. In 2003, Tierney should join a prospect-studded Wilmington rotation that includes Kansas City's last three first-round picks: Stodolka, Colt Griffin and Zack Greinke.

Year	Club (League)	Class	W	L	ERA	G	GS	CG	SV	IP	H	R	ER	HR	BB	SO	AVG
2001	Royals (GCL)	R	0	2	6.65	8	3	0	0	22	31	19	16	1	8	21	.326
2002	Burlington (Mid)	A	9	14	3.25	27	27	2	0	166	179	86	60	9	41	89	.271
MINOR LEAGUE TOTALS			9	16	3.64	35	30	2	0	188	210	105	76	10	49	110	.278

27. Adam Donachie, c

Born: March 3, 1984. **Ht.:** 6-2. **Wt.:** 180. **Bats:** R. **Throws:** R. **School:** Timber Creek HS, Orlando. **Career Transactions:** Selected by Royals in second round of 2002 draft; signed June 20, 2002.

Donachie led Florida high schoolers with 15 home runs as a senior, including one blast off first-round pick Zack Grienke. Nevertheless, he was considered more advanced defensively than offensively when he signed as a second-round pick for $800,000. That proved true as Donachie struggled at the plate in his first taste of pro ball. He was slowed by a high ankle sprain and failed to find a rhythm while splitting time with two other catchers. Nonetheless, he still packs plus power and the potential to hit for a solid average into his line-drive swing. He hit some impressive homers in a fall batting-practice session at Kauffman Stadium. A natural righthanded hitter, he switch-hit as a high school senior but the Royals have yet to decide whether he'll do so as a pro. Defensively, Donachie has sure hands, fine blocking and game-calling skills and a plus arm with a quick release (1.9 seconds from home plate to second base). He already has added 15 pounds to his durable frame since high school and still can get stronger as he blossoms into a frontline catcher capable of batting sixth or seventh in the order. He'll begin 2002 in low Class A.

Year	Club (League)	Class	AVG	G	AB	R	H	2B	3B	HR	RBI	BB	SO	SB	SLG	OBP
2002	Royals (GCL)	R	.206	21	68	7	14	3	0	0	3	9	12	0	.250	.304
MINOR LEAGUE TOTALS			.206	21	68	7	14	3	0	0	3	9	12	0	.250	.304

28. Dusty Wrightsman, rhp

Born: Dec. 7, 1979. **Ht.:** 6-4. **Wt.:** 220. **Bats:** R. **Throws:** R. **School:** Faulkner State (Ala.) JC. **Career Transactions:** Selected by Royals in 26th round of 2000 draft; signed June 13, 2000.

Wrightsman hit .597 as a high school senior to get nominated for Indiana's Mr. Baseball award, but his bat and his mid-80s fastball never drew much attention from scouts. The Royals drafted him after he earned second-team all-America honors at Faulkner State CC, but he did little to impress in his first two years as a pro. Wrightsman spent last offseason adding muscle and honing his command, and his entire repertoire became more crisp in 2002. He led the Royals system with a 2.38 ERA. Wrightsman succeeds with excellent control and trust in his stuff. He keeps the ball down in the zone as well as any pitcher in the organization. He throws his 88-92 mph fastball with an easy, deceptive motion that allows it to get in on hitters quickly. He also throws a quality slider. The development of his changeup will determine whether Wrightsman becomes a middle reliever or starter. Back spasms cut short his stint in the Arizona Fall League. He should have a rotation spot in Double-A this year.

Year	Club (League)	Class	W	L	ERA	G	GS	CG	SV	IP	H	R	ER	HR	BB	SO	AVG
2000	Royals (GCL)	R	1	3	5.64	8	5	0	0	22	25	14	14	3	12	15	.278
2001	Burlington (Mid)	A	5	6	4.29	34	4	0	0	80	90	43	38	6	22	54	.286
2002	Wilmington (Car)	A	9	4	2.38	39	10	0	5	106	99	36	28	5	18	85	.240
MINOR LEAGUE TOTALS			15	13	3.46	81	19	0	5	208	214	93	80	14	52	154	.262

29. Danny Tamayo, rhp

Born: June 3, 1979. **Ht.:** 6-1. **Wt.:** 240. **Bats:** R. **Throws:** R. **School:** University of Notre Dame. **Career Transactions:** Selected by Royals in 10th round of 2001 draft; signed June 12, 2001.

Tamayo worked in the same Notre Dame rotation with Mets 2001 first-round pick Aaron Heilman. He had Tommy John surgery in 1999, but returned as strong as ever in 2000, throwing a three-hit shutout against Mississippi State in the NCAA regionals. Tamayo consistently throws in the high 80s, sometimes touching 90 mph. He also works with an average curveball and a plus changeup. As with Ian Ferguson, Tamayo's feel for pitching is his best asset. He battles hitters from the mound, using his above-average command to move the ball to all quadrants of the strike zone. He tied for second in the organization with 14 wins last year and was undefeated in his final nine decisions. He profiles as a back-of-the-rotation starter or middle reliever, and should start 2003 at Double-A.

Year	Club (League)	Class	W	L	ERA	G	GS	CG	SV	IP	H	R	ER	HR	BB	SO	AVG
2001	Spokane (NWL)	A	3	3	4.54	14	14	1	0	67	60	39	34	7	16	64	.234
2002	Wilmington (Car)	A	14	4	2.77	23	20	0	0	123	121	48	38	13	32	108	.259
MINOR LEAGUE TOTALS			17	7	3.40	37	34	1	0	191	181	87	72	20	48	172	.250

30. Micah Kaaihue, 1b

Born: March 29, 1984. **Ht.:** 6-3. **Wt.:** 210. **Bats:** L. **Throws:** R. **School:** Iolani HS, Honolulu. **Career Transactions:** Selected by Royals in 15th round of 2002 draft; signed June 24, 2002.

While scouting premium Hawaiian prospects Bronson Sardinha (first round, Yankees) and Brandon League (second, Blue Jays) in 2001, Royals scouting director Deric Ladnier saw Kaaihue as a high school junior. Kaaihue's power potential impressed Ladnier and made him the island's top prospect for the 2002 draft. A subpar senior season and Kaaihue's commitment to the University of Nebraska combined to knock him down to the 15th round. He physically resembles David Segui, and like Segui he has baseball bloodlines. Kaaihue's father Kala caught in the minors for six years with the Pirates and Cardinals. Kaaihue possesses the best raw power in the Royals system, with emphasis on the word "raw." He showed good patience in the Gulf Coast League but also struck out in one-fourth of his at-bats. Elbow and biceps problems limited him to DH duties after he signed, so the Royals don't really have a take on Kaaihue's defensive prowess yet. He showed below-average range and speed in high school, but had good enough hands and arm strength that the Royals worked him out at third base. Kaaihue probably isn't ready for full-season ball at this point.

Year	Club (League)	Class	AVG	G	AB	R	H	2B	3B	HR	RBI	BB	SO	SB	SLG	OBP
2002	Royals (GCL)	R	.259	43	139	15	36	8	0	3	21	26	35	0	.381	.381
MINOR LEAGUE TOTALS			.259	43	139	15	36	8	0	3	21	26	35	0	.381	.381

LOS ANGELES
DODGERS

TOP 30 PROSPECTS

1. James Loney, 1b
2. Jonathan Figueroa, lhp
3. Edwin Jackson, rhp
4. Reggie Abercrombie, of
5. Joey Thurston, 2b/ss
6. Koyie Hill, c
7. Alfredo Gonzalez, rhp
8. Joel Hanrahan, rhp
9. Joel Guzman, ss
10. Chin-Feng Chen, of/1b
11. Hong-Chih Kuo, lhp
12. Victor Diaz, 3b/2b
13. Greg Miller, lhp
14. Andrew Brown, rhp
15. Derek Thompson, lhp
16. Franklin Gutierrez, of
17. Willy Aybar, 3b
18. Jonathan Broxton, rhp
19. Wilkin Ruan, of
20. Mike Nixon, c
21. Orlando Rodriguez, lhp
22. Zach Hammes, rhp
23. Steve Colyer, lhp
24. Jason Romano, of/2b
25. Jason Repko, of
26. Brian Pilkington, rhp
27. Mike Megrew, lhp
28. Jose Diaz, rhp
29. Franquelis Osoria, rhp
30. Delwyn Young, 2b

By Josh Boyd

In Dan Evans' first season as general manager, the Dodgers improved by six games and contended in the National League West despite facing several obstacles. Perennial malcontent Gary Sheffield demanded a trade last winter and claimed he had been lied to by the rookie GM. Evans solved the problem by dealing Sheffield to Atlanta in January for Brian Jordan, Odalis Perez and Andrew Brown. Jordan emerged as one of the team's emotional leaders. Perez completed his comeback from Tommy John surgery to become Los Angeles' ace. Brown, who also has recovered from Tommy John surgery, had a breakthrough season in high Class A.

Former GM Kevin Malone saddled the Dodgers with several bad contracts that Evans had to work around. Kevin Brown (seven years, $115 million) was hurt for the second straight season, while Darren Dreifort (five years, $55 million) never took the mound. Evans got rid of Eric Karros and Mark Grudzielanek in December, though the deal was a financial wash because he had to take Todd Hundley in return from the Cubs.

More significant, Evans has bolstered the front office and shifted the focus in Los Angeles back to scouting and player development. He has surrounded himself with a braintrust of veterans, such as assistant GM Kim Ng, farm director Bill Bavasi, scouting director Logan White, senior adviser John Boles, minor league field coordinator Terry Collins, international scouting director Rene Francisco and long-time scout Al LaMacchia.

The Dodgers farm system had withered in recent years, but the new regime started to rebuild the depth in the lower minors. There were positive developments at the top as well. Homegrown closer Eric Gagne emerged in his first season in the bullpen with 52 saves, the fifth-highest total in major league history. The Dodgers outbid other clubs for Japanese big leaguer Kazuhisa Ishii, a solid addition to the rotation. Second baseman Joey Thurston led Triple-A Las Vegas to the best record in the Pacific Coast League, and he has a clear opening to a starting job thanks to Grudzielanek's departure.

Evans also used the farm system to bolster the club with role players Tyler Houston and Paul Shuey. Neither was particularly effective, and the Dodgers may rue giving up four pitching prospects (Ricardo Rodriguez and Francisco Cruceta to Cleveland, Ben Diggins and Shane Nance to Milwaukee) for them.

Organization Overview

General Manager: Dan Evans. Farm Director: Bill Bavasi. Scouting Director: Logan White.

2002 PERFORMANCE

Class	Farm Team	League	W	L	Pct.	Finish*	Manager
Majors	Los Angeles	National	92	70	.568	5th (16)	Jim Tracy
Triple-A	Las Vegas 51s	Pacific Coast	85	59	.590	1st (16)	Brad Mills
Double-A	Jacksonville Suns	Southern	77	62	.554	2nd (10)	Dino Ebel
High A	Vero Beach Dodgers	Florida State	72	63	.533	4th (12)	Juan Bustabad
Low A	South Georgia Waves	South Atlantic	75	63	.543	5th (16)	Scott Little
Rookie	†Great Falls Dodgers	Pioneer	47	28	.627	+1st (8)	Dann Bilardello
Rookie	GCL Dodgers	Gulf Coast	33	27	.550	5th (14)	Luis Salazar
OVERALL MINOR LEAGUE RECORD			389	302	.563	3rd (30)	

*Finish in overall standings (No. of teams in league). +League champion. †Affiliate will be in Ogden (Pioneer) in 2003.

ORGANIZATION LEADERS

BATTING
*Minimum 250 At-Bats

*AVG	Mike Kinkade, Las Vegas	.341
R	Joe Thurston, Las Vegas	106
H	Joe Thurston, Las Vegas	196
TB	Joe Thurston, Las Vegas	297
2B	Joe Thurston, Las Vegas	39
3B	Joe Thurston, Las Vegas	13
	Reggie Abercrombie, Jacksonville/Vero Beach	13
HR	Chin-Feng Chen, Las Vegas	26
RBI	Chin-Feng Chen, Las Vegas	84
BB	Koyie Hill, Jacksonville	76
SO	Chin-Feng Chen, Las Vegas	160
SB	Shane Victorino, Jacksonville	45

PITCHING
#Minimum 75 Innings

W	Heath Totten, Jacksonville/Vero Beach	12
L	Ben Diggins, Vero Beach	10
	Andrew Brown, Vero Beach	10
#ERA	Jonathan Figueroa, South Georgia/Great Falls	1.42
G	Steve Colyer, Jacksonville	59
CG	Francisco Cruceta, South Georgia	3
SV	Lino Urdaneta, Jacksonville/Vero Beach	32
IP	Robert Ellis, Las Vegas	173
BB	Scott Proctor, Jacksonville	85
SO	Joel Hanrahan, Jacksonville/Vero Beach	149

BEST TOOLS

Best Hitter for Average	James Loney
Best Power Hitter	James Loney
Fastest Baserunner	Travis Ezi
Best Athlete	Mike Nixon
Best Fastball	Hong-Chih Kuo
Best Curveball	Jonathan Figueroa
Best Slider	Joel Hanrahan
Best Changeup	Alfredo Gonzalez
Best Control	Brian Pilkington
Best Defensive Catcher	Edwin Bellorin
Best Defensive Infielder	Brennan King
Best Infield Arm	Joel Guzman
Best Defensive Outfielder	Wilkin Ruan
Best Outfield Arm	Reggie Abercrombie

PROJECTED 2006 LINEUP

Catcher	Koyie Hill
First Base	James Loney
Second Base	Joey Thurston
Third Base	Adrian Beltre
Shortstop	Cesar Izturis
Left Field	Chin-Feng Chen
Center Field	Reggie Abercrombie
Right Field	Shawn Green
No. 1 Starter	Odalis Perez

Mike Kinkade **Heath Totten**

No. 2 Starter	Jonathan Figueroa
No. 3 Starter	Edwin Jackson
No. 4 Starter	Kazuisha Ishii
No. 5 Starter	Joel Hanrahan
Closer	Eric Gagne

TOP PROSPECTS OF THE DECADE

1993	Mike Piazza, c
1994	Darren Dreifort, rhp
1995	Todd Hollandsworth, of
1996	Karim Garcia, of
1997	Paul Konerko, 3b
1998	Paul Konerko, 1b
1999	Angel Pena, c
2000	Chin-Feng Chen, of
2001	Ben Diggins, rhp
2002	Ricardo Rodriguez, rhp

TOP DRAFT PICKS OF THE DECADE

1993	Darren Dreifort, rhp
1994	Paul Konerko, c
1995	David Yocum, lhp
1996	Damian Rolls, 3b
1997	Glenn Davis, 1b
1998	Bubba Crosby, of
1999	Jason Repko, ss/of
2000	Ben Diggins, rhp
2001	Brian Pilkington, rhp (2)
2002	James Loney, 1b

ALL-TIME LARGEST BONUSES

Joel Guzman, 2001	$2,250,000
Ben Diggins, 2000	$2,200,000
Hideo Nomo, 1995	$2,000,000
Kazuhisha Ishii, 2002	$1,500,000
James Loney, 2002	$1,500,000

MinorLeague**Depth**Chart

LOS ANGELES DODGERS

The Dodgers are heading in the right direction again after spiraling downward in the aftermath of the Kevin Malone regime. They have become the antithesis of the trendy Athletics philosophy, in that the Dodgers are relying primarily on traditional scouting methods with a focus on tools prospects from the prep ranks and Latin America. Logan White's first draft as scouting director established the trend as he tabbed eight high schoolers with his first 10 picks, including first-rounder James Loney, who jumped straight to the front of the system's prospects. The system is rich in lefthanders, unproven power arms and athletes.

Note: Depth charts prepared by Josh Boyd. Numbers in parentheses indicate prospect rankings.

LF
Chin-Feng Chen (10)
Jason Repko (25)
Lamont Mathews
Travis Ezi

CF
Reggie Abercrombie (4)
Wilkin Ruan (19)
Jason Romano (24)

RF
Franklin Gutierrez (16)
Jose Garcia

3B
Joel Guzman (9)
Willy Aybar (17)
David Bagley
Brennan King
Ricky Bell

SS

2B
Joe Thurston (5)
Victor Diaz (12)
Delwyn Young (30)

1B
James Loney (1)
Derek Michaelis

C
Koyie Hill (6)
Mike Nixon (20)
David Ross
Edwin Bellorin
Russell Martin

RHP

Starters	Relievers
Edwin Jackson (3)	Alfredo Gonzalez (7)
Joel Hanrahan (8)	Jose Diaz (28)
Andrew Brown (14)	Franquelis Osoria (29)
Jonathan Broxton (18)	Marcos Carvajal
Zach Hammes (22)	Will McCrotty
Brian Pilkington (26)	Jose Diaz
Jose Rojas	Kole Strayhorn
Reyes Soto	Agustin Montero
Jarod Plummer	Lino Urdaneta
Scott Proctor	Nate Ruhl
Heath Totten	

LHP

Starters	Relievers
Jonathan Figueroa (2)	Orlando Rodriguez (21)
Hong-Chih Kuo (11)	Steve Colyer (23)
Greg Miller (13)	Victor Alvarez
Derek Thompson (15)	Rick Roberts
Mike Megrew (27)	Edgar Ahumada
Eric Stults	

DraftAnalysis

2002 Draft

Best Pro Debut: Almost every high pick the Dodgers sent to the Rookie-level Pioneer League fared well, none better than 1B James Loney (1), whom most teams preferred as a pitcher. He was the league's top prospect and hit .350-5-35 between there and the high Class A Florida State League. LHP Eric Stults (15) spent time at both stops and reached Double-A, going 4-1, 2.82 overall.

Best Athlete: Arizona State and Notre Dame recruited C Mike Nixon (3) as a quarterback before he committed to play safety at UCLA. He gave that up when he signed for $950,000, the highest bonus in the third round last year. Stults played basketball at Bethel (Ind.) College.

Best Pure Hitter: Loney has a pretty swing that should allow him to hit for average. 2B Delwyn Young (4) was the top hitter in the California community college circuit.

Best Raw Power: Young gets the edge over 3B David Bagley (7).

Fastest Runner: Nixon is a 6.7-second runner in the 60. Draft-and-follow OF Jereme Milons is even faster.

Best Defensive Player: The Dodgers say Loney will win Gold Gloves at first base. Nixon's agility and arm strength give him a high ceiling as a catcher.

Best Fastball: RHP **Jonathan Broxton's** (2) 6-foot-3, 260-pound build is as imposing as his 94-96 mph fastball. LHP Greg Miller (1), RHP Zach Hammes (2) and LHP Marshall Looney (6) all work in the low 90s.

Best Breaking Ball: Miller's curveball. Draft-and-follow RHP Mike Rodriguez'

knuckle-curve is a plus-plus pitch at times.

Most Intriguing Background: RHP Ryan Tracy's (21) father Jim manages the Dodgers, and 3B Jon Riggleman's (37) dad Jim is his bench coach. Both players opted not to sign. RHP Ross Hawley (31) pitched with his identical twin Ryan at Kansas State. Unsigned 1B James McDonald's (11) father James was an NFL tight end. McDonald also is a cousin of Royals outfielder Donzell McDonald and Orioles minor league outfielder Darnell McDonald. OF **Broxton**

Sambu Ndungidi's (16) brother Ntema is an Orioles minor league outfielder.

Closest To The Majors: If Loney hadn't broken his left wrist, he would have gone to the Arizona Fall League as a high school draftee, which doesn't happen often. Stults did go to the AFL, which should hasten his development. A plus slider is his best pitch.

Best Late-Round Pick: RHP Jarod Plummer (26) boosted his fastball to 92-93 mph and improved his breaking ball after signing.

The One Who Got Away: RHP Robert Ray (28) and LHP Danny Forrer (38) are projectable but went to Texas A&M and Auburn.

Assessment: The Dodgers wanted to add productive bats to their system, and it's hard to argue with the early returns on Logan White's first draft as scouting director. Los Angeles didn't skimp on power arms either.

2001 Draft

The Dodgers didn't have a first-round pick, and RHP Brian Pilkington (2), the top choice, injured his shoulder. RHP Edwin Jackson (6) has developed rapidly, however. **Grade: C**

2000 Draft

RHP Ben Diggins (1) was mildly disappointing before being traded. RHP Joel Hanrahan (2), converted C Koyie Hill (4) and draft-and-follow 3B/2B Victor Diaz (37) look like keepers, with Diaz winning two batting titles in two years. **Grade: B**

1999 Draft

Sense a pattern here? OF Jason Repko (1) has moved slowly while SS Drew Meyer (2) didn't sign and became a 2002 first-rounder. Two later picks, 2B Joey Thurston (4) and draft-and-follow OF Reggie Abercrombie (23), have been much more impressive. **Grade: C+**

1998 Draft

C David Ross (7) homered off Mark Grace last September. That will be the legacy of a draft that started off badly with OF Bubba Crosby (1) and never got better. **Grade: F**

Note: Draft analysis prepared by Jim Callis. Numbers in parentheses indicate draft rounds.

... Loney's picturesque stroke reminds scouts of Shawn Green.

James
Loney 1b

Born: May 7, 1984.
Ht.: 6-3. **Wt.:** 200.
Bats: L. **Throws:** L.
School: Elkins HS, Missouri City, Texas.
Career Transactions: Selected by Dodgers in first round (19th overall) of 2002 draft; signed June 11, 2002.

Loney's name jumped up the follow lists of Houston area scouts last spring. Most teams were enticed by his left arm and projected him as a supplemental first- to second-rounder as a pitcher. The Dodgers, however, grabbed Loney as a first baseman with the 19th pick. After passing up a Baylor scholarship to sign for $1.5 million, he tore up the Rookie-level Pioneer League, where managers rated him the No. 1 prospect. He had no trouble making a late-season jump to high Class A Vero Beach. The only glitch came when he was hit by a pitch that broke his left wrist. That nixed plans to send him to the Arizona Fall League. Demonstrating his passion for the game, Loney was back swinging a bat with one hand within two weeks. He won a gold medal with the U.S. 16-and-under team at the 2000 Pan American Youth Games and the national high school title with Elkins High last spring. Loney was a high school All-American, batting .509-8-58 and going 12-1, 1.51 with 120 strikeouts in 69 innings. He got plenty of exposure playing for the best team in the country and in the same region as fellow first-rounders Clint Everts (Expos) and Scott Kazmir (Mets) of Cypress Falls High. Against Everts in a scrimmage, Loney drilled a 93 mph fastball out of the park to the opposite field.

Loney has outstanding bat control, and his picturesque lefthanded stroke reminds scouts of Shawn Green. He uses a pronounced leg lift as a timing mechanism, drawing comparisons to David Justice. Loney stays inside the ball well and his swing path keeps the bat head in the zone for a long time. He has grown four inches since his junior year, and projects to hit 35-plus home runs in the majors. He generates natural loft and raw power already. He's also a future Gold Glover as a first baseman. His instincts for the position make up for average range, and his soft hands will help save wild throws. On the mound, he reached 93 mph. Some scouts worried about Loney's durability as a position player because he had arthroscopic knee surgery after his junior season. His injury last year was a freak occurrence, but any time the wrist is involved, there are concerns about how it will affect his swing mechanics. Loney is an aggressive baserunner but will have below-average speed as he fills out.

Loney jumped on the fast track and only injury can slow him. He could beat out Kazmir as the first high schooler from the 2002 draft to reach the majors. He'll play first at high Class A this year—if the Dodgers can resist promoting him.

Year	Club (League)	Class	AVG	G	AB	R	H	2B	3B	HR	RBI	BB	SO	SB	SLG	OBP
2002	Great Falls (Pio)	R	.371	47	170	33	63	22	3	5	30	25	18	5	.624	.457
	Vero Beach (FSL)	A	.299	17	67	6	20	6	0	0	5	6	10	0	.388	.356
MINOR LEAGUE TOTALS			.350	64	237	39	83	28	3	5	35	31	28	5	.557	.430

2. Jonathan Figueroa, lhp

Born: Sept. 15, 1983. **Ht.:** 6-5. **Wt.:** 220. **Bats:** L. **Throws:** L. **Career Transactions:** Signed out of Venezuela by Dodgers, Jan. 22, 2002.

Figueroa burst onto the prospect scene in December 2000 at the Perfect Game World Showcase in Fort Myers, Fla., and he spent the majority of 2001 touring the showcase circuit. He also played in the Perfect Game Fall Scout League in Iowa, going 6-1 with 65 strikeouts in 33 innings that summer. The Dodgers got a bargain when they signed him for $500,000 last January. Figueroa fires an 89-94 mph fastball from a deceptive three-quarters slot, creating outstanding arm-side run. His curveball is the best in the organization. He'll drop down for a low three-quarters release to get a slider break against lefthanders—who managed a .141 average against him—and throw a hard, downward-biting curve against righties. He honed his changeup and toned his developing body in instructional league. Figueroa's mechanics are solid, though he occasionally rushes his arm. That causes him to lose his balance, affecting his command. Figueroa could get lefties out in the big leagues right now, and the Dodgers will move him along aggressively. His next stop is the high Class A rotation.

Year	Club (League)	Class	W	L	ERA	G	GS	CG	SV	IP	H	R	ER	HR	BB	SO	AVG
2002	Great Falls (Pio)	R	2	1	1.42	7	7	0	0	32	16	7	5	0	19	48	.147
	South Georgia (SAL)	A	5	2	1.42	8	8	0	0	44	22	10	7	1	20	57	.148
MINOR LEAGUE TOTALS			7	3	1.42	15	15	0	0	76	38	17	12	1	39	105	.147

3. Edwin Jackson, rhp

Born: Sept. 9, 1983. **Ht.:** 6-3. **Wt.:** 190. **Bats:** R. **Throws:** R. **School:** Shaw HS, Columbus, Ga. **Career Transactions:** Selected by Dodgers in sixth round of 2001 draft; signed June 18, 2001.

Jackson's story is the opposite of James Loney's. Most teams coveted Jackson's bat when he was in high school, but the Dodgers drafted him as a pitcher. They allowed him to DH between starts during his pro debut in the Rookie-level Gulf Coast League. They wanted his athleticism on the mound, however, and he began concentrating solely on pitching last spring. He started the season in extended spring training, joined low Class A South Georgia in May and was named the organization's minor league pitcher of the year. Jackson throws 91-94 mph with a picture-perfect arm action, and he can get to 96 with heavy, late action up and in on righthanders. His slider has slurvy action, showing hard, tight spin and late bite at times. He's one of the best athletes in the system, with the makings of an easy, repeatable delivery. Though he throws two types of breaking balls, Jackson might be better off abandoning the curve to help him improve his slider. The Dodgers say he'll be more efficient with his pitch counts once he gains consistency with his mechanics. His changeup has potential but still needs more work. The Dodgers project Jackson as a frontline starter. After an impressive showing in instructional league, he might make a move to Double-A this year.

Year	Club (League)	Class	W	L	ERA	G	GS	CG	SV	IP	H	R	ER	HR	BB	SO	AVG
2001	Dodgers (GCL)	R	2	1	2.45	12	2	0	0	22	14	12	6	1	19	23	.173
2002	South Georgia (SAL)	A	5	2	1.98	19	19	0	0	105	79	34	23	2	33	85	.206
MINOR LEAGUE TOTALS			7	3	2.06	31	21	0	0	127	93	46	29	3	52	108	.200

4. Reggie Abercrombie, of

Born: July 15, 1980. **Ht.:** 6-3. **Wt.:** 210. **Bats:** R. **Throws:** R. **School:** Lake City (Fla.) CC. **Career Transactions:** Selected by Dodgers in 23rd round of 1999 draft; signed May 24, 2000.

Abercrombie has blossomed from a raw draft-and-follow into, in the minds of some club officials, the organization's best prospect. Also a football and basketball standout in high school, Abercrombie hit .096 with 41 strikeouts in 96 at-bats in April. After getting contact lenses on May 1 he hit .315-10-53 with 23 walks and 117 strikeouts the rest of the way. Abercrombie doesn't just possess above-average tools; he grades out near the top of the charts for his raw power, speed, arm strength and defense. He's an aggressive hitter with a lightning-quick bat. He is a premium athlete, which prompts comparisons ranging from Preston Wilson to Torii Hunter to Reggie Sanders to Eric Davis. Statistical analysts argue Abercrombie won't hit because his plate discipline is so unrefined. Most scouts beg to differ because they say his flaws will be correctable with experience. He occasionally gets overanxious at the plate and the barrel of the bat gets out in front of his hands, causing him to hit around the ball. Abercrombie finished 2002 as Double-A Jacksonville's top hitter in the postseason, with a .303 average and five strikeouts in 33 at-bats. He'll spend the entire year there in 2003. If everything clicks, he profiles as a five-tool right fielder.

Year	Club (League)	Class	AVG	G	AB	R	H	2B	3B	HR	RBI	BB	SO	SB	SLG	OBP
2000	Great Falls (Pio)	R	.273	54	220	40	60	7	1	2	29	22	66	32	.341	.360
2001	Wilmington (SAL)	A	.226	125	486	63	110	17	3	10	41	19	154	44	.335	.272
2002	Vero Beach (FSL)	A	.276	132	526	80	145	23	13	10	56	27	158	41	.426	.321
	Jacksonville (SL)	AA	.250	1	4	1	1	0	0	0	0	0	1	1	.250	.250
MINOR LEAGUE TOTALS			.256	312	1236	184	316	47	17	22	126	68	379	118	.375	.309

5. Joey Thurston, 2b/ss

Born: Sept. 29, 1979. **Ht.:** 5-11. **Wt.:** 170. **Bats:** L. **Throws:** R. **School:** Sacramento CC. **Career Transactions:** Selected by Dodgers in fourth round of 1999 draft; signed June 6, 1999.

Thurston has earned a reputation as a winner by winning championships in junior college and the minors. In 2002, he won his second organization minor league player of the year award in three seasons and led Triple-A Las Vegas to the best record in the Pacific Coast League, topped the minors in hits and total bases (297) and all Dodgers farmhands in runs, doubles and triples. "Joey Ballgame" earned his nickname for his instincts and passion, which is evident in the way he carries himself. He doesn't employ classic swing mechanics as he dives into the plate and looks out of sync, but he has outstanding bat control and has developed more gap power as he has matured. He's the best baserunner in the system and has solid-average speed. Because he lacks soft hands, Thurston moved from shortstop to second base in 2001 with promising results. He rarely draws walks, which means he'll have to hit for a high average to have a good on-base percentage. He doesn't always make it look easy and his tools aren't overwhelming, leading some PCL scouts to project him as a utilityman instead of a regular. One of the Dodgers' most sought-after players in trades, Thurston is penciled in as their everyday second baseman following the offseason trade of Mark Grudzielanek. Thurston is a prime rookie of the year candidate.

Year	Club (League)	Class	AVG	G	AB	R	H	2B	3B	HR	RBI	BB	SO	SB	SLG	OBP
1999	Yakima (NWL)	A	.285	71	277	48	79	10	3	0	32	27	34	27	.343	.387
	San Bernardino (Cal)	A	.000	2	3	0	0	0	0	0	0	0	1	0	.000	.250
2000	San Bernardino (Cal)	A	.303	138	551	97	167	31	8	4	70	56	61	43	.410	.380
2001	Jacksonville (SL)	AA	.267	134	544	80	145	25	7	7	46	48	65	20	.377	.338
2002	Las Vegas (PCL)	AAA	.334	136	587	106	196	39	13	12	55	25	60	22	.506	.372
	Los Angeles (NL)	MAJ	.462	8	13	1	6	1	0	0	1	0	1	0	.538	.429
MAJOR LEAGUE TOTALS			.462	8	13	1	6	1	0	0	1	0	1	0	.538	.429
MINOR LEAGUE TOTALS			.299	481	1962	331	587	105	31	23	203	156	221	112	.419	.367

6. Koyie Hill, c

Born: March 9, 1979. **Ht.:** 6-0. **Wt:** 190. **Bats:** B. **Throws:** R. **School:** Wichita State University. **Career Transactions:** Selected by Dodgers in fourth round of 2000 draft; signed June 22, 2000.

Hill batted .354 as a three-year starting third baseman at Wichita State and led the Missouri Valley Conference with a .391 average as a junior. He was converted to catcher after signing in 2000. He led Jacksonville with 11 homers last year, then batted .307 in the Arizona Fall League. Hill has a pretty line-drive stroke with quick hands, and a disciplined approach from both sides of the plate. He shows the ability to drive the ball from the left side and projects to hit for average power. Hill has improved his game-calling and throwing, erasing 33 percent of basestealers last year. His arm strength and receiving skills are above-average. His makeup and feel for the game are on par with Joey Thurston's as the best in the organization. Hill is a well-rounded player without any glaring deficiencies. Still inexperienced as a catcher, he committed a Southern League-leading 17 errors after making 16 in 2001. Hill skipped a level a year ago and will move to Triple-A this season. With Paul LoDuca signed for two more years, the Dodgers have enviable catching depth. They won't need to rush Hill, who profiles as an everyday backstop.

Year	Club (League)	Class	AVG	G	AB	R	H	2B	3B	HR	RBI	BB	SO	SB	SLG	OBP
2000	Yakima (NWL)	A	.259	64	251	26	65	13	1	2	29	25	47	0	.343	.324
2001	Wilmington (SAL)	A	.301	134	498	65	150	20	2	8	79	49	82	21	.398	.368
2002	Jacksonville (SL)	AA	.271	130	468	67	127	25	1	11	64	76	88	5	.400	.368
MINOR LEAGUE TOTALS			.281	328	1217	158	342	58	4	21	172	150	217	26	.387	.359

7. Alfredo Gonzalez, rhp

Born: Sept. 17, 1979. **Ht.:** 5-11. **Wt.:** 160. **Bats:** R. **Throws:** R. **Career Transactions:** Signed out of Dominican Republic by Dodgers, Sept. 18, 1997.

Like Ricardo Rodriguez, the organization's top prospect a year ago before he was traded to Cleveland, Gonzalez pitched in the Rookie-level Dominican Summer League for three years. Signed for $75,000, he grew three inches along the way. His fastball grew as well. Gonzalez' change-up is graded as a top-of-the-charts 80 pitch (on the 20-80 scale) by some scouts and elicits comparisons to Eric Gagne's. It acts like a screwball or splitter with wicked late fade. After throwing 87-90 mph when he came to the United States two years ago, he effortlessly dials his fastball up to 93 with plus boring life now. He repeats his delivery and works to both sides of the plate. Because he has pitched in relief, Gonzalez hasn't had much opportunity to develop a breaking ball. He made strides with a slider pitching as a starter this winter in the Dominican. Gonzalez blitzed through three levels last year and was added to the 40-man roster. He'll get a long look this spring and should secure a middle-relief role in Los Angeles at some point in 2003.

Year	Club (League)	Class	W	L	ERA	G	GS	CG	SV	IP	H	R	ER	HR	BB	SO	AVG
1998	Dodgers (DSL)	R	3	0	2.92	15	2	1	0	37	37	21	12	0	15	30	.257
1999	Dodgers (DSL)	R	4	6	3.95	13	13	1	0	73	71	41	32	0	26	73	.251
2000	Dodgers (DSL)	R	8	1	2.32	12	11	0	0	74	67	24	19	3	12	89	.228
2001	Great Falls (Pio)	R	3	4	3.56	11	8	0	0	48	43	26	19	1	12	56	.234
	Wilmington (SAL)	A	1	0	3.00	2	1	0	0	9	10	4	3	0	3	12	.270
2002	Vero Beach (FSL)	A	2	1	1.57	17	0	0	1	34	20	6	6	3	11	47	.171
	Jacksonville (SL)	AA	0	1	1.35	13	0	0	3	20	13	4	3	0	2	18	.191
	Las Vegas (PCL)	AAA	2	3	2.91	14	0	0	1	22	23	10	7	1	9	23	.280
MINOR LEAGUE TOTALS			23	16	2.87	97	35	2	5	317	284	136	101	8	90	348	.235

8. Joel Hanrahan, rhp

Born: Oct. 6, 1981. **Ht.:** 6-3. **Wt.:** 210. **Bats:** R. **Throws:** R. **School:** Norwalk (Iowa) Community HS. **Career Transactions:** Selected by Dodgers in second round of 2000 draft; signed June 22, 2000.

Despite a light workload as an amateur in Iowa, where high schools don't play a spring season, Hanrahan has responded to aggressive promotions and established himself as a workhorse. He tossed nine- and six-inning no-hitters last year before earning a promotion to Double-A. Hanrahan displays a feel for three solid pitches. His 90-92 mph sinker and slider are plus offerings, and he also throws a straight changeup. He does an effective job at changing speeds and pitching inside aggressively. He has a strong, durable frame and clean arm action. Hanrahan has good command, but his delivery occasionally gets out of whack and hinders his location in the zone. The key is for him to stay on top of the ball through his delivery. Otherwise he flies off toward first base, causing his arm slot to drop and stuff to flatten out. He made progress working with pitching instructor Ken Howell. Hanrahan projects as a middle-of-the-rotation starter, but he still needs two full seasons in the minors to accumulate innings and experience. He'll return to Jacksonville, where he got hit hard in three starts.

Year	Club (League)	Class	W	L	ERA	G	GS	CG	SV	IP	H	R	ER	HR	BB	SO	AVG
2000	Great Falls (Pio)	R	3	1	4.75	12	11	0	0	55	49	32	29	4	23	40	.231
2001	Wilmington (SAL)	A	9	11	3.38	27	26	0	0	144	136	71	54	13	55	116	.250
2002	Vero Beach (FSL)	A	10	6	4.20	25	25	2	0	144	129	74	67	11	51	139	.242
	Jacksonville (SL)	AA	1	1	10.64	3	3	0	0	11	15	14	13	2	7	10	.326
MINOR LEAGUE TOTALS			23	19	4.15	67	65	2	0	354	329	191	163	30	136	305	.247

9. Joel Guzman, ss

Born: Nov. 24, 1984. **Ht.:** 6-5. **Wt.:** 220. **Bats:** R. **Throws:** R. **Career Transactions:** Signed out of Dominican Republic by Dodgers, July 2, 2001.

Coming off a one-year ban in the Dominican Republic for illegally signing Adrian Beltre, Los Angeles outbid 20 teams to sign Guzman for $2.25 million, a club record and the biggest bonus ever for a player from that nation. The Dodgers didn't have a first-round pick in 2001 and viewed Guzman as the equivalent. Guzman exhibits rare light-tower power in batting practice. He has the potential for five above-average tools, though his only present pluses are arm strength and raw pop. He has the bat speed and strength to develop well above-average game power in time. Guzman has yet to adjust to breaking pitches. He bails and his knees buckle at the sight of the slightest wrinkle. He needs to learn to trust his hands. Most scouts question whether he'll have the quickness to stay at shortstop and think a move to third base is on the horizon. Guzman is still immature at times. While the Dodgers have to keep him motivated, they won't hasten his timetable. It might be 2006 before he makes a big league appearance, but the end result could be special.

Year	Club (League)	Class	AVG	G	AB	R	H	2B	3B	HR	RBI	BB	SO	SB	SLG	OBP
2002	Dodgers (GCL)	R	.212	10	33	4	7	2	0	0	2	5	8	1	.273	.316
	Great Falls (Pio)	R	.252	43	151	19	38	8	2	3	27	18	54	5	.391	.331
MINOR LEAGUE TOTALS			.245	53	184	23	45	10	2	3	29	23	62	6	.370	.329

10. Chin-Feng Chen, of/1b

Born: Oct. 28, 1977. **Ht.:** 6-1. **Wt.:** 180. **Bats:** R. **Throws:** R. **Career Transactions:** Signed out of Taiwan by Dodgers, Jan. 4, 1999.

Rated as the No. 1 prospect in the organization after turning in an unprecedented 30-30 season in the high Class A California League during his 1999 pro debut, Chen hasn't displayed the same explosiveness on the bases or at the plate since shoulder surgery in 2000. He moved to first base last year, but didn't take to the new position and will head back to left field in 2003. Chen has quick wrists and generates raw power with plus bat speed. He shows well-above-average juice to the opposite field. While he doesn't get a good jump out of the box, Chen is a smooth, athletic runner once he gets under way. Chen is a streak hitter, and when he's not on he swings and misses a lot. His first move is away at the plate, leaving him vulnerable to pitches on the outer half. Defense isn't his strong suit. Chen's footwork around first base was horrendous, and he's a tentative outfielder with a below-average arm. Chen can still be a productive major league corner outfielder. The questions are whether it will be in Los Angeles and whether a club will tolerate his lofty strikeout totals. Unless he's traded or an injury creates an opening, he's headed back to Triple-A. By playing in three games with the Dodgers in 2002, Chen became the first player from Taiwan to play in the big leagues.

Year	Club (League)	Class	AVG	G	AB	R	H	2B	3B	HR	RBI	BB	SO	SB	SLG	OBP
1999	San Bernardino (Cal)	A	.316	131	510	98	161	22	10	31	123	75	129	31	.580	.404
2000	San Antonio (TL)	AA	.277	133	516	66	143	27	3	6	67	61	131	23	.376	.355
2001	Vero Beach (FSL)	A	.268	62	235	38	63	15	3	5	41	28	56	2	.421	.359
	Jacksonville (SL)	AA	.313	66	224	47	70	16	2	17	50	41	65	5	.629	.422
2002	Las Vegas (PCL)	AAA	.284	137	511	90	145	26	4	26	84	58	160	1	.503	.352
	Los Angeles (NL)	MAJ	.000	3	5	1	0	0	0	0	0	1	3	0	.000	.167
MAJOR LEAGUE TOTALS			.000	3	5	1	0	0	0	0	0	1	3	0	.000	.167
MINOR LEAGUE TOTALS			.292	529	1996	339	582	106	22	85	365	263	541	62	.494	.375

11. Hong-Chih Kuo, lhp

Born: July 23, 1981. **Ht.:** 6-0. **Wt.:** 200. **Bats:** L. **Throws:** L. **Career Transactions:** Signed out of Taiwan by Dodgers, June 19, 1999.

Kuo was one of Jack Zduriencik's last significant signings as the Dodgers' international scouting director before he left in 2000 to become Brewers scouting director. But since Kuo signed for $1.25 million, injuries have kept him from showcasing his high-octane arm. He needed Tommy John surgery following his first pro start in 2000. After missing most of 2001, he made one rehab appearance in the Gulf Coast League last June, but reported discomfort in his elbow and didn't pitch again until August. Each time out, he flirted with upper-90s velocity. He pitched for Taiwan in the Asian Games, but was wild and ineffective in two relief outings. Upon his return to the United States, doctors discovered scar tissue was irritating the nerves in his elbow. Though Kuo hasn't stayed healthy long enough to pitch in more than five consecutive games, Los Angeles officials insist he is one of the most promising prospects in the organization. Kuo has a free and easy arm action that makes it look like he's just playing catch with 97 mph heat. He creates a lot of his power with a strong leg drive in his delivery. He also spins a big breaking ball and shows an effective straight change. There's still time for him, but 2003 is a critical year in his development. He was able to participate in winter workouts at Dodger Stadium.

Year	Club (League)	Class	W	L	ERA	G	GS	CG	SV	IP	H	R	ER	HR	BB	SO	AVG
2000	San Bernardino (Cal)	A	0	0	0.00	1	1	0	0	3	0	0	0	0	0	7	.000
2001	Dodgers (GCL)	R	0	0	2.33	7	6	0	0	19	13	5	5	0	4	21	.186
2002	Dodgers (GCL)	R	0	0	4.50	3	3	0	0	6	4	3	3	0	1	9	.200
	Vero Beach (FSL)	A	0	1	6.75	4	4	0	0	8	11	6	6	0	2	8	.324
MINOR LEAGUE TOTALS			0	1	3.47	15	14	0	0	36	28	14	14	0	7	45	.211

12. Victor Diaz, 3b/2b

Born: Dec. 10, 1981. **Ht.:** 6-0. **Wt.:** 200. **Bats:** R. **Throws:** R. **School:** Grayson County (Texas) JC. **Career Transactions:** Selected by Dodgers in 37th round of 2000 draft; signed May 19, 2001.

Born in the Dominican Republic, Diaz went to high school in Chicago and was selected as a draft-and-follow pick before his freshman season at Grayson County (Texas) CC, which also produced John Lackey. Diaz has won batting titles in the Gulf Coast and South Atlantic leagues in his first two pro seasons. While he has a slightly unorthodox, free-swinging approach at the plate, he has plus bat speed and bat-head control. He can drive the ball into the alleys but probably won't hit for above-average home run power. Though he's stocky with a thick lower half, he's an above-average runner when he puts forth full effort. Scouts have questioned his work ethic since high school. He appears lackadaisical, especially in the field. He enjoys hitting so much that some scouts believe he just blows off working on his defensive skills. The Dodgers moved him from third to second to first base last year, and still aren't sure where he'll end up. He has plenty of arm strength, but lacks the hands and the first-step quickness for third base. Los Angeles would like to see him handle second base. He'll try to take home a third batting title in Double-A this season.

Year	Club (League)	Class	AVG	G	AB	R	H	2B	3B	HR	RBI	BB	SO	SB	SLG	OBP
2001	Dodgers (GCL)	R	.354	53	195	36	69	22	2	3	31	16	23	6	.533	.414
2002	South Georgia (SAL)	A	.350	91	349	64	122	26	2	10	58	27	69	20	.521	.407
	Jacksonville (SL)	AA	.211	42	152	22	32	7	0	4	24	7	42	7	.336	.258
MINOR LEAGUE TOTALS			.320	186	696	122	223	55	4	17	113	50	134	33	.484	.377

13. Greg Miller, lhp

Born: Nov. 3, 1984. **Ht.:** 6-5. **Wt.:** 190. **Bats:** L. **Throws:** L. **School:** Esperanza HS, Yorba Linda, Calif. **Career Transactions:** Selected by Dodgers in first round (31st overall) of 2002 draft; signed June 14, 2002.

Miller was on most Southern California area scouts' follow lists heading into last spring, and some thought he'd make a nice draft-and-follow pick. Then his low-80s velocity improved to the upper 80s, which coupled with his plus breaking ball caused his stock to soar. "He got better in March instead of the following spring," one American League cross-checker said. By draft day, that scout wasn't the only one making Chuck Finley comparisons. One of the youngest players in the draft at 17, Miller operates with an 89 mph fastball with sink down in the zone. He tops out at 92 and has projectability. His knuckle-curve is an above-average pitch with hard, downward break, though he needs to sharpen his command of the pitch. He demonstrates a feel for his rudimentary circle changeup, which projects as an average offering. Miller's delivery is a little choppy and needs some minor tinkering, but it also adds to his deception. He has a high leg kick and short stride, which helps him to snap off his nasty knuckle-curve, so the Dodgers won't lengthen it too much. Spring training will determine whether he's ready to jump into a full-season league.

Year	Club (League)	Class	W	L	ERA	G	GS	CG	SV	IP	H	R	ER	HR	BB	SO	AVG
2002	Great Falls (Pio)	R	3	2	2.37	11	7	0	0	38	27	14	10	1	13	37	.199
MINOR LEAGUE TOTALS			3	2	2.37	11	7	0	0	38	27	14	10	1	13	37	.199

14. Andrew Brown, rhp

Born: Feb. 17, 1981. **Ht.:** 6-6. **Wt.:** 230. **Bats:** R. **Throws:** R. **School:** Trinity Christian Academy, Jacksonville. **Career Transactions:** Selected by Braves in sixth round of 1999 draft; signed June 3, 1999 . . . On disabled list, June 19-Sept. 6, 2000 . . . Traded by Braves with OF Brian Jordan and LHP Odalis Perez to Dodgers for OF Gary Sheffield, Jan. 15, 2002.

Brown was something of an unknown when he was acquired as a throw-in in the Gary Sheffield deal with the Braves. Credit Los Angeles' pro scouting staff for uncovering a gem. Brown had Tommy John surgery and missed the 2000 season, but was touching the mid-90s by instructional league in 2001. He made a good impression on his new organization by ranking second in the Florida State League in strikeouts and third in average allowed last year. Brown can be overpowering with an 89-93 mph fastball, and his hammer curveball is a strikeout pitch. He mixes in a below-average slider and average changeup. He reminds some of a young Jack McDowell. He has a long, loose arm action, and just needs to repeat his delivery and release point to sharpen the command of his fastball. Brown's next challenge will be Double-A. He should move one level at a time.

Year	Club (League)	Class	W	L	ERA	G	GS	CG	SV	IP	H	R	ER	HR	BB	SO	AVG
1999	Braves (GCL)	R	1	1	2.34	11	11	0	0	42	40	15	11	4	16	57	.247
2000								Did Not Play—Injured									
2001	Jamestown (NY-P)	A	3	4	3.92	14	12	0	0	64	50	29	28	5	31	59	.215
2002	Vero Beach (FSL)	A	10	10	4.11	25	24	1	0	127	97	63	58	13	62	129	.215
MINOR LEAGUE TOTALS			14	15	3.74	50	47	1	0	234	187	107	97	22	109	245	.221

15. Derek Thompson, lhp

Born: Jan. 8, 1981. **Ht.:** 6-2. **Wt.:** 180. **Bats:** L. **Throws:** L. **School:** Land O'Lakes (Fla.) HS. **Career Transactions:** Selected by Indians in first round (37th overall) of 2000 draft; signed June 15, 2000 . . . Selected by Cubs from Indians in major league Rule 5 draft, Dec. 16, 2002 . . . Contract purchased by Dodgers from Cubs, Dec. 16, 2002.

When Cleveland's 2001 draft class was loaded with pitchers, Thompson went from a promising 2000 supplemental first-rounder to buried in a deep system. Knee surgery that limited him to just 12 innings in 2001 didn't help his cause. Still overshadowed, he emerged last spring throwing harder than ever. Thompson showed his best stuff in the high Class A Carolina League playoffs and, in what essentially turned out to be a showcase for Dodgers scouts, during instructional league last fall. In need of a lefthanded reliever, Los Angeles worked out a deal with the Cubs, who took Thompson in the major league Rule 5 draft and then sold him to the Dodgers. His 89-94 mph fastball, nasty two-plane slider and changeup spelled troubles for lefties, who hit .225 against him last year. The heavy sink on his fastball makes it difficult for hitters to lift the ball, resulting in loads of grounders. He has an athletic delivery with minimal effort. He'll have to throw lights-out for Los Angeles manager Jim Tracy in spring training, as it will be tough for a contending club to carry an extra arm. But the Dodgers project Thompson as a starter down the road and would like to find a way to keep him on their 25-man roster.

Year	Club (League)	Class	W	L	ERA	G	GS	CG	SV	IP	H	R	ER	HR	BB	SO	AVG
2000	Burlington (Appy)	R	0	4	5.82	12	12	0	0	43	50	38	28	2	14	40	.273
2001	Columbus (SAL)	A	0	2	9.75	2	2	0	0	12	16	13	13	2	3	5	.320
2002	Columbus (SAL)	A	3	4	3.42	14	14	0	0	74	71	39	28	2	27	50	.253
	Kinston (Car)	A	2	3	3.87	13	13	0	0	74	72	36	32	1	32	41	.259
MINOR LEAGUE TOTALS			5	13	4.47	41	41	0	0	203	209	126	101	8	76	136	.264

16. Franklin Gutierrez, of

Born: Feb. 21, 1983. **Ht.:** 6-2. **Wt.:** 170. **Bats:** R. **Throws:** R. **Career Transactions:** Signed out of Venezuela by Dodgers, Nov. 18, 2000.

Signed by Venezuelan scout Camilo Pascual as a 17-year-old, Gutierrez is a true projection prospect. He has average tools across the board with a chance to add a few pluses as he matures. Still lean and underdeveloped, he has a good frame to fill out. He shows tremendous raw power in batting practice, though he didn't mash in games last year. The Dodgers were pleased with the way he handled himself in his first taste of full-season ball, however. Gutierrez displays strong hitting mechanics and a lightning-quick bat. The wrist action in his swing creates good backspin carry off the bat. There are some holes in his swing he needs to address, though the Dodgers think his aggressiveness is one of his strongest assets. He's not a burner, but he's an athletic runner with a good stride from first to third. His arm strength is average and he's a solid defensive outfielder. He's expected to spend the season in high Class A.

Year	Club (League)	Class	AVG	G	AB	R	H	2B	3B	HR	RBI	BB	SO	SB	SLG	OBP
2001	Dodgers (GCL)	R	.269	56	234	38	63	16	0	4	30	16	39	9	.389	.324
2002	South Georgia (SAL)	A	.283	92	361	61	102	18	4	12	45	31	88	13	.454	.344
	Las Vegas (PCL)	AAA	.300	2	10	2	3	2	0	0	2	1	4	0	.500	.364
MINOR LEAGUE TOTALS			.278	150	605	101	168	36	4	16	77	48	131	22	.430	.337

17. Willy Aybar, 3b

Born: March 9, 1983. **Ht.:** 6-0. **Wt.:** 170. **Bats:** B. **Throws:** R. **Career Transactions:** Signed out of Dominican Republic by Dodgers, Jan. 31, 2000.

Aybar was No. 7 on the Dodgers prospect list in each of the first two years after he signed for a then-Dominican record $1.4 million in January 2000. (The mark since has been shattered by Joel Guzman's $2.25 million deal.) Aybar, whose brother Eric is a rising prospect in the Angels organization, got off to an inauspicious start last spring when he wasn't allowed into the United States because he couldn't produce documents to verify his identity. He didn't join the Dodgers until the end of spring training and it was the end of April before he was in the Vero Beach lineup. The good news was that his age was confirmed. The bad news was that he missed significant development time playing the waiting game with the U.S. consulate, though he did work out at the Dodgers' Dominican complex. Young and immature, Aybar is a high-maintenance prospect. He has developed a patient approach at the plate, perhaps at the expense of his aggressiveness. He doesn't identify pitches well and gives away too many at-bats. His swing is smooth and effortless from both sides of the plate, and he can drive the ball to all fields. An amateur shortstop, Aybar shows swift actions at third base but his lower half is getting thicker. He also has soft hands and a plus arm. His performance doesn't merit a promotion to Double-A and he'd be best served with another year in high Class A.

Year	Club (League)	Class	AVG	G	AB	R	H	2B	3B	HR	RBI	BB	SO	SB	SLG	OBP
2000	Great Falls (Pio)	R	.263	70	266	39	70	15	1	4	49	36	45	5	.372	.349
2001	Wilmington (SAL)	A	.237	120	431	45	102	25	2	4	48	43	64	7	.332	.307
	Vero Beach (FSL)	A	.286	2	7	0	2	0	0	0	0	1	2	0	.286	.375
2002	Vero Beach (FSL)	A	.215	108	372	56	80	18	2	11	65	69	54	15	.363	.339
MINOR LEAGUE TOTALS			.236	300	1076	140	254	58	5	19	162	149	165	27	.352	.329

18. Jonathan Broxton, rhp

Born: June 16, 1984. **Ht.:** 6-4. **Wt.:** 240. **Bats:** R. **Throws:** R. **School:** Burke County HS, Waynesboro, Ga. **Career Transactions:** Selected by Dodgers in second round of 2002 draft; signed June 30, 2002.

Nicknamed "The Bull," Broxton reminds scouts of Angels prospect Bobby Jenks for his large frame and power-pitcher mentality. Broxton turned down a Georgia Southern scholarship to sign for $685,000 as a 2002 second-round pick. A big-boned kid at 6-foot-4 and 260 pounds, he'll have to keep his weight under control. If he can, the Dodgers view his size as a plus because he's strong and durable. Broxton has a textbook delivery, with an effortless action and good arm speed. He pours 94-95 mph fastballs into the zone and tops out at an explosive 97. He threw four pitches in high school, including a slider and curveball, but the Dodgers say he'll be more effective if he focuses on one breaking ball. His curve shows more promise, with good velocity and late depth. Broxton made impressive progress on his changeup with roving instructor Mark Brewer last fall. He also made an adjustment to speed up his times to the plate with a new slide step. He throws strikes and can blow the ball by hitters. Broxton remains a starter for now, and he can fall back on being a quality set-up man or potential closer if he can't stay in the rotation for the long term.

Year	Club (League)	Class	W	L	ERA	G	GS	CG	SV	IP	H	R	ER	HR	BB	SO	AVG
2002	Great Falls (Pio)	R	2	0	2.76	11	6	0	2	29	22	9	9	0	16	33	.212
MINOR LEAGUE TOTALS			2	0	2.76	11	6	0	2	29	22	9	9	0	16	33	.212

19. Wilkin Ruan, of

Born: Sept. 18, 1978. **Ht.:** 6-0. **Wt.:** 170. **Bats:** R. **Throws:** R. **Career Transactions:** Signed out of Dominican Republic by Expos, Nov. 15, 1996 . . . Traded by Expos with RHP Guillermo Mota to Dodgers for RHP Matt Herges and SS Jorge Nunez, March 23, 2002.

In one of Omar Minaya's first moves as Expos general manager, he looked to stabilize his bullpen by acquiring Matt Herges from the Dodgers. The price proved to be steep, as Los Angeles came away with Guillermo Mota and Ruan. Mota made progress in middle relief and is a possible 97-98 mph set-up man for Eric Gagne. Ruan is more of a mystery. Last spring, he turned out to be a year older than previously believed. Scouts are split on his profile. Those who like him project him as a Gold Glove center fielder with a chance to develop power. Those who don't dispute his hitting potential but acknowledge that his defense will carry him to the big leagues. A free swinger with an overaggressive approach, Ruan made adjustments last year to iron out flaws in his swing. By lowering his hands in his stance, he takes a more direct path to the ball, and it paid off in Triple-A. His productivity still is below that of a quality outfielder. Ruan doesn't make enough contact or have enough discipline to hit at the top of the order, and he doesn't hit for enough power to bat in the middle. He uses his blazing speed well on the bases--where he improved his jumps on steals last year—and in center field. Ruan reminds scouts of Andruw Jones with his range and he has an above-average arm to boot. He needs more time in Triple-A to work on his approach at the plate.

Year	Club (League)	Class	AVG	G	AB	R	H	2B	3B	HR	RBI	BB	SO	SB	SLG	OBP
1997	Expos (DSL)	R	.348	69	293	53	102	16	5	4	46	31	34	33	.478	.414
1998	Jupiter (FSL)	A	.167	5	18	2	3	0	0	0	0	1	3	2	.167	.211
	Expos (GCL)	R	.239	54	201	22	48	9	3	1	19	5	43	13	.328	.262
1999	Cape Fear (SAL)	A	.224	112	397	43	89	16	4	1	47	18	79	29	.292	.268
2000	Cape Fear (SAL)	A	.287	134	574	95	165	29	10	0	51	24	75	64	.373	.323
2001	Jupiter (FSL)	A	.283	72	293	41	83	8	2	2	26	10	35	25	.345	.313
	Harrisburg (EL)	AA	.248	30	117	14	29	7	0	0	6	3	18	6	.308	.279
2002	Jacksonville (SL)	AA	.253	78	324	44	82	16	6	3	34	17	33	23	.367	.306
	Las Vegas (PCL)	AAA	.327	40	153	18	50	7	3	0	29	2	17	12	.412	.335
	Los Angeles (NL)	MAJ	.273	12	11	2	3	1	0	0	3	0	2	0	.364	.273
MAJOR LEAGUE TOTALS			.273	12	11	2	3	1	0	0	3	0	2	0	.364	.273
MINOR LEAGUE TOTALS			.275	594	2370	332	651	108	33	11	258	111	337	207	.362	.315

20. Mike Nixon, c

Born: Aug. 17, 1983. **Ht.:** 6-3. **Wt.:** 210. **Bats:** R. **Throws:** R. **School:** Sunnyslope HS, Phoenix. **Career Transactions:** Selected by Dodgers in third round of 2002 draft; signed June 8, 2002.

Questions over Nixon's signability kept him out of the top two rounds. One of the top athletes in the draft, he was recruited as a quarterback by Arizona State and Notre Dame after setting the Arizona high school record for career passing yards, and he committed to UCLA as a safety. Arizona's 2001 prep football player of the year kicked and punted as well, and he led Sunnyslope to a basketball championship. Nixon left his multisport aspirations behind when he signed a baseball-only contract worth $950,000, the third-highest bonus outside 2002's first round. His obvious athleticism aside, the Dodgers were enamored with Nixon's leadership and believe he'll translate it into superior game-calling skills. He still has a lot of room for improvement behind the plate. His feet don't work in sync with his upper body yet, which often causes his arm slot to drop, and he throws sliders down to second. He nabbed just eight of 74 basestealers (11 percent) in his first pro summer. Nixon has the agility to shift his weight and block pitches in the dirt. Despite his background as a quarterback, his arm is fringe average. At the plate, he hits line drives with a short, compact swing. He does a good job of staying inside the ball. Like most young players, he still needs to learn the strike zone. Not all scouts believe Nixon will be able to remain behind the plate, but he can handle the outfield, the position he played in high school. He'll make his full-season debut in low Class A this year.

Year	Club (League)	Class	AVG	G	AB	R	H	2B	3B	HR	RBI	BB	SO	SB	SLG	OBP
2002	Great Falls (Pio)	R	.311	55	219	33	68	10	0	1	31	11	36	7	.370	.355
MINOR LEAGUE TOTALS			.311	55	219	33	68	10	0	1	31	11	36	7	.370	.355

21. Orlando Rodriguez, lhp

Born: Nov. 28, 1980. **Ht.:** 5-10. **Wt.:** 150. **Bats:** L. **Throws:** L. **Career Transactions:** Signed out of Dominican Republic by White Sox, Jan. 12, 2000 . . . Traded by White Sox with RHP Gary Majewski and RHP Andre Simpson to Dodgers for RHP Antonio Osuna and LHP Carlos Ortega, March 22, 2001.

As in the cases of Andrew Brown, Derek Thompson and Ruddy Lugo, the Dodgers' pro scouting staff did a fine job identifying Rodriguez to get him thrown in as part of the Antonio Osuna trade with the White Sox in 2001. After he spent the first year in their organization as a starter, the Dodgers decided his two-pitch repertoire was better suited for the bullpen. He went 1-1, 1.13 in eight relief innings for the Dominican national team in the 2001 World Cup in Taiwan. Then Rodriguez didn't allow a run in 27 outings covering 35 innings last year, though his breakthrough season was interrupted by a bout with elbow tendinitis. He has a sneaky fastball that he can add and subtract velocity from. He can throw it by hitters at 95 mph. He sets up his fastball with a second plus pitch, a tight spinning curveball. Rodriguez was healthy by instructional league. Los Angeles pitching instructors think he could move fast if he didn't rely so heavily on his fastball. He should reach Double-A for the first time in 2003.

Year	Club (League)	Class	W	L	ERA	G	GS	CG	SV	IP	H	R	ER	HR	BB	SO	AVG
2000	White Sox (AZL)	R	2	5	4.20	16	5	0	0	41	36	30	19	3	32	53	.234
	White Sox (DSL)	R	1	1	4.20	3	3	0	0	15	11	8	7	3	4	25	.177
2001	Great Falls (Pio)	R	3	3	4.15	15	10	0	1	61	58	41	28	11	26	79	.240
2002	South Georgia (SAL)	A	3	0	0.00	20	0	0	5	28	12	0	0	0	10	42	.135
	Vero Beach (FSL)	A	0	0	0.00	7	0	0	1	7	6	0	0	0	3	10	.240
MINOR LEAGUE TOTALS			9	9	3.20	61	18	0	7	152	123	79	54	17	75	209	.215

22. Zach Hammes, rhp

Born: May 15, 1984. **Ht.:** 6-6. **Wt.:** 220. **Bats:** R. **Throws:** R. **School:** Iowa City (Iowa) HS. **Career Transactions:** Selected by Dodgers in second round of 2002 draft; signed June 21, 2002.

Like Joel Hanrahan, Hammes was signed out of Iowa by area scout Mitch Webster. Hammes is a giant on the mound, with more of an overpowering approach than Hanrahan. Hammes throws a power curveball rather than Hanrahan's nasty slider. Hammes' fastball features more explosive late life with projectable velocity. He already tops out in the 92-93 mph range. Without a spring high school season in Iowa, he has low mileage on his arm, though he did show his stuff for scouts in the Perfect Game spring scout league and various showcase events. He established himself as a premium pick at the predraft showcase last April. Because of his frame, effortless arm action and limited experience, he should reach the mid-90s. Dodgers pitching instructors will focus on improving Hammes' lower half in his delivery, which also should produce more power. He shows a feel for a straight change-up. Hanrahan jumped straight to a full-season Class A league in his second season, but

Hammes might be better served staying in extended spring training to work on his delivery and offspeed stuff.

Year	Club (League)	Class	W	L	ERA	G	GS	CG	SV	IP	H	R	ER	HR	BB	SO	AVG
2002	Dodgers (GCL)	R	2	2	3.27	10	8	0	0	33	26	14	12	0	15	27	.217
MINOR LEAGUE TOTALS			2	2	3.27	10	8	0	0	33	26	14	12	0	15	27	.217

23. Steve Colyer, lhp

Born: Feb. 22, 1979. **Ht.:** 6-4. **Wt.:** 200. **Bats:** L. **Throws:** L. **School:** Meramec (Mo.) JC. **Career Transactions:** Selected by Dodgers in second round of 1997 draft; signed May 23, 1998.

After spending the first four years of his career primarily as a starter, Colyer's aggressive mound presence and power arsenal prompted his move to the bullpen last year—as did his lack of control. Along with Colyer, the Dodgers have cultivated a promising group of left-handed bullpen arms in the upper levels including Derek Thompson, Orlando Rodriguez, Victor Alvarez, Rick Roberts and 2002 15th-rounder Eric Stults. Colyer has the best arm strength of the group and one of the best fastballs in the system. He pitched at 94-96 mph in every outing last year, maxing out at 97 with explosive late life. His feel for the strike zone is limited because he has a full-effort delivery that's hard to repeat. Colyer flashes a solid-average slider, but it's inconsistent because his release point is as well. He has the ideal mentality to pitch in tough late-inning situations, and not many lefthanders in baseball can match his pure velocity. He just needs the command to go with it. He'll move up to Triple-A this year.

Year	Club (League)	Class	W	L	ERA	G	GS	CG	SV	IP	H	R	ER	HR	BB	SO	AVG
1998	Yakima (NWL)	A	2	2	4.96	15	12	0	0	65	72	46	36	2	36	75	.277
1999	San Bernardino (Cal)	A	7	9	4.70	27	25	1	0	146	145	82	76	12	86	131	.269
2000	Vero Beach (FSL)	A	5	7	5.76	26	18	1	0	95	97	74	61	9	68	80	.272
2001	Vero Beach (FSL)	A	4	8	3.96	24	24	0	0	120	101	62	53	16	77	118	.234
2002	Jacksonville (SL)	AA	5	4	3.45	59	0	0	21	63	50	29	24	6	40	68	.214
MINOR LEAGUE TOTALS			23	30	4.60	151	79	2	21	489	465	293	250	45	307	472	.255

24. Jason Romano, of/2b

Born: June 24, 1979. **Ht.:** 6-0. **Wt.:** 180. **Bats:** R. **Throws:** R. **School:** Hillsborough HS, Tampa. **Career Transactions:** Selected by Rangers in first round (39th overall) of 1997 draft; signed July 11, 1997 . . . Traded by Rangers with OF Gabe Kapler to Rockies for OF Todd Hollandsworth and LHP Dennys Reyes, July 31, 2002 . . . Traded by Rockies to Dodgers for OF Luke Allen, Jan. 27, 2003.

Drafted out of the same Hillsborough High program that produced Dwight Gooden, Gary Sheffield and Carl Everett, Romano was often compared to Craig Biggio during his first few years in the Rangers system. After being passed by second baseman Mike Young in Texas and moved to the outfield, he came to the Rockies last summer. The Dodgers like his potential as a utilityman and traded for him in January. His bat has tailed off since he left high Class A in 1999, and Romano has established a reputation as more of a scrappy, versatile player. Drafted as a third baseman, he was moved to second base after his first season but never refined his footwork there. He has shown dramatic improvement in the outfield, utilitzing his instincts and aggressiveness. He has a compact, line-drive stroke and a sparkplug mentality, though his extra-base power has been absent at the upper levels. Romano has plus speed and runs the bases well. He should get consideration for playing time at second base in Los Angeles, but more likely will settle in as a versatile option off the bench. He also could be a righthanded complement to Dave Roberts in center field.

Year	Club (League)	Class	AVG	G	AB	R	H	2B	3B	HR	RBI	BB	SO	SB	SLG	OBP
1997	Rangers (GCL)	R	.257	34	109	27	28	5	3	2	11	13	19	13	.413	.349
1998	Savannah (SAL)	A	.271	134	524	72	142	19	4	7	52	46	94	40	.363	.336
	Charlotte (FSL)	A	.208	7	24	3	5	1	0	0	1	2	2	1	.250	.259
1999	Charlotte (FSL)	A	.312	120	459	84	143	27	14	13	71	39	72	34	.516	.376
2000	Tulsa (TL)	AA	.271	131	535	87	145	35	2	8	70	56	84	25	.389	.343
2001	Tulsa (TL)	AA	.242	46	186	19	45	9	1	1	19	16	31	8	.317	.304
	Oklahoma (PCL)	AAA	.315	41	149	32	47	6	1	4	13	20	28	3	.450	.394
	Rangers (GCL)	R	.143	5	21	2	3	0	0	0	0	1	8	1	.143	.182
	Charlotte (FSL)	A	.400	3	10	3	4	2	0	0	1	4	1	1	.600	.571
2002	Oklahoma (PCL)	AAA	.270	48	196	28	53	8	1	4	28	19	41	10	.383	.329
	Texas (AL)	MAJ	.204	29	54	8	11	4	0	0	4	4	13	2	.278	.254
	Colorado Springs (PCL)	AAA	.310	31	129	20	40	7	2	0	9	6	27	8	.395	.338
	Colorado (NL)	MAJ	.324	18	37	9	12	0	1	0	1	3	11	4	.378	.375
MAJOR LEAGUE TOTALS			.253	47	91	17	23	4	1	0	5	7	24	6	.319	.303
MINOR LEAGUE TOTALS			.280	600	2342	377	655	119	28	39	275	222	407	144	.404	.346

25. Jason Repko, of

Born: Dec. 27, 1980. **Ht.:** 5-11. **Wt.:** 170. **Bats:** R. **Throws:** R. **School:** Hanford HS, Richland, Wash. **Career Transactions:** Selected by Dodgers in first round (37th overall) of 1999 draft; signed June 3, 1999.

Repko showed the capability for all-around stardom as a first-team high school All-American in 1999, when he batted .581 with 18 home runs and 14 steals. A pulled hamstring and recurring back problems hampered his progress throughout the 2000-01 seasons, but he was healthy enough last year to play in a career-high 120 games. Instead of the five-tool projections and Paul Molitor comparisons from early in his career, Repko now projects as more of a versatile, reserve player in the Jason Romano mold. Repko moved to center field last year after committing 67 errors in 134 games at shortstop. He's one of the fastest players in the system—a 70 runner on the 20-80 scouting scale—with plus arm strength and solid baseball instincts, so the transition went smoothly. His power doesn't project as a plus tool anymore, though he can drive the ball into the alleys with some authority. He has a quick bat that should produce a good average if he can develop more selectivity at the plate. He chases too many pitches out of the zone. Repko could get a shot at Double-A this year.

Year	Club (League)	Class	AVG	G	AB	R	H	2B	3B	HR	RBI	BB	SO	SB	SLG	OBP
1999	Great Falls (Pio)	R	.304	49	207	51	63	9	9	8	32	21	43	12	.551	.375
2000	Yakima (NWL)	A	.294	8	17	3	5	2	0	0	1	1	7	0	.412	.333
2001	Wilmington (SAL)	A	.220	88	337	36	74	17	4	4	32	15	68	17	.329	.257
2002	Vero Beach (FSL)	A	.272	120	470	73	128	29	5	9	53	25	92	29	.413	.319
MINOR LEAGUE TOTALS			.262	265	1031	163	270	57	18	21	118	62	210	58	.413	.311

26. Brian Pilkington, rhp

Born: Sept. 17, 1982. **Ht.:** 6-5. **Wt.:** 210. **Bats:** R. **Throws:** R. **School:** Santiago HS, Garden Grove, Calif. **Career Transactions:** Selected by Dodgers in second round of 2001 draft; signed June 14, 2001.

In 2001, Ed Creech's last draft as Dodgers scouting director, he tabbed high school pitchers with his first six picks including Pilkington with his first choice in the second round. Pilkington, a nephew of 287-game winner Bert Blyleven, was shut down with a sore shoulder that required arthroscopic surgery after just five pro outings in 2001. Pilkington was ready to go from Opening Day last year, working shorter pitch-restricted stints until stretching out deeper into starts later in the summer. Like his uncle, Pilkington has a curveball that's a go-to pitch. It has good three-quarters break through the zone. He has outstanding command and control of three pitches. As a high school senior, he issued just seven walks in 72 innings. His fastball is average, sitting around 88-91 mph and topping out at 92, and his changeup has late fading action. Because he relies on location and changing speeds more than overpowering hitters, some scouts think Pilkington is around the strike zone too much. He demonstrates an advanced feel for pitching for his age and just needs to be more careful with his location. He's ready for a full season in high Class A in 2003.

Year	Club (League)	Class	W	L	ERA	G	GS	CG	SV	IP	H	R	ER	HR	BB	SO	AVG
2001	Great Falls (Pio)	R	0	1	5.63	5	2	0	0	16	19	11	10	2	2	17	.297
2002	South Georgia (SAL)	A	8	4	3.45	20	18	1	0	112	129	61	43	8	13	78	.283
	Vero Beach (FSL)	A	2	1	2.37	3	3	0	0	19	16	7	5	2	3	10	.235
MINOR LEAGUE TOTALS			10	6	3.54	28	23	1	0	147	164	79	58	12	18	105	.279

27. Mike Megrew, lhp

Born: Jan. 29, 1984. **Ht.:** 6-6. **Wt.:** 210. **Bats:** L. **Throws:** L. **School:** Chariho Regional HS, Hope Valley, R.I. **Career Transactions:** Selected by Dodgers in 5th round of 2002 draft; signed June 5, 2002.

Logan White is developing a good track record of evaluating young, projectable lefties. As an area scout, he signed Kevin Walker for the Padres. As an Orioles crosschecker he was so confident he said he would have put his job on the line for Rommie Lewis. His first draft class as Dodgers scouting director yielded at least three southpaws with similar qualifications: Greg Miller, McGrew and 15th-round gem Eric Stults. McGrew's delivery and quick arm reminded White of Walker and Lewis, who both enjoyed rapid jumps in velocity from the mid-80s. Area scout John Kosciak clocked McGrew at 84-87 mph in the spring. After signing, Megrew reached 88-93, also spinning a good curveball and mixing in a deceptive changeup. He gave the Dodgers a scare when he strained a ligament in his elbow last August. All the ingredients—projectable velocity, feel for secondary stuff and repeatable delivery—are in place for a rapid ascent. The Dodgers believe he'll be healthy for spring training and a potential trip to low Class A.

Year	Club (League)	Class	W	L	ERA	G	GS	CG	SV	IP	H	R	ER	HR	BB	SO	AVG
2002	Dodgers (GCL)	R	1	1	2.03	5	4	0	0	13	8	4	3	0	3	12	.178
MINOR LEAGUE TOTALS			1	1	2.03	5	4	0	0	13	8	4	3	0	3	12	.178

28. Jose Diaz, rhp

Born: Feb. 27, 1984. **Ht.:** 6-4. **Wt.:** 240. **Bats:** R. **Throws:** R. **Career Transactions:** Signed out of Dominican Republic by Dodgers, May 14, 2001.

Not to be confused with the Jose Diaz who made last year's Dodgers prospect list and now is known as Joselo Soriano, this Diaz is simply known as "Jumbo" throughout the organization. Both fire mid- to upper-90s heat, but Jumbo demonstrates a better feel for pitching. Originally signed for $100,000, he's physically imposing and can overpower hitters with one of the best fastballs in the system. He tops out at 97 mph and pitches at 94-95. He also has some aptitude for a slider which distinguishes him from other live arms in the lower levels. Diaz needs to get innings and experience, though he'll move up the ladder as a reliever. He has the build of a tight end, drawing obvious parallels to Armando Benitez. Diaz could close in low Class A this year and has a shot to advance higher.

Year	Club (League)	Class	W	L	ERA	G	GS	CG	SV	IP	H	R	ER	HR	BB	SO	AVG
2001	Dodgers (DSL)	R	8	3	3.66	28	0	0	5	32	28	15	13	2	24	32	.233
2002	Dodgers (GCL)	R	3	1	1.95	10	6	0	0	32	19	11	7	0	12	26	.174
	South Georgia (SAL)	A	1	1	3.94	3	3	0	0	16	16	7	7	0	10	7	.281
	Great Falls (Pio)	R	1	1	3.65	3	3	0	0	12	11	6	5	1	6	14	.224
MINOR LEAGUE TOTALS			13	6	3.11	44	12	0	5	93	74	39	32	3	52	79	.221

29. Franquelis Osoria, rhp

Born: Sept. 12, 1981. **Ht.:** 6-0. **Wt.:** 160. **Bats:** R. **Throws:** R. **Career Transactions:** Signed out of Dominican Republic by Dodgers, Dec. 28, 1999.

Another highly regarded young gun from Pablo Peguero's scouting efforts in the Dominican Republic, Osoria emerged as a prospect last year after two years as a starter in the Dominican Summer League. The Dodgers have a plethora of promising young arms who already have been restricted to relief roles. It's surprising that they've limited some of those prospects to the bullpen instead of developing stamina and encouraging a complete repertoire by making them starters. Osoria differs from the radar-gun monsters in that his fastball has average velocity, but no pitcher in the system can top his plus-plus movement. He keeps hitters off balance with a low three-quarters arm slot that borders on sidearm. Osoria operates primarily with a two-pitch, sinker-slider attack. He doesn't throw anything straight and hitters have little chance of lifting the ball against him. Florida State League hitters slugged just .260 against him, and righthanders managed a .181 average with one extra-base hit in 105 at bats. Praised for his work ethic, he could move through the system in a hurry.

Year	Club (League)	Class	W	L	ERA	G	GS	CG	SV	IP	H	R	ER	HR	BB	SO	AVG
2000	Dodgers (DSL)	R	3	4	2.52	13	12	0	0	64	58	33	18	1	23	46	.230
2001	Dodgers (DSL)	R	4	4	3.16	15	11	0	0	77	69	38	27	5	16	67	.237
2002	Vero Beach (FSL)	A	0	1	2.45	3	0	0	0	7	4	2	2	0	2	10	.154
	South Georgia (SAL)	A	2	2	3.32	21	1	0	1	43	40	22	16	1	13	30	.226
MINOR LEAGUE TOTALS			9	11	2.95	52	24	0	1	192	171	95	63	7	54	153	.229

30. Delwyn Young, 2b

Born: June 30, 1982. **Ht.:** 5-10. **Wt.:** 180. **Bats:** B. **Throws:** R. **School:** Santa Barbara (Calif.) CC. **Career Transactions:** Selected by Dodgers in fourth round of 2002 draft; signed June 12, 2002.

Selected by the Braves as a 29th-round draft-and-follow in 2001, Young emerged as one of the top junior college hitters in California last spring. He was expected to sign with Atlanta, but negotiations fell through and the Dodgers redrafted him in the fourth round. He intrigued Los Angeles brass with an impressive hitting display during a predraft workout at Dodger Stadium. After finishing among the Pioneer League leaders in doubles, home runs, slugging and extra-base hits, he continued to shine as the most impressive player at the club's winter workouts at Chavez Ravine. Young can put a charge into the ball from both sides of the plate. He showed signs of getting too homer-conscious, getting himself into trouble by trying to lift everything. He has plus arm strength and good hands, but his footwork needs improvement. The Dodgers want him to stay at second base, and that's where he'll play for one of their Class A affiliates this year.

Year	Club (League)	Class	AVG	G	AB	R	H	2B	3B	HR	RBI	BB	SO	SB	SLG	OBP
2002	Great Falls (Pio)	R	.300	59	240	42	72	18	1	10	41	27	60	4	.508	.380
MINOR LEAGUE TOTALS			.300	59	240	42	72	18	1	10	41	27	60	4	.508	.380

MILWAUKEE
BREWERS

TOP 30 PROSPECTS

1. Brad Nelson, 1b/of
2. Mike Jones, rhp
3. Prince Fielder, 1b
4. Ben Hendrickson, rhp
5. Corey Hart, 3b/1b
6. J.J. Hardy, ss
7. David Krynzel, of
8. Manny Parra, lhp
9. Ben Diggins, rhp
10. Matt Ford, lhp
11. Enrique Cruz, 3b/ss
12. Pedro Liriano, rhp
13. Keith Ginter, 3b
14. Ozzie Chavez, ss
15. Shane Nance, lhp
16. Steve Moss, of
17. Jayson Durocher, rhp
18. Bill Hall, ss
19. Eric M. Thomas, rhp
20. Mike Adams, rhp
21. Johnny Raburn, 2b/ss
22. Luis Martinez, lhp
23. Matt Childers, rhp
24. J.M. Gold, rhp
25. David Pember, rhp
26. Chris Morris, of
27. Cristian Guerrero, of
28. Khalid Ballouli, rhp
29. Jason Belcher, c/of
30. Josh Murray, ss

By Drew Olson

During the darkest days of their worst season, Brewers officials looked at their improving farm system as a source of inspiration and encouragement. Of course, what choice did they have?

Though the sometimes leaky roof above Miller Park was a source of embarrassment and frustration, it was no match for what happened on the field: 106 losses, a 10th straight losing season, two managerial changes, an All-Star Game debacle that will live in infamy, and the unpopular decision to sit shortstop Jose Hernandez in the final week to avoid having him set the major league record for strikeouts.

Under those bleak circumstances, positive reports about minor leaguers provided a welcome diversion. They weren't enough, however, to prevent a sweeping organizational overhaul. Wendy Selig-Prieb, the daughter of commissioner Bud Selig, stepped down as club president and was replaced by Ulice Payne Jr. On the same day, general manager Dean Taylor was fired and replaced by former Rangers GM Doug Melvin, who brought assistant Gord Ash and farm director Reid Nichols along as aides in his attempt to turn things around.

The first two years of Taylor's tenure coincided with the final year in County Stadium and the first year at Miller Park, which meant he faced pressure to win immediately while trying to rebuild a farm system haunted by first-round busts such as Antone Williamson and Chad Green. That double play is virtually impossible to turn. Taylor's most positive legacy is that the farm system is in better shape than when he came aboard during the fall of 1999. That's thanks primarily to scouting director Jack Zduriencik, who was retained by Melvin. Taylor also peddled veterans in the weeks before his forced exit, adding another infusion of solid prospects.

Under Taylor, the Brewers aggressively promoted their top prospects. In order to show disgruntled fans that a youth movement indeed was under way, he promoted a handful of young players to the big leagues in September. By then, it was too late.

With a four-year contract in his pocket and a solid track record in player development, Melvin may choose to let players develop at a slower pace. If he succeeds, he may owe a debt of gratitude to Taylor and the glaring reality that Brewers' fortunes can't sink much lower.

OrganizationOverview

General Manager: Doug Melvin. **Farm Director:** Reid Nichols. **Scouting Director:** Jack Zduriencik.

2002 PERFORMANCE

Class	Farm Team	League	W	L	Pct.	Finish*	Manager(s)
Majors	Milwaukee	National	55	106	.346	16th (16)	Davey Lopes/Jerry Royster
Triple-A	Indianapolis Indians	International	67	76	.469	9th (14)	Ed Romero
Double-A	Huntsville Stars	Southern	70	69	.509	5th (10)	Frank Kremblas
High A	High Desert Mavericks	California	60	80	.429	9th (10)	Mike Caldwell
Low A	Beloit Snappers	Midwest	57	82	.410	12th (14)	Don Money
Rookie	†Ogden Raptors	Pioneer	40	35	.533	2nd (8)	Wendell Kim
Rookie	AZL Brewers	Arizona	26	30	.464	6th (7)	Carlos Lezcano
OVERALL 2002 MINOR LEAGUE RECORD			320	372	.462	26th (30)	

*Finish in overall standings (No. of teams in league). †Affiliate will be in Helena (Pioneer) in 2003.

ORGANIZATION LEADERS

BATTING   *Minimum 250 At-Bats
*AVG	Callix Crabbe, Ogden	.328
R	Brad Nelson, High Desert/Beloit	94
H	Brad Nelson, High Desert/Beloit	150
TB	Brad Nelson, High Desert/Beloit	263
2B	Brad Nelson, High Desert/Beloit	49
3B	Dave Krynzel, Huntsville/High Desert	15
HR	Israel Alcantara, Indianapolis	27
RBI	Brad Nelson, High Desert/Beloit	116
BB	Three tied at	68
SO	Jeff Deardorff, Huntsville	131
SB	Dave Krynzel, Huntsville/High Desert	42

PITCHING   #Minimum 75 Innings
W	Paul Stewart, Huntsville	12
	Dan Hall, Beloit	12
L	Gerry Oakes, Beloit	14
#ERA	Ben Hendrickson, Huntsville/High Desert	2.74
G	Jack Krawczyk, Indianapolis/Huntsville	52
CG	Jimmy Osting, Indianapolis	3
SV	Brian Mallette, Indianapolis	25
IP	Pete Smart, High Desert	180
BB	Gerry Oakes, Beloit	84
SO	Mike Jones, Beloit	132

BEST TOOLS

Best Hitter for Average	Brad Nelson
Best Power Hitter	Prince Fielder
Fastest Baserunner	David Krynzel
Best Athlete	David Krynzel
Best Fastball	Mike Jones
Best Curveball	Ben Hendrickson
Best Slider	Pedro Liriano
Best Changeup	Jose Mieses
Best Control	Manny Parra
Best Defensive Catcher	Brian Moon
Best Defensive Infielder	J.J. Hardy
Best Infield Arm	J.J. Hardy
Best Defensive Outfielder	Steve Moss
Best Outfield Arm	Cristian Guerrero

2006 LINEUP

Catcher	Javier Valentin
First Base	Prince Fielder
Second Base	Enrique Cruz
Third Base	Corey Hart
Shortstop	J.J. Hardy
Left Field	Brad Nelson
Center Field	David Krynzel
Right Field	Richie Sexson
No. 1 Starter	Ben Sheets

Jeff Deardorff   Jack Krawczyk

No. 2 Starter	Nick Neugebauer
No. 3 Starter	Mike Jones
No. 4 Starter	Ben Hendrickson
No. 5 Starter	Manny Parra
Closer	Ben Diggins

TOP PROSPECTS OF THE DECADE

1993	Tyrone Hill, lhp
1994	Jeff D'Amico, rhp
1995	Antone Williamson, 3b
1996	Jeff D'Amico, rhp
1997	Todd Dunn, of
1998	Valerio de los Santos, lhp
1999	Ron Belliard, 2b
2000	Nick Neugebauer, rhp
2001	Ben Sheets, rhp
2002	Nick Neugebauer, rhp

TOP DRAFT PICKS OF THE DECADE

1993	Jeff D'Amico, rhp
1994	Antone Williamson, 3b
1995	Geoff Jenkins, of
1996	Chad Green, of
1997	Kyle Peterson, rhp
1998	J.M. Gold, rhp
1999	Ben Sheets, rhp
2000	David Krynzel, of
2001	Mike Jones, rhp
2002	Prince Fielder, 1b

ALL-TIME LARGEST BONUSES

Ben Sheets, 1999	$2,450,000
Prince Fielder, 2002	$2,400,000
Mike Jones, 2001	$2,075,000
David Krynzel, 2000	$1,950,000
J.M. Gold, 1998	$1,675,000

MinorLeagueDepthChart
MILWAUKEE BREWERS

16 RANK

When Dean Taylor took over as general manager before the 2000 season, the Brewers system ranked dead last among the 30 big league organizations. Considering where they were—they also ranked 30th heading into the 2001 season—the system is making tremendous strides. Taylor was fired late in the 2002 season, but scouting director Jack Zduriencik was retained. He deserves credit for hitting on his first-rounders and uncovering mid-round gems like Corey Hart. Most of the Brewers' prospects are at least two years away, and it will take time to develop depth and balance. The organization is expected to address those shortcomings by tapping the college ranks under a revamped front office headed by new GM Doug Melvin.

Note: Depth charts prepared by Josh Boyd. Numbers in parentheses indicate prospect rankings.

LF
Jason Belcher (29)
Peter Zoccolillo
D.J. Clark
Kade Johnson
Bill Scott

CF
David Krynzel (7)
Steve Moss (16)
Chris Morris (26)
Scott Podsednik
Nic Carter
Manuel Melo
Francisco Plasencia

RF
Cristian Guerrero (27)
Mario Mendez

3B
Corey Hart (5)
Enrique Cruz (11)
Keith Ginter (13)
Richard Paz

SS
J.J. Hardy (6)
Ozzie Chavez (14)
Bill Hall (18)
Josh Murray (30)

2B
Johnny Raburn (21)
Callix Crabbe

1B
Brad Nelson (1)
Prince Fielder (3)
Brandon Gemoll

C
Manny Ramirez
Cody McKay
Florian Villanueva

RHP

Starters	Relievers
Mike Jones (2)	Ben Diggins (9)
Ben Hendrickson (4)	Jayson Durocher (17)
Pedro Liriano (12)	Mike Adams (20)
Eric Thomas (19)	Matt Childers (23)
J.M. Gold (24)	Khalid Ballouli (28)
David Pember (25)	Roberto Giron
Tom Wilhelmsen	Carl Michaels
Jose Mieses	Mike Penney
Calvin Carpenter	
Jose Garcia	
Jon Steitz	

LHP

Starters	Relievers
Manny Parra (8)	Shane Nance (15)
Matt Ford (10)	Luis Martinez (22)
	John Foster

DraftAnalysis

2002 Draft

Best Pro Debut: 1B Prince Fielder's (1) doughy body made him a risk as the No. 7 overall pick, but he chased the Rookie-level Pioneer League triple crown before getting promoted to low Class A. He hit a combined .326-13-51. LHP Craig Breslow (26) went 6-2, 1.82 with 56 strikeouts in 54 PL innings.

Best Athlete: OFs Nic Carter (4) or Steve Moss (29). Carter was an all-state basketball player as a West Virginia high schooler.

Best Pure Hitter: Fielder's calling card is power, but he's not just a masher. As Cecil Fielder's son, Prince grew up in major league clubhouses and has an advanced approach.

Best Raw Power: Fielder's biggest payoff will come with home run production. He has a chance to become part of the first father-son tandem to each hit 50 homers in a big league season.

Fastest Runner: The Brewers clocked Carter from the left side of home to first base in 3.7 seconds, which is Ichiro territory.

Best Defensive Player: Moss glides to balls in either gap and unlike most center fielders, he has a plus arm. SS Josh Murray (2) has rebounded after missing 2001 following Tommy John surgery.

Best Fastball: String-bean RHP Tom Wilhelmsen (7) touched 97 mph in the 2001 American Legion World Series. Six-foot-9 RHP Eric Thomas (3) reached 96 in the spring before getting shoulder tendinitis.

Best Breaking Ball: LHP Manny Parra, the best talent on the draft-and-follow market last year, has a plus curveball and has hit 95 mph with his fastball. From the draft,

Thomas and RHP Bo Hall (19) have curves that aren't quite the equal of Parra's.

Most Intriguing Background: Fielder's dad led the American League in homers twice and RBIs three times. RHP Khalid Ballouli's (6) grandfather Dick Fowler and unsigned C Tim Dillard's (34) father Steve both had lengthy big league careers. C John Vanden Berg's (25) father Gary is the head groundskeeper at Miller Park. Unsigned RHP Simon Beresford (32) pitched for the Australian national team. And just to confuse themselves, the Brewers took another RHP Eric Thomas (28).

Carter

Closest To The Majors: Fielder was slowed by a groin pull in low Class A. He has worked hard to get into better shape, and when he's healthy he'll be hard to hold back. Parra could beat him to the majors.

Best Late-Round Pick: Moss, whose desire to attend UCLA scared off most teams.

The One Who Got Away: The Brewers couldn't beat UCLA for athletic SS Jarrad Page (5), who played safety for the Bruins.

Assessment: New general manager Doug Melvin astutely retained scouting director Jack Zduriencik, whose drafts over the last three years have provided most of Milwaukee's prospects. Fielder, Thomas and Parra give the Brewers the equivalent of three first-rounders.

2001 Draft

RHP Mike Jones (1), SS J.J. Hardy (2) and 1B Brad Nelson (4) quickly asserted themselves as the hope for Milwaukee's future. LHP Manny Parra (26) became the most coveted draft-and-follow of 2002 and signed for $1.55 million. **Grade: A**

2000 Draft

OF Dave Krynzel (1) and 3B/1B Corey Hart (11) are two more pieces to the Brewers' puzzle. They may regret trading RHP Matt Yeatman (13) for Twins retreads this offseason. **Grade: B+**

1999 Draft

RHP Ben Sheets (1) went from Olympic hero in 2000 to all-star as a rookie in 2001. RHP Ben Hendrickson (10) will join him in the big league rotation soon. **Grade: B+**

1998 Draft

If RHP Nick Neugebauer (2) can avoid the injuries that have plagued RHP J.M. Gold (1), he could become Milwaukee's ace. SS Bill Hall's (6) stock rose meteorically in 2001 and fell just as quickly last year. **Grade: B**

Note: Draft analysis prepared by Jim Callis. Numbers in parentheses indicate draft rounds.

... Few players can drive the ball the other way as far as Nelson can.

Brad
Nelson 1b/of

Born: Dec. 23, 1982.
Ht.: 6-2. **Wt.:** 220.
Bats: L. **Throws:** R.
School: Bishop Garrigan HS, Algona, Iowa.
Career Transactions: Selected by Brewers in fourth round of 2001 draft; signed July 25, 2001.

Nelson was considered one of the top high school power hitters in 2001, and he put on an impressive batting-practice display during a predraft workout for the Brewers. He also showed a low-90s fastball from the mound, but he nevertheless lasted until the fourth round of the draft. He failed to homer in 105 at-bats in Rookie ball that summer. Well, his adjustment to wood bats is over. A strong Iowa farmboy, Nelson was Milwaukee's 2002 minor league player of the year after leading the minors with 49 doubles and 116 RBIs. He did seem to run out of gas a little after he was promoted to high Class A High Desert at age 19.

Nelson is the best all-around hitter in the system. He has good actions at the plate and has earned comparisons to Sean Casey. Managers rated Nelson, and not Marlins slugger Jason Stokes, as the top power hitter in the low Class A Midwest League last year. While scouts disagreed, they did concede that Nelson had better pop to the opposite field. Few players can drive the ball as far the other way as Nelson can. His willingness to use the entire field enabled him to put up a strong first full season despite his youth and experience against inferior high school competition. Nelson's arm remains strong and he has good hands, though each is less of an asset at first base than it was when he played third base as an amateur. Class A Beloit manager Don Money considered Nelson a favorite because of his attitude and work ethic.

Pitchers are going to be loathe to challenge Nelson, so Money encouraged him to work the strike zone and take more walks. That lesson hasn't taken yet, at least not to the extent needed. Nelson lacks speed and range, which prompted his move from the hot corner and makes him no more than an ordinary defender. He has a thick body and will have to work to stay in shape, though no one questions his willingness to do so.

Nelson probably will return to the California League at the start of 2003 and could reach Miller Park as early as 2005. The big question is where he'll fit into Milwaukee's lineup. A move to left field could be in Nelson's future.

Year	Club (League)	Class	AVG	G	AB	R	H	2B	3B	HR	RBI	BB	SO	SB	SLG	OBP
2001	Brewers (AZL)	R	.302	17	63	10	19	6	1	0	13	8	18	0	.429	.392
	Ogden (Pio)	R	.262	13	42	5	11	4	0	0	10	3	9	0	.357	.298
2002	Beloit (Mid)	A	.297	106	417	70	124	38	2	17	99	34	86	4	.520	.353
	High Desert (Cal)	A	.255	26	102	24	26	11	0	3	17	12	28	4	.451	.333
MINOR LEAGUE TOTALS			.288	162	624	109	180	59	3	20	139	57	141	4	.489	.350

2. Mike Jones, rhp

Born: April 23, 1983. **Ht.:** 6-4. **Wt.:** 200. **Bats:** R. **Throws:** R. **School:** Thunderbird HS, Phoenix. **Career Transactions:** Selected by Brewers in first round (12th overall) of 2001 draft; signed June 27, 2001.

Of all the stats Jones compiled in his first full pro season, one stands out: 27. That's the number of starts he made at Beloit. Nagging shoulder problems and a reduction in velocity caused some clubs to shy away from Jones early in the 2001 draft, but the Brewers rolled the dice and could be rewarded with a top-of-the-rotation starter. Though he probably could have blown Midwest League hitters away with a low-90s fastball that touches 96 mph, Jones followed orders and worked hard to improve his curveball, which he releases from a three-quarters arm angle. Besides velocity, his fastball also has life to both sides of the plate. Scouts love his stuff, fluid delivery and athletic ability, but Milwaukee may be most pleased by his makeup. He competes intensely, shows good poise on the mound and works hard between starts. After the season, Jones went to instructional league to work on his changeup. If it improves as much as his curve, he'll move up the system quickly. He's still refining his command as well. Jones will spend this year in high Class A. The Brewers hope he'll eventually help form an impressive front three in their big league rotation with Ben Sheets and Nick Neugebauer.

Year	Club (League)	Class	W	L	ERA	G	GS	CG	SV	IP	H	R	ER	HR	BB	SO	AVG
2001	Ogden (Pio)	R	4	1	3.74	9	7	0	0	34	29	17	14	1	10	32	.236
2002	Beloit (Mid)	A	7	7	3.12	27	27	0	0	139	135	63	48	3	62	132	.256
MINOR LEAGUE TOTALS			11	8	3.24	36	34	0	0	172	164	80	62	4	72	164	.252

3. Prince Fielder, 1b

Born: May 9, 1984. **Ht.:** 6-0. **Wt.:** 260. **Bats:** L. **Throws:** R. **School:** Eau Gallie HS, Melbourne, Fla. **Career Transactions:** Selected by Brewers in first round (seventh overall) of 2002 draft; signed June 17, 2002.

Though they already have a potential logjam of first basemen starting with Richie Sexson, the Brewers surprised a lot of people by selecting another with the seventh overall pick last June. Fielder, however, isn't just another first baseman. The son of former American League home run king Cecil Fielder, Prince has power so rare that scouting director Jack Zduriencik said it was impossible to pass up. Not only was Fielder once of the best power bats available in the 2002 draft, but he also has a sweet lefthanded swing, an advanced hitting approach and solid plate discipline. The Brewers weren't afraid to promote him to low Class A two months after he left high school. They knew he wouldn't be overwhelmed because he grew up around big league parks. The question that has dogged Fielder thus far is his weight. After ballooning to more than 300 pounds in high school, he worked with a personal trainer and slimmed down to about 265. He has some agility but doesn't project to be more than an average first baseman. The Brewers toyed with the idea of trying Fielder in left field during instructional league, but a groin injury kept him off the field. He should be fine for spring training and will open the year back in Beloit.

Year	Club (League)	Class	AVG	G	AB	R	H	2B	3B	HR	RBI	BB	SO	SB	SLG	OBP
2002	Ogden (Pio)	R	.390	41	146	35	57	12	0	10	40	37	27	3	.678	.531
	Beloit (Mid)	A	.241	32	112	15	27	7	0	3	11	10	27	0	.384	.320
MINOR LEAGUE TOTALS			.326	73	258	50	84	19	0	13	51	47	54	3	.550	.448

4. Ben Hendrickson, rhp

Born: Feb. 4, 1981. **Ht.:** 6-4. **Wt.:** 190. **Bats:** R. **Throws:** R. **School:** Jefferson HS, Bloomington, Minn. **Career Transactions:** Selected by Brewers in 10th round of 1999 draft; signed Sept. 1, 1999.

Hendrickson pitched so well in low Class A in 2001 that the Brewers considered jumping him all the way to Double-A Huntsville last year. He started in the hitter-friendly California League instead, pitched well, and didn't skip a beat after a midseason promotion. Of the Brewers' top eight prospects, he's the only one who wasn't drafted by scouting director Jack Zduriencik. Hendrickson has one of the best curveballs in the minors, a spike curve with a 12-to-6 drop. It reminds many scouts of the late Darryl Kile's bender. He also throws an 89-92 mph fastball with running action. He has a clean delivery and nice arm action. Hendrickson's changeup still needs work. His control also needs tweaking. He has a skinny frame, though he has been durable in the minors and pitched a career-high 151 innings last year without missing a start. With a new regime in place, it's not certain whether Hendrickson will open 2003 in Huntsville or Triple-A Indianapolis. Either way, his future as a middle-of-the-rotation starter looks bright. He could be ready for a callup in September.

Year	Club (League)	Class	W	L	ERA	G	GS	CG	SV	IP	H	R	ER	HR	BB	SO	AVG
2000	Ogden (Pio)	R	4	3	5.68	13	7	0	1	51	50	37	32	7	29	48	.245
2001	Beloit (Mid)	A	8	9	2.84	25	25	1	0	133	122	58	42	3	72	133	.246
2002	High Desert (Cal)	A	5	5	2.55	14	14	0	0	81	61	31	23	3	41	70	.209
	Huntsville (SL)	AA	4	2	2.97	13	13	0	0	70	57	31	23	2	35	50	.231
MINOR LEAGUE TOTALS			21	19	3.22	65	59	1	1	335	290	157	120	15	177	301	.234

5. Corey Hart, 3b/1b

STEVE MOORE

Born: March 24, 1982. **Ht.:** 6-6. **Wt.:** 200. **Bats:** R. **Throws:** R. **School:** Greenwood HS, Bowling Green, Ky. **Career Transactions:** Selected by Brewers in 11th round of 2000 draft; signed June 12, 2000.

Hart had a breakthrough season in 2002, earning a trip to the Futures Game at Miller Park. He may be a year or two removed from Milwaukee, but he already has a big league nickname. His High Desert teammates last year started calling the laid-back Kentucky native "Hee Haw." There's nothing laid back about Hart's approach at the plate. Already 6-foot-5 and still growing, he's drawing comparisons to Richie Sexson. Though his arms are long, Hart has a quick, compact stroke and is developing the ability to pull his hands in and hit inside pitches with authority, a la Sexson. Power is Hart's calling card. If Hart continues to improve his pitch selection and recognition, he could be a .300 hitter. The Brewers' wealth of first-base prospects grew once they drafted Prince Fielder, so they decided to see if Hart could handle a move to third base. The jury is still out, because his size, somewhat clunky footwork and lack of experience work against him. A move to the outfield is a possibility for Hart, whose best position may still be first base. Look for him to begin 2003 in Double-A, where he'll join J.J. Hardy and David Krynzel to form the nucleus of what could be a championship-caliber team.

Year	Club (League)	Class	AVG	G	AB	R	H	2B	3B	HR	RBI	BB	SO	SB	SLG	OBP
2000	Ogden (Pio)	R	.287	57	216	32	62	9	1	2	30	13	27	6	.366	.332
2001	Ogden (Pio)	R	.340	69	262	53	89	18	1	11	62	26	47	14	.542	.395
2002	High Desert (Cal)	A	.288	100	393	76	113	26	10	22	84	37	101	24	.573	.356
	Huntsville (SL)	AA	.266	28	94	16	25	3	0	2	15	7	16	3	.362	.340
MINOR LEAGUE TOTALS			.299	254	965	177	289	56	12	37	191	83	191	47	.497	.360

6. J.J. Hardy, ss

JOHN SPEAR

Born: Aug. 19, 1982. **Ht.:** 6-2. **Wt.:** 180. **Bats:** R. **Throws:** R. **School:** Sabino HS, Tucson. **Career Transactions:** Selected by Brewers in second round of 2001 draft; signed July 16, 2001.

Forced into a big league exhibition game when the Brewers were shorthanded last spring, the 19-year-old Hardy collected three hits and played flawless defense against the Athletics. That moment in the sun set the tone for a positive year. Despite his youth, Hardy skipped a level to turn in a solid first half in high Class A, then held his own in Double-A and the Arizona Fall League. At this point in his career, Hardy's defensive ability is running considerably ahead of his offense. Though he's not exceptionally quick, his keen instincts allow him to get good jumps on balls. He covers ground with long strides, has soft hands and delivers the ball across the diamond with authority. Offensively, he's a gap-to-gap hitter and the Brewers are confident his power will increase as he matures. His work ethic and personality are outstanding. With his first full pro season complete, Hardy embarked on a weightlifting program designed to increase strength. Learning to draw walks also would help boost his offensive productivity. He also could add some loft to his swing. The Brewers consider Hardy their shortstop of the future, and the future is approaching rapidly. Though he may return to Double-A to start the year, a September callup isn't out of the question.

Year	Club (League)	Class	AVG	G	AB	R	H	2B	3B	HR	RBI	BB	SO	SB	SLG	OBP
2001	Brewers (AZL)	R	.250	5	20	6	5	2	1	0	1	1	2	0	.450	.286
	Ogden (Pio)	R	.248	35	125	20	31	5	0	2	15	15	12	1	.336	.326
2002	High Desert (Cal)	A	.293	84	335	53	98	19	1	6	48	19	38	9	.409	.327
	Huntsville (SL)	AA	.228	38	145	14	33	7	0	1	13	9	19	1	.297	.269
MINOR LEAGUE TOTALS			.267	162	625	93	167	33	2	9	77	44	71	11	.370	.312

7. David Krynzel, of

Born: Nov. 7, 1981. **Ht.:** 6-1. **Wt.:** 180. **Bats:** L. **Throws:** L. **School:** Green Valley HS, Henderson, Nev. **Career Transactions:** Selected by Brewers in first round (11th overall) of 2000 draft; signed June 12, 2000.

After watching Krynzel for 2½ seasons, the Brewers aren't sure whether they are looking at the next Steve Finley or Kenny Lofton. Either way, they like what they see. Returning to high Class A in 2002, he continued to improve in just about all facets of his game. Though he's being groomed for leadoff duty, Krynzel likes to flex his power muscles regularly and the Brewers haven't discouraged him. He realizes, however, that skills working counts, drawing walks and bunting will expedite his trip to the big leagues. He has plus tools as a center fielder (both his range and arm strength) and basestealer. For all his physical gifts, Krynzel's instincts on the bases and in the outfield are below-average. Like many first-round picks, he seems to put extra pressure on himself at times and tries to force things, rather than letting the game come to him. His mental toughness isn't in question, though. Krynzel just needs to increase his grasp of the game's subtleties. Slated to play in Double-A this year, he's on track to take over Milwaukee's center-field job in 2005, if not sooner.

Year	Club (League)	Class	AVG	G	AB	R	H	2B	3B	HR	RBI	BB	SO	SB	SLG	OBP
2000	Ogden (Pio)	R	.359	34	131	25	47	8	3	1	29	16	23	8	.489	.442
2001	Beloit (Mid)	A	.305	35	141	22	43	1	1	1	19	9	28	11	.348	.364
	High Desert (Cal)	A	.277	89	383	65	106	19	5	5	33	27	122	34	.392	.329
2002	High Desert (Cal)	A	.268	97	365	76	98	13	12	11	45	64	100	29	.460	.391
	Huntsville (SL)	AA	.240	31	129	13	31	2	3	2	13	4	30	13	.349	.269
MINOR LEAGUE TOTALS			.283	286	1149	201	325	43	24	20	139	120	303	95	.414	.361

8. Manny Parra, lhp

Born: Oct. 30, 1982. **Ht.:** 6-3. **Wt.:** 200. **Bats:** L. **Throws:** L. **School:** American River (Calif.) JC. **Career Transactions:** Selected by Brewers in 26th round of 2001 draft; signed May 27, 2002.

The idea of the budget-conscious Brewers signing a 26th-round pick for $1.55 million may seem far-fetched. Parra, however, represented an exceptional case. In his second junior college season, he blossomed into the premium draft-and-follow prospect from the 2001 draft and might have been a first-rounder had he gone back into the draft pool. By working diligently with weights, Parra boosted his fastball from the upper 80s in 2001 to a high of 95 mph last year. He throws three different varieties of the pitch: a two-seamer, a four-seamer and a cutter that often is mistaken for a slider. He has plus command of his five-pitch repertoire and a competitive streak that impressed Rookie-level Ogden manager Tim Blackwell. Milwaukee officials praise Parra's lanky body, smooth delivery and unflappable mound demeanor. The Brewers want Parra to work the inner half of the plate more often, and his reluctance to do so will likely disappear as he gets used to facing hitters with wood bats. His secondary pitches, a curveball and changeup, need refinement. Once Parra makes the necessary adjustments, he should move quickly through the system. He'll probably start 2003 in low Class A.

Year	Club (League)	Class	W	L	ERA	G	GS	CG	SV	IP	H	R	ER	HR	BB	SO	AVG
2002	Brewers (AZL)	R	0	0	4.50	1	0	0	0	2	1	1	1	1	0	4	.143
	Ogden (Pio)	R	3	1	3.21	11	10	0	0	48	59	30	17	3	10	51	.298
MINOR LEAGUE TOTALS			3	1	3.26	12	11	0	0	50	60	31	18	4	10	55	.293

9. Ben Diggins, rhp

Born: June 13, 1979. **Ht.:** 6-7. **Wt.:** 230. **Bats:** R. **Throws:** R. **School:** University of Arizona. **Career Transactions:** Selected by Dodgers in first round (17th overall) of 2000 draft; signed Aug. 23, 2000 . . . Traded by Dodgers with LHP Shane Nance to Brewers for 3B Tyler Houston and a player to be named, July 23, 2002; Dodgers acquired RHP Brian Mallete to complete trade (Oct. 16, 2002).

Acquiring Diggins and Shane Nance from the Dodgers for Tyler Houston and Brian Mallette last July may go down as one of the highlights of Dean Taylor's three-year tenure as general manager. Diggins was a supplemental first-round pick of the Cardinals in 1998, but spent two years at Arizona before signing for a then-Dodgers-record $2.2 million as the 17th overall pick in 2000. Diggins has an electric arm, consistently throwing in the mid-90s and peaking at 98 mph at Arizona, but his velocity and control have fluctuated as a pro.

He has thrown more in the low to mid-90s since signing. Some scouts think he'd have more success and regain his old velocity if he moved to the bullpen. Getting hammered during a September callup taught Diggins he can't rely on just his fastball and a mediocre curveball. He has been slow to pick up a changeup or to master his command. The Brewers think if he can refine a slider, that pitch could put him over the top. Diggins will have a chance to crack the Brewers rotation in spring training but may be better served by some time in Triple-A. Some Milwaukee officials think his future is as a closer, though there are no immediate plans to change his role.

Year	Club (League)	Class	W	L	ERA	G	GS	CG	SV	IP	H	R	ER	HR	BB	SO	AVG
2001	Wilmington (SAL)	A	7	6	3.58	21	21	0	0	106	88	49	42	5	48	79	.224
2002	Vero Beach (FSL)	A	6	10	3.63	20	19	0	0	114	103	54	46	8	41	101	.238
	Huntsville (SL)	AA	2	1	1.91	7	7	0	0	38	26	13	8	0	15	34	.208
	Milwaukee (NL)	MAJ	0	4	8.63	5	5	0	0	24	28	24	23	4	18	15	.298
MAJOR LEAGUE TOTALS			0	4	8.63	5	5	0	0	24	28	24	23	4	18	15	.298
MINOR LEAGUE TOTALS			15	17	3.36	48	47	0	0	257	217	116	96	13	104	214	.228

10. Matt Ford, lhp

Born: April 8, 1981. **Ht.:** 6-1. **Wt.:** 170. **Bats:** B. **Throws:** L. **School:** Taravella HS, Coral Springs, Fla. **Career Transactions:** Selected by Blue Jays in third round of 1999 draft; signed June 2, 1999 . . . Selected by Brewers from Blue Jays in major league Rule 5 draft, Dec. 16, 2002.

The Brewers selected two players in the major league Rule 5 draft, and both Ford and infielder Enrique Cruz have strong chances of sticking with Milwaukee this year. Ford didn't begin his 2002 season until May 7 because of a spring-training illness, but he showed what he could do when healthy by leading the high Class A Florida State League in ERA. Ford's best attributes are an 89-92 mph fastball and the wherewithal to use it. He stopped nibbling last year and attacked hitters with his heater, throwing it to both sides of the plate. He also can throw his curveball and changeup for strikes. Ford has gotten stronger over the last couple of years, allowing him to keep his velocity deeper into games. Though he commands them well, Ford still needs to improve his secondary pitches. His curveball gets slurvy at times. His durability is still in question after last year's illness and previous shoulder problems. Ford was the top lefty in the Blue Jays system, so they'd undoubtedly want him back if he can't stay on the Brewers' roster. He projects as an end-of-the-rotation starter but probably will spend this year as a middle reliever in Milwaukee.

Year	Club (League)	Class	W	L	ERA	G	GS	CG	SV	IP	H	R	ER	HR	BB	SO	AVG
1999	Medicine Hat (Pio)	R	4	0	2.05	13	7	0	0	48	31	11	11	0	23	68	.182
2000	Hagerstown (SAL)	A	5	3	3.87	18	14	1	0	84	81	42	36	5	36	86	.261
2001	Dunedin (FSL)	A	2	7	5.85	13	12	0	0	60	67	41	39	8	37	48	.294
	Charleston (SAL)	A	4	4	2.42	11	11	1	0	71	62	28	19	2	22	69	.237
2002	Dunedin (FSL)	A	9	5	2.37	21	18	0	0	114	100	43	30	7	42	85	.240
MINOR LEAGUE TOTALS			24	19	3.23	76	62	2	0	377	341	165	135	22	160	356	.246

11. Enrique Cruz, 3b/ss

Born: Nov. 21, 1981. **Ht.:** 6-1. **Wt.:** 180. **Bats:** R. **Throws:** R. **Career Transactions:** Signed out of Dominican Republic by Mets, Aug. 5, 1998 . . . Selected by Brewers from Mets in major league Rule 5 draft, Dec. 16, 2002.

Cruz was the first pick in the major league Rule 5 draft at the Winter Meetings. Though he needs at-bats at this stage of his career and probably won't get many if he sticks with Milwaukee this year, he could factor into the Brewers' second-base mix after they dumped Ron Belliard and don't have an obvious frontrunner for the job. Primarily a third baseman and shortstop in the Mets organization, Cruz had his best full season last year in high Class A. He's on the verge of becoming a real threat with the bat as he continues to grow into his body, though he has yet to show much power or aptitude for drawing walks. He's an above-average athlete with good range to his left and a plus arm. He made 33 errors in 2002, many because of poor footwork that resulted in errant throws. Following his strong performance in instructional league, the Mets planned on using Cruz as an everyday shortstop in Double-A. Milwaukee seems determined to retain him by keeping him on its roster all season, and New York likely will snatch him back if that doesn't happen.

Year	Club (League)	Class	AVG	G	AB	R	H	2B	3B	HR	RBI	BB	SO	SB	SLG	OBP
1999	Mets (GCL)	R	.306	54	183	34	56	14	2	4	24	28	41	0	.470	.399
2000	Capital City (SAL)	A	.185	49	157	19	29	12	0	1	12	25	44	1	.280	.299
	Kingsport (Appy)	R	.251	63	223	35	56	14	0	9	39	26	56	19	.435	.335
2001	Capital City (SAL)	A	.251	124	438	60	110	20	2	9	59	59	106	33	.368	.346
2002	St. Lucie (FSL)	A	.291	124	467	69	136	21	2	6	45	32	76	33	.383	.336
MINOR LEAGUE TOTALS			.264	414	1468	217	387	81	6	29	179	170	323	86	.386	.343

12. Pedro Liriano, rhp

Born: Oct. 23, 1980. **Ht.:** 6-2. **Wt.:** 160. **Bats:** R. **Throws:** R. **Career Transactions:** Signed out of Dominican Republic by Angels, Nov. 10, 1998 . . . Traded by Angels to Brewers, Sept. 20, 2002, completing trade in which Brewers sent OF Alex Ochoa and C Sal Fasano to Angels for C Jorge Fabregas and two players to be named (July 31, 2002); Brewers also acquired 2B Johnny Raburn (Aug. 14, 2002).

Introduced to scouts by his cousin, Angels starter Ramon Ortiz, and often confused with a Cubs second-base prospect of the same name, Liriano is trying to carve his own identity with the Brewers, who picked him up last July in the Alex Ochoa trade. After starring for three years in Rookie ball, including being named Pioneer League pitcher of the year in 2001, he jumped to high Class A last year and continued to thrive. His best pitch is a deceptive slider, though some scouts wonder if more advanced hitters will chase it. If they don't, Liriano could be in trouble because he rarely breaks 90 mph with his fastball and still needs to improve his changeup and command. As with many Latin players, there are rumblings that Liriano is older than his listed age of 22. If he continues to get hitters out, that won't be an issue with the Brewers. He'll start 2003 in Double-A.

Year	Club (League)	Class	W	L	ERA	G	GS	CG	SV	IP	H	R	ER	HR	BB	SO	AVG
1999	Angels (DSL)	R	7	2	1.83	17	9	3	0	79	46	23	16	3	23	61	.172
2000	Angels (DSL)	R	5	1	1.25	12	11	1	0	79	36	19	11	3	29	78	.132
2001	Provo (Pio)	R	11	2	2.78	15	14	0	0	78	80	39	24	3	31	76	.265
2002	Rancho Cucamonga (Cal)	A	10	14	3.60	28	28	1	0	167	129	86	67	14	74	176	.212
MINOR LEAGUE TOTALS			33	19	2.64	72	62	5	0	403	291	167	118	23	157	391	.201

13. Keith Ginter, 3b

Born: May 5, 1976. **Ht.:** 5-10. **Wt.:** 190. **Bats:** R. **Throws:** R. **School:** Texas Tech. **Career Transactions:** Selected by Astros in 10th round of 1998 draft; signed June 7, 1998 . . . Traded by Astros with LHP Wayne Franklin to Brewers, Sept. 5, 2002, completing trade in which Brewers sent 2B Mark Loretta and cash to Astros for two players to be named (Aug. 31, 2002).

Acquired along with lefty Wayne Franklin in a deal that sent Mark Loretta to Houston, Ginter impressed the Brewers during the final weeks of the season with a compact, powerful hitting stroke and a knack for getting on base. Though he once resisted a move to third base in the Astros system, he seemed comfortable there in September and made some nice plays. On most teams he'd be vying for a backup spot, but he'll get a chance to start at the hot corner in Milwaukee. Ginter had trouble following up on his breakthrough 2000 season, when he was the batting champion and MVP in the Double-A Texas League. He's purely an offensive player, using a short stroke to hit line drives and generate occasional pop, as well as showing consistent on-base ability. He's no more than an adequate defender, considered too stiff to play second base and not looking particularly comfortable in the outfield. He'll have to hit to win and then keep the third-base job, and may be better suited for a bench role.

Year	Club (League)	Class	AVG	G	AB	R	H	2B	3B	HR	RBI	BB	SO	SB	SLG	OBP
1998	Auburn (NY-P)	A	.315	71	241	55	76	22	1	8	41	60	68	10	.515	.461
1999	Kissimmee (FSL)	A	.263	103	376	66	99	15	4	13	46	61	90	9	.428	.381
	Jackson (TL)	AA	.382	9	34	9	13	1	0	1	6	4	6	0	.500	.463
2000	Round Rock (TL)	AA	.333	125	462	108	154	30	3	26	92	82	127	24	.580	.457
	Houston (NL)	MAJ	.250	5	8	3	2	0	0	1	3	1	3	0	.625	.300
2001	New Orleans (PCL)	AAA	.269	132	457	76	123	31	5	16	70	61	147	8	.464	.380
	Houston (NL)	MAJ	.000	1	1	0	0	0	0	0	0	0	0	0	.000	.000
2002	New Orleans (PCL)	AAA	.264	121	435	70	115	28	1	12	54	56	97	3	.416	.362
	Houston (NL)	MAJ	.200	7	5	1	1	1	0	0	0	2	1	0	.400	.500
	Milwaukee (NL)	MAJ	.237	21	76	6	18	8	0	1	8	15	14	0	.382	.363
MAJOR LEAGUE TOTALS			.233	34	90	10	21	9	0	2	11	18	18	0	.400	.364
MINOR LEAGUE TOTALS			.289	561	2005	384	580	127	14	76	309	324	535	54	.480	.406

14. Ozzie Chavez, ss

Born: July 13, 1983. **Ht.:** 6-1. **Wt.:** 150. **Bats:** B. **Throws:** R. **Career Transactions:** Signed out of Dominican Republic by Brewers, Aug. 1, 1999.

For a skinny 19-year-old in low Class A, Chavez fared about as well as could be expected in 2002. Signed out of the Dominican by longtime scout Eppy Guerrero and named Ozzie Smith Chavez in honor of the Hall of Fame shortstop, Chavez showed flashes of potential but will need to improve his offense to move up the ladder. His .323 on-base percentage wasn't impressive, but he worked to improve his strike-zone judgment and his 46 walks led Beloit. Though he made 29 errors, scouts were impressed by his smooth motions and soft hands at shortstop. With experience and better infields, he'll likely play tighter defense. Chavez is still learning how to bunt and to use his speed on the bases. The basic tools are there. With time, the Brewers hope Chavez will physically mature and refine his game. He hasn't set the world on fire yet, but his potential bears watching. He'll probably move up to high Class A this year.

Year	Club (League)	Class	AVG	G	AB	R	H	2B	3B	HR	RBI	BB	SO	SB	SLG	OBP
2000	Brewers (DSL)	R	.273	64	187	44	51	5	1	1	29	41	33	14	.326	.407
2001	Brewers (AZL)	R	.305	52	210	38	64	12	6	0	27	13	36	9	.419	.346
2002	Beloit (Mid)	A	.255	128	463	55	118	13	6	1	36	46	86	10	.315	.323
MINOR LEAGUE TOTALS			.271	244	860	137	233	30	13	2	92	100	155	33	.343	.349

15. Shane Nance, lhp

Born: Sept. 7, 1977. **Ht.:** 5-8. **Wt.:** 180. **Bats:** L. **Throws:** L. **School:** University of Houston. **Career Transactions:** Selected by Dodgers in 11th round of 2000 draft; signed June 12, 2000 . . . Traded by Dodgers with RHP Ben Diggins to Brewers for 3B Tyler Houston and a player to be named, July 23, 2002; Dodgers acquired RHP Brian Mallette to complete trade (Oct. 16, 2002).

Nance's first trip to the big leagues had an unhappy ending in an unusual place: the batter's box. Picked up along with Ben Diggins in a deal that sent Tyler Houston and Brian Mallette to Los Angeles, Nance threw 17 shutout innings in Triple-A after switching organizations to earn his first callup. In his fourth game with Milwaukee, he tore his right (non-pitching) biceps tendon while swinging a bat and needed surgery to have it reattached. He's expected to be fine by the time camp opens and will compete for a job in the Brewers bullpen. If they're judging by heart, Nance has a good chance. After setting Houston career records for wins (32) and strikeouts (388), he was passed over by many clubs who were put off by his size. He's listed at 5-foot-8 and might be shorter. He has pitched well at virtually every level, including a stint with Team USA during the 2001 World Cup, and was the winning pitcher in last year's Triple-A all-star game. While Nance doesn't have an overpowering pitch, his fastball jumped into the low 90s in 2002 and he has always gotten outs with his plus changeup. He also mixes in a curveball. Though he'll probably never be an all-star, Nance definitely has a chance to stick in the majors for a few years.

Year	Club (League)	Class	W	L	ERA	G	GS	CG	SV	IP	H	R	ER	HR	BB	SO	AVG
2000	Yakima (NWL)	A	2	4	2.48	12	9	0	0	58	41	19	16	1	22	66	.203
2001	Vero Beach (FSL)	A	6	3	2.63	21	0	0	4	48	28	15	14	3	21	63	.164
	Jacksonville (SL)	AA	7	0	1.59	28	0	0	1	45	31	11	8	4	17	44	.195
2002	Las Vegas (PCL)	AAA	11	3	4.17	37	0	0	1	58	58	32	27	5	26	53	.260
	Indianapolis (IL)	AAA	3	0	0.00	9	0	0	0	17	12	0	0	0	6	10	.207
	Milwaukee (NL)	MAJ	0	0	4.26	4	0	0	0	6	4	3	3	1	4	5	.174
MAJOR LEAGUE TOTALS			0	0	4.26	4	0	0	0	6	4	3	3	1	4	5	.174
MINOR LEAGUE TOTALS			29	10	2.58	107	9	0	6	226	170	77	65	13	92	236	.209

16. Steve Moss, of

Born: Jan. 12, 1984. **Ht.:** 6-2. **Wt.:** 180. **Bats:** R. **Throws:** R. **School:** Notre Dame HS, Sherman Oaks, Calif. **Career Transactions:** Selected by Brewers in 29th round of 2002 draft; signed July 13, 2002.

The Brewers broke even after going head-to-head with UCLA for two players in the 2002 draft. Fifth-round shortstop Jarrad Page, a physical player who resembles Torii Hunter, didn't sign and had two interceptions last fall as a safety on the Bruins' football team. But Milwaukee did sign Moss, another talented athlete who lasted until the 29th round because of an ankle injury and his commitment to UCLA. Though he played in just 35 games, Moss made a huge impression with his kamikaze play in center field. More than one scout was wowed when he dived for balls on the warning track and made plays all over the field. He runs with a long stride and has a build like Steve Finley. As a bonus, he also has a strong arm. Offensively, Moss had a solid debut in the Rookie-level Arizona League and showed that he has a decent idea at the plate. He still has a long way to go, but Moss looks like a sleeper.

Year	Club (League)	Class	AVG	G	AB	R	H	2B	3B	HR	RBI	BB	SO	SB	SLG	OBP
2002	Brewers (AZL)	R	.292	30	106	20	31	8	2	1	20	22	32	3	.434	.414
	Ogden (Pio)	R	.500	5	8	3	4	2	1	0	3	1	1	0	1.000	.538
MINOR LEAGUE TOTALS			.307	35	114	23	35	10	3	1	23	23	33	3	.474	.425

17. Jayson Durocher, rhp

Born: Aug. 12, 1974. **Ht.:** 6-3. **Wt.:** 190. **Bats:** R. **Throws:** R. **School:** Horizon HS, Scottsdale, Ariz. **Career Transactions:** Selected by Expos in ninth round of 1993 draft; signed July 8, 1993 . . . Selected by White Sox from Expos in major league Rule 5 draft, Dec. 9, 1996 . . . Returned to Expos, March 31, 1997 . . . Granted free agency, Oct. 15, 1999 . . . Signed by Padres, Nov. 10, 1999 . . . Granted free agency, Oct. 15, 2000 . . . Signed by Rangers, Nov. 10, 2000 . . . Granted free agency, Oct. 15, 2001 . . . Signed by Brewers, Nov. 16, 2001

The name on the back of his jersey was instantly recognizable, but Durocher was virtually unknown to Brewers fans when he was called up to the majors June 9. Durocher, whose grandfather was a cousin of Hall of Fame manager Leo Durocher, pitched nine seasons in the minors before being called up to replace injured Chad Fox. Making his big league debut at Oakland, the burly righthander pitched the Brewers out of a bases-loaded jam. The following day, he relieved Ben Sheets and gave up a homer to Eric Chavez on the first pitch he threw. That blast led some to believe Durocher's first outing was a fluke, but a stiff back was really the culprit. Durocher, who had felt tight warming up, was throwing on back-to-back days for the first time and impressed his teammates and coaches by remaining in the game and retiring the next three men in order and three of four he faced the following inning. His heavy 94-95 mph fastball gives hitters trouble, and he augments it with a hard slider and inconsistent splitter. The Brewers resisted the urge to overuse and overwhelm him, allowing him to pitch in low-stress stints. Based on his performance, Durocher will be considered a favorite to win a setup job in front of closer Mike DeJean. He'll likely see more pressure-packed situations than in the past.

Year	Club (League)	Class	W	L	ERA	G	GS	CG	SV	IP	H	R	ER	HR	BB	SO	AVG
1993	Expos (GCL)	R	2	3	3.46	7	7	3	0	39	32	23	15	0	13	21	.242
1994	Vermont (NY-P)	A	9	2	3.09	15	15	3	0	99	92	40	34	0	44	74	.247
1995	Albany (SAL)	A	3	7	3.91	24	22	1	0	122	105	67	53	5	56	88	.234
1996	W. Palm Beach (FSL)	A	7	6	3.34	23	23	1	0	129	118	65	48	5	44	101	.236
1997	W. Palm Beach (FSL)	A	6	4	3.83	25	17	0	0	87	84	58	37	6	39	71	.250
1998	Jupiter (FSL)	A	2	1	4.21	23	0	0	5	36	47	21	17	3	8	27	.313
	Harrisburg (EL)	AA	0	1	3.97	10	0	0	1	11	10	8	5	0	6	12	.250
1999	Harrisburg (EL)	AA	1	3	3.48	29	1	0	4	52	44	29	20	5	25	36	.233
	Ottawa (IL)	AAA	1	3	1.51	17	0	0	4	36	17	12	6	2	20	22	.140
2000	Las Vegas (PCL)	AAA	3	5	4.95	31	0	0	7	40	44	25	22	2	25	38	.284
	Mobile (SL)	AA	1	1	2.08	27	0	0	14	30	26	7	7	4	12	43	.228
2001	Tulsa (TL)	AA	0	0	0.00	3	0	0	0	4	0	0	0	0	3	4	.000
	Oklahoma (PCL)	AAA	4	1	4.99	31	0	0	6	40	34	25	22	5	23	52	.231
2002	Indianapolis (IL)	AAA	1	0	2.73	20	0	0	2	26	19	9	8	3	15	39	.194
	Milwaukee (NL)	MAJ	1	1	1.88	39	0	0	0	48	27	13	10	3	21	44	.164
MAJOR LEAGUE TOTALS			1	1	1.88	39	0	0	0	48	27	13	10	3	21	44	.164
MINOR LEAGUE TOTALS			40	37	3.52	285	85	8	43	751	672	389	294	40	333	628	.239

18. Bill Hall, ss

Born: Dec. 28, 1979. **Ht.:** 6-0. **Wt.:** 170. **Bats:** R. **Throws:** R. **School:** Nettleton (Miss.) HS. **Career Transactions:** Selected by Brewers in sixth round of 1998 draft; signed June 7, 1998.

After being named the Brewers' minor league player of the year in 2001, Hall took a step backward last season despite being selected to play in the Futures Game at Miller Park. It really wasn't all his fault. The losing at the big league level induced former general manager Dean Taylor to fast-track players to Milwaukee, and Hall was hurt by the approach. Despite not hitting well in Double-A the previous year, he was moved to Triple-A in 2002 and struggled in almost every facet of the game. The negative atmosphere that permeated the Indianapolis clubhouse also didn't help. Hall has strong raw tools, including range, speed and solid pop for a middle infielder. But he still has a lot of learning to do. He doesn't control the strike zone, hasn't adjusted to advanced pitching and makes too many careless errors. Former Brewers manager Jerry Royster was surprised at how raw Hall was during his September callup, working with him to correct a fundamental throwing flaw and wondering why he hadn't been told to work on his bunting. J.J. Hardy has supplanted him as Milwaukee's shortstop of the future, and Hall needs to make some improvements quickly.

Year	Club (League)	Class	AVG	G	AB	R	H	2B	3B	HR	RBI	BB	SO	SB	SLG	OBP
1998	Helena (Pio)	R	.176	29	85	11	15	3	0	0	5	9	27	5	.212	.263
1999	Ogden (Pio)	R	.289	69	280	41	81	15	2	6	31	15	61	19	.421	.329
2000	Beloit (Mid)	A	.262	130	470	57	123	30	6	3	41	18	127	10	.370	.287
2001	High Desert (Cal)	A	.303	89	346	61	105	21	6	15	51	22	78	18	.529	.348
	Huntsville (SL)	AA	.256	41	160	14	41	8	1	3	14	5	46	5	.375	.279
2002	Indianapolis (IL)	AAA	.228	134	465	35	106	20	1	4	31	25	105	17	.301	.272
	Milwaukee (NL)	MAJ	.194	19	36	3	7	1	1	1	5	3	13	0	.361	.256
MAJOR LEAGUE TOTALS			.194	19	36	3	7	1	1	1	5	3	13	0	.361	.256
MINOR LEAGUE TOTALS			.261	492	1806	219	471	97	16	31	173	94	444	74	.384	.300

19. Eric M. Thomas, rhp

Born: March 24, 1981. **Ht.:** 6-9. **Wt.:** 230. **Bats:** R. **Throws:** R. **School:** University of South Alabama. **Career Transactions:** Selected by Brewers in third round of 2002 draft; signed June 23, 2002.

Not to be confused with fellow 2002 Brewers draftee Eric A. Thomas, a 28th-rounder, Eric M. Thomas may prove to be a steal as a third-rounder. He spent his first two college seasons at NCAA Division II New Haven (Conn.), where he worked three innings, and Briarcliffe

(N.Y.) Junior College, where he was drafted in the 11th round by the Tigers after reaching 93 mph. With an imposing 6-foot-9 frame, Thomas touched 96 mph during the spring and was projected to be a first-rounder until shoulder tendinitis shelved him for two months. He was given a clean bill of health by Dr. James Andrews, who found no structural damage. But Thomas hasn't thrown as well since returning, and while he's intriguing some scouts question his secondary stuff and his ability to move quickly through the minors. He showed a sharp curve at times in college but still needs to develop a changeup and throw more strikes. He might develop more quickly as a closer.

Year	Club (League)	Class	W	L	ERA	G	GS	CG	SV	IP	H	R	ER	HR	BB	SO	AVG
2002	Ogden (Pio)	R	0	3	9.90	12	6	0	0	30	46	39	33	5	17	32	.341
MINOR LEAGUE TOTALS			0	3	9.90	12	6	0	0	30	46	39	33	5	17	32	.341

20. Mike Adams, rhp

Born: July 29, 1978. **Ht.:** 6-5. **Wt.:** 190. **Bats:** R. **Throws:** R. **School:** Texas A&M University Kingsville. **Career Transactions:** Signed as nondrafted free agent by Brewers, May 15, 2001.

Adams reached Double-A in his first full season after signing as a fifth-year college senior out of Texas A&M-Kingsville. He went to college as a two-sport athlete, but his basketball career was derailed by a broken ankle. Since turning pro, he has pitched well at each of four levels. Hitters haven't been able to make consistent contract against his 92-94 mph fastball and slider. Already 24, Adams has been older than his competition and still has to prove himself. His command slipped once he reached Huntsville, and his changeup is nothing more than a show-me pitch. But if he continues his success in Triple-A this year, he'll carve out a place for himself in the Milwaukee bullpen.

Year	Club (League)	Class	W	L	ERA	G	GS	CG	SV	IP	H	R	ER	HR	BB	SO	AVG
2001	Ogden (Pio)	R	2	2	2.81	23	0	0	12	32	26	10	10	4	6	44	.220
2002	Beloit (Mid)	A	0	0	2.93	11	0	0	5	15	13	6	5	1	2	21	.228
	High Desert (Cal)	A	2	1	2.57	10	0	0	5	14	9	6	4	2	7	23	.173
	Huntsville (SL)	AA	1	0	3.38	13	0	0	1	19	14	11	7	3	12	17	.209
MINOR LEAGUE TOTALS			5	3	2.93	57	0	0	23	80	62	33	26	10	27	105	.211

21. Johnny Raburn, 2b/ss

Born: Feb. 16, 1979. **Ht.:** 6-1. **Wt.:** 160. **Bats:** B. **Throws:** R. **School:** University of South Florida. **Career Transactions:** Selected by Angels in 16th round of 2000 draft; signed June 13, 2000 . . . Traded by Angels to Brewers, Aug. 14, 2002, as part of trade in which Brewers sent OF Alex Ochoa and C Sal Fasano to Angels for C Jorge Fabregas and two players to be named (July 31, 2002); Brewers acquired RHP Pedro Liriano to complete trade (Sept. 20, 2002).

The Angels sent Raburn to the Brewers in the Alex Ochoa trade because, well, they already had a David Eckstein. Raburn is taller than the Anaheim sparkplug but is a scrappy overachiever out of the same mold. His brother Ryan is a promising third baseman in the Tigers system. Though Johnny has virtually no power, he takes his walks, gets on base and is a threat to steal. His defense is ordinary. His quickness gives him good range, and he has an average if erratic arm. His arm has average strength, but is a bit erratic. Raburn played second base, shortstop, third base and the outfield in 2002. That versatility helps him project as a utilityman.

Year	Club (League)	Class	AVG	G	AB	R	H	2B	3B	HR	RBI	BB	SO	SB	SLG	OBP
2000	Boise (NWL)	A	.254	72	280	49	71	12	4	0	34	54	72	28	.325	.375
2001	Cedar Rapids (Mid)	A	.315	68	235	56	74	2	1	0	12	63	43	37	.332	.467
2002	Rancho Cucamonga (Cal)	A	.292	115	448	71	131	20	5	1	36	77	88	35	.366	.397
	High Desert (Cal)	A	.212	16	66	8	14	3	1	0	3	7	13	5	.288	.288
MINOR LEAGUE TOTALS			.282	271	1029	184	290	37	11	1	85	201	216	105	.342	.402

22. Luis Martinez, lhp

Born: Jan. 20, 1980. **Ht.:** 6-6. **Wt.:** 200. **Bats:** L. **Throws:** L. **Career Transactions:** Signed out of Dominican Republic by Brewers, Oct. 12, 1996.

It's not unusual for minor league players to endure ups and downs, but Martinez' six-year roller-coaster ride through the system has Brewers officials scratching their heads. Is he a starter or a situational reliever? Hard worker or pretender? Prospect or suspect? Martinez has an excellent body, fluid throwing motion and good command. His arsenal includes a 92-93 mph fastball, an above-average changeup and a curveball that needs work. Milwaukee officials compare him to Valerio de los Santos, but Martinez could be better because of his changeup. Then again, he has yet to post an ERA lower than 5.19 since leaving low Class A. Martinez lacks confidence and consistency, and he doesn't throw nearly enough strikes. Just when the Brewers think he has turned a corner, he'll turn in a string of rocky outings. He was more effective in relief last year, but he moved back to starting in the final two months.

Year	Club (League)	Class	W	L	ERA	G	GS	CG	SV	IP	H	R	ER	HR	BB	SO	AVG
1997	Brewers (DSL)	R	0	2	12.96	11	2	0	0	17	21	27	24	3	24	17	.288
1998	Helena (Pio)	R	0	9	10.13	17	10	0	0	48	64	73	54	5	66	47	.318
1999	Ogden (Pio)	R	0	7	6.97	15	7	0	1	50	66	65	39	3	34	43	.304
2000	Beloit (Mid)	A	5	7	3.79	28	13	0	0	93	71	49	39	8	61	77	.209
2001	High Desert (Cal)	A	8	9	5.19	22	22	0	0	113	112	67	65	9	64	121	.263
	Huntsville (SL)	AA	0	0	6.75	7	0	0	0	9	13	7	7	0	9	13	.333
2002	Huntsville (SL)	AA	8	8	5.20	29	18	0	1	109	114	70	63	6	65	106	.277
MINOR LEAGUE TOTALS			21	42	5.97	129	72	0	2	439	461	358	291	34	323	424	.270

23. Matt Childers, rhp

Born: Dec. 3, 1978. **Ht.:** 6-5. **Wt.:** 190. **Bats:** R. **Throws:** R. **School:** Westside HS, Augusta, Ga. **Career Transactions:** Selected by Brewers in ninth round of 1997 draft; signed June 6, 1997.

Though his older brother Jason continues to outpitch him in the Brewers system, Matt continues to be regarded as the better prospect because he has more pure stuff. After a rough start in Double-A last year, Milwaukee moved him to the bullpen in hopes he would make better use of his fastball in a shorter role. His velocity jumped 2-3 mph to 94-95 when he worked in relief. As in the past, Childers struggled with his curveball and changeup, though his secondary pitches were less vital in his new role. Just as he was getting comfortable as a closer, Childers was promoted to the majors to work in long relief. He was overmatched against big league hitters but didn't seem to lose confidence. It's not certain where he'll start 2003 or what his role will be, but he made enough of an impression as a closer to earn a second chance at finishing games. If he continues to refine the splitter he has dabbled with, his chances of bullpen success will increase.

Year	Club (League)	Class	W	L	ERA	G	GS	CG	SV	IP	H	R	ER	HR	BB	SO	AVG
1997	Helena (Pio)	R	1	4	6.20	14	10	0	1	61	81	49	42	5	24	19	.318
1998	Helena (Pio)	R	1	0	0.64	2	2	1	0	14	9	1	1	0	4	4	.184
	Beloit (Mid)	A	3	7	5.10	14	12	3	0	67	89	55	38	5	20	49	.325
1999	Beloit (Mid)	A	3	10	5.94	20	19	0	0	100	129	72	66	9	30	52	.317
2000	Beloit (Mid)	A	8	2	2.71	12	12	1	0	73	64	33	22	4	17	47	.227
	Mudville (Cal)	A	3	9	4.75	15	15	0	0	85	103	59	45	10	32	43	.295
2001	High Desert (Cal)	A	6	11	6.44	20	20	0	0	117	155	95	84	19	29	76	.320
	Huntsville (SL)	AA	2	2	3.43	7	7	0	0	39	41	19	15	3	12	21	.268
2002	Huntsville (SL)	AA	2	5	4.50	35	10	0	12	82	103	47	41	6	27	57	.308
	Milwaukee (NL)	MAJ	0	0	12.00	8	0	0	0	9	13	12	12	2	8	6	.342
	Indianapolis (IL)	AAA	0	0	0.00	3	0	0	0	5	1	0	0	0	2	4	.063
MAJOR LEAGUE TOTALS			0	0	12.00	8	0	0	0	9	13	12	12	2	8	6	.342
MINOR LEAGUE TOTALS			29	50	4.95	142	107	5	13	644	775	430	354	61	197	372	.298

24. J.M. Gold, rhp

Born: April 10, 1980. **Ht.:** 6-5. **Wt.:** 240. **Bats:** R. **Throws:** R. **School:** Toms River North HS, Toms River, N.J. **Career Transactions:** Selected by Brewers in first round (13th overall) of 1998 draft; signed June 24, 1998.

If the Brewers hadn't taken Gold 13th overall and handed him a $1.6 million bonus in 1998, he might have been filtered out of the organization by now. They are intent on getting a return for their investment, however. Remember, they drafted him ahead of Nick Neugebauer. Gold, who has pitched just 68 innings since having Tommy John surgery in 2000, has inspiring stuff when he's 100 percent. He has a mid-90s fastball and a sharp curveball. His delivery is so fluid and easy that it's hard to figure out how he has been hurt so much, though the same was true of another injury-prone Brewers first-rounder, Jeff D'Amico. Gold needs to stay healthy so he can work on his changeup and command. He's expected to be good to go at the start of spring training, but it's doubtful he'll advance past high Class A in 2003.

Year	Club (League)	Class	W	L	ERA	G	GS	CG	SV	IP	H	R	ER	HR	BB	SO	AVG
1998	Ogden (Pio)	R	1	0	2.61	5	5	0	0	21	21	13	6	1	7	15	.256
1999	Beloit (Mid)	A	6	10	5.40	21	21	2	0	112	120	82	67	16	54	93	.273
2000	Beloit (Mid)	A	3	1	2.91	7	7	0	0	34	27	13	11	0	16	33	.218
2001	Brewers (AZL)	R	0	1	7.56	4	4	0	0	8	17	7	7	0	2	7	.447
	Ogden (Pio)	R	1	1	2.17	7	7	0	0	29	20	12	7	1	9	42	.192
2002	High Desert (Cal)	A	1	3	7.63	7	7	0	0	31	33	29	26	4	22	33	.292
MINOR LEAGUE TOTALS			12	16	4.76	51	51	2	0	234	238	156	124	22	110	223	.264

25. David Pember, rhp

Born: May 24, 1978. **Ht.:** 6-5. **Wt.:** 220. **Bats:** R. **Throws:** R. **School:** Western Carolina University. **Career Transactions:** Selected by Brewers in eighth round of 1999 draft; signed Aug. 15, 1999.

Milwaukee officials often talk about Pember's mental toughness, but what the young righthander went through in the final two months of his 2002 season would shake even a grizzled veteran. Nearing the end of a satisfying Double-A season, Pember was promoted to Milwaukee and thrust into a starting assignment at Wrigley Field. He gave up four hits and five walks, allowing three earned runs in 3⅔ innings while taking a 10-1 loss. Pember pitched better in a mop-up role, then headed to the Arizona Fall League. It was clear that his career-high 165 innings and whirlwind tour of the majors had taken their toll, as he got creamed on a regular basis. The Brewers are confident that his confidence won't be rattled, but they don't belief in his stuff as much as his makeup. With an 88-89 mph fastball, Pember doesn't have much margin for error. His secondary pitches, a curveball and change, are average, so he needs fine command to succeed. He's a diabetic but has dealt with the condition since he was 17 and it hasn't held him back. He'll get some time in Triple-A to open 2003.

Year	Club (League)	Class	W	L	ERA	G	GS	CG	SV	IP	H	R	ER	HR	BB	SO	AVG
2000	Beloit (Mid)	A	2	10	4.68	17	16	0	0	98	118	56	51	9	25	70	.299
2001	Beloit (Mid)	A	3	4	3.27	8	8	0	0	44	49	20	16	3	10	39	.285
	High Desert (Cal)	A	9	6	4.82	20	20	0	0	121	135	73	65	12	35	96	.280
2002	Huntsville (SL)	AA	10	6	3.17	27	27	2	0	156	157	69	55	13	53	111	.262
	Milwaukee (NL)	MAJ	0	1	5.19	4	1	0	0	9	7	6	5	1	6	5	.219
MAJOR LEAGUE TOTALS			0	1	5.19	4	1	0	0	9	7	6	5	1	6	5	.219
MINOR LEAGUE TOTALS			24	26	4.01	72	71	2	0	419	459	218	187	37	123	316	.279

26. Chris Morris, of

Born: July 1, 1979. **Ht.:** 5-8. **Wt.:** 180. **Bats:** B. **Throws:** R. **School:** The Citadel. **Career Transactions:** Selected by Cardinals in 15th round of 2000 draft; signed June 16, 2000 . . . Traded by Cardinals with a player to be named to Brewers for RHP Jamey Wright and cash, Aug. 29, 2002; Brewers acquired LHP Mike Matthews to complete trade (Sept. 11, 2002).

Another late-season pickup, Morris came from the Cardinals in the Jamey Wright deal. He's a more talented version of Chad Green, another speedster who was a bust as Milwaukee's 1996 first-round pick. Unlike Green, Morris knows he's not a power hitter, has developed into a decent bunter and appreciates the value of a walk. Though he still whiffs far too often, Morris capitalizes on his blazing speed, which rates a 75 on the 20-to-80 scouting scale. He led NCAA Division I with 84 steals in 94 attempts in 2000, and topped all minor leaguers with 111 swipes in 135 tries in 2001. Despite his wheels, Morris' outfield defense isn't a significant asset. He lacks strength and got the bat knocked out of his hands too often in 2002. He's going to have to adjust and become an on-base machine to warrant big league playing time.

Year	Club (League)	Class	AVG	G	AB	R	H	2B	3B	HR	RBI	BB	SO	SB	SLG	OBP
2000	New Jersey (NY-P)	A	.170	63	182	34	31	2	1	0	15	50	48	42	.192	.356
2001	Peoria (Mid)	A	.294	134	480	89	141	11	9	2	39	83	101	111	.367	.398
2002	Potomac (Car)	A	.249	114	422	68	105	17	2	0	38	58	92	55	.299	.348
	Beloit (Mid)	A	.357	4	14	3	5	2	0	0	1	1	3	1	.500	.400
MINOR LEAGUE TOTALS			.257	315	1098	194	282	32	12	2	93	192	244	209	.313	.371

27. Cristian Guerrero, of

Born: July 12, 1980. **Ht.:** 6-5. **Wt.:** 200. **Bats:** R. **Throws:** R. **Career Transactions:** Signed out of Dominican Republic by Brewers, Aug. 28, 1997.

Guerrero has great bloodlines as the cousin of Vladimir and Wilton Guerrero, and youth is still on his side—though his age was revised upward nine months last year. But the Brewers are tiring of waiting for him to live up to his promise. With a 6-foot-5 frame, a strong arm and a powerful swing, he has the tools scouts covet but hasn't been able to put everything together. He's fun to watch in batting practice, when his moonshots draw oohs from the crowd, but not as enjoyable when the games begin. Guerrero's swing is long and he lacks plate discipline, a deadly combination. Too often, he gets tied up with inside pitches and chases breaking balls in the dirt. Though his defense has improved, he still has work to do in that area. In one memorable sequence during a big league spring-training game in 2002, he muffed a routine liner, then caught a fly on the next play and threw the runner out at the plate. That's the way things have gone for Guerrero, who needs to show consistency before he can be considered a true prospect. He'll repeat Double-A this season.

Year	Club (League)	Class	AVG	G	AB	R	H	2B	3B	HR	RBI	BB	SO	SB	SLG	OBP
1998	Brewers (DSL)	R	.268	64	213	45	57	9	3	5	37	43	54	5	.408	.395
1999	Ogden (Pio)	R	.310	65	226	51	70	7	3	5	28	23	59	26	.434	.377
2000	Beloit (Mid)	A	.164	15	55	5	9	4	0	2	8	1	18	1	.345	.190
	Ogden (Pio)	R	.341	66	255	56	87	14	4	12	54	37	42	24	.569	.431
2001	High Desert (Cal)	A	.312	85	327	50	102	18	2	7	41	18	79	22	.443	.349
2002	Huntsville (SL)	AA	.223	111	394	47	88	17	1	8	48	26	101	21	.332	.274
MINOR LEAGUE TOTALS			.281	406	1470	254	413	69	13	39	216	148	353	99	.425	.350

28. Khalid Ballouli, rhp

Born: March 20, 1980. **Ht.:** 6-2. **Wt.:** 190. **Bats:** R. **Throws:** R. **School:** Texas A&M University. **Career Transactions:** Selected by Brewers in sixth round of 2002 draft; signed June 12, 2002.

Ballouli missed all of 2001 at Texas A&M after elbow surgery, but bounced back strong to go in the sixth round last year. While his injury history undoubtedly caused many teams to look elsewhere, the Brewers were impressed by Ballouli's 91-94 mph fastball, his tight slider and deceptive changeup. Though his delivery is far from smooth, he works both sides of the plate pretty well. Ballouli had no problem throwing strikes in his pro debut but was hittable, so he'll need to locate his pitches better within the zone. The grandson of former big lea-guer Dick Fowler, Ballouli probably will start 2003 in low Class A.

Year	Club (League)	Class	W	L	ERA	G	GS	CG	SV	IP	H	R	ER	HR	BB	SO	AVG
2002	Ogden (Pio)	R	4	0	4.37	15	12	0	0	60	78	31	29	6	11	65	.317
MINOR LEAGUE TOTALS			4	0	4.37	15	12	0	0	60	78	31	29	6	11	65	.317

29. Jason Belcher, c/of

Born: Jan. 13, 1982. **Ht.:** 6-1. **Wt.:** 190. **Bats:** L. **Throws:** R. **School:** Walnut Ridge (Ark.) HS. **Career Transactions:** Selected by Brewers in fifth round of 2000 draft; signed June 30, 2000.

The Brewers haven't had a lot of luck developing catchers since B.J. Surhoff and David Nilsson. Belcher once seemed like a good bet to stop the drought, but his stock is plum-meting. Though he has a solid bat, Belcher hasn't shown that he can handle everyday catch-ing duties. Much like Kade Johnson, a second-round pick a year ahead of him, Belcher isn't nearly as valuable when he plays another position. He spent almost as much time in the outfield last year as he did catching. He threw out just four of 53 (8 percent) basestealers, the worst rate in the Midwest League. Belcher also is limited in the outfield. He does have some pop and plate discipline, and Milwaukee hasn't given up on him behind the plate. He'll move to high Class A this year.

Year	Club (League)	Class	AVG	G	AB	R	H	2B	3B	HR	RBI	BB	SO	SB	SLG	OBP
2000	Helena (Pio)	R	.333	46	162	30	54	18	2	4	36	20	25	3	.543	.403
2001	Beloit (Mid)	A	.326	38	144	23	47	6	0	2	23	15	16	0	.410	.394
2002	Beloit (Mid)	A	.261	98	348	44	91	19	0	6	38	45	42	3	.368	.348
MINOR LEAGUE TOTALS			.294	182	654	97	192	43	2	12	97	80	83	6	.420	.372

30. Josh Murray, ss

Born: Aug. 12, 1984. **Ht.:** 6-2. **Wt.:** 180. **Bats:** R. **Throws:** R. **School:** Jesuit HS, Tampa. **Career Transactions:** Selected by Brewers in second round of 2002 draft; signed June 27, 2002.

The Brewers' selection of Murray in the second round of the 2002 draft was a swing for the fences. He is a polished defender who handles the bat well for his age and shows good poise on the field. After missing the entire 2001 season while recovering from Tommy John surgery, Murray dropped on most teams' draft boards and some people were shocked when Milwaukee scouting director Jack Zduriencik announced the pick. Though the Brewers are confident Murray will blossom into a first-rate player, the early returns weren't overwhelm-ing. He hit .255 in Rookie ball, struck out 48 times in 157 at-bats and committed 22 errors in 48 games. At a price of $825,000, Murray could turn out to be a shrewd pick or an expen-sive mistake.

Year	Club (League)	Class	AVG	G	AB	R	H	2B	3B	HR	RBI	BB	SO	SB	SLG	OBP
2002	Ogden (Pio)	R	.255	48	157	18	40	7	0	2	19	14	48	3	.338	.328
MINOR LEAGUE TOTALS			.255	48	157	18	40	7	0	2	19	14	48	3	.338	.328

MINNESOTA
TWINS

TOP 30 PROSPECTS

1. Joe Mauer, c
2. Justin Morneau, 1b
3. Michael Cuddyer, of
4. Michael Restovich, of
5. Denard Span, of
6. Scott Tyler, rhp
7. J.D. Durbin, rhp
8. Jason Kubel, of
9. Lew Ford, of
10. Adam Johnson, rhp
11. Dusty Gomon, 1b
12. Jesse Crain, rhp
13. Alex Romero, of
14. Matt Yeatman, rhp
15. Brad Thomas, lhp
16. Sandy Tejada, rhp
17. Beau Kemp, rhp
18. Trent Oeltjen, of
19. Grant Balfour, rhp
20. Matt Vorwald, rhp
21. Brent Hoard, lhp
22. Juan Rincon, rhp
23. Todd Sears, 1b
24. Kevin Frederick, rhp
25. Travis Bowyer, rhp
26. Jose Morban, ss
27. Alexander Smit, lhp
28. Angel Garcia, rhp
29. Mike Ryan, of
30. B.J. Garbe, of

By Josh Boyd

T he Twins went from the brink of extinction following the 2001 season to the 2002 American League Championship Series.

While they certainly were motivated by commissioner Bud Selig and owner Carl Pohlad's offseason plans to eliminate the 101-year-old franchise, the Twins aren't a one-hit wonder. Thanks to a stable front office led by general manager Terry Ryan, Baseball America's 2002 Organization of the Year has the pieces in place to contend for some time.

Burgeoning with homegrown talent in the majors—including six starting pitchers and four outfielders who played more than 100 games last season—Ryan could trade surplus players to bolster the roster. Scouting director Mike Radcliff, who has the longest tenure at his position in baseball, has stocked the farm system from Triple-A to Rookie ball with promising prospects.

The Twins can stack their upper-level prospects against anyone in baseball, and catcher Joe Mauer ranks among the top 10 in the game. Three of the system's five top outfield prospects played for Pacific Coast League champion Edmonton last season.

Michael Cuddyer started six games in the postseason, hitting .333, and he'll head into spring training as the favorite to win the right-field job. He'll contend for Rookie of the Year after hitting a combined .304 with 50 home runs in the minors the last two years. Michael Restovich might need more seasoning in Triple-A before he becomes a dangerous power hitter in the middle of the lineup. Lew Ford is on the cusp after a breakthrough season when he led the minors in runs.

Other than the Matt Lawton-Rick Reed trade in 2001, Ryan hasn't been in a position to deal homegrown players to supplement the Twins. As the Cuddyers, Restoviches and Fords develop, big leaguers such as Jacque Jones, Bobby Kielty and Dustan Mohr could become expendable.

Despite Minnesota's survival and success last year, Ryan is still forced to operate on a limited budget. That's why he might opt to move Jones, who is coming off a career year, in favor of less expensive prospects.

Because the Twins have stayed true to their scouting and player development roots, they can make such a move without a significant dropoff. The strength of the farm system will help them sustain their success and give them a chance to improve.

OrganizationOverview

General Manager: Terry Ryan. **Farm Director:** Jim Rantz. **Scouting Director:** Mike Radcliff.

2002 PERFORMANCE

Class	Farm Team	League	W	L	Pct.	Finish*	Manager
Majors	Minnesota	American	94	67	.584	4th (14)	Ron Gardenhire
Triple-A	†Edmonton Trappers	Pacific Coast	81	59	.579	+2nd (16)	John Russell
Double-A	New Britain Rock Cats	Eastern	67	72	.482	8th (12)	Stan Cliburn
High A	Fort Myers Miracle	Florida State	77	62	.554	3rd (12)	Jose Marzan
Low A	Quad City River Bandits	Midwest	71	65	.522	6th (14)	Jeff Carter
Rookie	Elizabethton Twins	Appalachian	37	30	.552	4th (10)	Ray Smith
Rookie	GCL Twins	Gulf Coast	35	25	.583	4th (14)	Rudy Hernandez
OVERALL 2002 MINOR LEAGUE RECORD			368	313	.540	4th (30)	

*Finish in overall standings (No. of teams in league). +League champion. †Affiliate will be in Rochester (International) in 2003.

ORGANIZATION LEADERS

BATTING *Minimum 250 At-Bats
*AVG	Jason Kubel, Quad City	.321
R	Lew Ford, Edmonton/New Britain	121
H	Lew Ford, Edmonton/New Britain	180
TB	Lew Ford, Edmonton/New Britain	286
2B	Lew Ford, Edmonton/New Britain	38
3B	Michael Cuddyer, Edmonton	9
HR	Mike Ryan, Edmonton	31
RBI	Mike Ryan, Edmonton	101
BB	Lew Ford, Edmonton/New Britain	62
SO	Michael Restovich, Edmonton	151
SB	Lew Ford, Edmonton/New Britain	28

PITCHING #Minimum 75 Innings
W	Scott Randall, Edmonton/New Britain	14
L	Brad Thomas, Edmonton	12
#ERA	Willie Eyre, New Britain/Fort Myers	2.90
G	Beau Kemp, Fort Myers	59
CG	Juan Rincon, Edmonton	3
SV	Juan Padilla, New Britain	29
	Beau Kemp, Fort Myers	29
IP	Brent Hoard, New Britain	161
	J.D. Durbin, Quad City	161
BB	Jon Pridie, New Britain/Fort Myers	76
SO	J.D. Durbin, Quad City	163

BEST TOOLS

Best Hitter for Average	Joe Mauer
Best Power Hitter	Justin Morneau
Fastest Baserunner	Denard Span
Best Athlete	Denard Span
Best Fastball	Scott Tyler
Best Curveball	Josh Hill
Best Slider	J.D. Durbin
Best Changeup	Adam Johnson
Best Control	Joe Foote
Best Defensive Catcher	Joe Mauer
Best Defensive Infielder	Angelo Fermin
Best Infield Arm	Omar Burgos
Best Defensive Outfielder	Lew Ford
Best Outfield Arm	B.J. Garbe

PROJECTED 2006 LINEUP

Catcher	Joe Mauer
First Base	Justin Morneau
Second Base	Luis Rivas
Third Base	Corey Koskie
Shortstop	Cristian Guzman
Left Field	Jacque Jones
Center Field	Torii Hunter
Right Field	Michael Cuddyer
Designated Hitter	Michael Restovich
No. 1 Starter	Eric Milton

ROBERT GURGANUS

Mike Ryan   **Willie Eyre**

No. 2 Starter	Johan Santana
No. 3 Starter	Joe Mays
No. 4 Starter	Brad Radke
No. 5 Starter	Scott Tyler
Closer	Eddie Guardado

TOP PROSPECTS OF THE DECADE

1993	David McCarty, of
1994	Rich Becker, of
1995	LaTroy Hawkins, rhp
1996	Todd Walker, 3b
1997	Todd Walker, 3b
1998	Luis Rivas, ss
1999	Michael Cuddyer, 3b
2000	Michael Cuddyer, 3b
2001	Adam Johnson, rhp
2002	Joe Mauer, c

TOP DRAFT PICKS OF THE DECADE

1993	Torii Hunter, of
1994	Todd Walker, 3b
1995	Mark Redman, lhp
1996	*Travis Lee, 1b
1997	Michael Cuddyer, ss
1998	Ryan Mills, lhp
1999	B.J. Garbe, of
2000	Adam Johnson, rhp
2001	Joe Mauer, c
2002	Denard Span, of

*Did not sign.

ALL-TIME LARGEST BONUSES

Joe Mauer, 2001	$5,150,000
B.J. Garbe, 1999	$2,750,000
Adam Johnson, 2000	$2,500,000
Ryan Mills, 1998	$2,000,000
Michael Cuddyer, 1997	$1,850,000

MinorLeagueDepthChart

MINNESOTA TWINS

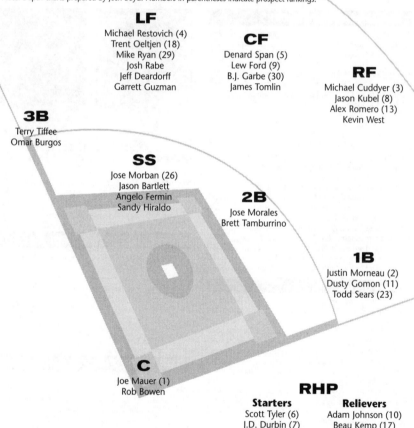

RANK 4

Not only did the Twins go from the brink of extinction to the American League Championship Series in 2002, but they also have one of the best-stocked farm systems in the game. Michael Cuddyer had an extended trial in right field in 2002 and will get every opportunity to win the job in spring training. A future lineup with Cuddyer, Joe Mauer, Justin Morneau and Michael Restovich would provide wallop not seen in Minnesota since Kirby Puckett and Kent Hrbek. Even with a small budget, the Twins have done an excellent job of combining winning with development. If there is a weakness it's in the middle infield, which the organization addressed in the Rule 5 draft with Jose Morban, and a deal with the Padres for shortstop Jason Bartlett.

Note: Depth charts prepared by Josh Boyd. Numbers in parentheses indicate prospect rankings.

LF
Michael Restovich (4)
Trent Oeltjen (18)
Mike Ryan (29)
Josh Rabe
Jeff Deardorff
Garrett Guzman

CF
Denard Span (5)
Lew Ford (9)
B.J. Garbe (30)
James Tomlin

RF
Michael Cuddyer (3)
Jason Kubel (8)
Alex Romero (13)
Kevin West

3B
Terry Tiffee
Omar Burgos

SS
Jose Morban (26)
Jason Bartlett
Angelo Fermin
Sandy Hiraldo

2B
Jose Morales
Brett Tamburrino

1B
Justin Morneau (2)
Dusty Gomon (11)
Todd Sears (23)

C
Joe Mauer (1)
Rob Bowen

RHP

Starters	Relievers
Scott Tyler (6)	Adam Johnson (10)
J.D. Durbin (7)	Beau Kemp (17)
Jesse Crain (12)	Grant Balfour (19)
Matt Yeatman (14)	Matt Vorwald (20)
Sandy Tejada (16)	Juan Rincon (22)
Angel Garcia (28)	Kevin Frederick (24)
Colby Miller	Travis Bowyer (25)
Brian Wolfe	Jon Pridie
Josmir Romero	Wille Eyre
Joe Foote	Pat Neshek
Tim Henkenjohann	Josh Hill
	Ronnie Corona
	Mike Nakamura
	Juan Padilla

LHP

Starters	Relievers
Alexander Smit (27)	Brad Thomas (15)
Ricky Barrett	Brent Hoard (21)
	Alex Merricks
	J.C. Contreras
	Ken Holubec
	Jason Miller

DraftAnalysis

2002 Draft

Best Pro Debut: LHP Ricky Barrett (7) doesn't have a true out pitch but led the Rookie-level Appalachian League with a 1.27 ERA, going 7-1 with 79 strikeouts in 64 innings. RHPs **Jesse Crain** (2) and Pat Neshek (6) both had sub-1.00 ERAs.

Best Athlete: OF Denard Span (1) was an all-Florida wide receiver in high school and could have played college football. Crain starred as a closer and shortstop at Houston.

Best Pure Hitter: Span doesn't have a classic stroke like Joe Mauer's, but his style and approach play to his strengths and should make him a catalyst atop a batting order. He can get on base by beating out routine grounders to shortstop.

Best Raw Power: The Twins didn't look for sluggers last year. OFs Doug Deeds (9) and Javier Lopez (18) are average to slightly above. Deeds, who hit .325-7-32 in the Appy League, is the better all-around hitter.

Fastest Runner: Span can cover 60 yards in 6.4 seconds and go from the left side of home to first in 4.0 seconds. OFs Ronald Perodin (27) and Tarrence Patterson (35) are also plus-plus runners.

Best Defensive Player: Span covers center field like a young Kenny Lofton.

Best Fastball: Crain, Neshek and RHP Adam Harben (15) can pump their fastballs to the mid-90s. Crain sustains it more easily than the other two. Neshek's deceptive delivery makes him more difficult to hit.

Best Breaking Ball: Crain's slider is better than Neshek's.

Most Intriguing Background: Unsigned C Jeff Clement (12) broke Drew Henson's national high school record with 75 career homers. Unsigned SS Toby Gardenhire's (38) father Ron is Minnesota's manager. RHP T.J. Prunty (21) went to the University of Miami as a quarterback. For the second straight year, the Twins drafted their state's best QB prospect, following Mauer with RHP John Stocco (45). They control Stocco's rights because he's at a school (Wisconsin) without a baseball program. LHP Alex Merricks' (4) brothers Charles and Matt are lefties in the Rockies and Braves organizations.

Crain

Closest To The Majors: Crain and Neshek are relievers who already have two plus pitches. Crain added a changeup last summer, and the Twins may be tempted to see how he does as a starter.

Best Late-Round Pick: Harben, RHP K.C. Jones (16) and Prunty are all tall youngsters with projectable arms.

The One Who Got Away: Minnesota was disappointed not to sign RHP Mark Sauls (3, at Florida State), OF Clete Thomas (5, Auburn), Clement (Southern California) and RHP Garrett Mock (14, Houston).

Assessment: The Twins usually have trouble signing top players–they signed only 10 of their first 20 picks–but Span adds to their enviable outfield depth, and they collected several promising pitchers.

2001 Draft

No. 1 overall pick Joe Mauer is showing that first-round catchers out of high school don't have to fail. RHP Scott Tyler (2) and 1B Dusty Gomon (9) are also quality prospects. SS/RHP Matt Macri (17), now at Notre Dame, would have been a first-rounder had he been considered signable.   **Grade: A**

2000 Draft

The Twins hurt themselves by not signing RHP Aaron Heilman (1) and 1B Tagg Bozied (2). At least they came away with RHPs Adam Johnson (1) and J.D. Durbin (2) and OF Jason Kubel (12).   **Grade: C+**

1999 Draft

Minnesota couldn't sign seven of its top 15 picks and spent $2.75 million it would love to have back on OF B.J. Garbe (1). But 1B Justin Morneau (3) looks like the real deal.   **Grade: B**

1998 Draft

The Twins were split on whether to take LHP Ryan Mills or Austin Kearns sixth overall. They made the wrong call and this crop never recovered.   **Grade: F**

Note: Draft analysis prepared by Jim Callis. Numbers in parentheses indicate draft rounds.

... Mauer is a natural hitter who makes consistent, hard contact to all fields.

Joe
Mauer c

Born: April 19, 1983.
Ht.: 6-4. **Wt.:** 220.
Bats: L. **Throws:** R.
School: Cretin-Derham Hall, St. Paul, Minn.
Career Transactions: Selected by Twins in first round (first overall) of 2001 draft; signed July 17, 2001.

Holding the No. 1 pick in the 2001 draft, the Twins opted for Baseball America High School Player of the Year Joe Mauer instead of consensus top talent Mark Prior, who was out of their price range. Mauer was hardly a consolation prize, though. He was one of the top quarterback recruits in the nation and nearly followed fellow Cretin-Derham Hall product Chris Weinke to Florida State. Mauer also starred on the basketball court, averaging nearly 20 points a game. He led Cretin-Derham to state titles in all three sports. The Twins signed Mauer to a franchise-record $5.15 million deal, and he started his pro career by hitting .400 for Rookie-level Elizabethton. He raked for low Class A Quad City in his first full season, which ended early thanks to double-hernia surgery. He was back by the end of instructional league following six weeks on the sideline. His older brother Jake played second base for Quad City last year.

Mauer shows outstanding balance at the plate and generates outstanding bat speed with a smooth, classic lefthanded stroke. A natural hitter, he covers the plate well, understands the strike zone and makes consistent, hard contact to all fields. He has a knack for finding the sweet spot when he connects with the ball. The ball carries well off his bat, and he'll develop above-average power as he continues to bulk up his loose, athletic frame and learns which pitches to turn on. He already shows plus power in batting practice. Mauer's arm is near the top of the scale, but more important, he's mechanically sound with a quick release and his throws are right on the bag. Mauer benefited from working with veteran catcher Tom Prince in spring training.

Mauer needs to learn the nuances of the game, including working with pitchers during a game. With his makeup and feel, he'll be a complete receiver. More at-bats will help him understand counts and when to attack pitches.

Mauer is primed for a speedy ascent. A.J. Pierzynski's emergence will help the Twins bide their time, though it will be tempting to promote him aggressively and he might not last the season at high Class A Fort Myers. He'll own the top spot on this list until he takes over in Minnesota.

Year	Club (League)	Class	AVG	G	AB	R	H	2B	3B	HR	RBI	BB	SO	SB	SLG	OBP
2001	Elizabethton (Appy)	R	.400	32	110	14	44	6	2	0	14	19	10	4	.491	.492
2002	Quad City (Mid)	A	.302	110	411	58	124	23	1	4	62	61	42	0	.392	.393
MINOR LEAGUE TOTALS			.322	142	521	72	168	29	3	4	76	80	52	4	.413	.414

2. Justin Morneau, 1b

Born: May 15, 1981. **Ht.:** 6-4. **Wt.:** 200. **Bats:** L. **Throws:** R. **School:** New Westminster (B.C.) SS. **Career Transactions:** Selected by Twins in third round of 1999 draft; signed June 17, 1999.

Drafted as a catcher out of the North Delta Blue Jays program in the B.C. Premier League, Morneau has settled in at first base after experimenting in the outfield during instructional league in 2001. Injuries have hampered him throughout his career. Last spring, he lost 25 pounds due to an intestinal infection and missed the first week of the season at Double-A New Britain. Morneau's lefthanded stroke is one of the sweetest in the minors. He produces outstanding power with a classic finish. He shows the ability to cover the plate and center the ball. His plus-plus bat speed propels the ball off his bat, and he has the best game power of any prospect in the system. As a first baseman, Morneau will be adequate but won't be an asset like incumbent Doug Mienkiewicz, a Gold Glover. Morneau worked on his hands and footwork in the Arizona Fall League. Morneau should produce well-above-average power and average. Mienkiewicz' job won't be in jeopardy until 2004, though Morneau could force his way into the Twins lineup as a DH by the all-star break in 2003.

Year	Club (League)	Class	AVG	G	AB	R	H	2B	3B	HR	RBI	BB	SO	SB	SLG	OBP
1999	Twins (GCL)	R	.302	17	53	3	16	5	0	0	9	2	6	0	.396	.333
2000	Twins (GCL)	R	.402	52	194	47	78	21	0	10	58	30	18	3	.665	.478
	Elizabethton (Appy)	R	.217	6	23	4	5	0	0	1	3	1	6	0	.348	.250
2001	Quad City (Mid)	A	.356	64	236	50	84	17	2	12	53	26	38	0	.597	.420
	Fort Myers (FSL)	A	.294	53	197	25	58	10	3	4	40	24	41	0	.437	.385
	New Britain (EL)	AA	.158	10	38	3	6	1	0	0	4	3	8	0	.184	.214
2002	New Britain (EL)	AA	.298	126	494	72	147	31	4	16	80	42	88	7	.474	.356
MINOR LEAGUE TOTALS			.319	328	1235	204	394	85	9	43	247	128	205	10	.507	.386

3. Michael Cuddyer, of

Born: March 27, 1979. **Ht.:** 6-2. **Wt.:** 210. **Bats:** R. **Throws:** R. **School:** Great Bridge HS, Chesapeake, Va. **Career Transactions:** Selected by Twins in first round (ninth overall) of 1997 draft; signed Aug. 19, 1997.

A high school shortstop, Cuddyer moved to third base in 1999 after committing 61 errors at short in low Class A in 1998, then to right field in 2001 as Corey Koskie emerged at third for Minnesota. Cuddyer was the Twins top prospect in 1999 and 2000. He has the juice to be a potent middle-of-the-order force. He generates well-above-average bat speed and rakes to all fields because he can drive even the best fastballs and keep his hands back on offspeed stuff. He has the leadership abilities to fit right in with the home-grown Twins. He has plenty of arm strength for right field. Though he has made progress in the outfield, Cuddyer is still learning to make proper routes and reads on fly balls. He looked a little rough during his late-season audition with Minnesota. The Bobby Kielty-Dustan Mohr platoon worked well for the Twins, but Cuddyer is still expected to claim the right-field job and hit in the heart of the order. He's a top candidate for Rookie of the Year in 2003.

Year	Club (League)	Class	AVG	G	AB	R	H	2B	3B	HR	RBI	BB	SO	SB	SLG	OBP
1998	Fort Wayne (Mid)	A	.276	129	497	82	137	37	7	12	81	61	107	16	.451	.364
1999	Fort Myers (FSL)	A	.298	130	466	87	139	24	4	16	82	76	91	14	.470	.403
2000	New Britain (EL)	AA	.263	138	490	72	129	30	8	6	61	55	93	5	.394	.351
2001	New Britain (EL)	AA	.301	141	509	95	153	36	3	30	87	75	106	5	.560	.395
	Minnesota (AL)	MAJ	.222	8	18	1	4	2	0	0	1	2	6	1	.333	.300
2002	Edmonton (PCL)	AAA	.309	86	330	70	102	16	9	20	53	36	79	12	.594	.379
	Minnesota (AL)	MAJ	.259	41	112	12	29	7	0	4	13	8	30	2	.429	.311
MAJOR LEAGUE TOTALS			.254	49	130	13	33	9	0	4	14	10	36	3	.415	.310
MINOR LEAGUE TOTALS			.288	624	2292	406	660	143	31	84	364	303	476	52	.487	.378

4. Michael Restovich, of

Born: Jan. 3, 1979. **Ht.:** 6-4. **Wt.:** 240. **Bats:** R. **Throws:** R. **School:** Mayo HS, Rochester, Minn. **Career Transactions:** Selected by Twins in second round of 1997 draft; signed Aug. 15, 1997.

Drafted a round after Michael Cuddyer, Restovich has been a step behind in his development ever since. Restovich headed to the Arizona Fall League for the second straight year to catch up, but he was exhausted by November and his performance reflected it. A gifted athlete who's built like a linebacker, Restovich has the unique ability for someone his size to combine pure strength with a short swing. His raw power, which rates a 70 on the 20-80 scouting scale, produces home runs that don't come down for a while. His arm strength and speed are average. Restovich understands the strike zone and has solid average bat speed, but he can be beat with good heat and needs to learn to lay off breaking balls away. A high school third baseman who has played left field for five years, he is still learning the finer points of defense, throwing and baserunning. With nine outfielders on the 40-man roster, the Twins can afford to start Restovich at Triple-A Rochester in 2003. He could be ready for a regular spot in the lineup by 2004, when he'll be just 25.

Year	Club (League)	Class	AVG	G	AB	R	H	2B	3B	HR	RBI	BB	SO	SB	SLG	OBP
1998	Elizabethton (Appy)	R	.355	65	242	68	86	20	1	13	64	54	58	5	.607	.489
	Fort Wayne (Mid)	A	.444	11	45	9	20	5	2	0	6	4	12	0	.644	.490
1999	Quad City (Mid)	A	.312	131	493	91	154	30	6	19	107	74	100	7	.513	.412
2000	Fort Myers (FSL)	A	.263	135	475	73	125	27	9	8	64	61	100	19	.408	.350
2001	New Britain (EL)	AA	.269	140	501	69	135	33	4	23	84	54	125	15	.489	.345
2002	Edmonton (PCL)	AAA	.286	138	518	95	148	32	7	29	98	53	151	11	.542	.353
	Minnesota (AL)	MAJ	.308	8	13	3	4	0	0	1	1	1	4	1	.538	.357
MAJOR LEAGUE TOTALS			.308	8	13	3	4	0	0	1	1	1	4	1	.538	.357
MINOR LEAGUE TOTALS			.294	620	2274	405	668	147	29	92	423	300	546	57	.505	.382

5. Denard Span, of

Born: Feb. 27, 1984. **Ht.:** 6-1. **Wt.:** 170. **Bats:** L. **Throws:** L. **School:** Tampa Catholic HS. **Career Transactions:** Selected by Twins in first round (20th overall) of 2002 draft; signed Aug. 15, 2002.

Span transferred from Hillsborough High (the alma mater of Carl Everett, Dwight Gooden and Gary Sheffield) to help Tampa Catholic win a Florida 3-A state title as a junior. He hit .456 as a senior and led the county in receiving yards for the football team. Span was a key member of the U.S. junior team that finished second in a Pan American tournament in Cuba in 2001. After signing for $1.7 million in August, he got his first pro exposure in instructional league. Span's profile and mindset are those of a classic top-of-the-order catalyst like Kenny Lofton. He puts pressure on the defense with his speed and has been clocked at 6.4 seconds in the 60-yard dash. He has a live, athletic frame with first-step quickness and average arm strength for center field. He makes solid contact and will drive the ball to the gaps with more authority as he fills out. Span is raw. He doesn't have a classic stroke, and the Twins altered his spread-out approach at the plate in the fall. He won't hit for plus power and needs to understand his limitations. Span will make his pro debut in low Class A. He's the Twins' leadoff hitter of the future.

Year	Club (League)	Class	AVG	G	AB	R	H	2B	3B	HR	RBI	BB	SO	SB	SLG	OBP
			Has Not Played—Signed 2003 Contract													

6. Scott Tyler, rhp

Born: Aug. 20, 1982. **Ht.:** 6-6. **Wt.:** 220. **Bats:** R. **Throws:** R. **School:** Downingtown (Pa.) HS. **Career Transactions:** Selected by Twins in second round of 2001 draft; signed July 8, 2001.

After signing for $875,000 in 2001, Tyler was so raw in instructional league that coaches had to stop innings before he recorded three outs. He learned to harness his power arsenal in extended spring training before leading the Rookie-level Appalachian League in strikeouts. His father Toby was an all-America basketball player at Cheyney (Pa.) University and was selected in the ABA draft. Physically imposing, Tyler mows batters down with a 95 mph fastball that has heavy, boring life and is delivered from a three-quarters arm slot. He shows the ability to spin a hard slider, though he needs to refine the pitch, and his changeup has become more reliable. At his size, Tyler has high-maintenance mechanics. He has worked to make his delivery compact but struggles to keep everything in sync, which affects his command. He has to tighten his slurvy breaking ball. Tyler has a powerhouse body and the overpowering stuff to develop into a frontline starter. He'll move to low Class A in 2003. The Twins like to move their starters one level at a time, but he could hasten that timetable by continuing to dominate.

Year	Club (League)	Class	W	L	ERA	G	GS	CG	SV	IP	H	R	ER	HR	BB	SO	AVG
2001	Twins (GCL)	R	0	1	6.75	5	3	0	0	11	11	8	8	0	2	14	.256
2002	Elizabethton (Appy)	R	8	1	2.93	14	13	0	0	68	37	23	22	5	46	92	.161
MINOR LEAGUE TOTALS			8	2	3.45	19	16	0	0	78	48	31	30	5	48	106	.176

7. J.D. Durbin, rhp

Born: Feb. 24, 1982. **Ht.:** 6-0. **Wt.:** 180. **Bats:** R. **Throws:** R. **School:** Coronado HS, Scottsdale, Ariz. **Career Transactions:** Selected by Twins in second round of 2000 draft; signed July 18, 2000.

A two-way stud as a righthander/outfielder in high school, Durbin also was recruited as a wide receiver. A $722,500 bonus kept him away from his Arizona State commitment. After signing in 2000, he was limited to two innings by a sore elbow, which gave him trouble again in 2001. An adjustment to Durbin's approach helped him develop into a prospect. Instead of trying to strike out every hitter, he learned to trust his stuff and pitch. He still led the Midwest League in whiffs, as hitters had a difficult time catching up to his 91-92 mph fastball and his darting slider, the best breaking pitch in the system. He can reach back for more velocity and touched 95 every time he took the mound. With his track record and size, Durbin's durability will be monitored closely. His changeup has improved but isn't consistently average yet. One scout who saw him in the MWL thought he had a long arm action and might be better suited for the bullpen. After making progress with his command, control and mound presence, Durbin could move quickly. He'll advance to high Class A in 2003.

Year	Club (League)	Class	W	L	ERA	G	GS	CG	SV	IP	H	R	ER	HR	BB	SO	AVG
2000	Twins (GCL)	R	0	0	0.00	2	0	0	0	2	2	0	0	0	0	4	.222
2001	Elizabethton (Appy)	R	3	2	1.87	8	7	0	0	34	23	13	7	2	17	39	.190
2002	Quad City (Mid)	A	13	4	3.19	27	27	0	0	161	144	66	57	14	51	163	.239
MINOR LEAGUE TOTALS			16	6	2.93	37	34	0	0	197	169	79	64	16	68	206	.231

8. Jason Kubel, of

Born: May 25, 1982. **Ht.:** 5-11. **Wt.:** 190. **Bats:** L. **Throws:** R. **School:** Highland HS, Palmdale, Calif. **Career Transactions:** Selected by Twins in 12th round of 2000 draft; signed June 13, 2000.

Kubel earned preseason third-team High School All-America recognition in 2000 from Baseball America and turned down an offer to go to Long Beach State. He enjoyed a breakthrough season in 2002 after a pair of obscure campaigns in the Rookie-level Gulf Coast League. He made the Midwest League all-star team despite being bothered by back problems. By shortening his stroke and learning which pitches he could handle, Kubel took a huge step forward. He's an aggressive contact hitter who can hit for power with a quick swing. Kubel pitched in high school and shows plus arm strength suitable for right field. He has a chance to be a solid-average defender. He held his own against lefties in 2002, but Kubel connected for just four extra-base hits in 105 at-bats against southpaws. He's a below-average runner, though he won't clog the bases. Kubel really impressed the Twins with his progress and is destined for high Class A in 2003. He could develop into a poor man's Brian Giles if he continues to develop power as he moves up the ladder.

Year	Club (League)	Class	AVG	G	AB	R	H	2B	3B	HR	RBI	BB	SO	SB	SLG	OBP
2000	Twins (GCL)	R	.282	23	78	17	22	3	2	0	13	10	9	0	.372	.367
2001	Twins (GCL)	R	.331	37	124	14	41	10	4	1	30	19	14	3	.500	.422
2002	Quad City (Mid)	A	.321	115	424	60	136	26	4	17	69	41	48	3	.521	.380
MINOR LEAGUE TOTALS			.318	175	626	91	199	39	10	18	112	70	71	6	.498	.387

9. Lew Ford, of

Born: Aug. 12, 1976. **Ht.:** 6-0. **Wt.:** 190. **Bats:** R. **Throws:** R. **School:** Dallas Baptist University. **Career Transactions:** Selected by Red Sox in 12th round of 1999 draft; signed June 7, 1999 . . . Traded by Red Sox to Twins for RHP Hector Carrasco, Sept. 10, 2000.

Originally drafted by the Red Sox, Ford had teamed with Boston prospect Freddy Sanchez to take Dallas Baptist to the NAIA World Series in 1999. The Red Sox dealt Ford to the Twins for journeyman reliever Hector Carrasco in September 2000. Ford led the minors in runs in 2002. Ford put his name on the map by homering four times in a 2001 game, and again showed his sneaky power by winning the home run derby at the 2002 Double-A all-star game. He's a plus runner with the instincts to work the count and draw walks. He has an average arm and shows fine range in center field. While he won't develop into a perennial all-star, Ford doesn't show many flaws in his game. His biggest obstacle is Minnesota's depth of quality outfielders. Ford capped the 2002 season with the MVP award in the Triple-A Pacific Coast League playoffs, and he was placed on the 40-man roster in November. After hitting well in the Venezuelan League (.302-5-15), he could crack the Opening Day roster as an extra outfielder.

Year	Club (League)	Class	AVG	G	AB	R	H	2B	3B	HR	RBI	BB	SO	SB	SLG	OBP
1999	Lowell (NY-P)	A	.280	62	250	48	70	17	4	7	34	19	35	15	.464	.339
2000	Augusta (SAL)	A	.315	126	514	122	162	35	11	9	74	52	83	52	.479	.390
2001	Fort Myers (FSL)	A	.298	67	265	42	79	15	2	2	24	21	30	19	.392	.373
	New Britain (EL)	AA	.218	62	252	30	55	9	3	7	25	20	35	5	.361	.289
2002	New Britain (EL)	AA	.311	93	373	81	116	27	2	15	51	49	47	17	.515	.401
	Edmonton (PCL)	AAA	.332	47	193	40	64	11	2	5	24	13	21	11	.487	.390
MINOR LEAGUE TOTALS			.296	457	1847	363	546	114	24	45	232	174	251	119	.456	.370

10. Adam Johnson, rhp

Born: July 12, 1979. **Ht.:** 6-2. **Wt.:** 210. **Bats:** R. **Throws:** R. **School:** Cal State Fullerton. **Career Transactions:** Selected by Twins in first round (second overall) of 2000 draft; signed June 19, 2000.

Known as a fiery competitor, Johnson made national headlines during spring training for his angry reaction to being sent to minor league camp. Then he went out and had a disappointing season at Triple-A Edmonton. He was the No. 2 overall pick in 2000, when he was the Big West Conference pitcher of the year and led NCAA Division I in strikeouts. Johnson is a different pitcher than he was at Cal State Fullerton, where he dominated opponents with a hard slider. His fastball sits in the 90-92 mph range and touches 94. His changeup has developed into an occasional plus offering as he has smoothed out his mechanics. The Pacific Coast League can be unkind to pitchers, and Johnson didn't help himself with his inconsistent location in the strike zone. His slider doesn't have the same bite it once did. He has been more of a control/command pitcher as a starter, while as a reliever he could have more of a power arsenal. Despite his struggles, Johnson will have a chance to claim a big league bullpen job in spring training. Many scouts project him to throw in the mid-90s and flourish as a potential closer prospect.

Year	Club (League)	Class	W	L	ERA	G	GS	CG	SV	IP	H	R	ER	HR	BB	SO	AVG
2000	Fort Myers (FSL)	A	5	4	2.47	13	12	1	0	69	45	21	19	2	20	92	.186
2001	New Britain (EL)	AA	5	6	3.82	18	18	0	0	113	105	53	48	10	39	110	.248
	Minnesota (AL)	MAJ	1	2	8.28	7	4	0	0	25	32	25	23	6	13	17	.323
	Edmonton (PCL)	AAA	1	1	5.70	4	4	0	0	24	19	15	15	0	10	25	.226
2002	Edmonton (PCL)	AAA	13	8	5.47	27	27	1	0	151	182	96	92	25	55	112	.304
MAJOR LEAGUE TOTALS			1	2	8.28	7	4	0	0	25	32	25	23	6	13	17	.323
MINOR LEAGUE TOTALS			24	19	4.38	62	61	2	0	357	351	185	174	37	124	339	.260

11. Dusty Gomon, 1b

Born: Sept. 3, 1982. **Ht.:** 6-3. **Wt.:** 200. **Bats:** R. **Throws:** R. **School:** Terry Parker HS, Jacksonville. **Career Transactions:** Selected by Twins in ninth round of 2001 draft; signed June 7, 2001.

Despite hailing from the talent hotbed of Florida, Gomon was an unknown commodity before the 2001 draft. Area scout Brad Weitzel and other members of the Twins' staff scouted every game Gomon played as a senior and noted the lack of interest from other scouts, allowing Minnesota to wait until the ninth round to pick him. Gomon broke his arm during his 2001 debut, but managed to make the most out of an emergency promotion to high Class A less than three months out of high school. He broke another bone—this time a hand—when he was hit by a pitch late in the 2002 season. Gomon has tremendous raw power and the strength to hit the ball out to all fields. He shows good instincts at the plate and uses his hands well to adjust to offspeed stuff. He still needs to work on recognizing breaking pitches. A soccer goalie in high school, Gomon shows surprising athleticism for his size and has worked hard to improve his footwork around the bag. The hand injury caused him to miss instructional league, but he should make the jump to low Class A this year.

Year	Club (League)	Class	AVG	G	AB	R	H	2B	3B	HR	RBI	BB	SO	SB	SLG	OBP
2001	Twins (GCL)	R	.324	19	74	13	24	6	0	2	10	5	15	1	.486	.367
	Fort Myers (FSL)	A	.278	6	18	2	5	0	0	1	3	0	6	0	.444	.278
2002	Elizabethton (Appy)	R	.302	53	199	43	60	7	2	14	41	22	54	1	.568	.372
MINOR LEAGUE TOTALS			.306	78	291	58	89	13	2	17	54	27	75	2	.540	.366

12. Jesse Crain, rhp

Born: July 5, 1981. **Ht.:** 6-1. **Wt.:** 200. **Bats:** R. **Throws:** R. **School:** University of Houston. **Career Transactions:** Selected by Twins in second round of 2002 draft; signed July 13, 2002.

After spending a semester at the University at Texas, Crain transferred to San Jacinto

(Texas) Junior College before continuing on to Houston for his junior season. Expected to play shortstop and do a little pitching, he emerged as an All-America two-way star. Crain started all 65 of Houston's games at short, batting .309-11-47, and didn't allow an earned run until the final game of the season, going 4-0, 0.23 with 10 saves. While he'll focus on pitching for the Twins, Crain can use his athleticism on the mound. His fastball has registered as high as 97 mph and typically sits around 92-94. His sharp slider is one of the best breaking pitches in the system, featuring late depth in the zone. He has demonstrated a feel for a changeup and a knuckle-curve as offspeed pitches, which will help him as he makes a move to the rotation. Crain has good control. Because Crain doesn't have much pitching experience, the Twins will exercise a cautious approach with his workload. He still could blitz through the system, becoming the first player from Minnesota's 2002 draft class to reach the majors.

Year	Club (League)	Class	W	L	ERA	G	GS	CG	SV	IP	H	R	ER	HR	BB	SO	AVG
2002	Elizabethton (Appy)	R	2	1	0.57	9	0	0	2	16	4	2	1	0	7	18	.082
	Quad City (Mid)	A	1	1	1.50	9	0	0	1	12	6	3	2	0	4	11	.154
MINOR LEAGUE TOTALS			3	2	0.98	18	0	0	3	28	10	5	3	0	11	29	.114

13. Alex Romero, of

Born: Sept. 9, 1983. **Ht.:** 6-0. **Wt.:** 170. **Bats:** B. **Throws:** R. **Career Transactions:** Signed out of Venezuela by Twins, July 2, 2002.

The Twins are loaded with outfield depth, and Romero is the low man on the totem pole in terms of experience. But scouts agree he has a chance to move up fast when he gets to show his stuff outside of Rookie ball. Signed by Venezuelan scout Jose Leon, Romero finished fifth in the Rookie-level Venezuelan Summer League in hitting in 2001 before finishing fourth in the Gulf Coast League last year. His advanced approach at the plate is unusual for his age, and the Twins thought enough of his maturity to send him to winter ball as one of the youngest players in Venezuela over the winter. International scouts there were impressed with Romero's presence and his tools, which consist of above-average wheels he uses well in center field, a plus arm and a line-drive bat with gap power. Romero's projects to have plus tools across the board except for his speed, which will regress as he gets stronger. While Romero has the instincts to play center field, he'll likely outgrow the position and move to right field. He'll get his first taste of full-season ball in Quad City this year, where he'll try to maintain his .340 career average.

Year	Club (League)	Class	AVG	G	AB	R	H	2B	3B	HR	RBI	BB	SO	SB	SLG	OBP
2001	San Joaquin (VSL)	R	.347	49	167	22	58	9	0	2	30	11	9	10	.437	.388
2002	Twins (GCL)	R	.333	56	186	31	62	13	2	2	42	29	14	16	.457	.423
MINOR LEAGUE TOTALS			.340	105	353	53	120	22	2	4	72	40	23	26	.448	.407

14. Matt Yeatman, rhp

Born: Aug. 2, 1982. **Ht.:** 6-4. **Wt.:** 200. **Bats:** R. **Throws:** R. **School:** Tomball (Texas) HS. **Career Transactions:** Selected by Brewers in 13th round of 2000 draft; signed Aug. 9, 2000 . . . Traded by Brewers with RHP Gerry Oakes to Twins for RHP Matt Kinney and C Javier Valentin, Nov. 15, 2002.

Pressed with 40-man roster issues, the Twins took an opportunity to swap two young players on the bubble (catcher Javier Valentin and righthander Matt Kinney) but without clear big league jobs for a pair of Class A righthanders: Yeatman and Gerry Oakes. Though Yeatman signed late in 2000 and didn't debut until midseason 2001, he quickly became one of Milwaukee's better pitching prospects. His fastball sits at 89-91 mph and touches 92-93, and there's room for more projection as he firms up his 6-foot-4 frame. His curveball is his best pitch at the moment. He made strides incorporating his changeup into his repertoire after operating almost strictly with a fastball/curveball attack in 2001. He has drawn comparisons to a young Kevin Millwood, but Yeatman might eventually thrive in the back of a bullpen with two power pitches. He sometimes throws across his body, which causes him to leave his fastball up in the strike zone. He'll move to high Class A in 2003.

Year	Club (League)	Class	W	L	ERA	G	GS	CG	SV	IP	H	R	ER	HR	BB	SO	AVG
2001	Ogden (Pio)	R	2	4	4.95	13	8	0	1	60	72	40	33	6	27	61	.301
2002	Beloit (Mid)	A	11	7	2.48	25	25	1	0	127	101	51	35	4	77	127	.219
MINOR LEAGUE TOTALS			13	11	3.27	38	33	1	1	187	173	91	68	10	104	188	.247

15. Brad Thomas, lhp

Born: Oct. 22, 1977. **Ht.:** 6-4. **Wt.:** 220. **Bats:** L. **Throws:** L. **Career Transactions:** Signed out of Australia by Dodgers, July 2, 1995 . . . Released by Dodgers, May 9, 1997 . . . Signed by Twins, May 12, 1997.

The Twins narrowly lost out to the Dodgers in a bidding war for Thomas when he was a 17-year-old Australian with little pitching experience in 1995. When visa problems forced

Los Angeles to release him two years later, Minnesota jumped at the second chance to sign him. He made his major league debut and had the third-lowest ERA in the minors in 2001, but he was torched in Triple-A last season. Thomas, who had run his fastball up into the mid-90s in the past, regularly works around 90 mph and touches 93 with good movement. He took a step in the wrong direction with his mechanics last season, causing his curveball to become inconsistent and his control to suffer. Thomas has the mentality to blow hitters away, but he struggles when he finds himself in a jam. His changeup is average. He has had his way with lefthanders in the past, but even they got in on the hit parade last season, batting .301 against him. The Twins already have more established lefties Eddie Guardado, J.C. Romero and Johan Santana virtually guaranteed spots on the staff. Thomas, entering his eighth pro season, is likely headed for a repeat of Triple-A.

Year	Club (League)	Class	W	L	ERA	G	GS	CG	SV	IP	H	R	ER	HR	BB	SO	AVG
1996	Great Falls (Pio)	R	3	2	6.31	11	5	0	0	36	48	27	25	2	11	28	.320
1997	Elizabethton (Appy)	R	3	4	4.48	14	13	0	0	70	78	43	35	5	21	53	.279
1998	Fort Wayne (Mid)	A	11	8	2.95	27	26	1	0	152	146	68	50	9	45	126	.248
1999	Fort Myers (FSL)	A	8	11	4.78	27	27	1	0	153	182	99	81	11	46	108	.300
2000	Fort Myers (FSL)	A	6	2	1.66	12	12	0	0	65	62	33	12	3	16	57	.239
	New Britain (EL)	AA	6	6	4.06	14	13	1	0	75	80	47	34	3	46	66	.277
2001	New Britain (EL)	AA	10	3	1.96	19	19	1	0	119	91	37	26	4	26	97	.206
	Minnesota (AL)	MAJ	0	2	9.37	5	5	0	0	16	20	17	17	6	14	6	.303
2002	Edmonton (PCL)	AAA	6	12	5.74	28	27	1	0	152	175	112	97	20	54	97	.291
MAJOR LEAGUE TOTALS			0	2	9.37	5	5	0	0	16	20	17	17	6	14	6	.303
MINOR LEAGUE TOTALS			53	48	3.94	152	142	5	0	823	862	466	360	57	265	632	.268

16. Sandy Tejada, rhp

Born: April 16, 1982. **Ht.:** 6-1. **Wt.:** 190. **Bats:** R. **Throws:** R. **Career Transactions:** Signed out of Dominican Republic by Twins, Sept. 17, 1998.

Signed for just $10,000 by Johnny Sierra, who hopes to spearhead a Twins resurgence in the Dominican, Tejada has one of the most exciting power arms in the system—when he's healthy. His 2002 season didn't start until mid-May because of shoulder soreness, and he wore down in August before having his labrum cleaned up in a relatively minor surgery. Scouts who only chart velocities during the first couple of innings of ballgames easily could be fooled by Tejada, who typically starts a game throwing 85-88 mph but dials it up to the mid-90s by the middle innings. Hitters have a difficult time generating any loft against his heavy fastball, though he isn't sharp enough with his command to always keep it down in the strike zone. He does have good control and finds the zone regularly with all three of his offerings, including a decent curveball and changeup. Tejada's delivery and arm action can be a little rough, which could have contributed to his shoulder problems. The Twins were encouraged by Tejada's offseason work and his willingness to stay near their minor league complex in Fort Myers. He could be ready to go by spring and needs to prove his stamina to move into the upper echelon of the system's prospects.

Year	Club (League)	Class	W	L	ERA	G	GS	CG	SV	IP	H	R	ER	HR	BB	SO	AVG
1999	Twins (DSL)	R	2	3	4.77	20	11	0	3	77	93	58	41	9	27	86	.293
2000	Twins (GCL)	R	6	2	4.53	15	10	1	0	58	57	30	29	3	20	49	.261
2001	Quad City (Mid)	A	0	1	4.50	4	2	0	0	10	7	8	5	1	9	13	.194
	Elizabethton (Appy)	R	5	3	3.20	11	10	0	0	56	43	26	20	6	20	87	.209
2002	Quad City (Mid)	A	9	4	2.76	14	14	1	0	91	70	32	28	9	23	78	.210
MINOR LEAGUE TOTALS			22	13	3.78	64	47	2	3	293	270	154	123	28	99	313	.243

17. Beau Kemp, rhp

Born: Oct. 31, 1980. **Ht.:** 6-0. **Wt.:** 180. **Bats:** R. **Throws:** R. **School:** Saddleback (Calif.) CC. **Career Transactions:** Selected by Twins in 31st round of 2000 draft; signed June 19, 2000.

Kemp was one of Oklahoma's best high school quarterbacks and considered a potential first- to third-round pick in the 1999 baseball draft, but off-the-field problems caused him to slip to the Orioles in the 22nd round. He opted for a year at Saddleback to get himself together. He didn't move up in the draft, though, and hasn't exactly been a model citizen since the Twins took a flier on him, as he ran into more troubles with the law last spring. On the mound, Kemp has been downright nasty. He blows hitters away with a full-effort delivery and a high-octane fastball that reaches 95 mph, allowing earned runs in just four of 59 appearances last year. He has a good, hard slider and can locate both pitches to either side of the plate. Sometimes the downward plane of his pitches becomes an issue because of his size, but he didn't allow a home run and keeps the ball low in the zone. Kemp must keep his focus as he continues to move one level at a time toward a short-relief role in Minnesota.

Yer	Club (League)	Class	W	L	ERA	G	GS	CG	SV	IP	H	R	ER	HR	BB	SO	AVG
2000	Twins (GCL)	R	0	1	3.12	7	0	0	1	9	6	5	3	0	3	10	.188
	Elizabethton (Appy)	R	1	0	2.18	17	0	0	7	21	12	6	5	2	6	28	.162
2001	Quad City (Mid)	A	0	1	2.51	31	0	0	4	43	29	17	12	4	15	46	.191
2002	Fort Myers (FSL)	A	3	2	0.66	59	0	0	29	68	49	14	5	0	18	49	.202
MINOR LEAGUE TOTALS			4	4	1.60	114	0	0	41	141	96	42	25	6	42	133	.192

18. Trent Oeltjen, of

Born: Feb. 28, 1983. **Ht.:** 6-2. **Wt.:** 185. **Bats:** L. **Throws:** L. **Career Transactions:** Signed out of Australia by Twins, Feb. 7, 2001.

Scouting director Mike Radcliff and international scout Howard Norsetter first saw Oeltjen at an Australia tournament when he was 15 and fell in love with his bat. In a year and a half, Oeltjen has blossomed into the top Australian position prospect in the system, while the Twins also have high hopes for Aussie pitchers Brad Thomas, Grant Balfour, Josh Hill and Mike Nakamura. Oeltjen has a loose, classic stroke with line-drive power. He has good control of the bat head in the zone and makes consistent contact. He has added strength to a lean frame since signing, growing a couple of inches and putting on about 25 pounds without sacrificing his plus speed. He had Tommy John surgery before he signed, leaving his arm strength as his weakest tool. He shows solid fundamentals on routes in the outfield. He's ready for full-season ball and will play in low Class A at age 20 this year.

Year	Club (League)	Class	AVG	G	AB	R	H	2B	3B	HR	RBI	BB	SO	SB	SLG	OBP
2001	Twins (GCL)	R	.321	45	134	21	43	7	3	0	18	14	16	10	.418	.387
	Elizabethton (Appy)	R	.233	9	30	4	7	1	0	0	4	0	6	2	.267	.226
2002	Elizabethton (Appy)	R	.298	54	215	36	64	7	2	3	18	16	34	7	.391	.363
	Quad City (Mid)	A	.240	10	25	4	6	1	0	0	1	3	2	1	.280	.321
MINOR LEAGUE TOTALS			.297	118	404	65	120	16	5	3	41	33	58	20	.384	.359

19. Grant Balfour, rhp

Born: Dec. 30, 1977. **Ht.:** 6-2. **Wt.:** 170. **Bats:** R. **Throws:** R. **Career Transactions:** Signed out of Australia by Twins, Jan. 19, 1997.

First scouted as a scrawny 5-foot-10 catcher at an under-16 tourney in Australia, Balfour made the transition to the mound shortly afterward. He barely broke the 80 mph barrier, but scouts liked his free, easy arm action and his arm speed. Before long he developed into a hard thrower capable of consistent 91-94 mph fastballs and devastating sliders. Like fellow Australian Brad Thomas, Balfour has been on a slow but steady climb up the organization ladder. He has been handled carefully along the way, but did log a career-best 58 games last year. His command and control are just average, which might keep him out of late-inning situations. He also needs to develop a more effective offspeed pitch to combat lefties, who batted .282 off him last year. Balfour heads into spring with a shot at a bullpen role, but a return to Triple-A to hone his command is more likely.

Year	Club (League)	Class	W	L	ERA	G	GS	CG	SV	IP	H	R	ER	HR	BB	SO	AVG
1997	Twins (GCL)	R	2	4	3.76	13	12	0	0	67	73	31	28	1	20	43	.292
1998	Elizabethton (Appy)	R	7	2	3.36	13	13	0	0	78	70	36	29	7	27	75	.240
1999	Quad City (Mid)	A	8	5	3.53	19	14	0	1	92	66	39	36	7	37	95	.204
2000	Fort Myers (FSL)	A	8	5	4.25	35	10	0	6	89	91	46	42	8	34	90	.263
2001	New Britain (EL)	AA	2	1	1.08	35	0	0	13	50	26	6	6	1	22	72	.149
	Minnesota (AL)	MAJ	0	0	13.50	2	0	0	0	3	3	4	4	2	3	2	.333
	Edmonton (PCL)	AAA	2	2	5.51	11	0	0	0	16	18	11	10	2	10	17	.305
2002	Edmonton (PCL)	AAA	2	4	4.16	58	0	0	8	71	60	34	33	3	30	88	.231
MAJOR LEAGUE TOTALS			0	0	13.50	2	0	0	0	3	3	4	4	2	3	2	.333
MINOR LEAGUE TOTALS			31	23	3.58	184	49	0	28	463	404	203	184	29	180	480	.237

20. Matt Vorwald, rhp

Born: Nov. 29, 1979. **Ht.:** 6-2. **Wt.:** 180. **Bats:** R. **Throws:** R. **School:** University of Illinois. **Career Transactions:** Selected by Twins in seventh round of 2001 draft; signed June 9, 2001.

Vorwald's attorney sent a lengthy letter, which included information from different counselors Vorwald had visited, to all 30 teams before the 2001 draft. The report painted a picture of a young man dealing with a number of psychological issues, and it prompted many teams to remove Vorwald from their draft boards. Twins area scout Billy Milos had built a relationship with Vorwald since his junior year of high school, however, so the Twins took a chance on him. Vorwald is very intelligent, and he's also a high-maintenance guy that Minnesota monitors closely. A year and a half into his career, the results have been encouraging. He reaches 93-95 mph with his lively fastball. His hard slider can be a plus pitch and his changeup features sink and diving action, though it doesn't always have enough separation in velocity from his fastball. Vorwald will be relegated to relief because of his maximum-effort delivery, which he has trouble repeating because of his low elbow slot. His makeup is best suited for the bullpen in any case, because it keeps him focused on every game. Barring any setbacks, Vorwald should follow Jesse Crain on the fast track to Minnesota.

Year	Club (League)	Class	W	L	ERA	G	GS	CG	SV	IP	H	R	ER	HR	BB	SO	AVG
2001	Elizabethton (Appy)	R	6	1	1.16	23	0	0	4	47	31	12	6	0	22	60	.180
2002	Quad City (Mid)	A	5	3	2.33	46	0	0	6	66	43	20	17	4	28	77	.189
MINOR LEAGUE TOTALS			11	4	1.84	69	0	0	10	112	74	32	23	4	50	137	.185

21. Brent Hoard, lhp

Born: Nov. 3, 1976. **Ht.:** 6-4. **Wt.:** 210. **Bats:** R. **Throws:** L. **School:** Stanford University. **Career Transactions:** Selected by Twins in third round of 1998 draft; signed July 15, 1998.

Pitching in the same Stanford rotation as Jeff Austin and Chad Hutchinson, with Jason Young and Justin Wayne in the pen, Hoard posted a disappointing 3-3, 6.05 record with 49 walks in 58 innings as a junior. He went in the third round anyway, and though it's been a slow climb through the Twins system, he's on the cusp of breaking into the big leagues. He has improved his control to the point that it's now one of his strengths. A confident competitor on the mound, Hoard believes he has what it takes to win as a starter, and so do the Twins. He commands three average or better pitches. His fastball, which was 87 mph in college when he threw nearly 50 percent changeups, is now clocked in the 90-92 mph range. His curveball sweeps through the zone with a tough two-plane break and his changeup, while not the same go-to pitch it once was, is average and has improved over the last season. After setting a career high in innings in 2002, Hoard was one of the most effective left-handers in the Arizona Fall League. His AFL stint may have increased his chances at getting a look from the Twins this spring, and it piqued other teams' interest, which could be important with the crowded pitching situation in Minnesota.

Year	Club (League)	Class	W	L	ERA	G	GS	CG	SV	IP	H	R	ER	HR	BB	SO	AVG
1998	Fort Wayne (Mid)	A	2	1	5.23	15	2	0	0	31	32	19	18	0	20	37	.264
1999	Quad City (Mid)	A	12	7	3.43	28	28	1	0	150	143	68	57	9	64	139	.251
2000	Fort Myers (FSL)	A	5	9	4.30	19	18	0	0	92	98	57	44	6	44	55	.272
	Quad City (Mid)	A	0	3	5.40	6	6	1	0	28	34	22	17	5	11	14	.286
2001	Fort Myers (FSL)	A	7	4	3.36	17	15	0	0	80	78	31	30	5	28	70	.263
	New Britain (EL)	AA	1	0	0.00	1	1	0	0	6	2	1	0	0	1	2	.105
2002	New Britain (EL)	AA	11	8	3.69	31	26	2	0	161	153	80	66	11	52	126	.253
MINOR LEAGUE TOTALS			38	32	3.81	117	96	4	0	548	540	278	232	36	220	443	.258

22. Juan Rincon, rhp

Born: Jan. 23, 1979. **Ht.:** 5-11. **Wt.:** 190. **Bats:** R. **Throws:** R. **Career Transactions:** Signed out of Venezuela by Twins, Nov. 4, 1996.

Rincon had a rough, brief major league debut in 2001, but it looked good compared to how he pitched in 2002. He performed like he was in front of a firing squad last year, unable to establish any sense of consistency. As a spot starter for the Twins in June and July, Rincon pitched just four times during a 26-day period before returning to Triple-A in August. He rejoined Minnesota as a reliever in September. Though Rincon has spent most of his career as a starter, scouts now project him as more of a reliever. He looks more comfortable pitching in shorter outings, where he can rely on his two best pitches—a fastball that tops out at 94 mph and a nasty slider—and less on his below-average changeup. Rincon will have a tough time getting a spot on a crowded staff in spring training, but he has provided glimpses of dominance in the past. It's now a matter of showing consistency from outing to outing.

Year	Club (League)	Class	W	L	ERA	G	GS	CG	SV	IP	H	R	ER	HR	BB	SO	AVG
1997	Twins (GCL)	R	3	3	2.95	11	10	1	0	58	55	21	19	0	24	46	.259
	Elizabethton (Appy)	R	0	1	3.86	2	1	0	0	9	11	4	4	0	3	7	.289
1998	Fort Wayne (Mid)	A	6	4	3.83	37	13	0	6	96	84	51	41	6	54	74	.232
1999	Quad City (Mid)	A	14	8	2.92	28	28	0	0	163	146	67	53	8	66	153	.239
2000	Fort Myers (FSL)	A	5	3	2.12	13	13	0	0	76	67	26	18	3	23	55	.238
	New Britain (EL)	AA	3	9	4.65	15	15	2	0	89	96	55	46	9	39	79	.267
2001	New Britain (EL)	AA	14	6	2.88	29	23	2	0	153	130	60	49	9	57	133	.226
	Minnesota (AL)	MAJ	0	0	6.35	4	0	0	0	6	7	5	4	1	5	4	.318
2002	Edmonton (PCL)	AAA	7	4	4.78	19	16	3	0	102	111	56	54	12	35	75	.278
	Minnesota (AL)	MAJ	0	2	6.28	10	3	0	0	29	44	23	20	5	9	21	.352
MAJOR LEAGUE TOTALS			0	2	6.29	14	3	0	0	34	51	28	24	6	14	25	.347
MINOR LEAGUE TOTALS			52	38	3.42	154	119	8	6	747	700	340	284	47	301	622	.247

23. Todd Sears, 1b

Born: Oct. 23, 1975. **Ht.:** 6-5. **Wt.:** 210. **Bats:** R. **Throws:** R. **School:** University. of Nebraska. **Career Transactions:** Selected by Rockies in third round of 1997 draft; signed July 3, 1997 . . . Traded by Rockies with cash to Twins for 2B Todd Walker and OF Butch Huskey, July 17, 2000.

Sears was one of Iowa's top high school athletes, starring in baseball, basketball and track, when the Angels drafted him in the 19th round in 1994. He opted to attend Nebraska, where he compiled the second-highest average (.374) in school history. The Rockies took Sears two years after drafting Todd Helton, so they moved him to third base before dealing him to the Twins in 2000. As he has moved up the ladder Sears has developed power, and he enjoyed the hitter-friendly parks in the Pacific Coast League. He has some loft to his swing and is content to serve most balls to the opposite field. The mechanics and length of his swing prevent him from turning on pitches with much authority. Not unlike incumbent Twins first baseman Doug Mientkiewicz, Sears can handle himself around the bag like a Gold Glover. Some scouts compare Sears' offensive potential to that of Dave Magadan. He could settle into the same type of role, especially because Justin Morneau is Minnesota's first baseman of the future. Sears could earn a job on the Twins' bench this spring.

Year	Club (League)	Class	AVG	G	AB	R	H	2B	3B	HR	RBI	BB	SO	SB	SLG	OBP
1997	Portland (NWL)	A	.270	55	200	37	54	13	1	2	29	41	49	2	.375	.393
1998	Asheville (SAL)	A	.290	130	459	71	133	26	2	11	82	72	89	10	.427	.387
1999	Salem (Car)	A	.281	109	385	58	108	21	0	14	59	58	99	11	.444	.379
2000	Carolina (SL)	AA	.301	86	299	54	90	21	0	12	72	72	76	12	.492	.434
	New Britain (EL)	AA	.314	40	140	15	44	8	1	3	15	18	40	1	.450	.396
	Salt Lake (PCL)	AAA	.364	3	11	2	4	1	0	1	4	1	2	0	.727	.417
2001	Edmonton (PCL)	AAA	.311	118	408	61	127	25	2	13	50	41	71	2	.478	.376
2002	Edmonton (PCL)	AAA	.310	129	484	88	150	36	4	20	100	59	142	2	.525	.388
	Minnesota (AL)	MAJ	.333	7	12	2	4	2	0	0	0	0	1	0	.500	.333
MAJOR LEAGUE TOTALS			.333	7	12	2	4	2	0	0	0	0	1	0	.500	.333
MINOR LEAGUE TOTALS			.298	670	2386	386	710	151	10	76	411	362	568	40	.465	.392

24. Kevin Frederick, rhp

Born: Nov. 4, 1976. **Ht.:** 6-1. **Wt.:** 210. **Bats:** L. **Throws:** R. **School:** Creighton University. **Career Transactions:** Selected by Twins in 34th round of 1998 draft; signed June 3, 1998.

A two-way player at Creighton, Frederick turned down the Twins as a 17th-rounder in 1997 following his junior season. A 34th-round senior sign a year later for $1,000, he's coming off the second shoulder operation of his career. He had an operation to repair a detached labrum last spring. But after five seasons in the minors, he'll head into spring training with a legitimate chance to make the big league staff. He didn't get out of Class A until he was 24, but he broke out in Double-A in 2001 and earned a spot on the 40-man roster. He's strictly a fastball/slider pitcher with 90-94 mph heat. To make the Twins he'll have to show better command and durability than he has in the past.

Year	Club (League)	Class	W	L	ERA	G	GS	CG	SV	IP	H	R	ER	HR	BB	SO	AVG
1998	Elizabethton (Appy)	R	1	4	4.25	17	0	0	1	30	28	21	14	4	10	46	.237
1999	Twins (GCL)	R	0	0	15.43	2	0	0	0	2	6	5	4	0	1	3	.500
2000	Quad City (Mid)	A	5	0	2.35	27	0	0	4	46	34	17	12	1	23	51	.210
	Fort Myers (FSL)	A	2	1	2.70	19	0	0	3	30	20	11	9	0	14	37	.189
2001	Fort Myers (FSL)	A	2	0	1.00	9	0	0	1	18	9	2	2	1	3	19	.145
	New Britain (EL)	AA	6	2	1.63	44	0	0	7	83	56	17	15	5	28	109	.195
2002	Edmonton (PCL)	AAA	3	6	4.58	46	2	0	22	55	63	31	28	8	21	47	.289
	Minnesota (AL)	MAJ	0	0	10.03	8	0	0	0	12	13	13	13	3	10	5	.283
MAJOR LEAGUE TOTALS			0	0	10.03	8	0	0	0	12	13	13	13	3	10	5	.283
MINOR LEAGUE TOTALS			19	13	2.87	164	2	0	38	264	216	104	84	19	100	312	.224

25. Travis Bowyer, rhp

Born: Aug. 3, 1981. **Ht.:** 6-3. **Wt.:** 225. **Bats:** R. **Throws:** R. **School:** Liberty HS, Bedford, Va. **Career Transactions:** Selected by Twins in 20th round of 1999 draft; signed June 9, 1999.

Three years into his career, Bowyer wasn't considered much of a prospect. He was floundering in Rookie ball with mediocre stuff. But a rigorous offseason of conditioning created a thick, 225-pound frame—he weighed 180 pounds when he was drafted—and he came into last spring with added velocity. A move to the bullpen helped him maintain it and his stock began to soar. Mostly an upper-80s pitcher in the past, Bowyer reached as high as 96 mph. His fastball is heavy, and his changeup is becoming a dependable second pitch. His breaking ball is a work in progress and could determine his ultimate role. He was moved back to the rotation near the end of last season and continued to start in instructional league. He'll be promoted to pitcher-friendly Fort Myers this year.

Year	Club (League)	Class	W	L	ERA	G	GS	CG	SV	IP	H	R	ER	HR	BB	SO	AVG
1999	Twins (GCL)	R	1	0	0.00	1	0	0	0	1	0	0	0	0	0	1	.000
2000	Twins (GCL)	R	3	5	4.07	12	12	1	0	55	55	31	25	2	22	36	.255
2001	Elizabethton (Appy)	R	2	5	6.10	9	8	0	0	38	38	30	26	3	20	34	.266
2002	Quad City (Mid)	A	4	4	2.16	39	9	0	3	92	74	28	22	2	46	90	.224
MINOR LEAGUE TOTALS			10	14	3.53	61	29	1	3	186	167	89	73	7	88	161	.241

26. Jose Morban, ss

Born: Dec. 2, 1979. **Ht.:** 6-1. **Wt.:** 170. **Bats:** R. **Throws:** R. **Career Transactions:** Signed out of Dominican Republic by Rangers, Dec. 15, 1996 . . . Selected by Twins from Rangers in major league Rule 5 draft, Dec. 16, 2002.

The Twins addressed an organization weakness by plucking Morban from the Rangers in the major league Rule 5 draft. They hope he can provide the same lift as a defensive middle infielder/pinch-runner that 2001 Rule 5 pick Luis Ugueto did for the Mariners last year. Despite Morban's five-tool potential and pure shortstop actions, he didn't fit in with the Rangers' new philosophies on plate discipline. He has struggled to improve his pitch recognition and two-strike approach, and it will be much more difficult to adapt at the big league level. He frustrated Texas with his inconsistency. While he improved his basestealing technique in 2002, he topped 100 strikeouts for the third consecutive season and made 34 errors. Minnesota will try to be more patient.

Year	Club (League)	Class	AVG	G	AB	R	H	2B	3B	HR	RBI	BB	SO	SB	SLG	OBP
1997	Rangers (DSL)	R	.313	13	16	5	5	0	0	0	2	4	7	3	.313	.450
1998	Rangers (DSL)	R	.232	54	168	31	39	10	5	4	25	24	35	13	.423	.338
1999	Rangers (GCL)	R	.283	54	205	45	58	10	5	4	18	31	70	19	.439	.378
2000	Savannah (SAL)	A	.220	80	273	44	60	8	4	4	28	41	79	27	.322	.330
	Pulaski (Appy)	R	.225	30	120	21	27	3	2	3	17	12	35	6	.358	.293
2001	Savannah (SAL)	A	.251	122	474	71	119	20	11	8	47	42	119	46	.390	.313
2002	Charlotte (FSL)	A	.260	126	485	75	126	27	12	8	66	46	111	21	.414	.326
MINOR LEAGUE TOTALS			.249	479	1741	292	434	78	39	31	203	200	456	135	.392	.330

27. Alexander Smit, lhp

Born: Oct. 2, 1985. **Ht.:** 6-3. **Wt.:** 190. **Bats:** L. **Throws:** L. **Career Transactions:** Signed out of Netherlands by Twins, July 14, 2002.

The Twins outbid the Yankees and Mariners for Smit last summer, signing him for $800,000. Smit, who was named the best junior (16-18 years old) pitcher in the Netherlands for two straight years, pitched in the World Junior Championship before reporting to instructional league for his first taste of pro ball. Minnesota is betting on Smit developing into a big, physical and athletic lefty in the mold of unsigned Orioles first-rounder Adam Loewen. The Twins believe Smit has the arm and delivery to fulfill their projection. Smit pitched in the mid- to upper 80s and topped out at 91 mph in instructional league. His changeup and ability to keep the ball down in the zone were particularly impressive to scouts. Smit has a chance to establish himself as one of the top lefties in the organization and one of the few who could remain a starter. The Twins have a good track record with helping foreign players adapt and will develop him cautiously, probably keeping him in extended spring training before sending him to one of their short-season clubs for his professional debut in 2003.

Year	Club (League)	Class	W	L	ERA	G	GS	CG	SV	IP	H	R	ER	HR	BB	SO	AVG
		Has Not Played—Signed 2003 Contract															

28. Angel Garcia, rhp

Born: Oct. 28, 1983. **Ht.:** 6-7. **Wt.:** 210. **Bats:** R. **Throws:** R. **School:** Nicolas Sevilla HS, Dorado, P.R. **Career Transactions:** Selected by Twins in fourth round of 2001 draft; signed June 19, 2001.

Garcia converted from catcher to the mound only months before the 2001 draft, yet he was still regarded as the top pitching prospect in Puerto Rico. His velocity steadily increased leading up to the draft, but after he signed for $310,000 the Twins overhauled his delivery and watched his velocity dip in 2002. It should be to his benefit in the long run. Garcia was hitting 95 mph with his fastball, but he was throwing directly over the top with no deception to hitters and no life on his stuff. He dropped down to a traditional three-quarters arm slot and added movement. He worked around 89-90 mph last year, and Minnesota expected his velocity to creep back into the plus range. His breaking ball has improved and his deceptive changeup—which was taught to him by fellow countryman and former big leaguer Edwin Correa—has the makings of an above-average pitch. Garcia is a work in progress and will be handled with kid gloves during his slow ascent. He might not make his full-season debut until 2004.

Year	Club (League)	Class	W	L	ERA	G	GS	CG	SV	IP	H	R	ER	HR	BB	SO	AVG
2001	Twins (GCL)	R	0	3	5.60	9	6	0	0	18	20	15	11	0	12	22	.286
2002	Twins (GCL)	R	4	4	3.40	13	7	0	0	53	41	24	20	0	31	63	.217
MINOR LEAGUE TOTALS			4	7	3.95	22	13	0	0	71	61	39	31	0	43	85	.236

29. Mike Ryan, of

Born: July 6, 1977. **Ht.:** 6-0. **Wt.:** 180. **Bats:** L. **Throws:** R. **School:** Indiana (Pa.) HS. **Career Transactions:** Selected by Twins in fifth round of 1996 draft; signed June 7, 1996.

After six undistinguished seasons in the Twins system, Ryan emerged as an intriguing prospect in his second tour of the Pacific Coast League. He had earned a reputation as a one-dimensional hitter with limited versatility, before he tied Diamondbacks prospect Scott Hairston for the minor league lead in extra-base hits and launched a career-best 31 home runs. Ryan drove in 101 runs primarily hitting out of the leadoff spot. A converted infielder, Ryan was drafted as a third baseman and move to second base in 1999 because he didn't hit for enough power. Last year was his first full season in the outfield. Ryan hit 27 of his homers against righties and slugged just .439 against lefties, so he has been labeled as a platoon player. Still, that kind of juice from the left side of the plate isn't easy to come by. Strong wrists enable him to turn on hard inside stuff and drive the ball. Ryan also impressed the Twins by turning up his aggressiveness after playing tentatively early in his career. Ryan's running, throwing and fielding grade out as below-average, likely limiting him to a reserve role. He'll be hard-pressed to win a job in the Twins' crowded outfield and could be headed for another season of Triple-A ball.

Year	Club (League)	Class	AVG	G	AB	R	H	2B	3B	HR	RBI	BB	SO	SB	SLG	OBP
1996	Twins (GCL)	R	.197	43	157	12	31	8	2	0	13	13	20	3	.274	.260
1997	Elizabethton (Appy)	R	.300	62	220	44	66	10	0	3	29	38	39	2	.386	.404
1998	Fort Wayne (Mid)	A	.318	113	412	68	131	24	6	9	72	44	92	7	.471	.381
1999	Fort Myers (FSL)	A	.274	131	507	85	139	26	5	8	71	63	60	3	.393	.356
2000	New Britain (EL)	AA	.277	122	481	64	133	23	8	11	69	34	79	4	.426	.323
	Salt Lake (PCL)	AAA	.222	3	9	1	2	0	0	0	2	3	2	0	.222	.417
2001	Edmonton (PCL)	AAA	.288	135	527	89	152	36	7	18	73	52	121	1	.486	.353
2002	Edmonton (PCL)	AAA	.261	131	540	92	141	36	6	31	101	55	124	4	.522	.330
	Minnesota (AL)	MAJ	.091	7	11	3	1	0	0	0	0	0	2	0	.091	.091
MAJOR LEAGUE TOTALS			.091	7	11	3	1	0	0	0	0	0	2	0	.091	.091
MINOR LEAGUE TOTALS			.279	740	2853	455	795	163	34	80	430	302	537	24	.444	.348

30. B.J. Garbe, of

Born: Feb. 3, 1981. **Ht.:** 6-2. **Wt.:** 190. **Bats:** R. **Throws:** R. **School:** Moses Lake (Wash.) HS. **Career Transactions:** Selected by Twins in first round (fifth overall) of 1999 draft; signed July 7, 1999.

Garbe was the gem of the nationally acclaimed trio of Moses Lake High prospects in 1999. He went fifth overall, while Jason Cooper (now with the Indians) and Ryan Doumit (Pirates) were taken in the second round. Garbe, who also was a top quarterback recruit after rushing and passing for more than 1,000 yards during his senior year, hasn't been able to translate his natural athleticism into baseball skills in his first four years in pro ball. The Twins hope he can turn the corner as did Torii Hunter, another first-rounder and pure athlete who struggled in the minors before figuring it out. Like Hunter, Garbe's strongest tools are his fly-chasing ability and his plus arm strength. Of course, Garbe's .619 on-base plus slugging percentage while repeating high Class A has skeptics wondering how he'll ever develop into a major league-caliber hitter. While he showcases plus-plus bat speed and generates above-average raw power, Garbe's approach is unrefined and he usually finds himself behind in the count. He hasn't made the adjustments at the plate to lay off off-speed stuff in the dirt because his pitch recognition hasn't improved. This will be a pivotal season for him in Double-A.

Year	Club (League)	Class	AVG	G	AB	R	H	2B	3B	HR	RBI	BB	SO	SB	SLG	OBP
1999	Elizabethton (Appy)	R	.316	41	171	33	54	8	0	3	32	20	34	4	.415	.391
2000	Quad City (Mid)	A	.233	133	476	62	111	12	3	5	51	63	91	14	.303	.333
2001	Fort Myers (FSL)	A	.242	127	463	55	112	14	4	6	61	50	86	13	.328	.331
2002	Fort Myers (FSL)	A	.239	115	427	46	102	13	2	5	45	36	89	18	.314	.305
MINOR LEAGUE TOTALS			.247	416	1537	196	379	47	9	19	189	170	300	49	.326	.331

MONTREAL
EXPOS

TOP 30 PROSPECTS

1. Clint Everts, rhp
2. Mike Hinckley, lhp
3. Josh Karp, rhp
4. Zach Day, rhp
5. Seung Song, rhp
6. Darrell Rasner, rhp
7. Claudio Vargas, rhp
8. Chris Young, rhp
9. Scott Hodges, 3b
10. Larry Broadway, 1b
11. Eric Good, lhp
12. Brandon Watson, of
13. Luke Lockwood, lhp
14. Rich Rundles, lhp
15. Cristobal Rodriguez, rhp
16. Ron Calloway, of
17. Terrmel Sledge, of
18. Val Pascucci, of
19. Rob Caputo, rhp
20. Matt Cepicky, of
21. Chad Bentz, lhp
22. Josh Labandeira, ss
23. Shawn Hill, rhp
24. Nick Long, rhp
25. David Thorne, rhp
26. Reg Fitzpatrick, of
27. Josh Girdley, lhp
28. Ignacio Puello, rhp
29. Greg Thissen, 2b
30. Ron Chiavacci, rhp

By Michael Levesque

For the first time in recent memory, the Expos utilized their farm system to bolster their major league club during the 2002 season. Despite all the upheaval with ownership, the front office and the roster, Montreal went 83-79 and finished second in the National League East–the team's best finish since 1996.

Unfortunately for the Expos, their minor league system now lacks premium position prospects and overall depth. In midseason blockbusters that brought in Bartolo Colon and Cliff Floyd, plus a spring trade for Matt Herges, general manager Omar Minaya dealt six players (Brandon Phillips, Grady Sizemore, Justin Wayne, Cliff Lee, Don Levinski, Wilkin Ruan) who entered 2002 rated among Montreal's top 13 prospects. The purge didn't stop there, as former No. 1 prospect Donnie Bridges (trade) and shortstop Wilson Valdez (waivers) went to the Marlins and Phil Seibel, Matt Watson, Jason Bay and Jim Serrano went to the Mets in minor deals.

It was still a successful year for Montreal's player-development system, though. In addition to having the prospects to acquire players the stature of Colon and Floyd, two homegrown players played key roles in the major league club's success. Outfielder/first baseman Brad Wilkerson broke the team record for homers by a rookie with 20, and righthander T.J. Tucker made a solid contribution out of the bullpen before a lower back strain in August rendered him ineffective. Minaya also recouped some of the lost talent by trading Floyd and Colon away again.

Montreal started the year with both the front office and coaching staff being put together by Major League Baseball–which assumed the ownership of the Expos–less than two weeks before spring training began. With just nine full-time scouts, scouting director Dana Brown's department did a fine job. The draft yielded promising righthanders Clint Everts and Darrell Rasner, and brought-much needed power with first baseman Larry Broadway and outfielder Chad Chop.

Adam Wogan, one of the few holdovers from the Jeffrey Loria regime, has climbed the organizational ladder quickly. He did a standout job in his first year as farm director, especially under the circumstances. He put together an impressive staff that included pitching guru Brent Strom and 288-game winner Tommy John. Wogan also instilled a sense of calm among the ranks.

OrganizationOverview

General Manager: Omar Minaya. **Farm Director:** Adam Wogan. **Scouting Director:** Dana Brown.

2002 PERFORMANCE

Class	Farm Team	League	W	L	Pct.	Finish*	Manager(s)
Majors	Montreal	National	83	79	.512	7th (16)	Frank Robinson
Triple-A	†Ottawa Lynx	International	80	61	.567	3rd (14)	Tim Leiper
Double-A	Harrisburg Senators	Eastern	79	63	.556	2nd (12)	Dave Huppert
High A	Brevard County Manatees	Florida State	50	85	.370	12th (12)	Bob Didier/Tony Torchia
Low A	#Clinton Lumber Kings	Midwest	61	75	.449	11th (14)	Dave Machemer
Short-season	Vermont Expos	New York-Penn	30	45	.400	12th (14)	Dave Barnett
Rookie	GCL Expos	Gulf Coast	28	32	.467	t-8th (14)	Andy Skeels
OVERALL 2002 MINOR LEAGUE RECORD			329	361	.476	20th (30)	

*Finish in overall standings (No. of teams in league). †Affiliate will be in Edmonton (Pacific Coast) in 2003. #Affiliate will be in Savannah (South Atlantic) in 2003.

ORGANIZATION LEADERS

BATTING   *Minimum 250 At-Bats
*AVG	Endy Chavez, Ottawa	.343
R	Terrmel Sledge, Ottawa/Harrisburg	86
H	Scott Hodges, Harrisburg	143
TB	Joe Vitiello, Ottawa	224
2B	Luis Ortiz, Ottawa	38
3B	Terrmel Sledge, Ottawa/Harrisburg	8
HR	Val Pascucci, Harrisburg	27
RBI	Joe Vitiello, Ottawa	82
	Val Pascucci, Harrisburg	82
BB	Val Pascucci, Harrisburg	93
SO	Lorvin Louisa, Clinton/Vermont	121
SB	Danny Rombley, Brevard County/Clinton	28

PITCHING   #Minimum 75 Innings
W	Julio Manon, Ottawa/Harrisburg	13
L	Ignacio Puello, Clinton	14
#ERA	Bryan Hebson, Ottawa/Harrisburg	2.00
G	David Maust, Brevard County/Clinton	49
CG	Julio Manon, Ottawa/Harrisburg	2
SV	Todd Williams, Ottawa	24
IP	Darwin Marrero, Harrisburg/Brevard County	160
BB	Ignacio Puello, Clinton	66
SO	Julio Manon, Ottawa/Harrisburg	132

BEST TOOLS

Best Hitter for Average	Terrmel Sledge
Best Power Hitter	Larry Broadway
Fastest Baserunner	Brandon Watson
Best Athlete	Brandon Watson
Best Fastball	Cristobal Rodriguez
Best Curveball	Clint Everts
Best Slider	Ron Chiavacci
Best Changeup	Josh Karp
Best Control	Mike Hinckley
Best Defensive Catcher	Drew McMillan
Best Defensive Infielder	Scott Hodges
Best Infield Arm	Felix Diaz
Best Defensive Outfielder	Brandon Watson
Best Outfield Arm	Lorvin Louisa

PROJECTED 2006 LINEUP

Catcher	Michael Barrett
First Base	Larry Broadway
Second Base	Jose Vidro
Third Base	Scott Hodges
Shortstop	Orlando Cabrera
Left Field	Brad Wilkerson
Center Field	Endy Chavez
Right Field	Vladimir Guerrero
No. 1 Starter	Javier Vazquez
No. 2 Starter	Clint Everts

Endy Chavez   **Bryan Hebson**

No. 3 Starter	Tony Armas
No. 4 Starter	Mike Hinckley
No. 5 Starter	Josh Karp
Closer	Zach Day

TOP PROSPECTS OF THE DECADE

1993	Cliff Floyd, 1b/of
1994	Cliff Floyd, 1b/of
1995	Ugueth Urbina, rhp
1996	Vladimir Guerrero, of
1997	Vladimir Guerrero, of
1998	Brad Fullmer, 1b
1999	Michael Barrett, 3b/c
2000	Tony Armas, rhp
2001	Donnie Bridges, rhp
2002	Brandon Phillips, ss

TOP DRAFT PICKS OF THE DECADE

1993	Chris Schwab, of
1994	Hiram Bocachica, ss
1995	Michael Barrett, ss
1996	*John Patterson, rhp
1997	Donnie Bridges, rhp
1998	Josh McKinley, ss
1999	Josh Girdley, lhp
2000	Justin Wayne, rhp
2001	Josh Karp, rhp
2002	Clint Everts, rhp

*Did not sign.

ALL-TIME LARGEST BONUSES

Justin Wayne, 2000	$2,950,000
Josh Karp, 2001	2,650,000
Clint Everts, 2002	2,500,000
Grady Sizemore, 2000	2,000,000
Josh Girdley, 1999	1,700,000

MinorLeague**Depth**Chart

MONTREAL EXPOS

29
RANK

If any organization traded one-third of its top 30 prospects, the cupboard would be pretty bare. That's exactly what general manager Omar Minaya has done to the Expos since Major League Baseball took over the Montreal franchise. Shortstop Brandon Phillips and lefthander Cliff Lee would have ranked Nos. 1-2 had they not been sent to Cleveland with outfielder Grady Sizemore, another top 10 lock, to rent Bartolo Colon last season. The return for Colon, who was dealt to the White Sox, didn't come close to replenishing the system's depth. Scouting director Dana Brown did a noble job on the fly in his first draft, but as long as MLB operates the Expos, it is clear the system will be sacrificed without regard for the future.

Note: Depth charts prepared by Josh Boyd. Numbers in parentheses indicate prospect rankings.

LF
Terrmel Sledge (17)
Matt Cepicky (20)
Roger Bernadina
Dominic Ambrosini

CF
Brandon Watson (12)
Ron Calloway (16)
Reg Fitzpatrick (26)

RF
Danny Rombley
Frank Diaz
Antonio Sucre

3B
Scott Hodges (9)
Felix Diaz

SS
Josh Labandeira (22)
Jose Contreras

2B
Greg Thissen (29)
Henry Mateo
Josh McKinley
Albenis Machado

1B
Larry Broadway (10)
Val Pascucci (18)
Chad Chop
Jeff Bailey

C
Drew McMillan
Saloman Manriquez

LHP
Starters	**Relievers**
Mike Hinckley (2)	Chad Bentz (21)
Eric Good (11)	Anthony Ferrari
Luke Lockwood (13)	Ben Dequin
Rich Rundles (14)	
Josh Girdley (27)	
Hector Cerezo	
Pierre-Luc Marceau	
Jon Felfoldi	
Brett Nyquist	
Tyler Kirkman	

RHP
Starters	**Relievers**
Clint Everts (1)	Cristobal Rodriguez (15)
Josh Karp (3)	David Thorne (25)
Zach Day (4)	Ignacio Puello (28)
Seung Song (5)	Ron Chiavacci (30)
Darrell Rasner (6)	Julio Manon
Claudio Vargas (7)	Luis Ayala
Chris Young (8)	Chris Schroeder
Rob Caputo (19)	Pat Collins
Shawn Hill (23)	
Nick Long (24)	
Stockton Davis	
Anthony Pearson	
Gustavo Mata	
Jason Bergmann	

DraftAnalysis

2002 Draft

Best Pro Debut: LHP Mike O'Connor (7) limited hitters to a .174 average and struck out 66 in 43 innings, and RHP Stockton Davis (21) had a 2.15 ERA and 81 whiffs in 71 innings. RHP **Jason Bergmann** (11) also had a strong performance, going 7-4, 2.89. All three pitched in the short-season New York-Penn League.

Best Athlete: RHP Clint Everts (1), the fifth overall pick, could have gone in the first three rounds as a shortstop. He repeats his delivery so easily that the command and quality of his stuff rarely waver.

Best Pure Hitter: The Expos selected only two hitters in the first 15 rounds. 1B Chad Chop (6) spent two years at San Diego State before transferring to little-known Vanguard (Calif.) and becoming the highest draft pick in school history.

Best Raw Power: 1B Larry Broadway (3) was one of the most dangerous longball threats in the Cape Cod League in 2001, but he's had a power outage since. He hit .315 in the NY-P and there's still plenty of strength in his 6-foot-4, 230-pound frame.

Fastest Runner: OF Anthony Brown (18) runs the 60-yard dash in 6.6 seconds.

Best Defensive Player: Broadway moves well around the bag at first base and has a strong arm. 2B Jason Conlisk (17) is the best among the up-the-middle players.

Best Fastball: Everts, who turned 18 in August, already throws 90-94 mph. And at times his fastball is his third-best pitch.

Best Breaking Ball: Everts had the draft's best curveball. He throws it as hard as 84

mph, and it gets a true 12-to-6 break. He also has aptitude for his changeup, which sometimes rates a 65 on the 20-80 scouting scale.

Most Intriguing Background: Everts and the Mets' Scott Kazmir made Houston's Cypress Falls High the fourth high school to produce two first-rounders in the same June draft. RHP Chris Barlow's (9) father Mike pitched in parts of seven big league seasons.

RICH ABEL

Bergmann

Closest To The Majors: RHP Darrell Rasner (2) combines pitching savvy, deception and four solid pitches. Everts held out all summer but could close on Rasner fast.

Best Late-Round Pick: Davis split time between DH and pitching at Oral Roberts and came cheap as a senior sign. He responded by touching 91 mph every time out, and his top pitch is a mid-80s slider.

The One Who Got Away: RHP Sean White (35) looked good in the Cape League last summer, but the Expos didn't have the money to spend on him. He returned to Washington.

Assessment: First-year scouting director Dana Brown had just nine scouts, and they didn't hit the road until mid-March. Radar guns and computers weren't available until mid-April. And yet the Expos had a credible draft, signing 23 of their first 26 picks, and landed a potential superstar pitcher.

2001 Draft

The Expos already have traded their best selection, RHP Don Levinski (2). RHP Josh Karp (1) and LHP Mike Hinckley (3) look like they'll help Montreal.   **Grade: B**

2000 Draft

All the best players from a strong draft have been dealt away: RHP Justin Wayne (1), OFs Grady Sizemore (3) and Jason Bay (22) and LHPs Cliff Lee (4) and Phil Seibel (8).   **Grade: B+**

1999 Draft

Same story: SS/2B Brandon Phillips (2) looks like a star, but he's now in Cleveland. LHP Josh Girdley (1) hasn't stayed healthy.   **Grade: B+**

1998 Draft

SS Josh McKinley (1) was a failed signability pick. At least the Expos had the sense to hold onto OF Brad Wilkerson (1).   **Grade: B**

Note: Draft analysis prepared by Jim Callis. Numbers in parentheses indicate draft rounds.

. . . Everts had the best curveball in the 2002 draft, a power curve that falls off the table.

Clint Everts rhp

Born: Aug. 10, 1984.
Ht.: 6-2. **Wt.:** 170.
Bats: R. **Throws:** R.
School: Cypress Falls HS, Houston.
Career Transactions:
Selected by Expos in first round (fifth overall) of 2002 draft; signed Aug. 24, 2002.

With the selection of Everts fifth overall, the Expos have taken a pitcher with their first pick in six of the last seven drafts. Everts and Scott Kazmir, who went 15th overall to the Mets, became the fourth pair of high school teammates to be chosen in the first round of the same draft. There were rumors that Everts had agreed to a predraft deal, but he held out throughout the summer. He finally signed in late August for $2.5 million, passing on a scholarship to Baylor. A two-way player in high school, Everts also attracted interest as a shortstop. He pitched for the U.S. national youth team in 2000, earning a gold medal at the Pan American Championships in Monterrey, Mexico.

Everts has the potential to be a front-of-the-rotation starter. He's an outstanding athlete with a slender frame that projects to fill out as he matures. He has a loose, quick, smooth arm action, using a high three-quarters arm slot and a balanced delivery to produce three above-average pitches. Everts had the best curveball in the 2002 draft. It's a 78-84 mph power curve that falls off the table with good spin, bite and two-plane break. His curve gets top marks on the 20-80 scouting scale, with one National League scouting director saying, "If that's not an 80 curveball, I'll never see one." Everts' fastball arrives at 90-94 mph with late movement. At times his circle changeup is his second-best pitch. He throws it at 78-81 mph with deception, sink, tumbling action and excellent arm speed. He has command of all his pitches, is a strong fielder, and has a good feel for pitching and plus makeup.

The Expos didn't hold instructional league, so Everts lost his first chance to gain what he needs most: experience. He has thrown an awful lot of curveballs at an early age, but hasn't had arm problems. All he seems to need are repetitions and added strength.

Though many expected Montreal to draft a collegian, Expos scouting director Dana Brown was ecstatic to select Everts. He should make his pro debut at Montreal's new low Class A Savannah affiliate. Though high school pitchers are a risky demographic, Everts could zoom through the system.

Year	Club (League)	Class	W	L	ERA	G	GS	CG	SV	IP	H	R	ER	HR	BB	SO	AVG
					Has Not Played—Signed 2003 Contract												

2. Mike Hinckley, lhp

Born: Oct. 5, 1982. **Ht.:** 6-3. **Wt.:** 170. **Bats:** R. **Throws:** L. **School:** Moore (Okla.) HS.
Career Transactions: Selected by Expos in third round of 2001 draft; signed July 5, 2001.

Hinckley came on strong as a high school senior before the 2001 draft, emerging from obscurity to become a third-rounder. After a lackluster debut, he led the short-season New York-Penn league in ERA and innings last season. Hinckley already touches 94 mph and sits in the low 90s, and some scouts project him to add more consistent velocity as he fills out his lean frame. He works with a low-stress arm action and delivery, allowing him to command all his pitches. He generates good sink, and his 79-82 mph changeup is an effective pitch against righthanders. Hinckley's curveball, a 74-78 mph bender with tight rotation, already is a plus pitch and should get better. He also has the best work ethic in the organization. Hinckley just needs to add strength and innings. He showed improvement in all areas of his game last year, doing a better job of pitching inside and improving the overall quality of his stuff. He learned to channel his intensity so he wouldn't overthrow and cost himself control and life with his pitches. The Expos envision Hinckley developing into a frontline starter. He'll make his full-season debut at Savannah in 2003.

Year	Club (League)	Class	W	L	ERA	G	GS	CG	SV	IP	H	R	ER	HR	BB	SO	AVG
2001	Expos (GCL)	R	2	2	5.24	8	5	0	0	34	46	23	20	1	12	28	.329
2002	Vermont (NY-P)	A	6	2	1.37	16	16	0	0	92	60	19	14	4	30	66	.188
MINOR LEAGUE TOTALS			8	4	2.43	24	21	0	0	126	106	42	34	5	42	94	.231

3. Josh Karp, rhp

Born: Sept. 21, 1979. **Ht.:** 6-5. **Wt.:** 210. **Bats:** R. **Throws:** R. **School:** UCLA. **Career Transactions:** Selected by Expos in first round (sixth overall) of 2001 draft; signed Sept. 27, 2001.

The sixth overall pick in 2001, Karp signed for $2.65 million and made his pro debut last year. He needed just seven starts at high Class A Brevard County to earn a promotion to Double-A Harrisburg. He missed a month with shoulder tendinitis, but returned to represent the Expos at the Futures Game. When everything is working for Karp, some scouts grade out his raw stuff equal to that of former Pacific-10 Conference rival Mark Prior. He has a prototypical pitcher's body and three plus pitches: a 91-94 mph fastball with good life, a tight downer curveball and a circle changeup. He has a balanced delivery and a quick, easy arm action. The Expos have urged Karp to use his fastball more. He'll have to find a way to battle lefthanders after they hit .331 against him in Double-A. He needs to improve the consistency of all his pitches, as he sometimes loses his mechanics and then overcompensates. Montreal plans to take it slow with Karp, who struggled in the Arizona Fall League while sick with strep throat. He could return to Double-A to begin 2003.

Year	Club (League)	Class	W	L	ERA	G	GS	CG	SV	IP	H	R	ER	HR	BB	SO	AVG
2002	Brevard County (FSL)	A	4	1	1.59	7	7	0	0	45	31	9	8	1	11	43	.190
	Harrisburg (EL)	AA	7	5	3.84	16	16	0	0	87	83	43	37	6	34	69	.256
MINOR LEAGUE TOTALS			11	6	3.07	23	23	0	0	132	114	52	45	7	45	112	.234

4. Zach Day, rhp

Born: June 15, 1978. **Ht.:** 6-4. **Wt.:** 180. **Bats:** R. **Throws:** R. **School:** LaSalle HS, Cincinnati. **Career Transactions:** Selected by Yankees in fifth round of 1996 draft; signed July 14, 1996 . . . Traded by Yankees with RHP Jake Westbrook to Indians, July 24, 2000, completing trade in which Indians sent OF David Justice to Yankees for OF Ricky Ledee and two players to be named (June 29, 2000) . . . Traded by Indians to Expos for OF Milton Bradley, July 31, 2001.

Day spent his first full season in the Expos system after coming over from the Indians in a July 2001 trade for Milton Bradley. After starting the season with Triple-A Ottawa, he beat the Blue Jays to become the first pitcher in big league history to win his debut on his birthday. Day threw his fastball in the 87-90 mph range early last season, but in September he was working out of the Montreal bullpen and pumping 93-97 mph four-seamers with outstanding arm-side action. He also did an excellent job of changing planes by mixing in a heavy 88-92 mph sinker, a plus 79-83 mph curveball and an improving changeup. Day has a strong pitcher's body, and the Expos also praise his demeanor and intelligence. Occasionally, Day will fly open with his front shoulder in his delivery. When that happens, he loses command and leaves his pitches high in the strike zone. With his strong performance in Montreal, Day earned the right to compete for a spot in the rotation. He could become a No. 1 or 2 starter, though he also could be their closer of the future.

Year	Club (League)	Class	W	L	ERA	G	GS	CG	SV	IP	H	R	ER	HR	BB	SO	AVG
1996	Yankees (GCL)	R	5	2	5.61	7	5	0	0	34	41	26	21	3	3	23	.311
1997	Oneonta (NY-P)	A	7	2	2.15	14	14	0	0	92	82	26	22	2	23	92	.240
1998	Tampa (FSL)	A	5	8	5.49	18	17	0	0	100	142	89	61	5	32	69	.326
	Greensboro (SAL)	A	1	2	2.75	7	6	1	0	36	35	22	11	1	6	37	.245
1999	Yankees (GCL)	R	1	1	3.78	5	4	0	0	17	20	10	7	1	4	17	.290
	Greensboro (SAL)	A	0	1	2.25	2	2	0	0	8	14	11	2	0	1	4	.359
2000	Greensboro (SAL)	A	9	3	1.90	13	13	1	0	85	72	29	18	6	31	101	.232
	Tampa (FSL)	A	2	4	4.19	7	7	0	0	34	33	22	16	2	15	36	.246
	Akron (EL)	AA	4	2	3.52	8	8	0	0	46	38	20	18	1	21	43	.232
2001	Akron (EL)	AA	9	10	3.10	22	22	2	0	137	123	57	47	8	45	94	.237
	Buffalo (IL)	AAA	1	0	1.50	1	1	0	0	6	3	1	1	0	1	4	.143
	Ottawa (IL)	AAA	2	2	7.43	6	5	0	0	27	38	23	22	2	8	15	.349
2002	Ottawa (IL)	AAA	5	6	3.50	17	16	1	0	90	77	38	35	5	32	68	.231
	Montreal (NL)	MAJ	4	1	3.62	19	2	0	1	37	28	18	15	3	15	25	.207
MAJOR LEAGUE TOTALS			4	1	3.62	19	2	0	1	37	28	18	15	3	15	25	.207
MINOR LEAGUE TOTALS			51	43	3.56	127	120	5	0	711	718	374	281	36	222	603	.261

5. Seung Song, rhp

Born: June 29, 1980. **Ht.:** 6-1. **Wt.:** 190. **Bats:** R. **Throws:** R. **Career Transactions:** Signed out of Korea by Red Sox, Feb. 2, 1999 . . . Traded by Red Sox with RHP Sun-Woo Kim to Expos for OF Cliff Floyd, July 30, 2002.

Song entered 2002 as Boston's top prospect and pitched in the Futures Game for the second consecutive year. But after coming to Montreal in a trade for Cliff Floyd, he finished the summer under the care of the Expos' medical staff. Trying to impress his new organization, he overthrew in his first start and missed the remainder of the season with a shoulder injury that didn't require surgery. Song has uncanny command of two plus pitches: a 90-94 mph fastball with arm-side tail and a 77-78 mph curveball. His changeup is effective. He has a good idea how to pitch, mix speeds and throw strikes. His arm stroke is a bit long, but he maintains his release point and does a good job of hiding the ball. Song puts a lot of stress on his shoulder with his corkscrew delivery. The Expos addressed it before he began to rehabilitate his injury. He also had elbow problems before the trade. Song could form a devastating one-two punch with Josh Karp in Double-A. Barring any more health problems, Song could make his big league debut after the all-star break.

Year	Club (League)	Class	W	L	ERA	G	GS	CG	SV	IP	H	R	ER	HR	BB	SO	AVG
1999	Red Sox (GCL)	R	5	5	2.30	13	9	0	0	55	47	29	14	2	20	61	.227
2000	Lowell (NY-P)	A	5	2	2.60	13	13	0	0	73	63	26	21	1	20	93	.233
2001	Augusta (SAL)	A	3	2	2.04	14	14	0	0	75	56	24	17	3	18	79	.208
	Sarasota (FSL)	A	5	2	1.68	8	8	0	0	48	28	11	9	1	18	56	.164
2002	Trenton (EL)	AA	7	7	4.39	21	21	0	0	109	106	61	53	11	37	116	.256
	Harrisburg (EL)	AA	0	0	0.00	1	1	0	0	5	5	2	0	0	0	5	.250
MINOR LEAGUE TOTALS			25	18	2.82	70	66	0	0	364	305	153	114	18	113	410	.226

6. Darrell Rasner, rhp

Born: Jan. 13, 1981. **Ht.:** 6-3. **Wt.:** 210. **Bats:** R. **Throws:** R. **Career Transactions:** Selected by Expos in second round of 2002 draft; signed July 2, 2002.

After taking Clint Everts in the first round, the Expos focused on college players for the rest of the 2002 draft. Rasner set Nevada's single-season win mark with 14 as a freshman in 2000, and two years later he had claimed Wolf Pack career records for victories (28), strikeouts (302) and innings (341). After signing for $800,000, he allowed two runs or less in six of his 10 pro starts, including back-to-back one-hit outings. Rasner gets heavy sink and run on his 90-94 mph fastball. He complements it with an 84-85 mph slider with good tilt. He also throws a circle changeup and a downer curveball. Rasner is a physical pitcher. He has an athletic frame with a strong upper half and wide shoulders. His balanced delivery includes a quick arm action, plus good follow-through and extension. Rasner scuffles with his command because he has an inconsistent release point. When he keeps his front side closed, he's able to throw strikes with greater ease. Look for Rasner to jump on the fast track in 2003. With a good spring, he could open the season in high Class A.

Year	Club (League)	Class	W	L	ERA	G	GS	CG	SV	IP	H	R	ER	HR	BB	SO	AVG
2002	Vermont (NY-P)	A	2	5	4.33	10	10	0	0	44	44	27	21	1	18	49	.262
MINOR LEAGUE TOTALS			2	5	4.33	10	10	0	0	44	44	27	21	1	18	49	.262

7. Claudio Vargas, rhp

Born: May 19, 1979. **Ht.:** 6-3. **Wt.:** 210. **Bats:** R. **Throws:** R. **Career Transactions:** Signed out of Dominican Republic by Marlins, Aug. 25, 1995 . . . Traded by Marlins with OF Cliff Floyd, 2B Wilton Guerrero and cash to Expos for RHP Carl Pavano, LHP Graeme Lloyd, RHP Justin Wayne, 2B Mike Mordecai and a player to be named, July 11, 2002; Marlins acquired RHP Don Levinski to complete trade (Aug. 5, 2002).

Considered one of the Marlins' top pitching prospects, Vargas was shellacked in his first taste of Triple-A in 2002. Florida included him in the July trade that brought Cliff Floyd back to Montreal. Vargas pitched better after a demotion to Double-A, but he wasn't as effective at that level as he had been the year before, when he ranked second in the Eastern League in strikeouts. Vargas has unlimited potential and one of the best arms in the system. His prototypical pitcher's body and quick arm help him generate an overpowering 94-97 mph fastball and a power curve. Both have the potential to be plus major league pitches. His fastball is fairly straight but can be deceptive at times. Vargas needs to refine his delivery so he can throw more strikes. He also must improve the consistency of his curveball and utilize it more often. If he's going to remain a starter, he'll have to come up with a better changeup. The Expos haven't decided whether Vargas' long-term role is in the rotation or bullpen. He'll give Triple-A another try in 2003.

Year	Club (League)	Class	W	L	ERA	G	GS	CG	SV	IP	H	R	ER	HR	BB	SO	AVG
1996	Marlins (DSL)	R	2	3	3.09	15	4	0	0	47	41	25	16	1	26	37	.230
1997	Marlins (DSL)	R	6	2	2.50	13	10	3	0	72	62	32	20	3	31	81	.232
1998	Brevard County (FSL)	A	0	1	4.66	2	2	0	0	10	15	5	5	1	4	9	.366
	Marlins (GCL)	R	0	4	4.08	5	4	0	0	29	24	15	13	1	7	27	.226
1999	Kane County (Mid)	A	5	5	3.88	19	19	1	0	100	97	47	43	8	41	88	.255
2000	Brevard County (FSL)	A	10	5	3.28	24	23	0	0	145	126	64	53	10	44	143	.234
	Portland (EL)	AA	1	1	3.60	3	2	0	0	15	16	9	6	1	6	13	.276
2001	Portland (EL)	AA	8	9	4.19	27	27	0	0	159	122	77	74	25	67	151	.211
2002	Calgary (PCL)	AAA	4	11	6.72	17	16	1	0	76	88	63	57	18	35	61	.291
	Harrisburg (EL)	AA	2	2	4.64	8	8	0	0	33	38	17	17	2	9	34	.286
MINOR LEAGUE TOTALS			38	43	3.99	133	115	5	0	685	629	354	304	70	270	644	.244

8. Chris Young, rhp

Born: May 25, 1979. **Ht.:** 6-10. **Wt.:** 250. **Bats:** R. **Throws:** R. **School:** Princeton University. **Career Transactions:** Selected by Pirates in third round of 2000 draft; signed Sept. 6, 2000 . . . Traded by Pirates with RHP Jon Searles to Expos for RHP Matt Herges, Dec. 20, 2002.

Expos scouting director Dana Brown signed Young for the Pirates as an area scout. Pittsburgh paid Young $1.65 million to buy him away from a potential NBA career after he was an all-Ivy League performer as a basketball center. He fell somewhat out of favor with the new Pirates regime, which included him in a deal for Matt Herges in December. Young added velocity to his fastball after having arthroscopic elbow surgery following the 2001 season, throwing 93 mph last year. He has the potential to throw harder, though his inability to do so frustrated the Pirates. His long arms and legs create plenty of deception in his delivery. Young is looking to develop a good second pitch. He scrapped his slider last season in favor of a curveball, and he's refining his changeup. He needs to clean up his mechanics and throw on more of a downhill plane to take full advantage of his height. Young didn't make his pro debut until June 2001 because he was working toward his Princeton degree. The Pirates made him repeat low Class A, and he's ready to move up a level in 2003. He's going to be a long-term project.

Year	Club (League)	Class	W	L	ERA	G	GS	CG	SV	IP	H	R	ER	HR	BB	SO	AVG
2001	Hickory (SAL)	A	5	3	4.12	12	12	2	0	74	79	39	34	6	20	72	.269
2002	Hickory (SAL)	A	11	9	3.11	26	26	1	0	145	127	57	50	11	34	136	.234
MINOR LEAGUE TOTALS			16	12	3.45	38	38	3	0	219	206	96	84	17	54	208	.246

9. Scott Hodges, 3b

Born: Dec. 26, 1978. **Ht.:** 6-0. **Wt.:** 190. **Bats:** L. **Throws:** R. **School:** Henry Clay HS, Lexington, Ky. **Career Transactions:** Selected by Expos in first round (38th overall) of 1997 draft; signed June 5, 1997.

Hodges' weight dropped from 220 to 178 in six weeks and he missed the last 51 games of the 2001 season because he had colitis, an inflammation of the large intestine. That came on the heels of a breakout 2000 performance. He didn't regain form last year as he continued to return to full health. Hodges has a smooth, compact lefthanded stroke and above-average bat speed. He's an aggressive hitter but makes decent contact, driving the ball hard from gap to gap. He projects as a legitimate middle-of-the-order threat with plus power. Defensively, he has a strong and accurate arm and solid hands. Hodges still hasn't regained all his strength and wore down in the second half last year. He needs to do a better job of not lunging at pitches. His range is just adequate at the hot corner. Hodges has drawn criticism at times for his lack of hustle, but he has improved in that area. The Expos would love to dump Fernando Tatis, but his $6 million salary makes that difficult. After gaining Triple-A experience, Hodges should be ready to take over for Tatis in 2004.

Year	Club (League)	Class	AVG	G	AB	R	H	2B	3B	HR	RBI	BB	SO	SB	SLG	OBP
1997	Expos (GCL)	R	.235	57	196	26	46	13	2	2	23	23	47	2	.352	.317
1998	Vermont (NY-P)	A	.278	67	266	35	74	13	3	3	35	11	59	8	.383	.305
1999	Cape Fear (SAL)	A	.258	127	449	62	116	31	2	8	59	45	105	8	.390	.324
2000	Jupiter (FSL)	A	.306	111	422	75	129	32	1	14	83	49	66	8	.486	.373
	Harrisburg (EL)	AA	.176	6	17	2	3	0	0	1	5	2	4	1	.353	.238
2001	Harrisburg (EL)	AA	.275	85	305	30	84	11	2	5	32	25	56	3	.374	.328
2002	Harrisburg (EL)	AA	.272	135	526	79	143	35	2	9	68	63	102	2	.397	.351
MINOR LEAGUE TOTALS			.273	588	2181	309	595	135	12	42	305	218	439	32	.403	.337

10. Larry Broadway, 1b

Born: Dec. 17, 1980. **Ht.:** 6-4. **Wt.:** 230. **Bats:** L. **Throws:** L. **School:** Duke University. **Career Transactions:** Selected by Expos in third round of 2002 draft; signed June 13, 2002.

Broadway is a product of Wellington (Fla.) High, where he played with Pirates first-round picks Bobby Bradley and Sean Burnett. Broadway began his career at Duke as a two-way player before an elbow injury made him a full-time first baseman. After displaying tremendous pop with wood bats in the Cape Cod League in 2001, he didn't hit as well with aluminum last spring. Broadway's best tool is his bat. He has a smooth left-handed stroke with natural loft that produces top-of-the-scale raw power, which he showed off with a mammoth homer in his first pro at-bat. He has the ability to hit the ball a long way without making sweet-spot contact. He moves well for a big man, and his arm and hands are solid. Broadway has made strides but must refine his approach at the plate. He relied on pure ability in college. He missed time at short-season Vermont because of a pulled muscle in his back. The Expos system desperately needs power prospects, so Broadway should be put on the fast track. He'll open the season with one of Montreal's Class A affiliates.

Year	Club (League)	Class	AVG	G	AB	R	H	2B	3B	HR	RBI	BB	SO	SB	SLG	OBP
2002	Vermont (NY-P)	A	.315	35	127	13	40	3	0	4	23	13	33	0	.433	.379
	Expos (GCL)	R	.250	4	8	1	2	0	0	0	0	4	4	0	.250	.500
MINOR LEAGUE TOTALS			.311	39	135	14	42	3	0	4	23	17	37	0	.422	.388

11. Eric Good, lhp

Born: April 10, 1980. **Ht.:** 6-3. **Wt.:** 180. **Bats:** R. **Throws:** L. **School:** Mishawaka (Ind.) HS. **Career Transactions:** Selected by Expos in second round of 1998 draft; signed June 15, 1998 . . . On disabled list, April 5-Sept. 4, 2002.

After just missing leading the Florida State League in ERA in 2001 because he fell four innings short of qualifying, Good missed all of last season following minor elbow surgery. Fully healthy again, he should start this year in Double-A. Good has an easy arm stroke, solid mechanics and, at times, three above-average pitches. He'll get his fastball up to 93 mph and usually pitches at 88-91 mph with sink and run. His curveball has hard bite and two-plane break. His best pitch is a changeup that moves down in the zone with late fade and tumbling action. Good has a tendency to leave his fastball up at times when he gets poor extension on his pitches. He needs to show more consistency with his curveball and do a better job of staying on top of it. Good also missed much of 2000 with a sprained nerve in his elbow, so his biggest task is remaining healthy.

Year	Club (League)	Class	W	L	ERA	G	GS	CG	SV	IP	H	R	ER	HR	BB	SO	AVG
1998	Expos (GCL)	R	1	2	2.08	6	3	0	0	17	11	4	4	0	8	20	.177
1999	Vermont (NY-P)	A	5	5	5.79	15	15	0	0	70	77	49	45	3	30	59	.277
2000	Cape Fear (SAL)	A	1	2	2.75	8	8	0	0	36	31	15	11	1	12	32	.226
2001	Jupiter (FSL)	A	5	5	2.82	21	20	1	0	108	104	42	34	4	26	70	.248
2002	Did Not Play—Injured																
MINOR LEAGUE TOTALS			12	14	3.65	50	46	1	0	232	223	110	94	8	76	181	.249

12. Brandon Watson, of

Born: Sept. 30, 1981. **Ht.:** 6-1. **Wt.:** 170. **Bats:** L. **Throws:** R. **School:** Westchester HS, Los Angeles. **Career Transactions:** Selected by Expos in ninth round of 1999 draft; signed June 7, 1999.

Watson had a breakthrough season in 2001 but tailed off in high Class A last year. He did earn a late-season promotion to Harrisburg, where he sustained a sprain and a hairline fracture in his right ankle. A high school second baseman who immediately moved to the outfield after turning pro, Watson is the best athlete in the system. His speed makes him the fastest runner and best defensive outfielder among Expos farmhands, and he's the best bunter. He's a potential Gold Glvoe center fielder who takes good routes to fly balls and has a strong, accurate arm. He's a top-of-the-scale burner who gets down the first-base line in 3.7 seconds on drag bunts. Watson is a contact hitter with excellent hand-eye coordination. He has a compact, line-drive stroke and uses the entire field. To be a top-of-the-order threat in the majors, Watson needs to draw more walks and get on base on a more consistent basis. The only tool he's truly lacking is power. He has an unconventional style at the plate, similar to Ichiro's, and sometimes lunges and gets out in front of pitches. He'll start this season in Double-A.

Year	Club (League)	Class	AVG	G	AB	R	H	2B	3B	HR	RBI	BB	SO	SB	SLG	OBP
1999	Expos (GCL)	R	.303	33	119	15	36	2	0	0	12	11	11	4	.319	.361
2000	Vermont (NY-P)	A	.291	69	278	53	81	9	1	0	30	25	38	26	.331	.354
2001	Clinton (Mid)	A	.327	117	489	74	160	16	9	2	38	29	35	33	.409	.364
2002	Brevard County (FSL)	A	.267	111	424	57	113	16	2	0	24	27	53	22	.314	.314
	Harrisburg (EL)	AA	.333	2	6	2	2	0	0	0	0	1	0	0	.333	.429
MINOR LEAGUE TOTALS			.298	332	1316	201	392	43	12	2	104	93	167	85	.353	.346

13. Luke Lockwood, lhp

Born: July 21, 1981. **Ht.:** 6-3. **Wt.:** 170. **Bats:** L. **Throws:** L. **School:** Silverado HS, Victorville, Calif. **Career Transactions:** Selected by Expos in eighth round of 1999 draft; signed June 3, 1999.

The Expos have lefthanded pitching depth throughout the system, and Lockwood is one of their most projectable southpaws. He put together a winning record for the first time in 2002, though he had pitched well in the past. Lockwood has a wiry strong body. He's not a flamethrower, but with his clean arm action he should throw harder once he matures more physically. Lockwood does a good job of commanding both sides of the plate with his 86-90 mph fastball, and his curve is becoming impressive. His changeup is an above-average major league pitch. Lockwood needs to continue to add weight and strength. He has difficulty throwing first-pitch strikes and sometimes slows his arm speed on his changeup. Lockwood has pitched a total of 310 innings the last two seasons at a young age, so the Expos will have to be cautious with his workload this year in Double-A.

Year	Club (League)	Class	W	L	ERA	G	GS	CG	SV	IP	H	R	ER	HR	BB	SO	AVG
1999	Expos (GCL)	R	1	2	4.57	11	7	0	0	41	46	21	21	3	13	32	.275
2000	Jupiter (FSL)	A	0	1	10.93	3	3	0	0	14	24	17	17	3	5	2	.407
	Vermont (NY-P)	A	1	0	2.25	2	2	0	0	12	12	3	3	1	1	8	.279
	Cape Fear (SAL)	A	2	4	4.50	9	9	0	0	48	49	32	24	3	20	33	.271
2001	Clinton (Mid)	A	5	10	2.70	26	26	3	0	163	152	78	49	8	49	114	.248
2002	Brevard County (FSL)	A	10	7	3.37	26	26	0	0	147	155	69	55	13	38	86	.274
MINOR LEAGUE TOTALS			19	24	3.57	77	73	3	0	426	438	220	169	31	126	275	.269

14. Rich Rundles, lhp

Born: June 3, 1981. **Ht.:** 6-5. **Wt.:** 180. **Bats:** L. **Throws:** L. **School:** Jefferson County HS, Dandridge, Tenn. **Career Transactions:** Selected by Red Sox in third round of 1999 draft; signed July 9, 1999 . . . Traded by Red Sox with RHP Tomo Ohka to Expos for RHP Ugueth Urbina, July 31, 2001.

When the Expos traded Ugueth Urbina to the Red Sox at the 2001 trade deadline, they received Tomo Ohka, who won 13 games and finished seventh in the National League in ERA last year, and Rundles. Montreal would make that deal again in a heartbeat. The good news for Rundles, who tired shortly after switching organizations and saw his fastball dip to 84-86 mph, was that he got his velocity back in 2002. He consistently threw 88-91 mph with good run and sink. He commanded the pitch well to both sides of the plate. The bad news was that he made just 11 starts because of elbow tendinitis and a cut finger, though neither injury is a long-term concern. Rundles also has a curveball with two-plane change and late break. He rounds out his repertoire with an above-average changeup that he throws with fastball arm speed. Rundles has a good feel for pitching and shows good composure on the mound. With Eric Good and Luke Lockwood, Rundles could give Harrisburg a lefty-laden rotation in 2003.

Year	Club (League)	Class	W	L	ERA	G	GS	CG	SV	IP	H	R	ER	HR	BB	SO	AVG
1999	Red Sox (GCL)	R	1	0	2.13	5	1	0	0	13	13	3	3	1	1	11	.255
2000	Red Sox (GCL)	R	3	1	2.45	9	6	0	0	40	31	15	11	3	10	32	.218
2001	Augusta (SAL)	A	7	6	2.43	19	19	0	0	115	109	46	31	5	10	94	.247
	Clinton (Mid)	A	1	1	2.33	4	4	0	0	27	26	10	7	0	3	20	.248
2002	Brevard County (FSL)	A	2	7	4.08	12	11	0	0	57	66	34	26	5	16	31	.296
MINOR LEAGUE TOTALS			14	15	2.78	49	41	0	0	252	245	108	78	14	40	188	.255

15. Cristobal Rodriguez, rhp

Born: Jan. 27, 1979. **Ht.:** 6-4. **Wt.:** 210. **Bats:** R. **Throws:** R. **Career Transactions:** Signed out of Venezuela by Expos, Feb. 14. 1996.

Nicknamed "Chi-Chi" after the former professional golfer, Rodriguez ranked third in the Gulf Coast League in ERA in his U.S. debut in 1997. He has the best arm in the system—not that he has been able to showcase it much. He has pitched a total of just 30⅓ innings the last two years while battling a shoulder injury. Rodriguez has a prototype pitcher's body with long arms and legs, and a quick arm action. He has a 95-96 mph fastball that explodes out of his hand and has been clocked as high as 101. His heater has late running action up in the zone. His out pitch is a splitter that drops off the table, and he throws a slider that remains inconsistent. He still needs to work on the command of his pitches and improve his delivery by coming straighter toward to the plate. He peels off toward first base, causing his pitches to sit high in the strike zone and placing undue stress on his shoulder. Rodriguez' rehabilitation went well and the Expos expect him to be a 100 percent for spring training.

Year	Club (League)	Class	W	L	ERA	G	GS	CG	SV	IP	H	R	ER	HR	BB	SO	AVG
1996	Expos (DSL)	R	0	5	6.59	15	6	0	1	41	43	32	30	5	22	29	.270
1997	Expos (GCL)	R	3	3	1.65	13	10	0	1	55	45	15	10	1	16	61	.224
1998	Expos (GCL)	R	1	1	2.45	8	8	0	0	40	30	16	11	2	11	48	.199
	Vermont (NY-P)	A	0	0	4.91	6	2	0	0	15	6	8	8	1	14	14	.122
1999	Cape Fear (SAL)	A	5	8	4.17	26	25	0	0	121	100	68	56	12	65	128	.224
2000	Cape Fear (SAL)	A	5	6	5.31	14	14	1	0	76	77	53	45	9	35	70	.259
2001	Jupiter (FSL)	A	1	0	3.29	14	0	0	7	14	11	5	5	0	7	19	.220
2002	Brevard County (FSL)	A	2	3	1.62	11	0	0	2	17	11	4	3	2	4	21	.193
MINOR LEAGUE TOTALS			17	26	4.00	107	65	1	11	378	323	201	168	32	174	390	.229

16. Ron Calloway, of

Born: Sept. 4, 1976. **Ht.:** 6-1. **Wt.:** 210. **Bats:** L. **Throws:** L. **School:** Canada (Calif.) JC. **Career Transactions:** Selected by Diamondbacks in eighth round of 1997 draft; signed June 3, 1997 . . . Traded by Diamondbacks to Expos, July 5, 1999, completing trade in which Expos sent C John Pachot to Diamondbacks for future considerations (May 21, 1999).

Calloway had an outstanding spring training and came close to making Montreal's Opening Day roster last year. While he never surfaced in the majors during the season, the Expos' outfield situation remained unresolved and he'll battle Endy Chavez, Peter Bergeron, Terrmel Sledge and Matt Cepicky for a spot on the roster in 2003. Now 26, he needs to step forward this year. A late bloomer who didn't start playing baseball until he was a teenager, Calloway is a good athlete with average to plus tools across the board. He's an aggressive hitter with a line-drive stroke that allows him to spray balls to the gaps. He has average power and projects to hit 20 homers annually in the majors, but he still needs to improve his plate discipline. He is a skilled center fielder with an above-average arm and range. A long strider, Calloway has plus speed and baserunning instincts. He's also an accomplished bunter.

Year	Club (League)	Class	AVG	G	AB	R	H	2B	3B	HR	RBI	BB	SO	SB	SLG	OBP
1997	Lethbridge (Pio)	R	.250	43	148	23	37	5	0	0	9	14	29	5	.284	.323
	South Bend (Mid)	A	.280	9	25	3	7	1	0	0	1	2	8	1	.320	.333
1998	South Bend (Mid)	A	.263	69	251	29	66	12	2	3	33	25	50	6	.363	.331
	High Desert (Cal)	A	.282	44	156	30	44	8	2	3	27	12	38	2	.417	.337
1999	High Desert (Cal)	A	.316	60	196	41	62	14	1	3	23	30	34	22	.444	.412
	El Paso (TL)	AA	.219	11	32	4	7	0	0	0	1	7	7	1	.219	.359
	Jupiter (FSL)	A	.270	54	211	30	57	8	4	3	25	15	45	5	.389	.325
2000	Jupiter (FSL)	A	.277	135	530	78	147	24	6	6	65	55	89	34	.379	.346
2001	Harrisburg (EL)	AA	.330	74	279	48	92	22	4	9	47	24	46	25	.534	.385
	Ottawa (IL)	AAA	.264	61	239	27	63	12	0	10	35	16	64	11	.439	.323
2002	Ottawa (IL)	AAA	.264	128	447	72	118	21	5	14	60	44	89	16	.427	.335
MINOR LEAGUE TOTALS			.278	688	2514	385	700	127	24	51	326	244	499	128	.409	.346

17. Terrmel Sledge, of

Born: March 18, 1977. **Ht.:** 6-0. **Wt.:** 180. **Bats:** L. **Throws:** L. **School:** Long Beach State University. **Career Transactions:** Selected by Mariners in eighth round of 1999 draft; signed June 18, 1999 . . . Traded by Mariners to Expos, Sept. 27, 2000, completing deal in which Expos sent C Chris Widger to Mariners for two players to be named (Aug. 8, 2000); Expos also acquired LHP Sean Spencer (Aug. 10, 2000).

Sledge won the California League batting title in 2000, though his season ended in early August because he strained his right shoulder. A month later, he went to the Expos as a player to be named for Chris Widger. Because of the injury, Sledge spent most of 2001 playing first base before returning to the outfield last year. Despite an unorthodox trigger mechanism in his swing, Sledge has batted .302 in the minors and is the best pure hitter in the system. He has a short stroke and gap power, and he uses the entire field. He has solid speed and is a heady baserunner who projects to steal 20-30 bases a year in the majors. Sledge profiles as a left fielder in the majors, and he may not have the power to be an everyday player at that position. He has good range but his arm never has bounced back from his shoulder injury.

Year	Club (League)	Class	AVG	G	AB	R	H	2B	3B	HR	RBI	BB	SO	SB	SLG	OBP
1999	Everett (NWL)	A	.318	62	233	43	74	8	3	5	32	27	35	9	.442	.406
2000	Wisconsin (Mid)	A	.217	7	23	5	5	2	2	0	3	3	3	1	.478	.333
	Lancaster (Cal)	A	.339	103	384	90	130	22	7	11	75	72	49	35	.518	.458
2001	Harrisburg (EL)	AA	.277	129	448	66	124	22	6	9	48	51	72	30	.413	.359
2002	Harrisburg (EL)	AA	.301	102	396	74	119	18	6	8	43	55	70	11	.437	.401
	Ottawa (IL)	AAA	.263	24	80	12	21	5	2	1	11	11	15	1	.413	.359
MINOR LEAGUE TOTALS			.302	427	1564	290	473	77	26	34	212	219	244	87	.450	.402

18. Val Pascucci, of

Born: Nov. 17, 1978. **Ht.:** 6-6. **Wt.:** 230. **Bats:** R. **Throws:** R. **School:** University of Oklahoma. **Career Transactions:** Selected by Expos in 15th round of 1999 draft; signed June 2, 1999.

Pascucci led the Eastern League with 27 homers last year, but it wasn't a totally impressive season. He was repeating the EL, had only 15 other extra-base hits and hit just .235. Then again, Pascucci contributes to an offense far beyond his batting average. He draws lots of walks and uses his lanky frame to generate excellent leverage and power to all fields. He has good plate coverage and doesn't strike out as much as his batting average and homer totals might indicate. Defensively, he has one of the strongest outfield arms in the system. He has average speed. Because the Expos have a void at first base, they'll give Pascucci more time there this year while he's at their new Triple-A Edmonton affiliate.

Year	Club (League)	Class	AVG	G	AB	R	H	2B	3B	HR	RBI	BB	SO	SB	SLG	OBP
1999	Vermont (NY-P)	A	.351	72	259	62	91	26	1	7	48	53	46	17	.541	.482
2000	Cape Fear (SAL)	A	.319	20	69	17	22	4	0	3	10	16	15	5	.507	.442
	Jupiter (FSL)	A	.284	113	405	70	115	30	2	14	66	66	98	14	.472	.394
2001	Harrisburg (EL)	AA	.244	138	476	79	116	17	1	21	67	65	114	8	.416	.344
2002	Harrisburg (EL)	AA	.235	137	459	73	108	14	1	27	82	93	115	2	.447	.374
MINOR LEAGUE TOTALS			.271	480	1668	301	452	91	5	72	273	293	388	46	.461	.391

19. Rob Caputo, rhp

Born: Nov. 7, 1979. **Ht.:** 6-7. **Wt.:** 200. **Bats:** R. **Throws:** R. **School:** University of Alabama-Birmingham. **Career Transactions:** Selected by Expos in 18th round of 2001 draft; signed June 9, 2001.

Former Expos scouting director Jim Fleming thought Caputo was a sleeper when he drafted him in 2001, and the assessment seems accurate after the way Caputo performed last season. He opened 2002 at low Class A Clinton before being sent back to extended spring training in April to rework his delivery and mechanics. Once he returned, he pitched well out of the bullpen before minor league pitching coordinator Brent Strom decided he warranted a shot in the rotation. Caputo went 2-0, 2.67 in six starts with 43 strikeouts in 27 innings. His command improved after he switched roles. Caputo has an outstanding pitcher's body, standing 6-foot-7 with plenty of room remaining for projection at 200 pounds. His fastball sits at 91-95 mph and sinks, and his 81-84 mph slider also has a chance to be a plus pitch. He's also developing a changeup. Caputo will try to build on his progress this year in high Class A.

Year	Club (League)	Class	W	L	ERA	G	GS	CG	SV	IP	H	R	ER	HR	BB	SO	AVG
2001	Vermont (NY-P)	A	0	2	4.75	20	1	0	3	30	32	20	16	5	16	28	.264
	Clinton (Mid)	A	0	2	0.00	4	0	0	0	5	4	4	0	0	5	8	.190
2002	Clinton (Mid)	A	3	0	2.63	21	6	0	1	48	32	15	14	1	36	69	.186
	Brevard County (FSL)	A	0	1	10.80	2	0	0	0	2	3	2	2	0	3	1	.375
MINOR LEAGUE TOTALS			3	5	3.39	47	7	0	4	85	71	41	32	6	60	106	.220

20. Matt Cepicky, of

Born: Nov. 10, 1977. **Ht.:** 6-2. **Wt.:** 210. **Bats:** L. **Throws:** R. **School:** Southwest Missouri State University. **Career Transactions:** Selected by Expos in fourth round of 1999 draft; signed June 12, 1999.

Cepicky was leading the Eastern League in RBIs when he was promoted to Montreal on July 31 and made his major league debut, striking out in his first at-bat against Randy Johnson. He didn't perform well with the Expos, yet his work ethic made him a favorite of manager Frank Robinson. Cepicky is a heavy-hitting outfielder who frequently draws comparisons to Ryan Klesko because of his tool set and body type. His lefthander power grades out at 70 on the 20-80 scale, though he has yet to truly tap into it because of his mediocre strike-zone judgment. Cepicky runs well for a man his size, but he's limited to left field. He has moderate range and a below-average but accurate arm. He should start the year in Triple-A but could serve the Expos as a left fielder (if they decide to move Brad Wilkerson to first base) or as a power bat off the bench.

Year	Club (League)	Class	AVG	G	AB	R	H	2B	3B	HR	RBI	BB	SO	SB	SLG	OBP
1999	Vermont (NY-P)	A	.307	74	323	50	99	15	5	12	53	20	49	10	.495	.349
2000	Jupiter (FSL)	A	.299	131	536	61	160	32	7	5	88	24	64	32	.412	.328
2001	Harrisburg (EL)	AA	.264	122	459	59	121	23	8	19	77	21	97	5	.473	.296
2002	Harrisburg (EL)	AA	.277	109	419	54	116	25	2	16	76	33	94	7	.461	.327
	Montreal (NL)	MAJ	.216	32	74	7	16	3	0	3	15	4	21	0	.378	.256
MAJOR LEAGUE TOTALS			.216	32	74	7	16	3	0	3	15	4	21	0	.378	.256
MINOR LEAGUE TOTALS			.286	436	1737	224	496	95	22	52	294	98	304	54	.455	.323

21. Chad Bentz, lhp

Born: May 5, 1980. **Ht.:** 6-2. **Wt.:** 210. **Bats:** R. **Throws:** L. **School:** Long Beach State University. **Career Transactions:** Selected by Expos in seventh round of 2001 draft; signed June 10, 2001.

Bentz was born without a complete right hand, similar to Jim Abbott. His thumb is functional, but the rest of the fingers on the hand are knuckle-like stumps. Originally drafted by the Yankees out of Juneau-Douglas (Alaska) High, where he played with current NBA rookie Carlos Boozer as the shortstop, Bentz turned down football scholarships from several Pacific-10 Conference schools. He thrived out of the bullpen at Long Beach State, started in his first pro summer and moved back to relief last year. He pitched well enough to be selected for the Florida State League all-star game, but a recurring nerve problem in the third toe on his left foot ended his season before the contest. Bentz is praised for his bulldog mentality and composure on the mound. With a balanced delivery and strong frame, he throws a 91-93 mph fastball with explosive life. He also throws a cutter to get inside on righthanders. His slider is a plus pitch at times, and his changeup is effective against righthanders but still needs improvement. For the most part, Bentz gets good downhill angle on his fastball, but at times he will overthrow and leave it up in the zone.

Year	Club (League)	Class	W	L	ERA	G	GS	CG	SV	IP	H	R	ER	HR	BB	SO	AVG
2001	Vermont (NY-P)	A	1	3	4.91	8	8	0	0	37	39	23	20	2	11	38	.264
2002	Brevard County (FSL)	A	0	1	3.64	23	0	0	5	30	30	14	12	1	14	34	.259
MINOR LEAGUE TOTALS			1	4	4.34	31	8	0	5	66	69	37	32	3	25	72	.261

22. Josh Labandeira, ss

Born: Feb. 25, 1979. **Ht.:** 5-7. **Wt.:** 180. **Bats:** R. **Throws:** R. **School:** Fresno State University. **Career Transactions:** Selected by Expos in sixth round of 2001 draft; signed June 13, 2001.

After Brandon Phillips was traded to Cleveland, Labandeira became the best shortstop prospect in the system. After winning the Western Athletic Conference player-of-the-year award and nearly the triple crown in 2001, he signed as a sixth-round pick but injured his knee in his first pro game. He returned last year to perform solidly in low Class A. A four-sport (baseball, football, soccer, wrestling) star in high school, he incorporates that athleticism on the diamond. He's not tall but he's solidly built, and while his swing can get a bit long he generates gap power. He has average speed and is capable of making spectacular defensive plays, though he's also error-prone. Labandeira has a strong arm, soft hands and a tick above-average range. He'll move to high Class A in 2003.

Year	Club (League)	Class	AVG	G	AB	R	H	2B	3B	HR	RBI	BB	SO	SB	SLG	OBP
2001	Vermont (NY-P)	A	.333	1	3	2	1	0	0	0	0	0	0	0	.333	.333
2002	Clinton (Mid)	A	.286	129	493	60	141	27	3	8	67	45	73	15	.402	.350
MINOR LEAGUE TOTALS			.286	130	496	62	142	27	3	8	67	45	73	15	.401	.350

23. Shawn Hill, rhp

Born: April 28, 1981. **Ht.:** 6-2. **Wt.:** 180. **Bats:** R. **Throws:** R. **School:** Bishop Reding HS, Georgetown, Ontario. **Career Transactions:** Selected by Expos in sixth round of 2000 draft; signed June 16, 2000.

Hill was one of the system's most consistent pitchers in 2002, winning 12 games and making the low Class A Midwest League all-star game in his first taste of full-season ball. He was primarily a shortstop as a Canadian amateur, not moving to the mound until 1998. He's polished in all facets of pitching despite his relative inexperience. Hill has a long, loose arm and solid mechanics. He throws a heavy 88-92 mph sinker that induces lots of ground balls. He doesn't beat himself because he throws strikes. When he doesn't have his best stuff, he's resourceful enough to get by on what he has. Hill also commands a sharp curveball and has a good feel for his changeup. He throws both his offspeed pitches at 73-78 mph. Montreal will continue moving him one level at a time, promoting him to high Class A this year.

Year	Club (League)	Class	W	L	ERA	G	GS	CG	SV	IP	H	R	ER	HR	BB	SO	AVG
2000	Expos (GCL)	R	1	3	4.81	7	7	0	0	24	25	17	13	0	10	20	.250
2001	Vermont (NY-P)	A	2	2	2.27	7	7	0	0	36	22	12	9	0	8	23	.172
2002	Clinton (Mid)	A	12	7	3.44	25	25	0	0	147	149	75	56	7	35	99	.261
MINOR LEAGUE TOTALS			15	12	3.40	39	39	0	0	207	196	104	78	7	53	142	.245

24. Nick Long, rhp

Born: Nov. 24, 1982. **Ht.:** 6-3. **Wt.:** 180. **Bats:** R. **Throws:** R. **School:** Shaw HS, Columbus, Ga. **Career Transactions:** Selected by Expos in fourth round of 2001 draft; signed July 21, 2001.

A former two-way player, Long was the right fielder on the Brooklyn team that won the 2000 Continental Amateur Baseball Association High School World Series. Set to play with his brother Brandon at the University of Georgia, Long's plans changed when the Expos took him in the fourth round of the 2001 draft. He has yet to reach full-season ball and was hammered in the New York-Penn League, but his potential remains evident. He has a thin, athletic body that projects to add plenty of strength. His best pitch right now is an 88-92 mph fastball that moves down and to the right as it reaches the plate. He should throw harder as he matures. Long also has a nice 77-80 mph curveball, but his changeup needs a lot of work. He also needs to improve the command of all his pitches, and he might not be quite ready for low Class A.

Year	Club (League)	Class	W	L	ERA	G	GS	CG	SV	IP	H	R	ER	HR	BB	SO	AVG
2001	Expos (GCL)	R	1	1	3.32	4	3	0	0	19	24	8	7	0	4	12	.324
2002	Expos (GCL)	R	5	2	1.67	8	6	0	0	38	34	15	7	3	12	37	.234
	Vermont (NY-P)	A	1	3	7.92	6	6	0	0	25	36	30	22	0	14	16	.336
MINOR LEAGUE TOTALS			7	6	3.97	18	15	0	0	82	94	53	36	3	30	65	.288

25. David Thorne, rhp

Born: Sept. 18, 1981. **Ht.:** 6-3. **Wt.:** 180. **Bats:** R. **Throws:** R. **Career Transactions:** Signed out of Australia by Expos, Jan. 25, 1999 . . . On voluntarily retired list, May 8, 2000-March 19, 2002.

Signed in January 1999 out of a tryout camp by noted scout Fred Ferreira, Montreal's former director of international operations, Thorne was set to make his pro debut the following year. Then doctors discovered bone chips in his elbow, and the grind of rehab and his homesickness for Australia caused him to quit in May 2000. His desire came back when he pitched in the Claxton Shield tournament for the Australian national championship in February 2002, and he rejoined the Expos a month later. He showed one of the better arms in the lower levels of the system. He throws a fastball, splitter and curveball from a high three-quarters arm slot. He can run his fastball to 93-95 mph, and his splitter is a strikeout pitch. He has a solid frame but needs to build his arm strength back up. Thorne also must improve his consistency and command. He should open 2003 with one of the Expos' Class A clubs.

Year	Club (League)	Class	W	L	ERA	G	GS	CG	SV	IP	H	R	ER	HR	BB	SO	AVG
2002	Expos (GCL)	R	3	2	1.50	9	9	0	0	42	33	12	7	1	19	45	.214
MINOR LEAGUE TOTALS			3	2	1.50	9	9	0	0	42	33	12	7	1	19	45	.214

26. Reg Fitzpatrick, of

Born: Feb. 28, 1983. **Ht.:** 5-11. **Wt.:** 180. **Bats:** L. **Throws:** L. **School:** McNair HS, Atlanta. **Career Transactions:** Selected by Expos in fifth round of 2001 draft; signed July 15, 2001.

Fitzpatrick struggled as a high school senior and again last year, but the Expos are still excited by his raw tools and huge upside. Nicknamed "The Train," he's a gifted athlete and a true burner. Fitzpatrick can run the 60-yard dash in 6.5-6.6 seconds. He shows major league range and outstanding flychasing skills in center field. He still has a ways to go in other areas of the game. Fitzpatrick's swing has length to it, but the ball comes off his bat well. He needs a better feel for the strike zone and for stealing bases. Fitzpatrick's arm is currently below-average but should improve with repetitions and added strength. Like Nick Long, a fellow Georgia high school product, Fitzpatrick may not be ready for full-season ball at the outset of his third pro season.

Year	Club (League)	Class	AVG	G	AB	R	H	2B	3B	HR	RBI	BB	SO	SB	SLG	OBP
2001	Expos (GCL)	R	.280	31	118	17	33	1	0	0	7	9	28	5	.288	.331
	Vermont (NY-P)	A	.125	4	16	2	2	0	0	0	1	0	2	1	.125	.125
2002	Vermont (NY-P)	A	.237	71	270	34	64	10	0	2	16	27	59	15	.296	.310
MINOR LEAGUE TOTALS			.245	106	404	53	99	11	0	2	24	36	89	21	.287	.309

27. Josh Girdley, lhp

Born: Aug. 29, 1980. **Ht.:** 6-3. **Wt.:** 180. **Bats:** L. **Throws:** L. **School:** Jasper (Texas) HS. **Career Transactions:** Selected by Expos in first round (sixth overall) of 1999 draft; signed June 2, 1999.

Girdley went sixth overall in the 1999 draft because he was willing to accept a below-market $1.7 million bonus. After a positive start to his career, he has missed the majority of the past two years and is starting to lose his luster. He was involved in a motorcycle accident after the 2000 season and has had shoulder problems. Girdley still has considerable talent, but 2003 is a huge year for him as he needs to prove he can pitch a full season and get back on track toward the majors. He's a projectable lefthander with an easy arm stroke and the potential for three above-average pitches. He's still building up his arm strength and threw his fastball at 85-91 mph with late life last year. He also has a tight 74-76 mph curveball with excellent two-plane break, and a solid changeup. He'll open the season in low Class A for the third straight year, as the Expos wait for him to get healthy and pitch to his ability.

Year	Club (League)	Class	W	L	ERA	G	GS	CG	SV	IP	H	R	ER	HR	BB	SO	AVG
1999	Expos (GCL)	R	0	2	3.32	12	11	0	1	43	41	19	16	2	16	49	.253
2000	Vermont (NY-P)	A	5	0	2.95	14	14	0	0	79	60	32	26	4	28	70	.214
2001	Clinton (Mid)	A	0	2	3.68	6	6	0	0	29	28	15	12	2	18	21	.248
2002	Clinton (Mid)	A	0	3	6.85	7	5	0	1	24	33	19	18	2	13	14	.340
MINOR LEAGUE TOTALS			5	7	3.69	39	36	0	2	176	162	85	72	10	75	154	.248

28. Ignacio Puello, rhp

Born: Oct. 16, 1980. **Ht.:** 6-1. **Wt.:** 170. **Bats:** R. **Throws:** R. **Career Transactions:** Signed out of Dominican Republic by Expos, May 14, 1998.

Puello is an enigma who hasn't yet produced numbers indicative of his talent. He had three mediocre seasons in the Rookie-level Dominican Summer League and hasn't been any better since coming to the United States. He had a horrendous first half in low Class A in 2002, losing eight consecutive starts with a 6.87 ERA during that span, before rebounding somewhat. Puello has the body of an NFL cornerback. He's a fast-twitch athlete with a wide back, big hands and a lean, athletic frame. He has a natural high three-quarters arm slot, but inconsistent mechanics lead to stretches where his control abandons him. He throws an explosive 92-95 mph fastball that tops out at 97 and has arm-side sink. Puello complements his fastball with an above-average power curveball. At times, he'll drop his elbow when throwing his curve, causing it to flatten out and stay up in the zone. His changeup has some promise. Unless Puello has a standout spring, he'll head back for a third stint in low Class A. He may have the highest ceiling of any pitcher in the organization, so the Expos are trying to be patient with him.

Year	Club (League)	Class	W	L	ERA	G	GS	CG	SV	IP	H	R	ER	HR	BB	SO	AVG
1998	Expos (DSL)	R	0	3	5.59	13	9	0	0	37	34	31	23	3	47	20	.266
1999	Expos (DSL)	R	1	2	3.75	11	5	0	0	24	17	15	10	1	31	21	.215
2000	Expos (DSL)	R	2	4	5.02	11	11	0	0	43	37	38	24	2	44	55	.220
	Expos (GCL)	R	1	1	6.06	4	3	0	0	16	20	13	11	0	12	13	.286
2001	Expos (GCL)	R	1	3	2.06	8	8	0	0	35	28	11	8	0	10	37	.214
	Clinton (Mid)	A	3	3	5.57	7	7	0	0	32	29	21	20	4	26	21	.244
2002	Clinton (Mid)	A	7	14	4.77	27	26	0	0	140	155	95	74	5	66	91	.278
MINOR LEAGUE TOTALS			15	30	4.67	81	69	0	0	327	320	224	170	15	236	258	.255

29. Greg Thissen, 2b

Born: June 1, 1981. **Ht.:** 6-4. **Wt.:** 185. **Bats:** R. **Throws:** R. **School:** Triton (Ill.) JC. **Career Transactions:** Selected by Expos in eighth round of 2001 draft; signed June 12, 2001.

After starring at Triton JC, the alma mater of Hall of Famer Kirby Puckett, Thissen turned down a Louisiana State scholarship to sign with the Expos. In his first full pro season, he played in the Midwest League all-star game and spent most of his time at second base. At 6-foot-4 and 185 pounds, he projects as a run-producing third baseman. Starting from an open stance with good balance, Thissen has a tension-free swing that generates alley power. He has quick wrists and some length to his swing, but the ball comes off his bat well and he should develop over-the-fence power when he adds more weight and strength. He has a lithe, athletic body with average to plus tools across the board. He needs to show more discipline at the plate so he can hit for a better average. Defensively, he has quick feet and good hands. Thissen grades out as a 60 runner on the 20-80 scale but has an unconventional running stride. Thissen, who needs to get stronger, struggles to keep weight on his body. He wore down over the 2002 season, losing more than 15 pounds. He'll play in high Class A this year.

Year	Club (League)	Class	AVG	G	AB	R	H	2B	3B	HR	RBI	BB	SO	SB	SLG	OBP
2001	Vermont (NY-P)	A	.235	59	221	27	52	13	0	1	19	20	43	9	.308	.306
2002	Clinton (Mid)	A	.255	129	486	69	124	27	1	13	68	48	101	13	.395	.327
MINOR LEAGUE TOTALS			.249	188	707	96	176	40	1	14	87	68	144	22	.368	.321

30. Ron Chiavacci, rhp

Born: Sept. 5, 1977. **Ht.:** 6-2. **Wt.:** 220. **Bats:** R. **Throws:** R. **School:** Kutztown (Pa.) University. **Career Transactions:** Selected by Expos in 44th round of 1998 draft; signed June 9, 1998.

After leading the Eastern League in strikeouts in 2001 while setting the Harrisburg franchise record, Chiavacci regressed in 2002. That led to Montreal's decision to designate him for assignment when it needed roster space after picking up three big leaguers for Bartolo Colon in January. A stocky righthander with a strong lower half, he struggled with his control and was converted from a starter to a reliever in June. Chiavacci has a power arm and all four of his pitches are better than average at times. He has a lively 91-95 mph fastball and uses a late-breaking slider as his out pitch. He also throws a downer curveball and a changeup. Chiavacci runs into trouble because he has a lengthy arm action that leads to an inconsistent release point and command. He'll try to smooth out his mechanics this year in Triple-A.

Year	Club (League)	Class	W	L	ERA	G	GS	CG	SV	IP	H	R	ER	HR	BB	SO	AVG
1998	Expos (GCL)	R	6	3	2.13	13	6	0	0	55	43	17	13	1	13	42	.215
	Jupiter (FSL)	A	0	1	2.35	4	0	0	1	8	5	2	2	0	2	5	.217
1999	Cape Fear (SAL)	A	5	3	3.59	20	8	0	1	63	60	39	25	5	34	67	.241
	Jupiter (FSL)	A	4	4	2.23	8	8	0	0	48	36	15	12	5	17	32	.205
2000	Jupiter (FSL)	A	11	11	3.65	28	26	1	0	158	145	80	64	12	59	131	.243
2001	Harrisburg (EL)	AA	3	11	3.97	25	25	2	0	147	137	77	65	12	76	161	.248
2002	Harrisburg (EL)	AA	6	9	4.27	35	10	0	0	112	105	70	53	6	65	98	.250
MINOR LEAGUE TOTALS			35	42	3.57	133	83	3	2	591	531	300	234	41	266	536	.239

NEW YORK
METS

TOP 30 PROSPECTS

1. Jose Reyes, ss
2. Scott Kazmir, lhp
3. Aaron Heilman, rhp
4. David Wright, 3b
5. Justin Huber, c
6. Matt Peterson, rhp
7. Pat Strange, rhp
8. Jaime Cerda, lhp
9. Bob Keppel, rhp
10. Craig Brazell, 1b
11. Phil Seibel, lhp
12. Neal Musser, lhp
13. Jason Phillips, c
14. Jeremy Griffiths, rhp
15. David Mattox, rhp
16. Prentice Redman, of
17. Jeff Duncan, of
18. Heath Bell, rhp
19. Angel Pagan, of
20. Tyler Walker, rhp
21. Tim Lavigne, rhp
22. Jake Joseph, rhp
23. Jae Seo, rhp
24. Wayne Lydon, of
25. Ty Wigginton, 3b
26. Haj Turay, of
27. Tyler Yates, rhp
28. Adam Elliot, rhp
29. Corey Ragsdale, ss
30. Ross Peeples, lhp

**By Bill
Ballew**

The Mets provided endless copy for the New York tabloids in 2002, little of it complimentary.

Roberto Alomar, Jeromy Burnitz, Roger Cedeno and Mo Vaughn were brought in at great expense and to much fanfare, but none lived up to his billing. A 15-game home losing streak in August was followed by reports of marijuana use by several players, including published photographs of Grant Roberts using the drug. The soap opera between general manager Steve Phillips and manager Bobby Valentine ended with Valentine's firing after the club finished in last place for the first time since 1993.

The local media showed little restraint in criticizing the hiring of former Athletics manager Art Howe to replace Valentine. Howe comes with an impressive track record, however, including three straight postseason appearances and 103 wins last season. More important, his calm and confident demeanor could prove to be the perfect change of pace.

Howe inherits an aging major league roster that figures to remain in a state of flux. To patch some of the Mets' numerous holes, Phillips signed Cliff Floyd, Tom Glavine and Mike Stanton as free agents. The farm system should be able to provide reinforcements soon.

Despite losing several early picks in recent years as compensation for free agents, Gary LaRocque has overseen five productive drafts, first as scouting director and now as assistant GM. His initial effort in 1998 has produced five major leaguers (Jason Tyner, Pat Strange, Ty Wigginton, Jaime Cerda, Earl Snyder) and a Top 10 Prospect in Craig Brazell. LaRocque and director of amateur scouting Jack Bowen got the steal of the 2002 draft when lefthander Scott Kazmir fell to them at 15th overall. The Mets surrendered their second- and third-rounders to sign David Weathers and Cedeno, but found promising players in later rounds, including outfielders Bobby Malek and Jon Slack, righthander Adam Elliot and third baseman/catcher Shawn Bowman. New York also is encouraged by the progress of outfielder Jamar Hill, who signed as a draft-and-follow.

The Mets are improving as an organization. Their system is deep with middle-of-the-rotation starters, catchers and athletic outfielders. Even after losing Enrique Cruz in the major league Rule 5 draft, they also have upgraded at the infield corners after being thin there a couple of years ago.

OrganizationOverview

General Manager: Steve Phillips. **Farm Director:** Jim Duquette. **Scouting Director:** Jack Bowen.

2002 PERFORMANCE

Class	Farm Team	League	W	L	Pct.	Finish*	Manager
Majors	New York	National	75	87	.466	11th (16)	Bobby Valentine
Triple-A	Norfolk Tides	International	70	73	.490	8th (14)	Bobby Floyd
Double-A	Binghamton Mets	Eastern	73	68	.518	6th (12)	Howie Freiling
High A	St. Lucie Mets	Florida State	71	69	.507	6th (12)	Ken Oberkfell
Low A	Capital City Bombers	South Atlantic	75	64	.540	6th (16)	Tony Tijerina
Short-season	Brooklyn Cyclones	New York-Penn	38	38	.500	7th (14)	Howard Johnson
Rookie	Kingsport Mets	Appalachian	23	44	.343	9th (10)	Joey Cora
OVERALL 2002 MINOR LEAGUE RECORD			350	356	.496	17th (30)	

*Finish in overall standings (No. of teams in league).

ORGANIZATION LEADERS

BATTING   *Minimum 250 At-Bats
*AVG	Jeff Duncan, St. Lucie/Capital City	.373
R	Jose Reyes, Binghamton/St. Lucie	104
H	Jose Reyes, Binghamton/St. Lucie	162
TB	Craig Brazell, Binghamton/St. Lucie	252
2B	Prentice Redman, Binghamton	35
3B	Jose Reyes, Binghamton/St. Lucie	19
HR	Aaron McNeal, Norfolk/Binghamton	22
	Craig Brazell, Binghamton/St. Lucie	22
RBI	Craig Brazell, Binghamton/St. Lucie	101
BB	David Wright, Capital City	76
SO	Andy Tracy, Norfolk	123
SB	Wayne Lydon, Capital City	87

PITCHING   #Minimum 75 Innings
W	Harold Eckert, Capital City	13
L	Wayne Ough, Capital City/Brooklyn	11
#ERA	Jason Scobie, Capital City/Brooklyn	2.84
G	Jim Serrano, Norfolk	53
CG	Four tied at	2
SV	Tim Lavigne, Binghamton/St. Lucie	16
IP	Pat Stange, Norfolk	165
BB	Nick Maness, Norfolk/Binghamton	80
SO	Matt Peterson, St. Lucie/Capital City	158

BEST TOOLS

Best Hitter for Average	Craig Brazell
Best Power Hitter	Craig Brazell
Fastest Baserunner	Wayne Lydon
Best Athlete	Jose Reyes
Best Fastball	Scott Kazmir
Best Curveball	Scott Kazmir
Best Slider	Aaron Heilman
Best Changeup	Pat Strange
Best Control	Aaron Heilman
Best Defensive Catcher	Jason Phillips
Best Defensive Infielder	Jose Reyes
Best Infield Arm	Corey Ragsdale
Best Defensive Outfielder	Jeff Duncan
Best Outfield Arm	Angel Pagan

PROJECTED 2006 LINEUP

Catcher	Justin Huber
First Base	Mike Piazza
Second Base	Roberto Alomar
Third Base	David Wright
Shortstop	Jose Reyes
Left Field	Cliff Floyd
Center Field	Prentice Redman
Right Field	Jeromy Burnitz
No. 1 Starter	Scott Kazmir

Jeff Duncan   **Nick Maness**

No. 2 Starter	Aaron Heilman
No. 3 Starter	Pedro Astacio
No. 4 Starter	Matt Peterson
No. 5 Starter	Pat Strange
Closer	Armando Benitez

TOP PROSPECTS OF THE DECADE

1993	Bobby Jones, rhp
1994	Bill Pulsipher, lhp
1995	Bill Pulsipher, lhp
1996	Paul Wilson, rhp
1997	Jay Payton, rhp
1998	Grant Roberts, rhp
1999	Alex Escobar, of
2000	Alex Escobar, of
2001	Alex Escobar, of
2002	Aaron Heilman, rhp

TOP DRAFT PICKS OF THE DECADE

1993	Kirk Presley, rhp
1994	Paul Wilson, rhp
1995	Ryan Jaroncyk, ss
1996	Robert Stratton, of
1997	Geoff Goetz, lhp
1998	Jason Tyner, of
1999	Neal Musser, lhp (2)
2000	Billy Traber, lhp
2001	Aaron Heilman, rhp
2002	Scott Kazmir, lhp

ALL-TIME LARGEST BONUSES

Scott Kazmir, 2002	$ 2,150,000
Geoff Goetz, 1997	$ 1,700,000
Paul Wilson, 1994	$ 1,550,000
Aaron Heilman, 2001	$ 1,508,750
Jason Tyner, 1998	$ 1,070,000

MinorLeagueDepthChart

NEW YORK METS

RANK 13

Based on the strength of their frontline prospects, the Mets have taken a leap forward in the last year. Shortstop Jose Reyes has established himself as one of the brightest prospects in the game, and he could be an altering force in the Mets lineup by midseason. Power lefthander Scott Kazmir fell into their laps with the 15th pick in the draft last year, as other teams passed on his price tag—and some worried about the durability of his undersized frame. David Wright and Justin Huber developed at the low Class A level, showing plus bat and power potential. The Mets' track record for developing pitchers is abysmal, but Aaron Heilman looks like a keeper. The organization's main weakness is depth.

Note: Depth charts prepared by Josh Boyd. Numbers in parentheses indicate prospect rankings.

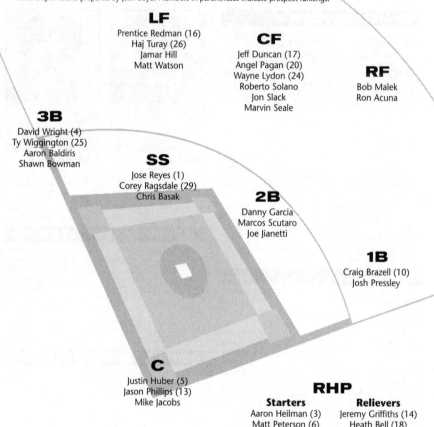

LF
Prentice Redman (16)
Haj Turay (26)
Jamar Hill
Matt Watson

CF
Jeff Duncan (17)
Angel Pagan (20)
Wayne Lydon (24)
Roberto Solano
Jon Slack
Marvin Seale

RF
Bob Malek
Ron Acuna

3B
David Wright (4)
Ty Wiggington (25)
Aaron Baldiris
Shawn Bowman

SS
Jose Reyes (1)
Corey Ragsdale (29)
Chris Basak

2B
Danny Garcia
Marcos Scutaro
Joe Jianetti

1B
Craig Brazell (10)
Josh Pressley

C
Justin Huber (5)
Jason Phillips (13)
Mike Jacobs

RHP

Starters	Relievers
Aaron Heilman (3)	Jeremy Griffiths (14)
Matt Peterson (6)	Heath Bell (18)
Pat Strange (7)	Tim Lavigne (21)
Bob Keppel (9)	Tyler Yates (27)
David Mattox (15)	P.J. Bevis
Tyler Walker (19)	Franklin Nunez
Jake Joseph (22)	Orlando Roman
Jae Seo (23)	Eric Cammack
Adam Elliot (28)	Saturo Komiyama
Nick Maness	Ryan Jamison

LHP

Starters	Relievers
Scott Kazmir (2)	Jaime Cerda (8)
Phil Seibel (11)	Jason Saenz
Neal Musser (12)	
Ross Peeples (30)	
Len Dinardo	

DraftAnalysis

2002 Draft

Best Pro Debut: LHP Scott Kazmir (1) signed late and pitched just 18 innings in the short-season New York-Penn League. Nevertheless he produced spectacular numbers: 1 ER (0.50 ERA), 5 H, 7 BB, 34 SO. 3B/2B **Blake Whealy** (13) hit .289-10-34 to earn NY-P all-star honors.

Best Athlete: OF Tyler Davidson (8) has a body (6-foot-5, 240 pounds) that scouts love, and speed and arm strength to go with his obvious offensive potential. He hurt his wrist taking batting practice before his first pro game and required surgery.

Best Pure Hitter: OF Bob Malek (4) hit .427 and .402 in his last two seasons at Michigan State, but teams backed off after he blew out his right elbow in May. He hit just .207 in the NY-P while playing through the pain, then had Tommy John surgery.

Best Raw Power: Davidson can put on a show in batting practice.

Fastest Runner: OF Jon Slack (5) runs a 6.5-second 60-yard dash. He's a stronger version of former Mets prospect Jason Tyner.

Best Defensive Player: 3B Shawn Bowman (12) signed after starring for Canada at the World Junior Championship. A converted shortstop, he's rangy with a strong arm.

Best Fastball: Kazmir had the most electric arm of any pitcher who signed out of the draft. He sat at 93-94 mph all year and touched 96-97 with regularity. And remember, he's lefthanded. RHP Adam Elliot (6) touched 93-94 mph in high school.

Best Breaking Ball: Kazmir's slider gives him a second plus-plus pitch, and he can change speeds off it. He also has a feel for a changeup. The only knock is that he's just 6 feet tall. Ron Guidry, whose size never worked against him, was a similar pitcher.

Most Intriguing Background: Kazmir teamed with the Expos' Clint Everts to give Houston's Cypress Falls High two first-rounders in the same June draft, just the fourth time a high school has accomplished the feat.

RICH ABEL

Whealy

Closest To The Majors: The Mets will try to avoid zipping Kazmir through the minors, but he's not going to make it easy on them. Would anyone be surprised if he's pitching at Shea Stadium in September?

Best Late-Round Pick: Bowman. Among players who have made their pro debuts, Whealy and RHP Bryan King (19) stand out. King gets good riding action on his 90-91 mph fastball.

The One Who Got Away: The Mets liked Canadian C Chris Robinson's (30) makeup, bat and live body, but his price tag got too high to buy him away from Illinois.

Assessment: Kazmir's rumored bonus demands caused him to drop to the 15th pick. Not only did the Mets steal him there, but they also didn't have to break the bank, signing him for $2.15 million. That easily soothed the sting of not having a second- or third-round pick.

2001 Draft

The Mets scored big with their two first-round picks, RHP Aaron Heilman and 3B David Wright. **Grade: B+**

2000 Draft

New York again did well at the top with LHP Billy Traber (1) and RHPs Bob Keppel (1) and Matt Peterson (2). Traber was sent to Cleveland in the Roberto Alomar trade. **Grade: C+**

1999 Draft

The Mets didn't have a first-rounder and didn't find an overwhelming prospect. LHP Neal Musser (2), RHP Jeremy Griffiths (3) and OF Prentice Redman (10) have potential. **Grade: D**

1998 Draft

No high ceilings here, but New York got useful players in RHP Pat Strange (2), 1B Craig Brazell (5), 3B Ty Wigginton (17) and draft-and-follow LHP Jaime Cerda (23). It also has used OF Jason Tyner (1) and 1B/3B Earl Snyder (36) as trade bait. The best player of all might have been OF Brian Cole (13), but he was killed in a March 2001 car accident. **Grade: C**

Note: Draft analysis prepared by Jim Callis. Numbers in parentheses indicate draft rounds.

... Reyes is the Mets' best everyday prospect since Darryl Strawberry blazed through the system in the early 1980s.

MARC LEVINE

Jose Reyes ss

Born: June 11, 1983.
Ht.: 6-0. **Wt.:** 160.
Bats: B. **Throws:** R.
Career Transactions:
Signed out of Dominican
Republic by Mets, Aug. 16, 1999.

After finishing fifth in the low Class A South Atlantic League batting race in 2001, when he was the youngest regular in any full-season league, Reyes was even better in 2002. He stood out in big league camp before reporting to the high Class A Florida State League, where he earned a quick promotion to the Double-A Eastern League. Managers in both leagues rated him the top defensive shortstop, strongest infield arm and most exciting player. He also was MVP at the Futures Game after stroking a bases-loaded triple, appropriate, as Reyes led all minor leaguers with 19 triples while ranking fifth in runs and sixth in steals. He went to the Dominican League for the winter and was rated as the league's top prospect, reinforcing his emergence as the best shortstop prospect in the game.

Reyes surprises people with his solid physique. His dedication to improving his strength, along with natural maturation, have transformed him from a skinny kid into an impressive specimen. He drives the ball more consistently to all fields. Reyes' plate discipline improved in high Class A before slipping after he reported to Double-A. He's an excellent baserunner with plus speed. He has demonstrated Gold Glove ability throughout his career, with a strong arm and tremendous range. Reyes needs to make improvements that should come with experience. He'll need more consistent strike-zone discipline to succeed against better pitching and to become the true leadoff hitter the Mets need. Reyes also is prone to making youthful mistakes in the field, though part of that stems from his exuberance. While he's a prolific basestealer, he can become more effective after getting caught 24 times last year.

Reyes is the Mets' best everyday prospect since Darryl Strawberry blazed through the system in the early 1980s. Though the organization shuns comparisons to other players, Reyes' all-around ability and athleticism remind scouts of Alfonso Soriano. The Mets unloaded Rey Ordonez to the Devil Rays in December, clearing the way for Reyes in the long term. The club did sign Rey Sanchez as a stopgap to give Reyes some time in Triple-A to make final preparations for New York, if he needs it.

Year	Club (League)	Class	AVG	G	AB	R	H	2B	3B	HR	RBI	BB	SO	SB	SLG	OBP
2000	Kingsport (Appy)	R	.250	49	132	22	33	3	3	0	8	20	37	10	.318	.359
2001	Capital City (SAL)	A	.307	108	407	71	125	22	15	5	48	18	71	30	.472	.337
2002	St. Lucie (FSL)	A	.288	69	288	58	83	10	11	6	38	30	35	31	.462	.353
	Binghamton (EL)	AA	.287	65	275	46	79	16	8	2	24	16	42	27	.425	.331
MINOR LEAGUE TOTALS			.290	291	1102	197	320	51	37	13	118	84	185	98	.439	.343

2. Scott Kazmir, lhp

Born: Jan. 24, 1984. **Ht.:** 6-1. **Wt.:** 170. **Bats:** L. **Throws:** L. **School:** Cypress Falls HS, Houston. **Career Transactions:** Selected by Mets in first round (15th overall) of 2002 draft; signed Aug. 2, 2002.

Kazmir may have had the best arm in the 2002 draft. His reported bonus demands scared off several teams before the Mets got him with the 15th overall pick, and signed him for a reasonable $2.15 million. After breaking Josh Beckett's Texas prep record for strikeouts and earning Baseball America's High School Player of the Year award, he overpowered hitters in the short-season New York-Penn League in 18 stirring innings. Kazmir has two plus-plus pitches: an electric fastball that sits in the 93-95 mph range and hits 97, plus a hard slider that he throws at different speeds. He shows an excellent feel for his changeup. Kazmir is a superb athlete with an easy delivery, superior arm quickness and strong leg drive. The Mets focused on speeding up Kazmir's delivery in instructional league. He has been so successful that he has little experience dealing with baserunners. His small frame is the only concern raised by scouts, but he has been durable and injury-free so far. The Mets say they are determined not to push Kazmir too fast, though that may be easier said than done. He's ticketed for low Class A Capital City in 2003.

Year	Club (League)	Class	W	L	ERA	G	GS	CG	SV	IP	H	R	ER	HR	BB	SO	AVG
2002	Brooklyn (NY-P)	A	0	1	0.50	5	5	0	0	18	5	2	1	0	7	34	.089
MINOR LEAGUE TOTALS			0	1	0.50	5	5	0	0	18	5	2	1	0	7	34	.089

3. Aaron Heilman, rhp

Born: Nov. 12, 1978. **Ht.:** 6-5. **Wt.:** 220. **Bats:** R. **Throws:** R. **School:** University of Notre Dame. **Career Transactions:** Selected by Mets in first round (18th overall) of 2001 draft; signed July 17, 2001.

A two-time first-round pick who spurned the Twins in 2000, Heilman has progressed rapidly since going 15-0, 1.74 as a senior at Notre Dame. He began his first full pro season at Double-A Binghamton and needed just three months to earn a promotion to Triple-A Norfolk–where he threw eight shutout innings in his first start. Heilman is an excellent competitor with good command and a loose three-quarters delivery. He throws a heavy 92-93 mph fastball that he keeps down in the strike zone. His strikeout pitch is a nasty splitter. His slider has a good downward slant when thrown properly. Heilman needs to become more consistent with his changeup, though he has made major strides with the pitch since signing. Better command of his splitter and more consistency with his potentially nasty slider would allow him to dominate more frequently. Heilman has the ingredients to be a quality No. 3 starter in the major leagues. He probably needs another half-season in Triple-A, but that could change with a strong showing in spring training.

Year	Club (League)	Class	W	L	ERA	G	GS	CG	SV	IP	H	R	ER	HR	BB	SO	AVG
2001	St. Lucie (FSL)	A	0	1	2.35	7	7	0	0	38	26	11	10	0	13	39	.190
2002	Binghamton (EL)	AA	4	4	3.82	17	17	0	0	97	85	43	41	7	28	97	.237
	Norfolk (IL)	AAA	2	3	3.28	10	7	0	0	49	42	18	18	3	16	35	.240
MINOR LEAGUE TOTALS			6	8	3.37	34	31	0	0	184	153	72	69	10	57	171	.228

4. David Wright, 3b

Born: Dec. 20, 1982. **Ht.:** 6-0. **Wt.:** 190. **Bats:** R. **Throws:** R. **School:** Hickory HS, Chesapeake, Va. **Career Transactions:** Selected by Mets in first round (38th overall) of 2001 draft; signed July 12, 2001.

Considered one of the purest hitters in the 2001 draft, Wright has lived up to that billing. After hitting .235 last April, he went on to tie for the Capital City lead in homers and ranked third in the South Atlantic League in RBIs. Wright is supremely confident in his abilities without coming across as arrogant. His makeup is off the charts and his determination is unmatched. His smooth and easy swing produces outstanding bat speed and hard line drives to all fields. His speed is barely average, but he's an excellent baserunner. Wright has a strong and accurate arm at third base. He also has steady hands, good lateral movement and the ability to charge bunts. Natural maturity and more experience should boost Wright's home run totals. He'll take pitchers deep more often when he learns to punish hanging breaking balls and other mistakes instead of taking them for balls. Wright is at least two full years from the major leagues, but he has all the ingredients to be the long-term answer at third base for the Mets. He'll open 2003 at high Class A St. Lucie.

Year	Club (League)	Class	AVG	G	AB	R	H	2B	3B	HR	RBI	BB	SO	SB	SLG	OBP
2001	Kingsport (Appy)	R	.300	36	120	27	36	7	0	4	17	16	30	9	.458	.391
2002	Capital City (SAL)	A	.266	135	496	85	132	30	2	11	93	76	114	21	.401	.367
MINOR LEAGUE TOTALS			.273	171	616	112	168	37	2	15	110	92	144	30	.412	.371

5. Justin Huber, c

RODGER WOOD

Born: July 1, 1982. **Ht.:** 6-2. **Wt.:** 190. **Bats:** R. **Throws:** R. **Career Transactions:** Signed out of Australia by Mets, July 26, 2000.

Huber jumped on the fast track last year and emerged as one of the minors' better catching prospects. He became the first unanimous selection in the South Atlantic League's midseason all-star game since Mike Hargrove in 1973. He continued to produce after a mid-July promotion to high Class A but looked exhausted in the Arizona Fall League. The Mets focused on Huber's defense last year, so everything he accomplished at the plate was a credit to him. Strong and intense, he has the bat speed and power to hit 25-30 homers a year. Huber understands the strike zone. He shows quick feet and excellent mobility behind the plate. Huber threw out just 24 percent of basestealers in 2002. He has average arm strength and accuracy and needs to improve his release. He worked with Capital City coach John Stephenson, a former big league receiver, on the finer aspects of game-calling. Huber is on track to be the eventual replacement for Mike Piazza behind the plate in New York. A return to St. Lucie is likely in 2003, with a midseason promotion to Double-A a possibility.

Year	Club (League)	Class	AVG	G	AB	R	H	2B	3B	HR	RBI	BB	SO	SB	SLG	OBP
2001	St. Lucie (FSL)	A	.000	2	6	0	0	0	0	0	0	0	2	0	.000	.000
	Kingsport (Appy)	R	.314	47	159	24	50	11	1	7	31	17	42	4	.528	.415
	Brooklyn (NY-P)	A	.000	3	9	0	0	0	0	0	0	0	4	0	.000	.000
2002	Capital City (SAL)	A	.291	95	330	49	96	22	2	11	78	45	81	1	.470	.408
	St. Lucie (FSL)	A	.270	28	100	15	27	2	1	3	15	11	18	0	.400	.370
MINOR LEAGUE TOTALS			.286	175	604	88	173	35	4	21	124	73	147	5	.462	.395

6. Matt Peterson, rhp

DAVID SCHOFIELD

Born: Feb. 11, 1982. **Ht.:** 6-5. **Wt.:** 210. **Bats:** R. **Throws:** R. **School:** Rapides HS, Alexandria, La. **Career Transactions:** Selected by Mets in second round of 2000 draft; signed Aug. 9, 2000.

Peterson was disappointed he was sent back to Capital City at the start of 2002, after making 18 appearances there in his 2001 pro debut. He put pressure on himself by trying to do too much before regaining his confidence in June, with a streak of allowing two earned runs or less in eight straight starts. Peterson has great size and throws his lively 92-93 mph fastball on a fine downhill plane. His overhand curveball, which has a sharp 11-to-5 drop, has the makings of becoming a plus pitch. When he finds his rhythm, Peterson shows why he projects as a dominating pitcher who could become a middle-of-the-rotation starter or better. Peterson's focus wanders at times on the mound, and he needs to be more dedicated in his preparation. His changeup is still in the developmental stages. Peterson made an emergency start at St. Lucie on Aug. 1 and allowed one run in six innings to earn the victory. He'll return to high Class A in 2003 and could climb the ladder quickly if a few intangibles fall into place.

Year	Club (League)	Class	W	L	ERA	G	GS	CG	SV	IP	H	R	ER	HR	BB	SO	AVG
2001	Capital City (SAL)	A	2	6	4.99	18	14	0	0	79	87	46	44	9	29	72	.275
	Brooklyn (NY-P)	A	2	2	1.62	6	6	0	0	33	26	7	6	0	14	19	.217
2002	Capital City (SAL)	A	8	10	3.86	26	26	1	0	138	109	67	59	13	61	153	.221
	St. Lucie (FSL)	A	1	0	1.50	1	1	0	0	6	5	2	1	0	2	5	.217
MINOR LEAGUE TOTALS			13	18	3.86	51	47	1	0	256	227	122	110	22	106	249	.238

7. Pat Strange, rhp

Born: Aug. 23, 1980. **Ht.:** 6-5. **Wt.:** 240. **Bats:** R. **Throws:** R. **School:** Central HS, Springfield, Mass. **Career Transactions:** Selected by Mets in second round of 1998 draft; signed July 29, 1998.

Strange has reached double figures in wins in each of his four full pro seasons, including 14 in 2000, when he was the Mets' minor league pitcher of the year. Last year, he tied for the Norfolk lead in victories and strikeouts before making an impressive major league debut in September. Strange has solid overall stuff, with the size and stamina to be a workhorse. When at his best, he keeps the ball down in the strike zone with a

91-94 mph sinker. He can throw his plus changeup in any count. His command is another asset. Despite his size and the quality of his pitches, Strange can be more of a finesse pitcher than a strikeout pitcher. His mechanics are inconsistent and have hurt the development of his breaking ball. His maximum-effort delivery raises health concerns. Strange has thrown more than 140 innings in the last four seasons, including a career-high 173 last year. A starter for most of his career, he did an excellent job out of the bullpen in New York. He'll be a strong candidate to make the big league staff this spring.

Year	Club (League)	Class	W	L	ERA	G	GS	CG	SV	IP	H	R	ER	HR	BB	SO	AVG
1998	Mets (GCL)	R	1	1	1.42	4	4	0	0	19	18	3	3	0	7	19	.254
1999	Capital City (SAL)	A	12	5	2.63	28	21	2	1	154	138	57	45	4	29	113	.238
2000	St. Lucie (FSL)	A	10	1	3.58	19	13	2	0	88	78	48	35	4	32	77	.240
	Binghamton (EL)	AA	4	3	4.55	10	10	0	0	55	62	30	28	2	30	36	.287
2001	Binghamton (EL)	AA	11	6	4.87	26	24	1	0	153	171	94	83	18	52	106	.288
	Norfolk (IL)	AAA	1	0	0.00	1	1	0	0	6	4	0	0	0	1	6	.182
2002	Norfolk (IL)	AAA	10	10	3.82	29	25	2	0	165	165	77	70	12	59	109	.265
	New York (NL)	MAJ	0	0	1.13	5	0	0	0	8	6	1	1	0	1	4	.207
MAJOR LEAGUE TOTALS			0	0	1.13	5	0	0	0	8	6	1	1	0	1	4	.207
MINOR LEAGUE TOTALS			49	26	3.71	117	98	7	1	641	636	309	264	40	210	466	.262

8. Jaime Cerda, lhp

Born: Oct. 26, 1978. **Ht.:** 6-0. **Wt.:** 170. **Bats:** L. **Throws:** L. **School:** Fresno CC. **Career Transactions:** Selected by Mets in 23rd round of 1998 draft; signed May 25, 1999 . . . Contract voided, July 20, 1999 . . . Signed by Mets, July 25, 1999 . . . On disabled list, July 25-Sept. 4, 1999.

Cerda had his original contract voided when the Mets discovered that he needed Tommy John surgery. He signed a new deal five days later and made his pro debut in 2000. After allowing one earned run in 21 Triple-A innings to lower his career minor league ERA to 1.35, Cerda was effective in his big league debut. Cerda has a deceptive delivery and gets ahead in the count with his fearless approach. He does an excellent job of working both sides of the plate with his 89-91 mph sinker. Cerda can cut his fastball to lock up righthanders, who hit just .204 against him in the majors. Because he's not overpowering, Cerda needs to become more consistent with the fade on his changeup and the command of his breaking ball. While he has moved rapidly through the organization, he must continue to make adjustments as major league hitters become more familiar with him. Cerda is a leading candidate to fill one of the lefty roles in the New York bullpen in 2003.

Year	Club (League)	Class	W	L	ERA	G	GS	CG	SV	IP	H	R	ER	HR	BB	SO	AVG
1999					Did Not Play—Injured												
2000	Pittsfield (NY-P)	A	4	1	0.57	20	1	0	5	47	33	6	3	0	6	51	.198
2001	St. Lucie (FSL)	A	2	1	0.97	28	0	0	6	56	40	8	6	3	12	56	.204
	Binghamton (EL)	AA	1	0	3.10	12	0	0	3	20	17	7	7	1	6	22	.233
	Norfolk (IL)	AAA	0	0	3.86	3	0	0	0	5	2	2	2	0	2	4	.125
2002	Binghamton (EL)	AA	5	1	2.27	14	0	0	0	32	21	8	8	0	10	33	.193
	Norfolk (IL)	AAA	0	0	0.43	12	0	0	1	21	10	2	1	0	7	17	.143
	New York (NL)	MAJ	0	0	2.45	32	0	0	0	26	22	7	7	0	14	21	.232
MAJOR LEAGUE TOTALS			0	0	2.45	32	0	0	0	26	22	7	7	0	14	21	.232
MINOR LEAGUE TOTALS			12	3	1.35	89	1	0	15	180	123	33	27	4	43	183	.195

9. Bob Keppel, rhp

Born: June 11, 1982. **Ht.:** 6-5. **Wt.:** 200. **Bats:** R. **Throws:** R. **School:** DeSmet HS, St. Louis. **Career Transactions:** Selected by Mets in first round (36th overall) of 2000 draft; signed July 7, 2000.

Keppel has put together back-to-back steady performances in his first two full seasons in pro ball since signing as the 36th overall pick in 2000. One of the youngest starting pitchers in the Florida State League last year, he led the St. Lucie staff in starts and innings while ranking second in wins. Keppel has impressive poise, a solid repertoire and good command of all his pitches. He has good sinking action on his low-90s fastball and throws it to both sides of the plate. He also throws his changeup for strikes and has made significant progress over the past year with his curveball. The Mets appreciate Keppel's maturity and work ethic. Keppel needs to continue developing his secondary pitches by locating them better within the strike zone. He can lose the feel for his curve on occasion. His slider continues to look like a cutter at times and hasn't been as consistent as it was earlier in his career. Keppel's progress is unmistakable and encouraging, which could lead to bigger things in a hurry. A move to Double-A is on his immediate horizon.

Year	Club (League)	Class	W	L	ERA	G	GS	CG	SV	IP	H	R	ER	HR	BB	SO	AVG
2000	Kingsport (Appy)	R	1	2	6.83	8	6	0	0	29	31	22	22	1	13	29	.261
2001	Capital City (SAL)	A	6	7	3.11	26	20	1	0	124	118	58	43	6	25	87	.249
2002	St. Lucie (FSL)	A	9	7	4.32	27	26	0	0	152	162	83	73	13	43	109	.277
MINOR LEAGUE TOTALS			16	16	4.07	61	52	1	0	305	311	163	138	20	81	225	.264

10. Craig Brazell, 1b

Born: May 10, 1980. **Ht.:** 6-3. **Wt.:** 210. **Bats:** L. **Throws:** R. **School:** Jeff Davis HS, Montgomery, Ala. **Career Transactions:** Selected by Mets in fifth round of 1998 draft; signed June 4, 1998.

Drafted as a catcher, Brazell moved to first base in 1999 and has earned team MVP honors in the last two seasons in Class A. He boosted his performance after his July promotion to Double-A last year, and continued to excel with a strong showing in the Arizona Fall League. Brazell makes hard, consistent contact, and managers rated him the best power-hitting prospect in the Florida State League last year. His home run totals have increased as he has learned which pitches he's capable of driving. Brazell has a knack for rising to the occasion, which helped him record a 10-game RBI streak last season. The Mets want Brazell to work deeper counts after he walked just 14 times last year. That will not only increase his on-base percentage, but it will also make him more productive if he looks for a hitter's pitch. While he has made steady progress at first base, he needs to get better at making difficult plays. New York officials consider Brazell the most promising lefthanded hitter they've developed in years. He should be a candidate for the big league club in 2004.

Year	Club (League)	Class	AVG	G	AB	R	H	2B	3B	HR	RBI	BB	SO	SB	SLG	OBP
1998	Mets (GCL)	R	.298	13	47	6	14	3	1	1	6	2	13	0	.468	.340
1999	Kingsport (Appy)	R	.385	59	221	27	85	16	1	6	39	7	34	6	.548	.422
2000	Capital City (SAL)	A	.241	112	406	35	98	28	0	8	57	15	82	3	.369	.279
2001	Capital City (SAL)	A	.308	83	331	51	102	25	5	19	72	15	74	0	.586	.343
2002	St. Lucie (FSL)	A	.266	100	402	38	107	25	3	16	82	13	78	2	.463	.292
	Binghamton (EL)	AA	.308	35	130	14	40	8	0	6	19	1	28	0	.508	.343
MINOR LEAGUE TOTALS			.290	402	1537	171	446	105	10	56	275	53	309	11	.481	.324

11. Phil Seibel, lhp

Born: Jan. 28, 1979. **Ht.:** 6-1. **Wt.:** 190. **Bats:** L. **Throws:** L. **School:** University of Texas. **Career Transactions:** Selected by Expos in eighth round of 2000 draft; signed Aug. 7, 2000 . . . Traded by Expos with RHP Scott Strickland and OF Matt Watson to Mets for LHP Bruce Chen, RHP Dicky Gonzalez, SS Luis Figueroa and a player to be named, April 5, 2002; Expos acquired RHP Saul Rivera to complete trade (July 14, 2002).

The Mets obtained Seibel from Montreal last spring when Bruce Chen was shipped to the Expos. A member of Team USA's college squad in 1999, Seibel strained an elbow tendon the following year during his final season at Texas in 2000. Now that he has completely recovered, he's making rapid progress. He spent all of last year at Binghamton and led the team in wins. Seibel is a classic crafty lefthander with good command of four pitches. He throws a high-80s fastball and a plus changeup. His stuff can border on nasty when both of his breaking balls—a good slider and an improving curveball—are working and complementing his fastball. Seibel has a good feel against lefthanders and is aggressive against hitters from both sides of the plate. He also does the little things well, such as holding runners on base and fielding his position. Seibel's greatest needs are to repeat his delivery in order to maintain his command, and to master the finer points of pitching. Seibel could contribute in the majors as either a starter or reliever, and he'll pitch in Triple-A this season.

Year	Club (League)	Class	W	L	ERA	G	GS	CG	SV	IP	H	R	ER	HR	BB	SO	AVG
2001	Jupiter (FSL)	A	10	7	3.95	29	21	0	0	134	144	70	59	12	28	88	.273
2002	Binghamton (EL)	AA	10	8	3.97	28	25	2	0	150	147	78	66	17	49	114	.263
MINOR LEAGUE TOTALS			20	15	3.96	57	46	2	0	284	291	148	125	29	77	202	.268

12. Neal Musser, lhp

Born: Aug. 25, 1980. **Ht.:** 6-2. **Wt.:** 200. **Bats:** L. **Throws:** L. **School:** Benton Central HS, Oxford, Ind. **Career Transactions:** Selected by Mets in second round of 1999 draft; signed June 23, 1999.

Musser missed much of 2002 with a stress fracture in his left foot that occurred during the 2001 season. He made three starts at St. Lucie in April, four more at short-season Brooklyn and another in high Class A in July, then was shut down after totaling just 28 innings. He returned to pitch in relief in the Arizona Fall League, though he wasn't nearly as effective as he had been in the minors. The Mets' top pick (second round) in 1999, Musser has a 2.53 career ERA but hasn't been durable, making just 49 appearances in 3½ seasons. He succeeds by getting ahead of hitters, and his command has improved immensely since he turned pro.

His fastball is average but he locates it well. His changeup is his most effective pitch, while his curveball continues to show more consistency and depth. If he could stay healthy, Musser could move fast through the minors. A jump to Double-A this spring is a strong possibility.

Year	Club (League)	Class	W	L	ERA	G	GS	CG	SV	IP	H	R	ER	HR	BB	SO	AVG
1999	Mets (GCL)	R	2	1	2.01	8	7	0	0	31	26	13	7	1	18	22	.224
2000	Kingsport (Appy)	R	3	2	2.10	7	7	0	0	34	33	10	8	1	6	21	.252
2001	Capital City (SAL)	A	7	4	2.84	17	17	1	0	95	86	38	30	3	18	98	.240
	St. Lucie (FSL)	A	3	4	3.55	9	9	0	0	46	45	24	18	2	19	40	.257
2002	St. Lucie (FSL)	A	2	0	1.42	4	4	0	0	19	20	4	3	1	5	12	.274
	Brooklyn (NY-P)	A	0	0	0.69	4	4	0	0	13	7	2	1	0	5	12	.163
MINOR LEAGUE TOTALS			17	11	2.53	49	48	1	0	238	217	91	67	8	71	205	.242

13. Jason Phillips, c

Born: Sept. 27, 1976. **Ht.:** 6-1. **Wt.:** 170. **Bats:** R. **Throws:** R. **School:** San Diego State University. **Career Transactions:** Selected by Mets in 24th round of 1997 draft; signed June 11, 1997.

The Mets could upgrade their defense significantly if they named Phillips their starter and moved Mike Piazza to first base, but Mo Vaughn's weighty $10 million salary this year makes that an impossibility. Regardless, Phillips is knocking on the door of the majors. A solid receiver who continues to improve in all aspects of the game, Phillips had his best power season to date in his first extended Triple-A stint. He hits for a decent average, though his walk rate dipped last year. He's not a basestealing threat, but he doesn't clog the bases like most catchers. Phillips' strengths are his catch-and-throw skills and his game-calling ability. He threw out an uncharacteristically low 22 percent of basestealers in 2002, but he has a better arm than that. He moves well behind the plate and has a take-charge attitude that can be infectious for the pitching staff. With Piazza determined to remain a catcher and Vance Wilson establishing a foothold as a big league backup, Phillips has no clear path to the big leagues in 2003. A return to Norfolk remains likely, but he's ready for the majors.

Year	Club (League)	Class	AVG	G	AB	R	H	2B	3B	HR	RBI	BB	SO	SB	SLG	OBP
1997	Pittsfield (NY-P)	A	.206	48	155	15	32	9	0	2	17	15	24	4	.303	.282
1998	Capital City (SAL)	A	.271	69	251	36	68	15	1	5	37	23	35	5	.398	.343
	St. Lucie (FSL)	A	.464	8	28	4	13	2	0	0	2	2	1	0	.536	.500
1999	St. Lucie (FSL)	A	.258	81	283	36	73	12	1	9	48	23	28	0	.403	.327
	Binghamton (EL)	AA	.227	39	141	13	32	5	0	7	23	13	20	0	.411	.304
2000	St. Lucie (FSL)	A	.276	80	297	53	82	21	0	6	41	23	19	1	.407	.343
	Binghamton (EL)	AA	.388	27	98	16	38	4	0	0	13	7	9	0	.429	.435
2001	Binghamton (EL)	AA	.293	93	317	42	93	21	0	11	55	31	25	0	.464	.362
	Norfolk (IL)	AAA	.303	19	66	8	20	2	0	2	14	7	8	0	.424	.365
	New York (NL)	MAJ	.143	6	7	2	1	1	0	0	0	0	1	0	.286	.143
2002	Norfolk (IL)	AAA	.282	88	323	35	91	22	1	13	65	24	29	1	.477	.327
	New York (NL)	MAJ	.368	11	19	4	7	0	0	1	3	1	1	0	.526	.409
MAJOR LEAGUE TOTALS			.308	17	26	6	8	1	0	1	3	1	2	0	.462	.345
MINOR LEAGUE TOTALS			.277	552	1959	258	542	113	3	55	315	166	198	11	.422	.341

14. Jeremy Griffiths, rhp

Born: March 22, 1978. **Ht.:** 6-6. **Wt.:** 240. **Bats:** R. **Throws:** R. **School:** University of Toledo. **Career Transactions:** Selected by Mets in third round of 1999 draft; signed June 9, 1999.

Griffiths was added to New York's 40-man roster in November after he put together a strong showing in Double-A during the second half, then continued to throw well in the Arizona Fall League. After posting just one victory during the first three months of the season, he won his next five starts and was even better down the stretch, allowing three earned runs in his final 36 innings. His career 27-31 record conceals the steady progress that he has made. At 6-foot-6, he has ironed out many of the kinks he had in his delivery early in his career. His low-90s fastball has an excellent downward plane, while he continues to show more consistency within the strike zone with his slider and changeup. The Mets are working with Griffiths on improving his mound presence so he can better use his size and stuff to his advantage. He was more aggressive going after hitters in the AFL, where he had a 1.91 ERA and a 5-1 strikeout-walk ratio. He'll get at least a cursory look in big league camp before heading to Triple-A.

Year	Club (League)	Class	W	L	ERA	G	GS	CG	SV	IP	H	R	ER	HR	BB	SO	AVG
1999	Kingsport (Appy)	R	3	5	3.30	14	14	1	0	76	68	40	28	6	36	74	.243
2000	Capital City (SAL)	A	7	12	4.34	26	26	0	0	129	120	78	62	12	39	138	.242
2001	St. Lucie (FSL)	A	7	8	3.75	23	20	2	0	132	126	63	55	9	35	95	.253
	Binghamton (EL)	AA	2	0	0.69	2	2	0	0	13	8	3	1	0	4	12	.174
2002	Binghamton (EL)	AA	8	6	3.89	27	26	2	0	153	157	75	66	12	54	126	.272
MINOR LEAGUE TOTALS			27	31	3.80	92	88	6	0	503	479	259	212	39	168	445	.252

15. David Mattox, rhp

Born: May 24, 1980. **Ht.:** 6-2. **Wt.:** 180. **Bats:** R. **Throws:** R. **School:** Anderson (S.C.) College. **Career Transactions:** Selected by Mets in 11th round of 2001 draft; signed June 8, 2001.

There is no question that Mattox has the talent to pitch in the major leagues. The Mets simply are waiting for natural maturity to run its course and make him a more complete pitcher. Mattox was the most consistent starter at Capital City last season and was named the team's pitcher of the year. Though not overpowering, he has four useful pitches that he throws for strikes. He produces excellent sinking movement on his 90 mph fastball. He switches speeds well with his changeup and keeps hitters off balance. Mattox also is capable of throwing his curveball for strikes at any time in the count, while his 79-80 mph slider is effective when he has the feel for it. New York is confident Mattox will take a major step forward when his focus and all-around preparation catch up with his ability. That would help improve his command. He'll return to high Class A, with a Double-A promotion a possibility later in the year.

Year	Club (League)	Class	W	L	ERA	G	GS	CG	SV	IP	H	R	ER	HR	BB	SO	AVG
2001	Kingsport (Appy)	R	5	1	2.40	14	8	1	0	56	48	22	15	3	19	58	.225
	Brooklyn (NY-P)	A	1	0	0.90	2	2	0	0	10	5	2	1	0	3	12	.147
2002	Capital City (SAL)	A	8	2	3.55	17	17	0	0	91	78	42	36	3	42	92	.234
	St. Lucie (FSL)	A	4	4	2.82	9	9	2	0	51	46	21	16	2	24	34	.245
MINOR LEAGUE TOTALS			18	7	2.93	42	36	3	0	209	177	87	68	8	88	196	.230

16. Prentice Redman, of

Born: Aug. 23, 1979. **Ht.:** 6-3. **Wt.:** 180. **Bats:** R. **Throws:** R. **School:** Bevill State (Ala.) CC. **Career Transactions:** Selected by Mets in 10th round of 1999 draft; signed June 4, 1999.

Redman continues to rise to the level of his competition and is the Mets' best homegrown hope to fill their void in center field. The brother of Pirates outfield prospect Tike Redman, Prentice was named Binghamton's MVP after his best all-around full season as a pro. Redman is a late bloomer who's becoming more comfortable as his body matures and gets stronger. An excellent baserunner who didn't hit into a double play last season, he has outstanding athleticism that allows him to steal bases. He succeeded in 43 of 52 attempts last year. Redman has the range and arm to handle all three outfield positions. His improved performance at the plate can be attributed to hitting the ball to all fields instead of trying to pull every pitch. The more he hit, the more confidence he gained. Redman, who continues to have difficulty against lefthanders (.228 last year), has exceeded many expectations and projects as a possible No. 2 hitter in the majors. Provided his development persists in Triple-A, he could make his major league debut by the end of this year.

Year	Club (League)	Class	AVG	G	AB	R	H	2B	3B	HR	RBI	BB	SO	SB	SLG	OBP
1999	Kingsport (Appy)	R	.295	58	200	40	59	14	1	6	29	24	42	16	.465	.373
2000	Capital City (SAL)	A	.260	131	497	60	129	19	1	3	46	52	90	26	.320	.332
2001	St. Lucie (FSL)	A	.261	132	495	70	129	18	1	9	65	42	91	29	.356	.322
2002	Binghamton (EL)	AA	.283	135	491	79	139	35	2	11	63	59	112	43	.430	.367
MINOR LEAGUE TOTALS			.271	456	1683	249	456	86	5	29	203	177	335	114	.380	.345

17. Jeff Duncan, of

Born: Dec. 9, 1978. **Ht.:** 6-2. **Wt.:** 180. **Bats:** L. **Throws:** L. **School:** Arizona State University. **Career Transactions:** Selected by Mets in seventh round of 2000 draft; signed June 24, 2000.

If Prentice Redman can't become the Mets' center fielder of the future, perhaps Duncan can. He's more of a leadoff hitter than Redman, so Duncan possibly could fill two voids. A quality athlete who was an all-Illinois hockey player in high school, he earned a spot on the 40-man roster this winter after making some major adjustments during 2002. He couldn't shake his aluminum-bat swing during his first two pro seasons, but redeveloped his approach at the plate last year. He started to use the lower half of his body after swinging primarily with his arms earlier in his career. He also stayed through the ball and drove pitches to all fields, enabling him to hit .373 between two Class A affiliates. While his bat has solid pop, Duncan also has small-ball skills. He draws lots of walks, has gone 86 for 96 (90 percent) as a pro basestealer and has improved his bunting. A smart baserunner and excellent defensive outfielder, Duncan was old for Class A at 23 and must prove his performance was no fluke when he steps up to Double-A this year. He also needs to stay healthy. Duncan broke his arm when hit by a pitch in 2001, then broke his nose last year when he walked into a bat being swung during pregame drills.

Year	Club (League)	Class	AVG	G	AB	R	H	2B	3B	HR	RBI	BB	SO	SB	SLG	OBP
2000	Pittsfield (NY-P)	A	.242	53	186	39	45	3	5	2	13	34	46	20	.344	.371
2001	Capital City (SAL)	A	.217	88	318	49	69	16	8	3	23	46	97	41	.346	.320
2002	St. Lucie (FSL)	A	.343	29	102	20	35	5	0	2	10	24	15	10	.451	.472
	Capital City (SAL)	A	.393	40	150	33	59	13	3	4	17	18	34	15	.600	.468
MINOR LEAGUE TOTALS			.275	210	756	141	208	37	16	11	63	122	192	86	.410	.383

18. Heath Bell, rhp

Born: Sept. 29, 1977. **Ht.:** 6-2. **Wt.:** 240. **Bats:** R. **Throws:** R. **School:** Rancho Santiago (Calif.) JC. **Career Transactions:** Signed as nondrafted free agent by Mets, June 16, 1998.

Undrafted out of Rancho Santiago JC, the Mets signed Bell while he was pitching in the summer Alaska League. Bell posted a 2.57 ERA and saved 56 games in his first 2½ seasons, but hit the wall hard in 2001 with a 6.02 ERA in Double-A. He opened eyes again in 2002, dominating the Eastern League in the first half to earn a promotion to Triple-A. Bell has a live low-90s fastball and a consistent slider, but his changeup has been his best pitch for most of his pro career. He works both sides of the plate, possesses plus command and has an excellent idea of what he wants to accomplish on the mound. He also keeps his pitches down in the strike zone, allowing just two homers last year. The Mets were impressed with the way Bell bounced back and added him to the 40-man roster in November. His mechanics and control went slightly awry at Norfolk last year. If he can iron that out, he'll be ready for his first major league promotion.

Year	Club (League)	Class	W	L	ERA	G	GS	CG	SV	IP	H	R	ER	HR	BB	SO	AVG
1998	Kingsport (Appy)	R	1	0	2.54	22	0	0	8	46	40	15	13	5	11	61	.231
1999	Capital City (SAL)	A	1	7	2.60	55	0	0	25	62	47	23	18	3	17	68	.203
2000	St. Lucie (FSL)	A	5	1	2.55	48	0	0	23	60	43	19	17	4	21	75	.201
2001	Binghamton (EL)	AA	3	1	6.02	43	0	0	4	61	82	44	41	13	19	55	.320
2002	Binghamton (EL)	AA	1	0	1.18	24	0	0	6	38	22	6	5	0	6	49	.168
	Norfolk (IL)	AAA	3	4	4.26	22	0	0	5	32	38	15	15	2	9	28	.302
MINOR LEAGUE TOTALS			14	13	3.28	214	0	0	71	299	272	122	109	27	83	336	.240

19. Angel Pagan, of

Born: July 2, 1981. **Ht.:** 6-1. **Wt.:** 180. **Bats:** B. **Throws:** R. **School:** Indian River (Fla.) JC. **Career Transactions:** Selected by Mets in fourth round of 1999 draft; signed June 1, 2000.

Though Pagan's body is less than impressive, his tools are unmistakable. As a center fielder, he shows excellent range, good reactions and a strong, accurate arm. His plus speed allowed him to steal 62 bases, which ranked fifth in the minors and first in the system last year. Possessing minimal power, Pagan makes consistent contact at the plate as a slap-and-run hitter who has attracted comparisons to Luis Castillo. In order for Pagan to become a big leaguer, he must develop more of a leadoff mentality. The Mets stressed the importance of on-base percentage to him, but his walk rate only declined. He's a free swinger who gets himself out as often as the pitchers do. A full season in high Class A, where he was spectacular last August, is next on Pagan's agenda.

Year	Club (League)	Class	AVG	G	AB	R	H	2B	3B	HR	RBI	BB	SO	SB	SLG	OBP
2000	Kingsport (Appy)	R	.361	19	72	13	26	5	1	0	8	6	8	6	.458	.410
2001	Capital City (SAL)	A	.298	15	57	4	17	1	1	0	5	6	5	3	.351	.365
	Brooklyn (NY-P)	A	.315	62	238	46	75	10	2	0	15	22	30	30	.374	.388
2002	Capital City (SAL)	A	.279	108	458	79	128	14	5	1	36	32	87	52	.338	.325
	St. Lucie (FSL)	A	.343	16	67	12	23	2	1	1	7	7	9	10	.448	.405
MINOR LEAGUE TOTALS			.302	220	892	154	269	32	10	2	71	73	139	101	.367	.358

20. Tyler Walker, rhp

Born: May 15, 1976. **Ht.:** 6-3. **Wt.:** 230. **Bats:** R. **Throws:** R. **School:** University of California. **Career Transactions:** Selected by Mets in second round of 1997 draft; signed July 29, 1997.

Walker had a breakthrough season in 2000, but it ended badly as he tore his labrum in the Arizona Fall League and required shoulder surgery. He didn't get back to full strength until he pitched in Venezuela after the 2001 season. His command has improved since he got hurt. He lost 40 pounds in order to put less stress on his arm, and he also has found it easier to repeat his delivery and throw strikes. The velocity on his fastball has returned to the low 90s, and he also has a plus changeup and reliable curveball. Walker no longer is a maximum-effort pitcher and does a better job of keeping his pitches low in the strike zone. He's working on a slider that shows promise. Though Walker had arthroscopic surgery to clean out his right knee after the 2002 season, it was considered a minor procedure and he'll be 100 percent for spring training. Capable of starting or relieving, he'll get a chance to make the Mets in spring training and will be on call in Triple-A if he doesn't.

Year	Club (League)	Class	W	L	ERA	G	GS	CG	SV	IP	H	R	ER	HR	BB	SO	AVG
1997	Mets (GCL)	R	0	0	1.00	5	0	0	3	9	8	1	1	0	2	9	.235
	Pittsfield (NY-P)	A	0	0	13.50	1	0	0	0	1	2	2	1	1	1	1	.400
1998	Capital City (SAL)	A	5	5	4.12	34	13	0	1	116	122	63	53	9	38	110	.268
1999	St. Lucie (FSL)	A	6	5	2.94	13	13	2	0	80	64	31	26	6	29	64	.219
	Binghamton (EL)	AA	6	4	6.22	13	13	0	0	68	78	49	47	11	32	59	.292
2000	Binghamton (EL)	AA	7	6	2.75	22	22	0	0	121	82	43	37	3	55	111	.191
	Norfolk (IL)	AAA	1	3	2.39	5	5	0	0	26	29	7	7	0	9	17	.290
2001	St. Lucie (FSL)	A	0	2	8.04	4	4	0	0	16	19	14	14	0	3	11	.288
	Binghamton (EL)	AA	1	0	0.40	4	3	0	0	22	9	2	1	1	13	13	.127
	Norfolk (IL)	AAA	3	2	4.02	8	8	0	0	40	34	19	18	7	8	35	.230
2002	Norfolk (IL)	AAA	10	5	3.99	28	25	1	1	142	152	65	63	13	38	109	.275
	New York (NL)	MAJ	1	0	5.91	5	1	0	0	11	11	7	7	3	5	7	.250
MAJOR LEAGUE TOTALS			1	0	5.91	5	1	0	0	11	11	7	7	3	5	7	.250
MINOR LEAGUE TOTALS			39	32	3.76	137	106	3	5	641	599	296	268	51	228	539	.247

21. Tim Lavigne, rhp

Born: July 4, 1978. **Ht.:** 5-11. **Wt.:** 180. **Bats:** R. **Throws:** R. **School:** University of Virginia. **Career Transactions:** Selected by Mets in 32nd round of 2000 draft; signed June 16, 2000.

A former shortstop at the University of Virginia who moved to the mound toward the end of his college career, Lavigne has made rapid progress during his first two full seasons as a pro. At 5-foot-11, he doesn't have the size scouts want in a righthander, and his overall stuff is far from overpowering. But he gets outs by spotting four pitches all around the strike zone. Lavigne ties up hitters with a changeup that's nearly a plus pitch. He also has an average fastball, a curveball and a slider. The Mets like the way Lavigne challenges hitters and never strays from his determined approach. He gets results, and his bulldog mentality could make him an effective set-up man in the majors if he can walk the fine line between throwing strikes and not giving batters too good a pitch to hit. His performance in spring training will determine whether Lavigne opens 2003 in Double-A or Triple-A.

Year	Club (League)	Class	W	L	ERA	G	GS	CG	SV	IP	H	R	ER	HR	BB	SO	AVG
2000	Pittsfield (NY-P)	A	2	1	2.70	15	0	0	6	17	11	5	5	1	7	15	.196
2001	Capital City (SAL)	A	5	3	2.29	33	0	0	12	63	51	24	16	1	21	44	.216
	St. Lucie (FSL)	A	1	0	0.00	4	0	0	0	5	4	2	0	0	2	2	.211
2002	St. Lucie (FSL)	A	0	2	3.76	22	0	0	7	26	21	11	11	3	9	25	.214
	Binghamton (EL)	AA	2	3	2.86	23	0	0	9	35	29	11	11	1	15	25	.236
MINOR LEAGUE TOTALS			10	9	2.65	97	0	0	34	146	116	53	43	6	54	111	.218

22. Jake Joseph, rhp

Born: Jan. 24, 1978. **Ht.:** 6-1. **Wt.:** 210. **Bats:** R. **Throws:** R. **School:** Cosumnes River (Calif.) JC. **Career Transactions:** Selected by Mets in second round of 1999 draft; signed July 7, 1999.

Joseph bounced back from a disastrous 2001 season to pitch effectively in Double-A, where he beat his childhood idol Roger Clemens, who was making a rehab start, 1-0 in August. Joseph doesn't miss a lot of bats, but he learned the hard way that he can't nibble and fall behind in the count. He still relies too much on his low-90s sinker and his slider, but he went after hitters much more aggressively last year. He must develop an offspeed pitch to have a chance to start in the majors, and he worked toward that goal in the Arizona Fall League. His 7.36 ERA in the AFL didn't detract from the fact that he has re-established himself with the Mets. He's a candidate for the Triple-A rotation this year and projects as more of a middle reliever in the majors.

Year	Club (League)	Class	W	L	ERA	G	GS	CG	SV	IP	H	R	ER	HR	BB	SO	AVG
1999	Pittsfield (NY-P)	A	3	2	2.91	11	6	0	1	43	35	19	14	1	27	26	.217
2000	Capital City (SAL)	A	4	3	2.85	15	15	0	0	85	81	45	27	2	29	59	.249
2001	St. Lucie (FSL)	A	4	12	5.34	25	24	0	0	128	162	93	76	6	52	69	.315
2002	St. Lucie (FSL)	A	3	3	3.59	13	13	0	0	73	75	33	29	1	13	47	.262
	Binghamton (EL)	AA	6	4	2.91	14	14	0	0	87	79	37	28	4	24	42	.248
	Norfolk (IL)	AAA	0	1	12.27	1	1	0	0	4	8	5	5	0	3	1	.421
MINOR LEAGUE TOTALS			20	25	3.84	79	73	0	1	420	440	232	179	14	148	244	.271

23. Jae Seo, rhp

Born: May 24, 1977. **Ht.:** 6-1. **Wt.:** 210. **Bats:** R. **Throws:** R. **Career Transactions:** Signed out of Korea by Mets, Jan. 6, 1998.

Seo's stock has dropped as much as any player's in the Mets system over the past year. Once considered at least a middle-of-the-rotation starter in the major leagues, Seo has yet to regain the velocity he had prior to having Tommy John surgery in 1999. His fastball used to sit at 93-95 mph but he rarely touched 92 last year in Triple-A. As a result, his plus changeup has lost effectiveness because it doesn't contrast his fastball as much as it once did. His best pitch at this point is a hard splitter. Seo rarely gives up walks but is too hittable and would be better served by trying to get hitters to chase more pitches. Besides his elbow surgery, there also are concerns about his conditioning. He reported to spring training considerably out of shape in 2001. Last year he was losing strength after a couple of innings until the Mets discovered he was not eating prior to starts. If Seo can put the pieces back together, he has a chance to be a fourth or fifth starter in the majors. He'll get a look in big league camp but is likely to open 2003 back in Triple-A.

Year	Club (League)	Class	W	L	ERA	G	GS	CG	SV	IP	H	R	ER	HR	BB	SO	AVG
1998	St. Lucie (FSL)	A	3	1	2.31	8	7	0	0	35	26	13	9	2	10	37	.206
	Mets (GCL)	R	0	0	0.00	2	0	0	0	5	4	0	0	0	0	5	.235
1999	St. Lucie (FSL)	A	2	0	1.84	3	3	0	0	15	8	3	3	0	2	14	.154
2000	Did Not Play—Injured																
2001	St. Lucie (FSL)	A	2	3	3.55	6	5	0	0	25	21	11	10	2	6	19	.221
	Binghamton (EL)	AA	5	1	1.94	12	10	0	0	60	44	14	13	3	11	47	.206
	Norfolk (IL)	AAA	2	2	3.42	9	9	0	0	47	53	18	18	4	6	25	.296
2002	Norfolk (IL)	AAA	6	9	3.99	26	24	1	0	129	145	66	57	14	22	87	.284
	Binghamton (EL)	AA	0	0	5.40	1	0	0	0	5	5	3	3	1	1	6	.250
	New York (NL)	MAJ	0	0	0.00	1	0	0	0	1	0	0	0	0	0	1	.000
MAJOR LEAGUE TOTALS			0	0	0.00	1	0	0	0	1	0	0	0	0	0	1	.000
MINOR LEAGUE TOTALS			20	16	3.16	67	58	1	0	321	306	128	113	26	58	240	.252

24. Wayne Lydon, of

Born: April 17, 1981. **Ht.:** 6-2. **Wt.:** 190. **Bats:** B. **Throws:** R. **School:** Valley View HS, Archbald, Pa. **Career Transactions:** Selected by Mets in ninth round of 1999 draft; signed June 4, 1999.

A former Penn State football recruit who gave up the gridiron to sign as a ninth-round pick in 1999, Lydon had to wonder if he made the right decision after batting .202 in his first 2½ pro seasons. He tried to be all things to all people instead of playing to his strengths and realizing his limitations. He opened last season as a low Class A reserve, but made the most of his opportunity for playing time when he received it. He batted a career-high .294 and stole 87 bases, one shy of the minor league lead. An intense player but one who shows little emotion on the field, Lydon started switch-hitting in 2001 to take advantage of his plus speed. While still feeble from his natural right side with a .234 average, he hit .314 batting lefthanded last year. He bunts well to both baselines and records numerous infield hits. Lydon also has the ability to drive the ball to the gaps on occasion, though power isn't expected to be part of his game. His defense improved considerably last year, with Lydon getting better jumps by reading the ball off the bat. His arm strength is average at best, which might limit him to left field, but he does have a quick release and good accuracy. Lydon needs to keep working on his on-base skills and defense this year in high Class A.

Year	Club (League)	Class	AVG	G	AB	R	H	2B	3B	HR	RBI	BB	SO	SB	SLG	OBP
1999	Mets (GCL)	R	.183	37	60	13	11	3	0	0	5	7	13	0	.233	.279
2000	Kingsport (Appy)	R	.203	55	172	34	35	4	1	3	20	24	47	35	.291	.300
2001	Kingsport (Appy)	R	.184	26	98	14	18	7	0	0	8	11	35	15	.255	.266
	Brooklyn (NY-P)	A	.246	21	57	12	14	1	1	0	1	7	18	10	.298	.348
2002	Capital City (SAL)	A	.294	127	473	93	139	9	5	0	46	54	104	87	.334	.368
MINOR LEAGUE TOTALS			.252	266	860	166	217	24	7	3	80	103	217	147	.307	.335

25. Ty Wigginton, 3b

Born: Oct. 11, 1977. **Ht.:** 6-0. **Wt.:** 200. **Bats:** R. **Throws:** R. **School:** UNC Asheville. **Career Transactions:** Selected by Mets in 17th round of 1998 draft; signed June 3, 1998.

Wigginton made the most of his first opportunity in the big leagues last year and surprised the Mets in the process. A career .273 hitter in four minor league seasons entering 2002, he received a promotion to New York in May when John Valentin went on the 15-day disabled list. He returned to the Mets in July and finished the season hitting .302-6-18 in 116 major league at-bats. The first player from UNC Asheville to reach the majors, Wigginton is a productive line-drive hitter with above-average gap power. An overachiever, he's an aggressive player and a hard worker. He has improved his strike-zone judgment. His defense, particularly with routine plays, can be a liability. A shortstop in college, he moved to second base during his first two professional seasons before shifting to third at Double-A in 2000. While his footwork and hands are adequate, consistency remains his biggest hurdle. He's a strong candidate to earn a utility role with New York this season and could compete for the starting job at third base after hitting .280-9-31 this winter in the Dominican Republic.

Year	Club (League)	Class	AVG	G	AB	R	H	2B	3B	HR	RBI	BB	SO	SB	SLG	OBP
1998	Pittsfield (NY-P)	A	.239	70	272	39	65	14	4	8	29	16	72	11	.408	.284
1999	St. Lucie (FSL)	A	.292	123	456	69	133	23	5	21	73	56	82	9	.502	.373
2000	Binghamton (EL)	AA	.285	122	453	64	129	27	3	20	77	24	107	5	.490	.319
2001	Norfolk (IL)	AAA	.250	78	260	29	65	12	0	7	24	27	66	3	.377	.323
	St. Lucie (FSL)	A	.333	3	9	1	3	1	0	0	1	4	2	0	.444	.571
	Binghamton (EL)	AA	.286	8	28	5	8	3	0	0	0	5	5	1	.393	.394
2002	Norfolk (IL)	AAA	.300	104	383	49	115	26	3	6	48	43	50	5	.431	.366
	New York (NL)	MAJ	.302	46	116	18	35	8	0	6	18	8	19	2	.526	.354
MAJOR LEAGUE TOTALS			.302	46	116	18	35	8	0	6	18	8	19	2	.526	.354
MINOR LEAGUE TOTALS			.278	508	1861	256	518	106	15	62	252	175	384	34	.451	.341

26. Haj Turay, of

Born: Sept. 22, 1982. **Ht.:** 6-0. **Wt.:** 200. **Bats:** R. **Throws:** R. **School:** Auburn (Wash.) HS. **Career Transactions:** Selected by Mets in second round of 2001 draft; signed July 5, 2001.

Turay ranked third in the New York-Penn League batting race in late August when the Mets sent him home because of his attitude. He had alienated teammates, opponents and fans with his behavior, which included deterring autograph seekers by pretending he didn't speak English and by signing Tom Hanks' name. He also cursed at a fan and destroyed a dugout water cooler. New York hopes the punishment will serve as a wakeup call for the hard-hitting Turay. After focusing on football for most of his high school career, he has shown raw offensive tools. His swing has a slight uppercut that allows him to drive the ball and get the necessary loft for homers. He needs to refine his approach at the plate, where his poor strike-zone judgment is a handicap. His lack of extensive experience is obvious in the outfield, where he's a marginal defender with a weak arm that will limit him to left field. He does have plus speed and athleticism. If Turay can get straightened out, he could become an impact player in the middle of the lineup. He'll open 2003 in low Class A.

Year	Club (League)	Class	AVG	G	AB	R	H	2B	3B	HR	RBI	BB	SO	SB	SLG	OBP
2001	Kingsport (Appy)	R	.245	43	163	21	40	8	3	2	20	9	46	8	.368	.286
2002	Brooklyn (NY-P)	A	.327	40	153	21	50	10	1	4	19	11	48	7	.484	.380
MINOR LEAGUE TOTALS			.285	83	316	42	90	18	4	6	39	20	94	15	.424	.331

27. Tyler Yates, rhp

Born: Aug. 7, 1977. **Ht.:** 6-4. **Wt.:** 220. **Bats:** R. **Throws:** R. **School:** University of Hawaii-Hilo. **Career Transactions:** Selected by Athletics in 23rd round of 1998 draft; signed June 10, 1998 . . . Traded by Athletics with LHP Mark Guthrie to Mets for OF David Justice and cash, Dec. 14, 2001.

After being acquired in a trade with Oakland during the offseason, Yates showed the Mets everything they hoped during the first half of 2002. He was untouchable while sharing closer duties in Triple-A, until he blew out his elbow and needed Tommy John surgery. A starter in college at Hawaii-Hilo, Yates refined his mechanics and emerged as a power reliever as a pro. He complements a mid-90s fastball with a mid-80s slider. When he begins pitching again in mid-2003, Yates will have to refine his command in addition to regaining his strength. If he hadn't gotten hurt, he would have fit nicely in the New York bullpen this year.

Year	Club (League)	Class	W	L	ERA	G	GS	CG	SV	IP	H	R	ER	HR	BB	SO	AVG
1998	Athletics (AZL)	R	0	0	3.91	15	0	0	2	23	28	12	10	0	14	20	.304
	S. Oregon (NWL)	A	0	0	0.00	2	0	0	1	2	2	0	0	0	0	1	.222
1999	Visalia (Cal)	A	2	5	5.47	47	1	0	4	82	98	64	50	12	35	74	.290
2000	Modesto (Cal)	A	4	2	2.86	30	0	0	1	57	50	23	18	2	23	61	.237
	Midland (TL)	AA	1	1	6.15	22	0	0	0	26	28	20	18	2	15	24	.275
2001	Midland (TL)	AA	4	6	4.31	56	0	0	17	63	66	39	30	4	27	61	.261
	Sacramento (PCL)	AAA	1	0	0.00	4	0	0	1	5	3	0	0	0	1	3	.167
2002	Norfolk (IL)	AAA	2	2	1.32	24	0	0	6	34	29	10	5	1	13	34	.227
MINOR LEAGUE TOTALS			14	16	4.03	200	1	0	32	293	304	168	131	21	128	278	.264

28. Adam Elliot, rhp

Born: March 27, 1984. **Ht.:** 6-2. **Wt.:** 200. **Bats:** B. **Throws:** R. **School:** Clayton Valley HS, Concord, Calif. **Career Transactions:** Selected by Mets in sixth round of 2002 draft; signed June 10, 2002.

The Mets clearly got a steal when Scott Kazmir fell to the 15th overall pick in the 2002 draft, and they pulled a less obvious coup when they grabbed Elliot in the sixth round. After forgoing his commitment to Nevada-Las Vegas, Elliot went from high school to low Class A at age 18. Along the way, he showed an aggressive disposition, a love for competition and total confidence. He throws straight over the top with a low-90s fastball that features good movement. His circle changeup is effective, and he's working on gaining consistency with his overhand curveball. He still has to harness all of his pitches and learn to do the little things associated with pitching, such as holding runners and fielding. Elliot will remain a starter for now to maximize his innings, but he could be a late-inning reliever down the road. He'll begin 2003 in low Class A.

Year	Club (League)	Class	W	L	ERA	G	GS	CG	SV	IP	H	R	ER	HR	BB	SO	AVG
2002	Kingsport (Appy)	R	2	2	3.16	11	8	0	0	43	27	16	15	6	14	37	.182
	Capital City (SAL)	A	0	1	10.80	1	1	0	0	5	6	6	6	1	1	8	.333
	Brooklyn (NY-P)	A	0	0	1.50	3	0	0	0	6	3	2	1	0	1	6	.136
MINOR LEAGUE TOTALS			2	3	3.69	15	9	0	0	54	36	24	22	7	16	51	.191

29. Corey Ragsdale, ss

Born: Nov. 10, 1982. **Ht.:** 6-4. **Wt.:** 170. **Bats:** R. **Throws:** R. **School:** Nettleton HS, Jonesboro, Ark. **Career Transactions:** Selected by Mets in second round of 2001 draft; signed July 26, 2001.

Ragsdale has hit .174 since turning pro, but the Mets remain hopeful that his bat will come around enough so they eventually can use him as an above-average defender at shortstop. His lack of production led the Mets to try him as a switch-hitter during the offseason. A natural righthanded hitter, Ragsdale got some hits from the left side in game action during the final week of instructional league. That left several Mets coaches re-energized about his long-term potential. Ragsdale easily is one of the best pure defensive players and top athletes in the system. While he can be inconsistent at times with the leather, he has easy, fluid actions and a powerful arm. Some scouts even think New York should try him on the mound. He'll head back to low Class A this year and try to figure out how to hit. Getting stronger would help, as would tightening his strike zone.

Year	Club (League)	Class	AVG	G	AB	R	H	2B	3B	HR	RBI	BB	SO	SB	SLG	OBP
2001	Kingsport (Appy)	R	.141	23	71	9	10	3	2	1	5	10	38	4	.282	.256
2002	Capital City (SAL)	A	.177	37	124	15	22	1	0	1	12	15	45	8	.210	.262
	Brooklyn (NY-P)	A	.183	66	224	35	41	7	2	2	19	23	72	26	.259	.277
MINOR LEAGUE TOTALS			.174	126	419	59	73	11	4	4	36	48	155	38	.248	.269

30. Ross Peeples, lhp

Born: Feb. 20, 1980. **Ht.:** 6-4. **Wt.:** 190. **Bats:** L. **Throws:** L. **School:** Middle Georgia CC. **Career Transactions:** Selected by Mets in 45th round of 1999 draft; signed May 25, 2000.

Peeples led the New York-Penn League in wins in 2001 and gave up just one earned run in his first three starts at low Class A last year, earning a rapid promotion in April. The Florida State League proved to be too much, too soon for Peeples, who got going again once he returned to the South Atlantic League. Signed as a draft-and-follow out of Middle Georgia, Peeples works as fast as any pitcher in the minors, keeping his fielders on their toes and opposing hitters off balance. While he doesn't have a plus pitch, he refuses to give in to hitters and mixes his offerings well. He throws a high-80s fastball, a sharp slider and a changeup. Improving his curveball would give another weapon. Peeples will get a second chance at high Class A this year.

Year	Club (League)	Class	W	L	ERA	G	GS	CG	SV	IP	H	R	ER	HR	BB	SO	AVG
2000	Kingsport (Appy)	R	1	2	2.61	15	2	0	0	31	25	15	9	1	10	29	.216
2001	Brooklyn (NY-P)	A	9	3	1.34	16	15	1	0	80	63	19	12	1	29	67	.214
2002	Capital City (SAL)	A	7	7	2.43	20	19	0	1	115	104	49	31	3	25	98	.241
	St. Lucie (FSL)	A	2	3	5.59	6	6	0	0	29	33	24	18	2	13	26	.284
MINOR LEAGUE TOTALS			19	15	2.47	57	42	1	1	255	225	107	70	7	77	220	.235

NEW YORK
YANKEES

TOP 30 PROSPECTS

1. Jose Contreras, rhp
2. Hideki Matsui, of
3. Juan Rivera, of
4. Bronson Sardinha, of
5. Brandon Claussen, lhp
6. Drew Henson, 3b
7. Chien-Ming Wang, rhp
8. Robinson Cano, 2b/ss
9. Danny Borrell, lhp
10. Julio DePaula, rhp
11. Rudy Guillen, of
12. Sean Henn, lhp
13. Ferdin Tejada, ss
14. Charlie Manning, lhp
15. Andy Phillips, 2b
16. Joaquin Arias, 2b/ss
17. Jason Anderson, rhp
18. Javier Ortiz, rhp
19. Brandon Weeden, rhp
20. Jose Valdez, rhp
21. Dioner Navarro, c
22. Alex Graman, lhp
23. Kevin Reese, of
24. Erick Almonte, ss
25. Marcus Thames, of
26. Ryan Bicondoa, rhp
27. Adrian Hernandez, rhp
28. Deivi Mendez, ss
29. Yhency Brazoban, rhp
30. Kevin Thompson, of

By Josh Boyd

After their earliest postseason exit since 1997, it figured to be a tumultuous offseason for George Steinbrenner's Yankees. And we were quickly reminded that these are *George Steinbrenner's* Yankees.

With their American League Division Series loss, the new labor agreement and an aging pitching staff, the Yankees began the offseason with talk of limiting payroll. General manager Brian Cashman was trying to find new homes for the contracts of Raul Mondesi, Rondell White and Sterling Hitchcock.

Not only did the Yankees not unload their excess, but they stayed true to their track record and spent more, signing Japanese superstar Hideki Matsui and Cuban defector Jose Contreras for a combined $53 million before Christmas. It didn't stop there, even as the payroll approached $160 million, more than $40 million over the luxury tax threshold. Instead of trimming excess the Yankees seemed to add to it by signing 37-year-old Todd Zeile after already re-signing 35-year-old Robin Ventura, then inking righthander Jon Lieber to a two-year deal even though he won't pitch again until 2004.

The highlight of all the moves was the Contreras signing, which may have had more to do with Steinbrenner's orders to keep the Cuban righthander away from the Red Sox than Contreras' talent. Never mind that manager Joe Torre had expressed his concerns about how to handle an overflowing rotation. The Yankees already had re-signed Andy Pettitte and Roger Clemens for another $21.6 million, with Mike Mussina, Contreras, David Wells, Jeff Weaver and Hitchcock also in the picture. If seven starters weren't enough, Steinbrenner kept the Bartolo Colon talks alive with the Expos, again to drive up the price for the Red Sox, and then helped drive a three-way deal that landed Colon in Chicago.

Though Steinbrenner hasn't gone back to firing managers at a Billy Martin-like pace, reports of him running amok in the front office were more frequent. Senior vice president of baseball operations Mark Newman, who headed the Yankees' minor league complex in Tampa and had duties ranging from player personnel decisions and pro and amateur scouting, was forced to step into a lesser role in January. International scouting director Gordon Blakeley, another respected talent evaluator, was promoted to Newman's position.

Organization**Overview**

General manager: Brian Cashman. **Farm director:** Rob Thomson. **Scouting director:** Lin Garrett.

2002 PERFORMANCE

Class	Farm Team	League	W	L	Pct.	Finish*	Manager(s)
Majors	New York	American	103	58	.640	1st (14)	Joe Torre
Triple-A	Columbus Clippers	International	59	83	.415	12th (14)	B. Butterfield/S. Merrill
Double-A	†Norwich Navigators	Eastern	76	64	.543	+3rd (12)	S. Merrill/L. Sojo
High A	Tampa Yankees	Florida State	71	62	.534	5th (12)	Mitch Seoane
Low A	#Greensboro Bats	South Atlantic	75	65	.535	7th (16)	Bill Masse
Short-season	Staten Island Yankees	New York-Penn	48	26	.649	+1st (14)	Derek Shelton
Rookie	GCL Yankees	Gulf Coast	36	24	.600	3rd (14)	Manny Crespo
OVERALL MINOR LEAGUE RECORD			365	324	.530	6th (30)	

*Finish in overall standings (No. of teams in league). +League champion. †Affiliate will be in Trenton (Eastern) in 2003. #Affiliate will be in Battle Creek (Midwest) in 2003.

ORGANIZATION LEADERS

BATTING
*Minimum 250 At-Bats
*AVG	Juan Rivera, Columbus/GCL Yankees	.324
R	Andy Phillips, Columbus/Norwich	90
H	Robinson Cano, Greensboro/Staten Island	155
TB	Andy Phillips, Columbus/Norwich	262
2B	Mitch Jones, Norwich/Tampa	35
	Andy Phillips, Columbus/Norwich	35
3B	Robinson Cano, Greensboro/Staten Island	10
HR	Andy Phillips, Columbus/Norwich	28
RBI	Mike Cervenak, Norwich	91
BB	Brian Myrow, Norwich/Tampa	83
SO	Drew Henson, Columbus	151
	Andy Brown, Tampa	151
SB	Kevin Thompson, Tampa/Greensboro/SI	31

PITCHING
#Minimum 75 Innings
W	Julio DePaula, Norwich	14
L	Matt Smith, Norwich/Tampa	12
#ERA	Danny Borrell, Norwich/Tampa	2.32
G	Jay Tessmer, Columbus	63
CG	Julio DePaula, Norwich	6
SV	Mathew Brumit, Staten Island	22
IP	Javier Ortiz, Tampa/Greensboro	177
BB	Jeremy King, Greensboro	66
SO	Julio DePaula, Norwich	152

BEST TOOLS

Best Hitter for Average	Hideki Matsui
Best Power Hitter	Hideki Matsui
Fastest Baserunner	Ferdin Tejada
Best Athlete	Brandon Weeden
Best Fastball	Jose Contreras
Best Curveball	Charlie Manning
Best Slider	Jose Contreras
Best Changeup	Ryan Bicondoa
Best Command	Jose Contreras
Best Defensive Catcher	Michel Hernandez
Best Defensive Infielder	Ferdin Tejada
Best Infield Arm	Robinson Cano
Best Defensive Outfielder	Kevin Thompson
Best Outfield Arm	Marcus Thames

PROJECTED 2006 LINEUP

Catcher	Jorge Posada
First Base	Nick Johnson
Second Base	Alfonso Soriano
Third Base	Drew Henson
Shortstop	Derek Jeter
Left Field	Hideki Matsui
Center Field	Bernie Williams
Right Field	Juan Rivera
Designated Hitter	Jason Giambi
No. 1 Starter	Jose Contreras

Andy Phillips   **Matt Smith**

No. 2 Starter	Mike Mussina
No. 3 Starter	Brandon Claussen
No. 4 Starter	Jeff Weaver
No. 5 Starter	Chien-Ming Wang
Closer	Mariano Rivera

TOP PROSPECTS OF THE DECADE

1993	Brien Taylor, lhp
1994	Derek Jeter, ss
1995	Ruben Rivera, of
1996	Ruben Rivera, of
1997	Ruben Rivera, of
1998	Eric Milton, lhp
1999	Nick Johnson, 1b
2000	Nick Johnson, 1b
2001	Nick Johnson, 1b
2002	Drew Henson, 3b

TOP DRAFT PICKS OF THE DECADE

1993	Matt Drews, rhp
1994	Brian Buchanan, of
1995	Shea Morenz, of
1996	Eric Milton, lhp
1997	*Tyrell Godwin, of
1998	Andy Brown, of
1999	David Walling, rhp
2000	David Parrish, c
2001	John-Ford Griffin, of
2002	Brandon Weeden, rhp (2)

*Did not sign.

ALL-TIME LARGEST BONUSES

Hideki Irabu, 1997	$8,500,000
Jose Contreras, 2002	$6,000,000
Wily Mo Pena, 1999	$2,440,000
Drew Henson, 1998	$2,000,000
Chien-Ming Wang, 2000	$1,900,000

MinorLeague**Depth**Chart

NEW YORK YANKEES

RANK

The outlook for the Yankees was much bleaker before they outbid everyone to sign international superstars Jose Contreras (Cuba) and Hideki Matsui (Japan) in December. But the system can't take credit for developing either player, as they aren't likely to ever see a day in the minors. The farm system was decimated by injuries, trades and disappointing performances in 2002 and much of the Yankees' hope for the future has been pinned on inexperienced, low-level prospects with high ceilings. Which direction Drew Henson's career heads in 2003 could be a major factor in the system's direction.

Note: Depth charts prepared by Josh Boyd. Numbers in parentheses indicate prospect rankings.

LF
Hideki Matsui (2)
Bronson Sardinha (4)
Jason Grove
Shelley Duncan
Erold Andrus
Mitch Jones

CF
Kevin Reese (23)
Kevin Thompson (30)
Richard Brown

RF
Juan Rivera (3)
Rudy Guillen (11)
Marcus Thames (25)
Matt Carson

3B
Drew Henson (6)
Elvis Corporan
Juan Camacho

SS
Ferdin Tejada (13)
Erick Almonte (24)
Deivi Mendez (28)

2B
Robinson Cano (8)
Andy Phillips (15)
Joaquin Arias (16)
Teuris Olivares

1B
Aaron Rifkin

C
Dioner Navarro (21)
Michel Hernandez
David Parrish

RHP

Starters
Jose Contreras (1)
Chien-Ming Wang (7)
Brandon Weeden (19)
Jose Valdez (20)
Ryan Bicondoa (26)
Jon Skaggs
Bryan Grace
Alan Bomer

Relievers
Julio DePaula (10)
Jason Anderson(17)
Javier Ortiz (18)
Adrian Hernandez (27)
Yhency Brazoban (29)
Manny Acosta
Edison Reynoso
Delvis Lantigua
Jeremy Blevins
Mathew Brumit
Adam Roller
Anderson Garcia
Christian Mendoza

LHP

Starters
Brandon Claussen (5)
Danny Borrell (9)
Sean Henn (12)
Charlie Manning (14)
Alex Graman (22)
Andy Beal
David Martinez
Matt Smith
Brad Halsey
Chase Wright
Edgar Soto

Relievers
Carlos Artiles

DraftAnalysis

2002 Draft

Best Pro Debut: RHP Mathew Brumit (44) caught the Yankees' attention during a predraft workout at Triple-A Columbus. He led the short-season New-York Penn League with 33 appearances and 22 saves, posting a 2.21 ERA and a 40-8 strikeout-walk ratio in 37 innings. New York's NY-P affiliate in Staten Island had a 2.57 team ERA. Other contributors included two of the Yankees' four signees from College World Series champion Texas: LHP **Brad Halsey** (8), who went 6-1, 1.93, and RHP Ray Clark (14), who went 3-0, 1.97. RHP Ryan Bicondoa, signed as a fifth-year senior before the draft, went 6-4, 1.90 with a 94-7 K-BB ratio.

Best Athlete: RHP Brandon Weeden (2) did it all for his Oklahoma high school. He was a football quarterback, basketball forward and a pitcher/shortstop. His frame (6-foot-4, 190 pounds), arm action and athleticism fit the mold of a true power pitcher.

Best Pure Hitter: 1B Ross Michelsen (7) reminds the Yankees of Nick Johnson when they took him in the third round in 1996. He has the same approach and discipline, uses the whole field and should add power.

Best Raw Power: OF Matt Carson (5) has a quick bat but was bothered by a knee he banged up during the Mountain West Conference tournament.

Fastest Runner: The Yankees didn't draft much speed. OF Jon Sheaffer (19) is above-average but not a burner.

Best Defensive Player: Carson has the arm and range to be a standout in right field.

Best Fastball: RHP Brandon Harmsen (6)

pitches at 90-93 mph. Weeden and RHP Alan Bomer (4), another Longhorn, top out at 93 also.

Best Breaking Ball: Weeden's slider.

Most Intriguing Background: Unsigned OF Skyler Fulton (22) is a wide receiver for Arizona State. The Yankees drafted LHP/OF Ben King (20), their fourth Longhorn, though he didn't pitch in 2001 because of a shoulder injury and missed all of 2002 after Tommy John surgery. King should be ready to take the mound by mid-2003.

Halsey

Closest To The Majors: Halsey hits his spots with an average fastball and tough splitter. Though radar guns usually catch him at 86-88 mph, Bicondoa could move quickly as well. His fastball has plenty of sink, his curveball is his out pitch, and he can throw his changeup in any count.

Best Late-Round Pick: Brumit has a plus fastball and solid slider, and throws strikes.

The One Who Got Away: The Yankees signed everyone through 21 rounds. Fulton is the only one they tried and failed to sign.

Assessment: Though cost is no object for the big league roster, the Yankees have been conservative in recent drafts. They gave up their first three picks in 2002 as free-agent compensation–and got a second-rounder (Weeden) for the loss of Tino Martinez–but didn't take any risks on expensive players.

2001 Draft

RHP Jason Arnold (1) and OF John-Ford Griffin (2) were traded and could reach the majors quickly with Toronto. OF Bronson Sardinha (1) is the most promising hitter in the lower levels. RHP Jon Skaggs (1) hurt his elbow in his debut and hasn't pitched since.   **Grade: B+**

2000 Draft

C David Parrish was a surprising first-round pick who has proven to be a reach. LHP Danny Borrell (2) has had the most minor league success. LHP Sean Henn (26) had Tommy John surgery after signing for a draft-and-follow record $1.701 million.   **Grade: C**

1999 Draft

RHP David Walling's (1) career has stalled, but there's hope for 2B Andy Phillips (7), who started hitting for power last summer.   **Grade: D**

1998 Draft

This crop looked a lot better before 3B Drew Henson hit .240 in Triple-A and draft-and-follow lefthander Brandon Claussen (34) succumbed to Tommy John surgery last year. OF Andy Brown (1) is a strikeout machine. Signing RHP Mark Prior (1) would have made all that easy to forget.   **Grade: C+**

Note: Draft analysis prepared by Jim Callis. Numbers in parentheses indicate draft rounds.

... Contreras is mature and competitive and has the work ethic to get considerably better.

Jose
Contreras rhp

Born: June 12, 1971.
Ht.: 6-4. **Wt.:** 230.
Bats: R. **Throws:** R.
Career Transactions: Signed out of Cuba by Yankees, Dec. 24, 2002.

Contreras defected from the Cuban national team during the Americas Series tournament in Saltillo, Mexico, last October. He sought asylum in the United States, but to avoid becoming subject to the draft he then established residency in Nicaragua. Major League Baseball declared him a free agent in December. The Yankees, Red Sox, Mariners and Dodgers sent officials to Nicaragua to negotiate with Contreras and agent Jaime Torres. Boston had a four-year, $27 million offer on the table and was willing to go higher when New York vice president of international scouting Gordon Blakeley and Latin American scouting supervisor Carlos Rios closed a deal at owner George Steinbrenner's behest. The Yankees signed Contreras to a four-year, $32 million major league contract that included a $6 million bonus. He was considered the best amateur pitcher in the world, and Blakeley opined that he might be the best ever.

Contreras earned his reputation by consistently dominating in international competition. At the last three major international tournaments—the 1999 Pan American Games, 2000 Olympics and 2001 World Cup—Contreras went 7-0, 0.59 with 66 strikeouts in 61 innings, facing mostly professional hitters. His most notable performance came against the Orioles in a 1999 exhibition in Havana. Contreras threw eight shutout innings in relief, striking out 10. In Cuban league play, Contreras had a career 127-50, 2.82 record, including a 13-4, 1.76 mark last season. Contreras regularly throws 94-96 mph with his fastball and tops out at 98. An impressive physical specimen with a rock-solid frame, he's able to maintain his velocity deep into games. His power arsenal is rounded out by two more plus pitches, a slider and a splitter, and he has the confidence and savvy to throw all three pitches in any count. He keeps lefties and righties alike off balance by varying the speed (81-89 mph) and shape (sweeping action on a short, biting cutter) of his slider, and he can throw his splitter for strikes or bury it in the dirt. His delivery is clean and powerful, and he creates deception with his lead arm. He also has toyed with a changeup, which has been effective.

The only test for Contreras is to prove he can rise to the occasion in major league venues with the burden of his huge contract and huge expectations in New York. He hasn't sustained any known injuries, but he has shouldered a heavy workload in Cuba. While many Cubans face questions about their age, no one has challenged Contreras' birthdate. He has all the makings of a No. 1 starter and will be expected to pitch to that standard in New York right away.

Year	Club (League)	Class	W	L	ERA	G	GS	CG	SV	IP	H	R	ER	HR	BB	SO	AVG
							Has Not Played—Signed 2003 Contract										

2. Hideki Matsui, of

Born: June 12, 1974. **Ht.:** 6-1. **Wt.:** 210. **Bats:** L. **Throws:** R. **Career Transactions:** Signed out of Japan by Yankees, Dec. 19, 2002.

A fan favorite in Japan, Matsui has been known more commonly as "Godzilla" since his days at Seiryo High in Japan's Ishikawa perfecture. He won the Central League MVP award for the third time last year, finishing seven points in batting average shy of a triple crown. After leading the Giants to their second Japan Series championship in three years, and the third of his career, he wasted little time in declaring his intentions to pursue a career in the U.S. The Yankees signed him to a three-year contract worth $21 million. Squarely built with a solid, muscular frame, Matsui employs a classic Japanese swing. He pulls off pitches with a slight spin but is able to generate plus-plus power. He should enjoy the short right-field porch in Yankee Stadium, and as one of the strongest players in Japan he displayed the raw power to drive the ball the other way as well. He has above-average bat speed and crushes mistakes over the plate. He's a patient hitter capable of working the count, and he's dangerous even with two strikes against him. For all of Matsui's home run prowess, he hit just .261 with four home runs in 119 at-bats in four years against touring U.S. major leaguers. Some scouts doubt his power will translate because of his unorthodox approach. Matsui feasted on the 361-foot alleys in Yomiuri's home park, the Tokyo Dome. He can be vulnerable to breaking balls in the dirt and there are questions whether he'll be able to catch up to the best major league fastballs. He won three Gold Gloves as a center fielder in Japan, though that was more for his popularity than for his defensive skills. His fringy arm and limited range will likely land him in left field in New York. Japanese scouts thought he might end up at first base, which is not a viable option, and Matsui couldn't handle third base when Yomiuri experimented with him there two years ago. The media circus that has followed Japanese players such as Ichiro and Hideo Nomo will be multiplied in New York, but Matsui has thrived under a microscope. His even-keeled approach should help him, and he'll also benefit from hitting behind Bernie Williams and Jason Giambi.

Year	Club (League)	Class	AVG	G	AB	R	H	2B	3B	HR	RBI	BB	SO	SB	SLG	OBP
1993	Yomiuri (CL)	JPN	.223	57	184	27	41	9	0	11	27	17	50	1	.451	.296
1994	Yomiuri (CL)	JPN	.294	130	503	70	148	23	4	20	66	57	101	6	.475	.368
1995	Yomiuri (CL)	JPN	.283	131	501	76	142	31	1	22	80	62	93	9	.481	.363
1996	Yomiuri (CL)	JPN	.314	130	487	97	153	34	1	38	99	71	98	7	.622	.401
1997	Yomiuri (CL)	JPN	.298	135	484	93	144	18	0	37	103	100	84	9	.564	.419
1998	Yomiuri (CL)	JPN	.292	135	487	103	142	24	3	34	100	104	101	3	.563	.421
1999	Yomiuri (CL)	JPN	.304	135	471	100	143	24	2	42	95	93	99	0	.631	.416
2000	Yomiuri (CL)	JPN	.316	135	474	116	150	32	1	42	108	106	108	5	.654	.438
2001	Yomiuri (CL)	JPN	.333	140	481	107	160	23	3	36	104	120	96	3	.617	.463
2002	Yomiuri (CL)	JPN	.334	140	500	112	167	27	1	50	107	114	104	3	.692	.461
JAPANESE LEAGUE TOTALS			.304	1268	4572	901	1390	245	16	332	889	844	934	46	.582	.413

3. Juan Rivera, of

Born: July 3, 1978. **Ht.:** 6-2. **Wt.:** 170. **Bats:** R. **Throws:** R. **Career Transactions:** Signed out of Venezuela by Yankees, April 12, 1996.

Rivera nearly won the Rookie-level Gulf Coast League triple crown with a .333-12-45 effort in 1998. He re-emerged at Double-A Norwich in 2001. On his way to his first game at Yankee Stadium last June, he got lost on the subway. Then he broke his right kneecap when he ran into a golf cart during pregame drills, which knocked him out for two months. He looked more like a veteran the second time around, finishing the season as a regular in left and right field and starting in all four games against the Angels in the American League Division Series. While Rivera doesn't employ a prototypical swing—his front foot bails a la Roberto Clemente—he crushes fastballs and covers the outer half of the plate when he keeps his hands back. He has above-average raw power, though his power production has been average at best. Rivera's defense may have been the deciding factor in his postseason starts. He has 65 arm strength on the 20-80 scouting scale. He makes good reads off the bat and takes good routes to the ball. Rivera could produce more power with improved selectivity, and he can be susceptible to offspeed stuff away. Rivera has a thick lower half and is an average runner. As he continues to fill out, his speed will diminish. In spite of his playoff experience, Rivera could be squeezed out of New York with the signing of Hideki Matsui and the team's inability to unload Raul Mondesi and Rondell White, and it's not clear whether the club considers him a long-term answer in the outfield.

Year	Club (League)	Class	AVG	G	AB	R	H	2B	3B	HR	RBI	BB	SO	SB	SLG	OBP
1996	Yankees (DSL)	R	.167	10	18	0	3	0	0	0	2	0	1	0	.167	.158
1997	Maracay 2(VSL)	R	.282	52	142	25	40	9	0	0	14	12	16	12	.345	.331
1998	Yankees (GCL)	R	.333	57	210	43	70	9	1	12	45	26	27	8	.557	.408
	Oneonta (NY-P)	A	.278	6	18	2	5	0	0	1	3	1	4	1	.444	.316
1999	Tampa (FSL)	A	.263	109	426	50	112	20	2	14	77	26	67	5	.418	.308
	Yankees (GCL)	R	.333	5	18	7	6	0	0	1	4	4	1	0	.500	.455
2000	Norwich (EL)	AA	.226	17	62	9	14	5	0	2	12	6	15	0	.403	.294
	Tampa (FSL)	A	.276	115	409	62	113	26	1	14	69	33	56	11	.447	.336
2001	Norwich (EL)	AA	.320	77	316	50	101	18	3	14	58	15	50	5	.528	.353
	Columbus (IL)	AAA	.327	55	199	39	65	11	1	14	40	15	31	4	.603	.372
	New York (AL)	MAJ	.000	3	4	0	0	0	0	0	0	0	0	0	.000	.000
2002	Columbus (IL)	AAA	.325	65	265	40	86	21	1	8	47	13	39	5	.502	.355
	New York (AL)	MAJ	.265	28	83	9	22	5	0	1	6	6	10	1	.361	.311
	Yankees (GCL)	R	.308	4	13	1	4	2	0	0	4	2	3	0	.462	.438
MAJOR LEAGUE TOTALS			.253	31	87	9	22	5	0	1	6	6	10	1	.345	.298
MINOR LEAGUE TOTALS			.295	572	2096	328	619	121	9	80	375	153	310	51	.476	.344

4. Bronson Sardinha, of

RODGER WOOD

Born: April 6, 1983. **Ht.:** 6-1. **Wt.:** 190. **Bats:** L. **Throws:** R. **School:** Kamehameha HS, Honolulu. **Career Transactions:** Selected by Yankees in first round (34th overall) of 2001 draft; signed June 13, 2001.

Bronson was named for his mother's favorite actor, Charles Bronson. His brothers Dane (named after a Hawaiian surfer) and Duke (named for John Wayne) play in the minors for the Reds and Rockies. Sardinha signed with the Yankees for $1 million, turning down the chance to be the third Sardinha to play at Pepperdine. Sardinha has a quiet, professional approach at the plate. He's short to the ball and has learned to stay back and trust his hands. He uses the whole field and hit for surprising power in his first full pro season. He worked hard to make himself an above-average runner, and his arm strength is a plus. Scouts weren't sold on Sardinha's ability to stay at shortstop, so the Yankees sent him back to short-season Staten Island to learn to play left field. Now the question is whether he projects to hit for enough power to man a corner outfield spot. Quiet by nature, Sardinha is a baseball rat who showed tremendous progress in a short period of time. The Yankees are contemplating moving him to center field at high Class A Tampa in 2003.

Year	Club (League)	Class	AVG	G	AB	R	H	2B	3B	HR	RBI	BB	SO	SB	SLG	OBP
2001	Yankees (GCL)	R	.303	55	188	42	57	14	3	4	27	28	51	15	.473	.398
2002	Greensboro (SAL)	A	.263	93	342	49	90	13	0	12	44	34	78	15	.406	.334
	Staten Island (NY-P)	A	.323	36	124	25	40	8	0	4	16	24	36	4	.484	.433
MINOR LEAGUE TOTALS			.286	184	654	116	187	35	3	20	87	86	165	30	.440	.372

5. Brandon Claussen, lhp

Born: May 1, 1979. **Ht.:** 6-2. **Wt.:** 200. **Bats:** L. **Throws:** L. **School:** Howard (Texas) JC. **Career Transactions:** Selected by Yankees in 34th round of 1998 draft; signed May 20, 1999.

Signed as a draft-and-follow in 1999, Claussen emerged as one of the game's top lefthanded pitching prospects by leading the minors with 220 strikeouts in 2001. He also topped the organization with 187 innings, and the workload took a toll on his arm in 2002, as he had Tommy John surgery in June. The Yankees say Claussen's bulldog mentality and work ethic will help him return on schedule and to his previous form. He's expected to regain his plus velocity and sharp breaking ball. His fastball was in the 88-94 mph range, and his slider, the best breaking pitch in the system, was effective against lefties and righties. He had made significant progress with his changeup. After breaking down, Claussen needs to build his stamina and avoid further injury. His pitch counts will be monitored closely when he returns. He throws four pitches, but his curveball is no more than a show-me pitch. Claussen should be back sometime in the second half of 2003.

Year	Club (League)	Class	W	L	ERA	G	GS	CG	SV	IP	H	R	ER	HR	BB	SO	AVG
1999	Yankees (GCL)	R	0	1	3.18	2	2	0	0	11	7	4	4	2	2	16	.175
	Staten Island (NY-P)	A	6	4	3.38	12	12	1	0	72	70	30	27	4	12	89	.253
	Greensboro (SAL)	A	0	1	10.50	1	1	1	0	6	8	7	7	1	2	5	.296
2000	Greensboro (SAL)	A	8	5	4.05	17	17	1	0	98	91	49	44	9	44	98	.251
	Tampa (FSL)	A	2	5	3.10	9	9	1	0	52	49	24	18	1	17	44	.245
2001	Tampa (FSL)	A	5	2	2.73	8	8	0	0	56	47	21	17	2	13	69	.224
	Norwich (EL)	AA	9	2	2.13	21	21	1	0	131	101	42	31	6	55	151	.210
2002	Columbus (IL)	AAA	2	8	3.28	15	15	0	0	93	85	47	34	4	46	73	.242
MINOR LEAGUE TOTALS			32	28	3.15	85	85	5	0	520	458	224	182	29	191	545	.235

6. Drew Henson, 3b

Born: Feb. 13, 1980. **Ht.:** 6-5. **Wt.:** 220. **Bats:** R. **Throws:** R. **School:** Brighton (Mich.) HS. **Career Transactions:** Selected by Yankees in third round of 1998 draft; signed July 24, 1998 . . . Traded by Yankees with OF Jackson Melian, LHP Ed Yarnall and RHP Brian Reith to Reds for LHP Denny Neagle and OF Mike Frank, July 12, 2000 . . . Traded by Reds with OF Michael Coleman to Yankees for OF Wily Mo Pena, March 20, 2001.

As a quarterback at Michigan, Henson projected as a potential first-round pick in the NFL draft. The Yankees traded him to the Reds in July 2001 and reacquired him the following spring, giving him a six-year, $17 million contract to give up the gridiron. Few prospects can match Henson's size, strength and athleticism. He can mash fastballs down in the zone and hit mistakes a long way. He also has an above-average arm and good lateral agility. His take-charge mentality makes him a favorite of Yankees brass. Henson's bat speed is only fair, though, and he tends to muscle the bat through the zone. His swing is long and he struggles to recognize offspeed pitches. His September callup ended early when he was sent to Tampa to work on defense. Henson has been rushed to the majors, yet he didn't get 400 at-bats in a season until 2002 because of football and injuries. His struggles in the Arizona Fall League underscored he's not ready for New York. He's headed back to Triple-A Columbus.

Year	Club (League)	Class	AVG	G	AB	R	H	2B	3B	HR	RBI	BB	SO	SB	SLG	OBP
1998	Yankees (GCL)	R	.316	10	38	5	12	3	0	1	2	3	9	0	.474	.366
1999	Tampa (FSL)	A	.280	69	254	37	71	12	0	13	37	26	71	3	.480	.345
2000	Tampa (FSL)	A	.333	5	21	4	7	2	0	1	1	1	7	0	.571	.364
	Norwich (EL)	AA	.287	59	223	39	64	9	2	7	39	20	75	0	.439	.347
	Chattanooga (SL)	AA	.172	16	64	7	11	8	0	1	9	4	25	2	.344	.221
2001	Tampa (FSL)	A	.143	5	14	2	2	0	0	1	3	2	7	1	.357	.316
	Norwich (EL)	AA	.368	5	19	2	7	1	0	0	2	1	4	0	.421	.429
	Columbus (IL)	AAA	.222	71	270	29	60	6	0	11	38	10	85	2	.367	.249
2002	Columbus (IL)	AAA	.240	128	471	68	113	30	4	18	65	37	151	2	.435	.301
	New York (AL)	MAJ	.000	3	1	1	0	0	0	0	0	0	1	0	.000	.000
MAJOR LEAGUE TOTALS			.000	3	1	1	0	0	0	0	0	0	1	0	.000	.000
MINOR LEAGUE TOTALS			.253	368	1374	193	347	71	6	53	196	104	434	10	.429	.308

7. Chien-Ming Wang, rhp

Born: March 31, 1980. **Ht.:** 6-3. **Wt.:** 200. **Bats:** R. **Throws:** R. **Career Transactions:** Signed out of Taiwan by Yankees, May 5, 2000.

Signed to a $1.9 million bonus, Wang came to the United States with high expectations. His 2000 pro debut was solid, but a shoulder injury knocked him out for all of the following year. He returned in 2002, tossing eight shutout innings to clinch the New York-Penn championship for Staten Island, then earned the MVP award for Taiwan at the Asian Games. Wang is polished in spite of his relative inexperience. He maintains 90-95 mph velocity on his fastball with a clean delivery and free arm action. His splitter and hard, late slider give him two more knockout pitches, and his changeup is a reliable option. He can command all four pitches in the strike zone. While Wang looked to be back to 100 percent, he hasn't pitched a full season yet. If Wang stays healthy, the Yankees are prepared to put him on the fast track. He could start 2003 in high Class A and reach Double-A Trenton before the end of the season.

Year	Club (League)	Class	W	L	ERA	G	GS	CG	SV	IP	H	R	ER	HR	BB	SO	AVG
2000	Staten Island (NY-P)	A	4	4	2.48	14	14	2	0	87	77	34	24	2	21	75	.233
2001						Did Not Play—Injured											
2002	Staten Island (NY-P)	A	6	1	1.72	13	13	0	0	78	63	23	15	2	14	64	.219
MINOR LEAGUE TOTALS			10	5	2.12	27	27	2	0	165	140	57	39	4	35	139	.226

8. Robinson Cano, 2b/ss

Born: Oct. 22, 1982. **Ht.:** 6-0. **Wt.:** 170. **Bats:** L. **Throws:** R. **Career Transactions:** Signed out of Dominican Republic by Yankees, Jan. 5, 2001.

Cano's father Jose signed with the Yankees in 1980 and reached the big leagues with the Astros in 1989. Robinson played baseball and basketball at his Dominican high school, and from the first time he worked out for the Yankees has shown an advanced approach. Like Bronson Sardinha, he went to Staten Island after opening the 2002 season at Class A Greensboro. Cano's bat is his greatest strength. He generates plus bat speed and has a knack for making adjustments with his hands to put the barrel of the bat on balls in different zones. He covers the plate well with a good idea of the strike zone, makes consistent hard contact and projects to hit for power. Defensively, Cano offers versatility, though he'll likely end up at second or third base or even right field with Ferdin Tejada and Joaquin Arias in the system. Cano has the actions, above-average arm and quick hands to play shortstop, and most of his errors were due to inexperience. He's a below-average runner. Cano finished third in the system in RBIs and should make the jump to high Class A in 2003.

Year	Club (League)	Class	AVG	G	AB	R	H	2B	3B	HR	RBI	BB	SO	SB	SLG	OBP
2001	Yankees (GCL)	R	.230	57	200	37	46	14	2	3	34	28	27	11	.365	.330
	Staten Island (NY-P)	A	.250	2	8	0	2	0	0	0	2	0	2	0	.250	.250
2002	Greensboro (SAL)	A	.276	113	474	67	131	20	9	14	66	29	78	2	.445	.321
	Staten Island (NY-P)	A	.276	22	87	11	24	5	1	1	15	4	8	6	.391	.308
MINOR LEAGUE TOTALS			.264	194	769	115	203	39	12	18	117	61	115	19	.416	.322

9. Danny Borrell, lhp

Born: Jan. 24, 1979. **Ht.:** 6-3. **Wt.:** 200. **Bats:** L. **Throws:** L. **School:** Wake Forest University. **Career Transactions:** Selected by Yankees in second round of 2000 draft; signed June 19, 2000.

When they drafted Borrell, the Yankees envisioned another physical lefty in the mold of their 1996 first-rounder, Eric Milton. Unlike the polished Milton, who needed just one season in the minors, Borrell was raw after splitting his college career between hitting and pitching. Borrell mixes speeds and throws strikes. He's athletic, which allows him to repeat his delivery. He has an average fastball that sits at 87-91 mph but tops out at 94, so he can reach back when he needs a little extra. His changeup is among the best in the system and he shows good rotation on his curveball. Borrell can locate his stuff to either side of the plate, but without a plus pitch to put hitters away, he must be perfect. His curveball lags behind his other two pitches. His arm has low mileage, and Borrell could throw harder with more innings. After leading the Eastern League in ERA, Borrell should begin 2003 in Triple-A. The age of New York's rotation will make him an attractive option soon.

Year	Club (League)	Class	W	L	ERA	G	GS	CG	SV	IP	H	R	ER	HR	BB	SO	AVG
2000	Yankees (GCL)	R	0	1	0.00	1	1	0	0	3	2	1	0	0	0	2	.182
	Staten Island (NY-P)	A	4	2	3.20	10	10	0	0	56	39	21	20	2	19	44	.194
2001	Tampa (FSL)	A	7	9	3.97	22	20	0	0	111	109	58	49	6	38	84	.259
2002	Tampa (FSL)	A	4	1	2.33	7	6	0	0	39	33	11	10	0	10	44	.239
	Norwich (EL)	AA	9	4	2.31	21	20	1	0	128	116	44	33	5	39	91	.239
MINOR LEAGUE TOTALS			24	17	2.99	61	57	1	0	337	299	135	112	13	106	265	.238

10. Julio DePaula, rhp

Born: July 27, 1979. **Ht.:** 6-1. **Wt.:** 160. **Bats:** R. **Throws:** R. **Career Transactions:** Signed out of Dominican Republic by Rockies, Jan. 13, 1997 . . . Traded by Rockies to Yankees, April 20, 2001, completing trade in which Yankees sent RHP Craig Dingman to Rockies for a player to be named (March 29, 2001).

It wasn't that the Rockies didn't think highly of DePaula when they traded him to the Yankees for Dingman, a minor league reliever. They just expected more of Dingman, who pitched just seven games in Colorado before leaving as a free agent. Meanwhile, DePaula has gone 29-12 and averaged nearly a strikeout an inning since the deal. The slight DePaula fools hitters with lightning-quick arm speed that generates 91-95 mph fastballs. He made strides last year in conserving pitches, which allowed him to work deeper into his starts. Never short on confidence, DePaula began throwing his low-80s slider and plus changeup when behind in the count. DePaula was able to channel his intensity to become more efficient on the mound. He must continue to keep his emotions in check to avoid losing control of the game. Though DePaula has been a durable strikeout artist, he might fit better as a dynamic short reliever in the majors. After being added to the 40-man roster for the first time, he'll attend his first big league camp and should open 2003 in Triple-A.

Year	Club (League)	Class	W	L	ERA	G	GS	CG	SV	IP	H	R	ER	HR	BB	SO	AVG
1997	Rockies (DSL)	R	3	6	4.75	15	11	1	0	66	77	46	35	4	28	59	.292
1998	Rockies (AZL)	R	5	5	3.81	17	9	0	2	54	54	30	23	1	18	62	.252
1999	Portland (NWL)	A	6	6	6.01	16	16	0	0	85	97	67	57	8	43	77	.290
2000	Asheville (SAL)	A	8	13	4.70	28	27	1	0	155	151	90	81	16	62	187	.260
2001	Asheville (SAL)	A	1	1	3.78	3	3	0	0	17	19	13	7	3	2	26	.268
	Greensboro (SAL)	A	6	1	2.75	8	8	0	0	56	35	19	17	2	21	67	.179
	Tampa (FSL)	A	9	5	3.58	16	13	0	0	83	65	43	33	3	53	77	.212
2002	Norwich (EL)	AA	14	6	3.45	27	26	6	0	175	141	74	67	11	52	152	.221
MINOR LEAGUE TOTALS			52	43	4.17	130	113	8	2	691	639	382	320	48	279	707	.245

11. Rudy Guillen, of

Born: Nov. 23, 1983. **Ht.:** 6-3. **Wt.:** 190. **Bats:** R. **Throws:** R. **Career Transactions:** Signed out of Dominican Republic by Yankees, July 2, 2000.

When baseball people talk about a Rookie-level prospect, they typically are reserved. While the Yankees try to temper their enthusiasm, Guillen's ability is too much to ignore. Signed for just over $100,000, Guillen led the Rookie-level Dominican Summer League with 11 home runs in 2001, and was the No. 2 prospect in the GCL in 2002. Guillen might have the highest ceiling in the organization. With a strong family background and education, he should continue to pick things up quickly. He projects as a power-hitting right fielder, though he plays center field now. Once timed as a 7.6-second runner in the 60-yard dash, he soon improved to 6.8–reminiscent of former Yankees farmhand Cristian Guzman at the same age. While Guillen has five-tool potential, his ability to hit for average will be tested against more advanced competition. He doesn't show the patience Yankees hitters are known for. Already blessed with a strong frame, Guillen is expected to fill out and develop into a prototype corner outfielder. He's at least four years away, but by that time he could be atop this list.

Year	Club (League)	Class	AVG	G	AB	R	H	2B	3B	HR	RBI	BB	SO	SB	SLG	OBP
2001	Yankees (DSL)	R	.281	62	231	38	65	13	2	11	41	15	50	11	.498	.337
2002	Yankees (GCL)	R	.306	59	219	38	67	7	2	3	35	14	39	7	.397	.351
MINOR LEAGUE TOTALS			.293	121	450	76	132	20	4	14	76	29	89	18	.449	.344

12. Sean Henn, lhp

Born: April 23, 1981. **Ht.:** 6-5. **Wt.:** 200. **Bats:** R. **Throws:** L. **School:** McLennan (Texas) JC. **Career Transactions:** Selected by Yankees in 26th round of 2000 draft; signed May 25, 2001.

The Yankees drafted Henn twice, but it wasn't until his velocity jumped two grades that they signed him to a $1.701 million bonus, a record for a draft-and-follow. Henn went down with a sore elbow nine games into his pro debut and needed Tommy John surgery that wiped out his entire 2002 season. Henn threw 86-89 mph as a junior-college freshman, and didn't show the breaking ball or maturity to handle the daily grind of pro ball. He blossomed by his sophomore season and was touching 99 mph in the months leading up to the draft. His arm action is clean, and his changeup is an effective secondary pitch. Rehab allowed Henn to focus on refining his delivery. He worked out in Tampa with pitching coordinators Billy Connors and Steve Webber, focusing on his stride and release point. His breaking ball was a work in progress before the injury. Henn threw simulated batting-practice sessions in Tampa during the fall. His rehab has been encouraging and the Yankees expect him to be ready by spring training, 18 months after his surgery.

Year	Club (League)	Class	W	L	ERA	G	GS	CG	SV	IP	H	R	ER	HR	BB	SO	AVG
2001	Staten Island (NY-P)	A	3	1	3.00	9	8	0	1	42	26	15	14	3	15	49	.178
2002					Did Not Play—Injured												
MINOR LEAGUE TOTALS			3	1	3.00	9	8	0	1	42	26	15	14	3	15	49	.178

13. Ferdin Tejada, ss

Born: Sept. 15, 1982. **Ht.:** 5-11. **Wt.:** 170. **Bats:** R. **Throws:** R. **Career Transactions:** Signed out of Dominican Republic by Yankees, Feb. 12, 2000.

Instead of continuing to target big-ticket players such as Wily Mo Pena and Jackson Melian, the Yankees are trying to spread out their bonus money in Latin America by signing more players for smaller amounts. Tejada could turn out to be the best bargain of all, as he signed for just $35,000 in 2002. With improved diet, instruction and overall conditioning, he has progressed in all facets of the game over the last two years. Dominican scout Victor Mata, who signed Cristian Guzman in 1994, gives Tejada's tools the edge across the board, save Guzman's top-of-the-line hands. Tejada emerged in the Dominican Summer League in 2001 by finishing second in the circuit in hitting. Both his speed and arm are plus-plus tools, and he has quick, sure hands. He can handle the bat from both sides of the plate, with a more advanced approach from the left. Power will never be his forte, though increased extra-base ability should develop with physical maturity. Tejada knows his limitations, uses all fields and is an outstanding bunter. With a career .303 average, he'll likely head to low Class A Michigan in 2003 for his first taste of full-season action.

Year	Club (League)	Class	AVG	G	AB	R	H	2B	3B	HR	RBI	BB	SO	SB	SLG	OBP
2001	Yankees (DSL)	R	.330	46	188	41	62	7	7	1	19	26	30	13	.457	.411
2002	Yankees (GCL)	R	.300	16	60	13	18	3	0	0	2	10	9	3	.350	.394
	Staten Island (NY-P)	A	.276	47	181	29	50	7	2	0	18	11	33	11	.337	.316
MINOR LEAGUE TOTALS			.303	109	429	83	130	17	9	1	39	47	72	27	.392	.370

14. Charlie Manning, lhp

Born: March 31, 1979. **Ht.:** 6-2. **Wt.:** 180. **Bats:** L. **Throws:** L. **School:** University of Tampa. **Career Transactions:** Selected by Yankees in ninth round of 2001 draft; signed June 11, 2001.

The Brewers drafted Manning in the 22nd round out of high school in 1997, but he headed to Polk (Fla.) CC and was drafted twice more before transferring to Tampa. The Mariners took a shot at signing him as a ninth-rounder following his junior season, but he returned to become the Sunshine State Conference pitcher of the year as a senior before finally signing with the Yankees. Manning finished second in the organization in strikeouts as he transformed himself into a prospect in 2002. He never will be overpowering, but the Yankees like his ability to fill the strike zone with four pitches. His repertoire consists of an 87-89 mph fastball, a late-breaking curveball, a slider and a changeup. His fastball peaks at 92. He's making his changeup a more effective weapon. Manning induces a lot of groundouts and allowed just five home runs by keeping the ball down in the zone. He already exceeded the organization's expectations, and other clubs were asking for him around the trade deadline in July. He should start 2003 in Double-A, where he finished his first full pro season.

Year	Club (League)	Class	W	L	ERA	G	GS	CG	SV	IP	H	R	ER	HR	BB	SO	AVG
2001	Staten Island (NY-P)	A	8	4	3.49	14	14	0	0	80	73	33	31	4	21	87	.245
2002	Tampa (FSL)	A	6	4	3.24	17	16	0	0	100	82	48	36	4	31	85	.221
	Norwich (EL)	AA	4	2	3.57	11	11	1	0	63	55	27	25	1	26	61	.235
MINOR LEAGUE TOTALS			18	10	3.41	42	41	1	0	243	210	108	92	9	78	233	.233

15. Andy Phillips, 2b

Born: April 6, 1977. **Ht.:** 6-0. **Wt.:** 200. **Bats:** R. **Throws:** R. **School:** University of Alabama. **Career Transactions:** Selected by Yankees in seventh round of 1999 draft; signed June 25, 1999.

Phillips entered the minors without fanfare despite a standout college career at Alabama. He rewrote the Crimson Tide record books, earned recognition as a third-team All American as a senior and had a Southeastern Conference-record 37-game hit streak snapped in the 1999 College World Series. Phillips continued to hit for average as a pro, but it wasn't until he showed the ability to hit for power in 2002 that his stock soared. After he led the Yankees system in homers, Phillips convinced scouts his power surge is legitimate. The ball jumps off his bat and he has the ability to drive the ball out to right-center, which is a graveyard at Norwich. Phillips draws high praise for his work ethic, and he spent last offseason on a strict conditioning program to build strength and increase his quickness and explosiveness. A shortstop in college, he moved to third base after signing and committed 48 errors in two years. That and Drew Henson's presence prompted Phillips to shift to second base in 2001. His hands and arm are suitable for the position, though he lacks the range of a middle infielder. Phillips projects as an offensive second baseman who will catch what he gets to.

Year	Club (League)	Class	AVG	G	AB	R	H	2B	3B	HR	RBI	BB	SO	SB	SLG	OBP
1999	Staten Island (NY-P)	A	.322	64	233	35	75	11	7	7	48	37	40	3	.519	.417
2000	Tampa (FSL)	A	.287	127	478	66	137	33	2	13	58	46	98	2	.446	.346
	Norwich (EL)	AA	.250	7	28	5	7	2	1	0	3	3	11	1	.393	.323
2001	Norwich (EL)	AA	.268	51	183	23	49	9	2	6	25	21	54	1	.437	.340
	Tampa (FSL)	A	.302	75	288	43	87	17	4	11	50	25	55	3	.503	.353
2002	Norwich (EL)	AA	.305	73	272	58	83	24	2	19	51	33	56	4	.618	.381
	Columbus (IL)	AAA	.263	51	205	32	54	11	1	9	36	10	46	0	.459	.296
MINOR LEAGUE TOTALS			.292	448	1687	262	492	107	19	65	271	175	360	14	.493	.357

16. Joaquin Arias, 2b/ss

Born: Sept. 21, 1984. **Ht.:** 6-2. **Wt.:** 170. **Bats:** R. **Throws:** R. **Career Transactions:** Signed out of Dominican Republic by Yankees, July 12, 2001.

When a bird-dog scout brought Arias to then-Latin American coordinator Victor Mata in 2000, Arias was a scrawny 140 pounds and Mata nearly walked away. Then he saw Arias swing the bat and it sounded like a 200-pounder was hitting the ball. The Yankees had him in their Dominican academy for nearly a year before signing him for $300,000. Alfonso Soriano is the new standard for middle-infield prospects, and as unfair as the comparisons might be, Arias has been compared to Soriano. Most were based on a physical resemblance. Arias has quick hands that trigger outstanding bat speed and surprising power, which projects as above-average as he matures. Since his first days at the academy, his arm strength has jumped a full grade to solid-average, his hands have improved and his 60-yard dash time has been cut to 6.5 seconds. Though he has all the tools for short, the Yankees moved him to second in the GCL because of shortstops Robinson Cano, Ferdin Tejada and Deivi Mendez in the lower levels. Arias started his career in the GCL instead of the Dominican Summer League. The Yankees will move him to the short-season New York-Penn League in 2003.

Year	Club (League)	Class	AVG	G	AB	R	H	2B	3B	HR	RBI	BB	SO	SB	SLG	OBP
2002	Yankees (GCL)	R	.300	57	203	29	61	7	6	0	21	12	16	2	.394	.338
MINOR LEAGUE TOTALS			.300	57	203	29	61	7	6	0	21	12	16	2	.394	.338

17. Jason Anderson, rhp

Born: June 9, 1979. **Ht.:** 6-0. **Wt.:** 170. **Bats:** L. **Throws:** R. **School:** University of Illinois. **Career Transactions:** Selected by Yankees in 10th round of 2000 draft; signed June 13, 2000.

Anderson was drafted by the Royals in the sixth round out of high school in 1997, but the honor student opted for college instead. He joined Cardinals prospect Jimmy Journell to go a combined 16-3 for Illinois as a freshmen. Anderson was the Big 10 Conference pitcher of the year and tournament MVP in 2000, finishing his career with a 29-5 record. After spending his entire career as a starter, including his first 18 games as a pro, Anderson didn't jump on the fast track until the Yankees tried him in the bullpen in the 2000 New York-Penn League playoffs. His fastball jumped from 88-91 mph to the mid-90s. He topped out at 97 in 2002. His slider has above-average potential, and he'll mix in a changeup for strikes. Anderson needs to develop more confidence in his secondary pitches, especially his changeup and cutter, which both can be quality major league offerings. At his size, there's some effort to his delivery upon release, yet he still manages to repeat his mechanics and throw strikes. He was shut down with a sore arm in the Arizona Fall League, renewing concerns about his durability. Anderson took a step backward in 2001 when he finished the year in Staten Island, but he headed in the right direction in 2002 as he blitzed through the upper levels of the system. Provided he's healthy, Anderson will battle for a big league bullpen job.

Year	Club (League)	Class	W	L	ERA	G	GS	CG	SV	IP	H	R	ER	HR	BB	SO	AVG
2000	Staten Island (NY-P)	A	6	5	4.03	15	15	0	0	80	84	41	36	1	25	73	.273
2001	Greensboro (SAL)	A	7	9	3.76	23	19	1	1	124	127	68	52	9	40	101	.267
	Staten Island (NY-P)	A	5	1	1.70	7	7	0	0	48	32	9	9	2	12	56	.190
2002	Tampa (FSL)	A	4	2	4.07	12	3	0	1	24	27	13	11	2	3	22	.281
	Norwich (EL)	AA	1	1	0.93	16	0	0	2	19	14	2	2	1	5	21	.212
	Columbus (IL)	AAA	5	1	3.15	26	0	0	7	34	26	13	12	3	11	28	.211
MINOR LEAGUE TOTALS			28	19	3.32	99	44	1	11	330	310	146	122	18	96	301	.251

18. Javier Ortiz, rhp

Born: Nov. 28, 1979. **Ht.:** 6-0. **Wt.:** 150. **Bats:** R. **Throws:** R. **Career Transactions:** Signed out of Dominican Republic by Yankees, July 2, 1996.

In the first five years of his career, Ortiz didn't endear himself to the organization with his maturity level or his performance. He didn't get past Rookie ball until late in the 2001 season, after missing the majority of 2000-01 with back and knee strains. But in 2002, he became a leader for the system's young Latin American players. His fastball ranges from 89-94 mph and averages 90-92 with occasional boring action from a high three-quarters release point. He has a good curveball, with 12-to-6 downward bite. His best pitch is a straight change with late fade. He still needs to solve lefthanders, who batted .286 against him in 2002. After all the injuries over the last couple of years, Ortiz was a workhorse in 2002, leading the organization with 177 innings. With command of three quality pitches, he should advance more rapidly now. He's ticketed for the Double-A rotation after finishing strong in high Class A. Some scouts project him as a middle reliever in the big leagues.

Year	Club (League)	Class	W	L	ERA	G	GS	CG	SV	IP	H	R	ER	HR	BB	SO	AVG
1997	Yankees (DSL)	R	3	2	4.47	9	9	0	0	44	50	29	22	4	16	28	.284
1998	Yankees (DSL)	R	6	3	2.32	12	12	0	0	66	50	30	17	3	30	66	.209
1999	Yankees (GCL)	R	3	2	5.68	12	10	1	0	51	63	40	32	4	35	46	.309
2000	Yankees (GCL)	R	0	0	7.71	1	0	0	0	2	3	2	2	0	1	2	.300
2001	Yankees (GCL)	R	0	0	0.00	2	0	0	0	4	1	0	0	0	1	2	.083
	Staten Island (NY-P)	A	1	1	1.98	3	3	0	0	14	11	4	3	1	4	12	.216
2002	Greensboro (SAL)	A	9	5	4.11	18	18	3	0	127	128	66	58	8	25	63	.263
	Tampa (FSL)	A	4	3	2.52	9	9	1	0	50	47	20	14	1	13	35	.250
MINOR LEAGUE TOTALS			26	16	3.72	66	61	5	0	358	353	191	148	21	125	254	.258

19. Brandon Weeden, rhp

Born: Oct. 14, 1983. **Ht.:** 6-4. **Wt.:** 190. **Bats:** R. **Throws:** R. **School:** Santa Fe HS, Edmond, Okla. **Career Transactions:** Selected by Yankees in second round of 2002 draft; signed June 12, 2002.

When the Yankees took Weeden with their first pick (albeit in the second round) in 2002, they broke from tradition. Not since 1998 had they started a draft with a high school player (Andy Brown), and it had been even longer since they had opened with a prep pitcher (Matt Drews, 1993). Scouting Weeden on the mound was a chore because he was his high school's starting shortstop and pitched almost exclusively out of the bullpen. The Oklahoma State recruit saved nine games and struck out 68 in 40 innings while hitting .373-5-32. Just

5-foot-10 as a freshman, Weeden blossomed into a mature athlete who starred at quarterback in football and small forward in basketball. He has a prototypical pitcher's frame, with a quick, loose arm and a clean delivery. There's plenty of room for projection on his lively 88-93 mph fastball. His slider features tight three-quarters bite in the strike zone and grades out as a future plus pitch. With his limited pitching experience, Weeden will advance slowly after starting 2003 in extended spring training.

Year	Club (League)	Class	W	L	ERA	G	GS	CG	SV	IP	H	R	ER	HR	BB	SO	AVG
2002	Yankees (GCL)	R	2	1	2.86	11	7	0	1	35	29	13	11	1	16	30	.228
MINOR LEAGUE TOTALS			2	1	2.86	11	7	0	1	35	29	13	11	1	16	30	.228

20. Jose Valdez, rhp

Born: Jan. 22, 1983. **Ht.:** 6-4. **Wt.:** 190. **Bats:** R. **Throws:** R. **Career Transactions:** Signed out of Dominican Republic by Yankees, Oct. 5, 2000.

Valdez gave the Yankees plenty of reasons to get excited about his Rookie-level performance. When Carlos Rios and Victor Mata signed him for $100,000, he was throwing 87-88 mph and touching 90, showing potential but not distinguishing himself. But Valdez separated himself from the pack, increasing his velocity to 92-94, and he now touches 96-97 with regularity. He has added a nasty splitter to his fastball/slider/changeup combo. Pitching instructors Billy Connors and Steve Webber received a lot of credit for refining his mechanics, though Valdez' delivery is still a little funky and he has trouble repeating it. He dropped his arm slot from high three-quarters to a traditional three-quarters in 2002. His ceiling is the highest of any pitcher in the system, and he could catapult himself into the top 10 after 2003, when he could make his full-season debut.

Year	Club (League)	Class	W	L	ERA	G	GS	CG	SV	IP	H	R	ER	HR	BB	SO	AVG
2001	Yankees (DSL)	R	3	4	1.94	15	10	0	1	70	60	21	15	1	11	50	.230
2002	Staten Island (NY-P)	A	1	3	5.40	4	4	0	0	20	19	14	12	0	9	21	.250
	Yankees (GCL)	R	1	4	3.35	8	7	0	0	40	45	19	15	2	10	28	.283
MINOR LEAGUE TOTALS			5	11	2.91	27	21	0	1	130	124	54	42	3	30	99	.250

21. Dioner Navarro, c

Born: Feb. 9, 1984. **Ht.:** 5-10. **Wt.:** 180. **Bats:** B. **Throws:** R. **Career Transactions:** Signed out of Venezuela by Yankees, Aug. 21, 2000.

Signed by scouts Carlos Rios, Ricardo Finol and Hector Rincones in Venezuela for $260,000, Navarro impressed Yankees officials in his 2001 debut as a 17-year-old. Built like a young Ivan Rodriguez, who was 5-foot-9 and 160 pounds when he signed out of Puerto Rico in 1988, Navarro is known as "Pudgito." Unlike Rodriguez, Navarro isn't likely to blitz through the minors in 2½ seasons. The similarities are more evident behind the plate, where Navarro used a quick release and above-average arm to erase 35 percent of basestealers for the second consecutive season. The Yankees moved him aggressively to low Class A in 2002, and the teenager ran out of gas in the second half. Navarro has a compact, direct stroke and has a solid idea of the strike zone. He uses the whole field and projects to hit for gap power, but needs to improve his approach from the left side. Navarro should climb the ladder one level at a time.

Year	Club (League)	Class	AVG	G	AB	R	H	2B	3B	HR	RBI	BB	SO	SB	SLG	OBP
2001	Yankees (GCL)	R	.280	43	143	27	40	10	1	2	22	17	23	6	.406	.345
2002	Greensboro (SAL)	A	.238	92	328	41	78	12	2	8	36	39	61	1	.360	.326
	Tampa (FSL)	A	.500	1	2	1	1	0	0	0	0	0	0	0	.500	.500
MINOR LEAGUE TOTALS			.252	136	473	69	119	22	3	10	58	56	84	7	.374	.333

22. Alex Graman, lhp

Born: Nov. 17, 1977. **Ht.:** 6-4. **Wt.:** 200. **Bats:** L. **Throws:** L. **School:** Indiana State University. **Career Transactions:** Selected by Yankees in third round of 1999 draft; signed June 5, 1999.

Just a couple of years ago, Graman was regarded as the leader of an impressive crop of up-and-coming Yankees southpaws that also included Randy Keisler, Brandon Claussen, David Martinez, Danny Borrell and Ted Lilly. Keisler, Claussen and Martinez missed the majority of 2002 with injuries, Borrell has made progress and Lilly was traded to the Athletics. Graman hasn't shown the improvement scouts expected. He has been the subject of trade requests because of his four-pitch mix and command. His fastball is average at 87-91 mph and he'll occasionally reach back for a little more. He'll also vary speeds and movement between his two-seamer and four-seamer. His splitter is a potential out pitch, and he keeps hitters guessing with a slider and changeup. Graman must take a step forward in the Triple-A rotation if he's going to figure into New York's plans.

Year	Club (League)	Class	W	L	ERA	G	GS	CG	SV	IP	H	R	ER	HR	BB	SO	AVG
1999	Staten Island (NY-P)	A	6	3	2.99	14	14	0	0	81	74	30	27	7	16	85	.244

2000	Tampa (FSL)	A	8	9	3.65	28	28	3	0	143	120	64	58	6	58	111	.226
	Norwich (EL)	AA	0	1	11.81	1	1	0	0	5	6	7	7	3	4	3	.300
2001	Norwich (EL)	AA	12	9	3.52	28	28	1	0	166	174	83	65	10	60	138	.267
2002	Norwich (EL)	AA	5	2	2.88	8	8	2	0	50	46	19	16	2	13	31	.242
	Columbus (IL)	AAA	6	9	4.65	20	20	1	0	124	141	74	64	11	37	98	.284
MINOR LEAGUE TOTALS			37	33	3.74	99	99	7	0	570	561	277	237	39	188	466	.256

23. Kevin Reese, of

Born: March 11, 1978. **Ht.:** 5-11. **Wt.:** 190. **Bats:** L. **Throws:** L. **School:** University of San Diego. **Career Transactions:** Selected by Padres in 27th round of 2000 draft; signed June 13, 2000 . . . Traded by Padres to Yankees for 2B Bernie Castro, Dec. 18, 2001.

Reese helped lead Mission Bay High to a championship as a senior and was a two-way player at the University of San Diego before he focused on hitting and set several Toreros offensive records. He tore a ligament in his thumb during his senior season, though, knocking him down in the draft. The Yankees acquired Reese from the Padres following the 2001 season. He exercises a solid understanding of the strike zone, yet still has an aggressive approach. Reese skipped a level to Double-A in 2002 and still had the third-best average in the system. He's a pure hitter who sprays line drives to all fields with a compact stroke. He shows occasional pull power but can be beaten inside by good fastballs. His baseball instincts and above-average speed make him a threat to steal or take an extra base. Reese played center for Norwich and probably could handle all three outfield spots in the major leagues. His arm is average and accurate and he shows playable range. There aren't many holes in Reese's game, but his lack of power might relegate him to a future as a reserve.

Year	Club (League)	Class	AVG	G	AB	R	H	2B	3B	HR	RBI	BB	SO	SB	SLG	OBP
2000	Idaho Falls (Pio)	R	.358	53	201	51	72	14	4	2	36	43	30	12	.498	.474
2001	Fort Wayne (Mid)	A	.329	125	459	84	151	30	6	13	73	54	62	30	.505	.402
2002	Norwich (EL)	AA	.290	138	514	80	149	24	6	4	45	77	87	22	.383	.385
MINOR LEAGUE TOTALS			.317	316	1174	215	372	68	16	19	154	174	179	64	.451	.408

24. Erick Almonte, ss

Born: Feb. 1, 1978. **Ht.:** 6-2. **Wt.:** 180. **Bats:** R. **Throws:** R. **Career Transactions:** Signed out of Dominican Republic by Yankees, Feb. 12, 1996.

Almonte's brother Hector reached the majors with the Marlins in 1999 and has spent the last two years in Japan. Erick has drawn comparisons to Derek Jeter with the raw tools to boot, but he might have to settle for a role as Jeter's backup. Almonte took a step backward after a dismal start in Triple-A. One of the best pure athletes in the system, he has frustrated the Yankees with his lack of progress. Columbus manager Stump Merrill got fed up with Almonte, who reportedly demanded a trade before he was demoted to Norwich. What's more aggravating about Almonte's season was that he had a tremendous showing in spring training. He did manage to hit a career-high 17 home runs, but he hasn't adjusted to the Yankees' plate-discipline philosophies, and pitch recognition is an issue with his long swing. Almonte, who also had a poor performance in the Dominican League in the offseason, might need a change of scenery. With his athleticism and strength, someone will give him a shot, possibly as a utilityman in the mold of Hiram Bocachica.

Year	Club (League)	Class	AVG	G	AB	R	H	2B	3B	HR	RBI	BB	SO	SB	SLG	OBP
1996	Yankees (DSL)	R	.282	58	216	37	61	7	0	8	36	15	30	3	.426	.333
1997	Yankees (GCL)	R	.283	52	180	32	51	4	4	3	31	21	27	8	.400	.355
1998	Greensboro (SAL)	A	.209	120	450	53	94	13	0	6	33	29	121	6	.278	.260
1999	Tampa (FSL)	A	.257	61	230	36	59	8	2	5	25	18	49	3	.374	.313
	Yankees (GCL)	R	.300	9	30	5	9	2	0	2	9	3	10	1	.567	.343
2000	Norwich (EL)	AA	.271	131	454	56	123	18	4	15	77	35	129	12	.427	.326
2001	Columbus (IL)	AAA	.287	97	345	55	99	19	3	12	55	44	90	4	.464	.369
	Norwich (EL)	AA	.250	3	12	2	3	0	0	0	1	1	6	1	.250	.308
	New York (AL)	MAJ	.500	8	4	0	2	1	0	0	0	0	1	2	.750	.500
2002	Columbus (IL)	AAA	.235	66	221	25	52	10	1	9	28	15	60	2	.412	.282
	Norwich (EL)	AA	.241	53	187	28	45	7	0	8	33	30	59	10	.406	.342
MAJOR LEAGUE TOTALS			.500	8	4	0	2	1	0	0	0	0	1	2	.750	.500
MINOR LEAGUE TOTALS			.256	650	2325	329	596	88	14	68	327	211	581	50	.394	.319

25. Marcus Thames, of

Born: March 6, 1977. **Ht.:** 6-2. **Wt.:** 200. **Bats:** R. **Throws:** R. **School:** East Central (Miss.) CC. **Career Transactions:** Selected by Yankees in 30th round of 1996 draft; signed May 16, 1997.

Marcus Thames hammered a 95 mph Randy Johnson fastball into the monuments at Yankee Stadium in his first at-bat in the big leagues. Overall, though, he took a step back from a monster 2001 campaign. Thames hit .275 with three home runs during spring training, but the signing of free agent Rondell White and trades for Raul Mondesi and John Vander Wal limited his opportunities. He displayed his strength and bat speed by homering against Johnson, but Thames is probably closer to a .229 hitter (his composite average in 1999-2000 and 2002) than the one who smacked 78 extra-base hits in his third year in Double-A in 2001. Thames, who joined the National Guard as an 18-year-old to help support his family, has the work ethic the Yankees covet. He could develop into a serviceable reserve outfielder.

Year	Club (League)	Class	AVG	G	AB	R	H	2B	3B	HR	RBI	BB	SO	SB	SLG	OBP
1997	Yankees (GCL)	R	.344	57	195	51	67	17	4	7	36	16	26	6	.579	.394
	Greensboro (SAL)	A	.313	4	16	2	5	1	0	0	2	0	3	1	.375	.313
1998	Tampa (FSL)	A	.284	122	457	62	130	18	3	11	59	24	78	13	.409	.328
1999	Norwich (EL)	AA	.225	51	182	25	41	6	2	4	26	22	40	0	.346	.316
	Tampa (FSL)	A	.244	69	266	47	65	12	4	11	38	33	58	3	.444	.332
2000	Norwich (EL)	AA	.241	131	474	72	114	30	2	15	79	50	89	1	.407	.313
2001	Norwich (EL)	AA	.321	139	520	114	167	43	4	31	97	73	101	10	.598	.410
2002	Columbus (IL)	AAA	.207	107	386	51	80	21	3	13	45	43	71	5	.378	.297
	New York (AL)	MAJ	.231	7	13	2	3	1	0	1	2	0	4	0	.538	.231
MAJOR LEAGUE TOTALS			.231	7	13	2	3	1	0	1	2	0	4	0	.538	.231
MINOR LEAGUE TOTALS			.268	680	2496	424	669	148	22	92	382	261	466	39	.456	.342

26. Ryan Bicondoa, rhp

Born: Jan. 26, 1979. **Ht.:** 6-3. **Wt.:** 190. **Bats:** R. **Throws:** R. **School:** Western Kentucky University. **Career Transactions:** Signed as nondrafted free agent by Yankees, May 28, 2002.

A cousin of Darryl Kile, Bicondoa signed as a fifth-year senior before the 2002 draft. He went 11-2, 2.55 with a Western Kentucky-record 150 strikeouts and just 23 walks in 124 innings to earn Sun Belt Conference pitcher of the year honors. His success translated immediately to the pro ranks as he led the New York-Penn League in strikeouts and complete games. One of the system's sleepers, Bicondoa generates plus-plus life on an 86-92 mph sinker from a true three-quarters release. He keeps the ball down in the zone and can paint the corners as well as anyone in the system. While he's not overpowering, he uses an outstanding changeup to keep hitters off-balance. Bicondoa's curveball has slurvy action and is occasionally average, but it's a work in progress and needs to be tightened up. The curve could be the difference between a future in the rotation or the bullpen. He could enjoy a similar ascent to Charlie Manning and reach Double-A in his first full pro season.

Year	Club (League)	Class	W	L	ERA	G	GS	CG	SV	IP	H	R	ER	HR	BB	SO	AVG
2002	Staten Island (NY-P)	A	6	4	1.90	14	14	3	0	85	64	25	18	3	7	94	.203
MINOR LEAGUE TOTALS			6	4	1.90	14	14	3	0	85	64	25	18	3	7	94	.203

27. Adrian Hernandez, rhp

Born: March 25, 1975. **Ht.:** 6-1. **Wt.:** 180. **Bats:** R. **Throws:** R. **Career Transactions:** Signed out of Cuba by Yankees, June 2, 2000.

He earned the nickname "El Duquecito" for similarities to countryman Orlando Hernandez (no relation), but Adrian needs to develop a style of his own. While he's provided glimpses of a pitcher worthy of the four-year, $4 million contract he signed in 2000, his 5.39 ERA in Triple-A illustrates his inconsistency. He tries to get too fancy at times, varying his arm angle and speed, but he tends to nibble when he does that. When he employs a more traditional delivery and stays at a three-quarters release, Hernandez challenges hitters with a 90-93 mph fastball with arm-side movement. He has yet to come up with an effective weapon against lefties, who have hit .303 against him at Columbus. His curveball, slider and changeup are average pitches, and he lacks a true out pitch. The revelation that he was more than four years older than previously believed didn't help his prospect status. Hernandez was outrighted from the 40-man roster and will have to battle for a bullpen spot in 2003.

Year	Club (League)	Class	W	L	ERA	G	GS	CG	SV	IP	H	R	ER	HR	BB	SO	AVG
2000	Tampa (FSL)	A	1	0	1.35	1	1	0	0	7	3	1	1	0	1	13	.130
	Norwich (EL)	AA	5	1	4.04	6	6	1	0	36	34	17	16	1	18	44	.248
	Columbus (IL)	AAA	2	1	4.40	5	5	2	0	31	24	18	15	2	18	29	.218
2001	Columbus (IL)	AAA	8	7	5.51	21	21	0	0	118	116	75	72	13	60	97	.265
	New York (AL)	MAJ	0	3	3.68	6	3	0	0	22	15	10	9	7	10	10	.190
2002	Columbus (IL)	AAA	6	7	5.25	20	20	0	0	110	114	67	64	9	45	109	.270
	New York (AL)	MAJ	0	1	12.00	2	1	0	0	6	10	8	8	2	6	9	.357
MAJOR LEAGUE TOTALS			0	4	5.46	8	4	0	0	28	25	18	17	9	16	19	.234
MINOR LEAGUE TOTALS			22	16	5.03	53	53	3	0	300	291	178	168	25	142	292	.258

28. Deivi Mendez, ss

Born: June 24, 1983. **Ht.:** 6-1. **Wt.:** 160. **Bats:** R. **Throws:** R. **Career Transactions:** Signed out of Dominican Republic by Yankees, July 2, 1999.

A holdup at the U.S. consulate in the Dominican Republic couldn't have come at a worse time for Mendez. An influx of middle-infield talent including Robinson Cano, Ferdin Tejada and Joaquin Arias pushed him down the Yankees' depth chart as he missed all of spring training and showed up out of shape. Nagging injuries hampered his progress throughout 2002, and he never really got untracked. The good news is that Mendez' date of birth didn't change, which means he's still younger than Cano and Tejada. After the season, the Yankees put him in a special conditioning program at their Dominican academy. He has a chance to develop into a plus defender with a strong arm. Offensively, the ball jumps off his bat to the alleys. He'll need to regroup and make up for lost time in 2003.

Year	Club (League)	Class	AVG	G	AB	R	H	2B	3B	HR	RBI	BB	SO	SB	SLG	OBP
2000	Yankees (GCL)	R	.300	56	210	37	63	20	1	2	25	26	39	4	.433	.382
2001	Greensboro (SAL)	A	.215	49	172	25	37	6	0	2	15	14	35	5	.285	.279
	Staten Island (NY-P)	A	.231	53	186	23	43	10	2	1	21	9	31	2	.323	.272
2002	Yankees (GCL)	R	.233	31	90	9	21	6	0	2	11	10	16	1	.367	.324
	Tampa (FSL)	A	.333	2	6	2	2	0	0	1	1	0	1	0	.833	.333
MINOR LEAGUE TOTALS			.250	191	664	96	166	42	3	8	73	59	122	12	.358	.317

29. Yhency Brazoban, rhp

Born: June 11, 1980. **Ht.:** 6-1. **Wt.:** 170. **Bats:** R. **Throws:** R. **Career Transactions:** Signed out of Dominican Republic by Yankees, July 10, 1997.

As an outfielder, Brazoban idolized Vladimir Guerrero. After switching to pitching in the middle of his fifth pro season, he'll need to find a new player to emulate. The Yankees grew tired of waiting for his bat to develop, so Brazoban, who had 80 arm strength on the 20-80 scouting scale, moved to the mound in mid-July. He hit 97 mph the first time he stepped on the mound and flashed a darting 87 mph slider. He produced encouraging results in his short Gulf Coast League stint before getting shut down with a sore arm. He continued to make progress by pitching in the Dominican instructional league after the season. His fastball sat between 91-97 and he threw his slider for strikes at 83 mph. Brazoban has surprisingly good mechanics with a fast, loose arm, though he was working on repeating his release point and getting extension out front. Brazoban could move fast because he has two plus pitches and good command. The Yankees will monitor his workload and move him slowly, hoping he can develop into into a dynamic reliever at the back of the bullpen.

Year	Club (League)	Class	AVG	G	AB	R	H	2B	3B	HR	RBI	BB	SO	SB	SLG	OBP
1998	Yankees (DSL)	R	.319	68	251	51	80	19	2	9	46	31	75	10	.518	.399
1999	Yankees (GCL)	R	.320	56	200	33	64	14	5	1	26	12	47	7	.455	.367
2000	Greensboro (SAL)	A	.188	12	48	6	9	3	0	0	8	3	15	1	.250	.231
	Yankees (GCL)	R	.303	54	201	36	61	14	4	5	28	11	28	2	.488	.349
2001	Greensboro (SAL)	A	.273	124	469	51	128	23	3	6	52	19	98	6	.373	.311
	Columbus (IL)	AAA	.200	1	5	2	1	1	0	0	0	0	2	0	.400	.200
2002	Greensboro (SAL)	A	.242	69	252	33	61	11	2	3	28	15	74	0	.337	.290
MINOR LEAGUE TOTALS			.283	384	1426	212	404	85	16	24	188	91	339	26	.416	.334

Year	Club (League)	Class	W	L	ERA	G	GS	CG	SV	IP	H	R	ER	HR	BB	SO	AVG
2002	Yankees (GCL)	R	0	0	4.50	6	0	0	0	6	3	3	3	0	4	11	.136
MINOR LEAGUE TOTALS			0	0	4.50	6	0	0	0	6	3	3	3	0	4	11	.136

30. Kevin Thompson, of

Born: Sept. 18, 1979. **Ht.:** 5-10. **Wt.:** 180. **Bats:** R. **Throws:** R. **School:** Grayson County (Texas) JC. **Career Transactions:** Selected by Yankees in 31st round of 1999 draft; signed June 7, 2000.

Another draft-and-follow project signed by Texas area scout Mark Batchko, who also landed Brandon Claussen and Sean Henn, Thompson was a shortstop/second baseman in junior college. He played on Grayson County's back-to-back Junior College World Series championship teams with the Angels' John Lackey. Thompson played seven games at second base in his 2000 pro debut before moving to center field, where he has emerged as one of the best defensive outfielders in the system along with Marcus Thames and Matt Carson. A plus runner (65 on the 20-80 scouting scale), Thompson led the organization in steals while getting caught just seven times in 2002. He makes consistent contact with a direct stroke and solid bat control, and shows an advanced understanding of strike-zone judgment. He should fare much better in his second attempt at high Class A and profiles as a versatile fourth outfielder.

Year	Club (League)	Class	AVG	G	AB	R	H	2B	3B	HR	RBI	BB	SO	SB	SLG	OBP
2000	Yankees (GCL)	R	.267	20	75	13	20	7	1	2	9	10	14	2	.467	.356
2001	Staten Island (NY-P)	A	.262	68	260	46	68	11	4	6	33	36	48	11	.404	.360
2002	Greensboro (SAL)	A	.283	62	226	44	64	24	3	3	31	37	42	14	.456	.396
	Tampa (FSL)	A	.184	25	87	10	16	5	0	0	7	13	15	11	.241	.298
	Staten Island (NY-P)	A	.302	36	139	25	42	5	2	4	14	17	24	6	.453	.376
MINOR LEAGUE TOTALS			.267	211	787	138	210	52	10	15	94	113	143	44	.416	.366

OAKLAND
ATHLETICS

TOP 30 PROSPECTS

1. Rich Harden, rhp
2. John Rheinecker, lhp
3. Bobby Crosby, ss
4. Jeremy Brown, c
5. Mike Wood, rhp
6. Joe Valentine, rhp
7. Marcus McBeth, of
8. Freddie Bynum, 2b/ss
9. Joe Blanton, rhp
10. Ben Fritz, rhp
11. Nick Swisher, of
12. Jason Grabowski, of/c
13. Chad Harville, rhp
14. Matt Allegra, of
15. Mark Teahen, 3b
16. Esteban German, 2b
17. Steve Obenchain, rhp
18. Adam Morrissey, 3b/2b
19. Dan Johnson, 1b
20. John McCurdy, ss
21. Mike Rouse, ss
22. J.T. Stotts, ss
23. Shane Bazzell, rhp
24. Andy Dickinson, lhp
25. Eddie Yarnall, lhp
26. Bill Murphy, lhp
27. Edwardo Sierra, rhp
28. Steve Stanley, of
29. Bert Snow, rhp
30. Brian Stavisky, of

By Casey Tefertiller

It's a feat that may never be matched. In 2002, the Athletics' player-development program could claim the American League MVP (Miguel Tejada) and Cy Young Award winner (Barry Zito) and Baseball America's Rookie of the Year (Eric Hinske), plus a third baseman who won both Silver Slugger and Gold Glove honors (Eric Chavez).

Tejada, Zito and Chavez all were purely homegrown, while Hinske was acquired from the Cubs and traded to the Blue Jays. Their accolades show how the A's have managed to make the playoffs for three straight years despite a limited payroll: identifying and developing talent, using the farm system both to stock the major league team and to deal for additional help.

General manager Billy Beane, BA's Major League Executive of the Year, has been the architect of the plan and overseen its progression. Even with the departures of scouting director Grady Fuson to the Rangers and adviser J.P. Ricciardi to the Blue Jays, the A's haven't been slowed, thanks to the continuing efforts of farm director Keith Lieppman.

After the 2002 season, Oakland lost manager Art Howe to the Mets and replaced him with bench coach Ken Macha. Beane considered an offer from the Red Sox before deciding to remain with his heart in Oakland.

A series of trades weakened the farm system after the 2001 season, when Beane acquired players who would help win the AL West. The system bounced back in 2002 as the cumulative record of Oakland's minor league affiliates topped .500 for the seventh time in eight years. Second baseman Mark Ellis and starting pitcher Aaron Harang also emerged to make significant contributions to the major league club.

First-year scouting director Eric Kubota had seven selections before the second round of the 2002 draft with compensation picks for losing free agents. He continued the Fuson-fused concept of valuing baseball instincts over tools, and helped to restock the lower levels of the system.

The organization's strength is pitching, with top prospects Rich Harden and John Rheinecker potential front-of-the-rotation performers. The two significant weaknesses are catchers and center fielders, and Oakland addressed both in the draft. The A's still are lacking in middle-of-the-order hitters.

Amid all the changes, Oakland has managed to stay the course by developing from within. The formula remains a success.

OrganizationOverview

General Manager: Billy Beane. **Farm Director:** Keith Lieppman. **Scouting Director:** Eric Kubota.

2002 PERFORMANCE

Class	Farm Team	League	W	L	Pct.	Finish*	Manager
Majors	Oakland	American	103	59	.636	2nd (14)	Art Howe
Triple-A	Sacramento RiverCats	Pacific Coast	66	78	.458	14th(16)	Bob Geren
Double-A	Midland RockHounds	Texas	75	64	.540	3rd (8)	Tony DeFrancesco
High A	Modesto A's	California	78	62	.557	2nd (10)	Greg Sparks
High A	†Visalia Oaks	California	70	71	.496	5th (10)	Webster Garrison
Short-season	Vancouver Canadians	Northwest	37	39	.487	6th (8)	Orv Franchuk
Rookie	AZL Athletics	Arizona	28	28	.500	t-3rd (7)	Ruben Escalera
OVERALL 2002 MINOR LEAGUE RECORD			354	342	.509	14th (30)	

*Finish in overall standings (No. of teams in league).   †Low Class A affiliate will be in Kane County (Midwest) in 2003.

ORGANIZATION LEADERS

BATTING   *Minimum 250 At-Bats
*AVG	Carlos Mendez, Sacramento	.324
R	Caonabo Cosme, Modesto	90
H	Freddie Bynum, Visalia	165
TB	Daylan Holt, Midland/Visalia	244
2B	Larry Sutton, Sacramento	40
3B	Kirk Asche, Midland	10
HR	Jorge Soto, Visalia	31
RBI	Graham Koonce, Midland	96
BB	Graham Koonce, Midland	133
SO	Jorge Soto, Visalia	195
SB	Freddie Bynum, Visalia	41

PITCHING   #Minimum 75 Innings
W	Mike Wood, Midland/Modesto	14
L	Chris Enochs, Sacramento/Midland	13
#ERA	Brad Weis, Sacramento/Modesto	2.27
G	Claudio Galva, Midland	62
CG	Chris Enochs, Sacramento/Midland	3
SV	Mike Frick, Modesto	23
IP	John Rheinecker, Midland/Visalia	179
BB	Neal Cotts, Modesto	87
SO	Rich Harden, Midland/Visalia	187

BEST TOOLS

Best Hitter for Average	Bobby Crosby
Best Power Hitter	Jorge Soto
Fastest Baserunner	Marcus McBeth
Best Athlete	Marcus McBeth
Best Fastball	Rich Harden
Best Curveball	John Rheinecker
Best Slider	Joe Valentine
Best Changeup	Rich Harden
Best Control	Mike Wood
Best Defensive Catcher	Jeremy Brown
Best Defensive Infielder	Bobby Crosby
Best Infield Arm	Francis Gomez Alfonseca
Best Defensive Outfielder	Marcus McBeth
Best Outfield Arm	Marcus McBeth

PROJECTED 2006 LINEUP

Catcher	Jeremy Brown
First Base	Nick Swisher
Second Base	Mark Ellis
Third Base	Eric Chavez
Shortstop	Miguel Tejada
Left Field	Bobby Crosby
Center Field	Marcus McBeth
Right Field	Jermaine Dye
Designated Hitter	Erubiel Durazo
No. 1 Starter	Tim Hudson

Graham Koonce   Neal Cotts

No. 2 Starter	Barry Zito
No. 3 Starter	Mark Mulder
No. 4 Starter	Rich Harden
No. 5 Starter	John Rheinecker
Closer	Keith Foulke

TOP PROSPECTS OF THE DECADE

1993	Todd Van Poppel, rhp
1994	Steve Karsay, rhp
1995	Ben Grieve, of
1996	Ben Grieve, of
1997	Miguel Tejada, ss
1998	Ben Grieve, of
1999	Eric Chavez, 3b
2000	Mark Mulder, lhp
2001	Jose Ortiz, 2b
2002	Carlos Pena, 1b

TOP DRAFT PICKS OF THE DECADE

1993	John Wasdin, rhp
1994	Ben Grieve, of
1995	Ariel Prieto, rhp
1996	Eric Chavez, 3b
1997	Chris Enochs, rhp
1998	Mark Mulder, lhp
1999	Barry Zito, lhp
2000	Freddie Bynum, ss (2)
2001	Bobby Crosby, ss
2002	Nick Swisher, of

ALL-TIME LARGEST BONUSES

Mark Mulder, 1998	$3,200,000
Nick Swisher, 2002	$1,780,000
Barry Zito, 1999	$1,625,000
Joe Blanton, 2002	$1,400,000
John McCurdy, 2002	$1,375,000

MinorLeagueDepthChart

OAKLAND ATHLETICS

RANK

Oakland doesn't have the same talent pool it did two years ago, but that's not because of the departures of former scouting director Grady Fuson (Rangers) and director of player personnel J.P. Ricciardi (Blue Jays). General manager Billy Beane has used the farm system's depth to help acquire talent for the parent club. Four prospects were sent to Texas a year ago, and righthanders Jeremy Bonderman and Franklyn German were dealt to Detroit last summer in a three-team deal for Ted Lilly, Jason Arnold and John-Ford Griffin. Arnold and Griffin were, in turn, shipped to Toronto. The A's replenished with seven of the top 39 picks in last year's draft, though they overdrafted several players with budget considerations in mind.

Note: Depth charts prepared by Josh Boyd. Numbers in parentheses indicate prospect rankings.

LF
Brian Stavisky (30)
Chris Tritle
Brian Sellier

CF
Marcus McBeth (7)
Nick Swisher (11)
Steve Stanley (28)
Rontrez Johnson
Gary Thomas

RF
Matt Allegra (14)
Austin Nagle

3B
Jason Grabowski (12)
Mark Teahen (15)
John McCurdy (20)

SS
Bobby Crosby (3)
Mike Rouse (21)
J.T. Stotts (22)
Francis Gomez

2B
Freddie Bynum (8)
Esteban German (16)
Adam Morrissey (18)
Mark Kiger

1B
Dan Johnson (19)
Graham Koonce
Brant Colamarino

C
Jeremy Brown (4)
Casey Myers
John Baker
Jorge Soto

RHP

Starters	Relievers
Rich Harden (1)	Joe Valentine (6)
Mike Wood (5)	Ben Fritz (10)
Joe Blanton (9)	Chad Harville (13)
Steve Obenchain (17)	Shane Bazzell (23)
Edwardo Sierra (27)	Bert Snow (29)
Darvin Withers	Mike Frick
Luke Robertson	Buddy Hernandez
Justin Duchscherer	Roy Smith
Mike Ziegler	Chris Mowday
Jeff Bruksch	Mike Neu
Shane Komine	Jack Krawczyk
Derell McCall	Kyle Crowell
	Jared Burton

LHP

Starters	Relievers
John Rheinecker (2)	Juan Pena
Andy Dickinson (24)	Claudio Galva
Eddie Yarnall (25)	
Bill Murphy (26)	

DraftAnalysis

2002 Draft

Best Pro Debut: The Athletics say they valued C Jeremy Brown (1) as a supplemental first-round pick, but part of his appeal was that he signed for $350,000. Regardless, the bad-body senior surpassed all expectations by hitting .310-10-40 in high Class A.

Best Athlete: 3B **Mark Teahen** (1) has the best chance of becoming a five-tool player. He has a plus arm and defensive skills, runs slightly above-average and has a chance to hit for power. If RHP Ben Fritz (1) had his way, he'd play every day as a power-hitting catcher. RHP Steve Schilsky (25) played defensive end at Illinois Wesleyan.

Best Pure Hitter: OF Brian Stavisky (6) has a quick bat and hit .294 in short-season ball. The A's also believe Brown and OF Steve Swisher (1) will produce for average.

Best Raw Power: Stavisky or 1B Brant Colamarino (7).

Fastest Runner: Oakland doesn't focus on speed as much as most organizations do. 2B Lloyd Turner (16) is a 60 runner on the 20-80 scouting scale.

Best Defensive Player: OF Steve Stanley (2) is only 5-foot-8, but he has tremendous instincts that serve him well in center field and as a leadoff catalyst.

Best Fastball: RHP Joseph Blanton (1) hit 95 mph while striking out 16 in a classic college duel with No. 1 overall pick Bryan Bullington, then touched 97 at the beginning of the summer before tiring. Fritz still was reaching 96 at the end of his pro debut. RHP Jared Burton (8) works at 93-94 mph when he's used out of the bullpen.

Best Breaking Ball: LHP Bill Murphy's (3) curveball.

Most Intriguing Background: Swisher's father Steve was a 1973 first-round pick of the White Sox and a 1976 all-star for the Cubs. LHP Curtis White (43) has been drafted for four consecutive years without signing and will try to make it five after returning to Oklahoma.

Closest To The Majors: Brown. Fritz is also advanced and Blanton has the stuff to accelerate his timetable.

JOHN SPEAR

Teahen

Best Late-Round Pick: C Jed Morris (36) was one of college baseball's best-hitting catchers last spring, but clubs knew he would need surgery to repair an Achilles tendon. LHP Andy Dickinson (28), who shares the University of Illinois career record for wins, vowed to the A's that he'll prove he's the next Jamie Moyer.

The One Who Got Away: Oakland would have made a stronger run at athletic SS Trevor Crowe (20) if he had been healthy, but his shoulder problems flared up again last summer. He's now at Arizona.

Assessment: The A's put more stock in performance than pure tools, so it's not the most encouraging sign that most of their seven first-rounders had mediocre debuts. Oakland has depleted its system with recent trades, so the organization will challenge several players to develop quickly.

2001 Draft

The Athletics scored with their first four picks—SS Bobby Crosby (1), RHP Jeremy Bonderman (1) and LHPs John Rheinecker (1) and Neal Cotts (2)—though they've traded Bonderman and Cotts. OF Marcus McBeth (4) and RHP Mike Wood (10) also look good.   **Grade: A**

2000 Draft

Without a first-rounder, Oakland still came away with 2B/SS Freddie Bynum (10) and draft-and-follow RHP Rich Harden (17). Harden has emerged quickly as the system's top prospect.   **Grade: B**

1999 Draft

LHP Barry Zito (1) alone makes this a great draft. OF Ryan Ludwick (2) reached the majors last summer after being dealt to Texas in the Carlos Pena deal. The A's have hopes for draft-and-follow OF Matt Allegra (16).   **Grade: A**

1998 Draft

LHP Mark Mulder (1) did for this draft what Zito did for 1999. Draft-and-follow C Gerald Laird (2) and 1B Jon Hart (5) joined Ludwick with the Rangers. OF Eric Byrnes (8) is a serviceable fourth outfielder. Unsigned 2B Michael Woods (31) became a first-rounder. **Grade: A**

Note: Draft analysis prepared by Jim Callis. Numbers in parentheses indicate draft rounds.

. . . With a fastball that hits 95 mph and a deceptive changeup, Harden has two outstanding pitches.

Rich
Harden rhp

Born: Nov. 30, 1981.
Ht.: 6-1. **Wt.:** 180.
Bats: L. **Throws:** R.
School: Central Arizona JC.
Career Transactions: Selected by Athletics in 17th round of 2000 draft; signed May 18, 2001.

The hard-throwing Harden emerged as a top prospect in 2002, making the leap from high Class A Visalia to Double-A Midland with hardly a struggle. He dominated after the promotion, and it was all the more impressive because he was 20 and in his first full season as a pro. Harden grew up in Victoria, B.C., and played mostly outfield in summer-league competition. He did pitch enough to catch the attention of the Mariners, who drafted him in the 38th round in 1999. He opted instead for Central Arizona JC because he didn't believe he was ready for pro ball. Athletics scout John Kuehl kept his eye on Harden and persuaded Oakland to call his name in the 17th round in 2000 as a draft-and-follow. Harden returned to Central Arizona and led all juco pitchers in strikeouts as a sophomore before signing in May. He tied for the short-season Northwest League lead in strikeouts in his pro debut, but he had a problem–his curveball was below pro standards. So Harden and the A's agreed to scrap it in favor of a slider. The results came almost instantly.

With a fastball that hits 95 mph and a deceptive changeup, Harden has two outstanding pitches as the foundation of his arsenal. He also throws the slider and a splitter, which can be above-average at times. While the slider isn't an exceptional pitch, it provides an effective balance to the fastball and changeup, keeping hitters off-balance. He has added a two-seam fastball, a mid-80s sinker that gives hitters something else to worry about. Harden has a calm demeanor on the mound and is rarely flustered with runners on base. He has shown the ability to work out of jams. Harden's pitch counts are too high. He has yet to learn to retire batters early in the count to allow him to go deeper into games. He sometimes reaches his pitch limit in the fifth or sixth inning. While his slider has shown dramatic improvement, it still needs more consistency.

Harden's combination of power and deception is intriguing. He has the potential to become a legitimate No. 1 starter. Harden is ticketed to begin 2003 at Triple-A Sacramento and could contribute in the majors by season's end

Year	Club (League)	Class	W	L	ERA	G	GS	CG	SV	IP	H	R	ER	HR	BB	SO	AVG
2001	Vancouver (NWL)	A	2	4	3.39	18	14	0	0	74	47	29	28	3	38	100	.179
2002	Visalia (Cal)	A	4	3	2.93	12	12	1	0	68	49	27	22	4	24	85	.201
	Midland (TL)	AA	8	3	2.95	16	16	1	0	85	67	33	28	2	52	102	.217
MINOR LEAGUE TOTALS			14	10	3.09	46	42	2	0	227	163	89	78	9	114	287	.200

2. John Rheinecker, lhp

Born: May 29, 1979. **Ht.:** 6-2. **Wt.:** 210. **Bats:** L. **Throws:** L. **School:** Southwest Missouri State University. **Career Transactions:** Selected by Athletics in first round (37th overall) of 2001 draft; signed June 30, 2001.

Rheinecker spent his first two college seasons at Belleville Area (Ill.) CC, throwing in the high 80s and playing in the outfield. When he moved to Southwest Missouri State, he developed a quality slider and added velocity as he matured. Projected as an early pick in the 2000 draft, he tore the anterior cruciate ligament in his right knee in an outfield collision. He made a full recovery as a senior. As a lefthander with a fastball that touches 91 mph and plus breaking stuff (he throws a curveball to go with his slider), Rheinecker excites the A's. He's refining a cutter that has been effective against righthanders and is an exceptional competitor on the mound. Rheinecker has a tendency to leave the ball up in the strike zone, making him too hittable at times. He must improve his changeup. He's still learning pitch sequences to set up batters. Reducing his pitch counts is another point of emphasis. The A's believe Rheinecker has the potential to emerge as a frontline big league starter, perhaps as early as 2004. He'll pitch in Triple-A in 2003, working on keeping his fastballs at the knees.

Year	Club (League)	Class	W	L	ERA	G	GS	CG	SV	IP	H	R	ER	HR	BB	SO	AVG
2001	Vancouver (NWL)	A	0	1	1.59	6	5	0	0	23	13	5	4	0	4	17	.160
	Modesto (Cal)	A	0	1	6.30	2	2	0	0	10	10	7	7	1	5	5	.256
2002	Visalia (Cal)	A	3	0	2.31	9	9	0	0	51	41	16	13	2	10	62	.216
	Midland (TL)	AA	7	7	3.38	20	20	1	0	128	137	63	48	7	24	100	.274
MINOR LEAGUE TOTALS			10	9	3.07	37	36	1	0	211	201	91	72	10	43	184	.248

3. Bobby Crosby, ss

Born: Jan. 12, 1980. **Ht.:** 6-3. **Wt.:** 200. **Bats:** R. **Throws:** R. **School:** Long Beach State University. **Career Transactions:** Selected by Athletics in first round (25th overall) of 2001 draft; signed July 3, 2001.

Crosby is the son of former A's scout and big leaguer Ed Crosby, who signed Jason Giambi and is now with the Diamondbacks. Bobby was the Big West Conference player of the year in 2001 and made an immediate impression by hitting .395 in his 11-game pro debut. He followed with a hot start at high Class A Modesto before moving on to Double-A to complete a solid first full season. Thanks to his background, Crosby has exceptional baseball instincts. He's consistent on defense, has a strong arm, reads balls well and makes all the plays. He should become a solid offensive performer, hitting for average with decent power. Crosby missed most of instructional league in 2001 with a hip flexor, and badly sprained his ankle at the start of the Arizona Fall League season in 2002. At 6-foot-3, he raises questions about whether he'll have the range to remain at shortstop. Crosby is Oakland's fallback if it loses Miguel Tejada, a free agent after the 2003 season. Crosby's spring-training performance will decide whether he returns to Double-A or heads to Triple-A.

Year	Club (League)	Class	AVG	G	AB	R	H	2B	3B	HR	RBI	BB	SO	SB	SLG	OBP
2001	Modesto (Cal)	A	.395	11	38	7	15	5	0	1	3	3	8	0	.605	.439
2002	Modesto (Cal)	A	.307	73	280	47	86	17	2	2	38	33	43	5	.404	.393
	Midland (TL)	AA	.281	59	228	31	64	16	0	7	31	19	41	9	.443	.335
MINOR LEAGUE TOTALS			.302	143	546	85	165	38	2	10	72	55	92	14	.434	.372

4. Jeremy Brown, c

Born: Oct. 25, 1979. **Ht.:** 5-10. **Wt.:** 210. **Bats:** R. **Throws:** R. **School:** University of Alabama. **Career Transactions:** Selected by Athletics in first round (35th overall) of 2002 draft; signed June 7, 2002.

Brown spent his first two years at Alabama as a corner infielder before moving behind the plate, where he had played occasionally in youth leagues. After turning down the Red Sox as a 19th-round pick in 2001, he won the 2002 Johnny Bench award as college baseball's best catcher. While his $350,000 bonus was easily the lowest in the top 66 picks, he proved himself offensively and defensively in high Class A after signing. Brown combines catch-and-throw abilities with a talent for hitting. His arm is slightly above-average. He hits for both power and average, with the plate discipline the A's covet. He set the Alabama career record for walks. Brown's short, squat body turned off many scouts and doesn't fit the mold of the more athletic modern big league catcher. But as A's general manager Billy Beane said, "We're not selling jeans here." Brown needs to improve his footwork and blocking skills, and he devoted instructional league to making the changes. Brown has a chance to jump to Double-A in 2003. If he continues to perform well, he'll be on a fast track to the majors.

Year	Club (League)	Class	AVG	G	AB	R	H	2B	3B	HR	RBI	BB	SO	SB	SLG	OBP
2002	Vancouver (NWL)	A	.286	10	28	7	8	1	0	0	1	10	5	1	.321	.487
	Visalia (Cal)	A	.310	55	187	36	58	14	0	10	40	44	49	1	.545	.444
MINOR LEAGUE TOTALS			.307	65	215	43	66	15	0	10	41	54	54	2	.516	.451

5. Mike Wood, rhp

Born: April 26, 1980. **Ht.:** 6-3. **Wt.:** 190. **Bats:** R. **Throws:** R. **School:** University of North Florida. **Career Transactions:** Selected by Athletics in 10th round of 2001 draft; signed June 10, 2001.

BILL NICHOLS

Undrafted out of high school, Wood attended NCAA Division II North Florida as a walk-on. He was a backup infielder as a freshman, moved into the rotation as a sophomore and became the team's closer as a junior. He has made a huge impression since joining the A's, using his dominant sinker to get outs at every level. Oakland calls Wood's out pitch a "super sinker" and compares it favorably to Tim Hudson's. Hitters repeatedly beat Wood's sinker into the ground or swing over the top of it. He pitches off his sinker with a slider, splitter and changeup. Velocity remains a concern. Wood reached 91 mph in college but has pitched in the mid-80s as a pro. There are some questions whether his sinker, which is slower than Hudson's, will be effective against major league hitters. His slider also needs work. Should Wood improve his velocity and slider, he could become a front-of-the-rotation starter. Because Oakland has plenty of starters and Wood has bullpen experience, his long-term role could be relief. He'll go to spring training with a chance to win a Triple-A job.

Year	Club (League)	Class	W	L	ERA	G	GS	CG	SV	IP	H	R	ER	HR	BB	SO	AVG
2001	Vancouver (NWL)	A	2	0	1.25	5	2	0	0	22	17	4	3	0	4	24	.210
	Modesto (Cal)	A	4	3	3.09	10	9	0	0	58	46	22	20	6	10	52	.211
2002	Modesto (Cal)	A	3	3	3.48	7	7	0	0	41	41	17	16	4	6	50	.265
	Midland (TL)	AA	11	3	3.15	17	17	0	0	106	103	41	37	8	29	63	.259
MINOR LEAGUE TOTALS			20	9	3.01	39	35	0	0	227	207	84	76	18	49	189	.243

6. Joe Valentine, rhp

Born: Dec. 24, 1979. **Ht.:** 6-2. **Wt.:** 190. **Bats:** R. **Throws:** R. **School:** Jefferson Davis (Ala.) JC. **Career Transactions:** Selected by White Sox in 26th round of 1999 draft; signed June 26, 1999 . . . Selected by Expos from White Sox in major league Rule 5 draft, Dec. 13, 2001 . . . Contract purchased by Tigers from Expos, Dec. 13, 2001 . . . Returned to White Sox, April 5, 2002 . . . Traded by White Sox with RHP Keith Foulke, C Mark Johnson and cash to Athletics for RHP Billy Koch and two players to be named, Dec. 3, 2002; White Sox acquired LHP Neal Cotts and OF Daylan Holt to complete trade (Dec. 16, 2002).

STEVE MOORE

The White Sox lost Valentine to the Tigers in the 2001 Rule 5 draft, then got him back when he showed little command in spring training with Detroit. He led the minors with 36 saves in 2002, then came to Oakland in the Keith Foulke/Billy Koch trade. Valentine held opponents to a .173 average and has allowed just 89 hits in 160 innings over the last three seasons. There's no subtlety with Valentine. He's a fastball/slider pitcher who can hit 96 mph, and he keeps hitters off balance by busting heat inside when they appear too comfortable. There are nights when his slider is filthy, and his pitches complement each other well. Valentine can be wild and has averaged nearly a walk per two innings as a pro. Because he is so tough to hit, the walks rarely come back to haunt him. Few minor league closers turn into major league closers, but Valentine could be an exception. Foulke becomes a free agent after the 2003 season, so Oakland could look to Valentine as soon as 2004. He should make his big league debut at some point in 2003.

Year	Club (League)	Class	W	L	ERA	G	GS	CG	SV	IP	H	R	ER	HR	BB	SO	AVG
1999	White Sox (AZL)	R	0	0	0.00	3	0	0	0	4	2	0	0	0	1	2	.154
	Bristol (Appy)	R	0	0	7.02	11	0	0	0	17	27	17	13	2	9	14	.360
2000	Bristol (Appy)	R	2	1	2.88	19	0	0	7	25	14	10	8	1	12	30	.163
2001	Kannapolis (SAL)	A	2	2	2.93	30	0	0	14	31	21	10	10	0	10	33	.194
	Winston-Salem (Car)	A	5	1	1.01	27	0	0	8	45	18	7	5	0	27	50	.122
2002	Birmingham (SL)	AA	4	1	1.97	55	0	0	36	59	36	16	13	1	30	63	.173
MINOR LEAGUE TOTALS			13	5	2.44	145	0	0	65	181	118	60	49	4	89	192	.185

7. Marcus McBeth, of

Born: Aug. 23, 1980. **Ht.:** 6-1. **Wt.:** 180. **Bats:** R. **Throws:** R. **School:** University of South Carolina. **Career Transactions:** Selected by Athletics in fourth round of 2001 draft; signed Aug. 16, 2001.

McBeth returned kicks for the football team and played center field for the baseball team at South Carolina. He signed late in 2001 and when he arrived in instructional league, the A's discovered a separation in his left shoulder. The injury affected his swing, and he has worked to strengthen his shoulder during the past year. McBeth has four standout tools. He's an outstanding center fielder who could handle defensive responsibilities in the majors today. His arm grades out as a legitimate 8 on the 2-to-8 scouting scale, and he has exceptional speed. He has shown impressive raw power in college and the pros, but McBeth has never put up impressive numbers. The shoulder separation may have been part of the problem, but he also had a lackluster 2002. He was the A's most improved hitter during instructional league, showing better pitch recognition and plate discipline. The A's hope McBeth will develop into a leadoff hitter, learning to reach base so he can use his speed. He'll start 2003 in high Class A and could advance to Double-A later in the season.

Year	Club (League)	Class	AVG	G	AB	R	H	2B	3B	HR	RBI	BB	SO	SB	SLG	OBP
2002	Visalia (Cal)	A	.227	76	255	45	58	7	3	10	39	29	73	14	.396	.318
	Athletics (AZL)	R	.333	4	9	5	3	0	0	0	0	3	0	3	.333	.500
MINOR LEAGUE TOTALS			.231	80	264	50	61	7	3	10	39	32	73	17	.394	.325

8. Freddie Bynum, 2b/ss

Born: March 15, 1980. **Ht.:** 6-1. **Wt.:** 180. **Bats:** L. **Throws:** R. **School:** Pitt County (N.C.) CC. **Career Transactions:** Selected by Athletics in second round of 2000 draft; signed June 19, 2000.

Bynum made the transition from a hopeful with tools to a skilled prospect with a breakthrough season in 2002. He made major strides in developing into a leadoff hitter and competent second baseman, then handled shortstop effectively in the Arizona Fall League. It was a nice comeback from a 2001 season ruined by ankle injuries. Bynum has the tools necessary to bat at the top of a lineup. He has excellent speed, hits well to the opposite field and, most important, has improved at getting on base. He owns a fine throwing arm and has proven he can handle second base. His performance at shortstop enhances his versatility. Because he came from a small junior college program, Bynum is still raw. He needs more at-bats and experience at higher levels of the minors. If he learned to bunt for hits, he could take greater advantage of his speed. His hands aren't the softest, though that's less of a problem at second base than it was at shortstop. If everything continues to come together, Bynum can become a quality leadoff hitter and middle infielder in the big leagues. He'll continue his development in Double-A in 2003.

Year	Club (League)	Class	AVG	G	AB	R	H	2B	3B	HR	RBI	BB	SO	SB	SLG	OBP
2000	Vancouver (NWL)	A	.256	72	281	52	72	10	1	1	26	31	58	22	.310	.341
2001	Modesto (Cal)	A	.261	120	440	59	115	19	7	2	46	41	95	28	.350	.325
2002	Visalia (Cal)	A	.306	135	539	83	165	26	5	3	56	64	116	41	.390	.385
MINOR LEAGUE TOTALS			.279	327	1260	194	352	55	13	6	128	136	269	91	.358	.355

9. Joe Blanton, rhp

Born: Dec. 11, 1980. **Ht.:** 6-3. **Wt.:** 220. **Bats:** R. **Throws:** R. **School:** University of Kentucky. **Career Transactions:** Selected by Athletics in first round (24th overall) of 2002 draft; signed July 20, 2002.

Blanton made his case as a top draft prospect when he led the Cape Cod League in strikeouts after his sophomore season. He outdueled No. 1 overall pick Bryan Bullington and struck out 16 in a 3-2 win over Ball State last spring. Oakland took him with a pick it received from the Yankees for losing Jason Giambi. Blanton has two power pitches in his fastball, which sits at 94 mph and tops out at 97, and his curveball. His slider and changeup are decent pitches, though they still need work. If he can refine his changeup, he could be a dynamic starter. He has a maximum-effort delivery, so the A's are trying to smooth out Blanton's mechanics. That will give him a better chance to repeat his delivery, which in turn will improve his command. He's still raw around the edges and developing a feel for pitching. Because of the changes he needs to make, Blanton isn't expected to move as quickly as some of Oakland's other college first-rounders. He'll probably start 2003 in high Class A, where he finished his first pro summer.

Year	Club (League)	Class	W	L	ERA	G	GS	CG	SV	IP	H	R	ER	HR	BB	SO	AVG
2002	Vancouver (NWL)	A	1	1	3.14	4	2	0	0	14	11	5	5	0	2	15	.216
	Modesto (Cal)	A	0	1	7.50	2	1	0	0	6	8	6	5	1	6	6	.296
MINOR LEAGUE TOTALS			1	2	4.43	6	3	0	0	20	19	11	10	1	8	21	.244

10. Ben Fritz, rhp

Born: March 29, 1981. **Ht.:** 6-4. **Wt.:** 220. **Bats:** R. **Throws:** R. **School:** Fresno State University. **Career Transactions:** Selected by Athletics in first round (30th overall) of 2002 draft; signed June 28, 2002.

A do-everything player, Fritz started all 59 games for Fresno State in 2002, seeing time at pitcher, catcher, first base and DH. His usual routine was to pitch on Friday, play first base on Saturday and catch on Sunday. The 2002 Western Athletic Conference pitcher of the year, he'd play every day if the decision were up to him. He has the arm, agility and power to make it as a catcher, but the A's decided that once he limits his workload to pitching, he has the potential to become a star. He has a great feel for the mound, with a true understanding of how to pitch. His stuff isn't bad, either. Fritz has a 90-94 mph fastball that touches 96, and his slider and changeup should become at least average pitches. He has good command and is a tenacious competitor. Some scouts have compared him to catcher-turned-pitcher Troy Percival and think Fritz' future may be in the bullpen. He excelled in that role during the summer of 2001, closing games for the Anchorage Glacier Pilots as they won the National Baseball Congress World Series championship. Along with Joe Blanton, Fritz is the most advanced of the pitchers Oakland drafted last year. He'll probably open this year in high Class A but could reach Double-A by season's end.

Year	Club (League)	Class	W	L	ERA	G	GS	CG	SV	IP	H	R	ER	HR	BB	SO	AVG
2002	Vancouver (NWL)	A	1	4	2.95	9	9	0	0	40	29	16	13	1	14	33	.199
	Visalia (Cal)	A	1	0	3.71	3	3	0	0	17	15	7	7	1	6	16	.242
MINOR LEAGUE TOTALS			2	4	3.18	12	12	0	0	57	44	23	20	2	20	49	.212

11. Nick Swisher, of

Born: Nov. 25, 1980. **Ht.:** 6-0. **Wt.:** 190. **Bats:** B. **Throws:** L. **School:** Ohio State University. **Career Transactions:** Selected by Athletics in first round (16th overall) of 2002 draft; signed June 14, 2002.

The A's coveted Swisher from the beginning of his junior season in 2002. He has the quality strike-zone knowledge they prize so highly, and they believe he'll hit for power and average while playing outstanding defense. He's the son of Steve Swisher, a former big league all-star who also was a first-round pick 29 years before Oakland took Nick 16th overall. A's scouting director Eric Kubota describes Swisher's defensive skills at first base as magical, but the organization wants to keep him in the outfield. He appears a step or two slow to be a center fielder, but he has ample speed and arm strength to be a plus defender on one of the corners. Some scouts question whether he has the true power to play there or at first base. But Swisher set the West Virginia high school record for single-season homers with 17, and he tied for the Big 10 Conference lead with 15 as a sophomore before hitting 10 last spring. He's a hard worker who's driven to become a major league star. The A's actually may have to convince Swisher to diminish his workload, as his extensive pregame workouts sometimes left him worn out by gametime.

Year	Club (League)	Class	AVG	G	AB	R	H	2B	3B	HR	RBI	BB	SO	SB	SLUG	OBP
2002	Vancouver (NWL)	A	.250	13	44	10	11	3	0	2	12	13	11	3	.455	.433
	Visalia (Cal)	A	.240	49	183	22	44	13	2	4	23	26	48	3	.399	.340
MINOR LEAGUE TOTALS			.242	62	227	32	55	16	2	6	35	39	59	6	.410	.360

12. Jason Grabowski, of/c

Born: May 24, 1976. **Ht.:** 6-3. **Wt.:** 200. **Bats:** L. **Throws:** R. **School:** University of Connecticut. **Career Transactions:** Selected by Rangers in second round of 1997 draft; signed June 12, 1997 . . . Claimed on waivers by Mariners from Rangers, Dec. 18, 2000 . . . Selected by Athletics from Mariners in major league Rule 5 draft, Dec. 13, 2001 . . . Granted free agency, March 26, 2002; re-signed by Athletics, March 28, 2002.

The path to the major leagues has taken many twists for Grabowski, but he'll come to spring training with an excellent chance to win a bench job. After playing catcher and short-stop at Connecticut, he signed with the Rangers as a catcher. Bouts with tendinitis in both knees led Grabowski to move to third base, and he primarily played the outfield in 2002. The Athletics got him in the 2001 major league Rule 5 draft but weren't able to keep him on their 25-man roster. They outrighted him to the minors, and because he had been outrighted previously that made him a free agent—and he immediately re-signed with Oakland. By mutual decision, Grabowski received some duty behind the plate last season. He needs better footwork at catcher, but he has enough arm strength for the position. He's also versatile enough to be a viable backup at the corner infield and outfield spots. As a hitter, Grabowski offers solid power and the ability to draw walks. He had the best offensive season of his career in 2002, though it was shortened when he broke the hamate bone in his wrist.

Year	Club (League)	Class	AVG	G	AB	R	H	2B	3B	HR	RBI	BB	SO	SB	SLG	OBP
1997	Pulaski (Appy)	R	.293	50	174	36	51	14	0	4	24	40	32	6	.443	.423
1998	Savannah (SAL)	A	.270	104	352	63	95	13	6	14	52	57	93	16	.460	.372
1999	Charlotte (FSL)	A	.313	123	434	68	136	31	6	12	87	65	66	13	.495	.407
	Tulsa (TL)	AA	.167	2	6	1	1	0	0	0	0	2	2	0	.167	.375
2000	Tulsa (TL)	AA	.274	135	493	93	135	33	5	19	90	88	106	8	.477	.383
2001	Tacoma (PCL)	AAA	.297	114	394	60	117	32	3	9	58	61	94	7	.462	.390
2002	Sacramento (PCL)	AAA	.294	73	265	50	78	22	3	12	52	39	56	6	.536	.387
	Oakland (AL)	MAJ	.375	4	8	3	3	1	1	0	1	3	1	0	.750	.545
MAJOR LEAGUE TOTALS			.375	4	8	3	3	1	1	0	1	3	1	0	.750	.545
MINOR LEAGUE TOTALS			.289	601	2118	371	613	145	23	70	363	352	449	56	..479	.391

13. Chad Harville, rhp

Born: Sept. 16, 1976. **Ht.:** 5-9. **Wt.:** 180. **Bats:** R. **Throws:** R. **School:** University of Memphis. **Career Transactions:** Selected by Athletics in second round of 1997 draft; signed June 19, 1997.

Almost from the day he signed, the A's looked upon Harville as their closer of the future. But a series of injuries keeps pushing the future further away. He burst into the majors in 1999, but he couldn't stick in Oakland when his 98 mph fastball stayed too high in the strike zone. He went to spring training in 2001 expecting to land a bullpen job, then wound up on the 60-day disabled list with tendinitis in his rotator cuff. He could have made the A's bullpen last year, but Oakland's depth forced him back to Triple-A, where he went down with a sore arm at midseason. If Harville can manage to remain healthy, he still owns the talent to become a dominant big league reliever, but he's no longer a young phenom. He still hits 95 mph regularly, though he's relying more on his sinking two-seamer than on his four-seamer. He has added a slow curveball so hitters have more trouble reading the speed on his fastball. He'll try once again to make the Oakland bullpen this spring, with his health and command the keys to his success.

Year	Club (League)	Class	W	L	ERA	G	GS	CG	SV	IP	H	R	ER	HR	BB	SO	AVG
1997	S. Oregon (NWL)	A	1	0	0.00	3	0	0	0	5	3	0	0	0	3	6	.176
	Visalia (Cal)	A	0	0	5.79	14	0	0	0	19	25	14	12	2	13	24	.325
1998	Visalia (Cal)	A	4	3	3.00	24	7	0	4	69	59	25	23	0	31	76	.230
	Huntsville (SL)	AA	0	0	2.45	12	0	0	8	15	6	4	4	0	13	24	.122
1999	Midland (TL)	AA	2	0	2.01	17	0	0	7	22	13	6	5	1	9	35	.165
	Vancouver (PCL)	AAA	1	0	1.75	22	0	0	11	26	24	5	5	0	11	36	.240
	Oakland (AL)	MAJ	0	2	6.91	15	0	0	0	14	18	11	11	2	10	15	.310
2000	Sacramento (PCL)	AAA	5	3	4.50	53	0	0	9	64	53	35	32	8	35	77	.222
2001	Modesto (Cal)	A	0	0	3.00	2	1	0	0	3	2	2	1	0	0	3	.182
	Visalia (Cal)	A	0	0	0.00	1	1	0	0	3	3	0	0	0	0	3	.250
	Sacramento (PCL)	AAA	5	2	3.98	33	0	0	8	41	35	20	18	5	12	55	.230
	Oakland (AL)	MAJ	0	0	0.00	3	0	0	0	3	2	0	0	0	0	2	.182
2002	Sacramento (PCL)	AAA	1	0	5.40	24	0	0	5	30	32	19	18	5	13	26	.274
MAJOR LEAGUE TOTALS			0	2	5.71	18	0	0	0	17	20	11	11	2	10	17	.290
MINOR LEAGUE TOTALS			19	10	3.59	205	9	0	52	296	255	130	118	21	140	365	.230

14. Matt Allegra, of

Born: July 10, 1981. **Ht.:** 6-3. **Wt.:** 210. **Bats:** R. **Throws:** R. **School:** Manatee (Fla.) CC. **Career Transactions:** Selected by Athletics in 16th round of 1999 draft; signed June 2, 2000.

Allegra remains a raw player, but the improvements he has made excite the A's. He made considerable progress in instructional league following the 2000 season, then bombed in high Class A in 2001. When he returned there last year, he hit a career-high .281 and unleashed his considerable power. Allegra is still far from a finished product, as evidenced by his 160 strikeouts last year and his 369 whiffs in 289 career games. Yet he has legitimate five-tool potential, with above-average skills across the board. He has enough speed to play center field in a pinch but is probably best suited for a corner job, with the arm and instincts to become an above-average defender. Allegra will work on making more consistent contact when he moves up to Double-A this season.

Year	Club (League)	Class	AVG	G	AB	R	H	2B	3B	HR	RBI	BB	SO	SB	SLG	OBP
2000	Athletics (AZL)	R	.270	42	141	26	38	7	3	0	13	25	44	15	.362	.384
2001	Modesto (Cal)	A	.209	51	153	19	32	3	2	17	21	61	3	.294	.315
	Vancouver (NWL)	A	.220	71	273	36	60	16	2	11	39	30	104	5	.414	.307
2002	Visalia (Cal)	A	.281	125	494	74	139	35	3	20	93	47	160	9	.486	.352
MINOR LEAGUE TOTALS			.254	289	1061	155	269	61	10	33	162	123	369	32	.423	.340

15. Mark Teahen, 3b

Born: Sept. 6, 1981. **Ht.:** 6-3. **Wt.:** 210. **Bats:** L. **Throws:** R. **School:** St. Mary's (Calif.) College. **Career Transactions:** Selected by Athletics in first round (39th overall) of 2002 draft; signed June 9, 2002.

One of Oakland's seven-first round picks in the 2002 draft, Teahen hit .404 at short-season Vancouver before finding high Class A more challenging. Pitchers learned to jam him inside, but he worked hard on making adjustments during instructional league and showed distinct improvement. He's a polished hitter who uses the opposite field well. He has always hit for average and shown outstanding hand-eye coordination, and the A's expect that will continue. The rap against him in college was his failure to consistently hit for power, but Oakland believes he'll show more pop as he learns to turn on pitches. He has average speed and good baseball instincts. An outstanding defender at third base, he has good hands and a strong arm. He reminds a lot of scouts of Bill Mueller, though the A's hope he'll have more home run power. Teahen should be better prepared for the California League in 2003.

Year	Club (League)	Class	AVG	G	AB	R	H	2B	3B	HR	RBI	BB	SO	SB	SLG	OBP
2002	Vancouver (NWL)	A	.404	13	57	10	23	5	1	0	6	5	9	4	.526	.444
	Modesto (Cal)	A	.239	59	234	25	56	9	1	1	26	21	53	1	.299	.307
MINOR LEAGUE TOTALS			.271	72	291	35	79	14	2	1	32	26	62	5	.344	.334

16. Esteban German, 2b

Born: Jan. 26, 1978. **Ht.:** 5-9. **Wt.:** 160. **Bats:** R. **Throws:** R. **Career Transactions:** Signed out of Dominican Republic by Athletics, July 4, 1996.

German's 2002 didn't begin auspiciously and it never got better. He didn't arrive in spring training until mid-March because of visa problems related to his falsified age. It turned out that German was 11 months older than previously believed. The A's gave him a look as their regular second baseman at the end of May, but he didn't do much in a brief stint before returning to Triple-A. He wasn't nearly as electric at Sacramento as he had been in 2001, when he was the organization's minor league player of the year. German's defense, never a strong suit, was shoddy in the major leagues. He's limited to playing second base, where Mark Ellis emphatically claimed the starting job last year. During his breakthrough season in 2001, German used the entire field and collected many of his hits by going the other way. He became pull-conscious again last year and wasn't as selective. German has little power, so he must get on base and use his speed to be of value. He'll start 2003 in Triple-A, trying to get back on track for another shot at the majors.

Year	Club (League)	Class	AVG	G	AB	R	H	2B	3B	HR	RBI	BB	SO	SB	SLG	OBP
1997	Athletics East (DSL)	R	.317	69	249	69	79	17	1	2	29	73	30	58	.418	.474
1998	Athletics West (DSL)	R	.313	10	32	9	10	1	1	0	4	7	2	1	.406	.436
	Athletics (AZL)	R	.307	55	202	52	62	3	10	2	28	33	43	40	.450	.413
1999	Modesto (Cal)	A	.311	128	501	107	156	16	12	4	52	102	128	40	.415	.428
2000	Midland (TL)	AA	.213	24	75	13	16	1	0	1	6	18	21	5	.267	.379
	Visalia (Cal)	A	.264	109	428	82	113	14	10	2	35	61	86	78	.357	.361
2001	Midland (TL)	AA	.284	92	335	79	95	20	3	6	30	63	66	31	.415	.415
	Sacramento (PCL)	AAA	.373	38	150	40	56	8	0	4	14	18	20	17	.507	.457
2002	Sacramento (PCL)	AAA	.275	121	458	72	126	16	4	2	43	78	66	26	.341	.390
	Oakland (AL)	MAJ	.200	9	35	4	7	0	0	0	0	4	11	1	.200	.300
MAJOR LEAGUE TOTALS			.200	9	35	4	7	0	0	0	0	4	11	1	.200	.300
MINOR LEAGUE TOTALS			.293	646	2430	523	713	96	41	23	241	453	462	296	..395	.412

17. Steve Obenchain, rhp

Born: July 29, 1981. **Ht.:** 6-5. **Wt.:** 200. **Bats:** R. **Throws:** R. **School:** University of Evansville. **Career Transactions:** Selected by Athletics in first round (37th overall) of 2002 draft; signed June 10, 2002.

Obenchain wasn't drafted out of Evansville's Memorial High, the same school that produced Don Mattingly. He stayed home to attend college at Evansville, where he was used primarily as a reliever and led the Missouri Valley Conference with a 1.38 ERA and 12 saves in 2002. The A's immediately made him a starter because of his variety of pitches. His plus changeup is his top pitch, though he's still learning to use it more often in his new role. Obenchain also throws an average fastball and a decent curveball. He's also working on a modified sinker that's still under construction. With four pitches, the A's want to see him start for a full season, possibly at their new low Class A Kane County affiliate, before determining his long-term role. If he returns to relieving, his resilient arm and ability to enter games and immediately throw strikes are huge assets.

Year	Club (League)	Class	W	L	ERA	G	GS	CG	SV	IP	H	R	ER	HR	BB	SO	AVG
2002	Vancouver (NWL)	A	2	3	2.85	11	10	0	0	41	35	18	13	1	10	29	.226
	Visalia (Cal)	A	2	0	3.00	4	4	0	0	24	23	8	8	2	3	10	.256
MINOR LEAGUE TOTALS			4	3	2.91	15	14	0	0	65	58	26	21	3	13	39	.237

18. Adam Morrissey, 3b/2b

Born: June 8, 1981. **Ht.:** 5-11. **Wt.:** 180. **Bats:** R. **Throws:** R. **Career Transactions:** Signed out of Australia by Cubs, Feb. 18, 1999 . . . Traded by Cubs to Athletics for 2B Mark Bellhorn, Nov. 2, 2001.

The November 2001 trade that sent Mark Bellhorn to the Cubs hasn't provided any immediate return for the A's, while Bellhorn set a Chicago club record for homers by a switch-hitter with 27 in 2002. Nevertheless, Oakland still thinks the deal could pay off, as some team officials view Morrissey as one of the system's highest-ceiling players. At 21, he already hit breaking balls quite well and displays considerable offensive potential. His power is still developing and he struggled in Double-A, but he reasserted himself with a strong performance in the Arizona Fall League. More questions surround his defense. He played second base, shortstop and the outfield during the regular season, and spent most of his time in the AFL at third base. He's not proficient at any of those positions, a major reason the Cubs decided to trade him and a stumbling block in Morrissey's quest to become a big league regular. He's expected to start the season at third base in Double-A, and he'll get more time at second base as well.

Year	Club (League)	Class	AVG	G	AB	R	H	2B	3B	HR	RBI	BB	SO	SB	SLG	OBP
1999	Cubs (AZL)	R	.296	44	169	23	50	7	3	2	23	21	28	4	.408	.376
2000	Eugene (NWL)	A	.275	73	269	32	74	16	2	7	36	42	50	12	.428	.374
2001	Lansing (Mid)	A	.309	122	418	88	129	26	11	14	62	80	82	10	.524	.427
2002	Midland (TL)	AA	.235	90	302	39	71	15	1	2	22	38	71	4	.311	.323
	Modesto (Cal)	A	.291	36	141	23	41	7	1	3	26	20	28	4	.418	.383
MINOR LEAGUE TOTALS			.281	365	1299	205	365	71	18	28	169	201	259	34	.428	.381

19. Dan Johnson, 1b

Born: Aug. 10, 1979. **Ht.:** 6-2. **Wt.:** 220. **Bats:** L. **Throws:** R. **School:** University of Nebraska. **Career Transactions:** Selected by Athletics in seventh round of 2001 draft; signed June 18, 2001.

Johnson was big and strong to begin with, and he devoted himself to the A's offseason conditioning program after he was drafted in 2001. He reported to spring training in great shape last year, setting the stage for an eye-opening season. He was tremendous down the stretch, hitting .374-12-38 in his final 33 games. Johnson continued to make adjustments during instructional league, closing a hole in his swing. He doesn't move well on defense and is a below-average first baseman. He's limited to first base or DH, and he'll have to generate plenty of power in order to advance. He did that during his two seasons at Nebraska, where he set school records for homers in a game (three) and season (25) while narrowly missing the career mark (two shy at 46). Johnson has a tendency to put extreme pressure on himself, and he must learn to deal with the rigors of the long season. He's ticketed for Double-A this year.

Year	Club (League)	Class	AVG	G	AB	R	H	2B	3B	HR	RBI	BB	SO	SB	SLG	OBP
2001	Vancouver (NWL)	A	.283	69	247	36	70	15	2	11	41	27	63	0	.494	.354
2002	Modesto (Cal)	A	.293	126	426	56	125	23	1	21	85	57	87	4	.500	.371
MINOR LEAGUE TOTALS			.290	195	673	92	195	38	3	32	126	84	150	4	.498	.364

20. John McCurdy, ss

Born: April 17, 1981. **Ht.:** 6-2. **Wt.:** 190. **Bats:** R. **Throws:** R. **School:** University of Maryland. **Career Transactions:** Selected by Athletics in first round (26th overall) of 2002 draft; signed June 30, 2002.

McCurdy put together one of the great offensive seasons for a shortstop in college baseball history, batting .443-19-77 at Maryland in 2002 before the A's drafted him 26th overall. Oakland had coveted another Atlantic Coast Conference shortstop, Clemson's Khalil Greene, but he went 13th to the Padres—three spots before the A's picked. While some scouts said McCurdy's breakout junior year was an aberration, the A's believe he has the potential to become a mighty offensive threat. After signing, he got off to a hot start with Vancouver, then saw his numbers fall as he attempted to adjust to the wood bat. He has to tighten his strike zone to take advantage of his strength and swing. There's some doubt whether he can remain a middle infielder after he made 20 errors in 51 games at shortstop. He has arm strength, but his hands and feet are ordinary and he's inconsistent. McCurdy often is compared to Jeff Kent as both an infielder and hitter—capable defensively and outstanding offensively. The A's will leave him at shortstop in 2003 as he advances to Class A.

Year	Club (League)	Class	AVG	G	AB	R	H	2B	3B	HR	RBI	BB	SO	SB	SLG	OBP
2002	Vancouver (NWL)	A	.242	56	223	33	54	9	1	3	29	12	57	5	.332	.282
MINOR LEAGUE TOTALS			.242	56	223	33	54	9	1	3	29	12	57	5	.332	.282

21. Mike Rouse, ss

Born: April 25, 1980. **Ht.:** 5-11. **Wt.:** 180. **Bats:** L. **Throws:** R. **School:** Cal State Fullerton. **Career Transactions:** Selected by Blue Jays in fifth round of 2001 draft; signed July 2, 2001 . . . Traded by Blue Jays to Athletics with RHP Chris Mowday for RHP Cory Lidle, Nov. 16, 2002.

The A's acquired Rouse in the offseason from the Blue Jays, as GM Billy Beane and former assistant J.P. Ricciardi, now Toronto's GM, got together for another deal. In doing so, the A's completed their set of Big West Conference shortstops, as Rouse (Cal State Fullerton), Bobby Crosby (Long Beach State) and J.T. Stotts (Cal State Northridge) all played in the league in 2001. Crosby was the league's player of the year and is the best prospect of the trio. Rouse has had a quick trajectory, though, already having some Double-A success as a Blue Jay. He had a strong pro debut in 2001 and his bat has been his best tool. Rouse has good power, especially pull power, for a shortstop from the left side. He's fairly disciplined by other organizations' standards but could use more patience to fit in with the A's. His swing can get long at times, though when he shortens up and is more consistent, he's an above-average offensive player. He hit well after missing time in 2002 with to a broken hamate bone in his right wrist. His range at shortstop is the question defensively. He has a solid arm but doesn't cover enough ground to play short on turf. The presence of former rivals Crosby and Stotts should push Rouse to second base.

Year	Club (League)	Class	AVG	G	AB	R	H	2B	3B	HR	RBI	BB	SO	SB	SLG	OBP
2001	Dunedin (FSL)	A	.272	48	180	27	49	17	2	5	24	13	45	3	.472	.327
2002	Tennessee (SL)	AA	.260	71	231	35	60	11	0	9	43	29	47	7	.424	.342
MINOR LEAGUE TOTALS			.265	119	411	62	109	28	2	14	67	42	92	10	.445	.335

22. J.T. Stotts, ss

Born: January 21, 1980. **Ht.:** 5-11. **Wt.:** 185. **Bats:** R. **Throws:** R. **School:** Cal State Northridge. **Career Transactions:** Drafted by A's in 3rd round, 2001.

Stotts was something of a Southern California prep legend at Newhall's William Hart High, winning league MVP honors in both baseball and basketball as a senior. When he and fellow A's shortstop prospects Bobby Crosby and Mike Rouse were all in the Big West Conference in 2001, Stotts topped the trio with a .409 batting average and tied Rouse for the lead with 12 homers. However, Stotts rarely has shown the ability to hit for power as a pro and best profiles as a singles-hitting, defensive-oriented shortstop. He does help himself by drawing walks and knowing how to use his plus speed on the bases. A gifted and graceful defender, Stotts has shown the hands, range and arm to play shortstop at the major league level. He still makes too many mistakes, with 56 errors in 195 pro games, though the A's expect his inconsistency to be resolved by experience. If Crosby returns to Double-A and/or Rouse remains at shortstop, Stotts will head back to high Class A to start 2003.

Year	Club (League)	Class	AVG	G	AB	R	H	2B	3B	HR	RBI	BB	SO	SB	SLG	OBP
2001	Vancouver (NWL)	A	.270	62	241	35	65	5	2	0	17	26	34	19	.307	.348
2002	Visalia (Cal)	A	.275	133	483	66	133	20	3	2	64	65	75	13	.342	.363
MINOR LEAGUE TOTALS			.273	195	724	101	198	25	5	2	81	91	109	32	.330	.358

23. Shane Bazzell, rhp

Born: March 22, 1979. **Ht.:** 6-2. **Wt.:** 180. **Bats:** L. **Throws:** R. **School:** New Hope HS, Columbus, Miss. **Career Transactions:** Selected by Athletics in 16th round of 1998 draft; signed June 29, 1998.

Bazzell needed three tries at high Class A before finding success in 2001. He hit the wall again in Double-A last year, surrendering 17 runs in his first two starts and posting a 6.02 ERA before the A's moved him into the bullpen in mid-June. Suddenly, he was a changed man. In relief, Bazzell could challenge hitters without having to worry about pacing himself or maintaining concentration for several innings. He hit 95 mph with his fastball, which he complements with a slider and splitter. As a starter, he tried to use seven different pitches, but from the bullpen he limits himself to his three best weapons. His fastball and slider are both plus pitches. He may just be starting to find himself as a pitcher. He could move rapidly, though he'll return to Double-A at the start of 2003 to work on his command.

Year	Club (League)	Class	W	L	ERA	G	GS	CG	SV	IP	H	R	ER	HR	BB	SO	AVG
1998	Athletics (AZL)	R	4	2	3.27	12	8	0	0	41	30	19	15	1	15	51	.197
1999	S. Oregon (NWL)	A	3	1	1.86	5	5	0	0	29	27	15	6	1	9	18	.239
	Visalia (Cal)	A	2	4	5.13	8	8	0	0	40	50	27	23	4	19	29	.311
2000	Modesto (Cal)	A	3	4	5.75	32	5	0	1	72	91	57	46	6	30	71	.310
2001	Modesto (Cal)	A	10	4	2.73	28	20	0	0	135	116	51	41	9	38	129	.231
	Midland (TL)	AA	0	2	19.64	2	2	0	0	7	20	17	16	2	2	4	.476
2002	Midland (TL)	AA	5	7	4.61	39	12	0	3	98	101	59	50	3	47	88	.269
MINOR LEAGUE TOTALS			27	24	4.19	126	60	0	4	423	435	245	197	26	160	390	.265

24. Andy Dickinson, lhp

Born: Dec. 13, 1979. **Ht.:** 6-2. **Wt.:** 170. **Bats:** L. **Throws:** L. **School:** University of Illinois. **Career Transactions:** Selected by Athletics in 28th round of 2002 draft; signed June 9, 2002.

Dickinson had exceptional success at Illinois, winning Big 10 Conference pitcher of the year honors in 2001 and tying the Illini career record for victories with 30. He carried that over into his first taste of pro ball, overmatching the Northwest League and holding his own in the California League. The problem is that Dickinson doesn't throw hard. He rarely boosts his fastball to 85 mph, and he sometimes pitches in the high 70s. He does know how to turn the ball over, cut it and use every imaginable trick to retire hitters. He also throws a curveball, slider and changeup, and he'll vary the speeds on all of those pitches. Hitters get bad swings against him and often look worse than they do when they face 95 mph fastballs. Because of his utter lack of velocity, Dickinson is difficult to project. Some in the organization say he could emerge as the next Jamie Moyer, others think he might be best suited to a lefty specialist role, while still others consider his chances of success exceedingly slim. What is certain is that Dickinson possesses outstanding command and gets the most out of his abilities. The A's wanted him to work on his conditioning during the offseason and plan on sending him back to high Class A this year.

Year	Club (League)	Class	W	L	ERA	G	GS	CG	SV	IP	H	R	ER	HR	BB	SO	AVG
2002	Vancouver (NWL)	A	4	0	2.06	11	10	0	0	48	37	11	11	1	12	40	.216
	Visalia (Cal)	A	1	1	3.38	4	4	0	0	24	32	9	9	1	6	14	.340
MINOR LEAGUE TOTALS			5	1	2.50	15	14	0	0	72	69	20	20	2	18	54	.260

25. Eddie Yarnall, lhp

Born: Dec. 4, 1975. **Ht.:** 6-3. **Wt.:** 230. **Bats:** L. **Throws:** L. **School:** Louisiana State University. **Career Transactions:** Selected by Mets in third round of 1996 draft; signed Aug. 12, 1996 . . . Traded by Mets with OF Preston Wilson and a player to be named to Marlins for C Mike Piazza, May 22, 1998; Marlins acquired LHP Geoff Goetz to complete deal (July 3, 1998) . . . Traded by Marlins with RHP Todd Noel and RHP Mark Johnson to Yankees for 3B Mike Lowell, Feb. 1, 1999 . . . Traded by Yankees with 3B Drew Henson, OF Jackson Melian and RHP Brian Reith to Reds for LHP Denny Neagle, July 12, 2000 . . . Released by Reds, April 2, 2001 . . . Signed by Orix (Japan), 2001 . . . Signed by Athletics, Jan. 17, 2003.

The well-traveled Yarnall returned to the United States when he signed with Oakland in January. After agreeing to a one-year deal worth $600,000 plus a possible $335,000 in incentives, he'll compete for a big league job in spring training. A Mets third-round pick in 1996, he was used in three trades for all-stars. He went to the Marlins for Mike Piazza, the Yankees for Mike Lowell and the Reds for Denny Neagle. Yarnall was all but handed a spot in the Yankees' 2000 rotation after being named Triple-A International League pitcher of the year in 1999, but handed it back with a wretched performance in spring training. He didn't impress Cincinnati the following spring and was sold to Japan's Orix Blue Wave for $300,000. In Japan, he ranked 10th in the Pacific League in ERA last season. Yarnall has solid stuff but is more deceptive than overpowering. His fastball reaches the low 90s, and he also throws a slider, curveball and changeup. His command never has been better than average, and he can't afford to fall behind in the count. Yarnall could factor into the back of the rotation or the middle of the bullpen.

Year	Club (League)	Class	W	L	ERA	G	GS	CG	SV	IP	H	R	ER	HR	BB	SO	AVG
1997	St. Lucie (FSL)	A	5	8	2.48	18	18	2	0	105	93	33	29	5	30	114	.233
	Norfolk (IL)	AAA	0	1	14.40	1	1	0	0	5	11	8	8	1	7	2	.500
	Binghamton (EL)	AA	3	2	3.06	5	5	0	0	32	20	11	11	2	11	32	.177
1998	Binghamton (EL)	AA	7	0	0.39	7	7	0	0	47	20	5	2	0	17	52	.127
	Portland (EL)	AA	2	0	2.93	2	2	0	0	15	9	5	5	2	4	15	.170
	Charlotte (IL)	AAA	4	5	6.20	15	13	2	0	70	79	60	48	11	39	47	.281
1999	Columbus (IL)	AAA	13	4	3.47	23	23	1	0	145	136	61	56	5	57	146	.252
	New York (AL)	MAJ	1	0	3.71	5	2	0	0	17	17	8	7	1	10	13	.254
2000	Columbus (IL)	AAA	2	1	4.56	10	10	1	0	49	43	27	25	4	26	34	.249
	New York (AL)	MAJ	0	0	15.00	2	1	0	0	3	5	5	5	1	3	1	.417
	Louisville (IL)	AAA	3	4	3.86	11	11	0	0	68	72	32	29	7	34	59	.270
2001	Orix (PL)	JPN	4	3	3.93	15	14	1	0	73	52	35	32	7	47	82	—
	Surpass (WL)	JPN	5	1	2.75	10	7	0	0	39	36	12	12	0	21	35	—
2002	Orix (PL)	JPN	6	13	3.61	25	25	1	0	164	149	70	66	13	62	120	—
MAJOR LEAGUE TOTALS			1	0	5.40	7	3	0	0	20	22	13	12	2	13	14	.278
MINOR LEAGUE TOTALS			39	25	3.57	92	90	6	0	537	483	242	213	37	225	501	.241

26. Bill Murphy, lhp

Born: May 9, 1981. **Ht.:** 6-0. **Wt.:** 190. **Bats:** L. **Throws:** L. **School:** Cal State Northridge. **Career Transactions:** Selected by Athletics in third round of 2002 draft; signed June 26, 2002.

A high school teammate of Brewers fireballer Nick Neugebauer, Murphy went to Cal State Northridge as a two-way player before focusing on pitching as a sophomore. He has an 88-92 mph fastball that touches 94 and features electric movement, and his curveball buckles hitters' knees. He began to add a changeup last spring, though it still needs work. Murphy's arm was tired when he signed, so he wasn't at his best in the Northwest League. His command, concentration and confidence all require improvement. He nibbles around the plate rather than going right after hitters. Murphy spent instructional league shortening his stride and slowing his delivery in order to achieve better control of his pitches. The results won't be known until he starts pitching in Class A this season.

Year	Club (League)	Class	W	L	ERA	G	GS	CG	SV	IP	H	R	ER	HR	BB	SO	AVG
2002	Vancouver (NWL)	A	1	4	4.57	13	9	0	0	41	28	23	21	2	35	46	.192
MINOR LEAGUE TOTALS			1	4	4.57	13	9	0	0	41	28	23	21	2	35	46	.192

27. Edwardo Sierra, rhp

Born: April 15, 1982. **Ht.:** 6-3. **Wt.:** 185. **Bats:** R. **Throws:** R. **Career Transactions:** Signed out of Dominican Republic by Athletics, February 15, 1999.

Sierra has yet to reach full-season ball after four years in the system, but he signed at 16 and his dazzling stuff still intrigues the A's. His fastball already hits 95 mph, and he's still growing and filling out his lanky frame. He also throws a slider, which isn't overly effective, and is working on adding a splitter to his repertoire. He lacks a true offspeed pitch, and Oakland expects to eventually move him to the bullpen, where he can just focus on throwing heat. He still must improve his command and learn to keep his hot fastball down in the strike zone. How Sierra performs in spring training will determine if he'll move up to Class A for the first time.

Year	Club (League)	Class	W	L	ERA	G	GS	CG	SV	IP	H	R	ER	HR	BB	SO	AVG
1999	Athletics East (DSL)	R	1	3	5.02	6	5	0	0	29	32	24	16	1	19	27	.288
	Athletics West (DSL)	R	1	1	3.18	8	1	0	1	28	26	18	10	1	13	27	.248
2000	Athletics West (DSL)	R	4	2	2.22	10	9	1	0	65	56	27	16	1	24	50	.230
	Athletics East (DSL)	R	1	2	3.57	4	4	0	0	23	21	9	9	0	9	19	.263
2001	Athletics (AZL)	R	2	1	3.02	12	6	0	1	45	45	19	15	1	9	41	.262
2002	Vancouver (NWL)	A	0	2	6.11	9	7	0	0	28	42	24	19	0	17	23	.336
	Athletics (AZL)	R	2	1	4.64	6	6	0	0	33	29	19	17	2	10	35	.240
MINOR LEAGUE TOTALS			11	12	3.67	55	38	1	2	250	251	140	102	6	101	222	.262

28. Steve Stanley, of

Born: Dec. 23, 1979. **Ht.:** 5-8. **Wt.:** 150. **Bats:** L. **Throws:** L. **School:** University of Notre Dame. **Career Transactions:** Selected by Athletics in second round of 2002 draft; signed June 25, 2002.

A's officials invoke the name of David Eckstein whenever Stanley is discussed. He plays well beyond his size and skill level because of his intensity, instincts and intangibles. Speed is probably Stanley's only legitimate tool, and he uses it to make himself a solid center fielder, chasing down virtually every fly ball hit his way. He also employs it on offense, bunting for hits and beating out infield rollers, and he shows excellent discipline at the plate. Oakland has no doubts that he'll get everything from his ability. His strong pro debut was no surprise considering his previous success with wood bats, as he won the Cape Cod League batting title in 2000 and was the Great Lakes League MVP the following summer. The only repeat winner of the Big East Conference player-of-the-year award, Stanley was one of two outfielders drafted by the A's off Notre Dame's 2002 College World Series team. Left fielder Brian Stavisky is a line-drive machine who may prove to be a steal as a sixth-rounder.

Year	Club (League)	Class	AVG	G	AB	R	H	2B	3B	HR	RBI	BB	SO	SB	SLG	OBP
2002	Modesto (Cal)	A	.286	63	262	48	75	11	1	1	17	39	46	4	.347	.382
MINOR LEAGUE TOTALS			.286	63	262	48	75	11	1	1	17	39	46	4	.347	.382

29. Bert Snow, rhp

Born: March 23, 1977. **Ht.:** 6-1. **Wt.:** 200. **Bats:** R. **Throws:** R. **School:** Vanderbilt University. **Career Transactions:** Selected by Athletics in 10th round of 1998 draft; signed June 20, 1998 . . . On disabled list, April 5-Sept. 4, 2001.

Snow led minor league relievers by averaging 13.1 strikeouts per nine innings in 2000 but missed all of 2001 following Tommy John surgery. He got back on the mound last year, though his focus was on recovery not results. He continued to miss bats but wasn't nearly as dominant in Double-A as he had been before. Snow hasn't regained the devastating slider that allowed him to blow hitters away. Snow sets up his slider with a sinker that keeps hitters off balance, and he has toyed with a splitter in the past. His command can be spotty at times. If his slider bounces all the way back, Snow could move quickly toward Oakland.

Year	Club (League)	Class	W	L	ERA	G	GS	CG	SV	IP	H	R	ER	HR	BB	SO	AVG
1998	S. Oregon (NWL)	A	1	3	5.64	11	8	0	0	45	52	38	28	2	18	35	.284
	Modesto (Cal)	A	1	1	3.12	2	2	0	0	9	12	8	3	1	6	12	.308
1999	Visalia (Cal)	A	3	2	5.15	31	3	0	5	65	55	43	37	4	40	90	.224
	Midland (TL)	AA	1	1	1.71	21	0	0	13	21	14	4	4	3	9	32	.187
	Vancouver (PCL)	AAA	1	0	3.86	2	0	0	0	2	3	1	1	0	1	3	.333
2000	Sacramento (PCL)	AAA	0	0	4.50	3	0	0	0	2	1	1	1	0	3	3	.143
	Midland (TL)	AA	1	7	3.59	59	0	0	27	68	58	33	27	6	36	98	.231
2001					Did Not Play—Injured												
2002	Visalia (Cal)	A	0	0	1.00	12	1	0	5	18	8	2	2	1	7	25	.131
	Midland (TL)	AA	0	3	4.98	24	0	0	8	22	21	12	12	1	11	29	.250
MINOR LEAGUE TOTALS			8	17	4.13	165	14	0	58	251	224	142	115	18	131	327	.235

30. Brian Stavisky, of

Born: July 6, 1980. **Ht.:** 6-3. **Wt.:** 230. **Bats:** L. **Throws:** R. **School:** University of Notre Dame. **Career Transactions:** Selected by Athletics in sixth round of 2002 draft; signed July 20, 2002.

The A's drafted not one but two outfielders off Notre Dame's 2002 College World Series team. Stavisky, who hit a dramatic walkoff homer to beat Rice in the second round of the CWS, finished second to Fighting Irish teammate Steve Stanley (Oakland's second-round pick) in the 2000 Cape Cod League batting race. Stavisky has seen his stock drop since that summer. He didn't sign with the Cubs as a 33rd-round draft-eligible sophomore in 2001, and may prove to be a steal as a sixth-round pick last June. Stavisky is a pure hitter with a quick bat and power potential that he'll start to realize once he adds some loft to his swing. He also has a good sense of plate discipline, which endears him to Oakland. His defense is a huge drawback, however, as he has a terrible arm that may make playing even left field a stretch. Stavisky played half of his first pro summer at DH and was scheduled to get some time at first base during instructional league. But he chose not to attend instructional league, which precluded further progress. He's expected to spend this year with one of the A's Class A affiliates.

Year	Club (League)	Class	AVG	G	AB	R	H	2B	3B	HR	RBI	BB	SO	SB	SLG	OBP
2002	Vancouver (NWL)	A	.294	32	102	12	30	10	1	1	15	15	30	5	.441	.407
MINOR LEAGUE TOTALS			.294	32	102	12	30	10	1	1	15	15	30	5	.441	.407

PHILADELPHIA
PHILLIES

TOP 30 PROSPECTS

1. Gavin Floyd, rhp
2. Chase Utley, 2b/3b
3. Marlon Byrd, of
4. Taylor Buchholz, rhp
5. Cole Hamels, lhp
6. Ryan Madson, rhp
7. Anderson Machado, ss
8. Ryan Howard, 1b
9. Elizardo Ramirez, rhp
10. Zach Segovia, rhp
11. Seung Lee, rhp
12. Jorge Padilla, of
13. Keith Bucktrot, rhp
14. Juan Richardson, 3b
15. Carlos Cabrera, rhp
16. Erick Arteaga, rhp
17. Carlos Rodriguez, ss
18. Brad Baisley, rhp
19. Eric Valent, of
20. Jake Blalock, of/3b
21. Josh Hancock, rhp
22. Franklin Perez, rhp
23. Robinson Tejeda, rhp
24. Danny Gonzalez, ss
25. Jean Machi, rhp
26. Eric Junge, rhp
27. Jeremy Wedel, rhp
28. Martire Franco, rhp
29. Esteban de los Santos, ss
30. Yoel Hernandez, rhp

By Will Kimmey

The Phillies open a new baseball-only stadium in 2004, but they already opened their wallets in hopes of fielding a winner there immediately.

General manager Ed Wade replaced Scott Rolen by signing free agent David Bell for four seasons at $17 million. He made a huge upgrade at first base by luring Jim Thome away from the Indians with a six-year, $85 million contract. And when Kevin Millwood's potential salary became too much for the Braves, Wade swooped in and stole him for the low, low price of backup catcher Johnny Estrada.

Even after their runs at Tom Glavine and Jamie Moyer failed, Philadelphia still has the talent to return to the playoffs for the first time since its 1993 World Series appearance. Plugging Thome into a heart of the order that already featured Bobby Abreu and Pat Burrell should make the Phillies potent. Millwood becomes the No. 1 starter, relieving the pressure on Vicente Padilla and Randy Wolf and giving Brett Myers time to grow into that role.

Despite being the nation's sixth-largest market, Philadelphia hasn't drawn well and will receive money in Major League Baseball's new revenue-sharing plan. The Indians pay into the fund and thus will indirectly subsidize Thome's contract.

The additions marked a significant payroll increase for Philadelphia–roughly $33 million in salaries and bonuses for 2003 alone–but the hope is a contending team and a move from Veterans Stadium will win back fans. The Phillies won six National League East titles from 1976-83 but have enjoyed just three winning seasons since–largely because the player-development system was ignored for years. Now there's a legitimate cause for optimism and sustained success.

Aside from the flashy moves, the bulk of the roster is homegrown. There's more talent on the way in a system that has been rebuilt under the watch of assistant general manager Mike Arbuckle.

Myers, Jimmy Rollins and Brandon Duckworth have graduated to the majors over the last two seasons, and center fielder Marlon Byrd is ready to take the next step. The Phillies still have pitching and hitting talent throughout the system.

The only possible downfall could come in the later years of Thome's and Bell's deals, as their skills diminish while they still eat up a large portion of the payroll.

Organization Overview

General Manager: Ed Wade. **Farm Director:** Steve Noworyta. **Scouting Director:** Marti Wolever.

2002 PERFORMANCE

Class	Farm Team	League	W	L	Pct.	Finish*	Manager(s)
Majors	Philadelphia	National	80	81	.497	8th (16)	Larry Bowa
Triple-A	Scranton/W-B Red Barons	International	91	53	.632	1st (14)	Marc Bombard
Double-A	Reading Phillies	Eastern	76	66	.535	4th (12)	Greg Legg
High A	Clearwater Phillies	Florida State	57	79	.419	11th (12)	John Morris/Roly deArmas
Low A	Lakewood BlueClaws	South Atlantic	69	70	.496	9th (16)	Jeff Manto
Short-season	Batavia Muckdogs	New York-Penn	34	42	.447	8th (14)	Ron Ortegon
Rookie	GCL Phillies	Gulf Coast	39	21	.650	+1st (14)	Ruben Amaro Sr.
OVERALL 2002 MINOR LEAGUE RECORD			366	331	.525	9th (30)	

*Finish in overall standings (No. of teams in league). +League champion.

ORGANIZATION LEADERS

BATTING
*Minimum 250 At-Bats
*AVG	Troy McNaughton, Reading/Clearwater	.312
R	Marlon Byrd, Scranton	103
H	Dave Doster, Scranton	171
TB	Marlon Byrd, Scranton	256
2B	Chase Utley, Scanton	39
3B	Dave Doster, Scranton	10
HR	Ryan Howard, Lakewood	19
RBI	Dave Doster, Scranton	91
BB	Nick Punto, Scranton	76
SO	Ryan Howard, Lakewood	145
SB	Nick Punto, Scranton	42

PITCHING
#Minimum 75 Innings
W	Ryan Madson, Reading	16
L	Yoel Hernandez, Clearwater	16
#ERA	Seung Lee, Reading/Clearwater/Lakewood	2.77
G	Pete Zamora, Scranton	55
CG	Seung Lee, Reading/Clearwater/Lakewood	6
SV	Josh Miller, Lakewood	17
IP	Taylor Buchholz, Reading/Clearwater	182
BB	Keith Bucktrot, Clearwater	78
SO	Taylor Buchholz, Reading/Clearwater	146

BEST TOOLS

Best Hitter for Average	Chase Utley
Best Power Hitter	Ryan Howard
Fastest Baserunner	Anderson Machado
Best Athlete	Chris Roberson
Best Fastball	Jean Machi
Best Curveball	Taylor Buchholz
Best Slider	Zach Segovia
Best Changeup	Ryan Madson
Best Control	Elizardo Ramirez
Best Defensive Catcher	Tim Gradoville
Best Defensive Infielder	Anderson Machado
Best Infield Arm	Anderson Machado
Best Defensive Outfielder	Eric Valent
Best Outfield Arm	Eric Valent

PROJECTED 2006 LINEUP

Catcher	Mike Lieberthal
First Base	Jim Thome
Second Base	Chase Utley
Third Base	David Bell
Shortstop	Jimmy Rollins
Left Field	Pat Burrell
Center Field	Marlon Byrd
Right Field	Bobby Abreu
No. 1 Starter	Brett Myers
No. 2 Starter	Gavin Floyd

Troy McNaughton   Seung Lee

No. 3 Starter	Kevin Millwood
No. 4 Starter	Vicente Padilla
No. 5 Starter	Randy Wolf
Closer	Zach Segovia

TOP PROSPECTS OF THE DECADE

1993	Tyler Green, rhp
1994	Tyler Green, rhp
1995	Scott Rolen, 3b
1996	Scott Rolen, 3b
1997	Scott Rolen, 3b
1998	Ryan Brannan, rhp
1999	Pat Burrell, 1b
2000	Pat Burrell, 1b
2001	Jimmy Rollins, ss
2002	Marlon Byrd, of

TOP DRAFT PICKS OF THE DECADE

1993	Wayne Gomes, rhp
1994	Carlton Loewer, rhp
1995	Reggie Taylor, of
1996	Adam Eaton, rhp
1997	*J.D. Drew, of
1998	Pat Burrell, 1b
1999	Brett Myers, rhp
2000	Chase Utley, 2b
2001	Gavin Floyd, rhp
2002	Cole Hamels, lhp

*Did not sign.

ALL-TIME LARGEST BONUSES

Gavin Floyd, 2001	$4,200,000
Pat Burrell, 1998	$3,150,000
Brett Myers, 1999	$2,050,000
Cole Hamels, 2002	$2,000,000
Chase Utley, 2000	$1,780,000

MinorLeague**Depth**Chart

PHILADELPHIA PHILLIES

RANK

The Phillies opened their checkbooks this offseason and landed marquee free agent Jim Thome as well as David Bell, then stole frontline starter Kevin Millwood from the Braves, their division rival. While the Phillies expect to have a new look about them just one year before moving into a new ballpark, those moves would not have been made had the farm system not been flourishing and ready to fill in the missing pieces. Marlon Byrd should be an offensive upgrade over the departed Doug Glanville in center, and Brett Myers took the first step toward fulfilling young Curt Schilling comparisons by joining a young rotation of Vicente Padilla, Randy Wolf and Brandon Duckworth. The system is rich in pitching talent, particularly righthanders.

Note: Depth charts prepared by Josh Boyd. Numbers in parentheses indicate prospect rankings.

LF
Jason Michaels
Chris Roberson

CF
Marlon Byrd (3)
Jay Sitzman

RF
Jorge Padilla (12)
Eric Valent (19)

3B
Juan Richardson (14)
Jake Blalock (20)
Kiel Fisher
Terry Jones
Jeff Phelps

SS
Anderson Machado (7)
Carlos Rodriguez (17)
Danny Gonzalez (24)
Esteban de los Santos (29)
Nick Punto

2B
Chase Utley (2)

1B
Ryan Howard (8)
Bryan Hansen
Nate Espy
Ryan Barthelemy

C
G.G. Sato
Tim Gradoville

RHP

Starters	Relievers
Gavin Floyd (1)	Zach Segovia (10)
Taylor Buchholz (4)	Franklin Perez (22)
Ryan Madson (6)	Jean Machi (25)
Elizardo Ramirez (9)	Eric Junge (26)
Seung Lee (11)	Jeremy Wedel (27)
Keith Bucktrot (13)	Elio Serrano
Carlos Cabrera (15)	Carlos Silverio
Erick Arteaga (16)	Geoff Geary
Brad Baisley (18)	Cary Hiles
Josh Hancock (21)	Darin Naatjes
Robinson Tejada (23)	Victor Menocal
Martire Franco (28)	
Yoel Hernandez (30)	
Ezequiel Astacio	
Taft Cable	
Lee Gwaltney	
Robby Read	
Francisco Butto	

LHP

Starters	Relievers
Cole Hamels (5)	Greg Kubes
Ryan Carter	
Nick Bourgeois	
Vinny DeChristofaro	

DraftAnalysis

2002 Draft

Best Pro Debut: Strong-bodied RHP Zach Segovia (2) went 3-2, 2.10 with a 30-3 strike-out-walk ratio in 34 innings in the Rookie-level Gulf Coast League. C Tim Gradoville (37) was a GCL all-star, more for his defense (he threw out a league-best 58 percent of basestealers) than his bat (.267-0-4).

Best Athlete: RHP **Darin Naatjes** (14) played two seasons of football for Stanford as a tight end and began his college baseball career as an outfielder. He since has converted to the mound to take advantage of his 94-95 mph fastball. Six-foot-5 RHP Rob Harrand (9) starred in volleyball and basketball as a Canadian high schooler.

Best Pure Hitter: 3B Jake Blalock (5) has been compared to his brother, Rangers third baseman Hank, who's one of the best young hitters in the game. The Phillies also like 3B Kiel Fisher (3), who came from a less advanced high school program.

Best Raw Power: Blalock has more power than his older brother at the same age.

Fastest Runner: The Phillies didn't sign a plus runner. OF Karl Nonemaker (20) is a bit above-average and had 13 steals in the GCL.

Best Defensive Player: Nonemaker plays a fine center field.

Best Fastball: LHP Cole Hamels (1), Blalock's teammate at national high school power Rancho Bernardo of San Diego, can match Naatjes' velocity. RHP Lee Gwaltney (6) touched 94 mph last spring.

Best Breaking Ball: Hamels' curveball consistently grades as a 60 or 70 on the 20-80 scouting scale.

Most Intriguing Background: As a high school sophomore, Hamels broke the humerus bone in his arm while pitching in a game and missed all of 2001. But Hamels apparently hurt his arm before taking the mound in a pick-up football game. Besides his brother connection, Blalock is the nephew of Rancho Bernardo coach Sam Blalock. C Trent Pratt's (11) brother Scott is an Indians minor league infielder. Unsigned 3B Brad McCann's (22) brother Brian signed with the Braves as a second-rounder; their father Howard is the former baseball coach at Marshall. Unsigned 3B Brett McMillan's (21) father Doug scouts for the Giants.

Naatjes

RICH ABEL

Closest To The Majors: Gwaltney, whose plus-plus splitter is better than his fastball.

Best Late-Round Pick: Naatjes.

The One Who Got Away: The Phillies liked McMillan's offensive potential but lost him to UCLA. LHP Clay Dirks (42) took his plus fastball and power curveball to Louisiana State.

Assessment: At least one club rated Hamels as the top pitcher available and most team doctors cleared him, but several teams passed him over for players with less risky medical backgrounds. If he stays healthy, getting him 17th overall could be one of the draft's biggest coups.

2001 Draft

RHP Gavin Floyd (1) could be the next Brett Myers. 1B Ryan Howard (5) has massive power potential. **Grade: B+**

2000 Draft

2B Chase Utley (1) and RHPs Keith Bucktrot (2) and Taylor Buchholz (6) rank among the system's best prospects. Unsigned LHP Kyle Bakker (37) projects as a 2003 first-round pick. **Grade: C+**

1999 Draft

RHP Brett Myers (1) cracked the Phillies rotation last year and Marlon Byrd (10) will be their starting center fielder in 2003. This would have been an even stronger effort had they signed LHP Joe Saunders (5), a 2002 first-rounder. **Grade: A**

1998 Draft

After failing to sign J.D. Drew as the No. 2 pick in 1997, Philadelphia made sure it signed the No. 1 guy in 1998. The club got the right guy, too, in OF Pat Burrell (1). **Grade: A**

Note: Draft analysis prepared by Jim Callis. Numbers in parentheses indicate draft rounds.

... Floyd throws his fastball 89-92 mph, peaking at 94-95 mph, with rapid arm action and a smooth delivery.

Gavin
Floyd rhp

Born: Jan. 27, 1983.
Ht.: 6-5. **Wt.:** 210.
Bats: R. **Throws:** R.
School: Mount St. Joseph HS, Baltimore.
Career Transactions: Selected by Phillies in first round (fourth overall) of 2001 draft; signed Aug. 24, 2001.

As a freshman on Mount St. Joseph High's junior-varsity team, Floyd watched his older brother Mike and Mark Teixeira, both seniors, play for the varsity. Three years later, Gavin and Teixeira were selected with the fourth and fifth overall picks in the 2001 draft, with Philadelphia also taking Mike in the 22nd round. The Floyd brothers were on the South Carolina campus ready to attend class before both agreed to last-minute deals with the Phillies, with Gavin receiving a club-record $4.2 million bonus. He made a strong pro debut in 2002, ranking among the low Class A South Atlantic League leaders in several categories. Managers rated him the league's top prospect. The Phillies handled Floyd cautiously, starting his pitch count at 70 and stretching it to 100 as he gained strength and durability.

Floyd came to the Phillies with two plus pitches: his fastball and hard, sharp curveball. He throws the fastball 89-92 mph, peaking at 94-95 mph, with rapid arm action and a smooth delivery, and he used it almost exclusively to no-hit Lexington on July 24. Nevertheless, his knee-buckling curve is his best pitch because it can be unhittable at times. The organization asked Floyd to lay off his curve last season, urging him to develop the changeup that he never needed in high school. He has a nice feel for it now, and it could become a third plus offering. While Floyd's stuff compares favorably to that of Brett Myers, he has a more laid-back personality. That doesn't mean Floyd isn't a strong competitor, though. His makeup and work ethic should allow him to maximize his talents. Floyd just needs innings and work in game situations. He's learning which pitches to throw in certain counts and how to read hitters. He throws strikes to both sides of the plate but is refining his command in the strike zone. Floyd must use his fastball more and not rely so much on his curveball.

Though he's as polished as any prep pitcher after one year in the minors, Floyd won't be rushed. The Phillies' minor league pitching depth will allow them to move him one level at a time. He can expect to start 2003 at high Class A Clearwater. Floyd profiles as a No. 1 starter.

Year	Club (League)	Class	W	L	ERA	G	GS	CG	SV	IP	H	R	ER	HR	BB	SO	AVG
2002	Lakewood (SAL)	A	11	10	2.77	27	27	3	0	166	119	59	51	13	64	140	.200
MINOR LEAGUE TOTALS			11	10	2.77	27	27	3	0	166	119	59	51	13	64	140	.200

2. Chase Utley, 2b/3b

Born: Dec. 17, 1978. **Ht.:** 6-1. **Wt.:** 170. **Bats:** L. **Throws:** R. **School:** UCLA. **Career Transactions:** Selected by Phillies in first round (15th overall) of 2000 draft; signed July 29, 2000.

While his Little League teammate Sean Burroughs' move from third base to second failed in 2002, Utley's switch from second to third was successful. He also improved his offensive numbers while making the jump from high Class A to Triple-A. Utley's sweet line-drive stroke and alley-to-alley power produced an International League-leading 39 doubles last year. He displayed a solid approach and handled breaking pitches well, especially for a player skipping Double-A. He moved closer to the plate and showed the ability to drive the ball hard to the opposite field. Utley's makeup allowed him to handle the position switch and skip a level at the same time. Utley never was a Gold Glove-caliber second baseman, and he won't win the award at the hot corner either. There are questions about his footwork and arm strength at third base. With hard work, he can be an average defender at either position. Until the Phillies signed David Bell, Utley was a natural choice to replace Scott Rolen. It's unclear where Utley will play in Triple-A, but he'd make a lot of sense as an offensive second baseman.

Year	Club (League)	Class	AVG	G	AB	R	H	2B	3B	HR	RBI	BB	SO	SB	SLG	OBP
2000	Batavia (NY-P)	A	.307	40	153	21	47	13	1	2	22	18	23	5	.444	.383
2001	Clearwater (FSL)	A	.257	122	467	65	120	25	2	16	59	37	88	19	.422	.324
2002	Scranton/W-B (IL)	AAA	.263	125	464	73	122	39	1	17	70	46	89	8	.461	.352
MINOR LEAGUE TOTALS			.267	287	1084	159	289	77	4	35	151	101	200	32	.442	.344

3. Marlon Byrd, of

Born: Aug. 30, 1977. **Ht.:** 6-0. **Wt.:** 220. **Bats:** R. **Throws:** R. **School:** Georgia Perimeter JC. **Career Transactions:** Selected by Phillies in 10th round of 1999 draft; signed June 4, 1999.

Don't let his Kirby Puckett build fool you. Byrd has 30-30 potential. He's a gym rat who has worked hard to reshape his body after ballooning to 315 pounds following an accident as a Georgia Tech freshman. Byrd severely injured his right leg after karate-kicking a door in jest, and required three surgeries. Byrd has above-average speed, can hit for average and will show power. He has a working knowledge of the strike zone and uses the entire field. He makes good reads and shows solid range in center field. He works as hard as any player to improve his game every day. Byrd focused too much on homers while hitting in the middle of the Triple-A Scranton/Wilkes Barre order. He needs to cut down on his strikeouts and be more aggressive on the bases. He was charged with assault after an August confrontation with his girlfriend. The matter was resolved, and the club hopes he'll learn from it. Byrd will be an upgrade over Doug Glanville and Ricky Ledee in center fieldr. His experience, maturity and minor league accomplishments should allow him to make the jump to the majors.

Year	Club (League)	Class	AVG	G	AB	R	H	2B	3B	HR	RBI	BB	SO	SB	SLG	OBP
1999	Batavia (NY-P)	A	.296	65	243	40	72	7	6	13	50	28	70	8	.535	.376
2000	Piedmont (SAL)	A	.309	133	515	104	159	29	13	17	93	51	110	41	.515	.379
2001	Reading (EL)	AA	.316	137	510	108	161	22	8	28	89	52	93	32	.555	.386
2002	Scranton/W-B (IL)	AAA	.297	136	538	103	160	37	7	15	63	46	98	15	.476	.362
	Philadelphia (NL)	MAJ	.229	10	35	2	8	2	0	1	1	1	8	0	.371	.250
MAJOR LEAGUE TOTALS			.229	10	35	2	8	2	0	1	1	1	8	0	.371	.250
MINOR LEAGUE TOTALS			.306	471	1806	355	552	95	34	73	295	177	371	96	.517	.375

4. Taylor Buchholz, rhp

Born: Oct. 13, 1981. **Ht.:** 6-4. **Wt.:** 220. **Bats:** R. **Throws:** R. **School:** Springfield (Pa.) HS. **Career Transactions:** Selected by Phillies in sixth round of 2000 draft; signed June 19, 2000.

Buchholz' commitment to North Carolina caused him to slip in the 2000 draft, but the Phillies persuaded the local product to sign by offering him $365,000, equivalent to fourth-round money. After starting his pro career with a 3-13 record, Buchholz rebounded to go 18-12 since. Like Brett Myers and Gavin Floyd, Buchholz has developed into a durable pitcher with the potential for three above-average pitches. He throws two- and four-seam fastballs, generating plus life and sitting at 88-93 mph with a high of 96. Buchholz learned a new curveball grip at low Class A Lakewood in 2001, and now his breaking ball has more velocity than Floyd's and equal bite. His conditioning, athleticism and sound delivery have made him durable. Like Floyd, Buchholz needs to refine his command in the strike zone. He tends to overthrow, causing him to leave his pitches up. His circle changeup is a work in progress. Buchholz was knocked around a bit in four late-season starts at Double-A Reading, and will head back there in 2003. He gives the Phillies another potential front-of-the rotation starter.

Year	Club (League)	Class	W	L	ERA	G	GS	CG	SV	IP	H	R	ER	HR	BB	SO	AVG
2000	Phillies (GCL)	R	2	3	2.25	12	7	0	0	44	46	22	11	2	14	41	.269
2001	Lakewood (SAL)	A	9	14	3.36	28	26	5	0	177	165	83	66	8	57	136	.250
2002	Clearwater (FSL)	A	10	6	3.29	23	23	4	0	159	140	66	58	11	51	129	.233
	Reading (EL)	AA	0	2	7.43	4	4	0	0	23	29	19	19	5	6	17	.315
MINOR LEAGUE TOTALS			21	25	3.44	67	60	9	0	402	380	190	154	26	128	323	.249

5. Cole Hamels, lhp

Born: Dec. 27, 1983. **Ht.:** 6-3. **Wt.:** 170. **Bats:** L. **Throws:** L. **School:** Rancho Bernardo HS, San Diego. **Career Transactions:** Selected by Phillies in first round (17th overall) of 2002 draft; signed Aug. 28, 2002.

Some clubs considered Hamels the best pitcher in the 2002 draft, but his medical history allowed the Phillies to get him with the 17th overall pick. He broke the humerus in his left arm as a high school sophomore, but it's not the same injury that ended the careers of major league lefthanders Tom Browning, Dave Dravecky and Tony Saunders. Hamels first injured the arm in an off-field accident before aggravating it while he was pitching. He had surgery performed by the Padres' team doctor and rehabbed with pitching guru Tom House, sitting out his junior year but pitching well as a senior. Hamels' fastball reaches 93-94 mph with good lefthanded life, though he often pitches closer to 90. He shows exceptional control of his curveball and already has a solid changeup. Hamels has an easy delivery and an advanced feel for pitching. The Phillies aren't worried about his arm, yet Hamels will have to establish his durability. In any case, he must get stronger. Hamels might have a better feel for pitching than Gavin Floyd and Brett Myers did at the same stage of their careers. He could make his pro debut in low Class A and move quickly from there.

Year	Club (League)	Class	W	L	ERA	G	GS	CG	SV	IP	H	R	ER	HR	BB	SO	AVG
						Has Not Played—Signed 2003 Contract												

6. Ryan Madson, rhp

Born: Aug. 28, 1980. **Ht.:** 6-6. **Wt.:** 180. **Bats:** L. **Throws:** R. **School:** Valley View HS, Moreno Valley, Calif. **Career Transactions:** Selected by Phillies in ninth round of 1998 draft; signed June 10, 1998.

Madson followed a breakout 2000 season with a less impressive encore in 2001, missing time with a tired shoulder. He bounced back last year to lead the Double-A Eastern League in victories, ranking second in strikeouts and third in ERA and innings. Despite his size, Madson reaches only the low 90s with his fastball. He struggled in 2001 as he tried to pitch around hitters, but he became more aggressive and worked inside more last season. That made his overhand curveball and changeup, which rates as the organization's best and is a major league out pitch, even more effective. Madson keeps the ball down in the zone, enticing groundouts and preventing homers. Madson is growing into his 6-foot-6 frame, but still could stand to add some more muscle, especially in his lower half. There's nothing specific for him to work on mechanically. He just needs the experience of facing hitters at the highest levels. Madson doesn't blow hitters away with electric stuff, but he stays around the plate and keeps the ball in the park. He figures to slide into the big league rotation after spending 2003 in Triple-A.

Year	Club (League)	Class	W	L	ERA	G	GS	CG	SV	IP	H	R	ER	HR	BB	SO	AVG
1998	Martinsville (Appy)	R	3	3	4.83	12	10	0	0	54	57	38	29	5	20	52	.265
1999	Batavia (NY-P)	A	5	5	4.72	15	15	0	0	88	80	51	46	5	43	75	.247
2000	Piedmont (SAL)	A	14	5	2.59	21	21	2	0	136	113	50	39	5	45	123	.225
2001	Clearwater (FSL)	A	9	9	3.90	22	21	1	0	118	137	68	51	4	49	101	.291
2002	Reading (EL)	AA	16	4	3.20	26	26	2	0	171	150	68	61	11	53	132	.242
MINOR LEAGUE TOTALS			47	26	3.59	96	93	5	0	566	537	275	226	30	210	483	.252

7. Anderson Machado, ss

Born: Jan. 25, 1981. **Ht.:** 5-11. **Wt.:** 160. **Bats:** B. **Throws:** R. **Career Transactions:** Signed out of Venezuela by Phillies, Jan. 14, 1998.

Machado's defense has always been first-rate, as he has drawn Dave Concepcion comparisons for his build and actions. The Phillies have waited patiently for his bat to develop, and they were rewarded with his best offensive season in 2002. He has been among the youngest regulars in his league for the last three years. Machado has the hands, arm, range and instincts to play shortstop in the majors right now. He reads the ball off the bat well. His 28 errors last year caused little concern because most were the result of his aggressive nature and confidence in his arm. Machado's best offensive tool is plus-plus speed that he easily translates into steals. He also showed improved plate discipline and power in 2002. Machado has to prove that his offensive performance wasn't a fluke. His swing mechanics are fine, but he needs to add strength to increase his bat speed and drive balls more often. With Jimmy Rollins in place, the Phillies have no need to rush Machado. He'll spend 2003 in Triple-A. He could be the second baseman of the future if Chase Utley can't move back there.

Year	Club (League)	Class	AVG	G	AB	R	H	2B	3B	HR	RBI	BB	SO	SB	SLG	OBP
1998	Phillies (DSL)	R	.201	68	219	26	44	7	0	0	17	30	44	4	.233	.313
1999	Phillies (GCL)	R	.259	43	143	26	37	6	3	2	12	15	38	6	.385	.335
	Clearwater (FSL)	A	.000	1	2	0	0	0	0	0	0	0	1	0	.000	.000
	Piedmont (SAL)	A	.233	20	60	7	14	4	2	0	7	7	20	2	.367	.324
2000	Clearwater (FSL)	A	.245	117	417	55	102	19	7	1	35	54	103	32	.331	.330
	Reading (EL)	AA	.364	3	11	2	4	1	0	1	2	0	4	0	.727	.364
2001	Clearwater (FSL)	A	.261	82	272	49	71	5	8	5	36	31	66	23	.393	.342
	Reading (EL)	AA	.149	31	101	13	15	2	0	1	8	12	25	5	.198	.237
2002	Reading (EL)	AA	.251	126	450	71	113	24	3	12	77	72	118	40	.398	.353
MINOR LEAGUE TOTALS			.239	491	1675	249	400	68	23	22	194	221	419	112	.346	.331

8. Ryan Howard, 1b

Born: Nov. 19, 1979. **Ht.:** 6-4. **Wt.:** 230. **Bats:** L. **Throws:** L. **School:** Southwest Missouri State University. **Career Transactions:** Selected by Phillies in fifth round of 2001 draft; signed July 2, 2001.

Following Rangers prospect Jason Hart as a slugging first baseman at Southwest Missouri State, Howard projected as a 2001 first-round pick. Then he succumbed to draft pressure and batted just .271-13-54 with a school-record 74 strikeouts, so the Phillies landed him that year as a fifth-rounder. Howard shows plus raw power from left-center field to the right-field corner, and he can drive low pitches. He blasted a homer off the batter's eye behind the center-field wall 400 feet from home plate in Lakewood. He did a good job of making adjustments during his first full pro season. Howard has good hands and agility for a big man and should become at least an average first baseman. Howard's swing tends to get long, giving him trouble with breaking balls. He draws walks but must adjust his approach to make more consistent contact. A shorter stroke could boost both his power and average. The signing of Jim Thome means Howard will get plenty of time to develop. The large ballparks in the Class A Florida State League will provide a stiff test for Howard and his power in 2003.

Year	Club (League)	Class	AVG	G	AB	R	H	2B	3B	HR	RBI	BB	SO	SB	SLG	OBP
2001	Batavia (NY-P)	A	.272	48	169	26	46	7	3	6	35	30	55	0	.456	.384
2002	Lakewood (SAL)	A	.280	135	493	56	138	20	6	19	87	66	145	5	.460	.367
MINOR LEAGUE TOTALS			.278	183	662	82	184	27	9	25	122	96	200	5	.459	.372

9. Elizardo Ramirez, rhp

Born: Jan. 28, 1983. **Ht.:** 6-0. **Wt.:** 180. **Bats:** R. **Throws:** R. **Career Transactions:** Signed out of Dominican Republic by Phillies, July 2, 1999.

Ramirez carries the nickname "Easy" because of his arm action and ability to throw strikes. He led the Rookie-level Gulf Coast League with a 1.10 ERA and tossed a two-hit shutout in the playoffs. He has the same body type and command as Pedro Martinez, but he doesn't have nearly the same stuff. Ramirez has an exceptional approach, shown by his 73-2 strikeout-walk ratio. He can throw any of his three pitches–a fastball that touches 92 mph, a solid curveball and an average changeup–for strikes. Better yet, Ramirez can place them wherever he wants in the strike zone. He's unflappable on the mound and demonstrates a great feel for a pitcher his age–which isn't questioned, except by those who believe the baby-faced pitcher is still a teenager. The Phillies want Ramirez to bulk up his slight frame, improving his velocity and durability. He also would benefit from working off his fastball more and using it to set up his offspeed pitches. Ramirez has demonstrated the savvy to succeed in the FSL, though the organization's pitching depth may dictate that he at least begins 2003 at Lakewood.

Year	Club (League)	Class	W	L	ERA	G	GS	CG	SV	IP	H	R	ER	HR	BB	SO	AVG
2000	Phillies (DSL)	R	5	2	1.88	11	9	0	1	57	47	19	12	1	5	67	.216
2001	Phillies (DSL)	R	10	1	1.26	14	14	1	0	93	71	26	13	0	9	81	.208
2002	Phillies (GCL)	R	7	1	1.10	11	11	2	0	73	44	18	9	3	2	73	.165
MINOR LEAGUE TOTALS			22	4	1.37	36	34	3	1	223	162	63	34	4	16	221	.196

10. Zach Segovia, rhp

Born: April 11, 1983. **Ht.:** 6-1. **Wt.:** 220. **Bats:** R. **Throws:** R. **School:** Forney (Texas) HS. **Career Transactions:** Selected by Phillies in second round of 2002 draft; signed July 2, 2002.

Segovia outpitched Mets first-rounder Scott Kazmir on the 2001 U.S. junior national team, striking out 15 and not allowing an earned run in eight innings at a tournament in Cuba. By getting into better shape as a high school senior, Segovia pitched himself into the second round of the 2002 draft and signed for $712,500. The Phillies hired his high school coach, Ron Ortegon, to manage short-season Batavia in 2002. Segovia's fastball sits at 92-93 mph. His best pitch is a tight-breaking slider, but Segovia used it so much that the Phillies took it away from him in the Gulf Coast League. They wanted him to refine his changeup, which improved rapidly. He got his slider back in instructional league, where he dominated by going after hitters with all three pitches. While the Phillies like Segovia's strength, he's on the thick side and must monitor his weight so he doesn't get soft. He needs to improve his changeup and work off his fastball more often. Segovia will spend his first full pro season at Lakewood. If he gets blocked by the starting pitchers ahead of him, he has the approach and stuff to become a future closer.

Year	Club (League)	Class	W	L	ERA	G	GS	CG	SV	IP	H	R	ER	HR	BB	SO	AVG
2002	Phillies (GCL)	R	3	2	2.10	8	8	0	0	34	21	11	8	0	3	30	.174
MINOR LEAGUE TOTALS			3	2	2.10	8	8	0	0	34	21	11	8	0	3	30	.174

11. Seung Lee, rhp

Born: June 2, 1979. **Ht.:** 6-4. **Wt.:** 220. **Bats:** R. **Throws:** R. **Career Transactions:** Signed out of Korea by Phillies, March 6, 2001.

Lee threw 95 mph as a Korean amateur before signing for $1.2 million in March 2001. A disc problem in his back and trouble adjusting to the United States limited his effectiveness that season. He enjoyed a more successful second year as his medical and mental outlooks improved. Lee went from introvert to extrovert and became a clubhouse clown, according to Lakewood manager Jeff Manto. He learned Spanish from his Latin teammates and made strides in English. Lee's back problems cut his velocity down to 92 mph. That's fine, because his changeup is solid and his backdoor slider has developed into a money pitch. He can throw it in any count and commands it as well as he does his fastball. Because of Lee's feel for pitching and ability to work both sides of the plate, the Phillies have encouraged him to pitch backward at times. Lee still is cleaning up his mechanics, paring down superfluous motion from his traditional Asian delivery where he pulls his hands above his head and then pauses before driving plateward. The Phillies worry that Lee's big, Paul Wilson-type body could pose a problem if he doesn't watch his conditioning. He was quite hittable in the Arizona Fall League, but the Phillies chalk that up to fatigue. Lee projects as a No. 3 or 4 starter at the major league level. While he had success in low Class A, he was old for the South Atlantic League. He should get a truer test in 2003 in Double-A, where he made a strong late-season start.

Year	Club (League)	Class	W	L	ERA	G	GS	CG	SV	IP	H	R	ER	HR	BB	SO	AVG
2001	Phillies (GCL)	R	1	0	3.00	3	3	0	0	9	12	7	3	0	0	4	.308
	Batavia (NY-P)	A	0	3	7.65	4	4	0	0	20	31	24	17	3	4	14	.341
2002	Lakewood (SAL)	A	7	10	3.24	23	22	5	1	147	132	64	53	8	46	112	.244
	Clearwater (FSL)	A	2	0	0.00	3	3	1	0	19	6	1	0	0	2	16	.095
	Reading (EL)	AA	0	1	0.00	1	1	0	0	6	5	2	0	1	0	6	.217
MINOR LEAGUE TOTALS			10	14	3.26	34	33	6	1	201	186	98	73	12	52	152	.246

12. Jorge Padilla, of

Born: Aug. 11, 1979. **Ht.:** 6-2. **Wt.:** 200. **Bats:** R. **Throws:** R. **School:** Florida Air Academy, Melbourne, Fla.
Career Transactions: Selected by Phillies in third round of 1998 draft; signed July 19, 1998.

A hamstring injury forced Padilla to miss 40 games and a chance at a 20-20 season in 2001. He also missed time with a foot injury in 2000. He remained healthy throughout 2002, but the rigors of playing a full season caught up to him. Mentally, Padilla found it difficult to deal with playing tired and fighting through slumps at the same time. He was hitting .297 through May, but struggled to make adjustments and batted just .224 the rest of the way. Double-A pitchers took advantage of his aggressive approach and got him to chase pitches. Padilla drives the ball well and possesses the strength to hit for power, but has yet to show it in game action. His top hand-dominated swing generates so much topspin that balls often dive into the alleys rather than carrying over the wall. He should develop a better feel for lofting the ball with time. Padilla rates as a plus runner and steals bases as much because of his instincts as his speed. He reads balls well off the bat and has plus arm strength, but still won't push Bobby Abreu out of right field. While previous comparisons to Magglio Ordonez might be a bit off base now, Padilla still flashes the tools to become a solid major league outfielder. He's capable of hitting .280 and being a 20-20 man. He'll start 2003 in Triple-A.

Year	Club (League)	Class	AVG	G	AB	R	H	2B	3B	HR	RBI	BB	SO	SB	SLG	OBP
1998	Martinsville (Appy)	R	.356	23	90	10	32	3	0	5	25	4	24	2	.556	.378
1999	Piedmont (SAL)	A	.208	44	168	13	35	10	1	3	17	5	44	0	.333	.247
	Batavia (NY-P)	A	.252	65	238	28	60	10	1	3	30	22	79	2	.340	.331
2000	Piedmont (SAL)	A	.305	108	413	62	126	24	8	11	67	26	89	8	.482	.346
2001	Clearwater (FSL)	A	.260	100	358	62	93	13	2	16	66	40	73	23	.441	.343
2002	Reading (EL)	AA	.256	127	484	71	124	30	2	7	65	40	77	32	.370	.322
MINOR LEAGUE TOTALS			.268	467	1751	246	470	90	14	45	270	137	386	67	.413	.329

13. Keith Bucktrot, rhp

Born: Nov. 27, 1980. **Ht.:** 6-3. **Wt.:** 190. **Bats:** L. **Throws:** R. **School:** Claremore (Okla.) HS. **Career Transactions:** Selected by Phillies in third round of 2000 draft; signed June 26, 2000.

Inconsistency has plagued Bucktrot throughout his career. He didn't even have consistent scouting reports as a prep player, as some teams liked him better as a hitter. He struggles to repeat his delivery, pitch to pitch and outing to outing. And there's not one clear problem. Sometimes Bucktrot rushes his delivery. Sometimes his front side flies open. At other times, he throws across his body. Bucktrot's future success is directly related to mastering his mechanics. When's he's on, he can dominate. His fastball sits between 92-94 mph, his power curveball can be a plus pitch at times and his changeup rates as at least average. But he's pretty hittable despite his stuff, and he walks nearly as many batters as he strikes out. Bucktrot had it all working in early August, when he tossed back-to-back complete games, allowing four hits in one and two in the other. In his next start, he displayed his mercurial approach by surrendering 10 hits and five runs in six innings. He figures to repeat high Class A at least at the start of 2003, which has as much to do with his need to refine his delivery as it does the depth of pitching in the system.

Year	Club (League)	Class	W	L	ERA	G	GS	CG	SV	IP	H	R	ER	HR	BB	SO	AVG
2000	Phillies (GCL)	R	3	2	4.78	11	7	0	0	38	39	21	20	5	19	40	.267
2001	Lakewood (SAL)	A	6	11	5.28	24	24	3	0	135	139	93	79	16	58	97	.269
2002	Clearwater (FSL)	A	8	9	4.88	27	24	2	0	160	167	101	87	10	78	84	.276
MINOR LEAGUE TOTALS			17	22	5.03	62	55	5	0	333	345	215	186	31	155	221	.272

14. Juan Richardson, 3b

Born: Jan. 27, 1979. **Ht.:** 6-1. **Wt.:** 170. **Bats:** R. **Throws:** R. **Career Transactions:** Signed out of Dominican Republic by Phillies, July 1, 1998.

Richardson turned out to be two years older than previously thought, but kept crushing baseballs like he always had. The age change moved him from among the Florida State League's younger players to the same age as its veterans. Nonetheless, Richardson's considerable power potential still makes him one of the Phillies' better prospects. A year after socking 22 home runs in low Class A, he stroked 15 in the FSL's humid air and spacious ballparks. He tied for fourth in home runs and fifth in RBIs. He improved his approach at the plate by using the whole field and showed the ability to adjust against breaking pitches. He's not going to hit for a better average until he tightens his strike zone. An average defender, Richardson displays a plus arm along with good hands at third base. He's an average runner. Richardson progressed enough to make the move to Double-A in 2003. With his age adjustment, it's now important that he moves fast—and it's also worth wondering where his career heads if he begins to struggle.

Year	Club (League)	Class	AVG	G	AB	R	H	2B	3B	HR	RBI	BB	SO	SB	SLG	OBP
1999	Phillies (GCL)	R	.226	46	164	27	37	14	0	5	23	11	46	7	.402	.290
	Piedmont (SAL)	A	.167	4	12	0	2	1	0	0	2	1	5	0	.250	.231
	Batavia (NY-P)	A	.125	7	24	1	3	0	0	1	2	2	8	0	.250	.222
2000	Piedmont (SAL)	A	.242	43	149	19	36	11	0	2	15	17	43	0	.356	.327
	Batavia (NY-P)	A	.154	10	39	0	6	2	0	0	2	3	15	0	.205	.214
2001	Lakewood (SAL)	A	.240	137	505	68	121	31	2	22	83	51	147	7	.440	.325
2002	Clearwater (FSL)	A	.257	122	456	52	117	21	2	18	83	44	122	0	.430	.339
MINOR LEAGUE TOTALS			.239	369	1349	167	322	80	4	48	210	129	386	14	.411	.320

15. Carlos Cabrera, rhp

Born: Feb. 19, 1983. **Ht.:** 6-4. **Wt.:** 195. **Bats:** R. **Throws:** R. **Career Transactions:** Signed out of Dominican Republic by Phillies, July 2, 1999.

After strong seasons in the Rookie-level Dominican Summer League and Gulf Coast League, Cabrera took another step up the ladder to the short-season New York-Penn League in 2002. Each year Cabrera has added strength and weight, going from 174 pounds after signing to 183 in 2001 and 195 last year. As he fills out his 6-foot-4 frame, Cabrera reminds the Phillies more and more of Carlos Silva. Like Silva, Cabrera has a strong arm and can be a durable starter. His fastball sits between 90-92 mph, can get up to 94 and bores in on hitters. His curveball is progressing nicely and should become an average to plus pitch, though now it still varies from crisp to flat. Cabrera just learned to throw a changeup but has picked it up quickly, giving him another solid offering. He struggled with his release point last season, which affects his command. The rest of his delivery is clean, so he shouldn't need a major adjustment. He'll continue to refine his secondary stuff while continuing his transition from thrower to pitcher in the Lakewood rotation in 2003. Cabrera is advanced for his age, which should expedite his rise through the system.

Year	Club (League)	Class	W	L	ERA	G	GS	CG	SV	IP	H	R	ER	HR	BB	SO	AVG
2000	Phillies (DSL)	R	0	0	1.46	4	4	0	0	12	6	3	2	0	9	10	.136
2001	Phillies (GCL)	R	2	2	2.91	10	8	0	0	43	35	23	14	2	23	40	.220
2002	Batavia (NY-P)	A	9	2	3.59	15	14	0	0	90	79	44	36	5	46	77	.237
MINOR LEAGUE TOTALS			11	4	3.21	29	26	0	0	146	120	70	52	7	78	127	.224

16. Erick Arteaga, rhp

Born: April 2, 1981. **Ht.:** 6-7. **Wt.:** 230. **Bats:** R. **Throws:** R. **Career Transactions:** Signed out of Venezuela by Phillies, July 18, 1998 . . . On restricted list, May 19, 1999-May 1, 2000.

There's not a significant difference between Arteaga and Carlos Cabrera. They bear a strong resemblance, both physically and as pitchers, with Cabrera just a bit further along. At 6-foot-7, Arteaga is an imposing figure on the mound and works hitters aggressively. He's taller and thicker than Cabrera, but not quite as strong. Arteaga throws his 92 mph fastball on a steep downhill plane. It's his best pitch and he needs to make more use of it rather than relying on his secondary stuff, which rates just a tick behind Cabrera's. Arteaga employs a curveball and changeup, which both eventually can become average or better. He shows solid command, but at times struggles to maintain a consistent release point and can get wild. He'll work on repeating his delivery as he joins Cabrera in low Class A.

Year	Club (League)	Class	W	L	ERA	G	GS	CG	SV	IP	H	R	ER	HR	BB	SO	AVG
1999						Did Not Play											
2000	La Victoria (VSL)	R	4	0	0.83	15	0	0	5	33	21	4	3	0	5	32	.191
2001	Phillies (GCL)	R	4	1	3.63	10	9	0	0	52	58	28	21	0	7	28	.278
2002	Batavia (NY-P)	A	3	1	2.79	12	12	0	0	81	61	27	25	5	21	44	.211
MINOR LEAGUE TOTALS			11	2	2.67	37	21	0	5	165	140	59	49	5	33	104	.230

17. Carlos Rodriguez, ss

Born: Oct. 4, 1983. **Ht.:** 6-0. **Wt.:** 180. **Bats:** B. **Throws:** R. **Career Transactions:** Signed out of Dominican Republic by Phillies, Oct. 13, 2000.

Then known as Carlos Rosario, Rodriguez signed with the Phillies for $700,000 shortly after emerging as a prospect at the 2000 Area Code Games. He's a raw player with plenty of tools who needs a lot of repetitions to refine all aspects of his game. For now, defense remains his calling card. Rodriguez' hands, arm, agility and range all rate as plus tools and he has proven a better fielder than his 18 errors at Batavia would suggest. Offensively, Rodriguez hasn't struggled as much as many other slick-fielding infield prospects. He generates good bat speed and his mechanics at the plate steadily have improved in each of the last two seasons. A plus runner, Rodriguez stands to learn more about stealing bases, as he was successful in just 21 of his 32 attempts last year. Rodriguez has better tools and more promise than Danny Gonzalez, who has played a level above him the last two seasons, but still faces a numbers crunch in Philadelphia with Jimmy Rollins there and Anderson Machado on the doorstep. Rodriguez will get his first taste of full-season ball at Lakewood in 2003.

Year	Club (League)	Class	AVG	G	AB	R	H	2B	3B	HR	RBI	BB	SO	SB	SLG	OBP
2001	Phillies (GCL)	R	.297	35	128	22	38	10	1	3	23	11	25	6	.461	.368
2002	Batavia (NY-P)	A	.290	61	248	29	72	7	3	0	15	19	48	21	.343	.351
MINOR LEAGUE TOTALS			.293	96	376	51	110	17	4	3	38	30	73	27	.383	.357

18. Brad Baisley, rhp

Born: Aug. 24, 1979. **Ht.:** 6-9. **Wt.:** 200. **Bats:** R. **Throws:** R. **School:** Land O' Lakes (Fla.) HS. **Career Transactions:** Selected by Phillies in second round of 1998 draft; signed July 16, 1998.

Arm injuries have wrecked the development of Baisley, who once was considered the Phillies' best pitching prospect after Brett Myers and now profiles as a back-of-the-rotation starter. The elbow tenderness that shortened Baisley's 2000 season also ate into his performance the following year, when he missed most of spring training and didn't get to Double-A until mid-May. He then struggled through his worst pro season. A frayed labrum held Baisley back in 2002. It wasn't a tear and minor surgery in the fall cleaned it up. He should return at 100 percent for 2003. He offers three solid-average pitches: a 90 mph fastball, a curveball and a changeup. The curve rates as a potential out pitch. The 6-foot-9 Baisley needs to stay on top of the ball and throw downhill more, as he often drops his arm angle, losing control and velocity. Though he pitched better last year, he didn't intimidate Eastern League hitters. While the injuries might have frustrated a lot of players, Baisley's background—his dad is a high school coach—and makeup have kept him focused on returning. The Phillies will take it slow with Baisley, starting him at Double-A again this year.

Year	Club (League)	Class	W	L	ERA	G	GS	CG	SV	IP	H	R	ER	HR	BB	SO	AVG
1998	Martinsville (Appy)	R	3	2	3.58	7	7	0	0	28	27	12	11	2	4	14	.255
1999	Piedmont (SAL)	A	10	7	2.26	23	23	3	0	148	116	56	37	5	55	110	.220
2000	Clearwater (FSL)	A	3	9	3.74	16	15	2	1	89	95	47	37	9	34	60	.270
2001	Clearwater (FSL)	A	2	4	3.78	11	9	0	0	64	59	31	27	4	18	43	.246
	Reading (EL)	AA	5	4	6.50	12	10	0	0	62	82	50	45	14	14	37	.314
2002	Reading (EL)	AA	7	9	4.17	21	21	1	0	117	111	69	54	12	51	64	.253
MINOR LEAGUE TOTALS			30	35	3.74	90	85	6	1	508	490	265	211	46	176	328	.255

19. Eric Valent, of

Born: April 4, 1977. **Ht.:** 6-0. **Wt.:** 190. **Bats:** L. **Throws:** L. **School:** UCLA. **Career Transactions:** Selected by Phillies in first round (42nd overall) of 1998 draft; signed July 1, 1998.

Valent played with Troy Glaus, Jim Parque and Eric Byrnes at UCLA, where he broke Glaus' career home run record. A player with Valent's talents might have ranked as the Phillies' top prospect five years ago. Instead, he has become a victim of the organization's depth, especially in the outfield. He spent time in Philadelphia in 2001, when he was promoted to serve as a DH during interleague play, but struggled and hasn't been back since. He got off to a slow start in 2002 spring training, which prevented him from making the big league roster, and it carried over into the beginning of the season. By the time Valent got things going again, Jason Michaels had usurped his spot as Philadelphia's fifth outfielder. While Valent might never hit for a high average, he always has been a run producer. He tied for fourth in the International League with in 84 RBIs, the fourth straight season in which he drove in at least 79 runs. He has quick hands and above-average power to drive balls into the gaps and over fences. Defensively, Valent rates as the best outfielder in the system and also boasts the best arm. With the ability to become a solid major league corner outfielder, Valent could serve as trade fodder as Philadelphia searches for the final pieces to put a winner in place.

Year	Club (League)	Class	AVG	G	AB	R	H	2B	3B	HR	RBI	BB	SO	SB	SLG	OBP
1998	Piedmont (SAL)	A	.427	22	89	24	38	12	0	8	28	14	19	0	.831	.500
	Clearwater (FSL)	A	.264	34	125	24	33	8	1	5	25	16	29	1	.464	.359
1999	Clearwater (FSL)	A	.288	134	520	91	150	31	9	20	106	58	110	5	.498	.359
2000	Reading (EL)	AA	.258	128	469	81	121	22	5	22	90	70	89	2	.467	.356
2001	Scranton/W-B (IL)	AAA	.272	117	448	65	122	30	2	21	78	49	105	0	.489	.352
	Philadelphia (NL)	MAJ	.098	22	41	3	4	2	0	0	1	4	11	0	.146	.196
2002	Scranton/W-B (IL)	AAA	.251	140	546	69	137	34	2	9	84	49	94	0	.370	.311
	Philadelphia (NL)	MAJ	.200	7	10	1	2	0	0	0	0	0	3	0	.200	.200
MAJOR LEAGUE TOTALS			.118	29	51	4	6	2	0	0	1	4	14	0	.157	.196
MINOR LEAGUE TOTALS			.274	575	2197	354	601	137	19	85	411	256	446	8	.469	.351

20. Jake Blalock, of/3b

Born: Aug. 6, 1983. **Ht.:** 6-4. **Wt.:** 220. **Bats:** R. **Throws:** R. **School:** Rancho Bernardo HS, San Diego. **Career Transactions:** Selected by Phillies in fifth round of 2002 draft; signed July 25, 2002.

The younger brother of Rangers prospect Hank Blalock received plenty of hype during his senior season at Rancho Bernardo High, where he played for his uncle Sam Blalock. Despite rumors that Blalock could be a supplemental first-round pick of the Athletics—Oakland general manager Billy Beane also played for Sam Blalock in high school—he fell to the fifth round and landed with the Phillies and high school teammate Cole Hamels, their first-round pick. Blalock is an impressive physical specimen, bigger than his brother and possessing more raw power. He hit a ball so hard in the Gulf Coast League that he left one side flat. He takes a solid approach to the plate, where he sees breaking balls well for a young hitter and uses the whole field. Owing to his baseball bloodlines, Blalock's makeup and work ethic are impressive. Defensively, he has yet to settle into a position. A high school shortstop, he has seen time at the outfield corners and third base since turning pro. At best, he'll be an adequate defender, as Blalock doesn't have the hands his brother does. His arm and range are average. A strong spring could earn him a spot in low Class A.

Year	Club (League)	Class	AVG	G	AB	R	H	2B	3B	HR	RBI	BB	SO	SB	SLG	OBP
2002	Phillies (GCL)	R	.250	25	88	13	22	6	0	1	13	10	15	3	.352	.317
MINOR LEAGUE TOTALS			.250	25	88	13	22	6	0	1	13	10	15	3	.352	.317

21. Josh Hancock, rhp

Born: April 11, 1978. **Ht.:** 6-3. **Wt.:** 210. **Bats:** R. **Throws:** R. **School:** Auburn University. **Career Transactions:** Selected by Red Sox in fifth round of 1998 draft; signed June 15, 1998 . . . Traded by Red Sox to Phillies for 1B Jeremy Giambi, Dec. 15, 2002.

Hancock came from the Red Sox in a Winter Meetings trade for Jeremy Giambi, who became expendable once the Phillies signed Jim Thome. Hancock is probably best known for getting the Pedro Martinez stamp of approval. Martinez skipped his last start of the 2002 season, nominating Hancock to replace him. He was as close to major league-ready as any pitcher in the Boston system, but his chances of making Philadelphia's Opening Day roster were diminished by his November surgery to repair a small tear in his pelvic wall. He should be able to bounce back, however. Hancock had his jaw broken by a line drive last June but returned after a month, cutting his expected recovery time in half. He doesn't have a true out pitch, but all three of his pitches are above-average at times. He commands his 91-94 mph fastball to both sides of the plate, and he also throws a curveball and changeup. Hancock just needs to show greater consistency with his secondary pitches. He throws across his body a little bit, but the Red Sox never thought his delivery would lead to injury. Hancock pitched well in three major league appearances in September and could join the Phillies bullpen at some point in 2003. He should be able to pitch in games by the end of March. Down the road, he could get a chance to crack the back end of the rotation.

Year	Club (League)	Class	W	L	ERA	G	GS	CG	SV	IP	H	R	ER	HR	BB	SO	AVG
1998	Red Sox (GCL)	R	1	1	3.38	5	1	0	0	13	9	5	5	1	3	21	.196
	Lowell (NY-P)	A	0	1	2.25	1	1	0	0	4	5	2	1	0	4	4	.333
1999	Augusta (SAL)	A	6	8	3.80	25	25	0	0	140	154	79	59	12	46	106	.279
2000	Sarasota (FSL)	A	5	10	4.45	26	24	1	0	144	164	89	71	9	37	95	.286
2001	Trenton (EL)	AA	8	6	3.65	24	24	0	0	131	138	60	53	8	37	119	.273
2002	Trenton (EL)	AA	3	4	3.61	15	14	2	1	85	82	40	34	9	18	69	.250
	Pawtucket (IL)	AAA	4	2	3.45	8	8	0	0	44	39	20	17	2	26	29	.235
	Boston (AL)	MAJ	0	1	3.68	3	1	0	0	7	5	3	3	1	2	6	.200
MAJOR LEAGUE TOTALS			0	1	3.68	3	1	0	0	7	5	3	3	1	2	6	.200
MINOR LEAGUE TOTALS			27	32	3.85	104	97	3	1	560	591	295	240	41	171	443	.270

22. Franklin Perez, rhp

Born: June 10, 1978. **Ht.:** 6-2. **Wt.:** 170. **Bats:** R. **Throws:** R. **Career Transactions:** Signed out of Dominican Republic by Phillies, Dec. 11, 1997.

Perez has made strides each year since his U.S. debut at 18. That progress was interrupted in October, when he had Tommy John surgery that will put him out through the 2003 season. Despite his elbow injury, the Phillies added him to their 40-man roster in November. Perez employs a heavy fastball with good sink. He improved his velocity in 2002, going from 88-91 mph to sitting at 93-94. Hitters have a tough time lifting it, so Perez gets a lot of grounders. For that reason, the Phillies see his future being in the bullpen rather than the rotation. Perez also seems to work better in relief, posting a 2.52 ERA in that role last year compared to 4.48 as a starter. The Phillies envision Perez being similar to Carlos Silva, eventually replacing him in the middle innings as Silva goes deeper into games. Perez' slider continues to improve but isn't an average pitch yet. He needs to work on his consistency within the strike zone, not so much throwing more strikes but better ones.

Year	Club (League)	Class	W	L	ERA	G	GS	CG	SV	IP	H	R	ER	HR	BB	SO	AVG
1998	Phillies (DSL)	R	4	5	3.39	17	11	0	0	64	54	42	24	2	38	43	.230
1999	Phillies (GCL)	R	3	4	6.31	12	7	0	0	41	44	36	29	2	27	35	.280
2000	Piedmont (SAL)	A	5	5	3.04	36	9	0	2	98	85	47	33	3	39	64	.239
2001	Clearwater (FSL)	A	4	2	3.52	31	0	0	3	64	58	29	25	2	26	45	.245
2002	Reading (EL)	AA	3	2	3.72	40	12	0	5	102	98	48	42	8	36	68	.255
MINOR LEAGUE TOTALS			19	18	3.74	136	39	0	10	368	339	202	153	17	166	255	.248

23. Rob Tejeda, rhp

Born: March 24, 1982. **Ht.:** 6-3. **Wt.:** 180. **Bats:** R. **Throws:** R. **Career Transactions:** Signed out of Dominican Republic by Phillies, Nov. 24, 1998.

Tejeda turned potential into performance in low Class A in 2001 and followed it up with a strong first half in high Class A last year. He ended up being shut down in mid-July with a tender shoulder, and the Phillies began to rework his mechanics in instructional league. Tejeda used a long arm action and also flew open quite a bit with his delivery, causing him to wrap his arm behind his body and then throw across it. The motion led to the shoulder soreness as well as some wildness on the mound. His health is no longer a question. Tejeda's breaking ball improved with the new delivery and he also offers an average changeup to go along with his 92-93 mph fastball. His unrefined secondary stuff and sore shoulder contributed to Tejeda's 14 home runs allowed, which ranked fifth in the Florida State League though he didn't throw a pitch over the last two months. He looks like an end-of-the-rotation pitcher. A return to Clearwater awaits.

Year	Club (League)	Class	W	L	ERA	G	GS	CG	SV	IP	H	R	ER	HR	BB	SO	AVG
1999	Phillies (GCL)	R	1	3	4.27	12	9	0	0	46	47	27	22	5	27	39	.273
2000	Phillies (GCL)	R	2	5	5.54	10	6	1	0	39	44	30	24	3	12	22	.273
2001	Lakewood (SAL)	A	8	9	3.40	26	24	1	0	151	128	74	57	10	58	152	.228
2002	Clearwater (FSL)	A	4	8	3.97	17	17	1	0	100	73	48	44	14	48	87	.204
MINOR LEAGUE TOTALS			15	25	3.94	65	56	3	0	336	292	179	147	32	145	300	.233

24. Danny Gonzalez, ss

Born: Nov. 20, 1981. **Ht.:** 6-0. **Wt.:** 180. **Bats:** B. **Throws:** R. **School:** Florida Air Academy, Melbourne, Fla. **Career Transactions:** Selected by Phillies in fourth round of 2000 draft; signed Aug. 25, 2000.

Like Jorge Padilla, Gonzalez is a Puerto Rican who spent his high school years in the United States playing for the Florida Air Academy in Melbourne. Like Eric Valent, Gonzalez gets lost in a deep Phillies system. Jimmy Rollins and Anderson Machado are ahead of him and Carlos Rodriguez is nipping at his heels. Gonzalez made the jump to full-season ball successfully in 2002. He's a slap hitter with a decent swing, but his bat must improve if he's to continue advancing through the system. Defensively, Gonzalez plays a solid shortstop and displays average arm strength and range. His hands are soft and he shows good actions around the bag. Gonzalez possesses average speed and runs the bases aggressively, though his 11 stolen bases in 32 attempts suggest he's too aggressive. Gonzalez is built similarly to Minnesota's Cristian Guzman, a frame that lends itself to durability but also one that worries the Phillies that he might get too thick for the position. He's headed to high Class A this year.

Year	Club (League)	Class	AVG	G	AB	R	H	2B	3B	HR	RBI	BB	SO	SB	SLG	OBP
2001	Batavia (NY-P)	A	.238	73	281	33	67	9	4	0	20	18	52	1	.299	.289
2002	Lakewood (SAL)	A	.270	131	493	58	133	14	4	4	43	55	88	11	.339	.349
MINOR LEAGUE TOTALS			.258	204	774	91	200	23	8	4	63	73	140	12	.324	.328

25. Jean Machi, rhp

Born: Feb. 1, 1983. **Ht.:** 6-0. **Wt.:** 200. **Bats:** R. **Throws:** R. **Career Transactions:** Signed out of Venezuela by Phillies, Feb. 22, 2000.

Sal Agostinelli and Jim Fregosi Jr. signed Machi for $58,000 out of a tryout camp in February 2000. Like many Latin players, Machi had his age corrected before the 2002 season, gaining a year in the process. A strong-bodied pitcher with solid command and a clean delivery, Machi has drawn comparisons to Bartolo Colon. He has dominated Rookie ball simply by relying on his mid- to high-90s fastball. Despite that heat, the Phillies want to break Machi's belief that harder is better, believing he'd be more successful if he works at 94-96 mph with a quality secondary pitch. He's still learning how to throw a curveball and changeup, both of which are new to him. He projects as a possible closer, but he likely will be used as a starter or long reliever this season at Batavia or Lakewood. That way he can get more innings in and will be forced to develop his full repertoire.

Year	Club (League)	Class	W	L	ERA	G	GS	CG	SV	IP	H	R	ER	HR	BB	SO	AVG
2000	La Victoria (VSL)	R	2	2	4.13	11	3	0	1	24	21	15	11	1	14	23	.241
2001	Mariara (VSL)	R	8	3	2.86	14	7	1	2	57	40	23	18	0	30	56	—
2002	Mariara (VSL)	R	2	0	0.00	11	0	0	7	12	5	0	0	0	3	13	.132
	Phillies (GCL)	R	2	0	1.00	10	2	0	1	27	11	4	3	0	16	22	.129
MINOR LEAGUE TOTALS			14	5	2.41	46	12	1	11	119	77	42	32	1	63	114	—

26. Eric Junge, rhp

Born: Jan. 5, 1977. **Ht.:** 6-5. **Wt.:** 210. **Bats:** R. **Throws:** R. **School:** Bucknell University. **Career Transactions:** Selected by Dodgers in 11th round of 1999 draft; signed June 5, 1999 . . . Traded by Dodgers with RHP Jesus Cordero to Phillies for LHP Omar Daal, Nov. 9, 2001.

When the Phillies dumped Omar Daal rather than pay him $4.5 million for 2002, Junge was the best of the two prospects they received from the Dodgers. Junge spent his first season in the system in Triple-A, where he led the International League in walks while finishing second in innings and fifth in strikeouts. The Phillies sent him to the Arizona Fall League to change him from an innings-eating starter into a reliever. He made four appearances there before shutting it down because he was physically and mentally exhausted from the long season. At 6-foot-5, Junge could emerge as an imposing figure coming out of the bullpen. His 91-94 mph fastball has good life and he has added a splitter that rates as an average to above average pitch. He also throws a changeup and curveball, but lacks consistency with them, leading to deep counts. Junge has a legitimate chance to make the Phillies this year as a swingman or long reliever.

Year	Club (League)	Class	W	L	ERA	G	GS	CG	SV	IP	H	R	ER	HR	BB	SO	AVG
1999	Yakima (NWL)	A	5	7	5.82	15	15	0	0	82	98	60	53	10	31	55	.303
2000	San Bernardino (Cal)	A	8	1	3.36	29	24	0	1	158	159	69	59	8	53	116	.267
2001	Jacksonville (SL)	AA	10	11	3.46	27	27	1	0	164	143	72	63	19	56	116	.237
2002	Scranton/W-B (IL)	AAA	12	6	3.54	29	29	1	0	181	170	77	71	16	67	126	.249
	Philadelphia (NL)	MAJ	2	0	1.42	4	1	0	0	13	14	3	2	0	5	11	.286
MAJOR LEAGUE TOTALS			2	0	1.42	4	1	0	0	13	14	3	2	0	5	11	.286
MINOR LEAGUE TOTALS			35	25	3.79	100	95	2	1	585	570	278	246	53	207	413	.259

27. Jeremy Wedel, rhp

Born: Nov. 27, 1976. **Ht.:** 6-0. **Wt.:** 190. **Bats:** R. **Throws:** R. **School:** Armstrong Atlantic (Ga.) State University. **Career Transactions:** Selected by Phillies in 20th round of 1998 draft; signed June 8, 1998.

Wedel always has had the odds stacked against him, especially in an organization as deep in pitching as the Phillies. He was a 20th-round pick from an NCAA Division II program and doesn't dominate with his stuff. But he's always competed tenaciously, and that's been enough to keep his door to the majors from being slammed shut. The Phillies rewarded him for a solid Triple-A season by adding him to the 40-man roster for the first time in November. Wedel is quick to the plate and has a resilient arm. A gutsy pitcher, he goes after hitters by changing speeds and mixing pitches. He has an 88-89 mph sinker that reaches 92 mph, plus a solid slider and changeup. He needs to stay on top of the slider to prevent it from spinning flatly toward the plate. Wedel sometimes gets too hyper on the mound and subsequently has mechanical problems. He'll get a shot at making the Philadelphia bullpen in spring training, but he most likely will repeat Triple-A.

Year	Club (League)	Class	W	L	ERA	G	GS	CG	SV	IP	H	R	ER	HR	BB	SO	AVG
1998	Batavia (NY-P)	A	7	6	4.38	16	15	1	0	88	102	48	43	3	15	65	.287
1999	Clearwater (FSL)	A	0	0	1.69	4	0	0	0	5	4	1	1	0	1	3	.200
	Piedmont (SAL)	A	5	3	2.16	23	0	0	3	50	46	19	12	2	8	40	.243
2000	Clearwater (FSL)	A	5	4	2.13	39	0	0	9	72	43	19	17	1	30	45	.178
2001	Reading (EL)	AA	5	3	3.71	45	0	0	5	63	67	33	26	4	16	43	.265
2002	Scranton/W-B (IL)	AAA	7	1	2.69	43	0	0	1	60	60	24	18	1	20	34	.262
MINOR LEAGUE TOTALS			29	17	3.11	170	15	1	18	339	322	144	117	11	90	230	.250

28. Martire Franco, rhp

Born: Feb. 25, 1978. **Ht.:** 6-0. **Wt.:** 170. **Bats:** R. **Throws:** R. **Career Transactions:** Signed out of Dominican Republic by Phillies, July 1, 1998.

Franco had three years and three months added to his age before the 2002 season, and then got slapped around a bit in his first stop in Double-A. He struggles to find the strike zone at times and ends up elevating his pitches, then running to back up third base. Maintaining a consistent release point would go a long way to alleviating his problems. Franco remains intriguing because of his 93-94 mph fastball with heavy sink. He gets it right in on hitters, leaving them with broken bats or stingers in their hands. With a little more polish, his slider can be an average or even plus pitch. His changeup is coming along as well. The Phillies think he'll be able to pull his repertoire together because of his strong work ethic and aptitude for pitching. Franco also tends to thrive in difficult situations because he's such a tough competitor. That makes him an eventual candidate for the bullpen, but for now he'll likely stay in the rotation to get more work in. His feel for pitching will serve as the ultimate factor in deciding where his future lies. Depending on how many young arms get sent back to Triple-A after spring training, Franco could pitch in either role there or start in Double-A.

Year	Club (League)	Class	W	L	ERA	G	GS	CG	SV	IP	H	R	ER	HR	BB	SO	AVG
1998	Phillies (DSL)	R	3	2	2.93	14	2	0	0	28	19	14	10	3	7	29	.179
1999	Phillies (DSL)	R	3	0	1.50	23	0	0	5	24	18	7	4	2	10	31	.209
2000	Piedmont (SAL)	A	8	6	4.13	24	23	2	0	126	146	70	58	7	57	89	.290
2001	Clearwater (FSL)	A	11	8	4.13	26	24	4	0	161	178	84	74	12	41	97	.281
2002	Reading (EL)	AA	4	8	5.76	16	16	2	0	89	109	62	57	13	25	50	.304
MINOR LEAGUE TOTALS			29	24	4.24	103	65	8	5	431	470	237	203	37	140	296	.279

29. Esteban de los Santos, ss

Born: Dec. 26, 1982. **Ht.:** 6-1. **Wt.:** 160. **Bats:** B. **Throws:** R. **Career Transactions:** Signed out of Dominican Republic by Phillies, Aug.12, 1999 . . . On restricted list, Aug. 24, 2001-June 16, 2002.

The Phillies' shortstop prospect train rolls on with de los Santos, who began his career as a third baseman. He possesses solid shortstop instincts and average range and arm strength. His inconsistent bat also helped force the move off the hot corner. De los Santos epitomizes streaky at the plate. He hit well over .400 in extended spring training last year before plummeting to .222 once he repeated the Gulf Coast League. De los Santos plays with a lot of emotion, and sometimes it takes over. If he strikes out in his first at-bat of a game, he's a good bet to add a few more K's to the boxscore in subsequent plate appearances. As he matures and learns to deal with the successes and failures inherent in baseball, he could come around at the plate. He might never become a .300 hitter, but the Phillies would settle for his consistent glovework and a .260 average with 10 homers. How he handles short-season ball in 2003 should be telling.

Year	Club (League)	Class	AVG	G	AB	R	H	2B	3B	HR	RBI	BB	SO	SB	SLG	OBP
2000	Phillies (DSL)	R	.244	55	193	81	47	14	3	3	24	22	49	9	.383	.323
2001	Phillies (GCL)	R	.195	38	123	18	24	6	4	2	13	8	27	3	.358	.254
2002	Phillies (GCL)	R	.222	50	167	24	37	6	3	5	29	15	50	6	.383	.302
MINOR LEAGUE TOTALS			.224	143	483	123	108	24	10	10	66	45	126	18	.377	.298

30. Yoel Hernandez, rhp

Born: April 15, 1982. **Ht.:** 6-2. **Wt.:** 170. **Bats:** R. **Throws:** R. **Career Transactions:** Signed out of Venezuela by Phillies, Nov. 5, 1998.

Like many pitchers in the Philadelphia system, Hernandez has a tall, slender frame. Unlike the others, he doesn't possess a plus pitch or the same ceiling. Using an 86-88 mph fastball and a curveball, changeup and sinker, he makes his living through precision. He can throw any pitch to any location in any count. His command is an asset, but because he's always around the plate Hernandez has been very hittable. He led the Florida State League in losses last year, but threw better than that stat suggests. Hernandez has shown the ability to be a workhorse, topping the FSL in innings pitched after a full winter's work in Venezuela. He'll pitch in the Double-A rotation this year.

Year	Club (League)	Class	W	L	ERA	G	GS	CG	SV	IP	H	R	ER	HR	BB	SO	AVG
1999	La Victoria (VSL)	R	2	2	3.32	14	11	0	1	60	48	27	22	3	29	57	.226
2000	Phillies (GCL)	R	4	1	1.35	10	9	2	0	60	39	10	9	2	17	46	.183
2001	Lakewood (SAL)	A	6	9	3.47	25	25	1	0	161	153	94	62	7	42	111	.243
2002	Clearwater (FSL)	A	7	16	3.54	28	28	3	0	170	176	76	67	6	54	116	.271
MINOR LEAGUE TOTALS			19	28	3.20	77	73	6	1	451	416	207	160	18	142	330	.244

PITTSBURGH PIRATES

TOP 30 PROSPECTS

1. John Van Benschoten, rhp
2. Sean Burnett, lhp
3. Bryan Bullington, rhp
4. Jose Castillo, ss
5. Duaner Sanchez, rhp
6. Tony Alvarez, of
7. Jose Bautista, 3b
8. J.J. Davis, of
9. Mike Gonzalez, lhp
10. Ian Oquendo, rhp
11. Humberto Cota, c
12. Ryan Doumit, c
13. Ryan Vogelsong, rhp
14. Bobby Bradley, rhp
15. J.R. House, c
16. Zach Duke, lhp
17. Walter Young, 1b
18. Matt Guerrier, rhp
19. Blair Johnson, rhp
20. Alex Hart, rhp
21. Nate McLouth, of
22. Leo Nunez, rhp
23. Mike Connolly, lhp
24. Chris Duffy, of
25. Carlos Rivera, 1b
26. Vic Buttler, of
27. Henry Owens, rhp
28. Josh Bonifay, of/2b
29. Shawn Garrett, of
30. Jason Sharber, rhp

By John Perrotto

The Pirates have become synonymous with losing over the past decade. Since winning three straight division titles from 1990-92, Pittsburgh has suffered through 10 straight losing seasons, the longest stretch of futility in the franchise's 116-year history.

At least their long history of losing in the minors came to an end last season. General manager Dave Littlefield hired Brian Graham as farm director prior to last season, telling him to change the mindset in the system. Graham, a former minor league manager for the Indians and a big league coach for Baltimore and Cleveland, did just that. The Pirates broke an incredible string in which their farm clubs had an overall losing record in 32 of the previous 33 years. Pittsburgh affiliates didn't just win. They won big. The six clubs went a combined 399-300 (.571), the second-best mark in baseball behind Cleveland's .577. The Pirates were one of just two organizations, along with the Dodgers, to have each of their six affiliates finish with winning records. Four of Pittsburgh's farm clubs went to the playoffs, and both of its full-season Class A teams won league championships.

"We are proud of the year we had," Littlefield said, "and feel this will help in laying the foundation for the future."

The Pirates made more of an effort to win by keeping most of their players at the same level throughout the season. That was a marked contrast to previous regimes that seemingly shuffled minor league rosters on a daily basis. "It's easier to develop players on a winning team," Graham said. "Winning also builds confidence, regardless of what level of baseball you're on. It creates a better atmosphere and I firmly believe you learn better habits when you're winning, and those carry with a player from the minor leagues to the major leagues."

While the farm system has improved since Littlefield took over for Cam Bonifay in June 2001, it still isn't producing players for the major league club yet. The Pirates stocked Triple-A Nashville with veteran free agents last season. Neither the Sounds nor Double-A Altoona had any players ranked among their league's top 20 prospects.

The Pirates have assembled talent at Class A and below after three good drafts by former scouting director Mickey White from 1999-2001 and a solid one by Ed Creech, his replacement, last year.

OrganizationOverview

General Manager: Dave Littlefield. **Farm Director:** Brian Graham. **Scouting Director:** Ed Creech.

2002 PERFORMANCE

Class	Farm Team	League	W	L	Pct.	Finish*	Manager
Majors	Pittsburgh	National	72	89	.447	13th (16)	Lloyd McClendon
Triple-A	Nashville Sounds	Pacific Coast	72	71	.503	t-8th (16)	Marty Brown
Double-A	Altoona Curve	Eastern	72	69	.511	7th (12)	Dale Sveum
High A	Lynchburg Hillcats	Carolina	87	53	.621	+2nd (8)	Pete Mackanin
Low A	Hickory Crawdads	South Atlantic	83	56	.597	+1st (16)	Tony Beasley
Short-season	Williamsport Crosscutters	New York-Penn	48	28	.632	3rd (14)	Andy Stewart
Rookie	GCL Pirates	Gulf Coast	37	23	.617	2nd (14)	Woody Huyke
OVERALL 2002 MINOR LEAGUE RECORD			399	300	.571	2nd (30)	

*Finish in overall standings (No. of teams in league)   +League champion.

ORGANIZATION LEADERS

BATTING
*Minimum 250 At-Bats
- *AVG Chris Shelton, Hickory .... .340
- R Chris Duffy, Lynchburg 85
- H Ray Navarrette, Lynchburg 169
- TB Walter Young, Hickory 277
- 2B Ray Navarrette, Lynchburg 41
- 3B Shawn Garrett, Altoona 8
- HR Josh Bonifay, Lynchburg 26
- RBI Walter Young, Hickory 103
- BB Jose Bautista, Hickory 67
- SO Humberto Cota, Nashville 106
- SB Manny Ravelo, Hickory 42

PITCHING
#Minimum 75 Innings
- W Sean Burnett, Lynchburg 13
-    Jeff Miller, Hickory 13
- L Tony McKnight, Nashville 14
- #ERA Ben Shaffar, Nashville/Altoona 3.17
- G D.J. Carrasco, Lynchburg 55
- CG Bronson Arroyo, Nashville 3
- SV D.J. Carrasco, Lynchburg 29
- IP Tony McKnight, Nashville 175
- BB Adrian Burnside, Altoona 67
- SO Ian Oquendo, Hickory 149

BEST TOOLS

- Best Hitter for Average .... Tony Alvarez
- Best Power Hitter .... Walter Young
- Fastest Baserunner .... Manny Ravelo
- Best Athlete .... J.J. Davis
- Best Fastball .... Duaner Sanchez
- Best Curveball .... Ian Oquendo
- Best Slider .... Mike Johnston
- Best Changeup .... Sean Burnett
- Best Control .... Mike Connolly
- Best Defensive Catcher .... Humberto Cota
- Best Defensive Infielder .... Jose Castillo
- Best Infield Arm .... Jose Castillo
- Best Defensive Outfielder .... Chris Duffy
- Best Outfield Arm .... Jeremy Harts

PROJECTED 2006 LINEUP

- Catcher .... Jason Kendall
- First Base .... Aramis Ramirez
- Second Base .... Pokey Reese
- Third Base .... Jose Bautista
- Shortstop .... Jose Castillo
- Left Field .... Brian Giles
- Center Field .... Tony Alvarez
- Right Field .... J.J. Davis
- No. 1 Starter .... Kris Benson

JOHN SPEAR   RODGER WOOD

Josh Bonifay   D.J. Carrasco

- No. 2 Starter .... John VanBenschoten
- No. 3 Starter .... Kip Wells
- No. 4 Starter .... Sean Burnett
- No. 5 Starter .... Bryan Bullington
- Closer .... Duaner Sanchez

TOP PROSPECTS OF THE DECADE

- 1993 .... Kevin Young, 1b
- 1994 .... Midre Cummings, of
- 1995 .... Trey Beamon, of
- 1996 .... Jason Kendall, c
- 1997 .... Kris Benson, rhp
- 1998 .... Kris Benson, rhp
- 1999 .... Chad Hermansen, of
- 2000 .... Chad Hermansen, of
- 2001 .... J.R. House, c
- 2002 .... J.R. House, c

TOP DRAFT PICKS OF THE DECADE

- 1993 .... Charles Peterson, of
- 1994 .... Mark Farris, ss
- 1995 .... Chad Hermansen, ss
- 1996 .... Kris Benson, rhp
- 1997 .... J.J. Davis, rhp
- 1998 .... Clint Johnston, lhp/of
- 1999 .... Bobby Bradley, rhp
- 2000 .... Sean Burnett, lhp
- 2001 .... John VanBenschoten, rhp/of
- 2002 .... Bryan Bullington, rhp

ALL-TIME LARGEST BONUSES

- Bryan Bullington, 2002 .... $4,000,000
- John VanBenschoten, 2001 .... $2,400,000
- Bobby Bradley, 1999 .... $2,225,000
- Kris Benson, 1996 .... $2,000,000
- J.J. Davis, 1997 .... $1,675,000

MinorLeagueDepthChart

PITTSBURGH PIRATES

RANK 18

The Pirates have been maligned for their lack of success in player development over the last few seasons, but 2002 saw considerable improvement. New farm director Brian Graham deserves a lot of credit for instilling a winning attitude throughout the system in his first year on the clock. Both Class A clubs won championships. Ed Creech's first draft shows promise, but the previous scouting regime, led by Mickey White, is responsible for eight of the Pirates top 10 prospects. Even with devastating injuries to J.R. House and Bobby Bradley, the Pirates are confident their talent pool has several quality major leaguers on the verge of breaking through.

Note: Depth charts prepared by Josh Boyd. Numbers in parentheses indicate prospect rankings.

LF
Josh Bonifay (28)
Shawn Garrett (29)
Jorge Cortes
Manny Ravelo
Bobby Kingsbury

CF
Tony Alvarez (6)
Nate McLouth (21)
Chris Duffy (24)
Vic Buttler (26)
Rajai Davis

RF
J.J. Davis (8)
Jeremy Harts
B.J. Barns

3B
Jose Bautista (7)
Yurendell DeCaster
Kody Kirkland

SS
Jose Castillo (4)
Javier Guzman
Taber Lee
Tomas de la Rosa

2B
Jeff Keppinger
Domingo Cuello

1B
Walter Young (17)
Carlos Rivera (25)
Brad Eldred
Ray Navarrette
Chris Shelton

C
Humberto Cota (11)
Ryan Doumit (12)
J.R. House (15)

RHP

Starters
John VanBenschoten (1)
Bryan Bullington (3)
Ian Oquendo (10)
Bobby Bradley (14)
Matt Guerrier (18)
Blair Johnson (19)
Alex Hart (20)
Leo Nunez (22)
Jason Sharber (30)
Jonathan Albaladejo
Ben Shaffar
Patrick O'Brien
Landon Jacobsen
Justin Reid

Relievers
Duaner Sanchez (5)
Ryan Vogelsong (13)
Henry Owens (27)
Casey Shumaker
Jeff Miller
Pedro Arias
Matt Capps
Kurt Shafer

LHP

Starters
Sean Burnett (2)
Zach Duke (16)
Josh Shortslef

Relievers
Mike Gonzalez (9)
Mike Connolly (23)
John Grabow
Shane Youman

DraftAnalysis

2002 Draft

Best Pro Debut: RHP Alex Hart (5) had Tommy John surgery in 2000 and didn't enjoy much college success until last spring. He carried it over, going 7-0, 1.85 with 73 strikeouts in 68 innings in the short-season New York-Penn League. NY-P all-star 1B Brad Eldred (6) hit .283-10-48 with 10 steals.

Best Athlete: OFs Bobby Kingsbury (8), Joseph Hicks (9) and Chaz Lytle (42). Kingsbury is compared to Steve Finley, while Hicks has been likened to Juan Pierre. They pale, however, next to RHP/OF Wardell Starling (4), who has a 95 mph fastball, tape-measure power and plus speed. Also a star high school wide receiver, Starling passed up San Diego State for Odessa (Texas) JC, so the Pirates still control his rights.

Best Pure Hitter: Kingsbury or OF Anthony Bocchino (11), who hit a combined .437 the last two years at Marist. Draft-and-follow 3B Kody Kirkland might have a better bat than either.

Best Raw Power: Eldred's 6-foot-5, 245-pound frame generates huge power.

Fastest Runner: Lytle takes 4.0 seconds from the left side of the plate to first base, while Hicks takes 4.1 from the right side.

Best Defensive Player: SS Taber Lee (3) has plus arm strength and range, and he gets good jumps on the ball.

Best Fastball: RHP Blair Johnson (2) was still maxing out at 94-96 mph in instructional league. RHP Bryan Bullington (No. 1 overall) has the same velocity, but signed late and has yet to play. Now that RHP Matt Capps (7) no longer spends part of his time

catching, he reaches 94-95 consistently.

Best Breaking Ball: Johnson's hard slurve sits in the low 80s. Bullington tightened his slider last spring.

Most Intriguing Background: Lytle's father Charlie was a musician who toured with Dick Clark in the 1960s and worked with bands such as the Allman Brothers and Rolling Stones as a representative of a company that manufactures instruments. He also has rented RVs to groups such as Aerosmith and Tiger Woods'

Hart

entourage. Lee's brother Travis played for the Phillies. Unsigned RHP Chris Toneguzzi (30) is a cousin of NHL star Chris Pronger.

Closest To The Majors: Given Bullington's holdout, Hart could beat him to Pittsburgh.

Best Late-Round Pick: Lytle. The Pirates also have hopes for projectable LHPs David Davidson (10), Brian Holliday (11) and John Hummel (16).

The One Who Got Away: Toneguzzi, who has a low-90s fastball, changed his mind about junior college and went to Purdue.

Assessment: The success of this draft depended on Pittsburgh's ability to sign Bullington, who sought Joe Mauer money ($5.15 million), and Starling. The Pirates ended up getting Bullington for the price they originally offered: $4 million.

2001 Draft

The Pirates shocked people by taking RHP John VanBenschoten (1) for his arm rather than his bat, but it's hard to argue with the results. They didn't sign RHP Jeremy Guthrie (3), a 2002 first-rounder, and SS Stephen Drew (11), a likely first-rounder in 2004.   **Grade: B**

2000 Draft

LHP Sean Burnett (1) has done nothing but win, while draft-and-follow 3B Jose Bautista (20) has been solid. RHP Chris Young (3) was mildly disappointing before being traded to Montreal this offseason.   **Grade: B**

1999 Draft

RHP Bobby Bradley (1) and Cs Ryan Doumit (2) and J.R. House (5) all elicit a lot of hope in Pittsburgh, but they haven't been able to stay healthy. Both Bradley and House have had Tommy John surgery.   **Grade: C**

1998 Draft

Most teams preferred Clint Johnston (1) as an outfielder, and he proved to be a bust as a pitcher. All the Pirates have to show from this draft is RHP Joe Beimel (18).   **Grade: F**

Note: Draft analysis prepared by Jim Callis. Numbers in parentheses indicate draft rounds.

... His fastball reaches the mid-90s with good movement and sits comfortably at 93 mph.

John
VanBenschoten rhp

Born: April 14, 1980.
Ht.: 6-4. **Wt.:** 210.
Bats: R. **Throws:** R.
School: Kent State University.
Career Transactions: Selected by Pirates in first round (eighth overall) of 2001 draft; signed July 3, 2001.

When VanBenschoten led NCAA Division I with 31 home runs as a junior at Kent State in 2001, most clubs projected him as a power-hitting right fielder. The Pirates watched VanBenschoten serve as the Golden Flashes' closer, however, and were intrigued enough by his mound work to surprise many by drafting him as a pitcher. VanBenschoten split time between pitcher and DH at short-season Williamsport in 2001 but stayed strictly on the mound last season and ranked as the No. 2 prospect in the low Class A South Atlantic League. He anchored the rotation as Hickory won the league championship.

VanBenschoten has a power arm that wasn't abused by overwork in college. His fastball reaches the mid-90s with good movement and sits comfortably at 93 mph. At the behest of the Pirates, VanBenschoten began throwing his curveball more last year and it became a plus pitch by the end of the season. He also has a slider with hard, late movement. Pittsburgh has made sure not to overextend VanBenschoten but believes he'll develop into a workhorse once he gets settled into the majors. While he won't get a chance to swing a bat again until he reaches Double-A, VanBenschoten's power stroke figures to make him one of the game's better hitting pitchers. He's intelligent and takes instruction well. One Pirates executive calls VanBenschoten "the total package, everything you would want in a pitching prospect."

VanBenschoten was a college prospect as a pitcher in high school but hasn't faced many advanced hitters. He tends to give up too many hits for a pitcher with his stuff, though that should change as he gains experience. Like most young pitchers, his changeup is erratic. He needs to refine it to have something to keep hitters off balance.

VanBenschoten will move to high Class A Lynchburg this season. While the Pirates were criticized in some circles for not pushing him, they're mindful of his lack of experience. He has the talent to be a No. 1 starter and could skip a level and arrive in Pittsburgh by 2005.

Year	Club (League)	Class	AVG	G	AB	R	H	2B	3B	HR	RBI	BB	SO	SB	SLG	OBP
2001	Williamsport (NY-P)	A	.227	32	75	9	17	5	0	0	8	7	23	3	.293	.302
MINOR LEAGUE TOTALS			.227	32	75	9	17	5	0	0	8	7	23	3	.293	.302

Year	Club (League)	Class	W	L	ERA	G	GS	CG	SV	IP	H	R	ER	HR	BB	SO	AVG
2001	Williamsport (NY-P)	A	0	2	3.51	9	9	0	0	26	23	11	10	0	10	19	.247
2002	Hickory (SAL)	A	11	4	2.80	27	27	0	0	148	119	57	46	6	62	145	.219
MINOR LEAGUE TOTALS			11	6	2.90	36	36	0	0	174	142	68	56	6	72	164	.223

2. Sean Burnett, lhp

Born: Sept. 17, 1982. **Ht.:** 6-1. **Wt.:** 170. **Bats:** L. **Throws:** L. **School:** Wellington (Fla.) Community HS. **Career Transactions:** Selected by Pirates in first round (19th overall) of 2000 draft; signed July 7, 2000.

The Pirates selected Burnett in the first round of the 2000 draft from Wellington Community High, a year after they took righthander Bobby Bradley in the first round from the same school. Burnett has been Pittsburgh's minor league pitcher of the year each of the past two seasons and was the high Class A Carolina League's pitcher of the year in 2002. His ERA last year was second in the minor leagues behind Bubba Nelson of the Braves. Bradley has improved the velocity on his heavy fastball to the point that it hit 93 mph in the Futures Game last year, though it sits more comfortably at 88-89. He also has become more willing to throw his fastball inside to hitters. Bradley's best pitch is a Tom Glavine-like changeup that hitters continually beat into the ground. He also has a good slider. Burnett doesn't have overpowering velocity, which sometimes limits him in situations when he needs a strikeout. He's also on the smallish side, raising mild concerns about his durability. Burnett mastered Class A in his teens and now will go to try Double-A Altoona. He's on track to take a spot in the major league rotation in 2005.

Year	Club (League)	Class	W	L	ERA	G	GS	CG	SV	IP	H	R	ER	HR	BB	SO	AVG
2000	Pirates (GCL)	R	2	1	4.06	8	6	0	0	31	31	17	14	0	3	24	.250
2001	Hickory (SAL)	A	11	8	2.62	26	26	1	0	161	164	63	47	11	33	134	.265
2002	Lynchburg (Car)	A	13	4	1.80	26	26	2	0	155	118	46	31	4	33	96	.210
MINOR LEAGUE TOTALS			26	13	2.38	60	58	3	0	348	313	126	92	15	69	254	.240

3. Bryan Bullington, rhp

Born: Sept. 30, 1980. **Ht.:** 6-5. **Wt.:** 220. **Bats:** R. **Throws:** R. **School:** Ball State University. **Career Transactions:** Selected by Pirates in first round (first overall) of 2002 draft; signed Oct. 30, 2002.

After winning Mid-American Conference player of the year honors by going 11-3, 2.84 at Ball State and setting a league record with 139 strikeouts in 105 innings, Bullington was the No. 1 overall pick in the 2002 draft. He finally signed in late October for a club-record $4 million, but missed the minor league season and instructional league while negotiating. Bullington dominated college hitters by throwing a heavy 95 mph fastball. He also has a sharp slider to complement his heater. Bullington won plenty of admiration for his toughness in the 2001 MAC tournament, when he was hit in the face by a line drive in the opening round and came back to pitch two days later. It remains to be seen how much of an effect sitting out all of last summer will have on Bullington in 2003. He needs to tighten his curveball and refine his changeup in order to have something to offset his hard stuff. The Pirates will start Bullington off in low Class A. He could be on the fast track and likely will be ready to break into majors in 2005, along with touted prospects John VanBenschoten and Sean Burnett.

Year	Club (League)	Class	W	L	ERA	G	GS	CG	SV	IP	H	R	ER	HR	BB	SO	AVG
	Has Not Played—Signed 2003 Contract																

4. Jose Castillo, ss

Born: March 19, 1981. **Ht.:** 6-1. **Wt.:** 190. **Bats:** R. **Throws:** R. **Career Transactions:** Signed out of Venezuela by Pirates, July 2, 1997.

Castillo repeated high Class A after having arthroscopic wrist surgery following the 2001 season. Though he was disappointed to be back at Lynchburg, he helped lead the Hillcats to the league championship. Managers named him the Carolina League's most exciting player and best defensive infielder. Castillo can hit for both average and power, with scouts estimating he'll hit 20-25 homers a year in the majors. He has plus range at shortstop and an outstanding arm, which enables him to make plays from deep in the hole. Castillo is a slightly above-average runner, though he doesn't project as a big basestealer. Castillo needs to improve his plate discipline and cut down on trying to make too many flashy plays in the field. He has a thick lower body, leaving some to wonder if he may eventually have to move to third base. With nothing left to prove at Class A, Castillo will move to Double-A this season. The Pirates have a young shortstop in Jack Wilson, but if he doesn't improve his hitting then Castillo will be ready to take over in 2005.

Year	Club (League)	Class	AVG	G	AB	R	H	2B	3B	HR	RBI	BB	SO	SB	SLG	OBP
1998	Montalban (VSL)	R	.291	55	179	31	52	9	1	1	13	20	30	23	.369	.380
1999	Pirates (GCL)	R	.266	47	173	27	46	9	0	4	30	11	23	8	.387	.316
2000	Hickory (SAL)	A	.299	125	529	95	158	32	8	16	72	29	107	16	.480	.346
2001	Lynchburg (Car)	A	.245	125	485	57	119	20	7	7	49	21	94	23	.359	.288
2002	Lynchburg (Car)	A	.300	134	503	82	151	25	2	16	81	49	95	27	.453	.370
MINOR LEAGUE TOTALS			.281	486	1869	292	526	95	18	44	245	130	349	97	.422	.339

5. Duaner Sanchez, rhp

Born: Oct. 14, 1979. **Ht.:** 6-0. **Wt.:** 190. **Bats:** R. **Throws:** R. **Career Transactions:** Signed out of Dominican Republic by Diamondbacks, Aug. 30, 1996 . . . Traded by Diamondbacks to Pirates for RHP Mike Fetters, July 6, 2002.

Sanchez was a struggling starter until the Diamondbacks converted him into a reliever last spring and watched his fastball reach 102 mph on the radar gun at Double-A El Paso early in the season. Arizona traded Sanchez to the Pirates last July for veteran reliever Mike Fetters. Sanchez' fastball gained velocity and movement once he was used in shorter bursts. The heater normally sits in the 93-94 mph range, though he can dial it up to 97 when necessary. Sanchez also has a plus slider, though the Pirates asked him to shelve it in favor a curveball after he was called up in September. He has experience throwing a changeup from his days as a starter. Sanchez has extremely thin legs, which causes some to wonder about his long-term durability. His command also needs work. He's a bit of a free spirit who has yet to totally accept that he is now a reliever instead of a starter. Sanchez will compete for a middle-relief job in the Pittsburgh bullpen this spring, though he may need a few more months at Triple-A. He looks like the heir apparent to closer Mike Williams.

Year	Club (League)	Class	W	L	ERA	G	GS	CG	SV	IP	H	R	ER	HR	BB	SO	AVG
1997	Diamondbacks (DSL)	R	4	4	5.13	21	6	0	1	60	57	50	34	3	48	44	.250
1998	Diamondbacks (DSL)	R	2	3	1.79	14	8	1	1	50	36	19	10	0	24	44	.203
1999	High Desert (Cal)	A	0	0	7.53	3	3	0	0	14	15	13	12	2	9	9	.288
	Missoula (Pio)	R	5	3	3.13	13	11	0	0	63	54	34	22	3	23	51	.224
2000	South Bend (Mid)	A	8	9	3.65	28	28	4	0	165	152	80	67	6	54	121	.243
2001	El Paso (TL)	AA	3	7	6.78	13	13	0	0	70	92	56	53	5	25	41	.324
	Lancaster (Cal)	A	2	4	4.58	10	10	1	0	59	65	44	30	7	18	49	.274
2002	El Paso (TL)	AA	4	3	3.03	31	0	0	13	36	31	16	12	1	13	37	.223
	Arizona (NL)	MAJ	0	0	4.91	6	0	0	0	4	3	2	2	1	5	4	.214
	Tucson (PCL)	AAA	1	1	6.75	4	0	0	1	5	6	4	4	1	1	9	.261
	Nashville (PCL)	AAA	0	3	4.76	20	0	0	6	23	23	12	12	2	11	20	.274
	Pittsburgh (NL)	MAJ	0	0	15.43	3	0	0	0	2	3	4	4	1	2	2	.300
MAJOR LEAGUE TOTALS			0	0	9.00	9	0	0	0	6	6	6	6	2	7	6	.250
MINOR LEAGUE TOTALS			29	37	4.22	157	79	6	22	546	531	328	256	30	226	425	.254

6. Tony Alvarez, of

Born: May 10, 1978. **Ht.:** 6-1. **Wt.:** 200. **Bats:** R. **Throws:** R. **Career Transactions:** Signed out of Venezuela by Pirates, Sept. 27, 1995.

Alvarez burst onto the scene as the short-season New York-Penn League's MVP in 1999 at Williamsport and has continued to blossom into a prospect. He was second in the Double-A Eastern League in hits and batting last season while ranking third in doubles. Alvarez also impressed during a September callup, his first major league action. Alvarez can hit for average and find the gaps with his line-drive swing. He has the potential to blossom into a power hitter with more strength and experience. Alvarez also has speed and basestealing ability. He has good range and a decent arm in center field. Alvarez plays with great enthusiasm but sometimes gets out of control and overswings or dives for balls he has no chance of catching. He's a good two-strike hitter but needs to learn to work counts better and stay back on breaking balls. Though the Pirates never did find a regular center fielder last season, they'll resist the temptation to move Alvarez into the lineup at the start of 2003. He'll begin this season at Triple-A Nashville and challenge for a major league roster spot in 2004.

Year	Club (League)	Class	AVG	G	AB	R	H	2B	3B	HR	RBI	BB	SO	SB	SLUG	OBP
1996	Pirates (DSL)	R	.138	39	109	12	15	2	0	1	9	8	12	6	.183	.203
1997	Guacara 1 (VSL)	R	.220	38	91	15	20	3	0	0	6	9	10	3	.253	.282
1998	Pirates (GCL)	R	.247	50	190	27	47	13	1	4	29	13	24	19	.389	.299
1999	Williamsport (NY-P)	A	.321	58	196	44	63	14	1	7	45	21	36	38	.510	.418
2000	Hickory (SAL)	A	.285	118	442	75	126	25	4	15	77	39	93	52	.462	.357
2001	Lynchburg (Car)	A	.344	25	93	10	32	4	0	2	11	7	11	7	.452	.390
	Altoona (EL)	AA	.319	67	254	34	81	16	1	6	25	9	30	17	.461	.359

Year	Club (League)	Class	AVG	G	AB	R	H	2B	3B	HR	RBI	BB	SO	SB	SLG	OBP
2002	Altoona (EL)	AA	.318	125	507	79	161	37	1	15	59	27	71	29	.483	.361
	Pittsburgh (NL)	MAJ	.308	14	26	6	8	2	0	1	2	3	5	1	.500	.379
MAJOR LEAGUE TOTALS			.308	14	26	6	8	2	0	1	2	3	5	1	.500	.379
MINOR LEAGUE TOTALS			.290	520	1882	296	545	114	8	50	261	133	287	171	.438	.349

7. Jose Bautista, 3b

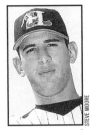

Born: Oct. 19, 1980. **Ht.:** 6-0. **Wt.:** 180. **Bats:** R. **Throws:** R. **School:** Chipola (Fla.) JC. **Career Transactions:** Selected by Pirates in 20th round of 2000 draft; signed May 19, 2001.

The Pirates selected Bautista, a native of the Dominican Republic, as a draft-and-follow in 2000 and signed him prior to the 2001 draft after he was Florida's junior college player of the year. He has led short-season Williamsport and Hickory to league titles in his first two pro seasons. With a quick bat, Bautista has hit for average while also flashing power and RBI potential as a pro. He has a good eye for a young hitter and should develop into a high on-base percentage guy with experience. Bautista is a good defensive third baseman with above-average range, arm and athleticism. To add versatility, he played center field in the Dominican League. Bautista hasn't been able to translate his bat speed into power yet, though that should come as his body fills out. He doesn't have great speed but also doesn't clog the bases. Bautista will continue his climb up the ladder this season in high Class A. He's on course to reach the major leagues in 2006.

Year	Club (League)	Class	AVG	G	AB	R	H	2B	3B	HR	RBI	BB	SO	SB	SLG	OBP
2001	Williamsport (NY-P)	A	.286	62	220	43	63	10	3	5	30	21	41	8	.427	.364
2002	Hickory (SAL)	A	.301	129	438	72	132	26	3	14	57	67	104	3	.470	.402
MINOR LEAGUE TOTALS			.296	191	658	115	195	36	6	19	87	88	145	11	.456	.390

8. J.J. Davis, of

Born: Oct. 25, 1978. **Ht.:** 6-5. **Wt.:** 250. **Bats:** R. **Throws:** R. **School:** Baldwin Park (Calif.) HS. **Career Transactions:** Selected by Pirates in first round (eighth overall) of 1997 draft; signed June 3, 1997.

Davis was highly regarded as a pitcher and hitter in high school, and the Pirates took him as an outfielder. He was considered an underachiever until a heart-to-heart talk with Altoona manager Dale Sveum last May turned his career around. By September, Davis made his major league debut. Davis has plenty of tools, most notably a power bat and a cannon arm in right field. Eastern League runners quit trying to take extra bases on him last year. He has above-average speed, though he's awkward on the bases. Davis needs a better understanding of the strike zone and discipline in chasing bad pitches. He tends to get late jumps and takes bad routes on fly balls. Davis' future has never been brighter after he adjusted his attitude and quit lobbying for a switch to the mound. A good Triple-A season would put him in position to give Pittsburgh much-needed power in the outfield in 2004.

Year	Club (League)	Class	AVG	G	AB	R	H	2B	3B	HR	RBI	BB	SO	SB	SLG	OBP
1997	Pirates (GCL)	R	.255	45	165	19	42	10	2	1	18	14	44	0	.358	.315
	Erie (NY-P)	A	.077	4	13	1	1	0	0	0	0	0	4	0	.077	.077
1998	Augusta (SAL)	A	.198	30	106	11	21	6	0	4	11	3	24	1	.368	.220
	Erie (NY-P)	A	.270	52	196	25	53	12	2	8	39	20	54	4	.474	.341
1999	Hickory (SAL)	A	.265	86	317	58	84	26	1	19	65	44	99	2	.533	.360
2000	Lynchburg (Car)	A	.243	130	485	77	118	36	1	20	80	52	171	9	.445	.319
2001	Altoona (EL)	AA	.250	67	228	21	57	13	3	4	26	21	79	2	.386	.317
	Pirates (GCL)	R	.471	4	17	3	8	1	0	2	6	1	2	0	.882	.500
2002	Altoona (EL)	AA	.287	101	348	51	100	17	3	20	62	33	101	7	.526	.351
	Pittsburgh (NL)	MAJ	.100	9	10	1	1	0	0	0	0	0	4	0	.100	.182
MAJOR LEAGUE TOTALS			.100	9	10	1	1	0	0	0	0	0	4	0	.100	.182
MINOR LEAGUE TOTALS			.258	519	1875	266	484	121	12	78	307	188	578	25	.460	.329

9. Mike Gonzalez, lhp

Born: May 23, 1978. **Ht.:** 6-2. **Wt.:** 210. **Bats:** R. **Throws:** L. **School:** San Jacinto (Texas) JC. **Career Transactions:** Selected by Pirates in 30th round of 1997 draft; signed June 24, 1997.

Gonzalez made slow progress through the system and had arthroscopic shoulder surgery after the 2000 season. He earned a spot on the 40-man roster following an outstanding Arizona Fall League in 2001. Gonzalez missed two months last season because of arthroscopic knee surgery, but finished the season in Double-A before shining again in the AFL. Gonzalez throws hard for a lefthander, with his fastball routinely reaching 95 mph. He also has a slider with good late life and an adequate changeup. Gonzalez isn't afraid to pitch inside and knock hitters off the plate. Gonzalez needs to improve the command of his pitches and polish up his changeup if he's to stay in the rotation. He was skittish facing major leaguers during exhibition games last spring, a sign he could use a shot of confidence. Gonzalez probably will go to Triple-A this season, though he'll have an outside shot to make the big league club in the spring. Gonzalez initially will pitch in relief once he reaches the majors and could become a rare lefthanded closer.

Year	Club (League)	Class	W	L	ERA	G	GS	CG	SV	IP	H	R	ER	HR	BB	SO	AVG
1997	Pirates (GCL)	R	2	0	2.48	7	3	0	0	29	21	9	8	0	8	33	.200
	Augusta (SAL)	A	1	1	1.86	4	3	0	0	19	11	5	4	1	8	22	.164
1998	Augusta (SAL)	A	4	2	2.84	11	9	0	0	51	43	24	16	2	26	72	.231
	Lynchburg (Car)	A	0	3	6.67	7	7	0	0	28	40	21	21	5	13	22	.351
1999	Lynchburg (Car)	A	10	4	4.02	20	20	0	0	112	98	55	50	10	63	119	.240
	Altoona (EL)	AA	2	3	8.10	7	5	0	0	27	34	25	24	4	19	31	.312
2000	Pirates (GCL)	R	1	0	4.50	2	1	0	0	6	8	6	3	1	4	7	.267
	Lynchburg (Car)	A	4	3	4.66	12	10	0	0	56	57	34	29	6	34	53	.269
2001	Lynchburg (Car)	A	2	2	2.93	14	2	0	0	31	28	14	10	3	7	32	.241
	Altoona (EL)	AA	5	4	3.71	14	14	1	0	87	81	38	36	5	36	66	.251
2002	Altoona (EL)	AA	8	4	3.80	16	16	0	0	85	77	38	36	4	47	82	.244
	Pirates (GCL)	R	2	0	0.00	2	2	0	0	13	5	1	0	0	3	14	.114
MINOR LEAGUE TOTALS			41	26	3.92	116	92	1	0	545	503	270	237	41	268	553	.248

10. Ian Oquendo, rhp

Born: Oct. 30, 1981. **Ht.:** 5-11. **Wt.:** 160. **Bats:** R. **Throws:** R. **School:** Caesar Rodney HS, Camden, Del. **Career Transactions:** Selected by Pirates in 26th round of 2000 draft; signed June 21, 2000.

Known as Ian Snell when drafted by the Pirates, Oquendo took his wife's surname when he got married after the 2000 season. By any name, Oquendo is a winner as he has compiled a 22-6 record as a pro, including 11-0 in his first two seasons. Oquendo is a battler who challenges hitters. His fastball routinely reaches 95 mph and looks deceptively faster because of his smooth delivery. He also throws an outstanding curveball, along with a changeup. Oquendo is considered one of the top athletes in the system and fields his position well. Oquendo occasionally loses focus in games and can be prone to big innings. Maturity is an issue with him, though the Pirates hope he can grow out of it. He's also on the smallish side, causing some to wonder if he can handle a starter's workload over the long haul. Oquendo will move up to high Class A, where Pittsburgh wants to see him take another step forward. Because of his youth, the Pirates won't rush Oquendo and he may not see the majors until 2006.

Year	Club (League)	Class	W	L	ERA	G	GS	CG	SV	IP	H	R	ER	HR	BB	SO	AVG
2000	Pirates (GCL)	R	1	0	2.35	4	0	0	0	8	5	2	2	1	1	8	.200
2001	Pirates (GCL)	R	3	0	0.47	3	3	0	0	19	12	2	1	0	5	13	.185
	Williamsport (NY-P)	A	7	0	1.39	10	9	1	0	65	55	16	10	2	10	56	.230
2002	Hickory (SAL)	A	11	6	2.71	24	22	0	0	140	127	49	42	8	45	149	.243
MINOR LEAGUE TOTALS			22	6	2.14	41	34	1	0	231	199	69	55	11	61	226	.234

11. Humberto Cota, c

Born: Feb. 7, 1979. **Ht.:** 6-0. **Wt.:** 200. **Bats:** R. **Throws:** R. **Career Transactions:** Signed out of Mexico by Braves, Dec. 22, 1995 . . . Loaned by Braves to Mexico City Tigers (Mexican), June 23-Sept. 23, 1996 . . . Released by Braves, Jan. 27, 1997 . . . Signed by Devil Rays, May 22, 1997 . . . Traded by Devil Rays with C Joe Oliver to Pirates for OF Jose Guillen and RHP Jeff Sparks, July 23, 1999.

After winning the Pirates' 2001 minor league player of the year award and appearing in the Futures Game, Cota got off to a horrid start last season. He was hitting .189 on June 12 while bothered by a strained right shoulder. As Cota's shoulder improved, so did his batting average and he wound up spending a second straight September in the major leagues. Cota continues to improve as a hitter and has learned to hit the ball hard to all fields. He can turn on balls when necessary but hits more for average at this stage of his career. He's good at blocking pitches and has gotten much better at calling games. Cota needs to be more persistent with his conditioning as he tends to pack on extra weight. His throwing has never been better than average, and teams with speed take advantage him. More plate discipline would make him more productive offensively. Cota figures to stick in Pittsburgh this season, as he's out of options and longtime backup Keith Osik signed with the Brewers as a free agent. Though Cota broke the hamate bone in his wrist playing winter ball in Mexico, he shouldn't miss much time in spring training. His big league playing time will be limited behind Jason Kendall.

Year	Club (League)	Class	AVG	G	AB	R	H	2B	3B	HR	RBI	BB	SO	SB	SLG	OBP
1997	Devil Rays (GCL)	R	.241	44	133	14	32	6	1	2	20	17	27	3	.346	.333
	Hudson Valley (NY-P)	A	.222	3	9	0	2	0	0	0	2	0	1	0	.222	.222
1998	Princeton (Appy)	R	.310	67	245	48	76	13	4	15	61	32	59	4	.580	.399
1999	Charleston, SC (SAL)	A	.280	85	336	42	94	21	1	9	61	20	51	1	.429	.320
	Hickory (SAL)	A	.271	37	133	28	36	11	2	2	20	21	20	3	.429	.365
2000	Altoona (EL)	AA	.261	112	429	49	112	20	1	8	44	21	80	6	.368	.297
2001	Nashville (PCL)	AAA	.297	111	377	61	112	22	2	14	72	25	74	7	.477	.351
	Pittsburgh (NL)	MAJ	.222	7	9	0	2	0	0	0	1	0	5	0	.222	.222
2002	Nashville (PCL)	AAA	.267	118	404	51	108	27	1	9	54	31	106	5	.406	.321
	Pittsburgh (NL)	MAJ	.294	7	17	2	5	1	0	0	0	1	4	0	.353	.333
MAJOR LEAGUE TOTALS			.269	14	26	2	7	1	0	0	1	1	9	0	.308	.296
MINOR LEAGUE TOTALS			.277	577	2066	293	572	120	12	59	334	167	418	29	.432	.335

12. Ryan Doumit, c

Born: April 3, 1981. **Ht.:** 6-0. **Wt.:** 190. **Bats:** B. **Throws:** R. **School:** Moses Lake (Wash.) HS. **Career Transactions:** Selected by Pirates in second round of 1999 draft; signed June 16, 1999.

Doumit has performed well when healthy, but his bugaboo has been injuries. He was slowed by a strained lower back in 2001, then missed the second half of 2002 with a broken pinky on his throwing hand. Doumit can hit for average, and he has the ability to blossom into a 20-homer man as his body fills out. He has started to take greater pride in his defense and handling of pitchers. Doumit has a plus arm and runs well for a catcher. He has had a hard time staying on the field, though it seems more a case of bad luck than poor conditioning. He needs to improve his plate discipline, though he did a better job of laying off bad pitches last season. Considering he has played just 211 games in four pro seasons, Doumit likely will start this season in low Class A. Switch-hitting catchers with power potential are hard to find, but he needs to get on the field more. Because of the time he has missed, it's hard to project Doumit reaching the majors before 2006.

Year	Club (League)	Class	AVG	G	AB	R	H	2B	3B	HR	RBI	BB	SO	SB	SLG	OBP
1999	Pirates (GCL)	R	.282	29	85	17	24	5	0	1	7	15	14	4	.376	.410
2000	Williamsport (NY-P)	A	.313	66	246	25	77	15	5	2	40	23	33	2	.439	.371
2001	Hickory (SAL)	A	.270	39	148	14	40	6	0	2	14	10	32	2	.351	.333
	Pirates (GCL)	R	.235	7	17	2	4	2	0	0	3	2	0	0	.353	.316
	Altoona (EL)	AA	.250	2	4	0	1	0	0	0	2	1	1	0	.250	.400
2002	Hickory (SAL)	A	.322	68	258	46	83	14	1	6	47	18	40	3	.453	.377
MINOR LEAGUE TOTALS			.302	211	758	104	229	42	6	11	113	69	120	11	.417	.370

13. Ryan Vogelsong, rhp

Born: July 22, 1977. **Ht.:** 6-3. **Wt.:** 200. **Bats:** R. **Throws:** R. **School:** Kutztown (Pa.) University. **Career Transactions:** Selected by Giants in fifth round of 1998 draft; signed June 7, 1998 . . . Traded by Giants with OF Armando Rios to Pirates for RHP Jason Schmidt and OF John Vander Wal, July 30, 2001.

Vogelsong was ready to move into the Pirates rotation after he was acquired from the Giants, but he blew out his elbow in his second start and needed Tommy John surgery. He returned to the mound last July. Erratic performances kept him from getting called back to Pittsburgh, though he did post a 2.78 ERA in his last four Double-A starts. Vogelsong has four pitches he can throw for strikes, including a 94 mph fastball he spots on both sides of the plate. His slider has good tilt and his curveball is solid while he continues to refine his changeup. He's a bright guy with a good grasp of how to pitch. Vogelsong is still a bit of a question mark after major surgery. He tends to get down on himself and lose confidence when things aren't going his way. He likely will begin 2003 in Triple-A but could move into the big league rotation when an opening arises. He needs a strong spring training to keep from getting lost in the shuffle of the organization's increasing pool of young arms.

Year	Club (League)	Class	W	L	ERA	G	GS	CG	SV	IP	H	R	ER	HR	BB	SO	AVG
1998	Salem-Keizer (NWL)	A	6	1	1.77	10	10	0	0	56	37	15	11	5	16	66	.186
	San Jose (Cal)	A	0	0	7.58	4	4	0	0	19	23	16	16	3	4	26	.307
1999	San Jose (Cal)	A	4	4	2.45	13	13	0	0	70	37	26	19	3	27	86	.154
	Shreveport (TL)	AA	0	2	7.31	6	6	0	0	28	40	25	23	7	15	23	.336
2000	Shreveport (TL)	AA	6	10	4.23	27	27	1	0	155	153	82	73	15	69	147	.260
	San Francisco (NL)	MAJ	0	0	0.00	4	0	0	0	6	4	0	0	0	2	6	.182
2001	Fresno (PCL)	AAA	3	3	2.79	10	10	0	0	58	35	18	18	6	18	53	.170
	San Francisco (NL)	MAJ	0	3	5.65	13	0	0	0	29	29	21	18	5	14	17	.257
	Pittsburgh (NL)	MAJ	0	2	12.00	2	2	0	0	6	10	10	8	1	6	7	.357
	Nashville (PCL)	AAA	2	3	3.98	6	6	0	0	32	26	15	14	2	15	33	.230
2002	Lynchburg (Car)	A	1	1	8.04	4	4	0	0	16	19	14	14	0	7	20	.297
	Altoona (EL)	AA	1	5	5.56	8	8	0	0	44	47	27	27	5	10	35	.278
MAJOR LEAGUE TOTALS			0	5	5.75	19	2	0	0	41	43	31	26	6	22	30	.264
MINOR LEAGUE TOTALS			23	29	4.05	88	88	1	0	477	417	238	215	46	181	489	.235

14. Bobby Bradley, rhp

Born: Dec. 15, 1980. **Ht.:** 6-1. **Wt.:** 190. **Bats:** R. **Throws:** R. **School:** Wellington (Fla.) Community HS.
Career Transactions: Selected by Pirates in first round (eighth overall) of 1999 draft; signed July 7, 1999 . . .
On disabled list, April 5-Sept. 11, 2002.

The eighth overall pick in the 1999 draft, Bradley was the Pirates' top pitching prospect before he had Tommy John surgery in October 2001. He missed the entire 2002 season, though he was able to pitch in instructional league and is expected to be 100 percent by spring training. Bradley has a tremendous curveball with late bite that buckles hitters' knees and is often unhittable. He has great command of his curve, along with a fastball that usually tops out in the high 80s and a changeup. He knows how to pitch and sets up hitters well. Bradley has been able to make just 29 starts in four pro seasons because of arm trouble and will have to be handled with care. The strain he puts on his elbow in throwing his curveball makes Bradley an injury risk. Once on the fast track to the major leagues, he has been slowed considerably and will start this season in high Class A. Bradley has the talent to get to the majors quickly, but his health will determine when he reaches that destination.

Year	Club (League)	Class	W	L	ERA	G	GS	CG	SV	IP	H	R	ER	HR	BB	SO	AVG
1999	Pirates (GCL)	R	1	1	2.90	6	6	0	0	31	31	13	10	2	4	31	.258
2000	Hickory (SAL)	A	8	2	2.29	14	14	3	0	83	62	31	21	3	21	118	.203
2001	Lynchburg (Car)	A	1	2	3.12	9	9	0	0	49	44	23	17	3	20	46	.238
2002					Did Not Play—Injured												
MINOR LEAGUE TOTALS			10	5	2.66	29	29	3	0	163	137	67	48	8	45	195	.224

15. J.R. House, c

Born: Nov. 11, 1979. **Ht.:** 5-10. **Wt.:** 200. **Bats:** R. **Throws:** R. **School:** Seabreeze HS, Daytona Beach, Fla.
Career Transactions: Selected by Pirates in fifth round of 1999 draft; signed June 12, 1999.

House was the organization's top prospect the past two years but has endured two subpar seasons in Double-A along with three surgeries in 2002. House had a hernia repaired in May and a follow-up operation in June to remove related scar tissue. He had Tommy John surgery in September, which will cause him to miss at least half of this season. His elbow reconstruction ended talk that he'd play quarterback at West Virginia, a constant subject of speculation since he set national high school records with 5,526 single-season and 14,457 career passing yards (both marks were surpassed in 2002). House has a good bat with power potential. He's a fine situational hitter and is adept at taking outside pitches the other way. He has an outstanding work ethic and confident personality, which leaves little doubt he'll put in the necessary work to recover from surgery. House has been overmatched at times by Double-A pitching and occasionally become passive at the plate. He also hasn't progressed behind the plate as much as the Pirates hoped, and his elbow surgery could lead to a position change. House will head back to Altoona when healthy and likely won't catch until late in the season. He probably won't reach Pittsburgh before 2005.

Year	Club (League)	Class	AVG	G	AB	R	H	2B	3B	HR	RBI	BB	SO	SB	SLG	OBP
1999	Pirates (GCL)	R	.327	33	113	13	37	9	3	5	23	11	23	1	.593	.394
	Williamsport (NY-P)	A	.300	26	100	11	30	6	0	1	13	9	21	0	.390	.358
	Hickory (SAL)	A	.273	4	11	1	3	0	0	0	0	0	3	0	.273	.273
2000	Hickory (SAL)	A	.348	110	420	78	146	29	1	23	90	46	91	1	.586	.414
2001	Altoona (EL)	AA	.258	112	426	51	110	25	1	11	56	37	103	1	.399	.323
2002	Altoona (EL)	AA	.264	30	91	9	24	6	0	2	11	13	21	0	.396	.349
	Pirates (GCL)	R	.313	5	16	3	5	2	0	1	2	3	1	0	.625	.421
MINOR LEAGUE TOTALS			.302	320	1177	166	355	77	5	43	195	119	263	3	.485	.369

16. Zach Duke, lhp

Born: April 19, 1983. **Ht.:** 6-2. **Wt.:** 210. **Bats:** L. **Throws:** L. **School:** Midway HS, Clifton, Texas. **Career Transactions:** Selected by Pirates in 20th round of 2001 draft; signed July 31, 2001.

Duke quickly has become a lower-round find for the Pirates. He signed too late to play in the minors in 2001 but made a big impression in instructional league. After staying behind in extended spring training last year, he made his professional debut by leading the rookie-level Gulf Coast League in wins while finishing fifth in ERA. Duke has an outstanding fastball/curveball combination. His heater reaches 92 mph and should gain velocity as his body fills out. His curveball baffled the young hitters in the GCL. Duke has a great desire to learn and has an outstanding attitude. He can be inconsistent with his mechanics, causing his fastball to dip down in the 85 mph range at times. His changeup is rudimentary and he needs to refine it in order to have something slow in his arsenal. The new Pirates regime doesn't believe in rushing young players, so Duke likely will spend all of

2003 in low Class A and move up the ladder one rung at a time.

Year	Club (League)	Class	W	L	ERA	G	GS	CG	SV	IP	H	R	ER	HR	BB	SO	AVG
2002	Pirates (GCL)	R	8	1	1.95	11	11	1	0	60	38	15	13	2	18	48	.185
MINOR LEAGUE TOTALS			8	1	1.95	11	11	1	0	60	38	15	13	2	18	48	.185

17. Walter Young, 1b

Born: Feb. 18, 1980. **Ht.:** 6-5. **Wt.:** 290. **Bats:** L. **Throws:** R. **School:** Purvis (Miss.) HS. **Career Transactions:** Selected by Pirates in 31st round of 1999 draft; signed June 3, 1999.

The Pirates took a flier on Young in 1999 and persuaded him to forgo a football scholarship to play defensive end at Louisiana State. He was stuck in short-season ball for three years until being promoted in 2002 to low Class A, where he took off. Young was named Pirates minor league player of the year and South Atlantic League MVP as he led the circuit in hits, homers, total bases (277) and extra-base hits (61). Young is big and strong with light-tower power. He can pull inside pitches a mile and can take outside pitches over the fence to the opposite field. He's personable and popular in the clubhouse. Young has lost weight since turning pro but needs to shed some more pounds. He's a slow runner and a poor defensive first baseman who lacks range and proper footwork. Young got his career on track last season and his lefthanded power is intriguing. He's still a project, though, and the Pirates want to see how he does in high Class A this year.

Year	Club (League)	Class	AVG	G	AB	R	H	2B	3B	HR	RBI	BB	SO	SB	SLG	OBP
1999	Pirates (GCL)	R	.231	37	130	9	30	6	2	0	15	4	34	2	.308	.270
2000	Pirates (GCL)	R	.296	45	162	32	48	11	1	10	34	8	29	3	.562	.357
	Williamsport (NY-P)	A	.185	24	92	5	17	4	0	2	12	1	26	0	.293	.200
2001	Williamsport (NY-P)	A	.289	66	232	40	67	10	1	13	47	19	43	1	.509	.353
2002	Hickory (SAL)	A	.333	132	492	84	164	34	2	25	103	36	102	2	.563	.390
MINOR LEAGUE TOTALS			.294	304	1108	170	326	65	6	50	211	68	234	8	.499	.349

18. Matt Guerrier, rhp

Born: Aug. 2, 1978. **Ht.:** 6-3. **Wt.:** 180. **Bats:** R. **Throws:** R. **School:** Kent State University. **Career Transactions:** Selected by White Sox in 10th round of 1999 draft; signed June 17, 1999 . . . Traded by White Sox to Pirates for LHP Damaso Marte and 2B Edwin Yan, March 27, 2002.

Guerrier led the minor leagues in wins in 2001, going a combined 18-4 in Double-A and Triple-A for the White Sox. The Pirates acquired him during the final week of spring training last year in a trade for Damaso Marte and second baseman Edwin Yan. While Marte became an effective late-inning reliever in Chicago and Yan led the minors in steals, Guerrier didn't come close to duplicating his success. He did rebound to go 3-1, 2.04 in his last six starts. Guerrier has a nice feel for pitching. He knows how to mix up his offerings, change speeds and attack hitters' weaknesses. He has good command of a fastball that sinks and tops out at 92 mph. His slider is above-average. Guerrier was hurt by big innings last season and has a hard time stopping the bleeding when the opposition starts stringing hits together. He could stand to tighten his curveball and refine his changeup. Guerrier will go back to Triple-A, where he needs to improve in order to avoid getting lost in the shuffle as the Pirates stockpile pitching talent.

Year	Club (League)	Class	W	L	ERA	G	GS	CG	SV	IP	H	R	ER	HR	BB	SO	AVG
1999	Bristol (Appy)	R	5	0	1.05	21	0	0	10	26	18	9	3	1	14	37	.196
	Winston-Salem (Car)	A	0	0	5.40	4	0	0	2	3	3	2	2	0	0	5	.214
2000	Winston-Salem (Car)	A	0	3	1.30	30	0	0	19	35	25	13	5	0	12	35	.194
	Birmingham (SL)	AA	3	1	2.70	23	0	0	7	23	17	9	7	1	12	19	.207
2001	Birmingham (SL)	AA	11	3	3.10	15	15	1	0	99	85	42	34	8	32	75	.237
	Charlotte (IL)	AAA	7	1	3.54	12	12	3	0	81	75	33	32	7	18	43	.250
2002	Nashville (PCL)	AAA	7	12	4.59	27	26	2	0	157	154	88	80	20	47	130	.253
MINOR LEAGUE TOTALS			33	20	3.46	132	53	6	38	424	377	196	163	37	135	344	.238

19. Blair Johnson, rhp

Born: March 25, 1984. **Ht.:** 6-4. **Wt.:** 200. **Bats:** R. **Throws:** R. **School:** Washburn HS, Topeka, Kan. **Career Transactions:** Selected by Pirates in second round of 2002 draft; signed June 24, 2002.

Johnson was a relative unknown until having a big summer following his junior year of high school. He continued to improve as a senior, and by the time the 2002 draft rolled around, he was known by all the clubs and selected by the Pirates with the first pick of the second round. He signed for $885,000, then was limited to just three innings by a tender shoulder. Johnson has a power arm and routinely reaches 95 mph with his fastball. He also has an above-average curveball and a changeup that has the makings of being a solid third pitch. Johnson basically had a lost summer last year, missing out on valuable experience. He needs innings as he's still raw in some of the finer points of the games, such as learning to work hitters. While Johnson's shoulder woes aren't considered serious, they do raise a red flag and the Pirates will take it slow with him. He probably will repeat Rookie ball this year before pitching in a full-season league in 2004.

Year	Club (League)	Class	W	L	ERA	G	GS	CG	SV	IP	H	R	ER	HR	BB	SO	AVG
2002	Pirates (GCL)	R	0	1	8.10	2	1	0	0	3	4	6	3	0	3	4	.286
MINOR LEAGUE TOTALS			0	1	8.10	2	1	0	0	3	4	6	3	0	3	4	.286

20. Alex Hart, rhp

Born: Jan. 10, 1980. **Ht.:** 6-6. **Wt.:** 220. **Bats:** R. **Throws:** R. **School:** University of Florida. **Career Transactions:** Selected by Pirates in fifth round of 2002 draft; signed June 15, 2002.

Drafted by the Orioles in the second round out of high school in 1998, Hart didn't sign and later blew out his elbow at Florida. Tommy John surgery cost him most of 2000 and he struggled as a redshirt sophomore in 2001. Armed with a new cut fastball, he blossomed last year, going 13-3 for the Gators and winning his first seven pro decisions while finishing third in the New York-Penn League in ERA. He tied up NY-P hitters with his slow, big-breaking curveball and improved his changeup, making his average fastball look better. Hart is lauded for his makeup and doesn't rattle in tight situations. He has lost some zip off his fastball since having surgery. It usually tops out around 90 mph. He tends to get under his curveball at times, and he must stay on top of it to get the 12-to-6 movement necessary for it to be a dominant pitch. Hart has an advanced knowledge of pitching and could move quickly. He'll begin this season in low Class A but should be knocking on the door to the majors sometime in 2005.

Year	Club (League)	Class	W	L	ERA	G	GS	CG	SV	IP	H	R	ER	HR	BB	SO	AVG
2002	Williamsport (NY-P)	A	7	0	1.85	15	10	0	2	68	52	15	14	1	20	73	.211
MINOR LEAGUE TOTALS			7	0	1.85	15	10	0	2	68	52	15	14	1	20	73	.211

21. Nate McLouth, of

Born: Oct. 28, 1981. **Ht.:** 5-11. **Wt.:** 170. **Bats:** L. **Throws:** R. **School:** Whitehall (Mich.) HS. **Career Transactions:** Selected by Pirates in 25th round of 2000 draft; signed Aug. 29, 2000.

McLouth was Michigan's Mr. Baseball in 2000. The Pirates gambled a 25th-round pick on him that year and lured him away from a scholarship to Michigan. He went straight to low Class A to make his pro debut in 2001, a rare leap for such a young player. McLouth is a high-energy guy who gets his uniform dirty on a daily basis and often draws comparisons to Lenny Dykstra. He makes consistent contact, is tough to strike out and has at least moderate power potential. He has plus speed and is good enough defensively to play center field, though left was his primary position last season. McLouth is a leadoff hitter in the making but needs to develop more patience at the plate to excel at that job. He tends to try to pull everything and must learn to hit outside pitches the opposite way. McLouth has climbed the ladder rapidly, so the Pirates may slow him down by sending him back to high Class A to start 2003.

Year	Club (League)	Class	AVG	G	AB	R	H	2B	3B	HR	RBI	BB	SO	SB	SLG	OBP
2001	Hickory (SAL)	A	.285	96	351	59	100	17	5	12	54	43	54	21	.464	.371
2002	Lynchburg (Car)	A	.244	114	393	58	96	23	4	9	46	41	48	20	.392	.324
MINOR LEAGUE TOTALS			.263	210	744	117	196	40	9	21	100	84	102	41	.426	.347

22. Leo Nunez, rhp

Born: Aug. 14, 1983. **Ht.:** 6-1. **Wt.:** 150. **Bats:** R. **Throws:** R. **Career Transactions:** Signed out of Dominican Republic by Pirates, Feb. 16, 2000.

Nunez burst onto the scene in 2000, going 5-3, 2.19 in 14 starts in the Rookie-level Dominican Summer League after signing that February. He was slow to adjust to the United States in 2001 and repeated the Gulf Coast League last year. Nunez throws hard, his fastball topping out at 96 mph and averaging 94. He has a smooth delivery and the ball appears to jump out of his hand as it gets on top of hitters in a hurry. Nunez has the potential to throw even harder once his body matures, but he needs to get over his reluctance to throw anything but his fastball. The Pirates want him to learn a breaking pitch and changeup but he's hesitant. Nunez obviously will need to add at least one more pitch and gain strength. His command has been impressive, though it remains to be seen how well he'll throw his secondary pitches for strikes. It's not out of the question that Nunez will stay in extended spring this year before reporting to short-season ball in June.

Year	Club (League)	Class	W	L	ERA	G	GS	CG	SV	IP	H	R	ER	HR	BB	SO	AVG
2000	Pirates (DSL)	R	5	3	2.19	14	14	1	0	86	69	26	21	0	27	82	—
2001	Pirates (GCL)	R	2	2	4.39	10	7	1	0	53	62	28	26	4	9	34	.284

2002	Pirates (GCL)	R	4	2	3.43	11	11	0	0	60	54	23	23	5	5	52	.238
	Hickory (SAL)	A	0	0	0.00	1	1	0	0	4	5	0	0	0	3	1	.333
MINOR LEAGUE TOTALS			11	7	3.09	36	33	2	0	204	190	77	70	9	44	169	—

23. Mike Connolly, lhp

Born: June 2, 1982. **Ht.:** 6-0. **Wt.:** 160. **Bats:** L. **Throws:** L. **School:** Oneonta (N.Y.) HS. **Career Transactions:** Selected by Pirates in 19th round of 2000 draft; signed June 9, 2000.

Connolly didn't get a lot of exposure in high school because he pitched in upstate New York. Nevertheless, he passed up a scholarship to East Carolina to sign as a 19th-round pick, and he has made swift progress as a pro. He pitched in high Class A last year as a teenager and drew comparisons to touted Lynchburg teammate Sean Burnett. Connolly doesn't have exceptional stuff but he's intelligent and a quick learner. He has a good idea of how to pitch and above-average command of four pitches: a fastball that usually tops out at 90 mph but has good movement, a curveball, slider and changeup. Connolly is on the smallish side and probably won't add much velocity to his fastball. His slight build also leaves some concern about his long-term durability as a starter. Connolly has met every challenge so far and will get a chance to tackle Double-A this season.

Year	Club (League)	Class	W	L	ERA	G	GS	CG	SV	IP	H	R	ER	HR	BB	SO	AVG
2000	Pirates (GCL)	R	1	2	2.29	11	0	0	2	20	20	6	5	0	6	25	.267
2001	Hickory (SAL)	A	11	7	3.94	33	15	2	0	121	116	59	53	10	41	107	.256
2002	Lynchburg (Car)	A	10	3	2.94	29	19	0	0	122	111	46	40	5	46	100	.251
MINOR LEAGUE TOTALS			22	12	3.35	73	34	2	2	263	247	111	98	15	93	232	.254

24. Chris Duffy, of

Born: April 20, 1980. **Ht.:** 5-10. **Wt.:** 180. **Bats:** B. **Throws:** L. **School:** Arizona State University. **Career Transactions:** Selected by Pirates in eighth round of 2001 draft; signed June 8, 2001.

The Pirates moved few players two levels in the farm system last season, but Duffy was an exception. He jumped to high Class A to begin 2002 after earning all-star honors in the short-season New York-Penn League in his pro debut. Following a slow start, Duffy shone in the Carolina League as he finished second in hits, third in runs and seven in batting. He's a scrapper and hustles all the time, routinely taking the extra base and diving for balls. He's an outstanding defensive center fielder with great instincts, above-average range and a decent arm. Duffy has a good line-drive stroke with power potential. He would be the prototypical leadoff hitter, except for one fundamental problem: He strikes out too much and rarely walks. Duffy needs to develop a better eye at the plate. If he does, he has the ability to be a .300 hitter in the majors. Duffy is moving fast and a major league debut sometime in 2004 isn't out of the question. His progress hinges on his ability to command the strike zone.

Year	Club (League)	Class	AVG	G	AB	R	H	2B	3B	HR	RBI	BB	SO	SB	SLG	OBP
2001	Williamsport (NY-P)	A	.317	64	221	50	70	12	4	1	24	33	33	30	.421	.440
2002	Lynchburg (Car)	A	.301	132	539	85	162	27	5	10	52	33	101	22	.425	.353
MINOR LEAGUE TOTALS			.305	196	760	135	232	39	9	11	76	66	134	52	.424	.380

25. Carlos Rivera, 1b

Born: June 20, 1978. **Ht.:** 5-11. **Wt.:** 230. **Bats:** L. **Throws:** L. **School:** Rio Grande (P.R.) HS. **Career Transactions:** Selected by Pirates in 10th round of 1996 draft; signed June 6, 1996.

Rivera made painfully slow progress through the Pirates system before bursting through in Double-A last year during his seventh pro season. In his second year in the Eastern League, he made the postseason all-star team as he finished second in home runs and 10th in batting. Rivera went through a rigorous conditioning program following the 2001 season, losing 25 pounds while adding upper-body strength. That enabled him to gain both power and bat speed, and he obliterated his previous career high of 13 homers. Rivera also is an outstanding fielder with great hands, good range for a big man and a knack for turning the 3-6-3 double play. He still has problems commanding the strike zone and needs to take an occasional walk. He's a slow runner who goes station to station and is a prime candidate to hit into a double play. The Pirates added Rivera to the 40-man roster at the end of last season and would like him to spend this year in Triple-A. However, he could land in the majors at some point in 2003 because the Pirates have a glaring need for power.

Year	Club (League)	Class	AVG	G	AB	R	H	2B	3B	HR	RBI	BB	SO	SB	SLG	OBP
1996	Pirates (GCL)	R	.284	48	183	24	52	8	3	3	26	15	22	1	.410	.338
1997	Augusta (SAL)	A	.272	120	415	52	113	16	5	9	65	19	82	4	.400	.316
1998	Augusta (SAL)	A	.285	87	316	38	90	17	1	5	53	11	46	3	.392	.318
	Lynchburg (Car)	A	.230	29	113	11	26	4	0	4	16	0	19	0	.372	.235

Year	Club (League)	Class	AVG	G	AB	R	H	2B	3B	HR	RBI	BB	SO	SB	SLG	OBP
1999	Hickory (SAL)	A	.322	119	457	63	147	30	1	13	86	15	45	2	.477	.355
2000	Lynchburg (Car)	A	.270	64	233	20	63	17	0	5	47	6	34	0	.408	.284
	Pirates (GCL)	R	.292	6	24	2	7	0	0	0	0	1	2	0	.292	.320
2001	Altoona (EL)	AA	.234	111	389	44	91	30	0	10	50	13	71	0	.388	.258
2002	Altoona (EL)	AA	.302	128	494	67	149	28	2	22	84	27	75	1	.500	.345
MINOR LEAGUE TOTALS			.281	712	2624	321	738	150	12	71	427	107	396	11	.429	.316

26. Vic Buttler, of

Born: Aug. 12, 1980. **Ht.:** 6-0. **Wt.:** 160. **Bats:** L. **Throws:** L. **School:** El Camino (Calif.) JC. **Career Transactions:** Selected by Pirates in 14th round of 2000 draft; signed June 21, 2000.

Buttler signed with the University of Arkansas out of high school but went to El Camino JC after breaking a hamate bone as a freshman. He repeated low Class A last season, his third year in pro ball, and performed solidly. Buttler is a great athlete who is beginning to translate his raw tools into baseball skills. He's outstanding defensively with tremendous range in center field, particularly coming in on balls. He didn't commit an error last season until August. He also has plus speed and is learning how to use it on the bases. Though he made strides as a hitter last year, Buttler can be a little overeager at times and get himself out on pitcher's pitches. While he puts the ball in play consistently and has power potential, he'll need to walk more to keep hitting at the top of the order. Buttler showed improvement last season and the Pirates are anxious to see how he handles high Class A this year.

Year	Club (League)	Class	AVG	G	AB	R	H	2B	3B	HR	RBI	BB	SO	SB	SLG	OBP
2000	Pirates (GCL)	R	.133	4	15	1	2	0	0	0	1	1	0	0	.133	.188
	Williamsport (NY-P)	A	.298	36	131	22	39	3	2	1	9	9	13	9	.374	.383
2001	Hickory (SAL)	A	.244	92	299	38	73	10	2	2	23	15	49	11	.311	.287
2002	Hickory (SAL)	A	.285	124	460	77	131	15	3	7	64	45	65	30	.376	.353
MINOR LEAGUE TOTALS			.271	256	905	138	245	28	7	10	105	76	127	50	.350	.334

27. Henry Owens, rhp

Born: April 23, 1979. **Ht.:** 6-3. **Wt.:** 230. **Bats:** R. **Throws:** R. **School:** Barry (Fla.) University. **Career Transactions:** Signed as nondrafted free agent by Pirates, June 7, 2001.

Owens truly has been a diamond in the rough. He was a catcher at NCAA Division II Barry when the Pirates signed him as a nondrafted free agent in 2001. They loved his strong arm and immediately converted him into a pitcher. Owens has dominated ever since and led Williamsport in saves last season. His fastball has been clocked as high as 98 mph and routinely sits at 95, though it will sometimes dip to 91 when his mechanics break down. He likes the challenge of closing games. Owens often short-arms the ball and his delivery needs work, not surprising for a pitcher with so little experience. His curveball tends to be too flat and he might be better served learning a slider. Owens is an intriguing case as he has as much raw talent as anyone in the system. He has "future closer" stamped all over him but is unpolished on the mound. He won't be rushed.

Year	Club (League)	Class	W	L	ERA	G	GS	CG	SV	IP	H	R	ER	HR	BB	SO	AVG
2001	Pirates (GCL)	R	1	0	1.29	6	0	0	1	7	5	1	1	0	2	8	.192
2002	Williamsport (NY-P)	A	0	3	2.62	23	0	0	7	45	26	18	13	4	16	63	.166
MINOR LEAGUE TOTALS			1	3	2.44	29	0	0	8	52	31	19	14	4	18	71	.169

28. Josh Bonifay, of/2b

Born: July 30, 1978. **Ht.:** 6-0. **Wt.:** 180. **Bats:** R. **Throws:** R. **School:** UNC Wilmington. **Career Transactions:** Selected by Pirates in 24th round of 1999 draft; signed June 5, 1999.

The son of former Pirates general manager and current Devil Rays farm/scouting director Cam Bonifay, Josh had a breakthrough year in 2002 for the organization that fired his father the previous summer. He led the Carolina League in homers, RBIs and extra-base hits (63). Bonifay has a live bat with power and crushes mistake pitches. He improved his plate discipline last season. As the son of a baseball man, he has a good feel for the nuances of the game. Bonifay isn't a good defensive player, however, as he lacks range and has a below-average arm. The Pirates moved him from second base to left field for the final month of last season. While his performance opened some eyes, he also was repeating the Carolina League and was old for high Class A. Bonifay will play left field in Double-A this season and go as far as his bat will take him. His best bet at a major league career is as a utility player with some thump in his bat.

Year	Club (League)	Class	AVG	G	AB	R	H	2B	3B	HR	RBI	BB	SO	SB	SLG	OBP
1999	Williamsport (NY-P)	A	.260	52	200	42	52	10	2	4	17	25	55	2	.390	.348
2000	Hickory (SAL)	A	.281	106	377	62	106	17	2	14	62	48	104	11	.448	.364
2001	Hickory (SAL)	A	.323	17	65	10	21	4	0	2	10	5	15	2	.477	.380
	Lynchburg (Car)	A	.297	85	323	42	96	14	1	13	41	26	87	5	.467	.355

2002	Lynchburg (Car)	A	.307	126	463	83	142	36	1	26	102	63	97	3	.557	.388
MINOR LEAGUE TOTALS			.292	386	1428	239	417	81	6	59	232	167	358	23	.481	.369

29. Shawn Garrett, of

Born: Nov. 2, 1978. **Ht.:** 6-3. **Wt.:** 190. **Bats:** B. **Throws:** R. **School:** Olney Central (Ill.) JC. **Career Transactions:** Selected by Padres in 29th round of 1997 draft; signed May 27, 1998 . . . Traded by Padres with RHP Shawn Camp to Pirates for OF Emil Brown, July 10, 2001.

The Pirates acquired Garrett and reliever Shawn Camp from San Diego in a July 2001 trade for outfielder Emil Brown, whom they had designated for assignment. While the deal didn't generate much publicity, it could turn out to be a steal for Pittsburgh. Garrett turned in a fine season and played in the Double-A all-star game in 2002. He has an outstanding work ethic and is always one of the first players to the park each day. He's a good competitor and enjoys hitting in RBI situations. Garrett has a consistent stroke from both sides of the plate, though he flashes more power lefthanded. He can play all three outfield spots but is only an adequate defender with a slightly below-average arm. He needs to show more power to play every day in the outfield in the majors. Though Garrett steals some bases, he possesses only average speed. He opened eyes last season and will get the chance to prove himself again this year in Triple-A. He could win a bench job in Pittsburgh in 2004.

Year	Club (League)	Class	AVG	G	AB	R	H	2B	3B	HR	RBI	BB	SO	SB	SLG	OBP
1998	Padres (AZL)	R	.333	49	186	36	62	13	2	0	29	16	36	5	.425	.393
1999	Idaho Falls (Pio)	R	.307	53	192	46	59	14	1	7	33	21	46	5	.500	.384
2000	Fort Wayne (Mid)	A	.272	123	438	59	119	28	3	10	55	47	79	6	.418	.341
2001	Lake Elsinore (Cal)	A	.313	77	275	41	86	16	8	7	44	24	57	16	.505	.373
	Lynchburg (Car)	A	.294	52	194	28	57	13	0	9	28	17	64	6	.500	.360
2002	Altoona (EL)	AA	.290	131	489	71	142	24	8	11	73	33	88	19	.440	.342
MINOR LEAGUE TOTALS			.296	485	1774	281	525	108	22	44	262	158	370	57	.456	.359

30. Jason Sharber, rhp

Born: Feb. 24, 1982. **Ht.:** 6-3. **Wt.:** 220. **Bats:** R. **Throws:** R. **School:** Oakland HS, Mufreesboro, Tenn. **Career Transactions:** Selected by Pirates in fifth round of 2000 draft; signed Aug. 29, 2000.

Jeffrey Jason Sharber has had an identity crisis since entering pro ball. He goes by Jason, though many sources continue to refer to him as Jeff. Sharber was considered a tough sign because of a scholarship from Vanderbilt, which is why he fell to the fifth round in 2000. When the Pirates failed to sign fourth-rounder Patrick Boyd (who went to Clemson and is now with the Rangers), they used that money to sign Sharber and 25th-rounder Nate McLouth. Sharber has an outstanding curveball for a young pitcher, as it buckles knees and serves as his out pitch. He also has a good changeup and throw strikes. Sharber's fastball is only average at this stage and lacks movement. He also throws a slider, though the Pirates may have him ditch it in order to concentrate more on his curve. Sharber has a tendency to get heavy and must continually stay on top of his conditioning. He went 56 days without a win toward the end of last season, so he may need more time at the high Class A level.

Year	Club (League)	Class	W	L	ERA	G	GS	CG	SV	IP	H	R	ER	HR	BB	SO	AVG
2001	Pirates (GCL)	R	1	0	0.50	3	3	0	0	18	5	1	1	1	4	19	.091
	Hickory (SAL)	A	2	2	1.99	7	7	0	0	45	34	13	10	2	19	57	.207
2002	Lynchburg (Car)	A	7	6	3.71	22	21	0	0	104	109	52	43	7	37	96	.270
MINOR LEAGUE TOTALS			10	8	2.90	32	31	0	0	168	148	66	54	10	60	172	.238

ST. LOUIS
CARDINALS

TOP 30 PROSPECTS

1. Dan Haren, rhp
2. Jimmy Journell, rhp
3. Chris Narveson, lhp
4. Justin Pope, rhp
5. Blake Hawksworth, rhp
6. Shaun Boyd, 2b
7. Rhett Parrott, rhp
8. John Nelson, ss
9. Tyler Johnson, lhp
10. Yadier Molina, c
11. Scotty Layfield, rhp
12. Kyle Boyer, ss/2b
13. John Gall, 1b
14. Travis Hanson, 3b
15. David Williamson, lhp
16. Gabe Johnson, 3b
17. Reid Gorecki, of
18. Shane Reedy, rhp
19. John Santor, 1b
20. John Novinsky, rhp
21. Josh Pearce, rhp
22. Dee Haynes, of
23. Skip Schumaker, of
24. Tyler Adamczyk, rhp
25. Josh Axelson, rhp
26. Rick Asadoorian, of
27. Nick Stocks, rhp
28. Chance Caple, rhp
29. Chris Duncan, 1b
30. So Taguchi, of

By Will Lingo

In recent years, the Cardinals have consistently ranked near the bottom of Baseball America's rankings of minor league talent. They've also finished first in the National League Central for three straight years, so they're obviously doing something right.

Like the Giants, the Cardinals have been at least as successful using minor league players in trades to bring in major league veterans as developing their own major leaguers. General manager Walt Jocketty's approach generally has been to hold on to a few of the best prospects but willingly trade any of the others.

The results are hard to argue with. Such players as Jim Edmonds, Edgar Renteria and Scott Rolen have come in at the cost of such prospects as Adam Kennedy, Pablo Ozuna, Braden Looper and Bud Smith. It's hard to find a case when you think the Cardinals wouldn't make the same deals again in a heartbeat.

Similarly, the prospects the Cardinals haven't traded have generally panned out, with J.D. Drew, Matt Morris and Albert Pujols as the best examples. One notable failure has been Rick Ankiel, perhaps the organization's most promising prospect of the last decade, whose control left a couple of years ago and shows no signs of returning.

Of course, Ankiel's struggles were the least of the organization's worries in 2002. Aside from Ankiel, the Cardinals had to deal with a worse-than-usual rash of injuries to their pitching staff. Then staff leader Darry Kile, 33, died in his sleep in a Chicago hotel room in June. That was only days after franchise icon Jack Buck passed away at 77.

Somehow, the Cardinals overcame all that, winning 26 of their final 33 games. Manager Tony La Russa used 14 different pitchers in a patchwork rotation, with Morris the ace in spite of his injuries. Pujols led the offense again, and Jocketty made his annual contribution, bringing in Chuck Finley to bolster the rotation and Rolen to bolster the lineup.

When Rolen was injured in the Division Series win over the Diamondbacks, the starch finally went out of the Cardinals and they lost to the Giants in the NL Championship Series. Rolen signed a long-term deal after the season, however, and there's no reason to think the Cardinals won't be back in the playoffs. Though the farm system still looks thin, the organization will use it to fill holes in the big leagues again, one way or another.

Organization Overview

General Manager: Walt Jocketty. **Farm Director:** Bruce Manno. **Scouting Director:** Marty Maier.

2002 PERFORMANCE

Class	Farm Team	League	W	L	Pct.	Finish*	Manager
Majors	St. Louis	National	97	65	.599	3rd (16)	Tony La Russa
Triple-A	Memphis Redbirds	Pacific Coast	71	71	.500	10th (16)	Gaylen Pitts
Double-A	†New Haven Ravens	Eastern	74	65	.532	5th (12)	Mark DeJohn
High A	#Potomac Cannons	Carolina	59	81	.421	6th (8)	Joe Cunningham
Low A	Peoria Chiefs	Midwest	85	53	.616	+1st (14)	Danny Sheaffer
Short-season	New Jersey Cardinals	New York-Penn	39	37	.513	6th (14)	Tommy Shields
Rookie	Johnson City Cardinals	Appalachian	29	38	.433	7th (10)	Brian Rupp
OVERALL MINOR LEAGUE RECORD			357	345	.509	15th (30)	

*Finish in overall standings (No. of teams in league). +League champion. †Affiliate will be in Tennessee (Southern) in 2003. #Affiliate will be in Palm Beach (Florida State) in 2003.

ORGANIZATION LEADERS

BATTING
Minimum 250 At-Bats

*AVG	John Gall, New Haven	.316
R	Shaun Boyd, Peoria	91
H	John Gall, New Haven	166
TB	John Gall, New Haven	277
2B	John Gall, New Haven	45
3B	Reid Gorecki, New Jersey	13
HR	Ivan Cruz, Memphis	35
RBI	Ivan Cruz, Memphis	100
BB	Johnny Hernandez, Potomac	67
SO	Tim Lemon, Peoria	165
SB	Chris Morris, Potomac	55

PITCHING
#Minimum 75 Innings

W	Tyler Johnson, Peoria	15
L	B.R. Cook, New Haven	13
#ERA	Rich Burgess, Potomac/Peoria	2.72
G	Jason Karnuth, Memphis/New Haven	59
CG	Rhett Parrott, New Haven/Potomac	5
SV	Scotty Layfield, New Haven	24
IP	Dan Haren, Potomac/Peoria	194
BB	Les Walrond, Memphis/New Haven	73
SO	Dan Haren, Potomac/Peoria	171

BEST TOOLS

Best Hitter for Average	John Gall
Best Power Hitter	Dee Haynes
Fastest Baserunner	Kyle Boyer
Best Athlete	John Nelson
Best Fastball	Shane Reedy
Best Curveball	Tyler Johnson
Best Slider	Matt Duff
Best Changeup	Blake Hawksworth
Best Control	Dan Haren
Best Defensive Catcher	Yadier Molina
Best Defensive Infielder	John Nelson
Best Infield Arm	John Nelson
Best Defensive Outfielder	Rick Asadoorian
Best Outfield Arm	Rick Asadoorian

PROJECTED 2006 LINEUP

Catcher	Yadier Molina
First Base	John Gall
Second Base	Shaun Boyd
Third Base	Scott Rolen
Shortstop	Edgar Renteria
Left Field	Albert Pujols
Center Field	Jim Edmonds
Right Field	J.D. Drew
No. 1 Starter	Matt Morris
No. 2 Starter	Dan Haren

Reid Gorecki

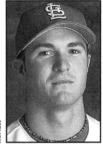

Scotty Layfield

No. 3 Starter	Jim Journell
No. 4 Starter	Chris Narveson
No. 5 Starter	Blake Hawksworth
Closer	Jason Isringhausen

TOP PROSPECTS OF THE DECADE

1993	Allen Watson, lhp
1994	Brian Barber, rhp
1995	Alan Benes, rhp
1996	Alan Benes, rhp
1997	Matt Morris, rhp
1998	Rick Ankiel, lhp
1999	J.D. Drew, of
2000	Rick Ankiel, lhp
2001	Bud Smith, lhp
2002	Jimmy Journell, rhp

TOP DRAFT PICKS OF THE DECADE

1993	Alan Benes, rhp
1994	Bret Wagner, lhp
1995	Matt Morris, rhp
1996	Braden Looper, rhp
1997	Adam Kennedy, ss
1998	J.D. Drew, of
1999	Chance Caple, rhp
2000	Shaun Boyd, of
2001	Justin Pope, rhp
2002	Calvin Hayes, ss (3)

ALL-TIME LARGEST BONUSES

J.D. Drew, 1998	$3,000,000
Rick Ankiel, 1997	$2,500,000
Chad Hutchinson, 1998	$2,300,000
Shaun Boyd, 2000	$1,750,000
Braden Looper, 1996	$1,675,000

MinorLeague**Depth**Chart

ST. LOUIS CARDINALS

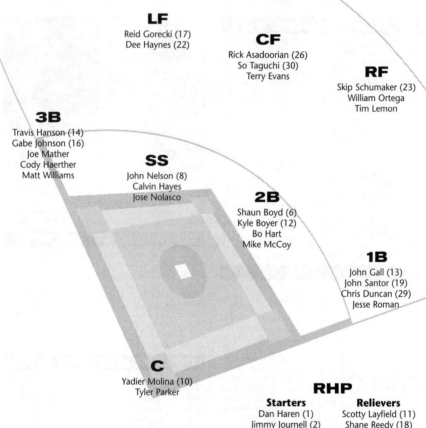

28 RANK

St. Louis' depth has improved only marginally over the last few years, and 2002 did little to change that. Though they lacked first- and second-round picks last year because of free-agent compensation, the Cardinals signed a first-round talent, Blake Hawksworth, to a $1.475 million draft-and-follow deal before the draft. Most of the organization's top pitching prospects have had their progress stunted by injuries, but the biggest hope in the system is riding on young arms like Dan Haren, Jimmy Journell, Chris Narveson, Justin Pope and Hawksworth. There is a distinct absence of impact bats in the organization.

Note: Depth charts prepared by Josh Boyd. Numbers in parentheses indicate prospect rankings.

LF
Reid Gorecki (17)
Dee Haynes (22)

CF
Rick Asadoorian (26)
So Taguchi (30)
Terry Evans

RF
Skip Schumaker (23)
William Ortega
Tim Lemon

3B
Travis Hanson (14)
Gabe Johnson (16)
Joe Mather
Cody Haerther
Matt Williams

SS
John Nelson (8)
Calvin Hayes
Jose Nolasco

2B
Shaun Boyd (6)
Kyle Boyer (12)
Bo Hart
Mike McCoy

1B
John Gall (13)
John Santor (19)
Chris Duncan (29)
Jesse Roman

C
Yadier Molina (10)
Tyler Parker

LHP

Starters	Relievers
Chris Narveson (3)	Ben Julianel
Tyler Johnson (9)	Josh Brey
David Williamson (15)	
Les Walrond	

RHP

Starters	Relievers
Dan Haren (1)	Scotty Layfield (11)
Jimmy Journell (2)	Shane Reedy (18)
Justin Pope (4)	John Novinsky (20)
Blake Hawksworth (5)	Josh Axelson (25)
Rhett Parrott (7)	Jeremy Lambert
Josh Pearce (21)	Matt Duff
Tyler Adamczyk (24)	Kevin Joseph
Nick Stocks (27)	Gabe Molina
Chance Caple (28)	Roberto Batista
Cristobal Correa	
Wilson Ciprian	
Julio Villalon	
Cheyenne Janke	

DraftAnalysis

2002 Draft

Best Pro Debut: OF Reid Gorecki (13) hit .281-8-52 with 22 steals and led the short-season New York-Penn League with 55 runs and 13 triples. 2B Mike McCoy (34) was a Rookie-level Appalachian League all-star after hitting .312-4-22 with 18 steals. OFs Matt Lemanczyk (10) and Joey Vandever (43) couldn't hit .240 but each was able to steal 31 bases to lead the Appy League and NY-P.

Best Athlete: SS Calvin Hayes (3), St. Louis' top pick, is compared to Ray Durham and was a star tailback for his high school football team. SS **Kyle Boyer** (4) shows glimpses of all five tools and re-established himself after playing little in the previous three years. He sat on Kansas State's bench in 1999, then went on a Mormon mission.

Best Pure Hitter: Hayes or 3B Travis Hanson (9), who batted .294-4-40 in the NY-P.

Best Raw Power: C Tyler Parker (8), though he may have to shorten his swing to make more contact.

Fastest Runner: Hayes and Lemanczyk are both 6.5-second runners in the 60-yard dash. Lemanczyk is more of a long strider, while Hayes is more compact.

Best Defensive Player: Gorecki or McCoy.

Best Fastball: Draft-and-follow RHP Shane Reedy has the best fastball in the organization, throwing 95-97 mph. Another draft-and-follow, RHP Blake Hawksworth, showed a 93-94 mph fastball after signing for $1.475 million. The best arm the Cardinals got from the 2002 draft was RHP David Brockman (11), who has a 90-91 mph heater.

Best Breaking Ball: LHP David Williamson's (7) curveball.

Most Intriguing Background: Unsigned 1B/OF Chris Gibson's (47) father Bob had a Hall of Fame career with the Cardinals. Lemanczyk's father Dave was an all-star pitcher for the Blue Jays. 2B Melvin Falu (28) is a cousin of Royals second baseman Luis Alicea, who was originally signed by St. Louis scouting director Marty Maier.

RICH ABEL

Boyer

Closest To The Majors: Williamson or Gorecki, though neither is on the fast track.

Best Late-Round Pick: Gorecki was solid in all phases and could be an enticing lead-off man if he tightens his strike zone.

The One Who Got Away: C Josh Bell (5) has a powerful bat and arm. Several schools recruited him as a pitcher, but he'll focus on catching at Auburn. RHP Chad Clark (17), who transferred from Southern California to Fresno State, has a live arm but little command. He could be a first-round pick next year if he can find the plate, but that may be asking too much.

Assessment: The Cardinals didn't have picks in the first two rounds, reached a little to take Hayes in the third and didn't sign their fifth-rounder. Landing Hawksworth and Reedy helps make up for failing to sign a high-ceiling pitcher from the draft.

2001 Draft

The first two picks—RHPs Justin Pope (1) and Dan Haren (2)—helped restock a thin farm system. So did three later finds, SS John Nelson (8) and RHPs Rhett Parrott (9) and Blake Hawksworth (23, draft-and-follow).   **Grade: B**

2000 Draft

This crop looked better before RHP Blake Williams (1) and LHP Chris Narveson (2) got hurt, then Williams was lost in the Rule 5 draft. Many of the system's better position players came from this group, led by 2B Shaun Boyd (1) and C Yadier Molina (4).   **Grade: C+**

1999 Draft

All three first-rounders, RHPs Chance Caple and Nick Stocks plus 1B Chris Duncan, have been hurt and/or disappointing. But OF Albert Pujols (13) has driven in 257 runs in two major league seasons and RHP Jimmy Journell (4) is one of their best prospects.   **Grade: A**

1998 Draft

OF J.D. Drew (1) might not be a superstar, but he's very good. LHP Bud Smith (4) and SS Jack Wilson (9) showed promise before getting traded. RHP Chad Hutchinson (2) jumped to the NFL. RHP Ben Diggins (1) didn't sign and was a first-rounder again two years later. **Grade: B+**

Note: Draft analysis prepared by Jim Callis. Numbers in parentheses indicate draft rounds.

. . . Haren's biggest strength is that he has no glaring weakness.

Dan
Haren rhp

Born: Sept. 17, 1980.
Ht.: 6-5. **Wt.:** 220.
Bats: R. **Throws:** R.
School: Pepperdine University.
Career Transactions: Selected by Cardinals in second round of 2001 draft; signed June 20, 2001.

Haren came out of Pepperdine in 2001 with teammate Noah Lowry, a lefthander who was drafted ahead of him but endured a season of shoulder problems in 2002. Haren, meanwhile, led the minor leagues in innings and jumped up the Cardinals' prospect list. He was West Coast Conference player of the year his junior season at Pepperdine, where he also was a DH. Haren showed flashes in his first professional summer but wore down, losing 15-20 pounds in the process. There was no such problem last season. Haren was a workhorse and finished the year with 22 quality starts in 28 games. He opened as the ace of the staff at Peoria, which featured many of the organization's most promising prospects and won the Midwest League title. But he quickly earned a promotion to high Class A Potomac, where he held his own for a mediocre team.

Haren's biggest strength is that he has no glaring weakness. At 6-foot-4 he has the frame of a workhorse and clean mechanics. He has three solid pitches and can command them all, and his big body allows him to generate a good downward plane on his pitches. His fastball is 88-92 mph, with a lot of 90s and 91s, and he can occasionally touch the mid-90s. He got better tilt on his slider last season and used his changeup more. He also throws a splitter that was one of his better pitches in college, though the Cardinals asked him to keep it in his back pocket for now. If he brings it back, it would be another effective weapon. Haren works quickly and pitches inside, going after hitters with a good understanding of how to attack their weaknesses. He also has a little bit of funk in his delivery, which creates deception.

Haren tired at the end of the season, understandable under a 194-inning workload. The organization says its goal is to protect arms while getting pitchers to the big leagues, and that Haren's frame and mechanics allowed him to pile up more innings than another pitcher might. Given the organization's injury history, though, that bears watching. Otherwise, he just needs experience against more advanced hitters. He still projects as a middle-of-the-rotation starter, but now it looks like Haren will reach the big leagues more quickly than expected. He'll open the season in Double-A and could move up if he pitches well there.

Year	Club (League)	Class	W	L	ERA	G	GS	CG	SV	IP	H	R	ER	HR	BB	SO	AVG
2001	New Jersey (NY-P)	A	3	3	3.10	12	8	0	1	52	47	22	18	6	8	57	.239
2002	Peoria (Mid)	A	7	3	1.95	14	14	1	0	102	89	32	22	6	12	89	.234
	Potomac (Car)	A	3	6	3.62	14	14	1	0	92	90	43	37	8	19	82	.252
MINOR LEAGUE TOTALS			13	12	2.82	40	36	2	1	246	226	97	77	20	39	228	.242

2. Jimmy Journell

Born: Dec. 29, 1977. **Ht.:** 6-4. **Wt.:** 200. **Bats:** R. **Throws:** R. **School:** University of Illinois. **Career Transactions:** Selected by Cardinals in fourth round of 1999 draft; signed Aug. 12, 1999.

Journell bounced back beautifully from Tommy John surgery just before the draft in 1999, becoming the organization's pitcher of the year in 2001 and top prospect a year ago. He took a small step back last year, opening the season in extended spring after having bone chips removed from his elbow, then getting shut down at Triple-A Memphis because of weakness in the back of his shoulder. Journell still has the great arm and pitches that made him a prospect: an electric fastball that was 91-94 mph last year, a hard slider and an improved changeup. He goes after hitters and showed good command in Double-A before his shoulder started bothering him. The Cardinals just want to see consistency from Journell. His arm slot has moved between where he's comfortable (low three-quarters) and where the organization would like him (a bit higher). When the old mechanics caused him pain and the new ones didn't, he went back where the Cardinals moved him. The higher arm slot also keeps Journell on top of his slider. The organization doesn't want to rush Journell and would like to see him stay healthy and dominate at Triple-A for a season before he breaks into the big leagues. But if he pitches well early and there's a need, he could be the first pitcher called. It's still possible he could end up in the bullpen if his arm doesn't hold up to starting, but that's on the back burner for now.

Year	Club (League)	Class	W	L	ERA	G	GS	CG	SV	IP	H	R	ER	HR	BB	SO	AVG
2000	New Jersey (NY-P)	A	1	0	1.97	13	1	0	0	32	12	12	7	0	24	39	.111
2001	Potomac (Car)	A	14	6	2.50	26	26	0	0	151	121	54	42	8	42	156	.220
	New Haven (EL)	AA	1	0	0.00	1	1	1	0	7	0	0	0	0	3	6	.000
2002	New Haven (EL)	AA	3	3	2.70	10	10	2	0	67	50	22	20	3	18	66	.206
	Memphis (PCL)	AAA	2	4	3.68	7	7	0	0	37	38	16	15	3	18	32	.264
MINOR LEAGUE TOTALS			21	13	2.58	57	45	3	0	293	221	104	84	14	105	299	.208

3. Chris Narveson, lhp

Born: Dec. 20, 1981. **Ht.:** 6-3. **Wt.:** 180. **Bats:** L. **Throws:** L. **School:** T.C. Roberson HS, Skyland, N.C. **Career Transactions:** Selected by Cardinals in second round of 2000 draft; signed June 27, 2000.

Narveson had Tommy John surgery in August 2001 but was back in game action by last June, starting in short stints in the Appalachian League and gradually stretching out as he moved up to Peoria. He pitched 12 innings in the Midwest League playoffs and allowed just two earned runs. At full strength, Narveson has three pitches that are major league average to slightly above-average. His fastball touches 90 mph and he works to both sides of the plate with it, and his slider has good bite. He needs to get more consistent with his changeup, but some in the organization say it's his best pitch. He can command all three pitches. Narveson's mechanics were a mess at times last year, as he pushed the ball more than before his injury, when he had a free and easy delivery. The organization attributes the problems to the layoff but says he shows no other ill effects. The numbers don't show it, but last year was promising for a pitcher less than a year removed from Tommy John surgery. Narveson was letting the ball go at the end of the season, so the Cardinals will send him to high Class A Palm Beach and see if he can get back on the fast track.

Year	Club (League)	Class	W	L	ERA	G	GS	CG	SV	IP	H	R	ER	HR	BB	SO	AVG
2000	Johnson City (Appy)	R	2	4	3.27	12	12	0	0	55	57	33	20	7	25	63	.263
2001	Peoria (Mid)	A	3	3	1.98	8	8	0	0	50	32	14	11	3	11	53	.185
	Potomac (Car)	A	4	3	2.57	11	11	1	0	67	52	22	19	4	13	53	.212
2002	Johnson City (Appy)	R	0	2	4.91	6	6	0	0	18	23	12	10	2	6	16	.307
	Peoria (Mid)	A	2	1	4.46	9	9	0	0	42	49	24	21	5	8	36	.283
MINOR LEAGUE TOTALS			11	13	3.14	46	46	1	0	232	213	105	81	21	63	221	.241

4. Justin Pope, rhp

Born: Nov. 8, 1979. **Ht.:** 6-0. **Wt.:** 180. **Bats:** B. **Throws:** R. **School:** University of Central Florida. **Career Transactions:** Selected by Cardinals in first round (28th overall) of 2001 draft; signed June 8, 2001.

Pope is a product of Wellington (Fla.) High, which has produced several pro prospects including Pirates lefthander Sean Burnett, and his father Walt is the pitching coach there. He missed more than two months last season after having a bone spur removed from his elbow, but was lights-out whenever he pitched and ended the season with three 10-strikeout games in his last five starts. Pope has average stuff but is a prospect because of his bulldog mentality and advanced approach to pitching. His fastball was 88-89 mph after his injury, though the Cardinals expect it to improve by spring training. He has good control of his slider and changeup and really goes after hitters. What you see is what you get with Pope. He's not going to get much better than he is right now and he's a bit undersized. He needs to continue to polish his overall package and vary the speed on his changeup more. Pope dominated the Midwest League, but at his age and experience level he should have. He'll move up to Palm Beach, where the Cardinals would like to see him dominate again and possibly move up to Double-A during the season.

Year	Club (League)	Class	W	L	ERA	G	GS	CG	SV	IP	H	R	ER	HR	BB	SO	AVG
2001	New Jersey (NY-P)	A	2	4	2.60	15	15	0	0	69	64	32	20	6	14	66	.241
2002	Peoria (Mid)	A	8	1	1.38	12	12	2	0	78	48	15	12	3	12	72	.174
MINOR LEAGUE TOTALS			10	5	1.95	27	27	2	0	148	112	47	32	9	26	138	.207

5. Blake Hawksworth, rhp

Born: March 1, 1983. **Ht.:** 6-3. **Wt.:** 190. **Bats:** R. **Throws:** R. **School:** Bellevue (Wash.) CC. **Career Transactions:** Selected by Cardinals in 28th round of 2001 draft; signed May 30, 2002.

A high school teammate of Cubs pitching prospect Andy Sisco in Sammamish, Wash., Hawksworth fell in the 2001 draft because of his commitment to Cal State Fullerton. But he decided to stay close to home and go to junior college instead. He improved significantly and the Cardinals gave him a $1.475 million bonus to keep him from going back into the draft, where he was a likely first-round pick. The Cardinals call Hawksworth a potentially special pitcher. He has a power arm and already has command of three potentially plus pitches, including a fastball that ranges from 90-92 mph and a developing curveball. He's mature for his age, both physically and mentally, and he has a good feel for pitching and accepts instruction well. Hawksworth's changeup is off the charts, but it's so good that it causes him to pitch backward. Cardinals scouts saw him throw 75 pitches in one amateur start, and they estimated 55 of the pitches were offspeed. With his arm, he's clearly better off establishing his fastball first. It's not clear yet what Hawksworth's ceiling might be. He'll open his first full season at Peoria but could move fast. He should make up for the Cardinals' lack of a first- or second-round pick last year.

Year	Club (League)	Class	W	L	ERA	G	GS	CG	SV	IP	H	R	ER	HR	BB	SO	AVG
2002	Johnson City (Appy)	R	2	4	3.14	13	12	0	0	66	58	31	23	8	18	61	.232
	New Jersey (NY-P)	A	1	0	0.00	2	2	0	0	10	6	0	0	0	2	8	.171
MINOR LEAGUE TOTALS			3	4	2.74	15	14	0	0	76	64	31	23	8	20	69	.225

6. Shaun Boyd, 2b

Born: Aug. 15, 1981. **Ht.:** 5-10. **Wt.:** 170. **Bats:** R. **Throws:** R. **School:** Vista HS, Oceanside, Calif. **Career Transactions:** Selected by Cardinals in first round (13th overall) of 2000 draft; signed June 26, 2000.

Boyd lingered on the fringes of prospect status for his first two years in the organization based more on draft status and potential than anything he did on the field. After a pitch broke his jaw and ended his 2001 season early, Boyd went back to the Midwest League and had a breakout season, finishing among the league leaders in several offensive categories. With his speed and quick bat, Boyd is an exciting offensive prospect. He has good bat discipline and uses the whole field, rarely getting pull-happy. He profiles as a No. 2 hitter and could even hit from the three hole if his power continues to develop. The only category Boyd led outright in the MWL was errors by a second baseman, with 40. He moved from the outfield after signing, and though the Cardinals think he'll stay there, he needs a lot of work. He was usually OK on bang-bang plays, but on other plays his throwing mechanics got out of whack. He also needs work on turning the double play. Boyd does-n't profile nearly as well as an outfielder, but if he stays at second base he could be a pre-mium player. The Cardinals will give him plenty of time to work out those bugs if he keeps hitting. He'll move up a step to Palm Beach in 2003.

Year	Club (League)	Class	AVG	G	AB	R	H	2B	3B	HR	RBI	BB	SO	SB	SLG	OBP
2000	Johnson City (Appy)	R	.263	43	152	15	40	9	0	2	15	10	22	6	.362	.315
2001	Peoria (Mid)	A	.282	81	277	42	78	12	2	5	27	33	42	20	.394	.357
2002	Peoria (Mid)	A	.313	129	520	91	163	36	5	12	60	54	78	32	.471	.379
MINOR LEAGUE TOTALS			.296	253	949	148	281	57	7	19	102	97	142	58	.431	.363

7. Rhett Parrott, rhp

Born: Nov. 12, 1979. **Ht.:** 6-2. **Wt.:** 190. **Bats:** R. **Throws:** R. **School:** Georgia Tech.
Career Transactions: Selected by Cardinals in ninth round of 2001 draft; signed July 11, 2001.

Like Shaun Boyd, Parrott had gotten attention more for his promise than performance before last year. He had a disappointing career at Georgia Tech and a mediocre debut but put together a strong season in 2002, making the Carolina League all-star team before earning a promo-tion to New Haven. Parrott is a smart pitcher with great makeup and an aggressive, competitive approach. He isn't afraid to pitch inside and works to both sides of the plate. His fastball sits at 88-91 mph, and his curveball started to come on last year. His changeup is improving. Parrott had a good slider in college but has-n't used it much as a pro. Parrott must work ahead in the count to be successful. A mechan-ical adjustment after the 2001 season helped his command, and he'll have to continue to work on it to get better hitters out. Already someone who competes hard, Parrott seemed to work even harder after getting promoted to Double-A. He'll return to that level to open the season (at the Cardinals' new Tennessee affiliate) and see if he can earn another midseason promotion.

Year	Club (League)	Class	W	L	ERA	G	GS	CG	SV	IP	H	R	ER	HR	BB	SO	AVG
2001	New Jersey (NY-P)	A	1	3	4.93	11	11	0	0	46	45	27	25	3	28	58	.262
2002	Potomac (Car)	A	8	5	2.71	19	19	2	0	113	91	42	34	6	41	82	.221
	New Haven (EL)	AA	4	1	2.86	9	9	3	0	66	53	24	21	3	13	38	.223
MINOR LEAGUE TOTALS			13	9	3.20	39	39	5	0	225	189	93	80	12	82	178	.230

8. John Nelson, ss

Born: March 3, 1979. **Ht.:** 6-1. **Wt.:** 190. **Bats:** R. **Throws:** R. **School:** University of Kansas. **Career Transactions:** Selected by Cardinals in eighth round of 2001 draft; signed June 17, 2001.

Because of visa problems with several Latin American prospects dur-ing spring training, the Cardinals needed an extra shortstop for the Peoria team. Nelson played the position at Kansas and scout Dave Karaff said he could play there, so Nelson went to a side field and worked with organization guru George Kissell, who gave him the thumbs-up. He ended the year as the Midwest League's all-star at short. Nelson's tools actually profile well at shortstop, but the Cardinals thought of him more as a poor-man's Larry Walker in right field because of his arm, which rates a 7 on the 2-8 scouting scale. He turned out to be fearless around the bag and got better at short as the year wore on. At the plate, he hits to all fields and can sting the ball. Nelson needs work on both offense and defense, but showed the ability to make adjustments last year. He raised his average near-ly 100 points from the beginning of May and improved his hands and footwork at short, though he still committed 33 errors. His approach and makeup mean Nelson is real easy to like. His stock jumped exponentially last year, so the Cardinals will challenge him with a jump to Double-A.

Year	Club (League)	Class	AVG	G	AB	R	H	2B	3B	HR	RBI	BB	SO	SB	SLG	OBP
2001	New Jersey (NY-P)	A	.238	66	252	43	60	16	3	8	26	35	76	14	.421	.332
2002	Peoria (Mid)	A	.274	132	481	85	132	28	5	16	63	54	123	16	.453	.349
MINOR LEAGUE TOTALS			.262	198	733	128	192	44	8	24	89	89	199	30	.442	.343

9. Tyler Johnson, lhp

Born: June 7, 1981. **Ht.:** 6-2. **Wt.:** 180. **Bats:** B. **Throws:** L. **School:** Moorpark (Calif.) JC. **Career Transactions:** Selected by Cardinals in 34th round of 2000 draft; signed May 15, 2001.

Johnson earned a scholarship to Washington State out of high school, but academic problems kept him off the field there and later at Moorpark. National crosschecker Chuck Fick stayed on him, though, and Steve Gossett, a Cardinals scout who had been the pitching coach at Cal State Northridge, worked with Johnson while he was ineligible in junior college. It paid off in a breakthrough year at Peoria, as Johnson was among the minor league leaders in wins and ERA. Johnson's true 12-to-6 curveball is the best breaking pitch in the organization, and when it's on it's unhittable. He also throws an 87-88 mph fastball that touches 91 mph and has great life, with natural lefthanded tail. He has a loose arm and already knows how to beat hitters from either side of the plate. Something you might expect to be a weakness—maturity—no longer is. Johnson wants to pitch in the big leagues. He needs to improve his changeup, especially his arm speed when he throws it. He missed a few starts last year with biceps tendinitis, but it's not a long-term problem. Johnson is just learning to pitch, but the early returns are exciting. He at least looks like the next Steve Kline, but he might be much more than that. The next step is to Palm Beach.

Year	Club (League)	Class	W	L	ERA	G	GS	CG	SV	IP	H	R	ER	HR	BB	SO	AVG
2001	Johnson City (Appy)	R	1	1	2.66	9	9	0	0	41	26	17	12	1	21	58	.181
	Peoria (Mid)	A	0	1	3.95	3	3	0	0	14	14	9	6	1	10	15	.255
2002	Peoria (Mid)	A	15	3	2.00	22	18	0	0	121	96	35	27	7	42	132	.218
MINOR LEAGUE TOTALS			16	5	2.31	34	30	0	0	176	136	61	45	9	73	205	.213

10. Yadier Molina, c

Born: July 13, 1982. **Ht.:** 5-11. **Wt.:** 180. **Bats:** R. **Throws:** R. **School:** Maestro Ladi HS, Vega Alta, P.R. **Career Transactions:** Selected by Cardinals in fourth round of 2000 draft; signed Sept. 6, 2000.

How loaded was Peoria in 2002? Just three players among the Cardinals' top 10 didn't play there. Molina, the brother of Angels catchers Benji and Jose Molina, handled a strong pitching staff that led the Midwest League in ERA. Molina has the catch-and-throw skills to join his brothers in the big leagues. He receives, throws and blocks the ball well, and he handles pitchers well for his age. He threw out 52 percent (49 of 94) of basestealers and turned nine double plays, showing the strength of his arm. Molina's ceiling depends on his offensive development. The Cardinals are preaching patience and were encouraged by his progress last year. He needs better plate discipline, must keep his strikeouts down and use the whole field. His swing still tends to get long. He doesn't run well. With defensive skills this good, Molina needs to be merely adequate on offense to be an everyday major league catcher. He was close to that last year, but now needs to prove it against better pitching at Palm Beach.

Year	Club (League)	Class	AVG	G	AB	R	H	2B	3B	HR	RBI	BB	SO	SB	SLG	OBP
2001	Johnson City (Appy)	R	.259	44	158	18	41	11	0	4	18	12	23	1	.405	.320
2002	Peoria (Mid)	A	.280	112	393	39	110	20	0	7	50	21	36	2	.384	.331
MINOR LEAGUE TOTALS			.274	156	551	57	151	31	0	11	68	33	59	3	.390	.328

11. Scotty Layfield, rhp

Born: Sept. 13, 1976. **Ht.:** 6-2. **Wt.:** 200. **Bats:** R. **Throws:** R. **School:** Valdosta State (Ga.) University. **Career Transactions:** Selected by Cardinals in 20th round of 1999 draft; signed June 4, 1999.

Layfield emerged in 2001 and earned a spot on the 40-man roster, and he solidified his spot in 2002, getting hitters out consistently in his first experience above Class A. In spite of battling a little tendinitis, Layfield led the Eastern League in appearances and games finished and dominated at times. Layfield has been a reliever almost from the time he signed with the Cardinals, and he appears born to the role. He loves to challenge hitters with his fastball and slider and wants the ball with the game on the line. His fastball ranges from 90-94 mph, and his hard, sharp-breaking slider is his best pitch. He can throw it from two different angles. He occasionally mixes in a changeup or splitter but is essentially a two-pitch pitcher. He's still working on a way to attack lefthanded hitters, who hit .284 against him last year (as opposed to .197 for righties). Layfield is such a physical specimen that he could be featured in a muscle magazine, but the Cardinals would like him to stay out of the weight room now. He has been working on his flexibility. Layfield should be the closer at Memphis this year, with a big league bullpen job just a phone call away.

Year	Club (League)	Class	W	L	ERA	G	GS	CG	SV	IP	H	R	ER	HR	BB	SO	AVG
1999	New Jersey (NY-P)	A	2	2	3.15	23	3	0	8	34	27	16	12	3	21	26	.216
2000	Peoria (Mid)	A	2	4	5.13	53	0	0	15	54	65	46	31	4	40	50	.284
2001	Potomac (Car)	A	1	2	1.84	47	0	0	31	54	36	13	11	1	18	66	.188
2002	New Haven (EL)	AA	6	4	2.35	58	0	0	24	65	54	22	17	5	24	63	.227
MINOR LEAGUE TOTALS			11	12	3.08	181	3	0	78	207	182	97	71	13	103	205	.232

12. Kyle Boyer, ss/2b

Born: March 5, 1980. **Ht.:** 6-0. **Wt.:** 180. **Bats:** R. **Throws:** R. **School:** Dixie (Utah) JC. **Career Transactions:** Selected by Cardinals in fourth round of 2002 draft; signed June 25, 2002.

It took awhile, but the Cardinals finally got their man. They drafted Boyer out of high school in 1998, but he decided to attend Kansas State instead. He left there after the 1999 season and went on a two-year Mormon mission. When he returned, he played the 2002 college season at Dixie JC in Utah. The Cardinals drafted him again and didn't let him get away. Because of a broken bone in his hand, he couldn't play until July, but he still made an impression. He showed an ability to turn on balls and is a plus-plus runner who also has a good arm. He showed surprising strength with the bat and should be an offensive middle infielder. Whether that's at short or second remains to be seen. His hands improved last year and he has enough arm for short, but he has holes. The Cardinals will wait to see him play more before they decide where he's better suited. Boyer has a lot of tools and just needs to play. He'll fit at one of Peoria's middle-infield positions this year and could move fast if he plays well.

Year	Club (League)	Class	AVG	G	AB	R	H	2B	3B	HR	RBI	BB	SO	SB	SLG	OBP
2002	New Jersey (NY-P)	A	.292	49	178	27	52	10	3	0	19	14	49	20	.382	.357
MINOR LEAGUE TOTALS			.292	49	178	27	52	10	3	0	19	14	49	20	.382	.357

13. John Gall, 1b

Born: April 2, 1978. **Ht.:** 6-0. **Wt.:** 190. **Bats:** R. **Throws:** R. **School:** Stanford University. **Career Transactions:** Selected by Cardinals in 11th round of 2000 draft; signed June 22, 2000.

Gall has been hitting for years, and set Pacific-10 Conference records for at-bats (1,027), hits (368) and doubles (80) at Stanford, where his name is all over the record book. He's been nearly as consistent since signing with the Cardinals, and his latest accomplishment was making the Eastern League all-star team at New Haven and hitting 20 home runs, double the number he had hit in his first season and a half in the organization. The people of New Haven will remember him for something else, though: the Gall Mobile, a 1989 Cadillac El Dorado. Gall bought it in New Haven but didn't want to drive it back home to California after the season, so he and the team sold foam baseballs for $2 and once each game, someone drove the car around the park. People tried to throw the balls in the car, and those who got one in got a chance to win the car. Gall got a cut of the money and used his share to buy an engagement ring for his fiancée after the season. On the field, Gall improved his profile again by adding power, which had been the missing part of his offensive game. He'll need power because he'll probably have to play first base. He can't play third and probably couldn't play in left field either, and he still needs work at first. Gall's bat will have to carry him as far as he goes, and he'll get a chance to win a job in Triple-A in spring training.

Year	Club (League)	Class	AVG	G	AB	R	H	2B	3B	HR	RBI	BB	SO	SB	SLG	OBP
2000	New Jersey (NY-P)	A	.239	71	259	28	62	10	0	2	27	25	37	16	.301	.304
2001	Peoria (Mid)	A	.302	57	205	27	62	23	0	4	44	16	18	0	.473	.353
	Potomac (Car)	A	.317	84	319	44	101	25	0	4	33	24	40	5	.433	.369
2002	New Haven (EL)	AA	.316	135	526	82	166	45	3	20	81	38	75	4	.527	.362
MINOR LEAGUE TOTALS			.299	347	1309	181	391	103	3	30	185	103	170	25	.451	.351

14. Travis Hanson, 3b

Born: Jan. 24, 1981. **Ht.:** 6-2. **Wt.:** 190. **Bats:** L. **Throws:** R. **School:** University of Portland. **Career Transactions:** Selected by Cardinals in ninth round of 2002 draft; signed June 9, 2002.

Hanson was more decorated as a student than a baseball player coming out of South Kitsap High in Port Orchard, Wash., just across Puget Sound from Seattle. He was valedictorian of his graduating class in 1999 and won numerous academic honors, including German student of the year, at the largest secondary school in the Pacific Northwest. He was a three-year starter at Portland and figures to start earning baseball honors now. He started slowly at New Jersey but came on strong to become the all-star third baseman in the New York-Penn League in his professional debut. He moved to third after playing shortstop as an amateur and profiles well there, with the arm, actions and instincts to play defense and the frame and swing to provide enough offense. He showed he could be a run producer at New Jersey, and the Cardinals expect him to add power. He's a work in progress and a below-average runner. His upside would probably make him comparable to former Cardinals farmhand Adam Kennedy. He'll spend his first full season as the third baseman at Peoria.

Year	Club (League)	Class	AVG	G	AB	R	H	2B	3B	HR	RBI	BB	SO	SB	SLG	OBP
2002	New Jersey (NY-P)	A	.294	75	272	31	80	17	5	4	40	12	55	1	.438	.326
MINOR LEAGUE TOTALS			.294	75	272	31	80	17	5	4	40	12	55	1	.438	.326

15. David Williamson, lhp

Born: May 13, 1980. **Ht.:** 6-1. **Wt.:** 180. **Bats:** L. **Throws:** L. **School:** University of Massachusetts-Lowell. **Career Transactions:** Selected by Cardinals in seventh round of 2002 draft; signed June 14, 2002.

Williamson was an all-state soccer player in high school in New Hampshire and the captain of his high school basketball team in addition to being an all-state baseball player. He went to the University of Massachusetts out of high school but transferred to Division II UMass-Lowell after his sophomore season. He helped the River Hawks to the D-II College World Series in 2001 and 2002 and played center field when he wasn't pitching. He threw seven complete games as a senior, including a 154-pitch effort in a 7-2 win against Florida Southern in the CWS. So it wasn't a surprise when the Cardinals shut Williamson down after 24 innings at New Jersey with a shoulder strain. He was impressive in the short time people got to see him, though. He throws an 87-89 mph fastball with good sink, and his slider looks like a good pitch. He's gritty and has a good approach to pitching, and he's obviously a good athlete. He should open the season with one of the Cardinals' Class A clubs.

Year	Club (League)	Class	W	L	ERA	G	GS	CG	SV	IP	H	R	ER	HR	BB	SO	AVG
2002	New Jersey (NY-P)	A	2	1	2.25	6	6	0	0	24	12	8	6	1	19	27	.152
MINOR LEAGUE TOTALS			2	1	2.25	6	6	0	0	24	12	8	6	1	19	27	.152

16. Gabe Johnson, 3b

Born: Sept. 21, 1979. **Ht.:** 6-1. **Wt.:** 190. **Bats:** R. **Throws:** R. **School:** Atlantic HS, Delray Beach, Fla. **Career Transactions:** Selected by Cardinals in third round of 1998 draft; signed June 7, 1998.

Johnson played shortstop, but the Cardinals tried to make him a catcher after drafting him. He was making progress on defense, but he was struggling on offense, so the organization moved him to third base part-time in 2000 and full-time by 2001. He opened 2001 in high Class A and was sent down after striking out 113 times in 281 at-bats. The Cardinals were left with a player whose confidence was shattered, so they sent him back to Peoria in 2002 and decided to keep him there all year. He showed good power and got his career back on track. Johnson isn't huge but is a strong, well-proportioned athlete. His bat profiles at third base if he can cut down on his strikeouts and make more consistent contact. As his background shows, he has the tools to play just about anywhere. To succeed at third, he'll have to improve his range and footwork. He has plenty of arm for the position, as well as quick feet and good hands. Johnson is ready to move forward again after getting behind in his progress. He'll move to Palm Beach and try to catch up.

Year	Club (League)	Class	AVG	G	AB	R	H	2B	3B	HR	RBI	BB	SO	SB	SLG	OBP
1998	Johnson City (Appy)	R	.251	57	187	30	47	11	3	9	32	20	71	3	.487	.335
1999	New Jersey (NY-P)	A	.194	35	124	12	24	5	2	5	14	9	49	1	.387	.252
2000	Peoria (Mid)	A	.157	58	197	20	31	8	0	4	22	13	91	1	.259	.223
2001	Potomac (Car)	A	.189	86	281	24	53	14	0	4	22	21	113	2	.281	.250
	Peoria (Mid)	A	.224	36	134	17	30	10	4	2	17	16	49	1	.403	.312
2002	Peoria (Mid)	A	.248	134	516	76	128	32	0	26	93	57	153	6	.461	.324
MINOR LEAGUE TOTALS			.218	406	1439	179	313	80	9	50	200	136	526	14	.390	.290

17. Reid Gorecki, of

Born: Dec. 22, 1980. **Ht.:** 6-1. **Wt.:** 180. **Bats:** R. **Throws:** R. **School:** University of Delaware. **Career Transactions:** Selected by Cardinals in 13th round of 2002 draft; signed June 10, 2002.

Gorecki completed a strong career at Delaware with a standout junior season, as he batted .414-12-50 and stole 34 bases for the Blue Hens. He was team MVP and an all-Colonial Athletic Association outfielder, but he still wasn't a premium draft pick. The Cardinals think he could blossom into a premium player, though. He led the New York-Penn League in triples and tied for the league lead in runs. Gorecki has a nice swing and showed the ability to drive the ball to the gaps with occasional home run power. He's got good speed and an aggressive approach to the game, with a competitive drive matched by few players in the organization. He has the tools to play center field, and he goes back on the ball well and gets good jumps. If Gorecki can improve his approach at the plate and take more walks, he could be a legitimate leadoff hitter. He also needs to get stronger and better channel his aggression on the basepaths. After stealing 76 bases in 87 attempts in three college seasons, Gorecki was caught 11 times in 33 attempts in his first pro experience. He'll be the center fielder in Peoria this season.

Year	Club (League)	Class	AVG	G	AB	R	H	2B	3B	HR	RBI	BB	SO	SB	SLG	OBP
2002	New Jersey (NY-P)	A	.281	73	274	55	77	8	13	8	52	20	57	22	.493	.327
MINOR LEAGUE TOTALS			.281	73	274	55	77	8	13	8	52	20	57	22	.493	.327

18. Shane Reedy, rhp

Born: June 2, 1982. **Ht.:** 6-2. **Wt.:** 200. **Bats:** R. **Throws:** R. **School:** Utah Valley State JC. **Career Transactions:** Selected by Cardinals in 44th round of 2001 draft; signed May 27, 2002.

Reedy emerged as a prospect at Utah Valley State, where he worked out of the bullpen and had a 1.31 ERA as a sophomore. He had the organization's best fastball from the moment he signed, after working at 92-95 mph most times in college. In one outing the Cardinals scouted, though, Reedy pitched 1⅓ innings and didn't throw a pitch below 94 mph, touching 96-97 much of the time. He didn't pitch much after signing as a draft-and-follow because he pulled a ribcage muscle after reporting to extended spring camp in Florida. He was impressive on the side, though, and got into three games late in the season at Johnson City and pitched well even though the muscle bothered him all summer. A hard slider is Reedy's only other pitch at this point, and he'll have a lot of refinements to make. He may work as a starter to get more innings, but Reedy projects as a reliever long-term.

Year	Club (League)	Class	W	L	ERA	G	GS	CG	SV	IP	H	R	ER	HR	BB	SO	AVG
2002	Johnson City (Appy)	R	0	0	2.16	3	3	0	0	8	7	3	2	0	0	7	.212
MINOR LEAGUE TOTALS			0	0	2.16	3	3	0	0	8	7	3	2	0	0	7	.212

19. John Santor, 1b

Born: Nov. 16, 1981. **Ht.:** 6-1. **Wt.:** 210. **Bats:** B. **Throws:** R. **School:** Highland HS, Palmdale, Calif. **Career Transactions:** Selected by Cardinals in 35th round of 2000 draft; signed June 16, 2000.

Santor was a diamond in the rough, a late-round pick in 2000 who just looked rough in his first season and a half in the organization. But he added a lot of strength to a good frame and established himself as one of the better hitters in the lower levels of the organization in 2002. He led the New York-Penn League with 62 RBIs and earned a late promotion to Peoria for the Midwest League playoffs. In one stretch of the season he drove in 39 runs in 26 games. Santor is a switch-hitter with a nice swing, good balance and good hands from both sides of the plate. He understands how to hit and should be a run producer. The ball jumps off his bat. He should be an average first baseman, with good agility around the bag. Befitting his role as an underdog, Santor plays hard. In a best case, Santor would have a similar profile as Sean Casey, with good defense and a great hitting approach. He'll need to prove himself in full-season ball first, starting at Peoria.

Year	Club (League)	Class	AVG	G	AB	R	H	2B	3B	HR	RBI	BB	SO	SB	SLG	OBP
2000	Johnson City (Appy)	R	.174	14	46	3	8	3	0	0	4	2	13	1	.239	.208
2001	New Jersey (NY-P)	A	.227	54	185	17	42	12	2	2	26	22	64	3	.346	.308
2002	Peoria (Mid)	A	.000	1	4	0	0	0	0	0	0	0	1	0	.000	.000
	New Jersey (NY-P)	A	.293	68	239	44	70	24	1	13	62	32	62	4	.565	.380
MINOR LEAGUE TOTALS			.253	137	474	64	120	39	3	15	92	56	140	8	.443	.334

20. John Novinsky, rhp

Born: April 25, 1979. **Ht.:** 6-3. **Wt.:** 190. **Bats:** R. **Throws:** R. **School:** Iona College. **Career Transactions:** Selected by Cardinals in ninth round of 2000 draft; signed Sept. 7, 2000.

Novinsky was the Metro Atlantic Athletic Conference pitcher of the year in his junior season at Iona, going 8-1, 1.86 to establish himself as the best draft prospect in New York in 2000. After the Cardinals drafted him, Novinsky went to pitch in the Cape Cod League and put together a 3.11 ERA at Yarmouth-Dennis before signing in September for $70,000. After a mediocre debut in 2001, Novinsky got off to a great start last season before an inflamed ulnar never knocked him out for seven weeks. When he came back, the Cardinals made him the closer at Potomac, with promising results. He pitched very well in August, though his numbers were marred by one disastrous appearance when he gave up five runs and recorded just one out. Novinsky has an average fastball that ranges from 90-92 mph with good movement, as well as a slider and changeup that are solid pitches. He needs to work on his command and there are questions about his durability. In addition to last year's injury, he had Tommy John surgery when he was in high school. That could keep him in the bullpen, where he seemed to thrive last year, but the Cardinals have not made that decision yet.

Year	Club (League)	Class	W	L	ERA	G	GS	CG	SV	IP	H	R	ER	HR	BB	SO	AVG
2001	Peoria (Mid)	A	9	11	5.52	25	25	1	0	139	165	95	85	17	43	115	.296
2002	Potomac (Car)	A	7	6	4.27	30	7	0	11	59	66	42	28	6	20	55	.280
MINOR LEAGUE TOTALS			16	17	5.15	55	32	1	11	198	231	137	113	23	63	170	.291

21. Josh Pearce, rhp

Born: Aug. 20, 1977. **Ht.:** 6-3. **Wt.:** 210. **Bats:** R. **Throws:** R. **School:** University of Arizona. **Career Transactions:** Selected by Cardinals in second round of 1999 draft; signed June 18, 1999.

Pearce's shoulder finally broke down from years of heavy use last year. The Cardinals figured out that he had pitched nearly 300 innings from college fall ball in 1998 through instructional league in 1999. Yet he still threw 160 innings in 2000 and 185 in 2001. Perhaps it shouldn't have come as a surprise when Pearce broke down early last season with a torn labrum. He had surgery in May and is expected to be ready for spring training. A true gamer, he tried to pitch for Memphis early last season but clearly was hurt, giving up four home runs in four innings in his first start. When he finally went down in May, it was the first time he had missed a professional start. When healthy, Pearce throws his fastball in the 88-91 mph range with a slurve and changeup. He doesn't have anything electric but "competes his ass off," in the words of one Cardinals official, and has an advanced approach. He'll open the season at Memphis and if his shoulder is sound he could provide help in St. Louis at some point in 2003. Long term, he projects as a back-end starter or long man.

Year	Club (League)	Class	W	L	ERA	G	GS	CG	SV	IP	H	R	ER	HR	BB	SO	AVG
1999	New Jersey (NY-P)	A	3	7	4.98	14	14	1	0	78	78	45	43	8	20	78	.257
2000	Potomac (Car)	A	5	3	3.45	10	10	1	0	63	70	25	24	5	10	42	.283
	Arkansas (TL)	AA	5	6	5.46	17	17	0	0	97	117	68	59	13	35	63	.298
2001	New Haven (EL)	AA	6	8	3.75	18	18	0	0	115	111	55	48	11	34	96	.253
	Memphis (PCL)	AAA	4	4	4.26	10	10	0	0	70	72	43	33	11	12	36	.266
2002	Memphis (PCL)	AAA	0	4	7.65	4	4	0	0	20	28	18	17	8	3	17	.322
	St. Louis (NL)	MAJ	0	0	7.62	3	3	0	0	13	20	13	11	1	8	1	.377
MAJOR LEAGUE TOTALS			0	0	7.62	3	3	0	0	13	20	13	11	1	8	1	.377
MINOR LEAGUE TOTALS			23	32	4.55	73	73	2	0	443	476	254	224	56	114	332	.274

22. Dee Haynes, of

Born: Feb. 22, 1978. **Ht.:** 6-0. **Wt.:** 200. **Bats:** R. **Throws:** R. **School:** Delta State (Miss.) University. **Career Transactions:** Selected by Cardinals in 14th round of 2000 draft; signed June 12, 2000.

Haynes was a relative unknown, even in his own organization, before he broke out in Double-A last season. He did so on the strength of one scorching month in particular: Haynes hit .367-9-34 in May, accounting for more than one-third of his production for the year. Haynes has big-time power potential with a stroke that should produce plenty of doubles as well as home runs. He's quite muscular, though he has to work on his flexibility. He's a liability on defense now, though the move from right field to left field helped him last year and he has improved. He still needs to work on his jumps and his overall range. Haynes also has to improve his pitch recognition and learn how to take pitches and handle breaking balls. After his hot start, pitchers fed him a steady diet of breaking stuff when he showed he couldn't handle it. If Haynes' defense improves, he could be a big league regular and have similarities to Dante Bichette, albeit with an average arm. If not, he'd still be a good bat off the bench. He'll try to prove himself at Memphis this year.

Year	Club (League)	Class	AVG	G	AB	R	H	2B	3B	HR	RBI	BB	SO	SB	SLG	OBP
2000	New Jersey (NY-P)	A	.255	64	243	31	62	18	4	7	37	16	53	4	.449	.300
2001	Potomac (Car)	A	.290	114	417	45	121	24	3	13	72	14	82	5	.456	.329
2002	New Haven (EL)	AA	.312	131	504	75	157	29	4	21	98	25	67	3	.510	.355
MINOR LEAGUE TOTALS			.292	309	1164	151	340	71	11	41	207	55	202	12	.478	.334

23. Skip Schumaker, of

Born: Feb. 3, 1980. **Ht.:** 5-10. **Wt.:** 170. **Bats:** L. **Throws:** R. **School:** UC Santa Barbara. **Career Transactions:** Selected by Cardinals in fifth round of 2001 draft; signed June 26, 2001.

Schumaker transferred to UC Santa Barbara after spending his freshman year at Loyola Marymount, then he missed the 2000 season with a dislocated shoulder that required surgery. Some teams liked him as a pitcher in the 2001 draft, and he hit 92 mph in limited action with the Gauchos. The Cardinals wanted him strictly as an outfielder, though, and have been pleased with the early results. Schumaker has a nice stroke from the left side of the plate and has above-average speed. He should have doubles power with a good approach at the plate and profiles as a No. 1 or 2 hitter. He's an aggressive player and a good defender. He spent some time in center field but most of his time in right last season, though he hasn't shown the power for that position yet. He clearly has the arm for right, and it's no surprise managers rated his outfield arm the best in the Carolina League. Schumaker needs to draw more walks and improve his approach against lefthanders, who held him to a .219 average last season. A player with his speed should also be more successful as a basestealer; he stole 26 bases but was caught 16 times last year. He'll move up to Double-A this season.

Year	Club (League)	Class	AVG	G	AB	R	H	2B	3B	HR	RBI	BB	SO	SB	SLG	OBP
2001	New Jersey (NY-P)	A	.253	49	162	22	41	10	1	0	14	29	33	11	.327	.368
2002	Potomac (Car)	A	.287	136	551	71	158	22	4	2	44	45	84	26	.352	.342
MINOR LEAGUE TOTALS			.279	185	713	93	199	32	5	2	58	74	117	37	.346	.348

24. Tyler Adamczyk, rhp

Born: Nov. 9, 1982. **Ht.:** 6-6. **Wt.:** 190. **Bats:** R. **Throws:** R. **School:** Westlake HS, Westlake Village, Calif. **Career Transactions:** Selected by Cardinals in seventh round of 2001 draft; signed Aug. 17, 2001.

Adamczyk was one of the more intriguing arms in the 2001 draft, drawing interest for the first two rounds but ultimately falling to the seventh because of his reported price tag and a commitment to the University of California. The Cardinals signed him late in 2001 for $700,000 and were impressed with him in instructional league. He was less impressive in his professional debut. Adamczyk has a potential power arm, and he touched 95 mph as an amateur. But he was at 88-90 mph last year, and sometimes not even that good. The Cardinals attribute it to growing pains and expect his velocity to return as he improves his mechanics and adds strength to a lanky, 6-foot-6 frame. Adamczyk's slider is a potential plus pitch but needs work, and his changeup is in the rudimentary stages. He doesn't have confidence in his offspeed stuff at this point and overthrows his fastball, which straightens it out and takes away from its usual sink. Adamczyk was also inconsistent as a high school senior, so the Cardinals would like to see a solid year out of him at Peoria.

Year	Club (League)	Class	W	L	ERA	G	GS	CG	SV	IP	H	R	ER	HR	BB	SO	AVG
2002	Johnson City (Appy)	R	4	3	3.41	13	11	0	0	63	56	31	24	3	35	54	.232
MINOR LEAGUE TOTALS			4	3	3.41	13	11	0	0	63	56	31	24	3	35	54	.232

25. Josh Axelson, rhp

Born: Dec. 4, 1978. **Ht.:** 6-1. **Wt.:** 200. **Bats:** R. **Throws:** R. **School:** Michigan State University. **Career Transactions:** Selected by Cardinals in fifth round of 2000 draft; signed June 14, 2000.

Hard to believe, but Axelson's 4.09 ERA was a career best and was even better than the ERAs he posted in three seasons at Michigan State. He opened the 2002 season in the Potomac rotation but got sent to the bullpen at midseason before working his way back into a starting role. He finished strong, going 4-2, 3.12 in August, and ended up as Potomac's player of the year for his performance on and off the field. He worked as an instructor at community baseball clinics throughout the local area last season. On the field, the Cardinals say the proverbial light finally came on for Axelson. Pitching coordinator Mark Riggins made a small mechanical adjustment, taking Axelson back to an over-the-top delivery after he had slipped to a three-quarters arm slot. Axelson also started to compete harder and got his confidence back, after he was promoted too quickly in 2001 and regressed. Axelson doesn't throw anything electric, with a fastball at 89-91 mph, a hard slider and a changeup that he's just starting to make good use of. When he has his mechanics and command in hand, though, he gets hitters out. Axelson can take a big step forward in the organization's plans with a good season in Double-A.

Year	Club (League)	Class	W	L	ERA	G	GS	CG	SV	IP	H	R	ER	HR	BB	SO	AVG
2000	New Jersey (NY-P)	A	3	9	5.13	15	14	0	0	74	79	53	42	2	34	63	.275
2001	Peoria (Mid)	A	5	7	4.61	18	18	1	0	109	112	62	56	12	28	77	.264
	Potomac (Car)	A	2	5	5.56	10	10	1	0	57	61	41	35	10	19	38	.275
2002	Potomac (Car)	A	6	7	4.09	32	20	2	0	136	135	72	62	12	40	82	.259
MINOR LEAGUE TOTALS			16	28	4.67	75	62	4	0	376	387	228	195	36	121	260	.266

26. Rick Asadoorian, of

Born: July 23, 1980. **Ht.:** 6-2. **Wt.:** 180. **Bats:** R. **Throws:** R. **School:** Northbridge HS, Whitinsville, Mass. **Career Transactions:** Selected by Red Sox in first round (17th overall) of 1999 draft; signed Aug. 16, 1999 . . . Traded by Red Sox with 1B Dustin Brisson and 1B Luis Garcia to Cardinals for RHP Dustin Hermanson, Dec. 15, 2001.

Asadoorian came to the organization after the 2001 season after signing with the Red Sox for a club-record $1.7255 million bonus in 1999. In his first season with the Cardinals, he showed about what the Red Sox had seen: outstanding defensive tools and a suspect bat. Asadoorian could find a spot on many major league rosters now as a defensive replacement in the outfield. He has the best outfield tools in the organization, with a plus arm. He gets great jumps, has soft hands, takes charge from center field and runs balls down in the gaps.

His tools haven't translated at the plate yet, however. In his second season in low-A ball, Asadoorian improved marginally. The Cardinals like his line-drive stroke but want him to keep his swing short and try to hit the ball the other way. He still hasn't refined his approach at the plate and developed a good idea of the strike zone. Asadoorian also is a hard-nosed player who can be tough on himself. With his cold-weather background, the Cardinals are trying to exercise patience with him. He'll move up to high Class A to work on his hitting.

Year	Club (League)	Class	AVG	G	AB	R	H	2B	3B	HR	RBI	BB	SO	SB	SLUG	OBP
2000	Red Sox (GCL)	R	.264	54	197	43	52	9	3	5	31	26	56	22	.416	.362
2001	Augusta (SAL)	A	.212	116	406	50	86	13	6	6	40	47	139	13	.318	.299
2002	Peoria (Mid)	A	.265	137	445	70	118	12	11	8	55	44	96	14	.396	.340
MINOR LEAGUE TOTALS			.244	307	1048	163	256	34	20	19	126	117	291	49	.369	.329

27. Nick Stocks, rhp

Born: Aug. 27, 1978. **Ht.:** 6-2. **Wt.:** 180. **Bats:** R. **Throws:** R. **School:** Florida State University. **Career Transactions:** Selected by Cardinals in first round (36th overall) of 1999 draft; signed Aug. 29, 1999.

Stocks is the classic case of a pitcher with an exciting arm who can't stay healthy enough to actually get anyone excited. He had Tommy John surgery as an amateur with Florida State but still was a supplemental first-round pick. He has endured a series of back and shoulder woes since signing. His latest operations came in December 2001, on his shoulder, and in April, on his knee after a spring training injury. He rehabbed in Florida and didn't join an affiliate until July, pitching briefly in New Jersey before getting moved up to Peoria. He threw eight shutout innings in an August start and jokingly referred to himself as a finesse pitcher after he averaged 83 mph with his fastball for the night. At his best, Stocks is the opposite of a finesse pitcher, with a hard fastball that reaches 94-95 mph and a hammer curve. Rarely has he been seen at his best, though. He never got comfortable in 2002 but told the organization he felt great heading into spring training 2003. The Cardinals expect his velocity to return this year and hope it's a breakout season for Stocks. It's definitely an important season. You can only live on reputation for so long.

Year	Club (League)	Class	W	L	ERA	G	GS	CG	SV	IP	H	R	ER	HR	BB	SO	AVG
2000	Peoria (Mid)	A	10	10	3.78	25	24	1	0	150	133	88	63	4	52	118	.234
2001	New Haven (EL)	AA	2	12	5.16	16	15	1	0	82	89	52	47	10	33	63	.276
2002	New Jersey (NY-P)	A	0	2	5.73	7	7	0	0	22	28	14	14	0	13	24	.308
	Peoria (Mid)	A	1	0	2.25	1	1	0	0	8	6	2	2	0	1	3	.222
	Potomac (Car)	A	0	2	5.74	3	3	0	0	16	18	13	10	3	6	11	.277
MINOR LEAGUE TOTALS			13	26	4.41	52	50	2	0	278	274	169	136	17	105	219	.255

28. Chance Caple, rhp

Born: Aug. 9, 1978. **Ht.:** 6-6. **Wt.:** 210. **Bats:** R. **Throws:** R. **School:** Texas A&M University. **Career Transactions:** Selected by Cardinals in first round (30th overall) of 1999 draft; signed July 15, 1999 . . . On disabled list, April 6-Sept. 4, 2001.

Caple no doubt finds bitter irony in the fact that his first name is Chance. Because so far in his professional career, Caple has had no chance. He pitched in pain for some time before finally having Tommy John surgery in April 2001, which knocked him out for the entire season. He rehabbed in extended spring camp last year and was assigned to Peoria in May. He made two starts and was sitting in the dugout when a line drive broke a finger on his right hand, knocking him out for six weeks. When he came back, he was bothered by tendinitis and a possible strain in his elbow. So needless to say, Caple has had a hard time getting into a rhythm. He has a lot of ability, with an 89-93 mph fastball, a potentially above-average slider and a changeup that needs work. So his injuries have been frustrating for him and the organization. He's expected to be healthy for spring training, so he'll get a shot at a job in Palm Beach.

Year	Club (League)	Class	W	L	ERA	G	GS	CG	SV	IP	H	R	ER	HR	BB	SO	AVG
1999	New Jersey (NY-P)	A	0	4	4.38	7	7	0	0	37	35	24	18	4	18	36	.245
2000	Potomac (Car)	A	7	9	4.39	22	22	0	0	125	128	68	61	11	34	97	.266
2001							Did Not Play—Injured										
2002	Peoria (Mid)	A	1	1	4.00	5	5	0	0	18	16	8	8	3	14	9	.242
MINOR LEAGUE TOTALS			8	14	4.33	35	34	0	0	181	180	100	87	18	66	142	.261

29. Chris Duncan, 1b

Born: May 5, 1981. **Ht.:** 6-5. **Wt.:** 210. **Bats:** L. **Throws:** R. **School:** Canyon del Oro HS, Tucson. **Career Transactions:** Selected by Cardinals in first round (46th overall) of 1999 draft; signed June 23, 1999.

Duncan, the son of Cardinals pitching coach Dave and brother of Yankees prospect

Shelley, may finally have solved low Class A in his third trip. For the second year in a row, he finished with a flourish after a slow start, this time closing with an 11-game hitting streak that included four homers and 13 RBIs on a strong Peoria team. Duncan made great strides in his hitting approach last year, starting to use the whole field instead of trying to yank everything. He has legitimate above-average power and will naturally hit home runs if he just puts the bat on the ball. He's a hard-nosed player and a hard worker. His strike-zone judgment still leaves a lot to be desired, a problem he recognizes but has struggled to improve on. His defense at first is spotty, as he committed 19 errors last year. His hands got better, but his footwork needs work. He's not a good runner. Duncan will still be just 21 on Opening Day, so the Cardinals will continue to be patient with him. He'll open 2003 at Palm Beach.

Year	Club (League)	Class	AVG	G	AB	R	H	2B	3B	HR	RBI	BB	SO	SB	SLG	OBP
1999	Johnson City (Appy)	R	.214	55	201	23	43	8	1	6	34	25	62	3	.353	.300
2000	Peoria (Mid)	A	.256	122	450	52	115	34	0	8	57	36	111	1	.384	.318
2001	Potomac (Car)	A	.179	49	168	12	30	6	0	3	16	10	47	4	.268	.229
	Peoria (Mid)	A	.306	80	297	44	91	23	2	13	59	36	55	13	.529	.386
2002	Peoria (Mid)	A	.271	129	487	58	132	25	4	16	75	44	118	5	.437	.337
MINOR LEAGUE TOTALS			.256	435	1603	189	411	96	7	46	241	151	393	26	.411	.325

30. So Taguchi, of

Born: July 2, 1969. **Ht.:** 5-10. **Wt.:** 160. **Bats:** R. **Throws:** R. **Career Transactions:** Signed out of Japan by Cardinals, Jan. 9, 2002.

Taguchi was the Cardinals' first sign from the Far East, and the early returns weren't positive. Taguchi had a .277 average in 10 seasons in Japan's Pacific League and was known more for his defense. St. Louis signed him to a three-year deal and hoped he would compete for at least a backup outfield job, but he was clearly overmatched from the beginning of spring training. He spent most of the season at Memphis, getting acclimated to American culture and baseball. Taguchi is about as sound fundamentally as a ballplayer can be, especially on defense. But he'll have to improve at the plate to be more than a footnote to the history of Japanese players in the major leagues. He gets overmatched by good fastballs and seemed to have trouble adjusting to the mindset of American pitchers, who attack hitters with pure stuff more than Japanese pitchers do. The Cardinals are chalking up last year as a learning experience and will give Taguchi a close look in spring training, in hopes he can win a backup job in St. Louis.

Year	Club (League)	Class	AVG	G	AB	R	H	2B	3B	HR	RBI	BB	SO	SB	SLG	OBP
1992	Orix (PL)	JPN	.268	47	123	—	33	—	—	1	7	—	—	5	—	—
1993	Orix (PL)	JPN	.277	31	83	—	23	—	—	0	5	—	—	3	—	—
1994	Orix (PL)	JPN	.307	108	329	—	101	—	—	6	43	—	—	0	—	—
1995	Orix (PL)	JPN	.246	130	495	—	122	—	—	9	61	—	—	14	—	—
1996	Orix (PL)	JPN	.279	128	509	—	142	—	—	7	44	—	—	10	—	—
1997	Orix (PL)	JPN	.294	135	572	—	168	—	—	10	56	—	—	7	—	—
1998	Orix (PL)	JPN	.272	132	497	—	135	—	—	9	41	—	—	8	—	—
1999	Orix (PL)	JPN	.269	133	524	—	141	—	—	9	56	—	—	11	—	—
2000	Orix (PL)	JPN	.279	129	509	—	142	—	—	8	49	—	—	9	—	—
2001	Orix (PL)	JPN	.280	134	453	70	127	21	6	8	42	43	88	6	—	—
2002	Memphis (PCL)	AAA	.247	91	304	37	75	17	0	5	36	13	44	6	.352	.286
	St. Louis (NL)	MAJ	.400	19	15	4	6	0	0	0	2	2	1	1	.400	.471
	New Haven (EL)	AA	.308	26	107	21	33	10	0	1	15	9	15	3	.430	.375
MAJOR LEAGUE TOTALS			.400	19	15	4	6	0	0	0	2	2	1	1	.400	.471
MINOR LEAGUE TOTALS			.263	117	411	58	108	27	0	6	51	22	59	9	—	—

SAN DIEGO
PADRES

TOP 30 PROSPECTS

1. Xavier Nady, of
2. Khalil Greene, ss
3. Mark Phillips, lhp
4. Tagg Bozied, 1b
5. Jake Gautreau, 2b
6. Ben Howard, rhp
7. Josh Barfield, 2b
8. Mike Nicolas, rhp
9. Rusty Tucker, lhp
10. Cory Stewart, lhp
11. Javier Martinez, rhp
12. Jason Bay, of
13. Justin Germano, rhp
14. Mike Bynum, lhp
15. Ben Johnson, of
16. Eric Cyr, lhp
17. Kennard Jones, of
18. Vince Faison, of
19. Bernie Castro, 2b
20. David Pauley, rhp
21. Shane Victorino, of
22. Jon Knott, of/1b
23. Cliff Bartosh, lhp
24. Freddy Guzman, of/2b
25. Mike Wodnicki, rhp
26. Greg Sain, 3b
27. Brad Baker, rhp
28. Nick Trzesniak, c
29. Chris Oxspring, rhp
30. Marcus Nettles, of

By Jim Callis

A year ago, a deep and balanced Padres system ranked as the fourth-best in the game. San Diego fans got a good look at the talent as the club used a record 59 players in 2002, including 16 who made their big league debuts. The Padres' top three prospects entering the season all made their way to Qualcomm Stadium, with mixed results. Sean Burroughs, who ranked No. 1 for three years, was an initial disappointment after dislodging Phil Nevin from third base. He batted a soft .271, hurt his shoulder and went back to Triple-A to play second base. Burroughs still has considerable promise as a hitter, but he didn't answer questions about whether he'll hit for power.

Righthander Dennis Tankersley went 1-4, 8.06 in 17 games with the Padres and continued to regress when he was demoted. His performance, coupled with the team's wealth of young pitching, has scouts wondering if Tankersley will be more than a middle reliever for San Diego. The news was better for righthander Jake Peavy. With the Padres rotation ravaged by injuries, he was brought to the big leagues and responded with six innings of one-run ball against the Yankees and went 6-7, 4.52 overall.

Another pitcher who arrived at Qualcomm ahead of schedule—and a bigger surprise—was 20-year-old lefty Oliver Perez. After beginning the season in high Class A, Perez went 4-5, 3.50 to finish with the best ERA among San Diego's regular starters. Ramon Vazquez, acquired from the Mariners the previous offseason, came alive offensively in the second half but looks more like a utilityman than a regular shortstop.

Growing pains are to be expected, considering the Padres promoted most of those players before they wanted to. A side effect is the system has been thinned out, though it still has blue-chippers such as outfielder Xavier Nady, shortstop Khalil Greene and lefthander Mark Phillips.

All along, San Diego's long-term plan was to get a nucleus of young talent in place, then take advantage of the new revenue when much-delayed Petco Park opens in 2004. By then, if not before, Nady should give the lineup the extra power bat it needs while Greene could fill the void at short.

The Padres may have to endure a fifth straight losing season in which they finish no better than fourth in the National League West in 2003. By next year, they finally should be ready to contend again.

OrganizationOverview

General Manager: Kevin Towers. **Farm Director:** Tye Waller. **Scouting Director:** Bill Gayton.

2002 PERFORMANCE

Class	Farm Team	League	W	L	Pct.	Finish*	Manager
Majors	San Diego	National	66	96	.407	15th (16)	Bruce Bochy
Triple-A	Portland Beavers	Pacific Coast	72	71	.503	t-8th (16)	Rick Sweet
Double-A	Mobile BayBears	Southern	76	63	.547	3rd (10)	Craig Colbert
High A	Lake Elsinore Storm	California	75	65	.536	4th (10)	George Hendrick
Low A	Fort Wayne Wizards	Midwest	69	68	.504	8th (14)	Tracy Woodson
Short-season	Eugene Emeralds	Northwest	41	35	.539	t-3rd (8)	Jeff Gardner
Rookie	Idaho Falls Braves	Pioneer	32	44	.421	8th (8)	Don Werner
OVERALL MINOR LEAGUE RECORD			365	346	.513	11th (30)	

*Finish in overall standings (No. of teams in league)

ORGANIZATION LEADERS

BATTING
*Minimum 250 At-Bats
*AVG	John Knott, Lake Elsinore/Fort Wayne	.... .339
R	Marcus Nettles, Lake Elsinore	 97
H	John Knott, Lake Elsinore/Fort Wayne	 167
TB	John Knott, Lake Elsinore/Fort Wayne .	 267
2B	John Knott, Lake Elsinore/Fort Wayne	 46
3B	Kory DeHaan, Portland .	 14
HR	Tagg Bozied, Mobile/Lake Elsinore	 24
RBI	Tagg Bozied, Mobile/Lake Elsinore	 92
BB	Marcus Nettles, Lake Elsinore	 101
SO	Jeremy Owens, Portland/Lake Elsinore.	 157
SB	Pedro De los Santos, Lake Els./Ft. Wayne/Eug. .. 58

PITCHING
#Minimum 75 Innings
W	Justin Germano, Lake Elsinore/Fort Wayne	 14
L	Junior Herndon, Portland	 13
#ERA	Ian Harvey, Mobile/Lake Elsinore	.... 2.65
G	Mike Nicolas, Lake Elsinore	 65
CG	Junior Herndon, Portland	 2
	Jon Huber, Fort Wayne	 2
SV	Rusty Tucker, Lake Elsinore/Fort Wayne	 27
IP	Justin Germano, Lake Elsinore/Fort Wayne 175
BB	Mark Phillips, Lake Elsinore	 94
SO	Mark Phillips, Lake Elsinore	 156

BEST TOOLS

Best Hitter for Average	.... Khalil Greene
Best Power Hitter	.... Xavier Nady
Fastest Baserunner	.... Marcus Nettles
Best Athlete	.... Kennard Jones
Best Fastball	.... Mike Nicolas
Best Curveball	.... Chris Rojas
Best Slider	.... Mike Bynum
Best Changeup	.... Brad Baker
Best Control	.... Justin Germano
Best Defensive Catcher	.... Humberto Quintero
Best Defensive Infielder	.... Donaldo Mendez
Best Infield Arm	.... Alexander Garcia
Best Defensive Outfielder	.... Shane Victorino
Best Outfield Arm	.... Josh Carter

PROJECTED 2006 LINEUP

Catcher	.... Wiki Gonzalez
First Base	.... Ryan Klesko
Second Base	.... Jake Gautreau
Third Base	.... Sean Burroughs
Shortstop	.... Khalil Greene
Left Field	.... Xavier Nady
Center Field	.... Mark Kotsay
Right Field	.... Phil Nevin
No. 1 Starter	.... Jake Peavy

JOHN SPEAR   JOHN SPEAR

Marcus Nettles   Justin Germano

No. 2 Starter	.... Mark Phillips
No. 3 Starter	.... Oliver Perez
No. 4 Starter	.... Brian Lawrence
No. 5 Starter	.... Dennis Tankersley
Closer	.... Mike Nicolas

TOP PROSPECTS OF THE DECADE

1993	.... Ray McDavid, of
1994	.... Joey Hamilton, rhp
1995	.... Dustin Hermanson, rhp
1996	.... Ben Davis, c
1997	.... Derrek Lee, 1b
1998	.... Matt Clement, rhp
1999	.... Matt Clement, rhp
2000	.... Sean Burroughs, 3b
2001	.... Sean Burroughs, 3b
2002	.... Sean Burroughs, 3b

TOP DRAFT PICKS OF THE DECADE

1993	.... Derrek Lee, 1b
1994	.... Dustin Hermanson, rhp
1995	.... Ben Davis, c
1996	.... Matt Halloran, ss
1997	.... Kevin Nicholson, ss
1998	.... Sean Burroughs, 3b
1999	.... Vince Faison, of
2000	.... Mark Phillips, lhp
2001	.... Jake Gautreau, 3b
2002	.... Khalil Greene, ss

ALL-TIME LARGEST BONUSES

Mark Phillips, 2000	.... $2,200,000
Sean Burroughs, 1999	.... $2,100,000
Jake Gautreau, 2001	.... $1,875,000
Khalil Greene, 2002	.... $1,500,000
Vince Faison, 1999	.... $1,415,000

MinorLeagueDepthChart

SAN DIEGO PADRES

RANK 20

A year ago, the Padres boasted one of the strongest systems in baseball with a blend of premium bats and arms. Thanks to injuries and a lack of depth in the big leagues, though, the Padres had 16 players make their major league debuts last year, including half of the organization's top 10 list. Still, this is not a system devoid of prospects. Now that they've developed a corps of promising young pitchers, the Padres need everyday prospects like Xavier Nady, Khalil Greene, Tagg Bozied and Jake Gautreau to step forward and help an ailing offense that finished last in the National League in home runs last year.

Note: Depth charts prepared by Josh Boyd. Numbers in parentheses indicate prospect rankings.

LF
Xavier Nady (1)
Vince Faison (18)
Marcus Nettles (30)

CF
Kennard Jones (17)
Shane Victorino (21)
Freddy Guzman (24)
Todd Donovan
Kory DeHaan

RF
Jason Bay (12)
Ben Johnson (15)
Alex Fernandez

3B
Greg Sain (26)

SS
Khalil Greene (2)
Luis Garcia
Donaldo Mendez

2B
Jake Gautreau (5)
Josh Barfield (7)
Bernie Castro (19)
Brian Burgamy
Peeter Ramos

1B
Tagg Bozied (4)
Jon Knott (22)
Paul McAnulty

C
Nick Trzesniak (28)
Humberto Quintero
Omar Falcon

RHP
Starters	Relievers
Ben Howard (6)	Mike Nicolas (8)
Javier Martinez (11)	Chris Oxspring (29)
Justin Germano (13)	Gabe Ribas
David Pauley (20)	J.J. Trujillo
Mike Wodnicki (25)	Brandon Villafuerte
Brad Baker (27)	
Henry Perez	
Cesar Rojas	
Clay Condrey	
Carlos Garcia	
Aaron Coonrod	
Josh Reynolds	

LHP
Starters	Relievers
Mark Phillips (3)	Rusty Tucker (9)
Cory Stewart (10)	Cliff Bartosh (23)
Mike Bynum (14)	
Eric Cyr (16)	
Sean Thompson	
Nobuaki Yoshida	

DraftAnalysis

2002 Draft

Best Pro Debut: SS Khalil Greene (1) backed up his BA College Player of the Year and Golden Spikes awards by batting .317-9-32 in high Class A. 1B Paul McAnulty (12) hit .379-8-51 and led the Rookie-level Pioneer League in batting and doubles (29). RHP Gabe Ribas went 8-1, 1.97 with a 66-5 strikeout-walk ratio, topping the short-season Northwest League in wins and finishing second in saves (16). LHP David Krisch (22) tied for the PL lead with 16 saves.

Best Athlete: OF Kennard Jones (3) is one of the fastest runners in the system and a quality center fielder. The Padres like his line-drive swing and ability to draw walks.

Best Pure Hitter: It's clearly Greene. Two others who bear watching are McAnulty, a smaller version of John Kruk, and 2B Brian Burgamy (9), a switch-hitter with surprising pop from both sides of the plate.

Best Raw Power: OF Steve Baker (29) has light-tower power and slammed 11 homers in the NWL. He'll have to learn how to control the strike zone after whiffing 88 times and drawing 16 walks in 232 at-bats.

Fastest Runner: Jones has been clocked at 6.45 seconds in the 60-yard dash and 3.85 seconds from the left side of home to first.

Best Defensive Player: Jones. While Greene lacks pure shortstop tools, the Padres say his body control, quick first step and accurate arm will allow him to stay at short.

Best Fastball: RHP Aaron Coonrod (4) showed a 92-95 mph fastball and low-80s slider while pitching John A. Logan (Ill.) JC to the Junior College World Series, but did-

n't throw as hard after coming down with shoulder tendinitis during the summer.

Best Breaking Ball: LHP Sean Thompson's (5) devastating curve helped him fan 69 PL hitters in 56 innings.

Most Intriguing Background: RHP Greg Bochy's (36) father Bruce manages the Padres. Unsigned SS Andy LaRoche's (21) brother Adam is a first-base prospect in the Braves system, and their father Dave made two all-star teams in a 14-year big league career.

Jones

Closest To The Majors: Greene will begin 2003 in Double-A and could be in San Diego by the end of the year.

Best Late-Round Pick: Ribas, LHP Kevin Beavers (16) and Krisch all touch 93 mph.

The One Who Got Away: Negotiations with sweet-swinging 1B Michael Johnson (2) quickly turned acrimonious. San Diego still controls his rights because he's a fifth-year senior, but if Clemson makes the NCAA regionals next spring the Padres will lose their window to sign him. San Diego definitely lost out on the pitchability of LHP Matt Lynch (7), who's back at Florida State.

Assessment: If Greene can stay at shortstop, he'll fill a void the Padres have tried to plug for years. Adding his college teammate Johnson would have given San Diego yet another talented corner infielder/outfielder. The Padres went heavily for college talent.

2001 Draft

2Bs Jake Gautreau (1) and Josh Barfield (4) and 1B Tagg Bozied (3) have been productive bats, as expected. LHP Rusty Tucker's (21) emergence as a hard-throwing bullpen force has been a surprise. **Grade: B+**

2000 Draft

LHP Mark Phillips (1) is their top pitching prospect, while OF Xavier Nady (2) is the best prospect, period. RHP Justin Germano (13) could be the next Brian Lawrence. **Grade: B+**

1999 Draft

Stealing RHP Jake Peavy (15) makes up for not getting much out of six first-round picks. The Padres still like OF Vince Faison, LHP Mike Bynum and C Nick Trzesniak, but they've been slow to develop. RHP Gerik Baxter was killed in a 2001 auto accident, while RHPs Omar Ortiz and Casey Burns fizzled quickly. **Grade: B+**

1998 Draft

3B Sean Burroughs (1) still looks like a future batting champion, while RHP Brian Lawrence (17) is a mainstay in San Diego's rotation. Draft-and-follow LHP Eric Cyr (30) has some upside. **Grade: A**

Note: Draft analysis prepared by Jim Callis. Numbers in parentheses indicate draft rounds.

... Nady is an impact hitter who will produce for both power and average.

Xavier Nady of

Born: Nov. 14, 1978.
Ht.: 6-2. **Wt.:** 200.
Bats: R. **Throws:** R.
School: University of California.
Career Transactions: Selected by Padres in second round of 2000 draft; signed, Sept. 17, 2000.

Nady entered 2000 as the No. 1 prospect for the June draft, but he had a so-so .329-19-59 season at California and signability was a concern. As a result, he slid to the Padres, who signed him to a big league contract with a $1.1 million bonus. His deal mandated a September callup, and he singled off Eric Gagne in his lone at-bat. Nady hasn't been back to San Diego since, with injuries the main culprit. He tore a ligament in his elbow in the Arizona Fall League in 2000 and had Tommy John surgery after the 2001 season. Last year, he couldn't play in the field until mid-June and strained a quadriceps muscle in the AFL. Nady has an impressive offensive résumé. He eclipsed Mark McGwire's Pacific-10 Conference record with a .718 slugging percentage, and was the high Class A California League's MVP and home run leader in 2001.

The Padres envision Nady as an impact hitter who will produce for both power and average. He has the strength and stroke to hit 40 homers a year, and he has an advanced approach at the plate. After trying to do too much after his midseason promotion to Triple-A Portland, Nady adjusted and closed holes in his swing. He batted .316-4-19 in the final month, then hit .323 in the AFL before getting hurt. Nady drives the ball hard to all fields. He's a determined competitor and has worked hard on his defense. Injuries have hampered his defensive development. He was drafted as a third baseman, but Sean Burroughs had a claim to that position. The Padres talked about trying Nady at second base, but his elbow problems limited him to first base in 2001. Left field is his position du jour, but he was only healthy enough to play 63 games (including the AFL) there in 2002. With more experience, Nady should become an average left fielder. He can make the routine plays and has improved his jumps on fly balls. His arm isn't quite average now but should stretch out more as he gets healthier. The only offensive concern with Nady is his plate discipline.

Bubba Trammell and Brian Buchanan are all that stand between Nady and a big league job. The Padres will give Nady a long look in spring training, though he probably needs more time in Triple-A before he's fully ready. San Diego got just 20 homers out of its left fielders last season, and Nady could exceed that total as a rookie.

Year	Club (League)	Class	AVG	G	AB	R	H	2B	3B	HR	RBI	BB	SO	SB	SLG	OBP
2000	San Diego (NL)	MAJ	1.000	1	1	1	1	0	0	0	0	0	0	0	1.000	1.000
2001	Lake Elsinore (Cal)	A	.302	137	524	96	158	38	1	26	100	62	109	6	.527	.381
2002	Lake Elsinore (Cal)	A	.278	45	169	41	47	6	3	13	37	28	40	2	.580	.382
	Portland (PCL)	AAA	.283	85	315	46	89	12	1	10	43	20	60	0	.422	.329
MAJOR LEAGUE TOTALS			1.000	1	1	1	1	0	0	0	0	0	0	0	1.000	1.000
MINOR LEAGUE TOTALS			.292	267	1008	183	294	56	5	49	180	110	209	8	.503	.366

LARRY GOREN

2. Khalil Greene, ss

Born: Oct. 21, 1979. **Ht.:** 5-11. **Wt.:** 210. **Bats:** R. **Throws:** R. **School:** Clemson University. **Career Transactions:** Selected by Padres in first round (13th overall) of 2002 draft; signed June 30, 2002.

Greene was undrafted out of high school and a 14th-round pick of the Cubs after his junior season in 2001, but scouts finally began to believe in him last year. He won the BA College Player of the Year and the Golden Spikes awards, carrying Clemson to the College World Series semifinals. He signed for $1.5 million and had no trouble adapting to pro ball. All of Greene's tools are average or better, and he supplements them with excellent instincts. His bat speed, hand-eye coordination, pitch recognition and ability to adjust make him the best pure hitter in the system. He also has surprising power for his size. Scouts question whether he's a pure shortstop, but his hands, range, arm, first-step quickness and body control are all assets. Greene's range and arm earn 55 grades on the 20-80 scouting scale, which means they're above-average but not extraordinary for a shortstop. The Padres believe his total package will allow him to stay at short. His only drawback at the plate is that he makes contact so easily that he doesn't draw many walks. Ticketed for Double-A, Greene could be the first 2002 draftee to reach the majors, perhaps as early as this summer.

Year	Club (League)	Class	AVG	G	AB	R	H	2B	3B	HR	RBI	BB	SO	SB	SLG	OBP
2002	Eugene (NWL)	A	.270	10	37	5	10	1	0	0	6	5	6	0	.297	.400
	Lake Elsinore (Cal)	A	.317	46	183	33	58	9	1	9	32	12	33	0	.525	.368
MINOR LEAGUE TOTALS			.309	56	220	38	68	10	1	9	38	17	39	0	.486	.374

3. Mark Phillips, lhp

Born: Dec. 30, 1981. **Ht.:** 6-3. **Wt.:** 200. **Bats:** L. **Throws:** L. **School:** Hanover (Pa.) HS. **Career Transactions:** Selected by Padres in first round (ninth overall) of 2000 draft; signed July 6, 2000.

Oliver Perez passed him as the top lefthander in San Diego's pecking order last year, but he can't match Phillips' pure stuff. Few southpaws can. Raw when he signed in 2000, he started to put it all together last August, posting a 2.53 ERA and a 37-9 strikeout-walk ratio in his final 32 innings. When he maintains his arm slot, Phillips shows two plus-plus pitches at times. His fastball touches 97 mph and sits in the low 90s, and farm director Tye Waller describes his curveball as "dropping out of the sky." After arriving out of shape for his first spring training, Phillips now understands the commitment needed to be a professional. He has a clean, effortless arm action. It all comes down to mechanics for Phillips. When he repeats his delivery consistently, his stuff is sharp and finds the strike zone. When he doesn't, his pitches aren't as crisp and he falls behind in the count. His changeup is effective at times but still developing. Phillips will join most of the players on this list at Double-A Mobile in 2003. The Padres hope he's ready to follow Perez' express route to San Diego.

Year	Club (League)	Class	W	L	ERA	G	GS	CG	SV	IP	H	R	ER	HR	BB	SO	AVG
2000	Idaho Falls (Pio)	R	1	1	5.35	10	10	0	0	37	35	30	22	2	24	37	.254
2001	Eugene (NWL)	A	3	1	3.74	4	4	0	0	22	16	10	9	1	9	19	.208
	Fort Wayne (Mid)	A	4	1	2.64	5	5	0	0	31	19	11	9	1	14	27	.174
	Lake Elsinore (Cal)	A	2	1	2.57	5	5	0	0	28	19	8	8	0	14	34	.190
2002	Lake Elsinore (Cal)	A	10	8	4.19	28	26	0	0	148	123	81	69	9	94	156	.225
MINOR LEAGUE TOTALS			20	12	3.96	52	50	0	0	266	212	140	117	13	155	273	.219

4. Tagg Bozied, 1b

Born: July 24, 1979. **Ht.:** 6-3. **Wt.:** 220. **Bats:** R. **Throws:** R. **School:** University of San Francisco. **Career Transactions:** Signed by independent Sioux Falls (Northern), June, 2001 . . . Selected by Padres in third round of 2001 draft; signed Nov. 9, 2001.

Bozied batted .412-30-82 and led NCAA Division I with a .936 slugging percentage as a sophomore in 1999 before tailing off in his final two college seasons. He turned down the Twins as a 2000 second-rounder—he went seven picks before Xavier Nady—and went to the independent Northern League before signing with the Padres for $725,000 in 2001. He led the system in homers and RBIs while reaching Double-A in his pro debut, then set an Arizona Fall League record with 12 longballs. Bozied's power is nearly as good as Nady's, though he's not as polished a hitter and has more effort to his swing. He has a strong arm and moves well for his size, so it's possible he could play the outfield. After tearing up high Class A, Bozied didn't do nearly as much damage in Double-A. He has holes in his long swing, particularly against breaking balls on the outer half of the plate. Scouts who saw him in the AFL said he punished mistakes more than he hit quality pitches. He labors at first base. Assuming Nady becomes San Diego's left fielder, Bozied won't have a clear path to big league playing time. For now, he'll try to refine his game in Double-A.

Year	Club (League)	Class	AVG	G	AB	R	H	2B	3B	HR	RBI	BB	SO	SB	SLG	OBP
2001	Sioux Falls (NorC)	IND	.307	58	228	35	70	17	0	6	31	13	34	3	.461	.359
2002	Lake Elsinore (Cal)	A	.298	71	282	45	84	23	1	15	60	35	60	3	.546	.377
	Mobile (SL)	AA	.214	60	234	35	50	14	0	9	32	16	43	1	.389	.268
MINOR LEAGUE TOTALS			.260	131	516	80	134	37	1	24	92	51	103	4	.475	.329

5. Jake Gautreau, 2b

Born: Nov. 14, 1979. **Ht.:** 6-0. **Wt.:** 180. **Bats:** L. **Throws:** R. **School:** Tulane University. **Career Transactions:** Selected by Padres in first round (14th overall) of 2001 draft; signed June 21, 2001.

The Padres thought Gautreau might tear up the California League like Xavier Nady had in his first full season. Instead he found his strength sapped by ulcerative colitis, which was diagnosed in early July. Gautreau batted just .263-1-4 in his final 20 games and .225 in the Arizona Fall League. A national raquetball champion at ages 8 and 10, Gautreau says that sport helped him hone his swing and agility. After moving him from third base to second in instructional league in 2001, San Diego projected him as a left-handed-hitting Jeff Kent. Now that he has his colitis under control, Gautreau may tap into his raw power. While he has been better than expected at second base, he's still making the transition. He needs to charge grounders more aggressively, and he has an unorthodox release on his throws. He won't ever be a Gold Glover, but he should become at least adequate. Considering his pretty line-drive stroke, he strikes out more than he should. Gautreau will move up to Double-A in 2003. Though he's the organization's top second-base prospect, he faces stiff competition with Bernie Castro ahead of him and Josh Barfield behind.

Year	Club (League)	Class	AVG	G	AB	R	H	2B	3B	HR	RBI	BB	SO	SB	SLG	OBP
2001	Eugene (NWL)	A	.309	48	178	28	55	19	0	6	36	22	47	1	.517	.389
	Portland (PCL)	AAA	.286	2	7	2	2	0	0	1	2	2	2	0	.714	.444
2002	Lake Elsinore (Cal)	A	.286	93	371	43	106	20	1	10	62	42	86	2	.426	.358
MINOR LEAGUE TOTALS			.293	143	556	73	163	39	1	17	100	66	135	3	.459	.369

6. Ben Howard, rhp

Born: Jan. 15, 1979. **Ht.:** 6-2. **Wt.:** 190. **Bats:** R. **Throws:** R. **School:** Central Merry HS, Jackson, Tenn. **Career Transactions:** Selected by Padres in second round of 1997 draft; signed June 25, 1997.

After improving more than any player in the system in 2001, Howard endured a trying year in 2002. He was the sole survivor of the Feb. 15 car crash that killed Padres outfielder Mike Darr and former Phillies minor leaguer Duane Johnson. Howard made his big league debut 10 weeks later but was rocked in three outings. Demoted to Triple-A, he strained his elbow and tried to pitch through it with little success. Howard is a pure power pitcher. When he's right, he throws in the mid-90s and has been clocked as high as 99. He complements his heat with a hard slider, and his changeup can be a plus pitch at times. Howard put too much pressure on himself when he got to the majors and tried to overthrow. He lost his release point and his command deserted him—though not to the point where he led his minor league in walks in each of his first four pro seasons. He needs more consistency with his changeup. The best thing for Howard would be to begin 2003 with less stress in Triple-A. His ceiling remains as high as any pitcher in the organization.

Year	Club (League)	Class	W	L	ERA	G	GS	CG	SV	IP	H	R	ER	HR	BB	SO	AVG
1997	Padres (AZL)	R	1	4	7.45	13	12	0	0	54	54	53	45	3	63	59	.255
1998	Idaho Falls (Pio)	R	4	5	6.03	15	15	0	0	69	67	61	46	2	87	79	.260
1999	Fort Wayne (Mid)	A	6	10	4.73	28	28	0	0	145	123	100	76	17	110	131	.226
2000	Rancho Cucamonga (Cal)	A	5	11	6.37	32	19	0	0	107	88	87	76	8	111	150	.227
2001	Lake Elsinore (Cal)	A	8	2	2.83	18	18	0	0	102	86	37	32	4	32	107	.229
	Mobile (SL)	AA	2	0	2.40	7	5	0	0	30	17	9	8	3	15	29	.167
2002	Mobile (SL)	AA	3	1	2.18	6	6	0	0	33	26	10	8	2	16	30	.222
	San Diego (NL)	MAJ	0	1	9.28	3	2	0	0	11	13	11	11	4	14	10	.302
	Portland (PCL)	AAA	0	4	6.20	11	7	0	0	45	47	34	31	10	15	25	.266
MAJOR LEAGUE TOTALS			0	1	9.28	3	2	0	0	11	13	11	11	4	14	10	.302
MINOR LEAGUE TOTALS			29	37	4.96	130	110	0	0	585	508	391	322	49	449	610	.234

7. Josh Barfield, 2b

Born: Dec. 17, 1982. **Ht.:** 6-0. **Wt.:** 180. **Bats:** R. **Throws:** R. **School:** Klein HS, Spring, Texas. **Career Transactions:** Selected by Padres in fourth round of 2001 draft; signed June 15, 2001.

He's the son of former American League home run champion Jesse Barfield, so perhaps it should be no surprise how quickly Josh has adapted to pro ball. He hit .310 in the Rookie-level Pioneer League in his 2001 pro debut. In his first full season, he led the low Class A Midwest League in hits and shared organization player of the year honors with Jon Knott. Unlike his father, who was more of a dead-pull power hitter, Barfield already uses the entire field. He makes consistently hard contact and started making adjustments against breaking balls in 2002. He should develop average to plus power as he gets stronger and more experienced. A good athlete, he has soft hands and average speed. Barfield might outgrow second base, though he should have enough bat to play elsewhere. He needs to address his footwork and double-play pivot. Offensively, his swing can get loopy at times and he needs a tighter strike zone. Barfield is ready for high Class A. He's three years younger but just one level behind Jake Gautreau, and their future battle for San Diego's second-base job should be fun to watch.

Year	Club (League)	Class	AVG	G	AB	R	H	2B	3B	HR	RBI	BB	SO	SB	SLG	OBP
2001	Idaho Falls (Pio)	R	.310	66	277	51	86	15	4	4	53	16	54	12	.437	.350
2002	Fort Wayne (Mid)	A	.306	129	536	73	164	22	3	8	57	26	105	26	.403	.340
	Lake Elsinore (Cal)	A	.087	6	23	2	2	0	0	0	4	1	4	0	.087	.120
MINOR LEAGUE TOTALS			.301	201	836	126	252	37	7	12	114	43	163	38	.406	.337

8. Mike Nicolas, rhp

Born: Sept. 5, 1979. **Ht.:** 6-3. **Wt.:** 220. **Bats:** R. **Throws:** R. **Career Transactions:** Signed out of Dominican Republic by Padres, March 21, 2000.

Nicolas' age was revised upward 26 months during the crackdown on visas before the 2002 season. Unlike most players who were affected, he saw his prospect status improve. That's because he destroyed California League hitters and topped all upper-minors relievers by averaging 14.1 strikeouts per nine innings. He tied for the minor league lead in appearances. When Nicolas throws strikes, he's nearly unhittable. He threw 92-96 mph every time out last year and peaked at 100. His slider is a plus pitch at times and if he ever becomes consistent with it, he'd almost be unfair. Lefthanders have hit .161 with two homers in 174 at-bats against him the last two seasons. Nicolas threw only fastballs at the start of the year, and the Padres had to make him work on his slider and rudimentary changeup. He overthrows, which detracts from his command, not a strong suit to begin with. He's slow to the plate, making him vulnerable to basestealers. Given the opportunity to close in the final two weeks last year, Nicolas went 7-for-7 converting saves and fanned 24 in 11 innings. He projects as San Diego's closer of the future.

Year	Club (League)	Class	W	L	ERA	G	GS	CG	SV	IP	H	R	ER	HR	BB	SO	AVG
2000	Padres (DSL)	R	4	5	2.89	17	6	0	2	56	42	27	18	2	27	65	.198
2001	Fort Wayne (Mid)	A	1	5	3.45	54	0	0	7	63	44	30	24	4	34	70	.206
	Lake Elsinore (Cal)	A	0	1	5.25	8	0	0	0	12	11	7	7	2	5	15	.250
2002	Lake Elsinore (Cal)	A	3	2	2.91	65	0	0	9	77	49	32	25	4	42	121	.181
MINOR LEAGUE TOTALS			8	13	3.20	144	6	0	18	208	146	96	74	12	108	271	.197

9. Rusty Tucker, lhp

Born: July 15, 1980. **Ht.:** 6-1. **Wt.:** 190. **Bats:** R. **Throws:** L. **School:** University of Maine. **Career Transactions:** Selected by Padres in 21st round of 2001 draft; signed June 11, 2001.

Coming out of Maine as a 21st-round pick in 2001, Tucker was the America East Conference pitcher of the year but had fringe-average stuff. He touched the low 90s in his pro debut but was wild, leading the Pioneer League in walks, and lacked confidence. All of sudden, he threw 94-97 mph in his first 2002 appearance and never stopped. Managers rated him the best reliever in the Midwest League. The Padres aren't sure how Tucker started throwing in the mid-90s and touching 99, not that they're complaining. They tried to slow down his delivery so he could throw more strikes, but didn't expect this. His slider also improved, reaching 79-81 mph with nice bite. He has a fearless closer's mentality. There isn't much deception to Tucker's fastball. He's not tall and uses a drop-and-drive delivery, so his heater comes in on a flat plane and without much movement. He still needs to refine his command. Just as they did in the second half last year, Tucker and Mike Nicolas will form a nasty lefty-righty, late-inning combination in 2003, this time in Double-A. Tucker got most of the saves at high Class A Lake Elsinore but may have to share more this year.

Year	Club (League)	Class	W	L	ERA	G	GS	CG	SV	IP	H	R	ER	HR	BB	SO	AVG
2001	Idaho Falls (Pio)	R	0	2	7.13	30	0	0	0	35	41	41	28	4	50	43	.297
2002	Fort Wayne (Mid)	A	5	1	1.01	31	0	0	13	36	19	8	4	2	10	50	.150
	Lake Elsinore (Cal)	A	2	3	2.43	26	0	0	14	30	26	10	8	1	18	33	.226
MINOR LEAGUE TOTALS			7	6	3.58	87	0	0	27	101	86	59	40	7	78	126	.226

10. Cory Stewart, lhp

Born: Nov. 14, 1979. **Ht:** 6-4. **Wt.:** 180. **Bats:** L. **Throws:** L. **School:** Boerne (Texas) HS. **Career Transactions:** Selected by Reds in 27th round of 1998 draft, Aug. 17, 1998 . . . On disabled list, June 16-Sept. 27, 2000 . . . Released by Reds, March 24, 2001 . . . Signed by independent Amarillo (Texas-Louisiana), May 2001 . . . Signed by Padres, Oct. 15, 2001.

Stewart dropped in the 1998 draft because he was committed to Southwest Texas State, but the Reds signed him for a significant bonus. After he missed all of 2000 with a shoulder injury, Cincinnati released him and he spent 2001 in the independent Texas-Louisiana League. The Padres picked him up and he opened eyes by topping out at 94 mph last spring training. He began the season in the Fort Wayne bullpen but pitched his way into the rotation by mid-April. With a loose, easy delivery, Stewart throws 88-94 mph with so much movement that hitters rarely get a good swing against his fastball. His curveball is a solid second pitch, and his strong suit is his command. He's athletic, so repeating his delivery comes naturally. Stewart needs to improve his secondary pitches. He loses his curve at times, and his change-up is little more than a show pitch at this point. Though he's a classic free-spirited left-hander, his work habits are improving. Stewart is slated for the Double-A rotation this year. With Oliver Perez and Mark Phillips ahead of him, he may have to settle for relieving once he reaches San Diego.

Year	Club (League)	Class	W	L	ERA	G	GS	CG	SV	IP	H	R	ER	HR	BB	SO	AVG
1999	Billings (Pio)	R	2	0	3.14	10	10	0	0	49	50	25	17	2	21	37	.263
2000							Did Not Play—Injured										
2001	Amarillo (T-L)	IND	6	6	5.39	22	20	3	0	120	132	87	72	9	67	107	.276
2002	Fort Wayne (Mid)	A	6	3	2.39	17	11	0	0	64	46	21	17	4	18	86	.198
	Lake Elsinore (Cal)	A	5	3	3.20	12	12	0	0	65	60	29	23	3	29	69	.251
MINOR LEAGUE TOTALS			13	6	2.89	39	33	0	0	177	156	75	57	9	68	192	.236

11. Javier Martinez, rhp

Born: Dec. 9, 1982. **Ht.:** 6-3. **Wt.:** 170. **Bats:** B. **Throws:** R. **Career Transactions:** Signed out of Mexico by Padres, March 26, 2000.

The Padres believe they may have a righthanded version of Oliver Perez in Martinez, a fellow Mexican. After posting a 6.43 ERA in Rookie ball in 2001, Martinez replaced Cory Stewart in the Fort Wayne rotation last June and nearly cut his ERA in half. He already has a 90-95 mph fastball and backs it up with an improved curveball and solid changeup. His projectable build and loose arm mean that he'll probably add more velocity in the future. Martinez' secondary pitches still need more reliability, but he already has improved his repertoire by not overusing his splitter. His command improved last year, and so did his work habits after he saw Perez get promoted to San Diego. Because he's still just 20, Martinez may return to low Class A in 2003.

Year	Club (League)	Class	W	L	ERA	G	GS	CG	SV	IP	H	R	ER	HR	BB	SO	AVG
2000	Padres (AZL)	R	0	0	0.00	3	0	0	1	3	0	0	0	0	3	2	.000
2001	Idaho Falls (Pio)	R	1	4	6.43	10	8	0	0	42	42	35	30	6	26	38	.261
2002	Eugene (NWL)	A	0	0	4.50	2	2	0	0	10	4	5	5	2	5	6	.121
	Fort Wayne (Mid)	A	6	4	3.38	12	12	0	0	69	55	28	26	5	19	69	.211
MINOR LEAGUE TOTALS			7	8	4.40	27	22	0	1	125	101	68	61	13	53	115	.217

12. Jason Bay, of

Born: Sept. 20, 1978. **Ht.:** 6-2. **Wt.:** 200. **Bats:** R. **Throws:** R. **School:** Gonzaga University. **Career Transactions:** Selected by Expos in 22nd round of 2000 draft; signed June 16, 2000 . . . Traded by Expos with RHP Jim Serrano to Mets for SS Lou Collier, March 27, 2002 . . . Traded by Mets with LHP Bobby Jones and RHP Josh Reynolds to Padres for RHP Steve Reed and RHP Jason Middlebrook, July 31, 2002.

Bay won the 2001 Midwest League batting title in his first full pro season, and his reward was getting traded twice in 2002. First, he became one of several Expos prospects to be given away by general manager Omar Minaya, and then the Mets sent him to the Padres in a mid-season deal for Steve Reed. He's not as powerful as Xavier Nady nor as athletic as several of the outfielders who rank behind him, but Bay has a nice combination of tools and instincts. He obviously hits well for average, has gap power and draws walks. He has surprising speed for his size and has succeeded on 84 percent of his basestealing attempts as a pro. Bay is capable of playing all three outfield spots and fits best in right field with his strong arm. San Diego added Bay to its 40-man roster and may start him in Triple-A this year.

Year	Club (League)	Class	AVG	G	AB	R	H	2B	3B	HR	RBI	BB	SO	SB	SLG	OBP
2000	Vermont (NY-P)	A	.304	35	135	17	41	5	0	2	12	11	25	17	.385	.358
2001	Jupiter (FSL)	A	.195	38	123	12	24	4	1	1	10	18	26	10	.268	.306
	Clinton (Mid)	A	.362	87	318	67	115	20	4	13	61	48	62	15	.572	.449
2002	St. Lucie (FSL)	A	.272	69	261	48	71	12	2	9	54	34	54	22	.437	.363
	Binghamton (EL)	AA	.290	34	107	17	31	4	2	4	19	15	23	13	.477	.383
	Mobile (SL)	AA	.309	23	81	16	25	5	2	4	12	13	22	4	.568	.411
MINOR LEAGUE TOTALS			.300	286	1025	177	307	50	11	33	168	139	212	81	.466	.388

13. Justin Germano, rhp

Born: Aug. 6, 1982. **Ht.:** 6-3. **Wt.:** 200. **Bats:** R. **Throws:** R. **School:** Claremont (Calif.) HS. **Career Transactions:** Selected by Padres in 13th round of 2000 draft; signed June 13, 2000.

The Padres thought so much of Germano's approach to pitching that they sent him to low Class A at age 18 in 2001. He didn't fare well, but he did when he got a second chance as a teenager last year. Germano led the system with 14 victories and improved his career strikeout-walk ratio to 5.6. While he's not overpowering, he has three potential average-or-better pitches and the best command in the system. His top pitch is a curveball that has been compared to Roy Oswalt's. He also throws an 88-89 mph fastball that could pick up velocity because he has a lanky build, wide shoulders and a quick arm. His changeup is decent. At times, Germano becomes too hittable because he's around the plate so much. But the bottom line is he's advanced for his age. He was spectacular in three late-season starts at high Class A and will return there to begin 2003.

Year	Club (League)	Class	W	L	ERA	G	GS	CG	SV	IP	H	R	ER	HR	BB	SO	AVG
2000	Padres (AZL)	R	5	5	4.59	17	8	0	1	67	65	36	34	4	9	67	.249
2001	Fort Wayne (Mid)	A	2	6	4.98	13	13	0	0	65	80	47	36	7	16	55	.302
	Eugene (NWL)	A	6	5	3.49	13	13	2	0	80	77	35	31	5	11	74	.246
2002	Fort Wayne (Mid)	A	12	5	3.18	24	24	1	0	156	166	63	55	14	19	119	.269
	Lake Elsinore (Cal)	A	2	0	0.95	3	3	0	0	19	12	3	2	1	5	18	.174
MINOR LEAGUE TOTALS			27	21	3.68	70	61	3	1	386	400	184	158	31	60	333	.262

14. Mike Bynum, lhp

Born: March 20, 1978. **Ht.:** 6-4. **Wt.:** 200. **Bats:** L. **Throws:** L. **School:** University of North Carolina. **Career Transactions:** Selected by Padres in first round (19th overall) of 1999 draft; signed July 1, 1999.

Bynum was one of the system's top lefties before a disastrous 2001, then regained his standing and made his major league debut last season. Bynum hurt his right knee in spring training 2001, but didn't tell anyone and tried to pitch through the injury. He wound up altering his mechanics, pitching poorly and requiring arthroscopic surgery. When he returned in spring training last year, Bynum tried to do too much too soon and strained an elbow ligament. He didn't see any game action until June, but reached San Diego two months later. He made three decent starts followed by nine scoreless relief appearances for the Padres, then got shellacked in his final two outings. His trademark pitch is still his slider, which mangers rated the best breaking ball in the Double-A Southern League. He has a plus changeup that he's starting to use more often, and his fastball runs from 86-90 mph. The key for Bynum is to locate his pitches, especially his fastball, and maintain his delivery. His slider is most effective when he gets hitters down in the count. Bynum's ceiling doesn't appear as high as it was when he reached Double-A in his first full pro season, so his long-term fit in San Diego probably will be in the bullpen.

Year	Club (League)	Class	W	L	ERA	G	GS	CG	SV	IP	H	R	ER	HR	BB	SO	AVG
1999	Idaho Falls (Pio)	R	1	0	0.00	5	3	0	0	17	7	0	0	0	4	21	.127
	Rancho Cucamonga (Cal)	A	3	1	3.29	7	7	0	0	38	35	17	14	1	8	44	.238
2000	Rancho Cucamonga (Cal)	A	9	6	3.00	21	21	0	0	126	101	55	42	4	51	129	.224
	Mobile (SL)	AA	3	1	2.91	6	6	0	0	34	31	12	11	2	16	27	.252
2001	Mobile (SL)	AA	2	7	5.02	16	15	0	0	84	90	53	47	14	35	69	.279
2002	Mobile (SL)	AA	4	0	0.82	6	5	0	0	33	17	5	3	0	7	29	.150
	Portland (PCL)	AAA	3	2	3.51	7	7	0	0	41	36	19	16	6	7	35	.235
	San Diego (NL)	MAJ	1	0	5.27	14	3	0	0	27	33	16	16	3	15	17	.308
MAJOR LEAGUE TOTALS			1	0	5.27	14	3	0	0	27	33	16	16	3	15	17	.308
MINOR LEAGUE TOTALS			25	17	3.20	68	64	0	0	374	317	161	133	27	128	354	.232

15. Ben Johnson, of

Born: June 18, 1981. **Ht.:** 6-1. **Wt.:** 200. **Bats:** R. **Throws:** R. **School:** Germantown (Tenn.) HS. **Career Transactions:** Selected by Cardinals in fourth round of 1999 draft; signed June 24, 1999 . . . Traded by Cardinals with RHP Heathcliff Slocumb to Padres for C Carlos Hernandez and SS Nate Tebbs, July 31, 2000.

The Padres have been patient with Johnson since they got him from the Cardinals in exchange for overpriced catcher Carlos Hernandez in 2000. He always has been young for his league—he reached Double-A last year at age 20—and San Diego has taken his so-so numbers in the proper context. Johnson still is learning how to hit. After the season ended, he went to instructional league to tweak his swing before moving on to the Arizona Fall League. He's showing more patience at the plate, though he tends to overswing when he gets behind in the count, leading to strikeouts. He just needs to let his natural 20-20 ability take over. Johnson has improved in right field, where both his range and arm are plus tools. The Padres aren't sure if they'll keep him in Double-A at the start of 2003 so he can build off a fast start or send him to Triple-A.

Year	Club (League)	Class	AVG	G	AB	R	H	2B	3B	HR	RBI	BB	SO	SB	SLG	OBP
1999	Johnson City (Appy)	R	.330	57	203	38	67	9	1	10	51	29	57	14	.532	.423
2000	Peoria (Mid)	A	.242	93	330	58	80	22	1	13	46	53	78	17	.433	.353
	Fort Wayne (Mid)	A	.193	29	109	11	21	6	2	3	13	7	25	0	.367	.261
2001	Lake Elsinore (Cal)	A	.276	136	503	79	139	35	6	12	63	54	141	22	.441	.358
2002	Mobile (SL)	AA	.241	131	456	58	110	23	4	10	55	65	127	11	.375	.337
MINOR LEAGUE TOTALS			.260	446	1601	244	417	95	14	48	228	208	428	64	.427	.353

16. Eric Cyr, lhp

Born: Feb. 11, 1979. **Ht.:** 6-4. **Wt.:** 200. **Bats:** R. **Throws:** L. **School:** Seminole State (Okla.) JC. **Career Transactions:** Selected by Padres in 30th round of 1998 draft; signed May 31, 1999.

Like Ben Howard, Cyr had difficulty following up on his breakthrough 2001 performance. Both started last season pitching well in Double-A, then struggled and got hurt after getting summoned to San Diego. Cyr injured his elbow and had arthroscopic surgery to remove bone chips. He had a similar operation that cost him most of the 2000 season. The cousin of former NHL winger Paul Cyr, his best pitch is a heavy 90-92 mph fastball. His velocity and command were down last year because of his elbow woes. Cyr still needs to show more feel for his offspeed pitches. He used to throw a knuckle-curve that the Padres want him to transform into a slider, and he also fiddles with a curveball and changeup. If he can't develop reliable secondary pitches Cyr will head to the bullpen, but the Padres aren't ready to make that move yet. He'll be a starter this year in Triple-A.

Year	Club (League)	Class	W	L	ERA	G	GS	CG	SV	IP	H	R	ER	HR	BB	SO	AVG
1999	Padres (AZL)	R	2	1	3.26	11	5	0	0	39	34	19	14	2	15	39	.243
	Idaho Falls (Pio)	R	1	0	1.80	1	1	0	0	5	5	1	1	0	1	3	.278
2000	Fort Wayne (Mid)	A	2	2	4.68	9	6	0	0	33	28	18	17	2	15	31	.233
	Padres (AZL)	R	0	0	3.00	2	1	0	0	3	4	1	1	0	2	4	.333
2001	Lake Elsinore (Cal)	A	7	4	1.61	21	16	0	0	101	68	28	18	1	24	131	.184
2002	Mobile (SL)	AA	4	6	3.24	14	14	0	0	72	62	37	26	6	34	65	.233
	San Diego (NL)	MAJ	0	1	10.50	5	0	0	0	6	6	7	7	0	6	4	.286
	Portland (PCL)	AAA	0	0	3.14	9	2	0	0	14	14	6	5	0	10	11	.246
MAJOR LEAGUE TOTALS			0	1	10.50	5	0	0	0	6	6	7	7	0	6	4	.286
MINOR LEAGUE TOTALS			16	13	2.77	67	45	0	0	267	215	110	82	11	101	284	.219

17. Kennard Jones, of

Born: Sept. 8, 1981. **Ht.:** 5-11. **Wt.:** 180. **Bats:** L. **Throws:** L. **School:** University of Indiana. **Career Transactions:** Selected by Padres in third round of 2002 draft; signed July 18, 2002.

As if they weren't already stocked with athletic outfielders, the Padres signed Jones as a 2002 third-round pick. He wasn't drafted out of high school or Wallace State (Ala.) CC before sharing Big 10 Conference player of the year honors last spring. A cousin of basketball Hall of Famer Sam Jones, he's as lightning-quick as the former Celtics star was. Jones can get from home to first in 3.85 seconds and runs the 60-yard dash in 6.45 seconds. Compared to Kenny Lofton, he averaged nearly a walk per game after signing. He's disciplined and shortened his swing to enhance his chances of making contact. Jones isn't as weak as his .333 slugging percentage in his pro debut would indicate. That's more reflective of him focusing on putting the ball in play on the ground, because he has upper-body strength and some snap in his wrists. He needs to drive more balls into the gaps. Defensively, Jones has plus range and an average arm. He's still a bit raw in the outfield but soaks up instruction and should improve quickly. He'll begin 2003 in low Class A.

Year	Club (League)	Class	AVG	G	AB	R	H	2B	3B	HR	RBI	BB	SO	SB	SLG	OBP
2002	Eugene (NWL)	A	.295	16	61	15	18	2	0	0	3	10	12	12	.328	.411
	Fort Wayne (Mid)	A	.286	20	77	15	22	4	0	0	5	11	21	3	.338	.382
MINOR LEAGUE TOTALS			.290	36	138	30	40	6	0	0	8	21	33	15	.333	.395

18. Vince Faison, of

Born: Jan. 22, 1981. **Ht.:** 6-0. **Wt.:** 180. **Bats:** L. **Throws:** R. **School:** Toombs County HS, Lyons, Ga. **Career Transactions:** Selected by Padres in first round (20th overall) of 1999 draft; signed June 4, 1999.

Faison was one of the top defensive backs in the nation and had committed to play football at the University of Georgia before the Padres made him the first of their six first-round picks in 1999. As he has gotten stronger, he has lost some of the raw speed that used to be his best tool. Nevertheless, San Diego still envisions him as a potential Ray Lankford. Faison is learning to develop patience and power, and he set full-season career highs for batting average, on-base percentage and slugging in 2002. However, he still has a ways to go. It's important for him to not worry about hitting for power at the expense of using the whole field. Faison has accepted that baseball will be a challenge and his athleticism won't carry him, and he's working harder than he did earlier in his career. Because his range has diminished and he never has had a strong arm, he projects as a left fielder. The Padres keep expecting him to blossom, and 2003 would be a good time to start.

Year	Club (League)	Class	AVG	G	AB	R	H	2B	3B	HR	RBI	BB	SO	SB	SLG	OBP
1999	Padres (AZL)	R	.309	44	178	40	55	6	6	4	28	18	45	30	.478	.378
	Fort Wayne (Mid)	A	.208	11	48	10	10	2	0	0	1	6	18	7	.250	.309
2000	Fort Wayne (Mid)	A	.219	117	457	65	100	20	2	12	39	26	159	21	.350	.267
2001	Fort Wayne (Mid)	A	.200	41	140	14	28	5	0	1	8	18	35	10	.257	.302
	Lake Elsinore (Cal)	A	.233	73	275	27	64	11	3	7	36	24	94	12	.371	.297
2002	Mobile (SL)	AA	.253	100	359	40	91	23	5	7	44	39	103	5	.404	.339
MINOR LEAGUE TOTALS			.239	386	1457	196	348	67	16	31	156	131	454	85	.371	.310

19. Bernie Castro, 2b

Born: July 14, 1979. **Ht.:** 5-10. **Wt.:** 160. **Bats:** B. **Throws:** R. **Career Transactions:** Signed out of Dominican Republic by Yankees, Sept. 25, 1997 . . . On disabled list, June 5-Sept. 24, 1999 . . . Traded by Yankees to Padres for OF Kevin Reese, Dec. 18, 2001.

Since being acquired from the Yankees for outfielder Kevin Reese in a rare prospect-for-prospect trade, Castro has won consecutive batting titles in the Dominican League the last two winters. In between, however, he hit a soft .260 in Double-A and had two years added to his age. His best tool is his speed, as he led the Southern League in steals. Managers rated him the league's best and fastest baserunner, as well as its most exciting player. The Padres knew he was fast but were surprised he was this fast: 3.8 seconds down the line on bunts, 3.9-4.0 seconds on grounders. Marcus Nettles has more pure speed, but he can't get to first base as quick as Castro. Castro plays to his speed by making contact, drawing walks and keeping the ball on the ground. He only had 16 extra-base hits last year, though as with Kennard Jones, the Padres say that's because of his approach and not a lack of strength. General manager Kevin Towers touted Castro as the club's second baseman of the future, but it's hard to believe he'll hold off Jake Gautreau and Josh Barfield without showing some more pop. He has improved defensively and is an average second baseman. His age jumped two years last offseason, so Castro wasn't young for Double-A last year. He'll need to show more with the bat in Triple-A in 2003, or else Gautreau might beat him to San Diego.

Year	Club (League)	Class	AVG	G	AB	R	H	2B	3B	HR	RBI	BB	SO	SB	SLG	OBP
1998	Yankees (DSL)	R	.330	61	224	78	74	6	4	0	17	37	40	63	.393	.432
1999	Did Not Play—Injured															
2000	Yankees (DSL)	R	.348	55	210	69	73	9	2	2	13	36	24	56	.438	.450
	Yankees (GCL)	R	.441	9	34	7	15	4	1	0	6	6	4	3	.618	.525
2001	Greensboro (SAL)	A	.260	101	389	71	101	15	7	1	36	54	67	67	.342	.350
	Staten Island (NY-P)	A	.351	15	57	6	20	1	0	0	7	11	12	8	.368	.464
2002	Mobile (SL)	AA	.260	109	419	61	109	13	3	0	32	52	67	53	.305	.345
MINOR LEAGUE TOTALS			.294	350	1333	292	392	48	17	3	111	196	214	250	.362	.388

20. David Pauley, rhp

Born: June 17, 1983. **Ht.:** 6-2. **Wt.:** 170. **Bats:** R. **Throws:** R. **School:** Longmont (Colo.) HS. **Career Transactions:** Selected by Padres in eighth round of 2001 draft; signed June 7, 2001.

Considered Colorado's top draft prospect in 2001, Pauley had a tough time getting acclimated to pro ball after signing. He tied for the Pioneer League lead with nine losses and had a 6.03 ERA. After going through extended spring training, he emerged as a new pitcher last year at short-season Eugene. He was consistent throughout the summer, showing three major league pitches. His fastball sat at 88-90 mph and topped out at 93-94, and he projects to add another 2-3 mph. His curveball and changeup are both solid average pitches. Pauley throws strikes, has a feel for pitching and throws without effort. He just needs a few more seasons of experience and some added strength. He'll move up to low Class A this year.

Year	Club (League)	Class	W	L	ERA	G	GS	CG	SV	IP	H	R	ER	HR	BB	SO	AVG
2001	Idaho Falls (Pio)	R	4	9	6.03	15	15	0	0	69	88	57	46	8	24	53	.308
2002	Eugene (NWL)	A	6	1	2.81	15	15	0	0	80	81	32	25	6	18	62	.266
MINOR LEAGUE TOTALS			10	10	4.30	30	30	0	0	149	169	89	71	14	42	115	.286

21. Shane Victorino, of

Born: Nov. 30, 1980. **Ht.:** 5-9. **Wt.:** 160. **Bats:** R. **Throws:** R. **School:** St. Anthony HS, Wailuku, Hawaii. **Career Transactions:** Selected by Dodgers in sixth round of 1999 draft; signed June 8, 1999 . . . Selected from Dodgers by Padres in major league Rule 5 draft, Dec. 16, 2002.

An official from another team said the Padres landed the sleeper of the major league Rule 5 draft at the Winter Meetings when they got Victorino from the Dodgers. After he had a strong season in low Class A in 2001, Los Angeles decided to jump him to Double-A last year. He struggled but ultimately held his own while continuing to make contact, steal bases and playing a fine center field. He played better as the season wore on, hitting .305 in the final two months and then .330 in the Arizona Fall League. Victorino abandoned switch-hitting to bat solely righthanded in 2001, but may want to consider trying it again after hitting .213 against righties last year. He's the best defensive outfielder in the system and has an average arm. He projects as a leadoff man if he can bring his average up, though jumping two more levels won't hasten his development. If San Diego can't keep Victorino on its 25-man roster all season, he'll have to clear waivers and be offered back to the Dodgers for half his $50,000 draft price.

Year	Club (League)	Class	AVG	G	AB	R	H	2B	3B	HR	RBI	BB	SO	SB	SLG	OBP
1999	Great Falls (Pio)	R	.280	55	225	53	63	7	6	2	25	20	31	20	.391	.335
2000	Yakima (NWL)	A	.246	61	236	32	58	7	2	2	20	20	44	21	.318	.310
2001	Wilmington (SAL)	A	.283	112	435	71	123	21	9	4	32	36	61	47	.400	.344
	Vero Beach (FSL)	A	.167	2	6	2	1	0	0	0	0	3	1	0	.167	.444
2002	Jacksonville (SL)	AA	.258	122	481	61	124	15	1	4	34	47	49	45	.318	.328
MINOR LEAGUE TOTALS			.267	352	1383	219	369	50	18	12	111	126	186	133	.355	.332

22. Jon Knott, of/1b

Born: Aug. 4, 1978. **Ht.:** 6-3. **Wt.:** 220. **Bats:** R. **Throws:** R. **School:** Mississippi State University. **Career Transactions:** Signed as nondrafted free agent by Padres, Sept. 28, 2001.

Knott went from nondrafted free agent in 2001 to California League batting champion and Padres co-minor league player of the year in 2002. He probably would have been drafted after leading Mississippi State with a .359 average and eight homers as a senior, but he strained a tendon in his right leg late in the college season. He wasn't fully healthy until that September, when he signed with San Diego. Knott plays with the work ethic of someone grateful for the opportunity to play pro ball, and he has tools to go with his desire. He's a line-drive hitter with gap power and an understanding of the strike zone. Despite his size he has average speed and is a sneaky threat on the bases. He moves well in the outfield and may have enough arm to play right field. He also has seen time at first base, where he's solid, and played third base in instructional league. Knott has made himself into a prospect and will continue to progress toward San Diego in Double-A this year.

Year	Club (League)	Class	AVG	G	AB	R	H	2B	3B	HR	RBI	BB	SO	SB	SLG	OBP
2002	Fort Wayne (Mid)	A	.333	37	126	19	42	12	3	3	18	17	33	2	.548	.411
	Lake Elsinore (Cal)	A	.341	93	367	55	125	33	8	8	73	46	68	5	.540	.414
MINOR LEAGUE TOTALS			.339	130	493	74	167	45	11	11	91	63	101	7	.542	.413

23. Cliff Bartosh, lhp

Born: Sept. 5, 1979. **Ht.:** 6-2. **Wt.:** 170. **Bats:** L. **Throws:** L. **School:** Duncanville (Texas) HS. **Career Transactions:** Selected by Padres in 29th round of 1998 draft; signed July 3, 1998.

Mobile had a pair of southpaw relief prospects in Bartosh and independent league refugee Matt Hampton, with Bartosh getting the edge because he shows more consistent velocity. He also was the BayBears' choice as closer and responded with 25 saves in his first year in the role. It was his second year in Double-A, and he pitched better this time because he didn't try to overthrow. Bartosh's two main pitches are an 88-93 mph fastball and a good slider. He has the command to move the ball around the strike zone, though sometimes he gets too caught up in trying to make a perfect pitch and loses his release point. He needs to show more consistency with his slider. Bartosh, whose brother Craig turned down the Padres as a

46th-round pick in 2002 and now attends Oklahoma State, projects as a solid set-up man in the majors. He'll be one step away in Triple-A this year.

Year	Club (League)	Class	W	L	ERA	G	GS	CG	SV	IP	H	R	ER	HR	BB	SO	AVG
1998	Padres (AZL)	R	3	2	3.48	13	5	0	0	44	43	23	17	2	16	43	.257
1999	Fort Wayne (Mid)	A	5	12	4.44	35	20	1	0	130	136	76	64	14	49	100	.270
2000	Fort Wayne (Mid)	A	8	4	3.04	50	4	0	1	77	50	40	26	6	44	94	.178
2001	Lake Elsinore (Cal)	A	6	2	1.58	38	0	0	10	46	42	17	8	2	12	66	.237
	Mobile (SL)	AA	1	2	3.97	20	0	0	2	23	20	12	10	5	13	20	.233
2002	Mobile (SL)	AA	2	4	3.18	62	0	0	25	71	54	28	25	4	32	70	.211
MINOR LEAGUE TOTALS			25	26	3.46	218	29	1	38	390	345	196	150	33	166	393	.235

24. Freddy Guzman, of/2b

Born: Aug. 8, 1980. **Ht.:** 5-10. **Wt.:** 160. **Bats:** B. **Throws:** R. **Career Transactions:** Signed out of Dominican Republic by Padres, March 21, 2000.

Because the Immigration and Naturalization Service promised an even more stringent crackdown on falsified visa information this offseason, the Padres decided to conduct their own investigation. They uncovered an additional 18 players from the Dominican Republic playing under false names. The most prominent was Guzman, who was believed to be 31 months younger and was known as Pedro de los Santos when managers rated him the fastest baserunner in the Midwest League last year. He's one of several blazers with top-of-the-line speed in the system, joining the likes of Kennard Jones, Bernie Castro and Marcus Nettles. Though he has a nice stroke from both sides of the plate, he still needs to add strength and learn to hit breaking balls. Guzman made a nice transition from second base to center field last year, though his arm is below average. He's instinctive on the bases and was caught just 12 times in 81 steal attempts in 2002. The Padres felt Guzman had impact potential before they learned his true age, and now he's going to have to sink or swim in high Class A in 2003. He's raw for his revised age.

Year	Club (League)	Class	AVG	G	AB	R	H	2B	3B	HR	RBI	BB	SO	SB	SLG	OBP
2000	Padres (DSL)	R	.210	49	167	38	35	6	1	1	10	46	38	24	.275	.386
2001	Idaho Falls (Pio)	R	.348	12	46	11	16	4	1	0	5	2	10	5	.478	.388
2002	Lake Elsinore (Cal)	A	.259	21	81	13	21	3	0	1	6	8	12	14	.333	.326
	Fort Wayne (Mid)	A	.279	47	190	35	53	7	5	0	18	18	37	39	.368	.341
	Eugene (NWL)	A	.225	21	80	14	18	2	1	0	8	7	15	16	.275	.293
MINOR LEAGUE TOTALS			.254	150	564	111	143	22	8	2	47	81	112	98	.332	.351

25. Mike Wodnicki, rhp

Born: Jan. 17, 1980. **Ht.:** 6-3. **Wt.:** 210. **Bats:** R. **Throws:** R. **School:** Stanford University. **Career Transactions:** Selected by Cardinals in 16th round of 2001 draft; signed July 12, 2001 . . . Traded by Cardinals to Padres, Dec. 17, 2002, completing trade in which Padres sent RHP Brett Tomko to Cardinals for RHP Luther Hackman and a player to be named (Dec. 14, 2002).

At Stanford, Wodnicki went to the three College World Series in three years but was buried behind pitchers such as Mike Gosling, Jeremy Guthrie, Justin Wayne and Jason Young—all of whom became first- or second-round picks, signed for a total of $10.7 million in bonuses and became top pro prospects. Last year, on Peoria's Midwest League championship team, he was overshadowed by Dan Haren, Justin Pope and Tyler Johnson. But Wodnicki, acquired when Brett Tomko became too expensive for the Padres and was traded to St. Louis in December, is a legitimate prospect. He throws a lively low-90s fastball and tight slider with above-average command. He can get overexcited, which contributed to his 1-5, 4.37 start in 2002. But once he settled himself down and focused on throwing first-pitch strikes, he posted a 3.13 ERA for the remainder of the regular season and pitched well in two postseason starts. Peoria manager Danny Sheaffer insisted that Wodnicki would one day reach the majors. How well he develops his changeup will determine whether he does so as a starter or middle reliever. He'll be in the high Class A rotation this year.

Year	Club (League)	Class	W	L	ERA	G	GS	CG	SV	IP	H	R	ER	HR	BB	SO	AVG
2001	New Jersey (NY-P)	A	2	3	2.43	22	0	0	0	30	17	10	8	3	13	26	.170
2002	Peoria (Mid)	A	11	10	3.49	26	25	2	0	155	144	72	60	16	37	131	.245
MINOR LEAGUE TOTALS			13	13	3.32	48	25	2	0	184	161	82	68	19	50	157	.234

26. Greg Sain, 3b

Born: Dec. 26, 1979. **Ht.:** 6-2. **Wt.:** 200. **Bats:** R. **Throws:** R. **School:** University of San Diego. **Career Transactions:** Selected by Padres in fifth round of 2001 draft; signed June 14, 2001.

Sain won two home run crowns in 2001, leading the West Coast Conference and the short-season Northwest League with 16 each, but his shoulder ached by the end of the summer. An MRI revealed tears in the labrum and rotator cuff in his right shoulder, which required surgery that December. Sain, whose father Tom reached Triple-A in the late 1970s, missed the first month of the 2002 season and couldn't play the field until mid-May. His shoulder slowed his swing and he tired late in the season, but did show what he was capable of when he hit .286-7-20 in July. Once he gets his bat speed back in 2003, the Padres believe Sain can shoot up this list. His chances of doing so will be enhanced if he can return behind the plate, where he saw time in college. His catching potential was a major reason why San Diego drafted him. He showed an average to plus arm in college before he got hurt, and he has good receiving skills. Sain's arm looked strong by the end of last season, leading to hope that he can try catching again this year in high Class A.

Year	Club (League)	Class	AVG	G	AB	R	H	2B	3B	HR	RBI	BB	SO	SB	SLG	OBP
2001	Eugene (NWL)	A	.293	67	256	48	75	19	1	16	40	21	68	1	.563	.356
2002	Fort Wayne (Mid)	A	.245	105	387	54	95	29	0	13	57	35	77	2	.421	.323
MINOR LEAGUE TOTALS			.264	172	643	102	170	48	1	29	97	56	145	3	.477	.336

27. Brad Baker, rhp

Born: Nov. 6, 1980. **Ht.:** 6-2. **Wt.:** 180. **Bats:** R. **Throws:** R. **School:** Pioneer Valley HS, Northfield, Mass. **Career Transactions:** Selected by Red Sox in first round (40th overall) of 1999 draft; signed July 26, 1999 . . . Traded by Red Sox with RHP Dan Giese to Padres for LHP Alan Embree and RHP Andy Shibilo, June 23, 2002.

At first glance, acquiring Baker in a midseason deal with the Red Sox for Alan Embree had the potential to be as one-sided as the Dennis Tankersley-for-Ed Sprague heist San Diego perpetrated in 2000. But while Baker rebounded from a down 2001 season and pitched in the Futures Game, he hasn't regained the form that made him the Red Sox' top pitching prospect in 2000. Though he scrapped Boston's weightlifting program, which left him too bulky, and grew into his body, Baker no longer throws in the low 90s or reaches 95. He sits at 85-88 mph with little movement, and relies on his approach and a plus-plus changeup to survive. He also throws a curveball, and whether he can develop it into a solid average pitch may determine whether he reaches the majors. Baker needs to throw more two-seam fastballs rather than four-seamers, and he should use his curve more against lefthanders. His command deteriorated when he went to Double-A after the trade, which wasn't a good sign. He'll return there to begin 2003.

Year	Club (League)	Class	W	L	ERA	G	GS	CG	SV	IP	H	R	ER	HR	BB	SO	AVG
1999	Red Sox (GCL)	R	1	0	0.79	4	3	0	0	11	10	3	1	0	2	10	.227
2000	Augusta (SAL)	A	12	7	3.07	27	27	0	0	138	125	58	47	3	55	126	.245
2001	Sarasota (FSL)	A	7	9	4.73	24	23	0	0	120	132	77	63	8	64	103	.272
2002	Sarasota (FSL)	A	7	1	2.79	12	12	1	0	61	53	22	19	4	25	65	.233
	Mobile (SL)	AA	4	4	4.48	12	12	1	0	64	47	33	32	5	45	57	.208
MINOR LEAGUE TOTALS			31	21	3.69	79	77	2	0	395	367	193	162	20	191	361	.246

28. Nick Trzesniak, c

Born: Nov. 19, 1980. **Ht.:** 6-0. **Wt.:** 210. **Bats:** R. **Throws:** R. **School:** Andrew HS, Tinley Park, Ill. **Career Transactions:** Selected by Padres in first round (51st overall) of 1999 draft; signed July 6, 1999.

The weakest position in the organization is catcher, hands down. The Padres hope Trzesniak can help change that if he can continue to stay healthy. Back problems and a hand injury limited him to 122 games in his first three seasons after signing as a 1999 supplemental first-round pick, but he nearly matched that total in 2002. An all-Illinois linebacker in high school, Trzesniak and Josh Barfield were the best athletes on the Fort Wayne club last year. Trzesniak resembles a young Javy Lopez with his arm strength, power and speed, which is very good for a catcher and only slightly below-average. He still has work to do, as he muscles his swing and is too aggressive at the plate. While he has solid receiving skills, he needs to improve his footwork and release after throwing out just 22 percent of basestealers last year. Chosen by Fort Wayne fans as their favorite player in 2002, he'll move up to high Class A this year.

Year	Club (League)	Class	AVG	G	AB	R	H	2B	3B	HR	RBI	BB	SO	SB	SLG	OBP
1999	Padres (AZL)	R	.241	29	108	17	26	3	1	0	16	14	39	7	.287	.344
2000	Idaho Falls (Pio)	R	.341	36	132	32	45	6	2	7	30	23	30	4	.576	.453
2001	Eugene (NWL)	A	.233	57	193	24	45	8	1	2	21	22	59	0	.316	.324
2002	Fort Wayne (Mid)	A	.237	110	409	53	97	18	2	10	38	27	97	10	.364	.293
MINOR LEAGUE TOTALS			.253	232	842	126	213	35	6	19	105	86	225	21	.376	.334

29. Chris Oxspring, rhp

Born: May 13, 1977. **Ht.:** 6-1. **Wt.:** 180. **Bats:** L. **Throws:** R. **Career Transactions:** Signed by independent Cook County (Frontier), June 2000 . . . Signed by Padres, Oct. 31, 2000.

The Padres scout independent leagues as thoroughly as any organization, and their persistence paid off in September 2000. During a rain-soaked tryout for Frontier League players, they saw more than two dozen pitchers before Oxspring took the mound and popped 94 mph on the radar gun. Oxspring, who pitched for Australia at the 2001 World Cup, still touches 94 and works in the low 90s. His nasty curveball may be an even better pitch. San Diego wanted him to start last year, but he resisted that idea and spent most of the year in middle relief. As a result, he didn't get as much of a chance to develop his slider and changeup. Oxspring missed two months with shoulder problems but threw well after returning. He'll head back to Double-A in 2003. He's now open to the idea of starting, and likely will earn a spot in a Mobile rotation that already will include top lefties Mark Phillips and Cory Stewart.

Year	Club (League)	Class	W	L	ERA	G	GS	CG	SV	IP	H	R	ER	HR	BB	SO	AVG
2000	Cook County (Fron)	IND	1	0	3.10	13	2	0	1	29	29	18	10	1	15	29	.257
2001	Fort Wayne (Mid)	A	4	1	4.15	41	2	0	0	56	66	29	26	5	25	54	.297
	Lake Elsinore (Cal)	A	0	0	0.64	7	0	0	0	14	10	2	1	1	6	17	.200
2002	Lake Elsinore (Cal)	A	0	1	4.78	15	1	0	0	26	24	16	14	2	8	30	.238
	Mobile (SL)	AA	0	0	1.26	6	1	0	0	14	13	3	2	0	8	21	.245
MINOR LEAGUE TOTALS			4	2	3.49	69	4	0	0	111	113	50	43	8	47	122	.265

30. Marcus Nettles, of

Born: May 15, 1980. **Ht.:** 5-11. **Wt.:** 180. **Bats:** L. **Throws:** L. **School:** University of Miami. **Career Transactions:** Selected by Padres in 11th round of 2001 draft; signed July 7, 2001.

In an organization loaded with speedsters, no player has more pure speed than Nettles. With a 6.2-second time, he might be able to beat any player in baseball in a 60-yard dash. Nettles runs like a sprinter, lifting his legs high and taking a while to accelerate, so he's not quite as quick as Bernie Castro down the first-base line. But that hasn't stopped Nettles from leading the Northwest and California leagues in stolen bases in his first two pro seasons. Managers rated him the best and fastest baserunner in the Cal League last year. Nettles still needs to refine the art of basestealing after getting caught a minor league-high 26 times in 2002, and has a lot of learning to do in other facets of the game. His ground-ball approach and exceptional patience serve him well as a leadoff prospect. But he'll have to improve his .299 slugging percentage, and he can get too passive at the plate, leading to too many called third strikes. Improving his ability to bunt would make him more dangerous. Nettles has incredible range in the outfield, but it's offset by his very weak arm. He broke the humerus bone in his arm as a high schooler and hasn't thrown well since. He does get to balls quickly, which helps, but his arm still makes him a left fielder. He injured his right foot during the Cal League playoffs, costing him valuable developmental time in instructional league. Nettles will play in Double-A this season.

Year	Club (League)	Class	AVG	G	AB	R	H	2B	3B	HR	RBI	BB	SO	SB	SLG	OBP
2001	Eugene (NWL)	A	.300	55	213	37	64	3	0	0	10	27	54	35	.315	.385
2002	Lake Elsinore (Cal)	A	.254	125	485	97	123	18	2	0	38	101	132	58	.299	.386
MINOR LEAGUE TOTALS			.268	180	698	134	187	21	2	0	48	128	186	93	.304	.386

SAN FRANCISCO
GIANTS

TOP 30 PROSPECTS

1. Jesse Foppert, rhp
2. Kurt Ainsworth, rhp
3. Jerome Williams,rhp
4. Francisco Liriano, lhp
5. Todd Linden, of
6. Boof Bonser, rhp
7. Fred Lewis, of
8. Ryan Hannaman, lhp
9. Lance Niekro, 1b/3b
10. Erick Threets, lhp
11. Matt Cain, rhp
12. Deivis Santos, of/1b
13. Tony Torcato, of
14. Travis Ishikawa, 1b
15. Melvin Valdez, rhp
16. Noah Lowry, lhp
17. Jason Ellison, of
18. Carlos Valderrama, of
19. David Cash, rhp
20. Dan Ortmeier, of
21. Jeff Clark, rhp
22. Greg Bruso, rhp
23. Jesse English, lhp
24. Anthony Pannone, rhp
25. Angel Chavez, 3b/ss
26. R.D. Spiehs, rhp
27. Trey Lunsford, c
28. Cody Ransom, ss
29. John Thomas, lhp
30. Carlos Portorreal, rhp

**By Jeff
Fletcher**

In Game Seven of the World Series last fall, the Giants did not have a position player in the field younger than 30, leading to the assumption that things are bound to change around Pac Bell Park soon.

General manager Brian Sabean says the Giants need to get younger, and the time could be coming when the farm system is finally ready to start cranking out players who will be ready for the big leagues. The last position player who came out of the Giants system to get even semi-regular playing time quickly was Bill Mueller, who reached the majors in 1996 and was the platoon starter at third in '97. They've done a little better with pitchers, developing two of last year's five starters (Russ Ortiz and Ryan Jensen).

The Giants hope that will change, starting with the starters. Jesse Foppert, Kurt Ainsworth and Jerome Williams all finished 2002 at Triple-A and should be ready for the majors at some point in 2003, if only the Giants can find a place for them. The Giants also have layers of pitching a year or two behind those three, giving them an ample supply not only to fill jobs in San Francisco, but also to be fodder for trades.

Lately the weakness of the Giants system has been producing position players. Sabean said their philosophy is to draft all the pitching they can get because that's the most valuable commodity, then trade the leftovers to get position players. The current crop of position players looks better than in years past, with outfielders Todd Linden and Tony Torcato probably ready for the majors in 2003. Versatile Deivis Santos and corner infielder Lance Niekro are not far behind. Deeper in the system are corner outfielder Fred Lewis, who is still raw but talented, first baseman Travis Ishikawa and center fielder Dan Ortmeier.

The Giants have the perfect manager to handle the transition in Felipe Alou. Dusty Baker preferred for young players to break in slowly, but Alou worked with a faster learning curve (by necessity) in Montreal, so he could do the same with players like Foppert, Williams and Linden.

Don't expect the Giants to turn things over to the kids and try to become the Twins, because it's not their nature to give up any season as a rebuilding one. They will still fill holes with veterans—the organization is weak in catchers and middle infielders—but hope the farm system will leave them fewer holes to fill in years to come.

OrganizationOverview

General Manager: Brian Sabean. Farm Director: Jack Hiatt. Scouting Director: Dick Tidrow.

2002 PERFORMANCE

Class	Farm Team	League	W	L	Pct.	Finish*	Manager
Majors	San Francisco	National	95	66	.590	4th (16)	Dusty Baker
Triple-A	Fresno Grizzlies	Pacific Coast	57	87	.396	16th (16)	Lenn Sakata
Double-A	†Shreveport Swamp Dragons	Texas	60	79	.432	7th (8)	Mario Mendoza
High A	San Jose Giants	California	68	72	.486	7th (10)	Bill Hayes
Low A	Hagerstown Suns	South Atlantic	63	77	.450	13th (16)	Mike Ramsey
Short-season	Salem-Keizer Volcanoes	Northwest	41	35	.539	t-3rd (8)	Fred Stanley
Rookie	AZL Giants	Arizona	32	23	.582	2nd (7)	Bert Hunter
OVERALL MINOR LEAGUE RECORD			321	373	.463	25th (30)	

*Finish in overall standings (No. of teams in league).   †Affiliate will be in Norwich (Eastern) in 2003.

ORGANIZATION LEADERS

BATTING
*Minimum 250 At-Bats
*AVG	Lance Niekro, Shreveport	.310
R	Todd Linden, Fresno/Shreveport	82
H	Deivis Santos, Fresno/Shreveport	152
TB	Todd Linden, Fresno/Shreveport	227
2B	Deivis Santos, Fresno/Shreveport	36
3B	Jamie Athas, San Jose	7
	Carlos Valderrama, Shreveport/San Jose	7
HR	Carlos Valderrama, Shreveport/San Jose	19
RBI	Julian Benavidez, Hagerstown	72
BB	Todd Linden, Fresno/Shreveport	81
SO	Dan Trumble, San Jose	185
SB	Jason Ellison, Fresno/San Jose	25

PITCHING
#Minimum 75 Innings
W	Jeff Clark, Shreveport/San Jose	14
L	Luis Estrella, Fresno	13
	Wes Hutchison, Fresno/Shreveport	13
#ERA	Jeff Clark, Shreveport/San Jose	2.66
G	Troy Brohawn, Fresno	56
CG	Anthony Pannone, Hagerstown	2
	Jeff Clark, Shreveport/San Jose	2
SV	Manny Aybar, Fresno	24
IP	Jeff Clark, Shreveport/San Jose	176
BB	Boof Bonser, Shreveport/San Jose	84
SO	Jesse Foppert, Fresno/Shreveport	183

BEST TOOLS

Best Hitter for Average	Fred Lewis
Best Power Hitter	Todd Linden
Fastest Baserunner	Fred Lewis
Best Athlete	Fred Lewis
Best Fastball	Erick Threets
Best Curveball	Clay Hensley
Best Slider	Jerome Williams
Best Changeup	Francisco Liriano
Best Control	Kurt Ainsworth
Best Defensive Catcher	Trey Lunsford
Best Defensive Infielder	Cody Ransom
Best Infield Arm	Cody Ransom
Best Defensive Outfielder	Jason Ellison
Best Outfield Arm	Jason Ellison

PROJECTED 2006 LINEUP

Catcher	Yorvit Torrealba
First Base	Lance Niekro
Second Base	Ray Durham
Third Base	Edgardo Alfonzo
Shortstop	Rich Aurilia
Left Field	Tony Torcato
Center Field	Fred Lewis
Right Field	Todd Linden
No. 1 Starter	Jesse Foppert

Deivis Santos   Manny Aybar

No. 2 Starter	Jerome Williams
No. 3 Starter	Jason Schmidt
No. 4 Starter	Kurt Ainsworth
No. 5 Starter	Francisco Liriano
Closer	Robb Nen

TOP PROSPECTS OF THE DECADE

1993	Calvin Murray, of
1994	Salomon Torres, rhp
1995	J.R. Phillips, 1b
1996	Shawn Estes, lhp
1997	Joe Fontenot, rhp
1998	Jason Grilli, rhp
1999	Jason Grilli, rhp
2000	Kurt Ainsworth, rhp
2001	Jerome Williams, rhp
2002	Jerome Williams, rhp

TOP DRAFT PICKS OF THE DECADE

1993	Steve Soderstrom, rhp
1994	Dante Powell, of
1995	Joe Fontenot, rhp
1996	*Matt White, rhp
1997	Jason Grilli, rhp
1998	Tony Torcato, 3b
1999	Kurt Ainsworth, rhp
2000	Boof Bonser, rhp
2001	Brad Hennessey, rhp
2002	Matt Cain, rhp

*Did not sign

ALL-TIME LARGEST BONUSES

Jason Grilli, 1997	$1,875,000
Brad Hennessey, 2001	$1,380,000
Matt Cain, 2002	$1,375,000
Osvaldo Fernandez, 1996	$1,300,000
Kurt Ainsworth, 2000	$1,300,000

MinorLeagueDepthChart

SAN FRANCISCO GIANTS

RANK 11

The Giants farm system has improved significantly in recent years. It is well stocked with promising live arms, and Triple-A Fresno has a potential rotation of the future in righthanders Jesse Foppert, Kurt Ainsworth and Jerome Williams. All are on the cusp of breaking into the big leagues. Throw in power lefties Francisco Liriano and Ryan Hannaman, and the Giants have filled out a five-man rotation. As strong as their pitching is, though, there is a gaping hole in overall infield depth. Todd Linden's powerful bat provides potential for future offensive help.

Note: Depth charts prepared by Josh Boyd. Numbers in parentheses indicate prospect rankings.

LF
Todd Linden (5)
Deivis Santos (12)
Tony Torcato (13)
Dan Ortmeier (20)
Adam Shabala

CF
Fred Lewis (7)
Jason Ellison (17)
Carlos Valderrama (18)

RF
Carlos Sosa
Randy Walter

3B
Lance Niekro (9)
Angel Chavez (25)
Julian Benevidez

SS
Cody Ransom (28)
Jamie Athas

2B
Joe Jester
Aaron Sobieraj

1B
Travis Ishikawa (14)
Sean McGowan

C
Trey Lunsford (27)
Dayton Buller
Justin Knoedler
Guillermo Rodriguez

RHP

Starters
Jesse Foppert (1)
Kurt Ainsworth (2)
Jerome Williams (3)
Boof Bonser (6)
Matt Cain (11)
Melvin Valdez (15)
Jeff Clark (21)
Greg Bruso (22)
Anthony Pannone (24)
Carlos Portorreal (30)
Brion Treadway
Kevin Correia
Clay Hensley
Glenn Woolard
Brad Hennessey

Relievers
David Cash (19)
R.D. Spiehs (26)
Luke Anderson

LHP

Starters
Francisco Liriano (4)
Ryan Hannaman (8)
Noah Lowry (16)
Jesse English (23)
John Thomas (29)

Relievers
Erick Threets (10)
Jeff Urban

DraftAnalysis

2002 Draft

Best Pro Debut: Managers named OF Fred Lewis (2) the top position player in the short-season Northwest League, where he batted .322-1-23. RHP Greg Bruso (16) went 4-3 with a NWL-best 1.99 ERA. RHP Luke Nelson (17) went 7-0 and had a lower ERA (1.87) but not enough innings to qualify for the title. OF David Stone (36) hit .281-4-21 and led the NWL with a .435 on-base percentage. In the Rookie-level Arizona League, LHP **Jesse English** (6) went 4-1, 2.68 with 68 strikeouts in 47 innings.

Best Athlete: Lewis played more football than baseball at Mississippi Gulf Coast JC before transferring to Southern as a junior. His speed is his best tool. OF Randy Walter (9) also has five-tool potential.

Best Pure Hitter: Lewis. The Giants also like OF Dan Ortmeier (3), Walter, 2B Aaron Sobieraj (13) and 1B Travis Ishikawa (21), all of whom hit .283 or better in the NWL.

Best Raw Power: Once he fills out and learns to drive the ball, Ishikawa will surpass Ortmeier. Lewis is also developing power.

Fastest Runner: Lewis is a true burner with 6.4-second speed in the 60-yard dash and a 3.85-second home-to-first time from the left side.

Best Defensive Player: Lewis is refining his center-field skills, but his potential is obvious. SS Jake Wald (11) is a pure shortstop who needs to get stronger at the plate.

Best Fastball: RHP Matt Cain (1) continued to touch 94-95 mph through instructional league. RHP Kevin Correia (4) also has a resilient arm and sits in the low 90s.

Best Breaking Ball: Cain's curveball over Correia's slider and RHP Clay Hensley's (8) curve.

Most Intriguing Background: RHP Glenn Woolard (10) was the NCAA Division II player of the year last spring, going 14-2, 2.81 with 148 strikeouts in 106 innings at Kutztown (Pa.). Unsigned RHP Justin Gee (25) was MVP of the 1999 Babe Ruth World Series.

Closest To The Majors: When Lewis puts everything together, he'll rush toward San Francisco.

English

Best Late-Round Pick: Ishikawa's bonus demands were all that stood between him going in the first three rounds. A strong student who had a college commitment to Oregon State, he signed for $950,000, a record for a 21st-rounder. With a solid fastball/slider/changeup repertoire, Bruso is for real.

The One Who Got Away: Some clubs liked SS Neil Walton (23) better as a pitcher, but the Giants liked his offensive potential and lanky build. He opted for Cal State Fullerton over pro ball.

Assessment: The Giants continued to add to one of the game's more underrated farm systems. They got a frontline pitcher in Cain, a top athlete in Lewis and a potentially special bat in Ishikawa.

2001 Draft

Getting RHP Jesse Foppert (2) with the 74th overall pick was outright robbery. OF Todd Linden (1) reached Triple-A in his first pro season. Two other first-rounders, RHP Brad Hennessey and LHP Noah Lowry, have been set back by health problems. **Grade: A**

2000 Draft

Not many players in the system have higher ceilings than RHP Boof Bonser (1), 1B/3B Lance Niekro (2) and LHPs Ryan Hannaman (4) and Erick Threets (7). **Grade: B+**

1999 Draft

The Giants got 40 percent of their future rotation with two first-rounders, RHPs Kurt Ainsworth and Jerome Williams. **Grade: B+**

1998 Draft

San Francisco doesn't have much to show for five first-rounders. OF Tony Torcato (1) has leveled off somewhat, and he's still light years ahead of RHP Nate Bump (since traded), OF Arturo McDowell, who has retired, and LHPs Chris Jones and Jeff Urban. **Grade: C**

Note: Draft analysis prepared by Jim Callis. Numbers in parentheses indicate draft rounds.

. . . Foppert has a smooth motion, looking as if he's barely working, and the ball still jumps out of his hand.

Jesse
Foppert rhp

Born: July 10, 1980.
Ht.: 6-6. **Wt.:** 210.
Bats: R. **Throws:** R.
School: University of San Francisco.
Career Transactions: Selected by Giants in second round of 2001 draft; signed June 8, 2001.

Foppert is from San Rafael, just a ferry ride away from Pac Bell Park. He's not far away in a baseball sense either. Undrafted as a high school infielder, he barely pitched in his first two years at the University of San Francisco. When his Shenandoah Valley League team needed pitchers in the summer of 2000, he was persuaded to get on the mound. To say it turned out to be a good move is an understatement. After a solid junior year pitching for the Dons, he went in the second round of the 2001 draft and led the short-season Northwest League in ERA during his pro debut. Foppert was even more dominant during his first full pro season in 2002. He reached Triple-A, where he was rated the Pacific Coast League's No. 1 prospect, and led the minors by averaging 11.7 strikeouts per nine innings.

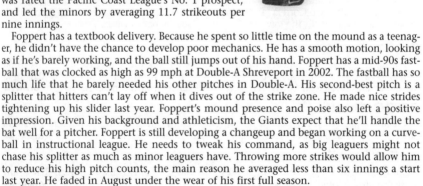

PAUL JASIENSKI

Foppert has a textbook delivery. Because he spent so little time on the mound as a teenager, he didn't have the chance to develop poor mechanics. He has a smooth motion, looking as if he's barely working, and the ball still jumps out of his hand. Foppert has a mid-90s fastball that was clocked as high as 99 mph at Double-A Shreveport in 2002. The fastball has so much life that he barely needed his other pitches in Double-A. His second-best pitch is a splitter that hitters can't lay off when it dives out of the strike zone. He made nice strides tightening up his slider last year. Foppert's mound presence and poise also left a positive impression. Given his background and athleticism, the Giants expect that he'll handle the bat well for a pitcher. Foppert is still developing a changeup and began working on a curveball in instructional league. He needs to tweak his command, as big leaguers might not chase his splitter as much as minor leaguers have. Throwing more strikes would allow him to reduce his high pitch counts, the main reason he averaged less than six innings a start last year. He faded in August under the wear of his first full season.

Foppert probably won't win a spot on the Opening Day roster. The Giants don't have a clear opening and he could use more time at Triple-A Fresno. But if he picks up where he left off, he could force a promotion quickly. Easing him into the majors in a long relief role also could be a possibility.

Year	Club (League)	Class	W	L	ERA	G	GS	CG	SV	IP	H	R	ER	HR	BB	SO	AVG
2001	Salem-Keizer (NWL)	A	8	1	1.93	14	14	0	0	70	35	18	15	7	23	88	.150
2002	Shreveport (TL)	AA	3	3	2.79	11	11	1	0	61	44	22	19	3	21	74	.199
	Fresno (PCL)	AAA	3	6	3.99	14	14	0	0	79	71	37	35	12	35	109	.244
MINOR LEAGUE TOTALS			14	10	2.95	39	39	1	0	210	150	77	69	22	79	271	.201

2. Kurt Ainsworth, rhp

Born: Sept. 9, 1978. **Ht.:** 6-3. **Wt.:** 190. **Bats:** R. **Throws:** R. **School:** Louisiana State University. **Career Transactions:** Selected by Giants in first round (24th overall) of 1999 draft; signed June 17, 1999.

Ainsworth recovered from Tommy John surgery at Louisiana State to become a first-round pick in 1999, and he won a gold medal with the U.S. Olympic team a year later. He sailed through his first two stops in the system before having a difficult time adjusting to Triple-A in the first half of 2001, but he has recovered nicely. He pitched well during two callups last year. Ainsworth is a complete pitcher with a solid five-pitch repertoire. He throws a 92-94 mph four-seam fastball, an 88-90 mph sinker, a slider, a curve and a changeup. He also developed a much better feel for setting up hitters his second time through Fresno. He missed a month last year with a pulled back muscle, but has otherwise been healthy since his elbow was rebuilt. While he's not overpowering, Ainsworth has the stuff and command to win. He needs to believe that, however, and go after hitters rather than trying to make the perfect pitch. The Giants believe Ainsworth has nothing left to gain in the minors. Unless he has a horrible spring, look for him to displace Ryan Jensen or possibly Livan Hernandez in the San Francisco rotation.

Year	Club (League)	Class	W	L	ERA	G	GS	CG	SV	IP	H	R	ER	HR	BB	SO	AVG
1999	Salem-Keizer (NWL)	A	3	3	1.61	10	10	1	0	45	34	18	8	1	18	64	.211
2000	Shreveport (TL)	AA	10	9	3.30	28	28	0	0	158	138	67	58	12	63	130	.233
2001	Fresno (PCL)	AAA	10	9	5.07	27	26	0	0	149	139	91	84	22	54	157	.247
	San Francisco (NL)	MAJ	0	0	13.50	2	0	0	0	2	3	3	3	1	2	3	.333
2002	San Francisco (NL)	MAJ	1	2	2.10	6	4	0	0	26	22	7	6	1	12	15	.237
	Fresno (PCL)	AAA	8	6	3.41	20	19	1	0	116	101	49	44	7	43	119	.238
MAJOR LEAGUE TOTALS			1	2	2.93	8	4	0	0	28	25	10	9	2	14	18	.245
MINOR LEAGUE TOTALS			31	27	3.73	85	83	2	0	468	412	225	194	42	178	470	.237

3. Jerome Williams, rhp

Born: Dec. 4, 1981. **Ht.:** 6-3. **Wt.:** 180. **Bats:** R. **Throws:** R. **School:** Waipahu (Hawaii) HS. **Career Transactions:** Selected by Giants in first round (39th overall) of 1999 draft; signed July 10, 1999.

After being rated the organization's top prospect the previous two years, Williams still is considered a potential star, though his stock dipped slightly in 2002. He sped through the system to reach Triple-A at 20, which made him the youngest regular starter in the Pacific Coast League, then dominated in the Arizona Fall League. Williams' athleticism is often compared to that of a young Dwight Gooden. He throws a 90-92 mph fastball and an outstanding changeup. He has a mound presence that helps him get out of jams. One of his catchers said he was great at improvising pitches during a game. His makeup came into question during a rough patch in the middle of 2002. Some Giants officials and PCL observers wondered why Williams couldn't translate his athleticism into better stuff, questioning his work ethic. He seemed to address those concerns by the end of the year, when he posted a 1.83 ERA in his final eight starts. Williams also needs to improve his slider and curveball. He may have more upside than Jesse Foppert or Kurt Ainsworth, but he's younger, less polished and less mature. He might pitch a second full season in Triple-A, like Ainsworth did last year.

Year	Club (League)	Class	W	L	ERA	G	GS	CG	SV	IP	H	R	ER	HR	BB	SO	AVG
1999	Salem-Keizer (NWL)	A	1	1	2.19	7	7	1	0	37	29	13	9	1	11	34	.213
2000	San Jose (Cal)	A	7	6	2.94	23	19	0	0	126	89	53	41	6	48	115	.201
2001	Shreveport (TL)	AA	9	7	3.95	23	23	2	0	130	116	69	57	14	34	84	.235
2002	Fresno (PCL)	AAA	6	11	3.59	28	28	0	0	161	140	76	64	16	50	130	.234
MINOR LEAGUE TOTALS			23	25	3.39	81	77	3	0	453	374	211	171	37	143	363	.224

4. Francisco Liriano, lhp

Born: Oct. 26, 1983. **Ht.:** 6-2. **Wt.:** 180. **Bats:** L. **Throws:** L. **Career Transactions:** Signed out of Dominican Republic by Giants, Sept. 9, 2000.

Liriano showed up at a Dominican tryout camp as an outfielder, but the Giants immediately moved him to the mound. He was just 18 when he began his first full season at low Class A Hagerstown last year. He pitched well and was selected for the Futures Game, but he didn't make the trip because of shoulder problems that prevented him from pitching after July 21. Liriano cranks his fastball up to 97 mph and throws consistently at 93-94 with good life. His slider and changeup are outstanding for his age, and he may have three big league-ready pitches right now. He's intelligent and mature beyond his years on the mound. The biggest issue for now is the health of his shoulder. Liriano will have to prove he can stay healthy and be durable after going more than five innings just five times in 16 starts last year. He needs more consistency with his secondary pitches and his control. He also needs to learn pitching strategy to better attack hitters. The Giants will be cautious with Liriano because he's so young and so talented. If he's healthy, he'll probably open 2003 at high Class A San Jose.

Year	Club (League)	Class	W	L	ERA	G	GS	CG	SV	IP	H	R	ER	HR	BB	SO	AVG
2001	Giants (AZL)	R	5	4	3.63	13	12	0	0	62	51	26	25	3	24	67	.232
	Salem-Keizer (NWL)	A	0	0	5.00	2	2	0	0	9	7	5	5	2	1	12	.206
2002	Hagerstown (SAL)	A	3	6	3.49	16	16	0	0	80	61	45	31	6	31	85	.210
MINOR LEAGUE TOTALS			8	10	3.64	31	30	0	0	151	119	76	61	11	56	164	.218

5. Todd Linden, of

Born: June 30, 1980. **Ht.:** 6-3. **Wt.:** 210. **Bats:** B. **Throws:** R. **School:** Louisiana State University. **Career Transactions:** Selected by Giants in first round (41st overall) of 2001 draft; signed Sept. 4, 2001.

The Giants had given up on signing Linden as a supplemental first-round pick in 2001, but then he dumped agent Tommy Tanzer and cut a deal for a $750,000 bonus on his own. Though his pro debut was delayed until 2002, he made up for it by tearing up Double-A and reaching Triple-A. Linden is a switch-hitter with 30-homer potential. Guys like that tend to move quickly, and he has. He sprays the ball around the field and is willing to draw walks, so he'll probably hit for average as well. He has a strong arm suited for right field. He runs well enough to get to balls in the oufield and steal bases if he's ignored. Linden's stroke can get long, and he occasionally overswings and gets herky-jerky with his mechanics. He needs work on his routes to fly balls. Linden finished 2002 in Triple-A and he'll probably start there this year. The Giants don't have a clear-cut right fielder, so it's possible he could break camp with them if he has a big spring. Realistically, he's another year away.

Year	Club (League)	Class	AVG	G	AB	R	H	2B	3B	HR	RBI	BB	SO	SB	SLG	OBP
2002	Shreveport (TL)	AA	.314	111	392	64	123	26	2	12	52	61	101	9	.482	.419
	Fresno (PCL)	AAA	.250	29	100	18	25	2	1	3	10	20	35	2	.380	.380
MINOR LEAGUE TOTALS			.301	140	492	82	148	28	3	15	62	81	136	11	.461	.411

6. Boof Bonser, rhp

Born: Oct. 14, 1981. **Ht.:** 6-4. **Wt.:** 230. **Bats:** R. **Throws:** R. **School:** Gibbs HS, St. Petersburg, Fla. **Career Transactions:** Selected by Giants in first round (21st overall) of 2000 draft; signed July 3, 2000.

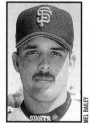

The owner of one of the best names in baseball, Bonser officially changed his name from John to Boof after his childhood nickname stuck. A bit of a surprise as the 21st overall pick in 2000, Bonser justified his selection by winning most valuable pitcher and top prospect recognition in the low Class A South Atlantic League in 2001. He struggled when rushed to Double-A to start last season and had to be demoted to work on his secondary pitches. Bonser showed a mid-90s fastball that was enough to dominate at Hagerstown, but it dropped to the low 90s last year at high Class A San Jose. Though he still must refine his curveball and changeup, they show promise. He has been unhittable as a pro, limiting opponents to a .203 average while averaging 10.7 strikeouts per nine innings. Bonser got pounded at Double-A because he couldn't throw his curve or changeup for strikes. He answered questions about his maturity and work ethic in 2001, but the Giants think he expected things to come too easily to him last season. Bonser still needs a lot of improvement on his pitches and command to reach his high ceiling, so it wouldn't be a shock if he started 2003 back in high Class A. He should reach the Giants' new Double-A Norwich affiliate by the end of the year.

Year	Club (League)	Class	W	L	ERA	G	GS	CG	SV	IP	H	R	ER	HR	BB	SO	AVG
2000	Salem-Keizer (NWL)	A	1	4	6.00	10	9	0	0	33	21	23	22	2	29	41	.188
2001	Hagerstown (SAL)	A	16	4	2.49	27	27	0	0	134	91	40	37	7	61	178	.192
2002	Shreveport (TL)	AA	1	2	5.55	5	5	0	0	24	30	15	15	3	14	23	.316
	San Jose (Cal)	A	8	6	2.88	23	23	0	0	128	89	44	41	9	70	139	.195
MINOR LEAGUE TOTALS			26	16	3.24	65	64	0	0	320	231	122	115	21	174	381	.203

7. Fred Lewis, of

Born: Dec. 9, 1980. **Ht.:** 6-2. **Wt.:** 190. **Bats:** L. **Throws:** R. **School:** Southern University. **Career Transactions:** Selected by Giants in second round of 2002 draft; signed June 20, 2002.

Lewis played more football than baseball at Mississippi Gulf Coast JC before transferring to Southern. He's part of a recent wave of Southern prospects that includes Tigers 2001 first-rounder Michael Woods and Rickie Weeks, the possible No. 1 overall pick in 2003. Lewis was the Northwest League's top position prospect in his pro debut. Though he's raw, Lewis is as close to a five-tool player as the Giants have in their system. He slashes the ball all over the field, which should help him maintain a high average, and he also has good patience for a player with his limited experience. He's the fastest player and best athlete in the system. Lewis has trouble tracking balls in center field, though his speed helps make up for some of that deficiency. He needs to learn how to steal bases and how to pull pitches for power. Lewis still has a lot of work to do, but the Giants rave about his potential and anticipate the day when he can cover center at Pacific Bell Park. He'll probably begin his first full season in low Class A.

Year	Club (League)	Class	AVG	G	AB	R	H	2B	3B	HR	RBI	BB	SO	SB	SLG	OBP
2002	Salem-Keizer (NWL)	A	.322	58	239	43	77	9	3	1	23	26	58	9	.397	.396
MINOR LEAGUE TOTALS			.322	58	239	43	77	9	3	1	23	26	58	9	.397	.396

8. Ryan Hannaman, lhp

Born: Aug. 28, 1981. **Ht.:** 6-3. **Wt.:** 200. **Bats:** L. **Throws:** L. **School:** Murphy HS, Mobile, Ala. **Career Transactions:** Selected by Giants in fourth round of 2000 draft; signed June 11, 2000.

The cream of the Giants system is the trio of polished righthanders at the top of the prospect list, but they also have collected an impressive group of power lefties, led by Francisco Liriano, Hannaman and Erick Threets. As with Liriano, San Francisco first saw Hannaman as a position player and immediately made him a full-time pitcher. Hannaman's lack of a pitching background was evident when he signed, and he's still raw, but one Giants official called him the most improved player in the system last year. As he got a better feel for his mechanics, he finished 2002 with 68 strikeouts in his last 49 innings. Batters can't get comfortable against his lively mid-90s fastball and tight slider. Hannaman doesn't have a consistent delivery, which causes his slider to flatten and his location to suffer. He's going to need time to come up with a changeup. He also requires plenty of work on the nuances of pitching, such as holding runners and fielding his position. If Hannaman can't smooth out his rough edges, he still could project as a nasty southpaw closer. He'll pitch this year in high Class A.

Year	Club (League)	Class	W	L	ERA	G	GS	CG	SV	IP	H	R	ER	HR	BB	SO	AVG
2000	Giants (AZL)	R	0	1	21.60	5	0	0	0	3	4	8	8	0	11	6	.333
	Salem-Keizer (NWL)	A	0	0	0.00	1	0	0	0	1	1	0	0	0	1	1	.250
2001	Giants (AZL)	R	4	1	2.00	11	11	0	0	54	34	14	12	1	31	67	.182
	Salem-Keizer (NWL)	A	1	1	2.08	3	3	0	0	13	8	5	3	1	8	19	.170
2002	Hagerstown (SAL)	A	7	6	2.80	24	24	1	0	132	129	54	41	9	46	145	.256
	San Jose (Cal)	A	0	0	3.00	1	1	0	0	6	3	2	2	1	3	7	.158
MINOR LEAGUE TOTALS			12	9	2.84	45	39	1	0	209	179	83	66	12	100	245	.232

9. Lance Niekro, 1b/3b

Born: Jan. 29, 1979. **Ht.:** 6-3. **Wt.:** 210. **Bats:** R. **Throws:** R. **School:** Florida Southern College. **Career Transactions:** Selected by Giants in second round of 2000 draft; signed June 3, 2000.

Yes, Niekro can throw a knuckleball just like his father Joe and uncle Phil, who won 539 games between them in the majors. Unlike them, his ticket to the majors is as a position player who first made his mark by nearly winning the 1999 Cape Cod League triple crown. He has risen quickly, though injuries have interrupted both his full seasons (shoulder in 2001, wrist in 2002). Niekro is a disciplined hitter who uses the whole field. He has good size and he knows how to use it to generate leverage. He has good range at third base and made a smooth adjustment to first base when the Giants wanted to give his shoulder a break following his 2001 surgery. Niekro should develop power, but so far he hasn't shown it. He makes good contact but has to draw more walks after totaling just 22 in 170 pro games. He's not much of a runner. Most of all, he has to stay healthy to get more experience. Niekro will start 2003 in Triple-A. The Giants still haven't decided if his future is at first or third base, though he'd prefer to go back to the hot corner.

Year	Club (League)	Class	AVG	G	AB	R	H	2B	3B	HR	RBI	BB	SO	SB	SLG	OBP
2000	Salem-Keizer (NWL)	A	.362	49	196	27	71	14	4	5	44	11	25	2	.551	.404
2001	San Jose (Cal)	A	.288	42	163	18	47	11	0	3	34	4	14	4	.411	.298
2002	Shreveport (TL)	AA	.310	79	297	33	92	20	1	4	34	7	32	0	.424	.327
MINOR LEAGUE TOTALS			.320	170	656	78	210	45	5	12	112	22	71	6	.459	.343

10. Erick Threets, lhp

Born: Nov. 4, 1981. **Ht.:** 6-5. **Wt.:** 240. **Bats:** L. **Throws:** L. **School:** Modesto (Calif.) JC. **Career Transactions:** Selected by Giants in seventh round of 2000 draft; signed Aug. 1, 2000.

Threets comes from Randy Johnson's hometown of Livermore, Calif., and has more heat than the five-time Cy Young Award winner. He reportedly hit 103 mph in instructional league following the 2001 season, and regularly reached triple digits last year. Poor mechanics have contributed to a sore arm and shoulder bursitis, limiting him to 150 innings as an amateur and pro over the last three years. Threets throws harder on a consistent basis than anyone in baseball, including the majors. He has a perfect build for a pitcher, at 6-foot-5 with wide shoulders and narrow hips. At times he'll show a nasty slider. At this point, Threets doesn't have much going for him besides velocity. He may have to sacrifice a few ticks to get more life and command. His delivery still needs smoothing out and his lack of control precludes using him as a starter. His slider is inconsistent and he has no semblance of an offspeed pitch. The Giants see Threets as a guy who can come in for an inning and blow hitters away. He'll advance quickly if he can lock in his mechanics and learn how to subtract a little when he gets behind in the count. If he can develop a second reliable pitch and throw more strikes, he has closer potential.

Year	Club (League)	Class	W	L	ERA	G	GS	CG	SV	IP	H	R	ER	HR	BB	SO	AVG
2001	San Jose (Cal)	A	0	10	4.25	14	14	0	0	59	49	34	28	2	40	60	.224
	Hagerstown (SAL)	A	2	0	0.75	12	0	0	1	24	13	3	2	1	9	32	.155
2002	San Jose (Cal)	A	0	1	6.67	26	0	0	0	28	23	24	21	2	28	43	.225
MINOR LEAGUE TOTALS			2	11	4.11	52	14	0	1	112	85	61	51	5	77	135	.210

11. Matt Cain, rhp

Born: Oct. 1, 1984. **Ht.:** 6-3. **Wt.:** 180. **Bats:** R. **Throws:** R. **School:** Houston HS, Germantown, Tenn. **Career Transactions:** Selected by Giants in first round (25th overall) of 2002 draft; signed June 26, 2002.

Cain was a 2002 first-round pick, but he didn't enter the year as the top prospect on his own team at Houston High. But Conor Lalor came down with a sore elbow—he's now at the University of South Carolina—and Cain seemed to get better with every start. He was just 17 when the Giants drafted him 25th overall, and his youth and his tall, slender build make him projectable. Cain threw 93-94 mph in the Rookie-level Arizona League, touched 95-96 and had his manager, Bert Hunter, predicting that he might one day reach 99-100. He had trouble throwing his curveball for strikes, so the Giants had him replace it with a slider. His overall command needs work, as his changeup is rudimentary and he tends to overthrow his fastball. San Francisco believes Cain is on the fast track because of his work ethic. He should be one of the youngest players in the South Atlantic League this season.

Year	Club (League)	Class	W	L	ERA	G	GS	CG	SV	IP	H	R	ER	HR	BB	SO	AVG
2002	Giants (AZL)	R	0	1	3.72	8	7	0	0	19	13	10	8	1	11	20	.197
MINOR LEAGUE TOTALS			0	1	3.72	8	7	0	0	19	13	10	8	1	11	20	.197

12. Deivis Santos, of/1b

Born: Feb. 9, 1980. **Ht.:** 6-1. **Wt.:** 170. **Bats:** L. **Throws:** L. **Career Transactions:** Signed out of Dominican Republic by Giants, May 30, 1997.

After signing with the Giants when he was just 17, Santos spent three years playing with the team's Rookie-level Dominican Summer League club. He has hit .300 since coming to the United States, employing a solid line-drive swing and making consistent contact. He's an outstanding defensive first baseman with plus speed for the position, so the Giants tried him in left field is 2002. He proved to be better than adequate in the outfield, and he could play either position in the majors. Santos has yet to show the power that teams want in a first baseman or lefthander, however. He also doesn't draw many walks, so his offensive value doesn't extend much beyond his batting average. He'll return to Triple-A after finishing last season there.

Year	Club (League)	Class	AVG	G	AB	R	H	2B	3B	HR	RBI	BB	SO	SB	SLG	OBP
1997	Giants (DSL)	R	.271	70	258	29	70	13	2	4	24	23	40	5	.384	.351
1998	Giants (DSL)	R	.281	60	221	26	62	17	0	1	22	24	22	5	.371	.351
1999	Giants (DSL)	R	.236	67	237	27	56	10	2	3	40	44	31	7	.333	.355
2000	Giants (AZL)	R	.372	12	43	13	16	2	1	2	10	7	6	4	.605	.460
	Salem-Keizer (NWL)	A	.000	2	7	0	0	0	0	0	0	0	0	0	.000	.000
2001	Hagerstown (SAL)	A	.290	131	520	64	151	27	3	12	80	25	91	16	.423	.325
2002	Shreveport (TL)	AA	.312	109	407	54	127	33	5	3	56	18	42	4	.440	.349
	Fresno (PCL)	AAA	.284	23	88	8	25	3	1	3	14	2	14	4	.443	.297
MINOR LEAGUE TOTALS			.285	474	1781	221	507	105	14	28	246	143	246	45	.407	.340

13. Tony Torcato, of

Born: Oct. 25, 1979. **Ht.:** 6-1. **Wt.:** 190. **Bats:** L. **Throws:** R. **School:** Woodland (Calif.) HS. **Career Transactions:** Selected by Giants in first round (19th overall) of 1998 draft; signed June 3, 1998.

Torcato had been a staple in the organization's top 10 since he was drafted in 1998. Expectations for him aren't quite as high now, though he still looks like he can be a productive big leaguer and will get a shot at making the Giants this spring. Torcato has been a solid hitter every step of the way, though he never has shown much power. During the 2002 season he made a concerted effort to try to pull the ball in certain situations. He hit 13 homers, nearly double his previous career high, and San Francisco hopes he'll eventually develop 20-homer power. Like Deivis Santos, he makes good contact but offsets that by not working many walks. He's no more than adequate as a left fielder, and his arm is nothing special. Drafted as a third baseman, he moved off the hot corner after a series of shoulder injuries. Torcato needs to build up his strength to get through the rigors of a full season.

Year	Club (League)	Class	AVG	G	AB	R	H	2B	3B	HR	RBI	BB	SO	SB	SLG	OBP
1998	Salem-Keizer (NWL)	A	.291	59	220	31	64	15	2	3	43	14	38	4	.418	.333
1999	Bakersfield (Cal)	A	.291	110	422	50	123	25	0	4	58	30	67	2	.379	.338
2000	San Jose (Cal)	A	.324	119	490	77	159	37	2	7	88	41	62	19	.451	.379
	Shreveport (TL)	AA	.500	2	8	1	4	0	0	0	2	0	1	0	.500	.500
2001	San Jose (Cal)	A	.341	67	258	38	88	21	2	2	47	17	40	9	.461	.381
	Shreveport (TL)	AA	.293	36	147	13	43	9	1	1	23	9	15	0	.388	.344
	Fresno (PCL)	AAA	.320	35	150	20	48	8	1	2	8	2	20	0	.427	.329
2002	Fresno (PCL)	AAA	.290	130	490	64	142	23	3	13	64	29	65	4	.429	.330
	San Francisco (NL)	MAJ	.273	5	11	0	3	1	0	0	0	0	2	0	.364	.273
MAJOR LEAGUE TOTALS			.273	5	11	0	3	1	0	0	0	0	2	0	.364	.273
MINOR LEAGUE TOTALS			.307	558	2185	294	671	138	11	32	333	142	308	38	.424	.350

14. Travis Ishikawa, 1b

Born: Sept. 24, 1983. **Ht.:** 6-3. **Wt.:** 190. **Bats:** L. **Throws:** L. **School:** Federal Way (Wash.) HS. **Career Transactions:** Selected by Giants in 21st round of 2002 draft; signed July 11, 2002.

Despite keeping a low profile before his high school senior year, Ishikawa emerged as a projected second- or third-round pick in the 2002 draft. But teams were scared off by his bonus demands and his declared intention to attend Oregon State, so the Giants got him in the 21st round. After a month of negotiations he signed for $950,000, an unprecedented bonus for a player that deep in the draft. Ishikawa draws John Olerud comparisons because of his smooth line-drive swing and defensive prowess. However, he has more power potential and athleticism. The way Ishikawa hits balls out of the park effortlessly in batting practice leads the Giants to believe he'll have at least 30-homer pop. His speed and agility allow him to play the outfield, where he saw some brief time in his pro debut. Though Ishikawa is slick at first base, he needs to be more aggressive pursuing grounders to his right instead of letting his second baseman handle everything. He'll probably begin his first full season in low Class A.

Year	Club (League)	Class	AVG	G	AB	R	H	2B	3B	HR	RBI	BB	SO	SB	SLG	OBP
2002	Giants (AZL)	R	.279	19	68	10	19	4	2	1	10	7	20	7	.441	.364
	Salem-Keizer (NWL)	A	.307	23	88	14	27	2	1	1	17	5	22	1	.386	.347
MINOR LEAGUE TOTALS			.295	42	156	24	46	6	3	2	27	12	42	8	.410	.355

15. Melvin Valdez, rhp

Born: Dec. 26, 1981. **Ht.:** 6-3. **Wt.:** 170. **Bats:** R. **Throws:** R. **Career Transactions:** Signed out of Dominican Republic by Braves, Nov. 18, 1999 . . . Traded with LHP Damian Moss to Giants for RHP Russ Ortiz, Dec. 16, 2002.

When the Giants decided to trim a little salary by trading Russ Ortiz to the Braves for Damian Moss in December, they also picked up Valdez, previously known as Melvin Mateo. In 2002, his first season in the United States, he led the Rookie-level Gulf Coast League in strikeouts and was rated as the league's top pitching prospect. For a youngster—though he's nine months older than previously believed—he has impressive maturity and desire. His stuff is noteworthy as well. Valdez gets ahead in the count with his lively 93-95 mph fastball. He shows a good feel for his slider and changeup but remains inconsistent with both, forcing him to rely too much on his fastball. His slider has good depth when thrown properly, and his changeup has a decent fade even though it remains in the developmental phase. Valdez, who has front-of-the-rotation potential, is expected to pitch in low Class A this year.

Year	Club (League)	Class	W	L	ERA	G	GS	CG	SV	IP	H	R	ER	HR	BB	SO	AVG
2000	Braves (DSL)	R	1	5	1.57	14	7	0	0	57	52	27	10	2	14	32	.234
2001	Braves 2 (DSL)	R	6	7	2.93	15	14	1	0	92	93	41	30	0	18	48	.258
2002	Braves (GCL)	R	7	3	1.98	12	8	1	0	68	47	18	15	0	12	76	.193
MINOR LEAGUE TOTALS			14	15	2.27	41	29	2	0	218	192	86	55	2	44	156	.233

16. Noah Lowry, lhp

Born: Oct. 10, 1980. **Ht.:** 6-2. **Wt.:** 190. **Bats:** L. **Throws:** L. **School:** Pepperdine University. **Career Transactions:** Selected by Giants in first round (30th overall) of 2001 draft; signed June 20, 2001.

Drafted in the first round ahead of Jesse Foppert in 2001, Lowry endured a frustrating first full season. Nagging shoulder problems caused him to spend half the year on the disabled list, and only twice was he allowed to pitch more than five innings. Nothing more than tendinitis ever was diagnosed, and he was successful when he was able to take the mound. Opponents batted just .186 against him. Lowry throws a 91-92 mph fastball and has an excellent changeup that constantly befuddles hitters. Some people say his curveball is even better than his changeup. He also throws a cutter, and all of his pitches have plus potential. He competes well and throws strikes with a smooth delivery, though he sometimes overthrows. If Lowry can stay healthy, he'll sail through the minors. He'll pitch in Double-A in 2003.

Year	Club (League)	Class	W	L	ERA	G	GS	CG	SV	IP	H	R	ER	HR	BB	SO	AVG
2001	Salem-Keizer (NWL)	A	1	1	3.60	8	7	0	0	25	26	15	10	2	8	28	.265
2002	San Jose (Cal)	A	6	5	2.15	15	12	0	0	59	38	21	14	4	20	62	.186
MINOR LEAGUE TOTALS			7	6	2.58	23	19	0	0	84	64	36	24	6	28	90	.212

17. Jason Ellison, of

Born: April 4, 1978. **Ht.:** 5-10. **Wt.:** 180. **Bats:** R. **Throws:** R. **School:** Lewis-Clark State (Idaho) College. **Career Transactions:** Selected by Giants in 22nd round of 2000 draft; signed June 11, 2000.

Ellison draws comparisons to Marvin Benard because both came out of NAIA powerhouse Lewis-Clark State—Ellison won two national championships in two years with the Warriors and was MVP of the 1999 NAIA World Series—and both play beyond their tools. Ellison, though, has better tools than Benard. One of the fastest players in the organization, he's an outstanding center fielder with a strong arm. His take-no-prisoners approach has made him a favorite of his minor league managers. The Giants have been searching for a true center fielder who can produce offensively for a decade. Ellison could be a prototype leadoff hitter if he were a bit more patient at the plate. He also needs to learn how to use his speed to steal bases. Ellison just needs to tighten up his swing to make the final jump to the big leagues. He'll start 2003 in Triple-A, where he finished last season after starting it in high Class A.

Year	Club (League)	Class	AVG	G	AB	R	H	2B	3B	HR	RBI	BB	SO	SB	SLG	OBP
2000	Salem-Keizer (NWL)	A	.300	74	300	67	90	15	2	0	28	29	45	13	.363	.374
2001	Hagerstown (SAL)	A	.291	130	494	95	144	38	3	8	55	71	68	19	.429	.388
2002	San Jose (Cal)	A	.270	81	322	40	87	13	0	5	40	25	37	9	.357	.325
	Fresno (PCL)	AAA	.311	49	196	31	61	8	1	3	8	21	28	16	.408	.389
MINOR LEAGUE TOTALS			.291	334	1312	233	382	74	6	16	131	146	178	57	.393	.370

18. Carlos Valderrama, of

Born: Nov. 30, 1977. **Ht.:** 6-0. **Wt.:** 180. **Bats:** R. **Throws:** R. **Career Transactions:** Signed out of Dominican Republic by Giants, Feb. 23, 1995.

Once considered the organization's lone true five-tool prospect, Valderrama was the talk of San Francisco's big league camp in 2001. Then he tore his right rotator cuff that May and has been battling the injury ever since. He was almost all the way back last spring, but he pushed himself too hard in spring training and suffered a setback. He never took the field in 2002, getting only DH duty. He had another operation to clean out his shoulder after the season and the Giants hope he'll be at full strength this year. If so, Valderrama still could become the power-hitting center fielder they once thought he was. How much his defensive instincts and arm strength have suffered remains to be seen. There's nothing wrong with his speed, and he's capable of turning walks into doubles. Problem is, he doesn't walk much. Valderrama often overswings, leading to too many strikeouts, but can really drive the ball when he connects. If he has fully recovered from his shoulder problems, he could make his big league debut in 2003.

Year	Club (League)	Class	AVG	G	AB	R	H	2B	3B	HR	RBI	BB	SO	SB	SLG	OBP
1995	Giants (DSL)	R	.228	22	57	7	13	1	0	0	4	6	10	1	.246	.302
1996	Giants (DSL)	R	.223	46	166	29	37	4	1	0	11	29	24	26	.259	.342
1997	Salem-Keizer (NWL)	A	.319	41	138	21	44	7	3	3	28	12	29	22	.478	.368
1998	Salem-Keizer (NWL)	A	.345	7	29	5	10	1	0	0	4	1	7	4	.379	.367
1999	San Jose (Cal)	A	.256	26	90	12	23	2	0	0	12	4	19	8	.278	.284
	Salem-Keizer (NWL)	A	.291	40	134	27	39	3	1	2	18	12	34	17	.373	.349
2000	Bakersfield (Cal)	A	.315	121	435	78	137	21	5	13	81	39	96	54	.476	.370
2001	Shreveport (TL)	AA	.308	41	159	29	49	12	2	1	8	18	29	11	.428	.379
2002	San Jose (Cal)	A	.314	74	299	65	94	19	6	15	45	34	60	14	.569	.384
	Shreveport (TL)	AA	.244	37	135	13	33	3	1	4	15	10	23	4	.370	.304
MINOR LEAGUE TOTALS			.292	455	1642	286	479	73	19	38	226	165	331	161	.429	.357

19. David Cash, rhp

Born: July 25, 1979. **Ht.:** 6-1. **Wt.:** 180. **Bats:** R. **Throws:** R. **School:** University of California. **Career Transactions:** Selected by Giants in sixth round of 2001 draft; signed June 19, 2001.

Cash spent one season at Modesto (Calif.) JC, where Erick Threets later pitched, before moving on to California for three years. Because he was drafted as a college senior, the Giants have pushed him quickly to see what they had. They sent him to Double-A to start his first full pro season in 2002, and then shipped him to the Arizona Fall League. San Francisco tried to make him a starter at the beginning of the year, but his slender build and high pitch counts weren't conducive to handling that workload. Cash moved back to relief, his role in his pro debut, and had a 1.82 ERA (compared to 4.05 in the rotation). He has a nice repertoire, led by a sinker. He also throws a 91 mph four-seam fastball, a slider, curveball and changeup. The Giants would love to get him stronger and throwing more strikes so he could try to start again. If Cash doesn't work his way back into the rotation, he still could make the majors as a ground-ball specialist out of the bullpen. He got roughed up in the AFL, an indication that he needs time in Triple-A this year.

Year	Club (League)	Class	W	L	ERA	G	GS	CG	SV	IP	H	R	ER	HR	BB	SO	AVG
2001	San Jose (Cal)	A	4	0	2.08	20	0	0	1	39	23	9	9	4	17	46	.170
2002	Shreveport (TL)	AA	5	8	3.05	34	12	0	5	109	94	41	37	9	39	88	.232
MINOR LEAGUE TOTALS			9	8	2.79	54	12	0	6	148	117	50	46	13	56	134	.217

20. Dan Ortmeier, of

Born: May 11, 1981. **Ht.:** 6-4. **Wt.:** 220. **Bats:** B. **Throws:** L. **School:** University of Texas-Arlington. **Career Transactions:** Selected by Giants in third round of 2002 draft; signed June 23, 2002.

Like Fred Lewis, Ortmeier was a raw college outfielder when the Giants grabbed him with an early pick (third round) in the 2002 draft. Ortmeier isn't quite as toolsy as Lewis but he's a little more polished. Ortmeier projects as a center fielder, which makes him a valuable commodity in the Giants system. Still, San Francisco didn't get to see him in center as much as it wanted after he signed. He injured his shoulder, which kept him in left field until he was shut down in mid-August and knocked him out of instructional league. Though his progress was slowed by the injury, Ortmeier should move quickly once he's healthy because he's a switch-hitter with size, speed and power. He's better as a lefthanded hitter at this point. If he plays alongside Lewis in low Class A this year, Ortmeier may see more time in right field than in center.

Year	Club (League)	Class	AVG	G	AB	R	H	2B	3B	HR	RBI	BB	SO	SB	SLG	OBP
2002	Salem-Keizer (NWL)	A	.292	49	195	32	57	9	1	5	31	18	37	3	.426	.352
MINOR LEAGUE TOTALS			.292	49	195	32	57	9	1	5	31	18	37	3	.426	.352

21. Jeff Clark, rhp

Born: May 6, 1980. **Ht.:** 6-6. **Wt.:** 240. **Bats:** R. **Throws:** R. **School:** University of Connecticut-Avery Point JC. **Career Transactions:** Selected by Giants in 20th round of 2000 draft; signed June 11, 2000.

After Ryan Jensen won 13 games for the Giants as a rookie last year despite underwhelming stuff, there's hope for Clark. He has won 14 games in each of his two full pro seasons, and he was the high Class A California League's 2002 pitcher of the year and ERA leader. He's considered a similar pitcher to Jensen but with a better body. Clark is 6-foot-6 and 240 pounds, yet doesn't crack 90 mph with his fastball. His biggest assets are his control and his curveball, both of which managers rated the best in the Cal League. He also throws a slider and changeup. He maintains his composure at all times. Guys who do it with smoke and mirrors often are exposed once they get to Double-A, and Clark did get hit hard in his first exposure at that level. That makes 2003 a critical season for Clark to show if he's got what it takes.

Year	Club (League)	Class	W	L	ERA	G	GS	CG	SV	IP	H	R	ER	HR	BB	SO	AVG
2000	Giants (AZL)	R	2	5	5.56	11	11	0	0	57	66	41	35	2	10	35	.295
	San Jose (Cal)	A	0	0	2.25	2	0	0	0	4	2	1	1	0	0	8	.143
2001	Hagerstown (SAL)	A	14	9	3.65	27	27	0	0	148	152	72	60	18	15	131	.266
2002	San Jose (Cal)	A	12	3	2.06	21	21	1	0	140	118	37	32	10	18	129	.224
	Shreveport (TL)	AA	2	2	5.05	6	6	1	0	36	45	21	20	5	2	20	.308
MINOR LEAGUE TOTALS			30	19	3.47	67	65	2	0	384	383	172	148	35	45	323	.258

22. Greg Bruso, rhp

Born: May 5, 1980. **Ht.:** 6-3. **Wt.:** 190. **Bats:** R. **Throws:** R. **School:** UC Davis. **Career Transactions:** Selected by Giants in 16th round of 2002 draft; signed June 10, 2002.

After three undistinguished seasons at NCAA Division II UC Davis, Bruso blossomed into the California Collegiate Athletic Association pitcher of the year as a senior. He also emerged as the most pleasant surprise from San Francisco's 2002 draft, leading the Northwest League in ERA while showing three big league average pitches. Afterward, he was named the top pitcher in the Giants' instructional league camp. Bruso throws a 91 mph fastball, a slider and a changeup. While many first-year pros tend to nibble at the strike zone, he was a strike-throwing machine. He takes the mound with the poise of a veteran. His performance in low Class A this year will determine just where he fits among the system's deep store of pitching prospects.

Year	Club (League)	Class	W	L	ERA	G	GS	CG	SV	IP	H	R	ER	HR	BB	SO	AVG
2002	Salem-Keizer (NWL)	A	4	3	1.99	14	13	0	0	81	58	23	18	5	17	78	.201
MINOR LEAGUE TOTALS			4	3	1.99	14	13	0	0	81	58	23	18	5	17	78	.201

23. Jesse English, lhp

Born: Sept. 13, 1984. **Ht.:** 6-3. **Wt.:** 220. **Bats:** L. **Throws:** L. **School:** Rancho Buena Vista HS, Vista, Calif. **Career Transactions:** Selected by Giants in sixth round of 2002 draft; signed June 9, 2002.

A two-way star as a pitcher/outfielder in high school, English resembles a smaller C.C. Sabathia. In his pro debut, English rated as the No. 4 prospect in the Arizona League. His potential is considerable because he's a lefty with movement on all his pitches. His fastball sits at 90 mph, and there's hope that he might gain more velocity as he firms up his body. He also can crank up the heat when he needs a strikeout. English's best pitch is his change-up, which greatly enhances his fastball. Those two pitches allowed him to average 13 strikeouts per nine innings in the AZL. His curveball is a bit slow, and if he can't tighten it the Giants will have him switch to a slider. The biggest adjustment he must make is learning what it takes to be a professional. There are concerns about his work ethic and weight. English will start 2003 in extended spring training and report to the Northwest League in June.

Year	Club (League)	Class	W	L	ERA	G	GS	CG	SV	IP	H	R	ER	HR	BB	SO	AVG
2002	Giants (AZL)	R	4	1	2.68	12	12	0	0	47	33	17	14	2	18	68	.194
MINOR LEAGUE TOTALS			4	1	2.68	12	12	0	0	47	33	17	14	2	18	68	.194

24. Anthony Pannone, rhp

Born: July 7, 1981. **Ht.:** 6-3. **Wt.:** 220. **Bats:** R. **Throws:** R. **School:** Seward County (Kan.) CC. **Career Transactions:** Selected by Giants in 16th round of 2000 draft; signed May 14, 2001.

A 16th-round pick in 2000, Pannone pitched for the National Baseball Congress World Series champion Liberal Bee Jays that summer and signed as a draft-and-follow the next May. Though overshadowed by Francisco Liriano and Ryan Hannaman, he pitched more consistently than either and led Hagerstown in wins and opponent batting average (.247) last year. Pannone doesn't throw hard (88-91 mph), but gets outs with the downward movement on his sinker. He also throws a slider, curveball and changeup and needs to improve his overall command. He has a pretty good idea of what he's doing on the mound, which puts him ahead of other young pitchers deep in the farm system. Pannone has a chance to be a big league starter but is more likely to find his way into a middle-relief role if he gets there. He's headed for high Class A in 2003.

Year	Club (League)	Class	W	L	ERA	G	GS	CG	SV	IP	H	R	ER	HR	BB	SO	AVG
2001	Salem-Keizer (NWL)	A	7	1	4.11	14	14	0	0	77	82	41	35	9	13	61	.272
2002	Hagerstown (SAL)	A	9	10	3.11	28	28	2	0	168	157	73	58	7	61	116	.247
MINOR LEAGUE TOTALS			16	11	3.42	42	42	2	0	245	239	114	93	16	74	177	.255

25. Angel Chavez, 3b/ss

Born: July 22, 1981. **Ht.:** 6-1. **Wt.:** 180. **Bats:** R. **Throws:** R. **Career Transactions:** Signed out of Panama by Giants, Oct. 30, 1998.

The Giants signed Chavez as a 17-year-old shortstop in 1998. He subsequently had knee surgery, so the Giants moved him to third base so he wouldn't have to move as much. He still has shortstop hands, though. Chavez is one of the best defensive infielders and has one of the best infield arms in the organization. He likes to show off his arm, too, waiting as long as possible before gunning throws across the diamond. He's good enough defensively that he still might move back to shortstop. At the plate, Chavez has some holes in his swing, though the ball jumps off his bat when he makes contact. He has a Gary Sheffield-like pump in his swing but lacks the bat speed to get away with it. His approach also needs some tinkering, as he rarely draws walks. A move to Double-A in 2003 will be a good test to see if Chavez can hit enough to reach the majors.

Year	Club (League)	Class	AVG	G	AB	R	H	2B	3B	HR	RBI	BB	SO	SB	SLG	OBP
1999	La Victoria (VSL)	R	.344	52	186	40	64	12	1	14	49	15	32	11	.645	.392
2000	Giants (AZL)	R	.276	7	29	2	8	0	1	1	7	1	5	1	.448	.300
2001	Hagerstown (SAL)	A	.189	13	37	5	7	2	0	2	3	1	12	1	.405	.231
	San Jose (Cal)	A	.244	84	316	37	77	22	2	3	28	16	60	10	.354	.280
2002	San Jose (Cal)	A	.257	130	471	61	121	20	5	8	62	28	83	21	.372	.303
MINOR LEAGUE TOTALS			.267	286	1039	145	277	56	9	28	149	61	192	44	.419	.310

26. R.D. Spiehs, rhp

Born: Oct. 18, 1979. **Ht.:** 6-3. **Wt.:** 210. **Bats:** R. **Throws:** R. **School:** University of Nebraska. **Career Transactions:** Selected by Giants in 33rd round of 2001 draft; signed Aug. 19, 2001.

The Giants took a flier on Spiehs in the 2001 draft, then signed him after he helped the Anchorage Glacier Pilots win the National Baseball Congress World Series. He pitched well enough in high Class A during his 2002 pro debut to earn an invitation to the Arizona Fall League, usually reserved for players with more experience. Spiehs usually pitches with average velocity and tops out at 93, but he gets by with a sinker/slider combination. Both pitches have hard downward movement when he's on, getting him lots of ground balls. He's still inconsistent with his sinker and occasionally hangs it up in the strike zone. Spiehs mixes in a few changeups, but he's essentially a two-pitch guy. He'll pitch in Double-A this year and projects as a middle reliever.

Year	Club (League)	Class	W	L	ERA	G	GS	CG	SV	IP	H	R	ER	HR	BB	SO	AVG
2002	San Jose (Cal)	A	6	6	3.66	47	0	0	11	84	86	36	34	13	32	80	.267
MINOR LEAGUE TOTALS			6	6	3.66	47	0	0	11	84	86	36	34	13	32	80	.267

27. Trey Lunsford, c

Born: May 25, 1979. **Ht.:** 6-1. **Wt.:** 200. **Bats:** R. **Throws:** R. **School:** Texas Tech. **Career Transactions:** Selected by Giants in 33rd round of 2000 draft; signed June 14, 2000.

Lunsford has been one of the organization's quickest risers. He earned an invitation to big league camp and progressed from high Class A to the majors last year. His strength is his defense behind the plate. He has outstanding catch-and-throw skills and threw out 35 percent of basestealers in 2002. Pitchers love throwing to him because of the way he calls a game and gets them through jams or nights when they don't have their best stuff. He and Yorvit Torrealba are the top two candidates from within the organization to take over after Benito Santiago retires. Right now the question is whether Lunsford can hit. He doesn't project as more than a .250 hitter with a handful of homers and a few walks in the majors. That might be enough, considering his defense. He'll be the everyday catcher in Triple-A this year.

Year	Club (League)	Class	AVG	G	AB	R	H	2B	3B	HR	RBI	BB	SO	SB	SLG	OBP
2000	Salem-Keizer (NWL)	A	.270	59	215	23	58	9	0	3	30	30	40	1	.353	.378
2001	Hagerstown (SAL)	A	.237	114	396	53	94	19	0	5	50	45	89	10	.323	.320
2002	San Jose (Cal)	A	.255	16	51	7	13	3	0	1	5	3	5	2	.373	.321
	Shreveport (TL)	AA	.281	66	210	26	59	13	0	1	20	29	42	5	.357	.379
	Fresno (PCL)	AAA	.175	19	57	3	10	0	0	2	9	6	15	0	.281	.258
	San Francisco (NL)	MAJ	.667	3	3	0	2	1	0	0	1	0	1	0	1.000	.667
MAJOR LEAGUE TOTALS			.667	3	3	0	2	1	0	0	1	0	1	0	1.000	.667
MINOR LEAGUE TOTALS			.252	274	929	112	234	44	0	12	114	113	191	18	.338	.343

28. Cody Ransom, ss

Born: Feb. 17, 1976. **Ht.:** 6-2. **Wt.:** 190. **Bats:** R. **Throws:** R. **School:** Grand Canyon (Ariz.) University. **Career Transactions:** Selected by Giants in ninth round of 1998 draft; signed June 4, 1998.

Ransom is 27 and coming off a year when he hit just .207 in his second stint in Triple-A. Yet he's so good defensively that he still has a chance to play in the big leagues, maybe even as a starter. Ransom is the kind of shortstop who can make a difference for a pitching staff. He has great range and an outstanding arm, making bullet throws with seemingly little effort. He could become a Rey Sanchez/Rey Ordonez type, sticking in the majors on his glove alone. Ransom has good power for a shortstop and has patience, but he has so many holes in his long swing that he's a career .227 hitter as a pro. He's athletic, so there's some hope he can make adjustments, but that also should have happened before now. His future probably isn't with the Giants, who have the much more productive Rich Aurilia as a starter. It's also possible they could try his strong arm on the mound. They did that with Ransom's brother Troy, drafting him as an outfielder before converting him to a pitcher. Ransom will give Triple-A another try in 2003.

Year	Club (League)	Class	AVG	G	AB	R	H	2B	3B	HR	RBI	BB	SO	SB	SLG	OBP
1998	Salem-Keizer (NWL)	A	.233	71	236	52	55	12	7	6	27	43	56	19	.419	.351
1999	Bakersfield (Cal)	A	.275	99	356	69	98	12	6	11	47	54	108	15	.435	.382
	Shreveport (TL)	AA	.122	14	41	6	5	0	0	2	4	4	22	0	.268	.208
2000	Shreveport (TL)	AA	.200	130	459	58	92	21	2	7	47	40	141	9	.301	.263
2001	Fresno (PCL)	AAA	.241	134	469	77	113	21	6	23	78	44	137	17	.458	.303
	San Francisco (NL)	MAJ	.000	9	7	1	0	0	0	0	0	0	5	0	.000	.000
2002	Fresno (PCL)	AAA	.207	135	449	53	93	18	4	13	46	47	151	6	.352	.283
	San Francisco (NL)	MAJ	.667	7	3	2	2	0	0	1	1	1	1	0	.667	.750
MAJOR LEAGUE TOTALS			.200	16	10	3	2	0	0	1	1	1	6	0	.200	.273
MINOR LEAGUE TOTALS			.227	583	2010	315	456	84	25	62	249	232	615	66	.386	.308

29. John Thomas, lhp

Born: July 24, 1981. **Ht.:** 6-3. **Wt.:** 200. **Bats:** L. **Throws:** L. **School:** Righetti HS, Santa Maria, Calif. **Career Transactions:** Selected by Giants in second round of 1999 draft; signed Sept. 27, 1999 . . . On disabled list, June 20-Sept. 5, 2000.

When the Giants drafted Thomas in 1999 and signed him for $565,000, they thought they had found another hard-throwing lefthander. But they soon discovered that he needed Tommy John surgery. They decided not to void his contract, even though he wouldn't make his pro debut until 2001. San Francisco is still waiting to see what a healthy Thomas might do, because he has pitched just 111 pro innings and spent two months on the disabled list last year with a shoulder injury. He had a strong instructional league, so there's still hope that he might blossom. Thomas throws one of the best changeups in the organization, though he's still learning how to take advantage of it. He has a 91-92 mph when he's healthy, and throws a curveball and cutter. He probably needs more time in high Class A.

Year	Club (League)	Class	W	L	ERA	G	GS	CG	SV	IP	H	R	ER	HR	BB	SO	AVG
2000							Did Not Play—Injured										
2001	Hagerstown (SAL)	A	3	3	4.16	15	15	0	0	71	70	40	33	5	22	65	.259
2002	San Jose (Cal)	A	1	5	6.08	11	11	0	0	40	56	32	27	7	22	29	.329
MINOR LEAGUE TOTALS			4	8	4.85	26	26	0	0	111	126	72	60	12	44	94	.286

30. Carlos Portorreal, rhp

Born: April 28, 1984. **Ht.:** 6-2. **Wt.:** 180. **Bats:** R. **Throws:** R. **Career Transactions:** Signed out of Dominican Republic by Giants, Oct. 17, 2001.

Portorreal made his U.S. debut as an 18-year-old in the Arizona League last year, earning league all-star honors and wowing the Giants with his 93 mph fastball and the makings of a plus curveball. He continued to impress in instructional league, and he should throw even harder once he fills out. Like many young pitchers out of the Dominican, Portorreal is skin and bones. A few years of weight training and proper nutrition could turn him into a monster. The Giants compare him to a young Lorenzo Barcelo, who came up in their system before being traded to the White Sox, but say he's further along than Barcelo was at this stage. Portorreal still needs to tighten up his curveball, which gets a little loopy, and develop a changeup. He'll move up to low Class A this year, when he'll be one of the younger starters in the South Atlantic League.

Year	Club (League)	Class	W	L	ERA	G	GS	CG	SV	IP	H	R	ER	HR	BB	SO	AVG
2002	Giants (AZL)	R	6	2	3.00	14	14	0	0	72	60	31	24	1	22	64	.232
MINOR LEAGUE TOTALS			6	2	3.00	14	14	0	0	72	60	31	24	1	22	64	.232

SEATTLE
MARINERS

TOP 30 PROSPECTS

1. Rafael Soriano, rhp
2. Chris Snelling, of
3. Jose Lopez, ss
4. Shin-Soo Choo, of
5. Clint Nageotte, rhp
6. Aaron Taylor, rhp
7. Travis Blackley, lhp
8. Rett Johnson, rhp
9. Greg Dobbs, 3b/of
10. Jamal Strong, of
11. Ryan Christianson, c
12. Luis Ugueto, ss
13. Willie Bloomquist, inf/of
14. Ismael Castro, 2b
15. Kevin Olore, rhp
16. Michael Garciaparra, ss
17. Kenny Kelly, of
18. Ryan Anderson, lhp
19. Jeff Heaverlo, rhp
20. J.J. Putz, rhp
21. Allan Simpson, rhp
22. Bobby Madritsch, lhp
23. Aaron Looper, rhp
24. Rene Rivera, c
25. Craig Anderson, lhp
26. Juan Done, rhp
27. Bobby Livingston, lhp
28. Jon Nelson, 1b/of
29. Troy Cate, lhp
30. Ryan Ketchner, lhp

By Jim Callis

Most teams would consider winning 93 games and getting three promising prospects to the majors a successful year. Yet the Mariners had to be disappointed in 2002.

A year after tying a 95-year-old record with 116 victories, the Mariners came up short of the playoffs. They led the American League West by five games at the all-star break but went 38-36 in the second half as the Athletics and Angels steamed past them. Manager Lou Piniella, who had become as much of a franchise icon as Ken Griffey, Randy Johnson and Alex Rodriguez, followed them out of town and went home to Tampa Bay.

Also coming off a banner 2001, the farm system fell back a little. After leading baseball with a .577 winning percentage in 2000 and ranking third at .560 in 2001, Seattle affiliates had a .471 mark last year to place 23rd. Where five of the six farm clubs reached the playoffs in 2001, just three qualified in '02.

More troubling than wins and losses was the rash of injuries that struck many of Seattle's top prospects. It started in spring training, when lefthander Ryan Anderson and righthander Jeff Heaverlo went down with torn labrums. Anderson missed all of 2001 with the same injury, and his career is now in doubt after he ranked atop the Mariners prospect list for five years running.

Righthander Rafael Soriano missed nearly a month with a strained shoulder, and outfielder Chris Snelling tore the anterior cruciate ligament in his left knee during his eighth big league game. Infielder Antonio Perez had wrist problems for the second straight year, then went to the Devil Rays in the Piniella-Randy Winn exchange. Catcher Ryan Christianson broke a bone in his foot and lost two months.

The draft didn't go well either. The Mariners knew first-round pick John Mayberry Jr. would be a tough sign, and he never backed off his $3 million price tag. They also failed to sign Eddy Martinez-Esteve, another outfielder with a premium bat.

None of this is to suggest Seattle will stop contending or developing talent. Just eight major league clubs won more games, and up-and-comers such as shortstop Jose Lopez, lefthander Travis Blackley and third baseman Greg Dobbs blossomed in 2002.

The Mariners have legitimate expectations of returning to the postseason in 2003. They also hope the sailing will be smoother than it was last year.

OrganizationOverview

General Manager: Pat Gillick. Farm Director: Benny Looper. Scouting Director: Frank Mattox.

2002 PERFORMANCE

Class	Farm Team	League	W	L	Pct.	Finish*	Manager(s)
Majors	Seattle	American	93	69	.611	T-5th (14)	Lou Piniella
Triple-A	Tacoma Rainiers	Pacific Coast	65	76	.461	13th (16)	Dan Rohn
Double-A	San Antonio Missions	Texas	68	72	.486	+6th (8)	Dave Brundage
High A	San Bernardino Stampede	California	77	63	.550	3rd (10)	Daren Brown
Low A	Wisconsin Timber Rattlers	Midwest	53	86	.381	13th (14)	Gary Thurman
Short-season	Everett AquaSox	Northwest	44	32	.579	2nd (8)	O. Munoz/R. Hansen
Rookie	AZL Mariners	Arizona	19	36	.345	7th (7)	Darrin Garner

OVERALL 2002 MINOR LEAGUE RECORD   326 365 .471   23rd (30)
*Finish in overall standings (No. of teams in league)   +League champion

ORGANIZATION LEADERS

BATTING   *Minimum 250 At-Bats
*AVG	Luis Figueroa, San Antonio/San Bernardino	.336
R	Shin-Soo Choo, San Bernardino/Wisconsin	83
H	Jose Lopez, San Bernardino	169
TB	John Lindsey, San Bernardino	248
2B	Jose Lopez, San Bernardino	39
3B	Kenny Kelly, Tacoma	10
	Jaime Bubela, San Bernardino	10
HR	John Lindsey, San Bernardino	22
RBI	John Lindsey, San Bernardino	93
BB	Shin-Soo Choo, San Bernardino/Wisconsin	79
SO	Craig Kuzmic, Tacoma/San Antonio	148
SB	Jamal Strong, San Antonio	46

PITCHING   #Minimum 75 Innings
W	Russ Morgan, San Bernardino	13
	Rett Johnson, San Antonio/San Bern.	13
L	J.J. Putz, Tacoma/San Antonio	14
#ERA	Ryan Ketchner, Tacoma/Wisconsin	2.70
G	Aaron Taylor, San Antonio	61
CG	Ken Cloude, Tacoma	3
	Juan Done, Wisconsin	3
SV	Jared Hoerman, San Bernardino	29
IP	Clint Nageotte, San Bernardino	165
BB	Juan Done, Wisconsin	75
SO	Clint Nageotte, San Bernardino	214

BEST TOOLS

Best Hitter for Average	Chris Snelling
Best Power Hitter	Jon Nelson
Fastest Baserunner	Jamal Strong
Best Athlete	Kenny Kelly
Best Fastball	Aaron Taylor
Best Curveball	Travis Blackley
Best Slider	Clint Nageotte
Best Changeup	Craig Anderson
Best Control	Brian Sweeney
Best Defensive Catcher	Ryan Christianson
Best Defensive Infielder	Luis Ugueto
Best Infield Arm	Ruben Castillo
Best Defensive Outfielder	Jamal Strong
Best Outfield Arm	Shin-Soo Choo

PROJECTED 2006 LINEUP

Catcher	Ryan Christianson
First Base	John Olerud
Second Base	Bret Boone
Third Base	Greg Dobbs
Shortstop	Jose Lopez
Left Field	Shin-Soo Choo
Center Field	Jamal Strong
Right Field	Ichiro Suzuki
Designated Hitter	Chris Snelling
No. 1 Starter	Freddy Garcia

Kenny Kelly   **Russ Morgan**

No. 2 Starter	Rafael Soriano
No. 3 Starter	Joel Pineiro
No. 4 Starter	Clint Nageotte
No. 5 Starter	Travis Blackley
Closer	Aaron Taylor

TOP PROSPECTS OF THE DECADE

1993	Marc Newfield, of
1994	Alex Rodriguez, ss
1995	Alex Rodriguez, ss
1996	Jose Cruz Jr., of
1997	Jose Cruz Jr., of
1998	Ryan Anderson, lhp
1999	Ryan Anderson, lhp
2000	Ryan Anderson, lhp
2001	Ryan Anderson, lhp
2002	Ryan Anderson, lhp

TOP DRAFT PICKS OF THE DECADE

1993	Alex Rodriguez, ss
1994	Jason Varitek, c
1995	Jose Cruz Jr., of
1996	Gil Meche, rhp
1997	Ryan Anderson, lhp
1998	Matt Thornton, lhp
1999	Ryan Christianson, c
2000	Sam Hays, lhp (4)
2001	Michael Garciaparra, ss
2002	*John Mayberry Jr., of

*Did not sign.

ALL-TIME LARGEST BONUSES

Ichiro Suzuki, 2000	$5,000,000
Ryan Anderson, 1997	$2,175,000
Ryan Christianson, 1999	$2,100,000
Kazuhiro Sasaki, 2000	$2,000,000
Michael Garciaparra, 2001	$2,000,000

MinorLeague**Depth**Chart

SEATTLE MARINERS

RANK 9

The Mariners' winning percentage in both the majors and minors suffered the greatest decline in baseball from 2001 to 2002. Of more significance, the talent level in the system slipped as lefthander Ryan Anderson, their top prospect five years running, was lost to injury for a second straight season and the Mariners failed to sign two premium draft picks. They were handicapped in the 2000 and 2001 drafts by losing picks to free-agent compensation but have been resourceful in their scouting efforts and still rank among the better systems in the game. Their top four prospects are international products, Aaron Taylor was a minor league Rule 5 pick, and Greg Dobbs was undrafted. Jose Lopez' emergence has also been a pleasant surprise.

Note: Depth charts prepared by Josh Boyd. Numbers in parentheses indicate prospect rankings.

LF
Greg Dobbs (9)
Jaime Bubela
John Cole
Carlos Arroyo
Josh Ellison

CF
Chris Snelling (2)
Shin-Soo Choo (4)
Jamal Strong (10)
Kenny Kelly (17)
Chris Colton
Michael Wilson
Josh Womack

RF
Gary Harris
T.J. Bohn

3B
Matt Hagen

SS
Jose Lopez (3)
Luis Ugueto (12)
Michael Garciaparra (16)
Ramon Castillo

2B
Willie Bloomquist (13)
Ismael Castro (14)
Evel Bastida-Martinez
Tim Merritt

1B
Jon Nelson (28)
Ruben Olguin

C
Ryan Christianson (11)
Rene Rivera (24)
John Castellano

RHP

Starters	Relievers
Rafael Soriano (1)	Aaron Taylor (6)
Clint Nageotte (5)	Kevin Olore (15)
Rett Johnson (8)	Allan Simpson (21)
Jeff Heaverlo (19)	Aaron Looper (23)
J.J. Putz (20)	Ryan Ketchner (30)
Juan Done (26)	Julio Mateo
Emiliano Fruto	Jared Hoerman
Cha Baek	
Phil Cullen	
Randy Frye	

LHP

Starters	Relievers
Travis Blackley (7)	Bobby Madritsch (22)
Ryan Anderson (18)	Miguel Martinez
Craig Anderson (25)	Justin Blood
Bobby Livingston (27)	
Troy Cate (29)	
Matt Thornton	
Glenn Bott	
Russ Morgan	
Kendall Bergdall	
Sam Hays	

DraftAnalysis

2002 Draft

Best Pro Debut: LHP Troy Cate (6) lacks an outstanding pitch but kept short-season Northwest League hitters off balance, going 6-1, 2.00 with a 95-11 strikeout-walk ratio in 85 innings. OF Gary Harris (18) batted .287-6-43 with a league-high eight triples to gain NWL all-star recognition.

Best Athlete: OF Josh Womack (2) was more of a football player in high school. He's not polished but projects to have four solid tools, with his power the only question. OFs Corey Harrington (17) and T.J. Bohn (30) are also promising athletes.

Best Pure Hitter: 3B Hunter Brown (22) has the best mechanics and approach of any hitter signed by the Mariners last year. While he hit .224 in his first pro summer, he showed more power than he had in the past and drew a healthy amount of walks. He has succeeded with wood in the past, batting .295 in the Cape Cod League in 2001.

Best Raw Power: 3B Matt Hagen (12), who hit .289-7-30 in the NWL.

Fastest Runner: Womack, Harrington and Harris are 6.6-6.7 runners in the 60.

Best Defensive Player: Harris can play all three outfield positions and shows an above-average arm at times.

Best Fastball: LHP Kendall Bergdall (5) touched 94 mph in 2001 but didn't show the same velocity last year. RHP Randy Frye's (4) sinker jumped to 89-93 mph last spring.

Best Breaking Ball: Frye's slider.

Most Intriguing Background: Unsigned OF John Mayberry Jr.'s (1) father John was a 1967 Astros first-rounder–current Mariners general manager Pat Gillick signed him for Houston–and a two-time all-star. 2B Evel Bastida-Martinez (7) survived a 3½-day trip across the Gulf of Mexico on a small boat crammed with more than two dozen people to defect from Cuba in December 2000. The Mariners pursued him as a free agent before Major League Baseball ruled he was subject to the draft.

JOHN SPEAR

Cate

Closest To The Majors: Seattle says Bastida-Martinez is an advanced player, even for a 23-year-old. He hit .350 in 11 low Class A games.

Best Late-Round Pick: Harris or Bohn.

The One Who Got Away: Mayberry, who reminds scouts of Jermaine Dye, told clubs he wanted $3 million to pass up going to Stanford, and the Mariners couldn't move him off that figure. Seattle also lost out on several other talented players who could be prominent picks when next eligible: OF Eddy Martinez-Esteve (3, now at Florida State), 3B Gaby Sanchez (15, Miami), SS Travis Buck (22, Arizona State) and RHP Kyle Patrick (33, Florida State).

Assessment: The Mariners missed their chance to land two high-ceiling bats in Mayberry and Martinez-Esteve, failing to sign a first-round pick for the first time since 1989. The players they did sign are going to need significant time to develop.

2001 Draft

The jury is still out on SS Michael Garciaparra (1). No player from this draft is on the upper half of the Mariners' top 30 list.

Grade: C

2000 Draft

Seattle didn't have picks in the first three rounds and hasn't seen much from its top choice, LHP Sam Hays (4). It recovered nicely, however, with OF Jamal Strong (6) and RHP Rett Johnson (8).

Grade: C+

1999 Draft

The Mariners found depth with C Ryan Christianson (1), INF/OF Willie Bloomquist (3) and RHPs Clint Nageotte (5), J.J. Putz (6) and Kevin Olore (20). RHP Jeff Heaverlo (1) was more advanced than any of the pitchers until he tore his labrum. Signing RHP Rich Harden (38), now Oakland's top prospect, would have been a huge bonus.

Grade: B

1998 Draft

LHP Matt Thornton (1) joined Seattle's parade of injured pitchers in 2002. LHP Andy Van Hekken (3) went to Detroit in a bad trade for Brian Hunter, while LHP John Rheinecker (30), now Oakland's No. 2 prospect, didn't sign.

Grade: C

Note: Draft analysis prepared by Jim Callis. Numbers in parentheses indicate draft rounds.

. . . Soriano is a true power pitcher, and his fastball/slider combination would allow him to close games.

Rafael
Soriano rhp

Born: Dec. 19, 1979.
Ht.: 6-1. **Wt.:** 170.
Bats: R. **Throws:** R.
Career Transactions: Signed out of Dominican Republic by Mariners, Aug. 30, 1996.

For a guy who didn't start pitching until 1999, Soriano has made remarkable progress. He spent his first two years in pro ball hitting .220 as an outfielder. After getting acclimated to the mound, Soriano ranked as one of the low Class A Midwest League's top pitching prospects in 2000 based primarily on his fastball, but he now projects as a three-pitch starter. Though his arrival at spring training in 2002 was delayed by three weeks while his identity and birthdate were being confirmed by immigration officials–none of Soriano's vital statistics changed–he pitched well enough at Double-A San Antonio to earn his first big league promotion in early May. After two scoreless relief appearances, he pitched well in five of his first six starts. Then he strained his shoulder and landed on the disabled list. Sent back to Double-A once he was healthy, Soriano won the Texas League championship game. He allowed one run and two hits in seven innings while striking out 14, including three against Rangers slugger Mark Teixeira.

The Mariners were encouraged by Soriano's playoff performance because he had all three of his pitches working. He threw in the mid-90s and topped out at 97 mph and showed his usual hard slider. Best of all, he threw 12-15 changeups to keep a predominantly lefthanded lineup at bay. When he made the transition to the mound, Soriano quickly demonstrated polish and smooth mechanics. He is a true power pitcher, and his fastball/slider combination would allow him to close games if Seattle needs him in that role.

Soriano missed the latter part of 2001 with an impingement in his shoulder, and the joint bothered him again last year. With a career high of just 137 innings, he has yet to prove he can handle a full-season grind. Soriano needs more consistency and trust in his changeup. He doesn't beat himself with walks but needs better command in the strike zone. The Mariners have two openings in their rotation, and Soriano is a prime candidate to fill one of them. Even if he starts 2003 at Triple-A Tacoma, Soriano will get called up before too long.

Year	Club (League)	Class	AVG	G	AB	R	H	2B	3B	HR	RBI	BB	SO	SB	SLG	OBP
1997	Mariners (AZL)	R	.269	38	119	19	32	3	2	0	12	14	31	7	.328	.351
1998	Mariners (AZL)	R	.167	32	108	17	18	4	0	0	6	11	34	5	.204	.250
MINOR LEAGUE TOTALS			.220	70	227	36	50	7	2	0	18	25	65	12	.269	.303

Year	Club (League)	Class	W	L	ERA	G	GS	CG	SV	IP	H	R	ER	HR	BB	SO	AVG
1999	Everett (NWL)	A	5	4	3.11	14	14	0	0	75	56	34	26	8	49	83	.209
2000	Wisconsin (Mid)	A	8	4	2.87	21	21	1	0	122	97	41	39	3	50	90	.225
2001	San Bernardino (Cal)	A	6	3	2.53	15	15	2	0	89	49	28	25	4	39	98	.164
	San Antonio (TL)	AA	2	2	3.35	8	8	0	0	48	34	18	18	5	14	53	.192
2002	San Antonio (TL)	AA	2	3	2.31	10	8	0	0	47	32	13	12	6	15	52	.190
	Seattle (AL)	MAJ	0	3	4.56	10	8	0	1	47	45	25	24	8	16	32	.243
MAJOR LEAGUE TOTALS			0	3	4.56	10	8	0	1	47	45	25	24	8	16	32	.243
MINOR LEAGUE TOTALS			23	16	2.83	68	66	3	0	382	268	134	120	26	167	376	.200

2. Chris Snelling, of

Born: Dec. 3, 1981. **Ht.:** 5-10. **Wt.:** 160. **Bats:** L. **Throws:** L. **Career Transactions:** Signed out of Australia by Mariners, March 2, 1999.

Since signing at 17, Snelling has done two things: rake line drives and get hurt. He was the Midwest League's best hitting prospect in 2000, when he broke his left hand and injured his left wrist. He won the high Class A California League batting title despite a stress fracture in his right ankle in 2001. Last year, he broke his right thumb in spring training and then blew out his left knee in his eighth big league game. Snelling is a pure hitter who has batted .316 as a pro despite annually being one of the youngest regulars in his league. He has average speed, but his tremendous instincts allow him to play center field. He has the arm for right field when he moves to a corner in the majors. His recklessness is exciting, but Snelling may have to tone it down. He has good gap power but may never hit more than 20 homers, below-average power for a corner outfielder. Snelling is expected to miss part of spring training as he completes his recovery from knee surgery. He's the best candidate for left field but may get some Triple-A seasoning.

Year	Club (League)	Class	AVG	G	AB	R	H	2B	3B	HR	RBI	BB	SO	SB	SLG	OBP
1999	Everett (NWL)	A	.306	69	265	46	81	15	3	10	50	33	24	8	.498	.388
2000	Wisconsin (Mid)	A	.305	72	259	44	79	9	5	9	56	34	34	7	.483	.386
2001	San Bernardino (Cal)	A	.336	114	450	90	151	29	10	7	73	45	63	12	.491	.418
2002	San Antonio (TL)	AA	.326	23	89	10	29	9	2	1	12	12	11	5	.506	.429
	Seattle (AL)	MAJ	.148	8	27	2	4	0	0	1	3	2	4	0	.259	.207
MAJOR LEAGUE TOTALS			.148	8	27	2	4	0	0	1	3	2	4	0	.259	.207
MINOR LEAGUE TOTALS			.320	278	1063	190	340	62	20	27	191	124	132	32	.492	.404

3. Jose Lopez, ss

Born: Nov. 24, 1983. **Ht.:** 6-2. **Wt.:** 190. **Bats:** R. **Throws:** R. **Career Transactions:** Signed out of Venezuela by Mariners, July 2, 2000.

Lopez held his own as the youngest player in the short-season Northwest League in 2001, and his bat took a quantum leap last year in the California League, where he was the second-youngest regular. He led all minor league shortstops in hitting and topped the Cal League in hits and doubles. He was Seattle's minor league player of the year. Lopez' defensive abilities have been apparent since he made his pro debut. Managers said he had the best infield arm in the Cal League, and he has fine hands, range and actions at shortstop. He has excellent instincts in all phases of the game, making him an adept hitter and a threat on the bases. He has plenty of pop for a middle infielder. Because he excels at making contact, Lopez rarely works deep counts or walks. He's filling out and may outgrow shortstop, though he'll still have enough bat for second or third base. Like most teenagers, he could be more consistent on a daily basis. Doctors have discovered an extra bone in Lopez' right foot, which may require surgery. Barring a major setback, he'll play in Double-A this year at 19.

Year	Club (League)	Class	AVG	G	AB	R	H	2B	3B	HR	RBI	BB	SO	SB	SLG	OBP
2001	Everett (NWL)	A	.256	70	289	42	74	15	0	2	20	13	44	13	.329	.309
2002	San Bernardino (Cal)	A	.324	123	522	82	169	39	5	8	60	27	45	31	.464	.360
MINOR LEAGUE TOTALS			.300	193	811	124	243	54	5	10	80	40	89	44	.416	.342

4. Shin-Soo Choo, of

Born: July 13, 1982. **Ht.:** 5-11. **Wt.:** 170. **Bats:** L. **Throws:** L. **Career Transactions:** Signed out of South Korea by Mariners, Aug. 14, 2000.

The Mariners gave seven-figure bonuses to the first two Koreans they signed, righthander Cha Seung Baek and Choo, who attended the same high school. While Baek has been sidetracked by Tommy John surgery, Choo has put together back-to-back all-star seasons in the low minors. He and Jose Lopez represented Seattle at the 2002 Futures Game. Like the hitters ahead of him on this list, Choo enhances his solid tools with superb instincts. He's a natural line-drive hitter, and his average speed plays better on the diamond than on a stopwatch. Choo's most impressive tool is his arm, which delivered 95 mph fastballs when he led Korea to the gold medal at the 2000 World Junior Championship. The question for Choo is how much power he'll develop. The Mariners have toned down their expecations, though they still point to his bat speed and leverage and envision 20-25 homers a year. He has a good eye at the plate but sometimes can be too passive. Choo probably won't play center field for Seattle, so he'll have to boost his power. He should reach Double-A by the end of 2003.

Year	Club (League)	Class	AVG	G	AB	R	H	2B	3B	HR	RBI	BB	SO	SB	SLG	OBP
2001	Mariners (AZL)	R	.302	51	199	51	60	10	10	4	35	34	49	12	.513	.420
	Wisconsin (Mid)	A	.462	3	13	1	6	0	0	0	3	1	3	2	.462	.533
2002	Wisconsin (Mid)	A	.302	119	420	69	127	24	8	6	48	70	98	34	.440	.417
	San Bernardino (Cal)	A	.308	11	39	14	12	5	1	1	9	9	9	3	.564	.460
MINOR LEAGUE TOTALS			.306	184	671	135	205	39	19	11	95	114	159	51	.469	.423

5. Clint Nageotte, rhp

Born: Oct. 25, 1980. **Ht.:** 6-4. **Wt.:** 210. **Bats:** R. **Throws:** R. **School:** Brooklyn (Ohio) HS. **Career Transactions:** Selected by Mariners in fifth round of 1999 draft; signed Aug. 18, 1999.

An all-state basketball player at his Ohio high school, Nageotte has seen his baseball career take off since he has focused on one sport. He won the championship game of the Rookie-level Arizona League playoffs in his 2000 pro debut, rated as the Midwest League's top pitching prospect as an encore, led the minors in strikeouts last year. Nageotte's out pitch is a slider that ranks among the best in the minors. It has allowed him to average 11.3 whiffs per nine innings as a pro and gives righthanders no chance against him. His 91-94 mph fastball gives him a second plus pitch. Though he has more than enough fastball, Nageotte doesn't locate it well in the strike zone and often scraps it and goes with his slider. His changeup isn't effective, so right now he just has one pitch that he trusts. With better command, he could lower his pitch counts and work deeper into games. If Nageotte can improve his pitch selection, command and offspeed pitch, he could move to the top of this list. He'll work on those facets of his game this year in Double-A.

Year	Club (League)	Class	W	L	ERA	G	GS	CG	SV	IP	H	R	ER	HR	BB	SO	AVG
2000	Mariners (AZL)	R	4	1	2.16	12	7	0	1	50	29	15	12	0	28	59	.167
2001	Wisconsin (Mid)	A	11	8	3.13	28	26	0	0	152	141	65	53	10	50	187	.246
2002	San Bernardino (Cal)	A	9	6	4.54	29	29	1	0	165	153	101	83	10	68	214	.241
MINOR LEAGUE TOTALS			24	15	3.63	69	62	1	1	367	323	181	148	20	146	460	.233

6. Aaron Taylor, rhp

Born: Aug. 20, 1977. **Ht.:** 6-5. **Wt.:** 200. **Bats:** R. **Throws:** R. **School:** Lowndes HS, Valdosta, Ga. **Career Transactions:** Selected by Braves in 11th round of 1996 draft; signed June 5, 1996 . . . Selected by Mariners from Braves in minor league Rule 5 draft, Dec. 13, 1999.

Taylor comes from Hahira, Ga., and Lowndes High, which also spawned the Drew brothers–big leaguers J.D. and Tim, and current Florida State star Stephen. Taylor's career was going nowhere when he quit during spring training 2001 after posting a 6.26 ERA in his first five seasons. Once he returned, he went from low A to the majors in 15 months. Pitchers don't come much more intimidating than Taylor, who's tall and features three dastardly pitches. His fastball reaches 94-97 mph every time out and peaks at 99. If hitters start looking for heat, he can cross them up with his slider and splitter. Taylor's secondary pitches require more consistency after deserting him at times during his September callup. His splitter is generally more effective than his slider, which flattens out if he drops his arm angle. Command has never been his strong suit. Spring training will determine whether Taylor opens the season in Seattle or Triple-A. He's the heir apparent to Mariners closer Kazuhiro Sasaki.

Year	Club (League)	Class	W	L	ERA	G	GS	CG	SV	IP	H	R	ER	HR	BB	SO	AVG
1996	Braves (GCL)	R	0	9	7.74	13	9	0	0	52	68	54	45	0	28	33	.315
1997	Danville (Appy)	R	1	8	5.53	15	7	0	0	55	65	49	34	4	31	38	.288
1998	Danville (Appy)	R	3	6	6.25	14	14	1	0	72	87	60	50	9	36	55	.300
1999	Macon (SAL)	A	6	7	4.88	27	8	0	1	79	86	56	43	9	27	78	.270
2000	Everett (NWL)	A	1	4	7.43	15	14	0	0	63	76	54	52	5	37	57	.304
2001	Wisconsin (Mid)	A	3	1	2.45	28	0	0	9	29	19	9	8	1	11	50	.184
2002	San Antonio (TL)	AA	4	3	2.34	61	0	0	24	77	51	28	20	5	34	93	.184
	Seattle (AL)	MAJ	0	0	9.00	5	0	0	0	5	8	5	5	2	0	6	.348
MAJOR LEAGUE TOTALS			0	0	9.00	5	0	0	0	5	8	5	5	2	0	6	.348
MINOR LEAGUE TOTALS			18	38	5.29	173	52	1	34	428	452	310	252	33	204	404	.269

7. Travis Blackley, lhp

Born: Nov. 4, 1982. **Ht.:** 6-3. **Wt.:** 190. **Bats:** L. **Throws:** L. **Career Transactions:** Signed out of Australia by Mariners, Oct. 29, 2000.

While closing in on Shin-Soo Choo at the 2000 World Junior Championship, the Mariners spotted Blackley, who lost to Korea in the semifinals as a member of the Australian team. After a promising pro debut in 2001, Blackley sustained a small fracture in his elbow while pitching in instructional league. He returned by the beginning of May, skipped a level and fared well as the California League's youngest starting pitcher. Blackley is similar to Craig Anderson, another Mariners left-hander from Australia: His best attributes are his changeup and his command, and he has a solid curveball. He has a higher ceiling because he's more projectable and throws in the high 80s, while Anderson works in the low 80s. Blackley's competitive nature has allowed him to handle every challenge thrown his way. With three pitches that should be average or better to go with an advanced feel for pitching, Blackley has no obvious shortcoming. Adding velocity would be nice, but plenty of lefties have been effective working in the high 80s. Double-A will provide Blackley's biggest test yet in 2003. At this point, he's on track to reach Seattle by 22.

Year	Club (League)	Class	W	L	ERA	G	GS	CG	SV	IP	H	R	ER	HR	BB	SO	AVG
2001	Everett (NWL)	A	6	1	3.32	14	14	0	0	79	60	34	29	7	29	90	.211
2002	San Bernardino (Cal)	A	5	9	3.49	21	20	1	0	121	102	52	47	11	44	152	.227
MINOR LEAGUE TOTALS			11	10	3.42	35	34	1	0	200	162	86	76	18	73	242	.220

8. Rett Johnson, rhp

Born: July 6, 1979. **Ht.:** 6-2. **Wt.:** 210. **Bats:** L. **Throws:** R. **School:** Coastal Carolina University. **Career Transactions:** Selected by Mariners in eighth round of 2000 draft; signed June 13, 2000.

Johnson was an eighth-round bargain after he set Coastal Carolina records for innings (133) and strikeouts (151) in 2000. The workload sapped his velocity, causing clubs to back off. He has bounced back and hasn't had any physical problems since signing. Johnson's 86-88 mph slider isn't far behind Clint Nageotte's. He complements it with a 91-93 mph fastball that has nice sink. Johnson thrives on pressure. His pitches seem to have a little extra when he gets into a jam, and he had a 1.80 postseason ERA as San Antonio won the Texas League title. Johnson's shortcomings also are similar to Nageotte's. He needs to refine his changeup and command, though he does a better job of establishing his fastball. While he's ticketed to start 2003 in Triple-A, Johnson could surface in Seattle during the summer. He's probably no lower than third behind Rafael Soriano and J.J. Putz among Mariners farmhands ready to help the big club as a starter, and Johnson's fastball/slider combo also would be an asset out of the bullpen.

Year	Club (League)	Class	W	L	ERA	G	GS	CG	SV	IP	H	R	ER	HR	BB	SO	AVG
2000	Everett (NWL)	A	5	4	2.07	17	8	0	0	70	51	26	16	1	21	88	.198
2001	Wisconsin (Mid)	A	5	5	2.27	16	16	2	0	99	92	33	25	4	30	96	.248
	San Bernardino (Cal)	A	6	2	4.09	12	12	0	0	66	56	36	30	5	33	70	.230
2002	San Bernardino (Cal)	A	3	1	3.65	7	7	0	0	37	27	17	15	1	11	34	.199
	San Antonio (TL)	AA	10	4	3.62	21	21	1	0	117	107	63	47	5	53	104	.242
MINOR LEAGUE TOTALS			29	16	3.08	73	64	3	0	389	333	175	133	16	148	392	.230

9. Greg Dobbs, 3b/of

Born: July 2, 1978. **Ht.:** 6-1. **Wt.:** 200. **Bats:** L. **Throws:** R. **School:** University of Oklahoma. **Career Transactions:** Signed as nondrafted free agent by Mariners, May 28, 2001.

Dobbs went from Riverside (Calif.) CC to Long Beach State to Oklahoma, earning all-conference honors four times. After sitting out 2000 when he was academically ineligible, he hit .428 to lead the Big 12 Conference and signed as a fifth-year senior before the 2001 draft. The Mariners drafted him in the 53rd round out of high school. Dobbs cemented his reputation for hitting everywhere he has gone with his Double-A performance; he hit .409 in the Texas League playoffs. He has power as well, and projects as a .280-.300 hitter with 20-25 homers. Seattle knew Dobbs' bat was ready for high Class A at the start of 2002, but sent him to the Midwest League so he could work on play-ing third base. He has adequate hands, range and arm strength, but his footwork and throwing angles are erratic and lead to wayward throws. He made 23 errors in 72 games at third last year. Dobbs has enough bat for first base or left field, but his value will be enhanced if he can stick at the hot corner. Considering Seattle's need there, he'll be given every opportunity to do so.

Year	Club (League)	Class	AVG	G	AB	R	H	2B	3B	HR	RBI	BB	SO	SB	SLG	OBP
2001	Everett (NWL)	A	.321	65	249	37	80	17	2	6	41	30	39	5	.478	.396
	San Bernardino (Cal)	A	.385	3	13	2	5	1	0	1	3	0	4	0	.692	.357
2002	Wisconsin (Mid)	A	.275	86	320	43	88	16	2	10	48	31	50	13	.431	.338
	San Antonio (TL)	AA	.365	27	96	13	35	2	0	5	15	9	17	1	.542	.425
MINOR LEAGUE TOTALS			.307	181	678	95	208	36	4	22	107	70	110	19	.469	.372

10. Jamal Strong, of

Born: Aug. 5, 1978. **Ht.:** 5-10. **Wt.:** 180. **Bats:** R. **Throws:** R. **School:** University of Nebraska. **Career Transactions:** Selected by Mariners in sixth round of 2000 draft; signed June 14, 2000.

Strong has run wild since turning pro, stealing 188 bases (at an 82 percent success rate) and scoring 241 runs in 334 games. He has won two stolen-base crowns, including last year in the Texas League, where managers also rated him the circuit's best and fastest baserunner. Strong's speed grades out as an 8 on the 2-to-8 scouting scale. Just as important, he realizes it's his ticket to the big leagues. He does what he can to get on base, drawing walks and hitting the ball on the ground. He has improved his reads as a basestealer and center fielder. His arm never has been strong, though it has improved and is playable in center. He does get to balls and get rid of them quickly. While Strong doesn't try to hit for power, he'll have to produce a few more extra-base hits. He has some strength but is still learning to deal with pitchers who bust him inside. With Mike Cameron sliding in the second half and Kenny Kelly struggling in Triple-A during 2002, Strong's chances to one day start for Seattle have increased. He'll be one step away in Tacoma this year.

Year	Club (League)	Class	AVG	G	AB	R	H	2B	3B	HR	RBI	BB	SO	SB	SLG	OBP
2000	Everett (NWL)	A	.314	75	296	63	93	7	3	1	28	52	29	60	.368	.422
2001	Wisconsin (Mid)	A	.353	51	184	41	65	12	1	0	19	40	27	35	.429	.478
	San Bernardino (Cal)	A	.311	81	331	74	103	11	2	0	32	51	60	47	.356	.411
2002	San Antonio (TL)	AA	.278	127	503	63	140	16	5	1	31	62	87	46	.336	.366
MINOR LEAGUE TOTALS			.305	334	1314	241	401	46	11	2	110	205	203	188	.361	.406

11. Ryan Christianson, c

Born: April 21, 1981. **Ht.:** 6-2. **Wt.:** 210. **Bats:** R. **Throws:** R. **School:** Arlington HS, Riverside, Calif. **Career Transactions:** Selected by Mariners in first round (11th overall) of 1999 draft; signed July 18, 1999.

Catcher remains a soft spot at both the major and minor league levels in the Mariners organization. Christianson is their best chance to reverse that trend. However, he took a step backward in 2002. After hitting .215 in Double-A, he was demoted to high Class A San Bernardino and just starting to heat up at the plate when he broke a bone in his left foot. After missing two months, he went back to Double-A and finished strong. Seattle still believes Christianson can become an above-average offensive catcher. To do so, he'll have to stop trying to pull and lift too many pitches. He has the strength to drive the ball with power to the opposite field. Christianson also needs to tighten his plate discipline, which has slipped a little. His throwing was questioned earlier in his career, but his arm strength and release have improved. He threw out 38 percent of basestealers last year. Christianson still needs work on the mental aspects of catching, such as handling pitchers and calling games. The Mariners hope he'll fare better in Double-A this year.

Year	Club (League)	Class	AVG	G	AB	R	H	2B	3B	HR	RBI	BB	SO	SB	SLG	OBP
1999	Mariners (AZL)	R	.263	11	38	3	10	8	0	0	7	2	12	2	.474	.300
	Everett (NWL)	A	.280	30	107	19	30	7	0	8	17	14	31	3	.570	.379
2000	Wisconsin (Mid)	A	.249	119	418	60	104	20	0	13	59	50	98	1	.390	.328
2001	San Bernardino (Cal)	A	.248	134	528	65	131	42	5	12	85	53	112	3	.415	.320
2002	San Antonio (TL)	AA	.253	52	190	20	48	11	0	5	17	16	36	0	.389	.317
	San Bernardino (Cal)	A	.282	21	71	12	20	5	1	1	8	4	17	1	.423	.346
MINOR LEAGUE TOTALS			.254	367	1352	179	343	93	6	39	193	139	306	10	.418	.328

12. Luis Ugueto, ss

Born: Feb. 15, 1979. **Ht.:** 5-11. **Wt.:** 170. **Bats:** B. **Throws:** R. **Career Transactions:** Signed out of Venezuela by Marlins, April 28, 1996 . . . Selected by Pirates from Marlins in major league Rule 5 draft, Dec. 13, 2001 . . . Contract purchased by Mariners from Pirates, Dec. 13, 2001.

Though the Mariners contended all of the 2002 season, they valued Ugueto so highly that they kept him on their 25-man roster almost the entire way (with the exception of some disabled-list time after he sprained his left wrist). Otherwise they would have had to put him on waivers and offer him back to the Marlins after acquiring him in the 2001 major league Rule 5 draft via the Pirates. After getting a total of 74 at-bats between the majors and Triple-A, Ugueto will need to make up for lost time in 2003. He's a true shortstop with pure speed. His instincts, range and hands make him the system's best defensive infielder—quite a compliment considering his competition includes Jose Lopez and Ruben Castillo. Ugueto is stronger than he looks, but he needs to forget about power and worry more about getting on base. Pitchers will keep pounding him inside until he proves he can turn on those offerings. Ugueto never had played above high Class A before 2002 and ideally would go to Double-A this year. But the presence of Jose Lopez likely means Ugueto instead will go to Tacoma.

Year	Club (League)	Class	AVG	G	AB	R	H	2B	3B	HR	RBI	BB	SO	SB	SLG	OBP
1996	Marlins (DSL)	R	.254	70	240	37	61	4	2	0	12	41	33	14	.288	.365
1997	Maracay 1 (VSL)	R	.180	50	111	17	20	3	2	0	17	18	16	7	.243	.288
1998	Brevard County (FSL)	A	.182	3	11	0	2	0	0	0	0	0	5	0	.182	.182
	Marlins (GCL)	R	.229	50	166	20	38	8	2	0	15	8	37	7	.301	.270
1999	Brevard County (FSL)	A	.133	12	30	1	4	0	0	0	3	7	5	1	.133	.297
	Marlins (GCL)	R	.000	1	3	0	0	0	0	0	2	1	0	0	.000	.200
	Utica (NY-P)	A	.276	56	217	33	60	11	2	1	26	18	46	9	.359	.335
2000	Kane County (Mid)	A	.234	114	393	43	92	13	2	1	32	28	83	12	.285	.291
2001	Brevard County (FSL)	A	.263	121	392	53	103	12	5	3	43	38	96	22	.342	.330
2002	Seattle (AL)	MAJ	.217	62	23	19	5	0	0	1	1	2	8	8	.348	.280
	Tacoma (PCL)	AAA	.255	12	51	5	13	1	0	0	5	3	13	2	.275	.291
MAJOR LEAGUE TOTALS			.217	62	23	19	5	0	0	1	1	2	8	8	.348	.280
MINOR LEAGUE TOTALS			.243	489	1614	209	393	52	15	5	155	162	334	74	.304	.315

13. Willie Bloomquist, inf/of

Born: Nov. 27, 1977. **Ht.:** 5-11. **Wt.:** 180. **Bats:** R. **Throws:** R. **School:** Arizona State University. **Career Transactions:** Selected by Mariners in third round of 1999 draft; signed June 10, 1999.

Bloomquist is a product of nearby Port Orchard, Wash. He has been an organization favorite from the day he signed because of his makeup, but his bat leveled off after he left high Class A in 2000. He bounced back last year, overcoming a bulging disc in his back and a case of vertigo to be named Tacoma's player of the year. After Bloomquist hit .455 during his September callup, the Mariners now envision him as another Mark McLemore. He's a David Eckstein overachiever with better tools than Eckstein, though none of Bloomquist's grade out above-average. He's a steady defender at second base, third base and shortstop, and he did a good job of learning the outfield in 2002. His instincts serve him well in all facets of the game and make him a threat on the basepaths. Bloomquist doesn't have much power, so he needs to get on base. He's good at making contact, which also hurts him somewhat because that cuts down on his walks. He's expected to make the big league club as a utilityman this year.

Year	Club (League)	Class	AVG	G	AB	R	H	2B	3B	HR	RBI	BB	SO	SB	SLG	OBP
1999	Everett (NWL)	A	.287	42	178	35	51	10	3	2	27	22	25	17	.410	.366
2000	Lancaster (Cal)	A	.379	64	256	63	97	19	6	2	51	37	27	22	.523	.456
	Tacoma (PCL)	AAA	.225	51	191	17	43	5	1	1	23	7	28	5	.277	.249
2001	San Antonio (TL)	AA	.255	123	491	59	125	23	2	0	28	28	55	34	.310	.294
2002	Tacoma (PCL)	AAA	.270	104	337	47	91	14	3	6	47	29	44	20	.383	.331
	Seattle (AL)	MAJ	.455	12	33	11	15	4	0	0	7	5	2	3	.576	.526
MAJOR LEAGUE TOTALS			.455	12	33	11	15	4	0	0	7	5	2	3	.576	.526
MINOR LEAGUE TOTALS			.280	384	1453	221	407	71	15	11	176	123	179	98	.372	.336

14. Ismael Castro, 2b

Born: Aug. 14, 1983. **Ht.:** 5-9. **Wt.:** 160. **Bats:** B. **Throws:** R. **Career Transactions:** Signed out of Colombia by Mariners, Sept. 24, 1999.

Castro was named Northwest League MVP and led the league in runs, hits, doubles, total bases and extra-base hits while making his U.S. debut in 2002. He doesn't rate higher on this list because of the skepticism about his listed birthdate. That would have made him 18 for much of his breakout season, but he's physically mature and looks at least a couple of years older. Castro is a purely offensive player whose bat will have to carry him. He's only average defensively and probably is limited to second base. He's a switch-hitter who uses a compact swing to generate pop to all fields. He uses a line-drive approach and lets his power come naturally. Castro is a solid average runner whose lone offensive weakness at this point is his inability to draw walks. He'll be tested with his first extensive stint in full-season ball in 2003. If he passes, he'll rank much higher a year from now.

Year	Club (League)	Class	AVG	G	AB	R	H	2B	3B	HR	RBI	BB	SO	SB	SLG	OBP
2000	San Felipe (VSL)	R	.302	35	116	24	35	10	0	2	28	10	20	1	.440	.351
2001	Aguirre (VSL)	R	.300	53	200	34	60	7	4	2	21	12	34	23	.405	.340
2002	San Bernardino (Cal)	A	.150	6	20	4	3	2	0	0	2	1	9	0	.250	.261
	Everett (NWL)	A	.313	66	284	55	89	26	1	9	46	16	41	13	.507	.356
MINOR LEAGUE TOTALS			.302	160	620	117	187	45	5	13	97	39	104	37	.453	.347

15. Kevin Olore, rhp

Born: Sept. 21, 1978. **Ht.:** 6-2. **Wt.:** 200. **Bats:** L. **Throws:** R. **School:** Marist College. **Career Transactions:** Selected by Mariners in 20th round of 1999 draft; signed June 13, 1999.

The lowest-drafted player signed by Seattle directly out of the 1999 draft, Olore has taken awhile to command respect. He pitched in relief in his first two years as pro, then won 13 games in his first shot as a starter in 2001. His reward? A trip back to the bullpen at the beginning of last year. He posted a 1.77 ERA in April, then missed five weeks with a sore shoulder. San Bernardino needed him in the rotation when Olore returned, and he was more than up to the task. Once his strict pitch counts were lifted, he went 7-0, 1.62 in his final nine starts and struck out 67 in 57 innings. Olore added 3 mph to his fastball, and it's now a solid-average offering at 89-92. His curveball is just as good, and his changeup is close. He throws strikes and is stingy with homers, allowing just four in 2002—and none to lefties in 156 at-bats. Olore doesn't have a significant out pitch, so he'll have to prove himself again in Double-A this year.

Year	Club (League)	Class	W	L	ERA	G	GS	CG	SV	IP	H	R	ER	HR	BB	SO	AVG
1999	Everett (NWL)	A	0	0	4.88	22	0	0	2	31	31	21	17	5	21	31	.263
2000	Wisconsin (Mid)	A	1	3	7.20	12	0	0	0	20	25	16	16	1	14	17	.309
	New Haven (EL)	AA	0	0	8.31	3	0	0	0	4	7	5	4	1	2	2	.368
	Everett (NWL)	A	1	3	2.95	26	0	0	2	55	50	28	18	5	28	64	.236
2001	Wisconsin (Mid)	A	13	4	3.32	27	27	0	0	155	134	70	57	14	40	158	.231
2002	San Bernardino (Cal)	A	10	3	2.73	25	18	0	1	105	89	37	32	4	41	128	.232
MINOR LEAGUE TOTALS			25	13	3.50	115	45	0	5	371	336	177	144	30	146	400	.241

16. Michael Garciaparra, ss

Born: April 2, 1983. **Ht.:** 6-1. **Wt.:** 160. **Bats:** R. **Throws:** R. **School:** Don Bosco Tech HS, Rosemead, Calif. **Career Transactions:** Selected by Mariners in first round (36th overall) of 2001 draft; signed Aug. 20, 2001.

As the younger brother of Nomar Garciaparra, Michael faces comparisons that are unfair yet inevitable. He's not as explosive offensively as Nomar and probably never will be, but Michael is as gifted with the glove. He also shares Nomar's considerable instincts and work ethic, and is participating in the same intensive offseason workouts. That will help Michael do what he needs most, which is to get stronger. A surprise supplemental first-round pick in 2001, Garciaparra didn't play baseball in high school or in the minors that summer while recovering from a knee injury. He blew out his anterior cruciate ligament making a tackle after kicking off for his prep football team. Garciaparra got a $2 million bonus to pass up the opportunity to play at the University of Tennessee, and the Mariners are happy with their investment after seeing his pro debut last year. He showed a solid arm and range at shortstop, and an advanced approach at the plate. If he can make more contact and mature physically, he'll be a possible No. 2 hitter. Seattle thinks Garciaparra has the aptitude for switch-hitting and may have him try that in the future. The current plan is to keep him batting righthanded this year in low Class A.

Year	Club (League)	Class	AVG	G	AB	R	H	2B	3B	HR	RBI	BB	SO	SB	SLG	OBP
2002	Mariners (AZL)	R	.275	46	160	27	44	8	5	0	20	20	42	13	.388	.383
	Everett (NWL)	A	.161	9	31	3	5	2	0	0	3	4	15	0	.226	.257
MINOR LEAGUE TOTALS			.257	55	191	30	49	10	5	0	23	24	57	13	.361	.363

17. Kenny Kelly, of

Born: Jan. 26, 1979. **Ht.:** 6-3. **Wt.:** 180. **Bats:** R. **Throws:** R. **School:** Tampa Catholic HS. **Career Transactions:** Selected by Devil Rays in second round of 1997 draft; signed June 12, 1997 . . . Sold by Devil Rays to Mariners, April 4, 2001.

Before Ken Dorsey made his near-flawless three-year run as the University of Miami's quarterback, Kelly took snaps for the Hurricanes. He gave up football in February 2000 to sign a four-year major league contract worth $2.2 million with the Devil Rays, who had signed him as a second-round pick three years earlier and let him play two sports. When Kelly was mediocre in his first year of focusing on baseball, Tampa Bay got out of the remaining three years of his contract by selling him to Seattle for $350,000 in April 2001. Kelly finally seemed to have turned the corner late that season, finishing strong in Double-A and starring in the Arizona Fall League. But he regressed in 2002, and if he doesn't make a strong rebound this season it may be time to write him off. His athleticism is unquestioned. Kelly has tremendous speed, pop in his bat and a decent arm. But he hasn't shown the ability to control the strike zone or make adjustments, nor the instincts to steal bases. He tends to dwell on bad at-bats, and he has plenty of them. It's time for him to turn his tools into skills. Kelly will be out of options after 2003, which he'll begin in Triple-A.

Year	Club (League)	Class	AVG	G	AB	R	H	2B	3B	HR	RBI	BB	SO	SB	SLG	OBP
1997	Devil Rays (GCL)	R	.212	27	99	21	21	2	1	2	7	11	24	6	.313	.304
1998	Charleston, SC (SAL)	A	.280	54	218	46	61	7	5	3	17	19	52	19	.399	.347
1999	St. Petersburg (FSL)	A	.277	51	206	39	57	10	4	3	21	18	46	14	.408	.346
2000	Orlando (SL)	AA	.252	124	489	73	123	17	8	3	29	59	119	31	.337	.338
	Tampa Bay (AL)	MAJ	.000	2	1	0	0	0	0	0	0	0	0	0	.000	.000
2001	San Antonio (TL)	AA	.262	121	478	72	125	20	5	11	46	45	111	18	.393	.326
2002	Tacoma (PCL)	AAA	.248	122	391	51	97	13	10	11	53	26	93	11	.417	.296
MAJOR LEAGUE TOTALS			.000	2	1	0	0	0	0	0	0	0	0	0	.000	.000
MINOR LEAGUE TOTALS			.257	499	1881	302	484	69	33	33	173	178	445	99	.382	.326

18. Ryan Anderson, lhp

Born: July 12, 1979. **Ht.:** 6-10. **Wt.:** 210. **Bats:** L. **Throws:** L. **School:** Divine Child HS, Dearborn, Mich. **Career Transactions:** Selected by Mariners in first round (19th overall) of 1997 draft; signed Sept. 10, 1997 . . . On disabled list, April 5-Sept. 30, 2001 . . . On disabled list, April 5-Sept. 30, 2002.

Anderson saw one impressive streak end in 2002 and another he'd like to avoid continue. His five-year run atop the Mariners' prospect list ended, not because he finally established himself in the majors, but because he tore the labrum in his left shoulder for the second straight spring. He has had two surgeries and hasn't pitched in a regular-season game since 2000. They hope he'll be ready for spring training. Before he got hurt, Anderson was as intimidating as any lefthander this side of Randy Johnson. At 6-foot-10 and possessing a 94-97 mph fastball, batters didn't relish facing him. But as overpowering as he could be, Anderson wasn't a finished product when his shoulder started acting up. He was still putting the final touches on a slider that was becoming a second plus pitch, and his changeup and command still needed work. And despite his size and stuff, Anderson never truly dominated at any level of the minors. He may not have worked as diligently as he should coming back from the first surgery, but he has learned his lesson. Anderson was able to pitch off a mound again last fall and should be ready to go for spring training. Seattle obviously will handle him carefully in hopes he can return to his previous form.

Year	Club (League)	Class	W	L	ERA	G	GS	CG	SV	IP	H	R	ER	HR	BB	SO	AVG
1998	Wisconsin (Mid)	A	6	5	3.23	22	22	0	0	111	86	47	40	4	67	152	.220
1999	New Haven (EL)	AA	9	13	4.50	24	24	0	0	134	131	77	67	9	86	162	.259
2000	Tacoma (PCL)	AAA	5	8	3.98	20	20	1	0	104	83	51	46	8	55	146	.218
2001	Did Not Play—Injured																
2002	Did Not Play—Injured																
MINOR LEAGUE TOTALS			20	26	3.94	66	66	1	0	349	300	175	153	21	208	460	.235

19. Jeff Heaverlo, rhp

Born: Jan. 13, 1978. **Ht.:** 6-1. **Wt.:** 210. **Bats:** R. **Throws:** R. **School:** University of Washington. **Career Transactions:** Selected by Mariners in first round (33rd overall) of 1999 draft; signed July 25, 1999 . . . On disabled list, April 5-Sept. 30, 2002.

Ryan Anderson didn't suffer the first torn labrum in Seattle's big league camp last spring. That distinction went to Heaverlo, who was on the verge of completing the first father-son tandem to pitch for the Mariners. His dad Dave, nicknamed "Kojak" for his shaved head, spent seven years in the majors. Jeff didn't have nearly the pure stuff that Anderson did, so he has to hope that shoulder surgery doesn't take too much away from him. His best pitch was a slider that was almost in the class of Clint Nageotte's, and it helped him lead the Texas League in strikeouts in 2001. Heaverlo's fastball was average in terms of both life and velocity, topping out at 92 mph. His command and savvy made him quite effective, and the one task that remained was improving his changeup to get lefthanders out. Heaverlo has progressed a little further on the comeback trail than Anderson and definitely will be ready to pitch again in spring training.

Year	Club (League)	Class	W	L	ERA	G	GS	CG	SV	IP	H	R	ER	HR	BB	SO	AVG
1999	Everett (NWL)	A	1	0	2.08	3	0	0	0	9	5	5	2	1	2	9	.161
	Wisconsin (Mid)	A	1	0	2.55	3	3	1	0	18	15	6	5	1	7	24	.227
2000	Lancaster (Cal)	A	14	6	4.22	27	27	0	0	156	170	84	73	18	52	159	.275
	Tacoma (PCL)	AAA	0	1	4.85	2	2	0	0	13	14	7	7	2	6	4	.298
2001	San Antonio (TL)	AA	11	6	3.12	27	27	4	0	179	164	75	62	12	40	173	.239
2002	Did Not Play—Injured																
MINOR LEAGUE TOTALS			27	13	3.59	62	59	5	0	374	368	177	149	34	107	369	.254

20. J.J. Putz, rhp

Born: Feb. 22, 1977. **Ht.:** 6-5. **Wt.:** 220. **Bats:** R. **Throws:** R. **School:** University of Michigan. **Career Transactions:** Selected by Mariners in sixth round of 1999 draft; signed June 17, 1999.

Putz had shoulder problems in 2002, though they were less serious than those of Ryan Anderson and Jeff Heaverlo. Putz missed the first three weeks of the season while recovering from tendinitis in extended spring training, and skipped the Arizona Fall League because his shoulder bothered him again. He didn't require surgery. Putz' 5-14 record last year was misleading, as he allowed three earned runs or less in 19 of his 24 starts. He had 14 quality starts but only a 4-5 record to show for those outings. Putz has a thick, strong frame and an easy arm action that allows him to maintain low-90s velocity on his fastball throughout a game. He also has a slider, which he needs to throw for strikes more consistently, and a changeup, which still requires some improvement. He'll probably open the year in Triple-A but could get a call to Seattle if reinforcements are needed early in the season. Putz projects as a back-of-the-rotation starter or a middle reliever.

Year	Club (League)	Class	W	L	ERA	G	GS	CG	SV	IP	H	R	ER	HR	BB	SO	AVG
1999	Everett (NWL)	A	0	0	4.84	10	0	0	2	22	23	13	12	2	11	17	.288
2000	Wisconsin (Mid)	A	12	6	3.15	26	25	3	0	143	130	71	50	4	63	105	.247
2001	San Antonio (TL)	AA	7	9	3.83	27	26	0	0	148	145	80	63	11	59	135	.259
2002	San Antonio (TL)	AA	3	10	3.64	15	15	1	0	84	84	41	34	7	28	60	.264
	Tacoma (PCL)	AAA	2	4	3.83	9	9	0	0	54	51	23	23	4	21	39	.258
MINOR LEAGUE TOTALS			24	29	3.63	87	75	4	2	451	433	228	182	28	182	356	.258

21. Allan Simpson, rhp

Born: Aug. 26, 1977. **Ht.:** 6-4. **Wt.:** 180. **Bats:** R. **Throws:** R. **School:** Taft (Calif.) JC. **Career Transactions:** Selected by Mariners in eighth round of 1997 draft; signed June 3, 1997.

Simpson shared minor league pitcher of the year honors in the organization with San Antonio bullpen mates Aaron Taylor and Aaron Looper, who helped the Missions win the Texas League championship. With Taylor promoted to Seattle before the TL finals, Simpson took over as closer and earned a win and two saves. Simpson's fastball sits at 92-95 mph, and he got up to 99 in the postseason. His second pitch is a slider, which has improved but still isn't more than an average pitch. He also has a changeup, but it's not as strong as his other two offerings and he doesn't use it much. Opponents batted just .189 against him in 2002, though he surrendered nearly as many walks (50) as hits (53). Simpson's future is cloudy after he was diagnosed with lupus, a chronic inflammatory disease, during the offseason. That led to the Mariners' decision to remove him from the 40-man roster and outright him to Triple-A when they needed a roster spot after re-signing Jamie Moyer in December.

Year	Club (League)	Class	W	L	ERA	G	GS	CG	SV	IP	H	R	ER	HR	BB	SO	AVG
1997	Everett (NWL)	A	0	3	6.84	16	0	0	0	26	26	23	20	1	24	26	.263
1998	Wisconsin (Mid)	A	3	5	4.44	19	19	0	0	93	89	52	46	5	61	86	.257
	Mariners (AZL)	R	1	0	0.96	3	0	0	1	9	8	2	1	1	3	12	.235
1999	Wisconsin (Mid)	A	2	9	4.38	24	13	1	0	90	83	56	44	4	48	88	.245
	Lancaster (Cal)	A	0	0	6.33	9	0	0	0	21	17	16	15	4	14	25	.218
2000	Lancaster (Cal)	A	3	2	2.08	46	0	0	6	52	34	17	12	1	27	67	.184
2001	San Bernardino (Cal)	A	1	0	1.80	16	0	0	1	30	19	7	6	1	12	40	.178
	San Antonio (TL)	AA	2	1	1.86	22	0	0	9	39	25	8	8	1	15	37	.184
2002	San Antonio (TL)	AA	10	5	3.06	56	0	0	7	82	53	33	28	4	50	99	.189
MINOR LEAGUE TOTALS			22	25	3.65	211	32	1	24	444	354	214	180	22	254	480	.221

22. Bobby Madritsch, lhp

Born: Feb. 28, 1976. **Ht.:** 6-2. **Wt.:** 190. **Bats:** L. **Throws:** L. **School:** Point Park (Pa.) College. **Career Transactions:** Selected by Reds in sixth round of 1998 draft; signed June 10, 1998 . . . On disabled list, April 5-Sept. 30, 1999 . . . Released by Reds, March 24, 2001 . . . Signed by independent Rio Grande (Texas-Louisiana), June 2001 . . . Signed by independent San Angelo (Texas-Louisiana), July 2001 . . . Signed by independent Chico (Western), August 2001 . . . Signed by independent Winnipeg (Northern), May 2002 . . . Signed by Mariners, Sept. 23, 2002.

Baseball America named Madritsch its 2002 Independent Player of the Year after he went 11-4, 2.30 and set a Northern League record with 153 strikeouts in 125 innings. After the season, the Mariners beat out several teams to sign him and added him to their 40-man roster. He originally signed with the Reds as sixth-round pick in 1998 and led the Rookie-level Pioneer League in strikeouts during his first pro summer. But after hurting his shoulder and having surgery, he missed all of 1999 and most of 2000 before the Reds released him the following spring. Madritsch's best pitch is a 92-94 mph fastball that has inconsistent life. He doesn't spin his curveball particularly well and his changeup still has a ways to go. Seattle plans on using him as a starter, though if he can't refine his secondary pitches he could settle for being a hard-throwing lefty reliever.

Year	Club (League)	Class	W	L	ERA	G	GS	CG	SV	IP	H	R	ER	HR	BB	SO	AVG
1998	Billings (Pio)	R	7	3	2.80	14	13	0	0	80	72	30	25	3	35	87	.240
1999					Did Not Play—Injured												
2000	Reds (GCL)	R	1	1	2.01	6	4	0	0	22	15	5	5	0	9	27	.192
	Dayton (Mid)	A	0	0	0.90	2	2	0	0	10	8	1	1	0	7	7	.222
2001	Rio Grande (T-L)	IND	3	4	3.15	10	9	3	0	60	55	25	21	1	34	58	.239
	San Angelo (T-L)	IND	0	2	1.73	3	3	1	0	26	14	8	5	2	6	27	.159
	Chico (West)	IND	0	1	11.74	5	0	0	0	8	14	12	10	2	6	12	.359
2002	Winnipeg (NorC)	IND	11	4	2.30	19	18	2	0	125	94	35	32	6	36	153	.205
MINOR LEAGUE TOTALS			8	4	2.48	22	19	0	0	113	95	36	31	3	51	121	.229

23. Aaron Looper, rhp

Born: Sept. 7, 1976. **Ht.:** 6-2. **Wt.:** 180. **Bats:** R. **Throws:** R. **School:** Indian Hills (Iowa) CC. **Career Transactions:** Selected by Mariners in 30th round of 1997 draft; signed May 29, 1998.

His main claim to fame entering the 2002 season was that he's the son of Mariners farm director Benny Looper, but he ended it as the system's co-minor league pitcher of the year. He earned the save in the final game of the Texas League playoffs by throwing two shutout innings. After the TL all-star break (including the postseason), he allowed just four earned runs in 58 innings for a 0.62 ERA. Unlike Aaron Taylor and Allan Simpson, his fellow pitchers of the year in the system, Looper can't just throw the ball by hitters. He relies instead on an 89-92 mph fastball with consistent plus sink, and an improved slider. When he moves to Triple-A this year, he'll work on improving his changeup.

Year	Club (League)	Class	W	L	ERA	G	GS	CG	SV	IP	H	R	ER	HR	BB	SO	AVG
1998	Everett (NWL)	A	4	5	6.86	14	14	0	0	59	72	52	45	8	31	40	.306
1999	Wisconsin (Mid)	A	9	6	4.10	38	7	0	3	90	89	47	41	8	26	73	.251
2000	Lancaster (Cal)	A	5	3	5.70	51	0	0	0	73	105	62	46	7	22	47	.329
2001	San Bernardino (Cal)	A	6	11	2.79	56	0	0	5	71	59	34	22	1	22	77	.224
2002	San Antonio (TL)	AA	6	1	2.28	57	0	0	0	91	76	33	23	4	30	73	.230
MINOR LEAGUE TOTALS			30	26	4.16	216	21	0	8	383	401	228	177	28	131	310	.267

24. Rene Rivera, c

Born: July 31, 1983. **Ht.:** 5-10. **Wt.:** 190. **Bats:** R. **Throws:** R. **School:** Papa Juan XXIII HS, Bayamon, P.R. **Career Transactions:** Selected by Mariners in second round of 2001 draft; signed June 14, 2001.

If Ryan Christianson can't become the Mariners' catcher of the future, they have hopes that Rivera can. Like Christianson, he has yet to tear up minor league pitching, though Rivera was named to the Northwest League's postseason all-star team in 2002. He got himself selected in the second round the year before with an impressive power display in a Puerto Rican predraft showcase. Rivera is still raw at the plate and needs to tighten his strike zone in order to be more productive. His catch-and-throw skills are more advanced than his bat at this point. Rivera moves well behind the plate, and his strong arm allowed him to lead the NWL in throwing out 38 percent of basestealers. Seattle also has been impressed at how quickly he has picked up English. Rivera will move to full-season ball for the first time in 2003.

Year	Club (League)	Class	AVG	G	AB	R	H	2B	3B	HR	RBI	BB	SO	SB	SLG	OBP
2001	Everett (NWL)	A	.089	15	45	3	4	1	0	2	3	1	19	0	.244	.106
	Mariners (AZL)	R	.338	21	71	13	24	4	0	2	12	2	11	0	.479	.360
2002	Everett (NWL)	A	.242	62	227	29	55	18	1	1	26	16	38	5	.344	.314
MINOR LEAGUE TOTALS			.242	98	343	45	83	23	1	5	41	19	68	5	.359	.297

25. Craig Anderson, lhp

Born: Oct. 30, 1980. **Ht.:** 6-3. **Wt.:** 180. **Bats:** L. **Throws:** L. **Career Transactions:** Signed out of Australia by Mariners, March 2, 1999.

Anderson earned one of Australia's two victories at the 2000 Olympics and led the California League in strikeouts in 2001, but he leveled off last year despite being named a Texas League all-star. He allowed more than three earned runs in just six of his 27 starts, but his fastball settled into the low 80s and he didn't miss many bats. His usually exemplary command slipped a notch too, as he didn't go after hitters as much as he had in the past. Anderson still has the best changeup in the system, and his curveball also is a useful pitch. He helps himself by doing all the little things well, such as fielding (only one error in 2002) and holding runners (59 percent of basestealers were caught while he was on the mound, the second-best rate in the TL). His carefree delivery not only allows him to throw strikes but keeps him healthy, as he hasn't missed a start in four pro seasons. If all goes well, Anderson can become another Jamie Moyer. But he'll need to come up with a little more juice on his fastball to make that happen.

Year	Club (League)	Class	W	L	ERA	G	GS	CG	SV	IP	H	R	ER	HR	BB	SO	AVG
1999	Everett (NWL)	A	10	2	3.20	15	15	2	0	90	81	42	32	7	13	82	.239
2000	Wisconsin (Mid)	A	11	8	3.71	26	26	1	0	158	161	81	65	14	40	131	.267
2001	San Bernardino (Cal)	A	11	4	2.26	28	28	0	0	179	142	65	45	16	39	178	.215
2002	San Antonio (TL)	AA	7	7	3.20	27	27	1	0	152	143	61	54	12	64	94	.254
MINOR LEAGUE TOTALS			39	21	3.05	96	96	4	0	579	527	249	196	49	156	485	.243

26. Juan Done, rhp

Born: Oct. 2, 1980. **Ht.:** 6-2. **Wt.:** 220. **Bats:** R. **Throws:** R. **School:** Broward (Fla.) CC. **Career Transactions:** Selected by White Sox in 19th round of 1999 draft; signed June 9, 1999 . . . Contract voided, Aug. 13, 1999 . . . Signed by Mariners, June 28, 2001.

Done signed out of Pace High in Miami with the White Sox in 1999, but his contract was voided because of a pre-existing injury that was discovered two months later. Because he was released within 90 days, he retained his junior college eligibility. Draft rules granted him free agency after he finished his career at Broward CC in 2001, and he signed with the Mariners. Done's upside is as huge as nearly any pitcher in the system, as is the amount of improvement he'll need to reach that ceiling. He has a 93-94 mph fastball and a hard slider, but he must work on nearly everything except arm strength. He tends to get excited and overthrow, muscling the ball and making his shaky command worse. His slider is inconsistent and his changeup is raw. He was up and down throughout 2002. In April he followed three straight quality starts with a three-inning, 11-run performance. After pitching scoreless ball with 10 strikeouts in each of two consecutive starts in late July, he allowed seven runs in 2⅔ innings in his next outing and didn't win again the rest of the year. With his profile, he could be converted into a late-inning reliever, though Seattle will keep him in the rotation and hope for a steadier season in 2003.

Year	Club (League)	Class	W	L	ERA	G	GS	CG	SV	IP	H	R	ER	HR	BB	SO	AVG
2001	Mariners (AZL)	R	0	0	1.00	5	0	0	2	9	5	3	1	0	6	12	.147
	Everett (NWL)	A	0	0	8.35	8	1	0	0	18	24	21	17	3	14	13	.316
2002	Wisconsin (Mid)	A	9	13	3.94	27	26	3	0	164	130	96	72	13	75	141	.215
MINOR LEAGUE TOTALS			9	13	4.23	40	27	3	2	192	159	120	90	16	95	166	.222

27. Bobby Livingston, lhp

Born: Sept. 3, 1982. **Ht.:** 6-3. **Wt.:** 190. **Bats:** L. **Throws:** L. **School:** Trinity Christian HS, Lubbock, Texas. **Career Transactions:** Selected by Mariners in fourth round of 2001 draft; signed Aug. 18, 2001.

Livingston threw in the low 90s as a high school senior, earning a Major League Scouting Bureau grade that trailed only 100 mph fastballer Colt Griffin among Texas prepsters in March 2001. His velocity dipped to 86-87 mph before the draft, though. Combined with his commitment to Texas Tech and some makeup concerns, it allowed the Mariners to get him in the fourth round. Livingston pitched mainly in the upper 80s during his pro debut last year. He has such a loose arm and projectable frame that he could get back up to the low 90s as he matures. While his fastball, slider, changeup and command still need development, Livingston pitched well for a 19-year-old in the Northwest League. He got better as the summer wore on, posting a 2.08 ERA and 33-4 strikeout-walk ratio over his final six starts. His awkward, deceptive delivery confuses hitters and he has the potential to have average to plus stuff across the board. He'll pitch in low Class A this season.

Year	Club (League)	Class	W	L	ERA	G	GS	CG	SV	IP	H	R	ER	HR	BB	SO	AVG
2002	Everett (NWL)	A	6	5	3.02	15	14	0	0	80	80	33	27	2	14	76	.255
MINOR LEAGUE TOTALS			6	5	3.02	15	14	0	0	80	80	33	27	2	14	76	.255

28. Jon Nelson, 1b/of

Born: Jan. 16, 1980. **Ht.:** 6-5. **Wt.:** 240. **Bats:** R. **Throws:** R. **School:** Dixie State (Utah) JC. **Career Transactions:** Selected by Mariners in 26th round of 2001 draft; signed Aug. 15, 2001.

Like Bobby Livingston, Nelson is a 2001 draft pick who signed late and had an impressive pro debut in the Northwest League last year. Nelson easily led the NWL in homers and RBIs as he continued to acclimate himself to the daily grind of baseball. He took two years off to serve a Mormon mission in South Florida, where he learned to speak Spanish well enough to serve as a translator for his Everett teammates. Nelson's raw power stands out in a system that isn't loaded with home run hitters. To make use of it at higher levels, he'll have to make much better contact after leading the NWL in strikeouts. If he doesn't find some plate discipline and stop chasing breaking balls, he'll be exploited by more advanced pitchers. Nelson played OK at first base after playing on the left side of the infield at Dixie State JC. Because he runs well and has a decent arm, he got a look in left field during instructional league. Nelson should split time between first and left in low Class A this year.

Year	Club (League)	Class	AVG	G	AB	R	H	2B	3B	HR	RBI	BB	SO	SB	SLUG	OBP
2002	Everett (NWL)	A	.234	66	274	37	64	8	0	17	64	14	96	4	.449	.289
MINOR LEAGUE TOTALS			.234	66	274	37	64	8	0	17	64	14	96	4	.449	.289

29. Troy Cate, lhp

Born: Oct. 21, 1980. **Ht.:** 6-1. **Wt.:** 200. **Bats:** L. **Throws:** L. **School:** Ricks (Idaho) JC. **Career Transactions:** Selected by Mariners in sixth round of 2002 draft; signed June 16, 2002.

Cate went on a two-year Mormon mission to England after graduating from high school, then pitched at Ricks JC. He set school records with a 2.35 ERA and 83 strikeouts last year and can rest assured that they'll never be broken: Ricks has become a four-year school, changing its name to Brigham Young-Idaho and dropped all intercollegiate sports. Cate was even more spectacular in his pro debut, finishing second in the Northwest League in ERA and strikeouts. His fastball ranges anywhere from 82-92 mph, and the Mariners aren't sure whether he really varies the speeds on purpose or if his velocity just fluctuates naturally. His curveball is his best pitch and he has an advanced changeup. Cate locates his pitches well and could be a find if he can keep his fastball in the upper 80s.

Year	Club (League)	Class	W	L	ERA	G	GS	CG	SV	IP	H	R	ER	HR	BB	SO	AVG
2002	Everett (NWL)	A	6	1	2.00	16	12	1	0	85	62	21	19	6	11	95	.203
MINOR LEAGUE TOTALS			6	1	2.00	16	12	1	0	85	62	21	19	6	11	95	.203

30. Ryan Ketchner, lhp

Born: April 19, 1982. **Ht.:** 6-1. **Wt.:** 190. **Bats:** L. **Throws:** L. **School:** John I. Leonard HS, Greenacres, Fla. **Career Transactions:** Selected by Mariners in 10th round of 2000 draft; signed June 19, 2000.

Born partially deaf, Ketchner has 40 percent of his hearing. He wears hearing aids in both of his ears, which allow him to pick up vibrations, and he reads lips. He's believed to be the only deaf pitcher in professional baseball, but Ketchner is notable for more than his handicap. He was the pitcher of the year at Wisconsin in 2002, limiting Midwest League hitters to a .190 average thanks to his command and crafty ability to mix pitches. Ketchner has an 83-88 mph fastball and a below-average slider, though both pitches have the potential to become average. His fastball has plenty of life and his delivery is deceptive, making him difficult to hit. His changeup is his best pitch. Ketchner never has been given a full season as a starter, though that may change as he has asserted himself as a lefty prospect in a system loaded with them. Besides the seven southpaws on the top 30 list, the Mariners also have hopes for: Matt Thornton, the 2001 California League pitcher of the year who's coming back from Tommy John surgery; former nondrafted free agents Glenn Bott and Russ Morgan (who tied for the Cal League lead in victories in 2002); and 2002 draftees Kendall Bergdall, Brandon Perry and Jared Thomas.

Year	Club (League)	Class	W	L	ERA	G	GS	CG	SV	IP	H	R	ER	HR	BB	SO	AVG
2000	Mariners (AZL)	R	1	2	4.21	9	1	0	0	26	22	14	12	0	3	27	.227
2001	Everett (NWL)	A	3	3	2.92	20	5	0	2	52	38	19	17	3	18	58	.199
2002	Wisconsin (Mid)	A	3	6	2.59	31	12	0	1	111	75	39	32	3	39	118	.190
	Tacoma (PCL)	AAA	0	1	4.76	1	1	0	0	6	9	3	3	0	0	6	.360
MINOR LEAGUE TOTALS			7	12	2.96	61	19	0	3	195	144	75	64	6	60	209	.203

TAMPA BAY
DEVIL RAYS

TOP 30 PROSPECTS

1. Rocco Baldelli, of
2. Josh Hamilton, of
3. B.J. Upton, ss
4. Dewon Brazelton, rhp
5. Seth McClung, rhp
6. Wes Bankston, of
7. Jon Switzer, lhp
8. Antonio Perez, ss/2b
9. Jason Pridie, of
10. Doug Waechter, rhp
11. Jason Standridge, rhp
12. Jonny Gomes, of
13. Chris Flinn, rhp
14. Chris Seddon, lhp
15. Gerardo Garcia, rhp
16. Pete LaForest, c
17. Delvin James, rhp
18. Elijah Dukes, of
19. Shawn Riggans, c
20. Matt White, rhp
21. Joey Gomes, of
22. Chad Gaudin, rhp
23. Romelio Lopez, rhp/of
24. Lance Carter, rhp
25. Josh Parker, rhp
26. Bobby Seay, lhp
27. Hector Luna, ss
28. Evan Rust, rhp
29. Joe Gathright, of
30. Carlos Hines, rhp

**By Bill
Ballew**

The Devil Rays hope 2002 will represent the bottom for the franchise. Financial woes and hints of contraction permeated the season, while a lifeless team inside lifeless Tropicana Field lost the most games (106) in the Rays' short history. But the franchise reaffirmed its plans to stick with developing talent, while trying to escape from the last of the crippling contracts from an ill-advised spending spree four years ago. General manager Chuck LaMar still takes a wait-and-see approach.

"It will be a year or two before you see a tremendous turn in wins and losses," he said. "Over the next two years, it will be a building process."

Heading the building at the major league level will be manager Lou Piniella, who returns to his hometown after a 10-year stint in Seattle. After taking the Mariners from mediocrity to consistent success, Piniella faces the daunting task in Tampa Bay of trying to build a winner while several young players receive on-the-job training.

The trend was obvious last spring when three players picked up from the major league Rule 5 draft made the Opening Day roster. Rookie catcher Toby Hall and outfielder Jason Tyner were deemed not ready for prime time and returned to Triple-A before bouncing back. Outfielder Carl Crawford debuted last July and stayed afloat, and righthander Dewon Brazelton received his first cup of coffee in September. Outfielder Rocco Baldelli, Baseball America's Minor League Player of the Year, leads the next wave.

In addition to Piniella's arrival, there were other bright spots. Triple-A Durham won the International League title, and the farm system is stocked with several intriguing pitchers and outfielders with both power and speed.

Prior to his departure to become Marlins vice president for player personnel, former scouting director Dan Jennings left the Rays with one of the best drafts of 2002, headed by second overall pick B.J. Upton. Tampa Bay has the first pick in 2003, to be made by former Pirates GM Cam Bonifay, who added player development and scouting responsibilities to his title of director of player personnel after Jennings' departure.

One other glimmer of hope comes from history. Tampa Bay played its 800th game in 2002. While the franchise's .395 winning percentage is dismal, it is better than the Blue Jays, Mariners, Mets, Padres and Rangers at the same point in their existence.

OrganizationOverview

General Manager: Chuck LaMar. **Farm/Scouting Director:** Cam Bonifay.

2002 PERFORMANCE

Class	Farm Team	League	W	L	Pct.	Finish*	Manager
Majors	Tampa Bay	American	55	106	.341	t-13th (14)	Hal McRea
Triple-A	Durham Bulls	International	80	64	.556	+5th (14)	Bill Evers
Double-A	Orlando Rays	Southern	58	79	.423	10th (10)	Mako Oliveras
High A	Bakersfield Blaze	California	69	72	.489	t-6th (10)	Charlie Montoyo
Low A	Charleston RiverDogs	South Atlantic	60	76	.441	14th (16)	Buddy Biancalana
Short-season	Hudson Valley Renegades	New York-Penn	26	49	.347	14th (14)	David Howard
Rookie	Princeton Devil Rays	Appalachian	19	49	.279	10th (10)	Edwin Rodriguez
OVERALL 2002 MINOR LEAGUE RECORD			312	329	.445	29th (30)	

*Finish in overall standings (No. of teams in league).   + League champion.

ORGANIZATION LEADERS

BATTING   *Minimum 250 At-Bats
*AVG	Jason Pridie, Hudson Valley/Princeton	.366
R	Jonny Gomes, Bakersfield	102
H	Rocco Baldelli, Durham/Orlando/Bakersfield	158
TB	Jonny Gomes, Bakersfield	256
2B	Jorge Cantu, Orlando	31
3B	Jason Pridie, Hudson Valley/Princeton	10
HR	Jonny Gomes, Bakersfield	30
RBI	Pete LaForest, Durham/Orlando	79
BB	Jonny Gomes, Bakersfield	91
SO	Jonny Gomes, Bakersfield	173
SB	Ryan Freel, Durham	37
	Fernando Cortez, Charleston	37

PITCHING   #Minimum 75 Innings
W	Lance Carter, Durham	12
L	Jim Magrane, Durham/Orlando	11
#ERA	Dewon Brazelton, Durham/Orlando	3.22
G	John Benedetti, Bakersfield	54
	Evan Rust, Orlando/Bakersfield	54
CG	Brandon Backe, Orlando	3
	Mark Malaska, Orlando/Bakersfield	3
SV	Evan Rust, Orlando/Bakersfield	31
IP	Jason Standridge, Durham	173
BB	Neal Frendling, Orlando/Bakersfield	80
SO	Doug Waechter, Orlando/Bakersfield/Charleston	155

BEST TOOLS

Best Hitter for Average	Jason Pridie
Best Power Hitter	Jonny Gomes
Fastest Baserunner	Joe Gathright
Best Athlete	B.J. Upton
Best Fastball	Seth McClung
Best Curveball	Seth McClung
Best Slider	Chris Seddon
Best Changeup	Dewon Brazelton
Best Control	Lance Carter
Best Defensive Catcher	Shawn Riggans
Best Defensive Infielder	B.J. Upton
Best Infield Arm	B.J. Upton
Best Defensive Outfielder	Rocco Baldelli
Best Outfield Arm	Josh Hamilton

PROJECTED 2006 LINEUP

Catcher	Toby Hall
First Base	Aubrey Huff
Second Base	Antonio Perez
Third Base	Jared Sandberg
Shortstop	B.J. Upton
Left Field	Carl Crawford

Jorge Cantu   **Jason Standridge**

Center Field	Rocco Baldelli
Right Field	Josh Hamilton
Designated Hitter	Wes Bankston
No. 1 Starter	Dewon Brazelton
No. 2 Starter	Joe Kennedy
No. 3 Starter	Seth McClung
No. 4 Starter	Jon Switzer
No. 5 Starter	Doug Waechter
Closer	Delvin James

TOP PROSPECTS OF THE DECADE

1997	Matt White, rhp
1998	Matt White, rhp
1999	Matt White, rhp
2000	Josh Hamilton, of
2001	Josh Hamilton, of
2002	Josh Hamilton, of

TOP DRAFT PICKS OF THE DECADE

1996	Paul Wilder, of
1997	Jason Standridge, rhp
1998	Josh Pressley, 1b (4)
1999	Josh Hamilton, of
2000	Rocco Baldelli, of
2001	Dewon Brazelton, rhp
2002	B.J. Upton, ss

ALL-TIME LARGEST BONUSES

Matt White, 1996	$10,200,000
Rolando Arrojo, 1997	$7,000,000
B.J. Upton, 2002	$4,600,000
Dewon Brazelton, 2001	$4,200,000
Josh Hamilton, 1999	$3,960,000

MinorLeague**Depth**Chart

TAMPA BAY DEVIL RAYS

RANK 10

While 1999 No. 1 overall draft pick Josh Hamilton spent another frustrating year battling injuries, the Devil Rays enhanced the deepest crop of outfielders in the game. Rocco Baldelli emerged as Baseball America's 2002 Minor League Player of the Year, and Dan Jennings' last draft as scouting director produced three high-ceiling players in Wes Bankston, Jason Pridie and Elijah Dukes. None of the other positions is as deep, but the Devil Rays are building a solid foundation for future success. Early gambles on Matt White and Bobby Seay haven't paid off yet, leaving the pitching ranks a little thin, but not many organizations can match the Devil Rays' collection of frontline prospects.

Note: Depth charts prepared by Josh Boyd. Numbers in parentheses indicate prospect rankings.

LF
Jonny Gomes (12)
Joey Gomes (21)
Blair Irvin
Adam Bonner

CF
Rocco Baldelli (1)
Jason Pridie (9)
Elijah Dukes (18)
Joey Gathright (29)
Irwin Centeno

RF
Josh Hamilton (2)
Wes Bankston (6)
Romelio Lopez (23)

3B
Juan Salas
Edgar Gonzalez

SS
B.J. Upton (3)
Hector Luna (27)
Jace Brewer
Jorge Cantu
Wilmy Caceres

2B
Antonio Perez (8)
Nestor Perez

1B
Aaron Clark

C
Pete LaForest (16)
Shawn Riggans (19)

RHP

Starters	Relievers
Dewon Brazelton (4)	Delvin James (17)
Seth McClung (5)	Lance Carter (24)
Doug Waechter (10)	Evan Rust (28)
Jason Standridge (11)	Carlos Hines (30)
Chris Flinn (13)	Brandon Backe
Gerardo Garcia (15)	Austin Coose
Matt White (20)	Lee Gardner
Chad Gaudin (22)	Jason Cromer
Josh Parker (25)	
Brian Stokes	
Jarod Mathews	
Scott Autrey	

LHP

Starters	Relievers
Jon Switzer (7)	Bobby Seay (26)
Chris Seddon (14)	Mark Malaska
	Hans Smith

DraftAnalysis

2002 Draft

Best Pro Debut: OF Wes Bankston (4) was the Rookie-level Appalachian League MVP, hitting .301-18-57 and leading the league in homers and RBIs. OF **Joey Gomes** (8) won the short-season New York-Penn League homer crown and batted .279-16-52. OF Jason Pridie (2) hit .366-8-34 and topped the Appy League with 105 hits and nine triples.

Best Athlete: The Rays got four blue-chip athletes with their first four choices. SS B.J. Upton's (1) arm and speed are plus-plus tools, and he has the actions of a young Derek Jeter. Pridie is a five-tool player who showed a 92 mph fastball in the Arizona 4-A championship game. OF Elijah Dukes' (3) size, speed and strength draw comparisons to Bo Jackson. Bankston is a prototype right fielder. All four were prep football stars.

Best Pure Hitter: Upton or Pridie.

Best Raw Power: Dukes has more pure strength than Bankston or Gomes. 3B/RHP Romelio Lopez (18), 6-foot-7 and 250 pounds, also has tape-measure power. The Devil Rays will give him a look as both a pitcher and hitter in spring training.

Fastest Runner: Upton has 6.5-second speed in the 60-yard dash, but he's not as fast as two high schoolers from Louisiana. OF Blair Irvin (12) and SS Shane Shelley (37) both run in the 6.35-6.45 range.

Best Defensive Player: Upton.

Best Fastball: Lopez threw 94-97 mph during the spring. Among those who have made pro debuts, RHPs Scott Autrey (7) and Brian Bulger (25) have 90-94 mph fastballs.

Best Breaking Ball: LHP Brandon Mann's (27) curve.

Most Intriguing Background: Upton's brother Justin, a shortstop, projects as the No. 1 pick for the 2005 draft. Lopez turned down $800,000 to sign out of Venezuela two years ago, then resurfaced after moving to Texas. Gomes' brother Jonny, an outfielder, and unsigned RHP Justin Standridge's (45) brother Jason, a righthander, are prospects in the Devil Rays system. Bulger's brother Jason, a righty, was a Diamondbacks 2001 first-round pick. Pridie's

RICH ABEL

Gomes

brother Jon pitches in the Twins system.

Closest To The Majors: Autrey has an edge over Gomes because Tampa Bay has a logjam of outfield prospects.

Best Late-Round Pick: Lopez. The Rays like the projection on lean RHPs Jason Hammel (10), Cole Smith (19) and Jarred Farrell (20), all of whom throw in the low 90s.

The One Who Got Away: LHP Mark Romanczuk (5) and RHP Mike Pelfrey (15) wanted big money and headed to Stanford and Wichita State. The fortunes of RHP Matt Harrington (13), a 2000 first-rounder, continue to plummet as he tours indy leagues.

Assessment: Dan Jennings provided a nice going-away present in his final draft before he joined the Marlins. Now the challenge is to develop these athletes into players who can help the dismal big league club.

2001 Draft

An outfield-heavy system added nice arms with RHPs Dewon Brazelton (1) and Chris Flinn (3) and LHPs Jon Switzer (2) and Chris Seddon (5). Unsigned RHP David Bush (4) would have been a welcome addition, too. **Grade: B**

2000 Draft

OF Rocco Baldelli (1), BA's 2002 Minor League Player of the Year, was an astute pick at No. 6 overall. The Devil Rays didn't have picks in the next three rounds and didn't do anything worthwhile afterward. **Grade: B+**

1999 Draft

Getting OF Josh Hamilton (1) to stay healthy would be huge. If not, Tampa Bay still could fall back on OF Carl Crawford (2) and RHP Seth McClung (5). 2B Mike Fontenot (21) and RHP Chadd Blasko (47) didn't sign and became future first-round picks. **Grade: A**

1998 Draft

The Devil Rays got off to a late start, owning no picks in the first three rounds and whiffing on their top choice, 1B Josh Pressley (4). But 1B Aubrey Huff (5) and Joe Kennedy (8) have become two of their few promising players in the majors. **Grade: B+**

Note: Draft analysis prepared by Jim Callis. Numbers in parentheses indicate draft rounds.

. . . Coaches and scouts rave about Baldelli's makeup and desire to become the best player he can be.

ROCCO
Baldelli of

Born: Sept. 25, 1981.
Ht.: 6-4. **Wt.:** 187.
Bats: R. **Throws:** R.
School: Warwick (R.I.) HS.
Career Transactions: Selected by Devil Rays in first round (sixth overall) of 2000 draft; signed June 19, 2000.

Few players made more progress in 2002 than Baldelli, the sixth overall pick in the 2000 draft and the recipient of a $2.25 million bonus. A career .237 hitter in his first two pro seasons, he opened at high Class A Bakersfield and closed by helping Triple-A Durham win the International League championship. Baldelli was Baseball America's Minor League Player of the Year and the top prospect in the California League. He was one of the youngest players in the Southern League during his three weeks at Double-A Orlando, where he batted .371 and hit safely in 14 of his 17 games. After jumping to Durham, Baldelli served as the Bulls' center fielder and leadoff hitter during their run to the title.

Baldelli is the total package and getting better. Considered the top athlete in the 2000 draft, he was a standout volleyball and basketball player in high school in addition to starring in baseball. Baldelli has excellent bat speed and uses his hands well to produce line drives. He can hit and hit for power, and he wasn't overmatched against veteran pitchers. A natural center fielder, he has plus speed and is an effortless runner who glides to the ball with a long stride. Coaches and scouts rave about his makeup and desire to become the best player he can be. Despite his natural athleticism, Baldelli isn't just a pure tools guy. The biggest question about Baldelli's readiness for Tampa Bay is his plate discipline, shown by his dearth of walks last season. He didn't draw a single walk in Triple-A, though he made strides in the Arizona Fall League. Baldelli also needs to work on the art of stealing bases. Somewhat inexperienced because he hails from a cold-weather state, Baldelli should continue to improve with time. His arm is his weakest tool, though most scouts think it will be close to major league average because of the accuracy of his throws.

After promoting a 20-year-old Carl Crawford last year, the Devil Rays will give Baldelli every opportunity in spring training to prove that he belongs in center field. Though he played well during the AFL, the consensus is that Baldelli needs a little more Triple-A seasoning.

Year	Club (League)	Class	AVG	G	AB	R	H	2B	3B	HR	RBI	BB	SO	SB	SLG	OBP
2000	Princeton (Appy)	R	.216	60	232	33	50	9	2	3	25	12	56	11	.310	.269
2001	Charleston, SC (SAL)	A	.249	113	406	58	101	23	6	8	55	23	89	25	.394	.303
2002	Bakersfield (Cal)	A	.333	77	312	63	104	19	1	14	51	18	63	21	.535	.382
	Orlando (SL)	AA	.371	17	70	10	26	3	1	2	13	5	11	3	.529	.413
	Durham (IL)	AAA	.292	23	96	13	28	6	1	3	7	0	23	2	.469	.292
MINOR LEAGUE TOTALS			.277	290	1116	177	309	60	11	30	151	58	242	62	.431	.324

2. Josh Hamilton, of

Born: May 21, 1981. **Ht.:** 6-4. **Wt.:** 220. **Bats:** L. **Throws:** L. **School:** Athens Drive HS, Raleigh, N.C. **Career Transactions:** Selected by Devil Rays in first round (first overall) of 1999 draft; signed June 3, 1999.

Hamilton has battled injuries and misfortune since entering the 2001 season as baseball's best prospect. He made three trips to the disabled list in 2002 before arthroscopic surgery in July to repair his left shoulder and remove a bone spur from his left elbow. When healthy, he showed why he was the No. 1 overall pick in the 1999 draft. Hamilton's instinctive ability to play the game is obvious. He has a classic lefthanded swing with the power to hit 30-plus home runs annually. A top pitching prospect in high school, he has one of the strongest outfield arms in the minors and the speed to handle any outfield position. His biggest improvement in 2002 came in making adjustments between at-bats. Injuries have kept Hamilton from playing a full season for three years. He would be in the major leagues otherwise. He showed better plate discipline but it still could get better. Hamilton is expected to be healthy for spring training. Though he's unproven above high Class A, Hamilton is close to receiving consideration for the majors if he stays on the field and could make the jump from Double-A at some point in 2003.

Year	Club (League)	Class	AVG	G	AB	R	H	2B	3B	HR	RBI	BB	SO	SB	SLG	OBP
1999	Princeton (Appy)	R	.347	56	236	49	82	20	4	10	48	13	43	17	.593	.378
	Hudson Valley (NY-P)	A	.194	16	72	7	14	3	0	0	7	1	14	1	.236	.213
2000	Charleston, SC (SAL)	A	.302	96	391	62	118	23	3	13	61	27	71	14	.476	.348
2001	Orlando (SL)	AA	.180	23	89	5	16	5	0	0	4	5	22	2	.236	.221
	Charleston, SC (SAL)	A	.364	4	11	3	4	1	0	1	2	2	3	0	.727	.462
2002	Bakersfield (Cal)	A	.303	56	211	32	64	14	1	9	44	20	46	10	.507	.359
MINOR LEAGUE TOTALS			.295	251	1010	158	298	66	8	33	166	68	199	44	.474	.338

3. B.J. Upton, ss

Born: Aug. 21, 1984. **Ht.:** 6-3. **Wt.:** 170. **Bats:** R. **Throws:** R. **School:** Greenbrier Christian Academy, Chesapeake, Va. **Career Transactions:** Selected by Devil Rays in first round (second overall) of 2002 draft; signed Sept. 16, 2002.

Considered the top position player in the 2002 draft, Upton went second overall and negotiated all summer with the Rays before coming to terms on a $4.6 million bonus in mid-September. After suffering a bout with dehydration during his first day in instructional league, Upton displayed the skills to suggest he's ready for the fast track. Upton is a premier athlete with pure five-tool potential. His cannon-strong arm is his most impressive asset. Upton has a fluid body, his range at shortstop is exceptional, and he has 6.5-second speed in the 60-yard dash. Upton hits to all fields and has excellent power potential. His wiry frame suggests more pop awaits. The only major item on Upton's to-do list is to get stronger so he can handle major league pitching. It's a minor concern, and scouts don't harbor any doubts that he'll be an effective hitter. Upton is the type of player who could help put the Rays on the major league map. Quiet yet supremely confident, he believes he can reach the big leagues in two years. His journey is expected to begin at low Class A Charleston in April.

Year	Club (League)	Class	AVG	G	AB	R	H	2B	3B	HR	RBI	BB	SO	SB	SLG	OBP
	Has Not Played—Signed 2003 Contract															

4. Dewon Brazelton, rhp

Born: June 16, 1980. **Ht.:** 6-4. **Wt.:** 200. **Bats:** R. **Throws:** R. **School:** Middle Tennessee State University. **Career Transactions:** Selected by Devil Rays in first round (third overall) of 2001 draft; signed Aug. 25, 2001.

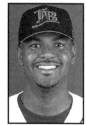

The third overall pick in the 2001 draft, Brazelton got off to a slow start at Double-A Orlando in his professional debut by winning just one of his first 20 starts. The former Team USA standout rebounded to go 5-0, 1.00 in his final seven minor league outings before reaching the majors in September. By adding a slider while discovering the nuances of pitching at the professional level, Brazelton showed he can adjust. His low- to mid-90s fastball has plus movement and complements his best pitch, a changeup. He works both sides of the plate and challenges hitters. Brazelton's struggles came after the club asked him to reduce his full windup. He returned to his old delivery at midseason and excelled. His curveball has a mediocre break with inconsistent depth. His overall command also needs improvement. Brazelton limited the Yankees to two runs over seven innings in his second start, proving he's not far from being ready. He'll compete for a job in the Tampa Bay rotation in the spring.

Year	Club (League)	Class	W	L	ERA	G	GS	CG	SV	IP	H	R	ER	HR	BB	SO	AVG
2002	Orlando (SL)	AA	5	9	3.33	26	26	1	0	146	129	69	54	7	67	109	.241
	Durham (IL)	AAA	1	0	0.00	1	1	0	0	5	5	0	0	0	1	6	.263
	Tampa Bay (AL)	MAJ	0	1	4.85	2	2	0	0	13	12	7	7	3	6	5	.279
MAJOR LEAGUE TOTALS			0	1	4.85	2	2	0	0	13	12	7	7	3	6	5	.279
MINOR LEAGUE TOTALS			6	9	3.22	27	27	1	0	151	134	69	54	7	68	115	.242

5. Seth McClung, rhp

Born: Feb. 7, 1981. **Ht.:** 6-6. **Wt.:** 230. **Bats:** R. **Throws:** R. **School:** Greenbrier East HS, Lewisburg, W.Va. **Career Transactions:** Selected by Devil Rays in fifth round of 1999 draft; signed June 21, 1999.

A seven-sport athlete in high school, McClung took another big step in his development by overpowering the Class A California League during the 2002 season's first month. He allowed two earned runs or fewer in eight of his first nine starts before hitting the skids in Double-A. At 6-foot-6, McClung is built like a power pitcher, with thick thighs and an aggressive approach. He has good command of a mid-90s fastball that has been clocked as high as 99 mph. He also possesses a plus hard curveball with excellent spin, and it's on the verge of becoming a second out pitch. The Rays love McClung's makeup and desire to succeed. McClung is still learning how to pitch. His changeup is nothing more than mediocre, which hurt him against Double-A hitters. McClung also needs to repeat his mechanics consistently while refining all aspects of his game, including his command. The Rays have hopes that McClung will develop into a special pitcher and have no desire to rush him. He'll return to Double-A to open 2003.

Year	Club (League)	Class	W	L	ERA	G	GS	CG	SV	IP	H	R	ER	HR	BB	SO	AVG
1999	Princeton (Appy)	R	2	4	7.69	13	10	0	0	46	53	47	39	3	48	46	.285
2000	Hudson Valley (NY-P)	A	2	2	1.85	8	8	0	0	44	37	18	9	0	17	38	.227
	Charleston, SC (SAL)	A	2	1	3.19	6	6	0	0	31	30	14	11	0	19	26	.246
2001	Charleston, SC (SAL)	A	10	11	2.79	28	28	2	0	164	142	72	51	6	53	165	.231
2002	Bakersfield (Cal)	A	3	2	2.92	7	7	0	0	37	35	16	12	1	11	48	.243
	Orlando (SL)	AA	5	7	5.37	20	19	0	0	114	138	74	68	12	53	64	.299
MINOR LEAGUE TOTALS			24	27	3.93	82	78	2	0	436	435	241	190	22	201	387	.257

6. Wes Bankston, of

Born: Nov. 23, 1983. **Ht.:** 6-4. **Wt.:** 200. **Bats:** R. **Throws:** R. **School:** Plano East HS, Plano, Texas. **Career Transactions:** Selected by Devil Rays in fourth round of 2002 draft; signed June 17, 2002.

Anyone who saw Bankston in his pro debut wondered how he lasted until the fourth round. He led the Rookie-level Appalachian League in home runs and RBIs. Managers rated him the league's second-best prospect, behind Braves first-rounder Jeff Francoeur. A prototype right fielder, Bankston has outstanding raw power. He's big and is a good athlete who rates at least average in all five tools. He has good side-to-side mobility and above-average arm strength that will enable him to play right field. His knowledge of the strike zone and plate discipline weren't as raw as expected. Appy managers were impressed with his ability to hit changeups as well as fastballs at any time in the count. Not unlike many young power hitters, Bankston tends to overswing at times. His swing can be a little long. He simply needs to face more advanced pitching and continue to make adjustments as he climbs the ladder. Bankston will go to Charleston in 2003 and should be one of the younger everyday players in the South Atlantic League.

Year	Club (League)	Class	AVG	G	AB	R	H	2B	3B	HR	RBI	BB	SO	SB	SLG	OBP
2002	Princeton (Appy)	R	.301	62	246	48	74	10	1	18	57	18	46	2	.569	.346
	Hudson Valley (NY-P)	A	.303	8	33	2	10	1	0	0	1	0	6	1	.333	.294
MINOR LEAGUE TOTALS			.301	70	279	50	84	11	1	18	58	18	52	3	.541	.340

7. Jon Switzer, lhp

Born: Aug. 13, 1979. **Ht.:** 6-3. **Wt.:** 190. **Bats:** L. **Throws:** L. **School:** Arizona State University. **Career Transactions:** Selected by Devil Rays in second round of 2001 draft; signed Aug. 13, 2001.

A projected first-round pick in 2001, Switzer fell to the second round (47th overall) because his velocity dropped from the low 90s to the high 80s. After pitching just 14 innings in the short-season New York-Penn League in 2001, he tied for fifth among starters in the minor leagues last year by averaging 11.24 strikeouts per nine innings. He was shut down in August with elbow tendinitis. Switzer recovered the velocity of his fast-ball by altering his arm slot and throwing the ball on more of a downhill plane. He mixed a solid 79-81 mph slider and added a straight changeup with good depth and fade. He works both sides of the plate and does a good job of moving the ball around the strike zone. He limited lefthanders to a .216 average, allowing one extra-base hit in 74 at-bats. Switzer's command can become inconsistent during the course of a game. He needs to repeat his mechanics to maintain his velocity while keeping his pitches from flattening out, especially against righthanders. Switzer will climb a step higher to Orlando. Tampa Bay officials say the mature lefthander isn't far from the majors.

Year	Club (League)	Class	W	L	ERA	G	GS	CG	SV	IP	H	R	ER	HR	BB	SO	AVG
2001	Hudson Valley (NY-P)	A	2	0	0.63	5	0	0	0	14	9	3	1	0	2	20	.173
2002	Bakersfield (Cal)	A	7	5	4.27	20	20	0	0	103	108	55	49	8	26	129	.269
MINOR LEAGUE TOTALS			9	5	3.82	25	20	0	0	118	117	58	50	8	28	149	.258

8. Antonio Perez, ss/2b

Born: Jan. 26, 1980. **Ht.:** 5-11. **Wt.:** 170. **Bats:** R. **Throws:** R. **Career Transactions:** Signed out of Dominican Republic by Reds, March 21, 1998 . . . Traded by Reds with RHP Jake Meyer, OF Mike Cameron and RHP Brett Tomko to Mariners for OF Ken Griffey Jr., Feb. 10, 2000 . . . Traded by Mariners to Devil Rays for OF Randy Winn, Oct. 28, 2002.

The Rays acquired Perez from the Mariners for Randy Winn in the compensation deal that brought manager Lou Piniella to Tampa Bay. After a breakthrough season in 2000, Perez was limited to five games in 2001 with a broken bone in his right wrist before a hamate bone injury in the same wrist caused him to miss two months in 2002. Perez is a potential five-tool shortstop. He's a plus fielder with soft hands, a strong arm and good range. He makes consistent contact and can hit for average and power, and he has above-average speed and ability to steal bases. In addition to losing time to injuries, Perez also added 18 months to his age in 2002. Maturity and improved dedication would help overcome those. He needs to improve his footwork in order to remain at shortstop and get better jumps on the basepaths. Perez was a key component in the deal that sent Ken Griffey to Cincinnati. His star has dimmed, but as thin as the Devil Rays are in the middle infield, the trade provides him a great opportunity to turn it around. He will go to Double-A or Triple-A to begin 2003.

Year	Club (League)	Class	AVG	G	AB	R	H	2B	3B	HR	RBI	BB	SO	SB	SLG	OBP
1998	Reds (DSL)	R	.255	63	212	57	54	11	0	2	24	53	33	58	.335	.408
1999	Rockford (Mid)	A	.288	119	385	69	111	20	3	7	41	43	80	35	.410	.376
2000	Lancaster (Cal)	A	.276	98	395	90	109	36	6	17	63	58	99	28	.527	.376
2001	San Antonio (TL)	AA	.143	5	21	3	3	0	0	0	0	0	7	0	.143	.143
2002	San Antonio (TL)	AA	.258	72	240	30	62	8	2	2	24	11	64	15	.333	.312
	Mariners (AZL)	R	.333	6	15	3	5	1	0	1	3	4	2	4	.600	.476
MINOR LEAGUE TOTALS			.271	363	1268	252	344	76	11	29	155	169	285	140	.417	.369

9. Jason Pridie, of

Born: Oct. 9, 1983. **Ht.:** 6-1. **Wt.:** 180. **Bats:** L. **Throws:** R. **School:** Prescott (Ariz.) HS. **Career Transactions:** Selected by Devil Rays in second round of 2002 draft; signed June 12, 2002.

The younger brother of Twins pitching prospect Jon Pridie, Jason was the 43rd overall pick in the 2002 draft. He led all short-season players with 116 hits, becoming only the sixth player in modern Appalachian League history to reach the century mark. Pridie is a pure baseball player with great instincts and the combination of speed and hitting ability to wreak havoc near the top of the lineup. He has been clocked at 4.0-4.1 seconds to first base from the left side of the plate, and blankets center field. He also is a capable middle infielder and has a plus arm that produced low-90s fastballs last spring in high school. He makes excellent contact and can drive the ball to all fields. A minor hitch in Pridie's swing could be exposed at higher levels. He needs to draw more walks in order to become a classic leadoff hitter. Several scouts compare Pridie to Boston's Johnny Damon and say he could progress through the minors at a similar rate. He got some work at third base in instructional league, which could provide a solution to the organization's outfield logjam, but he's ticketed for the outfield in Charleston in 2003.

Year	Club (League)	Class	AVG	G	AB	R	H	2B	3B	HR	RBI	BB	SO	SB	SLG	OBP
2002	Princeton (Appy)	R	.368	67	285	60	105	12	9	7	33	19	35	13	.547	.410
	Hudson Valley (NY-P)	A	.344	8	32	4	11	1	1	1	1	3	6	0	.531	.400
MINOR LEAGUE TOTALS			.366	75	317	64	116	13	10	8	34	22	41	13	.546	.409

10. Doug Waechter, rhp

Born: Jan 28, 1981. **Ht.:** 6-4. **Wt.:** 210. **Bats:** R. **Throws:** R **School:** Northeast HS, St. Petersburg, Fla., 1999. **Career Transactions:** Selected by Devil Rays in third round of 1999 draft; signed June 27, 1999.

A local product from St. Petersburg, Waechter experienced success at both Class A levels last year before getting a late taste of Double-A. After giving up the most hits and runs in the South Atlantic League in 2001, he led the Rays system with 155 strikeouts in 162 innings. Waechter is a pure athlete who was recruited to play quarterback at South Florida. He has a fastball that sits in the 92-93 mph range and a plus slider that's usually clocked at 82-86. The Devil Rays love his toughness and advanced maturity. Waechter has battled inconsistency throughout his career, especially with his mechanics and his tall frame. His command of the strike zone needs work, and he must be able to place his fastball and slider better. A changeup with more depth will be necessary against more experienced hitters. The Devil Rays say that Waechter can become a power-pitching workhorse once all the refinements are made. He'll open the 2003 season in Double-A.

Year	Club (League)	Class	W	L	ERA	G	GS	CG	SV	IP	H	R	ER	HR	BB	SO	AVG
1999	Princeton (Appy)	R	0	5	9.77	11	7	0	0	35	46	45	38	2	35	38	.317
2000	Hudson Valley (NY-P)	A	4	4	2.35	14	14	2	0	73	53	23	19	2	37	58	.205
2001	Charleston, SC (SAL)	A	8	11	4.34	26	26	1	0	153	179	97	74	14	38	107	.285
2002	Charleston, SC (SAL)	A	3	3	3.47	7	7	0	0	36	39	20	14	2	16	36	.277
	Bakersfield (Cal)	A	6	3	2.66	17	17	0	0	108	114	43	32	9	29	101	.267
	Orlando (SL)	AA	1	3	9.00	4	4	1	0	18	27	20	18	4	13	18	.338
MINOR LEAGUE TOTALS			22	29	4.14	79	75	4	0	424	458	248	195	33	168	358	.273

11. Jason Standridge, rhp

Born: Nov. 9, 1978. **Ht.:** 6-4. **Wt.:** 210. **Bats:** R. **Throws:** R. **School:** Hewitt-Trussville HS, Trussville, Ala. **Career Transactions:** Selected by Devil Rays in first round (31st overall) of 1997 draft; signed June 6, 1997.

Standridge had a difficult season in Triple-A in 2001, yet bounced back last year to put himself in contention for a spot in Tampa Bay's 2003 rotation. The former Auburn quarterback recruit gave up two earned runs or fewer in 19 of his 29 starts. After showing signs of being tentative following a brawl during the 2001 season, Standridge did a better job of pitching inside and using both sides of the plate last season. He continues to throw his fastball in the 92-94 mph range, and he has a hard curveball with a sharp break. His changeup continues to serve as his third pitch and will need to get a little better in order to be effective in the major leagues. A hard worker with outstanding makeup, Standridge has to work more consistently in the strike zone and deepen his repertoire. He has had a cup of coffee in the big leagues in each of the past two seasons and should be a candidate for a starting role at the end of the Tampa Bay rotation this spring. His brother Justin was drafted in the 45th round by the Rays in June but opted for junior college.

Year	Club (League)	Class	W	L	ERA	G	GS	CG	SV	IP	H	R	ER	HR	BB	SO	AVG
1997	Devil Rays (GCL)	R	0	6	3.59	13	13	0	0	58	56	30	23	3	13	55	.250
1998	Princeton (Appy)	R	4	4	7.00	12	12	0	0	63	82	61	49	4	28	47	.314
1999	Charleston, SC (SAL)	A	9	1	2.02	18	18	3	0	116	80	35	26	5	31	84	.197
	St. Petersburg (FSL)	A	4	4	3.91	8	8	0	0	48	49	21	21	0	20	26	.268
2000	St. Petersburg (FSL)	A	2	4	3.38	10	10	1	0	56	45	28	21	4	31	41	.214
	Orlando (SL)	AA	6	8	3.62	17	17	2	0	97	85	46	39	4	43	55	.237
2001	Durham (IL)	AAA	5	10	5.28	20	20	0	0	102	130	73	60	13	50	48	.315
	Tampa Bay (AL)	MAJ	0	0	4.66	9	1	0	0	19	19	10	10	5	14	9	.260
	Orlando (SL)	AA	0	2	5.59	2	2	0	0	10	12	6	6	0	4	7	.300
2002	Durham (IL)	AAA	10	9	3.12	29	29	0	0	173	168	71	60	12	64	111	.259
	Tampa Bay (AL)	MAJ	0	0	9.00	1	0	0	0	3	7	3	3	1	4	1	.500
MAJOR LEAGUE TOTALS			0	0	5.24	10	1	0	0	22	26	13	13	6	18	10	.299
MINOR LEAGUE TOTALS			40	48	3.80	129	129	6	0	723	707	371	305	45	284	474	.258

12. Jonny Gomes, of

Born: Nov. 22, 1980. **Ht.:** 6-1. **Wt.:** 200. **Bats:** R. **Throws:** R. **School:** Santa Rosa (Calif.) CC. **Career Transactions:** Selected by Devil Rays in 18th round of 2001 draft; signed June 13, 2001.

Gomes could end up giving Tampa Bay one of the biggest steals in the 2001 draft. After earning Appalachian League MVP honors and leading the circuit with 16 home runs in his pro debut, Gomes continued to impress in 2002 with his power potential. He ranked fifth in the minors with 30 home runs and a .574 slugging percentage. He fell one homer shy of the California League title as he and his brother Joey, Tampa Bay's eighth-round pick in June, nearly became the first siblings to win homer crowns in the same year since Danny and Ike Boone in 1929. Gomes has incredible bat speed that causes the lumber to whistle while whipping through the strike zone. Unlike many young power hitters, he does a good job of working counts, enabling him to draw 91 walks last year and finish second in the Cal League with a .431 on-base percentage. He's susceptible to strikeouts because his swing is a bit long and has a couple of holes. He's best suited for left field at higher levels. Former Tampa Bay scouting director Dan Jennings calls Gomes a throwback player because of his old-fashioned, hard-nosed approach. Though several aspects of his game remain raw, Gomes has polished many areas and is making impressive progress. He's scheduled to open the 2003 season in Double-A.

Year	Club (League)	Class	AVG	G	AB	R	H	2B	3B	HR	RBI	BB	SO	SB	SLG	OBP
2001	Princeton (Appy)	R	.291	62	206	58	60	11	2	16	44	33	73	15	.597	.442
2002	Bakersfield (Cal)	A	.278	134	446	102	124	24	9	30	72	91	173	15	.574	.432
MINOR LEAGUE TOTALS			.282	196	652	160	184	35	11	46	116	124	246	30	.581	.436

13. Chris Flinn, rhp

Born: Aug. 18, 1980. **Ht.:** 6-2. **Wt.:** 190. **Bats:** R. **Throws:** R. **School:** University at Stony Brook. **Career Transactions:** Selected by Devil Rays in third round of 2001 draft; signed June 13, 2001.

The Rays pushed Flinn at the beginning of 2002 after watching him put together a strong pro debut in 2001, along with solid showings during instructional league and spring training. After initially bypassing Charleston, he struggled during his six weeks at Bakersfield. Once he was sent back to low Class A, he ranked third in the South Atlantic League in ERA and limited opponents to a .222 batting average. Flinn tossed at least six innings in 18 of his 19 starts and allowed three earned runs or fewer in all but two outings. He throws three pitches, including a plus fastball in the 90-93 mph range and a mesmerizing knuckle-curve that serves as his out pitch. His straight changeup is average, and he does a good job of moving all of his pitches around in the strike zone. While Charleston pitching coach Xavier Hernandez did an excellent job with him, Flinn still needs to improve his overall command. He also must repeat his delivery and maintain the consistency of his release point. A return trip to high Class A is most likely for Flinn in 2003, with the possibility of a midseason promotion to Double-A.

Year	Club (League)	Class	W	L	ERA	G	GS	CG	SV	IP	H	R	ER	HR	BB	SO	AVG
2001	Hudson Valley (NY-P)	A	3	4	2.36	15	10	0	2	69	54	33	18	3	21	72	.209
2002	Bakersfield (Cal)	A	0	4	8.64	7	7	0	0	33	52	36	32	9	17	22	.359
	Charleston, SC (SAL)	A	8	6	2.31	19	19	2	0	128	103	44	33	6	41	116	.222
MINOR LEAGUE TOTALS			11	14	3.24	41	36	2	2	230	209	113	83	18	79	210	.241

14. Chris Seddon, lhp

Born: Oct. 13, 1983. **Ht.:** 6-3. **Wt.:** 170. **Bats:** L. **Throws:** L. **School:** Canyon HS, Santa Clarita, Calif. **Career Transactions:** Selected by Devil Rays in fifth round of 2001 draft; signed July 31, 2001.

Seddon was frustrated during the first half of the 2002 season in low Class A. His best pitch was a hard slider that explodes in on the hands of righthanders, but Tampa Bay brass didn't want him throwing it in games because of his previous shoulder problems. He was slowed by soreness and lingering bouts of tendinitis in 2001, which knocked him to the fifth round of the draft. Seddon got the go-ahead to throw the slider again in June, though it took him awhile to recapture his feel for the pitch. In the meantime, his changeup became his out pitch, followed shortly thereafter by the return of his slider. What's more, with a sound shoulder Seddon hit 93 mph with his sneaky fastball, and his curveball developed into an average pitch. He prompts the inevitable comparisons to Tom Glavine, but could become more of a power pitcher than Glavine. Thin and wiry, Seddon needs to continue to add strength. His stuff is heavy, resulting in a .218 opponent batting average, but he must improve his command and control. The Rays believe Seddon could be on the verge of making rapid progress, beginning in high Class A in 2003.

Year	Club (League)	Class	W	L	ERA	G	GS	CG	SV	IP	H	R	ER	HR	BB	SO	AVG
2001	Princeton (Appy)	R	1	2	5.11	4	2	0	0	12	15	7	7	2	6	18	.300
2002	Charleston, SC (SAL)	A	6	8	3.62	26	20	0	1	117	93	63	47	7	68	88	.218
MINOR LEAGUE TOTALS			7	10	3.76	30	22	0	1	129	108	70	54	9	74	106	.226

15. Gerardo Garcia, rhp

Born: Feb. 13, 1980. **Ht.:** 6-0. **Wt.:** 160. **Bats:** R. **Throws:** R. **Career Transactions:** Signed out of Mexico by Devil Rays, Jan. 20, 1999 . . . Loaned by Devil Rays to Mexico City Tigers (Mexican), March 15-Sept. 20, 1999 . . . Loaned by Devil Rays to Mexico City, June 18-21, 2000 . . . Released by Devil Rays, June 21, 2000; re-signed by Devil Rays, Feb. 20, 2002.

Garcia came out of nowhere in 2002 to emerge as a prospect. He actually was in Rays camp in 2000 but returned to Mexico because of arm problems and homesickness. After pitching for the Mexico City Tigers in 2001, he earned a spot in the Orlando rotation last spring. His season was full of highlights, including a Double-A no-hitter, a trip to the Futures Game and a victory with 6⅔ one-hit, shutout innings in the clinching game of the International League playoffs. Garcia's fastball has been clocked as high as 96 mph and resides in the 92-94 mph range. His curveball is considered a plus pitch, while his average changeup showed some improvement over the course of the season. Garcia had control problems in Triple-A, where lefthanders bashed him at a .348 clip because he tried to be too fine and left his pitches over the plate. His stuff can flatten out at times, making him very hittable. He's scheduled to return to Triple-A in 2003.

Year	Club (League)	Class	W	L	ERA	G	GS	CG	SV	IP	H	R	ER	HR	BB	SO	AVG
1999	M.C. Tigers (Mex)	AAA	5	1	4.60	22	3	0	0	45	55	30	23	0	31	25	.301
2000	M.C. Tigers (Mex)	AAA	2	2	4.75	15	1	0	0	30	27	16	16	0	18	16	.245
2001								Did Not Play									
2002	Orlando (SL)	AA	2	1	2.79	10	4	1	0	39	24	14	12	4	12	28	.174
	Durham (IL)	AAA	2	7	6.50	15	15	0	0	64	79	48	46	5	30	50	.312
MINOR LEAGUE TOTALS			11	11	4.91	62	23	1	0	178	185	108	97	9	91	119	.270

16. Pete LaForest, c

Born: Jan. 27, 1978. **Ht.:** 6-2. **Wt.:** 200. **Bats:** L. **Throws:** R. **School:** Gatineau (Quebec) HS. **Career Transactions:** Selected by Expos in 16th round of 1995 draft; signed June 5, 1995 . . . Contract voided, Aug. 15, 1995 . . . Signed by Devil Rays, May 10, 1997.

After missing most of the 2001 season with a right knee injury, LaForest emerged as a solid catching prospect. The Quebec native topped the system in RBIs and tied for the Southern League lead with 20 homers. Signed as a third baseman, LaForest has made significant strides during his conversion to catching but remains far from a polished product behind the plate. He does a decent job in calling a game and hustles behind the plate with a warrior mentality. His arm strength rates at least average, and he has good quickness with his footwork in making throws to second base. LaForest's greatest improvement has come with the bat. He makes solid contact and is able to drive the ball. By serving as Durham's every-day catcher in 2003, LaForest will have the opportunity to make the necessary refinements to make the final jump to the major leagues.

Year	Club (League)	Class	AVG	G	AB	R	H	2B	3B	HR	RBI	BB	SO	SB	SLG	OBP
1995	Expos (GCL)	R	.000	2	6	1	0	0	0	0	0	2	4	0	.000	.250
1996								Did Not Play								
1997	Devil Rays (GCL)	R	.262	34	107	21	28	7	2	3	21	10	18	4	.449	.328
1998	Princeton (Appy)	R	.275	25	91	18	25	7	1	2	14	12	18	4	.440	.365
1999	Charleston, SC (SAL)	A	.256	125	445	64	114	21	3	13	53	55	97	9	.404	.343
2000	St. Petersburg (FSL)	A	.270	129	474	85	128	28	7	14	70	56	108	2	.447	.351
2001	Orlando (SL)	AA	.095	7	21	3	2	0	0	1	1	5	9	0	.238	.269
2002	Orlando (SL)	AA	.270	106	359	57	97	18	1	20	64	60	94	9	.493	.374
	Durham (IL)	AAA	.258	17	66	7	17	3	0	3	15	3	28	0	.439	.290
MINOR LEAGUE TOTALS			.262	445	1569	256	411	84	14	56	238	203	376	28	.440	.349

17. Delvin James, rhp

Born: Jan. 3, 1978. **Ht.:** 6-4. **Wt.:** 220. **Bats:** R. **Throws:** R. **School:** Nacogdoches (Texas) HS. **Career Transactions:** Selected by Devil Rays in 14th round of 1996 draft; signed June 11, 1996.

James' biggest challenge in 2002 was off the field, as he was shot on Sept. 2 while eating at a Waffle House in Raleigh, N.C. After being struck by bullets in the left shoulder and neck, James had surgery and came back to pitch in relief in the International League playoffs. He then had two outings in September with the Rays, including an impressive relief appearance against the Yankees. It was a turbulent year for James, who debuted in the big leagues in April in his seventh pro season. He made five starts before going on the disabled list with a sore shoulder. In high school, James had the chance to play linebacker at Oklahoma State before signing with Tampa Bay for $50,000. One of the rawest prospects in franchise history, James has made impressive strides every season. His fastball sits in the low- to mid-90s, and his changeup continues to improve. He has worked on adding a breaking ball but has yet to find a consistent slider. Though his work ethic is exceptional and his command is good, James is unlikely to compete for a relief job in the major leagues until he develops a deeper repertoire.

Year	Club (League)	Class	W	L	ERA	G	GS	CG	SV	IP	H	R	ER	HR	BB	SO	AVG
1996	Devil Rays (GCL)	R	2	8	8.87	11	11	1	0	48	64	52	47	0	21	40	.320
1997	Princeton (Appy)	R	4	4	4.94	20	5	0	0	58	71	57	32	11	24	46	.290
1998	St. Petersburg (FSL)	A	0	0	10.80	1	0	0	0	2	2	2	2	0	0	0	.333
	Charleston, SC (SAL)	A	2	0	5.40	7	0	0	0	8	12	5	5	0	2	8	.343
	Hudson Valley (NY-P)	A	7	4	2.98	15	15	0	0	82	71	39	27	2	32	64	.232
1999	Charleston, SC (SAL)	A	8	8	3.64	25	25	1	0	158	142	76	64	13	33	106	.237
	St. Petersburg (FSL)	A	3	0	3.18	3	2	0	0	17	18	6	6	0	4	6	.281
2000	St. Petersburg (FSL)	A	7	9	4.26	22	22	3	0	137	142	74	65	10	27	74	.264
	Orlando (SL)	AA	1	3	2.92	6	6	1	0	37	31	15	12	3	7	26	.221
2001	Orlando (SL)	AA	2	0	1.65	7	7	0	0	44	25	8	8	1	9	31	.168
	Durham (IL)	AAA	3	7	4.80	31	9	1	0	84	99	51	45	8	27	51	.296
2002	Durham (IL)	AAA	2	1	3.93	7	7	0	0	34	41	15	15	4	4	26	.295
	Tampa Bay (AL)	MAJ	0	3	6.55	8	6	0	0	34	40	25	25	5	15	17	.301
	Orlando (SL)	AA	1	2	3.55	3	1	0	0	13	12	7	5	2	2	13	.235
MAJOR LEAGUE TOTALS			0	3	6.55	8	6	0	0	34	40	25	25	5	15	17	.301
MINOR LEAGUE TOTALS			42	46	4.15	158	110	7	0	722	730	407	333	54	192	491	.260

18. Elijah Dukes, of

Born: June 26, 1984. **Ht.:** 6-2. **Wt.:** 220. **Bats:** B. **Throws:** R. **School:** Hillsborough HS, Tampa. **Career Transactions:** Selected by Devil Rays in third round of 2002 draft; signed Aug. 21, 2002.

As if the Devil Rays didn't have enough athletic outfield prospects, they selected Dukes in the third round last June with the 74th overall pick. A product of Tampa's Hillsborough High, Dukes follows in the footsteps of such alumni as Carl Everett, Dwight Gooden and Gary Sheffield. A linebacker and running back on the gridiron, he turned down a football scholarship to North Carolina State and signed for $500,000. Dukes draws comparisons to Bo Jackson because of his impressive combination of size, speed and strength. He may be the strongest player in the organization, and he has been clocked at 4.0 seconds to first base from the right side of the plate. Dukes is a polished athlete and is not as raw as many players who focus on football in high school. While his entire game needs refinement as he devotes all of his time to baseball, Dukes' maturity is the biggest concern at this point. He attended four high schools in four years, and several off-the-field incidents bothered many schools and scouts. Based on his limited experience, Dukes should spend the first half of 2003 in extended spring training before reporting to Rookie-level Princeton.

Year	Club (League)	Class	AVG	G	AB	R	H	2B	3B	HR	RBI	BB	SO	SB	SLG	OBP
		Has Not Played—Signed 2003 Contract														

19. Shawn Riggans, c

Born: July 25, 1980. **Ht.:** 6-2. **Wt.:** 190. **Bats:** R. **Throws:** R. **School:** Indian River (Fla.) JC. **Career Transactions:** Selected by Devil Rays in 24th round of 2000 draft; signed May 7, 2001.

Riggans' time behind the plate has been limited to a handful of games since he signed in 2001 as a draft-and-follow. He got off to a great start in his pro debut, with eight homers and 17 RBIs in 15 games in Rookie ball before needing Tommy John surgery to repair his throwing elbow. He recovered in time to report to short-season Hudson Valley last June and started at catcher twice during the first four games. The lingering effects from his elbow surgery limited him to DH over the next two months before he caught five times during the last two weeks of the season. Riggans has solid defensive skills, moves well behind the plate and does a good job of blocking pitches in the dirt. His weakness comes in working with pitchers and refining his overall approach, which are parts of his game he has been unable to develop because of his arm problems. Offensively, Riggans is a good contact hitter with excellent bat speed and a compact swing that generates plus power. He has the makings of a run-producing receiver, provided his arm continues to recover during the 2003 season in low Class A.

Year	Club (League)	Class	AVG	G	AB	R	H	2B	3B	HR	RBI	BB	SO	SB	SLG	OBP
2001	Princeton (Appy)	R	.345	15	58	15	20	4	0	8	17	9	18	1	.828	.433
2002	Hudson Valley (NY-P)	A	.263	73	266	34	70	13	0	9	48	32	72	2	.414	.343
MINOR LEAGUE TOTALS			.278	88	324	49	90	17	0	17	65	41	90	3	.488	.360

20. Matt White, rhp

Born: Aug. 13, 1978. **Ht.:** 6-5. **Wt.:** 230. **Bats:** R. **Throws:** R. **School:** Waynesboro (Pa.) HS. **Career Transactions:** Selected by Giants in first round (seventh overall) of 1996 draft; granted free agency . . . Signed by Devil Rays, Nov. 25, 1996.

After shoulder surgery in May 2001, White began his rehabilitation in extended spring in 2002 before reporting to low Class A in June. He made 10 solid starts before earning a promotion and battling consistency with his command in Double-A. The Rays continue to hope to get something for their $10.2 million investment, a bonus that remains the largest ever for an amateur player. For that to happen, White will need to continue to reinvent himself. Once a power pitcher who blew away hitters with his mid-90s heat, he rarely broke 90 mph with his fastball last season. His sharp-breaking power curveball remains his best offering, and his changeup has the potential to be an above-average pitch. In addition to fine-tuning his repertoire, White must find consistency with his mechanics and discover the nuances of being a finesse pitcher, which include spotting his pitches, working both sides of the plate and altering the batter's eye level. He also must continue to improve his arm strength. Prior to the shoulder injury, White entered spring training in 2001 with a chance to earn a job in the Tampa Bay rotation. The Rays hope he will start this year in Triple-A and show enough progress to merit a promotion in 2003.

Year	Club (League)	Class	W	L	ERA	G	GS	CG	SV	IP	H	R	ER	HR	BB	SO	AVG
1997	Hudson Valley (NY-P)	A	4	6	4.07	15	15	0	0	84	78	44	38	3	29	82	.241
1998	Charleston, SC (SAL)	A	4	3	3.82	12	12	0	0	75	72	41	32	1	21	59	.253
	St. Petersburg (FSL)	A	4	8	5.55	17	17	1	0	96	107	70	59	10	41	64	.282
1999	St. Petersburg (FSL)	A	9	7	5.18	21	20	2	0	113	125	75	65	6	33	92	.278
2000	Orlando (SL)	AA	7	6	3.75	20	20	2	0	120	94	56	50	10	58	98	.221
	Durham (IL)	AAA	3	2	2.83	6	6	0	0	35	36	14	11	1	16	28	.269
2001	Durham (IL)	AAA	0	5	7.80	7	7	0	0	30	33	28	26	4	25	16	.300
2002	Charleston, SC (SAL)	A	3	4	3.15	10	10	0	0	54	48	21	19	5	15	38	.239
	Orlando (SL)	AA	1	2	5.56	7	7	0	0	34	33	22	21	7	19	20	.252
MINOR LEAGUE TOTALS			35	43	4.50	115	114	5	0	641	626	371	321	47	257	497	.257

21. Joey Gomes, of

Born: Nov. 2, 1979. **Ht.:** 6-2. **Wt.:** 210. **Bats:** R. **Throws:** R. **School:** Santa Clara University. **Career Transactions:** Selected by Devil Rays in eighth round of 2002 draft; signed June 12, 2002.

One year older than his brother Jonny, Joey was a third team All-American at Santa Clara last spring and led the New York-Penn League in homers during the summer. He reminded many observers of his brother with his ability to mash while showing solid athleticism for left field. Gomes is aggressive at the plate with excellent raw power and the ability to lift the ball for long home runs. He also makes consistent contact and should hit for a decent average at higher levels. While he tends to overswing on occasion, he's not out of control. He has a good idea of what he wants to accomplish and a mature approach at the plate. His speed is more than adequate for left field, and his arm rates slightly above-average. Gomes also proved to be durable, playing in Hudson Valley's first 68 games last season before a late promotion to high Class A. Gomes needs to continue to make adjustments while gaining experience against advanced pitching. Spring training will determine where he lands in 2003, with a return to Bakersfield most likely.

Year	Club (League)	Class	AVG	G	AB	R	H	2B	3B	HR	RBI	BB	SO	SB	SLG	OBP
2002	Hudson Valley (NY-P)	A	.283	68	276	45	78	14	4	15	48	21	50	4	.525	.344
	Bakersfield (Cal)	A	.227	5	22	1	5	0	0	1	4	0	4	0	.364	.227
MINOR LEAGUE TOTALS			.279	73	298	46	83	14	4	16	52	21	54	4	.513	.336

22. Chad Gaudin, rhp

Born: March 24, 1983. **Ht.:** 5-10. **Wt.:** 170. **Bats:** R. **Throws:** R. **School:** Crescent City Baptist HS, Metairie, La. **Career Transactions:** Selected by Devil Rays in 34th round of 2001 draft; signed Aug. 23, 2001.

After turning down a Louisiana State scholarship and tossing 38 innings without allowing an earned run during instructional league in 2001, Gaudin made his regular season debut in 2002 year and exceeded all expectations. He ranked 10th in the minors in ERA, limiting opponents to no more than one earned run in 16 of his 26 outings. Gaudin works quickly and goes right at hitters. His fastball sits at 92 mph, his curveball has a nice break, and his changeup is at least an average pitch. He also spots the ball well but needs more consistency in the strike zone. At 5-foot-11, Gaudin doesn't have great size for a righthander and is considered an overachiever. While his bulldog tenacity is a plus, he's hard on himself and needs to handle his emotions a little better. He is expected to start 2003 in high Class A at age 20.

Year	Club (League)	Class	W	L	ERA	G	GS	CG	SV	IP	H	R	ER	HR	BB	SO	AVG
2002	Charleston, SC (SAL)	A	4	6	2.26	26	17	0	1	119	106	43	30	5	37	106	.244
MINOR LEAGUE TOTALS			4	6	2.26	26	17	0	1	119	106	43	30	5	37	106	.244

23. Romelio Lopez, rhp/of

Born: Oct. 10, 1983. **Ht.:** 6-7. **Wt.:** 250. **Bats:** B. **Throws:** R. **School:** Conroe (Texas) HS. **Career Transactions:** Selected by Devil Rays in 18th round of 2002 draft; signed Aug. 22, 2002.

Lopez may be the most intriguing player ever signed by the Devil Rays, and that includes outfielder Toe Nash. Lopez turned down a reported $800,000 signing bonus out of Venezuela in 2000 before disappearing from scouts' radar screens. He re-emerged in Texas last spring and made two starts for Conroe High after his parents provided the proper residency documentation. Scouts who had seen Lopez previously were shocked at how he had grown into a 6-foot-6, 245-pounder. He produced tape-measure shots at the plate during the Perfect Game predraft showcase by putting his entire force into swings. Lopez also was clocked consistently at 94-97 mph on the mound during his two high school starts. The Rays are leaning toward using him as a pitcher, though they'll give him a look as a hitter during spring training. His mechanics are raw, with all of his heat produced with his plus arm strength. He appears to have a decent feel for pitching, though his fastball is his primary offering and his command needs work. Definitely a project, Lopez is likely to begin the 2003 season in extended spring training before reporting to Hudson Valley or Princeton.

Year	Club (League)	Class	W	L	ERA	G	GS	CG	SV	IP	H	R	ER	HR	BB	SO	AVG
	Has Not Played—Signed 2003 Contract																

24. Lance Carter, rhp

Born: Dec. 18, 1974. **Ht.:** 6-1. **Wt.:** 190. **Bats:** R. **Throws:** R. **School:** Manatee (Fla.) JC. **Career Transactions:** Selected by Royals in 21st round of 1994 draft; signed June 12, 1994 . . . On disabled list, June 12-Sept. 15, 1997 . . . Granted free agency, Oct. 15, 2000 . . . Signed by Devil Rays, Jan. 11, 2002.

The Rays signed Carter after the 27-year-old tried out for former Tampa Bay manager Hal McRae in January 2002. After two reconstructive elbow surgeries, Carter started and relieved in Triple-A and was the organization's pitcher of the year. He returned to the major leagues in September, three years after reaching that level with Royals. Carter had his first major elbow operation in 1997, and missed the entire 2001 season after his second. He's known for his excellent command, and he relies on changing speeds and getting ahead of hitters. His best pitch is his changeup, followed by his curveball and a fastball with below-average velocity. Carter also refuses to give in to hitters, and counts on his patience to frustrate opponents. His perseverance has enabled him to overcome long odds, which should help him compete for a relief job on the Rays' staff this spring.

Year	Club (League)	Class	W	L	ERA	G	GS	CG	SV	IP	H	R	ER	HR	BB	SO	AVG
1994	Eugene (NWL)	A	1	0	5.47	8	7	0	0	26	28	17	16	2	15	23	.286
	Royals (GCL)	R	3	0	0.29	5	5	0	0	31	19	1	1	1	3	36	.179
1995	Springfield (Mid)	A	9	5	3.99	27	24	1	0	138	151	77	61	14	22	118	.276
1996	Wilmington (Car)	A	3	6	6.34	16	12	0	0	65	81	50	46	8	17	49	.298
1997					Did Not Play—Injured												
1998	Lansing (Mid)	A	3	1	0.67	15	2	0	2	40	34	6	3	0	9	37	.231
	Wilmington (Car)	A	1	4	3.29	28	1	0	5	52	50	21	19	5	14	61	.262
1999	Wichita (TL)	AA	5	2	0.78	44	0	0	13	70	49	10	6	1	27	77	.195
	Kansas City (AL)	MAJ	0	1	5.06	6	0	0	0	5	3	3	3	2	3	3	.167
2000	Omaha (PCL)	AAA	2	8	4.95	34	6	0	5	76	88	46	42	13	18	51	.295
2001					Did Not Play												
2002	Durham (IL)	AAA	12	2	2.80	33	0	0	2	132	111	43	41	15	12	90	.230
	Tampa Bay (AL)	MAJ	2	0	1.33	8	0	0	2	20	15	3	3	2	5	14	.203
MAJOR LEAGUE TOTALS			2	1	2.10	14	0	0	2	26	18	6	6	4	8	17	.196
MINOR LEAGUE TOTALS			39	28	3.35	210	75	3	26	631	611	271	235	59	137	542	.255

25. Josh Parker, rhp

Born: Jan. 12, 1981. **Ht.:** 6-7. **Wt.:** 220. **Bats:** R. **Throws:** R. **School:** Wallace State (Ala.) CC. **Career Transactions:** Selected by Devil Rays in 29th round of 2001 draft; signed June 7, 2001.

Parker's 3-9 record wasn't indicative of how he pitched in 2002. He consistently showed a 93-94 mph fastball with heavy action, and a good changeup with nice fade. He also has an average slider that could be nasty if he can throw it with more consistency. Parker also worked on developing a splitter. He's an animal with a closer's mentality. His greatest need is to get ahead in the count and then put hitters away. While he does a decent job of spotting his pitches, Parker tends to leave them up in the strike zone, resulting in cheap hits. His coaches have told him he'll ascend quickly if he can pitch three inches lower in the zone.

If he learns how to use his natural sinking action to his advantage and avoid getting down on himself, Parker has the overall package to be a setup man and a possible closer. He's expected to begin 2003 in high Class A.

Year	Club (League)	Class	W	L	ERA	G	GS	CG	SV	IP	H	R	ER	HR	BB	SO	AVG
2001	Princeton (Appy)	R	2	1	2.35	22	0	0	5	31	29	12	8	0	6	34	.250
	Charleston, SC (SAL)	A	2	1	2.70	3	0	0	0	7	7	3	2	0	4	4	.269
2002	Charleston, SC (SAL)	A	3	7	2.85	45	0	0	15	60	75	29	19	3	22	64	.302
	Bakersfield (Cal)	A	0	2	9.00	8	0	0	1	9	18	9	9	1	6	8	.409
MINOR LEAGUE TOTALS			7	11	3.22	78	0	0	21	106	129	53	38	4	38	110	.297

26. Bobby Seay, lhp

Born: June 20, 1978. **Ht.:** 6-2. **Wt.:** 220. **Bats:** L. **Throws:** L. **School:** Sarasota (Fla.) HS. **Career Transactions:** Selected by White Sox in first round (12th overall) of 1996 draft; granted free agency . . . Signed by Devil Rays, Nov. 8, 1996.

Lefthanded pitchers with the ability to throw in the low 90s are always in demand, and Tampa Bay's perilous financial situation only adds to Seay's value. Signed for $3 million as a draft loophole free agent in 1996, Seay has yet to experience a breakthrough season, yet remains on the radar screen because he still has potential. The 2002 season represented another disappointment. After reaching the major leagues the year before, Seay developed a sore shoulder in spring training and landed in Double-A, where he was shelved with elbow trouble. He wound up falling short of 100 innings for the fifth time in six minor league seasons. Seay does have two plus pitches in his fastball and curveball, and he's not afraid to challenge hitters. Inconsistent command and a mediocre changeup have stunted his development nearly as much as Seay's inability to stay healthy. While he'll continue to receive serious consideration for the Tampa Bay bullpen, his opportunity to establish himself as a long-term answer is dwindling.

Year	Club (League)	Class	W	L	ERA	G	GS	CG	SV	IP	H	R	ER	HR	BB	SO	AVG
1997	Charleston, SC (SAL)	A	3	4	4.55	13	13	0	0	61	56	35	31	2	37	64	.249
1998	Charleston, SC (SAL)	A	1	7	4.30	15	15	0	0	69	59	40	33	10	29	74	.236
1999	St. Petersburg (FSL)	A	2	6	3.00	12	11	0	0	57	56	25	19	0	23	45	.271
	Orlando (SL)	AA	1	2	7.94	6	6	0	0	17	22	15	15	2	15	16	.319
2000	Orlando (SL)	AA	8	7	3.88	24	24	0	0	132	132	64	57	13	53	106	.265
2001	Orlando (SL)	AA	2	5	5.98	15	13	0	0	65	81	48	43	9	26	49	.310
	Tampa Bay (AL)	MAJ	1	1	6.23	12	0	0	0	13	13	11	9	3	5	12	.260
2002	Orlando (SL)	AA	2	0	3.28	15	3	0	0	36	31	16	13	2	15	24	.237
	Durham (IL)	AAA	0	0	6.00	10	0	0	0	15	15	10	10	1	2	14	.254
MAJOR LEAGUE TOTALS			1	1	6.23	12	0	0	0	13	13	11	9	3	5	12	.260
MINOR LEAGUE TOTALS			19	31	4.40	110	85	0	0	452	452	253	221	39	200	392	.266

27. Hector Luna, ss

Born: Feb. 1, 1980. **Ht.:** 6-1. **Wt.:** 170. **Bats:** R. **Throws:** R. **Career Transactions:** Signed out of Dominican Republic by Indians, Feb. 2, 1999 . . . Selected by Devil Rays from Indians in major league Rule 5 draft, Dec. 16, 2002.

The Devil Rays always have been desperate at shortstop—remember, this is the organization that traded Bobby Abreu for Kevin Stocker—and have a few years to wait before B.J. Upton is ready. They addressed the position this offseason by getting Rey Ordonez from the Mets in a trade and Luna from the Indians in the major league Rule 5 draft. Luna is athletic and has the range and arm to play any position in the infield. At times he tries to do too much and makes wild throws, which contributed to his high error total (32) last year. He's an above-average runner with basestealing ability, and as such would really benefit from improved plate discipline. His strikeout totals aren't outrageous, but he could benefit by being more selective and taking more walks. If he can learn to play more under control, Luna has a chance to be an everyday shortstop in the major leagues.

Year	Club (League)	Class	AVG	G	AB	R	H	2B	3B	HR	RBI	BB	SO	SB	SLG	OBP
1999	Indians (DSL)	R	.256	61	234	44	60	13	2	1	24	27	36	29	.342	.345
2000	Burlington (Appy)	R	.204	55	201	25	41	5	0	1	15	27	35	19	.244	.306
	Mahoning Valley (NY-P)	A	.316	5	19	2	6	2	0	0	4	1	3	0	.421	.350
2001	Columbus (SAL)	A	.266	66	241	36	64	8	3	3	23	23	48	15	.361	.339
2002	Kinston (Car)	A	.276	128	468	67	129	15	6	11	51	39	79	32	.404	.334
MINOR LEAGUE TOTALS			.258	315	1163	174	300	43	11	16	117	117	201	95	.355	.333

28. Evan Rust, rhp

Born: May 4, 1978. **Ht.:** 6-1. **Wt.:** 200. **Bats:** R. **Throws:** R. **School:** St. Mary's (Calif.) College. **Career Transactions:** Signed as nondrafted free agent by Devil Rays, June 15, 2000.

Rust wasn't drafted after going 1-11 at St. Mary's in 2000, but since has emerged as one of

Tampa Bay's top relief prospects. He succeeded in 23 of 25 save opportunities in high Class A in 2002 before earning eight more saves in Double-A to finish fourth in the minors with 31 overall. Managers rated him the top reliever in the Class A California League. Rust has the necessary makeup to close in the professional ranks. After trying to overpower hitters with his low-90s fastball in the past, Rust succeeded by keeping his pitches down in the strike zone and worrying about command more than velocity. A late bloomer, Rust could become the first homegrown closer in Rays' history if he continues to make progress like he has in his first three pro seasons. He'll start 2003 back at Orlando.

Year	Club (League)	Class	W	L	ERA	G	GS	CG	SV	IP	H	R	ER	HR	BB	SO	AVG
2000	Princeton (Appy)	R	5	2	2.89	26	0	0	1	44	37	17	14	3	13	34	.226
2001	Charleston, SC (SAL)	A	7	6	3.06	35	11	0	12	97	88	47	33	3	27	88	.238
2002	Bakersfield (Cal)	A	0	1	2.18	28	0	0	23	33	28	8	8	1	10	45	.233
	Orlando (SL)	AA	1	3	3.70	26	0	0	8	24	30	10	10	0	14	25	.294
MINOR LEAGUE TOTALS			13	12	2.95	115	11	0	44	198	183	82	65	7	64	192	.242

29. Joe Gathright, of

Born: April 22, 1982. **Ht.:** 5-10. **Wt.:** 170. **Bats:** L. **Throws:** R. **School:** Bonnabel HS, Metairie, La. **Career Transactions:** Selected by Devil Rays in 32nd round of 2001 draft; signed Aug. 29, 2001.

Gathright may be the fastest player in the minor leagues. The Devil Rays have clocked him at 6.18 seconds in the 60-yard dash, and some say he's one of the few players to possess truly game-changing speed. His natural athleticism has allowed him to make solid progress. His development was hindered last year when he lost two months after separating his shoulder while trying to make a diving catch. Gathright hails from the same area of Louisiana that produced Toe Nash, who produced more hype than production before the Rays released him. His approach at the plate is simple, with Gathright either bunting or butcher-chopping virtually every pitch. In fact, his first 50 hits last season were singles. He has a short swing and a good knowledge of the strike zone, but it's not clear he'll hit at higher levels. In addition to adding strength, Gathright must get better jumps and reads on fly balls in the outfield. He also must become a student of stealing bases, as his 22 swipes in 2002 came strictly on athletic talent. While Gathright has work to do to be another Quinton McCracken, he should make the jump to high Class A in 2003.

Year	Club (League)	Class	AVG	G	AB	R	H	2B	3B	HR	RBI	BB	SO	SB	SLG	OBP
2002	Charleston, SC (SAL)	A	.264	59	208	30	55	1	0	0	14	21	36	22	.269	.360
MINOR LEAGUE TOTALS			.264	59	208	30	55	1	0	0	14	21	36	22	.269	.360

30. Carlos Hines, rhp

Born: Sept. 26, 1980. **Ht.:** 6-4. **Wt.:** 190. **Bats:** R. **Throws:** R. **School:** Smithfield-Selma HS, Smithfield, N.C. **Career Transactions:** Selected by Reds in 24th round of 1999 draft; signed June 9, 1999 . . . Released by Reds, Aug. 25, 1999 . . . Signed by Devil Rays, June 20, 2001.

Signed out of a North Carolina high school in 1999 by the Reds, Hines was released for disciplinary reasons later that summer and didn't play pro ball in 2000. He resurfaced with the Devil Rays in 2001, earning pitcher of the year honors at Princeton. He struggled in 2002, though he showed good athleticism for a pitcher and a fastball that touches 94 mph. He also throws a decent slider, but most scouts agree he's a one-pitch pitcher at this point in his career. Because of his limited repertoire and mediocre movement on his fastball, Hines has difficulty when he goes through the lineup a second time. He needs to make more progress with his slider while developing a changeup. Added maturity would help the 22-year-old as well, as his makeup has been described as questionable at best. His potential lies as a set-up man and possibly a closer if he adds a little velocity to his heater. He'll probably spend 2003 with one of Tampa Bay's Class A affiliates.

Year	Club (League)	Class	W	L	ERA	G	GS	CG	SV	IP	H	R	ER	HR	BB	SO	AVG
1999	Reds (GCL)	R	0	0	8.10	5	0	0	0	10	15	12	9	0	8	7	.349
2000							Did Not Play										
2001	Princeton (Appy)	R	2	3	4.44	13	7	0	0	49	51	33	24	3	17	56	.260
2002	Charleston, SC (SAL)	A	1	3	5.21	24	7	0	2	48	54	29	28	1	15	26	.287
	Hudson Valley (NY-P)	A	2	2	3.96	5	5	0	0	25	28	13	11	3	7	12	.295
	Orlando (SL)	AA	0	0	16.20	3	0	0	0	3	8	9	6	0	5	3	.400
MINOR LEAGUE TOTALS			5	8	5.19	50	19	0	2	135	156	96	78	7	52	104	.288

TEXAS
RANGERS

TOP 30 PROSPECTS

1. Mark Teixeira, 3b
2. Colby Lewis, rhp
3. Ben Kozlowski, lhp
4. Laynce Nix, of
5. Gerald Laird, c
6. Drew Meyer, ss/2b
7. Ryan Ludwick, of
8. C.J. Wilson, lhp
9. Travis Hughes, rhp
10. Jason Bourgeois, 2b/ss
11. Jason Hart, of/1b
12. Marshall McDougall, inf
13. Jose Dominguez, rhp
14. Kelvin Jimenez, rhp
15. A.J. Murray, lhp
16. Ryan Dittfurth, rhp
17. Nick Regilio, rhp
18. John Barnett, rhp
19. Jermaine Clark, of/2b
20. Mario Ramos, lhp
21. Chris O'Riordan, 2b
22. Ramon Martinez, 2b
23. Erik Thompson, rhp
24. Patrick Boyd, of
25. Kiki Bengochea, rhp
26. Derrick Van Dusen, lhp
27. Jason Botts, of/1b
28. John Koronka, lhp
29. Nate Gold, 1b
30. Julin Charles, of

By John Manuel

I t's tough to thrive in the American League West. The Angels are the reigning World Series champion. The Mariners are a year removed from winning a record-tying 116 games. The Athletics are on a three-year playoff run and have back-to-back 100-win seasons.

Then there are the Rangers. They have the division's marquee player (Alex Rodriguez) and largest payroll ($130.6 million for the 40-man roster in 2002, $30 million more than any division rival). Owner Tom Hicks is willing to spend what it takes to compete, and his bankroll and track record–he owned the Dallas Stars when they won the Stanley Cup–lured John Hart from Cleveland to become general manager.

Hart's first acquisition was assistant GM Grady Fuson, Oakland's former scouting director. Fuson helped engineer the regime's first big trade, sending first baseman Carlos Pena to Oakland for four prospects. The supposed centerpiece of the deal, lefthander Mario Ramos, flopped in Triple-A.

The rest of the first year of Hart's regime didn't go much better. The club continued to spend on free agents, giving Chan Ho Park a five-year, $65 million contract and watching him turn into a bust. Juan Gonzalez, Jay Powell and Todd Van Poppel also didn't have much success. The Rangers finished 72-90, their third straight last-place finish. After the season, they said goodbye to catcher Ivan Rodriguez and faced the possible retirement of oft-injured Rusty Greer.

Fuson was hired in part to revamp the Rangers' scouting efforts, though all the free-agent signings cost the organization draft picks from rounds two through five. Fuson surprised many by drafting shortstop Drew Meyer 10th overall, and by giving righthander Kiki Bengochea, like many Rangers a client of Scott Boras, a hefty $550,000 bonus as an 11th-round pick. Fuson also brought a new philosophy for the minor league system, which should be able to handle the departures of farm director Trey Hillman and pitching coordinator Bob Cluck. As Fuson sees it, the key is minimizing risk. For hitters, that means working counts while being aggressive. For pitchers, it means efficiency and throwing strikes, emphasizing approach over radar-gun readings. For the draft, it means an emphasis on college players with a record of success.

The way Hart and Fuson see it, the AL West has enough risks as it is.

Organization Overview

General Manager: John Hart. Farm Director: Bob Miscik. Scouting Director: Grady Fuson.

2002 PERFORMANCE

Class	Farm Team	League	W	L	Pct.	Finish*	Manager
Majors	Texas	American	72	90	.444	10th (14)	Jerry Narron
Triple-A	Oklahoma RedHawks	Pacific Coast	75	69	.521	t-5th (16)	Bobby Jones
Double-A	†Tulsa Drillers	Texas	72	67	.518	5th (8)	Tim Ireland
High A	#Charlotte Rangers	Florida State	84	56	.600	1st (12)	Darryl Kennedy
Low A	&Savannah Sand Gnats	South Atlantic	49	89	.355	16th (16)	Paul Carey
Rookie	^Pulaski Rangers	Appalachian	34	32	.515	6th (10)	Pedro Lopez
Rookie	@GCL Rangers	Gulf Coast	28	32	.467	t-8th (14)	Carlos Subero
OVERALL MINOR LEAGUE RECORD			342	345	.498	16th (30)	

*Finish in overall standings (No. of teams in league)   †Affiliate will be in Frisco (Texas) in 2003.   #Affiliate will be in Stockton (California).   &Affiliate will be in Clinton (Midwest).   ^Affiliate will be in Spokane (Northwest).   @Affiliate will be in Arizona League.

ORGANIZATION LEADERS

BATTING
*Minimum 250 At-Bats

*AVG	Travis Hafner, Oklahoma	.342
R	Ramon Martinez, Charlotte	98
H	Laynce Nix, Charlotte	146
TB	Jason Hart, Oklahoma	244
2B	Jason Jones, Tulsa	33
3B	Jose Morban, Charlotte	12
HR	Jason Hart, Oklahoma	25
RBI	Laynce Nix, Charlotte	110
BB	Jason Jones, Tulsa	87
SO	Kelly Dransfeldt, Oklahoma	133
SB	Ramon Martinez, Charlotte	39

PITCHING
#Minimum 75 Innings

W	C.J. Wilson, Tulsa/Charlotte	11
	Spike Lundberg, Oklahoma/Tulsa	11
L	Kelvin Jimenez, Savannah	10
	David Mead, Savannah	10
#ERA	Ben Kozlowski, Tulsa/Charlotte	2.07
G	Greg Runser, Tulsa	61
CG	Three tied at	2
SV	Greg Runser, Tulsa	25
IP	Spike Lundberg, Oklahoma/Tulsa	164
BB	Travis Hughes, Tulsa	82
SO	Travis Hughes, Tulsa	137

BEST TOOLS

Best Hitter for Average	Mark Teixeira
Best Power Hitter	Mark Teixeira
Fastest Baserunner	Jason Bourgeois
Best Athlete	Drew Meyer
Best Fastball	Colby Lewis
Best Curveball	Ben Kozlowski
Best Slider	Travis Hughes
Best Changeup	John Barnett
Best Control	Erik Thompson
Best Defensive Catcher	Gerald Laird
Best Defensive Infielder	Ramon Martinez
Best Infield Arm	Drew Meyer
Best Defensive Outfielder	Patrick Boyd
Best Outfield Arm	Julin Charles

PROJECTED 2006 LINEUP

Catcher	Gerald Laird
First Base	Mark Teixeira
Second Base	Michael Young
Third Base	Hank Blalock
Shortstop	Alex Rodriguez
Left Field	Laynce Nix
Center Field	Drew Meyer
Right Field	Ryan Ludwick
Designated Hitter	Kevin Mench
No. 1 Starter	Joaquin Benoit

Jason Jones

Spike Lundberg

No. 2 Starter	Colby Lewis
No. 3 Starter	Ben Kozlowski
No. 4 Starter	Chan Ho Park
No. 5 Starter	C.J. Wilson
Closer	Travis Hughes

TOP PROSPECTS OF THE DECADE

1993	Benji Gil, ss
1994	Benji Gil, ss
1995	Julio Santana, rhp
1996	Andrew Vessel, of
1997	Danny Kolb, rhp
1998	Ruben Mateo, of
1999	Ruben Mateo, of
2000	Ruben Mateo, of
2001	Carlos Pena, 1b
2002	Hank Blalock, 3b

TOP DRAFT PICKS OF THE DECADE

1993	Mike Bell, 3b
1994	Kevin Brown, c (2)
1995	Jonathan Johnson, rhp
1996	R.A. Dickey, rhp
1997	Jason Romano, 3b
1998	Carlos Pena, 1b
1999	Colby Lewis, rhp
2000	Scott Heard, c
2001	Mark Teixeira, 3b
2002	Drew Meyer, ss

ALL-TIME LARGEST BONUSES

Mark Teixeira, 2001	$4,500,000
Drew Meyer, 2002	1,875,000
Carlos Pena, 1998	1,850,000
Scott Heard, 2000	1,475,000
Jonathan Johnson, 1995	1,100,000

MinorLeagueDepthChart

TEXAS RANGERS

RANK 19

It was difficult for assistant general manager/scouting director Grady Fuson to put his stamp on the farm system in his first year because the Rangers had only one draft pick in the first five rounds. He went off the board with the 10th overall pick, snagging athletic Drew Meyer, and didn't pick again until the sixth round. An organization-wide change in philosophy is in motion, however. Fuson has implemented many of the same player-development programs practiced by the Athletics, his former organization. While the Rangers' depth took a hit after they dealt Travis Hafner in the offseason, they still boast premium talent on the infield corners in Mark Teixeira and Hank Blalock, who have a chance to make an impact in 2003.

Note: Depth charts prepared by Josh Boyd. Numbers in parentheses indicate prospect rankings.

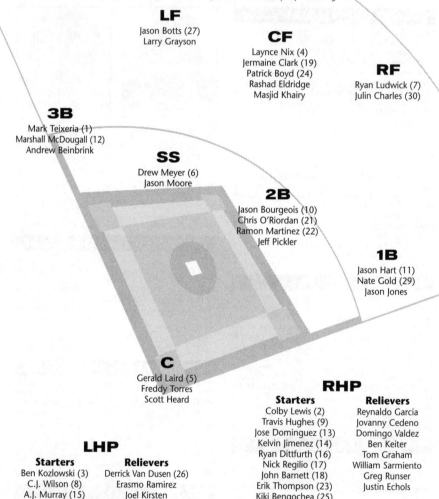

LF
Jason Botts (27)
Larry Grayson

CF
Laynce Nix (4)
Jermaine Clark (19)
Patrick Boyd (24)
Rashad Eldridge
Masjid Khairy

RF
Ryan Ludwick (7)
Julin Charles (30)

3B
Mark Teixeira (1)
Marshall McDougall (12)
Andrew Beinbrink

SS
Drew Meyer (6)
Jason Moore

2B
Jason Bourgeois (10)
Chris O'Riordan (21)
Ramon Martinez (22)
Jeff Pickler

1B
Jason Hart (11)
Nate Gold (29)
Jason Jones

C
Gerald Laird (5)
Freddy Torres
Scott Heard

RHP

Starters
Colby Lewis (2)
Travis Hughes (9)
Jose Dominguez (13)
Kelvin Jimenez (14)
Ryan Dittfurth (16)
Nick Regilio (17)
John Barnett (18)
Erik Thompson (23)
Kiki Bengochea (25)
Nick Masset
David Mead
Jason Andrew
Andrew Tisdale
Omar Beltre

Relievers
Reynaldo Garcia
Jovanny Cedeno
Domingo Valdez
Ben Keiter
Tom Graham
William Sarmiento
Greg Runser
Justin Echols

LHP

Starters
Ben Kozlowski (3)
C.J. Wilson (8)
A.J. Murray (15)
Mario Ramos (20)
John Koronka (28)
Sam Narron
Chris Russ

Relievers
Derrick Van Dusen (26)
Erasmo Ramirez
Joel Kirsten

DraftAnalysis

2002 Draft

Best Pro Debut: RHP John Barnett (6) advanced to high Class A, where he went 3-0, 1.44. Scrappy 2B **Chris O'Riordan** (8) was a Rookie-level Appalachian League all-star after finishing first in on-base percentage (.495) and second in hitting (.370). 2B/OF Cameron Coughlan (18) hit .291 and led the Rookie-level Gulf Coast League with 34 steals. RHP Erik Thompson (12) went 3-3, 2.38 between the two Rookie clubs.

Best Athlete: The Rangers love everything SS Drew Meyer (1) brings to the table, including plus speed and arm strength. Texas is refining his hitting approach and believes he'll be a valuable offensive player.

Best Pure Hitter: O'Riordan has a short stroke and knows the strike zone.

Best Raw Power: 1B Nate Gold (10) has plus-plus power and led NCAA Division I with 33 homers last spring. He hit .247-10-44 between Rookie ball and low Class A. Gold moves well for a big man and may get a shot at playing third base.

Fastest Runner: Meyer is a good bunter who can get to first in 3.7-3.8 seconds from the left side when he drags the ball, and in 4.0-4.1 seconds when he swings away.

Best Defensive Player: Meyer won't move Alex Rodriguez, but he has the tools to be a standout second baseman or center fielder. The Rangers will keep him at shortstop for now and let him focus on hitting.

Best Fastball: Thompson touched 95-96 mph during the spring, while Barnett throws 89-93 mph every time out.

Best Breaking Ball: RHP Andrew Tisdale

O'Riordan

(7) has a mid-80s slider. He was limited last summer by a minor shoulder problem.

Most Intriguing Background: LHP Sam Narron's (15) second cousin Jerry managed the Rangers until being replaced in October by Buck Showalter, and his grandfather Sam played briefly in the majors. Unsigned RHP Andy Myette's (41) brother Aaron pitched for the Rangers in 2002. RHP Gary Hogan's (32) father Gary is the former baseball coach at Arkansas-Little Rock.

Closest To The Majors: Barnett. The Rangers need pitching and Meyer will have to make more adjustments.

Best Late-Round Pick: RHP Kiki Bengochea (11) or Thompson. Bengochea figured to be a first-round pick entering his junior season at Miami, then bombed early on. After signing for $550,000, he went 3-4, 3.00 in low Class A.

The One Who Got Away: It's often difficult to sign juniors out of Rice. RHP Steven Herce (9), the only unsigned pick in the first 16 rounds, was no exception.

Assessment: In his first draft with the Rangers, scouting director Grady Fuson was handicapped by not having a pick between the first and sixth rounds. He placed a lot of faith in Meyer, though he did find some helpful arms in Barnett, Bengochea and Thompson later in the draft.

2001 Draft

3B Mark Teixeira (1) has been everything he's supposed to be so far. It doesn't matter that the Rangers didn't have second- or third-round picks, or failed to sign fourth-round RHP Josh Baker. **Grade: A**

2000 Draft

The Rangers missed with all three of their first-round picks. C Scott Heard can't hit, OF Tyrell Godwin didn't sign and RHP Chad Hawkins hasn't stayed healthy. OF Laynce Nix (4) has been a revelation. So has 3B Edwin Encarnacion (9), but he was traded. **Grade: C+**

1999 Draft

Texas scored three quality players with RHP Colby Lewis (1), 3B Hank Blalock (3), OF Kevin Mench (4). RHP Aaron Harang (6) has had his moments since being dealt to the A's. RHP David Mead (1) has gone 3-20 over the last two years in low Class A. **Grade: A**

1998 Draft

The Rangers regret not signing LHP Barry Zito (3). 1B Carlos Pena looked like a big part of their future before they abruptly traded him. The best thing to come out of this draft was turning LHP Andy Pratt (9) into Ben Kozlowski in a deal with the Braves. **Grade: B**

Note: Draft analysis prepared by Jim Callis. Numbers in parentheses indicate draft rounds.

. . . Teixeira's tools, approach and strength make him the best hitting prospect in the minor leagues.

Mark Teixeira 3b

Born: April 11, 1980.
Ht.: 6-3. **Wt.:** 220.
Bats: B. **Throws:** R.
School: Georgia Tech.
Career Transactions:
Selected by Rangers in first round (fifth overall) of 2001 draft; signed Aug. 24, 2001.

Under the prospect microscope since high school, Teixeira has always thrived when healthy. He was expected to be a first-round pick out of high school in 1998, but fell to the Red Sox in the ninth thanks to perceived bonus demands. Teixeira had a decorated career at Georgia Tech, where he was Baseball America's College Player of the Year in 2000. His junior season was interrupted by a broken right ankle. The injury, and again perceived bonus demands, contributed to his being available to the Rangers with the No. 5 overall pick in 2001. He signed a major league contract that guaranteed him $9.5 million, including a club-record $4.5 million bonus. A ruptured tendon in his left elbow and forearm sidelined him in spring training, but Teixeira bounced back to have a big season in his pro debut.

Teixeira's tools, approach and strength make him the best hitting prospect in the minor leagues. He has well-above-average power—40 homers a year is no stretch—and hitting ability from both sides of the plate, in part because he's in tune with his abilities and has sound fundamentals. Powerfully built, he has a short swing with leverage from both sides, excellent pitch recognition and an advanced two-strike approach. Athletic and instinctive, Teixeira also works hard on the deficiencies in his game. Teixeira takes pride in not being a base clogger, but speed is his weakest tool. Offensively, he can be stubborn and hasn't taken to the organization's take-a-strike philosophy, but his mindset stems from his success. Teixeira's range at third is average and he had throwing problems in 2002, which the Rangers attribute to injuries and rust. He worked on getting his body back into his throws, and by the Arizona Fall League his arm was again a plus instead of a problem.

Teixeira's AFL stint was cut short by a muscle strain in his torso, but BA still rated him the league's top prospect. His major league ETA depends solely on his health. He figures to start 2003 in Triple-A but should get big league at-bats soon at third base, first base (which he hasn't played since the Cape Cod League in 1999) or DH.

Year	Club (League)	Class	AVG	G	AB	R	H	2B	3B	HR	RBI	BB	SO	SB	SLG	OBP
2002	Charlotte (FSL)	A	.320	38	150	32	48	10	2	9	41	21	24	2	.593	.411
	Tulsa (TL)	AA	.316	48	171	31	54	11	3	10	28	25	36	3	.591	.415
MINOR LEAGUE TOTALS			.318	86	321	63	102	21	5	19	69	46	60	5	.592	.413

2. Colby Lewis, rhp

Born: Aug. 2, 1979. **Ht.:** 6-4. **Wt.:** 230. **Bats:** R. **Throws:** R. **School:** Bakersfield (Calif.) JC. **Career Transactions:** Selected by Rangers in first round (38th overall) of 1999 draft; signed June 15, 1999.

Lewis surprised the Rangers by making the big league club out of spring training, thanks in part to injuries to Jay Powell and Jeff Zimmerman. Lewis held opponents to a .200 average to earn a bullpen spot when Texas went with 13 pitchers. His mid-90s fastball ultimately wasn't enough for him to succeed in the majors his first time through, however. Lewis is a prototypical power righthander. He's strong and durable, has a fluid delivery and gets excellent leverage and downhill movement on his fastball, which can touch 97 mph. His curveball, slider and changeup all have been effective when he commands them, but Lewis needs to find an offspeed pitch he can consistently throw for strikes. He toyed with a splitter this offseason. If he develops more touch and feel with his curve or change he may not need the splitter. Lewis could start 2003 in Texas again, but this time it would be in the rotation. He'll enter spring training with a 50-50 shot at a big league job.

Year	Club (League)	Class	W	L	ERA	G	GS	CG	SV	IP	H	R	ER	HR	BB	SO	AVG
1999	Pulaski (Appy)	R	7	3	1.95	14	11	1	0	65	46	24	14	3	27	84	.189
2000	Charlotte (FSL)	A	11	10	4.07	28	27	3	0	164	169	83	74	11	45	153	.270
2001	Charlotte (FSL)	A	1	0	0.00	1	0	0	0	4	0	0	0	0	0	8	.000
	Tulsa (TL)	AA	10	10	4.50	25	25	1	0	156	150	85	78	15	62	162	.253
2002	Texas (AL)	MAJ	1	3	6.29	15	4	0	0	34	42	26	24	4	26	28	.304
	Oklahoma (PCL)	AAA	5	6	3.63	20	20	0	0	107	100	49	43	4	28	99	.245
MAJOR LEAGUE TOTALS			1	3	6.29	15	4	0	0	34	42	26	24	4	26	28	.304
MINOR LEAGUE TOTALS			34	29	3.80	88	83	5	0	495	465	241	209	33	162	506	.247

3. Ben Kozlowski, lhp

Born: Aug. 16, 1980. **Ht.:** 6-6. **Wt.:** 220. **Bats:** L. **Throws:** L. **School:** Santa Fe (Fla.) CC. **Career Transactions:** Selected by Braves in 12th round of 1999 draft; signed June 12, 1999 . . . Traded by Braves to Rangers for LHP Andy Pratt, April 9, 2002.

Major League Baseball stopped the Rangers from putting Ryan Dittfurth on the 60-day disabled list in April, so they had to act quickly to clear a spot on the 40-man roster. They were able to send Andy Pratt to the Braves for Kozlowski, who didn't need to be placed on the 40-man. Kozlowski went from high Class A to the majors by September. Start with a strong left arm attached to a big frame, then add the poise to handle a rapid rise through the system and it resulted in a breakthrough season. Kozlowski deals low-90s fastballs and has good arm speed on his changeup, one of the system's best. He uses his size to get depth on his curve, which can be a real hammer at times. Innings and experience will help Kozlowski repeat his mechanics and improve his fastball and changeup command. He'll have to become more consistent with his curve as well. Texas' rotation has openings, but Kozlowski has refinements to make and would be better off opening 2003 in the minors.

Year	Club (League)	Class	W	L	ERA	G	GS	CG	SV	IP	H	R	ER	HR	BB	SO	AVG
1999	Braves (GCL)	R	1	1	1.87	15	0	0	3	34	28	9	7	0	6	29	.222
2000	Macon (SAL)	A	3	8	4.21	15	14	0	0	77	76	53	36	6	39	67	.252
2001	Macon (SAL)	A	10	7	2.48	26	23	1	0	145	134	60	40	8	27	147	.248
	Myrtle Beach (Car)	A	0	2	3.77	2	2	0	0	14	15	7	6	1	3	13	.283
2002	Myrtle Beach (Car)	A	0	1	4.50	1	1	0	0	4	4	5	2	0	3	3	.235
	Charlotte (FSL)	A	4	4	2.05	21	12	0	0	79	63	31	18	2	25	76	.219
	Tulsa (TL)	AA	4	2	1.90	8	8	0	0	52	28	12	11	3	22	41	.155
	Texas (AL)	MAJ	0	0	6.30	2	2	0	0	10	11	7	7	3	11	6	.289
MAJOR LEAGUE TOTALS			0	0	6.30	2	2	0	0	10	11	7	7	3	11	6	.289
MINOR LEAGUE TOTALS			22	25	2.66	88	60	1	3	405	348	177	120	20	125	376	.231

4. Laynce Nix, of

Born: Oct. 30, 1980. **Ht.:** 6-0. **Wt.:** 190. **Bats:** L. **Throws:** L. **School:** Midland (Texas) HS. **Career Transactions:** Selected by Rangers in fourth round of 2000 draft; signed June 21, 2000.

A second-team baseball All-American and a star quarterback in high school, Nix has continued to achieve success since spurning a baseball scholarship from Louisiana State. His Arizona Fall League campaign was cut short by a ligament injury in his right thumb. His brother Jayson plays second base in the Rockies organization. Many compare Nix to Brian Giles because of his compact, muscular build and power potential. Nix' power has developed to the point that he has outstripped comparisons to Rusty Greer, though like Greer he has an excellent work ethic, a nice swing and a disciplined-yet-aggressive approach. He ranked third in the minor leagues in RBIs in 2002. While Nix played center field in 2002 and the Rangers have a need at the position, scouts see him as a corner outfielder. He's an average runner and probably will slow down. The thick Nix must be careful that he doesn't cost himself flexibility with his workouts. Nix should move up to Double-A Frisco and continue to play center field in 2003. A successful tour of his native Texas League should have Nix ready for a trip to Arlington in 2004.

Year	Club (League)	Class	AVG	G	AB	R	H	2B	3B	HR	RBI	BB	SO	SB	SLG	OBP
2000	Rangers (GCL)	R	.226	51	199	34	45	7	1	2	25	23	37	4	.302	.307
2001	Savannah (SAL)	A	.278	104	407	50	113	26	8	8	59	37	94	9	.440	.337
	Charlotte (FSL)	A	.297	9	37	4	11	3	1	0	2	1	13	0	.432	.316
2002	Charlotte (FSL)	A	.285	137	512	86	146	27	3	21	110	72	105	17	.473	.374
MINOR LEAGUE TOTALS			.273	301	1155	174	315	63	13	31	196	133	249	30	.430	.348

5. Gerald Laird, c

Born: Nov. 13, 1979. **Ht.:** 6-2. **Wt.:** 190. **Bats:** R. **Throws:** R. **School:** Cypress (Calif.) JC. **Career Transactions:** Selected by Athletics in second round of 1998 draft; signed June 1, 1999 . . . Traded by Athletics with LHP Mario Ramos, OF Ryan Ludwick and 1B Jason Hart to Rangers for 1B Carlos Pena and LHP Mike Venafro, Jan. 14, 2002.

Following an injury-plagued 2001, Laird was considered the least promising of the four players the Rangers netted from the Athletics in the Carlos Pena trade. He got healthy and had a breakout season, just in time for the Rangers to cut ties with Ivan Rodriguez. Laird got a then-record $1 million bonus as a draft-and-follow primarily because of his catch-and-throw skills, and they remain his strong suit. He's an above-average receiver with good balance and a solid, very accurate arm. With a quick release, he led the Texas League by throwing out 44 percent of basestealers in 2002. Laird's athletic ability allowed him to start 13 games in the outfield, including one in center. Laird is more of a grinder offensively, though he has started to develop power. He lacks the patience customary for a premium prospect who played in the A's system. He also has durability questions, as his 101 games at Tulsa marked a career high. Laird needs at least one season in Triple-A before challenging for the big league job, and the trade for Einar Diaz buys him that time. Laird eventually should relegate him to a backup role.

Year	Club (League)	Class	AVG	G	AB	R	H	2B	3B	HR	RBI	BB	SO	SB	SLG	OBP
1999	S. Oregon (NWL)	A	.285	60	228	45	65	7	2	2	39	28	43	10	.360	.361
2000	Visalia (Cal)	A	.243	33	103	14	25	3	0	0	13	14	27	7	.272	.333
	Athletics (AZL)	R	.300	14	50	10	15	2	1	0	9	6	7	2	.380	.379
2001	Modesto (Cal)	A	.255	119	443	71	113	13	5	5	46	48	101	10	.341	.337
2002	Tulsa (TL)	AA	.276	123	442	70	122	21	4	11	67	45	95	8	.416	.343
MINOR LEAGUE TOTALS			.269	349	1266	210	340	46	12	18	174	141	273	37	.367	.345

6. Drew Meyer, ss/2b

Born: Aug. 29, 1981. **Ht.:** 5-10. **Wt.:** 180. **Bats:** L. **Throws:** R. **School:** University of South Carolina. **Career Transactions:** Selected by Rangers in first round (10th overall) of 2002 draft; signed June 26, 2002.

Meyer was a second-round pick of the Dodgers out of high school, but not even a visit from Tommy Lasorda could dissuade him from playing for South Carolina. He followed first-rounders Adam Everett and Brian Roberts as the Gamecocks' shortstop and led them to the College World Series in 2002. Meyer oozes tools, has a strong body and never leaves a game with a clean uniform. He's an above-average runner who should steal bases. His plus arm and instincts allow him to make up for footwork deficiencies at second base, where he had limited experience before turning pro, and shortstop. His tools may profile better in center field. Meyer has never been a dominant hitter and struggled in two summers with wood bats in the Cape Cod League. He lacks a real plan at the plate and is too pull-conscious. The Rangers believe his instincts, strength and aggressiveness will help him succeed, though. Meyer was indoctrinated in the Rangers' philosophy during instructional league, where he showed more patience at the plate. He'll try to build on his progress at high Class A Stockton in 2003.

Year	Club (League)	Class	AVG	G	AB	R	H	2B	3B	HR	RBI	BB	SO	SB	SLG	OBP
2002	Savannah (SAL)	A	.243	54	214	15	52	5	4	1	24	10	53	7	.318	.274
	Tulsa (TL)	AA	.214	4	14	0	3	0	0	0	0	1	5	0	.214	.267
MINOR LEAGUE TOTALS			.241	58	228	15	55	5	4	1	24	11	58	7	.311	.274

7. Ryan Ludwick, of

Born: July 13, 1978. **Ht.:** 6-3. **Wt.:** 200. **Bats:** R. **Throws:** L. **School:** University of Nevada-Las Vegas. **Career Transactions:** Selected by Athletics in second round of 1999 draft; signed July 17, 1999 . . . Traded by Athletics with LHP Mario Ramos, 1B Jason Hart and C Gerald Laird to Rangers for 1B Carlos Pena and LHP Mike Venafro, Jan. 14, 2002.

Another part of the Carlos Pena trade, Ludwick made his big league debut in 2002, starting 21 games in center field for Texas. He became the second member of his family to reach the majors, joining his brother Eric, a righthanded pitcher. His season ended in August, however, when he had a screw inserted in his left hip to repair a stress fracture. Ludwick has quick hands that generate power at the plate. He's a good defensive outfielder, especially on the corners, with a strong arm and average speed. He's suited for the grind of pro ball and doesn't get too high or low. Ludwick doesn't do anything exceptionally well. He still doesn't get his lower half into his swing, leaving him with several holes, and his swing mechanics can get out of whack easily. He also needs to be more patient and develop a better two-strike approach. The Rangers' outfield situation is crowded by bad contracts (Carl Everett, Juan Gonzalez), but Ludwick could figure into it, if healthy, in 2003 as a low-cost reserve. A start back at Triple-A seems more likely.

Year	Club (League)	Class	AVG	G	AB	R	H	2B	3B	HR	RBI	BB	SO	SB	SLG	OBP
1999	Modesto (Cal)	A	.275	43	171	28	47	11	3	4	34	19	45	2	.444	.348
2000	Modesto (Cal)	A	.264	129	493	86	130	26	3	29	102	68	128	10	.505	.359
2001	Midland (TL)	AA	.269	119	443	82	119	23	3	25	96	56	113	9	.503	.356
	Sacramento (PCL)	AAA	.228	17	57	10	13	3	0	1	7	2	16	2	.333	.246
2002	Oklahoma (PCL)	AAA	.285	78	305	62	87	27	4	15	52	38	76	2	.548	.370
	Texas (AL)	MAJ	.235	23	81	10	19	6	0	1	9	7	24	2	.346	.295
MAJOR LEAGUE TOTALS			.235	23	81	10	19	6	0	1	9	7	24	2	.346	.295
MINOR LEAGUE TOTALS			.270	386	1469	268	396	90	13	74	291	183	378	25	.500	.355

8. C.J. Wilson, lhp

Born: Nov. 18, 1980. **Ht.:** 6-2. **Wt.:** 190. **Bats:** L. **Throws:** L. **School:** Loyola Marymount University. **Career Transactions:** Selected by Rangers in fifth round of 2001 draft; signed June 12, 2001.

A two-way player in college, Wilson was the California community college co-player of the year at Santa Ana in 2000. A student of the game, he keeps a notebook on opposing hitters now that he's become a full-time pitcher. He made the high Class A Florida State League's all-star game in his first full season. Wilson has above-average athleticism to go with his thirst for pitching knowledge. The Rangers laud his heart and focus. He knows the value of pitching inside with his 89-91 mph fastball and his changeup, which developed into an efficient out pitch last year. His natural sinker helps keep balls in the park. His breaking pitch, while effective when thrown down in the zone, is still slurvy and could use some tightening. Wilson should do that as he becomes more accustomed to pro ball and pitching. Wilson resembles Mario Ramos in his ability to carve up hitters with a fastball and changeup. Wilson has more juice on his fastball, which could give him a better chance to succeed at higher levels. The Rangers will find out in 2003, which he'll open in Double-A.

Year	Club (League)	Class	W	L	ERA	G	GS	CG	SV	IP	H	R	ER	HR	BB	SO	AVG
2001	Pulaski (Appy)	R	1	0	0.96	8	8	0	0	38	24	6	4	2	9	49	.178
	Savannah (SAL)	A	1	2	3.18	5	5	2	0	34	30	13	12	2	9	26	.252
2002	Charlotte (FSL)	A	10	2	3.06	26	15	0	1	106	86	48	36	4	41	76	.215
	Tulsa (TL)	AA	1	0	1.80	5	5	0	0	30	23	6	6	0	12	17	.211
MINOR LEAGUE TOTALS			13	4	2.51	44	33	2	1	208	163	73	58	8	71	168	.214

9. Travis Hughes, rhp

Born: May 25, 1978. **Ht.:** 6-5. **Wt.:** 230. **Bats:** R. **Throws:** R. **School:** Cowley County (Kan.) CC. **Career Transactions:** Selected by Rangers in 19th round of 1997 draft; signed June 1, 1998.

Hughes signed as a draft-and-follow out of junior-college power Cowley County (Kan.), which also produced Diamondbacks infielder Junior Spivey and former Rangers farmhand Travis Hafner. He overcame offseason knee problems and a midsummer slump to emerge from the Rangers' pack of Double-A righthanders. Hughes has a big body and uses it to throw one of the organization's best fastballs, a mid-90s sinker. He has started commanding it better and added bite to his slider. When he stays on top of it, it's the best slider in the organization. Three starts in the Texas League playoffs helped Hughes gain much-needed feel for his changeup, which was a plus pitch in the postseason. The organization leader in walks in 2002, Hughes still has major command issues. His mechanics can go awry and he's not a tremendous athlete, so he has trouble repeating his delivery. Hughes' experience as a starter helped him develop his raw power arm. He figures to stay in that role until the big league team needs him in the bullpen, where he still profiles best. He'll get a look in spring training but figures to open 2003 in the Triple-A rotation.

Year	Club (League)	Class	W	L	ERA	G	GS	CG	SV	IP	H	R	ER	HR	BB	SO	AVG
1998	Pulaski (Appy)	R	2	6	3.89	22	3	0	2	42	30	25	18	2	25	48	.189
1999	Savannah (SAL)	A	11	7	2.81	30	23	1	2	157	127	60	49	9	54	150	.221
2000	Charlotte (FSL)	A	9	9	4.42	39	14	1	9	126	122	76	62	9	54	96	.254
2001	Tulsa (TL)	AA	5	7	4.64	47	5	0	8	87	91	52	45	8	45	86	.270
2002	Tulsa (TL)	AA	9	7	3.52	26	26	1	0	143	139	68	56	11	82	137	.255
MINOR LEAGUE TOTALS			36	36	3.73	164	71	3	21	556	509	281	230	39	260	517	.243

10. Jason Bourgeois, 2b/ss

Born: Jan. 4, 1982. **Ht.:** 5-9. **Wt.:** 170. **Bats:** B. **Throws:** R. **School:** Forest Brook HS, Houston. **Career Transactions:** Selected by Rangers in second round of 2000 draft; signed June 19, 2000.

A second-team prep All-American, Bourgeois was part of an Arizona State recruiting class that included No. 7 overall pick Matt Harrington and 2002 minor league ERA champion Bubba Nelson. Like the others, he didn't end up in Tempe, signing for a $621,000 bonus. Bourgeois has a unique package of tools considering his size. He has average power and is a plus runner. His range and arm, a tick above-average, prompted a move to shortstop from second base, and Bourgeois showed he can handle the position. His overall package, including leadership and a gamer's makeup, draw comparisons to Jimmy Rollins and Harold Reynolds. Bourgeois' size remains an issue, as he wore down late in the 2002 season and hit just .210 in the final month. A more patient approach would allow him to make better use of his power and his speed. He still needs repetitions to acclimate himself to shortstop. At worst, Bourgeois could be a utilityman. With his tools, though, the ceiling is higher than that. He'll take it one step at a time and could move back to second base down the road.

Year	Club (League)	Class	AVG	G	AB	R	H	2B	3B	HR	RBI	BB	SO	SB	SLG	OBP
2000	Rangers (GCL)	R	.239	24	88	18	21	4	0	0	6	14	15	9	.284	.356
2001	Pulaski (Appy)	R	.311	62	251	60	78	12	2	7	34	26	47	21	.458	.387
2002	Savannah (SAL)	A	.255	127	522	72	133	21	5	8	49	40	66	22	.360	.318
	Charlotte (FSL)	A	.185	9	27	5	5	1	0	0	4	2	4	1	.222	.233
MINOR LEAGUE TOTALS			.267	222	888	155	237	38	7	15	93	82	132	53	.376	.339

11. Jason Hart, of/1b

Born: Sept. 5, 1977. **Ht.:** 6-4. **Wt.:** 230. **Bats:** R. **Throws:** R. **School:** Southwest Missouri State University. **Career Transactions:** Selected by Athletics in fifth round of 1998 draft; signed June 5, 1998 . . . Traded by Athletics with LHP Mario Ramos, OF Ryan Ludwick and C Gerald Laird to Rangers for 1B Carlos Pena and LHP Mike Venafro, Jan. 14, 2002.

Hart was a Missouri Valley Conference home run champ at Southwest Missouri State, which had a noted hitter's park, but has since established a track record as a legitimate pro power hitter. Hart clearly is a favorite of assistant general manager Grady Fuson, who drafted him for the Athletics and then had him included in the Carlos Pena trade. Hart has spent the last two years in Triple-A, and in some organizations would be thought of as a Four-A player, but Fuson and the Rangers consider him a strong big league option who could be a starter if not for Rafael Palmeiro's presence in Texas. Hart added versatility to his game by spending more than half of last season in left field—in part to accommodate the since-traded Travis Hafner, who was limited to first base—and playing it adequately. Hart's arm and speed are slightly below-average, but he hits enough for the position. Hart has holes in his swing, particularly on offspeed stuff away. But he can handle a good fastball, has pull power and is willing to work the count to get a pitch he can drive. The Rangers could keep him as a big league reserve depending on the makeup of their roster.

Year	Club (League)	Class	AVG	G	AB	R	H	2B	3B	HR	RBI	BB	SO	SB	SLG	OBP
1998	S. Oregon (NWL)	A	.258	75	295	58	76	19	1	20	69	36	67	0	.532	.336
1999	Modesto (Cal)	A	.305	135	550	96	168	48	2	19	123	56	105	2	.504	.370
2000	Midland (TL)	AA	.326	135	546	98	178	44	3	30	121	67	112	4	.582	.401
	Sacramento (PCL)	AAA	.278	5	18	4	5	1	0	1	4	3	7	0	.500	.381

2001	Sacramento (PCL)	AAA	.247	134	494	71	122	26	1	19	75	57	102	3	.419	.325
2002	Oklahoma (PCL)	AAA	.263	134	514	78	135	32	1	25	83	68	122	1	.475	.356
	Texas (AL)	MAJ	.267	10	15	2	4	3	0	0	0	2	7	0	.467	.353
MAJOR LEAGUE TOTALS			.267	10	15	2	4	3	0	0	0	2	7	0	.467	.353
MINOR LEAGUE TOTALS			.283	618	2417	405	684	170	8	114	475	287	515	10	.501	.361

12. Marshall McDougall, inf

Born: Dec. 19, 1978. **Ht.:** 6-1. **Wt.:** 200. **Bats:** R. **Throws:** R. **School:** Florida State University. **Career Transactions:** Selected by Athletics in ninth round of 2000 draft; signed June 28, 2000 . . . Traded by Athletics to Indians for LHP Ricardo Rincon, July 30, 2002 . . . Selected by Rangers from Indians in major league Rule 5 draft, Dec. 16, 2002.

Few minor leaguers have received the kind of notoriety McDougall dealt with as a collegian, when he hit six home runs in a game and was the Most Outstanding Player of the College World Series in 1999, his first season at Florida State. However, scouts doubted his power and athleticism, and he wasn't drafted until the 26th round by the Red Sox that year. He was offered $1,000 to sign and instead chose to return for his senior season, after which the Athletics drafted him in the ninth round. Assistant general manager Grady Fuson was Oakland's scouting director then and drafted McDougall again, this time in the major league phase of the Rule 5 draft. McDougall doesn't wow anyone with his tools, but he always has hit and has power. At worst, he's a 'tweener—a third baseman without enough power, or a second baseman whose range and athleticism leave him short defensively. At best, he's a hitter with on-base skills, some power and good enough footwork and hands to compensate for his athletic shortcomings. He figures to get more playing time at second base if he sticks with the Rangers this year.

Year	Club (League)	Class	AVG	G	AB	R	H	2B	3B	HR	RBI	BB	SO	SB	SLG	OBP
2000	Vancouver (NWL)	A	.275	27	102	17	28	4	2	0	11	18	19	5	.353	.380
2001	Visalia (Cal)	A	.257	134	534	79	137	43	7	12	84	46	110	14	.431	.321
2002	Midland (TL)	AA	.303	84	323	60	98	22	5	9	56	38	57	7	.486	.374
	Mahoning Valley (NY-P)	A	.200	2	5	0	1	0	0	0	0	1	1	0	.200	.333
	Akron (EL)	AA	.389	7	18	6	7	2	0	1	4	6	2	0	.667	.542
MINOR LEAGUE TOTALS			.276	254	982	162	271	71	14	22	155	109	189	26	.444	.350

13. Jose Dominguez, rhp

Born: Aug. 7, 1982. **Ht.:** 6-2. **Wt.:** 180. **Bats:** R. **Throws:** R. **Career Transactions:** Signed out of Dominican Republic by Rangers, Dec. 26, 1999.

Dominguez had visa issues to start the 2002 season, but instead of having his age revised upward, Dominguez just had his season delayed. He didn't return to the United States in time to start spring training, got going in extended spring and then finally got into his first game action in late June. Once he got started, he took to Texas' tandem-starter concept and showed a plus arm, with a low-90s fastball as well as one of the organization's best changeups. It's a circle change thrown with excellent arm action that helped him average more than a strikeout an inning. The changeup helps him neutralize lefthanded hitters, who hit just .204 against him with one home run in 98 at-bats. Dominguez still has much to learn in terms of carrying his stuff throughout a game, refining his slider (which came along during instructional league) and improving his fastball command. He'll also need to show he can pitch a full season, which he should get a chance to do in high Class A in 2003.

Year	Club (League)	Class	W	L	ERA	G	GS	CG	SV	IP	H	R	ER	HR	BB	SO	AVG
2000	Rangers (DSL)	R	1	6	4.52	14	14	0	0	68	69	49	34	2	38	56	.253
2001	Rangers (GCL)	R	4	2	4.01	11	9	1	0	58	56	29	26	4	12	55	.250
	Charlotte (FSL)	A	1	0	3.60	2	0	0	0	5	4	2	2	1	1	5	.235
2002	Rangers (DSL)	R	0	0	0.00	1	1	0	0	1	1	0	0	0	0	0	.250
	Savannah (SAL)	A	1	3	2.16	16	9	0	1	67	50	23	16	4	21	70	.209
MINOR LEAGUE TOTALS			7	11	3.53	44	33	1	1	199	180	103	78	11	72	186	.238

14. Kelvin Jimenez, rhp

Born: Oct. 27, 1980. **Ht.:** 6-2. **Wt.:** 150. **Bats:** R. **Throws:** R. **Career Transactions:** Signed out of Domincan Republic by Rangers, May 7, 2000.

The Rangers have been searching for pitching in the Dominican Republic for some time. Joaquin Benoit finally rewarded their patience with flashes of brilliance in the big leagues as a rookie in 2002, while Jovanny Cedeno has fallen by the wayside with injuries. Cedeno was protected on the 40-man roster, but became a free agent after being nontendered in December. Benoit and Jimenez were the most prominent Rangers to have their ages revised in the 2001-02 offseason—both added two years—but Jimenez' performance still has him on a solid trajectory for the big leagues. He has grown into a 6-foot-2 body (though he's still listed at 150 pounds) and emerged along with Jose Dominguez as one of the system's two fine Dominican pitching candidates at low Class A. Jimenez was Savannah's most consistent and durable starter, belying his 5-10 record. He was more effective out of the bullpen in the tandem-starter arrangement, showing better control of with his fastball, which reached the low 90s, slider and changeup. He'll move up to high Class A with Dominguez this year, when he'll try to further refine his command with the strike zone.

Year	Club (League)	Class	W	L	ERA	G	GS	CG	SV	IP	H	R	ER	HR	BB	SO	AVG
2000	Rangers (DSL)	R	3	6	4.62	17	9	0	0	64	70	47	33	1	32	60	.273
2001	Pulaski (Appy)	R	0	3	6.28	4	4	0	0	14	24	14	10	2	4	10	.353
	Rangers (GCL)	R	3	3	2.56	9	6	1	1	46	36	19	13	2	9	51	.214
2002	Savannah (SAL)	A	5	10	3.20	29	16	0	0	121	122	63	43	9	37	116	.259
MINOR LEAGUE TOTALS			11	22	3.63	59	35	1	1	245	252	143	99	14	82	237	.262

15. A.J. Murray, lhp

Born: March 17, 1982. **Ht.:** 6-3. **Wt.:** 200. **Bats:** B. **Throws:** L. **School:** Salt Lake CC. **Career Transactions:** Selected by Rangers in 19th round of 2000 draft; signed May 27, 2001.

The Rangers don't have outstanding pitching in the minors, but they do have depth, especially among lefthanders. Start with Ben Kozlowski, of course, but don't forget C.J. Wilson, Murray, Mario Ramos, Derrick Van Dusen and major league Rule 5 acquisition John Koronka. Other than Kozlowski, the rest of Texas' lefties share a common theme: decent arms, plus changeups and the need to throw quality strikes down in the zone. Murray did that consistently in 2002, his first full pro season. Rangers officials compare him to Kirk Rueter for his willingness to pitch inside with an 86-88 mph fastball, and because Murray spots his slider and changeup down in the zone, getting hitters off balance and reaching. Armed with a deceptive delivery, Murray pitched better in 2002 after a move up to high Class A and is in line for a promotion to Double-A. His slider's effectiveness helps separate him from some of the lefties below him on this list. He'll have to keep throwing it for strikes to remain a rotation candidate instead of being consigned to the bullpen.

Year	Club (League)	Class	W	L	ERA	G	GS	CG	SV	IP	H	R	ER	HR	BB	SO	AVG
2001	Rangers (GCL)	R	3	3	1.86	12	8	0	0	53	48	15	11	1	10	45	.247
2002	Savannah (SAL)	A	5	3	2.87	14	8	0	0	63	63	22	20	0	14	51	.270
	Charlotte (FSL)	A	3	3	3.02	19	14	0	2	83	77	31	28	4	20	68	.243
MINOR LEAGUE TOTALS			11	9	2.66	45	30	0	2	199	188	68	59	5	44	164	.253

16. Ryan Dittfurth, rhp

Born: Oct. 18, 1979. **Ht.:** 6-6. **Wt.:** 200. **Bats:** R. **Throws:** R. **School:** Tulsa Union HS. **Career Transactions:** Selected by Rangers in fifth round of 1998 draft; signed June 29, 1998.

Dittfurth ranked as the organization's No. 6 prospect a year ago, before a serious shoulder injury derailed his impressive march through the minors. He had October surgery to repair a torn rotator cuff, and while that injury no longer spells certain doom for a pitcher, it may keep him off the mound for the entire 2003 season. The Rangers protected him on their 40-man roster, then got him through waivers and outrighted him to Triple-A once the season was over. Texas was glad to hold on to Dittfurth because of his arm strength and makeup. He's driven and an excellent competitor on the mound. When healthy, Dittfurth pitches off his fastball, which has low-90s velocity and sinks. He also throws a curveball, slider and changeup. The Rangers now must hope Dittfurth's stuff returns when he comes back. They should get their first look late in the summer or in instructional league.

Year	Club (League)	Class	W	L	ERA	G	GS	CG	SV	IP	H	R	ER	HR	BB	SO	AVG
1998	Rangers (GCL)	R	3	2	1.34	8	6	0	0	34	25	8	5	0	11	33	.202
1999	Pulaski (Appy)	R	7	2	2.60	14	14	1	0	83	66	35	24	4	42	85	.218
2000	Savannah (SAL)	A	8	13	4.25	29	29	2	0	159	127	83	75	8	99	158	.220
2001	Charlotte (FSL)	A	9	6	3.48	27	24	2	0	147	123	66	57	9	66	134	.227
2002	Charlotte (FSL)	A	3	2	2.45	6	3	0	0	26	11	7	7	2	7	21	.129
	Tulsa (TL)	AA	1	3	5.66	9	9	0	0	41	42	29	26	1	23	32	.266
MINOR LEAGUE TOTALS			31	28	3.57	93	85	5	0	490	394	228	194	24	248	463	.220

17. Nick Regilio, rhp

Born: Sept. 4, 1978. **Ht.:** 6-2. **Wt.:** 180. **Bats:** R. **Throws:** R. **School:** Jacksonville University. **Career Transactions:** Selected by Rangers in second round of 1999 draft; signed June 11, 1999.

Regilio made steady progress in 2002, interrupted only by biceps tendinitis that required rest in July. It was the second straight year physical concerns had slowed him, as a ribcage injury helped spoil his 2001 season that included a perfect game in the Florida State League. Neither injury required surgery, but Regilio made just two starts for Double-A Tulsa after returning from the tendinitis, neither lasting past the third inning. Up to that point, he had made great advances and earned an emergency June start in Triple-A when Aaron Myette was promoted to Texas. He should return to Triple-A in 2003 based on merit, not need. Regilio first made the move to Double-A in 2001 but struggled. He stopped trying to be a strikeout pitcher in 2002 and had more success in the Texas League, letting his 89-92 mph sinker and slider do the work. He showed improved velocity early in the year, getting up to 93 mph, and has another weapon to work with down in the zone in his splitter. Regilio still needs to command his pitches better, but the Rangers credit him for having the work ethic that helped him improve in the last offseason. They expect more progress in 2003.

Year	Club (League)	Class	W	L	ERA	G	GS	CG	SV	IP	H	R	ER	HR	BB	SO	AVG
1999	Pulaski (Appy)	R	4	2	1.63	11	8	1	0	50	30	12	9	2	16	58	.172
2000	Charlotte (FSL)	A	4	3	4.52	20	20	0	0	86	94	54	43	8	29	63	.286
2001	Charlotte (FSL)	A	6	2	1.55	11	11	1	0	64	47	16	11	5	16	60	.200
	Tulsa (TL)	AA	1	3	5.54	10	10	0	0	52	62	34	32	2	20	40	.297
2002	Tulsa (TL)	AA	6	8	3.44	19	19	2	0	105	97	46	40	8	47	59	.245
	Oklahoma (PCL)	AAA	1	0	10.80	1	1	0	0	5	9	6	6	1	5	4	.391
MINOR LEAGUE TOTALS			22	18	3.52	72	69	4	0	361	339	168	141	26	133	284	.248

18. John Barnett, rhp

Born: Jan. 30, 1981. **Ht.:** 6-2. **Wt.:** 190. **Bats:** B. **Throws:** R. **School:** Florida Southern College. **Career Transactions:** Selected by Rangers in sixth round of 2002 draft; signed June 18, 2002.

A prep quarterback, Barnett was drafted out of high school by the Braves in the 46th round. Instead, he joined NCAA Division II powerhouse Florida Southern. Barnett had a consistent college career, winning MVP honors at the Division II South Regional in 2002, and was the first pitcher Grady Fuson drafted with the Rangers. Barnett has a durable frame, good arm action and a pro body, all of which project him as a workhorse. His size and stuff have drawn comparisons to Pat Hentgen. Barnett has a sinking 91-93 mph fastball that can touch the mid-90s, and he also employs an excellent changeup. He repeats his delivery well and has good athleticism, translating into plus command. He performed well in his pro debut and will continue to be pushed quickly if he shows similar results. The key as he moves up a level to high Class A in 2003 will be refining his slider, which needs tighter spin and better depth. Barnett missed some development time when he skipped instructional league to return to school in the fall, but the Rangers see his intelligence as an asset.

Year	Club (League)	Class	W	L	ERA	G	GS	CG	SV	IP	H	R	ER	HR	BB	SO	AVG
2002	Pulaski (Appy)	R	0	0	0.00	1	1	0	0	3	0	0	0	0	0	1	.000
	Savannah (SAL)	A	0	1	5.00	3	1	0	0	9	12	5	5	0	2	8	.353
	Charlotte (FSL)	A	3	0	1.44	9	7	0	0	44	21	7	7	3	8	28	.140
MINOR LEAGUE TOTALS			3	1	1.94	13	9	0	0	56	33	12	12	3	10	37	.171

19. Jermaine Clark, of/2b

Born: Sept. 29, 1976. **Ht.:** 5-10. **Wt.:** 170. **Bats:** L. **Throws:** R. **School:** University of San Francisco. **Career Transactions:** Selected by Mariners in fifth round of 1997 draft; signed June 10, 1997 . . . Selected by Tigers from Mariners in major league Rule 5 draft, Dec. 11, 2000 . . . Returned to Mariners, April 19, 2001 . . . Traded by Mariners with LHP Derrick Van Dusen to Rangers for RHP Ismael Valdes, Aug. 19, 2002.

After wandering unnoticed through the Mariners farm system for nearly six seasons, Clark is more valued by the Rangers. After they acquired him in a trade for Ismael Valdes, Clark had an excellent debut with his new organization and kept hitting in the Arizona Fall League. Though Clark wasn't protected on Texas' 40-man roster, he made it through the Rule 5 draft and could make the Rangers in a utility role. Exclusively a second baseman while with Seattle, Clark has moved to center field and taken to the switch. He has good speed and range for the position, but still needs to learn the intricacies of the outfield and has a below-average arm. His strengths are his speed, his ability to make consistent contact and his eye for drawing walks. The last trait is especially valued by Texas. Even after the signing of Doug Glanville, center field is still a trouble spot in the organization, and Clark could help the Rangers there this year.

Year	Club (League)	Class	AVG	G	AB	R	H	2B	3B	HR	RBI	BB	SO	SB	SLG	OBP
1997	Everett (NWL)	A	.337	59	199	42	67	13	2	3	29	34	31	22	.467	.437
1998	Wisconsin (Mid)	A	.324	123	448	81	145	24	13	6	55	57	64	40	.475	.402
1999	Lancaster (Cal)	A	.315	126	502	112	158	27	8	6	61	58	80	33	.436	.386
2000	New Haven (EL)	AA	.293	133	447	80	131	23	9	2	44	87	69	38	.394	.421
2001	Detroit (AL)	MAJ	.000	3	0	1	0	0	0	0	0	0	0	0	.000	.000
	Tacoma (PCL)	AAA	.250	74	216	35	54	7	3	1	26	27	39	13	.324	.340
2002	Tacoma (PCL)	AAA	.266	108	368	48	98	14	4	6	36	62	59	29	.375	.370
	Oklahoma (PCL)	AAA	.298	13	57	13	17	2	1	1	4	7	11	6	.421	.375
MAJOR LEAGUE TOTALS			.000	3	0	1	0	0	0	0	0	0	0	0	.000	.000
MINOR LEAGUE TOTALS			.300	636	2237	410	670	110	40	25	255	332	353	181	.418	.394

20. Mario Ramos, lhp

Born: Oct. 19, 1977. **Ht.:** 6-1. **Wt.:** 180. **Bats:** L. **Throws:** L. **School:** Rice University. **Career Transactions:** Selected by Athletics in sixth round of 1999 draft; signed Aug. 23, 1999 . . . Traded by Athletics with OF Ryan Ludwick, 1B Jason Hart and C Gerald Laird to Rangers for 1B Carlos Pena and LHP Mike Venafro, Jan. 14, 2002.

Few minor leaguers were as scrutinized as Ramos last season. He was the key player the Rangers acquired from the Athletics in the Carlos Pena trade, and Grady Fuson staked his personal reputation on the deal, but his 2002 season was a disaster. Luckily for Fuson, he has plenty of success stories to mitigate Ramos' failings, and there also is some hope to go with Ramos' disastrous numbers. He must pitch off his changeup to succeed, but the he got away from that in trying to justify the trade. Ramos succeeded in the past when he varied speeds off his 85-88 mph fastball and changeup and threw strikes with his curveball. However, he began last season trying to pound righthanders inside with his mediocre fastball and got destroyed in Triple-A. He posted an 8.20 ERA as a starter and didn't regain his confidence until a move to the bullpen late in the year. Ramos was protected on the 40-man roster, evidence the Rangers think he can regain his confidence and his ability to pitch, whether as a starter or back in the bullpen.

Year	Club (League)	Class	W	L	ERA	G	GS	CG	SV	IP	H	R	ER	HR	BB	SO	AVG
2000	Modesto (Cal)	A	12	5	2.90	26	24	1	0	152	131	63	49	6	50	134	.234
	Midland (TL)	AA	2	0	1.32	4	4	0	0	27	24	6	4	0	6	19	.242
2001	Midland (TL)	AA	8	1	3.07	15	15	0	0	94	71	37	32	7	28	68	.204
	Sacramento (PCL)	AAA	8	3	3.14	13	13	1	0	80	74	32	28	5	27	82	.241
2002	Oklahoma (PCL)	AAA	3	8	7.40	34	19	0	0	122	162	107	100	20	53	75	.321
MINOR LEAGUE TOTALS			33	17	4.04	92	75	2	0	475	462	245	213	38	164	378	.254

21. Chris O'Riordan, 2b

Born: Jan. 29, 1980. **Ht.:** 5-9. **Wt.:** 180. **Bats:** R. **Throws:** R. **School:** Stanford University. **Career Transactions:** Selected by Rangers in eighth round of 2002 draft; signed June 27, 2002.

O'Riordan didn't have as decorated a career as some San Diego prep players, but he is clearly a product of that city's outstanding quality of high school baseball. O'Riordan wasn't drafted out of high school and went on to a stellar career at Stanford, where he was a three-year starter and the Cardinal's most consistent hitter over that span. Short but solidly built and deceptively strong, O'Riordan has hit everywhere he has played. He proved his bat was his best tool in his debut, dominating the Rookie-level Appalachian League the way a college senior should and finishing second in the league batting race. O'Riordan is more than adequate at second base, though with his range and arm he'll never be confused for Roberto Alomar. He has good enough footwork on the double play and may have enough arm to spend some time at third base down the line. His key will be his performance. As long as he hits, he'll move up the ladder and could have a similar career to former Rangers utilityman Frank Catalanotto.

Year	Club (League)	Class	AVG	G	AB	R	H	2B	3B	HR	RBI	BB	SO	SB	SLG	OBP
2002	Pulaski (Appy)	R	.370	48	173	37	64	16	1	3	24	37	20	14	.526	.495
	Savannah (SAL)	A	.273	9	33	6	9	3	0	0	2	7	5	1	.364	.400
MINOR LEAGUE TOTALS			.354	57	206	43	73	19	1	3	26	44	25	15	.500	.481

22. Ramon Martinez, 2b

Born: Feb. 22, 1980. **Ht.:** 5-10. **Wt.:** 170. **Bats:** B. **Throws:** R. **Career Transactions:** Signed out of Dominican Republic by Rangers, Jan. 25, 1998.

Second base isn't supposed to be a prospect position, so maybe it's not a good sign that the Rangers' best depth in the minors appears to be there. Besides having possible second sackers in the top 10 with Drew Meyer and Jason Bourgeois, the Rangers also like the looks of Chris O'Riordan, Martinez and Jeff Pickler. Martinez got on the prospect map last season when he repeated high Class A with startling results. He improved his average by 64 points, cut down on his strikeouts and improved his stolen-base percentage. Martinez served as a catalyst at the top of the lineup for the best team in the Florida State League, was a league all-star and was named the best defensive second baseman by FSL managers. He made just eight errors in 100 games at second. Martinez' best tools are his speed, which rates a 70 on the 20-80 scale. He has an average arm and may play more shortstop now that Jose Morban is out of the organization. Martinez needs more strength and better plate discipline, and also has some swing mechanics to improve on, but he made enough strides in 2002 to make the Rangers think it's possible.

Year	Club (League)	Class	AVG	G	AB	R	H	2B	3B	HR	RBI	BB	SO	SB	SLG	OBP
1998	Rangers (DSL)	R	.285	54	179	23	51	13	0	3	21	8	7	2	.408	.328
1999	Rangers (DSL)	R	.359	50	195	43	70	19	2	7	44	9	16	7	.585	.409
2000	Charlotte (FSL)	A	.289	42	152	12	44	7	1	1	20	5	28	8	.368	.310
	Savannah (SAL)	A	.311	39	164	19	51	9	0	1	17	2	29	6	.384	.331
2001	Charlotte (FSL)	A	.241	128	515	69	124	20	1	2	32	28	65	28	.295	.286
2002	Charlotte (FSL)	A	.305	114	472	98	144	21	8	3	41	32	44	39	.403	.353
MINOR LEAGUE TOTALS			.289	427	1677	264	484	89	12	17	175	84	189	90	.386	.331

23. Erik Thompson, rhp

Born: June 23, 1982. **Ht.:** 5-11. **Wt.:** 180. **Bats:** R. **Throws:** R. **School:** Pensacola (Fla.) JC. **Career Transactions:** Selected by Rangers in 12th round of 2002 draft; signed June 21, 2002.

The Rangers drafted Thompson in the 43rd round out of high school, but had to wait two more years to land him as a 12th-rounder out of Pensacola JC. In between, the one-time Florida recruit had Tommy John surgery. While 2002 was his first full season back from the injury, Thompson maintained an 88-93 mph fastball throughout the season and showed the ability to spot it anywhere. He's a short righthander, but he has long arms and gets life on his pitches by throwing from a low three-quarters arm angle. Thompson touched 96 mph early last spring and he's aggressive early in the count with his fastball, helping him to have incredibly low walk totals—three in 32 pro innings, one in instructional league. He also has command of a curveball that can be a plus pitch. The Rangers brought Thompson along slowly last summer after he had a heavy workload in the spring, so a jump to high Class A in 2003 wouldn't be a surprise. A bulldog on the mound, he could move quickly.

Year	Club (League)	Class	W	L	ERA	G	GS	CG	SV	IP	H	R	ER	HR	BB	SO	AVG
2002	Rangers (GCL)	R	2	2	2.04	10	5	0	0	40	38	12	9	2	2	34	.250
	Pulaski (Appy)	R	1	1	3.18	3	3	0	0	17	19	6	6	0	2	16	.297
MINOR LEAGUE TOTALS			3	3	2.38	13	8	0	0	57	57	18	15	2	4	50	.264

24. Patrick Boyd, of

Born: Sept. 7, 1978. **Ht.:** 6-3. **Wt.:** 200. **Bats:** B. **Throws:** R. **School:** Clemson University. **Career Transactions:** Selected by Rangers in seventh round of 2001 draft; signed Jan. 16, 2002.

Boyd and Kiki Bengochea have similar stories. Both were highly drafted out of high school (second round by the Mariners in 1998 for Boyd, third round by the Royals in 1999 for Bengochea). Both had some college success, with Boyd a second-team All-American after a sterling sophomore season at Clemson. Both stumbled thereafter and had disappointing ends to their college careers. Both are represented by Scott Boras and signed with the Rangers for bonuses that surprised the industry. Boyd signed in January 2002 for $600,000, the second-highest bonus ever given to a seventh-round pick. But unlike Bengochea, who rebounded once he turned pro, Boyd has continued to be dogged by a string of injuries that began in 2000. He has been bothered by a thumb injury that forced him to leave the Cape Cod League early that summer, and a cracked vertebra in his back wiped out his 2001 season. Last year, he battled an Achilles tendon problem. In each case, the Rangers say, Boyd's diligence and desire to get back on the field actually hurt him because he hasn't allowed his injuries to properly heal. His tools remain tantalizing. He's a switch-hitter with a line-drive swing (it's better from the left side), gap power and above-average power. He's an excellent defender in center field with a plus arm and good range. He had a good instructional league performance, but will need to stay healthy to start turning his potential into reality.

Year	Club (League)	Class	AVG	G	AB	R	H	2B	3B	HR	RBI	BB	SO	SB	SLG	OBP
2002	Savannah (SAL)	A	.241	69	257	25	62	15	2	5	30	24	68	8	.374	.313
	Charlotte (FSL)	A	.250	4	12	0	3	1	0	0	3	1	3	0	.333	.308
MINOR LEAGUE TOTALS			.242	73	269	25	65	16	2	5	33	25	71	8	.372	.313

25. Kiki Bengochea, rhp

Born: Dec. 4, 1980. **Ht.:** 6-2. **Wt.:** 190. **Bats:** R. **Throws:** R. **School:** University of Miami. **Career Transactions:** Selected by Rangers in 11th round of 2002 draft; signed June 25, 2002.

Bengochea entered 2002 as a preseason first-team All-American, meaning that big league scouting directors considered him one of the top five pitchers in college baseball. He was anything but for the Hurricanes, getting lit up early in the season and needing a late rush to finish at 6-7, 5.63. However, Bengochea won 14 games and a national championship in his first two seasons at Miami, and in two summers with Team USA he went 6-1, 0.61. Assistant general manager Grady Fuson thought it worth the gamble to pick Bengochea in the 11th round and pay him a bonus worthy of a third-round pick, $550,000. Bengochea pitched effectively in his pro debut. He's a classic sinker/slider pitcher who must keep his

89-91 mph fastball down in the zone to be effective. His slider is his best pitch. He got hammered in college when he overthrew, trying to put up radar-gun numbers instead of just pitching. The Rangers have worked, successfully so far, with getting Bengochea to stay on top of his pitches and use his sinking changeup more frequently. While he's not projected as a frontline starter anymore, he could move quickly if he makes those adjustments.

Year	Club (League)	Class	W	L	ERA	G	GS	CG	SV	IP	H	R	ER	HR	BB	SO	AVG
2002	Savannah (SAL)	A	3	4	3.00	12	9	0	0	39	37	18	13	0	14	36	.252
MINOR LEAGUE TOTALS			3	4	3.00	12	9	0	0	39	37	18	13	0	14	36	.252

26. Derrick Van Dusen, lhp

Born: June 6, 1981. **Ht.:** 6-3. **Wt.:** 180. **Bats:** L. **Throws:** L. **School:** Riverside (Calif.) CC. **Career Transactions:** Selected by Mariners in fifth round of 2000 draft; signed June 19, 2000 . . . Traded by Mariners with 2B Jermaine Clark to Rangers for RHP Ismael Valdes, Aug. 19, 2002.

The Rangers acquired Van Dusen from the Mariners in the Ismael Valdes deal. Van Dusen isn't a premium pitching prospect, but he's lefthanded and has a slider that could be a plus major league pitch. He also has an above-average changeup that may be better than Mario Ramos'. Van Dusen has a deceptive delivery and, despite his unorthodox arm action, he has the ability to command his 84-87 mph fastball, slider and changeup. He pauses a bit during his windup, a change he made in 2002. He also shows a good feel for pitching. He sailed through the Mariners system, keeping hitters off balance and building his confidence, until he reached Double-A. Van Dusen bounced back after the trade and then reported to the Arizona Fall League, where he worked on his slider and got his first extended taste of relieving. The Rangers will keep him in the rotation this year in Double-A, but a move to the bullpen remains a possibility.

Year	Club (League)	Class	W	L	ERA	G	GS	CG	SV	IP	H	R	ER	HR	BB	SO	AVG
2000	Mariners (AZL)	R	6	0	2.63	10	2	0	0	41	38	14	12	1	6	58	.239
	Everett (NWL)	A	1	1	3.60	4	2	0	0	15	17	13	6	1	5	24	.270
2001	Wisconsin (Mid)	A	5	4	3.19	18	18	1	0	96	82	40	34	6	24	103	.224
	San Bernardino (Cal)	A	0	1	5.40	1	1	0	0	3	3	2	2	0	1	3	.231
2002	San Bernardino (Cal)	A	7	6	3.10	20	20	0	0	125	111	46	43	13	36	118	.237
	San Antonio (TL)	AA	1	2	7.20	5	4	0	0	25	31	21	20	4	12	17	.316
	Tulsa (TL)	AA	1	1	2.25	3	1	0	0	12	14	5	3	0	3	5	.304
MINOR LEAGUE TOTALS			21	15	3.41	61	48	1	0	317	296	141	120	25	87	328	.244

27. Jason Botts, of/1b

Born: July 26, 1980. **Ht.:** 6-6. **Wt.:** 240. **Bats:** B. **Throws:** R. **School:** Glendale (Calif.) JC. **Career Transactions:** Selected by Rangers in 46th round of 1999 draft; signed May 15, 2000.

Botts is good friends with Laynce Nix and spent a third straight season with him, but he fell behind his buddy in terms of development. Botts, whose cousin Carl Bacon is a college catcher at Santa Clara, is the most physically imposing player in the system. He has size and speed to go with it, once running a 6.55-second 60-yard dash, best in the organization at the time. With all that athleticism, the Rangers will be patient—and Botts is testing that patience. His raw power and selectivity at the plate should generate a lot of home runs, but he has yet to crack double digits as a pro, thanks in part to some serious holes in his swing. In his first full season as more of an outfielder than first baseman, Botts looked raw in right field last year. He should repeat high Class A in 2003, this time closer to family back at Stockton.

Year	Club (League)	Class	AVG	G	AB	R	H	2B	3B	HR	RBI	BB	SO	SB	SLG	OBP
2000	Rangers (GCL)	R	.319	48	163	36	52	12	0	6	34	26	29	4	.503	.440
2001	Savannah (SAL)	A	.309	114	392	63	121	24	2	9	50	53	88	13	.449	.416
	Charlotte (FSL)	A	.167	4	12	1	2	1	0	0	0	4	4	0	.250	.375
2002	Charlotte (FSL)	A	.254	116	401	67	102	22	5	9	54	75	99	7	.401	.387
MINOR LEAGUE TOTALS			.286	282	968	167	277	59	7	24	138	158	220	24	.436	.408

28. John Koronka, lhp

Born: July 3, 1980. **Ht.:** 6-1. **Wt.:** 180. **Bats:** L. **Throws:** L. **School:** South Lake HS, Groveland, Fla. **Career Transactions:** Selected by Reds in 12th round of 1998 draft; signed June 7, 1998.

Koronka adds to Texas' lefthanded depth after being plucked from the Reds in the major league Rule 5 draft. He got onto the prospect map last season by winning his first 11 decisions with Stockton, earning California League all-star honors. Koronka was much more hittable after his promotion to Double-A, but the Rangers saw enough potential to merit trying to keep him on their 25-man roster for all of this season. Koronka fits the bill of pitchers Grady Fuson looks for. He throws strikes (with a fastball in the high 80s) and has a good changeup, which Reds officials considered of major league caliber. He was effective with that combination in the Arizona Fall League, where he held hitters to a .212 average. Koronka's chances of sticking in the majors will be coming up with a breaking ball. His fastball/changeup combo doesn't faze lefthanders, who hit .355 against him last year. He'll have to improve on his slurvy curveball to stick as a situational reliever, the usual path for Rule 5 lefthanders.

Year	Club (League)	Class	W	L	ERA	G	GS	CG	SV	IP	H	R	ER	HR	BB	SO	AVG
1998	Billings (Pio)	R	0	3	8.04	12	3	0	0	31	47	43	28	2	26	36	.326
1999	Reds (GCL)	R	3	3	1.69	7	7	0	0	37	25	11	7	1	14	27	.194
	Billings (Pio)	R	2	3	5.58	7	7	0	0	40	41	26	25	1	17	34	.273
2000	Clinton (Mid)	A	4	13	4.33	20	18	4	0	104	123	65	50	7	38	74	.301
2001	Dayton (Mid)	A	3	1	0.75	5	5	0	0	24	23	12	2	0	8	25	.256
	Mudville (Cal)	A	5	2	4.94	12	12	0	0	71	78	44	39	10	39	66	.281
	Chattanooga (SL)	AA	1	5	5.73	9	9	0	0	55	62	37	35	7	28	44	.286
2002	Stockton (Cal)	A	11	0	3.07	12	12	0	0	73	59	36	25	4	35	69	.214
	Chattanooga (SL)	AA	2	8	4.99	16	15	0	0	96	109	56	53	10	52	69	.298
MINOR LEAGUE TOTALS			31	38	4.47	100	88	4	0	532	567	330	264	42	257	444	.275

29. Nate Gold, 1b

Born: June 12, 1980. **Ht.:** 6-3. **Wt.:** 220. **Bats:** R. **Throws:** R. **School:** Gonzaga University. **Career Transactions:** Selected by Rangers in 10th round of 2002 draft; signed June 15, 2002.

Gold led NCAA Division I in home runs in 2002 with 33 in just 56 games. If you're going to have one tool, power is a good one to have, and that's Gold's calling card. He has shown the ability to loft the ball, gets good extension in his uppercut swing and has as much raw power as any Rangers minor leaguer besides Mark Teixeira. How much of his power will translate from batting practice to the games is the question. He's big and strong, with a build the Major League Scouting Bureau compared to Lee Stevens'. Gold isn't a guy who will hit for high average because he tries to pull the ball too much, a weakness South Atlantic League pitchers exploited. However, the Rangers remain high on Gold, who figures to return to low Class A in 2003. He'll move slowly as he polishes his raw approach at the plate and his defensive play at first base.

Year	Club (League)	Class	AVG	G	AB	R	H	2B	3B	HR	RBI	BB	SO	SB	SLG	OBP
2002	Pulaski (Appy)	R	.319	30	113	19	36	9	1	5	30	17	20	2	.549	.405
	Savannah (SAL)	A	.190	37	142	12	27	7	0	5	14	11	38	0	.345	.258
MINOR LEAGUE TOTALS			.247	67	255	31	63	16	1	10	44	28	58	2	.435	.325

30. Julin Charles, of

Born: Oct. 31, 1982. **Ht.:** 6-1. **Wt.:** 170. **Bats:** R. **Throws:** R. **Career Transactions:** Signed out of Dominican Republic by Rangers, Jan. 25, 2000.

Grady Fuson calls Charles a "big dreams" guy, and he evoked comparisons to a former Rangers farmhand who also was raw and from the Dominican: Sammy Sosa. No one in the organization puts those kinds of expectations on Charles, however. They do compare his raw tools favorably to most any player in the organization, and are anxious to see what Charles can do in 2003, when he'll get his first taste of full-season ball. He has a good pro body that is still developing. He possesses the organization's strongest outfield arm, though he needs to be more accurate, and should develop into a good defensive right fielder. He gets good jumps on fly balls and is a plus runner. Offensively, he makes good use of his speed on the basepaths, stealing 35 bases in 40 tries over the last two seasons. A quick bat helps him crush fastballs and makes the ball jump off his bat, and he led Rookie-level Pulaski in homers in 2002. Charles' hitting approach, however, remains very unrefined. He struck out once every four at-bats and has little plate discipline, a commodity highly valued by the Rangers. Charles will be given time to hone the skills he needs to unleash his raw tools.

Year	Club (League)	Class	AVG	G	AB	R	H	2B	3B	HR	RBI	BB	SO	SB	SLG	OBP
2000	Rangers (DSL)	R	.274	66	263	28	72	10	3	2	32	17	44	19	.357	.325
2001	Rangers (GCL)	R	.241	52	187	23	45	15	4	1	22	12	41	17	.380	.287
2002	Savannah (SAL)	A	.161	8	31	4	5	0	1	0	0	2	11	0	.226	.212
	Pulaski (Appy)	R	.253	62	241	40	61	12	2	8	44	20	61	18	.419	.321
MINOR LEAGUE TOTALS			.253	188	722	95	183	37	10	11	98	51	157	54	.378	.309

TORONTO
BLUE JAYS

TOP 30 PROSPECTS

1. Dustin McGowan, rhp
2. Jayson Werth, of/c
3. Kevin Cash, c
4. Francisco Rosario, rhp
5. Jason Arnold, rhp
6. Brandon League, rhp
7. Alexis Rios, of
8. Russ Adams, ss/2b
9. John-Ford Griffin, of
10. Vinny Chulk, rhp
11. Gabe Gross, of
12. Guillermo Quiroz, c
13. Mark Hendrickson, lhp
14. David Bush, rhp
15. Dominic Rich, 2b
16. Miguel Negron, of
17. Chad Pleiness, rhp
18. D.J. Hanson, rhp
19. Tyrell Godwin, of
20. Tracy Thorpe, rhp
21. Mike Smith, rhp
22. Shawn Fagan, 1b/3b
23. Justin Maureau, lhp
24. Sandy Nin, rhp
25. Jason Perry, 1b
26. Manuel Mayorson, ss
27. Mike Snyder, 1b
28. Jordan DeJong, rhp
29. Eric Stephenson, lhp
30. John Wesley, rhp

**By John
Manuel**

Perhaps no team in the American League East has more potential than the Blue Jays. It has been a decade since Toronto won back-to-back World Series, but SkyDome was once again home to a hotbed of talent in 2002. Roy Halladay and Vernon Wells, the organization's top prospects for a combined five years, emerged as franchise cornerstones. Halladay led the AL in innings and won 19 games while Wells played a Gold Glove-caliber center field and drove in 100 runs. Eric Hinske won Baseball America's Rookie of the Year award, while fellow rookies Orlando Hudson, Josh Phelps, Mark Hendrickson, Justin Miller and Pete Walker all made contributions. The club found a new direction under Carlos Tosca, who replaced Buck Martinez and led the Jays to a 58-51 record.

The organization's 2002 draft was the best in the game, and first-year general manager J.P. Ricciardi made some fine moves, such as acquiring Hinske from the Athletics and dumping Raul Mondesi on the Yankees. "Looking back from November to now I think we're going in the right direction," Ricciardi said late in the season. "We're walking. We're not running."

Ricciardi's next move was to supplement the roster with minor league free-agent signings, a hallmark of his tenure with the Athletics. That was followed by three more trades with Oakland, getting Corey Lidle for the rotation and two prospects in righthander Jason Arnold and outfielder John-Ford Griffin.

For all Toronto's potential, though, things could also go wrong in a hurry. Ricciardi is a young GM and must find a way to move first baseman Carlos Delgado, whose contract eats up more than 20 percent of the Jays' projected payroll. He also must bring together his organization, part of which was alienated by the firing of several long-time scouts and minor league coaches in the offseason.

The graduation of talent to the majors has also left the Blue Jays with holes atop the minor league depth chart. Toronto still has future big leaguers in the pipeline, but finding a surefire impact player may be difficult.

Finally, the Blue Jays don't have a lot of money to spend any longer. As the Canadian dollar remains weak against its American counterpart, Toronto's financial picture remains murky at best. So Ricciardi and the Jays need to develop young, cheap talent more than ever.

OrganizationOverview

General Manager: J.P. Ricciardi. Farm Director: Dick Scott. Scouting Director: Chris Buckley.

2002 PERFORMANCE

Class	Farm Team	League	W	L	Pct.	Finish*	Manager(s)
Majors	Toronto	American	78	84	.481	8th (14)	Buck Martinez/Carlos Tosca
Triple-A	Syracuse SkyChiefs	International	64	80	.444	10th (14)	Omar Malave
Double-A	†Tennessee Smokies	Southern	69	71	.493	6th (10)	Rocket Wheeler
High A	Dunedin Blue Jays	Florida State	63	72	.467	9th (12)	Marty Pevey
Low A	Charleston Alley Cats	South Atlantic	61	79	.436	15th (16)	Paul Elliott
Short-season	Auburn Doubledays	New York-Penn	47	29	.618	4th (14)	Dennis Holmberg
Rookie	#Medicine Hat Blue Jays	Pioneer	37	38	.493	5th (8)	Rolando Pino

OVERALL 2002 MINOR LEAGUE RECORD   341 369 .480   19th (30)

*Finish in overall standings (No. of teams in league). †Affiliate will be in New Haven (Eastern) in 2003. #Affiliate will be in Pulaski (Appalachian) in 2003.

ORGANIZATION LEADERS

BATTING
*Minimum 250 At-Bats
*AVG	Dominic Rich, Tennessee/Dunedin	.326
R	Rich Thompson, Tennessee	109
H	Dominic Rich, Tennessee/Dunedin	166
TB	Gary Burnham, Syracuse	238
2B	Chad Mottola, Syracuse	35
3B	Alexis Rios, Dunedin	8
	Justin Singleton, Tennessee/Dunedin	8
HR	Josh Phelps, Syracuse	24
RBI	Gary Burnham, Syracuse	88
	Simon Pond, Dunedin	88
BB	Shawn Fagan, Tennessee	102
SO	Jayson Werth, Syracuse	125
SB	Rich Thompson, Tennessee	45

PITCHING
#Minimum 75 Innings
W	Diegomar Markwell, Tennessee	13
	Vinny Chulk, Tennessee	13
L	Peter Bauer, Tennessee	13
#ERA	Francisco Rosario, Dunedin/Charleston	1.94
G	Brian Bowles, Syracuse	59
CG	Peter Bauer, Tennessee	3
SV	John Ogiltree, Dunedin	26
IP	Peter Bauer, Tennessee	177
BB	Diegomar Markwell, Tennessee	60
SO	Dustin McGowan, Charleston	163

BEST TOOLS

Best Hitter for Average	John-Ford Griffin
Best Power Hitter	Mike Snyder
Fastest Baserunner	Tyrell Godwin
Best Athlete	Mark Hendrickson
Best Fastball	Dustin McGowan
Best Curveball	Justin Maureau
Best Slider	Brian Cardwell
Best Changeup	Francisco Rosario
Best Control	Brandon League
Best Defensive Catcher	Kevin Cash
Best Defensive Infielder	Manuel Mayorson
Best Infield Arm	Nom Siriveaw
Best Defensive Outfielder	Miguel Negron
Best Outfield Arm	Miguel Negron

PROJECTED 2006 LINEUP

Catcher	Kevin Cash
First Base	Josh Phelps
Second Base	Orlando Hudson
Third Base	Eric Hinske
Shortstop	Russ Adams
Left Field	Shannon Stewart
Center Field	Vernon Wells
Right Field	Jayson Werth
Designated Hitter	Carlos Delgado

Dominic Rich   **Peter Bauer**

RICK BATTLE   TYLER BOLDEN

No. 1 Starter	Roy Halladay
No. 2 Starter	Dustin McGowan
No. 3 Starter	Francisco Rosario
No. 4 Starter	Jason Arnold
No. 5 Starter	Brandon League
Closer	Kelvim Escobar

TOP PROSPECTS OF THE DECADE

1993	Carlos Delgado, c
1994	Alex Gonzalez, ss
1995	Shawn Green, of
1996	Shannon Stewart, of
1997	Roy Halladay, rhp
1998	Roy Halladay, rhp
1999	Roy Halladay, rhp
2000	Vernon Wells, of
2001	Vernon Wells, of
2002	Josh Phelps, c

TOP DRAFT PICKS OF THE DECADE

1993	Chris Carpenter, rhp
1994	Kevin Witt, ss
1995	Roy Halladay, rhp
1996	Billy Koch, rhp
1997	Vernon Wells, of
1998	Felipe Lopez, ss
1999	Alexis Rios, of
2000	Miguel Negron, of
2001	Gabe Gross, of
2002	Russ Adams, ss

ALL-TIME LARGEST BONUSES

Felipe Lopez, 1998	$2,000,000
Gabe Gross, 2001	$1,865,000
Russ Adams, 2002	$1,785,000
Vernon Wells, 1997	$1,600,000
Billy Koch, 1996	$1,450,000

MinorLeague**Depth**Chart

TORONTO BLUE JAYS

6
R A N K

While under orders to slash the budget, general manager J.P. Ricciardi is incorporating his own ideas into the Blue Jays' player-development and scouting operations that he developed while working in Oakland as Billy Beane's right-hand man. Ricciardi inherited a strong farm system and saw homegrown players Roy Halladay, Orlando Hudson, Josh Phelps and Vernon Wells blossom in his first year on the job. He added Baseball America Rookie of the Year Eric Hinske from Oakland before the 2002 season, and top prospects Jason Arnold and John-Ford Griffin in deals with the A's after the season. The Blue Jays' 2002 draft brought in a nice group of polished, college-level prospects and rated as the best in baseball at first glance.

Note: Depth charts prepared by Josh Boyd. Numbers in parentheses indicate prospect rankings.

LF
John-Ford Griffin (9)
Tyrell Godwin (19)
Randy Braun

CF
Alexis Rios (7)
Miguel Negron (16)
Dewayne Wise
Rich Thompson

RF
Jayson Werth (2)
Gabe Gross (11)
Jason Dubois
Justin Owens

3B
Shawn Fagan (22)
Glenn Williams
Jim Deschaine
Nom Siriveaw

SS
Russ Adams (8)
Manuel Mayorson (26)

2B
Dominic Rich (15)
Jorge Sequea
Lee Delfino

1B
Jason Perry (25)
Mike Snyder (27)
Jarad Mangioni

C
Kevin Cash (3)
Guillermo Quiroz (12)
Jose Yepez
John Schneider

RHP

Starters	**Relievers**
Dustin McGowan (1)	David Bush (14)
Francisco Rosario (4)	Sandy Nin (24)
Jason Arnold (5)	Jordan DeJong (28)
Brandon League (6)	John Wesley (30)
Vinny Chulk (10)	Aquilino Lopez
Chad Pleiness (17)	Gary Majewski
D.J. Hanson (18)	Brian Bowles
Tracy Thorpe (20)	Brian Cardwell
Mike Smith (21)	Willie Glen
Pascual Coco	Chris Baker
Juan Perez	
Neomar Flores	
Adam Peterson	
Vince Perkins	
Charles Talanoa	

LHP

Starters	**Relievers**
Mark Hendrickson (13)	Justin Maureau (23)
Eric Stephenson (29)	Scott Wiggins
Diegomar Markwell	
Gustvao Chacin	
Chris Leonard	

DraftAnalysis

2002 Draft

Best Pro Debut: RHP Jordan DeJong (18) topped the Rookie-level Pioneer League with 16 saves. He went 7-1, 1.30 with a 65-11 strikeout-walk ratio in 48 innings between the PL and the short-season New York-Penn League. 1B Jason Perry (6) batted .384-11-41 for the same two clubs. The NY-P team was loaded with successful pitchers, led by LHP Justin Maureau (3), who posted a 1.44 ERA. SS Russ Adams (1) was an NY-P all-star, hitting .354 before a promotion to high Class A, while 3B Scott Dragicevich (36) earned the same distinction in the PL, where he batted .296-6-37.

Best Athlete: Adams has every tool but power, yet his biggest assets may be his instincts and hustle. OF Randy Braun (17) could be a Paul O'Neill type. RHP Chad Pleiness (5) was a three-year starter for Central Michigan's basketball team.

Best Pure Hitter: Adams is a perfect lead-off man because he knows how to work counts, make contact and get on base.

Best Raw Power: Perry, who will see more time in the outfield in 2003.

Fastest Runner: Adams has a step above-average speed, but he's a proficient bases-stealer because he knows the game so well. He succeeded on 18 of his 21 attempts.

Best Defensive Player: Cs Paul Richmond (28) and John Schneider (13) finished 1-2 in the NY-P in throwing out basestealers at 53 and 52 percent. Schneider has the better defensive package, while Richmond is the superior hitter. Adams is at shortstop for now but projects to move to second base,

where he could be a Gold Glover.

Best Fastball: RHPs David Bush (2) and Adam Peterson (4) throw 91-94 mph. RHP John Wesley, who was often injured at South Carolina, reached 96 mph after signing as a nondrafted free agent.

Best Breaking Ball: Maureau had one of the best curveballs in the draft. Pleiness, who led NCAA Division I with 13.2 strikeouts per nine innings last spring, throws 88-92 mph and gets his whiffs with his curveball. Bush's slider can be dominant.

RICH ABEL

DeJong

Most Intriguing Background: SS/3B Brad Hassey's (19) father Ron and unsigned C Drew Butera's (48) father Sal both caught in the majors.

Closest To The Majors: Bush and Maureau could beat Adams to Toronto if they stay in the bullpen.

Best Late-Round Pick: DeJong, who showed a steady 90-92 mph fastball and solid breaking pitch all summer.

The One Who Got Away: RHP Matt Farnum (24) took his 91-95 mph fastball back to Texas A&M.

Assessment: Toronto's first six picks are college players who had immediate success. Bush, Maureau, Peterson and DeJong all could address the need for a closer. If LHP Chris Leonard (8) recovers from Tommy John surgery, a strong draft will look even better.

2001 Draft

OF Gabe Gross (1) took a step back in 2002 but should be able to recover. RHP Brandon League (2) has one of the system's most electric arms. **Grade: C+**

2000 Draft

OF Miguel Negron (1) was picked for signability rather than ability. RHP Dustin McGowan (1) has blossomed into the Blue Jays' best prospect. **Grade: C**

1999 Draft

OF Alexis Rios (1) was another signability choice, though he has shown more promise. LHP Matt Ford (3) won the 2002 Florida State League ERA title, then was lost in the major league Rule 5 draft. **Grade: C**

1998 Draft

SS Felipe Lopez (1) and OF/1B Jay Gibbons (14) will become big league regulars, but not in Toronto. **Grade: B**

Note: Draft analysis prepared by Jim Callis. Numbers in parentheses indicate draft rounds.

. . . When McGowan is on, he has front-of-the-rotation stuff. His fastball reaches anywhere from 92-97 mph.

Dustin
McGowan rhp

Born: March 24, 1982.
Ht.: 6-3. **Wt.:** 190.
Bats: R. **Throws:** R.
School: Long County HS, Ludowici, Ga.
Career Transactions: Selected by Blue Jays in first round (33rd overall) of 2000 draft; signed June 20, 2000.

The Blue Jays have a history of success when drafting high school righthanders in the first round, and McGowan is starting to fit the bill. The track record includes Steve Karsay (1990), Chris Carpenter (1993) and current Toronto ace Roy Halladay (1995). McGowan was a supplemental pick for the loss of free agent Graeme Lloyd, a trade the Jays would make every time. A standout basketball wing guard/forward as well as a shortstop and pitcher, McGowan helped Long County High to the Georgia state playoffs three years in a row and became the most decorated pitcher from south Georgia since Joey Hamilton. He struggled out of the gates in 2002 but started to right himself with a dominating 11-strikeout, five-inning outing at Savannah with hundreds of friends and family on hand to watch.

When McGowan is on, he has front-of-the-rotation stuff. His fastball ranks as his top pitch and the best in the organization. It's a heavy fastball that reaches anywhere from 92-97 mph. More important for a young pitcher, McGowan became more consistent with his fastball command late in the season. A true power pitcher, his breaking ball is a power curve with 11-to-7 break, thrown from a three-quarters release point, and he showed better control of the pitch in 2002. The combination helped him lead the low Class A South Atlantic League in strikeouts. A good fielder, he has an athletic pitcher's body and his arm works well. McGowan's changeup remains a work in progress, and he has yet to dominate his level of competition. He struggled with command and consistency of his delivery early in the season, when he tended to overstride. It resulted in too many pitches up in the strike zone and a 5.43 ERA through May. As with most young pitchers, though, his biggest need is innings and experience.

McGowan has stepped to the front of the Blue Jays' line of young power arms, in part because of injuries to Francisco Rosario and Tracy Thorpe, in part because of his stuff, and in part because of his experience edge compared to Brandon League. Pitching on the same staff with Rosario and Thorpe at Charleston provided a positive, competitive atmosphere for McGowan, but he'll have to make the next step to Class A Dunedin without them. His third pro year was his first in a full-season league, and the Jays figure to continue taking it slow with him.

Year	Club (League)	Class	W	L	ERA	G	GS	CG	SV	IP	H	R	ER	HR	BB	SO	AVG
2000	Medicine Hat (Pio)	R	0	3	6.48	8	8	0	0	25	26	21	18	2	25	19	.274
2001	Auburn (NY-P)	A	3	6	3.76	15	14	0	0	67	57	33	28	1	49	80	.234
2002	Charleston, WV (SAL)	A	11	10	4.19	28	28	1	0	148	143	77	69	10	59	163	.251
MINOR LEAGUE TOTALS			14	19	4.31	51	50	1	0	240	226	131	115	13	133	262	.249

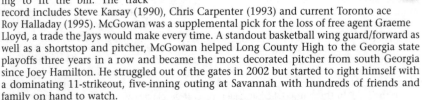

2. Jayson Werth, of/c

Born: May 20, 1979. **Ht.:** 6-5. **Wt.:** 210. **Bats:** R. **Throws:** R. **School:** Glenwood HS, Chatham, Ill. **Career Transactions:** Selected by Orioles in first round (22nd overall) of 1997 draft; signed June 13, 1997 . . . Traded by Orioles to Blue Jays for LHP John Bale, Dec. 11, 2000.

Werth started his career as a catcher but made the transition to the outfield in 2002, even playing a game in center field for Toronto at season's end. The Blue Jays got him from the Orioles for lefty John Bale (since traded away by Baltimore) and have seen Werth mature on and off the field into one of their top prospects. Werth has exceptional athletic ability and made the transition to the outfield look easy. He instantly took to reading fly balls and took excellent routes, and has the arm, speed and range for any outfield position. As he continues to fill out his long frame, he has developed above-average power. He has shown the ability to gear up for plus fastballs. Werth's swing path tends to get long, and he has some holes that he just can't close. He makes adjustments but always will strike out frequently. His ability to make adjustments will determine whether he's a 20-homer or a 30-homer guy. Werth could either be an above-average corner outfielder or the next Eli Marrero, a super-utility player who would be best served getting 400 at-bats a year. Werth figures to get more time to fine-tune his game at Triple-A Syracuse in 2003.

Yr	Club (League)	Class	AVG	G	AB	R	H	2B	3B	HR	RBI	BB	SO	SB	SLG	OBP
1997	Orioles (GCL)	R	.295	32	88	16	26	6	0	1	8	22	22	7	.398	.432
1998	Delmarva (SAL)	A	.265	120	408	71	108	20	3	8	53	50	92	21	.387	.364
	Bowie (EL)	AA	.158	5	19	2	3	2	0	0	1	2	6	1	.263	.238
1999	Frederick (Car)	A	.305	66	236	41	72	10	1	3	30	37	37	16	.394	.403
	Bowie (EL)	AA	.273	35	121	18	33	5	1	1	11	17	26	7	.355	.364
2000	Bowie (EL)	AA	.228	85	276	47	63	16	2	5	26	54	50	9	.355	.361
	Frederick (Car)	A	.277	24	83	16	23	3	0	2	18	10	15	5	.386	.347
2001	Dunedin (FSL)	A	.200	21	70	9	14	3	0	2	14	17	19	1	.329	.356
	Tennessee (SL)	AA	.285	104	369	51	105	23	1	18	69	63	93	12	.499	.387
2002	Syracuse (IL)	AAA	.257	127	443	65	114	25	2	18	82	67	125	24	.445	.354
	Toronto (AL)	MAJ	.261	15	46	4	12	2	1	0	6	6	11	1	.348	.340
MAJOR LEAGUE TOTALS			.261	15	46	4	12	2	1	0	6	6	11	1	.348	.340
MINOR LEAGUE TOTALS			.265	619	2113	336	561	113	10	58	312	339	485	103	.411	.371

3. Kevin Cash, c

Born: Dec. 6, 1977. **Ht.:** 6-0. **Wt.:** 185. **Bats:** R. **Throws:** R. **School:** Florida State University. **Career Transactions:** Signed as nondrafted free agent by Blue Jays, Aug. 7, 1999.

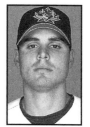

Cash's tale is one of the best in baseball. An average corner infielder at Florida State, he caught the Blue Jays' attention working as an emergency catcher in the Cape Cod League in 1999. He capped his rapid rise—2002 was just his second full season behind the plate—with a short stint in Toronto. Even in a one-game trial in the Cape, Cash showed the skills defensively that have made him one of the best catching prospects in the game. He has supreme catch-and-throw skills, throwing out 43 percent of minor league basestealers in 2002. He also shook off a bruised right hand to show solid power. He projects to hit 15-25 homers annually in the majors, and was leading the Double-A Southern League in RBIs when he was promoted. Cash never has been a great hitter. Even at Florida State, his best average was .319. He can be too pull-conscious and lost command of the strike zone after his promotion to Triple-A. He needs a better two-strike approach and more patience. Cash's defensive prowess allows the Jays to move Josh Phelps to DH or first base and Jayson Werth to the outfield. Cash will start 2003 back at Syracuse but is in line for a midseason promotion.

Year	Club (League)	Class	AVG	G	AB	R	H	2B	3B	HR	RBI	BB	SO	SB	SLG	OBP
2000	Hagerstown (SAL)	A	.245	59	196	28	48	10	1	10	27	22	54	5	.459	.323
2001	Dunedin (FSL)	A	.283	105	371	55	105	27	0	12	66	43	80	4	.453	.369
2002	Tennessee (SL)	AA	.277	55	213	38	59	15	1	8	44	36	44	5	.469	.381
	Syracuse (IL)	AAA	.220	67	236	27	52	18	0	10	26	25	72	0	.424	.299
	Toronto (AL)	MAJ	.143	7	14	1	2	0	0	0	0	1	4	0	.143	.200
MAJOR LEAGUE TOTALS			.143	7	14	1	2	0	0	0	0	1	4	0	.143	.200
MINOR LEAGUE TOTALS			.260	286	1016	148	264	70	2	40	163	126	250	14	.451	.347

4. Francisco Rosario, rhp

Born: Sept. 28, 1980. **Ht.:** 6-0. **Wt.:** 160. **Bats:** R. **Throws:** R. **Career Transactions:** Signed out of Dominican Republic by Blue Jays, Jan. 11, 1999.

JOHN SPEAR

Rosario spent his first two years as a reliever in the Rookie-level Dominican Summer League, then struggled in 2001 in his first effort as a starter. Everything game together in 2002 until he blew out his elbow in the Arizona Fall League. Rosario harnessed his power stuff, dominating two Class A levels with a 92-97 mph fastball, two variations on a plus changeup, and a breaking ball with slurvy action that at times was a plus pitch. Rosario's smallish frame proved unable to hold up under the torque he placed on his arm. He had reconstructive surgery and bone chips removed from his elbow. Full recovery from Tommy John surgery usually takes 12-18 months, and the Jays will proceed with caution with Rosario. If healthy, he might have ranked atop this list. Toronto officials compare his situation to that of Billy Koch, who had the same procedure in 1997 and came back as a closer. When Rosario returns in 2004, his career could take the same path.

Year	Club (League)	Class	W	L	ERA	G	GS	CG	SV	IP	H	R	ER	HR	BB	SO	AVG
1999	Blue Jays (DSL)	R	1	0	3.06	18	0	0	3	32	26	16	11	0	11	38	.208
2000	Blue Jays (DSL)	R	2	0	1.21	26	0	0	16	37	21	5	5	0	7	51	.160
2001	Medicine Hat (Pio)	R	3	7	5.59	16	15	0	0	76	79	61	47	8	38	55	.271
2002	Charleston, WV (SAL)	A	6	1	2.57	13	13	1	0	67	50	22	19	5	14	78	.206
	Dunedin (FSL)	A	3	3	1.29	13	12	0	0	63	33	10	9	3	25	65	.151
MINOR LEAGUE TOTALS			15	11	2.98	86	40	1	19	275	209	114	91	16	95	287	.207

5. Jason Arnold, rhp

Born: May 2, 1979. **Ht.:** 6-3. **Wt.:** 210. **Bats:** R. **Throws:** R. **School:** University of Central Florida. **Career Transactions:** Selected by Yankees in second round of 2001 draft; signed June 15, 2001 . . . Traded by Yankees with LHP Ted Lilly and OF John-Ford Griffin to Athletics as part of three-way trade in which Yankees received RHP Jeff Weaver from Tigers and Tigers received 1B Carlos Pena, RHP Franklyn German and a player to be named from Athletics, July 6, 2002; Tigers acquired RHP Jeremy Bonderman from Athletics to complete trade (Aug. 22, 2002) . . . Traded by Athletics to Blue Jays as part of four-way trade in which Athletics received 1B Erubiel Durazo from Diamondbacks, Diamondbacks received RHP Elmer Dessens from Reds, and Reds received SS Felipe Lopez from Blue Jays.

DAVID SCHOFIELD

Arnold has gone 20-6, 2.28, reached Double-A and been involved in two major trades involving seven teams in less than two years. Oakland gave up three of its best prospects to Detroit to get Arnold from the Yankees. Toronto got him from the Athletics for Felipe Lopez, who had played his way out of the Jays lineup. Arnold possesses superior game sense and instinctively knows how to vary his pitching patterns to set up hitters. In addition to his effective 88-91 mph fastball, he throws two different palmballs that serve as changeups. One floats and the other dives, and Arnold will throw them at any time in the count. He's also very aggressive at pitching inside. Arnold's slider is too flat and needs refinement. When he reported to the A's, there was some concern about his conditioning. However, he hired a personal trainer at the end of the season and engaged in strenuous workouts that showed quick results. Arnold was a reliever for his first three seasons in college, and some scouts believe his delivery will lead him back to the bullpen. The Jays will continue to use him as a starter, however, and he could get his first taste of the majors in late 2003.

Year	Club (League)	Class	W	L	ERA	G	GS	CG	SV	IP	H	R	ER	HR	BB	SO	AVG
2001	Staten Island (NY-P)	A	7	2	1.50	10	10	2	0	66	35	13	11	2	15	74	.158
2002	Tampa (FSL)	A	7	1	2.48	13	13	0	0	80	64	27	22	2	22	83	.217
	Norwich (EL)	AA	1	2	4.15	3	3	0	0	17	17	14	8	1	5	18	.254
	Midland (TL)	AA	5	1	2.33	10	10	0	0	58	42	22	15	2	24	53	.208
MINOR LEAGUE TOTALS			20	6	2.28	36	36	2	0	221	158	76	56	7	66	228	.201

6. Brandon League, rhp

Born: March 16, 1983. **Ht.:** 6-2. **Wt.:** 180. **Bats:** R. **Throws:** R. **School:** St. Louis HS, Honolulu. **Career Transactions:** Selected by Blue Jays in second round of 2001 draft; signed July 3, 2001.

RODGER WOOD

The Blue Jays continued their trend of taking it slow with high school pitchers, sending League to the short-season New York-Penn League in 2002 rather than full-season ball. His season almost ended before it started when he was hit in the right arm by a line drive during an exhibition game. He escaped with nothing more than a bruise. League has an electric, quick arm and one of the organization's best fastballs. He hit 97 mph at times in 2002 but pitched consistently from 94-96 mph, with natural sinking action generated by a low three-quarters release point. He also improved his changeup and showed a resilient arm, maintaining his stuff throughout the season. League has to stay on top of his slider, which tends to flatten out. He also needs to get stronger to keep his velocity deeper into games. Other refinements, such as improved fastball command and pitch efficiency, will come with experience. League should get his first shot at full-season Class A in 2003. If he improves his slider and trusts his fastball more while nibbling less, he could have a breakout year.

Year	Club (League)	Class	W	L	ERA	G	GS	CG	SV	IP	H	R	ER	HR	BB	SO	AVG
2001	Medicine Hat (Pio)	R	2	2	4.66	9	9	0	0	39	36	23	20	3	11	38	.245
2002	Auburn (NY-P)	A	7	2	3.15	16	16	0	0	86	80	42	30	2	23	72	.248
MINOR LEAGUE TOTALS			9	4	3.62	25	25	0	0	124	116	65	50	5	34	110	.247

7. Alexis Rios, of

Born: Feb. 18, 1981. **Ht.:** 6-6. **Wt.:** 202. **Bats:** R. **Throws:** R. **School:** San Pedro Martir HS, Guaynabo, P.R. **Career Transactions:** Selected by Blue Jays in first round (19th overall) of 1999 draft; signed June 4, 1999.

Rios' climb from surprise first-round pick to legitimate prospect is almost complete. He overcame a broken finger, bruised thumb and jammed wrist to rank fourth in the Florida State League in batting in 2002. Rios' swing path attracted the Jays to draft him in the first place as a low-cost, compromise choice, and he has rewarded them by becoming one of the organization's best hitters. He rarely strikes out and has an extraordinarily short swing for such a tall player. Rios runs well and has improved in center field, where he has an adequate, accurate arm and good range. Rios' power has yet to evolve in regular-season games, though he hit seven homers in spring training and showed similar pop in instructional league, once his hand and wrist had healed. He doesn't draw a lot of walks and needs to learn which pitches to lay off and which he can drive. Rios was protected on the 40-man roster this offseason, an intriguing decision given GM J.P. Ricciardi's affinity for walks and on-base percentage. Rios should move to Double-A New Haven in 2003, with improved power and patience his top priorities.

Year	Club (League)	Class	AVG	G	AB	R	H	2B	3B	HR	RBI	BB	SO	SB	SLG	OBP
1999	Medicine Hat (Pio)	R	.269	67	234	35	63	7	3	0	13	17	31	8	.325	.321
2000	Hagerstown (SAL)	A	.230	22	74	5	17	3	1	0	5	2	14	2	.297	.256
	Queens (NY-P)	A	.267	50	206	22	55	9	2	1	25	11	22	5	.345	.314
2001	Charleston, WV (SAL)	A	.263	130	480	40	126	20	9	2	58	25	59	22	.354	.296
2002	Dunedin (FSL)	A	.305	111	456	60	139	22	8	3	61	27	55	14	.408	.344
MINOR LEAGUE TOTALS			.276	380	1450	162	400	61	23	6	162	82	181	51	.362	.316

8. Russ Adams, ss/2b

Born: August 30, 1980. **Ht.:** 6-1. **Wt.:** 178. **Bats:** L. **Throws:** R. **School:** University of North Carolina. **Career Transactions:** Selected in first round (14th overall) in 2002 draft; signed June 7, 2002.

A quarterback at the same rural North Carolina high school that produced Rockies infielder Brent Butler, Adams blossomed at North Carolina and in the Cape Cod League, where he was the top prospect in the summer of 2001. He overcame a hairline fracture in his left thumb to have an All-America season for the Tar Heels in 2002. One of the organization's top athletes, Adams has solid average to plus tools across the board, with the exception of power. He plays the game instinctively, especially on the basepaths, where he uses his above-average speed well. At the plate, he has good bat speed, the ability to center the ball well and excellent plate discipline. Adams doesn't hit for much power now, but it wouldn't surprise the Jays if he ended up hitting 10-15 homers annually down the road. Though his arm may not be enough to play shortstop on artificial turf, he's going to remain at the position until he proves he can't handle it. He wore down from a long season in 2002 and needs to get stronger. Adams got off to a fast start at short-season Auburn and should return to high Class A for his first full year. He has all the makings of being a leadoff or No. 2 hitter, and if the power develops could see time at third base as well as second.

Year	Club (League)	Class	AVG	G	AB	R	H	2B	3B	HR	RBI	BB	SO	SB	SLG	OBP
2002	Auburn (NY-P)	A	.354	30	113	25	40	7	3	0	16	24	11	13	.469	.464
	Dunedin (FSL)	A	.231	37	147	23	34	4	2	1	12	18	17	5	.306	.321
MINOR LEAGUE TOTALS			.285	67	260	48	74	11	5	1	28	42	28	18	.377	.386

9. John-Ford Griffin, of

Born: Nov. 19, 1979. **Ht.:** 6-2. **Wt.:** 210. **Bats:** L. **Throws:** L. **School:** Florida State University. **Career Transactions:** Selected by Yankees in first round (23rd overall) of 2001 draft; signed June 14, 2001 . . . Traded by Yankees with LHP Ted Lilly and RHP Jason Arnold to Athletics as part of three-way trade in which Yankees received RHP Jeff Weaver from Tigers and Tigers received 1B Carlos Pena, RHP Franklyn German and a player to be named from Athletics, July 6, 2002; Tigers acquired RHP Jeremy Bonderman from Athletics to complete trade (Aug. 22, 2002) . . . Traded by Athletics to Blue Jays for a player to be named, Jan. 7, 2003.

After the three-team trade that took him from the Yankees to the Athletics, Griffin played two games in Double-A before being sidelined by a hand injury for the rest of the season. Then the A's traded him to the Blue Jays over the winter, as he continued to follow Jason Arnold from organization to organization. Griffin is a prolific hitter, having batted .400 in each of his three seasons at Florida State, where Seminoles coach Mike Martin called him the best hitter in the program's storied history. Griffin generates tremendous bat speed and has the makings of an outstanding hitter. While he has just 13 homers in 151 pro games, scouts say he has longball strength and will increase his power production as he matures. Griffin had surgery on his throwing arm after his sophomore year at Florida State and has not regained his arm strength. He has worked diligently, but it remains below-average. He could be limited to left field, moved to first base or even stuck as a DH. Griffin will return to Double-A, where he played just 20 games in 2002. He should be among the first players to reach the majors from the 2001 draft.

Year	Club (League)	Class	AVG	G	AB	R	H	2B	3B	HR	RBI	BB	SO	SB	SLG	OBP
2001	Staten Island (NY-P)	A	.311	66	238	46	74	17	1	5	43	40	41	10	.454	.413
2002	Tampa (FSL)	A	.267	65	255	32	68	16	1	3	31	29	45	1	.373	.344
	Norwich (EL)	AA	.328	18	67	17	22	3	0	5	10	8	13	0	.597	.400
	Midland (TL)	AA	.143	2	7	0	1	0	0	0	0	0	3	0	.143	.250
MINOR LEAGUE TOTALS			.291	151	567	95	165	36	2	13	84	77	102	11	.430	.379

10. Vinny Chulk, rhp

Born: Dec. 19, 1978. **Ht.:** 6-3. **Wt.:** 180. **Bats:** R. **Throws:** R. **School:** St. Thomas (Fla.) University. **Career Transactions:** Selected by Blue Jays in 12th round of 2000 draft; signed June 12, 2000.

Chulk got a tryout with NCAA Division II St. Thomas thanks to a recommendation from his future brother-in-law, the team's center fielder. It took 10 pitches in a bullpen session for coach Manny Mantrana to give Chulk a scholarship. The Blue Jays gambled Chulk had the four-pitch repertoire to move into the rotation while jumping to Double-A in 2002, and he rewarded that hunch by becoming the Southern League's pitcher of the year. Chulk's best pitch is a 91-94 mph sinker, and he does a good job of keeping it down in the zone. His slider, curveball and changeup are all solid offerings that he commands well. His competitiveness is a major asset, and Chulk showed he can pitch effectively without his best stuff. He's an above-average athlete who does little things (fielding, holding runners) well. Chulk doesn't have a strikeout pitch or the stuff to get by when he can't find the strike zone. He must refine his changeup to better combat lefthanders, who batted .272 against him. Chulk profiles as a No. 3 or No. 4 starter. He also has the resilient arm and command potential to be an effective middle reliever. He'll return to Triple-A in 2003.

Year	Club (League)	Class	W	L	ERA	G	GS	CG	SV	IP	H	R	ER	HR	BB	SO	AVG
2000	Medicine Hat (Pio)	R	2	4	3.80	14	13	0	0	69	75	36	29	5	20	51	.277
2001	Dunedin (FSL)	A	1	2	3.12	16	1	0	1	35	38	16	12	2	13	50	.271
	Syracuse (IL)	AAA	1	0	1.50	5	0	0	0	6	5	1	1	0	4	3	.238
	Tennessee (SL)	AA	2	5	3.14	24	1	0	2	43	34	15	15	5	8	43	.227
2002	Tennessee (SL)	AA	13	5	2.96	25	24	0	1	152	133	55	50	12	53	108	.236
	Syracuse (IL)	AAA	0	1	5.79	2	1	0	0	5	6	6	3	0	6	2	.316
MINOR LEAGUE TOTALS			19	17	3.20	86	40	0	4	309	291	129	110	24	104	257	.250

11. Gabe Gross, of

Born: Oct 21, 1979. **Ht.:** 6-3. **Wt.:** 205. **Bats:** L. **Throws:** R. **School:** Auburn University. **Career Transactions:** Selected by Blue Jays in first round (15th overall) of 2001 draft; signed July 1, 2001.

Gross' father Lee was an all-conference center at Auburn, and Gabe briefly followed in his dad's football footsteps, earning six starts as a freshman quarterback. His success at baseball, though, convinced him to give up the gridiron for his last two seasons with the Tigers. His first full year as a pro, 2002, brought his first failure on the diamond. Gross still has the plus tools to be a prototype right fielder. He has lefthanded power, a strong throwing arm and athleticism, and he's an above-average defender. He recovered from a slow start, hitting .282-8-35 in the last three months. Gross had a rough start in 2002, hitting .141 in April. He had trouble getting his hands started and through the zone, blocking off his own swing and leaving him unable to catch up to good fastballs. Shannon Stewart and Vernon Wells worked through similar woes during their minor league careers. Gross has the work ethic and ability to work though his swing problem and did so in the second half, as well as in the Arizona Fall League. He should spend his second full season repeating and conquering Double-A.

Year	Club (League)	Class	AVG	G	AB	R	H	2B	3B	HR	RBI	BB	SO	SB	SLG	OBP
2001	Dunedin (FSL)	A	.302	35	126	23	38	9	2	4	15	26	29	4	.500	.426
	Tennessee (SL)	AA	.244	11	41	8	10	1	0	3	11	6	12	0	.488	.373
2002	Tennessee (SL)	AA	.238	112	403	57	96	17	5	10	54	53	71	8	.380	.333
MINOR LEAGUE TOTALS			.253	158	570	88	144	27	7	17	80	85	112	12	.414	.357

12. Guillermo Quiroz, c

Born: Nov. 29, 1981. **Ht.:** 6-1. **Wt.:** 202. **Bats:** R. **Throws:** R. **Career Transactions:** Signed out of Venezuela by Blue Jays, Sept. 25, 1998.

Quiroz signed for $1.2 million, one of the largest bonuses ever for a Venezuelan player. He entered the 2002 season a career .205 hitter, but progressed enough to get an emergency Triple-A promotion when Kevin Cash hurt his hand. Quiroz has excellent athletic ability and agility behind the plate, and his catch-and-throw skills nearly match those of Cash. He has become fluent in English and handles pitching staffs well. Quiroz finally started to answer offensive concerns by showing better concentration and strike-zone judgment at the plate, unleashing his above-average power. His offensive approach is similar (though less potent) than Josh Phelps'. Quiroz' power comes with lots of strikeouts. He has a long, sweepy swing that constantly needs adjusting. He's never going to win a batting title and still needs to learn the strike zone better. With Phelps, Cash and Jayson Werth ahead of him, the Jays can afford to be patient with Quiroz. He'll move up to Double-A and could continue his offensive improvement as pitchers throw more strikes.

Year	Club (League)	Class	AVG	G	AB	R	H	2B	3B	HR	RBI	BB	SO	SB	SLG	OBP
1999	Medicine Hat (Pio)	R	.221	63	208	25	46	7	0	9	28	18	55	0	.385	.296
2000	Hagerstown (SAL)	A	.162	43	136	14	22	4	0	1	12	16	44	0	.213	.269
	Queens (NY-P)	A	.224	55	196	27	44	9	0	5	29	27	48	1	.347	.329
2001	Charleston, WV (SAL)	A	.199	82	261	25	52	12	0	7	25	29	67	5	.326	.294
2002	Dunedin (FSL)	A	.260	111	411	50	107	28	1	12	68	35	91	1	.421	.330
	Syracuse (IL)	AAA	.222	13	45	7	10	4	0	1	6	3	14	0	.378	.271
MINOR LEAGUE TOTALS			.224	367	1257	148	281	64	1	35	168	128	319	7	.360	.308

13. Mark Hendrickson, lhp

Born: June 23, 1974. **Ht.:** 6-9. **Wt.:** 230. **Bats:** L. **Throws:** L. **School:** Washington State University. **Career Transactions:** Selected by Blue Jays in 20th round of 1997 draft; signed May 22, 1998.

Forgoing an NBA career looks like the right decision for Hendrickson. He was a two-time first-team all-Pacific-10 Conference selection in basketball at Washington State, leading the Cougars to an NCAA tournament berth in 1994 as a power forward. He played parts of four seasons in the NBA with four teams, most recently the Cleveland Cavaliers in 2000. He was on non-guaranteed 10-day contracts and finally decided to give baseball a full-time shot. Drafted six different times in baseball by five organizations, Hendrickson signed with the Blue Jays in 1998. He made the most progress in 2002, when he finished the year in the major leagues and went 3-0, 2.45 for Toronto, making four effective starts to end the season. Hendrickson has more projection left than the average 28-year-old, given his inexperience and size. He has worked hard to stay tall in his delivery and has bumped his fastball velocity to 92-93 mph. He has developed a solid cut fastball and changeup, and is working on keeping good tilt on his 76-80 mph power curveball, which can be a plus pitch. As expected from an NBA veteran, Hendrickson wasn't phased by the big league atmosphere. His confidence and athleticism may have been the deciding factors in helping him persevere to this point, and he'll compete for a spot in the 2003 big league rotation.

Year	Club (League)	Class	W	L	ERA	G	GS	CG	SV	IP	H	R	ER	HR	BB	SO	AVG
1998	Dunedin (FSL)	A	4	3	2.37	16	5	0	1	49	44	16	13	2	26	38	.249
1999	Knoxville (SL)	AA	2	7	6.63	12	11	0	0	56	73	46	41	4	21	39	.319
2000	Dunedin (FSL)	A	2	2	5.61	12	12	1	0	51	63	34	32	7	29	38	.315
	Tennessee (SL)	AA	3	1	3.63	6	6	0	0	40	32	17	16	5	12	29	.216
2001	Syracuse (IL)	AAA	2	9	4.66	38	6	0	0	73	80	43	38	13	18	33	.274
2002	Syracuse (IL)	AAA	7	5	3.52	19	14	0	0	92	90	38	36	12	22	68	.254
	Toronto (AL)	MAJ	3	0	2.45	16	4	0	0	37	25	11	10	1	12	21	.202
MAJOR LEAGUE TOTALS			3	0	2.45	16	4	0	0	37	25	11	10	1	12	21	.202
MINOR LEAGUE TOTALS			20	27	4.38	103	54	1	1	361	382	194	176	43	128	245	.273

14. David Bush, rhp

Born: Nov. 9, 1979. **Ht.:** 6-2. **Wt.:** 210. **Bats:** R. **Throws:** R. **School:** Wake Forest University. **Career Transactions:** Selected by Blue Jays in second round of 2002 draft; signed June 17, 2002.

A catcher in high school, Bush was converted to the mound at Wake Forest and emerged as one of the nation's top closers at the end of his freshman year, when he put on a dominating performance at the Atlantic Coast Conference tournament. Bush ranked as one of the top seniors available for the 2002 draft after failing to come to terms as a 2001 fourth-round pick of the Devil Rays. His senior season almost ended before it started, as he was diagnosed with blood clots in his left leg in November 2001. Surgery and blood thinners took care of the problem, and though Bush got off to a slow start, he earned All-America honors. Having regained his strength and conditioning, Bush got off to a fast start in pro ball and joined Russ Adams in getting promoted to high Class A in their first pro summers. Bush could reach the major leagues by 2004 as a middle reliever or closer. He has a polished approach and throws strikes with a mid-to-high 80s power slider and a 91-92 mph fastball that can touch 94. His fastball command and changeup (still in its nascent stages) have some Jays officials believing Bush deserves a shot as a starter before consigning him to the bullpen. That decision will determine where he begins 2003.

Year	Club (League)	Class	W	L	ERA	G	GS	CG	SV	IP	H	R	ER	HR	BB	SO	AVG
2002	Auburn (NY-P)	A	1	1	2.82	18	0	0	10	22	13	9	7	1	7	39	.159
	Dunedin (FSL)	A	0	1	2.03	7	0	0	0	13	10	3	3	1	2	9	.222
MINOR LEAGUE TOTALS			1	2	2.52	25	0	0	10	36	23	12	10	2	9	48	.181

15. Dominic Rich, 2b

Born: Aug. 22, 1979. **Ht.:** 5-10. **Wt.:** 190. **Bats:** L. **Throws:** R. **School:** Auburn University. **Career Transactions:** Selected by Blue Jays in second round of 2000 draft; signed June 19, 2000.

Rich had always shown the ability to hit. An offensive catalyst at Auburn as a second baseman and center fielder, he had a productive college career that included a pair of .300 summers in the Cape Cod League, including a .341 mark in 1999. That's what puzzled the Blue Jays about Rich's first 1½ seasons as a pro. He had just a .272 career average going into 2002, though he had shown good plate discipline. A wrist injury short-circuited his 2001 season, and a healthy Rich showed the Blue Jays what he could do in 2002. He won the Florida State League batting championship while walking more than he struck out, and he held his own after a promotion to Double-A Tennessee. Rich recognizes what pitches he can hit and has decent gap power, with an offensive package that resembles Ray Durham's. However, his defense is also Durhamesque. Rich has hard hands and actions and heavy feet for the middle infield, and he won't ever be more than adequate at second base. Improved maturity and a better work ethic have helped him improve defensively, but he may never be cut out for artificial turf. Fortunately for him, he plays in an organization that values bat-first prospects. He'll return to Double-A to start 2003.

Year	Club (League)	Class	AVG	G	AB	R	H	2B	3B	HR	RBI	BB	SO	SB	SLG	OBP
2000	Queens (NY-P)	A	.263	67	236	37	62	11	4	0	25	38	33	10	.343	.372
2001	Charleston, WV (SAL)	A	.278	91	327	67	91	16	1	4	32	47	54	20	.370	.382
2002	Dunedin (FSL)	A	.345	95	377	72	130	14	5	8	50	57	49	8	.472	.437
	Tennessee (SL)	AA	.273	38	132	14	36	4	1	1	14	18	23	2	.341	.364
MINOR LEAGUE TOTALS			.291	.298	1072	190	319	45	11	13	121	160	159	40	.396	.397

16. Miguel Negron, of

Born: Aug. 22, 1982. **Ht.:** 6-2. **Wt.:** 170. **Bats:** L. **Throws:** L. **School:** Manuela Toro HS, Caguas, P.R. **Career Transactions:** Selected by Blue Jays in first round (18th overall) of 2000 draft; signed June 12, 2000.

The Blue Jays have been pleased with the progress of the first of their Puerto Rican first-round picks, protecting Alexis Rios on their 40-man roster this offseason. They'll face that decision with Negron after the 2003 season. Always grouped with Rios because of their common heritage and draft status, Negron is a completely different player. He made great improvements in maturity and in his approach in 2002. As one Toronto official put it, he tucked away his macho pride and focused on the smaller parts of the game. Negron is one of the faster players in the system and plays an excellent center field with a plus arm. He's getting stronger and making better use of his pull power, but he needs to tone down his swing, use the whole field and take better advantage of his speed. Negron will face a challenge in high Class A in 2003, and he's still young for that level. If he shows he can make consistent hard contact, he should follow Rios' path to the 40-man roster.

Year	Club (League)	Class	AVG	G	AB	R	H	2B	3B	HR	RBI	BB	SO	SB	SLG	OBP
2000	Medicine Hat (Pio)	R	.232	53	190	26	44	5	0	0	13	23	39	5	.258	.324

2001	Charleston, WV (SAL)	A	.192	25	99	11	19	1	0	0	2	6	21	5	.202	.238
	Auburn (NY-P)	A	.253	50	186	27	47	6	1	1	13	15	22	7	.312	.314
2002	Charleston, WV (SAL)	A	.255	118	420	56	107	15	2	5	41	35	77	20	.336	.312
MINOR LEAGUE TOTALS			.242	246	895	120	217	27	3	6	69	79	159	37	.299	.307

17. Chad Pleiness, rhp

Born: March 5, 1980. **Ht.:** 6-6. **Wt.:** 230. **Bats:** R. **Throws:** R. **School:** Central Michigan University. **Career Transactions:** Selected by Blue Jays in fifth round of 2002 draft; signed June 8, 2002.

A supreme athlete, Pleiness finally has picked a sport. He went to Central Michigan on a football scholarship as a tight end, but after redshirting as a freshman in the fall, joined the baseball team and showed promise on the diamond. He ditched football but took up basketball, a sport in which he set Mason County (Mich.) Central High's single-season scoring record and led his team to the state finals. (He also graduated with honors at Mason County.) Pleiness earned a basketball scholarship after leading the Mid-American Conference in free-throw percentage (88.4) in 2000-01, and in his last two seasons he averaged 11 points a game. He was much more dominant in baseball, though, striking out 100 in 68 innings last year to rank second (behind No. 1 overall pick Bryan Bullington) in the MAC. His 13.2 strikeouts per nine innings led Division I. Pleiness has used his athletic, long frame to become a hard-throwing pitcher. He also has a fresh arm and still is filling out physically. He maintains the velocity on his 88-92 mph fastball well and has an above-average curveball (his out pitch), as well as the makings of a solid changeup. Pleiness still has work to do on smoothing out his delivery, which can get away from him at times, but made excellent progress during instructional league.

Year	Club (League)	Class	W	L	ERA	G	GS	CG	SV	IP	H	R	ER	HR	BB	SO	AVG
2002	Auburn (NY-P)	A	8	3	2.42	16	9	0	0	74	48	23	20	2	32	70	.182
MINOR LEAGUE TOTALS			8	3	2.42	16	9	0	0	74	48	23	20	2	32	70	.182

18. D.J. Hanson, rhp

Born: Aug. 7, 1980. **Ht.:** 5-11. **Wt.:** 170. **Bats:** R. **Throws:** R. **School:** Richland (Wash.) HS. **Career Transactions:** Selected by Blue Jays in sixth round of 1999 draft; signed June 14, 1999 . . . On disabled list, June 16-Sept. 10, 2001.

The 1999 draft was a heady one for the state of Washington, with eight players—lefthander Ty Howington; righthanders Gerik Baxter, Jeff Heaverlo and Jason Stumm; catcher Ryan Doumit; infielder Jason Repko; and outfielders Jason Cooper and B.J. Garbe—drafted in the first two rounds. Because of injuries, ineffectiveness and Baxter's death in a car crash, Hanson might turn out to be better than any of them. Hanson missed 2001 after injuring his knee in a spring-training collision with Alvin Morrow (now on the practice squad of the NFL's Cleveland Browns) and had postseason surgery in 2002 to clean up scar tissue. His stuff, however, is undeniable. Hanson has a quick, strong arm and runs his fastball up to 95 mph. He pitches in the 92-94 range with explosive movement at times. His curveball is a power offering, thrown in the mid-80s, and has helped him average nearly a strikeout per inning as pro. If Hanson stays healthy, he has a chance to move up to low Class A with other members of Auburn's talented staff, such as Brandon League, David Bush and Sandy Nin.

Year	Club (League)	Class	W	L	ERA	G	GS	CG	SV	IP	H	R	ER	HR	BB	SO	AVG
1999	Medicine Hat (Pio)	R	1	2	5.32	14	7	0	0	46	64	33	27	1	21	35	.335
2000	Medicine Hat (Pio)	R	7	3	5.81	15	15	0	0	79	82	55	51	6	29	79	.262
2001						Did Not Play—Injured											
2002	Auburn (NY-P)	A	5	2	1.68	9	9	0	0	48	35	11	9	4	11	51	.203
MINOR LEAGUE TOTALS			13	7	4.53	38	31	0	0	173	181	99	87	11	61	165	.268

19. Tyrell Godwin, of

Born: July 10, 1979. **Ht.:** 6-0. **Wt.:** 200. **Bats:** L. **Throws:** R. **School:** University of North Carolina. **Career Transactions:** Selected by Blue Jays in third round of 2001 draft; signed July 2, 2001.

Godwin's background, which includes turning down the Yankees as their first-round pick in 1997, has been well-documented. Originally a two-sport athlete at North Carolina, he dropped football (where his highlight was a 100-yard kickoff return for a touchdown against Stanford) to concentrate on baseball. Drafted again as a supplemental first-rounder by the Rangers in 2000, he never signed after a physical revealed a pre-existing right knee injury. Instead of returning for his senior season at North Carolina, Godwin finished his degree in the fall (he was on a full academic scholarship) and sat out the spring, rehabbing his knee after reconstructive surgery. After signing with the Jays, he had an explosive debut, but tempered hopes with an injury-plagued followup in 2002. Shoulder and hamstring injuries kept him in extended spring training for most of April, and his season ended June 28 when he broke his hand sliding headfirst into home. Godwin made improvements, steadily strengthening his arm—though it's still below-average, making a move to left field necessary—and gaining better control of the strike zone. He still has excellent bat speed and some power potential. His speed and hitting ability lead to comparisons to former Braves first baseman Gerald Perry. But Godwin must stay healthy and show what he can do over a full season.

Year	Club (League)	Class	AVG	G	AB	R	H	2B	3B	HR	RBI	BB	SO	SB	SLG	OBP
2001	Auburn (NY-P)	A	.368	33	117	26	43	8	2	2	15	19	27	9	.521	.464
2002	Charleston, WV (SAL)	A	.281	48	185	31	52	8	5	0	16	20	23	10	.378	.364
MINOR LEAGUE TOTALS			.315	81	302	57	95	16	7	2	31	39	50	19	.434	.403

20. Tracy Thorpe, rhp

Born: Dec. 15, 1980. **Ht.:** 6-4. **Wt.:** 250. **Bats:** R. **Throws:** R. **School:** Melbourne (Fla.) HS. **Career Transactions:** Selected by Blue Jays in 11th round of 2000 draft; signed June 12, 2000.

A former Central Florida football recruit likened to Daunte Culpepper because of his size and arm strength, Thorpe played in the 2002 South Atlantic League all-star game, teaming with Francisco Rosario and Dustin McGowan to give Charleston three dynamic power pitchers. He was named the organization's man of the year for his off-field contributions while with Charleston. He became heavily involved in a school program in Charleston, reading to school children at schools and libraries, taking kids to the mall or out to lunch, and meeting with them before and after games at the ballpark. In short, Thorpe was having a breakthrough 2002 season. But it all came crashing down in June, when Thorpe injured his shoulder. He had surgery in August to repair two tears in his labrum and may not pitch in 2003. His upside was evident before the injury, though. Thorpe was touching 98 mph with his fastball and regularly gassing hitters with a 93-97 heater that was just wild enough to be effective. He also was starting to throw more consistent strikes with his curveball and changeup, and had toyed with a split-finger fastball. Thorpe was pursuing his rehabilitation program aggressively and hoped to be healthy enough to start soft tossing again in spring training.

Year	Club (League)	Class	W	L	ERA	G	GS	CG	SV	IP	H	R	ER	HR	BB	SO	AVG
2000	Medicine Hat (Pio)	R	0	4	8.54	11	6	0	0	26	28	28	25	3	17	15	.275
2001	Charleston, WV (SAL)	A	4	13	5.08	24	23	0	0	103	108	77	58	8	51	81	.271
2002	Charleston, WV (SAL)	A	5	7	4.18	20	19	1	0	103	96	55	48	6	31	70	.242
MINOR LEAGUE TOTALS			9	24	5.07	55	48	1	0	232	232	160	131	17	99	166	.259

21. Mike Smith, rhp

Born: Sept. 19, 1977. **Ht.:** 5-11. **Wt.:** 190. **Bats:** R. **Throws:** R. **School:** University of Richmond. **Career Transactions:** Selected by Blue Jays in fifth round of 2000 draft; signed June 15, 2000.

Like GM J.P. Ricciardi, Smith is a Massachusetts native. He played in Boston's Yawkey Baseball League as a youngster, and his sister is the daughter-in-law of former Red Sox president John Harrington. Smith played both ways at Richmond, often sharing time in the outfield with his twin brother Rich. He homered in his first college at-bat but soon settled on pitching and reached the big leagues within two years of signing with Toronto. However, his limitations started to show in the big leagues. Smith has one speed: fast. He throws a 92-95 mph fastball and a power slider in the high 80s, enough to handle Triple-A in his first try but not enough to get by as a starter in the big leagues. He has yet to master a changeup or anything else offspeed, and his lack of height keeps him from getting good leverage on his fastball. His power repertoire and competitiveness help him profile as a setup man. The Jays will give him at least one more look as a starter before moving him to the bullpen.

Year	Club (League)	Class	W	L	ERA	G	GS	CG	SV	IP	H	R	ER	HR	BB	SO	AVG
2000	Queens (NY-P)	A	2	2	2.29	14	12	0	0	51	41	18	13	1	17	55	.224
2001	Charleston, WV (SAL)	A	5	5	2.10	14	14	2	0	94	78	32	22	2	21	85	.224
	Tennessee (SL)	AA	6	2	2.42	14	14	1	0	93	80	32	25	7	26	77	.226
2002	Syracuse (IL)	AAA	8	4	3.48	20	20	1	0	122	106	51	47	10	43	76	.233
	Toronto (AL)	MAJ	0	3	6.62	14	6	0	0	35	43	28	26	3	20	16	.301
MAJOR LEAGUE TOTALS			0	3	6.62	14	6	0	0	35	43	28	26	3	20	16	.301
MINOR LEAGUE TOTALS			21	13	2.68	62	60	4	0	360	305	133	107	20	107	293	.228

22. Shawn Fagan, 1b/3b

Born: March 2, 1978. **Ht.:** 5-11. **Wt.:** 200. **Bats:** R. **Throws:** R. **School:** Penn State University. **Career Transactions:** Selected by Blue Jays in 13th round of 2000 draft; signed June 13, 2000.

One of the best players in Penn State history, Fagan excelled as a third baseman/closer and led the Nittany Lions to the NCAA super-regional round in 2000. He led the Big 10 Conference in RBIs that year as a senior after setting Penn State's single-season saves record as a sophomore with seven. The Blue Jays drafted him for his bat and he has delivered, improving at every level. Fagan has an advanced knowledge of the strike zone, showing an ability to lay off pitcher's pitches and working counts to his advantage, waiting for a fastball to crush. His 102 walks led the organization and surely grabbed the attention of Ricciardi, an on-base fanatic. An avid weight trainer, Fagan has gotten bulkier and stronger since signing and his power is now considered average. His swing, work ethic and versatility—he has played both corner spots and will see time in left field in spring training—have some in the organization comparing him to Greg Colbrunn. Fagan, who threw in the low 90s as a college closer, has lost some arm strength and flexibility as he has gotten thicker, and he doesn't have the arm or range to be an everyday third baseman anymore. He'll move up to Triple-A, where he'll again have to prove himself because of his average tools.

Year	Club (League)	Class	AVG	G	AB	R	H	2B	3B	HR	RBI	BB	SO	SB	SLG	OBP
2000	Queens (NY-P)	A	.289	25	90	17	26	6	1	2	13	12	22	0	.444	.387
	Hagerstown (SAL)	A	.279	45	172	20	48	8	1	2	23	18	28	5	.372	.351
2001	Dunedin (FSL)	A	.301	132	475	68	143	18	5	10	71	86	114	7	.423	.407
2002	Tennessee (SL)	AA	.268	127	421	71	113	24	0	12	69	102	87	6	.411	.411
MINOR LEAGUE TOTALS			.285	329	1158	176	330	56	7	26	176	218	251	18	.413	.399

23. Justin Maureau, lhp

Born: Dec. 17, 1980. **Ht.:** 6-1. **Wt.:** 170. **Bats:** R. **Throws:** L. **School:** Wichita State University. **Career Transactions:** Selected by Blue Jays in third round of 2002 draft; signed June 25, 2002.

Maureau was a seventh-round pick out of high school by the Diamondbacks after a decorated prep career in which he set the Colorado career strikeout record. He continued to be a strikeout pitcher at Wichita State, where he struck out 253 in 221 career innings. Maureau did it with a fastball in the 88-90 mph range, good changeup and one of the best curveballs in college baseball. He brought the same package to the Blue Jays and had a dominant debut as a reliever for Auburn, missing bats consistently and showing excellent command of all three pitches. The biggest questions surrounding Maureau are his future role and his durability. His slight build led even the Shockers to use him out of the bullpen quite a bit as a junior, and he excelled in that role in the Cape Cod League in 2001. Maureau's ability to throw his plus curve, which has excellent depth and bite, for consistent strikes and his lack of durability make him a perfect candidate to be a lefthanded reliever, and he could move quickly in that role. As a lefty with three plus pitches, though, expect Maureau to at least get a chance in a starting role, perhaps in high Class A in his first full pro season.

Year	Club (League)	Class	W	L	ERA	G	GS	CG	SV	IP	H	R	ER	HR	BB	SO	AVG
2002	Auburn (NY-P)	A	0	0	1.44	22	0	0	8	44	24	10	7	1	12	51	.158
MINOR LEAGUE TOTALS			0	0	1.44	22	0	0	8	44	24	10	7	1	12	51	.158

24. Sandy Nin, rhp

Born: Aug. 13, 1980. **Ht.:** 6-0. **Wt.:** 170. **Bats:** R. **Throws:** R. **Career Transactions:** Signed out of Dominican Republic by Blue Jays, July 11, 2000.

Known as Antonio Nin when he led the Dominican Summer League in victories and ranked fourth in strikeouts in 2001, Nin had a successful U.S. debut in 2002. His stuff was almost pedestrian by Auburn's staff standards, but like Brandon League, Dave Bush, Chad Pleiness, Adam Peterson, Vince Perkins and latecomer Juan Perez, Nin runs his fastball into the 90s. He sits in the 93-95 mph range and has an effective power slider. He generates explosive drive toward the plate thanks to strong legs and a thick torso. Nin was aggressive with his power stuff and also showed the makings of a decent changeup. Considering his age and it was his first year in the States, Nin maintained his composure well and made good adjustments. The biggest questions for him now concern experience, command of his fastball and changeup, and his ability to stay on top of his pitches. At his size, Nin always will have to work hard to keep his fastball from flattening out.

Year	Club (League)	Class	W	L	ERA	G	GS	CG	SV	IP	H	R	ER	HR	BB	SO	AVG
2001	Blue Jays (DSL)	R	11	1	1.12	14	14	3	0	97	70	23	12	1	19	105	.194
2002	Blue Jays (DSL)	R	2	0	1.25	3	2	1	0	22	10	4	3	2	1	25	.132
	Auburn (NY-P)	A	4	4	2.92	17	11	0	2	74	61	29	24	3	11	61	.225
MINOR LEAGUE TOTALS			17	5	1.82	34	27	4	2	193	141	56	39	6	31	191	.199

25. Jason Perry, 1b

Born: Aug. 18, 1980. **Ht.:** 6-0. **Wt.:** 200. **Bats:** L. **Throws:** R. **School:** Georgia Tech. **Career Transactions:** Selected by Blue Jays in sixth round of 2002 draft; signed June 22, 2002.

Part of the reason that teams like the Athletics and now the Blue Jays draft college players is because they have more of a track record than high school players. Perry has a track record for success and for hitting for power that includes a productive career at Georgia Tech, where he helped the Yellow Jackets reach the 2002 College World Series. He also put together an impressive résumé with wood bats, batting .287 and leading the Cape Cod League with eight home runs in 2001. Perry struggled with a bad ankle sprain during the 2002 college season, which contributed to him falling to the sixth round, but had one of the best minor league debuts among drafted players. He tore up the Rookie-level Pioneer League and held his own after a promotion to high Class A, thanks to a short, strong swing and good plate discipline. Perry's bat would play even more if he can handle left field, where he spent some time in college. He has a decent arm and may have the range for the position, though his ankle injury limited him to three games in the outfield after he signed. Perry should start 2003 back at Dunedin.

Year	Club (League)	Class	AVG	G	AB	R	H	2B	3B	HR	RBI	BB	SO	SB	SLG	OBP
2002	Medicine Hat (Pio)	R	.425	30	106	25	45	6	2	10	36	12	19	0	.802	.508
	Dunedin (FSL)	A	.289	13	45	7	13	3	0	1	5	5	11	0	.422	.389
MINOR LEAGUE TOTALS			.384	43	151	32	58	9	2	11	41	17	30	0	.689	.472

26. Manuel Mayorson, ss

Born: March 10, 1983. **Ht.:** 5-10. **Wt.:** 160. **Bats:** R. **Throws:** R. **Career Transactions:** Signed out of Dominican Republic by Blue Jays, July 5, 1999.

For Mayorson, the climb up the prospect charts may be an arduous one. One of Latin American coordinator Tony Arias' many signees in the organization, Mayorson predates the J.P. Ricciardi era. The new general manager figures to de-emphasize Latin American scouting because of the difficulty of establishing a track record for players and because it takes a while for prospects like Mayorson, a toolsy middle infielder, to develop. Defense always will be his calling card. He has natural shortstop actions, showing the arm and instincts for shortstop. But his supporters in the organization point out that considering his age and background, Mayorson had a solid 2002 season with the bat. He hit .163 in April but .296 thereafter. He'll never have much power and needs better plate discipline, but Mayorson also proved tough to strike out and ran the bases well, though he can improve on reading pitchers and getting jumps on stolen bases. A move up to high Class A is in order, where he may split time between second base and shortstop with first-round pick Russ Adams.

Year	Club (League)	Class	AVG	G	AB	R	H	2B	3B	HR	RBI	BB	SO	SB	SLG	OBP
2000	Medicine Hat (Pio)	R	.220	56	218	39	48	2	1	0	12	33	27	3	.239	.325
2001	Charleston, WV (SAL)	A	.000	1	2	0	0	0	0	0	0	0	1	0	.000	.000
	Dunedin (FSL)	A	.189	18	37	6	7	0	0	0	2	2	2	0	.189	.231
	Auburn (NY-P)	A	.263	62	247	28	65	5	0	0	18	21	19	25	.283	.325
2002	Charleston, WV (SAL)	A	.274	133	508	72	139	19	1	0	45	31	29	28	.315	.316
MINOR LEAGUE TOTALS			.256	270	1012	145	259	26	2	0	77	87	78	56	.286	.317

27. Mike Snyder, 1b

Born: Feb. 11, 1981. **Ht.:** 6-5. **Wt.:** 230. **Bats:** L. **Throws:** R. **School:** Ayala HS, Chino Hills, Calif. **Career Transactions:** Selected by Blue Jays in second round of 1999 draft; signed June 10, 1999.

On the verge of being considered a bust, Snyder had a breakthrough season in 2002, earning South Atlantic League all-star honors. After entering the season with a career .225 average and just 16 homers in 1,002 at-bats, he led Charleston in home runs and RBIs and ranked third in the Sally League in hits. Snyder's size led to his move from third base, the position he played in high school, across the diamond to first, and he had yet to translate his raw power into games prior to last season. His improved patience at the plate helped unlock his power. A sharp player who has started to pick up the nuances of the game, Snyder simply overpowers mistakes and has become more aggressive while at the same time increasing his walk rate. He wasn't placed on the 40-man roster after the season, but that could change in 2003 if he has another productive season. Lefthanded hitters with his raw power usually get several chances, and Snyder has earned at least one more.

Year	Club (League)	Class	AVG	G	AB	R	H	2B	3B	HR	RBI	BB	SO	SB	SLG	OBP
1999	Medicine Hat (Pio)	R	.209	62	196	30	41	7	0	3	19	31	47	3	.291	.320
2000	Hagerstown (SAL)	A	.182	54	165	26	30	8	1	1	13	32	48	4	.261	.318
	Queens (NY-P)	A	.278	57	227	28	63	11	3	4	34	22	49	4	.405	.343
2001	Charleston, WV (SAL)	A	.220	119	414	47	91	18	2	8	45	40	101	12	.331	.290
2002	Charleston, WV (SAL)	A	.286	136	518	67	148	21	4	16	87	76	107	5	.434	.378
MINOR LEAGUE TOTALS			.245	428	1520	198	373	65	10	32	198	201	352	28	.364	.335

28. Jordan DeJong, rhp

Born: April 12, 1979. **Ht.:** 6-2. **Wt.:** 170. **Bats:** R. **Throws:** R. **School:** Cal State Fullerton. **Career Transactions:** Selected by Blue Jays in 18th round of 2002 draft; signed June 4, 2002.

DeJong was out of baseball in 2001. He had struggled in his first two seasons at Cal State Fullerton and got knocked around after transferring to Tennessee in 2000. The Volunteers cut his scholarship and DeJong returned home to Southern California, returning to class at Fullerton but turning down an offer to return to the baseball team. In the fall of 2001, though, Titans assistant Dave Serrano convinced him to give baseball one last try, and DeJong did so with spectacular success. He tied for second in the Big West Conference with 11 victories last spring and got drafted in the 18th round, then overmatched hitters in his professional debut. A few mechanical adjustments pushed DeJong's fastball to 90-92 mph, and he varied his arm angles to run his fastball in on lefthanders. He also throws an overhand curve, tight slider and solid changeup, all average pitches that he can command. He repeats his delivery and competes well, giving him a chance to join the bigger names and stronger arms from the 2002 Auburn staff in Charleston's 2003 rotation.

Year	Club (League)	Class	W	L	ERA	G	GS	CG	SV	IP	H	R	ER	HR	BB	SO	AVG
2002	Medicine Hat (Pio)	R	6	1	1.43	33	0	0	16	44	23	10	7	1	10	62	.149
	Auburn (NY-P)	A	1	0	0.00	2	0	0	0	4	0	0	0	0	0	1	3	.000
MINOR LEAGUE TOTALS			7	1	1.30	35	0	0	16	48	23	10	7	1	11	65	.139

29. Eric Stephenson, lhp

Born: Sept. 3, 1982. **Ht.:** 6-4. **Wt.:** 180. **Bats:** R. **Throws:** L. **School:** Triton HS, Erwin, N.C. **Career Transactions:** Selected by Blue Jays in 15th round of 2000 draft; signed June 14, 2000.

Stephenson entered 2002 as one of the organization's better-regarded lefthanders but struggled to live up to billing on a talented Charleston rotation. His father Earl pitched in the big leagues, and it's not too late for Stephenson to do the same. He still has good stuff, starting with an 88-92 mph fastball. He's learning to command the pitch and needs to throw it more and rely less on his above-average curveball. His curve is one of the better breaking balls in the organization, but Stephenson needs to be more aggressive with the pitch and stop nibbling. That got him into trouble both in falling behind hitters and in lacking the efficiency to pitch deep into games. With more maturity, Stephenson will pitch inside more and realize that while his curve is a power pitch, his fastball is too. He could return to low Class A or earn a promotion to high Class A with a good spring-training showing.

Year	Club (League)	Class	W	L	ERA	G	GS	CG	SV	IP	H	R	ER	HR	BB	SO	AVG
2000	Medicine Hat (Pio)	R	1	1	8.33	19	0	0	0	27	41	28	25	2	13	21	.353
2001	Auburn (NY-P)	A	3	6	4.04	15	14	0	0	78	80	45	35	7	44	62	.272
2002	Charleston, WV (SAL)	A	6	12	4.32	23	23	0	0	127	143	80	61	6	56	70	.290
MINOR LEAGUE TOTALS			10	19	4.69	57	37	0	0	232	264	153	121	15	113	153	.292

30. John Wesley, rhp

Born: Oct. 14, 1980. **Ht.:** 6-6. **Wt.:** 230. **Bats:** R. **Throws:** R. **School:** University of South Carolina. **Career Transactions:** Signed as nondrafted free agent by Blue Jays, June 25, 2002.

Wesley's size and fastball made him an intriguing signing, much to the chagrin of South Carolina coaches who viewed him as their 2003 closer. His injury-plagued background helps explain why a big righthander with a dominating 96 mph fastball didn't get drafted. An accomplished auto mechanic, Wesley spent one year at Brevard (Fla.) Junior College (which no longer has a program) before joining the Gamecocks, where he overcame a knee injury to earn three saves as a sophomore. He got a medical redshirt in 2001, when he had arm problems stemming from looseness in his shoulder. His 2002 season also was affected, as he came back too soon from offseason surgery to tighten his shoulder capsule and didn't pitch from early March until mid-May. When he returned, he had lost his closer job but worked himself back into game shape and pitched critical, effective innings in regional and super-regional play. He threw in a dominating relief effort in the College World Series against Nebraska to further entice the Blue Jays. Wesley is yet another mid-90s arm if he can hold up, and Toronto plans to use him strictly in a relief role as he gets into better shape. His fastball has good life, and he also throws a curveball and good splitter. He uses his size and fastball to change planes well at the top and bottom of the strike zone.

Year	Club (League)	Class	W	L	ERA	G	GS	CG	SV	IP	H	R	ER	HR	BB	SO	AVG
2002	Medicine Hat (Pio)	R	3	0	1.88	19	0	0	2	29	21	12	6	1	8	38	.194
MINOR LEAGUE TOTALS			3	0	1.88	19	0	0	2	29	21	12	6	1	8	38	.194

Signing Bonuses

EVOLUTION OF THE BONUS RECORD
Domestic Players Only

Pre-Draft Record

Year	Team, Player, Pos., School	Bonus
1964	Angels. Rick Reichart, of, Wisconsin	$205,000

Draft Era Record

Year	Team, Player, Pos., School, Round	Bonus
1965	Athletics. Rick Monday, of, Arizona State (1)	$104,000
1966	Phillies. Steve Arlin, rhp, Ohio State (1/secondary)	105,000
1973	Rangers. David Clyde, lhp, HS—Houston (1)	125,000
1975	Angels. Danny Goodwin, c, Southern (1)	125,000
1978	Braves. Bob Horner, 3b, Arizona State (1)	175,000
	Tigers. Kirk Gibson, of, Michigan State (1)	200,000
1988	Padres. Andy Benes, rhp, Evansville (1)	235,000
1989	Braves. Tyler Houston, c, HS—Las Vegas (1)	241,000
	Orioles. #Ben McDonald, rhp, Louisiana State (1)	350,000
	Blue Jays. John Olerud, 1b, Washington State (3)	575,000
1991	Braves. Mike Kelly, of, Arizona State (1)	575,000
	Yankees. Brien Taylor, lhp, HS—Beaufort, N.C. (1)	1,550,000
1994	Mets. Paul Wilson, rhp, Florida State (1)	1,550,000
	Marlins. Josh Booty, 3b, HS—Shreveport, La. (1)	1,600,000
1996	Pirates. Kris Benson, rhp, Clemson (1)	2,000,000
	*Diamondbacks. Travis Lee, 1b, San Diego State U. (1)	10,000,000
	*Devil Rays. Matt White, rhp, HS—Chambersburg, Pa. (1)	10,200,000

Round indicated in parentheses.

*Declared free agent on contract tendering technicality.

#Signed major league contract (For players signed to major league contracts, the amount is only the stated bonus in the contract. For players signed to standard minor league contracts, the amount is the full compensation to be paid out over the life of the contract.).

LARGEST BONUSES IN DRAFT HISTORY
For players signing with the team that drafted them

Rank	Club, Year. Player, Pos., School	Bonus
1.	White Sox, 2000. Joe Borchard, of, Stanford	$5,300,000
2.	Twins, 2001. Joe Mauer, c, HS—St. Paul	5,150,000
3.	Devil Rays, 2002. B.J. Upton, ss, HS—Chesapeake, Va.	4,600,000
4.	Rangers, 2001. #Mark Teixeira, 3b, Georgia Tech	4,500,000
5.	Devil Rays, 2001. #Dewon Brazelton, rhp, Middle Tennessee State	4,200,000
	Phillies, 2001. Gavin Floyd, rhp, HS—Severna Park, Md.	4,200,000
7.	Cubs, 2001. #Mark Prior, rhp, Southern California	4,000,000
	Pirates, 2002. Bryan Bullington, rhp, Ball State	4,000,000
9.	Devil Rays, 1999. Josh Hamilton, of, HS—Raleigh, N.C.	3,960,000
10.	Cubs, 1998. Corey Patterson, of, HS—Kennesaw, Ga.	3,700,000
11.	Marlins, 1999. #Josh Beckett, rhp, HS—Spring, Texas	3,625,000
12.	Tigers, 1999. #Eric Munson, c, Southern California	3,500,000
13.	Athletics, 1998. Mark Mulder, lhp, Michigan State	3,200,000
14.	Phillies, 1998. #Pat Burrell, 1b, Miami	3,150,000
15.	Cardinals, 1998. #J.D. Drew, of, St. Paul/Northern	3,000,000
	Marlins, 2000. Adrian Gonzalez, 1b, HS—Chula Vista, Calif.	3,000,000
	Indians, 2002. #Jeremy Guthrie, rhp, Stanford	3,000,000
18.	Expos, 2000. Justin Wayne, rhp, Stanford	2,950,000
19.	Twins, 1999. B.J. Garbe, of, HS—Moses Lake, Wash.	2,750,000
	Cubs, 2000. Luis Montanez, ss, HS—Miami	2,750,000
	Rockies, 2000. Jason Young, rhp, Stanford	2,750,000

#Signed major league contract (For players signed to major league contracts, the amount is only the stated bonus in the contract. For players signed to standard minor league contracts, the amount is the full compensation to be paid out over the life of the contract).

Signing Bonuses
TOP 100 PICKS, 2002 DRAFT

FIRST ROUND

Order, Player, Pos.	Bonus
1. Pirates. Bryan Bullington, rhp	$4,000,000
2. Devil Rays. B.J. Upton, ss	4,600,000
3. Reds. Chris Gruler, rhp	2,500,000
4. Orioles. Adam Loewen, lhp	Unsigned
5. Expos. Clint Everts, rhp	2,500,000
6. Royals. Zack Greinke, rhp	2,475,000
7. Brewers. Prince Fielder, 1b	2,400,000
8. Tigers. Scott Moore, ss	2,300,000
9. Rockies. Jeff Francis, lhp	1,850,000
10. Rangers. Drew Meyer, ss	1,875,000
11. Marlins. Jeremy Hermida, of	2,012,500
12. Angels. Joe Saunders, lhp	1,825,000
13. Padres. Khalil Greene, ss	1,500,000
14. Blue Jays. Russ Adams, ss	1,785,000
15. Mets. Scott Kazmir, lhp	2,150,000
16. Athletics. Nick Swisher, of	1,780,000
17. Phillies. Cole Hamels, lhp	2,000,000
18. White Sox. Royce Ring, lhp	1,600,000
19. Dodgers. James Loney, 1b	1,500,000
20. Twins. Denard Span, of	1,700,000
21. Cubs. Bobby Brownlie, rhp	Unsigned
22. Indians. Jeremy Guthrie, rhp	3,000,000
23. Braves. Jeff Francoeur, rhp	2,200,000
24. Athletics. Joseph Blanton, rhp	1,400,000
25. Giants. Matt Cain, rhp	1,375,000
26. Athletics. John McCurdy, ss	1,375,000
27. Diamondbacks. Sergio Santos, ss	1,400,000
28. Mariners. John Mayberry Jr., of	Did not sign
29. Astros. Derick Grigsby, rhp	1,125,000
30. Athletics. Ben Fritz, rhp, Fresno State	1,200,000

SUPPLEMENTAL FIRST-ROUND

31. Dodgers. Greg Miller, lhp	1,200,000
32. Cubs. Luke Hagerty, lhp	1,150,000
33. Indians. Matt Whitney, 3b	1,125,000
34. Braves. Dan Meyer, lhp	1,000,000
35. Athletics. Jeremy Brown, c	350,000
36. Cubs. Chadd Blasko, rhp	1,050,000
37. Athletics. Steve Obenchain, rhp	750,000
38. Cubs. Matt Clanton, rhp	875,000
39. Athletics. Mark Teahen, 3b	725,000
40. Reds. Mark Schramek, 3b	200,000
41. Indians. Micah Schilling, 2b	915,000

SECOND ROUND

42. Pirates. Blair Johnson, rhp	885,000
43. Devil Rays. Jason Pridie, of	892,500
44. Reds. Joey Votto, c	600,000
45. Orioles. Corey Shafer, of	800,000
46. Expos. Darrell Rasner, rhp	800,000
47. Royals. Adam Donachie, c	800,000
48. Brewers. Josh Murray, ss	825,000
49. Tigers. Brent Clevlen, of	805,000

50. Rockies. Micah Owings, rhp	Did not sign
51. Dodgers. Zach Hammes, rhp	750,000
52. Marlins. Robert Andino, ss	750,000
53. Angels. Kevin Jepsen, rhp	745,000
54. Padres. Michael Johnson, 1b	Did not sign
55. Blue Jays. David Bush, rhp	450,000
56. Cubs. Brian Dopirak, 1b	740,000
57. Red Sox. Jon Lester, lhp	1,000,000
58. Phillies. Zach Segovia, rhp	712,500
59. White Sox. Jeremy Reed, of	650,000
60. Dodgers. Jonathan Broxton, rhp	685,000
61. Twins. Jesse Crain, rhp	650,000
62. Cubs. Justin Jones, lhp	625,000
63. Indians. Brian Slocum, rhp	625,000
64. Braves. Brian McCann, c	750,000
65. Braves. Tyler Greene, ss	Did not sign
66. Giants. Fred Lewis, of	595,000
67. Athletics. Steve Stanley, of	200,000
68. Diamondbacks. Chris Snyder, c	567,000
69. Mariners. Josh Womack, of	550,000
70. Astros. Mitch Talbot, rhp	550,000
71. Yankees. Brandon Weeden, rhp	565,000

SUPPLEMENTAL SECOND-ROUND

72. Indians. Pat Osborn, 3b	547,500

THIRD ROUND

73. Pirates. Taber Lee, ss	525,000
74. Devil Rays. Elijah Dukes, of	500,000
75. Reds. Kyle Edens, rhp	300,000
76. Orioles. Val Majewski, of	400,000
77. Expos. Larry Broadway, 1b	450,000
78. Royals. David Jensen, 1b	472,500
79. Brewers. Eric Thomas, rhp	470,000
80. Tigers. Curtis Granderson, of	469,000
81. Rockies. Ben Crockett, rhp	345,000
82. Indians. Jason Cooper, of	472,500
83. Marlins. Trevor Hutchinson, rhp	Unsigned
84. Angels. Kyle Pawelczyk, rhp	465,000
85. Padres. Kennard Jones, of	465,000
86. Blue Jays. Justin Maureau, lhp	455,000
87. Tigers. Matt Pender, rhp	450,000
88. Red Sox. Scott White, 3b	825,000
89. Phillies. Kiel Fisher, 3b	450,000
90. White Sox. Josh Rupe, rhp	440,000
91. Dodgers. Mike Nixon, c	950,000
92. Twins. Mark Sauls, rhp	Did not sign
93. Cubs. Billy Petrick, rhp	459,500
94. Indians. Daniel Cevette, lhp	400,000
95. Braves. Charlie Morton, rhp	415,000
96. Cubs. Matt Craig, ss	399,000
97. Giants. Dan Ortmeier, of	396,000
98. Athletics. Bill Murphy, lhp	410,000
99. Diamondbacks. Jared Doyle, lhp	390,000
100. Mariners. Eddy Martinez-Esteve, of	Did not sign

Signing Bonuses

TOP 100 PICKS, 2001 DRAFT

FIRST ROUND

Order. Player, Pos.	Bonus
1. Twins. Joe Mauer, c	$5,150,000
2. Cubs. Mark Prior, rhp	4,000,000
3. Devil Rays. Dewon Brazelton, rhp,	4,000,000
4. Phillies. Gavin Floyd, rhp	4,200,000
5. Rangers. Mark Teixeira, 3b	4,500,000
6. Expos. Josh Karp, rhp	2,650,000
7. Orioles. Chris Smith, lhp	2,175,000
8. Pirates. John VanBenschoten, rhp/1b	2,400,000
9. Royals. Colt Griffin, rhp	2,400,000
10. Astros. Chris Burke, 2b/ss	2,100,000
11. Tigers. Kenny Baugh, rhp	1,800,000
12. Brewers. Mike Jones, rhp	2,075,000
13. Angels. Casey Kotchman, 1b	2,075,000
14. Padres. Jake Gautreau, 3b	1,875,000
15. Blue Jays. Gabe Gross, of	1,865,000
16. White Sox. Kris Honel, rhp	1,500,000
17. Indians. Dan Denham, rhp	1,860,000
18. Mets. Aaron Heilman, rhp	1,508,750
19. Orioles. Mike Fontenot, 2b	1,300,000
20. Reds. Jeremy Sowers, lhp	Did not sign
21. Giants. Brad Hennessey, rhp	1,382,500
22. Diamondbacks. Jason Bulger, rhp	938,600
23. Yankees. John-Ford Griffin, of	1,200,000
24. Braves. Macay McBride, lhp	1,340,000
25. Athletics. Bobby Crosby, ss	1,350,000
26. Athletics. Jeremy Bonderman, rhp	1,350,000
27. Indians. Alan Horne, rhp	Did not sign
28. Cardinals. Justin Pope, rhp	900,000
29. Braves. Josh Burrus, ss	1,250,000
30. Giants. Noah Lowry, lhp	1,175,000

SUPPLEMENTAL FIRST ROUND

31. Orioles. Bryan Bass, ss	1,150,000
32. Tigers. Michael Woods, 2b	1,100,000
33. Angels. Jeff Mathis, c	850,000
34. Yankees. Bronson Sardinha, ss	1,000,000
35. Indians. J.D. Martin, rhp	975,000
36. Mariners. Michael Garciaparra, ss	2,000,000
37. Athletics. John Rheinecker, lhp	600,000
38. Mets. David Wright, 3b	960,000
39. White Sox. Wyatt Allen, rhp	872,500
40. Braves. Richard Lewis, 2b	850,000
41. Giants. Todd Linden, of	750,000
42. Yankees. Jon Skaggs, rhp	600,000
43. Indians. Michael Conroy, of	870,000
44. Rockies. Jayson Nix, ss	925,000

SECOND ROUND

45. Twins. Scott Tyler, rhp	875,000
46. Cubs. Andy Sisco, lhp	1,000,000
47. Devil Rays. Jon Switzer, lhp	850,000
48. Red Sox. Kelly Shoppach, c	737,500
49. Mariners. Rene Rivera, c	688,000
50. Expos. Donald Levinski, rhp	825,000
51. Indians. Jake Dittler, rhp	750,000
52. Braves. J.P. Howell, lhp	Did not sign
53. Royals. Roscoe Crosby, of	1,750,000
54. Astros. Mike Rodriguez, of	675,000
55. Tigers. Preston Larrison, rhp	685,000
56. Brewers. J.J. Hardy, ss	735,000
57. Angels. Dallas McPherson, 3b	660,000
58. Padres. Matt Harrington, rhp	Did not sign
59. Blue Jays. Brandon League, rhp	660,000
60. Marlins. Garrett Berger, rhp	795,000
61. Red Sox. Matt Chico, lhp	Did not sign
62. Yankees. Shelley Duncan, of	655,000
63. Yankees. Jason Arnold, rhp	400,000
64. Reds. Justin Gillman, rhp	625,000
65. Tigers. Matt Coenen, lhp	620,000
66. Diamondbacks. Mike Gosling, lhp	2,000,000
67. Mariners. Michael Wilson, of	900,000
68. Dodgers. Brian Pilkington, rhp	600,000
69. Athletics. Neal Cotts, lhp	525,000
70. Mets. Alhaji Turay, of	517,500
71. White Sox. Ryan Wing, lhp	575,000
72. Cardinals. Dan Haren, rhp	530,000
73. Braves. Cole Barthel, 3b	475,000
74. Giants. Jesse Foppert, rhp	520,000

SUPPLEMENTAL SECOND ROUND

75. Rockies. Trey Taylor, lhp	Did not sign
76. Mets. Corey Ragsdale, ss	480,000

THIRD ROUND

77. Twins. Jose Morales, ss	490,000
78. Cubs. Ryan Theriot, ss	485,000
79. Devil Rays. Chris Flynn, rhp	466,000
80. Mariners. Lazaro Abreu, c	400,000
81. Angels. Steven Shell, rhp	460,000
82. Expos. Mike Hinckley, lhp	425,000
83. Orioles. Dave Crouthers, rhp	425,000
84. Pirates. Jeremy Guthrie, rhp	Did not sign
85. Royals. Matt Ferrara, 3b	450,000
86. Astros. Kirk Saarloos, rhp	300,000
87. Tigers. Jack Hannahan, 3b	435,000
88. Brewers. Jon Steitz, rhp	460,000
89. Angels. Jacob Woods, lhp	442,500
90. Padres. Taggert Bozeid, 1b-3b	700,000
91. Blue Jays. Tyrell Godwin, of	480,000
92. Marlins. Allen Baxter, rhp	450,000
93. Red Sox. Jonathan DeVries, c	450,000
94. Rockies. Jason Frome, of	420,000
95. Yankees. Chase Wright, lhp	400,000
96. Reds. Alan Moye, of	400,000
97. Indians. Nick Moran, rhp	400,000
98. Diamondbacks. Scott Hairston, 2b	400,000
99. Mariners. Tim Merritt, ss	400,000
100. Dodgers. David Taylor, rhp	385,000

Signing Bonuses
TOP 100 PICKS, 2000 DRAFT

FIRST ROUND

Order. Player, Pos.	Bonus
1. Marlins. Adrian Gonzalez, 1b	$3,000,000
2. Twins. Adam Johnson, rhp	2,500,000
3. Cubs. Luis Montanez, ss	2,750,000
4. Royals. Mike Stodolka, lhp	2,500,000
5. Expos. Justin Wayne, rhp	2,950,000
6. Devil Rays. Rocco Baldelli, of	2,250,000
7. Rockies. Matt Harrington, rhp	Did not sign
8. Tigers. Matt Wheatland, rhp	2,150,000
9. Padres. Mark Phillips, lhp	2,200,000
10. Angels. Joe Torres, lhp	2,080,000
11. Brewers. David Krynzel, of	1,950,000
12. White Sox. Joe Borchard, of	5,300,000
13. Cardinals. Shaun Boyd, of	1,750,000
14. Orioles. Beau Hale, rhp	2,250,000
15. Phillies. Chase Utley, 2b	1,780,000
16. Mets. Billy Traber, lhp	400,000
17. Dodgers. Ben Diggins, rhp	2,200,000
18. Blue Jays. Miguel Negron, of	950,000
19. Pirates. Sean Burnett, lhp	1,650,000
20. Angels. Chris Bootcheck, rhp	1,800,000
21. Giants. Boof Bonser, rhp	1,245,000
22. Red Sox. Phil Dumatrait, lhp	1,275,000
23. Reds. David Espinosa, ss	None
24. Cardinals. Blake Williams, rhp	1,375,000
25. Rangers. Scott Heard, c	1,475,000
26. Indians. Corey Smith, ss	1,375,000
27. Astros. Robert Stiehl, rhp	1,250,000
28. Yankees. David Parrish, c	1,425,000
29. Braves. Adam Wainwright, rhp	1,250,000
30. Braves. Scott Thorman, 3b	1,225,000

SUPPLEMENTAL FIRST ROUND

31. Twins. Aaron Heilman, rhp	Did not sign
32. Orioles. Tripper Johnson, rhp	1,050,000
33. Blue Jays. Dustin McGowan, rhp	950,000
34. Reds. Dustin Moseley, rhp	930,000
35. Rangers. Tyrell Godwin, of	Did not sign
36. Mets. Bob Keppel, rhp	895,000
37. Indians. Derek Thompson, lhp	850,000
38. Braves. Kelly Johnson, ss	790,000
39. Rangers. Chad Hawkins, rhp	625,000
40. Braves. Aaron Herr, ss	850,000

SECOND ROUND

41. Marlins. Jason Stokes, 1b	2,027,000
42. Twins. Taggert Bozied, 1b	Did not sign
43. Cubs. Bobby Hill, ss	1,425,000
44. Royals. Mike Tonis, c	800,000
45. Blue Jays. Peter Bauer, rhp	800,000
46. Reds. Dane Sardinha, c	None
47. Rockies. Jason Young, rhp	2,750,000
48. Tigers. Chad Petty, lhp	600,000

49. Padres. Xavier Nady, 3b	1,100,000
50. Angels. Jared Abruzzo, c	687,500
51. Braves. Kenny Nelson, rhp	675,000
52. White Sox. Tim Hummel, ss	645,000
53. Cardinals. Chris Narveson, lhp	675,000
54. Twins. J.D. Durbin, rhp	722,500
55. Indians. Brian Tallet, lhp	595,000
56. Rangers. Jason Bourgeois, ss	621,000
57. Dodgers. Joel Hanrahan, rhp	615,000
58. Blue Jays. Dominic Rich, 2b	600,000
59. Pirates. David Beigh, rhp	635,000
60. Athletics. Freddie Bynum, ss	495,000
61. Giants. Lance Niekro, 3b	655,000
62. Red Sox. Manny Delcarmen, rhp	700,000
63. Reds. Ryan Snare, lhp	595,000
64. Rangers. Randy Truselo, rhp	600,000
65. Mets. Matt Peterson, rhp	575,000
66. Indians. Mark Folsom, of	700,000
67. Astros. Chad Qualls, rhp	415,000
68. Yankees. Danny Borrell, lhp	600,000
69. Diamondbacks. Mike Schultz, rhp	500,000
70. Braves. Bryan Digby, rhp	450,000

THIRD ROUND

71. Marlins. Rob Henkel, lhp	650,000
72. Twins. Colby Miller, rhp	480,000
73. Cubs. Aaron Krawiec, lhp	450,000
74. Royals. Scott Walter, c	447,500
75. Expos. Grady Sizemore, of	2,000,000
76. Cubs. Nic Jackson, of	425,000
77. Rockies. Chris Buglovsky, rhp	410,000
78. Tigers. Exavier Logan, ss	450,000
79. Padres. Omar Falcon, c	425,000
80. Angels. Tommy Murphy, ss	440,000
81. Brewers. Dane Artman, lhp	475,000
82. White Sox. Mike Morse, ss	365,000
83. Cardinals. Chase Voshell, ss	430,000
84. Orioles. Richard Bartlett, rhp	455,000
85. Phillies. Keith Bucktrot, rhp	435,000
86. Orioles. Tommy Arko, c	400,000
87. Dodgers. Jeff Tibbs, rhp	440,000
88. Blue Jays. Morrin Davis, of	440,000
89. Pirates. Chris Young, rhp	1,650,000
90. Athletics. Daylan Holt, of	450,000
91. Giants. Brion Treadway, rhp	410,000
92. Red Sox. Matt Cooper, 1b	400,000
93. Reds. David Gil, rhp	160,000
94. Rangers. Chris Russ, lhp	407,500
95. Mets. Josh Reynolds, rhp	400,000
96. Indians. Sean Swedlow, c	450,000
97. Astros. Anthony Pluta, rhp	450,000
98. Yankees. Jason Grove, of	400,000
99. Diamondbacks. Bill White, lhp	387,500
100. Braves. Blaine Boyer, rhp	375,000

College Class of 2003
TOP 100 DRAFT PROSPECTS

Rank	Player, Pos.	College	Hometown	Class	B-T	Ht.	Wt.	Last Drafted
1	Rickie Weeks, 2b	Southern	Altamonte Springs, Fla.	Jr.	R-R	5-11	195	Never drafted
2	Kyle Sleeth, rhp	Wake Forest	Westminster, Colo.	Jr.	R-R	6-5	185	Orioles '00 (18)
3	Brad Sullivan, rhp	Houston	Nederland, Texas	Jr.	R-R	6-1	190	Never drafted
4	Tim Stauffer, rhp	Richmond	Saratoga Springs, N.Y.	Jr.	R-R	6-2	205	Orioles '00 (36)
5	Michael Aubrey, of	Tulane	Shreveport, La.	Jr.	L-L	6-0	180	Never drafted
6	David Aardsma, rhp	Rice	Englewood, Colo.	Jr.	R-R	6-5	190	Never drafted
7	Landon Powell, c	South Carolina	Apex, N.C.	Jr.	B-R	6-3	225	Never drafted
8	Matt Murton, of	Georgia Tech	McDonough, Ga.	Jr.	R-R	6-1	214	Never drafted
9	Paul Maholm, lhp	Mississippi State	Holly Springs, Miss.	Jr.	L-L	6-3	214	Twins '00 (17)
10	Kyle Bakker, lhp	Georgia Tech	Omaha	Jr.	L-L	6-9	255	Phillies '00 (37)
11	Wes Littleton, rhp	Cal State Fullerton	Oceanside, Calif.	Jr.	R-R	6-3	200	Expos '00 (7)
12	Anthony Gwynn, of	San Diego State	Poway, Calif.	Jr.	L-L	6-0	185	Braves '00 (33)
13	Bob Zimmermann, rhp	SW Missouri State	Creve Coeur, Mo.	Jr.	R-R	6-5	225	Rockies '00 (14)
14	Carlos Quentin, of	Stanford	Chula Vista, Calif.	Jr.	R-R	6-2	215	Never drafted
15	Aaron Hill, ss/3b	Louisiana State	Visalia, Calif.	Jr.	R-R	6-0	200	Angels '00 (7)
16	David Purcey, lhp	Oklahoma	Addison, Texas	So.	L-L	6-5	235	Mariners '01 (20)
17	Conor Jackson, 3b/1b	California	Woodland Hills, Calif.	Jr.	R-R	6-3	190	Indians '00 (31)
18	Tony Richie, c	Florida State	Jacksonville, Fla.	Jr.	R-R	6-1	215	White Sox '00 (5)
19	Anthony Reyes, rhp	Southern California	Whittier, Calif.	Sr.	R-R	6-1	200	Tigers '02 (13)
20	Chris Ray, rhp	William & Mary	Tampa	Jr.	R-R	6-3	190	Never drafted
21	Matt Brown, rhp	California	Danville, Calif.	Jr.	R-R	6-5	220	Never drafted
22	Michael Johnson, 1b	Clemson	Georgetown, S.C.	Sr.	L-R	6-4	220	Padres '02 (2)
23	Javi Herrera, c	Tennessee	Miami	Jr.	R-R	6-2	195	Red Sox '00 (42)
24	Tim Moss, 2b	Texas	Lancaster, Texas	Jr.	R-R	5-11	177	Never drafted
25	Michael Bourn, of	Houston	Humble, Texas	Jr.	L-R	5-11	170	Astros '00 (19)
26	Scott Baker, rhp	Oklahoma State	Shreveport, La.	Jr.	R-R	6-4	190	Pirates '00 (36)
27	Ben Harrison, of	Florida	Key West, Fla.	Jr.	R-R	6-3	190	Never drafted
28	Vince Sinisi, 1b	Rice	The Woodlands, Texas	So.	L-L	6-0	195	Never drafted
29	Chad Cordero, rhp	Cal State Fullerton	Chino, Calif.	Jr.	R-R	6-1	195	Padres '00 (26)
30	Brian Wilson, rhp	Louisiana State	Londonderry, N.H.	Jr.	R-R	6-1	205	Indians '00 (30)
31	Shane Costa, of	Cal State Fullerton	Visalia, Calif.	Jr.	L-L	6-1	200	Devil Rays '00 (37)
32	Lee Mitchell, 3b	Georgia	Silver Creek, Ga.	Jr.	R-R	6-0	196	Never drafted
33	Daniel Moore, lhp	North Carolina	Spencer, N.C.	Jr.	R-L	6-5	205	Marlins '00 (23)
34	Jamie D'Antona, 3b	Wake Forest	Trumbull, Conn.	Jr.	R-R	6-2	205	Never drafted
35	Chad Corona, 3b	San Diego State	Carlsbad, Calif.	Jr.	R-R	6-3	208	Cubs '00 (16)
36	Sam Fuld, of	Stanford	Durham, N.H.	Jr.	L-L	5-10	180	Never drafted
37	Javon Moran, of	Auburn	Valdosta, Ga.	Jr.	R-R	5-11	174	Never drafted
38	Mitch Maier, c	Toledo	Novi, Mich.	Jr.	R-R	6-2	190	Never drafted
39	Rod Allen, of	Arizona State	Phoenix	Jr.	R-R	6-1	199	Reds '00 (34)
40	Matt Macri, ss	Notre Dame	Clive, Iowa	So.	R-R	6-1	185	Twins '01 (17)
41	Josh Banks, rhp	Fla. International	Arnold, Md.	Jr.	R-R	6-3	195	Orioles '00 (34)
42	Ryan Schroyer, rhp	Arizona State	Oracle, Ariz.	Jr.	R-R	6-2	216	Tigers '00 (16)
43	David Murphy, of	Baylor	Spring, Texas	Jr.	L-L	6-4	185	Angels '00 (50)
44	Matt Farnum, rhp	Texas A&M	Littleton, Colo.	Jr.	R-R	6-1	185	Blue Jays '02 (24)
45	Brian Snyder, 3b/2b	Stetson	Wellington, Fla.	Jr.	R-R	6-0	190	Never drafted
46	Clark Girardeau, rhp	South Alabama	Mobile, Ala.	Jr.	R-R	6-5	210	Never drafted

47	Abe Alvarez, lhp	Long Beach State	Fontana, Calif.	Jr.	L-L	6-3	185	Never drafted
48	Steven White, rhp	Baylor	League City, Texas	Sr.	R-R	6-4	195	Brewers '02 (18)
49	Michael Hollimon, ss	Texas	Dallas	So.	B-R	6-1	176	Dodgers '01 (32)
50	Myron Leslie, 3b	South Florida	Valrico, Fla.	Jr.	B-R	6-4	213	Rangers '00 (14)
51	Peter Stonard, 2b/of	San Diego State	Clayton, Mo.	Jr.	L-L	6-1	180	Yankees '01 (41)
52	Todd Nicholas, lhp	Mississippi State	Greenville, Ala.	So.	R-L	6-3	216	Mets '00 (22)
53	Robbie Van, lhp	Nevada-Las Vegas	Las Vegas, Nev.	Jr.	L-L	6-2	210	Never drafted
54	Colt Morton, c	North Carolina State	West Palm Beach, Fla.	Jr.	R-R	6-5	227	Devil Rays '00 (36)
55	Josh Smith, rhp	Texas	McGregor, Texas	Jr.	R-R	6-4	220	Yankees '01 (18)
56	Darric Merrell, rhp	Cal State Fullerton	Temecula, Calif.	Jr.	R-R	6-4	210	Yankees '00 (20)
57	Michael Moon, 2b-3b	Southern California	Alta Loma, Calif.	Jr.	L-R	6-0	205	Never drafted
58	Chris Pillsbury, rhp	Florida Atlantic	Jacksonville, Fla.	Jr.	R-R	6-4	194	Rangers '00 (37)
59	Frazer Dizard, lhp	Southern California	Edmonds, Wash.	Jr.	L-L	6-0	195	Orioles '00 (21)
60	Marc Kaiser, rhp/dh	Lewis-Clark State	Reno, Nev.	Jr.	R-R	6-1	185	Reds '00 (4)
61	Jim Brauer, rhp	Michigan	Carmel, Ind.	Jr.	R-R	6-4	192	Expos '00 (29)
62	Mateo Miramontes, rhp	Nevada	Pleasanton, Calif.	Jr.	R-R	6-4	190	Never drafted
63	Trey Webb, ss	Baylor	Mansfield, Texas	Jr.	B-R	5-11	160	Never drafted
64	Chris Snavely, 2b/of	Ohio State	Defiance, Ohio	Jr.	L-R	6-2	200	Never drafted
65	Steve Herce, rhp	Rice	Houston	Sr.	R-R	6-3	220	Rangers '02 (9)
66	Justin Hoyman, rhp	Florida	Melbourne, Fla.	So.	R-R	6-4	160	Rockies '02 (43)
67	Dennis Dove, rhp	Georgia Southern	Ocilla, Ga.	Jr.	R-R	6-3	205	Never drafted
68	Matt Foster, lhp	Navy	Ventura, Calif.	Sr.	L-L	6-3	205	Never
69	Aaron Marsden, lhp	Nebraska	Grand Forks, N.D.	Jr.	L-L	6-6	220	Indians '01 (34)
70	Brad Snyder, of	Ball State	Bellevue, Ohio	Jr.	L-R	6-3	190	Never drafted
71	Steven Jackson, rhp	Clemson	Summerville, S.C.	Jr.	R-R	6-5	195	Devil Rays '00 (38)
72	Christian Colonel, ss	Texas Tech	American Falls, Idaho	Jr.	R-R	6-2	200	Mets '02 (9)
73	Jeff Leise, of	Nebraska	Omaha	Sr.	L-L	5-11	165	Angels '02 (7)
74	Brian Barton, of	Miami (Fla.)	Los Angeles	So.	R-R	6-3	180	Dodgers '00 (38)
75	Logan Kensing, rhp	Texas A&M	Boerne, Texas	So.	R-R	6-1	185	Never drafted
76	Tim Cunningham, lhp	Stanford	Rocklin, Calif.	Sr.	L-L	6-3	190	Braves '02 (23)
77	Travis NeSmith, lhp	Florida Atlantic	Miami	Jr.	L-L	6-3	200	White Sox '00 (25)
78	Matt Lynch, lhp	Florida State	Fort Pierce, Fla.	Sr.	L-L	6-2	190	Padres '02 (7)
79	Jon Papelbon, rhp	Mississippi State	Jacksonville, Fla.	Jr.	R-R	6-3	232	Never drafted
80	Thomas Pauly, rhp	Princeton	Atlantic Beach, Fla.	Jr.	R-R	6-2	180	Never drafted
81	Rene Recio, rhp	Oral Roberts	Corpus Christi, Texas	Jr.	R-R	6-3	190	Never drafted
82	Brian Marshall, lhp	Va. Commonwealth	Chesterfield, Va.	Jr.	L-L	6-5	185	Never drafted
83	Shane Hawk, lhp	Oklahoma State	Midwest City, Okla.	Jr.	L-L	6-4	180	Braves '00 (41)
84	Andre Ethier, of	Arizona State	Phoenix	Jr.	L-L	6-3	175	Athletics '01 (37)
85	Tila Reynolds, ss	Washington	Renton, Wash.	Sr.	R-R	5-11	175	Brewers '02 (13)
86	Pat Misch, lhp	Western Michigan	Northbrook, Ill.	Sr.	R-L	6-2	170	Astros '02 (5)
87	Rob McCrory, rhp	Southern Mississippi	Columbus, Miss.	Jr.	R-R	6-0	205	Astros '00 (11)
88	Tom Oldham, lhp	Creighton	Fremont, Neb.	Jr.	L-L	6-2	210	Never drafted
89	Danny Zell, lhp	Houston	Houston	Jr.	L-L	6-5	210	Royals '01 (15)
90	John Hudgins, rhp	Stanford	Mission Viejo, Calif.	Jr.	R-R	6-2	200	Athletics '00 (20)
91	David Marchbanks, lhp	South Carolina	Simpsonville, S.C.	Jr.	L-L	6-3	202	Angels '00 (40)
92	Josh Anderson, of	Eastern Kentucky	Eubank, Ky.	Jr.	L-R	6-2	190	Never drafted
93	Brian Bannister, rhp	Southern California	Paradise Valley, Ariz.	Jr.	R-R	6-1	205	Red Sox '02 (45)
94	Josh Baker, rhp	Rice	Houston	So.	R-R	6-5	210	Rangers '01 (4)
95	Justin Simmons, lhp	Texas	DeSoto, Texas	Jr.	L-L	6-3	210	Never drafted
96	Ryan Goleski, of	Eastern Michigan	Lake Orion, Mich.	Jr.	R-R	6-3	220	Never drafted
97	Robert Ransom, rhp	Vanderbilt	Atlanta	Jr.	R-R	6-3	225	Never drafted
98	Casey McGehee, 3b	Fresno State	Aptos, Calif.	Jr.	R-R	6-1	186	Never drafted
99	T.J. Beam, rhp	Mississippi	Scottsdale, Ariz.	Sr.	R-R	6-7	215	Phillies '02 (11)
100	Ryan Mulhern, of	South Alabama	Highlands Ranch, Colo.	Sr.	R-R	6-2	200	Cardinals '02 (19)

Compiled by Allan Simpson.

NOTE: List does not include junior college players who remain under control to teams that drafted them in 2002.

High School Class of 2003
TOP 100 DRAFT PROSPECTS

Rank, Player, Pos.	High School	Hometown	B-T	HT	WT	Commitment
1 Delmon Young, of	Camarillo HS	Camarillo, Calif.	R-R	6-3	205	Arizona
2 Lastings Milledge, of	Lakewood Ranch HS	Sarasota, Fla.	R-R	6-0	185	
3 Andrew Miller, lhp	Buchholz HS	Gainesville, Fla.	L-L	6-6	192	North Carolina
4 Jared Hughes, rhp	Santa Margarita HS	Laguna Niguel, Calif.	R-R	6-6	220	Santa Clara
5 Chris Lubanski, of	Kennedy-Kenrick Catholic HS	Schwenksville, Pa.	L-L	6-3	180	Florida State
6 Ryan Harvey, of/rhp	Dunedin HS	Palm Harbor, Fla.	R-R	6-5	196	Florida
7 Jeff Allison, rhp	Veterans Memorial HS	Peabody, Mass.	R-R	6-2	195	Arizona
8 Chad Billingsley, rhp	Defiance HS	Defiance, Ohio	B-R	6-2	200	South Carolina
9 Jay Sborz, rhp	Langley HS	Great Falls, Va.	R-R	6-4	200	Arizona State
10 Ryan Sweeney, lhp/of	Xavier HS	Cedar Rapids, Iowa	L-L	6-5	200	San Diego State
11 James Houser, lhp/1b	Sarasota HS	Sarasota, Fla.	L-L	6-5	180	Florida
12 Craig Whitaker, rhp	Lufkin HS	Lufkin, Texas	R-R	6-4	180	Texas A&M
13 Jonathan Fulton, ss	George Washington HS	Danville, Va.	R-R	6-4	200	Virginia Tech
14 Jeff Manship, rhp	Ronald Reagan HS	San Antonio, Texas	R-R	6-1	165	Notre Dame
15 Colin Curtis, of	Issaquah HS	Sammamish, Wash.	L-L	6-0	190	Arizona State
16 Jarrod Saltalamacchia, c	Royal Palm Beach HS	West Palm Beach, Fla.	B-R	6-4	190	Florida State
17 Ryan Smith, rhp	Enumclaw HS	Enumclaw, Wash.	R-R	6-4	195	Arizona State
18 Robert Lane, 3b/rhp	Neville HS	Monroe, La.	R-R	6-4	215	Louisiana State
19 Drew Stubbs, of	Atlanta HS	Atlanta, Texas	R-R	6-3	185	Texas
20 John Danks, lhp	Round Rock HS	Round Rock, Texas	L-L	6-2	175	Texas
21 Ian Stewart, 3b	La Quinta HS	Garden Grove, Calif.	L-R	6-2	195	Southern California
22 Sean Rodriguez, of	Coral Park HS	Miami, Fla.	R-R	6-0	170	Florida International
23 Adam Hale, lhp/of	Bellaire HS	Houston, Texas	L-L	6-3	195	Rice
24 Scott Maine, lhp	Dwyer HS	Palm Beach Gardens, Fla.	L-L	6-3	170	Miami
25 Chuck Tiffany, lhp	Charter Oak HS	Covina, Calif.	L-L	6-1	205	Cal State Fullerton
26 Justin Brashear, c	Barbe HS	Lake Charles, La.	L-R	6-3	200	Mississippi
27 Jimmy Barthmaier, rhp	Roswell HS	Roswell, Ga.	R-R	6-4	210	
28 Cain Byrd, hp	Southwood HS	Shreveport, La.	R-R	6-3	185	Louisiana State
29 Andy D'Alessio, 1b/3b	Barron Collier HS	Naples, Fla.	L-R	6-4	195	Clemson
30 Ian Kennedy, rhp	LaQuinta HS	Garden Grove, Calif.	R-R	5-11	195	Southern California
31 Brennan Boesch, 1b/of	Harvard-Westlake HS	Los Angeles, Calif.	L-L	6-3	195	California
32 Robert Valido, ss	Coral Park HS	Miami, Fla.	R-R	6-1	175	Florida International
33 Michael Rogers, of/lhp	Del City HS	Del City, Okla.	L-L	5-10	160	Texas
34 Daric Barton, c	Marina HS	Huntington Beach, Calif.	L-R	5-11	195	Cal State Fullerton
35 Eric Duncan, 3b	Seton Hall Prep	Florham Park, N.J.	L-R	6-2	195	Louisiana State
36 Richie Lentz, rhp/of	Woodinville HS	Woodinville, Wash.	R-R	6-2	200	Washington
37 Daniel Bard, rhp	Charlotte Christian Academy	Charlotte, N.C.	R-R	6-3	175	North Carolina
38 Adam Jones, ss	Morse HS	San Diego, Calif.	R-R	6-1	180	San Diego State
39 Matt Moses, 3b/of	Mills Godwin HS	Richmond, Va.	L-R	6-1	205	Clemson
40 Philip Stringer, ss	Klein Oak HS	Spring, Texas	R-R	5-9	170	Tulane
41 Doug Frame, lhp	Tomball HS	Tomball, Texas	L-L	6-4	210	Texas A&M
42 Cory Van Allen, lhp	Clements HS	Sugar Land, Texas	L-L	6-2	170	Baylor
43 Jo Jo Reyes, lhp/1b	Poly HS	Riverside, Calif.	L-L	6-2	215	Southern California
44 Xavier Paul, of/rhp	Slidell HS	New Orleans, La.	L-R	5-10	195	Tulane
45 C.J. Bressoud, c	North Cobb HS	Kennesaw, Ga.	R-R	6-1	185	Alabama
46 Mickey Hall, of	Walton HS	Marietta, Ga.	B-R	6-0	175	Georgia Tech

47	Ryan Feierabend, lhp	Midview HS	Grafton, Ohio	L-L	6-3	190	
48	Miguel Vega, 3b	Carmen B. Huyke HS	Arroyo, P.R.	R-R	6-3	207	
49	Adam Miller, rhp	McKinney HS	McKinney, Texas	R-R	6-4	180	Arizona
50	Donald Veal, lhp	Buena HS	Hereford, Ariz.	L-L	6-2	185	Arizona
51	Lance Zawadzki, ss	St. John's Prep	Ashland, Mass.	B-R	5-11	180	Louisiana State
52	Tim Battle, of/rhp	McIntosh, HS	Peachtree City, Ga.	R-R	6-1	185	
53	Jordan Mayer, rhp/3b	Alexandria HS	Alexandria, La.	R-R	6-3	215	Louisiana State
54	Quentin Andes, rhp	Cibola HS	Albuquerque, N.M.	R-R	6-2	185	Arizona State
55	Chris Perez, rhp	Manatee HS	Holmes Beach, Fla.	R-R	6-4	245	Miami
56	Brandon Wood, ss	Horizon HS	Scottsdale, Ariz.	R-R	6-2	175	Texas
57	Kyle McCulloch, inf/rhp	Bellaire HS	Houston, Texas	R-R	6-2	170	Texas
58	Daniel Perales, of	Mater Dei HS	Anaheim Hills, Calif.	L-R	6-0	175	Southern California
59	Dennis Dixon, of	San Leandro HS	San Leandro, Calif.	R-R	6-3	185	Oregon
60	Jacob Stevens, lhp/1b	Cape Coral HS	Cape Coral, Fla.	L-L	6-3	215	Miami
61	Brad Depoy, rhp	The Woodlands HS	The Woodlands, Texas	R-R	6-1	195	Houston
62	Matthew Pike, rhp	Centennial HS	Pueblo, Colo.	R-R	6-6	190	Nebraska
63	Derik Olvey, rhp	Pelham HS	Pelham, Ala.	R-R	6-4	215	Notre Dame
64	Blair Erickson, rhp	Jesuit HS	Fair Oaks, Calif.	R-R	6-1	195	UC Irvine
65	Emeel Salem, of	Mountain Brook HS	Birmingham, Ala.	L-L	6-0	165	Alabama
66	Greg Reynolds, rhp	Terra Nova HS	Pacifica, Calif.	R-R	6-5	200	
67	Charles Benoit, lhp	Carroll HS	Southlake, Texas	L-L	6-2	225	Oklahoma
68	David Shinskie, rhp	Mt. Carmel Area HS	Kulpmont, Pa.	R-R	6-4	190	Delaware
69	Tim Gustafson, rhp/inf	Parkview HS	Lilburn, Ga.	R-R	6-3	185	Georgia Tech
70	Brant Rustich, rhp	Grossmont HS	El Cajon, Calif.	R-R	6-6	215	UCLA
71	Patrick Bresnehan, rhp	Dover-Sherborn HS	Sherborn, Mass.	R-R	6-1	190	Arizona State
72	Mark Krampitz, rhp	Sealy HS	Sealy, Texas	R-R	6-1	185	Rice
73	Sean Henry, inf	Armijo HS	Suisun City, Calif.	R-R	6-0	170	San Diego State
74	Jeremy Laster, of	Hunters Lane HS	Nashville, Tenn.	R-R	6-1	185	
75	Chris Worster, rhp	Dwyer HS	Palm Beach Gardens, Fla.	R-R	6-3	185	Tulane
76	Jason Donald, ss	Buchanan HS	Clovis, Calif.	R-R	6-1	185	Arizona
77	David Winfree, c/3b	First Colonial HS	Virginia Beach, Va.	R-R	6-2	195	Clemson
78	Scott Leffler, c	Dunedin HS	St. Petersburg, Fla.	R-R	6-2	175	North Carolina State
79	Bryan Opdyke, c	Catalina Foothills HS	Tucson, Ariz.	L-R	6-2	195	Arizona
80	Adrian Alaniz, of/rhp	Sinton HS	Sinton, Texas	R-R	6-2	190	Texas
81	David Cash, ss	Northside Christian HS	Odessa, Fla.	B-R	6-3	170	South Carolina
82	Alex Boston, of	Bartow HS	Bartow, Fla.	R-R	6-2	225	Florida State
83	Ryne Malone, 2b	P. K. Yonge HS	Gainesville, Fla.	L-R	6-0	175	Florida State
84	Asher Demme, rhp	South Lakes HS	Reston, Va.	R-R	6-2	195	
85	Darin Downs, lhp	Santaluces HS	Boynton Beach, Fla.	L-L	6-3	170	South Carolina
86	Dylan Gonzalez, rhp	American Heritage HS	Weston, Fla.	B-R	6-3	176	Florida
87	Paul Bacot, rhp	Lakeside HS	Atlanta, Ga.	R-R	6-5	190	Georgia
88	Jose Ronda, ss	Gabriela Mistral HS	San Juan, P.R.	B-R	6-1	170	
89	Patrick Freeman, rhp	Key West HS	Key West, Fla.	R-R	6-2	190	Miami
90	Jason Smith, rhp	Bourne HS	Bourne, Mass.	R-R	6-3	190	South Florida
91	Kenny Lewis, of	George Washington HS	Danville, Va.	L-L	5-9	180	Virginia Tech
92	Dallas Buck, rhp	Newberg HS	Newberg, Ore.	R-R	6-2	190	
93	Matt Nachreiner, rhp	Round Rock HS	Cedar Park, Texas	R-R	6-2	175	Arizona
94	Robert Coello, rhp	Lake Region HS	Winter Haven, Fla.	R-R	6-5	210	South Florida
95	Brett Lawler, 1b/of	A&M Consolidated HS	College Station, Texas	R-R	6-3	205	Arkansas
96	Brandon Rauch, of	El Capitan HS	El Cajon, Calif.	R-R	6-2	220	San Diego State
97	D.J. Lewis, c/of	San Fernando HS	North Hollywood, Calif.	R-R	6-0	190	
98	Ryan Marion, rhp	Glenn HS	Kernersville, N.C.	R-R	6-2	185	
99	Eddy Rodriguez, c	Coral Gables HS	Miami, Fla.	R-R	6-1	195	Miami
100	Andy Mudd, of	Scotland HS	Laurinburg, N.C.	L-R	6-3	185	

Compiled by Allan Simpson.

Minor League
TOP 20 PROSPECTS

A s a complement to our organizational prospect rankings, Baseball America also ranks prospects in every minor league right after each season. Like the organizational lists, they place more weight on potential than present performance and should not be regarded as minor league all-star teams.

The league lists do differ a little bit from the organizational lists, which are taken more from a scouting perspective. The league lists are based on conversations with league managers. They are not strictly polls, though we do try to talk with every manager. Some players on these lists, such as Carl Crawford and Sean Burroughs, were not eligible for our organization prospect lists because they are no longer rookie-eligible. Such players are indicated with an asterisk (*). Players who have been traded from the organizations they are listed with are indicated with a pound sign (#).

Remember that managers and scouts tend to look at players differently. Managers give more weight to what a player does on the field, while scouts look at what a player might eventually do. We think both perspectives are useful, so we give you both even though they don't always jibe with each other.

For a player to qualify for a league prospect list, he much have spent at least one-third of the season in a league. Position players must have one plate appearance per league game. Pitchers must pitch ⅓ inning per league game. Relievers must make at least 20 appearances in a full-season league or 10 appearances in a short-season league.

TRIPLE-A
INTERNATIONAL LEAGUE
1. *Carl Crawford, of, Durham (Devil Rays)
2. *Brett Myers, rhp, Scranton/Wilkes-Barre (Phillies)
3. *Orlando Hudson, 2b, Syracuse (Blue Jays)
4. Marlon Byrd, of, Scranton/Wilkes-Barre (Phillies)
5. Brandon Phillips, ss/2b, Buffalo (Indians)
6. *Josh Phelps, c/dh, Syracuse (Blue Jays)
7. Juan Rivera, of, Columbus (Yankees)
8. Joe Borchard, of, Charlotte (White Sox)
9. Eric Munson, 1b, Toledo (Tigers)
10. *Joe Crede, 3b, Charlotte (White Sox)
11. Franklyn German, rhp, Toledo (Tigers)
12. Wilson Betemit, ss, Richmond (Braves)
13. Drew Henson, 3b, Columbus (Yankees)
14. Chase Utley, 2b, Scranton/Wilkes-Barre (Phillies)
15. Brandon Larson, 3b, Louisville (Reds)
16. *Endy Chavez, of, Ottawa (Expos)
17. Omar Infante, ss, Toledo (Tigers)
18. Aaron Heilman, rhp, Norfolk (Mets)
19. *Willie Harris, 2b, Charlotte (White Sox)
20. Josh Bard, c, Buffalo (Indians)

PACIFIC COAST LEAGUE
1. Jesse Foppert, rhp, Fresno (Giants)
2. Michael Cuddyer, of, Edmonton (Twins)
3. *Hank Blalock, 3b, Oklahoma (Rangers)
4. *John Lackey, rhp, Salt Lake (Angels)
5. Michael Restovich, of, Edmonton (Twins)
6. *Sean Burroughs, 2b/3b, Portland (Padres)
7. Colby Lewis, rhp, Oklahoma (Rangers)
8. Hee Seop Choi, 1b, Iowa (Cubs)
9. *Bobby Hill, 2b, Iowa (Cubs)
10. Aaron Cook, rhp, Colorado Springs (Rockies)
11. #Travis Hafner, 1b, Oklahoma (Rangers)
12. Francisco Rodriguez, rhp, Salt Lake (Angels)
13. Kurt Ainsworth, rhp, Fresno (Giants)
14. *Dennis Tankersley, rhp, Portland (Padres)
15. Lyle Overbay, 1b, Tucson (Diamondbacks)
16. Jerome Williams, rhp, Fresno (Giants)
17. Angel Berroa, ss, Omaha (Royals)
18. Jason Young, rhp, Colorado Springs (Rockies)
19. Brad Lidge, rhp, New Orleans (Astros)
20. Joey Thurston, 2b, Las Vegas (Dodgers)

DOUBLE-A
EASTERN LEAGUE
1. Jose Reyes, ss, Binghamton (Mets)
2. #Brandon Phillips, ss, Harrisburg (Expos)
3. Victor Martinez, c, Akron (Indians)
4. Justin Morneau, 1b, New Britain (Twins)
5. Cliff Lee, lhp, Harrisburg/Akron (Expos/Indians)
6. Aaron Heilman, rhp, Binghamton (Mets)
7. Adrian Gonzalez, 1b, Portland (Marlins)
8. Kevin Youkilis, 3b, Trenton (Red Sox)
9. Erik Bedard, lhp, Bowie (Orioles)
10. Freddy Sanchez, ss/2b, Trenton (Red Sox)
11. Jimmy Journell, rhp, New Haven (Cardinals)
12. Billy Traber, lhp, Akron (Indians)
13. Brian Tallet, lhp, Akron (Indians)
14. Ryan Madson, rhp, Reading (Phillies)
15. Danny Borrell, lhp, Norwich (Yankees)
16. Seung Song, rhp, Trenton/Harrisburg (Red Sox/Expos)
17. Josh Karp, rhp, Harrisburg (Expos)
18. Julio DePaula, rhp, Norwich (Yankees)
19. Covelli Crisp, of, New Haven/Akron (Cardinals/Indians)
20. Jesus Medrano, 2b, Portland (Marlins)

SOUTHERN LEAGUE
1. *Jake Peavy, rhp, Mobile (Padres)
2. Aaron Cook, rhp, Carolina (Rockies)
3. Francis Beltran, rhp, West Tennessee (Cubs)
4. Jason Young, rhp, Carolina (Rockies)
5. #Ricardo Rodriguez, rhp, Jacksonville (Dodgers)
6. Miguel Olivo, c, Birmingham (White Sox)
7. Choo Freeman, of, Carolina (Rockies)
8. Vinnie Chulk, rhp, Tennessee (Blue Jays)
9. Ben Hendrickson, rhp, Huntsville (Brewers)
10. *Dennis Tankersley, rhp, Mobile (Padres)
11. Koyie Hill, c, Jacksonville (Dodgers)
12. Dewon Brazelton, rhp, Orlando (Devil Rays)
13. David Kelton, 1b, West Tennessee (Cubs)
14. Corwin Malone, lhp, Birmingham (White Sox)
15. Kevin Cash, c, Tennessee (Blue Jays)
16. #Joe Valentine, rhp, Birmingham (White Sox)
17. Jung Bong, lhp, Greenville (Braves)
18. Wily Mo Pena, of, Chattanooga (Reds)
19. Brett Evert, rhp, Greenville (Braves)
20. Steve Colyer, lhp, Jacksonville (Dodgers)

TEXAS LEAGUE
1. Mark Teixeira, 3b, Tulsa (Rangers)
2. Jesse Foppert, rhp, Shreveport (Giants)
3. Todd Linden, of, Shreveport (Giants)
4. Rafael Soriano, rhp, San Antonio (Mariners)
5. Francisco Rodriguez, rhp, Arkansas (Angels)
6. *Kirk Saarloos, rhp, Round Rock (Astros)
7. Mike Gosling, lhp, El Paso (Diamondbacks)
8. Rich Harden, rhp, Midland (Athletics)
9. Ben Kozlowski, lhp, Tulsa (Rangers)
10. Bobby Jenks, rhp, Arkansas (Angels)
11. *Runelvys Hernandez, rhp, Wichita (Royals)
12. Franklyn German, rhp, Midland (Athletics)
13. Alexis Gomez, of, Wichita (Royals)
14. Chad Tracy, 3b, El Paso (Diamondbacks)
15. Jeremy Hill, rhp, Wichita (Royals)
16. Aaron Taylor, rhp, San Antonio (Mariners)
17. Travis Hughes, rhp, Tulsa (Rangers)
18. John Buck, c, Round Rock (Astros)
19. Jamal Strong, of, San Antonio (Mariners)
20. Gerald Laird, c, Tulsa (Rangers)

HIGH CLASS A
CALIFORNIA LEAGUE
1. Rocco Baldelli, of, Bakersfield (Devil Rays)
2. *Oliver Perez, lhp, Lake Elsinore (Padres)
3. Clint Nageotte, rhp, San Bernardino (Mariners)
4. #Jeremy Bonderman, rhp, Modesto (Athletics)
5. Ben Hendrickson, rhp, High Desert (Brewers)
6. Xavier Nady, dh, Lake Elsinore (Padres)
7. Boof Bonser, rhp, San Jose (Giants)
8. Jose Lopez, ss, San Bernardino (Mariners)
9. Josh Hamilton, of, Bakersfield (Devil Rays)
10. J.J. Hardy, ss, High Desert (Brewers)
11. Dustin Moseley, rhp, Stockton (Reds)
12. Rich Harden, rhp, Visalia (Athletics)
13. Dave Krynzel, of, High Desert (Brewers)
14. Khalil Greene, ss, Lake Elsinore (Padres)
15. Corey Hart, 3b/1b, High Desert (Brewers)
16. Rich Fischer, rhp, Rancho Cucamonga (Angels)
17. Mark Phillips, lhp, Lake Elsinore (Padres)
18. Bobby Jenks, rhp, Rancho Cucamonga (Angels)
19. Travis Blackley, lhp, San Bernardino (Mariners)
20. Jake Gautreau, 2b, Lake Elsinore (Padres)

CAROLINA LEAGUE
1. Sean Burnett, lhp, Lynchburg (Pirates)
2. Jose Castillo, ss, Lynchburg (Pirates)
3. Adam Wainwright, rhp, Myrtle Beach (Braves)
4. Bubba Nelson, rhp, Myrtle Beach (Braves)
5. Chin-Hui Tsao, rhp, Salem (Rockies)
6. Brad Hawpe, 1b, Salem (Rockies)
7. Corey Smith, 3b, Kinston (Indians)
8. Dan Haren, rhp, Potomac (Cardinals)
9. Rhett Parrott, rhp, Potomac (Cardinals)
10. Grady Sizemore, of, Kinston (Indians)
11. Fernando Cabrera, rhp, Kinston (Indians)
12. Adam LaRoche, 1b, Myrtle Beach (Braves)
13. Josh Bonifay, 2b/of, Lynchburg (Pirates)
14. Chris Duffy, of, Lynchburg (Pirates)
15. Ryan Church, of, Kinston (Indians)
16. Daniel Curtis, rhp, Myrtle Beach (Braves)
17. Kelly Johnson, ss, Myrtle Beach (Braves)
18. Byron Gettis, of, Wilmington (Royals)
19. Richard Lewis, 2b, Myrtle Beach (Braves)
20. Skip Schumaker, of, Potomac (Cardinals)

FLORIDA STATE LEAGUE
1. Mark Teixeira, 3b, Charlotte (Rangers)
2. Jose Reyes, ss, St. Lucie (Mets)
3. Francisco Rosario, rhp, Dunedin (Blue Jays)
4. Taylor Buchholz, rhp, Clearwater (Phillies)
5. Miguel Cabrera, 3b, Jupiter (Marlins)
6. Laynce Nix, of, Charlotte (Rangers)
7. Alexis Rios, of, Dunedin (Blue Jays)

8. Joel Hanrahan, rhp, Vero Beach (Dodgers)
9. Ben Kozlowski, lhp, Charlotte (Rangers)
10. Reggie Abercrombie, of, Vero Beach (Dodgers)
11. Angel Guzman, rhp, Daytona (Cubs)
12. Andrew Brown, rhp, Vero Beach (Dodgers)
13. Preston Larrison, rhp, Lakeland (Tigers)
14. #Rob Henkel, lhp, Jupiter (Marlins)
15. Kelly Shoppach, c, Sarasota (Red Sox)
16. Beau Kemp, rhp, Fort Myers (Twins)
17. Kevin Youkilis, 3b, Sarasota (Red Sox)
18. Ruddy Lugo, rhp, Vero Beach (Dodgers)
19. #Jason Arnold, rhp, Tampa (Yankees)
20. Nook Logan, of, Lakeland (Tigers)

LOW CLASS A
MIDWEST LEAGUE
1. Joe Mauer, c, Quad City (Twins)
2. Jason Stokes, 1b, Kane County (Marlins)
3. Dontrelle Willis, lhp, Kane County (Marlins)
4. Donald Levinski, rhp, Clinton (Expos)
5. Brad Nelson, 1b, Beloit (Brewers)
6. Casey Kotchman, 1b, Cedar Rapids (Angels)
7. Scott Hairston, 2b, South Bend (Diamondbacks)
8. Shin-Soo Choo, of, Wisconsin (Mariners)
9. Jeff Mathis, c, Cedar Rapids (Angels)
10. Mike Jones, rhp, Beloit (Brewers)
11. Angel Guzman, rhp, Lansing (Cubs)
12. J.D. Durbin, rhp, Quad City (Twins)
13. Johan Santana, rhp, Cedar Rapids (Angels)
14. Dallas McPherson, 3b, Cedar Rapids (Angels)
15. Edwin Encarnacion, 3b/ss, Dayton (Reds)
16. Dan Haren, rhp, Peoria (Cardinals)
17. Shaun Boyd, 2b, Peoria (Cardinals)
18. Justin Pope, rhp, Peoria (Cardinals)
19. Josh Barfield, 2b, Fort Wayne (Padres)
20. Tyler Johnson, lhp, Peoria (Cardinals)

SOUTH ATLANTIC LEAGUE
1. Gavin Floyd, rhp, Lakewood (Phillies)
2. John VanBenschoten, rhp, Hickory (Pirates)
3. Macay McBride, lhp, Macon (Braves)
4. Andy Marte, 3b, Macon (Braves)
5. Francisco Rosario, rhp, Charleston (Blue Jays)
6. Francisco Liriano, lhp, Hagerstown (Giants)
7. Kris Honel, rhp, Kannapolis (White Sox)
8. #Francisco Cruceta, rhp, South Georgia (Dodgers)
9. Justin Huber, c, Capitol City (Mets)
10. David Wright, 3b, Capital City (Mets)
11. Edwin Jackson, rhp, South Georgia (Dodgers)
12. Carlos Duran, of, Macon (Braves)
13. Ryan Hannaman, lhp, Hagerstown (Giants)
14. Scott Thorman, 1b, Macon (Braves)
15. Walter Young, 1b, Hickory (Pirates)
16. Victor Diaz, 3b/2b, South Georgia (Dodgers)
17. Dustin McGowan, rhp, Charleston (Blue Jays)
18. Seung Lee, rhp, Lakewood (Phillies)
19. Travis Foley, rhp, Columbus (Indians)
20. Phil Dumatrait, lhp, Augusta (Red Sox)

SHORT-SEASON
NEW YORK-PENN LEAGUE
1. Hanley Ramirez, ss, Lowell (Red Sox)
2. Brandon League, rhp, Auburn (Blue Jays)
3. Mike Hinckley, lhp, Vermont (Expos)
4. Bronson Sardinha, of, Staten Island (Yankees)
5. Russ Adams, ss, Auburn (Blue Jays)
6. Chien-Ming Wang, rhp, Staten Island (Yankees)
7. D.J. Hanson, rhp, Auburn (Blue Jays)
8. Carlos Cabrera, rhp, Batavia (Phillies)
9. Alex Hart, rhp, Williamsport (Pirates)
10. Curtis Granderson, of, Oneonta (Tigers)
11. Robinson Cano, 2b, Staten Island (Yankees)
12. Henry Owens, rhp, Williamsport (Pirates)
13. Darrell Rasner, rhp, Vermont (Expos)
14. Josh Shortslef, lhp, Williamsport (Pirates)

15. Sandy Nin, rhp, Auburn (Blue Jays)
16. Chad Pleiness, rhp, Auburn (Blue Jays)
17. Ben Francisco, of, Mahoning Valley (Indians)
18. Brian Slocum, rhp, Mahoing Valley (Indians)
19. Joey Gomes, of, Hudson Valley (Devil Rays)
20. Roberto Novoa, rhp, Williamsport (Pirates)

NORTHWEST LEAGUE
1. Andy Sisco, lhp, Boise (Cubs)
2. Freddie Lewis, of, Salem-Keizer (Giants)
3. Ismael Castro, 2b, Everett (Mariners)
4. Luke Hagerty, lhp, Boise (Cubs)
5. Jae-Kuk Ryu, rhp, Boise (Cubs)
6. Ben Fritz, rhp, Vancouver (Athletics)
7. Steve Obenchain, rhp, Vancouver (Athletics)
8. Jerry Gil, ss, Yakima (Diamondbacks)
9. John McCurdy, ss, Vancouver (Athletics)
10. Travis Ishikawa, 1b, Salem-Keizer (Giants)
11. Marland Williams, of, Yakima (Diamondbacks)
12. Kevin Collins, 1b, Boise (Cubs)
13. Dan Ortmeier, of, Salem-Keizer (Giants)
14. Jon Nelson, 1b, Everett (Mariners)
15. Troy Cate, lhp, Everett (Mariners)
16. Ricky Nolasco, rhp, Boise (Cubs)
17. Jared Doyle, lhp, Yakima (Diamondbacks)
18. Brian Stavisky, of, Vancouver (Athletics)
19. Greg Aquino, rhp, Yakima (Diamondbacks)
20. Jason Fransz, of, Boise (Cubs)

ROOKIE
APPALACHIAN LEAGUE
1. Jeff Francoeur, of, Danville (Braves)
2. Wes Bankston, of, Princeton (Devil Rays)
3. Matt Whitney, 3b, Burlington (Indians)
4. Dusty Gomon, 1b, Elizabethton (Twins)
5. Jason Pridie, of, Princeton (Devil Rays)
6. Anthony Lerew, rhp, Danville (Braves)
7. Blake Hawksworth, rhp, Johnson City (Cardinals)
8. Dan Meyer, lhp, Danville (Braves)
9. Scott Tyler, rhp, Elizabethton (Twins)
10. Anthony Webster, of, Bristol (White Sox)
11. Daniel Cabrera, rhp, Bluefield (Orioles)
12. Luis Jimenez, of/1b, Bluefield (Orioles)
13. Osvaldo Fernando, ss, Martinsville (Astros)
14. Tommy Arko, c, Bluefield (Orioles)
15. Ricky Barrett, lhp, Elizabethton (Twins)
16. Julin Charles, of, Pulaski (Rangers)
17. Josh Rupe, rhp, Bristol (White Sox)
18. Chris de la Cruz, ss, Burlington (Indians)
19. Pedro Lopez, 2b, Bristol (White Sox)
20. Chris O'Riordan, 2b, Pulaski (Rangers)

ARIZONA LEAGUE
1. Felix Pie, of, Cubs
2. Micah Schnurstein, 3b, White Sox
3. Justin Jones, lhp, Cubs
4. Jesse English, lhp, Giants
5. Carlos Sosa, of, Giants
6. Daniel Haigwood, lhp, White Sox

7. Matt Brown, 3b, Angels
8. Travis Ishikawa, 1b, Giants
9. Billy Petrick, rhp, Cubs
10. Ryan Rodriguez, lhp, White Sox
11. Josh Womack, of, Mariners
12. Matt Cain, rhp, Giants
13. Chris Young, of, White Sox
14. Michael Garciaparra, ss, Mariners
15. Matt Creighton, 2b, Cubs
16. Rafael Rodriguez, rhp, Angels
17. Brandon McCarthy, rhp, White Sox
18. Jairo Garcia, rhp, Athletics
19. Steve Moss, of, Brewers
20. Alfredo Francisco, 3b, Cubs

GULF COAST LEAGUE
1. Hanley Ramirez, ss, Red Sox
2. Rudy Guillen, of, Yankees
3. Manuel Mateo, rhp, Braves
4. Leo Nunez, rhp, Pirates
5. Jose Diaz, rhp, Dodgers
6. Elizardo Ramirez, rhp, Phillies
7. Joaquin Arias, 2b, Yankees
8. Alex Romero, of, Twins
9. Luis Hernandez, ss, Braves
10. Brent Clevlen, of, Tigers
11. Javier Guzman, ss, Pirates
12. Victor Prieto, rhp, Marlins
13. Miguel Mota, of, Braves
14. Zach Segovia, rhp, Phillies
15. Joel Zumaya, rhp, Tigers
16. Scott Moore, ss, Tigers
17. Jake Blalock, of/3b, Phillies
18. Dustin Brown, of/c, Red Sox
19. Zach Duke, lhp, Pirates
20. Brian McCann, c, Braves

PIONEER LEAGUE
1. James Loney, 1b, Great Falls (Dodgers)
2. Jonathan Figueroa, lhp, Great Falls (Dodgers)
3. Manny Parra, lhp, Ogden (Brewers)
4. Prince Fielder, 1b, Ogden (Brewers)
5. Sergio Santos, ss, Missoula (Diamondbacks)
6. Alberto Callaspo, 2b, Provo (Angels)
7. Joel Guzman, ss, Great Falls (Dodgers)
8. Joe Saunders, lhp, Prove (Angels)
9. Greg Miller, lhp, Great Falls (Dodgers)
10. Dustin Nippert, rhp, Missoula (Diamondbacks)
11. Jonathan Broxton, rhp, Great Falls (Dodgers)
12. Eric Aybar, ss, Provo (Angels)
13. Ching-Lung Lo, rhp, Casper (Rockies)
14. William Bergolla, 2b, Billings (Reds)
15. Mike Nixon, c, Great Falls (Dodgers)
16. Ryan Shealy, 1b, Casper (Rockies)
17. Danny Mateo, ss, Billings (Reds)
18. Ubaldo Jimenez, rhp, Casper (Rockies)
19. Sean Thompson, lhp, Idaho Falls (Padres)
20. Quan Cosby, of, Provo (Angels)

Winter League
TOP PROSPECTS

These were the Top Prospects for the Arizona Fall League and the four leagues of the Caribbean confederation for the 2002-2003 offseason. The lists are based on discussions with scouts, managers and coaches who worked the leagues this winter, and include only players who have not exceeded the major league rookie standards of 130 at-bats and 50 innings. All the lists were compiled by Josh Boyd.

ARIZONA FALL LEAGUE
1. Mark Teixeira, 3b, Peoria (Rangers)
2. Rocco Baldelli, of, Grand Canyon (Devil Rays)
3. Brandon Phillips, 2b, Phoenix (Indians)
4. Bobby Jenks, rhp, Scottsdale (Angels)
5. Jerome Williams, rhp, Grand Canyon (Giants)
6. Justin Morneau, 1b, Peoria (Twins)
7. Hee Seop Choi, 1b, Mesa (Cubs)
8. Bobby Basham, rhp, Scottsdale (Reds)
9. Ken Harvey, 1b, Scottsdale (Royals)
10. Todd Wellemeyer, rhp, Mesa (Cubs)
11. Scott Hairston, 2b, Scottsdale (Diamondbacks)
12. Corey Hart, 3b, Maryvale (Brewers)
13. Chase Utley, 3b, Grand Canyon (Phillies)
14. Josh Karp, rhp, Maryvale (Expos)
15. Kyle Snyder, rhp, Scottsdale (Royals)
16. Horacio Ramirez, lhp, Grand Canyon (Braves)
17. Todd Linden, of, Grand Canyon (Giants)
18. Mike Gonzalez, lhp, Phoenix (Pirates)
19. Rett Johnson, rhp, Peoria (Mariners)
20. Tagg Bozied, 1b, Peoria (Padres)

DOMINICAN LEAGUE
1. Jose Reyes, ss, Gigantes (Mets)
2. Johan Santana, rhp, Estrellas (Angels)
3. Wilson Betemit, ss, Escogido (Braves)
4. Franklyn German, rhp, Escogido (Tigers)
5. Arnie Munoz, lhp, Aguilas (White Sox)
6. Rafael Soriano, rhp, Escogido (Mariners)
7. Alfredo Gonzalez, rhp, Azucareros (Dodgers)
8. Francis Beltran, rhp, Estrellas (Cubs)
9. Alexis Gomez, of, Aguilas (Royals)
10. Duaner Sanchez, rhp, Gigantes (Pirates)

MEXICAN LEAGUE
1. Edgar Gonzalez, rhp, Hermosillo (Diamondbacks)
2. Nic Jackson, of, Guasave (Cubs)
3. Jorge de la Rosa, lhp, Hermosillo (Red Sox)
4. Oscar Villarreal, rhp, Mexicali (Diamondbacks)
5. Freddy Sanchez, 2b, Navojoa (Red Sox)
6. Luis Garcia, of, Obregon (Indians)
7. David Kelton, 3b, Guasave (Cubs)
8. Alfredo Amezaga, 2b, Obregon (Angels)
9. Robb Quinlan, of, Obregon (Angels)
10. Jason Grabowski, of/1b, Hermosillo (Athletics)

PUERTO RICAN LEAGUE
1. Mike MacDougal, rhp, Mayaguz (Royals)
2. Travis Hafner, 1b, Carolina (Indians)
3. Zach Greinke, rhp, Mayaguez (Royals)
4. Joe Borchard, of, Mayaguez (White Sox)
5. Eric Munson, 1b/3b, Carolina (Tigers)
6. Andy Pratt, lhp, Mayaguez (Braves)
7. Fernando Cabrera, rhp, Ponce (Indians)
8. William Vazquez, rhp, Santurce (Rockies)
9. Javier Lopez, lhp, Santurce (Red Sox)
10. Gabby Martinez, ss, Ponce (Devil Rays)

VENEZUELAN LEAGUE
1. Miguel Cabrera, 3b, Aragua (Marlins)
2. Jose Castillo, ss, Caracas (Pirates)
3. Victor Martinez, c, Oriente (Indians)
4. Lew Ford, of, Aragua (Twins)
5. Alex Herrera, lhp, Oriente (Indians)
6. Beau Kemp, rhp, Aragua (Twins)
7. Rene Reyes, of, Caracas (Rockies)
8. Miguel Pinango, rhp, Magallanes (Mets)
9. Alejandro Machado, 2b/ss, Caracas (Royals)
10. Yoel Hernandez, rhp, Zulia (Phillies)

Index

A

Abercrombie, Reggie (Dodgers) 243
Abruzzo, Jared (Angels) 29
Adamczyk, Tyler (Cardinals) 395
Adams, Mike (Brewers) 266
Adams, Russ (Blue Jays) 485
Ainsworth, Kurt (Giants) 419
Albers, Matt (Astros) 220
Alfaro, Jason (Astros) 221
Allegra, Matt (Athletics) 343
Allen, Luke (Rockies) 171
Allen, Wyatt (White Sox) 123
Almonte, Edwin (White Sox) 122
Almonte, Erick (Yankees) 331
Alvarez, Tony (Pirates) 372
Ambres, Chip (Marlins) 199
Amezaga, Alfredo (Angels) 26
Anderson, Craig (Mariners) 443
Anderson, Jason (Yankees) 329
Anderson, Ryan (Mariners) 441
Anderson, Wes (Marlins) 204
Andino, Robert (Marlins) 201
Aquino, Greg (Diamondbacks) 44
Aramboles, Ricardo (Reds) 133
Arias, Joaquin (Yankees) 328
Arko, Tommy (Orioles) 75
Arnold, Jason (Blue Jays) 484
Arteaga, Erick (Phillies) 360
Atkins, Garrett (Rockies) 167
Asadoorian, Rick (Cardinals) 395
Austin, Jeff (Royals) 234
Axelson, Josh (Cardinals) 395
Aybar, Eric (Angels) 26
Aybar, Willy (Dodgers) 248

B

Baisley, Brad (Phillies) 361
Baker, Brad (Padres) 412
Baker, Jeff (Rockies) 165
Baldelli, Rocco (Devil Rays) 450
Balfour, Grant (Twins) 281
Ballouli, Khalid (Brewers) 269
Bankston, Wes (Devil Rays) 452
Bard, Josh (Indians) 152
Barden, Brian (Diamondbacks) 40
Barfield, Josh (Padres) 405
Barmes, Clint (Rockies) 170
Barnett, John (Rangers) 473
Barrett, Jimmy (Astros) 211
Bartlett, Richard (Orioles) 77
Bartosh, Cliff (Padres) 410
Basham, Bobby (Reds) 131
Bass, Bryan (Orioles) 70
Baugh, Kenny (Tigers) 184
Bautista, Denny (Marlins) 199
Bautista, Jose (Pirates) 373
Baxter, Allen (Marlins) 205
Bay, Jason (Padres) 406
Bazardo, Yorman (Marlins) 203
Bazzell, Shane (Athletics) 346
Bechler, Steve (Orioles) 72
Bedard, Erik (Orioles) 66
Belcher, Jason (Brewers) 269
Belisle, Matt (Braves) 61
Belizario, Ronald (Marlins) 199
Beltran, Francis (Cubs) 100

Bell, Heath (Mets) 313
Bengochea, Kiki (Rangers) 475
Bentz, Chad (Expos) 298
Berger, Garrett (Marlins) 204
Bergolla, William (Reds) 138
Berroa, Angel (Royals) 227
Betemit, Wilson (Braves) 51
Bicondoa, Ryan (Yankees) 332
Birkins, Kurt (Orioles) 71
Blackley, Travis (Mariners) 437
Blalock, Jake (Phillies) 362
Blanco, Andres (Royals) 229
Blanco, Gregor (Braves) 56
Blanco, Tony (Reds) 138
Blanton, Joe (Athletics) 341
Blasko, Chadd (Cubs) 106
Bloomquist, Willie (Mariners) 439
Bonderman, Jeremy (Tigers) 178
Bong, Jung (Braves) 56
Bonifay, Josh (Pirates) 380
Bonser, Boof (Giants) 420
Bonvechio, Brett (Red Sox) 92
Booker, Chris (Reds) 139
Bootcheck, Chris (Angels) 22
Borchard, Joe (White Sox) 114
Borrell, Danny (Yankees) 326
Botts, Jason (Rangers) 476
Bowyer, Travis (Twins) 283
Boyd, Patrick (Rangers) 475
Boyd, Shaun (Cardinals) 388
Boyer, Blaine (Braves) 58
Boyer, Kyle (Cardinals) 391
Bourgeois, Jason (Rangers) 470
Bozied, Tagg (Padres) 403
Bradley, Bobby (Pirates) 376
Brazell, Craig (Mets) 310
Brazelton, Dewon (Devil Rays) 451
Brazoban, Yhency (Yankees) 333
Brice, Thomas (White Sox) 125
Broadway, Larry (Expos) 294
Brousard, Ben (Indians) 155
Brown, Andrew (Dodgers) 247
Brown, Dustin (Red Sox) 86
Brown, Jeremy (Athletics) 339
Broxton, Jonathan (Dodgers) 249
Bruback, Matt (Cubs) 105
Brunet, Mike (Angels) 28
Bruney, Brian (Diamondbacks) 37
Bruso, Greg (Giants) 426
Buchholz, Taylor (Phillies) 355
Buck, John (Astros) 210
Bucktrot, Keith (Phillies) 359
Buglovsky, Chris (Rockies) 168
Bukvich, Ryan (Royals) 230
Bullington, Bryan (Pirates) 371
Burke, Chris (Astros) 212
Burnett, Sean (Pirates) 371
Burnside, Adrian (Tigers) 186
Bush, David (Blue Jays) 488
Buttler, Vic (Pirates) 380
Bynum, Freddie (Athletics) 341
Bynum, Mike (Padres) 407
Byrd, Marlon (Phillies) 355

C

Cabrera, Carlos (Phillies) 360
Cabrera, Daniel (Orioles) 67

Cabrera, Fernando (Indians) 154
Cabrera, Miguel (Marlins) 194
Cain, Matt (Giants) 422
Callaspo, Alberto (Angels) 27
Calloway, Ron (Expos) 296
Cano, Robinson (Yankees) 325
Caple, Chance (Cardinals) 396
Caputo, Rob (Expos) 297
Carrasco, D.J. (Royals) 235
Carter, Lance (Devil Rays) 459
Cash, David (Giants) 425
Cash, Kevin (Blue Jays) 483
Castillo, Jose (Pirates) 371
Castro, Bernie (Padres) 409
Castro, Ismael (Mariners) 439
Cate, Troy (Mariners) 445
Cedeno, Juan (Red Sox) 90
Cepicky, Matt (Expos) 298
Cerda, Jaime (Mets) 309
Chapman, Travis (Tigers) 186
Charles, Julin (Rangers) 477
Chavez, Angel (Giants) 427
Chavez, Ozzie (Brewers) 263
Chen, Chin-Feng (Dodgers) 246
Chiavacci, Ron (Expos) 301
Childers, Matt (Brewers) 267
Childress, Daylan (Reds) 137
Choi, Hee Seop (Cubs) 98
Choo, Shin-Soo (Mariners) 435
Christensen, Danny (Royals) 231
Christianson, Ryan (Mariners) 438
Chulk, Vinny (Blue Jays) 486
Church, Ryan (Indians) 155
Cintron, Alex (Diamondbacks) 43
Clark, Jeff (Giants) 426
Clark, Jermaine (Rangers) 473
Claussen, Brandon (Yankees) 324
Clevlen, Brent (Tigers) 182
Closser, J.D. (Rockies) 168
Coenen, Matt (Tigers) 183
Colina, Javier (Rockies) 171
Colyer, Steve (Dodgers) 251
Connolly, Mike (Pirates) 379
Conrad, Brooks (Astros) 221
Contreras, Jose (Yankees) 322
Cook, Aaron (Rockies) 162
Cormier, Lance (Diamondbacks) 44
Cosby, Quan (Angels) 25
Cota, Humberto (Pirates) 374
Cota, Jesus (Diamondbacks) 40
Cotts, Neal (White Sox) 119
Crain, Jesse (Twins) 278
Cresse, Brad (Diamondbacks) 41
Crisp, Covelli (Indians) 156
Crockett, Ben (Rockies) 172
Crosby, Bobby (Athletics) 339
Crosby, Roscoe (Royals) 234
Crouthers, Dave (Orioles) 71
Cruceta, Francisco (Indians) 151
Cruz, Enrique (Brewers) 262
Cuddyer, Michael (Twins) 275
Cust, Jack (Rockies) 169
Cyr, Eric (Padres) 408

D

Davis, Jason (Indians) 150
Davis, J.J. (Pirates) 373

Dawkins, Gookie (Reds)	138	Franco, Martire (Phillies)	364	Guzman, Joel (Dodgers)	245
Day, Zach (Expos)	291	Francoeur, Jeff (Braves)	52		
DeJesus, David (Royals)	233	Frederick, Kevin (Twins)	283		
DeJong, Jordan (Blue Jays)	493	Freeman, Choo (Rockies)	164	**H**	
De la Cruz, Chris (Indians)	156	Fritz, Ben (Athletics)	342	Hafner, Travis (Indians)	148
De la Rosa, Jorge (Red Sox)	85	Fuentes, Brian (Rockies)	169	Hagerty, Luke (Cubs)	101
Delcarmen, Manny (Red Sox)	84			Haigwood, Daniel (White Sox)	121
De los Santos, Esteban (Phillies)	365			Hairston, Scott (Diamondbacks)	34
Denham, Dan (Indians)	152	**G**		Hale, Beau (Orioles)	76
DePaula, Julio (Yankees)	326	Gabbard, Kason (Red Sox)	87	Hall, Bill (Brewers)	265
Diaz, Felix (White Sox)	117	Gall, John (Cardinals)	391	Hall, Josh (Reds)	134
Diaz, Jose (Dodgers)	253	Gamble, Jerome (Reds)	136	Hall, Victor (Astros)	217
Diaz, Victor (Dodgers)	247	Garbe, B.J. (Twins)	285	Hamels, Cole (Phillies)	356
Dickinson, Andy (Athletics)	347	Garcia, Angel (Twins)	284	Hamilton, Josh (Devil Rays)	451
Digby, Bryan (Braves)	55	Garcia, Gerardo (Devil Rays)	456	Hammes, Zach (Dodgers)	250
Diggins, Ben (Brewers)	261	Garcia, Luis (Indians)	154	Hammock, Robby (Diamondbacks)	42
Dittfurth, Ryan (Rangers)	472	Garciaparra, Michael (Mariners)	440	Hancock, Josh (Phillies)	362
Dobbs, Greg (Mariners)	437	Garrett, Shawn (Pirates)	381	Hannahan, Jack (Tigers)	184
Dominguez, Jose (Rangers)	471	Gathright, Joe (Devil Rays)	461	Hannaman, Ryan (Giants)	421
Donachie, Adam (Royals)	236	Gaudin, Chad (Devil Rays)	458	Hanrahan, Joel (Dodgers)	245
Done, Juan (Mariners)	444	Gautreau, Jake (Padres)	404	Hanson, D.J. (Blue Jays)	489
Donnelly, Brendan (Angels)	23	German, Esteban (Athletics)	344	Hanson, Travis (Cardinals)	391
Dopirak, Brian (Cubs)	106	German, Franklyn (Tigers)	179	Harden, Rich (Athletics)	338
Doumit, Ryan (Pirates)	375	German, Ramon (Astros)	219	Hardy, J.J. (Brewers)	260
Doyle, Jared (Diamondbacks)	42	Germano, Justin (Padres)	407	Haren, Dan (Cardinals)	386
DuBose, Eric (Orioles)	73	Gettis, Byron (Royals)	236	Harris, Brendan (Cubs)	101
Duffy, Chris (Pirates)	379	Gil, Jerry (Diamondbacks)	45	Hart, Alex (Pirates)	378
Duke, Zach (Pirates)	376	Gillman, Justin (Reds)	136	Hart, Corey (Brewers)	260
Dukes, Elijah (Devil Rays)	457	Gimenez, Hector (Astros)	213	Hart, Jason (Rangers)	470
Dumatrait, Phil (Red Sox)	84	Ginter, Keith (Brewers)	263	Harvey, Ken (Royals)	227
Duncan, Chris (Cardinals)	396	Girdley, Josh (Expos)	300	Harville, Chad (Athletics)	343
Duncan, Jeff (Mets)	312	Gobble, Jimmy (Royals)	227	Hawksworth, Blake (Cardinals)	388
Duran, Carlos (Braves)	53	Godwin, Tyrell (Blue Jays)	489	Hawpe, Brad (Rockies)	166
Durbin, J.D. (Twins)	277	Gold, J.M. (Brewers)	267	Haynes, Dee (Cardinals)	394
Durocher, Jayson (Brewers)	264	Gold, Nate (Rangers)	477	Haynes, Nathan (Angels)	24
		Gomes, Joey (Devil Rays)	458	Heaverlo, Jeff (Mariners)	441
		Gomes, Jonny (Devil Rays)	455	Heilman, Aaron (Mets)	307
E		Gomez, Alexis (Royals)	228	Hendrickson, Ben (Brewers)	259
Edens, Kyle (Reds)	140	Gomon, Dusty (Twins)	278	Hendrickson, Mark (Blue Jays)	487
Elliot, Adam (Mets)	316	Gonzalez, Adrian (Marlins)	195	Henkel, Rob (Tigers)	181
Ellison, Jason (Giants)	424	Gonzalez, Alfredo (Dodgers)	245	Henn, Sean (Yankees)	327
Encarnacion, Edwin (Reds)	131	Gonzalez, Andy (White Sox)	117	Henry, Paul (Orioles)	73
English, Jesse (Giants)	426	Gonzalez, Danny (Phillies)	363	Henson, Drew (Yankees)	325
Ennis, John (Braves)	60	Gonzalez, Edgar (Diamondbacks)	36	Hermida, Jeremy (Marlins)	196
Escobar, Alex (Indians)	151	Gonzalez, Mike (Pirates)	373	Hernandez, Adrian (Yankees)	332
Espinosa, David (Tigers)	187	Good, Andrew (Diamondbacks)	42	Hernandez, Anderson (Tigers)	182
Esposito, Mike (Rockies)	168	Good, Eric (Expos)	294	Hernandez, Yoel (Phillies)	365
Everett, Adam (Astros)	219	Gorecki, Reid (Cardinals)	392	Herrera, Alex (Indians)	154
Evert, Brett (Braves)	53	Gosling, Mike (Diamondbacks)	35	Hill, Koyie (Dodgers)	244
Everts, Clint (Expos)	290	Goss, Michael (Red Sox)	86	Hill, Jamar (Mets)	317
		Gotay, Ruben (Royals)	231	Hill, Jeremy (Royals)	230
		Grabowski, Jason (Athletics)	342	Hill, Shawn (Expos)	299
F		Gracesqui, Franklyn (Marlins)	205	Hinckley, Mike (Expos)	291
Fagan, Shawn (Blue Jays)	490	Graman, Alex (Yankees)	330	Hines, Carlos (Devil Rays)	461
Faison, Vince (Padres)	409	Granderson, Curtis (Tigers)	185	Hoard, Brent (Twins)	282
Farfan, Alex (Reds)	140	Gredvig, Doug (Orioles)	73	Hodges, Scott (Expos)	294
Ferguson, Ian (Royals)	233	Greene, Khalil (Padres)	403	Hodges, Trey (Braves)	57
Fielder, Prince (Brewers)	259	Greinke, Zack (Royals)	226	Holliday, Matt (Rockies)	167
Figgins, Chone (Angels)	28	Griffin, Colt (Royals)	229	Honel, Kris (White Sox)	116
Figueroa, Jonathan (Dodgers)	243	Griffin, John-Ford (Blue Jays)	486	Hooper, Kevin (Marlins)	200
Fischer, Rich (Angels)	21	Griffiths, Jeremy (Mets)	311	Houlton, D.J. (Astros)	220
Fitzpatrick, Reg (Expos)	299	Grigsby, Derick (Astros)	214	House, J.R. (Pirates)	376
Flinn, Chris (Devil Rays)	455	Gross, Gabe (Blue Jays)	486	Howard, Ben (Padres)	404
Floyd, Gavin (Phillies)	354	Gruler, Chris (Reds)	130	Howard, Ryan (Phillies)	357
Foley, Travis (Indians)	153	Guerrero, Cristian (Brewers)	268	Howington, Ty (Reds)	132
Fontenot, Mike (Orioles)	68	Guerrier, Matt (Pirates)	377	Huber, Justin (Mets)	308
Foppert, Jesse (Giants)	418	Guillen, Rudy (Yankees)	327	Hudson, Luke (Reds)	134
Ford, Lew (Twins)	277	Guthrie, Jeremy (Indians)	147	Hughes, Travis (Rangers)	469
Ford, Matt (Brewers)	262	Gutierrez, Franklin (Dodgers)	248	Hummel, Tim (White Sox)	120
Francis, Jeff (Rockies)	165	Gutierrez, Jesse (Reds)	140		
Francisco, Alfredo (Cubs)	104	Guzman, Angel (Cubs)	99	**I**	
Francisco, Franklin (White Sox)	124	Guzman, Freddy (Padres)	411	Infante, Omar (Tigers)	179

Ishikawa, Travis (Giants) 423

J

Jackson, Edwin (Dodgers) 243
Jackson, Nic (Cubs) 100
James, Delvin (Devil Rays) 456
Jenks, Bobby (Angels) 19
Jepsen, Kevin (Angels) 27
Jimenez, Kelvin (Rangers) 471
Jimenez, Ubaldo (Rockies) 166
Jimerson, Charlton (Astros) 220
Jiminez, Luis (Orioles) 67
Johnson, Adam (Twins) 278
Johnson, Ben (Padres) 408
Johnson, Blair (Pirates) 377
Johnson, Dan (Athletics) 345
Johnson, Gabe (Cardinals) 392
Johnson, J.J. (Cubs) 107
Johnson, Josh (Marlins) 204
Johnson, Kelly (Braves) 55
Johnson, Rett (Mariners) 437
Johnson, Tripper (Orioles) 69
Johnson, Tyler (Cardinals) 390
Jones, Justin (Cubs) 103
Jones, Kennard (Padres) 408
Jones, Mike (Brewers) 259
Jorgensen, Ryan (Marlins) 202
Joseph, Jake (Mets) 314
Journell, Jimmy (Cardinals) 387
Junge, Eric (Phillies) 364

K

Kaaihue, Micah (Royals) 237
Karp, Josh (Expos) 291
Kazmir, Scott (Mets) 307
Kelly, Kenny (Mariners) 440
Kelton, David (Cubs) 101
Kemp, Beau (Twins) 280
Keppel, Bob (Mets) 309
Ketchner, Ryan (Mariners) 445
Kibler, Ryan (Rockies) 172
Kimpton, Nick (Angels) 28
Knott, Jon (Padres) 410
Koronka, John (Rangers) 476
Kotchman, Casey (Angels) 19
Kozlowski, Ben (Rangers) 467
Kroeger, Josh (Diamondbacks) 44
Krynzel, David (Brewers) 261
Kubel, Jason (Twins) 277
Kuo, Hong-Chih (Dodgers) 246

L

Labandeira, Josh (Expos) 298
LaForest, Pete (Devil Rays) 456
Laird, Gerald (Rangers) 468
Lane, Jason (Astros) 211
Langerhans, Ryan (Braves) 57
Larrison, Preston (Tigers) 179
LaRoche, Adam (Braves) 55
Larson, Brandon (Reds) 133
Lavigne, Tim (Mets) 314
Layfield, Scotty (Cardinals) 390
League, Brandon (Blue Jays) 484
Ledezma, Wil (Tigers) 186
Lee, Cliff (Indians) 147
Lee, Seung (Phillies) 358
Leicester, Jon (Cubs) 109
Lerew, Anthony (Braves) 58
Lester, Jon (Red Sox) 85
Levinski, Don (Marlins) 196
Lewis, Colby (Rangers) 467
Lewis, Fred (Giants) 421

Lewis, Richard (Braves) 58
Lewis, Rommie (Orioles) 68
Lidge, Brad (Astros) 211
Linden, Todd (Giants) 420
Liriano, Francisco (Giants) 420
Liriano, Pedro (Brewers) 263
Livingston, Bobby (Mariners) 444
Lo, Ching-Lung (Rockies) 167
Lockwood, Luke (Expos) 295
Logan, Nook (Tigers) 181
Loney, James (Dodgers) 242
Long, Nick (Expos) 299
Looper, Aaron (Mariners) 443
Lopez, Gonzalo (Braves) 54
Lopez, Javier (Red Sox) 92
Lopez, Jose (Mariners) 435
Lopez, Pedro (White Sox) 121
Lopez, Romelio (Devil Rays) 459
Loux, Shane (Tigers) 189
Lowry, Noah (Giants) 424
Ludwick, Ryan (Rangers) 469
Lugo, Ruddy (Astros) 219
Luna, Hector (Devil Rays) 460
Lunsford, Trey (Giants) 427
Lydon, Wayne (Mets) 315

M

MacDougal, Mike (Royals) 228
Machado, Alejandro (Royals) 231
Machado, Anderson (Phillies) 357
Machi, Jean (Phillies) 363
Madritsch, Bobby (Mariners) 442
Madson, Ryan (Phillies) 356
Maine, John (Orioles) 69
Majewski, Val (Orioles) 71
Malone, Corwin (White Sox) 117
Manning, Charlie (Yankees) 328
Marte, Andy (Braves) 51
Martin, J.D. (Indians) 152
Martinez, Anastacio (Red Sox) 86
Martinez, Javier (Padres) 406
Martinez, Luis (Brewers) 266
Martinez, Ramon (Rangers) 474
Martinez, Victor (Indians) 147
Mateo, Aneudis (Red Sox) 86
Materano, Oscar (Rockies) 166
Mathis, Jeff (Angels) 19
Matsui, Hideki (Yankees) 323
Mattox, David (Mets) 312
Mauer, Joe (Twins) 274
Maureau, Justin (Blue Jays) 491
Mayorson, Manuel (Blue Jays) 492
McBeth, Marcus (Athletics) 341
McBride, Macay (Braves) 52
McCann, Brian (Braves) 60
McCarthy, Bill (Braves) 61
McClung, Seth (Devil Rays) 452
McCurdy, John (Athletics) 345
McDonald, Darnell (Orioles) 67
McDougall, Marshall (Rangers) 471
McGowan, Dustin (Blue Jays) 482
McLouth, Nate (Pirates) 378
McPherson, Dallas (Angels) 20
Medrano, Jesus (Marlins) 203
Megrew, Mike (Dodgers) 252
Mendez, Deivi (Yankees) 332
Meyer, Dan (Braves) 57
Meyer, Drew (Rangers) 468
Miller, Brian (White Sox) 120
Miller, Greg (Astros) 217
Miller, Greg (Dodgers) 247
Miller, Tony (Rockies) 167
Miner, Zach (Braves) 56

Miniel, Rene (Red Sox) 88
Molina, Yadier (Cardinals) 390
Montanez, Luis (Cubs) 103
Moore, Scott (Tigers) 180
Morban, Jose (Twins) 284
Morneau, Justin (Twins) 275
Morris, Chris (Brewers) 268
Morrissey, Adam (Athletics) 345
Moseley, Dustin (Reds) 132
Moss, Steve (Brewers) 264
Moye, Alan (Reds) 139
Munoz, Arnie (White Sox) 118
Munson, Eric (Tigers) 180
Murphy, Bill (Athletics) 348
Murphy, Tommy (Angels) 29
Murray, A.J. (Rangers) 472
Murray, Josh (Brewers) 269
Musser, Neal (Mets) 310

N

Nady, Xavier (Padres) 402
Nageotte, Clint (Mariners) 436
Nance, Shane (Brewers) 264
Narveson, Chris (Cardinals) 387
Navarro, Dioner (Yankees) 330
Neal, Blaine (Marlins) 197
Negron, Miguel (Blue Jays) 488
Nelson, Brad (Brewers) 258
Nelson, Bubba (Braves) 51
Nelson, John (Cardinals) 389
Nelson, Jon (Mariners) 444
Nettles, Marcus (Padres) 413
Nicolas, Mike (Padres) 405
Niekro, Lance (Giants) 422
Nieve, Fernando (Astros) 218
Nin, Sandy (Blue Jays) 491
Nippert, Dustin (Diamondbacks) 41
Nix, Jayson (Rockies) 164
Nix, Laynce (Rangers) 467
Nixon, Mike (Dodgers) 250
Nolasco, Ricky (Cubs) 105
Nova, Juan (Marlins) 203
Novoa, Roberto (Tigers) 188
Novinsky, John (Cardinals) 393
Nunez, Abraham (Marlins) 200
Nunez, Leo (Pirates) 378

O

Obenchain, Steve (Athletics) 344
Obermueller, Wes (Royals) 233
Oeltjen, Trent (Twins) 281
Olivo, Miguel (White Sox) 115
Olmedo, Rainer (Reds) 137
Olore, Kevin (Mariners) 440
Olsen, Scott (Marlins) 202
Olson, Tim (Diamondbacks) 38
Oquendo, Ian (Pirates) 374
O'Riordan, Chris (Rangers) 474
Ortiz, Javier (Yankees) 329
Ortmeier, Dan (Giant) 425
Osoria, Franquelis (Dodgers) 253
Overbay, Lyle (Diamondbacks) 35
Owens, Henry (Pirates) 380
Oxspring, Chris (Padres) 413
Ozuna, Pablo (Rockies) 170

P

Padilla, Jorge (Phillies) 359
Pagan, Angel (Mets) 313
Pahucki, David (Red Sox) 91
Pannone, Anthony (Giants) 427
Paradis, Mike (Orioles) 76

Parker, Josh (Devil Rays) 459
Parker, Zach (Rockies) 165
Parra, Manny (Brewers) 261
Parrott, Rhett (Cardinals) 389
Pascucci, Val (Expos) 297
Patterson, John (D'backs) 35
Pauley, David (Padres) 409
Paulino, Ronny (Royals) 234
Pearce, Josh (Cardinals) 394
Peeples, Ross (Mets) 317
Pelland, Tyler (Red Sox) 91
Pember, David (Brewers) 267
Pena, Wily Mo (Reds) 131
Pender, Matt (Tigers) 188
Penn, Hayden (Orioles) 76
Peralta, Johnny (Indians) 153
Perez, Antonio (Devil Rays) 453
Perez, Beltran (Diamondbacks) 43
Perez, Franklin (Phillies) 362
Perez, Miguel (Reds) 139
Perry, Jason (Blue Jays) 491
Peterson, Matt (Mets) 308
Petrick, Billy (Cubs) 104
Petty, Chad (Tigers) 182
Phillips, Andy (Yankees) 328
Phillips, Brandon (Indians) 146
Phillips, Heath (White Sox) 123
Phillips, Jason (Mets) 311
Phillips, Mark (Padres) 403
Pie, Felix (Cubs) 99
Pignatiello, Carmen (Cubs) 108
Pilkington, Brian (Dodgers) 252
Pinto, Renyel (Cubs) 107
Pleiness, Chad (Blue Jays) 489
Pluta, Anthony (Astros) 215
Pope, Justin (Cardinals) 388
Portorreal, Carlos (Giants) 429
Pratt, Andy (Braves) 59
Pridie, Jason (Devil Rays) 453
Prieto, Victor (Marlins) 201
Puello, Ignacio (Expos) 300
Putz, J.J. (Mariners) 442

Q

Qualls, Chad (Astros) 213
Quinlan, Robb (Angels) 25
Quiroz, Guillermo (Blue Jays) 487

R

Raburn, Johnny (Brewers) 266
Raburn, Ryan (Tigers) 187
Ragsdale, Corey (Mets) 316
Rakers, Aaron (Orioles) 72
Ramirez, Elizardo (Phillies) 357
Ramirez, Hanley (Red Sox) 82
Ramirez, Horacio (Braves) 54
Ramirez, Santiago (Astros) 214
Ramos, Mario (Rangers) 474
Ransom, Cody (Giants) 428
Rasner, Darrell (Expos) 292
Rauch, Jon (White Sox) 116
Redman, Prentice (Mets) 312
Reed, Eric (Marlins) 201
Reed, Jeremy (White Sox) 122
Reed, Keith (Orioles) 74
Reedy, Shane (Cardinals) 393
Reese, Kevin (Yankees) 331
Regilio, Nick (Rangers) 472
Repko, Jason (Dodgers) 252
Restovich, Michael (Twins) 275
Reyes, Jose (Mets) 306
Reyes, Rene (Rockies) 163

Rheinecker, John (Athletics) 339
Rich, Dominic (Blue Jays) 488
Richardson, Juan (Phillies) 359
Riggans, Shawn (Devil Rays) 457
Riley, Matt (Orioles) 75
Rincon, Juan (Twins) 282
Ring, Royce (White Sox) 118
Rios, Alexis (Blue Jays) 485
Rivas, Arturo (Orioles) 75
Rivera, Carlos (Pirates) 379
Rivera, Juan (Yankees) 323
Rivera, Rene (Mariners) 443
Robertson, Jeriome (Astros) 216
Rodriguez, Carlos (Phillies) 360
Rodriguez, Cristobal (Expos) 296
Rodriguez, Francisco (Angels) 18
Rodriguez, Orlando (Dodgers) 250
Rodriguez, Rafael (Angels) 12
Rodriguez, Ricardo (Indians) 148
Rogers, Ed (Orioles) 74
Rohlicek, Russ (Cubs) 108
Romano, Jason (Dodgers) 251
Romero, Alex (Twins) 279
Rosario, Adriano (D'backs) 39
Rosario, Francisco (Blue Jays) 484
Rosario, Rodrigo (Astros) 213
Ross, Cody (Tigers) 183
Rouse, Mike (Athletics) 346
Ruan, Wilkin (Dodgers) 249
Rundles, Rich (Expos) 295
Rupp, Josh (White Sox) 123
Rust, Evan (Devil Rays) 460
Ryan, Mike (Twins) 285
Ryu, Jae-Kuk (Cubs) 102

S

Sadler, Carl (Indians) 157
Sadler, Ray (Cubs) 108
Sain, Greg (Padres) 411
Saladin, Miguel (Astros) 216
Sanchez, Duaner (Pirates) 372
Sanchez, Felix (Cubs) 103
Sanchez, Freddy (Red Sox) 83
Sanchez, Humberto (Tigers) 185
Sanders, Dave (White Sox) 119
Santana, Johan (Angels) 20
Santillan, Manny (Astros) 216
Santor, John (Cardinals) 393
Santos, Angel (Red Sox) 93
Santos, Deivis (Giants) 423
Santos, Sergio (Diamondbacks) 37
Sardinha, Bronson (Yankees) 324
Sardinha, Dane (Reds) 136
Saunders, Joe (Angels) 21
Schilling, Micah (Indians) 156
Schnurstein, Micah (White Sox) 119
Schramek, Mark (Reds) 134
Schumaker, Skip (Cardinals) 394
Sears, Todd (Twins) 283
Seay, Bobby (Devil Rays) 460
Seddon, Chris (Devil Rays) 455
Segovia, Zach (Phillies) 358
Seibel, Phil (Mets) 310
Seo, Jae (Mets) 314
Shafer, Corey (Orioles) 70
Shanks, James (Royals) 235
Sharber, Jason (Pirates) 381
Shell, Steven (Angels) 22
Shibilo, Andy (Red Sox) 87
Shoppach, Kelly (Red Sox) 83
Shortell, Rory (Astros) 218
Sierra, Edwardo (Athletics) 348
Simon, Billy (Red Sox) 85

Simpson, Allan (Mariners) 442
Sing, Brandon (Cubs) 106
Sisco, Andy (Cubs) 99
Sizemore, Grady (Indians) 149
Sledge, Termel (Expos) 297
Slocum, Brian (Indians) 157
Smit, Alexander (Twins) 284
Smith, Chris (Orioles) 77
Smith, Chris (Red Sox) 88
Smith, Corey (Indians) 150
Smith, Mike (Blue Jays) 490
Smith, Sean (Indians) 155
Smith, Will (Marlins) 198
Smitherman, Stephen (Reds) 135
Smyth, Steve (Cubs) 104
Snare, Ryan (Marlins) 198
Snelling, Chris (Mariners) 435
Snow, Bert (Athletics) 348
Snyder, Chris (Diamondbacks) 39
Snyder, Earl (Red Sox) 90
Snyder, Kyle (Royals) 229
Snyder, Mike (Blue Jays) 492
Song, Seung (Expos) 292
Soriano, Rafael (Mariners) 434
Span, Denard (Twins) 276
Spann, Chad (Red Sox) 89
Specht, Brian (Angels) 26
Spiehs, R.D. (Giants) 427
St. Pierre, Maxim (Tigers) 188
Stahl, Richard (Orioles) 69
Standridge, Jason (Devil Rays) 454
Stanley, Henri (Astros) 214
Stanley, Steve (Athletics) 348
Stavisky, Brian (Athletics) 349
Stephenson, Eric (Blue Jays) 493
Stewart, Cory (Padres) 406
Stewart, Josh (White Sox) 122
Stewart, Paul (Red Sox) 90
Stocks, Nick (Cardinals) 396
Stokes, Jason (Marlins) 195
Stotts, J.T. (Athletics) 346
Strange, Pat (Mets) 308
Strong, Jamal (Mariners) 438
Stumm, Jason (White Sox) 121
Sullivan, Cory (Rockies) 172
Swisher, Nick (Athletics) 342
Switzer, Jon (Devil Rays) 453

T

Taguchi, So (Cardinals) 397
Talbot, Mitch (Astros) 218
Tallet, Brian (Indians) 150
Tamayo, Danny (Royals) 237
Taylor, Aaron (Mariners) 436
Teahen, Mark (Athletics) 344
Teixeira, Mark (Rangers) 466
Tejada, Ferdin (Yankees) 327
Tejada, Sandy (Twins) 280
Tejeda, Rob (Phillies) 363
Tejeda, Juan (Tigers) 189
Terrero, Luis (Diamondbacks) 38
Thames, Marcus (Yankees) 331
Thigpen, Josh (Reds) 135
Thissen, Greg (Expos) 301
Thomas, Brad (Twins) 279
Thomas, Eric M. (Brewers) 265
Thomas, John (Giants) 428
Thompson, Derek (Dodgers) 248
Thompson, Erik (Rangers) 475
Thompson, Kevin (Yankees) 333
Thorman, Scott (Braves) 53
Thorne, David (Expos) 299
Thorpe, Tracy (Blue Jays) 490

Threets, Erick (Giants)	422
Thurston, Joey (Dodgers)	244
Tiburcio, Hector (Reds)	141
Tierney, Chris (Royals)	236
Tonis, Mike (Royals)	232
Torcato, Tony (Giants)	423
Torres, Andres (Tigers)	184
Torres, Joe (Angels)	21
Touchstone, Nick (Angels)	25
Traber, Billy (Indians)	149
Tracy, Chad (Diamondbacks)	37
Trzesniak, Nick (Padres)	412
Tsao, Chin-Hui (Rockies)	163
Tucker, Rusty (Padres)	405
Turay, Haj (Mets)	315
Turnbow, Derrick (Angels)	23
Tussen, Denny (Red Sox)	91
Tyler, Scott (Twins)	276

U

Ugueto, Luis (Mariners)	438
Ulacia, Dennis (White Sox)	124
Upton, B.J. (Devil Rays)	451
Utley, Chase (Phillies)	355

V

Valderrama, Carlos (Giants)	425
Valdez, Jose (Yankees)	330
Valdez, Melkin (Giants)	424
Valent, Eric (Phillies)	361
Valentine, Joe (Athletics)	340
Valverde, Jose (Diamondbacks)	40
VanBenschoten, John (Pirates)	370

Vance, Cory (Rockies)	170
Van Dussen, Derrick (Rangers)	476
Van Hekken, Andy (Tigers)	183
Vargas, Claudio (Expos)	293
Vasquez, Jose (Rockies)	173
Victorino, Shane (Padres)	410
Villarreal, Oscar (D'backs)	39
Vogelsong, Ryan (Pirates)	375
Vorwald, Matt (Twins)	281
Votto, Joey (Reds)	136
Voyles, Brad (Royals)	232

W

Waechter, Doug (Devil Rays)	454
Wainwright, Adam (Braves)	50
Walker, Tyler (Mets)	313
Wang, Chien-Ming (Yankees)	325
Waters, Chris (Braves)	59
Watson, Brandon (Expos)	295
Wayne, Justin (Marlins)	197
Weatherby, Charlie (Red Sox)	92
Webb, Brandon (Diamondbacks)	36
Webb, John (Cubs)	105
Webster, Anthony (White Sox)	115
Wedel, Jeremy (Phillies)	364
Weeden, Brandon (Yankees)	329
Wellemeyer, Todd (Cubs)	102
Werth, Jayson (Blue Jays)	483
Wesley, John (Blue Jays)	493
West, Brian (White Sox)	120
White, Bill (Diamondbacks)	41
White, Matt (Devil Rays)	458
White, Matt (Red Sox)	89
White, Scott (Red Sox)	87

Whiteman, Tommy (Astros)	212
Whiteside, Eli (Orioles)	70
Whitney, Matt (Indians)	153
Williams, Blake (Reds)	141
Williams, Jerome (Giants)	419
Williams, Marland (D'backs)	42
Williamson, David (Cardinals)	392
Willingham, Josh (Marlins)	202
Willis, Dontrelle (Marlins)	195
Wilson, C.J. (Rangers)	469
Wilson, Josh (Marlins)	198
Wilson, Phil (Angels)	27
Wing, Ryan (White Sox)	120
Wodnicki, Mike (Padres)	411
Wood, Mike (Athletics)	340
Woods, Jake (Angels)	24
Woods, Michael (Tigers)	185
Wright, David (Mets)	307
Wright, Gavin (Astros)	215
Wright, Matt (Braves)	60
Wrightsman, Dusty (Royals)	237
Wylie, Jason (Cubs)	106

Y

Yan, Edwin (White Sox)	124
Yarnall, Eddie (Athletics)	347
Yates, Tyler (Mets)	316
Yeatman, Matt (Twins)	279
Youkilis, Kevin (Red Sox)	83
Young, Chris (Expos)	293
Young, Delwyn (Dodgers)	253
Young, Jason (Rockies)	163
Young, Walter (Pirates)	377